THE BRITISH YEAR BOOK OF
INTERNATIONAL LAW

THE
BRITISH YEAR BOOK OF
INTERNATIONAL LAW

2007

SEVENTY-EIGHTH YEAR OF ISSUE

OXFORD
AT THE CLARENDON PRESS
2008

OXFORD
UNIVERSITY PRESS

Great Clarendon Street, Oxford OX2 6DP

Oxford University Press is a department of the University of Oxford.
It furthers the University's objective of excellence in research, scholarship,
and education by publishing worldwide in

Oxford New York

Auckland Cape Town Dar es Salaam Hong Kong Karachi
Kuala Lumpur Madrid Melbourne Mexico City Nairobi
New Delhi Shanghai Taipei Toronto

With offices in

Argentina Austria Brazil Chile Czech Republic France Greece
Guatemala Hungary Italy Japan Poland Portugal Singapore
South Korea Switzerland Thailand Turkey Ukraine Vietnam

Oxford is a registered trade mark of Oxford University Press
in the UK and in certain other countries

Published in the United States
by Oxford University Press Inc., New York

© Oxford University Press, 2008

British Library Cataloguing in Publication Data

Data available

Library of Congress Cataloging in Publication Data

Data available

Typeset by Newgen Imaging Systems (P) Ltd., Chennai, India
Printed in Great Britain
on acid-free paper by
CPI Antony Rowe, Chippenham, Wiltshire

ISBN 978-0-19-954740-1

1 3 5 7 9 10 8 6 4 2

Editorial Communications should be addressed as follows:

Articles and Notes:
PROFESSOR JAMES CRAWFORD
Lauterpacht Centre for International Law,
5 Cranmer Road, Cambridge, CB3 9BL.
JRC1000@hermes.cam.ac.uk

Books for Review (from 2008):
PROFESSOR J. CRAIG BARKER
Sussex Law School, University of Sussex,
Brighton, East Sussex BN1 9QQ
J.C.Barker@sussex.ac.uk

The Editors and members of the Editorial Committee do not make themselves in any way responsible for the views expressed by contributors.

The British Year Book of International Law is indexed in *Current Law Index,* published by Information Access Company, and in *Legal Journals Index,* published by Legal Information Resources Limited.

CONTENTS

LIST OF ABBREVIATIONS

ACP	African, Caribbean or Pacific
AfDF	African Development Fund
A-G	Attorney General
AIDS	Acquired Immune Deficiency Syndrome
AIT	Asylum and Immigration Tribunal
ASCOBANS	Agreement on the Conservation of Small Cetaceans of the Baltic, North East Atlantic, Irish and North Seas
ASEAN	Association of Southeast Asian Nations
AU	African Union
BAE	British Aerospace
BDTC	British Dependent Territory Citizens
BGB	German Civil Code
BiH	Bosnia and Herzegovina
BIS	Bank for International Settlements
BNA (HK)	British Nationality (Hong Kong) Act
BN(O)	British National Overseas
BNSC	British National Space Centre
BOC	British Overseas Citizen
BoE	United Kingdom Bank of England base rate
BOTC	British Overseas Territories Citizen
BPP	British Protected Person
BS	British subject
BTWC	Biological and Toxin Weapons Convention
CAHDI	Committee of Legal Advisers on Public International Law
CBRN	Chemical, Biological, Radiological and Nuclear
CCAMLR	Commission for the Conservation of Antarctic Marine Living Resources
CCS	Carbon Capture and Storage
CD	Six month certificate of deposit
CDM	Clean Development Mechanism
CEMA	Customs and Excise Management Act
CFE	Conventional Forces in Europe Treaty
CFI	Court of First Instance
CFSP	Common Foreign and Security Policy
CIA	Central Intelligence Agency
CIDT	Centre for International Development & Training
CITES	Convention on International Trade in Endangered Species
CJ	Chief Justice
CJNA	Committee of Experts on Nationality
CLCS	United Nations Commission on the Limits of the Continental Shelf

CLVA	Colonial Laws Validity Act
CNC	Civil Nuclear Constabulary
COCON	EU Council Working Party on Consular Co-operation
CPA	Coalition Provisional Authority
CPI	Consumer Price Index
CPR	Civil Procedure Rule
CPS	Crown Prosecution Service
COREPER	Permanent Representatives Committee
CRC	Convention on the Rights of the Child
CRN	Coalition of Rainforest Nations
CSA	Comprehensive Safeguards Agreement
CSBA	Cyprus Sovereign Base Areas
CSD	Claims Settlement Declaration
CTBT	Comprehensive Nuclear Test Ban Treaty
CTD	Counter Terrorism Division of the Crown Prosecution Service
CUP	Cambridge University Press
CVL	Common Visa List
CWC	Chemical Weapons Convention
DEFRA	Department for Environment, Food and Rural Affairs
DFID	Department for International Development
DFS	Development-facilitation subsidy
DFT	Development Facilitation Tariff
DRC	Democratic Republic of the Congo
DSF	Debt Sustainability Framework
DSTL	Defence Science and Technology Laboratory
DTI	Department of Trade and Industry
DWA	Deportation with assurances
EC	European Community
ECA	Export Credit Agency
ECB	European Central Bank
ECE	Economic Commission for Europe
ECHR	European Convention on Human Rights and Fundamental Freedoms
ECHR	European Court of Human Rights
ECJ	European Court of Justice
ECO	Export Control Organization
ECOSOC	Economic and Social Council
ECOWAS	Economic Community of West African States
ECSC	European Coal and Steel Community
EEC	European Economic Community
EEZ	Exclusive Economic Zone
EIA	Environmental Impact Assessment
EIC	East India Company
EIDHR	European Instrument for Democracy and Human Rights

EITI	Extractive Industries Transparency Initiative
EMC	Ethnic Minority Citizenship
EPA	Economic Partnership Agreements
ETIS	Elephant Trade Information System
ETS	Emissions Trading Scheme
ETS	Europe Treaty Series
EU	European Union
EUFOR	European Union Force
EUI	European University Institute
EUSR	European Union Special Representative
FAC	Foreign Affairs Select Committee
FAO	Food and Agriculture Organization of the United Nations
FATF	Financial Action Task Force
FCC	Federal Communications Commission
FCO	Foreign and Commonwealth Office
FFR	United States Federal Reserve Fund
FFRP	Forum des Femmes Rwandaises Parliamentaires
FJA	Foreign Jurisdiction Act
FLEGT	Forest Law Enforcement, governance and Trade
FOC	Flags-of-convenience
FRY	Federal Republic of Yugoslavia
FTA	Free trade agreement
GATT	General Agreement on Tariffs and Trade
GCHQ	Government Communications Headquarters
GDO	Government Diamond Office
GHG	Greenhouse gas
GMT	Greenwich Mean Time
GSIF	Gibraltar Social Insurance Fund
GV3	Declaration of identity for Visa Purposes
HIPC	Heavily Indebted Poor Countries
HIV	Human Immunodeficiency Virus
HL	House of Lords
HM	Her Majesty
HMG	Her Majesty's Government
HMRC	Her Majesty's Revenue and Customs
HMS	Her Majesty's Ship
HRA	Human Rights Act
HRC	United Nations Human Rights Council
IAEA	International Atomic Energy Agency
IBRD	International Bank for Reconstruction and Development
ICAO	International Civil Aviation Organization
ICC	International Criminal Court
ICCAT	International Commission for the Conservation of Atlantic Tunas
ICCPR	International Covenant on Civil and Political Rights
ICJ	International Court of Justice

ICPS	International Centre for Prison Studies
ICRW	International Convention on the Regulation of Whaling
ICSID	International Convention for the Settlement of International Disputes
ICTR	International Criminal Tribunal for Rwanda
ICTY	International Criminal Tribunal for the Former Yugoslavia
IDA	International Development Association
IDP	Internally displaced person
IGC	Intergovernmental Conference
ILC	International Law Commission
ILO	International Labour Organization
IMF	International Monetary Fund
IND	Immigration and Nationality Directorate
INF	Irradiated Nuclear Fuel
ISC	Intelligence and Security Committee
ISAF	International Security Assistance Force
ISO	International Standards Organization
ITLOS	International Tribunal for the Law of the Sea
IUCN	International Union for Conservation of Nature
IWC	International Whaling Commission
IWRM	Integrated Water Resources Management Organization
J	Justice
JHA	Justice and Home Affairs
JJ	Justices
KC	King's Counsel
KFOR	'Kosovo Force'
KPCS	Kimberley Process Certification Scheme
LCIA	London Court of International Arbitration
LGB	Lesbians, gays and bisexuals
LIBOR	London Interbank Office Rate
LJ	Lord Justice
LJJ	Lords Justices
LLMC	Limitation of Liability for Maritime Claims
LSE	London School of Economics
LTTE	Liberation of Tigers Tamil Eelam
MDG	Millennium Development Goals
MDRI	Multilateral Debt Relief Initiative
MEA	Multilateral Environmental Agreement
MEP	Member of the European Parliament
MIKE	Monitoring of the Illegal Killing of Elephants
MINURCAT	United Nations Mission in the Central African Republic and Chad
MNF	Multi-National Force
MoD	Ministry of Defence

MoU	Memorandum of Understanding
MOX	Mixed Oxide Fuel
MR	Master of the Rolls
MSC	Mediterranean Shipping Company
MTCR	Missile Technology Control Regime
NAFTA	North American Free Trade Agreement
NAFO	Northwest Atlantic Fisheries Organisation
NATO	North Atlantic Treaty Organization
NDCS	National Drug control Strategy
NGO	Non-Governmental Organization
NPT	Nuclear Non-proliferation Treaty
NSG	Nuclear Suppliers Group
NWS	Nuclear Weapon States
NNWS	Non-nuclear-weapon States
OCT	Overseas Countries and Territories
OECD	Organization for Economic Co-operation and Development
OSPAR	Protection of the Marine Environment of the North-East Atlantic
OUP	Oxford University Press
PCA	Permanent Court of Arbitration
PCIJ	Permanent Court of International Justice
PIC	Convention on the Prior Informed Consent
PKK	Kurdistan Workers' Party
PNG	Papua New Guinea
QC	Queen's Counsel
QDF	Qadhafi Development Foundation
QMV	Qualified majority voting
RAF	Royal Air Force
RCPO	Revenue and Customs Prosecutions Office
RN	Royal Navy
RSPCA	Royal Society for the Prevention of Cruelty to Animals
SAA	Stabilisation and association agreement
SAP-FL	Special Action Programme on Forced Labour
SAR	Search and rescue
SCIF	Strategic Committee on Immigration, Frontiers and Asylum
SCM	WTO Agreement on Subsidies and Countervailing Measures
SCR	Security Council Resolution
SCSL	Special Court for Sierra Leone
SEIA	Strategic Environmental Impact Assessment
SFO	Serious Fraud Office
SFRY	Socialist Federal Republic of Yugoslavia
SIA	State Immunity Act
SIAC	Special Immigration Appeals Commission
SIS	Secret Intelligence Service
SMRU	Sea Mammal Research Unit
SOSREP	Secretary of State's Representative for Maritime Salvage and Intervention

START I	Strategic Arms Reduction Agreement
START II	Second Strategic Arms Reduction Agreement
TAC	Treaty of Amity and Co-operation in Southeast Asia
TBT	Technical Barriers to Trade
TEC	Treaty establishing the European Community
TRIPS	Trade Related Aspects of Intellectual Property Rights
TRG	Transitional Federal Government
TRNC	Turkish Republic of Northern Cyprus
UAE	United Arab Emirates
UK	United Kingdom
UN	United Nations
UNAMI	United Nations Assistance Mission in Iraq
UNCAT	United Nations Convention Against Torture and Other Cruel, Inhuman or Degrading Treatment or Punishment
UNCC	United Nations Compensation Commission
UNCITRAL	United Nations Commission on International Trade Law
UNCLOS	United Nations Convention on the Law of the Sea
UN ECE	United Nations Economic Commission for Europe
UNESCO	United Nations Educational, Scientific and Cultural Organization
UNFSA	United Nations Fish Stocks Agreement
UNGA	United Nations General Assembly
UNHCR	United Nations High Commissioner for Refugees
UNICEF	United Nations Children's Fund
UNIDROIT	United Nations International Institute for the Unification of Private Law
UNIIIC	United Nations Independent International Investigation Commission
UNMIK	United Nations Mission in Kosovo
UNMOVIC	United Nations Monitoring, Verification and Inspection Commission
UNSC	United Nations Security Council
UNSCR	United Nations Security Council Resolution
US	United States
USA	United States of America
VAT	Value Added Tax
VCDR	Vienna Convention on Diplomatic Relations
VCLT	Vienna Convention on the Law of Treaties
WGB	Working Group on Bribery
WHO	World Health Organization
WLR	Weekly Law Reports
WMD	Weapons of Mass Destruction
WTO	World Trade Organization

Sir Vincent Evans
(1915–2007)

SIR VINCENT EVANS (1915–2007)

Sir Vincent Evans, GCMG, QC, who died in 2007 at the age of 91, was the Legal Adviser to the Foreign Office for a period of eight years in the 1960s and 70s. It could however be said that the full flowering of his career as an international lawyer came only later, first with his election to the Human Rights Committee in 1977, and then during his 11-year spell as the British Judge on the European Court of Human Rights between 1980 and 1991.

Born in the London suburbs, though of a thoroughly Welsh ancestry affectionately reflected by his being widely known in Whitehall in later years as "Evans the law", Vincent Evans was a man of strong loyalties to the institutions that had nurtured him, and to which he gave unselfishly in return: his school (Merchant Taylors'), Wadham College, Oxford, where he took his first degree in law and then the BCL, the Foreign Office and Diplomatic Service, the United Nations, and the European human rights system centred around the Commission and Court in Strasbourg.

After the BCL, he read for the Bar on a Lincoln's Inn scholarship, and was called just before the outbreak of war in 1939. Despite his poor eyesight he served a full war in the Army, the last year of which as the legal adviser to the British Military Administration in Cyrenaica. He was demobbed in 1946 as Lieutenant-Colonel and MBE, and almost immediately afterwards joined the Foreign Office which was expanding its legal staff, until then surprisingly small in size, to cope with the challenges of post-War international organization. Promotion to the senior rank of Counsellor at the early age of 39 led to his posting as Legal Adviser to the UK Mission to the United Nations in the mid-50s, at a crucial period for the UN's development, and having to cope while there with the fallout from the Suez disaster. His tour of duty in New York was longer than would nowadays be the case, lasting for nearly six years, and the records of the General Assembly's Legal Committee show his patient influence in building up some of the UN's key institutions in the legal field. His careful hand can, for example, be seen both in securing acceptance of the need to create an external avenue for the review of staff appeals in the UN system, and (when the chosen route became through advisory opinions from the ICJ) in the attempt to head off in advance the procedural problems that dogged the system and contributed to its eventual demise some decades later.

On his return to the Foreign Office in 1959 Evans was made CMG, and further promotion followed rapidly. He served for a year as acting Legal Adviser in 1965–6, when Sir Francis Vallat was on sabbatical at McGill University, and shortly after that was appointed to the post substantively when Vallat took early retirement. This was however at the time of the successive amalgamation of the three external affairs ministries under the Wilson administration, beginning with the creation of a 'Commonwealth Office' out of the old Colonial and Commonwealth Relations Offices, and continuing after a short interval with its merger into the Foreign Office, to create the present-day 'Foreign and Commonwealth Office' (FCO). The full emergence of a unified Legal Adviser's Office inevitably took longer to achieve. After the second merger, Evans served for a brief period conjointly with Sir James McPetrie (the last Legal Adviser to the old Colonial Office) before becoming, in 1971, the sole Legal Adviser to the FCO. It was not simply a matter of taking over responsibility for the conduct of relations with the independent members of the Commonwealth, but that the new FCO inherited as well the still extensive responsibility for Colonial administration. Along with that came the administrative challenge of managing the amalgamation between the Foreign Office's quite small cadre of international lawyers and the considerable number of seasoned practitioners from the Colonial and Commonwealth service whose experience lay largely in constitutional and public law and in judicial administration. Evans's skill and tact, and his kindness at the personal level, conduced in a major way not just to making light work out of the potential awkwardnesses inherent in having conjoint Legal Advisers in one government ministry, but contributed more enduringly to the successful integration of three widely differing legal staffs into one close unit, with common practices and aspirations, and professional standards of the highest order. Moreover his own post-War experience in Libya stood the FCO in good stead in coping with the manifold practical, administrative, and legal problems as Britain's overseas commitments were harshly and hastily scaled down (e.g. in South-East Asia and the Gulf) and the trickle of decolonization turned into a torrent, all against the background of hostile barracking from within the UN. The present-day habit of concentrating on the few difficult problems that left an awkward legacy (such as Diego Garcia and the British Indian Ocean Territory) too easily obscures the myriad things that were done right, in a time of great turbulence. In all that, Evans stood as a monument of calm good sense, which meant in turn that his advice carried weight with his policy clients and with Ministers in the FCO. And, just as important, the regard in which Evans was held by his professional counterparts across the whole of Whitehall could hardly have been higher, which added weight to the FCO voice in matters of cross-Departmental interest. The responsibilities falling on the Legal Adviser across this vast range of business would have been more than any single individual could have managed, were it not for Evans's innate sense for encouraging and fostering the independent judgement of his staff, while being always available to them for support and guidance. Which is not to say that he was not himself a stickler for accuracy into the most minute detail, but never in a way that dimmed the affection in which he was held by all his staff!

This astute combination of delegation and supervision had the valuable side-effect of allowing Evans the space to put his standing and persistence behind other undertakings outside the FCO proper. He was an assiduous attender at the UN General Assembly for each autumn Session, delivering in 1970 a characteristically careful and meticulous statement of interpretation on the adoption of the Friendly Relations Declaration. He was a firm supporter of the codification process and took a particular interest in the development of the law on privileges and immunities. He lent Stavropoulos (the UN Legal Counsel) strong backing over his initiative that led to the establishment of the UN Commission on International Trade Law (UNCITRAL) in 1966. Closer to home, he was a staunch friend of the Council of Europe, and was one of the prime movers behind the original organization of its consultation meetings in the field of international law in general, later given institutional embodiment in the creation of its 'ad hoc committee' in this field (CAHDI), which continues to be the largest regular gathering of Foreign Ministry Legal Advisers outside the informal annual gathering at the UN each autumn.

By the time he left the FCO in 1975, other momentous changes had taken place as well, most notably of course UK entry into the European Communities (as they then were), and, although the main responsibility for the negotiations and their aftermath was carried by Ian Sinclair as Deputy Legal Adviser, Vincent Evans's open-mindedness and practical sense showed themselves not just in the legislative framework adopted for UK membership, but equally in the arrangements worked out for handling the UK's European business both in Whitehall and in Brussels. Knighted in 1970 (QC in 1973), he was advanced to GCMG on his retirement.

The picture given above misses, however, the key thread that human rights had played—and was still to play—in his professional life. He had been involved early on in the drafting of the UN Declaration on Human Rights, and his time in New York coincided with an important stage in the laborious negotiation of the two International Covenants on human rights, in respect of which he played a key role on his return in securing UK ratification with only a minimum of reservations. And the independence arrangements for colonial territories invariably involved Bills of Rights. So it was logical that, after his retirement from the FCO, he was nominated for and elected to the Human Rights Committee (the supervisory body under the International Covenant on Civil and Political Rights) in 1977, where he remained for seven years. These were the formative years of the Committee, when its all-important procedures were being developed. Evans used all his skill and patience in persuading the more reluctant members (and in particular those from the then Soviet bloc) to accept procedures that would be effective. He approached the substance of the Committee's work with equal care; his leading role in the production of General Comment No. 12 (declaring that the production, testing, possession, deployment and use of nuclear weapons should be prohibited and recognized as crimes against humanity) raised some eyebrows, but reflected a strong personal belief. On the European plane, he became a member and in due course chairman of the Council of Europe's Steering Committee on Human Rights. From that it was another logical step, and a popular one, when he was nominated to succeed Sir Gerald Fitzmaurice on the European Court of Human Rights in 1980.

Evans's style on the ECHR was however noticeably different from his predecessor's: less pugnacious, less prone to dissent, persuasive not by the brilliance of his reasoning but out of respect for his character and principles and his straightforward good sense, as well as his sheer hard work in mastering every detail of the cases with which he dealt. He epitomized the view that it was one of the expected functions of the national member of the Court (or as the case may be of the Commission) to have a complete command of his own country's laws and practices, and to be able to explain them where necessary to his colleagues. Conversely, the great respect in which Evans was held throughout government in his own country contributed materially to the acceptance of adverse decisions out of Strasbourg when they came, and he was wholeheartedly in favour of the incorporation of the Convention into UK law when in due course that occurred.

On the Court, Evans was most often with the majority, nudging the Court from within towards a realistically liberal view of the development of Convention rights. He was by nature careful, rather than cautious, and took it as self-evident that the duty of a judge was to deal with each case on its individual merits. It is thought that he was the first judge ever to put questions to the parties from the bench during oral hearings, so contributing to a livelier and more direct style of hearing. He was generally regarded, by colleagues and Council of Europe officials alike, as a kind and open person who could easily be approached for a talk, and was always ready to listen and to share his own views.

Exactly the same approachability, without distinction as to person or position, characterized Evans's relationships outside the Strasbourg institutions. Even when he was on the Court he would find time to come to meetings with students, and especially after his retirement from the Court he was a very regular attender at events at his own College in Oxford and elsewhere. His genial manner made it easy for students to have access to the working mind of the Court and to a realistic appraisal as much of the ECHR's problems and limits as of its potential.

In his first important case, *LeCompte, van Leuven and De Meyere v Belgium,* decided on 23 June 1981, over the guarantees of fair trial under Article 6 in professional disciplinary proceedings against medical practitioners, Evans in fact dissented, finding Article 6 inapplicable in a case which, to him, did not concern a "civil right or obligation" or a "criminal charge". So also in *Campbell and Fell v UK* of 28 June 1984 about disciplinary proceedings before the Board of Prison Visitors. His position was closer to that of the European Commission of Human Rights, in that he was stricter over the scope of application of Article 6, but more ready to find it to have been violated once it was applicable. By contrast, the majority on the Court was more ready to find Article 6 applicable in principle, but less apt to find a violation in fact.

Article 6 apart, Evans contributed significantly towards the evolution of the Court's case law on civil liberties, approaching the Convention as a 'living instrument' to be applied in cases where injustices occurred on the national level as a result of the application of legislation or jurisprudence that national courts were obliged to respect, but where the human rights court could legitimately assess matters differently on the international level.

Evidence for this approach can be seen as early as his second case on the Court, *Young, James and Webster,* decided on 18 August 1981, in which a 'closed shop' agreement between a trade union and British Rail was found to be in breach of Article 11, followed a short while later by *Dudgeon,* in which the law on homosexual offences in Northern Ireland was found to constitute an unjustified interference with the applicant's private life contrary to Article 8. Both of these were majority decisions, going against the UK, and in both Evans was with the majority. Similarly in two important Article 8 cases: *Silver and others v UK,* decided on 25 March 1983, the first case of its kind to come to the Court, over the stopping of prisoners' correspondence particularly with their lawyers; and *Malone v UK,* decided on 2 August 1984, concerning telephone tapping, the Court found the UK in breach, again with Evans voting with the majority.

Evans participated as well in *Abdulaziz, Cabales, and Balkandali v UK,* decided on 28 May 1985, concerning the rights of foreign spouses to enter the UK, where the Court found the distinction in UK law between male and female spouses to constitute discrimination in breach of Article 14 in combination with Article 8 of the Convention; and in the series of cases in 1987 in which applicants claimed that they had been unable to have the question of access to their children determined by a court, and the Court unanimously found breaches of Article 6.

Other landmark cases in which he sat included *Soering v UK,* decided on 7 July 1989, where the Court examined at length the human rights implications of the 'death row phenomenon' in the USA, before holding—in a decision that has echoed down the years—that the applicant's extradition without guarantees against a death sentence would be a violation of Article 3; and *Thynne, Wilson, and Gunnell v UK,* decided on 25 October 1990, where the Court found that discretionary life sentences, under which prisoners were not able to have the continued lawfulness of their detention decided by a court at reasonable intervals throughout their imprisonment, were in breach of Article 5.

Evans's final cases were the notorious "Spycatcher" cases, decided on 26 November 1991, brought by three leading British newspapers against an interlocutory injunction preventing them from publishing excerpts of a book written, without authorization, about the author's experiences as a member of the Security Service (MI5), the Court unanimously finding a violation on the basis that the interference was not "necessary" within the meaning of Article 10 once the information in question was already in the public domain.

Sir Vincent Evans left the ECHR in 1991. In final retirement he was a doyen of the UK human rights community, and gave his constant support to the creation of the Centre for International Human Rights Law at Essex, which conferred on him an honorary doctorate in 1986.

FRANK BERMAN

Sir Arthur Watts
(1931–2007)

SIR ARTHUR WATTS (1931–2007)

Sir Arthur Desmond Watts KCMG, QC, a member of the Editorial Committee of this *Year Book* from 1990, died on 16 November 2007, having collapsed suddenly a few days previously. He will be remembered as one of the most eminent, capable and constructive international lawyers of the second half of the 20th century and the opening years of this century. Despite the fact that he was already 76 when he died, he gave every impression of being able to continue indefinitely with his vigorous academic output and substantial practice as an international litigator and arbitrator. He will be sorely missed.

Born on 14 November 1931 in England, Arthur spent the first seven years of his life in India, where his father was a colonel in the British Army Education Corps. He was brought up in the strict, disciplined and structured social atmosphere surrounding the families of British army officers stationed in India. Nevertheless, there was no lack of affection in the family. In 1938 he was sent back to England to continue his education, first at preparatory school and then at Haileybury College from 1945–1949. There he became a prominent cricketer—a sport to which he remained much attached for the rest of his life and in which he captained the Shropshire county team in 1955. In his fifties, when he was much engaged in matters relating to Antarctica, he even organised and played in a cricket match in Antarctica at the Bowden Neve, between the Beardmore Casuals, captained by himself, and the Gondwanaland Casuals, led by Chris Beeby, a New Zealand ambassador, subsequently recorded in the *Guinness Book of Records* as the most southerly cricket match ever played.

From Haileybury he went in 1950 to the Royal Military College at Sandhurst for training as an army officer, but after one year he left the Army due to a problem with his right hip—a condition which dogged him throughout his life and led in later years to his constant use of a walking stick. Otherwise he was in good physical shape and so remained until the last year of his life.

In 1952 he entered Downing College, Cambridge, where he first read economics for a year and then changed to law. After completing the Law Tripos in 1954 he stayed on for a further year's specialist study of international law. He obtained a First in the LLB in 1955 and was awarded the Whewell Scholarship in International Law for special merit in that subject. He was also elected a scholar of his College. That summer he spent at the Hague Academy of International Law. In the year 1955–56 he did research which led to his first published work, a substantial note in the *International and Comparative Law Quarterly*, on 'Recent Decisions of the ILO Administrative Tribunal'[1] in which he examined the jurisdictional issues and control over the discretionary powers of those administering international organisations.

Shortly afterwards, well grounded in international law, he entered the Foreign Office, later to be renamed the Foreign and Commonwealth Office (FCO), as a Legal Assistant. His career there was to be outstandingly successful. As is usual, even for the lawyers in the Office, he had three foreign postings, all of them of interest and importance. The first was as Legal Adviser to the British Property Commission in Cairo immediately after the restoration of relations with Egypt following the "Suez" episode of 1956. His task there was to assist in the implementation of the Financial Agreement between the United Kingdom and Egypt,[2] handling the mass of British claims arising out of the seizure of British property by Egypt. In this task he was confronted by many difficult problems involving nationality of claims and the assessment of compensation. Nonetheless, busy though he was, he managed to find time to assist the editor of the *International Law Reports* as contributor of a number of cases from the British Commonwealth and British colonies and dependent territories. Although a seemingly simple task, it was a time-consuming one. This association continued until 1979.

In the years 1957–1960 he showed a special interest in the nationality of ships and the protection of seamen,[3] writing critical reviews[4] of an Italian work by Franco Florio on the nationality of ships and an article on 'The Maintenance of Public Order at Sea and the Nationality of Ships' by Professor McDougal, W T Burke and I A Vlasic.[5] These were followed in 1963 by a substantive review of McDougal and Burke's *The Public Order of the Oceans*.[6]

After three years in Cairo he returned to the Foreign Office in 1962 and spent five years there as an Assistant Legal Adviser engaged in general legal advising. During this period he found time to assist Lord McNair in the preparation of the fourth edition of McNair's classic work on *The Legal Effects of War*, in recognition of which McNair named Arthur as joint author. The edition was published in 1966 and Arthur must have been engaged on it at least from 1962. It expanded considerably on previous

---

[1] (1956) 5 *ICLQ* 483–490.

[2] UK Treaty Series, 1959 No. 35. The role of the British Property Commission was described by Arthur in a note on 'Jurisdictional Immunities of Special Missions: The French Property Commission in Egypt' (1963) 12 *ICLQ* 1383–1399.

[3] 'The Protection of Merchant Ships' (1957) 33 *BYIL* 52–84; 'The Protection of Alien Seamen' (1958) 7 *ICLQ* 691–711.

[4] In, respectively, (1958) 7 *ICLQ* 399–401 and (1960) 16 *Revue Egyptienne de Droit International* 4–10.

[5] (1960) 54 *American Journal of International Law* 25–116. But Arthur's focus was not narrow. It extended to a substantial and approbatory review of Louis Sohn's two volumes of *Cases and Materials on United Nations Law* (1956) and *Basic Documents of the United Nations* (1956) ((1959) 8 *ICLQ* 785–788) and included also a note on the Convention with Germany on the enforcement of judgments (1960) 36 *BYIL* 359–370.

[6] (1963) 19 *Revue Egyptienne de Droit International* 93–98.

editions prepared by McNair alone. The enlargement of the chapter on the meaning of "war", the developments resulting from the Suez crisis of 1956, the acts of governments dispossessed by belligerent occupation and the reflection of the enormous output of judicial decisions mentioned in the Preface, though not specifically attributed to Arthur, undoubtedly demonstrate his extensive collaboration.

In 1967 he received his second posting, this time to the British Embassy in Bonn as Legal Adviser, where he was required to deal with the many legal problems arising out of the continuing division of Germany, including in particular the application of the Bonn Convention of 1952, the status of Berlin and the boundaries of Germany. He remained there for three years (1967–1969) before returning to London to become an Assistant Solicitor in the Law Officers' Department for the period 1969–1970. There he was engaged on those questions of international law that arose in the work of the Attorney General and the Solicitor General, in particular those referred by the FCO to them for their Opinion.[7]

In 1970 he returned to the FCO with the rank of Legal Counsellor until, in 1973, he received his third overseas posting, this time to the United Kingdom Permanent Representation to the European Communities in Brussels. There, he became heavily involved in the legal issues arising out of Britain's recent entry into the Common Market. Following his time in Brussels, he returned to London, first as a Legal Counsellor, 1977–1982, then from 1982 to 1987 as Deputy Legal Adviser and finally as Legal Adviser from 1987 until his retirement in 1991.

In all these positions he acquitted himself with great merit. He is remembered as a leader of profound knowledge, understanding and kindliness, most approachable, and forthcoming with advice of the highest quality fully attuned to political realities. He described the work of the Legal Advisers' office in the note already referred to.[8] In 1980 he led the British delegation to the meeting in Manila of the UN Charter Review Committee. Two years later he became heavily involved in developments relating to Antarctica, an area which was to become one of his principal interests. Between 1982 and 1988 he led the UK delegations in the Antarctic Minerals Negotiations and the Antarctic Consultative Meetings in Canberra and Brussels. From this activity there emerged a number of articles[9] on Antarctica as well as, somewhat later, his lectures on *International Law and the Antarctic Treaty System* delivered in

---

[7] The nature of this work was described in Arthur's article on 'International Law and International Relations: United Kingdom Practice' (1991) 2 *European Journal of International Law* 157, 159.

[8] Ibid.

[9] Review of Auburn, *Antarctic Law and Politics* in *New Scientist* (22 July 1982) 255–256; 'Liability for Activities in Antarctica:Who Pays the Bill to Whom?' in Wolfrum (ed) *Antarctic Challenge II* (1986) 147–161; 'The Antarctic mineral resources: negotiations for a mineral resources regime' in Triggs (ed), *The Antarctic Treaty Regime—Law, Environment and Resources* (1987), 164–175; 'Lessons to be Learned from the Mineral Resources Negotiations' in Wolfrum (ed) *Antarctic Challenge III* (1988) 319–331; 'The Convention on the Regulation of Antarctic Mineral Resource Activities 1988' (1990) 39 *ICLQ* 169–182; 'The Present Antarctic System of Environmental Protection' in Francioni

Cambridge in the Hersch Lauterpacht Memorial Lecture series in 1992 and published in the same year—a substantial volume of 300 pages. As he noted in a letter seeking official consent to the publication of one of his articles, he and Dr Heap, the Head of the Polar Regions Section of the South America Department of the FCO, were "directly responsible for the conduct of our Antarctic policies". He also found time to prepare a number of case notes for an *Encyclopaedic Dictionary of International Law* originally conceived by Clive Parry but published only after his death.[10] Arthur's contributions were repeated in the second edition in 2003, but without being attributed to him.

In 1985–86 he was closely concerned with the preparation of the Australia Act, enacted in 1986, which terminated the power of the Parliament of the United Kingdom to legislate for Australia and removed restraints on the powers of the Australian State legislatures, leaving them only subject to the Commonwealth constitution.[11] From 1987 to 1989 he was a member of the Western European Union Appeals Board. In 1985 he led the UK Delegation to the Preparatory Meeting for the CSCE Human Rights meeting in Ottawa; from 1987 to 1989 he was Chairman of the Council of Europe Committee of Experts on Public International Law. He became well known in the United Nations when he was the UK Representative in the Sixth Committee of the General Assembly at the sessions in 1987–1990. In 1991 he was the leader of the UK Delegation at the CSCE meeting in Valletta on the Peaceful Settlement of Disputes. At the same time as all this, he was the Agent for the United Kingdom in the complex and extended arbitration with the United States regarding the level of user charges at Heathrow Airport under the bilateral "Bermuda 2" agreement. The dispute was eventually settled in May 1994 and the proceedings were discontinued.[12]

Retirement from the FCO in 1991 led to the opening up of new avenues of involvement in international law. Having become a QC in 1988, he immediately entered practice and joined Chambers at 20 Essex Street, London as an adviser and arbitrator in international litigation. His reputation as a compelling advocate was firmly established by his appearance in the oral proceedings before the International Court of Justice in the case unsuccessfully brought by New Zealand and Australia against France in 1995 in an attempt to reopen the proceedings in the 1974 *Nuclear Tests* case. France took the, for it unprecedented, step of enlisting the help of a non-French advocate, namely, Arthur. The elegance and persuasiveness of his performance occasioned the highest praise, not least from those against whom he appeared. This appearance in the ICJ

(ed), *International Environmental Law for Antarctica* (1992) 31–52 (This article is an updated version of a paper delivered at a symposium in Siena in June 1990).

[10] Parry and Grant (eds) (Oceana Publications, Inc, 1986).
[11] See his note on the Act in 'The Australia Act, 1986' (1987) 36 *ICLQ* 132–139.
[12] 102 *ILR* 215.

was followed by others: the *Case Concerning the Gabčíkovo-Nagymaros Project (Hungary/Slovakia)* on behalf of Slovakia, (for which he was awarded a high Slovak honour by the President of Slovakia (the Double White Cross);[13] the *Land and Maritime Boundary between Cameroon and Nigeria*[14] on behalf of Nigeria; the case between Indonesia and Malaysia concerning *Sovereignty over Pulau Ligitan and Pulau Sipadan* on behalf of Indonesia;[15] and the Advisory Opinion on *Legal Consequences of the Construction of a Wall in the Occupied Palestinian Territory* on behalf of Jordan.[16] At the time of his death, he was engaged in the preparatory stages of a number of other cases.

He was also an active arbitrator, notably in the *Saluka* case in the ICSID system. Particularly important, and extended, however, was his participation in the Eritrea-Ethiopia Boundary Commission established in 2001. Many parts of the Delimitation Decision produced by the Commission in April 2002 bear the stamp of his reasoning and style.[17] Then, between 2002 and 2007, he was closely involved in the attempts of the Commission to carry out the demarcation of the boundary as required by the treaty under which it was operating. Despite the fact that he had been nominated by Ethiopia, he brought to the work of the Commission a completely impartial approach. His contribution was informed by diplomatic wisdom and considerable drafting skill directed towards expressing the Commission's views in a manner most likely to be acceptable to both sides. He was much involved in the preparation of the Commission's Statement of November 2006[18] in which it resorted to the unusual, but in the circumstances unavoidable, device of demarcating the boundary by precise coordinates as opposed to the actual placement of boundary pillars.

His work in practice did not, however, stem the flow of his academic and related writing which was quite wide-ranging. His involvement in Antarctic matters had already led to a series of thoughtful analyses of the legal issues arising in that connection.[19]

A notable contribution of this period was his essay for the *Festschrift* in honour of Geraldo do Nascimento e Silva, published in 2000, on 'Negotiation and International Law'.[20] This examined the concept and form of negotiation, the obligation to negotiate, the requirements for negotiation and the legal implications of the conduct of negotiation.

---

[13] *ICJ Reports* 1997, p 7.

[14] Preliminary Objections, *ICJ Reports* 1998, p 275; Merits, *ICJ Reports* 2002, p 303.

[15] *ICJ Reports* 2002, p 625.

[16] *ICJ Reports* 2004, p 136.

[17] *Decision regarding Delimitation of the Border between the State of Eritrea and the Federal Democratic Republic of Ethiopia* (2002) 130 *ILR* 1.

[18] *Statement regarding Demarcation of the Border between the State of Eritrea and the Federal Democratic Republic of Ethiopia* (2006) 130 *ILR* 147.

[19] See above n 9.

[20] Casella (ed) *Dimensão Internacional do Direito, Estudos en Homenagen a G E do Nascimentto e Silva* (2000), 519–536.

Amongst other points raised in the article, he expressed doubts about the correctness of the extension by the ICJ in the Advisory Opinion on *Legality of the Threat or Use of Nuclear Weapons* of the obligation undertaken by the Parties in Article VI of the Treaty on the Non-Proliferation of Nuclear Weapons 1963 "to pursue negotiations in good faith on effective measures relating to cessation of the nuclear arms race" to one requiring them to bring such negotiations to a successful conclusion.

Many other publications followed during the 1990s and early 2000s, in part at a time when he was still busy on the ninth edition of Oppenheim.[21]

Most prominent amongst them was the substantial course of lectures that he delivered in 1994 at the Academy of International Law in The Hague on 'The Legal Position in International Law of Heads of State, Heads of Government and Foreign Ministers'.[22] His views were frequently referred to in the speeches in the House of Lords in the *Pinochet* extradition case in 1999.[23]

At about the same time, he became involved in an initiative then being promoted in the United Nations by Prince Hans Adam II of Liechtenstein for acknowledgement of the right of self-determination on what was called "the community level", as opposed to a "national" or "peoples" level. Although it is not clear from the available material whether Arthur was

[21] They included 'International Law and International Relations: United Kingdom Practice', above n 7; 'The International Court of Justice: Efficiency of Procedure and Working Methods' (with Bowett, Crawford and Sinclair) (1996) 45 *ICLQ Supplement* 1 and (with additional comments) in Bowett et al, *The International Court of Justice: Process, Practice and Procedure,* (1997) 27–84; 'The Present Antarctic System of Environmental Protection', above n 9; 'The International Rule of Law' (1993) 36 *German Yearbook of International Law,* 15–45; 'Delimitation in the Aegean Sea: Implications of Recent International Judgments' in *Aegean Issues: Problems—Legal and Political Matrix,* (Foreign Policy Institute, Ankara, 1995), 111–145; 'Nationality of Claims: some relevant concepts' in Lowe and Fitzmaurice (eds) *Fifty Years of the International Court* (1996), 242–439; 'The Relevance of International Law' in Glas CCCLXXXIII de l'Académie serbe des sciences et des arts, Classe des sciences sociales, No 28, 3–9 (This paper was based on a talk given on 24 April 1997 to the Serbian Academy of Arts and Science, Belgrade); 'The Importance of International Law' in Byres (ed) *The Role of Law in International Politics* (2000) 31–44; 'Enhancing the Effectiveness of Procedures of International Dispute Settlement' (2001) 5 *Max Planck Yearbook of United Nations Law* 21–39; 'The International Court and the Continuing Customary International Law of Treaties' in Ando, McWhinney and Wolfrum (eds), *Liber Amicorum Judge Shigeru Oda* (2002), 251–265; 'New Practice Directions of the International Court of Justice' (2002) 1 *The Law and Practice of International Courts and Tribunals* 247–256; 'The ICJ's Practice Directions of 30 July 2004' (2004) 3 *The Law and Practice of International Courts and Tribunals* 385–394; 'Physical Barriers to Armed Infiltration: Self-Defence and Israel's Wall in the Occupied Palestinian Territories' in Crnić-Grotić and Matulović (eds) *International Law and the Use of Force at the Turn of the Centuries: Essays in Honour of V D Degan* (2005), 239–253; 'The Art of Apology' in Ragazzi (ed) *International Responsibility Today: Essays in Honour of Oscar Schachter* (2005), 107–116; 'The Commonwealth and International Law' (2006) 15 *The Commonwealth Lawyer* 21–26 (This article was the main speech at the Commonwealth Lawyers' Association meeting in London, 22 June 2006); 'Observer Status for Taiwan's Health Entity in the World Health Assembly' (2007) 2 *London Law Review* 1119–1139 (A footnote by the author states: "The article is an adapted version of an Opinion prepared by the author and is published with the approval of those for whom the Opinion was prepared."); 'The ICJ's Practice Directions IX *bis* and IX *ter* (2006)', to be published in the forthcoming issue of *The Law and Practice of International Courts and Tribunals*.

[22] Subsequently published in (1994–III) 247 *Recueil des Cours* 9–130.

[23] See eg *R v Bow Street Metropolitan Stipendiary Magistrate, ex parte Pinochet Ugarte (No. 3)* [2000] 1 AC 147, 203–4 (Lord Browne-Wilkinson); 210–211 (Lord Goff of Chieveley, dissenting).

actually the draftsman of 'The Liechtenstein Draft Convention on Self-Determination Through Self-Administration', there can be little doubt that he played a major role in its formulation. By 1994 a full draft had been prepared and Arthur produced a detailed commentary on it.[24] A key idea in the draft was that of "self-administration". As stated by Arthur:

[I]t is the very essence of the Liechtenstein proposals that while independence can never be completely excluded, it is not their central aim. On the contrary, it is felt that by providing for self-administration, communities may feel their aspirations to self-determination are adequately met and they are no longer compelled to seek full independence.

For this purpose, a "community" was defined as meaning "the members of a distinct group which inhabits a limited area within a State and possesses a sufficient degree of organisation as such a group for the effective application of the relevant practises of this Convention". Arthur's Commentary provides important elaboration of the concept. Following on it, he prepared two substantial contributions for the *Princeton Encyclopedia of Self-Determination*[25] which he completed in October 2006. One was on 'Sovereignty', the other on 'Nation-State'. He also wrote four substantial pieces for the new edition of the *Max Planck Encyclopedia of Public International Law*. His last academic writing appears to have been his contribution to the *Liber Amicorum* for Judge Thomas Mensah on 'Preparation for International Litigation'.[26] At the time of his death he was planning two further books on 'The International Litigation Process' and 'The Work of the Eritrea-Ethiopia Boundary Commission'.

From March 1996 until June 2001 much of his time was taken up with the meetings, discussions, drafting and travel associated with his role as the High Representative's Special Negotiator for Succession Issues in respect of the States that had formed part of Yugoslavia prior to its break-up in 1991. In effect, Arthur acted as a mediator in arranging the distribution of the assets and some liabilities of the former Yugoslavia. The negotiation of a settlement of such delicate and divisive issues required the energetic application by Arthur of all his diplomatic acumen and drafting skills. The successful result was a great tribute to his dedicated performance.[27]

Alongside all of this he was busy preparing a collection of materials relating to the work of the International Law Commission of the United

---

[24] See Danspreckgruber (ed), *The Self-Determination of Peoples* (2001). Arthur's Commentary (undated) is printed in full as Appendix B, 365–381, of this volume. 1994 is given as the date of the draft Convention which is the subject of the Commentary.

[25] Not yet published.

[26] Ndiaye and Wolfrum (eds) *Law of the Sea, Environmental Law and Settlement of Disputes* (2007) 327–340.

[27] For a description of the background to the negotiation, see Arthur's article on 'State Succession: Some Recent Practical Legal Problems' in Götz, Selmer and Wolfrum (eds) *Liber Amicorum Günther Jaenicke—Zum 85. Geburtstag* (1999), 397–426, esp 405 et seq. For the Agreement on Succession Issues, signed in June 1992, with an introductory note by Arthur, see (2002) 41 *ILM* 1.

Nations (ILC) from its establishment in 1949 until 1998. This was published in 1999 in three substantial volumes[28] and comprised the treaties adopted on the basis of ILC draft articles, the final draft articles that had not by then resulted in the conclusion of a treaty and reports other than final draft articles. The value of the collection as a reference work was enhanced by a number of introductory notes by Arthur, of which the opening one was a particularly helpful history of the work of the ILC and an assessment of its role within the international legal system. In November 2004 he gave the Roche Lecture at New College, Oxford, on 'International Law for the Twenty-First Century'.[29]

Though much of his writing tended to be of an expository nature it was always accompanied by shrewd comment. Here and there are secreted gems with much broader implications. As an example, here is what he had to say about the possibility that a political department in the FCO might recommend a course of action inconsistent with the legal advice given to it:

It has already been stressed that it is extremely rare for a recommendation to be put forward which is inconsistent with the legal advice that has been given. But what if that were to happen? Where the British Government is concerned, and certainly in my own experience, this is a hypothetical question with respect to matters of any substance or importance. However, some indications can be given as to what would be likely to happen should these circumstances arise, as they reflect certain general procedural aspects of the way in which the FCO works. First, there would be no special authorisation procedure for such a course of action. What would happen is that the Department would, in the usual way, put forward its recommendation for the action to be taken, and when doing so would state that the legal advice was that that action would be contrary to international law. It would remain for those who are responsible for policy to decide whether to accept the recommendation or whether to reject it. Second, there is no particular level laid down at which such a decision would have to be taken. This would depend on the importance of the subject, including the significance of any unlawfulness which might be involved: in practice, however, such a decision on a matter of any importance would be taken by a Minister. Third, if a decision were taken to embark on a certain course of action notwithstanding the contrary legal advice, there would indeed be some negative internal reaction—mainly, perhaps, from the Legal Adviser, but also from others in the FCO. For it would be seen by all to be a very serious matter for the United Kingdom to act in a way which was contrary to its international obligations. However, as has already been noted, this is all hypothetical, and assumes that a decision to act unlawfully has been taken. In practice, long before matters reach that stage senior officials and Ministers would enquire whether there was not some other way, within the law, of achieving the same object. Fourth, and finally, if legal advice were given that proposed action contrary to international law, this would not in any special way be kept secret, although the general rule in the United Kingdom is that, under the Public Records Act, official papers are not open to the public for 30

---

[28] (Oxford University Press 1999). [29] Not yet published.

years. At the end of that period the papers generally become available for public inspection in the Public Record Office.[30]

Surveying the whole extent of his writing, one is bound to be impressed not only by the quality of the individual items, but also by the breadth of his knowledge, the scope of his interests and the clarity of his presentation. He was the very model of what a modern international lawyer should be—totally familiar with the whole subject, possessed of the skill to expound and comment on it in a readily understandable manner and able to draft in a truly professional style, all this combined with a full understanding of relevant political realities.

His was a most equable character. Not a man to be flustered or troubled by pressure, he responded to all the demands made upon him thoughtfully and skilfully. He was always ready to take on more work if he thought it was likely to be interesting and his help was needed. A strikingly modest man, he made no display of his considerable knowledge and professional standing. He never sought the academic recognition for which he was undoubtedly qualified. He did not look for a professorial appointment after his retirement from the FCO. He could have got a Cambridge LL.D. on the basis of his book on Antarctica, his work on the ninth edition of Oppenheim and the collection of his articles, but he appears never to have thought of these possibilities or, if he did, did not think it necessary to pursue them. Yet, though he was by no means self-assertive, he was firm in the expression of his opinions—and his positions were so soundly based and cogently expressed that they usually prevailed.

His standing and achievements were recognised by a number of important appointments. He became a CMG in 1977 and a KCMG in 1989. He was elected an Honorary Fellow of Downing College, Cambridge in 1999. In 1998 he became a Member of the Panel of Arbitrators under the UN Law of the Sea Convention and in 2003 a member of the British National Group of the Permanent Court of Arbitration. From 1992 to 1998 he was President of the British Branch of the International Law Association and thereafter sat on its Council of Management. In 2006 he was elected an Honorary Fellow of the Lauterpacht Centre for International Law in the University of Cambridge at which he had for some years led the special course in international law for FCO officials. Jordan honoured him with the Order of Independence in 2007.

He led a highly organised and stable private life. Of his interests outside the law, two were most prominent. In recent years he was much engaged in the task of reconstructing his home at Tortington Priory near Arundel in West Sussex and developing its gardens.[31] He became a trustee of the

---

[30] 'International Law and International Relations: United Kingdom Practice', above n 7, 162 [footnote omitted].
[31] See *Tortington and the Black Canons* (2002), written and compiled by the Boxgrove History Group.

Sussex Heritage Trust in 2002 and Chairman in 2006. And he retained an abiding love for cricket, the game in which he had excelled as a young man.

He married Iris Collier in 1957 and they had two children. In 1986 they separated amicably but remained good friends and continued to live near each other. Thereafter, Cecilia Gillette became his loyal and devoted partner for the rest of his life. He is buried in the churchyard of Boxgrove Priory.

ELIHU LAUTERPACHT

THE LAW AND PROCEDURE OF THE INTERNATIONAL COURT OF JUSTICE 1960–1989

SUPPLEMENT, 2007: PARTS FOUR, FIVE AND SIX

By HUGH THIRLWAY*

* © Visiting Professor, University of Leiden; Visiting Professor, University of Bristol; Former Principal Legal Secretary, International Court of Justice.

PART FIVE

III. Points of Substantive Law

Division A: The Law of the Sea

INTRODUCTION

The present article is the third supplemental article intended to complete and bring up to date the series published in this Year Book between 1989 and 2003. That series dealt with the jurisprudence of the International Court, beginning from the date of the last decisions dealt with by Sir Gerald Fitzmaurice in his earlier series of articles with the same title. Initially, the *terminus ad quem* was to be 1989, but as the years passed this became unrealistic, and each article dealt with the decisions given up to the date of publication. The structure of the series was however analytical rather than chronological. This produced, in the work as a whole, a lop-sided effect; the treatment of subjects dealt with in the earlier articles did not take account of later developments, while subjects reserved for later treatment benefited from examination of all the case-law up to that later date.

Some form of supplement was therefore required: the first such supplemental article appeared in the 2005 volume of the Year Book, and the second in the 2006 volume. In the latter article, it was explained that the writer had hoped 'that the present essay would complete the work of supplementing and updating the original articles, but this has not been possible, largely because of the amount of new material to be discussed, so a further instalment will be needed to round off the series'. This explan-ation has unfortunately to be renewed here; the acceleration in the work of the Court, which, as its President recently proudly recalled, means that there is no longer a backlog of undecided cases, and in particular judicial advances in the law of the sea, examined below, have afforded a consid-erable amount of material which could not be ignored. Hope, however, springs eternal: the 2008 Year Book may yet see the end of the series.

The present article supplements Parts Four,[1] Five,[2] and Six[3] of the original series of articles. The structure of that series (derived from that of the articles of Fitzmaurice) has been maintained so far as possible,[4] to facilitate comparison and confrontation with the earlier articles. Some new sections, indicated by underlined titles, have however had to be introduced. The most recent decision treated here is the Judgment of 8 October 2007 in the case concerning the *Territorial and Maritime Dispute between Honduras and Nicaragua in the Caribbean Sea*.[5]

---

[1] (1992) *BYIL* 1.   [2] (1993) *BYIL* 1.
[3] (1994) *BYIL* 1.
[4] Considerable rearrangement has however been necessary in the Division on the Law of the Sea.
[5] Some reference has been made to the decision of 13 December 2007 in the *Territorial Dispute (Nicaragua/Colombia)*, given just before the text of the present article was completed.

PART FOUR[6]

II. TREATY INTERPRETATION AND OTHER TREATY POINTS (CONTINUED)

Division B: Other Treaty Points

CHAPTER I: PRELIMINARY MATTERS

1. THE *PACTUM DE CONTRAHENDO* AND THE 'OBLIGATION TO NEGOTIATE'

It was suggested in the earlier article in this series that 'international law has acquired, on the impulsion of the *North Sea* decision, and now of the United Nations Convention on the Law of the Sea, a genuine *pactum de contrahendo*',[7] in the sense of an 'obligation to reach agreement'.[8] It was there explained that, although the obligation to negotiate a solution to a maritime delimitation dispute provided for in Articles 74 and 83 of the Convention does not clearly predefine its solution, so as to become, in effect, the end of the process rather than the beginning, it can nevertheless 'be judicially enforced by reference to the amorphous concept of equity'.[9] The exact manner in which it would be so enforced is not clear from the *North Sea* decision, but as also observed in the earlier article, that such was the intention of the Court emerges from, in particular, the dissent of Judge Morelli on the point.

In the case of the *Land and Maritime Boundary between Cameroon and Nigeria*, Nigeria in a preliminary objection invoked this obligation to negotiate, but the procedural consequence that it attributed to the alleged failure of Cameroon to comply with it was that the request for a delimitation by the Court should be *pro tanto* inadmissible. However, the decision of the Court appears clearly to have thrown over the idea of a general obligation to negotiate in customary law, in relation to maritime delimitation disputes, as conceived by the Court in the *North Sea* case, since it rejected the Nigerian objection on the ground that:

in this case, it has not been seised on the basis of Article 36, paragraph 1, of the Statute, and, in pursuance of it, in accordance with Part XV of the United Nations Convention on the Law of the Sea relating to the settlement of disputes arising between the parties to the Convention with respect to its interpretation or application. It has been seised on the basis of declarations made under

---

[6] This Part is a supplement to (1992) *BYIL* 1.

[7] Ibid, 10. Aust suggests that the term *pactum de contrahendo* is one of those Latin phrases that 'can conceal more than they reveal', and that its exact meaning is 'uncertain': A Aust, *Modern Treaty Law and Practice* (2007), 25 (hereinafter: Aust, *Modern Treaty Law and Practice*).

[8] Ibid, 8.   [9] Ibid, 10.

Article 36, paragraph 2, of the Statute, which declarations do not contain any condition relating to prior negotiations to be conducted within a reasonable time period.[10]

Nigeria did in fact refer in support of its objection to the provisions of Articles 74 and 83 of the Convention, as the Court noted;[11] but it is clear from its seventh preliminary objection that it was relying, not on the text of those articles as such, but on the wider principle identified in the *North Sea* case.[12] It argued that 'the position under the 1982 Convention is the same as that under general international law. Rather than adopting the formula of Article 6 of the 1958 Geneva Convention on the Continental Shelf, the 1982 Convention makes a *renvoi* to the rules of general international law, as developed by the Court.'[13]

The Court thus treated the matter as one of the specific conditions attached to the process of seising the Court under a given instrument, rather than as an element of the law of maritime delimitation.[14] The decision therefore tacitly declined to give effect to that element, and thus effectively reversed the *North Sea* decision on the point.

2. PRIVITY OF CONTRACT: PRIVATE LAW AGREEMENTS AND PARALLEL TREATIES

A problem that has arisen in a number of boundary delimitation cases (maritime or terrestrial) is that of the effect, if any, to be given to agreements made by persons or authorities not normally in a position to commit the State to which they belonged. In some circumstances such agreements might have legal effect by the process demonstrated in the *Barcelona Traction* case, discussed in the previous article, whereby 'contracts and agreements between private interests may lead to a subsequent inter-State agreement endorsing or referring to the terms thus privately agreed;'[15] or may operate in equity, or internationally within the limits of the responsibilities of the person concerned. Such a result may seem the more desirable in this context, since the agreements involved in boundary matters involve more than private interests, namely regional—or even national—arrangements in the interests of the States concerned. However, in practice these agreements (or alleged agreements) are rather such as to fall within the class of situations contemplated by Article 8 of the Vienna Convention on the Law

---

[10] [1998] ICJ Rep 321–322, para 109.
[11] Ibid, 320, para 104.
[12] Nigerian Preliminary Objections, paras 7.18–7.20.
[13] Ibid, para 7.26.
[14] As was pointed out by Judge *ad hoc* Ajibola in his dissent, it was 'not a question of jurisdiction under Article 36(2) of the Statute but one of admissibility': [1998] ICJ Rep 415.
[15] (1992) *BYIL* 1, 12 (footnote omitted).

of Treaties, referring to the performance, by a person not authorized to represent a State, of 'an act relating to the conclusion of a treaty'. The *Barcelona Traction* case on the other hand involved an agreement that at the time of making did not involve any State-to-State relationship. The cases referred to above will therefore be considered under the heading of the forms of conclusion of treaties, as a matter of representation of the State for this purpose.[16]

---

[16] See Chapter II, Section 3(2) below.

CHAPTER II: CONDITIONS OF THE FORMATION OF AGREEMENT

1. Private Law Analogies

(1) Offer and acceptance[17]

In the earlier article in this series, it was observed that '[i]n general, the formality of a treaty as an instrument for embodying or recording consent renders superfluous any enquiry into the steps by which its precise terms were arrived at', and it was suggested that for this reason 'the familiar common-law concepts of offer and acceptance, the backbone of the law of contracts, usually have no role to play in the law of treaties.'[18] Some exceptions to this were noted, including the jurisdictional problems in the *Monetary Gold* case.

A further situation in which the creation of an international legal agreement may be effected by a process analogous to offer and acceptance is the system of acceptances of the Court's jurisdiction under the optional clause of Article 36 of the Statute; and it was ably analysed in these terms by Vice-President Weeramantry at the preliminary objection stage of the case of the *Land and Maritime Boundary between Cameroon and Nigeria*. In his survey of the basic principles underlying the creation of consensual commitment, which he insisted are equally applicable in the field of international law, the following is a key passage:

> Since the so-called compulsory jurisdiction clause is consensual in its architecture, one must satisfy oneself that the results of the Court's Judgment are in conformity with the legal concept of consensus. A State lodging a declaration under Article 36, paragraph 2, performs a twofold juristic act. On the one hand, it is making an *offer* to every other State that has not already filed a declaration that it will be bound by its terms to such State, upon that State making a declaration in accordance with Article 36. On the other hand, a declaration made in terms of Article 36 is an *acceptance* of the offers made by other States which have already filed such a declaration. A declaration duly made under Article 36 is thus both an offer to some States and an acceptance of the offer already made by other States.[19]

The question before the Court, on the basis of a Nigerian preliminary objection, was whether the Court should follow the precedent of the *Right of Passage over Indian Territory* case, and base jurisdiction on an acceptance (by Cameroon) of the optional clause system of which the other party (Nigeria) had had no notice at the time that proceedings were instituted. The Court held that it did have jurisdiction on that basis;

---

[17] A reservation to a multilateral treaty may be seen as an offer to conclude a different convention with those parties willing to accept the reservation; *cf* Chapter II, Section 3(3), below.
[18] (1992) *BYIL* 1, 12.
[19] [1998] ICJ Rep 368.

Vice-President Weeramantry disagreed. On the basis of his analysis of the structure of the system as offer and acceptance, he proceeded to examine the question 'whether the acceptance needs to be communicated' for an agreement to come into existence.[20] His conclusion that this was so, that optional-clause declarations 'fall into the category in which the offeror must know that his offer has been accepted' for the agreement as to jurisdiction to be created;[21] and that the deposit of the declaration with the Secretary-General was insufficient, being 'clearly not tantamount to a notification to all the world'.[22]

Vice-President Weeramantry was in effect invoking an alleged 'general principle of law' to be derived from the consistent provisions of municipal legal systems; and outside the special system of the optional clause a good case can certainly be made for the existence of such a principle. The Court did not examine the question on that basis at all: it referred first to its own previous decision in the *Right of Passage* case, and stated that '[t]he real question is whether, in this case, there is cause not to follow the reasoning and conclusions of earlier cases.'[23] Having thus established, in effect, a presumption against any departure from the earlier ruling, it dealt with the matter merely by considering whether the adoption of the Vienna Convention on the Law of Treaties justified any such departure.[24] It noted that the International Law Commission had examined the question whether, in the case of the deposit of an instrument with the depositary of a treaty, 'the deposit itself establishes the legal nexus between the depositing State and other contracting States or whether the legal nexus arises only upon their being informed by the depositary'.[25] The Commission had in effect followed the Court's solution in the *Right of Passage*, that notification to other States was not necessary for the nexus to be established, and in 1998 the Court concluded that '[t]hat solution should be maintained'.[26]

The Court's finding does not however throw doubt on Vice-President Weeramantry's analysis of the role of offer and acceptance in the formation of contract, and its probable existence also in the background to the law of the conclusion of treaties. In 1957 the Court had found in effect that the optional clause of the Statute had established a special regime, in which States had accepted in advance that they would become linked to each other by the 'compulsory jurisdiction' system without having the right of refusal, as it were, as each new State joined the optional-clause group; and thirty years later the Court saw no reason to depart from that conclusion. What the Court had rejected in 1957 was not the offer-and-acceptance analysis of the optional clause system, but the thesis that

[20] Ibid, 370–373.   [21] Ibid, 373.
[22] Ibid, 372.   [23] Ibid, 292, para 28.
[24] Ibid, 293–294, paras 29–31.
[25] Ibid 294, para 31, quoting *ILC Yearbook 1966-II*, 201.
[26] Ibid.

this analysis entailed 'notification to the offeror that his offer has been accepted'.

In the case of the *Legal Consequences of the Construction of a Wall in the Occupied Palestinian Territory*, the Court referred to the position of Palestine in relation to the Fourth Geneva Convention in terms suggestive of offer and acceptance. On 7 June 1972 Palestine gave a unilateral undertaking to apply that Convention, and this was accepted as 'valid' (whatever that may mean) by Switzerland as the depositary State.[27] The Court mentioned this fact in the same breath as its recording that Israel and Jordan were parties to the Fourth Convention, with the apparent implied conclusion that the provisions of the Convention were in force as treaty-law between those three States or entities.[28]

(2) Consideration

No further mention has been made in the Court's decisions of the common law doctrine of consideration as a requirement for a valid contract, referred to in the *Fisheries Jurisdiction* case between the UK and Iceland, and discussed in the previous article.[29] Something analogous to, or reminiscent of, this doctrine is however to be found in a passage of the judgment in the case of the *Gabčíkovo-Nagymaros Project (Hungary/ Slovakia)*. A 1977 Treaty had provided for that Project to be carried out by Hungary and Czechoslovakia jointly, on the Danube where it formed the boundary between them; when Hungary in effect withdrew, and endeavoured to terminate the Treaty, Czechoslovakia went ahead with a modified version of its share of the works, known as Variant C. Hungary claimed that Variant C was a violation of the Treaty, and Czechoslovakia retorted that it was 'essentially no more than what Hungary had already agreed to' in the Treaty, and that 'the only modifications made were those which had become necessary' because of Hungary's backing-out.[30] The Court's ruling was as follows:

It is true that Hungary, in concluding the 1977 Treaty, had agreed to the damming of the Danube and the diversion of its waters into the bypass canal. But it was only in the context of a joint operation and a sharing of its benefits that Hungary had given its consent. The suspension and withdrawal of that consent constituted a violation of Hungary's legal obligations, demonstrating, as it did,

---

[27] [2004] ICJ Rep 173, para 91.

[28] The position of Jordan was relevant because of an argument by Israel that the territories occupied by it in 1967 were not at that time under the sovereignty of Jordan, and thus fell outside the precise terms of Article 2, paragraph 2, of the Convention: ibid, 174, para 93. The Court rejected this interpretation (ibid, 177, para 101), but did not explain in what respect the status of Palestine in relation to the Convention was relevant to the argument.

[29] (1992) *BYIL* 1, 16–18. That case may however be seen as rejecting the view of Judge Jessup that '[t]he doctrine of "consideration", which plays so large a part in Anglo-American contract law, has not been taken over into the international law of treaties': separate opinion in *South West Africa Cases,* [1962] ICJ Rep 403.

[30] [1997] ICJ Rep 54, para 78.

the refusal by Hungary of joint operation; but that cannot mean that Hungary forfeited its basic right to an equitable and reasonable sharing of the resources of an international watercourse.[31]

Thus before the Treaty was concluded, Hungary possessed certain rights in relation to the Danube; by the Treaty, it gave up or limited some of those rights, in exchange for benefits to be conferred by Czechoslovakia under the Treaty. Those benefits were not forthcoming, yet Czechoslovakia was claiming still to operate, in breach of the pre-Treaty rights of Hungary, in reliance on Hungary's commitments in the Treaty. This might be regarded as a failure of the consideration for Hungary's renunciation or limitation of its pre-Treaty rights; but it is curious that Hungary was entitled to insist on those rights even though the failure of consideration was the result of Hungary's own withdrawal from the Treaty.

In the earlier article it was observed that there is a link between this concept and that of 'fundamental change of circumstances' as a ground for termination of a treaty. Attention may also be drawn to the distinction made by the Court between bilateral treaties and multilateral law-making treaties, in relation to the *exceptio non adimpleti contractus*.

In the case of *Avena and Other Mexican Nationals (Mexico v United States of America)*, the Court rejected an objection made by the United States to the admissibility of the Mexican application on the ground that 'Mexico should not be allowed to invoke against the United States standards [of compliance with the Convention on Consular Relations] that Mexico does not follow in its own practice'.[32] In rejecting this objection, the Court invoked 'the nature of the Vienna Convention', which 'lays down certain standards to be observed by all States parties, with a view to the "unimpeded conduct of consular relations"'.[33] The underlying thought appears to be that, whereas in a bilateral treaty each State expects to obtain, in exchange for performance of its own commitments, performance by the other State of those which it has undertaken, acceptance of a multilateral treaty of the type of the Consular Relations Convention is related to the general desirability of the objective of the Convention, so that if one of the other parties fails to perform its obligations there has been no 'failure of consideration'. As the Court observed in the case of *Reservations to the Genocide Convention*:

In such a convention the contracting States do not have interests of their own; they merely have, one and all, a common interest, namely, the accomplishment of those high purposes which are the *raison d'être* of the convention.[34]

---

[31] Ibid.

[32] [2004] ICJ Rep 38, para 45. On this case, see further below, Chapter III, Section 2.

[33] Ibid, para 47.

[34] [1951] ICJ Rep 23. See also the Third Report on the Law of Treaties by Sir Gerald Fitzmaurice, *ILC Yearbook 1957-II*, 27 (Art 18(2)).

(3) Intention to create legal relations[35]

In the previous article on this subject,[36] this heading merely made a reference to a discussion in a previous article,[37] where the subject had been treated under the heading 'The Intent to Create Legal Obligations'. No further material was included in this section in the last previous article; but Section A, Preliminary, of Chapter II, Treaty Interpretation and other Treaty Points,[38] mentioned the case of *Maritime and Territorial Questions between Qatar and Bahrain,* which can also be viewed as raising the question of intent to create legal relations. Briefly, it may be recalled that Qatar invoked the Tripartite Minutes of meetings between representatives of the two parties and of Saudi Arabia, at which agreement was reached, at least in principle, for the dispute to be brought before the Court. Qatar relied on the status of the Minutes as a basis of title; Bahrain disputed this, contending that the Minutes 'were no more than a simple record of negotiations...; that accordingly they did not rank as an international agreement, and could not therefore serve as a basis for the jurisdiction of the Court'.[39]

The discussion in the previous article in this series focussed on the question whether the Minutes constituted an international agreement, since that was how the Court framed the question, answering it in the affirmative.[40] However one aspect of the question was the intention of the parties in signing the Minutes; the Foreign Minister of Bahrain stated that he did not consider that in signing the Minutes he was 'committing Bahrain to a legally binding instrument'; and that he did not in fact have the power constitutionally to do so. He was 'prepared to subscribe to a statement recording a political understanding, but not to sign a legally binding instrument'.[41] If this contention were accepted, then on at least one side there was no 'intention to create legal relations', and thus no agreement on which jurisdiction could be based.[42] The Court's

---

[35] On this subject, reference may be made to the conclusions of the Report of M Virally to the *Institut de droit international* at its Cambridge Session in 1983, *Annuaire de l'Institut, 1984,* Vol. 60-II, 138–143, contemplating a spectrum of 'hardness' of obligation created by treaty-like instruments, depending on the intentions of the parties. The Institut preferred to adopt only a formal resolution on the question: see S Rosenne, *Developments in the Law of Treaties 1945–1986* (1989), 104 ff (hereinafter: Rosenne, *Developments in the Law of Treaties*).

[36] (1992) *BYIL* 1, 18.

[37] (1991) *BYIL* 1, 8–15.

[38] Ibid, 4–6.

[39] [1994] ICJ Rep 120, para 22.

[40] Ibid, 121, para 25.

[41] Ibid, para 26. The importance of the reference to his constitutional powers was not to suggest that Article 46 of the Vienna Convention on the Law of Treaties was applicable, but a pointer to the state of mind of the Minister when he signed the Minutes.

[42] The Court found that there existed 'commitments to which the Parties have consented'; and from the fact that the Minutes 'enumerated' those commitments, it deduced that the Minutes 'thus' created rights and obligations in international law for the parties: ibid, 121, para 25. It would seem however that if the 'commitments' antedated their enumeration in the Minutes, it was not the Minutes that 'created' rights and obligations. On the significance of the word 'thus' in this context

finding on the point was quoted in the previous article, but should be repeated here:

> The Court does not find it necessary to consider what might have been the intentions of the Foreign Minister of Bahrain or, for that matter, those of the Foreign Minister of Qatar. The two Ministers signed a text recording commitments accepted by their Governments, some of which were to be given immediate application. Having signed such a text, the Foreign Minister of Bahrain is not in a position subsequently to say that he intended to subscribe only to a 'statement recording a political understanding', and not to an international agreement.[43]

Is this then a rejection of the principle that there must, for an international agreement to come into existence, be an intention on both sides to create treaty-like relations? It would not seem so; all the Court was saying, it appears, was that on that question of intention it preferred the evidence of the wording of the Minutes, which in the Court's view showed that it partook of the nature of a treaty, to the *ex post facto* repudiation by the Bahraini Minister of the intention suggested by his signature.[44]

Rosenne, who approves of the Court's decision on this point, urges a distinction between the intentions of the signatory, in this case the Foreign Minister, and the intention of the State party, ie the government that instructs the Minister. Drawing on his experience as ambassador, he observes that:

> In my experience, while I might have known in signing an agreement what my intentions were, and what my instructions were, I could never really be sure of the intentions of those who gave me my instructions. The interpretation of an international agreement is not concerned with the intentions of the signatories, whatever their rank and style.[45]

It is of course correct that it is the intention of the State that matters; but the distinction drawn by Rosenne may yet be regarded as too sharp, particularly in relation to the case in hand, where the Minister presumably had a hand in formulating the policy of his Government in relation to the dispute. Nor was it a question of signing an instrument denominated 'agreement', but of signing 'Minutes'; while the intention to be

---

cf M Fitzmaurice and O Elias, *Contemporary Issues in the Law of Treaties* (2005), 13 (hereinafter: Fitzmaurice and Elias, *Contemporary Issues in the Law of Treaties*).

[43] Ibid, 121–122, para 27.

[44] Writing some years before the *Qatar/Bahrain* case, J Klabbers suggested that 'courts, when deciding on whether or not a certain instrument is intended to be legally binding, start from the presumption that such an instrument is intended to be legally binding' and only 'refuse to give an instrument legal force when there is clear evidence that it was not so intended': *The Concept of Treaty in International Law* (1996), 253. Such a presumption is more than reasonable when the instrument on its face is of a kind that is usually, or even often, binding; the difficulty with the Doha Minutes was that they were not of that kind, even if they used language suggestive of commitment.

[45] S Rosenne, *Essays on International Law and Practice* (2007), 442 (hereinafter: Rosenne, *Essays on International Law and Practice*).

determined was that of the Government of Bahrain, the assessment of the nature of the instrument would have had to be made by the signatory on behalf of the Government (and presumably reported by him); if he thought that there was nothing of the nature of an agreement to be signed, how could the State have formulated the intention to enter into a binding treaty commitment?[46]

2. FORMS OF CONCLUSION OF TREATIES

(1) Are there legal requirements as to form?

The case concerning *Maritime Delimitation and Territorial Questions between Qatar and Bahrain* also involved the question of the form of international treaties. Since Bahrain maintained that the Tripartite Minutes were no more than a record of negotiations, and not an international agreement, the Court took the opportunity to observe that 'international agreements may take a number of forms and be given a diversity of names'; it quoted Article 2, paragraph 1 *(a)*, of the Vienna Convention on the Law of Treaties, and its own dictum in the *Aegean Sea Continental Shelf* case, to the effect that the Court

knows of no rule of international law which might preclude a joint communiqué from constituting an international agreement to submit a dispute to arbitration or judicial settlement.[47]

As observed in the previous article on this subject, the same conclusion, that international instruments, and in particular treaties, do not have to have any predetermined form, emerges from the 1961 decision in the *Temple of Preah Vihear* case.[48]

The *Qatar/Bahrain* judgment did however emphasize the question of form from a different angle: as noted above, the Foreign Minister of Bahrain claimed that he did not intend, and could not have intended, to sign a binding treaty-instrument. The Court commented on this that:

The two Ministers signed a text recording commitments accepted by their Governments, some of which were to be given immediate application. Having signed such a text, the Foreign Minister of Bahrain is not in a position subsequently to say that he intended to subscribe only to a 'statement recording a political understanding', and not to an international agreement.[49]

---

[46] It is also clear from Rosenne's book that he has doubts about the evidential value of 'a statement made some 12 months later by one of the signatories' (ibid). It is not clear from the Judgment at what point in time Qatar made it clear to Bahrain that it was treating the Doha Minutes as a treaty; until then, there was no reason for the Minister to make his statement.

[47] [1994] ICJ Rep 120–121, para 23, quoting [1978] ICJ Rep 39, para 96.

[48] (1992) *BYIL* 1, 18–19, quoting [1961] ICJ Rep 31.

[49] [1994] ICJ Rep 122, para 27.

In other words, if a State representative signs something that appears to be a treaty, he cannot be heard to say subsequently that he believed it was something else, and that therefore *non est factum*. However, the Court based this approach not on an appreciation of the outward forms adopted but on the implications of the text. The Court was not saying that the document was labelled 'Treaty', or provided for ratification, and thus looked like a treaty in form, but that the wording used was such as to 'enumerate the commitments to which the parties have consented'.[50] Nevertheless, there must be room for an instrument to be drawn up by States, recording negotiations and matters agreed in principle, which does not, for all that, constitute a binding agreement on those matters; and it would seem that the test for determining whether an instrument falls into this category or that of an international agreement is likely to be, if only to some extent, one of form.[51]

(2) Ancient treaties

The Court has not, in the period under review, had to deal with treaties of earlier date than the 19th century, so that the problems associated with the treaties relied on in the *Right of Passage* and *Western Sahara* cases[52] have not been repeated. In the *Frontier Dispute* case between Libya and Chad, the significance of some 19th century agreements might have been questioned, but they were 'adopted' by a 1955 Treaty as defining frontiers, and there was no need for the Court to go behind that Treaty.[53]

(3) Consent to be bound established by deposit of appropriate instrument

The rule laid down in the *Right of Passage* case, that a declaration under the optional clause of Article 36, paragraph 2, of the Statute, takes effect from the date of its deposit, even in relation to another State that has no knowledge of it, was confirmed in the preliminary objection stage of the case concerning *Land and Maritime Boundary between Cameroon and Nigeria*.[54] The Court rejected the contention of Nigeria that the Court's

---

[50] Ibid, 121, para 25.

[51] The case suggests the possible need in international negotiations of a formula akin to '[s]ubject to contract' hallowed in common law usage to prevent initial stages of a negotiation being found to have committed one or other of the parties. According to Aust (*Modern Treaty Law and Practice*, 17–18), many instruments are drawn up by foreign ministries 'which employ carefully chosen terminology to indicate that, rather than creating international rights and obligations, the intention of the participants is to record no more than mutual understandings as to how they will conduct themselves'.

[52] See the discussion in (1989) *BYIL* 1, 130–132; (1992) *BYIL* 1, 19–21.

[53] See (2006) *BYIL* 1, 69.

[54] [1998] ICJ Rep 275. The question was briefly examined in a previous article in this series: (2000) *BYIL* 1, 34–35.

interpretation of Article 36, paragraph 4, of the Statute should be reconsidered in the light of Article 78(c) of the Vienna Convention on the
Law of Treaties, which provides that notifications and communications
to the depositary under the Convention should be 'considered as received
by the State for which it was intended only when the latter State has been
informed by the depositary'. It observed that these were two different
régimes: but it also observed that

Article 78 of the Convention is only designed to lay down the modalities according to which notifications and communications should be carried out. It does
not govern the conditions in which a State expresses its consent to be bound by
a treaty and those under which a treaty comes into force, those questions being
governed by Articles 16 and 24 of the Convention.[55]

A similar provision in the Vienna Convention deals with withdrawal of
reservations to a treaty, which has the effect of enlarging the scope of
the existing commitment to be bound. Article 22, paragraph 3(a), of
the Convention provides that such a withdrawal becomes operative in
relation to another State party only 'when notice of it has been received
by that State'. The Court referred to a rule in this sense as having been
'expressed' in that Article, and applied it, in the *Case concerning Armed
Activities on the Territory of the Congo (New Application, 2002)*.[56] Rwanda
had indicated an intention to withdraw (inter alia) its reservation to
Article IX (the compromissory clause) of the Genocide Convention, and
the Democratic Republic of the Congo (DRC) relied on that Article to
support jurisdiction in the case. The Court noted that the UN Secretary-
General was the depositary of the Genocide Convention, and that

it is thus in principle through the medium of the Secretary-General that
[contracting] States must be informed both of the making of a reservation to
the Convention and of its withdrawal. Rwanda notified its reservation to Article
IX of the Genocide Convention to the Secretary-General. However, the Court
does not have any evidence that Rwanda notified the Secretary-General of the
withdrawal of this reservation.[57]

Accordingly, the Court regarded the reservation as still in force so as to
debar reliance on Article IX as a title of jurisdiction.

(4) Is ratification necessary?

In the case of the *Land and Maritime Boundary between Cameroon and
Nigeria*, a joint declaration of the two Heads of State, referred to as the
Maroua Declaration, was relied on by Cameroon as amounting to a treaty

---

[55] Ibid, 293, para 31.

[56] Judgment of 3 February 2006, see esp para 41. The wording chosen suggests that the Court
regarded the rule as one of customary law, not merely a convention provision, but it is less clear than,
for example, the term 'reflected' used in other contexts to describe incorporation of a customary rule
in a law-making convention (eg the VCLT).

[57] Ibid, para 43.

commitment. One of the arguments of Nigeria against this contention was that the Declaration 'was invalid under international law because it was signed by the Nigerian Head of State but never ratified.' The Court did not accept this, observing that

while in international practice a two-step procedure consisting of signature and ratification is frequently provided for in provisions regarding entry into force of a treaty, there are also cases where a treaty enters into force immediately upon signature. Both customary international law and the Vienna Convention on the Law of Treaties leave it completely up to States which procedure they want to follow.[58]

The Court did not refer expressly to Article 14, paragraph 1, of the Vienna Convention, under which it would have been necessary, since the Declaration did not indicate that it was 'subject to ratification', nor was it signed on that basis, for Nigeria to show that the intention of Nigeria to sign subject to ratification 'was expressed during the negotiation' of the Declaration, or that it was 'otherwise established that the negotiating States were agreed that ratification should be required'. As Aust observes, '[t]his may be evidenced by a collateral agreement or in the *travaux*', but '[t]oday that would be unusual: if a treaty is silent on the question of ratification it is presumed that it is not needed'.[59]

3. CONSENT AND DEFECTS IN CONSENT

(1) Who may give valid consent?

The Court has held on a number of occasions that

it is a well-established rule of international law that the Head of State, the Head of Government and the Minister for Foreign Affairs are deemed to represent the State merely by virtue of exercising their functions, including for the performance, on behalf of the said State, of unilateral acts having the force of international commitments. The Court moreover recalls that, in the matter of the conclusion of treaties, this rule of customary law finds expression in Article 7, paragraph 2, of the Vienna Convention on the Law of Treaties, which provides that "[i]n virtue of their functions and without having to produce full powers, the following are considered as representing their State: *(a)* Heads of State, Heads of Government and Ministers for Foreign Affairs, for the purpose of performing all acts relating to the conclusion of a treaty".[60]

---

[58] [2002] ICJ Rep 429, para 264.
[59] Aust, *Modern Treaty Law and Practice*, 82. The presumption is of course rebuttable.
[60] *Case concerning Armed Activities on the Territory of the Congo (New Application 2002)* (Judgment of 3 February 2006), para 46, citing the following decisions: *Nuclear Tests (Australia v. France)*, [1974] ICJ Rep 269–270, paras 49–51; *Application of the Convention on the Prevention and Punishment of the Crime of Genocide (Bosnia and Herzegovina v. Yugoslavia), Preliminary Objections*, [1996-II] ICJ Rep 622, para 44; *Arrest Warrant of 11 April 2000 (Democratic Republic of the Congo v. Belgium)*, [2002] ICJ Rep. 21–22, para 53; see also *Legal Status of Eastern Greenland (Denmark v Norway), Judgment, 1933, P.C.I.J., Series A/B, No. 53, 71.*

The Court had occasion in 2006 to recall this principle in the context of a case where a statement by a Minister of Justice was relied on as effecting a withdrawal of a reservation made to the Genocide Convention, an act which, as expressive of the State's consent in relation to the provisions of the Convention, would normally require application of the same rules as the consent expressed to be bound by the Convention itself.

A preliminary point is however the nature of the *acte juridique* involved. At the point in the judgment at which the Court made the observation above, it had already dealt with a claim that Rwanda had withdrawn its reservation by adopting an internal *décret-loi* providing for withdrawal of all reservations made by it 'at the accession approval and ratification of international instruments'. In that connection the Court drew attention to the

rule of international law, deriving from the principle of legal security and well established in practice, that, subject to agreement to the contrary, the withdrawal by a contracting State of a reservation to a multilateral treaty takes effect in relation to the other contracting States only when they have received notification thereof. This rule is expressed in Article 22, paragraph 3 *(a)*, of the Vienna Convention on the Law of Treaties, which provides as follows: "3. Unless the Treaty otherwise provides, or it is otherwise agreed: *(a)* the withdrawal of a reservation becomes operative in relation to another Contracting State only when notice of it has been received by that State." Article 23, paragraph 4, of that same Convention further provides that "[t]he withdrawal of a reservation or of an objection to a reservation must be formulated in writing".[61]

The Court thus recognized that the withdrawal of a reservation to a treaty, like the act of becoming bound by the treaty and the entering of a reservation to it, is a unilateral act the modalities of which are fixed in advance by international law; that it is an act which has its recognized place in the established legal structure.

The statement that was also relied on by the DRC as committing Rwanda had been made by the Minister of Justice of Rwanda, in that capacity, before the UN Human Rights Commission on 17 March 2005. The Court observed, in relation to the declaration, that '[i]n order to determine the legal effect of that statement,' it had to 'examine its actual content as well as the circumstances in which it was made', and the Court cited the *Nuclear Tests* and *Frontier Dispute* cases.[62] However, those case concerned unilateral acts in the narrow sense of the term: acts which are not made on the basis, or within the framework, of a set of legal relations laying down in advance what the effects are of those acts, and the conditions of their making. The effects of such 'pure' unilateral acts 'are defined, not by pre-existing legal rules, but by the simple intention of the State performing

---

[61] Ibid, 25–26, para 41.

[62] Ibid, para 49, citing *Nuclear Tests (Australia v. France)*, [1974] ICJ Rep 269, para 51; *Frontier Dispute (Burkina Faso/Republic of Mali)*, [1986] ICJ Rep 573–574, paras 39–40.

them'.[63] This is not to say that the Court was wrong in examining the content of the Minister's statement, and the context in which it was made, but that it is doubtful whether it was right, in the context of the withdrawal of a reservation, to follow the course outlined by the jurisprudence cited.

The Court appears to be saying that an act which can normally be done according to the established formulas of international law can also, in theory or in principle, be done by means of a unilateral act of the 'pure' type. The implications of this view suggest that it is questionable. If the unilateral act whereby a Head of State says *urbi et orbi* that, for example, 'the Government of Ruritania accepts the Genocide Convention' is sufficient to make Ruritania a party to that Convention, it is difficult to see why there are established rules and procedures for signifying consent to be bound by a treaty.

This is of course a question going to the analysis of the legal status and effects of 'pure' international unilateral acts, which is not here the subject of discussion. However, the Court's approach raises the question of the significance of the passage in its decision in which it took account of current State practice as to the possibility of a State being represented in its international relations by persons other than the Head of State or Foreign Minister.

The Court notes, however, that with increasing frequency in modern international relations other persons representing a State in specific fields may be authorized by that State to bind it by their statements in respect of matters falling within their purview. This may be true, for example, of holders of technical ministerial portfolios exercising powers in their field of competence in the area of foreign relations, and even of certain officials.[64]

Does this observation apply to the *formal* acts of, for example, ratification of a treaty, or only to the sort of informal unilateral declaration that was under discussion? If in the case of *Territorial Questions and Maritime Delimitation between Qatar and Bahrain*, the Tripartite Minute that the Court found equivalent to a treaty conferring jurisdiction had been signed, not by the Bahraini Minister for Foreign Affairs but by the Minister of Justice, would the conclusion have been the same? It would seem strange if a Minister of Justice could commit his State to a treaty obligation by an informal declaration of the *Nuclear Tests* type, but not by formally signing the treaty or the act of ratification. The question is perhaps one of the nature and extent of the State practice appealed to by the Court as justifying its view, cited above; but unfortunately the Court does not spell this out, and the Parties' pleadings are not helpful in this respect.

If however the Court's ruling signifies that the strict requirements for the performance of the *formal* acts of consent to a treaty are now relaxed, what then is the criterion for determining whether the act of a particular

---

[63] H Thirlway, 'The Sources of International Law' in Evans (ed), *International Law* (2nd edition, 2006), 135.
[64] [2006] ICJ Rep, para 47 of the Judgment of 3 February 2006.

person, other than the Head of State or Foreign Minister, has the legal effect of committing the State? This emerges from the Court's examination of the specific statement:

Ms Mukabagwiza spoke before the United Nations Commission on Human Rights in her capacity as Minister of Justice of Rwanda and that she indicated *inter alia* that she was making her statement "on behalf of the Rwandan people". The Court further notes that the questions relating to the protection of human rights which were the subject of that statement fall within the purview of a Minister of Justice. It is the Court's view that the possibility cannot be ruled out in principle that a Minister of Justice may, under certain circumstances, bind the State he or she represents by his or her statements.[65]

This is not an instance expressly contemplated by the Draft Guidelines under preparation by the International Law Commission on Reservations to Treaties. Paragraph 2 of Draft Guideline 2.1.3, on Formulation of Reservations, recognizes a number of persons as not needing to produce full powers (Heads of State, Heads of Mission, etc.,) but does not include specialised ministers. Paragraph 1 however states that 'a person is considered as representing a State or an international organization for the purpose of formulating a reservation if:

...

(b) It appears from practice *or other circumstances* that it was the intention of the States and international organizations concerned to consider that person as competent for such purposes without having to produce full powers.'[66]

(2) Representation of the State for the conclusion of treaties and agreements

In the case of the *Land and Maritime Boundary between Cameroon and Nigeria*, Cameroon relied on a Joint Communiqué issued by the Heads of State of the two parties in Maroua on 1 June 1975, indicating that the signatories had 'reached full agreement on the exact course of the maritime boundary' between them.[67] Nigeria contended that this Communiqué, referred to as the Maroua Declaration, lacked legal validity because it was not ratified by the Supreme Military Council after being signed by the Nigerian Head of State. The Vienna Convention on the Law of Treaties was applicable between the parties,[68] and it was in any event not disputed that the customary rule as to the treaty-making powers of a Head of State are as indicated in Article 7, paragraph 2(a), of that Convention, i.e., that a Head of State, in virtue of his functions and without having to produce full powers, represents the

---

[65] Ibid, para 48.

[66] *Report of the ILC, Fifty-Seventh Session*, 171–172 (emphasis added).

[67] The Maroua Declaration is not reproduced in full in the Judgment; it referred to and confirmed an earlier document known as the 'Yaoundé II Declaration' (also not quoted in full). See [2002] ICJ Rep 425–429.

[68] Ibid, 429, para 263.

State 'for the purpose of performing all acts relating to the conclusion of the treaty'. For Nigeria however, that provision 'is solely concerned with the way in which a person's function as a State's representative is established, but does not deal with the extent of that person's powers when exercising that representative function.'[69] In other words, if an instrument claimed to be a treaty is signed by a Head of State, it cannot be challenged on the ground that the State should, according to its constitution, have been represented by its Foreign Minister; but it does not follow that the effectiveness of the signature cannot be challenged on the grounds that the powers of the Head of State in this domain are subject to constitutional limitations. The constitution of Nigeria in force at the time provided that 'executive acts were in general to be carried out by the Supreme Military Council or subject to its approval.'[70]

The dispute over the validity of the Maroua Declaration as a treaty-instrument thus centred on the rule reflected in Article 46 of the Vienna Convention.[71] Nigeria in effect invoked 'the fact that its consent to be bound by a treaty has been expressed in violation of a provision of its internal law regarding competence to conclude treaties as invalidating its consent'; to meet the requirements indicated in Article 46, on the basis that these represented customary law, Nigeria had therefore to show that the 'violation was manifest and concerned a rule of its internal law of fundamental importance.' The question raised was thus that defined by Sinclair in 1984 as follows:

Does paragraph 2 of Article 7 raise an incontestable presumption as a matter of international law that the designated office-holders are *ex officio* entitled to perform the specified acts without the need to produce full powers notwithstanding that, as a matter of internal law, they are not empowered to do so?[72]

Sinclair's view, based on the *travaux préparatoires* of the Vienna Conference, was that '[i]t would seem that the presumption is incontestable.'[73]

The Court began by stating what appears to be its conclusion, that the Maroua Declaration 'constitutes an international agreement concluded between States in written form...; it is thus governed by international law and constitutes a treaty in the sense of the Vienna Convention on the

---

[69] Ibid, para 258.

[70] Ibid, 427, para 257.

[71] 1. A State may not invoke the fact that its consent to be bound by a treaty has been expressed in violation of a provision of its internal law regarding competence to conclude treaties as invalidating its consent unless that violation was manifest and concerned a rule of its internal law of fundamental importance.
2. A violation is manifest if it would be objectively evident to any State conducting itself in the matter in accordance with normal practice and in good faith.

[72] *The Vienna Convention on the Law of Treaties* (2nd edn, 1984), 32.

[73] Ibid. Cf. the way in which UK company law deals with a similar problem: Companies Act 2006, clause 40(1) (re-enacting earlier legislation): 'In favour of a person dealing with a company in good faith, the power of the directors to bind the company, or authorise others to do so, is deemed to be free of any limitation under the company's constitution.'

Law of Treaties...'[74] It then dealt with the argument that 'the Maroua Declaration was invalid because it was signed by the Nigerian Head of State at the time but never ratified.'[75] It noted the variety of international practice, and observed that '[b]oth customary international law and the Vienna Convention on the Law of Treaties leave it completely up to States which procedure they want to follow'. It quoted the key terms of the Declaration, and concluded that the Declaration 'entered into force immediately upon its signature.'[76] Curiously, it did not in this connection cite Article 14 of the Convention, defining the circumstances in which '[t]he consent of a State to be bound by a treaty is [to be regarded as] expressed by ratification...', and indicate specifically that these circumstances were not present.

The Court then dealt with the application of Articles 7 and 46 of the Vienna Convention. It rejected Nigeria's arguments on the basis of a different conception of the relationship between these texts. Under Article 46, the provision of internal law as to constitutional competence to conclude treaties which had allegedly been violated must be one of fundamental importance and its violation must have been 'manifest'.

The rules concerning the authority to sign treaties for a State are constitutional rules of fundamental importance. However, a limitation of a Head of State's capacity in this respect is not manifest in the sense of Article 46, paragraph 2, unless at least properly publicized. This is particularly so because Heads of State belong to the group of persons who, in accordance with Article 7, paragraph 2, of the Convention "[i]n virtue of their functions and without having to produce full powers" are considered as representing their State.[77]

The sense of this is clear if it is conceived negatively: if a treaty were signed on behalf of one of the parties by, say, the Minister of Agriculture, and the signature was then repudiated on the ground that the Minister had no constitutional power to conclude treaties, little or no publicization of the actual constitutional arrangements of the State concerned would be required, since it is, as it were, notorious that Ministers of Agriculture do not normally conclude treaties, and—more to the point—are not included in the list in Article 7, paragraph 2, of the Vienna Convention.

Thus the Court went on to say:

The Court cannot accept Nigeria's argument that Article 7, paragraph 2, of the Vienna Convention on the Law of Treaties is solely concerned with the way in which a person's function as a state's representative is established, but does not deal with the extent of that person's powers when exercising that representative function. The Court notes that the commentary of the International

---

[74] Ibid, 429, para 263. In fact this is probably not an anticipated conclusion; what is probably meant here is that, *prima facie* and subject to the question of the validity of the instrument under Articles 7 and 46 of the Vienna Convention, the Declaration was a treaty, so that the Convention was applicable to it.
[75] [2002] ICJ Rep 429, para 264; see below, Section 2 (4).
[76] Ibid, 429–430, para 264.   [77] [2002] ICJ Rep 430, para 265.

Law Commission on Article 7, paragraph 2, expressly States that "Heads of State...are considered as representing their State for the purpose of performing alı acts relating to the conclusion of a treaty".[78]

A finding of some practical importance for Foreign Ministries was made in response to Nigeria's argument that 'Cameroon knew, or ought to have known, that the Head of State of Nigeria had no power legally to bind Nigeria without consulting the Nigerian Government'.[79] The Court noted that

there is no general legal obligation for States to keep themselves informed of legislative and constitutional developments in other States which are or may become important for the international relations of these States.[80]

(3) Commitment by persons not regularly representing the State

As mentioned above, in a number of delimitation cases, in particular, the question has arisen whether agreements, of a more or less informal nature, entered into by officials of a State not specifically authorized to enter into commitments on its behalf, on the lines laid down in Article 7 of the Vienna Convention on the Law of Treaties, could be regarded as binding the State.

In the *Gulf of Maine* case, an issue raised was whether the United States had agreed to the use of a median line for the delimitation of the parties' respective continental shelves, and in this respect Canada relied on a letter of 14 May 1965 addressed to the Canadian Department of Northern Affairs and National Resources by a United States official of the Bureau of Land Management named Hoffman, and thus known as the 'Hoffman Letter'. The Chamber of the Court considered that the terms of the letter could not be invoked against the US Government. In the letter, Mr. Hoffman had explained that he was not authorized to commit the United States as to the *position* of a median line, so that it was suggested that he was accepting, on behalf of his Government, the *principle* of use of such a line. The Chamber apparently read the letter as reserving this point also, though its argument is not entirely clear.[81] The Chamber however continued:

Mr. Hoffman, like his Canadian counterpart, was acting within the limits of his technical responsibilities and did not seem aware that the question of principle

---

[78] Ibid. See ILC Commentary, Art. 6 (of what was then the draft Convention), para 4, *Yearbook of the International Law Commission*, 1966, Vol. II, 193. The sudden invocation of *travaux préparatoires* might be difficult to justify under Article 32 of the Convention!

[79] Ibid para 266; *sic*: the contention of Nigeria was that not mere consultation but approval by the Supreme Military Council was required.

[80] Ibid.

[81] In the authentic French text, the sentence reads: 'La réserve exprimée par M. Hoffman, suivant laquelle il n'était pas habilité à engager les États-Unis, ne concernait, il est vrai, que l'emplacement d'une ligne médiane; la ligne médiane en tant que méthode de délimitation ne paraissait pas être en cause, mais rien n'indique que cette méthode ait été adoptée à l'échelon gouvernemental.' [1984] ICJ Rep 307, para 139.

which the subject of the correspondence might imply had not been settled, and that the technical arrangements he was to make with his Canadian correspondents should not prejudge his country's position in subsequent negotiations between governments. This situation, however, being a matter of United States internal administration, does not authorize Canada to rely on the contents of a letter from an official of the Bureau of Land Management of the Department of the Interior, which concerns a technical matter, as though it were an official declaration of the United States Government on that country's international maritime boundaries.[82]

There seems to be some emphasis here on the subjective intentions of the author of the letter; insofar as it might relied upon on the basis of estoppel, this would be irrelevant, since what matters in that respect is the impression conveyed to the other party. The Chamber must therefore be taken to have been analyzing the letter as a purported agreement, and indicating its view that the purport of any such agreement was not as claimed by Canada. The last sentence quoted is however more sweeping, and seems to suggest simply that an agreement entered into at a level not generally authorized to conclude treaties, as contemplated by Article 7 of the Vienna Convention, could have no international legal effect, or at least no effect outside the field of the 'technical responsibilities' of its author.

In the *Frontier Dispute* case between Burkina Faso and Mali, the Chamber of the Court was supplied with an agreement concluded on 15 January 1965 between delegations from each State composed of '*commandants de cercle* and other administrators on each side.'[83] The agreement was to divide a particular pool by 'a perpendicular line dividing the pool of Soum in two and running through the centre...', and a sketch-map was attached. The administrator concerned on the Burkina Faso side transmitted the agreement with a report to the Ministry of the Interior, but no inter-governmental agreement endorsing it was ever concluded. The Court noted that

In its Memorial Mali emphasized that the only authority with jurisdiction at the time to make a definitive settlement of frontier problems was the Standing Joint Commission, on which sat the Ministers of the Interior of both countries. From this it argues that all the agreements concluded at the level of *commandants de cercle* which were not confirmed subsequently by that Commission must be treated as ineffectual. The Chamber agrees that such agreements, not approved by the competent authorities of each Party, do not have the binding force of a convention.[84]

The problem before the Chamber was thus that it could not apply the 1965 agreement; but it was required by the Special Agreement to fix the frontier throughout its length. It escaped the dilemma by appealing to the 'idea of equity *infra legem*, which both Parties have recognized as

---

[82] [1984] ICJ Rep 307–308, para 139.   [83] [1986] ICJ Rep 631, para 146.
[84] Ibid, 632, para 147.

being applicable in this case'.[85] It therefore divided the pool between the two parties 'in an equitable manner', which it found to be so as 'to divide the maximum area of the pool...in equal proportions between the two States'.[86] It is striking that the Chamber thus arrived at a solution other than that agreed at *cercle* level in 1965, although one view of equity would be that that solution, being the one favoured by the regional authorities directly interested, should be adopted.[87] To adopt this approach might however tend to weaken excessively the principle already stated by the Court as to the requirement that binding agreements be those 'approved by the competent authorities of each Party'.

Nevertheless, in the subsequent case of the *Land, Island and Maritime Frontier Dispute* between El Salvador and Honduras the Chamber seised of the case was prepared to adopt, in the name of equity *infra legem*, the terms of an a agreement reached at non-governmental level as to the position of a frontier line. In 1869 representatives of the two States had met and, having concluded that a particular river was the frontier, drew a delimitation line in the form of a straight line to a selected point on the river from an identified endpoint of an agreed sector of the frontier. The Chamber noted that '[n]o international agreement was however concluded to give effect to that delimitation'.[88] The Chamber cited the decision of its predecessor in the *Frontier Dispute* case, and considered that 'it can in this case resort to the line proposed in the 1869 negotiations...as a reasonable and fair solution in all the circumstances'. There was however an additional circumstance:

There is nothing in the records of the 1861 and 1869 negotiations to suggest that there was any fundamental disagreement between the Parties on that line; acceptance of it however was linked to the different question whether the river Negro-Quiagara did or did not form the provincial boundary. That question is resolved by the present Judgment, and the Chamber has no doubt that it is equitable, as a corollary, to allow the 1869 agreement to take effect on this specific point.[89]

This circumstance may be regarded as differentiating the case from the *Frontier Dispute* case, and as justifying an apparent infringement of the requirement mentioned above of approval by the 'competent authorities' in order for an agreement to be binding on States. The Chamber took it as a justifiable assumption that if the disputed question of the status of the river as provincial boundary could have been settled in 1869, in the sense that the river did have that status, then the 1869

---

[85] Ibid, 633, para 149.

[86] Ibid, para 150. The reference to the 'maximum area' is to be explained by the fact that the extent of the pool varied to a considerable extent according to the seasons.

[87] Cf. the reasoning in the case of the *Continental Shelf (Tnuisia/Libya)* as to the indications by the parties of the delimitation that they themselves would have regarded as equitable: [1982] ICJ Rep 84, para 118, discussed in a previous article: (1994) *BYIL*, 1, 20–23, 26–28. For subsequent developments in this respect in the law of the sea, see below, Heading III-A, Chapter II, Section 2(1).

[88] [1992] ICJ Rep 514, para 261.   [89] Ibid, 515, para 263.

agreement would have been formalized by both parties; and that the Chamber, having settled the question of the status of the river, was able, as a matter purely of equity, to treat as having been done what would and should have been done had that question been settled in the earlier case. It is of course true that, had the question of the river been resolved in 1869, neither party would at that moment have been *bound* to formalize the frontier agreement; but neither party had specifically disowned the 1869 agreement subsequently. In looking for 'a reasonable and fair solution in all the circumstances', the Chamber could therefore proceed as it did without prejudicing the general rule enabling a State to avoid being committed, behind its back, as it were, by officials not having status to represent the State.

The Chamber in the *Land, Island and Maritime Frontier Dispute* was also ready to endorse a delimitation line that had been adopted in a 1935 agreement between the parties, but by the El Salvador side only *ad referendum*.[90] This decision however was based on different reasoning, since the agreement was made at governmental level, by persons authorized to represent the State for that purpose, even if it was never perfected.

Outside the domain of delimitation agreements, a similar problem arose in the jurisdictional phase of the case of *Armed Activities on the Territory of the Congo (New Application, 2002)*. The title of jurisdiction relied on by the Democratic Republic of the Congo (DRC) in its claim against Rwanda was Article IX of the Genocide Convention; but on accession Rwanda had made a reservation excluding that Article. In 1995 a *décret-loi* had been adopted by the President of Rwanda which was directed to the withdrawal of, *inter alia*, the reservation to the Genocide Convention. When this instrument was invoked by the DRC before the Court, it decided that since no action at the international level had been taken by Rwanda to implement it, it did not effect a withdrawal of the reservation.[91] However, the DRC also relied on a statement made by the Rwandan Minister of Justice on 17 March 2005 in the UN Human Rights Commission. The Court dealt with this statement as, apparently, a unilateral act, stating that in order to determine its legal effect it had to 'examine its actual content as well as the circumstances in which it was made', citing the *Nuclear Tests* and *Frontier Dispute* cases.[92] This case has already been examined above in Section 3, subsection 1, in the context of consent in the conclusion of treaties.

(a) Error

One might be tempted to suppose that the commitment of Bahrain to a judicial settlement of its dispute with Qatar by reason of its signature of

---

[90] [1992] ICJ Rep 422, para 100.

[91] [2006] ICJ Rep, para 44 of the Judgment of 3 February 2006.

[92] Ibid, para 49, quoting *Nuclear Tests (Australia v. France)* [1974] ICJ Rep 269, para 51 and *Frontier Dispute (Burkina Faso/Republic of Mali)* [1986] ICJ Rep. 573–574, paras. 39–40.

the Doha Minutes could also be challenged by reference to the concept of error. Clearly, an error as to the nature of an instrument is fundamental, and in municipal law may well lead to nullity, by such a principle as that of *non est factum*. However, the Vienna Convention is more restrictive: it contemplates that '[a] State may invoke *an error in a treaty* as invalidating its consent to be bound by the treaty if the error relates to a fact or situation which was assumed by that State to exist at the time when the treaty was concluded and formed an essential basis of its consent to be bound by the treaty'.[93] The hypothesis is that the State has given a consent to be bound, but is entitled *ex post facto* to say that it was a not a valid consent, so that the treaty is invalid; but Bahrain was denying that any consent *to a treaty obligation* had ever been given at all. The question was not whether a treaty existed which was, however, invalid for error; it was whether any treaty existed at all.

(b) Fraud and duress

Any application by the Court of Articles 49 and 52 of the Vienna Convention on the Law of Treaties, concerning fraud would signify that it was concerned with a very regrettable state of affairs; fortunately no such situation has arisen.[94] There was a suggestion in the *Territorial Dispute* case between Libya and Chad that during the negotiation of the 1955 Treaty of Friendship that played a major role in the case, Libya had 'lacked the experience to engage in difficult negotiations with a Power [France] enjoying the benefit of long international experience', and that Libya was 'consequently placed at a disadvantage.'[95] However Libya merely suggested that this be taken into account for purposes of interpretation of the Treaty, and did not take 'this argument so far as to suggest it as a ground for invalidity of the Treaty itself.'[96] At least in terms of the Vienna Convention, it is in fact difficult to see what the precise ground of invalidity could have been, unless Libya could indicate some point on which it had been misled by the wily Gallic negotiators, such as to constitute a ground of error under Article 48.

As to coercion or duress, it was argued by Nicaragua in the *Territorial Dispute (Nicaragua/Colombia)* in connection with a 1928 Treaty between the parties that

at the time the Treaty was concluded, Nicaragua was under military occupation by the United States and was precluded from concluding treaties that ran contrary to the interests of the United States and from rejecting the conclusion of treaties that the United States demanded it to conclude. Nicaragua

---

[93] Article 48, paragraph 1, emphasis added.
[94] The deplorable affair of the forged documents in the *Qatar/Bahrain* case does spring to mind (see M Mendelson, 'The Curious Case of Qatar v. Bahrain in the International Court of Justice', (2001) *BYIL* 183, 197 ff.), but these were apparently designed to induce the Court to give a particular decision—equally heinous as fraud in the negotiation of a treaty, but not a matter of treaty-law.
[95] [1994] ICJ Rep 20, para 36.
[96] Ibid.

submits that Colombia was aware of this situation and "took advantage of the US occupation of Nicaragua to extort from her the conclusion of the 1928 Treaty."[97]

The Court did not examine the circumstances of the conclusion of the Treaty, since it found it sufficient to note that Nicaragua had not invoked the invalidity of the Treaty until long after any possible duress, resulting from the presence of US troops in Nicaragua until 1933, had ceased; 'it therefore cannot today be heard to assert that the 1928 Treaty was not in force in 1948',[98] the relevant date for the purposes of the case.

(c) Reservations to treaties, the 'object and purpose' of a treaty, and jus cogens

In two recent cases, the Court was concerned, though almost incidentally, with one of the most thorny problems of the law of treaties, one which has been the subject of fierce debate in the International Law Commission and elsewhere. Its contribution to this debate has however been no more than conservative, in the sense that, as a Court, it refrained from venturing into controversial territory, though some of its Members commented on the matter; it declined to deal with some problems in a situation in which, in the view of some commentators, it should have taken the opportunity to do so. The controversy is the effect, if any, of an objectionable reservation to a multilateral treaty, that is to say, one which is contrary to the 'object and purpose' of the treaty, the test indicated by the Court in the case of Reservations to the Genocide Convention, and adopted in Article 19(c) of the Vienna Convention. Such a reservation may be termed not 'admissible' (according to one school of thought) or 'opposable' according the other;[99] is such a reservation void ab initio, or is it only ineffective vis-à-vis States which do not accept it?[100] In terms of the Vienna Convention, Article 19(c) simply indicates that a State may formulate a reservation 'unless... the reservation is incompatible with the object and purpose of the treaty,' but does not indicate the consequences of such incompatibility, nor—a key question—how and by whom it is to be determined whether the reservation is compatible or incompatible. A second aspect of the problem is this: if the incompatible reservation is void, or is ineffective against a particular State, can it be severed from the accession to the treaty which it qualifies, or does the reservation, in falling, take the principal instrument, the accession, with it?

---

[97] [2007] ICJ Rep, para 75 of the Judgment of 13 December 2007.

[98] Ibid, paras. 79–80

[99] See the Reports of A Pellet to the ILC on Reservations to Treaties, particularly First Report (A/CN.4/470), para 115, and Second Report (A/CN.4/477, 1996), para 44.

[100] The Special Rapporteur of the ILC, A Pellet, proposed the use of the terms 'validiy/invalidity' specifically to adopt a neutral stance on this controversy: Report of the ILC, Fifty-Seventh Session, UN doc A/CN.4/588, 154, para 354. Doubts were however expressed whether neutrality was achieved by these terms: ibid, 154, para 391.

The context in which the problem has raised its head in cases before the Court is that of reservations to the compromissory clause of the Genocide Convention. In situations of dispute in which there exists a compromissory clause in a multilateral convention that would *prima facie* confer jurisdiction on the Court over the dispute, but the intended Respondent has entered a reservation to that clause, there would at first sight seem to be little point in instituting proceedings invoking that clause. Nevertheless in two recent cases involving the Convention on the Prevention and Punishment of the Crime of Genocide, Article IX of that Convention has been relied on as title of jurisdiction[101] despite the existence of a reservation to that Article by the Respondent State, so that the question of the validity of the reservation has been before the Court.

In the cases concerning the *Legality of the Use of Force* brought by Yugoslavia against the Member States of NATO, Article IX of the Genocide Convention was a jurisdictional title relied on against all Respondents. Spain had however entered a reservation excluding that Article, and the United States had also entered a reservation to the effect that, before any dispute to which the United States was a party might be submitted to the Court, 'the specific consent of the United States is required in each case'.[102] The US made it clear that no such consent would be forthcoming; and Yugoslavia did not, in either the case against Spain or in that against the United States, put forward any argument that, for example, the reservation might be invalid. The Court, in its Orders on the request of Yugoslavia for the indication of provisional measures, found as follows:

Whereas the Genocide Convention does not prohibit reservations; whereas Yugoslavia did not object to [Spain's] [the United States] reservation to Article IX; and whereas the said reservation had the effect of excluding that Article from the provisions of the Convention in force between the Parties;[103]

On this basis, the Court not only refused the request for provisional measures, but found that it 'manifestly lacks jurisdiction to entertain Yugoslavia's Application', and removed the case from the list.[104] Of the three judges who voted against this finding, Judge Vereshchetin conceded that the Court's jurisdiction in relation to the United States was 'non-existent'[105]; and Judge Parra-Aranguren simply indicated that he considered that it was

---

[101] The almost universal participation of States in the Genocide Convention, coupled with the existence of the compromissory clause of Article IX, makes it an attractive basis on which to assert jurisdiction in cases in which use of armed force can be equated, with a greater or lesser degree of plausibility, with genocide. The growth in popularity of ideas of *jus cogens* and *erga omnes* obligations, as a sort of trump card or joker in the pack, was bound to be invoked sooner or later to overcome the inconvenience of reservations to Article IX.

[102] Quoted in [1999] ICJ Rep 923, para 21.

[103] Ibid, 772, para 30; 924, para 24.

[104] Ibid, 773, para 35; 774, para 40(2); 925, para 29; 926, para 34(2). This is a step which has never been taken before at the provisional measures stage.

[105] Ibid, 779–780; 931–932.

an improper procedure to make a finding of jurisdiction, and remove a case from the list, at the provisional measures stage.[106] Only the Yugoslav judge *ad hoc*, Judge Kreča, argued that the US reservation was invalid as a matter of *jus cogens*;[107] no other judge agreed, or even suggested that the point should have been examined in the Order.

In the subsequent case of *Armed Activities on the Territory of the Congo (New Application, 2002)*, the Congo also relied upon (*inter alia*) Article IX of the Genocide Convention as basis of jurisdiction for its claim against Rwanda. The accession of Rwanda to the Convention was how-ever subject to a reservation whereby '[t]he Rwandan Republic does not consider itself as bound by Article IX of the Convention'.[108] The Congo endeavoured to overcome this difficulty by arguing that the reservation was 'inoperative', in view of the special nature of the Convention.[109] The Court examined the point to a limited extent at the stage of the request for the indication of provisional measures, and in more detail when deal-ing with the preliminary objections of Rwanda.

When dealing with the Congo's contention at the earlier stage, the Court first recalled that special nature of the Genocide Convention, referring in particular to the *erga omnes* character of 'the rights and obli-gations enshrined by the Convention.'[110] It then recalled its dictum in the *East Timor* case that 'the *erga omnes* character of a norm and the rule of consent to jurisdiction are two different things.'[111] It continued

whereas it does not follow from the mere fact that rights and obligations *erga omnes* are at issue in a dispute that the Court has jurisdiction to adjudicate upon that dispute; whereas. as the Court has noted above..., it has jurisdiction in respect of States only to the extent that they have consented thereto: and whereas, when a compromissory clause in a treaty provides for the Court's jur-isdiction, that jurisdiction exists only in respect of the parties to the treaty who are bound by that clause and within the limits set out in that clause.[112]

This part of the reasoning does not appear to correspond to any spe-cific contention of the Congo, which apparently recognized the principle stated in the last part of this passage, but nevertheless contended for the invalidity of the reservation.

The Court then dealt with this argument of the Congo:

Whereas the Genocide Convention does not prohibit reservations; whereas the Congo did not object to Rwanda's reservation when it was made; whereas that

---

[106] Ibid, 950.   [107] Ibid, 962–966, paras 8–10.
[108] Quoted in *Armed Activities on the Territory of the Congo (New Application, 2002)*, [2002] ICJ Rep 245, para 69.
[109] The arguments of the Congo on the point are summarised in paragraph 22 of the Court's Order of 10 July 2002: [2002] ICJ Rep 228–229.
[110] *Application of the Convention on the Prevention and Punishment of the Crime of Genocide, Preliminary Objections*, [1996-II] ICJ Rep. 616, para 31; quoted in [2001] ICJ Rep 245, para 71. For a criticism of this formulation, see the earlier article in this series at (2005) *BYIL* 1, 56–57.
[111] [1995] ICJ Rep 102, para 29.
[112] [2002] ICJ Rep 245, para 71.

reservation does not bear on the substance of the law, but only on the Court's jurisdiction; whereas it therefore does not appear contrary to the object and purpose of the Convention; ... [113]

This amounts to a rejection of the argument of the Congo that the effect of the Rwandan reservation was 'to exclude Rwanda from any mechanism for the monitoring and prosecution of genocide', although it had urged that 'the object and purpose of the Convention are the abolition of impunity for this serious violation of international law'.[114] The Congo had also argued that, whatever might have been the position when the Convention was adopted, international law had evolved, and pointed to Article 120 of the Statute of Rome for the International Criminal Court—which deals (inter alia) with genocide—, a text which expressly provides that no reservations may be made to the Statute. It also drew attention to the existence of the International Criminal Tribunal for crimes committed in Rwanda, and suggested that it was inconsistent for Rwanda, which had requested the establishment of such a tribunal to reject the Court's jurisdiction in the instant case. The Court rejected these arguments also

whereas it is immaterial that different solutions have been adopted for courts of a different character; whereas, specifically, it is immaterial that the International Criminal Tribunal for crimes committed in Rwanda was established at Rwanda's request by a mandatory decision of the Security Council or that Article 120 of the Statute of the international Criminal Court signed at Rome on 17 July 1998 prohibits all reservations to that Statute;[115]

The key question was thus whether, in the special case of the Genocide Convention, a reservation to the compromissory clause, which is not expressly forbidden by the Convention itself, could be regarded as contrary to the object and purpose of the Convention; and if so, whether the reservation would be invalid; and what effect this would have on the status in relation to the Convention of the party making the reservation, vis-à-vis a party having objected to the reservation, or generally. The Court's answer was simple and not unexpected; the reservation is valid, and the Court thus has no jurisdiction in relation to the party making it. Once again, the Court saw no need to enquire into any matters of jus cogens.

This is not however a view that has gone unchallenged. In particular, it has been argued by Orakhelashvili that in these two Orders the Court 'ignor[ed] the effects of peremptory norms embodied in a treaty and undermin[ed] the efficiency of the Genocide Convention'.[116] The Orders

---

[113] Ibid, 245–246, para 72. In the joint opinion of five judges attached to the Court's 2006 judgment in the same case, this paragraph is treated as the Court's own assessment of the compatibility of the reservation ([2006] ICJ Rep 70, para 20), with the implication that the Court was rejecting the idea that compatibility is a matter for each of the other States parties to judge for itself. See further the discussion of the joint opinion, below.

[114] Quoted in [2002] ICJ Rep 229, para 22.   [115] Ibid, 246.

[116] A Orakhelashvili, *Peremptory Norms in International Law* (2006), 514 (hereinafter: Orakhelashvili, *Peremptory Norms in International Law*).

in the *Use of Force* cases were decisions on provisional measures, and thus an exercise of preliminary jurisdiction; and in the cases against the United States and Spain, the Court proceeded to remove them from the list, so that no further argument on the jurisdictional point—regarded as open and shut—was possible. Before examining the criticisms of these Orders, and of that in the *Congo/Rwanda* case, we should note the more pondered views of the Court expressed in its decision of 3 February 2006 on the preliminary objections in the latter case. At that stage, the Court decided by an overwhelming majority that it had no jurisdiction, *inter alia* because the reservation of Rwanda to Article IX of the Genocide Convention was effective. An important separate opinion was appended jointly by Judges Higgins, Kooijmans, Elaraby, Owada and Simma, the reasoning of which will be examined below; but those judges did not disagree with the finding upholding the effectiveness of the reservation in the instant case.

The Court had first to deal with a contention, not here material, that Rwanda had withdrawn its reservation[117]; the Court found that contention unfounded, and proceeded to consider the question of validity. The arguments on both sides were essentially the same as those examined by the Court at the stage of the request for provisional measures. Nor did the Court vary its stance; it merely re-stated its findings in a little more detail. Again, it emphasized the *erga omnes* character of the 'rights and obligations' under the Convention; and again it recalled its dictum in the *East Timor* case, noted above, that 'the *erga* omnes character of a norm and the rule of consent to jurisdiction are two different things', adding that:

The same applies to the relationship between peremptory norms of general international law *(jus cogens)* and the establishment of the Court's jurisdiction: the fact that a dispute relates to compliance with a norm having such a character, which is assuredly the case with regard to the prohibition of genocide, cannot of itself provide a basis for the jurisdiction of the Court to entertain that dispute. Under the Court's Statute that jurisdiction is always based on the consent of the parties.[118]

Though this did not correspond precisely to a Congolese argument, it was probably right to include it as a sort of *pons asinorum* in this field of law.

The Court repeated the equally basic precept that '[w]hen a compromissory clause in a treaty provides for the Court's jurisdiction, that jurisdiction exists only in respect of the parties to the treaty who are bound by that clause and within the limits set out therein.' Dealing with the nub of the matter, the Court stated:

The Court notes, however, that it has already found that reservations are not prohibited under the Genocide Convention (Advisory Opinion in the case

---

[117] See above Chapter II, Section 3(3).   [118] [2006] ICJ Rep 32, para 64 *in fine*.

concerning *Reservations to the Convention on the Prevention and Punishment of the Crime of Genocide, I.C.J. Reports 1951*, pp. 22 *et seq.*). This legal situation is not altered by the fact that the Statute of the International Criminal Court, in its Article 120, does not permit reservations to that Statute, including provisions relating to the jurisdiction of the International Criminal Court on the crime of genocide. Thus, in the view of the Court, a reservation under the Genocide Convention would be permissible to the extent that such reservation is not incompatible with the object and purpose of the Convention.

Rwanda's reservation to Article IX of the Genocide Convention bears on the jurisdiction of the Court, and does not affect substantive obligations relating to acts of genocide themselves under that Convention. In the circumstances of the present case, the Court cannot conclude that the reservation of Rwanda in question, which is meant to exclude a particular method of settling a dispute relating to the interpretation, application or fulfilment of the Convention, is to be regarded as being incompatible with the object and purpose of the Convention.[119]

The Court also recalled that it had given effect to reservations to Article IX in the *Use of Force* cases, and that 'as a matter of the law of treaties, when Rwanda acceded to the Genocide Convention and made the reservation in question, the DRC made no objection to it.'[120] In passing, it may be noted that this observation is more significant than it appears, and perhaps even than the Court intended. Its immediate relevance is that if the DRC had objected to the reservation, then according to the Court's ruling in the case of *Interpretation of the Genocide Convention*, the Convention would not have been in force between the DRC and Rwanda, so that there would *a fortiori* have been no jurisdiction. The Court seems to be hinting at a sort of estoppel; that having failed to object in due time, the DRC had accepted the validity of the reservation. But if the reservation was invalid, objectively speaking, as contrary to the object and purpose of the Convention, could the consent or recognition of another party cure that invalidity *quoad hunc*?

The Court noted in 2006 that in 1951 it had decided that reservations to the Genocide Convention were not prohibited by the Convention itself. In the 1951 proceedings the Court rejected the view of the dissenting judges that the general rule in the matter was, according to 'the current practice of the United Nations, ... to the effect that, without the consent of all the parties, a reservation proposed in relation to a multilateral convention cannot become effective and the reserving State cannot become a party thereto'.[121] Nevertheless, the Court did not at that time indicate what reservations might, in the particular case of the Genocide Convention, be regarded as either compatible

---

[119] Ibid, paras 66–67.
[120] Ibid, para 68.
[121] Joint dissenting opinion of Judges Guerrero, McNair, Read and Hsu Mo, [1951] ICJ Rep 41. The reference to 'the United Nations' in contemporary usage refers to the Member States as a group, not to the Organization.

or incompatible with the object and purpose of the Convention. It had been powerfully argued before the Court in 1951 that Article IX had been conceived as an essential part of the Convention,[122] but the Court made no finding as to the possibility of reservations to that Article. This silence is understandable: the essence of the Court's advisory opinion was that compatibility with the object and purpose of the Convention was a matter for subjective assessment by each State in relation to each reservation advanced,[123] and it would have been inconsistent to assert *a priori* that a particular kind of reservation was objectively and essentially incompatible.[124] Articles 21 and 22 of the Vienna Convention on the Law of Treaties have of course adopted the Court's 1951 solution, and it would seem, as the Court has said of other provisions of that Convention, that these texts 'in many respects' reflect customary international law.[125]

Does that however mean that a reservation may nevertheless be objectively incompatible with the object and purpose of a convention? This is the contention of the 'permissibility' school of thought[126]; those holding the 'opposability' view consider that any reservation whatever may have validity between the reserving State and another State that accepts it. The 'permissibility' view signifies, in a practical sense, that the Court could, if seised of the specific question, qualify as objectionable and invalid a reservation that had been accepted by one or more other States parties, thereby annulling the convention relation between those parties and the reserving State.[127] In the 1951 Advisory Opinion, the Court considered the following possibility:

[I]t may be that certain parties who consider that the assent given by other parties to a reservation is incompatible with the purpose of the Convention, will decide to adopt a position on the jurisdictional plane in respect of this divergence and to settle the dispute which arises either by special agreement or by the procedure laid down in Article IX of the Convention.[128]

---

[122] See for example Sir Hartley Shawcross (UK), at *Pleadings, Oral Arguments, Documents*, 380. Orakhelashvili comments that '[t]he Court did not [in 1951] contradict that view' (*Peremptory Norms in International Law*, 509), but it did not need to for the purposes of its decision, and therefore no consequence can properly be drawn from its silence.

[123] In this sense I Brownlie, *Principles of Public International Law* (6th edn, 2003), 586.

[124] The UN Human Rights Committee was of course subsequently to assert the existence of objectively unacceptable reservations to human rights treaties, and to claim the power of making this 'objective' assessment: General Comment No. 24 (52), 2 November 1994, particularly paras. 19–20; but it is doubtful whether this ruling was soundly based in existing customary law: see the draft Resolution prepared by the International Law Commission on the reports of Prof. Pellet, A/CN.4/L.540 (4 July 1997), particularly paras. 2–4. The matter is discussed further below in the context of the joint opinion in the *Armed Activities (Congo/Rwanda)* case.

[125] For a list of references to dicta of the Court in this sense, see previous articles: (1991) *BYIL* 1, 3, fn 8; (2006) *BYIL* 1, 26, fn 103.

[126] An early example of this view is D Bowett, 'Reservations to Non-Restricted Multilateral Treaties' (1976–7) 48 *BYIL* 83.

[127] This is the contention of Orakhelashvili: *Peremptory Norms in International Law*, 511–512.

[128] [1951] ICJ Rep 27.

The Court appears to be saying that if it were judicially established that a reservation was incompatible with the Convention, then the reserving State would not be a party to it at all, even in relation to the States that had accepted the reservation. The passage cited above is preceded by the observation that the decision to object or not to object will, 'in the ordinary course of events,... only affect the relationship between the State making the reservation and the objecting State'; however the Court continued

on the other hand, as will be pointed out later, such a decision might aim at the complete exclusion from the Convention in a case where it was expressed by the adoption of a position on the jurisdictional plane.[129]

It is not however apparent how a power of the Court to resolve this 'divergence' can be reconciled with the entitlement of each party to the Convention 'to appraise the validity of the reservation... individually and from its own standpoint.'[130]

Furthermore, the acceptance of a reservation (or the lack of objection to be equated with acceptance) may take place at two stages: when the reservation is made; and when the issue is before the Court. In the *Use of Force* cases the Court did not pronounce on the question whether the Spanish and US reservations to Article IX were contrary to the object and purpose of the Convention, because Yugoslavia did not raise the issue. If, 'objectively' speaking, the reservation was so incompatible, should the Court not have gone into the matter *proprio motu*, on the basis that the Court must satisfy itself whether it has jurisdiction? Can there be *non-forum prorogatum*, i.e. implied agreement between the parties that the Court does *not* have jurisdiction? The principle of *Kompetenz-Kompetenz* would seem to suggest otherwise: that competence is conferred by the original agreement to (in the case of the ICJ) the Statute, and is not dependent on specific *ad hoc* consent.

It is suggested that the answer to this conundrum may be found, not in the idea of an 'objective' classification of reservations as compatible or incompatible with the object and purpose of a treaty, but in the concept of *jus cogens* itself. A reservation to an accession to a multilateral treaty is in effect an offer to conclude a slightly different treaty; those States that do not object to the reservation accept the offer, and the modified treaty operates between them and the reserving State. Between the reserving State and those State parties that object to the reservation, no treaty comes into operation at all. Thus the question is not the compatibility with the object and purpose of the original convention; it is whether the modified convention created by the reservation (coupled with acceptance or non-objection) contravenes a rule of *jus cogens*. This suffices to dispose of the problem of, for example, the hypothetical reservation to the effect that the Genocide Convention should not protect a specified

---

group, raised during the drafting of the Convention, and referred to by the Secretary-General and the UK in the 1951 proceedings;[131] such a reservation would clearly be contrary to *jus cogens*. This is essentially the system adopted by the United Nations Human Rights Committee in General Comment No. 24. The only reason why the legality of that Comment could be questioned was because it asserted the Committee's power itself to determine what reservations conflicted with peremptory norms, simply on the basis of 'someone must do it'; the incompatibility of a reservation, conflicting with such a norm, to a human rights treaty is practically self-evident.[132]

On this basis, it may be observed that the Court's 1951 ruling gave to Article IX a different slant from that which had been discussed during the proceedings before it. It could convincingly be advanced that, if certain reservations to the Genocide Convention were to be regarded as objectionable and invalid, irrespective of the attitude of the parties other than the reserving State, then an independent and objective observer was needed to indicate with authority which were such reservations: and this would imply that Article IX was, and had been conceived as, an essential part of the Convention structure.[133] The moment it was established, in the Court's advisory opinion, that the test of compatibility with the object and purpose was individual and subjective, then Article IX, whatever its other advantages, ceased to be vital to the determination of the validity of reservations. The test of validity of a reservation as between reserving State A and party State B was a simple matter of acceptance or non-acceptance by State B; no tribunal was required to apply the test, and no tribunal could over-ride that acceptance.

It has however been suggested that the system of the Vienna Convention, based on the 1951 Advisory Opinion, may be 'unworkable in practice', 'unless jurisdiction is vested in some international organ to determine, with an effect binding all parties, whether a reservation is compatible with the object of a treaty.'[134] This is somewhat surprising, as the Vienna

---

[131] *Pleadings, Oral Arguments, Documents*, 88, 381.

[132] The Committee appears however to have recognized that Optional Protocol No. 1 to the International Covenant on Civil and Political Rights, the equivalent of a compromissory clause in a Convention, while it could not be made a vehicle for a reservation to the Covenant, could be used to 'ensure that the State's compliance with [its Covenant] obligation may not be tested by the Committee': loc. cit, para 13.

[133] The argument of Sir Hartley Shawcross, counsel for the UK, was close to this, but not identical: for him, the machinery of appeal to the Court was necessary in case 'States choose to disregard the obligations that they have undertaken': *Pleadings, Oral Arguments, Documents*, 88, 380.

[134] *Oppenheim's International Law*, 9th edn by R Jennings and A Watts (1996), Vol. II, 1245, note 4 (hereinafter: Jennings and Watts, *Oppenheim's International Law*). The matter should be seen against the background of a trend, identified in particular by Rosenne, toward vesting in the ICJ the function of determining the precise scope of a novel rule of law incorporated in a convention, an approach earlier regarded by the ILC, for example, as an abdication of responsibility: see Rosenne, *Developments in the Law of Treaties*, 281 ff. Admittedly, assessment of the 'object and purpose' of a convention is in general a task for which the Court is well-fitted; but the fact that States parties may differ over the compatibility of a reservation suggests that the question is unlikely to be open-and-shut.

Convention system seems to have settled down satisfactorily in practice, even if to a tidy mind it is disturbing that 'a reserving State is a party in relation to some signatories [*sic*: parties] but not in relation to others', as the learned authors feared.[135]

Orakhelashvili also contends that '[t]o determine the consequences of reservations to Article IX [of the Genocide Convention], the Vienna Convention regime which is relevant to the process of reservation-acceptance/objection is not helpful as it applies only to compatible reservations in terms of Article 19 of the Vienna Convention and also only on the State-to-State decentralized plane.'[136] He thus interprets Article 19, paragraph *(c)*, as recognizing a class of reservations which are essentially and *ipso facto* incompatible with the convention to which they relate, so that the whole process of acceptance or objection is irrelevant or inoperative. As a justification for the view that an objective judicial assessment of compatibility is possible *ex post facto*, this interpretation proves too much. The difficulty with it is that there is no way of telling that a particular reservation, when made, has this status, and States will therefore treat all reservations in the same way, objecting to them if *they* consider the reservation incompatible with the object and purpose of the convention, or accepting them if not.[137]

The contention that the Court could and should have set aside the reservation made to Article IX of the Genocide Convention by Rwanda, and perhaps those of Spain and the United States, also encounters a further difficulty. The mere fact that the reservation is to the compromissory clause is not a problem: the *compétence de la compétence* suffices for the Court to consider whether the jurisdiction conferred by Article IX has been successfully cancelled by a reservation. But if the reservation is held to be improper, either as incompatible with the object and purpose of the Convention, or as in conflict with a rule of *jus cogens*, what is the consequence? The Court clearly envisaged in 1951 that it would be the total exclusion of the reserving State from participation in the Convention, even in relation to States which had not objected to the reservation. The result that would be that any complaint of non-compliance with the Convention by the reserving State would necessarily fail, both for lack of adherence of the reserving State to the compromissory clause, and because that State would have no obligation to comply with

[135] Jennings and Watts, *Oppenheim's International Law*, 1245, note 4.

[136] Orakhelashvili, *Peremptory Norms in International Law*, 511.

[137] O'Connell, writing in 1970, expressed the view that 'since the Court's judgment [*sic*: the 1951 advisory opinion is apparently meant] takes into account the possibility of a judicial over-ruling to any objection the criterion of compatibility is subjective only so long as the objection does not become the subject of a justiciable dispute': *International Law* (2nd edn, 1970), Vol I, 234. However he made clear in a later passage that in litigation in which a party relies on the treaty, 'it may be determined whether the objection to the reservation results in the reserving State not being a party to the treaty vis-à-vis the objecting State, and the answer to this question disposes of the question whether the reservation is compatible with the object of the treaty.' (at 237).

the substantive requirements of the Convention.[138] In response to this, Orakhelashvili simply states that '[t]o safeguard the object and purpose of the Convention, the Court has to disregard the will of an individual State and sever the reservation purporting to preclude the exercise of jurisdiction under Article IX'.[139] The inconsistency of this approach with the essential character of State consent as underlying not merely judicial jurisdiction but the whole law of treaties, will be evident.[140]

Another conundrum is as follows. State A, which has entered a reservation to Article IX, brings proceedings, invoking the Genocide Convention, against State B, which is a party without reservations, and which has not objected to the reservation of State A. The Convention is thus in force between States A and B, but with the exclusion of Article IX, so that *prima facie* there is no jurisdiction. State A however invokes the invalidity of its own reservation, on the grounds of incompatibility with the object and purpose of the Convention. Logically, if Orakhelashvili's view is correct, the reservation is indeed invalid, and the Convention is in force between the two States, with the inclusion of Article IX, and there is jurisdiction. It is however no longer a question of outlawing a reservation which would enable State A to avoid judicial scrutiny of its behaviour; and State B has never sought to avoid scrutiny. On the other hand, one point of the system of reservations established by the Vienna Convention is something parallel to the reciprocity system of Article 36 of the Court's Statute, that a State which makes a reservation can only be a party to the Convention as amended by the reservation, and the amendment operates for the benefit of, as well as against, all States which have accepted it.[141] State B was entitled to suppose that it was immune from suit under the Convention at the instance of State A; and whether it did or did not want such immunity is beside the point.

Although the Court did not explicitly address the issue, there is one element in its 2006 decision in the *Congo/Rwanda* case, and in its Orders

---

[138] It would of course remain subject to the customary law as to genocide, but its compliance with that law would be outside the Court's competence.

[139] Orakhelashvili, *Peremptory Norms in International Law*, 512.

[140] Orakhelashvili also advocates that in the future the Court should adopt 'a differential approach' and 'in cases involving plausible accusations of genocide, distinguish the decisions on *Kosovo* and *DRC–Rwanda* on the basis that the more credible the accusations of genocide the more likely the Court's disregard of reservations to Article IX' (*Peremptory Norms in International Law*, 514). This shows a complete misunderstanding of the relationship between matters of jurisdiction and matters of merits: jurisdiction depends simply on the presence of consent, and has no relation whatsoever to the rights and wrongs of the case on the merits, let alone to the 'plausibility' of the claims made. As the Court observed in the *East Timor* case, having found that it could not exercise jurisdiction the Court 'cannot rule on Portugal's claims on the merits, whatever the importance of the questions raised by those claims and of the rules of international law which they bring into play', which included matters of *jus cogens*: [1995] ICJ Rep 105, para 36. See also the present writer's 'Judicial Activism and the International Court of Justice' in N Ando et al (eds.), *Liber Amicorum Judge Shigeru Oda* (2002), 75, at 99 ff.

[141] It is tempting to argue that the general principle would apply that a party cannot take advantage of its own wrong; but is it a 'wrong' to make a reservation to a Convention, which is not forbidden by the Convention?

in that case and the *Use of Force* cases, that suggests that its attitude was on the lines of the 'opposability' view. It attached importance to the fact that 'when Rwanda acceded to the Genocide Convention and made the reservation in question, the DRC made no objection to it.'[142] If however the 'permissibility' approach is the correct one, the failure of the DRC to object would have no effect whatever on the validity of the reservation. It seems therefore permissible to conclude that these decisions of the Court are opposable to those scholars who consider that a reservation to a multilateral treaty may suffer from an invalidity such that it cannot be cured by the lack of objection, or even consent, of another State party to the Convention; that the Court, in short, was tacitly rejecting that view. When making the Orders on provisional measures in that case and the *Use of Force* cases, the Court could properly have considered that it was not appropriate to examine the controversial question of the possible invalidity of a reservation to Article IX in interlocutory proceedings, and therefore declined to follow the example of the Yugoslav judge *ad hoc*. The matter was however properly and fully before the Court in the preliminary objection phase, and since it is examined in the dissenting opinion of Judge Koroma,[143] it must presumably have figured in the deliberations. The fact that the Court dealt with it such a summary fashion is therefore a further indication that, with the exception of Judge Koroma, its Members were convinced of the correctness of the 'opposability' thesis.

Turning now to the joint opinion of Judges Higgins, Kooijmans, Elaraby, Owada and Simma, this can best be described as a holding operation. Its purpose essentially was to record the view that there was no inconsistency between the decision of the Court giving effect to the Rwandan reservation to Article IX of the Genocide Convention, on the one hand, and the developments in relation to international treaty-instruments relating to human rights, in particular General Comment No. 24 of the United Nations Human Rights Committee,[144] and the *Bellilos, Loizidou*, and *Rawle Stevens* cases, on the other. The authors of the opinion made it clear that they regarded these as sound law and desirable developments, and were anxious lest the decision in the *Armed Activities* case be read as a rejection thereof by the Court. Even on the specific point regarding the Rwandan reservation, they considered that:

It is thus not self-evident that a reservation to Article IX could not be regarded as incompatible with the object and purpose of the Convention [and therefore, presumably, to be set aside] and we believe that this is a matter that the Court should revisit for further consideration.[145]

---

[142] [2006] ICJ Rep 33, para 68.

[143] The judge *ad hoc* appointed by the DRC, Judge Mavungu, voted against the finding of lack of jurisdiction, but did not, in his dissenting opinion, rely on the argument that the Rwandan reservation to Article IX was ineffective: see [2006] ICJ Rep 95 ff.

[144] Adopted while President Higgins was a member of that Committee.

[145] [2006] ICJ Rep 72, para 29. Since the decision on the preliminary objections had put an end to the proceedings, there would be no further opportunity to examine the point in those proceedings.

It may be convenient to recall here the developments since the Vienna Convention that the authors of the joint opinion had in mind. On 2 November 1994 the United Nations Human Rights Committee issued General Comment No. 24, in which the Committee noted that a large number of reservations had been entered by States when adhering to the International Covenant on Civil and Political Rights, and that in very few instances had the other States parties made any objection to such reservations on the ground of incompatibility with the object and purpose of the Covenant. The Committee recalled the system established by the Vienna Convention for the treatment and effect of reservations to multilateral conventions, but considered that its provisions were 'inappropriate to address the problem of reservations to human rights treaties',[146] and that '[i]t necessarily falls to the Committee to determine whether a specific reservation is compatible with the object and purpose of the Covenant.'[147] It continued:

Because of the special character of a human rights treaty, the compatibility of a reservation with the object and purpose of the Covenant must be established objectively, by reference to legal principles, and the Committee is particularly well placed to perform this task. The normal consequence of an unacceptable reservation is not that the Covenant will not be in effect at all for a reserving party. Rather, such a reservation will generally be severable, in the sense that the Covenant will be operative for the reserving party without benefit of the reservation.[148]

This Comment was criticised both on the grounds that the fact that the Committee was 'particularly well-placed' to judge of the compatibility of reservations did not mean that it was legally authorized to do so; that the idea of an 'objective' assessment of compatibility was inconsistent with the Court's 1951 decision in the *Interpretation of the Genocide Convention* case and the system of the Vienna Convention; and that to hold a State bound to the obligations of a convention in disregard of a reservation, subject to which it had given its consent to be bound, was flatly in contradiction with the whole consensual principle of treaty relations.

In the cases of *Bellilos* v. *Switzerland* and *Loizidou* v. *Turkey*, the European Court of Human Rights was also willing, in the context of the European Human Rights Convention, to reject a reservation, but at the same time to

It is unclear in what circumstances the Court could or should 'revisit for further consideration' the question of the compatibility of a reservation to Article IX with the object and purpose of the Genocide Convention. In any other case in which the problem arose, the parameters would appear to be the same; the effect of the reservation would be identical, and the object and purpose of the Convention would remain unchanged. There is some hint in para 28 of the opinion that the situation might change if States did not fulfil their role as 'monitors of each other's compliance with [the] prohibition on genocide'; this would be consistent with the philosophy of General Comment No. 24. But the matter would only come before the Court again if proceedings had been brought against a State which had made a reservation to Article IX, and this would signify that at least one other State (the Applicant) was endeavouring to discharge this role.

[146] General Comment 24, para 17.
[147] Ibid, para 20.   [148] Ibid.

treat it as severable, so that the State concerned would still be a party to the relevant instrument, as though the reservation had never been made. In the *Loizidou* case, this meant that a reservation to the jurisdiction of the European Court itself was set aside, and the claim determined despite its exclusion, by the reservation, from the scope of the Court's jurisdiction.

The joint opinion approves of these approaches. In terms similar to those of General Comment No. 24, the authors observe that it would be 'too sweeping' to view the 1951 advisory opinion as having stipulated 'a régime of inter-State *laissez-faire* in the matter of reservations, in the sense that while the object and purpose of a convention should be borne in mind both by those making reservations and those objecting to them, everything in the final analysis is left to the States themselves.'[149] The opinion also stresses the intertemporal aspect: '[s]ince 1951 many other issues relating to reservations have emerged, that... were not and could not have been before the Court at that time'. Among these, the opinion noted, were the possible role 'as regards assessment of compatibility with object and purpose' of monitoring bodies like the Human Rights Committee, and 'the scope of powers given to courts at the centre of the great human rights treaties.'[150]

The practice of such bodies is not to be viewed as 'making an exception' to the law as determined in 1951 by the International Court; we take the view that it is rather a development to cover what the Court was never asked at that time, and to address new issues that have arisen subsequently.[151]

The true issue here is however not that of formal consistency with the 1951 opinion, but whether or not a development of customary law can be effected, not by the practice of States, but by the fiat of a monitoring body or an international tribunal of limited jurisdiction—or indeed any tribunal in the absence of an express authorisation to make, rather than apply, the relevant international law.[152] However, just as the Court in 1951 was not called upon to consider all the issues that might have been submitted to it, so in 2006 the Court was not called upon to pass judgment on General Comment No. 24 or the jurisprudence of the *Belilos* and *Loizidou* cases. In the *Armed Activities* case, the Court simply decided that a reservation excluding Article IX of the Genocide Convention was not contrary to the object and purpose of the Convention; this was thus

---

[149] [2006] ICJ Rep 65, para 4.
[150] Ibid, 68, para 12.   [151] Ibid, 69, para 16.
[152] A similar understatement of the essential role of State practice is found in the opinion's treatment of the successive human rights instruments and the reservations made to them. In order to show that the problem of reservations, particularly to human rights treaties, is much more extensive than would have appeared in 1951, the opinion cites the reservations entered to a number of human rights conventions, beginning with the Genocide Convention (1949), and continuing up the International Convention on the Rights of the Child (1989). An equally significant aspect of this historical account is that in none of the Conventions mentioned was any attempt made to adopt a different method for handling reservations: the draftsmen and the States parties appear to have regarded the general system deriving from the 1951 opinion, and reflected in the Vienna Convention, as adequate to the task.

a rejection of the view argued by Orakhelashvili and other scholars, but not of specific steps taken by the Human Rights Committee and human rights tribunals, invoked by those scholars in support of their more far-reaching contentions.

The joint opinion is impliedly hostile to the 'permissibility' approach to the question of validity of reservations. Referring to the wording of the Court's 2002 Order on provisional measures, the opinion noted that the Court had 'added its own assessment as to the compatibility' of the reservation with the Genocide Convention; and in the 2006 Judgment it had 'gone beyond noting a reservation by one State and a failure by the other to object.' Certainly the 'opposability' thesis in its purest form would seem to require the Court, once it had noted that a reservation by one party to a dispute had been accepted, or not objected to, by the other party, to conclude, simply on that basis, that the reservation was valid and effective as between the parties. On the other hand, the 'permissibility' thesis in its purest form would render the attitude of the other party legally irrelevant for determination of the validity of the reservation; yet, as mentioned above, the Court took note that, 'as a matter of the law of treaties,' the DRC had not objected to the reservation.[153]

The major innovation of General Comment No. 24 was of course on the question of severability of a reservation. It can be accepted without difficulty that a State that purports to accept the régime of a multilateral convention, particularly a human rights convention, while eviscerating it of content by substantial reservations, contrary to its object and purpose, should not be able simultaneously to hold itself out as a party to the convention, even if the other parties prefer not to 'rock the boat' by objecting to the reservations. It is therefore just that other parties should be able to say to that State: 'because of your reservation, you are not a party as far as I am concerned'; and if there is a judicial or other body empowered to rule on the question of compatibility, that body should be able to say to the errant State: you are not a party to the Convention *at all*. This would be consistent with the 1951 opinion and the Vienna Convention. But it is one thing for the State to be told by such a body, 'You only consented to your own private version of the Convention, and therefore we hold that you are not a party to the real Convention at all', and quite another for it to be told, 'You only consented to your own private version of the Convention, but since that is not permissible, you must be treated as having consented to the real and complete Convention, whether you like it or not'. The view of the Human Rights Committee seems to have been that the first sanction is insufficient to deter improper reservations, and that the second was therefore required; but that is not to say that such a desirable solution is part of international law, then or now.

---

[153] [2006] ICJ Rep 33, para 68. It is possible that the Court intended to hint at a distinction between the 'law of treaties' and wider legal considerations justifying rejection of the reservation; yet those considerations would also seem to be part of the 'law of treaties'.

The paradox is particularly marked when the reservation is, as in the *Loizidou* case before the ECHR and in the *Armed Activities* case, directed to the compromissory clause of the multilateral convention. The view expressed by Judge Sir Hersch Lauterpacht in the *Certain Norwegian Loans* case as to the effect of finding a reservation, *in casu* a reservation to an optional-clause acceptance of jurisdiction, to be invalid, was that '[t]he Court cannot properly uphold the validity of the Acceptance as a whole and at the same time treat as non-existent any such far-reaching, articulate and deliberate limitation of its jurisdiction.... The Court certainly cannot assume jurisdiction if there is a clearly expressed intention to deny it in special circumstances'.[154] This has generally been regarded as the most consistent with the nature of the Court's consensual jurisdiction; but commitment to a treaty obligation is also a consensual matter. If a State made a reservation to what could be viewed as a comparatively minor provision of a multilateral convention, there might be a question whether its consent to the convention as a whole was conditioned by the attachment of the reservation; but there must be a presumption that a State attaching reservations intended to accept the convention as modified by the reservation, and nothing else. Furthermore, unless the reservation were one contrary to the object and purpose of the convention, no question of validity would arise; and if it could be treated as contrary to the object and purpose, the provision the subject of the reservation could hardly be deemed 'comparatively minor'.

It is also worth reflecting on an observation made by the judge *ad hoc* nominated by the DRC in a separate opinion appended to the 2002 Order on provisional measures. He suggested that to declare a reservation to Article IX invalid would not only be inconsistent with previous case-law, but 'could result in State parties to the Convention which have excluded the Court's jurisdiction by making reservations to the jurisdictional clause denouncing the Convention under Article XIV'.[155]

The treatment by some Members of the Court of the issue of the effect of reservations to a compromissory clause is revelatory of an attitude to the role of the Court which is not the traditional one, and which is perhaps disturbing. This attitude is summed up in the joint opinion of five judges in these words:

It must be regarded as a very grave matter that a State should be in position to shield from international judicial scrutiny any claim that might be made against it concerning genocide.[156]

---

[154] *Certain Norwegian Loans*, separate opinion, [1957] ICJ Rep 58.

[155] Separate opinion of Judge Marungu, *Armed Activities on the Territory of the Congo*, [2002] ICJ Rep 287, para 57.

[156] [2006] ICJ Rep 71, para 25. This is echoed in the declaration made separately by one of the five authors of the opinion, Judge Elaraby: '... I do firmly believe that States, in general, should not be permitted to evade international judicial scrutiny regarding a crime as grave as genocide': ibid, 82, para 1.

A comment that springs immediately to mind is on the lines of *dura lex, sed lex*: the situation deprecated by these judges is the result of the drafting of the Genocide Convention, and so long as it is not amended, that is the conventional law. The choice was made in 1951 not to forbid reservations to Article IX, so as to oblige States, if they wished to make a real commitment to the outlawing of genocide, to accept 'international judicial scrutiny'.

There is however a more profound implication in the passage quoted, though it needs only to be touched on here, being a matter not of treaty law but of the nature of international judicial settlement, and the role of the Court in particular. The expression 'to shield from international judicial scrutiny' implies that such scrutiny is the norm, and that for a State to arrange its international commitments so that certain activities are not subject to international jurisdiction is an evasion, and is or should be impossible. This idea was however at the heart of the *Fisheries Jurisdiction* case between Spain and Canada, and in that case the Court did not accept the Spanish contention that Canada should not be permitted to 'shield from judicial scrutiny' its fishery protection activities in areas outside its regular jurisdiction, inasmuch as such activities were, it was suggested, admittedly unlawful. The Court was surely right to declare in the *Fisheries Jurisdiction* case that '[c]onditions or reservations [appended to optional-clause declarations] do not by their terms derogate from a wider acceptance already given'.[157] It was a dissenting judge, Judge Bedjaoui, who took the opposite view, and was prepared to go so far as to assert that the Court could 'declare null and void and invalid *ab initio* any reservation that prevents it from hearing proceedings concerning genocide, slavery, piracy, or any other international crime'.[158]

Secondly however, the role of the International Court is not 'judicial scrutiny' but settlement of disputes, as Article 38, paragraph 1, of the Statute expressly states. It is a false analogy to argue from the role of national courts of universal jurisdiction to that of international courts of consensual jurisdiction, and from the role of national courts as a means to the enforcement of the law to the role of international tribunals as a means of establishing what the law is, the consequences being essentially in the hands of the parties.

The idea of 'judicial scrutiny' is of course attractive when a claim is made that a State has committed genocide; but the principle is nevertheless that no activity of a State is subject to international judicial scrutiny unless and so far as accepted by the State concerned. If a State which has not accepted any ICJ jurisdiction commits genocide, it is in breach of international law, but its actions are subject to no judicial scrutiny. If a State deposits an optional-clause declaration with a reservation which, *de facto*, excludes, or turns out in the events which have happened to exclude, jurisdiction over alleged acts of genocide (eg

---

[157] [1998] ICJ Rep 453, para 44.
[158] Ibid, 534, para 44. *Cf.* Also the views of Judge Weeramantry, ibid 513, para 69.

exclusion of any dispute relating to the events of specified hostilities, or that occurred during a specified period of time), can that exclusion be over-ridden to assume jurisdiction on the grounds of nullity of the exclusion?

(d) Succession to treaties

The case of the *Gabčíkovo-Nagymaros Project* raised directly the question whether there exists any automatic rule of succession to a bilateral treaty on the dissolution of one of the States parties. The treaty in question had been concluded in 1977 between Hungary and Czechoslovakia; on 1 January 1993 the State of Czechoslovakia was replaced by the separate States of the Czech Republic and Slovakia. Had Slovakia succeeded to Czechoslovakia as a party to the treaty? No agreement had been concluded between Hungary and Slovakia to regulate the matter. Slovakia invoked Article 34 of the 1978 Vienna Convention on Succession of States in respect of Treaties, which provides that:

When a part or parts of the territory of a State separate to form one or more States, whether or not the predecessor State continues to exist...any treaty in force at the date of the succession of States in respect only of that part of the territory of the predecessor State which has become a successor State continues in force in respect of that successor State alone.

The Vienna Convention was not however in force between the parties, so that the rule laid down in Article 34 could only be relied on if it represented an existing rule of customary law.

The Court however declined to rule on the general question whether Article 34 represents a rule of customary law; it found that the matter was governed by the more specific rule stated in Article 12 of the Vienna Convention, to the effect that

A succession of States does not as such affect:

   (a) obligations relating to the use of any territory, or to restrictions upon its use, established by a treaty for the benefit of any territory of a foreign State and considered as attaching to the territories in question;...

The Court considered that 'Article 12 reflects a rule of customary law', and noted that 'neither of the Parties disputed this'.[159] However, Article 12 does not state, as does Article 34, that the relevant treaty continues in force in relation to the new State, but simply that the 'obligations...established by [the] treaty' are unaffected by the succession of States.[160] As the Court observed, this 'appears to lend support to the position of Hungary rather than that of Slovakia',[161] since it was essential to Slovakia's case

---

[159] [1997] ICJ Rep 72, para 123.

[160] This might be a serious objection as a matter of treaty-interpretation, but when applying a customary rule reflected in a treaty-provision, the same degree of nicety of assessment of the exact words used is perhaps not required.

[161] [1997] ICJ Rep 72, para 123.

that the 1977 Treaty continued to exist and to be effective in relation to Slovakia as a party by succession. As Judge Bedjaoui put it:

According to Hungary, that Party—Slovakia—did not inherit *the formal instrument* itself, but *its material content* made up of *"the rights and obligations"* which Slovakia allegedly derived from this—according to Hungary—now defunct Treaty.[162]

Citing the records of the International Law Commission relating to the drafting of the 1978 Convention, the Court concluded

that this formulation was devised rather to take account of the fact that, in many cases, treaties which had established boundaries or territorial régimes were no longer in force... Those that remained in force would nonetheless bind a successor State.[163]

Hungary disputed the territorial character of the 1977 Treaty for purposes of the application of Article 12, suggesting that it was more in the nature of a joint investment. The Court recognized that it did have such a character,[164] but noted that 'its major elements were the proposed construction and joint operation of a large, integrated and indivisible complex of structures and installations' along the Danube, and 'created a situation in which the interest of other users of the Danube were affected.'[165] The Court took into account that the ILC had indicated that 'treaties concerning water rights or navigation on rivers are commonly regarded as candidates for inclusion in the category of territorial treaties'.[166] The Court's conclusion was thus that

the content of the 1977 Treaty indicates that it must be regarded as establishing a territorial régime within the meaning of Article 12 of the 1978 Vienna Convention. It created rights and obligations "attaching to" the parts of the Danube to which it relates; thus the Treaty itself cannot be affected by a succession of States. The Court therefore concludes that the 1977 Treaty became binding upon Slovakia on 1 January 1993.[167]

A question of succession to treaties was at the heart of the litigation concerning the genocide committed, or alleged to have been committed, in Bosnia and Herzegovina. The jurisdiction of the Court in the case concerning *Application of the Genocide Convention*, and in the *Legality of the Use of Force* cases, depended on the status of the State eventually known as Serbia and Montenegro as a party to the Statute of the Court as the successor the Socialist Federal Republic of Yugoslavia. However that status depended on the question whether that State had or had not succeeded to the Membership of the SFRY in the United Nations; and the matter will therefore be examined in Division D, Chapter II, in a further instalment of this series, in relation to the law of the United Nations.

[162] Ibid, 126, para 24.

[163] Ibid, citing *Official Records of the United Nations Conference on the Succession of States in respect of Treaties*, Vol. III, doc. A/CONF.80/16/Add.2, 26–37.

[164] Ibid, 71, para 123.   [165] Ibid 71–72.

[166] Ibid, 72, citing Official Records of the United Nations Conference on the Succession of States in respect of Treaties, Vol. III, doc. A/CONF.80/16/Add.2, 33, para 26.

[167] Ibid, 72, para 123.

CHAPTER III. THE TREATY IN ACTION

1. WHAT IS MEANT BY SAYING THAT A TREATY IS 'IN FORCE'?

The discussion of this question in the earlier article[168] was directly related to the interpretation by the Court of the term 'in force' in Articles 36, paragraph 1, and 37 of the Statute; but it was there noted that the decisions of the Court in this context 'may also be read... to give some indication of the meaning of an important concept of treaty-law'. In the subsequent period, that concept has been relevant outside the narrow context of the Articles of the Statute referred to.

In the case concerning the *Gabčíkovo-Nagymaros Project*, a bilateral Treaty between Hungary and Slovakia (as successor to Czechoslovakia) was held to be still in force despite the fact that 'the Treaty has not been fully implemented for years, and indeed [the parties'] acts of commission and omission have contributed to creating [that] factual situation...',[169] and despite the fact that Hungary had purported to terminate the Treaty in 1992, and had argued before the Court that 'by their conduct both parties had repudiated the Treaty and that a bilateral treaty repudiated by both parties cannot survive.'[170]

On this second point, the Court's ruling is inspired by the need for the stability of treaties, and recognizes the importance of the element of consent, basic to the law of treaties:[171]

The Court is of the view, however, that although it has found that both Hungary and Czechoslovakia failed to comply with their obligations under the 1977 Treaty, this reciprocal wrongful conduct did not bring the Treaty to an end nor justify its termination. The Court would set a precedent with disturbing implications for treaty relations and the integrity of the rule *pacta sunt servanda* if it were to conclude that a treaty in force between States, which the parties have implemented in considerable measure and at great cost over a period of years, might be unilaterally set aside on grounds of reciprocal noncompliance. It would be otherwise, of course, if the parties decided to terminate the Treaty by mutual consent. But in this case, while Hungary purported to terminate the Treaty, Czechoslovakia consistently resisted this act and declared it to be without legal effect.[172]

The last sentence however refers back to the separate issue of Hungary's purported unilateral termination of the Treaty, which was a response to action by Czechoslovakia (the implementation of an operation known as 'Variant C') regarded by Hungary as contrary to the Treaty, and based

---

[168] (1992) *BYIL* 1, 32 ff.   [169] [1997] ICJ Rep 76, para 133.

[170] Ibid, 68, para 114.

[171] Cf the attitude expressed by some Members of the Court to the similar issue of the possibility of a treaty ceasing to have effect through desuetude, in the *Nuclear Tests* cases: below, Chapter V, Section 6.

[172] [1997] ICJ Rep 68, para 114.

on five legal grounds: the existence of a state of necessity; impossibility of performance; occurrence of a fundamental change of circumstances; material breach of the Treaty by Czechoslovakia; and the development of new norms of international environmental law.[173] Hungary's argument based on repudiation was different: it was that 'even on the hypothesis that the 1977 Treaty survived termination by Hungary on 19 May 1992, the implementation of Variant C amounted to a repudiation by Czechoslovakia of the Treaty'.[174] Thus the question was not one of a treaty being 'unilaterally set aside on grounds of reciprocal non-compliance', as the Court puts it; it was whether the 'reciprocal wrongful conduct' in the sense of conduct incompatible with the treaty, of both parties was such as to show that each of them either wished to put an end to the treaty-relationship, or regarded that relationship as ended. The Court's analysis of the matter as one of 'consent' is correct, though that consent might be separate rather than mutual, if both parties independently arrived at the conclusion that the treaty should be, or had been, repudiated, again by both parties. On the facts, there was ample ground for the Court's conclusion that no bilateral repudiation had occurred; but the use of the term 'unilaterally' is perhaps inappropriate, as is the reference to the lengthy and costly implementation of the 1977 Treaty, since if the parties chose to cast aside what had been achieved, they were free to do so, as long as it was by the consent of both of them.

A treaty that has been validly terminated is clearly no longer 'in force'; what of a treaty that has been suspended? And is there a distinction to be made between suspension of the treaty and suspension of performance of obligations under the treaty? The Vienna Convention on the Law of Treaties refers to 'suspension of the operation of a treaty' rather than to the suspension of the treaty itself.[175]

If a treaty has been validly suspended, performance cannot be demanded of the obligations that it imposes upon each party;[176] but does that of itself mean that the treaty is not 'in force'? If the matter is regarded as one of interpretation of the references in the Court's Statute to 'treaties in force', an answer was given by the Court in the *ICAO Appeal* case. India was arguing that the suspension of the Chicago Convention conferring jurisdiction on the Court deprived it of jurisdiction. The Court held that it had jurisdiction; but it gave a series of reasons for this, and on the particular point now under discussion its reasoning is a little obscure:

---

[173] Ibid, 58, para 92.

[174] Hungarian Memorial, para 10.104. The point that Czechoslovakia had repudiated the Treaty by conduct, and that the repudiation was 'adopted and intensified' when Slovakia came into existence, was developed by Prof. Crawford as counsel for Hungary, as an argument quite distinct from that of Hungary's termination of the Treaty: Verbatim Record of 7 March 1997, CR 97/6, 24 ff.

[175] Part V, Section 3 (Articles 57–60).

[176] An interesting question is whether performance, during the period of suspension, of acts that would have been required by the treaty, can be regarded as 'performance' of an obligation which is, for the time being, non-existent; but the question could probably only be answered in relation to a specific text, and a specific set of acts.

What India has affirmed is that the Treaties—which are multilateral ones—are suspended (or that their operation is suspended) as between herself and Pakistan. This is not the same thing as saying that they are not in force in the definitive sense, or even that they have wholly ceased to be in force as between the two Parties concerned.[177]

This does not really resolve the issue; but the problem was that it was Pakistan that was arguing that the Convention was suspended by the action of India; if it had been India that was claiming that its own suspension rendered the Convention 'not in force', then India could claim to define for itself what degree of suspension had been its intention, and consistency would suggest that it intended to exclude the Convention from the category of 'treaties in force' for purposes of the Statute. The Court does however apparently recognize that a suspension *could* have the effect that a treaty would become 'not in force in the definitive sense'—apparently, because it is not clear whether in the passage quoted the Court is saying that what matters is what India was claiming to do, or that a suspension never implies becoming 'not in force in the definitive sense'. A further complication is that the argument quoted is only one of a set which the Court uses to reject the challenge to jurisdiction, and one of the others is that a jurisdictional clause is in a special category, so as to be unaffected by a suspension of the treaty containing it;[178] which necessarily implies, in relation to the terms of Article 36 of the Statute, that the relevant treaty would, with this exception, have ceased to be 'in force'.

It may be that the necessary conclusion is that how far the effect of a particular act of suspension of a treaty is to render the treaty no longer 'in force' depends on the provisions of the treaty itself, and subject thereto, to the intention of the party effecting the suspension; in other words, that the term 'in force' in relation to a treaty is not one with a fixed and immutable content.

The effect of a suspension cannot however depend solely on the stated intention of the party declaring it. Whether a purported suspension of a treaty is lawful depends on the terms of the treaty, and general international law; but whether an act is a suspension, lawful or otherwise, or not, may also depend on the treaty and general international law. In the case concerning the *Gabčíkovo-Nagymaros Project*, Hungary claimed that when in 1989 it suspended works on the Project which it was required to carry out under the 1977 Treaty establishing the Project, 'although it did suspend or abandon certain works, on the contrary, it never suspended the application of the 1977 Treaty itself'.[179] The Court did not accept this contention, interpreting the relevant conduct of Hungary 'as

---

[177] [1972] ICJ Rep 53, para 16(a). The reference to the multilateral nature of the Treaties probably indicates that the Court had in mind the matters later dealt with in Article 58 of the Vienna Convention on the law of Treaties, ensuring that suspension of the operation of a multilateral treaty between certain parties does not prejudice the rights of other parties to it.

[178] Ibid, 53–54, para 16(b).

[179] [1997] ICJ Rep 35, para 40.

an expression of its unwillingness to comply with at least some of the provisions of the Treaty', and, more importantly, noting that its effect was 'to render impossible the accomplishment of the system of works [on both sides of the frontier] that the Treaty expressly described as "single and indivisible"'.[180] However, the Court went on from this finding to consider whether Hungary had been entitled to suspend the operation of the Treaty on grounds of necessity (as Hungary claimed) and found that it was not; in the light of this, it concluded 'that Hungary was not entitled to suspend and subsequently abandon, in 1989, the works' under the Treaty. Thus Hungary was found to have been in breach of the Treaty; but had the Treaty been suspended? The way in which the Court expressed itself suggested that it had been—wrongfully—suspended; but no conclusion was drawn from this, other than that Hungary was in breach of the Treaty.

Hungary's contention was that in 1989 the 1977 Treaty remained in force, but since 'the essential continuing obligation on the parties under the Treaty was to seek to resolve difficulties by negotiation in good faith', its provisions as to timetable of works were flexible and could be adjusted; it drew 'a distinction between the suspension and even the termination of works at Nagymaros and the continuation of the Treaty'.[181] The force of the distinction appears to be that, in Hungary's contention, the provisions for negotiation in the Treaty came into effect, so that 'it was a matter for the parties in good faith to negotiate with a view to resolving the difficulties, if possible, or if not, to adjusting the Project plans, and eventually the 1977 Treaty itself, accordingly'.[182] If the Treaty were terminated, and apparently also even if it were merely suspended, these provisions would not have effect. This contention became irrelevant, since in 1992 Hungary purported to terminate the Treaty, and no claim was made by either party the settlement of which turned on whether or not the Treaty was suspended between 1989 and 1992.

It is evident that if a treaty is 'in force' at a particular date for purposes of a reference in another treaty-instrument to 'treaties in force', that reference is satisfied even if the treaty in question ceases to be effective at some subsequent date. In the *Territorial Dispute (Nicaragua/Colombia)* the 1948 Pact of Bogotá excluded from its dispute-settlement provisions any matters 'governed by agreements or treaties in force' at the date of the Pact. Nicaragua argued that a 1928 Treaty between the Parties did not fall within this provision because it had been invalid; but the Court found that no claim or assertion of invalidity had been made by Nicaragua until 1980, long after the Pact came into force.[183]

---

[180] Ibid, 39, para 48.   [181] Hungarian Memorial, para 9.18.
[182] Ibid, para 9.24.
[183] [2007] ICJ Rep, para 79 of the Judgment of 13 December 2007.

2. The Claiming of Rights Entails Submission to the Corresponding Obligations

Mention has been made above[184] of the objection presented by the United States to the claim of Mexico in the case of *Avena and Other Mexican Nationals*, essentially on the basis of the *exceptio non adimpleti contractus*: the USA suggested that Mexico's own standards of compliance with the Vienna Convention on Contractual Relations should debar it from presenting a claim based on non-compliance by the United States. This may also be seen as an invocation of the principle discerned by Fitzmaurice and defined as in the title of this Section, which was discussed by him in relation to the *South West Africa* case.[185] As explained above, the Court rejected the objection on the basis that it was inappropriate to a convention of the type represented by the Consular Convention; but in connection with Fitzmaurice's principle it may also be observed that there must be an element of proportion in its application; a State cannot be debarred from asserting its rights under a treaty as a result of any breach thereof, however trivial, that it has itself committed. If there were cases of United States citizens arrested in Mexico who had not been given the full protection offered by the Convention, this should not in itself prevent Mexico from insisting on proper treatment for its nationals in the United States. It would be otherwise if it were shown that it was the policy of the Mexican authorities to deny the protection of the Convention to alien detainees, or detainees of a particular nationality. Any failure to comply with the Convention requirements would be a breach of the Convention; but a policy of this kind would be not merely a continuing breach, but in effect a repudiation of the Convention obligation, and it would be that that would, in principle, justify exclusion of the defaulting State from entitlement to claim its Convention rights.

In the particular case, however, of the Consular Convention, and *a fortiori* in the case of conventions of a humanitarian nature, considerations deriving from the nature of the Convention, as identified by the Court in the *Avena* case, would over-ride the *exceptio*: it would, it is suggested, be unacceptable to penalise the citizens of the defaulting State by depriving them of the benefit of the treatment guaranteed by the Convention as a sort of counter-measure because citizens of the receiving State were being denied that benefit in the defaulting State, even if that denial were not sporadic, but a matter of deliberate government policy.[186]

---

[184] Chapter II, Section 1(2).

[185] (1950) *BYIL* 8; (1951) *BYIL* 51; see the previous article in the present series, (1992) *BYIL* 1, 40–41.

[186] The case does not appear to fall squarely within the limitations laid down in Article 50, paragraph 1, of the International Law Commission's Articles on State Responsibility, but is comparable to those limitations and to the precedents in the matter, as recounted in the Commission's Commentary, paras. (1) to (8).

3. IMPLIED POWERS IN TREATY

In the previous article in this series,[187] note was taken of the view of Fitzmaurice that the doctrine of implied powers, as a qualification of the principle of speciality, was a matter of treaty interpretation—an application of Fitzmaurice's Principle of Effectiveness;[188] but the present writer ventured to doubt whether this was a correct analysis. It was suggested that the interpretation of a treaty is a process that involves placing oneself at the time when the treaty was concluded, and considering what the draftsmen meant in the light of what they foresaw, or may be deemed to have foreseen. The doctrine of implied powers, on the other hand, might be expressed in the adage, 'who wills the ends, wills the means'; and the consequence is that, if the alleged need for an implied power only reveals itself many years after the date of the treaty, it is not necessary to take account only of the text of the treaty and 'such intentions and expectations as might have been in the minds of its signatories'.[189]

In the case concerning the *Legality of the Use by a State of Nuclear Weapons in Armed Conflict*, the WHO requested of the Court an advisory opinion on the question whether '[i]n view of the health and environmental effects,... the use of nuclear weapons by a State in war or other armed conflict [would] be a breach of its obligations under international law including the WHO Constitution'.[190] In accordance with Article 96, paragraph 2, of the Charter, the Court had to be satisfied that that question was one which arose 'within the scope of [the] activities' of the WHO. After examining the organization's constitution, the Court concluded that the question put was not 'capable of being considered as "arising within the scope of [the] activities" of the WHO'.[191] The Court then proceeded to make a classic statement of the principle of speciality, and the doctrine of implied powers:

The Court need hardly point out that international organizations are subjects of international law which do not, unlike States, possess a general competence. International organizations are governed by the "principle of speciality", that is to say, they are invested by the States which create them with powers, the limits of which are a function of the common interests whose promotion those States entrust to them.[192]

...

The powers conferred on international organizations are normally the subject of an express statement in their constituent instruments. Nevertheless, the necessities of international life may point to the need for organizations, in order

---

[187] (1992) *BYIL* 1, 42–43.
[188] (1951) *BYIL* 18–19; *Collected Edition*, I 59–60.
[189] (1992) *BYIL* 1, 43.
[190] Quoted in [1996] ICJ Rep 68, para 1.
[191] Ibid, 77, para 22.
[192] Ibid, 78, para 25, citing *Jurisdiction of the European Commission of the Danube, Advisory Opinion*, P.C.I.J., Series B, No. 14, p. 64.

to achieve their objectives, to possess subsidiary powers which are not expressly provided for in the basic instruments which govern their activities. It is generally accepted that international organizations can exercise such powers, known as "implied" powers.[193]

The Court was not however prepared to find that the question was one arising within the activities of the WHO on the basis of the doctrine of implied powers.

In the opinion of the Court, to ascribe to the WHO the competence to address the legality of the use of nuclear weapons—even in view of their health and environmental effects—would be tantamount to disregarding the principle of speciality; for such competence could not be deemed a necessary implication of the Constitution of the Organization in the light of the purposes assigned to it by its member States.[194]

This is a curiously negative formulation: it would be natural to say that competence to address the legality of the use of nuclear weapons could not be deemed a necessary implication of the Constitution, and therefore the doctrine of implied powers had no application; but the opposite view would on this basis not be a 'disregard' of the principle of speciality, but a misapplication of it.

These findings may be said, at the least, not to conflict with the analysis presented in the previous article. In the first place, the Court makes no mention of the criteria for interpretation of treaties enunciated in the Vienna Convention, with which it regularly prefaces its discussions of the interpretation of a treaty text. Furthermore, the Court indicates as justification for the doctrine of implied powers the fact that 'the necessities of international life may point to the need for organizations, in order to achieve their objectives, to possess subsidiary powers...'—that is to say, the fact of such necessities arising, not the fact that the parties had contemplated, at the time of conclusion of the treaty, that such necessities might arise.[195]

On the other hand, the Court also examined the distribution of competences within the UN system, and found that, simply expressed, questions of public health were for the WHO, but questions of use of force and the regulation of armaments were for the Security Council. In this context it observed that:

The WHO Constitution can only be interpreted, as far as the powers conferred upon that Organization are concerned, by taking due account not only

---

[193] Ibid, 79, para 25, citing *Reparation for Injuries Suffered in the Service of the United Nations, Advisory Opinion*, [1949] ICJ Rep. 182–183, and *Effect of Awards of Compensation Made by the United Nations Administrative Tribunal, Advisory Opinion*, [1954] ICJ Rep 57.

[194] Ibid, 79, para 25.

[195] *Cf.* also the dissenting opinion of Judge Koroma in which he refers to 'implied powers, which without conflicting with [the relevant] constitution, are a logical incident of it and contribute to ensuring its effectiveness.': [1996] ICJ Rep 193–194.

of the general principle of speciality, but also of the logic of the overall system contemplated by the Charter.[196]

This is not however to say that the principle of speciality is itself a principle of interpretation, but simply that it is in the light of, *inter alia*, the results of applying the principle of speciality that the relevant constitutional text requires to be interpreted.

4. THIRD PARTIES AND TREATIES

(1) Pactum in favorem tertii

The previous article dealt, under this heading, with aspects of the situation contemplated by Article 36 of the Vienna Convention on the Law of Treaties, namely provision in a treaty giving rise to rights to be enjoyed by a third State, that is to say a State not a party to the treaty. This is not a situation that the Court has had to consider in the period since that article was published. The question was raised in the case of *Passage through the Great Belt*, in which Finland claimed the benefit of the 1857 Copenhagen Treaty on the Redemption of the Sound Dues, to which it had not been a party, in support of its claim to free passage through the Great Belt for oil drilling rigs;[197] that case was however withdrawn following agreement between the parties, and thus the Court was not called upon to rule on the matter.

(2) Treaties conferring rights on individuals

The Court has however had to deal with a parallel problem: that of a treaty alleged to have conferred rights not merely on the States parties to it, but on the nationals of those States—rights exercisable by those nationals in their own right, and capable of enforcement by diplomatic protection. The question of the nature of the 'rights' of a national capable of diplomatic protection was discussed extensively in the first of these articles, by reference to the *Barcelona Traction* decision.[198] Much of the difficulty of that decision arose from the distinction made by the Court between injury to the 'rights' of the shareholder and injury merely to his 'interests'; this provoked the question: given that a 'right' can only exist in the context of a legal system, by what law was the existence of a 'right', and its status as such, rather than an 'interest', to be determined?

---

[196] Ibid, 80, para 26.

[197] See the Finnish Memorial in that case, *ICJ Pleadings* 322–324, and the Danish response, ibid, 609–611, conceding Finland's right to the benefit of the 1857 Treaty in accordance with Article 36 of the VCLT. Neither party commented on the doctrinal controversy over whether the consent of the third party is necessary to the validity of a *stipulation pour autrui* (cf. the discussion in Fitzmaurice and Elias, *Contemporary Issues in the Law of Treaties*, 276–281), but clearly the use by Finnish ships of the Sound would indicate consent.

[198] (1989) *BYIL* 1, 117–125.

In view of (*inter alia*) the established principle that diplomatic protection involves the assertion by the protecting State of its own right (the principle enunciated in the *Mavrommatis Palestine Concessions* case[199]), it appeared that only a relevant system of national law could be applied to in order to determine these questions.

As the International Law Commission has noted, much has changed in international law in this respect. 'The individual is the subject of many primary rules of international law, both under custom and treaty, which protect him at home, against his own Government, and abroad, against foreign Governments.'[200] For this reason, the ILC in its Draft Articles on Diplomatic Protection formulated the text 'in such a way as to leave open the question whether the State exercising diplomatic protection does so in its own right or that of its national—or both'.[201] The ILC referred in this respect to the decisions of the Court in the *LaGrand* and *Avena* cases; however, both those cases involved the question whether rights were conferred by treaty on individuals, and it will be convenient to examine them here from the angle of conferral of rights by treaty on entities other than the parties to the treaty.

The treaty in question in these cases was the Vienna Convention on Consular Relations (the Consular Convention). Article 36, paragraph 1(b) of the Convention provided that, when the national of one contracting State was arrested in the territory of another, he was entitled to request the authorities of the arresting State to inform his national consular post; and the text added that '[t]he said authorities shall inform the person concerned without delay of his rights under this subparagraph.'[202] Furthermore, paragraph 2 of Article 36 provided that:

The rights referred to in paragraph 1 of this article shall be exercised in conformity with the laws and regulations of the receiving State, subject to the proviso, however, that the said laws and regulations must enable full effect to be given to the purposes for which the rights accorded under this article are intended.

Germany in the *LaGrand* case, and Mexico in the *Avena* case, relied on both of these provisions, in order to assert simultaneously a direct claim for breach of treaty and a claim of diplomatic protection of their injured nationals.

A first question that arose in the *LaGrand* case resulted from the request by Germany, granted by the Court, for the indication of provisional measures to restrain the United States authorities from executing Walter LaGrand, a German national who had been tried and condemned

---

[199] [1924] PCIJ, Series A, No. 2, p. 12.
[200] Commentary to ILC Draft Articles on State Responsibility, *ILC Report on the work of the 58th Session*, A/61/10, Article 1, commentary para 4.
[201] Ibid, para 5.
[202] Quoted in [2001] ICJ Rep 475, para 15.

to death without the German Consulate having been informed. In its Order, the Court recalled its consistent jurisprudence to the effect that:

the power of the Court to indicate provisional measures under Article 41 of its Statute is intended to preserve the respective rights of the parties pending its decision, and presupposes that irreparable prejudice shall not be caused to rights which are the subject of a dispute in judicial proceedings; whereas it follows that the Court must be concerned to preserve by such measures the rights which may subsequently be adjudged by the Court to belong either to the Applicant, or to the Respondent; . . . [203]

It then found that the execution of Walter LaGrand 'would cause irreparable harm to the rights claimed by Germany in this particular case'.[204] The Court was restricted by the jurisdictional title invoked—the Optional Protocol to the Consular Convention—to determining disputes concerning the interpretation and application of that Convention, and thus could only adjudge rights conferred by the Convention. The last-minute proceedings on the request aimed at saving a man's life were not the appropriate moment to raise legal niceties of this kind, and the Court cannot be criticized for having issued its Order; but *ex post facto* doubts may be permitted. What rights conferred by the Convention would be harmed by the execution? The German nationals concerned could claim the right to life, and the State could claim to restrain unlawful injury to one of its citizens; but these were not rights conferred by the Convention; and it was not immediately clear how the rights of notification under Article 36 would be breached by the execution of the national. The Court referred in its Order to 'the rights claimed *by Germany*'; could this refer to rights vested in the German national concerned, and protected on a basis of diplomatic protection?

At the stage of the merits, the Court had before it a submission by Germany that the United States, 'by failing to take all measures at its disposal' to prevent the execution of Walter LaGrand was in breach of an international obligation, but that obligation was attributed by Germany to the effect of the Order indicating provisional measures itself. Thus Germany did not assert the existence of any right, having existed at the time of its application to the Court, that would have been violated by the execution, let alone any right of that nature under the Consular Convention.

Setting aside the question of the rights arising out of the provisional measures Order itself, what rights were relevant in the case? It was clear—and conceded by the United States—that the non-notification to the LaGrand brothers (and to Avena and his fellow-citizens in the later case) constituted breaches by the United States of the Consular Convention vis-à-vis Germany and Mexico. The rights of these two claimant States had thus been infringed; it was argued by the United

---

[203] [1999] ICJ Rep 15, para 22.   [204] Ibid, para 24.

States in the *LaGrand* case that the claim to diplomatic protection added nothing, was inappropriate in the context of consular law, and was unsupported by precedent.[205] Its relevance was however essentially in connection with the reliance by the Applicants on paragraph 2 of Article 36, with its provision as to giving 'full effect to the purpose for which the rights accorded under this article are intended'. Once a failure to notify had occurred, a breach of paragraph 1 would be established; if the subsequent criminal proceedings were not such as to remedy the breach *ex post facto*, the rights of the State of the arrested national would not, it may be suggested, suffer any further diminution. Hence, even assuming (as was disputed by the United States) that paragraph 2 was intended to justify a separate claim for alleged breaches of it, nothing would be added. The original failure of notification would be both a breach of paragraph 1, and a failure to give full effect to the State's rights as required by paragraph 2.

For this reason the argument of Germany and Mexico was that Article 36, paragraph 1, conferred rights on the individual national, which would be breached by non-notification; that if the subsequent criminal proceedings in the national courts could nullify the effects of the breach (for example, by making it possible for the proceedings to be set aside, and only re-instated after the appropriate consular notification had been made), then 'full effect' would have been given to the rights conferred by the Convention on the individual national; but that if such were not the case, then there would have been a failure to give such 'full effect', and thus a breach of paragraph 2. This was the argument accepted by the Court, which enabled it to direct the United States, in any future case in which there might be a failure of consular notification, to 'allow the review and reconsideration of the conviction and sentence by taking account of the violation of the rights set forth in [the] Convention'.[206]

Further discussion of these cases will be more appropriate in a further article in the series, dealing with State responsibility; the *LaGrand* and *Avena* cases serve however in the present context to confirm both the possibility of conferring rights on individuals by treaty, and the difficulty that may arise in practice in distinguishing them in operation and effect from the rights of the parties to the treaty.

(3) *Treaties as* res inter alios acta

In the case of the *Land and Maritime Boundary between Cameroon and Nigeria* the question arose whether the maritime delimitation requested of the Court had to be geographically restricted to take account of the possible rights or interests of third States, specifically Equatorial Guinea (which was intervening in the case as a non-party) and Sao Tome and

---

[205] [2001] ICJ Rep 493, para 76.
[206] *LaGrand*, [2001] ICJ Rep 516, para 128(7).

Principe. Cameroon claimed that no delimitation could affect those States, 'as the Court's judgment will be *res inter alios acta* for all States other than itself and Nigeria'. It invoked the *Continental Shelf (Tunisia/ Libya)* case, and contended that

most of the maritime boundary agreements that are already in force would never have come into being if it had not been possible for the States concerned to reach a bilateral agreement on a maritime boundary without there being any prerequisite as to the participation of all such States as might potentially be involved in the area in question.[207]

It also referred to the *Frontier Dispute (Burkina Faso/Mali)* and the *Territorial Dispite (Libya/Chad)*, and argued that

the effect of the Court's Judgment would be the same as a bilateral maritime delimitation treaty, which will not be opposable as such to third States, but by which the two parties to the treaty may agree to fix their maritime boundary up to a tripoint decided bilaterally, without the participation of the third State concerned.[208]

In the *Frontier Dispute* case, the Court had found itself able to define the frontier between the two parties up to the tripoint with the neighbouring State, Niger, on the basis both of Article 59 of the Statute and of a parallel with boundary treaties:

The Parties could at any time have concluded an agreement for the delimitation of their frontier, according to whatever perception they might have had of it, and an agreement of this kind, although legally binding upon them by virtue of the principle *pacta sunt servanda,* would not be opposable to Niger. A judicial decision, which "is simply an alternative to the direct and friendly settlement" of the dispute between the Parties *(P.C.I.J., Series A, No. 22,* p. 13), merely substitutes for the solution stemming directly from their shared intention, the solution arrived at by a court under the mandate which they have given it. In both instances, the solution only has legal and binding effect as between the States which have accepted it, either directly or as a consequence of having accepted the Court's jurisdiction to decide the case.[209]

In that case, however, the Court drew a distinction between land boundaries and maritime delimitations; it recognized that in the case of the *Continental Shelf (Libya/Malta)* it had restricted the maritime delimitation so as not to encroach on areas claimed by Italy, for reasons connected with the nature of continental shelf rights.[210] In the *Cameroon/Nigeria* case, the Court followed this precedent, and therefore declined to 'rule on Cameroon's claims' to maritime areas 'in so far as they might affect rights of Equatorial Guinea and Sao Tome and Principe'.[211] It considered that

---

[207] [2002] ICJ Rep 418, para 232.
[208] Ibid, 419, para 233.
[209] [1986] ICJ Rep 577, para 46.
[210] Ibidm 578, para 47, citing [1985] ICJ Rep, 26, para 21.
[211] [2002] ICJ Rep 421, para 238.

the reasoning in the *Burkina Faso/Mali* case was not 'necessarily trans-posable to those concerning maritime boundaries'.[212] It would seem to follow that maritime boundary agreements that turn out to deal with areas to which legally a third State has entitlements are not merely non-opposable to the third State, but actually contrary to law and thus invalid; this indeed was the view expressed in the *Frontier Dispute* case.[213] This does not however prevent States in practice from concluding delimitation agreements defining a line right up to a tripoint, defined as such either specifically or by implication.[214] Since the principle is that *res inter alios acta nec nocet nec praestat*, it is the land boundary delimitation treaty that is the norm, and the maritime boundary delimitation treaty that is the exception in this regard.

---

[212] Ibid.

[213] [1986] ICJ Rep 578, para 47.

[214] Examples in C G Lathrop, 'Tripoint Issues in Maritime Boundary Delimitation', in D A Colson and R W Smith (eds), *International Maritime Boundaries* (2005), Vol V, 3313–3316.

CHAPTER IV: CONDUCT INCONSISTENT WITH A TREATY

1. DUTY NOT TO DEPRIVE A TREATY OF ITS OBJECT AND PURPOSE

In the earlier article on this subject, the decision in the case of *Military and Paramilitary Activities in and against Nicaragua* was discussed at some length; it was in that case that the Court declared the existence of a duty of a party to a treaty not to deprive the treaty of its object or purpose, not only pending ratification, as contemplated by Article 18 of the Vienna Convention on the Law of Treaties, but also during the currency of the treaty itself.[215]

Such a duty is not, the Court found, so open-ended, in the case of a treaty of friendship, as to cover any unfriendly act whatever: '[t]here must be a distinction, even in the case of a treaty of friendship, between the broad category of unfriendly acts, and the narrower category of acts tending to defeat the object and purpose of the Treaty.'[216] This finding was cited with approval by the Court in its decision in the *Oil Platforms* case, but in a different context. As explained in the most recent article in this series,[217] the question in that case was the identification of the 'object and purpose' of the Treaty between Iran and the United States, in order to apply it as a criterion for the interpretation of the text of the Treaty. It is thus only the distinction just quoted that has been re-confirmed by the Court; the innovation constituted by recognition (not to say, creation) of a duty not to defeat the object and purpose of a treaty, in parallel and in addition to the obligations stated in the treaty, has not been re-asserted by the Court. The contrary views expressed at the time by Judge Oda, and respectfully supported by the present writer,[218] have thus not so far been rejected on any re-examination of the question.

In the case of *Avena and Other Mexican Nationals* the Court interpreted the Vienna Convention on Consular Relations as incorporating an obligation closely resembling an obligation not to defeat the object and purpose of the Convention; this will however be discussed in the next section.

What might be the consequences of a breach of the obligation not to defeat the object and purpose of a treaty? This question is prompted by an observation in the judgment in the case concerning the *Gabčíkovo-Nagymaros Project*. Hungary had claimed that it was entitled to terminate the 1977 Treaty relating to the Project, between itself and Czechoslovakia,

---

[215] (1992) *BYIL* 1, 48–54, citing [1986] ICJ Rep 135–138.
[216] [1986] ICJ Rep 137, para 273.
[217] (2006) *BYIL* 1, 48–49.
[218] Ibid, 52–53, citing Judge Oda in [1986] ICJ Rep 250, para 81.

on the grounds (*inter alia*) of the breach by Czechoslovakia of a number of conventions other than the 1977 Treaty itself, and rules of general international law.[219] On this claim the Court ruled that 'it is only a material breach of the treaty itself, by a State party to that treaty, which entitles the other party to rely upon it as a ground for terminating the treaty'.[220]

As was noted in the previous article,[221] the obligation not to impede the object and purpose of a treaty 'is not a duty imposed by the treaty itself.'[222] Accordingly, a breach of the obligation is not, as such, a breach of the treaty; and therefore, on the basis of the *Gabčíkovo-Nagymaros* dictum, does not justify a termination of the treaty. In the circumstances contemplated by Article 18 of the Vienna Convention on the Law of Treaties, the treaty is not yet in force; but in the circumstances referred to in the *Nicaragua* case, it is; and a breach of the obligation not to impede the object and purpose might in fact be more disruptive of the continued operation of a treaty than a 'material breach' of the treaty itself. Since however this was not a point to which the Court was addressing itself in *Gabčíkovo-Nagymaros*, it may perhaps be regarded as an open question.

2. BREACH OF TREATY: THE RELEVANCE OF MUNICIPAL LAW

The interaction of a State's own municipal law with its treaty obligations was an issue that arose in the case of *LaGrand* and that of *Avena and Other Mexican Nationals*, in each case in relation to the obligations imposed by Article 36 of the Vienna Convention on Consular Relations.[223] In the latter case, the first issue that arose was however a very general one. The United States presented an objection to the jurisdiction of the Court, arguing that the claim of Mexico was 'fundamentally addressed to the treatment of Mexican nationals in the federal and state criminal justice system of the United States', rather than to breach of treaty-obligations.[224] The Court rejected the objection, on the ground that it related, not to jurisdiction, but to the merits:

If and so far as the Court may find that the obligations accepted by the parties to the Vienna Convention included commitments as to the conduct of their municipal courts in relation to the nationals of other parties, then in order to ascertain whether there have been breaches of the Convention, the Court must be able to examine the actions of those courts in the light of international law.[225]

---

[219] [1997] ICJ Rep 65, para 105.
[220] Ibid, para 106.   [221] (1992) *BYIL* 1, 50.
[222] *Military and Paramilitary Activities,* [1986] ICJ Rep 135, para 270.
[223] This Convention will be referred to as the 'Consular Convention', to avoid any confusion with other Vienna Conventions, particularly that on the Law of Treaties.
[224] [2004] ICJ Rep 30, para 27.
[225] Ibid, para 28.

In other words, while matters such as the criminal justice system of a State are in principle matters of 'domestic policy' which, as the Court observed in the *Military and Paramilitary Activities* case, 'fall within its exclusive jurisdiction, provided of course that it does not violate any obligation of international law', there remains 'the possibility of a State binding itself by agreement in relation to a question of domestic policy';[226] and whether or to what extent the Consular Convention had had that effect was one of the issues the Court was asked, and had jurisdiction, to decide.

Germany and Mexico each based their claims on Article 36 of the Consular Convention. Paragraph 1 of that Article lays upon contracting States the obligation to carry out various notifications whenever a foreign national is arrested, designed to ensure that he has the possibility of obtaining assistance from his consul. Paragraph 2 of the Article provides that:

The rights referred to in paragraph 1 of this article shall be exercised in conformity with the laws and regulations of the receiving State, subject to the proviso, however, that the said laws and regulations must enable full effect to be given to the purposes for which the rights accorded under this article are intended.

Germany, and subsequently Mexico, claimed that their nationals had not been given the necessary notifications, and that the United States was thus in breach not only of paragraph 1, but also of an obligation to ensure 'full effect' of the rights referred to in that paragraph, and thus a breach of paragraph 2. The relevance of United States internal law to the dispute was that the foreign nationals concerned had endeavoured to raise the issue of non-notification before appeals bodies, after they had been convicted of crimes without being aware of their consular rights, but had been met with the obstacle of the rule of US criminal procedure known as the 'procedural default rule'.

Since the argument turned on the effect to be given to paragraph 2 of Article 36, the issue was not one of general law governing the relationship between provisions of municipal law and the State's obligations under international law, but rather of interpretation of the Convention: did the municipal law complained of fail to 'give full effect' to the purpose of the rights referred to in paragraph 1?—a question which of course entailed ascertaining precisely what those rights were. The decisions in these two cases however clearly have a resonance going beyond the interpretation of the specific text, and it is thus appropriate to comment on them here.

The 'procedural default' rule, well-established in the criminal law of the United States (federal and at State level), was relevant in both cases, but it is convenient to refer to the definition of the rule cited by the Court

---

[226] *Military and Paramilitary Activities in and against Nicaragua,* [1986] ICJ Rep 131, paras 258, 259.

in the *Avena* case, which had been given by Mexico (the Applicant), and tacitly accepted by the United States:

a defendant who could have raised, but fails to raise, a legal issue at trial will generally not be permitted to raise it in future proceedings, on appeal or in a petition for a writ of *habeas corpus*. The rule requires exhaustion of remedies, *inter alia*, at the state level and before a *habeas corpus* motion call be filed with federal courts.[227]

In the *LaGrand* case, Germany contended that

the United States, by applying rules of its domestic law, in particular the doctrine of procedural default, which barred Karl and Walter LaGrand from raising their claims under the Vienna Convention on Consular Relations, and by ultimately executing them, violated its international legal obligation to Germany under Article 36 paragraph 2 of the Vienna Convention to give full effect to the purposes for which the rights accorded under Article 36 of the said Convention are intended.[228]

It was shown that after the LaGrand brothers who, unknown to themselves at the time of their trial, possessed German nationality, had been tried for murder and condemned to death, they had sought to have their convictions set aside on the ground, *inter alia*, that the United States authorities had failed to notify the German consulate of their arrest, as required by the Consular Convention. This claim was rejected on the basis of the 'procedural default' rule.[229]

The Court, following in this the German argument,[230] distinguished between the procedural default rule 'as such and its specific application in the present case', continuing:

In itself, the rule does not violate Article 36 of the Vienna [Consular] Convention. The problem arises when the procedural default rule does not allow the detained individual to challenge a conviction and sentence by claiming, in reliance on Article 36, paragraph 1, of the Convention, that the competent national authorities failed to comply with their obligation to provide the requisite consular information "without delay", thus preventing the person from seeking and obtaining consular assistance from the sending State.[231]

There is here an echo of the controversy which once existed round the question whether, as a general proposition, the enactment of a municipal law, the effect of which would be inconsistent with the international legal obligations of the State enacting it, would in itself constitute a breach of those obligations; or whether only the application of the law in a given case would constitute such a breach. Crawford has suggested that the principle of 'objective responsibility' adopted in the ILC Articles on State Responsibility, excluding the ideas of intention and fault from

---

[227] [2004] ICJ Rep 56, para 111, citing the Mexican Memorial.
[228] [2001] ICJ Rep 495, para 79.   [229] Ibid, 477, para 23.
[230] Ibid, 495, para 81.   [231] Ibid, 497, para 90.

the definition, has resolved this difficulty, inasmuch as no general rule is called for: what is determinative is the nature of the particular obligation in question. In some cases, 'actual harm or injury, eg to individuals, is of the essence of the wrong', while in others, for example in relation to uniform law conventions, there is an undertaking by a State 'that certain provisions be made part of its law'.[232]

Into which category does Article 36, paragraph 2, of the Consular Convention fall? That paragraph does not impose any obligation on States parties to enact any particular legislation; it is in the nature of a saving clause, permitting States to legislate as they see fit in this field, provided the obligations of the Convention are complied with (and as such a matter more *ex abundanti cautela* than prescriptive).[233] The Court nevertheless found in the *Avena* case that, 'by not permitting the review and reconsideration' of the cases of the Mexican nationals (as a result of the application of the procedural default rule), the United States 'breached the obligations incumbent upon it under Article 36, paragraph 2, of the Convention'; it thus treated that paragraph as incorporating an obligation distinct from the specific obligations stated in paragraph 1.[234] That obligation may be stated as being an obligation so to arrange its municipal law as to ensure that 'full effect' is given to the purposes for which the rights under paragraph 1 of Article 36 were intended.[235] In its lack of specificity and its emphasis on 'purpose' rather than conduct, this is an obligation strongly resembling the obligation not to defeat the object and purpose of a treaty, discussed above. But is it an obligation that is breached by the mere inconsistency of the municipal law with the treaty obligation[235a], or does a breach of it only occur when injury or damage results from breach of the obligation?

As indicated above, the Court in the *Avena* case distinguished between the existence of the 'procedural default rule' and its application, thereby opting for the second of the two possible analyses just stated. The case however suggests that the distinction may not be so sharp in practice as it might appear. If the United States had legislated to provide for the

---

[232] J Crawford, *The International Law Commission's Articles on State Responsibility* (2002) 13. As pointed out by Jennings and Watts (*Oppenheim's International Law*, 9th edn, Vol I, 86, fn 13), a good example is Article 5 of the Genocide Convention, whereby the parties expressly undertake to enact the necessary legislation to give effect to the Convention. Failure to do so would be a breach of the Convention whether or not any genocide had been committed to which the missing legislation would have applied.

[233] The United States argued in the *Avena* case that 'Article 36(2) recognizes the sovereign right of States to order their own affairs, and to implement their international obligations within the context of their own criminal justice systems, so long as these laws and regulations do not preclude giving full effect to the purposes of Article 36(1).' (US Counter-Memorial, para 6.59).

[234] Whether this was the proper interpretation of the text is not here to the purpose; the question is, on the basis that paragraph 2 imposed such an obligation, how did it relate to the municipal law of the States parties.

[235] A question that was of some importance in the *Avena* case was whether the 'rights' referred to were those of the State party or of the foreign national entitled to notification.

[235a] As, for example, the failure of a party to the Genocide Convention to exact laws against genocide: see above n 232.

notifications required by the Consular Convention to be given, but had included a provision that '[i]n no case shall failure to effect these notifications be invoked to invalidate the criminal proceedings against the foreign national', this would have defeated the object of Article 36, and would certainly not have amounted to giving 'full effect' to that Article under paragraph 2 thereof. Proceedings before the ICJ on the jurisdictional basis of the Optional Protocol could, it is suggested, have been brought in such a case by any other State party against the United States, even in the absence of any actual application of the law to a national of that State party. What then would be the position if the 'procedural default rule' had been incorporated in the municipal legislation, by a clause on the lines of '[f]ailure to effect these notifications may only be invoked on appeal if it had already been raised before the court of first instance'? The International Court, in the *LaGrand* and *Avena* cases, found that this was what in fact the United States courts had decided in relation to the German and Mexican nationals concerned, and that this, when applied in practice to the detriment of those nationals, amounted to a violation of the Consular Convention. Would a specific statutory provision to that effect also constitute a violation of the Treaty? The distinction between these two hypothetical US legislative provisions is perhaps a fine one.

The legal system of the United States being essentially of the common law type, by no means all positive law has its basis in legislation.[236] Once the 'procedural default rule' became established as law, and once it became established as applicable to complaints of non-compliance with Article 36 of the Consular Convention, there was no legal distinction between that situation and the situation that would have resulted from specific legislation bringing about the same effect.[237] The practical difference is of course the visibility of the legal position to the outside observer. One can well imagine the embassy of another State party to the Convention drawing its Government's attention to a Bill in Congress containing one or other of the objectionable provisions suggested as hypotheses above; it would be less likely that a jurisprudential development involving the same consequence would be noticed and signaled in the same way. When the first Mexican national found his path to relief against non-notification barred by the 'procedural default rule', his consul (on learning of this) might well have reported the matter to the Mexican Government; but there would then be a practical application of the law, so that the question

---

[236] For simplicity, no account is taken here of the existence in parallel of federal law and the law of the various states of the Union.

[237] It might be suggested that there is a distinction, as regards breach of treaty, between the deliberate act of a government in adopting a piece of legislation inconsistent with its obligations under the treaty, and the development of a rule by its courts (particularly a rule of judicial procedure); in the second case there is a lack of intention on the part of the central government. However, it is well established that a State is responsible for the acts of (inter alia) its judiciary: cf. for example the case of the *Arrest Warrant of 11 April 2000*, [2002] ICJ Rep 3.

whether the mere existence of the rule (as applicable to non-notification cases) amounted to a breach of treaty would be moot.

3. THE DOCTRINE OF APPROXIMATE APPLICATION FOLLOWING A BREACH OF TREATY

The only example, which was referred to in the earlier article on this subject,[238] of the doctrine to which this name has been given in the jurisprudence of the Court was a dictum in the separate opinion of Judge Sir Hersch Lauterpacht in the case concerning *Admissibility of Hearings of Petitioners by the Committee on SW Africa*. Judge Lauterpacht stated his view that:

It is a sound principle of law that whenever a legal instrument of continuing validity cannot be applied literally owing to the conduct of one of the parties, it must, without allowing that party to take advantage of its own conduct, be applied in a way approximating most closely to its primary object. To do that is to interpret and give effect to the instrument—not to change it.[239]

The legal instrument to which Judge Lauterpacht was referring was of course the Mandate for South-West Africa, the nature of which, at the time he was writing, had not yet been authoritatively established;[240] hence he did not refer to the point as one of the law of treaties. He did however base his argument on the concept of a régime created by multilateral treaty, arguing that '[t]he unity and the operation of [such a] régime . . . cannot be allowed to fail because of a breakdown or gap which may arise in consequence of an act of a party or otherwise'.[241] It does not therefore appear that, in Lauterpacht's thinking, the same considerations would apply to a bilateral treaty not of a law-making character. On the contrary, he contrasted the situation he had in view with that of 'the case of a breach of the provisions of an ordinary treaty'.[242]

The principle was however relied on by Slovakia in the case concerning the *Gabčíkovo-Nagymaros Project*, in order to justify actions complained of by Hungary as breaches of the 1977 Treaty concerning the Project. The background was that Hungary had first suspended and then abandoned the works which under the Treaty it was bound to carry out on the Danube. As the Court explained,

Czechoslovakia repeatedly denounced Hungary's suspension and abandonment of works as a fundamental breach of the 1977 Treaty and consequently could have invoked this breach as a ground for terminating the Treaty; but this would

---

[238] (1992) *BYIL* 1, 59–60. See also S Rosenne, *Breach of Treaty* (1984), Section III(*a*) (hereinafter: Rosenne, *Breach of Treaty*), the only full treatment of the question prior to the *Gabčíkovo-Nagymaros* decision.
[239] [1956] ICJ Rep 46.
[240] See Rosenne, *Breach of Treaty*, 95–96.
[241] [1956] ICJ Rep 48.   [242] Ibid, 48–49.

not have brought the Project any nearer to completion. It therefore chose to insist on the implementation of the Treaty by Hungary, and on many occasions called upon the latter to resume performance of its obligations under the Treaty. When Hungary steadfastly refused to do so—although it had expressed its willingness to pay compensation for damage incurred by Czechoslovakia—and when negotiations stalled owing to the diametrically opposed positions of the parties, Czechoslovakia decided to put the Gabčíkovo system into operation unilaterally, exclusively under its own control and for its own benefit.[243]

This was the operation referred to throughout the case as 'Variant C'.

Although the 1977 Treaty was bilateral, and thus outside the contemplation of Lauterpacht in 1956, it did, as the Court found in a different context, have to be 'regarded as establishing a territorial régime'.[244]

In response to the reliance by Slovakia on the principle defined by Lauterpacht, the Court ruled as follows.

It is not necessary for the Court to determine whether there is a principle of international law or a general principle of law of "approximate application" because, even if such a principle existed, it could by definition only be employed within the limits of the treaty in question. In the view of the Court, Variant C does not meet that cardinal condition with regard to the 1977 Treaty.[245]

The reasons why the Court took this view were essentially that the works contemplated by the Treaty provided for joint ownership and operation, which could not be achieved by unilateral action, so that 'Variant C thus differed sharply from [the project] in all its legal characteristics'.[246] Furthermore, the result of Variant C was that Czechoslovakia appropriated 'essentially for its use and benefit, between 80 and 90 per cent of waters' of a shared international watercourse.[247] The Court did not refer expressly to Lauterpacht's qualification of the principle as not allowing the party concerned to take advantage of its own conduct, but seems to have had that in mind.

It is however striking that, while at this stage in its judgment the Court left open the question whether there existed any such principle as that of 'approximate application', in framing its actual decision on the case it applied something which looks very like that principle. Writing long before the decision in the *Gabčíkovo-Nagymaros Project* case, this is how Rosenne, with remarkable foresight, interpreted the practical impact of the doctrine of 'approximate application':

...faced with a situation of established breach [of treaty]...the parties themselves in the first instance, renegotiate and apply the treaty in good faith and where they are not successful in doing this themselves, then acting through or with the assistance of a competent international organ, whether judicial or not,

[243] [1997] ICJ Rep 53, para 73.
[244] [1997] ICJ Rep 72, para 123. This was for the purpose of the rule as to succession to treaties stated in Article 12 of the Vienna Convention: see Chapter II, Section 3(3)(d).
[245] Ibid, para 76.   [246] Ibid, 54, para 77.
[247] Ibid, para 78.

are legally obliged to take steps to redraft the treaty or reformulate the subs-
system [sc. the part of the treaty that has been breached] so as to ensure its continued effective application.[248]

In the *Gabčíkovo-Nagymaros Project* case, after establishing the legal
situation as it resulted from the acts of the parties in relation to the 1977
Treaty, the Court indicated that it had to determine 'what the *future*
conduct of the Parties should be'.[249] In that respect it was 'of cardinal
importance' that 'the 1977 Treaty is still in force and consequently
governs the relationship between the Parties'; but the Court could not
'disregard the fact that the Treaty has not been fully implemented by
either party for years', and had to take account of that factual situation.[250]
The Court stated as its objective that

the factual situation as it has developed since 1989 shall be placed within the
context of the preserved and developing treaty relationship, in order to achieve
its object and purpose in so far as that is feasible. For it is only then that the
irregular state of affairs which exists as the result of the failure of both Parties
to comply with their treaty obligations can be remedied.[251]

How this was to be done turned out to be something that the parties had
to work out for themselves: the Court indicated that it was of the opinion that, in the negotiations for the implementation of the judgment to
which the parties had committed themselves in their Special Agreement,
they were 'under a legal obligation...to consider, within the context of
the 1977 Treaty, in what way the multiple objectives of the Treaty can
best be served, keeping in mind that all of them should be fulfilled'.[252]
It gave a number of hints and indications, such as, for example, stressing
the need to take account of environmental considerations, but ultimately
the parties were to work out their own salvation.[253]

It is, it is suggested, a fair assessment of the Court's handling of
this dispute to say that, while it declined formally to endorse Judge
Lauterpacht's *trouvaille*, and rejected Slovakia's attempt to rely on
the doctrine for its own benefit, the Court ultimately applied the core
of the concept. It recognized that the legal instrument could not be
'applied literally', owing to the conduct of one, or possibly both, parties;
it refused to let a party take advantage of its own breach of its treaty
obligations; but it directed the application of the Treaty 'in a way most

---

[248] Rosenne, *Breach of Treaty*, 99–100.
[249] [1997] ICJ Rep 75–76, para 131, emphasis original.
[250] Ibid, 76, para 133.   [251] Ibid.
[252] Ibid, 77, para 139.
[253] Which they have not so far succeeded in doing. The Judgment was given on 25 September
1997; on 3 September 1998 Slovakia came back to the Court under an enabling provision in the
Special Agreement to ask for an additional judgment aimed at getting the stalled negotiations moving again (ICJ Press Release 1998/28). The Court directed Hungary to file a written statement of
its position on this request, by 7 December 1998; since then, nothing seems to have occurred at The
Hague, though the case remains on the list of pending cases.

closely approximating to its primary object'. In the earlier article, it was suggested that '[t]he case for the inclusion of the [Lauterpacht] doctrine in positive international law must be regarded as, for the present, unproved';[254] the *Gabčíkovo-Nagymaros Project* case would seem now to have confirmed such inclusion.

4. Breach of Treaty and Implementation of Compromissory Clauses

The problem discussed under this heading in the previous article was that of the survival of the compromissory clause of a treaty which one party has claimed to have terminated. It has not arisen again in the period under review; while there have been claims for breach of treaty containing a compromissory clause (e.g. the *Oil Platforms* case), these did not involve an assertion that the treaty had for that reason been terminated; and there have been claims that a treaty has been terminated (*Gabčíkovo-Nagymaros Project* case), but the Court was seised under a special agreement, the disputed treaty not containing any compromissory provision. Since the publication of the previous article, the principle established in the *Appeal Relating to the Jurisdiction of the ICAO Council* and the case of the *Diplomatic and Consular Staff in Tehran* has however been noted by the International Law Commission as 'well-established', and relied on in support of the exclusion from the scope of counter-measures of the obligations of a State 'under any dispute settlement procedure applicable between it and the responsible State'.[255]

---

[254] (1992) *BYIL* 1, 60.

[255] ILC Articles on State Responsibility, Art. 50, para 2 (a); see also the ILC Commentary to that Article. The hypothesis is of course primarily counter-measures in response to an alleged internationally wrongful act constituted by a breach of a treaty containing the compromissory clause; it must be doubted whether repudiation of a commitment to dispute settlement of a general nature could ever be regarded as 'commensurate' with an allegedly wrongful act wholly unrelated to the instrument containing the commitment.

CHAPTER V: TERMINATION OF TREATIES

1. Termination of Treaties containing no Provision for Denunciation

In the case of the *Gabčíkovo-Nagymaros Project*, Hungary had claimed that a bilateral treaty with Czechoslovakia had been unilaterally terminated by Hungary in 1992, but Czechoslovakia (and subsequently Slovakia as successor State) claimed that the purported termination was invalid.[256] The Court began its analysis of the matter with a statement of principle:

> The 1977 Treaty does not contain any provision regarding its termination. Nor is there any indication that the parties intended to admit the possibility of denunciation or withdrawal. On the contrary, the Treaty establishes a long-standing and durable régime of joint investment and joint operation. Consequently, the parties not having agreed otherwise, the Treaty could be terminated only on the limited grounds enumerated in the Vienna Convention.[257]

Although the Vienna Convention was not applicable as such to the 1977 Treaty, the Court had already observed earlier in its judgment that the rules of the Convention 'which are declaratory of customary law' were nevertheless applicable, and decided that 'this is the case, in many respects, with Articles 60 to 62 of the Vienna Convention relating to termination or suspension of the operation of a treaty'.[258] It did not however make any finding as to the possible customary-law status of Article 65 of the Vienna Convention, laying down (*inter alia*) a minimum period of notice (three months) for the termination of a treaty; and this provision is of a procedural nature and thus not appropriate to be regarded as declaratory of existing law.[259]

The action complained of by Hungary as a ground for termination of the 1977 Treaty was the construction and putting into operation by Czechoslovakia of an alternative means of carrying out the part of the planned project that was to its benefit, in a form which became known as 'Variant C'. The Court held that by putting Variant C into operation, which involved diverting the shared waters of the Danube, Czechoslovakia did indeed commit a breach of the Treaty. The Court

---

[256] For the parallel claim by Hungary to have suspended the operation of the Treaty in 1989, see above, Chapter III, Section 1, and Section 2 of the present Chapter.

[257] [1997] ICJ Rep 62–63, para 100. This of course in fact amounts to a re-statement of Article 56 of the Vienna Convention itself, but with the omission of any reference to the possibility that 'a right of denunciation or withdrawal' might be 'implied by the nature of the treaty'. In view of the nature of the Project, the Court probably thought that the fact that this was not so in the case before it was too obvious to mention. On the background to Article 46, see Fitzmaurice and Elias, *Contemporary Issues in the Law of Treaties*, 354–358.

[258] Ibid, 62, para 99; the Court added '[o]n this, the Parties, too, were broadly in agreement.'

[259] See further on this, Section 5 below.

then rejected Hungary's claim to be entitled to terminate it, on a procedural ground—that at the date at which gave notice terminating the Treaty, all that Czechoslovakia had done was carry out works preliminary to a breach of the Treaty.[260] However, the Court also took account of the fact that, as it found, Czechoslovakia committed its unlawful act 'as a result of Hungary's own prior wrongful conduct',[261] in suspending operations under the Treaty; it remains slightly uncertain therefore which of these two grounds was determinative. The Court also made a rather mysterious allusion to good faith, in connection with the fact that the purported termination was effected with only six days' notice. While citing the advisory opinion on the *Interpretation of the Agreement of 25 March 1951 between the WHO and Egypt*, which mentioned that the question of the period of notice of termination to be given in the absence of any provision in the treaty was to be determined by the parties 'by consultation and negotiation in good faith',[262] the Court refrained from stating expressly either that six days' notice was insufficient, or that the absence of consultation before the notice was given was a fatal flaw.[263] Judge Herczegh recalled in his dissenting opinion that Article 65 of the Vienna Convention on the Law of Treaties qualified the provision there made for three months' notice with the words 'except in cases of special urgency', and suggested that this was such a case.[264] It may also be recalled that the *WHO Agreement* case concerned a situation in which no termination had yet been effected, and the intended termination was not on the basis of any breach or alleged breach of the agreement. The considerations regarded by the Court as appropriate in those circumstances might not necessarily be so where a State considered that its legal interests were seriously threatened as a result of a breach of a treaty by the other party, and that prompt action to terminate the treaty was required to limit the damage.[265]

Judge Herczegh also pointed out that Czechoslovakia was planning to carry out Variant C as an 'approximate application' of the Treaty. The lawfulness of its action on its own territory could not be challenged; but it could only lawfully carry out works on or affecting Hungarian territory by virtue of powers derived from the Treaty. By terminating the Treaty Hungary could therefore rob the Variant C works of any colour

---

[260] The distinction was not accepted by Judge Ranjeva (dissenting opinion, [1997] ICJ Rep 173).

[261] [1997] ICJ Rep 67, para 110.

[262] [1980] ICJ Rep 96, para 49.

[263] It seems that the latter may have been the main consideration, since the Court did not quote a slightly earlier passage in the *WHO Agreement* case, to the effect that the party which wished to terminate the agreement was under a duty 'to give a reasonable period of notice to the other party for the termination of the existing situation': ibid, 95–96, para 49.

[264] [1997] ICJ Rep 198.

[265] The argument of the duty of limitation of damage was in fact employed by Slovakia to argue that Czechoslovakia had been not merely entitled but obliged to carry out Variant C in order to mitigate the damage caused by Hungary's effective withdrawal from the Project ([1997] ICJ Rep 51–52). The Court held that '[w]hile this principle might thus provide a basis for the calculation of damages, it could not, on the other hand, justify an otherwise wrongful act' (ibid, 55).

of legality, and, he suggested, was thus 'the only means available to prevent Czechoslovakia diverting the Danube' in the Hungarian sector.[266] It might be objected that this argument assumes its conclusion: that it amounts to saying that Hungary's termination was valid because Variant C was a breach of the Treaty, but at the same time that it would only be a breach because the Treaty had been terminated. That however would be an over-simplification. The Court's argument was that the termination would only be lawful, and therefore effective in blocking Czechoslovakia's action, if a breach of the Treaty had already been committed; but on the other hand it did in fact find that the implementation of Variant C was a breach of the Treaty (and probably a 'material breach'—see below). This result does not seem very satisfactory, and there may be room for a doctrine of 'anticipatory breach' as a ground for termination. As has been noted above,[267] it is recognized that there are cases in which the lack of conformity of municipal legislation with the international law obligations of the State may constitute an internationally wrongful act. If there had existed Czechoslovak legislation as a basis for the Project works, including Variant C,[268] then on the hypothesis (subsequently confirmed) that Variant C was not authorized by the Treaty, that legislation would have provided for the commission of an internationally wrongful act. The situation called for a balancing of two principles, here conflicting: a State's right and duty to protect its territory and the interests of its inhabitants against wrongful prejudice caused by another State; and the interest of the international community, and of individual States, in the maintenance of the *pacta sunt servanda* principle and the sanctity of treaty obligations.

In the case of the *Armed Activities on the Territory of the Congo (DRC v Uganda)*, one of the arguments advanced by Uganda in response to the claims of the DRC concerning wrongful acts committed on the latter's territory was that, during a defined period, Ugandan troops were present in the territory with the consent of the Government of the DRC. This was advanced as a 'circumstance excluding responsibility' in the terminology of the ILC Articles on State Responsibility, and handled by the Court as such. However, a key question was whether, and if so with effect from what date, the DRC had withdrawn its consent, and this can therefore be seen, in addition or alternatively, as an issue of the termination of an informally-created treaty-relationship.

The parties were agreed that initially, from a date around May 1997 until around August 1998, the troops had been present in Congolese territory with the consent of the Congolese Government, but the precise terms of the consent, which might perhaps have been characterized

---

[266] [1997] ICJ Rep 198.   [267] Chapter IV, Section 2.
[268] According to counsel involved in the case (private communication), no such legislation existed, so that this line of argument was probably not available; but the general point, it is suggested, remains valid.

rather as an absence of objection, were obscure.[269] On 27 April 1998, the two States signed a Protocol on Security along the Common Border, providing that their respective armies would 'co-operate to insure security and peace along the common border'.[270] The Court found that '[t]he source of an authorization or consent to the crossing of the border by [the Ugandan] troops antedated the Protocol', and went on to find that, apparently as a consequence, 'this prior authorization or consent could *thus* be withdrawn at any time by the Government of the DRC, without further formalities being necessary'[271], i.e. without the need to denounce the Protocol formally.[272] The factual circumstances of the withdrawal of consent were almost as obscure as those of its original grant, but the Court was able to conclude that 'any earlier consent by the DRC to the presence of Ugandan troops on its territory had at the latest been withdrawn by 8 August 1998'.[273]

The application, by analogy or otherwise, of the provisions of the Vienna Convention on the Law of Treaties to this situation throws up a difficulty with the inter-relation of Articles 54 and 56 of that text. Could the termination of the agreement of the DRC to the presence of Ugandan troops be regarded as 'in conformity with the provisions of the treaty', or in this case, agreement, under Article 54(*a*)? In the absence of specific stipulation, the agreement must be taken to have contained an implied term authorising termination by the DRC at any time. As a matter of practical politics, there need be no difficulty about this; if the consent had been embodied in a formal treaty, such a clause would no doubt have been insisted on by the DRC Government. But the case would then apparently fall within the category where a right of denunciation or withdrawal was 'implied by the nature' of the agreement, under Article 56(1)(*b*); and where this is the case, Article 56(2) requires 12 months' notice of denunciation or withdrawal. It is doubtful whether such a precise requirement exists in the customary law which was in effect being codified by the Convention; and as the Court pointed out in its advisory opinion on *Interpretation of the Agreement of 25 March 1951 between the WHO and Egypt*, 'these provisions... are based on an obligation to act in good faith and have reasonable regard to the interests of the other party to the treaty'.[274] The situation was, it is suggested, that the implied terms of the agreement of 1997 were that the DRC could indeed

---

[269] [2005] ICJ Rep 196–197, para 45. The question of consent to the presence of troops also arose in relation to the period after 10 July 1999, the date of the conclusion of the Lusaka Agreement between the two parties. The issues there however did not relate to termination of consent, but to whether an agreement for orderly withdrawal of the troops constituted a consent to their presence, either retrospectively, or prospectively for the period laid down for the process of withdrawal. See ibid, 210–212, paras. 98–105.

[270] Ibid, 197, para 46.   [271] Ibid, emphasis added.

[272] Uganda had argued that such a denunciation was necessary to terminate the consent: ibid, 198, para 50.

[273] Ibid, 199, para 53.

[274] [1980] ICJ Rep 95, para 47

indicate at any time that its consent to the presence of Ugandan troops was withdrawn, and Uganda would thereupon come under an obligation to arrange their prompt departure; but their presence would only constitute an internationally unlawful act at the expiration of such a period as was reasonably necessary for the Ugandan Government, acting in good faith, to make the necessary arrangements for the withdrawal.[275] These were questions that did not in fact arise in the *Armed Activities* case, as Uganda did not proceed to withdraw its troops, claiming that their presence after the withdrawal of DRC consent was justified by considerations of self-defence.[276]

2. TERMINATION (OR SUSPENSION) OF TREATIES ON ACCOUNT OF MATERIAL BREACH

The question of termination for material breach cannot be entirely separated from the principle, discussed above, that 'the claiming of rights entails submission to the corresponding obligations';[277] it is related to the maxim *inadimplementi non est adimplendum*.[278] There is however a distinction to be made; 'a party which disowns or does not fulfil its own obligations cannot be recognized as retaining the rights which it claims to derive from the [relevant international] relationship'.[279] Nevertheless, some *acte juridique* must intervene if the relationship is to cease to exist either permanently (termination) or temporarily (suspension); and the non-fulfilment will not in all cases give rise to the right of the other party to perform that *acte*.[280]

It would seem axiomatic that where there are two or more treaties in force between the same two parties, even if they are *in pari materia*, the breach, or alleged breach, of one treaty by one of the parties cannot be invoked by the other party as a 'material breach' of a different treaty, as

[275] However, it should be noted that when in 1999 the Lusaka Agreement, two Disengagement Plans, and the Luanda Agreement of 6 September 2002 laid down precise arrangements for the withdrawal of the Ugandan troops, the Court was not willing to see in these instruments a consent to their presence during the period laid down for the withdrawal: ibid, 212, para 105. This finding was strongly and (it is suggested) rightly criticized by Judge Parra-Aranguren, [2005] ICJ Rep 294, para 8, who drew attention to the 'impossible legal situation' so created for Uganda. No practical consequences of the finding seem to have been drawn in the Judgment; but it may have implications in the field of reparations, to be dealt with, if necessary, in further proceedings. Cf. also the observations in the *Case Concerning the Gabčíkovo-Nagymaros Project* discussed in section 5 of this chapter, below.

[276] [2005] ICJ Rep 213 ff., paras 106 ff.

[277] See above Chapter III, Section 2.

[278] Cf. B Simma, 'Reflections on Article 60 of the Vienna Convention on the Law of Treaties and its Background in General International Law', 20 *Österreichische Zeitschrift für öffentliches Recht und Völkerrecht* (1970), 20.

[279] *Legal Consequences for States of the Continued Presence of South Africa in Namibia (South West Africa) notwithstanding Security Resolution 276 (1970)*, Advisory Opinion, [1971] ICJ Rep 46, para 91.

[280] For this reason it does not seem correct to present this dictum in the *South West Africa* case (previous note) as a pronouncement 'concerning material breach', as in Fitzmaurice and Elias, *Contemporary Issues in the Law of Treaties*, 363–364.

grounds for terminating or suspending the latter treaty.[281] It could of course happen that the relationship between the two treaties was such that the breach of the one necessarily involved a breach of the other, but in that case the claim to termination would be based on the breach of the treaty terminated. There is a contrast to be noted between termination of a treaty on the grounds of material breach *of the treaty*, and termination on the basis of fundamental change of circumstances: in the latter context, the party invoking the change will be debarred from doing so if the change results from that party's own breach either of the treaty or of 'any other international obligation owed to any other party to the treaty'.[282]

Nevertheless in the *Gabčíkovo-Nagymaros Project* case, Hungary maintained that it had been entitled to terminate the 1977 Treaty relating to the Project on the grounds that Czechoslovakia had breached not only that Treaty but other international conventions 'and general international law'.[283] The Court gave this argument short shrift:

As to that part of Hungary's argument which was based on other treaties and general rules of international law, the Court is of the view that it is only a material breach of the treaty itself, by a State party to that treaty, which entitles the other party to rely on it as a ground for terminating the treaty. The violation of other treaty rules or of rules of general international law may justify the taking of certain measures, including countermeasures, by the injured State, but it does not constitute a ground for termination under the law of treaties.[284]

The parallel between action under Article 60 of the Vienna Convention, or more precisely, under the customary rule codified in the Convention, and counter-measures—or, as they used to be termed, reprisals—has been noted in the past, and generally the view has been taken that they do not overlap. Article 16 of the Draft Articles on State Responsibility prepared by Special Rapporteur Riphagen, at the end of the Part of the Draft devoted to implementation of responsibility, reserved the position by providing that the provisions of that Part should 'not prejudice any question that may arise in regard to . . . the invalidity, termination and suspension of the operation of treaties'.[285]

The Court did not, in the *Gabčíkovo-Nagymaros Project* case, make any findings indicative of the definition of a 'material breach' justifying termination of a treaty, since it decided, as mentioned above, that Hungary's purported termination of the 1977 Treaty was invalid or ineffective for

---

[281] Note however the argument advanced by some States in the *Namibia* case that South Africa's mandate could be terminated on the ground of, inter alia, breaches of the UN Charter and the Universal Declaration of Human Rights: commented on by J Klabbers, 'Some Problems Regarding the Object and Purpose of Treaties' (1997) 8 *Finnish Yearbook of International Law* 142.

[282] Vienna Convention on the Law of Treaties, Article 62, para 2*(b)*.

[283] [1997] ICJ Rep 61, para 96.

[284] Ibid, 65, para 106.

[285] UN doc. A/CN/4/389, 15. At its 37th Session the ILC considered that the relationship between the draft and the Vienna Convention needed to be 'further clarified' (A/40/10, 24, para 156) and the draft Article was dropped in the Rapporteur's next Report (A/CN.4/397).

reasons not going to its justification. The Court had however found in an earlier part of its judgment that the action on the part of Czechoslovakia complained of by Hungary, once it was completed, did amount to a breach of the Treaty.[286] It refused however to see in Czechoslovakia's action a 'repudiation' of the Treaty, as had also been pleaded by Hungary;[287] thus it would presumably not have been willing to regard that action as falling within paragraph 3 (a) of Article 60 of the Vienna Convention, referring to 'a repudiation of the treaty not sanctioned by the present Convention' as a type of material breach. The other head of the definition, in paragraph 3 (b), is 'the violation of a provision essential to the accomplishment of the object and purpose of the treaty'.

3. TERMINATION ON THE GROUND OF FUNDAMENTAL CHANGE OF CIRCUMSTANCES

The case of the *Gabčíkovo-Nagymaros Project* also gave the Court the opportunity to make a general statement of the principles governing the termination of a treaty on the grounds of a fundamental change of circumstances, as recognized in Article 62 of the Vienna Convention.[288]

A fundamental change of circumstances must have been unforeseen; the existence of the circumstances at the time of the Treaty's conclusion must have constituted an essential basis of the consent of the parties to be bound by the Treaty. The negative and conditional wording of Article 62 of the Vienna Convention on the Law of Treaties is a clear indication moreover that the stability of treaty relations requires that the plea of fundamental change of circumstances be applied only in exceptional cases.[289]

The Court's actual decision on the specific claims made by Hungary on this head was however differently expressed:

The changed circumstances advanced by Hungary are, in the Court's view, not of such a nature, either individually or collectively, that their effect would radically transform the extent of the obligations still to be performed in order to accomplish the Project.[290]

The result seems to be that the Court has re-confirmed as customary law the provisions of Article 62, paragraph 1, of the Vienna Convention, expressly relied on as such by Hungary:[291]

---

[286] [1997] ICJ Rep 54, para 78.   [287] Ibid, 68, para 114.

[288] The existence and nature in customary law of the *clausula rebus sic stantibus* has been controversial, particularly as regards the question whether or not (as the term '*clausula*' implies), it is to be regarded as subjective, based on an implied term in treaties. On the practice prior to the adoption of the Vienna Convention, see for example D F Vagts, '*Rebus* Revisited: Changed Circumstances in Treaty Law' (2004–2005) 43 *Columbia Journal of Transnational Law* 459, and G Dahm, *Völkerrecht* (1988), II, 742.

[289] [1997] ICJ Rep 65, para 104.   [290] Ibid.

[291] See Ibid, 59–60, para 95. The Court had already held in the two Icelandic *Fisheries Jurisdiction* cases that Article 62 could be regarded 'in many respects' as codifying customary law: [1973] ICJ Rep 18, para 36; 63, para 36.

A fundamental change of circumstances which had occurred with regard to those existing at the time of the conclusion of a treaty, and which was not foreseen by the parties, may not be invoked as a ground for terminating or withdrawing form the treaty unless:

(a) the existence of those circumstances constituted an essential basis of the consent of the parties to be bound by the treaty; and

(b) the effect of the change is radically to transform the extent of obligations still to be performed under the treaty.

The actual changes specified by Hungary as grounds for termination were 'profound changes of a political nature, the Project's diminishing economic viability, the progress of environmental knowledge and the development of new norms and prescriptions of international environmental law'.[292] As regards political changes, it should be recalled that there was broad agreement at the Vienna Conference that 'a change in the attitude or policy of a Government could never be invoked' as a ground of termination of a treaty.[293]

The first two grounds were dismissed essentially on the facts; but the last is of more general interest. The position of Hungary can perhaps be simply summed up as 'if we'd known in 1977 what we now know about the environmental impact of the Project, we would never have adopted it'; a very reasonable position, but can it be made to fit the requirements of 'fundamental change of circumstances'? The Court rejected this particular contention for two reasons: first, that it did not consider 'that new developments in the state of environmental knowledge and of environmental law can be said to have been completely unforeseen'; and secondly '[w]hat is more, the formulation of Articles 15, 19, and 20 [of the 1977 Treaty], designed to accommodate change, made it possible for the parties to take account of such developments and to apply them when implementing the treaty provisions'.[294]

In the previous article on this subject, attention was drawn to a distinction which appeared to exist between the requirements for a termination on the basis of changed circumstances contemplated by the Court in the *Fisheries Jurisdiction* cases, and those of Article 62 of the Vienna Convention. The Convention refers to the 'change of circumstances' as one 'which was not foreseen by the parties'; but the *Fisheries Jurisdiction* judgment apparently contemplated a change of circumstances of which the *impact* on the obligations of the party affected had not been foreseen. In that article it was therefore observed that:

Clearly a change of circumstances which was totally unforeseeable, but which has occurred, may yet have no, or minimal, effect as regards the onerousness

---

[292] [1997] ICJ Rep 64, para 104, referring to ibid, 60, para 95.

[293] *ILC Yearbook 1966-II*, 259; and see I M Sinclair, *The Vienna Convention on the Law of Treaties* (1984), 194–195.

[294] Ibid, 64–65, para 104. However, one of the grounds on which Hungary claimed that Czechoslovakia had committed material breaches of the Treaty was precisely that it 'had violated Articles 15, 19 and 20 of the Treaty by refusing to enter into negotiations with Hungary' in order to adapt the Project to 'new scientific and legal developments regarding the environment': ibid, 65, para 107.

of the parties' obligations...; on the other hand, events which the parties could have foreseen, and perhaps even did foresee, might turn out to have an unexpected effect on their obligations.[295]

In that case the Court was not applying the Vienna Convention, nor even regarding Article 62 as an expression of customary law, so it was free to take this view of the foreseeability question. In the *Gabčíkovo-Nagymaros Project* case, the Court's options were more limited: '[a] fundamental change of circumstances must have been unforeseen'.[296] The Court recognized that, consistently with previous decisions, that the Convention had codified existing customary law, and that 'in many respects[297] this applies to the provisions of the Vienna Convention concerning the termination...of treaties, set forth in Articles 60 to 62'.[298] Nevertheless, it appears to have recognized the force of the distinction; the environmental changes were treated as not themselves 'completely unforeseen', but in summing up its attitude to all the changes relied on by Hungary (including the political and economic changes), it considered, as noted above, that they were 'not of such a nature...that their effect would radically transform *the extent of the obligations* still to be performed to accomplish the Project'.[299]

In its 1997 decision, the Court added another condition for the invocation of fundamental change of circumstances: that that change could not have been accommodated within the structure of the treaty, through mechanisms there provided for adjustment of the parties' rights and obligations.[300] This chimes well with the general policy of the law of regarding termination of a treaty as a last resort; but as the *Gabčíkovo-Nagymaros Project* case shows, there may well be difficulties if disagreements between the parties prevent the adjustment provisions from taking effect.

A question that remains unsettled is whether the 'circumstances' contemplated by Article 63 are purely factual, or whether a change in the relevant international law might also qualify as such. The text of the Article gives no guidance; but in the *travaux préparatoires* of the ILC, there are references to an intention not to exclude the possibility of a change of

---

[295] (1992) *BYIL* 1, 80–81.

[296] [1997] ICJ Rep 65, para 104.

[297] A formula which Rosenne calls 'an obscure form of phrase which may mean much or very little': *Breach of Treaty*, 32.

[298] [1997] ICJ Rep 38, para 46 (footnotes omitted).

[299] Ibid, 65, para 104, emphasis added.

[300] In the previous article on this subject, it was suggested that the concept formerly known as the *rebus sic stantibus* rule was subject to a qualification excluding its operation where the parties in their treaty had 'made other provision for the possible events which might justify invocation of the rule' (1992) *BYIL* 1, 79. For an analogous finding as to the relevance of the terms of the treaty to issues in some sense 'outside' it, cf. the Court's finding in the *Military and Paramilitary Activities* case that 'an act cannot be said to be one calculated to deprive a treaty of its object and purpose, or to impede its due performance, if the possibility of that act has been foreseen in the treaty itself, and it has been expressly agreed that the treaty 'shall not preclude' the act...': [1986] ICJ Rep 136, para 272.

legal regime impossible of performance.[301] There is of course a distinction between circumstances rendering a treaty impossible of performance (dealt with in Article 61 of the Vienna Convention) and a fundamental change of circumstances (dealt with in Article 62);[302] however, there does not appear to be any vital difference between the two situations as regards the possible impact of changes in the law.

It may be recalled that the Court in the *Fisheries Jurisdiction* cases was faced with a contention by Iceland that the relevant international law had developed since the 1961 Exchange of Notes was concluded; since Iceland was not appearing in the proceedings, this argument was not couched in formal legal terms. However the treaty instrument which, in Iceland's contention, was affected by the change, the 1961 Exchange of Notes, was purely a dispute settlement agreement; if the law on fisheries jurisdiction had changed, Iceland would be able to rely on the change as a matter of the merits of the dispute, but this would be irrelevant to the continuing force of the Exchange of Notes—and the Court made an express finding to that effect.[303] The Court examined the Icelandic position in the light of 'fundamental change of circumstances' as affecting the operation of the Exchange of Notes only in relation to factual changes, such as the development of new fishing techniques. Hungary in the *Project* case relied on 'changes in environmental knowledge and law' in support of its reliance on 'fundamental change of circumstances', but emphasized that these in themselves would not have been enough; it was the combination of political, economic, environmental and legal circumstances that was relied on.[304]

An argument against the inclusion of changes in the law in the category of relevant 'circumstances' for purposes of Article 62 of the Vienna Convention might be based on Article 64 of the Convention: if a treaty is terminated by the emergence of a peremptory norm of international law with which it is not consistent, can it be deduced *a contrario* that no other change in the law has any effect on the continued operation of the treaty?[305] Something of the sort was argued by Slovakia, but rather in

---

[301] See for example H Waldock in *ILC Yearbook 1963-I*, 248.

[302] There is of course a degree of overlap between the two concepts (cf. Jennings and Watts, *Oppenheim's International Law* II, 1304, fn.1). Cf. also the decision of the European Court of Justice in *A. Racke GmbH* v. *Hauptzollamt Mainz* (Case C-162/96), in which a suspension of tariff concessions under a treaty régime between Germany and Yugoslavia on the grounds of the outbreak of hostilities in Yugoslavia was challenged on the ground (inter alia) that 'a certain volume of trade had to continue with Yugoslavia and that the Community could have continued to grant tariff concessions'; the Court ruled that 'that application of the customary international law rules in question does not require an impossibility to perform obligations, and that there was no point in continuing to grant preferences, with a view to stimulating trade, in circumstances where Yugoslavia was breaking up' (para 57 of the Judgment).

[303] [1973] ICJ Rep 16, para 30; 61, para 30.

[304] See, e.g., Hungary's Reply, para 3.78.

[305] Hungary in fact originally argued that subsequent norms of environmental law took precedence over an earlier treaty on the basis of *lex posterior derogat priori*: see the Hungarian Declaration of Termination of the Treaty, Hungarian Memorial, Vol. 4, Annex 82, 182, para 6.

response to a contention by Hungary that the 1977 Treaty had become impossible of performance.[306] However, the characteristic (and controversial) feature of Article 64 is its automatic operation; it does not need to be invoked by either party, and the invalidity of the treaty is independent of the wishes or intentions of either party or both parties.[307] For this reason the decision in the *Gabčíkovo-Nagymaros Project* case has been criticized inasmuch as the Court declined to investigate *ex officio* whether any *jus cogens* rules of environmental law had emerged, contenting itself with noting that '[n]either of the Parties contended' that such was the case.[308] There seems no reason of principle why a change in the applicable international law, not having the quality of *jus cogens*, might not 'radically transform the obligations still to be performed' by a party to the treaty; the difficulty is to imagine circumstances in which this might be so.

In the case of the *Gabčíkovo-Nagymaros Project*, Hungary also presented an argument to the effect, as quoted by the Court, that 'subsequently imposed requirements of international law in relation to the protection of the environment precluded performance of the Treaty', because '[t]he previously existing obligation not to cause substantive damage to the territory of another State had . . . evolved into an *erga omnes* obligation of prevention of damage pursuant to the "precautionary principle"'.[309] The Court continued its statement of Hungary's argument: '[o]n this basis, Hungary argued, its termination was "forced by the other party's refusal to suspend work on Variant C".'[310] Since it was not argued that any damage would be caused by the Project works to any territories other than those of the parties, it is at first sight unclear how this assertion, even if correct, would affect the Treaty. However, Hungary in fact recalled in its Memorial that when terminating the Treaty it had invoked, *inter alia*, the fact that 'subsequently imposed requirements of international law in relation to protection of the environment precluded performance of the Treaty', and noted that this was 'relevant to' the other grounds relied on, particularly that of fundamental change of circumstances.[311] The Memorial then explained that the important development in international law was the recognition that it was *prevention* of harm that mattered[312] (the possible *erga omnes* character of the rule being apparently irrelevant in a bilateral relationship), and hence:

If Czechoslovakia was obliged under general international law not to carry out activities on its territory that would cause serious or substantial harm to

---

[306] [1997] ICJ Rep 62, para 97.

[307] This is clear from the modifications made by the ILC to the drafts of G Fitzmaurice and H Waldock, which had proposed a faculty for any party to call for the termination of the treaty: *ILC Yearbook 1963-II*, 211.

[308] [1997] ICJ Rep 67, para 112; for criticism see Orakhelashvili, *Peremptory Norms in International Law*, 498.

[309] [1997] ICJ Rep 62, para 97.   [310] Ibid.

[311] Hungarian Memorial, paras. 10.91–10.92.

[312] A point which is not made clear in the Court's summary of the argument, quoted above.

Hungary, then Hungary was entitled to take action to remove any pretext for such conduct.[313]

This is an argument that the Court did not deal with expressly, but it amounts to saying that fundamental change of circumstances may cover 'subsequently imposed requirements of international law', ie, that Article 62 of the Vienna Convention was not limited to physical changes.

3A. IMPOSSIBILITY OF PERFORMANCE

As though anxious to provide the Court with an opportunity of reviewing the full gamut of grounds for termination of treaties contemplated by the Vienna Convention, Hungary in the case of the *Gabčíkovo-Nagymaros Project* also relied on the principle of impossibility of performance (Article 61 of the Convention). Since the Vienna Convention was not as such applicable to the 1977 Treaty between the parties (which was concluded before the entry into force of the Vienna Convention between the parties), the Court was in fact being called upon to rule on the question of impossibility in customary law, in the light of the Convention. The Court however treated the matter as though Article 61 were the exclusive source of law on the point; it observed immediately that in the Convention this ground is limited to cases in which the impossibility 'results from the permanent disappearance or destruction of an object indispensable for the execution of the treaty'; and it is to be noted that the word 'object' here clearly has its sense of a tangible article, not—as in the hallowed phrase 'the object and purpose of the treaty'—a purposive sense.[314] Although Hungary argued that the 'object' did not have to be a physical object,[315] its claim, as summarised by the Court, does seem to hover between these two senses: it contended that

the essential object of the Treaty—an economic joint investment which was consistent with environmental protection and which was operated by the two contracting parties jointly—had permanently disappeared and that the Treaty had thus become impossible to perform.[316]

The term 'impossible' was also used in Hungary's contentions in a sense other than that of 'that which cannot be done', but something nearer to 'that which it would be absurd or unreasonable to do', since Hungary also complained that it could not be 'obliged to fulfill a *practically* impossible task, namely to construct a barrage system on its own territory that would cause irreparable environmental damage.'[317]

---

[313] Hungarian Memorial, para 10. 96.

[314] The ILC contemplated such examples as the disappearance of an island, the drying-up of a river, or the destruction of a dam.

[315] [1997] ICJ Rep 59, para 94.   [316] Ibid, para 103.

[317] Ibid, 59, para 94, emphasis added. For some commentators, the plea of impossibility of performance is an application of the concept of *force majeure* rendering non-performance 'non fautive' (see, e.g. P Daillier and A Pellet, *Droit International Public* (5th edn, 1999), 305, para 206).

The Court's ruling on this was as follows:

It is not necessary for the Court to determine whether the term "object" in Article 61 can also be understood to embrace a legal régime as in any event, even if that were the case, it would have to conclude that in this instance that régime had not definitively ceased to exist. The 1977 Treaty—and in particular its Articles 15, 19 and 20—actually made available to the parties the necessary means to proceed at any time, by negotiation, to the required readjustments between economic imperatives and ecological imperatives.[318]

Some lines earlier it had however already indicated a doubt whether the intention of the Convention text had been to contemplate anything other than the disappearance of a *physical* object, by noting that:

During the [Vienna] conference, a proposal was made to extend the scope of the article by including in it cases such as the impossibility to make certain payments because of serious financial difficulties...Although it was recognized that such situations could lead to a preclusion of the wrongfulness of non-performance by a party of its treaty obligations, the participating States were not prepared to consider such situations to be a ground for terminating or suspending a treaty, and preferred to limit themselves to a narrower concept.[319]

The Court however added a further reason why Hungary's reliance on supervening impossibility of performance could not be accepted:

The Court would add that, if the joint exploitation of the investment was no longer possible, this was originally because Hungary did not carry out most of the works for which it was responsible under the 1977 Treaty; Article 61, paragraph 2, of the Vienna Convention expressly provides that impossibility of performance may not be invoked for the termination of a treaty by a party to that treaty when it results from that party's own breach of an obligation flowing from that treaty.[320]

The phenomenon of multiplicity of reasons in a judgment in support of a single conclusion, which is probably to be attributed to the collegiate nature of the Court, sometimes makes it difficult to extract a true *ratio decidendi*; but in this case, the essential (and the most specific) reason employed would seem to be that performance of a treaty is not to be deemed impossible, for purposes of Article 61, if the treaty itself provides for its being adapted to the circumstances relied on as showing impossibility; in such case, at the very least, the onus is upon the party claiming impossibility to show that those provisions would not have rescued the achievement of compliance with the treaty.

---

[318] Ibid, 63–64.

[319] [1997] ICJ Rep 63, para 102, citing *Official Records of the United Nations Conference on the Law of' Treaties, First Session, Vienna, 26 March-24 May 1968*, A/CONF.39/11, Summary records of the plenary meetings and of the meetings of the Committee of the Whole, 62nd Meeting of the Committee of the Whole, 361–365.

[320] Ibid, 64, para 103.

4. FAILURE OF CONSIDERATION AS A GROUND FOR TERMINATION OF TREATIES?

Attention has been drawn above to an aspect of the *Gabčíkovo-Nagymaros Project* case which bears some resemblance to an application of the concept of failure of consideration in Anglo-American contract law.[321]

5. PROCEDURAL REQUIREMENTS ON TERMINATION OF TREATY

In the preceding article on this aspect, reference was made to the provisions (Articles 65 to 68) of the Vienna Convention concerning 'Procedure', and specifically 'Procedure to be followed with respect to invalidity, termination, withdrawal from or suspension of the operation of a treaty'. How rapidly the law has developed since that time, under the influence of the Convention itself is apparent from a comparison of the view stated in that article that '[i]t appears evident that, except to the extent that Article 33 of the Charter may be taken to reflect customary law, these provisions of the Vienna Convention are *de lege ferenda* ...',[322] with the Court's observation in the case of the *Gabčíkovo-Nagymaros Project* that:

Both Parties agree that Articles 65 to 67 of the Vienna Convention on the Law of Treaties, if not codifying customary law, at least generally reflect customary international law and contain certain procedural principles which are based on an obligation to act in good faith.[323]

The relevance of the rules of customary law that thus corresponded to these provisions was in view of the termination, or purported termination, by Hungary of the 1977 Treaty concerning the Project. This was effected by a Declaration transmitted to the Government of Czechoslovakia on 19 May 1992, accompanied by a letter explaining that the immediate cause for the termination was Czechoslovakia's refusal, expressed in a letter of 23 April 1992, to suspend works known as 'Variant C' during mediation efforts of the Commission of the European Communities.[324] The termination was stated to be effective as of 25 May 1992—a mere 6 days later.

When the Court considered the question of the length of notice of termination, in the light of the customary law corresponding to

---

[321] See above Chapter II, Section 1(2).

[322] (1992) *BYIL* 1, 86.

[323] [1997] ICJ Rep 66, para 109. The Court cited its advisory opinion in the case of the *Interpretation of the Agreement of 25 March 1951 between the WHO and Egypt*, [1980] ICJ Rep 96, para 49, relating to Article 56 of the Convention, discussed in the previous article.

[324] [1997] ICJ Rep 58, para 91.

Article 65 of the Vienna Convention, it had already, in the preceding paragraph of its judgment, concluded that 'the notification of termination by Hungary was premature', inasmuch as '[n]o breach of the Treaty by Czechoslovakia had yet taken place' and consequently 'Hungary was not entitled to invoke any such breach of the Treaty as a ground for terminating when it did'.[325] The notice of termination was therefore presumably a nullity; and one might question the usefulness of examining whether it might also be vitiated by shortness of the period of notice.[326] However, the Court did not in fact rule on the question whether the Declaration, had it been justified by Czechoslovakia's actions, might have been given to take effect on too short notice. The Court said:

The termination of the Treaty by Hungary was to take effect six days after its notification. On neither of these dates had Hungary suffered injury resulting from acts of Czechoslovakia. The Court must therefore confirm its conclusion that Hungary's termination of the Treaty was premature.[327]

The length of the notice given thus turns out to be quite irrelevant: if Hungary had given a much longer period of notice, one that would satisfy whatever the requirements of international law on the point may be, it would still have been premature and invalid if at the date of its expiry Hungary had not yet suffered 'injury resulting from acts of Czechoslovakia'. On the face of the judgment, the Court not only gives no ruling on what would be an adequate period of notice; its finding that, as the parties agreed, Article 65 of the Vienna Convention 'reflected customary international law' was otiose. However, it should not be overlooked that Judge Herczegh, in his dissenting opinion, took the point of alleged short notice, and drew attention to the qualification in Article 65, paragraph 2, of the Convention: that text requires effective termination to be 'after the expiration of a period which, except in cases of special urgency, shall not be less than three months after the receipt of the notification'. In Judge Herczegh's view, 'in the face of very visible progress in the building of Variant C, Hungary was manifestly in such a situation of "special urgency".'[328] The Court may thus be taken to have been tacitly rejecting Judge Herczegh's view on this point.

---

[325] Ibid, 66, para 108.

[326] The Court also proceeded to find that when Czechoslovakia did commit an internationally wrongful act by 'putting into operation Variant C', this was 'as a result of Hungary's own wrongful conduct', and that 'Hungary, by its own conduct, had prejudiced its right to terminate the Treaty': ibid, 67, para 110. This argument is introduced almost as an afterthought, but it would seem to have logical priority: if Hungary 'had prejudiced its right to terminate the Treaty', then whatever the formal validity of its notification, it would have been substantially a nullity.

[327] [1997] ICJ Rep 66–67, para 109.

[328] Ibid, para 198.

6. DESUETUDE

In the earlier article, under this heading, the contention of France in the *Nuclear Tests* cases was discussed, that the 1928 General Act could no longer serve as a basis for the jurisdiction of the Court, having fallen into desuetude.[329] While the Court made no finding on the point, the views of those judges who discussed it in their opinions tend to support the view of the International Law Commission that if a treaty can cease to be effective after a long lapse of time, it can only be because a tacit consent of the parties can be discerned in this circumstance. It was there observed that non-recourse to a jurisdictional title, for example a declaration under the Optional Clause of the Court's Statute, cannot be relied on to suggest that the title has fallen into desuetude, in view of the sporadic and tangential way in which such titles may be relied on.

In the case of the *Aerial Incident of 10 August 1999*, it was argued by Pakistan that a reservation in India's Optional Clause declaration was 'obsolete' and thus could not be relied on.[330] Such a reservation, and indeed a declaration under the optional clause, partakes of the nature of a unilateral act; but one which is embedded in a treaty relationship,[331] so that (for example) the rules of interpretation of treaties may *mutatis mutandis* be applied to the interpretation of declarations.[332] The Court did not consider whether desuetude or obsolescence was a concept applicable to declarations; Judge Al-Khasawneh in his dissenting opinion noted that it had been argued that 'the doctrine of obsolescence does not apply to unilateral acts', and suggested that that view might be questioned inasmuch as it was

based on the assumption that what starts as a unilateral undertaking goes on being so even when it is transformed into mutual arrangements, raising in other parties to the optional clause system reasonable expectations not dissimilar to those raised under treaty relations.[333]

The reservation was the Commonwealth clause, excluding from the acceptance of jurisdiction disputes between the declarant State and other members of the British Commonwealth. The suggestion that that clause 'could easily [be] regarded as obsolete' had been thrown out by Judge Ago in 1992 in his dissenting opinion in the case of *Certain Phosphate*

---

[329] (1992) *BYIL* 1, 94–96, citing ICJ Pleadings in the case, Vol. II, 354.

[330] [2000] ICJ Rep 30, para 41. A point the Court was not in the event called upon to decide was whether, if the reservation was ineffective for, as it were, desuetude, the result would be that the whole declaration would be invalid, as suggested by Judge Lauterpacht in respect of the Connally reservation in the *Certain Norwegian Loans* case [1957] ICJ Rep 57–59.

[331] *Cf. Military and Paramilitary Activities in and against Nicaragua*, [1984] ICJ Rep 418, para 60.

[332] See the case of *Fisheries Jurisdiction (Spain v. Canada)*, [1998] ICJ Rep 453, para 46, discussed in the previous article, (2006) *BYIL* 1, 27–28.

[333] [2000] ICJ Rep 50, para 5.

Lands in Nauru. The reason he gave, which was later to be invoked by Pakistan, was that the clause had 'originally been inserted in the [United Kingdom] declaration in anticipation of the establishment of a special court for the Commonwealth' and 'that expectation has never been fulfilled'.[334] In the case of the Indian declaration, as the Court noted, the reservation had been consistently included in successive declarations deposited by India following its independence,[335] the most recent dating from 1974, a date at which (though the Court did not spell this out) it had become undeniably evident that the special court for the Commonwealth was never going to be created.[336] Unsurprisingly, the Court rejected the argument of Pakistan, observing that:

While the historical reasons for the initial appearance of the Commonwealth reservation in the declarations of certain States under the optional clause may have changed or disappeared, such considerations cannot, however, prevail over the intention of a declarant State, as expressed in the actual text of its declaration. India has repeatedly made clear that it wishes to limit in this manner the scope *ratione personae* of its acceptance of the Court's jurisdiction. Whatever may have been the reasons for this limitation, the Court is bound to apply it.[337]

This decision, while undoubtedly correct and appropriate to the case before the Court, does not afford the assistance that might be hoped for on the question of desuetude. If India's declaration had stood unchanged since 1947, and if at that time the original justification for the inclusion of the Commonwealth reservation had been still in existence, what effect, if any, could the subsequent disappearance of that justification have on the declaration and the reservation? On the actual facts of the case, India's intentions had not altered and were not in doubt: to maintain the reservation. The purpose underlying it may perhaps have been no more than force of habit, or *ex abundanti cautela*; but perhaps also India maintained the clause in view of the political developments making disputes with Pakistan far from unlikely. This indeed was suggested by Pakistan as the reason for India's maintenance of the reservation[338], a contention accepted by Judge Al-Khasawneh.[339]

In view of the emphasis on consent in relation to desuetude of bilateral treaties, one may ask, not whether a reservation can fall into

---

[334] [1992] ICJ Rep 327, para 5.

[335] And in fact even before independence, when in 1929 the Commonwealth countries accepted the Optional Clause of the Statute of the Permanent Court (LNTS, Vol. 6, 379).

[336] The idea that the Judicial Committee of the Privy Council might serve as an inter-Commonwealth court was linked with the *inter se* doctrine, that relations between the Commonwealth countries were not relations governed by international law in the same way as those between States (cf. the Report of the 1926 Imperial Conference, British Command Papers, Cmd. 2768, Section V). For the background generally, see R Jennings, 'The Commonwealth and International Law', (1953) BYIL 320; W Dale, *The Modern Commonwealth* (1983).

[337] [2000] ICJ Rep 31, para 44.

[338] Ibid, 27, para 30 *in fine.*

[339] Ibid, 51, para 11.

desuetude, but rather whether a reservation could be abandoned by its maker; and whether such abandonment might be inferred even in the absence of formal withdrawal. Perhaps the only circumstances in which this particular reservation might have been treated as abandoned would be if on a number of occasions proceedings before the Court had been brought against India by other Commonwealth countries, and on each occasion India had refrained from relying on the reservation, and had made no statement reserving its position. The case would be even stronger if it could be shown that there was a general tacit consensus among Commonwealth States that the reservation should not be invoked. This however is somewhat speculative: what is clear is that in the field of Optional Clause reservations, and possibly generally in the field of treaty-law, the Court does not regard as applicable the maxim *cessat ratio legis, cessat lex ipsa.*

PART FIVE[340]

III. POINTS OF SUBSTANTIVE LAW

Division A: The Law of the Sea[341]

INTRODUCTION

Of all the fields of international law which the Court has had occasion to deal with, and which have been examined in the present series of articles, the law of the sea has perhaps developed to the greatest extent since the previous articles commenting upon it, as a result of a number of substantial decisions of the Court in maritime delimitation cases. While some other aspects of the law of the sea have been touched on in the Court's recent case-law, maritime delimitation has become one of its specialisations[342]; much of this Division will therefore concern delimitation cases. Perhaps unexpectedly, the International Tribunal for the Law of the Sea, which was created become of some dissatisfaction with the Court, has not so far been entrusted with cases of this kind[343]; and a considerable part of its work has been applications under Article 292 of the Law of the Sea Convention for prompt release of arrested vessels, for which the Tribunal has a special competence. This is not however to underrate the potential importance of arbitration under the provisions of the Law of the Sea Convention, which may constitute a more serious rival than ITLOS itself to the Court's quasi-monopoly of delimitation cases.[344] Before these are examined in any detail, it may be convenient to sketch out the broad lines of this development.

All the recent maritime delimitation cases, that is to say those decided subsequently to that of *Maritime Delimitation in the Area between Greenland and Jan Mayen* in 1993,[345] already examined in this series, have involved

---

[340] This Part is a supplement to (1993) *BYIL* 1.

[341] I am indebted to Dr Yoshifumi Tanaka for a number of perceptive comments on the draft of this part of the present article.

[342] This may indicate a greater degree of trust in the Court for settlement of this class of dispute. A slight pointer in the opposite direction is however Australia's exclusion of maritime disputes from its optional clause declaration of acceptance of jurisdiction (March 2002).

[343] Although the number of States expressing a preference for ITLOS under Article 287 of the Law of the Sea Convention slightly exceeds the number of those preferring the ICJ. For an insider's analysis of the comparative merits of the two tribunals, see T Treves, 'What have the United Nations Convention and the International Tribunal for the Law of the Sea to offer as regards Maritime Delimitation Disputes?', in R Lagoni and D Vignes (eds), *Maritime Delimitation* (2006) 63, and particularly 71–72; see also R Churchill, 'Some Reflections on the Operation of the Dispute Settlement System of the UN Convention on the Law of the Sea during its First Decade', in D Freestone, R Barnes and D M Ong (eds), *The Law of the Sea: Progress and Prospects* (2006), 388.

[344] In this sense, see M D Evans, 'Maritime Boundary Delimitation: Where Do We Go From Here?' in D Freestone, R Barnes and D M Ong (eds), *The Law of the Sea: Progress and Prospects* (2006) 137.

[345] [1993] ICJ Rep 38.

delimitation by a single maritime boundary, that is to say a line intended to mark the division not only of the seabed but also of the superjacent waters. In the *Greenland/Jan Mayen* case, there was no difference in the location of the line drawn by the Court for the continental shelf and for the fishery zones, but in the absence of agreement for a single boundary, these were two coincident lines, not a single maritime boundary.[346] Such a boundary is not provided for in the 1982 Law of the Sea Convention, or other multilateral treaty text, and, as the Court has made clear, can only be created by agreement; consequently, the Court is not empowered to draw such a boundary unless the two parties are agreed in requesting it. Absent such agreement, application of the law relating to the continental shelf, and of that relating to the EEZ or fishery zones, would involve drawing two lines, even if, as in the *Greenland/Jan Mayen* case, they coincided in location. Furthermore, most of the maritime delimitations requested of the Court during the period under consideration have included a delimitation of the territorial seas of the parties, either because of the geographical relationship between the parties' coasts (as in *Maritime Delimitation and Territorial Questions between Qatar and Bahrain*), or because of the close relationship between the azimuth of a territorial sea delimitation line and the line dividing the areas further from the coast, the position of which could be vital for purposes of sea-bed exploitation (*Territorial and Maritime Dispute between Nicaragua and Honduras in the Caribbean Sea*). The treaty-law concerning territorial sea entitlement is more specific (or, as the Court has put it, 'more articulated'[347]) than that relating to the other maritime areas; the Court has nevertheless carried out some degree of assimilation between them, so that the process of delimitation and the factors treated as relevant do not differ essentially from the one area to the other.

Despite the fact that the single maritime boundary incorporates the element of waters superjacent to the seabed, and consequently of the living resources of those waters, it is striking to what extent the tacit emphasis in recent delimitation cases has been on seabed delimitation; or perhaps it might be more accurate to say, to what extent considerations relating to the resources of the water column have been absent from the analysis of relevant circumstances. In the first case involving a single boundary, the *Gulf of Maine* case, the Chamber seised of the case noted the difficulty in finding any indication in customary law of the requirements of law as to the methods of delimitation; falling back on a very generally phrased 'fundamental norm', it observed that the methods employed had to be 'just as suitable for the delimitation of the sea-bed and its subsoil as for the delimitation of the superjacent waters and their fishery resources.'[348] In effect, this has in practice meant the use of a 'neutral criterion' or what the

[346] A distinction that has perhaps not always been appreciated: see below, Chapter II, Introduction B(b).
[347] *Territorial and Maritime Dispute between Nicaragua and Honduras in the Caribbean Sea* [2007] ICJ Rep, para 269.
[348] [1984] ICJ Rep 329, para 199.

Chamber called 'geometrical methods', ie methods involving essentially an examination of a map of the area, rather than investigation, for the continental shelf, of the nature of the seabed and its relationship to the coasts, and for the living resources of the waters, of any idea of 'equitable access' to fish stocks.[349] The 'neutral criterion' derives solely from what is fixed and visible, not from the mobile resources of the waters: as the *Greenland/Jan Mayen* case demonstrated, an impressively equitable-looking line on the map may look much less appropriate if the fishery resources are also plotted on the map—to the extent that such plotting is possible at all.[350] Possibly because of the absence of substantial fishery resources in the areas concerned, recent delimitation decisions of the Court have made little or no reference to their possible relevance for the delimitation.[351]

Consistently with this map-based approach, the most important element in maritime delimitation has unquestionably come to be the equidistance line, drawn on a provisional basis, and then adjusted, if and to the extent appropriate, to take account of various special or relevant circumstances, in order to achieve the 'equitable result' required by Articles 74 and 83 of the Law of the Sea Convention.[352] Historically, this process, which had already begun when the previous articles in this series were published, constitutes a *revirement de jurisprudence*,[353] since in the very first case concerning seabed areas, the *North Sea Continental Shelf* case in 1969, the Court refused to see Article 6 of the 1958 Geneva Convention on the Continental Shelf, providing for delimitation by an equidistance line, as corresponding to customary law; and as late as 1985 the Court similarly refused, in the case of the *Continental Shelf (Libya/Malta)*, 'to accept that, even as a preliminary and provisional step towards the drawing of a delimitation line, the equidistance line is one which *must* be used...'.[354]

Against this background, a number of the questions examined in the previous two articles in this series devoted to the law of the sea have now lost all or the greater part of their importance, and others now demand to be treated extensively. One practical consequence is that it has not been possible in the present supplemental article to preserve the original division by headings and sub-headings.

[349] See the *Greenland/Jan Mayen* decision, [1993] ICJ Rep 72, para 76.

[350] An interpenetration of seabed delimitation law and fishery resources division law was postulated in the decision in the case of the *Continental Shelf (Libya/Malta)*, suggesting that even in a case concerned solely with the continental shelf, 'greater importance must be attributed to elements, such as distance from the coast, which are common to both concepts', ie the continental shelf and the EEZ: [1985] ICJ Rep 33, para 33.

[351] In the *Nicaragua/Honduras* case, the Court examined evidence of fisheries activities, but solely in relation to the disputed sovereignty over offshore islands: [2007] ICJ Rep, paras. 190–198 of the Judgment of 8 October 2007.

[352] Article 15 of the Convention, applicable to delimitation of the territorial sea, does not mention this as the object in view, but has been read as directing it by implication.

[353] In this sense, D Anderson, 'Developments in Maritime Boundary Law and Practice', in D A Colson and R W Smith (eds) *International Maritime Boundaries* (2005), Vol V, 3209; Evans, above n 344, 138.

[354] [1985] ICJ Rep 37, para 43 (emphasis in original).

CHAPTER I: CLAIMS TO MARITIME SPACES: GENERAL SURVEY

'Il n'est guère usité d'étendre la déscription des limites
entre deux Etats au-delà du territoire et jusqu'en mer.'

Response of the Netherlands Foreign Ministry
to a Belgian proposal to delimit the territorial sea, 1934[355]

1. THE RELATIONSHIP OF TERRITORIAL SOVEREIGNTY TO RIGHTS OVER MARITIME SPACES: BASES OF TITLE

(1) Sovereignty over a coastal territory

As was observed in the previous article on this subject, '[r]ights over maritime areas are an adjunct of sovereignty over the coastal territory.'[356] The truth of this hardly original observation is evident from the trend to bring matters for judicial settlement involving both claims to sovereignty over coastal areas, and claims to maritime areas off the coasts, the title to the one governing the entitlement to the other.[357] In the case of *Maritime Delimitation and Territorial Questions between Qatar and Bahrain* the logical relationship between the questions before the Court was of course the reverse of the order given in the case title: the Court had to determine which of the two States had sovereignty over Zubarah, on the Qatar peninsula, and over the Hawar Islands, before it could establish what were the coasts of the parties on the basis of which a line of maritime delimitation could be constructed; it noted that '[i]t is thus the territorial situation that must be taken as starting point for the determination of the maritime rights of a coastal State'.[358] Similarly, in the case of the *Land and Maritime Boundary between Cameroon and Nigeria*, it is no exaggeration to say that, of the whole length of the land boundary that the Court was asked to delimit, the most vital element was the last section, where the boundary approached and met the coastline, namely the Bakassi Peninsula, since it was this that would govern at least the initial portion of the maritime delimitation. In the case of the *Territorial and Maritime Dispute between Nicaragua and Honduras in the Caribbean Sea* the course

---

355 Cited in G Gidal, *Le Droit International Public de la Mer* (1934), t.III, 765–766.
356 (1993) *BYIL* 1, 5.
357 *Cf* the Arbitration Agreement in the *Eritrea/Yemen* dispute, Art 2(3), whereby the Tribunal was to decide the maritime delimitation dispute 'taking into account the opinions that it will have formed on questions of territorial sovereignty...' The dispute between Indonesia and Malaysia over the islands of Sipadan and Ligitan 'crystallized in the context of discussions concerning the delimitation of the respective continental shelves of the two States', though only the dispute over the islands themselves was brought before the Court: [2002] ICJ Rep 642, para 31.
358 [2001] ICJ Rep 97, para 185.

of the delimitation was affected by the presence of a number of islets or cays of undetermined sovereignty, so that the Court had first to resolve the dispute over these.

In the *Cameroon/Nigeria* case, Nigeria, whose claim to the Peninsula was in fact rejected by the Court, endeavoured to argue that, in the particular circumstances of the case, the link between sovereignty at the terminal point of the land boundary and, at least, the first section of the maritime boundary, was severed by the agreement or acquiescence of the parties. Professor Crawford, for Nigeria, argued that in the maritime areas off the coast of the Peninsula there had been 'long-standing activity and acquiescence by both Parties', and that this 'must have legal consequences on vested rights and legitimate expectations in the maritime domain, however the issue of sovereignty over the Bakassi Peninsula may be resolved', and Professor Crawford emphasized the last phrase,[359] which for him was 'the essential point'. The Court did not deal with this contention specifically; it simply stated what the Nigerian contention was as to the line of the maritime boundary, and continued '[s]ince the Court has already found that sovereignty over the Bakassi Peninsula lies with Cameroon and not with Nigeria..., it is unnecessary to deal any further with this argument of Nigeria.'[360] The Court may well have been unconvinced by the evidence of activities suggesting acquiescence in a particular line; but it is a pity that it did not comment on the matter. Although the land boundary between the two States was disputed right up to its meeting with the coastline, they were able to agree a maritime delimitation starting from a chosen point some little way offshore. If the line so agreed was inconsistent with the later judicial finding on sovereignty over the land territory at the endpoint of the frontier, it was perfectly arguable that this pointed to a joint intention to agree a delimitation independent of the land frontier, and that this agreement was intended to govern beyond the seaward extent of the line actually adopted.

In the *Gulf of Maine* case, the Chamber of the Court was asked, by the parties' special agreement, to decide the question of maritime delimitation starting, not from the endpoint of the land boundary,[361] but from a point offshore referred to as point A, which was 'the point where the lines then [ie at the date of the special agreement] representing in graphical

---

[359] CR 2002/13, 62. I am obliged to Dr Y Tanaka for drawing my attention to this passage.

[360] [2002] ICJ Rep 427, para 255.

[361] In the case of the *Continental Shelf (Tunisia/Libya)*, the delimitation indicated by the Court also started some way offshore, but this was because the Court was asked to delimit only the continental shelf, and not the territorial waters of the parties. In fact this put the Court in a difficulty, since there was no agreed delimitation of the territorial sea, so that the starting point of the shelf delimitation was undefined: [1982] ICJ Rep 65, para 82. The Court got round this difficulty by defining the delimitation line landwards from a point defined by the intersection of oil exploration concessions granted by the parties, on a bearing defined primarily by the relationship between those concessions, the intersection of that bearing with the outer limit of the territorial sea constituting the starting point of the shelf delimitation: ibid, 85, para 120.

terms the Parties' respective claims happened to intersect'.[362] The terminal point of the land boundary was undisputed; but point A, as the Chamber noted, was not derived from basepoints on the coasts of the two parties, and could not therefore 'be located on the path of any equidistance line traced by the Chamber or constitute the starting point of any such line'.[363] The Chamber not only started its line from point A (since it could not otherwise comply with the special agreement by which it was seised), but chose, for the first part of the delimitation, a method other than equidistance which, the judgment seem to suggest, the Chamber would otherwise have favoured.[364]

In the *Gulf of Maine* case, the agreement of the parties was evident, and binding on the Chamber as part of the *compromis*. In the *Cameroon/Nigeria* case, whether or not there was acquiescence amounting to an agreement as to the initial course of the line, it would seem very difficult to establish that that agreement was to operate independently of the delimitation to be effected by the Court.[365] It remains true, however—and it is for this reason that it is regrettable that the Court did not touch on the point—that while the principle that 'the land dominates the sea' remains fundamental, its working-out in a particular case must be a matter primarily of agreement; and that therefore an agreed delimitation which is not that which the geographical circumstances might appear to dictate remains valid and over-rides such hypothetical delimitation.

The voting in the *Cameroon/Nigeria* case also illustrates the operation of the principle that rights over maritime spaces depend upon or derive from sovereignty over land territory: those judges who disagreed with the Court's finding that the Bakassi Peninsula was under the sovereignty of Cameroon also voted against the clause of the judgment defining the line, to the extent that this was dictated by the sovereignty finding.[366]

In that case there was also some indication, if not of the reverse principle, that sovereignty over a land feature might depend on an entitlement to a maritime area, at least of the possible relevance of an *agreed* maritime

---

[362] [1984] ICJ Rep 332, para 211.
[363] Ibid.   [364] See ibid, 332–333, para 212.
[365] If the case had been brought by special agreement, any prior agreement as to delimitation would certainly have been mentioned in the special agreement, so that absence of such mention would make the point virtually unarguable. However, the *Cameroon/Nigeria* case was brought on the basis of optional-clause declarations.
[366] See the voting on paragraphs III(B) and IV(B) of the operative clause (para 325) at [2002] ICJ Rep 455–456. It is arguable that this was incorrect: that once the Court had determined, by majority, that sovereignty was with Cameroon, it became the duty of the minority judges to accept that finding for the purposes of the issues still to be decided, and vote on the delimitation line on its own merits as an implementation of the decision on sovereignty. This point might have been clearer had the Court chosen to deal specifically with the Nigerian argument severing the (alleged) agreement as to the maritime boundary from the sovereignty issue, and resolved it with, presumably, the same division of votes. In general, any other course in a situation of this kind could lead to deadlock: if the decision on sovereignty were adopted, say, by 10 votes to 5, and of the majority 7 judges favoured delimitation line A, and the 3 others line B, no majority could be found if the 5 judges who had dissented on sovereignty were free to vote against *any* delimitation line based on the sovereignty finding.

delimitation to a disputed question of sovereignty. It may well be that sovereignty over a land territory is in fact determined in the course of the process of effecting a maritime delimitation, e.g., for purposes of determining the 'relevant coasts' of the parties.[367] When examining the question of sovereignty over the Bakassi peninsula, the Court mentioned the fact that

Cameroon and Nigeria participated from 1971 to 1975 in the negotiations lead-ing to the Yaoundé, Kano and Maroua Declarations [which, as the Court found, had produced an agreed delimitation line up to point G], with the maritime delimitation line clearly being predicated upon Cameroon's title to Bakassi.[368]

At this point in its judgment, the Court was considering the claim of Nigeria to base sovereignty over Bakassi on 'manifestations of sover-eignty by Nigeria together with acquiescence by Cameroon in Nigerian sovereignty over the Bakassi Peninsula',[369] and in particular the alleged 'acquiescence' of Cameroon.[370] It therefore does not appear to be saying that the absence of sovereignty of Nigeria over Bakassi can be deduced from its participation in these negotiations, but rather that any lack of zeal by Cameroon in enforcing its claims to Bakassi can be understood against the background of apparent Nigerian acceptance of those claims.

Nevertheless, it is conceivable that where determination of sovereignty over a particular geographical area or feature would have a far-reaching effect on the delimitation of disputed maritime areas, the conclusion of a delimitation agreement consistent only with attribution of sovereignty over that feature to party A might be interpreted as recognition or acqui-escence by party B in the claim of party A.[371] Obviously such a conclu-sion would be subject to any express disclaimer by party B, and would in any event have to be treated with caution in view of the fact that States evidently always are free to negotiate and agree a maritime boundary that is not identical with the boundary that would have been 'dictated' by the geographical and other factors that a Court would have taken into account.[372] Whether the mere participation in negotiations, the unspoken premise of which appeared to be recognition of the other party's sover-eignty over the land feature, would suffice may be more doubtful.[373] The

---

[367] Cf B Kwiatowska, 'The World Court and Peaceful Settlement of Oceans Disputes', in D Freestone, R Barnes and D M Ong (eds), *The Law of the Sea: Progress and Prospects* (2006) 433, 449–450.

[368] [2002] ICJ Rep 416, para 223.

[369] Ibid, 412, para 218 (iii).

[370] Ibid, 415, para 223, second sub-paragraph.

[371] Tanaka interprets the dictum in *Cameroon/Nigeria* in this sense: 'Reflections on Maritime Delimitation in the *Cameroon/Nigeria* case' (2004) 53 *ICLQ* 404.

[372] In this sense, M D Evans, 'Delimitation and the Common Maritime Boundary' (1993) *BYIL* 283, 293; implied also by *North Sea Continental Shelf* [1969] ICJ Rep 50, para 93.

[373] In the *Factory at Chorzów* case the PCIJ held that it was not open to it to take account of 'dec-larations, admissions or proposals' made in the course of negotiations, as being 'made without preju-dice': *PCIJ Series A, No. 9*, 19. However in the case of the *Land, Island and Maritime Boundary* case the ICJ Chamber appeared to distinguish between contentions advanced 'in principle, which

phenomenon is in any event not a reversal of the principle that maritime title depends on territorial sovereignty, but rather a deduction from it: to recognize maritime title as an incident of sovereignty may, if the relation is unambiguous, amount to recognition of that sovereignty.

In the *Qatar/Bahrain* case, discussed below, the Court acted in a manner that could be interpreted as deducing sovereignty from a maritime delimitation effected by the Court itself: see Chapter II, Section 1(3)(c)(i) below.

The Court has also re-asserted the principle that 'the land dominates the sea' in the context of the treatment, for purposes of maritime delimitation, of islands over which sovereignty was disputed.[374] In the case of the *Territorial and Maritime Dispute between Nicaragua and Honduras in the Caribbean Sea*, there were a number of uninhabited islets or cays in the area in which the delimitation would have to be made. Honduras laid claim to these, and also claimed a 12-mile territorial sea around them; Nicaragua disputed the claim of Honduras, and presented some material in support of a claim itself to have sovereignty over them. However, it argued in favour of a maritime delimitation using a bisector of the angle of coastal fronts, and proposed that 'sovereignty over [the islands] could be attributed to either party depending on the position of the feature involved with respect to the bisector line'.[375] It was agreed between the parties that the islands had at the time of Spanish decolonization been *terra nullius*, and the Nicaraguan proposal was explained as follows:

Nicaragua's position on the question of the cays and rocks located in or around the area in dispute is that these features have never been susceptible of effective occupation by any sovereign. As indicated before, these minor incidents located barely above water in an area of very heavy seas and rains and yearly hurricane threats have never been the object of permanent use by anybody. That is why Nicaragua considered that by using a bisector as a method of delimitation, sovereignty over these features could be attributed to either Party depending on the position of the feature involved with respect to the bisector line.[376]

The Court however responded by citing the principle that 'the land dominates the sea',[377] and continued:

To draw a single maritime boundary line in an area of the Caribbean Sea where a number of islands and rocks are located the Court would have to consider what influence these maritime features might have on the course of that line. To plot

thus define the extent of the dispute', and subsequent 'suggestions for mutual concessions', to conclude that '[i]f no agreement is reached, neither party can be held to such suggested concessions': [1992] ICJ Rep 406, para 73. If the whole negotiations were conducted on the basis (even if unspoken) that sovereignty over the disputed feature was with party A, a court would, it is suggested, be entitled to take that fact into account as possible evidence of a recognition by party B.

374 On the role of islands in maritime delimitation, see further Chapter II, Section 1(3)(d) below.

375 [2007] ICJ Rep, para 112 of the Judgment of 8 October 2007: see also the Nicaraguan Agent in CR 2007/1, 17, para 7.

376 CR 2007/1, 38, para 77 (Agent of Nicaragua).

377 Ibid, para 113, citing *North Sea Continental Shelf, Aegean Sea,* and the *Qatar/Bahrain* case.

that line the Court would first have to determine which State has sovereignty over the islands and rocks in the disputed area. The Court is bound to do so whether or not a formal claim has been made in this respect.[378]

This amounts to an implied rejection of the Nicaraguan argument, but that argument in fact contains an ambiguity or contradiction. Nicaragua contended that the features were not 'susceptible of effective occupation by any sovereign', meaning presumably that sovereignty could not be acquired over them; yet at the same time it was claiming that they would be 'attributed' to the one party or the other by the delimitation, ie attributed *to the sovereignty* of the one party or the other.[379]

The principle would seem to be that a coastal or maritime feature which is capable of appropriation in sovereignty must necessarily have an effect, appropriate to its geographical position, on a maritime delimitation in its vicinity, and that any feature not so capable of appropriation in principle has no such effect unless it is itself situated in the territorial sea of a State. This qualification is required for consistency with Article 7, paragraph 4, of the Law of the Sea Convention, and the Court's treatment of low-tide elevations in the *Qatar/Bahrain* case,[380] where the question whether low-tide elevations were capable of appropriation in sovereignty was left undetermined. This conclusion may be regarded as a corollary of the principle that the land dominates the sea, or as an element underlying it.

The link between territorial disputes and maritime delimitations was also emphasized by the controversy between the parties to the case entitled *Territorial Dispute* between Nicaragua and Colombia over the nature of the subject of the dispute. Colombia asserted, by way of preliminary objection, that there was no extant dispute between itself and Nicaragua, since the issues raised had been settled by a 1928 Treaty and a 1930 Protocol concluded between them; if it could convince the Court that this was so, then not only would the Court dismiss the case for lack of jurisdiction, but under Article XXXIV of the Pact of Bogotá (the jurisdictional basis relied on by Nicaragua), the 'controversy' submitted to the Court would have to be 'declared ended'.[381] The 1928 Treaty had contained reciprocal recognitions of sovereignty of each party by the other, relating to various territories and islands; the 1930 Protocol declared that the 'San Andrés and Providencia Archipelago' referred to in the Treaty did not 'extend west of the 82nd degree of longitude

---

[378] [2007] ICJ Rep, para 114 of the Judgment.

[379] Nicaragua's approach was two-pronged: it claimed that either the islands should be allocated to it by the effect of the bisector delimitation line, or 'in the event that the Court determines that the method of delimitation to be used cannot decide the issue of sovereignty over these features then Nicaragua claims that the factual evidence points to Nicaraguan sovereignty over them': CR 2007/1, 39, para 80 (Agent of Nicaragua).

[380] Discussed in Chapter II, Section 1(3)(c)(i) below.

[381] Though, as the Court noted, this would only be so 'within the framework of the Pact itself', leaving open the possibility of invoking other jurisdictional titles: [2007] ICJ Rep, para 129 of the Judgment of 13 December 2007.

west of Greenwich'. Contrary to the contentions of Colombia, the Court found that 'the 1928 Treaty and 1930 Protocol did not effect a general delimitation of the maritime boundary between Colombia and Nicaragua'.[382]

(2) Inherent rights over 'maritime spaces'

The distinction between those rights over maritime spaces which exist *ipso facto* and *ab initio*, as the Court put it in the *North Sea* case, and those which exist when and to the extent that they have been expressly claimed by the coastal State, has become of less importance now that most States have laid claims to the maximum areas off their coasts that the law permits.[383] The pre-existing rights of States to the areas of continental shelf appertaining to their coasts have been defined by claims, and the potential rights of States to EEZ, fishery zones, and indeed enlarged territorial seas, have been actualised by express claims.

The Court was concerned in the case of *Maritime Delimitation between Greenland and Jan Mayen* with conflicting claims to fishery zones, which are not dealt with in the 1982 Convention on the Law of the Sea, but which have in fact been claimed and respected in State practice. As the Court observed,

there appears to be no decision of an international tribunal that has been concerned only with a fishery zone; but there are cases involving a single dual-purpose boundary asked for by the parties in a special agreement, for example the *Gulf of Maine* case . . . [384]

The Court noted the relationship of fishery zones to the concept of the EEZ in the 1982 Convention, and continued:

Whatever that relationship may be, the Court takes note that the Parties adopt in this respect the same position, in that they see no objection, for the settlement of the present dispute, to the boundary of the fishery zones being determined by the law governing the boundary of the exclusive economic zone, which is customary law . . . [385]

Accordingly, though the Court did not comment expressly on the point, the existence of a fishery zone as of an EEZ, was dependent on the proclamation of a claim to it, unlike the continental shelf.

---

[382] Ibid, para 120.

[383] And indeed further: cf. the disputed claims of the Russian Federation to areas of the Arctic extending to the North Pole, and similar claims said to be imminent in the Antarctic.

[384] [1993] ICJ Rep 59, para 47. Attention has been drawn elsewhere ((2005) *BYIL* 1, 116, citing P Weil, *Perspectives du droit de la délimitation maritime* (1988), 12 (hereinafter: Weil, *Perspectives du droit de la délimitation maritime*)) to the Court's invocation of previous jurisprudence rather than State practice; *cf* also L Lucchini, 'La délimitation des frontières maritimes dans la jurisprudence internationale: vue d'ensemble' in R Lagoni and D Vignes (eds), *Maritime Delimitation* (2006), 8–9, who considers that the judicial decisions in this field are creative of law.

[385] Ibid.

At a later stage in the judgment, however, the Court referred, as an element relevant to the delimitation, to a 'particular feature' of 'maritime boundary claims'—without distinguishing between types of claim—namely that 'there is an area of overlapping entitlements, in the sense of overlap between the areas which each State would have been able to claim had it not been for the presence of the other State'.[386] Thus for the Court, international law confers on each coastal State what one might call a vested but inchoate right to certain areas, the extent and boundaries thereof being, at least in theory, already defined by the law, whether those areas are continental shelf or EEZ or fishery zones. In the case of all areas other than the continental shelf, these pre-determined boundaries presumably yield to those actually claimed, if the State concerned claims less than its 'entitlement'. If therefore there is any distinction between the areas which a State is entitled to claim by way of EEZ, and the *ipso facto* and *ab initio* entitlement to continental shelf, it would presumably have to be that a claim to a lesser area of continental shelf than that entitlement leaves the full entitlement still existing in some legal limbo. This is however an unrealistic conclusion, at least to the extent that a delimitation, agreed or judicial, between two areas of shelf must be final and determinative;[387] one party could not claim to re-open the matter on the basis that it had, in ignorance, failed to insist on everything the law gives it.[388]

In the *Qatar/Bahrain* case the Court had to deal with the question of entitlement existing prior to a claim being made, in relation to a form of maritime right that had not, prior to the proceedings, been claimed by the State concerned, but to the incidents of which it nonetheless claimed to be entitled. The 1982 Law of the Sea Convention created a new legal concept, that of the 'archipelagic State', and authorised States falling within the Convention definition, *inter alia*, to draw 'straight archipelagic baselines' around the outermost points of the islands composing the archipelago, and to measure the breadth of the territorial sea, the continental shelf and the EEZ outwards from those baselines.[389] Bahrain argued

that, as a *de facto* archipelagic State, it is entitled to declare itself an archipelagic State under Part IV of the 1982 Law of the Sea Convention and to draw the

---

[386] Ibid, 64, para 59.

[387] As regards an agreed delimitation, it was regarded as axiomatic in the *Cameroon/Nigeria* case that, if the Maroua Declaration had effected an agreed delimitation, that was binding and had to be respected in the delimitation operation carried out by the Court. Nigeria's argument for a complete delimitation *de novo* was based on the contention that no delimitation had yet been agreed: [2002] ICJ Rep 426, para 254. A judicial delimitation by the Court will be the subject of a judgment, revision of which is only possible on narrowly defined grounds: *Application for Revision of the Judgment of 11 September 1992*, [2003] ICJ Rep 399, para 20.

[388] Cf. the previous article (1993) *BYIL* 1, 46 and the article by R Jennings there referred to. Such a claim would also raise issues of treaty-law, for example on the effect of a treaty concluded on the basis of an error of law: see another earlier article in this series: (1992) *BYIL* 1, 27–28.

[389] UNCLOS 1982, Articles 47 and 48.

permissive baselines of Article 47 of that Convention, i.e., "straight archipelagic baselines joining the outermost points of the outermost islands and drying reefs of the archipelago".[390]

Qatar disputed this claim on the grounds that

Part IV has not become customary law, and that consequently it is not opposable to it. Moreover, Bahrain has never produced a claim of archipelagic status, either as regards its relations with Qatar or with respect to other States; the basic reason for this is that Bahrain would have difficulty in proving that it meets the relevant requirements of the 1982 Convention...[391]

Bahrain was claiming, in effect, that the status of archipelagic State existed in law (under the Convention or customary law) on the basis of geographical circumstances, *ipso facto* and *ab initio* as it were, so that the fact that it had not made a formal claim to this status in accordance with the Convention[392] did not prevent it asserting the rights attaching to that status.

The Court's handling of the matter was as follows:

With regard to Bahrain's claim that it is entitled to the status of archipelagic State in the sense of the 1982 Convention on the Law of the Sea, the Court observes that Bahrain has not made this claim one of its formal submissions and that the Court is therefore not requested to take a position on this issue. What the Court, however, is called upon to do is to draw a single maritime boundary in accordance with international law.[393]

It continued, however, with a passage that appears at first sight to reject the idea of any *ab initio* or *ipso facto* right:

The Court can carry out this delimitation only by applying those rules and principles of customary law which are pertinent under the prevailing circumstances. The Judgment of the Court will have binding force between the Parties, in accordance with Article 59 of the Statute of the Court, and consequently could not be put in issue by the unilateral action of either of the Parties, and in particular, by any decision of Bahrain to declare itself an archipelagic State.[394]

However, all this is saying is that a subsequent declaration by Bahrain that it is an archipelagic State in accordance with the 1982 Convention will not affect the existing delimitation. As was observed above in relation to continental shelf rights, a delimitation once established prevails over any rights, even *ipso facto* and *ab initio* rights, that may have existed previously. Bahrain might be able to claim, in general terms, that it is, and always has been, an archipelagic State; but vis-à-vis Qatar the

---

[390] [2001] ICJ Rep 96, para 181.

[391] Ibid, para 182.

[392] Bahrain did claim that it had asserted its archipelagic claims in its diplomatic correspondence with other States—not, apparently, including Qatar, the State most concerned—and during multilateral negotiations 'over the course of the last century' (ibid, para 181); this seems clearly to suggest a contention that the 1982 Convention was, as regards archipelagic States, in some respects declaratory of customary law.

[393] [2001] ICJ Rep 96–97, para 183.

[394] Ibid.

delimitation (at root, an agreed delimitation[395]) cannot be affected by such a declaration.

2. THE RELATIONSHIP OF LAND TERRITORY TO SEA-BED AREAS: 'NATURAL PROLONGATION' AND DISTANCE[396]

The previous article examined the efforts made, particularly by parties to successive cases before the Court, to establish an underlying principle by virtue of which States would be entitled to claim, as they had been doing since the Truman Proclamation, sovereign rights over submarine areas off their coasts, which should be a principle of such a nature that it would, if not dictate the method of delimitation of such areas vis-à-vis neighbouring States, at least provide a basis for reasoning to establish the appropriate delimitation.[397] To some extent, the Court itself also endeavoured to find such a principle: in 1969, the Court saw it as the principle of 'natural prolongation' of the land territory; but until very recently subsequent decisions appeared, if not to have rejected that concept, at least to have discarded it in the geophysical form in which it was employed in the *North Sea* case, for the purposes of the delimitations in hand. A candidate for the successorship in this role was the distance criterion: in the *Libya/Malta* case, the Court observed that 'so far as [the relevant areas] are situated at a distance of under 200 miles from the coasts in question, title depends solely on the distance from the coasts of the claimant States of any areas of sea-bed claimed by way of continental shelf'.[398] As was explained in the previous article, neither principle in itself served to define a method of delimitation; but in a broader sense the idea of natural prolongation, expressed *inter alia*, in a criterion of

---

[395] A judicial determination is in effect an agreed determination because the parties have agreed that the line that the judicial body pronounces shall be accepted.

[396] This section was originally entitled 'The Relationship of Land Territory to Sea-bed Areas: the Avatars of 'Natural Prolongation''.

[397] It was the view of Judge Morelli in the *North Sea* case that '[o]nce the existence of a rule of general international law which confers certain rights over the continental shelf on various States considered individually is admitted, the necessity must be recognized for such a rule to determine the subject-matter of the rights which it confers': [1969] ICJ Rep 200, para3; i.e. that the entitlement must dictate the method of entitlement. The majority of the Court did not accept this view. A similar argument by Honduras in the *Land, Island and Maritime Frontier Dispute*, that 'a legal title without delimitation of its scope is a title without any real substance', was also unsuccessful: [1992] ICJ Rep 584, para 375.

[398] [1985] ICJ Rep 35, para 39. The Court thus virtually reversed its finding in the *North Sea Continental Shelf* cases that 'adjacency' of a maritime area to a coast was not the same as 'proximity' (nearness), and proximity may not in all circumstances be the only, or the most appropriate test to determine title: [1969] ICJ Rep 30, para 42, and the dictum in the Gulf of Maine case: 'Regarding adjacency, the Chamber acknowledges that in most cases this concept can be credited with the ability to express, perhaps better than that of natural prolongation, the link between a State's sovereignty and its sovereign rights to [sic; over] adjacent submerged land'. [1984] ICJ Rep 296, para 103.

distance from the coasts, continued to underlie judicial approaches to maritime delimitation.[399]

Since the previous article was published, the United Nations Convention on the Law of the Sea has come into force, and the articles of that Convention dealing with the delimitation of the EEZ and of the continental shelf, Articles 74 and 83, provide in identical terms that such delimitation 'shall be effected by agreement on the basis of international law ... in order to achieve an equitable solution'. But it is evident that this does not signify that the equitable solution for the delimitation of the shelf is necessarily the equitable solution for the EEZ. The effect of the Convention is that whatever rules or criteria may be relevant to the delimitation of the one area or the other now operate as pointers to an 'equitable solution'; but what they are must, it seems, be determined by the nature of the area to be delimited; or at least that they should be 'consistent with the concepts underlying the attribution of legal title.'[400] It would not therefore be inconsistent with the provisions of UNCLOS to argue that in a particular maritime area the 'equitable solution' for the delimitation of the continental shelf might be governed, or at least influenced, by the idea of 'natural prolongation' or that of 'distance'. Yet already in the *Libya/Malta* case, the Court had recognized that the fact that the EEZ includes a continental shelf component must mean that the EEZ must be taken into account in a delimitation of the continental shelf.[401]

However, even when the previous article was published, the knell of the 'natural prolongation' concept had probably already been sounded, in particular by the *Libya/Malta* decision. Case-law since that date had not seen any resurrection of the natural prolongation principle until the case of the *Territorial and Maritime Dispute between Nicaragua and Honduras in the Caribbean Sea*, discussed below; but, so far as the Court was concerned, this was not to be expected since the two major decisions, in the case of *Maritime Delimitation and Territorial Questions between Qatar and Bahrain* and *Land and Maritime Boundary between Cameroon and Nigeria*, have each involved a single maritime boundary, that is to say, a boundary valid both for the continental shelf and for the EEZ.

In the *Qatar/Bahrain* case, the Court made no attempt to derive any rules or methods of delimitation from first principles; nor did it cite any State practice, in the form of delimitation agreements. It simply offered a series of quotations from its own case-law, the *Gulf of Maine* case, the case of the *Continental Shelf (Libya/Malta)*, and the *Jan Mayen* case, on the basis of which it decided that

For the delimitation of the maritime zones beyond the 12-mile [territorial sea] zone it will first provisionally draw an equidistance line and then consider

---

[399] As was explained in the previous article, while natural prolongation and the distance criterion are two independent and distinguishable approaches, the use of distance, indeed of equidistance, amounts to asking 'how far does natural prolongation prolong?': see (1993) *BYIL* 1, 29–30.

[400] [1985] ICJ Rep 47, para 61.

[401] [1985] ICJ Rep 33, para 33; cited in (1993) *BYIL* 1, 28.

whether there are circumstances which must lead to an adjustment of that line.[402]

In the *Jan Mayen* case, it will be recalled, the circumstances pointing to an adjustment of the equidistance line were considered from two successive viewpoints: that of the adjustment of the continental shelf boundary, and that of the adjustment of the fishery zones. To the extent that the EEZ involves an element of living resources, it would seem that this process is equally necessary when what is to be drawn is not a coincident line, as in the *Jan Mayen* case, but a true 'single maritime boundary'. The originality of the *Jan Mayen* decision lay in its endorsement of a rule requiring the initial adoption of the equidistance method both for the continental shelf and for the fishery zones. For the shelf, the appropriateness of this step could be justified both on the basis of practice and of its reasonableness for an area defined, in one dimension, by the coast of each State; but the only evident justification of it for fisheries delimitation was convenience, since the distribution of fish stocks might well be geographically erratic or uneven.[403] This was however a consideration which could come back into play at the 'relevant circumstances' phase, as it did in the *Jan Mayen* case. The way in which the Court in the *Qatar/Bahrain* case applied the circumstances relevant to shelf or to fish will be examined below: for the moment, we may note that the Court did not feel the need, any more than it had in *Jan Mayen*, to explain the underlying legal philosophy of equidistance as applied to delimitation of the water column.

In the *Cameroon/Nigeria* case, the Court followed the example of the *Qatar/Bahrain* decision, citing previous jurisprudence, and quoting finally the passage from *Qatar/Bahrain* quoted above.

In both cases, however, the actual method of delimitation used was to begin with an equidistance line, and then adjust it as appropriate in the light of 'circumstances'; this could be understood as a recognition that the 'distance' principle, of which an equidistance line is perhaps the most perfected expression, is still governing. As regards the continental shelf (and the seabed component of the EEZ), this is, *pace* the *North Sea* decision, the most appropriate approach; but there seems much less logic in its application for the delimitation as regards the resources of the water column. The *Jan Mayen* case showed that an adjusted equidistance line *can* be reconciled with the available information as to the distribution of fish stocks, but is far from proving that this is possible in every case.

However, in the case of the *Territorial and Maritime Dispute between Nicaragua and Honduras in the Caribbean Sea,* natural prolongation, or something very like it, was one of the doctrines invoked by Nicaragua

---

[402] [2001] ICJ Rep 111, para 230.

[403] For this reason an agreement on a total allowable catch for each party may be preferable to a delimitation: *cf* the Agreement of 28 May 1980 between Norway (for Jan Mayen) and Iceland, Art. 4.

to support its contention that the delimitation should be effected by a bisector of the angle of the coastal fronts of the two States: it relied on 'the principle of non-encroachment' and the principle of preventing 'any cut-off of the seaward projection of the coast of either of the States'.[404] The Court does not appear to have specifically rejected these ideas;[405] it expressed its own thinking on the point as follows:

The justification for the application of the bisector method in maritime delimitation lies in the configuration of and relationship between the relevant coastal fronts and the maritime areas to be delimited. In instances where, as in the present case, any base points that could be determined by the Court are inherently unstable, the bisector method may be seen as an approximation of the equidistance method.[406]

The Court quoted from the *Gulf of Maine* case to explain that the bisector method was a geometrical approach that can be used to give legal effect to the

criterion long held to be as equitable as it is simple, namely that in principle, while having regard to the special circumstances of the case, one should aim at an equal division of areas where the maritime projections of the coasts of the States...converge and overlap.[407]

The use of a bisector has some claim to be in fact a better implementation of this criterion. In many geographical circumstances, equidistance—at least if unmodified or uncorrected in the name of equity—is far from ensuring an *equal* division of areas of seabed; the whole objection to equidistance, from the *North Sea* judgment on, is that the division of areas can be distorted by the effects of a concave coast, or the presence of capes or protrusions on one coast, producing one or more basepoints that will govern the equidistance line through all or a considerable part of its length.

As noted above,[408] no arguments are adduced to show that the bisector is appropriate to ensure an equitable result as regards any fishery component of the EEZ; there were, apparently no particular fishery interests to be provided for, or at least none were asserted by the parties.[409] This

---

[404] [2007] ICJ Rep, para 290 of the Judgment.

[405] The 'reasons' advanced by Nicaragua are set out in paragraph 290 of the Judgment; then in paragraph 291 the Court explains that '[t]o demonstrate the equitable character of its own proposed bisector line Nicaragua also refers to a number of relevant circumstances..'; and in paragraph 292 it states that '[t]he Court is not persuaded in the present case as to the pertinence of these factors and does not find them legally determinative for the purposes of the delimitation to be effected. Rather, the key elements are the geographical configuration of the coast, and the geomorphological features of the area where the endpoint of the land boundary is located.' The implication seems to be that it is only the 'factors' mentioned in para 291 that are rejected.

[406] [2007] ICJ Rep, para 287 of the Judgment.

[407] [1984] ICJ Rep 327, para 195, quoted ibid.

[408] In the Introduction to this Chapter.

[409] Honduras relied on its granting of fishing licences as acts of governmental authority justifying a claim to sovereignty over the offshore islands, and this was one of the elements taken into account by the Court in upholding Honduras's claim to sovereignty: [2007] ICJ Rep, paras. 190–195 and 208

raises a question of principle: if a single maritime boundary has to ensure an 'equitable result' both in respect of the continental shelf (Article 83 of the Law of the Sea Convention) and in respect of the EEZ (Article 74 of the Convention), is the equitableness of the line affected by the known or probable position of resources of the one kind or the other? In the North Sea case, one of the elements which the Court held had legally to be taken into account in a delimitation was, 'so far as known or readily ascertainable, the physical and geological structure, and natural resources, of the continental shelf areas involved.'[410] Subsequent jurisprudence has reduced this element in the equation of equitableness to vanishing point;[411] the delimitation assumes a homogeneous shelf in this respect, since it is effected essentially by reference to maps. What then is the position as to fishery resources? Are they also to be assumed to be evenly distributed over the area of EEZ involved? The decision in the Greenland/Jan Mayen case suggests the contrary, with its employment of the concept of 'equitable access' to fish-stocks as a relevant factor in the drawing of the delimitation line.

of the Judgment. The fishing in question took place 'in the waters around the islands' (para 195); sufficient protection of these interests may thus have been afforded by the recognition of a 12-mile territorial sea around the islands (para 302), though there is no mention of the matter in the decision.

[410] [1969] ICJ Rep 54, para 101(D)(2).

[411] The question has become confused with that of the relevance of seabed exploration activities of the parties, and that of the significance of such activities as evidence of agreement: see Chapter II, Section 1(2) below.

PART SIX[412]

CHAPTER II: MARITIME DELIMITATION: LEGAL AND PRACTICAL ASPECTS

INTRODUCTION

A. Areas to be Delimited and Applicable Law

The maritime areas which may require to be delimited by a judicial decision are the territorial sea, the continental shelf, the exclusive economic zones, and fishery zones. A preliminary question is the degree to which the rules and principles governing delimitation are common to all of these, or are peculiar to a particular category.

In terms of the applicable multilateral treaty texts, delimitation of the territorial sea is governed by Article 12 of the 1958 Geneva Convention on the Territorial Sea and the Contiguous Zone, or by Part II, Section 2 (Articles 2–16) of the 1982 Law of the Sea Convention, which reproduces the texts of the 1958 Convention with only minor changes of wording. Delimitation of the continental shelf is governed by Article 6 of the 1958 Geneva Convention on the Continental Shelf and Article 83 of the Law of the Sea Convention; delimitation of the EEZ is governed by Article 74 of the latter Convention. There is no treaty text specifically applying to the delimitation of fishery zones, nor to delimitation of several zones effected by a 'single maritime boundary'. Where there is no agreement for such a boundary, however, it remains possible to draw a single coincident line delimiting the continental shelf and fishery zones, if the application of the law governing each of these produces, or can be persuaded to produce, the same line for each, as was achieved in the case of *Maritime Delimitation in the Area between Greenland and Jan Mayen*.

In terms of the convention texts, an obvious distinction is between those which give explicit preference to the median or equidistance line, and those which do not. In the case of the territorial sea, the median or equidistance line is to be excluded only in case of 'historic title or other special circumstances', and in the case of the continental shelf under the regime of the 1958 Geneva Convention, the delimitation is to be the subject of agreement, but if not agreed is to be the median or equidistance line 'unless another boundary line is justified by special circumstances'.[413] The texts in the 1982 Law of the Sea Convention are much less specific, and indeed contain little more than a *renvoi* to customary

---

[412] This Part is a supplement to (1994) *BYIL* 1.
[413] 1958 Geneva Convention on the Territorial Sea and the Contiguous Zone, Article 12; 1982 Law of the Sea Convention, Article 15; 1958 Geneva Convention on the Continental Shelf, Article 6.

law: the delimitation is to be effected 'by agreement on the basis of international law ... in order to achieve an equitable solution'.[414]

As a result, save where the 1958 Geneva Convention on the Continental Shelf is applicable, there is *ex definitione* no difference between the 1982 Convention law and customary law for the delimitation of the continental shelf and EEZ; and for a delimitation by a single maritime boundary, only customary law is available. For the territorial sea, the extent to which customary law follows the convention texts on delimitation is not entirely clear. In the case of *Maritime Delimitation and Territorial Questions between Qatar and Bahrain*, the Court noted that the parties to that case agreed that the provisions of Article 15 of the Law of the Sea Convention (which, as the Court noted, are virtually identical to those of Article 12, paragraph 1, of the 1958 Convention) were 'part of customary law'. The Court proceeded to apply those provisions as such; even though, technically, this could be regarded as a *lex specialis* deriving from the agreement of the parties, it is unlikely that in any future case the Court would be persuaded that the provisions in question do not represent customary law.[415]

There has been no recent case in which the Court has been asked to delimit a continental shelf independently of the EEZ, or vice-versa, the trend now being in favour of agreement between the parties to ask for the drawing of a 'single maritime boundary'.[416] In the *Greenland/Jan Mayen* case, this boundary was to define the continental shelf and the fishery zones, but not the territorial sea, since the two coasts were opposite, and the distance between them considerably in excess of the total of 24 nautical miles ranking as territorial sea. In both the *Qatar/Bahrain* case and the *Territorial and Maritime Dispute between Nicaragua and Honduras in the Caribbean Sea*, the single maritime boundary asked for was to delimit both the territorial sea and the areas beyond it, as continental shelf and EEZ. In the case of the *Land and Maritime Boundary between Cameroon and Nigeria*, the parties were in agreement that the maritime delimitations should be by a 'single' line, applicable to the respective continental shelves and areas of EEZ; the area in dispute lay outside the territorial seas of the two States.[417] The case-law of the Court during the period

---

[414] 1982 Law of the Sea Convention, Articles 74 and 83.

[415] In the case of the *Land and Maritime Boundary between Cameroon and Nigeria*, the Court noted that the areas it was asked to delimit lay outside the territorial seas of the parties: [2002] ICJ Rep 440, para 285; in the case of the *Territorial and Maritime Dispute between Nicaragua and Honduras in the Caribbean Sea*, the delimitation, so far as it concerned territorial sea, was governed by Article 15 of the Law of the Sea Convention, to which both States were parties: [2007] ICJ Rep, para 267 of the Judgment.

[416] *Cf* Anderson, 'Developments in Maritime Boundary Law & Practice', above n 353, 3210, who notes that the only recent agreements limited to the shelf have related to areas beyond the 200 nautical mile limit. On the other hand, there are in existence a number of agreements simultaneously delimiting continental shelf and EEZ with the same boundaries, but treating them as separate regimes: see C Yacouba and D McRae, 'The Legal Regime of Maritime Boundary Agreements', in D A Colson and R W Smith (eds) *International Maritime Boundaries* (2005), Vol V, 3284–3287.

[417] [2002] ICJ Rep 440, para 285.

now under consideration is therefore limited, according to its terms, to the drawing of a single maritime boundary, applicable in all cases considered, to the continental shelf and the EEZ, and in some cases to the territorial sea. It is however clear from the way that the Court has expressed the motivation of its decisions, including observations that may strictly be regarded as *obiter*, that it would regard the principles and rules that it has defined as applicable also to the delimitation of the continental shelf and the EEZ *ut singuli*; as regards the territorial sea, whether or not its delimitation forms part of a single-line delimitation, the same principles and rules apply.[418]

B. THE SINGLE MARITIME BOUNDARY

(a) Single boundary and coincident boundary

The term 'single maritime boundary' has become part of the commonly used terminology in the field of maritime boundary delimitation, but attention should perhaps be paid to its definition. Where the same areas of sea and/or seabed are subject to the claims of two or more coastal States to territorial sea, continental shelf, fisheries zones or to exclusive economic zones (EEZ), boundaries have to be drawn to indicate where each claim to a particular class of rights meets a rival claim to the same class of rights: where the territorial sea of State A meets the territorial sea of State B, or the EEZ of State X meets the EEZ of State Y. However, the parallel development of the law governing entitlement to these different classes of rights, and the difference between exploitation of the (fixed) resources of the sea-bed and that of the (motile) resources of the water-column, has meant that the boundaries may fall in different places; that the continental shelf of one State may extend further, or less far, towards the coast of another State than does its entitlement to EEZ. It is however usually more convenient if the boundaries can coincide, so that the extent of each State's EEZ and the extent of its continental shelf are bounded by a single line: this was the sense of the decision in the *Greenland/Jan Mayen* case, but as has been powerfully urged by Professor Evans, the parties were given satisfaction at the expense of a consistent development of the law concerning the two regimes.[419]

Until the case of *Maritime Delimitation and Territorial Questions between Qatar and Bahrain*, the Court had not had to delimit the territorial sea. However, in the context of such a delimitation, the problem does not arise; or, to put the point another way, the boundary is necessarily a single multi-purpose boundary. As the Court observed in that case, 'delimitation of territorial seas does not present comparable problems [to

---

[418] See further on this Section B below.
[419] M D Evans, 'Delimitation and the Common Maritime Boundary' (1993) *BYIL* 283.

those encountered further seaward], since the rights of the coastal State in the area concerned are not functional but territorial, and entail sovereignty over the sea-bed and the superjacent waters and air column'.[420] Since territorial rights are the most complete rights possible over a land or marine area, a boundary between territorial areas is necessary a single one; there are no separate rights, the extent of which, being governed by different criteria, may vary within the same area, but one bundle of rights with its own governing rules and criteria. If a judicial determination of territorial seas alone were asked for, there would be no need to refer to a 'single maritime boundary' in the sense of one combining different claims; but in practice a 'single maritime boundary' may be asked for and determined in areas where, for part of its extent, the boundary divides territorial seas.[421]

In such a case, however, is it still the 'pure' law of territorial sea delimitation that applies; or some form of 'single maritime boundary-law' that extends also, in certain cases, to territorial sea delimitation? In the *Qatar/Bahrain* case, the Court defined its task as 'to apply *first and foremost* the principles and rules of international customary law which refer to the delimitation of the territorial sea', while taking into account that 'its ultimate task is to draw a single maritime boundary *that serves other purposes as well*'.[422] This seems to suggest that by asking for a 'single maritime boundary' in an area including territorial sea areas, the parties enabled or required the Court to apply a different set of rules than those of the 'pure' law of territorial sea delimitation.[423]

In the previous article on this subject in the present series, attention was drawn to the difficulty in establishing the law applicable to the drawing of a single maritime boundary, in the absence (at that time) of sufficient State practice to support an established customary law; and note was taken of the solution to the problem adopted in the *Gulf of Maine* case, that of recourse to what were regarded as 'purely neutral criteria', involving the rejection of the established law governing the component parts of the line, that is to say the law of the continental shelf and the law of fishery zones. Comparison of that case with the subsequent case of *Maritime Delimitation in the Area between Greenland and Jan Mayen* brought out the distinction between a single maritime boundary and

---

[420] [2001] ICJ Rep 93, para 174.

[421] As, for example, in the *Eritrea/Yemen Arbitration* and in the *Qatar/Bahrain* case. Tanaka (*Predictability and Flexibility in the Law of Maritime Delimitation*, 2006) lists seven delimitation agreements between 1957 and 1989 which delimit both the territorial sea and the continental shelf or EEZ (Appendix, 358-359).

[422] [2001] ICJ Rep 93, para 174.

[423] In this sense G Despeux, 'Das IGH-Urteil *Katar gegen Bahrein* vom 16. März 2001', 61 *Zeitschrift für Ausländisches Offentliches Recht und Völkerrecht* (2001), 491-492 (hereinafter: Despeux, , 'Das IGH-Urteil *Katar gegen Bahrein* vom 16. März 2001') who considers that the Court should have interpreted the agreement of the parties as requiring a continuous line dividing the territorial seas in the South and the shelf and EEZ in the North, since even though territorial sea rights apply both to seabed and water-column, this means only that one maritime boundary, but not a 'single maritime boundary', can be drawn ('zwar eine einzige, aber keine 'einheitliche' Seegrenze').

a coincident maritime boundary, since it was the latter that the Court drew in the *Jan Mayen* case. One party had asked the Court for a single maritime boundary, and the other asked for two distinct boundaries to be drawn, one for the continental shelf and the other for the fisheries zones, and the Court had decided that, in the absence of agreement of the parties to ask for a single boundary, it was obliged to apply separately the law governing the shelf and the law governing the fisheries.[424] It was however able to find that the considerations relevant under each of these systems of law produced, or could be encouraged to produce, the same line. Legally, however, this was a coincident line, not strictly a 'single maritime boundary'.[425] Rather surprisingly the distinction is overlooked in the *Qatar/Bahrain* judgment, which states that in the *Jan Mayen* case the Court 'was...asked to draw a single maritime boundary.'[426]

In the same case, two judges commented on the definition of the term. Judge Oda considered that it had been misused in the judgment. In his view:

The term "single" boundary has come to mean an *identical* boundary, being a single line for the two different régimes of the continental shelf and the exclusive economic zone, and was referred to in this sense in the 1984 case concerning the *Delimitation of the Maritime Boundary in the Gulf of Maine Area,* the 1985 case concerning the *Continental Shelf (Libyan Arab Jamahiriya),* and the 1993 case concerning the *Maritime Delimitation in the Area between Greenland and Jan Mayen.* The term "single" boundary does not mean anything else, despite the Court's use of this word in a different sense in the present Judgment.[427]

How then did the Court use the term? According to Judge Oda, the Court pronounced a decision on a single maritime boundary 'despite the fact that both Qatar and Bahrain presented in their submissions individual claims to a boundary line'.[428] The Court however interpreted the submissions of each of the parties as asking for a 'single maritime boundary',[429] and the 'Bahraini formula', by which the Court (as it had found) was given jurisdiction, called upon it to 'draw a single maritime boundary'.[430] In each case, the term seems to have been intended to mean 'a single line for the two different régimes of the continental shelf and the exclusive economic zone'. Unless therefore it was the inclusion of the territorial sea in the definition that he objected to, Judge Oda unfortunately does not make clear what the difference was that he saw between the Court's usage and his own.

It was the inclusion of the territorial seas in the areas to be delimited that caused Judge *ad hoc* Torres Bernárdez to comment on the use of

---

[424] *Maritime Delimitation in the Area between Greenland and Jan Mayen* [1993] ICJ Rep 57, para 43.
[425] Ibid, 79, para 90. Denmark did indeed ask for a single boundary, but Norway asked for two distinct, but coincident, lines: ibid, 56–57, para 41.
[426] [2001] ICJ Rep 110, para 227.
[427] [2001] ICJ Rep 127, para 12; see also ibid, 139, para 35.
[428] Ibid.   [429] Ibid, 91, para 168.
[430] Quoted at ibid, 63, para 67.

the term 'single maritime boundary'. He pointed out that in none of the previous jurisprudence cited by the Court when considering the law applicable to the single maritime boundary had the territorial sea been involved; he added the commonsense observation that '[n]evertheless, the boundary must be a *single maritime boundary* because this is what the Parties requested'. It followed that it was 'a single maritime boundary independently of the maritime jurisdictions divided in the different sectors of its course'.[431] Judge Torres Bernárdez's objection was not to the use of the term, but to the fact that, in his view, the Court had not taken sufficient account of the 'singleness' of the boundary in its reasoning.

In the case of the *Land and Maritime Boundary between Cameroon and Nigeria*, the Court seems to have deliberately avoided the term 'single maritime boundary': it stated that the parties had agreed 'that the delimitation between their maritime areas should be effected by a single line'.[432] While the operative clause of the *Qatar/Bahrain* judgment decided 'that the single maritime boundary that divides the various maritime zones' of each party should be as there indicated,[433] the operative clause in the *Cameroon/Nigeria* case defines 'the boundary of the maritime areas appertaining respectively' to Cameroon and to Nigeria.[434] However, since the parties were agreed in requesting a single line, it is suggested that this was a case of a single maritime boundary, not a coincident boundary. In the *Territorial and Maritime Dispute between Nicaragua and Honduras in the Caribbean Sea*, both the parties in their submissions and the Court in its judgment (including the operative clause) used the expression 'single maritime boundary'.

(b) The law applicable to the single maritime boundary

It is inherent in the nature of the single maritime boundary that for such a boundary to be drawn at all between the entitlements of any two States, the operation, if not the line, must be a matter of agreement between those two States. In this it differs from single-purpose boundaries. The delimitation between two entitlements to continental shelf, since it is between areas which in law exist *ipso facto* and *ab intiio*, as declared by the Court in the *North Sea* case,[435] is presumably pre-determined and also exists *ipso facto, ab initio* and (for that matter) *in gremio legis*, even though it has to be determined in such a way as to produce an equitable result.[436] The delimitation between two claims to EEZ or fishery zones may result from the meeting of claims, or from agreement, or may be determined on the basis of customary law so as to produce an equitable

---

[431] [2001] ICJ Rep 426, para 483, emphasis original.
[432] [2002] ICJ Rep 440, para 286.
[433] [2001] ICJ Rep 117, para 252(6).
[434] Ibid, 456, para 325 (IV)(B).
[435] [1969] ICJ Rep 22, para 19.
[436] See the discussion in the previous article: (1993) *BYIL* 1, 43–54.

result. However, these are two equitable results, one for the shelf and the other for the EEZ, not one: since, as noted above, the circumstances relevant to the determination of an equitable continental shelf boundary may well not be the same as those relevant to the determination of an equitable EEZ boundary.

There may well be a temptation in such circumstances to 'flatten out' the effect of any element relevant to the one or the other maritime area which is irrelevant, or less relevant, to the other. This is in fact suggested by a finding in the judgment in the *Qatar/Bahrain* case. While the two States were still under the protection of the British Government, that Government had in 1947 taken a decision, supplementing a 1939 decision on certain disputed land territories, which drew, or purported to draw, a line dividing the seabed entitlements of the two States. Qatar invoked this decision as a relevant circumstance, though it did not go so far as to suggest that it was a decision binding on the two States; Bahrain contested the relevance of the 1947 line on a number of grounds. The Court decided that it did not need to determine the legal character of the 1947 decision, since 'neither of the Parties has accepted it as a binding decision and...they have invoked only parts of it to support their arguments.'[437] However, the Court went on to say:

The Court further observes that the British decision only concerned the division of the sea-bed between the Parties. The delimitation to be effected by the Court, however, is partly a delimitation of the territorial sea and partly a combined delimitation of the continental shelf and the exclusive economic zone. The 1947 line cannot therefore be considered to have direct relevance for the present delimitation process.[438]

The Court here seems to be saying that even if the British decision had been binding on the parties, it would not have had 'direct relevance' for the determination of a single maritime boundary.[439] A decision of this kind, if binding, would surely have been as effective *inter partes* as an agreed delimitation, so the situation would be that the delimitation of the seabed had already been effected. Unless the parties had expressly indicated their intention not to abide by that delimitation (or were, for example, held to have done so implicitly by agreeing to ask for a single boundary), it should presumably have been a circumstance of the highest relevance to the situation as a whole, and to the position of a single maritime boundary. Unless the same line appeared equitable as delimitation of the water-column, it would however complicate considerably the task of the Court in finding a result that was equitable in respect of both kinds of entitlement.

---

[437] [2001] ICJ Rep 113, para 239

[438] Ibid, 113–114, para 240.

[439] On the other hand, this may be a case where a judgment, perhaps to satisfy different views within the Court, uses more than one argument in parallel, making it difficult for the observer to discern what the relationship is, if any, between them.

C. THE TERRITORIAL SEA

As a result of the survival, virtually unchanged, of the provisions of the 1958 Geneva Convention on the Territorial Sea and the Contiguous Zone into the 1982 Law of the Sea Convention, the conventional law on territorial sea delimitation is still dominated by the equidistance principle. Article 15 of the 1982 Convention provides that, between opposite or adjacent States, the maximum territorial sea each of them can claim is up to the median line drawn in relation to the baselines of each State.[440] As regards the continental shelf, the equidistance principle as employed in Article 6 of the 1958 Geneva Convention on the Continental Shelf was present up to a very late stage in the drafts of the 1982 Convention, including those relating to the EEZ, only to disappear at the last minute, giving place to the *renvoi* to customary law effected by the empty formula of Articles 74 and 83. Nevertheless, any apparent distinction between the law applicable to the delimitation of the territorial sea, where the relevant treaty text expressly provides for the use of a median line (or equidistance line), and the law applicable to the delimitation of continental shelf or EEZ, is weakened almost to effacement by the judicial development of the customary law[441] to which Articles 74 and 83 refer. In the view of the Tribunal in the *Eritrea/Yemen Arbitration,* treaty law coincides with customary law in the field of maritime delimitation; and that customary law favours the median line, particularly between opposite coasts.[442]

The Court has had to deal with delimitations extending to the territorial seas of the parties in the three most recent delimitation cases: *Maritime Delimitation and Territorial Questions between Qatar and Bahrain; Land and Maritime Boundary between Cameroon and Nigeria;* and *Territorial and Maritime Dispute between Nicaragua and Honduras in the Caribbean Sea.* In the *Cameroon/Nigeria* case, the Court found that the delimitation had already been effected by what amounted to a binding international agreement, so that no enquiry was needed into the principles and rules of conventional or customary law governing such a delimitation.[443] Nigeria, which did not accept the status and validity of the agreement, had argued in favour of a median line, and since the parties were both parties to the 1982 Convention, this would seem to have been fully justified, absent the existing delimitation agreement.[444] The *Qatar/Bahrain* case was more

---

[440] Similarly, under Article 4, the outer limit of the territorial sea towards the open sea is in effect a unilateral equidistance line defined by the 'breadth of the territorial sea'.

[441] On the judicial nature of the law of maritime delimitation, see the earlier articles in this series, (1993) *BYIL* 2–54 and (1994) *BYIL* 2–87, and Weil, *Perspectives du droit de la délimitation maritime,* 11–13.

[442] *Award,* paras. 130, 131. Part, but only part, of the maritime boundary in that case was in fact a territorial sea boundary (see footnote 430 below). The observation is *obiter* since the Tribunal was asked to apply the 1982 Convention.

[443] [2002] ICJ Rep 426–427, para 255.

[444] Note also the *Eritrea/Yemen Arbitration,* where the 1982 Convention was applicable by virtue of a provision to that effect in the special Agreement; part of the boundary to be drawn, which the

complex, but the underlying principle of equidistance was reflected in the judgment. In the *Nicaragua/Honduras* case, equidistance was not used for the delimitation of the territorial seas of the parties (nor for their other maritime entitlements, except for the purpose of delimitation between opposite islands off the coasts[445]).

In the *Qatar/Bahrain* case the Court not only applied the same considerations to the delimitation of the territorial sea as to the delimitation of continental shelf and EEZ, but made the general statement of principle that 'the equidistance/special circumstances rule' applicable to the territorial sea, and the 'equitable principles/relevant circumstances rule' applicable to shelf and EEZ, 'are closely interrelated'—which means, apparently, that their workings and effects are identical.[446]

1. THE 'FUNDAMENTAL NORM' REQUIRING RECOURSE TO EQUITY

(1) The demise of 'subjective equity'

In the field of the application of equity or 'equitable principles' to maritime delimitation, or the determination of what is the 'equitable result' required of a delimitation, the period now under examination has seen the virtual disappearance of one category of equity that featured largely in the first delimitation effected by the Court,[447] the case of the *Continental Shelf (Tunisia/Libya)*. In the previous article on the subject in this series,[448] this was called 'subjective equity'; it was expressed in the 1982 judgment in that case as follows: the question being 'what method of delimitation would ensure an equitable result',

it is evident that the Court must take into account whatever indicia are available of the line or lines which the Parties themselves may have considered equitable or acted upon as such—if only as an interim solution affecting part of the area to be delimited.[449]

On that basis, the Court regarded a *de facto* line dividing oil concessions granted by one party from those granted by the other as an indication of the equitable line, and incorporated it into its decision.[450] The Court

---

Tribunal decided should be 'a single all-purpose boundary', was in fact a territorial sea boundary; the Tribunal's line was a median line, subject to verification and possible modification: see para 132 of the Award of 17 December 1999.

[445] See below, Section 1(3)(d)(iii).

[446] [2001] ICJ Rep 111, para231. Despeux comments: 'Dies ist wahrscheinlich einer der entscheidenden Sätze des Urteils': 'Das IGH-Urteil *Katar gegen Bahrein* vom 16. März 2001', 495.

[447] In the *North Sea Continental Shelf* case, the Court was merely asked to indicate the applicable principles and rules, and did not attempt to draw a delimitation line.

[448] (1994) *BYIL* 1, 20–23, 26–28.

[449] [1982] ICJ Rep 84, para 118.

[450] No decision since the *North Sea* case has recognized the presence of oil resources, or the position of exploitation activities, as a circumstance affecting in itself the position of an equitable

however took care to indicate that this was not on the basis that the line represented a tacit *agreement* between the parties, as this 'in view of their more extensive and firmly maintained claims, would not be possible'.

In subsequent cases, attempts were made by the one party or the other to assert the existence of similar 'indicia' of a mutually recognized equitable solution; the Court did not accept any of these claims, but did not reverse its jurisprudence by suggesting that such indicia, or the idea of 'subjective equity', were irrelevant.[451] In the case of the *Maritime Delimitation and Territorial Questions between Qatar and Bahrain*, Judge *ad hoc* Torres Bernárdez accepted an argument of Qatar that the conduct of the parties in relation to a 1947 division of the sea-bed by the British authorities could be taken into account as providing 'some clues to what the Parties themselves may have considered at certain times to be an equitable delimitation line',[452] but his colleagues did not agree.

In the case of the *Land and Maritime Boundary between Cameroon and Nigeria*, however, Nigeria contended that 'State practice with regard to oil concessions is a decisive factor in the establishment of maritime boundaries', and in response to this claim the Court reviewed its jurisprudence on the relevance of oil concessions, including the *Tunisia/Libya* case. Unfortunately however, it did not accurately recount the content of that decision. In its 2002 Judgment, the Court said:

On that occasion [the *Tunisia/Libya* case] the Court did not take into consideration 'the direct northward line asserted as boundary of the Libyan petroleum zones' *(ICJ Reports* 1982, p 83, para 117), because that line had 'been found...to be wanting in those respects [that would have made it opposable] to the other Party' *(ibid.)*; however, the Court found that close to the coasts the concessions of the parties showed and confirmed the existence of a *modus vivendi (ibid.,* p 84, para 119).[453]

This quotation omits the most important part of the 1982 decision; having found that the 'northward line' claimed by Libya was not relevant for the reason stated, the Court went on to consider 'the history of the enactment of petroleum licensing legislation by each party, and the grant of successive petroleum concessions',[454] which in its view resulted in 'the appearance on the map of a *de facto* line dividing concession areas

line; but see the observation in the *Eritrea/Yemen* decision on petroleum contracts and resources: Phase II Award, para75–83 and 132, 119 ILR 417. For examples of clauses in delimitation treaties providing for treatment of unity of deposits, see B Kwiatowska, 'Resource, Navigational and Environmental Factors in Equitable Maritime Boundary Delimitation', in D A Colson and R W Smith (eds), *International Maritime Boundaries* (2005), Vol V, 3228–3229.

[451] See *Gulf of Maine*, [1984] ICJ Rep 310, para 150; *Continental Shelf (Libya/Malta)*, [1985] ICJ Rep 29, para 25; cf. also *Maritime Delimitation in the Area between Greenland and Jan Mayen*, [1993] ICJ Rep 53, para 33. The same concept was mentioned in *Sovereignty over Pulau Sipadan and Pulau Ligitan*, in the slightly different context of a dispute over the interpretation of a treaty which, on one view, might have provided for a delimitation allocating certain islands to one State or the other: [2002] ICJ Rep 664, paras. 78–79.

[452] [2001] ICJ Rep 429, para 493.   [453] [2002] ICJ Rep 447, para 304.
[454] [1982] ICJ Rep 83, para 117.

which were the subject of active claims, in the sense that exploration activities were authorized by one Party, without interference, or (until 1977) protests, by the other'.[455] It was this line that the Court regarded as an *indicium* of the parties' views as to the position of an equitable delimitation. The *modus vivendi* referred to in the 2002 decision in this connection was in fact a *modus vivendi* concerning *fishery limits*, not oil concessions, and the Court cited it simply in support of its reliance on the oil concessions line.

The Court in 2002 continued by reviewing the subsequent *Gulf of Maine* and *Libya/Malta* cases, as well as the *St. Pierre and Miquelon* decision, in order to arrive at this conclusion:

Overall, it follows from the jurisprudence that, although the existence of an express or tacit agreement between the parties on the siting of their respective oil concessions may indicate a consensus on the maritime areas to which they are entitled, oil concessions and oil wells are not in themselves to be considered as relevant circumstances justifying the adjustment or shifting of the provisional delimitation line. Only if they are based on express or tacit agreement between the parties may they be taken into account. In the present case there is no agreement between the Parties regarding oil concessions.[456]

This must, it seems, be read as an abandonment of the concept referred to here as 'subjective equity'.[457] Whatever the value of this conclusion generally, it cannot however be based on the *Tunisia/Libya* decision, and is in fact contradicted by that decision, since, as indicated above, the Court in that case was very careful to make clear that it was *not* relying on the idea of tacit agreement.[458]

It may of course be doubted whether the Court was wise, or legally justified, in the *Tunisia/Libya* decision, in making the distinction between tacit agreement and mutual, or independent, recognition that a certain line would be a fair, and thus 'equitable', dividing line. It is also probable that the decision has been noted in Foreign Ministries, and care taken to avoid any action that might later be interpreted in this sense; so that the concept of 'subjective equity' probably has no further role to play in maritime delimitation law. It is nonetheless to be regretted that the Court seems to have been unaware of what it was doing in the *Cameroon/Nigeria* case, as a result of having misunderstood, or misremembered, its own earlier decision; the more so since the Court adopted a line which did in fact to a very large extent respect what emerged from the practice of the parties.

---

[455] ibid, 84, para 117.

[456] [2002] ICJ Rep 447, para 304.

[457] In this sense, R Bundy, 'Preparing for a delimitation case: the practitioner's view', in R Lagoni and D Vignes (eds), *Maritime Delimitation* (2006), 110: the author nevertheless advises, *ex abundanti cautela*, presenting to the tribunal any available material pointing in this direction.

[458] As was in fact pointed out by Nigeria in its pleadings: Nigerian Counter-Memorial, 583, para 21.25; see also Nigerian Rejoinder, para 13.23.

(2) What is it that must be equitable?

A major simplification in the terminology of the law of maritime delimitation has come about since the publication of the previous article on the subject in the present series. It was there pointed out[459] that decisions on maritime delimitations were consistent in making frequent use of the word 'equitable', but applying that adjective to different nouns, such as 'delimitation', 'determination', 'principles', 'procedures' and 'solution'. Consistency now appears to have been achieved, in the sense that the delimitation operation is to be carried out so as to achieve 'an equitable result'. For example, in the case of the *Land and Maritime Boundary between Cameroon and Nigeria*, the Court added, only to exclude, a fresh formula—'delimiting in equity'—, but then opted firmly for the 'equitable result'.

> The Court is bound to stress... that delimiting with a concern to achieve an equitable result, as required by current international law, is not the same as delimiting in equity. The Court's jurisprudence shows that, in disputes relating to maritime delimitation, equity is not a method of delimitation, but solely an aim that should be borne in mind in effecting the delimitation.[460]

When a formula is as carefully chosen as this evidently is, it is legitimate, and appropriate, to scrutinise it carefully; and two points may be noted. First, the Court does not refer to '*the* equitable result' but to '*an* equitable result', thus suggesting that there is not one single correct delimitation for any given set of circumstances. Secondly, a tribunal carrying out a delimitation is to show 'a concern' to achieve such a result, and to 'bear in mind' equity in that process; these terms fall well short of a directive, and almost suggest that equity is only one element among others to determine, or affect, the delimitation, which in turn would imply the existence of some superior element to determine what the relevant elements are, and how they are to be balanced—a sort of super-equity or delimitation-*Grundnorm*. Whether this was the Court's intention is however far from clear.

On the other hand, the process followed has become established as involving the establishment of a provisional equidistance line, and then considering whether there are 'circumstances' or 'reasons' that 'might make it *necessary* to adjust the equidistance line in order to achieve an equitable result',[461] which suggests that the objective of an equitable result is over-riding. If the result is not equitable, then the law of delimitation has not been applied correctly. But what is an 'equitable result', and how is it to be distinguished from a result that is not equitable? As was observed in the previous article:

---

[459] (1994) *BYIL* 1, 6 ff.   [460] [2002] ICJ Rep 443, para 294.

[461] *Maritime Delimitation and Territorial Questions between Qatar and Bahrain*, [2001] ICJ Rep 111, para 232; virtually the same formula in *Land and Maritime Boundary between Cameroon and Nigeria*, [2002] ICJ Rep 448, para 305.

If one speaks of an "equitable delimitation", or the "equitable result" of a delimitation process, then these expressions, taken in isolation, may mean no more than that the delimitation is "fair", that it corresponds to generalized feelings of justice, regardless of whether or not the correct legal principles and processes have been followed in achieving it.[462]

If the only rule in maritime delimitation is that the result must be equitable, then there are no 'correct' legal principles and procedures to achieve it. It is therefore hardly surprising that the Court in the *Cameroon/Nigeria* case found it necessary to deny this conclusion in advance, by distinguishing the process from 'delimiting in equity'.

The advantage of such a concept as 'equitable principles' or 'procedures' is that it could embrace principles that could be defined in sufficiently general terms to be independent of the particular geographical and other circumstances, while still leaving room for allowing special circumstances their say, as a separate operation. Proportionality between areas of seabed and coastal lengths was one such principle, as was the notion of 'natural prolongation' and even of 'coastal fronts'. There seems now to be only one first-stage principle, or method, or concept: that of equidistance: which implies that the equidistance is by definition *the* equitable solution, subject to possible adjustment in special cases.

As long ago as the *Tunisia/Libya* case in 1982, however, the Court had already indicated that the terminology then in use

is not entirely satisfactory because it employs the term equitable to characterize both the result to be achieved and the means to be applied to reach this result. It is, however, the result which is predominant; the principles are subordinate to the goal. The equitableness of a principle must be assessed in the light of its usefulness for the purpose of arriving at an equitable result.[463]

This is reflected also in the terms of Articles 74 and 83 of the 1982 Law of the Sea Convention, which give no indication of methods (unlike Article 6 of the 1958 Conventions on the Continental Shelf and on the Territorial Sea and the Contiguous Zone, and indeed the drafts of Article 74 and 83 up to a very late stage), but simply indicate that what has to be achieved is an 'equitable result'. In the *Libya/Malta* case the Court repeated the observations it had made in the *Tunisia/Libya* case as to the relationship between 'equitable principles' and the 'equitable result', and added: 'It is the goal—the equitable result—and not the means used to achieve it, that must be the primary element in this duality of characterization.'[464]

The decision in the case concerning the *Territorial and Maritime Dispute between Nicaragua and Honduras in the Caribbean Sea* however prompts reflection on this simplification. In that case the Court for the

---

[462] (1994) *BYIL* 1, 7.   [463] [1982] ICJ Rep 59, para 70.
[464] [1985] ICJ Rep 38–39, para 45.

first time put aside the equidistance method, even as a preliminary step toward the establishment of an equitable line, and adopted a system based on a bisector of the angle formed by the coastal fronts of the two States. One of the reasons it gave for doing so is of considerable interest as suggesting a particular, and perhaps novel, view of the relationship between the equitable nature of the methods used and the equitableness of the result.

The terminal point of the land boundary, from which any maritime delimitation had to begin (initially for the territorial sea, and thereafter, by agreement between the parties, as a single maritime boundary), was formed by the mouth of the River Coco, as a result of the 1906 Arbitral Award of the King of Spain; and in 1962 a Mixed Commission had determined that the land boundary should begin at a point identified by co-ordinates of latitude and longitude. The mouth of the River Coco is however a delta, and there is a continuous process of movement of the river in its bed, whereby a main channel becomes a subsidiary one, and vice versa, and islands are created and subsequently disappear. By the time of the proceedings before the Court, the point identified by the Mixed Commission was no longer in the mouth of the river, but on the Nicaraguan bank; and there were a number of small islands sovereignty over which was undetermined.

There was therefore a problem in determining the position of appropriate base-points from which to construct an equidistance line, even on a provisional basis. Before considering this problem, however, the Court first took note of another consideration:

Cape Gracias a Dios, where the Nicaragua-Honduras land boundary ends, is a sharply convex territorial projection abutting a concave coastline on either side to the north and south-west. Taking into account Article 15 of UNCLOS[465] and given the geographical configuration described above, the pair of base points to be identified on either bank of the River Coco at the tip of the Cape would assume a considerable dominance in constructing an equidistance line, especially as it travels out from the coast. Given the close proximity of these base points to each other, any variation or error in situating them would become disproportionately magnified in the resulting equidistance line. The Parties agree, moreover, that the sediment carried to and deposited at sea by the River Coco have caused its delta, as well as the coastline to the north and south of the Cape, to exhibit a very active morpho-dynamism. Thus continued accretion at the Cape might render any equidistance line so constructed today arbitrary and unreasonable in the near future.[466]

The Court noted that, because of the configuration of the coast, where Cape Gracias a Dios protruded into the sea from a coastline which was

---

[465] The first part of the line being a delimitation of the territorial sea, this provision of UNCLOS was applicable, and, unlike Articles 74 and 83 on the EEZ and the continental shelf, it requires the use of an equidistance line save in the presence of 'special circumstances'.

[466] [2007] ICJ Rep; para 277 of the Judgment, available online at http://www.icj-cij.org/docket/files/120/14075.pdf.

otherwise very convex, the whole equidistance line would be governed by the initial two basepoints, one on the coast of each party.[467]

Similarly, the Court noted that

the Parties are in disagreement as to title over the unstable islands having formed in the mouth of the River Coco, islands which the Parties suggested during the oral proceedings could be used as base points. It is recalled that because of the changing conditions of the area the Court has made no finding as to sovereignty over these islands... Moreover, whatever base points would be used for the drawing of an equidistance line, the configuration and unstable nature of the relevant coasts, including the disputed islands formed in the mouth of the River Coco, would make these base points (whether at Cape Gracias a Dios or elsewhere) uncertain within a short period of time.[468]

These considerations formed part of the 'set of circumstances' making it 'impossible' for the Court to 'identify basepoints and draw a provisional equidistance line'[469], and which constituted 'special circumstances' justifying non-application of the equidistance method called for by Article 15 of the Law of the Sea Convention. Furthermore, there is some indication that it was the instability of the basepoints, rather than the difficulty in discerning them in the first place, that was the major factor in the decision.[470]

It is curious that no mention is made of the various islands already adjudged to be under Honduran sovereignty,[471] and to which, at a later stage in its decision, the Court attributes areas of territorial sea.[472] It would appear from the maps attached to the judgment that an equidistance line could have been constructed using as basepoints first whatever points could be established as appropriate at the mouth of the River Coco, and subsequently, as the line extended seaward, basepoints on the Honduran islands and appropriate basepoints on the Nicaraguan coast (probably the same used for the initial line); an equidistance line using the basepoints on the islands was in fact proposed by Honduras at one stage.[473] Because of the use of the islands, such a line would apparently be less open to the criticism that it would not, at some future time, be the same as the line that might then be drawn from basepoints taking into account a shifting of the river mouth in the meantime.

It is implicit in the Court's decision that any judicial delimitation of maritime areas, while it can only speak from the date at which it is

[467] Ibid; Judge Torres Bernádez considered that this was simply an element of the situation that the Court had before it, and not a 'facteur d'inéquité': separate opinion, para 132. He pointed out that the same situation had been encountered in the Cameroon/Nigeria case, [2002] ICJ Rep 443, para 292.

[468] Ibid, para 280. Judge Ranjeva, who dissented from this part of the decision, suggested that the problem of shifting basepoints could be overcome by choosing two suitable points equidistant from the point identified by the Mixed Commission as the terminus of the land boundary: separate opinion, para 10.

[469] Ibid.   [470] See para 287 of the Judgment:

[471] [2007] ICJ Rep, para 227 of the Judgment.

[472] Ibid, paras. 299–305.   [473] Ibid, para 276.

given,[474] must, of its nature, be final and definitive.[475] Apart from the effect of Article 60 of the Statute, a judicial delimitation is a substitute for a delimitation by agreement, and enjoys its status by virtue of the consent of the parties to jurisdiction.[476] Just as a treaty establishing a land frontier is exempt from termination on the grounds of the *exceptio rebus sic stantibus*, so a delimitation would not be. affected by any political changes. Changes of this kind can however easily be imagined which would radically alter the basis for the delimitation; if, for example, Germany were to annex Denmark, the delimitation indicated by the Court in 1969 between Germany and the Netherlands, which took into account the effect of the convergence of the coastlines of Denmark and the Netherlands, would no longer rest on the considerations of equity that had inspired it. Nevertheless it would remain valid and binding.[477]

More delicate is the question of delimitations with or between third parties: the Court in 1969 indicated, in relation to the concept of proportionality, that a delimitation should take account 'of the effects, *actual or prospective, of* any other continental shelf delimitation between adjacent States in the same region.'[478] Presumably if such other delimitation was carried out in an unexpected way, so that the account taken of it *in posse* by the Court turned out to have been inappropriate, this would not affect the validity of the Court's delimitation. In subsequent cases, the matter has been seen from the opposite angle, and the Court has taken care not to indicate a delimitation line that might intrude into areas claimed by third States, and which might be attributed to them once a delimitation were effected between the third State and one or both of the parties.[479]

In the *Nicaragua/Honduras* case the Court was applying similar reasoning to prospective changes in the coastline around the terminus of the land boundary. The position of an equidistance line drawn from basepoints appropriate today, whether provisionally or definitively, might, because of the shifting nature of the coastline, differ markedly from the position of an equidistance line drawn next year, on the basis of

---

[474] In the *Qatar/Bahrain* case, Judge *ad hoc* Torres Bernárdez drew attention to the fact that some of the waters treated in the judgment had, at the time the Court was seised of the case, been high seas: [2001] ICJ Rep 424, para 478. He suggested that this raised a jurisdictional issue, but it is not clear what conclusion he drew: it does not seem that he would have the Court decide as it would have done at the time of the seisin, ignoring subsequent developments.

[475] See above n 387 and n 388 and accompanying text.

[476] Sir Robert Jennings drew attention in 1989 to the difficulties that would arise 'if a treaty establishing a maritime boundary could subsequently be called in question by a dissatisfied party alleging that the agreed boundary is not in accordance with equitable principles': 'The Principles Governing Maritime Boundaries', *Staat und Völkerrechtsordnung, Festschrift für Karl Doehring* (1989), 402: see also (1993) *BYIL* 1, 46.

[477] The Court of course did no more than indicate the applicable legal rules and principles, and the actual delimitation was effected by treaty, which would have the definitive status attached to boundary treaties; but this does not detract from the point here being made.

[478] [1969] ICJ Rep 54, para 101(D)(3).

[479] Cf. the cases of *Continental Shelf (Tunisia/Libya)* [1982] ICJ Rep 18; *Continental Shelf (Libya/Malta)* [1985] ICJ Rep 13; *Land and Maritime Boundary between Cameroon and Nigeria* [2002] ICJ Rep 303.

basepoints regarded as appropriate to the configuration of the coastline as it had developed in the meantime. That is why the Court considered that '[t]he continued accretion at the Cape [the land boundary terminus] might render any equidistance line so constructed today arbitrary and unreasonable in the near future.'[480] It therefore invoked the 'special circumstances' contemplated by Article 15 of the Law of the Sea Convention, while hastily adding that '[a]t the same time, equidistance remains the general rule.'[481]

The argument is thus that if an equidistance line is constructed from basepoints on a shifting coast, and adopted as delimitation line on the grounds of its equitable character, it may become 'arbitrary and unreasonable', that is to say inequitable, if the coast changes in such a way that an equidistance line constructed from the new available basepoints would be markedly different. This implies that if the original equidistance line is equitable, it is so because of the choice of the basepoints. It is clear however that the situation is not so simple; having constructed the equidistance line, the Court must see whether there are any circumstances that require its adjustment; and at that stage it will presumably consider whether the line is equitable taking account of the whole geographical situation. If the equidistance line today is equitable in relation to the whole geographical situation, presumably it will take more than a small shifting of the mouth of the river to render it inequitable, even if as a result of the shifting the basepoints from which the line was derived are no longer available, or supplanted by new ones.

The Court in the *Nicaragua/Honduras* case seems to have departed from the principle enunciated in previous case-law, and mentioned above, that what counts is the equitable result, not the equitableness of the method applied to produce the result. The line actually drawn by the Court in the case was based on quite different methods (bisector of the angle of coastal fronts); the Court seems to have started out with the idea that the resulting line was to be considered equitable because it was so constructed, but in application of Articles 74 and 83 of the Law of the Sea Convention it could only be the proper line, or a proper line, because its effect was regarded as equitable. Curiously enough, the Court does not say so: again, its emphasis is on the nature of the bisector method and the justification for it, but the Court does observe that it 'could adjust the line' created by that method 'so as to achieve an equitable result,'[482] which implies that, in the absence of adjustment, the line is to be regarded as equitable.

It could well occur, depending on the shifting of the coast around the mouth of the river, that the basepoints would turn out to be so placed as to produce an equidistance line approximating closely to the bisector line. Whichever method produces the line, that line must in itself be equitable in relation to the whole geographical situation. Why then

---

[480] [2007] ICJ Rep, para 277 of the Judgment.
[481] Ibid, para 281.   [482] Ibid, para 294.

should a line produced by the equidistance method suddenly cease to be equitable if the basepoints have shifted, whereas an essentially identical line, produced by the bisector method, would be unaffected by such minor changes in the coastline? The answer can only be, because the line derives its equitable nature from the method by which it was produced, which seems to be a departure from previous jurisprudence, and an unconvincing innovation.

The Court did not refer to one of the provisions in the Law of the Sea Convention that does envisage the problem of shifting coastlines, in the context of the delimitation of the territorial sea. Article 7, dealing with straight baselines drawn by the coastal State, provides in paragraph 2:

Where because of the presence of a delta and other natural conditions the coastline is highly unstable, the appropriate points may be selected along the furthest seaward extent of the low-water line and, notwithstanding subsequent regression of the low-water line, the straight baselines shall remain effective until changed by the coastal State in accordance with this Convention.

This of course refers to delimitation of the territorial sea in relation to the high seas, not to delimitation between the territorial seas of two States, but it does constitute a recognition in the regime of the Convention that a delimitation based on the shape assumed by a coastline at the moment that the delimitation is effected does not necessarily have to change because the shape of the coastline has altered.[483]

More generally, it is interesting to consider the position if two basepoints on Cape Gracias a Dios could have been easily identified, and were situated on stable territorial features. The circumstances invoked by the Court for putting aside the equidistance method would have been absent. Nevertheless, the equidistance line would still have been open to criticism as a *definitive* delimitation line: it would have been reduced to a line drawn from a point halfway along the line joining the two basepoints, and perpendicular to that line. If such a line had been drawn, as a first step, it would have been appropriate to adjust it in the light of such circumstances as, for example, the angle of the coastal fronts. This suggests that the difficulties of identifying stable basepoints were not necessarily so influential as the Court permitted them to be.

(3) Equidistance and after: the methods of attaining the equitable result

(a) Introduction

More perhaps in this field of international law than in any other, the intellectual process involved in settling a delimitation dispute is likely

---

[483] The reference to the drawing of fresh baselines by the State concerned is not expressed as an obligation, but rather as a faculty, so that, at least vis-à-vis the high seas, the coastal State is entitled to continue enjoying an extent of territorial sea beyond that to which it would be entitled if it were to draw new baselines along the modified coastline.

to be, whether the decision-maker realises it or not, a leap to the sort of solution that looks and feels right on a basis of equitableness as fairness, followed by the construction of an intellectual process to support it. This underlies the popularity both of the equidistance method, which provides the basis from which the leap can be made, and of the idea of adjustment for 'relevant circumstances', which meets the need for a corrective if the line does not 'look right' because of an unusual shape of the coastlines or for some other reason.

The 'equidistance line' is, as it were, the all-purpose tool of maritime delimitation: a tool which can be employed effectively in virtually all circumstances so as to produce a useful result, either as an initial stage to be subsequently adapted by fine-tuning in the light of special circumstances, or as in itself affording an equitable result.[484] It is therefore unexpected to find an experienced judge stating its nature in a somewhat loose manner. In his dissenting opinion in the case of *Maritime Delimitation and Territorial Questions between Qatar and Bahrain*, Judge Torres Bernárdez complained of the method of delimitation employed by the Court, stating that:

An "equidistance line" is by definition a line between two lines, but there is no trace in the Judgment of those two *lines* required for the construction of the "equidistance line". Normally, those baselines are the mainline coasts or coastal front lines of the two States concerned.[485]

An equidistance line is constructed, not from lines, but from basepoints on the coast: as the delimitation proceeds, each point defines the line until another point on the same coast is nearer the point that the line has reached: from then on the new point governs the course of the line until it is displaced by another.[486]

It was observed in an earlier article in this series that application of the equidistance line is the only rule which 'has been—or, it seems, could be—devised which could ensure total predictability of result'.[487] Mention

---

[484] Eighteen out of twenty-three agreed delimitations effected between 1993 and 2001 were based on the equidistance model: see the list in Despreux, 'Das IGH-Urteil *Katar gegen Bahrein* vom 16. März 2001', 497, fn. 113. In the recent arbitral decision in the *Guyana/Suriname* case, the Tribunal referred to the use of equidistance tempered by special circumstances as 'the methodology... which has been practised by international courts and tribunals during the last two decades', and declined to adopt a methodology 'at variance' with it on account of geographical peculiarities which could be taken into account as 'relevant circumstances': Award of 17 September 2007, 120, para 372.

[485] [2001] ICJ Rep 432, para 506.

[486] It is thus possible for an equidistance line between two extensive coasts to be dictated by a very small number of basepoints situated on salient coastal features, as indeed occurred in the *Libya/Malta* case: see [1985] ICJ Rep 50–51, para 70. The same looseness of terminology is however found (e.g.) in the Report of the Committee of Experts to the International Law Commission of 18 May 1953, reproduced in *North Sea Continental Shelf, Pleadings, Oral Arguments, Documents*, Vol. I, 257, para VI, referring, in the English version, to 'the median line, every point on which is equidistant from the baselines of the States concerned'. (The French text has 'chaque point est équidistant des deux côtes': ibid, 252). The Court in 1969 correctly referred to the effect of an equidistance line as leaving to each party 'all those portions of the continental shelf that are nearer to *a point* on its own coast than they are to any *point* on the coast of the other party': [1969] ICJ Rep 17, para 6 (emphasis added).

[487] (1993) *BYIL* 1, 41.

may however be made here of a technique for adjusting an equidistance line which does not seem so far to have been employed in judicial delimitations, which does ensure some degree of predictability or automaticity, provided recognition of appropriate areas can be achieved. The equidistance line is constructed on the basis that every point is an equal distance from the nearest point on each of the two coastlines; but it is equally possible to construct a line where the relationship of the two distances is not equality, but a defined ratio. For example, if the equidistance line gives too much to State A and too little to State B, a line could be constructed such that the distance (a) of every point on it from the nearest point on the coast of State A, and the distance (b) of every point on it from the nearest point on the coast of State B would be such that the ratio of (a) to (b) would be, for example 1.5:1. This technique—the *equiratio* line—would have the advantage that it could reflect in precise arithmetical terms the ratio of inequality that the judge found between the results each side of an equidistance line. So far as the present writer is aware, however, it has not hitherto been so employed.

The method of equidistance is closely linked with the notion of 'special' or 'relevant' circumstances. If in given circumstances the equidistance line 'looks right', then it will not be difficult to explain why other possibly relevant circumstances put forward by the one party or the other do not, in the instant case, operate to disturb the equidistance line. If the equidistance line seems to give too much to the one party and too little to the other, then it will normally not be difficult to choose from the palette of circumstances those that will swing or transpose the line in the direction desired. An example of this perfectly defensible process is visible in the decision in the case of *Maritime Delimitation in the Area between Greenland and Jan Mayen*, where the median line was regarded as attributing too much of the seabed areas to Norway. If the Court had simply adopted the same course as it had in the *Libya/Malta* case, of transposing the line towards the coast of Jan Mayen in a direction at right angles to its general course, shifting it sideways, as it were, so that the delimitation line would be parallel to the median line, then, in the Court's view, this would not give both parties in the *Jan Mayen* case 'equitable access' to the fish stocks.[488] The Court accordingly adopted a more complex geometrical operation, the essence of which was to reconcile the purely proportional adjustment of the median line required for an equitable delimitation of the seabed, with the means of affording equitable access to the fish stocks required for the equitable delimitation of the fishery zones.[489]

(b) The delimitation process: circumstances generating the line and circumstances adjusting the line

The process of judicial delimitation by the use of an equidistance line may be thought of as a dialogue between the judge and the cartographer,

---

[488] On this curious concept, see the previous article: (1994) *BYIL* 1, 13–14.
[489] The whole process is set out in [1993] ICJ Rep 79–81, paras. 90–93, illustrated by a sketch-map.

the latter representing the objective scientific aspect of the process, and the former the subjective element. Having identified the area relevant for the delimitation, itself not necessarily evident,[490] the judge asks the cartographer to draw an equidistance line; the cartographer replies, By all means; but between which coasts? The first exercise of judicial assessment is thus the identification of the 'relevant' coastlines, which may exclude some considerable part of the coasts employed by each party as basis for its claims.[491] This step may also have to be preceded, as observed above, by an inquiry into and determination of sovereignty over certain land features that may prove to be part of the relevant coasts. The cartographer then identifies the appropriate basepoints on which to construct his equidistance line; theoretically these are dictated by the nature and contours of the two coastlines, but here again he may have to go back to the judge for further instructions: if there are straight baselines, are these legitimate so that he should take them into account? There may be questions of mixed law and fact: is this feature, which appears to constitute a basepoint, an island, a low-tide elevation, or a mere sandbank?[492] As a matter of law, does it constitute a basepoint or basepoints?[493]

A line may then be produced and exhibited to the judge, and at this point the most openly subjective stage begins. Independently of the geographical picture, are there special historical or other circumstances that should be taken into account in such a way as to affect the delimitation?[494] In regard to the continental shelf, and looking at the relationship between the 'relevant' coasts and the areas of seabed, is the proportionality test satisfied?[495] Here and there a basepoint situated on a particular feature, a small promontory, for example, has a marked influence on the course of the line; taking account of the importance of the feature, is that influence excessive, so as to make that part of the line inequitable? In these circumstances, the judge will go back to the cartographer, and ask him to

---

[490] Cf L Lucchini, 'La délimitation des frontières maritimes dans la jurisprudence internationale' in R Lagoni and D Vignes (eds), Maritime Delimitation (2006), 11–12.

[491] As in Continental Shelf (Libya/Malta) and Territorial and Maritime Dispute between Nicaragua and Honduras in the Caribbean Sea.

[492] It is also possible to construct an equidistance line by the so-called 'mainland to mainland method' (strongly supported by Judge ad hoc Torres Bernárdez in the case of Maritime Delimitation and Territorial Questions between Qatar and Bahrain: [2001] ICJ Rep 433–434, par. 513), disregarding islands and similar features, but this will not necessarily make the line a purely objective cartographical exercise.

[493] Even (for example) the definition of an island in the Law of the Sea Convention as 'above water at high tide' may prompt the enquiry from the experts: which high tide? See R Bundy, 'Preparing for a Delimitation Case: the Practitioner's View' in R Lagoni and D Vignes (eds), Maritime Delimitation (2006), 106–107.

[494] E.g. an existing partial delimitation, as in Land and Maritime Boundary between Cameroon and Nigeria; or the division of the seabed between Qatar and Bahrain by the British in 1947, was not in fact accepted as relevant in the case of Maritime Delimitation and Territorial Questions between Qatar and Bahrain.

[495] See the discussion in the earlier article: (1994) BYIL 1, 54–60.

adjust his basic data: ignore the promontory, or in cases of greater ambit, move his whole line.[496]

However, it is also possible that, even before the initial provisional line is drawn, the judge considers that to give effect, or full effect, to a particular feature will, *a priori*, produce an inequitable effect, and tell the cartographer to adjust accordingly: for example, by leaving out of account a basepoint on a small feature that, legally and in theory may be employed as a basepoint, but seems inappropriate in the circumstances.[497] If it seems inappropriate because its anticipated effect on the line would be excessive, this may be regarded as a compression of the process, as though the cartographer had drawn a line using that feature, and been told to go back and draw another, ignoring it, because its effect was too distorting. For this reason, it would not normally seem to matter much whether the feature is allowed to influence the initial line, and is later excluded, or whether a decision is taken at the earlier stage to ignore it for purposes of construction of the line. Perhaps less defensible is a process of excluding a feature at the stage of the construction of the equidistance line, and subsequently giving it effect for purposes of adjustment of the line in the interests of equity.[498]

In the *Gulf of Maine* case, however, the Chamber seised of the case, in the course of an explanation why it did not find it appropriate to employ the equidistance method, suggested that there was a difference:

[T]he Chamber likewise would point out the potential disadvantages inherent in any method which takes tiny islands, uninhabited rocks or low-tide elevations, sometimes lying at a considerable distance from terra firma, as basepoint for the drawing of a line intended to effect an equal division of a given area. If any of these geographical features possess some degree of importance, there is nothing to prevent their subsequently being assigned whatever limited corrective effect may equitably be ascribed to them, but that is an altogether different operation from making a series of such minor features the very basis for the determination of the dividing line, or from transforming them into a succession of basepoints for the geometrical construction of the entire line.[499]

The thinking of the Chamber however appears to be that reference to the minor geographical features mentioned might, or might not, as appropriate,

---

[496] As in *Continental Shelf (Libya/Malta)* and *Maritime Delimitation in the Area between Greenland and Jan Mayen*.

[497] For example the islet or rock of Filfla in the *Libya/Malta* case, the position of which meant that an 'immediate qualification' had to be made to the first provisional median line: [1985] ICJ Rep 48, para 6.

[498] The *Qatar/Bahrain* decision is criticized on this point by Despeux, 'Das IGH-Urteil *Katar gegen Bahrein* vom 16. März 2001', 519–520. Judge Torres Bernárdez in that case however specifically defended the process as in accordance with case-law: [2001] ICJ Rep 423, para 475.

[499] [1984] ICJ Rep 329–330, para 201. The idea that the objective should be an *equal* division rather than an *equitable* division is a source of confusion found in other passages written around this time; see also the previous article, (1994) *BYIL* 1, 29–30.

be used to adjust or correct a line drawn by some other method than equidistance; whereas if the equidistance method were used, these features would necessarily have an impact, even though, presumably that impact could itself then be corrected, backwards, as it were, in order that the final result might be equitable.

In the *Qatar/Bahrain* case, Judge *ad hoc* Torres Bernárdez cited this passage in connection with what he identified as a divergence of approach between himself and the majority over the proper application of the 1982 Law of the Sea Convention to a territorial sea delimitation. He considered that the Court had accepted the following proposition

that when the maritime boundary line divides 'territorial seas' the delimitation operation concerned should take into account from the very beginning of the process all minor or tiny maritime features without excluding low-tide elevations for the purpose of defining 'basepoints'.[500]

In his view, these were, on the contrary, 'special circumstances' within the meaning of Article 15 of the 1982 Convention, that were 'supposed to intervene in the delimitation operation *after* the establishment of the 'median line'...*and not before or simultaneously*, as the Judgment does.'[501]

In view of the provisions of the 1982 Convention concerning the establishment of baselines for the territorial sea, this seems at least a counter-intuitive interpretation of the text; but that is not here the question. Can it be shown that, in certain cases, the inclusion of reference to geographical features of this kind in the process of establishment of the equidistance line has an effect that cannot be undone by adjustment of that line *ex post facto* in order to ensure equitableness? Since the judge, if dissatisfied with the effect of a particular feature, may ask the cartographer to draw a fresh line ignoring it, there would seem to be no difference in the ultimate result, though ignoring the feature at the outset may perhaps save some time.

Judge Torres Bernárdez suggests that the process followed by the Court amounts to 'the definition by Court of the maritime frontiers of Bahrain as a State', by which he apparently means the legally appropriate baselines along the coast of Bahrain.[502] While there is some force in this criticism, at the end of the day his opinion does not make clear how, independently of the other arguments he employs against the Court's solution, the result of the delimitation process is affected or prejudiced by taking into account from the outset all features that, cartographically speaking, may affect the course of an equidistance line.

---

[500] [2001] ICJ Rep 424, para 476. For simplicity, the present discussion is leaving aside an additional or alternative proposition that the Judge attributes to the majority, concerning the nature of Bahrain as an archipelago.

[501] Ibid, 427, para 488, emphasis original.

[502] ibid, 424, para 477.

*(c) The circumstances invoked as appropriate for
adjusting the provisional delimitation*

There does not yet appear to be a *numerus clausus* of circumstances
which may need to be taken into account to render a delimitation line
appropriate as an 'equitable result'. In the *North Sea Continental Shelf*
case, the Court famously stated that there was 'no limit to the considerations which States may take account of' for this purpose[503], though in
the *Libya/Malta* case it noted that a court does not have the same freedom in this regard as the parties.[504]

The circumstances referred to in each case during the period under
consideration will be examined here, case by case; with the exception of
the Court's treatment of islands, to be examined in a separate section.

(i) Maritime Delimitation and Territorial Questions
between Qatar and Bahrain

The single delimitation line required in this case was for a considerable
part of its length a delimitation of the territorial seas of the two States.
Since the parties agreed (and the Court accepted) that 'most of the provisions of the 1982 [Law of the Sea] Convention which are relevant for
the present case reflect customary law', the Court was to this extent following the provisions of Part II, Section 2, of the Convention; the Court
was called upon to draw a 'single maritime boundary', but in this region
there was only one kind of maritime space to delimit, which had its own
delimitation rules. In particular, Article 15 of the Convention imposes the
median line as delimitation of the territorial sea, except where 'it is necessary by reason of historic title or other special circumstances' to adopt a
different delimitation. It may be noted that in the subsequent decision in
Land and Maritime Boundary between Cameroon and Nigeria, the Court
observed that the method required by international law for delimitation
by a single line 'is very similar to the equidistance/special circumstances
method applicable in the delimitation of the territorial sea.'[505]

For the remainder of the delimitation, it followed the established procedure of drawing an equidistance line and then investigating possible
special circumstances, which had been defined in the *Jan Mayen* case as
'circumstances which might modify the result produced by an unquali-
fied application of the equidistance principle.'[506]

The first of these was the presence of pearling banks to the north of
the Qatar peninsula, claimed to 'have appertained to Bahrain since time

---

[503] [1969] ICJ Rep 50, para 93.

[504] [1985] ICJ Rep 40, para 48; see also the *Jan Mayen* case, [1993] ICJ Rep 63, para 57. The
Arbitral Tribunal in the *Guyana/Suriname* case took the view that 'special circumstances that may
affect a delimitation are to be assessed on a case-by-case basis, with reference to international jurisprudence and State practice', and accepted navigational considerations as capable of inclusion:
Award of 17 September 2007, 95–96, paras. 303–304.

[505] [2002] ICJ Rep 441, para 288.

[506] [1993] ICJ Rep 62, para 55, quoted in [2001] ICJ Rep 111, para 229.

immemorial.'[507] The Court disregarded this as a special circumstance; noting that the pearling industry had ceased to exist half a century before, it based its decision on the fact that pearl diving had traditionally been considered as a right which was common to the coastal population, and had never led to recognition of an exclusive quasi-territorial right to the pearl fishing grounds or superjacent waters.[508]

The Court next considered the suggestion that a British 'decision' of 1947 concerning the division of the seabed was a relevant circumstance; this point was of course peculiar to the case, and not apparently capable of general application. The decision in question was a follow-up to an earlier decision of 1939, by which the British Government decided that the Hawar Islands belonged to the State of Bahrain, and not to the State of Qatar. This decision was given on the basis of an agreement between the two States that the issue would be decided by the British Government; but since 'it was left to the latter to determine how that decision would be arrived at and by which officials', the decision did not (as the Court found) 'constitute an international arbitral award'.[509] In 1947, the British Government informed the Rulers of Qatar and Bahrain of a delimitation of the seabed that it had drawn around these islands, the effect of which was to exclude a feature known as Hadd Janan.

These decisions had already been given effect by the Court before it reached the stage in its Judgment of effecting the maritime delimitation, in order to decide first that the Hawar Islands were under the sovereignty of Bahrain, and secondly that Hadd Janan did not form part of those islands. As regards the seabed, Qatar relied on the British 1947 line, though in rather unspecific terms; Bahrain denied that it had any relevance whatsoever.

The Court noted that 'neither of the Parties has accepted' the British delimitation 'as a binding decision' (presumably in respect of the seabed, as distinct from in relation to Hadd Janan), and that 'they have invoked only parts of it to support their arguments'. It continued as follows:

The Court further observes that the British decision only concerned the division of the sea-bed between the Parties. The delimitation to be effected by the: Court, however, is partly a delimitation of the territorial sea and partly a combined delimitation of the continental shelf and the exclusive economic zone. The 1947 line cannot therefore be considered to have direct relevance for the present delimitation process.[510]

Applying first principles, one would say that a seabed delimitation by a third party, entrusted with the task by the agreement of the States concerned, ranks the same as an agreed delimitation, which would normally have to be taken into account in any subsequent judicial delimitation. The Court seems to have read the attitude of the parties as waiving this

---

[507] [2001] ICJ Rep 112, 235.
[509] Ibid, 77, para 114.

[508] Ibid, 112–113, para 236.
[510] Ibid, 113–114, para 240.

point, or as agreement that the earlier seabed delimitation should be disregarded; and this is legally sound enough. However, that conclusion would follow whatever the precise subject-matter of the earlier delimitation; and if two parties had effected, or were bound by, an earlier delimitation of their continental shelves, it would seem that, absent a waiver of this kind, a subsequent delimitation by a single maritime boundary should necessarily take that delimitation into account.

It was next suggested that there was a significant disparity in the coastal lengths of the two States; the Court was apparently ready in principle to take this element into account, consistently with previous case-law,[511] but in fact the claimed disparity rested on an assumption by Qatar that the disputed Hawar Islands were under its sovereignty, and once the Court had decided that this was not so, the disparity disappeared.[512]

The final circumstance examined was one which had a negative or self-excluding effect. This was the location of a 'sizeable maritime feature' known as Fasht al Jarim, partly situated in the territorial sea of Bahrain. What Fasht al Jarim actually was—island, sandbank, low-tide elevation or whatever—was disputed, and the Court found it unnecessary to decide. If it were regarded as a projection of Bahrain's coastline, the Court considered, it would 'distort the boundary and have disproportionate effects.'[513]

In the view of the Court, such a distortion, due to a maritime feature located well out to sea and of which at most a minute part is above water at high tide, would not lead to an equitable solution which would be in accord with all other relevant factors referred to above. In the circumstances of the case considerations of equity require that Fasht al Jarim should have no effect in determining the boundary line in the northern sector.[514]

The result was that the equidistance line was 'adjusted' to take account of the absence of effect given to Fasht al Jarim, which presumably is in practice means that it was drawn as an equidistance line generated by basepoints elsewhere, as though Fasht al Jarim did not exist. Thus the Court could, it is suggested, have decided at an earlier stage of its reasoning to exclude the basepoints on Fasht al Jarim for purposes of drawing the provisional line, as was done for Filfla in the *Libya/Malta* case.

Turning to the delimitation of the territorial sea, the *Qatar/Bahrain* case revealed the existence of a situation unforeseen and unprovided-for

[511] Most notably, of course, in the *North Sea* cases, [1969] ICJ Rep 50, para 93; see also *Continental Shelf (Tunisia/Libya)* [1982] ICJ Rep 72, para 103; *Continental Shelf (Libya/Malta)* [1985] ICJ Rep 49, para 66. A similar approach was employed in the *Anglo-French Arbitration*, Decision, paras. 100–101, and the *St. Pierre and Miquelon Arbitration*, Decision, paras. 60–63 and 92–93. The matter is discussed in the previous article at (1994) *BYIL* 1, 54–60.

[512] [2001] ICJ Rep 114, paras. 241–243.

[513] ibid, 114–115, para 247; the phrase is quoted, with acknowledgment, from the *Anglo-French* Decision, para 244.

[514] [2001] ICJ Rep 115, para 248. The first sentence is slightly obscure, since at this stage of the Court's reasoning the line is still the provisional equidistance line, no 'circumstance' having yet been found justifying departing from it.

in the successive multilateral treaty provisions applicable to the territorial sea and its delimitation. The system established by the 1958 Geneva Convention on the Territorial Sea and the Contiguous Zone, taken over virtually unchanged by the 1982 Convention on the Law of the Sea, was briefly as follows. Every coastal State is entitled to claim a territorial sea of a breadth determined by international law currently in force; the extent of that sea is determined by measuring seawards to the extent thus permitted (or claimed, if less) from baselines established by the State concerned; the actual line is thus a unilateral 'distance' line, 'the line every point of which is at a distance from the nearest point of the baseline equal to the breadth of the territorial sea', in the words of Article 4 of the 1982 Convention. Where the areas seaward of the claimed territorial sea are part of the high seas, the claim could still be challenged by other States on the grounds that the baselines drawn, or the basepoints used to establish them, were not in accordance with international law. Since the areas in dispute would not be extensive, and no economic interests would normally be involved,[515] such disputes would be unlikely to require third party settlement.

Where however the coasts of two States are sufficiently close to each other, laterally or opposite, for there to be insufficient sea areas to allow each of them the full entitlement of territorial sea, Article 15 of the 1982 Convention provides that

neither of the two States is entitled, failing agreement between them to the contrary, to extend its territorial sea beyond the median line every point of which is equidistant from the nearest points on the baselines from which the breadth of the territorial sea of each of the two States is measured...

and continues by adding a saving clause 'where it is necessary by reason of historic title or other special circumstances' to use a different method of delimitation. In the event of dispute between two States in this situation, the validity of the baselines drawn by each could be tested against the requirements of international law, and the median line then drawn by reference to baselines found to be legally valid. The intellectual process involved would thus logically be: define the correct baselines, then draw the median line.

Such a system would seem to cover all foreseeable cases. However, as Judge Oda pointed out in the *Qatar/Bahrain* case,[516] it was designed for system of 3-mile territorial seas, in which problems of conflicting claims would only arise in a limited number of actual geographical situations. With the extension of the permitted breadth of the territorial sea, first to 6,

---

[515] Because the areas outside the claimed territorial sea would be part of the entitlement of the coastal State to continental shelf or EEZ; the exact position of the outward limit of the territorial sea would only be relevant to questions of passage, and since *ex hypothesi* there would be no other terrestrial features in the vicinity, the exact limits of free passage and innocent passage would not be of any practical importance.

[516] [2001] ICJ Rep 124–125, para 7.

then to 12 miles, the possibilities of conflict increased, and the unforeseen problem presented itself: what is the position if there is a geographical feature, *in casu* a low-tide elevation, so positioned that each of the two States can make an arguable case for using it as a basepoint for the drawing of baselines? Article 13 of the 1982 Convention provides that if such an elevation 'is situated wholly or partly at a distance not exceeding the breadth of the territorial sea from the mainland or an island', then its low-water line may be used as a baseline.[517] If however the distance between two opposite coasts is less than 24 miles, such a low-tide elevation may be within 12 miles of the mainland of each of the two States, and each of them may claim it as providing a baseline.[518]

In the *Qatar/Bahrain* case, there was a low-tide elevation known as Fasht ad Dibal in this situation. The Court's examination of the problem is bedevilled, as Judge Torres Bernárdez pointed out,[519] by a confusion of terminology. It refers several times to the an overlap between the *territorial seas* of the parties,[520] when what is meant is clearly either an overlap between their *claims*, or an overlap between their *potential* territorial seas, i.e. the areas each of them would have been able to claim if the land territory of the other State had not existed, or been positioned further off.[521] This was a concept employed by the Court in the case of the *Maritime Boundary between Greenland and Jan Mayen*, but in that case it was explained that the 'overlapping entitlements' were constituted by 'overlap between the areas which each State *would have been able to claim* had it not been for the presence of the other State.'[522]

Unfortunately the Court in the *Qatar/Bahrain* case was not provided with clear-cut geographical bases for the claims by each party: neither of them specified the baselines that it claimed should be used for the

---

[517] Judge Torres Bernárdez argues that since Article 13 of the 1982 Convention provides that the low-water line on a low-tide elevation 'may be used as the baseline', this is an option for the State concerned, but not an obligation, which is incontrovertible. However he goes on to argue that similarly when the Court is asked to delimit the territorial sea, it 'may', but need not, draw the baseline from a low-tide elevation: [2001] ICJ Rep 427, para 490; but contrast the same judge's views at ibid, 434, para 514. This seems a superficial interpretation. If the State concerned claims, as it *may* do, a baseline drawn from the elevation, then either it is justified in international law in doing so, or it is not. The Court is under an obligation to find accordingly; the freedom of choice offered to the State by the wording of the Article is *not* available to the Court.

[518] It is of course possible that the same situation could arise in a delimitation between two adjacent States.

[519] [2001] ICJ Rep 422–423, para 474.

[520] [2001] ICJ Rep 93, para 172; 101, para 202. Elsewhere it refers more accurately to areas 'within the 12-mile limit of both States' (ibid, 99, para 197), or to a 'zone of overlapping claims' (ibid, 102, para 209).

[521] There is even here a further complication: Fasht ad Dibal lay within the area that could have been claimed by each party as territorial sea if Fasht ad Dibal itself had not existed; but its existence meant that, in the hypothetical absence of the opposite State, it would itself have generated a further 12 miles of territorial sea—for each of the two States taken in isolation!

[522] [1993] ICJ Rep 64, para 59. See the discussion in a previous article in this series at (1993) *BYIL* 1, 17–18, where it was observed that the unspoken premise underlying the concept is something resembling the notion of the 'just and equitable share' out forward by the Federal Republic of Germany in the *North Sea* case: see [1969] ICJ Rep 20, para 15.

determination of the territorial sea.[523] The Court stated as a general rule that

When a low-tide elevation is situated in the overlapping area of the territorial sea of two States, whether with opposite or with adjacent coasts, both States in principle are entitled to use its low-water line for the measuring of the breadth of their territorial sea. The same low-tide elevation then forms part of the coastal configuration of the two States. That is so even if the low-tide elevation is nearer to the coast of one State than that of the other, or nearer to an island belonging to one party than it is to the mainland coast of the other.[524]

It is striking that the Court does not merely say that each State in these circumstances is entitled to *claim* the low-tide elevation as a base-point, but that both States are entitled to *use* it for that purpose, which suggests that the two conflicting median lines drawn by the two parties on that basis would be equally valid. This is apparently confirmed by the following sentence. There must however be some provisional element in the status of such lines, since international law could not tolerate a situation of two valid claims to sovereignty over the same territory.

The parties were agreed that the provisions of the 1982 Law of the Sea Convention concerning the territorial sea (effectively re-enacting those of the 1958 Geneva Convention) represented customary law.[525] The terms of Article 13 of the 1982 Convention are certainly consistent with the Court's reading: a low-tide elevation so situated 'may be used' for delimitation purposes, presumably by any State the coastline of which is within the defined distance; at the same time, for the reason just stated, this can be only a provisional solution. Bahrain argued that the issue was resolved by *effectivités*, by the fact that its display of sovereign authority over the low-tide elevations meant that it could treat Fasht ad Dibal as though it were an island under Bahraini sovereignty;[526] this of course would not resolve the general problem, but would enable the Court to leave it aside. The Court however found that the Bahraini claim raised another unsolved problem of international law: 'the question whether low-tide elevations are territory and can be appropriated in conformity with the rules and principles of territorial acquisition'.[527] Finding no help either in treaty-law or in practice capable of giving rise to customary law,[528] the Court found that the law of the sea contained 'a number

---

[523] [2001] ICJ Rep 94, para 177.

[524] Ibid, 101, para 202. The last sentence would seem to be an *obiter dictum*, as Fasht ad Dibal lies only slightly closer to Qatar than to Bahrain; but see note 523 below.

[525] [2001] ICJ Rep 91, para 167, which refers to 'most of' the Convention provisions, but the subsequent discussion proceeds on the basis that Article 15 of the 1982 Convention was among them.

[526] Ibid, 101, para 203.

[527] Ibid, para 204.

[528] The Court did not refer to the finding in the *Minquiers and Ecrehos* case, [1953] ICJ Rep 53, recognising that there are islets and rocks that are incapable of appropriation; see the discussion of the case by Fitzmaurice in (1955–56) *BYIL* 46, or the finding on the status of Meanguerita in the *Land, Island and Maritime Frontier* case, all of which were brought to its attention by counsel: CR 2000/9, para 44 (Quéneudec). In the latter case, the Court said of Meanguerita that it was

of permissive rules... with regard to low-tide elevations' near the coast, which did not 'justify a general assumption that [such elevations] are territory in the same sense as islands'.[529] Referring to the requirement in Article 7, paragraph 4, of the 1982 Convention, excluding the drawing of straight baselines to and from low-tide elevations unless lighthouses or similar installations have been built on them, it refused to assimilate such elevations to islands.[530] This of course left the problem unresolved; and the Court's conclusion was that

in the present case there is no ground for recognizing the right of Bahrain to use as a baseline the low-water line of those low-tide elevations which are situated in the zone of overlapping claims, or for recognizing Qatar as having such a right. The Court accordingly concludes that for the purposes of drawing the equidistance line, such low-tide elevations must be disregarded.[531]

The provisional entitlement, stated earlier by the Court, of each party to use low-tide elevations as basepoints, thus evaporates; such a conclusion seems inescapable if any delimitation were ever to be made in the area, but it is legally somewhat unsatisfying. Furthermore, as Despeux points out, the fact that low-tide elevations are dependent features, which cannot as such confer rights on the coastal State, does not make them any the less territorial, which must make them capable of appropriation.[532]

Having reached this point in the Court's judgment, the reader might assume that nothing more would be heard of Fasht ad Dibal. However, the Court also had problems in determining whether another feature, known as Fasht al Azm, was part of a larger island or a separate low-tide elevation, and decided to leave the matter open and draw two possible median lines, based on each of these two interpretations of the status of the feature. Having done so, it then considered the effect of each line on Fasht ad Dibal: one of the two lines 'cut through Fasht ad Dibal leaving the greater part of it on the Qatari side'; the other line 'runs west of Fasht ad Dibal', i.e. between that feature and Bahrain. The Court concluded:

'undoubted' that it was 'capable of appropriation', adding that 'it is not a low-tide elevation, and is covered by vegetation, though it lacks fresh water': [1992] ICJ Rep 570, para 356. This is however more of an unexamined assumption—that low-tide elevations are not capable of appropriation— than a finding on the point which was not, as such, in issue.

[529] [2001] ICJ Rep 102, paras. 205–206. It is interesting that the Court, faced with the risk of a *non-liquet*, adopted the approach of requiring Bahrain to show a permissive rule, rather than adopting a *Lotus*-type approach of State freedom of action.

[530] This aspect of the Judgment is strongly criticized by Despeux, 'Das IGH-Urteil *Katar gegen Bahrein* vom 16. März 2001', 483–485; he suggests that there is no logical link between the legal status of a geographical feature and the legal rules as to its appropriation. While it is correct that low-tide elevations are dependent, non-autonomous elements which cannot confer rights on the coastal State, it does not follow that they do not constitute territory that can be appropriated by a State. Despeux also suggests that the Court was misinformed as to the role of low-tide elevations in State practice in the form of delimitation agreements.

[531] [2001] ICJ Rep 102–103, para 209.

[532] Despeux, 'Das IGH-Urteil *Katar gegen Bahrein* vom 16. März 2001', 483.

In view of the fact that under both hypotheses, Fasht ad Dibal is largely or totally on the Qatari side of the adjusted equidistance line, the Court considers it appropriate to draw the boundary line between Qit'at Jaradah and Fasht ad Dibal. As Fasht ad Dibal thus is situated in the territorial sea of Qatar, it falls for that reason under the sovereignty of that State.[533]

As Tanaka observes, by making sovereignty depend on a maritime delimitation, rather than the other way round, 'it is conceivable that the Court assimilated low-tide elevation to the ocean, not to land', since '[i]f not, the Court's solution would run counter to the fundamental principle of 'the land dominates the sea''.[534] Although the Court refers to what is 'appropriate' rather than what is 'equitable', the procedure emphasizes the extent to which the intervention of equity in maritime delimitation at times verges on the *ex aequo et bono* (which, of course, may be no bad thing in view of the varied and unpredictable circumstances of each delimitation).

The Court's treatment of the low-tide elevation Fasht ad Dibal has been examined; but there were other maritime features whose possible relevance or effect had to be determined: a low-tide elevation called Fasht al Azm and a feature called Qit'at Jaradah. The problem with the first of these was that it could be regarded as part of an island called Sitrah, and therefore only relevant as part of the island, or separated from it by a natural channel, and therefore to be taken into account in itself as a low-tide elevation within the appropriate distance from the main coastline. This problem the Court declined to resolve: as already mentioned, it drew two alternative median lines, one for each interpretation of the character of Fasht al Azm, and then chose between them by reference to the position of Fasht ad Dibal. What is not at all clear from the Judgment is why, if Fasht al Azm was no more than a low-tide elevation, it could not nevertheless furnish basepoints for the construction of the median line on the basis of the rule codified in Article 13 of the 1982 Convention, recalled by the Court in its discussion of Fasht ad Dibal.[535] The answer appears to be given by Judge Torres Bernardez, who was strongly of the view that Fasht al Azm was separate from the island of Sitrah: it could not be used to provide basepoints 'because it is a low-tide elevation which is not located in the territorial sea of one State only but of the two States parties.'[536] Judge Torres Bernárdez does not spell out the conclusion that, like Fasht ad Dibal, it would have to be left out of account altogether.[537]

---

[533] [2001] ICJ Rep 109, para 220.

[534] Y Tanaka, 'Reflections on Maritime Delimitation in the *Qatar/Bahrain* case' (2003) 52 *ICLQ* 72. The author cites the 1978 Torres Strait Treaty between Australia and Papua New Guinea as apparently adopting a similar approach to low-tide elevations: ibid, 73.

[535] [2001] ICJ Rep 100, para 201.

[536] Dissenting Opinion, [2001] ICJ Rep 440, para 533 (italicised in original).

[537] However, it may be with an eye to this conclusion that the Court mentioned, in relation to Fasht ad Dibal, that the nearness of a 'shared' low-tide elevation to the one or the other State is

As to Qit'at Jadarah, the parties disagreed over its status as an island or as a mere low-tide elevation; the Court, after examining the evidence and recalling the definition in Article 121 of the 1982 Convention, decided that Qit'at Jedarah was an island.[538] It then concluded, on the basis of certain activities carried out there by Bahrain that it was under Bahraini sovereignty.[539] It therefore employed two basepoints on the low-water mark of the island to generate the median line.[540]

(ii) Land and Maritime Boundary between Cameroon and Nigeria

Cameroon and Nigeria being both parties to the UN Convention on the Law of the Sea, the Court had explicitly to apply Articles 74 and 83 to the delimitation of the continental shelf and the exclusive economic zone, and noted that those Articles both provide that the delimitation must be effected in such a way as to 'achieve an equitable solution'.[541] The parties had however agreed that the delimitation should be effected by a single line; thus, with some apparent inconsistency, the Court went on to quote its finding in the *Qatar/Bahrain* case that 'the concept of a single maritime boundary does not stem from multilateral treaty law but from State practice', i.e. customary law.[542] While there is therefore some ambiguity as to the source of the applicable law, the Court was clear that the applicable method of delimitation 'involves first drawing an equidistance line, then considering whether there are factors calling for the adjustment or shifting of that line in order to achieve an 'equitable result'.'[543] The elements which might affect the line are thus no longer 'circumstances', but 'factors', but this appears to be no more than a semantic distinction.[544]

The first factor advanced by one party was the nature and form of the relevant coastlines of the parties. Cameroon contended that 'the concavity of the Gulf of Guinea in general, and of Cameroon's coastline in particular, creates a virtual enclavement of Cameroon', and suggested that this constituted a special circumstance to be taken into account.[545] The Court accepted that such a concavity could in principle be a special circumstance, and cited the *North Sea* case and the arbitral decision in the *Guinea/Guinea-Bissau* case, but continued:

Nevertheless the Court stresses that this can only be the case when such concavity lies within the area to be delimited. Thus, in the *Guinea/Guinea-Bissau* case, the

---

irrelevant; Fasht ad Dibal is more or less centrally situated, while Fasht al Azm is very close to the island of Sitrah.

[538] [2001] ICJ Rep 99, para 195.
[539] Ibid, 100, para 197.
[540] See Sketch-Map No. 6 at [2001] ICJ Rep. 108.
[541] [2002] ICJ Rep 440, para 285.
[542] ibid, para 286.   [543] Ibid, 441, para 288.
[544] As noted above, 'factors' was a term apparently first used in the *Jan Mayen* case: [1993] ICJ Rep 62, para 54, and subsequently in the *Qatar/Bahrain* case, [2001] ICJ Rep 111, para 229–230.
[545] [2002] ICJ Rep 445, para 296.

Arbitral Tribunal did not address the disadvantage resulting from the concavity of the coast from a general viewpoint, but solely in connection with the precise course of the delimitation line between Guinea and Guinea.Bissau (*ILM*, Vol. 25 (1986), p. 295, para. 104). In the present case the Court has already determined that the coastlines relevant to delimitation between Cameroon and Nigeria do not include all of the coastlines of the two States within the Gulf of Guinea. The Court notes that the sectors of coastline relevant to the present delimitation exhibit no particular concavity. Thus the concavity of Cameroon's coastline is apparent primarily in the sector where it faces [the island of] Bioko.[546]

As will be evident from the maps attached to the Judgment, Cameroon's difficulty was the presence of Bioko off its coasts, under the sovereignty of Equatorial Guinea. If the island were disregarded, the position of Cameroon in the Gulf would strongly resemble that of Germany in the *North Sea* case, and equidistance lines drawn from the termini of the land boundaries with Nigeria and Equatorial Guinea would certainly present the cut-off effect observed in that case.

The Court's finding on the point demonstrates the importance of the initial stage of the delimitation process: the identification of the relevant coasts. The Court does not assert specifically that, once these have been selected, no feature outside the area so defined can have any influence on the delimitation, even as a factor affecting the assessment of the equitableness of the line drawn by reference solely to the 'relevant' coasts, but the passage quoted certainly suggests this conclusion. If so, it would appear not to be consistent with the view taken in, for example, the *Continental Shelf (Libya/Malta)* case. There, the Court drew a median line between Malta and the limited stretch of Libyan coastline immediately opposite to it, in order to limit the delimitation to areas in which there were no claims by third States. It noted the disparity of lengths of coasts within this area as an element to be taken into account, and in fact requiring an adjustment of the median line.[547] It was also contemplating the application, later in its judgment, of the test of proportionality of coasts and areas of shelf, and explained that 'the question of the coasts and areas to be taken into account for application of the proportionality test is one which only arises at later stage in the delimitation process',[548] i.e. that these would not necessarily be the same as the coasts already identified as relevant. The Court specifically stated that '[i]n the present case, the Court has also to look beyond the area concerned in the case, and consider the general geographical context in which the delimitation will have to be effected'.[549] When the Court turned to the application

---

[546] Ibid, para 297. The last sentence is somewhat obscure: Cameroon was drawing attention to the concavity of the whole Gulf; and its coast directly opposite Bioko shows no more concavity than does the coast identified by the Court as relevant to the delimitation with Nigeria (from the land boundary terminus to Debundsha).

[547] [1985] ICJ Rep 50, para 68.

[548] Ibid, para 67.

[549] Ibid, para 69.

of the proportionality test, it found itself unable to 'achieve a predetermined arithmetical ration', but did conclude as follows:

The relationship between the lengths of the relevant coasts of the Parties has of course already been taken into account in the determination of the delimitation line; if the Court turns its attention to the extent of the areas of shelf lying on each side of the line, it is possible for it to make a broad assessment of the equitableness of the result, without seeking to define the equities in arithmetical terms. The conclusion to which the Court comes in this respect is that there is certainly no evident disproportion in the areas of shelf attributed to each of the Parties respectively such that it could be said that the requirements of the test of proportionality as an aspect of equity were not satisfied.[550]

The next element suggested as relevant to the equitableness of the provisional equidistance line was the island of Bioko itself: this will be dealt with in the section below concerning the significance of islands in delimitation.

Cameroon finally invoked the disparity of the length of coastlines of the two States in the Gulf of Guinea. Again, the Court recognized that, in general, 'a substantial difference in the lengths of the parties' respective coastlines may be a factor to be taken into consideration in order to adjust or shift the provisional delimitation line'; but again, it confined its attention to the part of the coastline of Cameroon regarded as relevant, i.e. the part not cut off by Bioko.

A further question, raised by Nigeria, was that whether 'the oil practice of the Parties provides helpful indications for the purposes of the delimitation';[551] this aspect has already been discussed above,[552] under the heading of 'subjective equity'. The Court's conclusion was, contrary to that of the *Tunisia/Libya* case, that oil concessions can only be taken into account 'if they are based on express or tacit agreement'.[553] As M. D. Evans has pointed out[554] this implies that such concessions are never a relevant circumstance, since if there is an agreed line, the whole equidistance plus adjustment system becomes inoperative.

(iii) Territorial and Maritime Dispute between Nicaragua and Honduras in the Caribbean Sea

As already noted, the decision in this case differs from the others studied in that the provisional delimitation line drawn was not an equidistance line—even though the Court placed on record its view that 'equidistance remains the general rule'—, but a line devised as a bisector of the angle represented by the coastal fronts, as identified by the Court. The only adjustment of the line effected was as a result of the presence of islands, over which Honduran sovereignty had been recognized, but which would lie on the Nicaraguan side of the line; this matter is discussed in

550 Ibid, 55, para 75.
551 Ibid, 447, para 303.
552 Chapter II, section 1(3)(c)(ii).
553 [2002] ICJ Rep 447–448, para 304.
554 Evans, above n 344, 158.

Section 1(3)(d)(iii) below. The Court stated in the course of its reasoning that '[i]f necessary in the circumstances, the Court could adjust the line so as to achieve an equitable result (see UNCLOS, Arts 74, para 1, and 83, para 1).'[555] This was however in the context of the choice of the endpoints of the coastal fronts which would dictate the angle to be bisected; the sentence quoted is immediately preceded by the observation that

the co-ordinates of the endpoints of the chosen coastal fronts need not at this juncture be specified with exactitude for present purposes; one of the practical advantages of the bisector method is that a minor deviation in the exact position of endpoints, which are at a reasonable distance from the shared point [sc., the point where the parties' coastal fronts meet] will have only a relatively minor influence on the course of the entire coastal front line.[556]

The possibility of adjustment mentioned may therefore perhaps have been visualized simply as involving pushing the chosen endpoints this way and that, so as to make the angle to be bisected more obtuse or more acute, an operation which was not performed, being presumably regarded as unnecessary. However, the Court did in fact adjust the bisector line in the sense that it superimposed upon it the limits of the areas of territorial sea attributed to the Honduran islands, so that the eventual line bellies out, or sags southward, in order to accommodate these areas (see sketch-map No. 7 attached to the judgment). In the judgment, this process, which did no more than respect the entitlement of Honduras under Article 3 of the Law of the Sea Convention, is not explicitly treated as an 'adjustment'; the Court, having established 'the appropriate method and procedures for the delimitation from the mainland', turns to the 'separate task of delimiting the waters around and between [the] islands.'[557] That 'separate task' is not however something to be embarked upon at or as the geographical end of the bisector line: that line continues on the same azimuth after the limits of the islands' territorial waters have been drawn.

The judgment therefore leaves uncertain whether, in a case in which the initial provisional line is not an equidistance line, but constructed on a geometrical basis, it is open to adjustment in the light of the same, or similar, special circumstances that would be relevant to the equitableness of an equidistance line; and if so, whether the method of such adjustment would be limited to tinkering with the geometrical bases of the construction of the line. Once it is decided that the circumstances of a particular case require the delimitation to be effected by some method other than that of first drawing, then adjusting, an equidistance line, it should theoretically be possible to proceed directly to the drawing of a line that is equitable in itself, requiring no adjustment. However, it would seem that any line other than equidistance would be, like that drawn in the *Nicaragua/Honduras* case, geometrical, or at least would possess a

---

[555] [2007] ICJ Rep, para 294 of the Judgment.   [556] Ibid.
[557] Ibid, paragraph 299 of the Judgment.

considerable geometrical component.[558] In many foreseeable cases, it would be a straight line on a defined azimuth. Since nature tends not to employ straight lines, adjustment to the untidy pattern of coasts may still be needed for the result to look equitable.

(d) The effect of islands

In each of the delimitations effected by the Court in the period under review, the presence of one or more islands (or islets) has complicated the operation.[559] In the earlier cases also the Court had had to take account of such geographical features: the Kerkennah Islands in the *Tunisia/Libya* case, and the islet or rock of Filfla in the *Libya/Malta* case. In the case of the *Land, Island and Maritime Frontier* case, the Chamber seised of the case had first to determine sovereignty over the islands in the Gulf of Fonseca, and then to proceed to resolve the question of the rights of the riparian States in the Gulf, but the special status of the Gulf meant that in this respect it was not the general law of the sea that was applicable. In the *Tunisia/Libya* case, the Court was not using an equidistance line, but a line at a fixed angle determined by the angular relation between the direction of the mainland coasts of the parties, and it then had to consider what effect to give to the Kerkennah Islands off the Tunisian coast. Essentially it decided that to treat that coast as defined by those islands would push the line too far away from Tunisia, while ignoring the islands would swing the line too far the other way. It therefore devised a means of giving 'half-effect' to the islands.[560] In the *Libya/Malta* case, Malta had claimed on the basis of an equidistance line calculated from basepoints that included the uninhabited Maltese islet of Filfla; the Court however constructed a provisional median line ignoring that islet, ruling as follows:

The Court does not express any opinion on whether the inclusion of Filfla in the Maltese baselines was legally justified; but in any event the baselines as determined by coastal States are not *per se* identical with the points chosen on a coast to make it possible to calculate the area of continental shelf appertaining to that State. In this case, the equitableness of an equidistance line depends on whether the precaution is taken of eliminating the disproportionate effect of certain "islets, rocks and minor coastal projections", to use the language of the Court in its 1969 Judgment, quoted above. The Court thus finds it equitable not to take account of Filfla in the calculation of the provisional median line between Malta and Libya.[561]

---

[558] *Cf.* the lines drawn in the *Tunisia/Libya* case: the ZV 45° line and the line reflecting the change of direction of the coasts.

[559] See generally on this aspect, V Prescott and G Triggs, 'Islands and Rocks and their Role in Maritime Delimitation', in D A Colson and R W Smith (eds), *International Maritime Boundaries* (2005), Vol V, 3245.

[560] See the discussion in the previous article on this subject, (1994) *BYIL* 1, 24–25.

[561] [1985] ICJ Rep 48, para 64.

(i) Maritime Delimitation and Territorial Questions between Qatar and Bahrain

In its judgment in this case, the Court had to deal with a number of geographical features which might or might not be classified as 'islands', within the meaning of Article 121, paragraph 1, of the Law of the Sea Convention.[562] There were first of all the Hawar Islands: here the dispute was simply one of territorial sovereignty, both parties recognizing that they were islands in the full sense of the term, and thus to be taken into account as such in the delimitation—this indeed being the reason for the dispute over sovereignty, rather than any intrinsic value of the islands themselves. Having determined that Bahrain had sovereignty over the islands,[563] the Court first drew the appropriate conclusion as regards 'what constitutes Bahrain's relevant coasts' for establishing baselines from which to draw a provisional equidistance line.[564] At a later stage in its reasoning, it also drew the appropriate conclusion as to the relative lengths of the coastlines of the two States: that, once the Hawar Islands were included as part of Bahrain, 'the disparity in length of the coastal fronts of the Parties cannot be considered such as to necessitate an adjustment of the [provisional] equidistance line.'[565] Nearby there was another island, or pair of islands, called Janan and Hadd Janan, claimed by both parties; the Court decided that sovereignty was with Qatar.[566] There were also 'islands which are at high tide very small in size, but at low tide have a surface which is considerably larger', named Jazirat Mashtan and Umm Jalid; these were claimed by Bahrain, and this claim was not contested by Qatar.[567]

A problem was however posed by a feature called Fasht al Azam, which could be 'deemed to be part of the island of Sitrah', which was recognized as under the sovereignty of Bahrain, or 'a low-tide elevation which has always been separated from Sitrah Island by a natural channel.'[568] The Court in fact found it possible to carry out the delimitation without determining this particular dispute. A similar problem of categorization arose in respect of a feature called Qit'at Jaradah: was it an island, as claimed by Bahrain, or a low-tide elevation, as claimed by Qatar? The Court recalled the legal definition of an island in the 1958 Convention on the Territorial Sea and the 1982 Law of the Sea Convention,[569] as

---

[562] Despeux draws attention to the fact that international maritime law allocates all maritime features to a closed class of seven categories (mainland, islands, low-tide elevations, rocks, coral reefs and atolls), and that consequently, there being no room for an intermediate feature, it has to be squeezed into, for example, the 'island' category: 'Das IGH-Urteil *Katar gegen Bahrein* vom 16. März 2001', 480–481.

[563] [2001] ICJ Rep 85, para 147.
[564] Ibid, 97, paras. 186–187.
[565] Ibid, 114, para 243.
[566] Ibid, 90–91, para 165.
[567] Ibid, 97, para 187.
[568] Ibid 97–98, paras. 188–189.

[569] 1958 Convention, Art. 10, para 1; 1982 Convention, Art. 121, para 1. The Court stated later in its decision, in a different context, that in this respect the provisions of the 1982 Convention as to low-tide elevations (Article 13, para 1) 'reflect customary law': [2001] ICJ Rep 100, para 201. By implication, it seems that the Court took the same view of the provisions concerning islands.

'a naturally formed area of land, surrounded by water, which is above water at high tide'; on the basis of the expert and other evidence submitted, the Court found that Qit'at Jaradah did satisfy the Convention criteria to be classified as an island.[570]

The outcome of these findings was, apparently,[571] that the provisional equidistance line drawn by the Court as a first step toward the delimitation was drawn, where appropriate, from basepoints or baselines on those features that had been identified as islands, as part of the coastline of the State enjoying sovereignty over them. The question of the effect of the various islands was then taken up in the context of an examination of the question whether 'there are special circumstances which make it necessary to adjust the equidistance line...to obtain an equitable result.'[572] Qit'at Jaradah proved to be a case of a 'special circumstance':

The Court observes that Qit'at Jaradah is a very small island, uninhabited and without any vegetation. This tiny island, which—as the Court has determined...comes under Bahraini sovereignty, is situated about midway between the main island of Bahrain and the Qatar peninsula. Consequently, if its low-water line were to be used for determining a basepoint in the construction of the equidistance line, and this line taken as the delimitation line, a disproportionate effect would be given to an insignificant maritime feature... In similar situations the Court has sometimes been led to eliminate the disproportionate effect of small islands (see *North Sea Continental Shelf*, I.C.J. Reports 1969, p. 36, para. 57; *Continental Shelf (Libyan Arab Jamahiriyal Malta), Judgment*, I.C.J. Reports 1985, p. 48, para. 64). The Court thus finds that there is a special circumstance in this case warranting the choice of a delimitation line passing immediately to the east of Qit'at Jaradah.[573]

The justice of this finding is unquestionable, but its wording illustrates the difficulty in maritime delimitation in finding language to express the reasons for taking full account, less account, or no account of a particular feature, which does not ultimately convey more than a subjective assessment. The terms 'disproportionate' and 'insignificant' perhaps suggest a greater degree of precision in definition than they can really bear. It is also not clear which of the characteristics of the island are relevant and determinative: its size, its position, its lack of inhabitants or even its lack of vegetation. Probably one must conclude that all these contribute to the general conclusion that the island ought not to be allowed the effect it would 'normally' have on the delimitation, an effect which can probably be defined as generating, through basepoints on its coastline, part of the equidistance line exactly as though it were part of the mainland coast.

---

[570] [2001] ICJ Rep 99. para 195.

[571] The Court does not at any point in the decision indicate exactly on what basis its provisional equidistance line was drawn; it was severely criticised, in the dissenting opinion of Judge *ad hoc* Torres Bernárdez, for using selected basepoints rather than the baselines claimed by the parties, which had not in fact been made clear to the Court: [2001] ICJ Rep 434–435, paras. 514–518.

[572] Ibid, 104, para 217.

[573] Ibid, 104–105, para 219.

How then is the 'disproportionate effect' avoided? Not, apparently, by drawing the equidistance line as though the island were not there at all, as was done for Filfla in the *Libya/Malta* case,[574] nor by any sort of 'half-effect' as adopted in the *Tunisia/Libya* case; but rather by pushing the equidistance line westward to become a line 'passing immediately'—that is to say, judging from the map attached to the judgment, at a distance of about a kilometre—to the east of Qit'at Jaradah.

(ii) Land and Maritime Boundary between Cameroon and Nigeria

The area in which a maritime delimitation was required between Cameroon and Nigeria had one unusual feature: the presence of a large island under the sovereignty of neither party but of a third State, Equatorial Guinea, which had been permitted to intervene in the case as a non-party.[575] The island of Bioko lies off the coast of Cameroon rather than off the mainland coast of Equatorial Guinea, thus in effect cutting off Cameroon from any protrusion of rights or claims over areas seaward of the island.

The presence of the island of Bioko raised two problems. The first was the extent to which the delimitation between Cameroon and Nigeria had to be limited in order not to encroach on the rights of, or the areas claimed by, Equatorial Guinea, the problem which had arisen in the *Libya/Malta* case, and which had been solved by confining the delimitation to the 'safe' area, in which no claims had been made by Italy, the third State concerned. The *Cameroon/Nigeria* case however differed from that earlier case in that Equatorial Guinea was present in the proceedings, even if not as a party. This aspect of the case raises issues as to the effect of Article 59 of the Statute and its relationship with intervention, and will therefore not be dealt with here.

The second issue to which the presence of the island was relevant was the question of the definition of the area in which the delimitation was to be effected, and the relevant coasts to be taken into account. Cameroon asked the Court in effect to look at the shape of the whole Gulf of Guinea, including the coast of Equatorial Guinea and part of the coast of Gabon, from Akasso in Nigeria to Cape Lopez in Gabon.[576] It suggested a line which it contended was an equidistance line 'adjusted to take account of the relevant circumstances so as to produce an equitable solution', these circumstances including the concavity of the Gulf, the relevant lengths of the coastlines of the parties, and the presence of

---

[574] Tanaka ('Reflections on Maritime Delimitation in the *Qatar/Bahrain* case', 52 *ICLQ* (2003), 78) suggests that 'approximately no effect was given' to the island. In the absence of indications by the Court as to how its provisional equidistance line was constructed, which would make it possible to estimate the position of an equidistance line ignoring the island, this must remain a matter of opinion.

[575] Order of 21 October 1999, [1999] ICJ Rep 1029.

[576] See the map on [2002] ICJ Rep 444.

Bioko Island,[577] which would be situated within an enclave on the analogy of the treatment of the Channel Isles in the United Kingdom/France arbitration.[578]

The Court did not accept this contention. It held first that the boundary could only be determined 'by reference to points on the coastlines of' the parties, not of third States. It continued:

Secondly, the presence of Bioko makes itself felt from Debundsha, at the point where the Cameroon coast turns south-south-east. Bioko is not an island belonging to either of the two Parties. It is a constituent part of a third State, Equatorial Guinea. North and east of Bioko the maritime rights of Cameroon and Equatorial Guinea have not yet been determined. The part of the Cameroon coastline beyond Debundsha Point faces Bioko. It cannot therefore be treated as facing Nigeria so as to be relevant to the maritime delimitation between Cameroon and Nigeria... [579]

It of course indisputable as a matter of fact that 'the part of the Cameroon coastline beyond Debundsha Point faces Bioko', in the sense that it does not 'face' any part of the Nigerian coast because Bioko is in the way. To say however that 'the presence of Bioko makes itself felt from Debundsha' seems to be a statement of law rather than fact; and as a reply to the suggestion that Bioko could be dealt with, in an equitable way, by enclaving, seems rather to assume its conclusion. The attempt of Cameroon to have Bioko done away with, so as to 'make use of' its own coastline beyond Debunsha (not to mention the coastlines of the neighbouring States) was probably asking too much of a Court entrusted with finding an equitable solution; and, to be fair to the Court, it is difficult to see what other, more precise, formula could be found to convey the decision in a way that would indicate an underlying rule or principle.

Probably all one can say is that, where the situation of the Channel Isles lent itself to equitable settlement by enclaving, that of Bioko, taking into account its size and importance[580] and its relationship with the mainland coasts, did not. However, the Court had at an earlier stage in its judgment decided as a matter of principle that 'it cannot rule on Cameroon's claims in so far as they might affect rights of Equatorial Guinea and Sao Tome and Principe.'[581] This would seem to rule out any possibility of adopting a prospective enclaving solution for Bioko; the most that the Court could do, following the *Libya/Malta* precedent, would be to devise a delimitation between Cameroon and Nigeria that left open *all* possibilities as regards delimitation between Cameroon and

---

[577] Ibid, 433, para 272.

[578] Ibid, 434, para 274, citing *UNRIAA*, Vol. XVIII, 3.

[579] Ibid, 442–443. para 291.

[580] Nigeria mentioned in its arguments against the Cameroonian contention that Bioko is 'an island substantial in area and population and the seat of the capital of the Republic of Equatorial Guinea' ([2002] ICJ Rep 435, para 279), but it is not clear whether the Court attached any real significance, in the context of delimitation, to this last circumstance.

[581] [2002] ICJ Rep 421, para 238.

Equatorial Guinea. Since the enclave solution would apparently necessarily limit what Equatorial Guinea might reasonably claim, it is difficult to see how this could be done.

(iii) Territorial and Maritime Dispute between Nicaragua and Honduras in the Caribbean Sea

In this case also, the Court had first to resolve the question of sovereignty over a number of islands off the relevant coasts—islands that one would once have called 'insignificant', but which had acquired considerable significance in view of the possible seabed resources to which title to the islands might prove to be the key. They were claimed by Honduras primarily on the basis of the principle of *uti possidetis*; but while the application of that principle to islands was recognized by the Court as possible, it found that in the case of these particular islands 'there was no clear-cut demarcation' attributing them to one Spanish administrative division rather than another.[582] Nevertheless, Honduran sovereignty was recognized on the basis of various acts exercised there by Honduras *à titre de souverain*, even though these were not many in number, and of comparatively recent date.[583]

What influence the islands might have had on an equidistance line must remain unknown, as the Court opted to depart from what had become the standard procedure of drawing an equidistance line and then assessing it for equitableness, for reasons explained above in Chapter II, section 1(2). Neither party had in the first instance proposed an equidistance line, but Honduras had at one stage put such a line forward as a possible solution, subsidiary to its main claim of a historic line following a parallel of latitude.

Honduras did not use the islands north and south of the 15th parallel as base points for constructing this line but did adjust the line both to allow a full 12-mile territorial sea for these islands where possible and to follow a median line where their opposite-facing territorial seas overlap (mostly to the south of the 15th parallel).[584]

The provisional line adopted by the Court—a bisector of the angle between lines representing the coastal fronts of the two States—was based solely on the mainland coasts, treated as 'adjacent' coasts, and had clearly to be adjusted to take account of the islands. It had the effect of leaving the islands, found to be Honduran, on the 'wrong' side, the Nicaraguan side, and their coasts were treated as 'opposite' in relation to the mainland coast of Nicaragua.[585] This did not however involve the creation of an equidistance line, even a provisional line, between the islands and the mainland coast;[586] the Court decided that each island was

---

[582] [2007] ICJ Rep, para 162 of the Judgment.
[583] Ibid, para 208.   [584] Ibid, para 276.
[585] Ibid, para 299.
[586] The Court alludes to the 'problems' that would have been presented by the drawing of such a line (ibid, para 304); it does not explain what these were, but presumably it had in mind the problem

entitled to a full territorial sea of 12 miles,[587] and the consequent arcs of circles constituting the outer limits of such areas of territorial sea created a 'bite' out of the bisector line in favour of Honduras (see the maps attached to the Judgment).

Nicaragua recognized that the islands were entitled to their own areas of territorial sea, but suggested that this should be limited to three miles on the ground that a twelve-mile sea 'would result in giving a disproportionate amount of the maritime areas in dispute to Honduras'[588], in other words that this would not amount to the 'equitable solution' required by the Law of the Sea Convention. The Court did not comment on this contention, but merely cited Article 3 of the Convention as entitling Honduras 'to establish the breadth of its territorial sea up to a limit of 12 nautical miles be that for its mainland or for islands under its sovereignty', and noting that Honduras had made such a claim[589] (One may in fact speculate what territorial sea would have been attributed to the islands if Honduras, whose claim to sovereignty over them was upheld, had not made a specific declaration claiming a 12-mile territorial sea around them). If, despite the wording of Article 3 of UNCLOS, the Court had attributed only a 3-mile territorial sea, as suggested by Nicaragua, would Honduras have been entitled to assert its rights under Article 3 at a later date, thereby upsetting (presumably) the equitableness of the overall delimitation?

The Court thus did not comment on the possible application of Article 15, with its reference to 'special circumstances' as a reason for departing from the median line; nor on the inter-relation between Article 3 and Articles 74 and 83 of the Convention concerning the equitableness of the delimitation of the continental shelf and EEZ, and consequently of a single maritime boundary. Despite the absolute terms of Article 3 of the Convention, under Article 15, where the distance between opposite coasts is 24 nautical miles or less, the presence of 'special circumstances' would justify one State having a sea of a breadth less than 12 miles. The Court seems to have concluded tacitly that when the distance between the coasts is more than 24 miles, Article 15 has no application. That which is certainly the appropriate interpretation in terms of territorial sea delimitation, since this circumstance means that a reduction of one State's territorial sea to less than 12 miles would mean extending that of the other to a greater breadth, and incorporating within it the band, however narrow,

of identification of basepoints at the mouth of the River Coco, and the shifting nature of these points: see above Chapter II, section 1(2).

[587] In fact, by the time it came in the judgment to deal with the question of their territorial sea, it had already stated the principle of a full 12-mile entitlement in connection with the procedural question of a 'new' claim by Nicaragua in the proceedings: [2007] ICJ Rep, para 302 of the Judgment.

[588] Ibid, para 300. Nicaragua argued for a 3-mile territorial sea, claiming that the features in question were cays that could not sustain human habitation, and concluding that they were not automatically entitled to 12 miles, so that 'this question...must be decided in the context of maritime delimitation and on the basis of equitable criteria': written reply to question put by Judge Simma, 22 March 2007.

[589] Ibid, para 302.

of sea and seabed between the two territorial seas, which is not itself territorial sea, and cannot, apparently, be transformed into territorial sea by circumstances, be they never so special. The question raised by the Nicaraguan contention is whether, where the territorial sea of one State is bounded by the continental shelf and/or EEZ of another, the over-riding requirement of an equitable delimitation of the latter could justify the reduction of the territorial sea entitlement conferred by Article 3 of the Convention. Articles 55 and 76 of the Convention make it clear that the EEZ and continental shelf begin where the territorial sea ends, rather than the other way round; and outside the situation contemplated by Article 15, there is nothing in the text to qualify Article 3. Nevertheless, it is perhaps a pity that the Court did not comment on this aspect of the matter.

As between the Honduran islands and the one Nicaraguan island in the vicinity (Edinburgh Cay), the Court drew a provisional equidistance line, and found that there were no 'legally relevant 'special circumstances' in this area that would warrant adjusting this provisional line.'[590] The reference to special circumstances in quotation marks clearly alludes to Article 15 of the Law of the Sea Convention; again, the question whether the overall delimitation of the continental shelf and EEZ by a single maritime boundary might involve wider considerations of equity is not mentioned.

There was however another island in the area the presence of which was invoked by the parties in support of their claims, which the Court handled differently—or rather, declined to handle at all.

A claim was also made during the oral proceedings by each Party to an island in an entirely different location, namely, the island in the mouth of the River Coco. For the last century the unstable nature of the river mouth has meant that larger islands are liable to join their nearer bank and the future of smaller islands is uncertain. Because of the changing conditions of the area, the Court makes no finding as to sovereign title over islands in the mouth of the River Coco.[591]

This could be read as implying that, because of the 'changing conditions of the area', no sovereignty was possible over such an ephemeral feature; or that while sovereignty was possible, none had ever been established, i.e. that the island was to be taken to be *terra nullius*; or it could be read as meaning that the Court saw no necessity to decide the question for the purposes of the maritime delimitation which was the object of the case. It is noteworthy that the Court refers to the feature as an 'island', not as a low-tide elevation or bank, which suggests that it did regard it as susceptible of appropriation in sovereignty. Given that the island in all probability did not exist, or existed in a quite different form, at the time of decolonization, the principle of *uti possidetis* would not in itself be likely to resolve the problem; but since the River Coco was the established colonial boundary and international frontier, research into the possible application of the principles of accretion and avulsion might have supplied an answer.[592]

590 Ibid, para 304.   591 Ibid, para 145.
592 Cf *Land, Island and Maritime Frontier Dispute*, [1992] ICJ Rep 546–547, paras. 308–311.

Was it then open to the Court, on the basis of the nature of the dispute submitted to it, to leave the matter open, as not essential to the process of reaching a decision on the delimitation? If not, would it be justified, in view of the uncertainty of the information available to it, to declare a form of *non liquet*?[593] The latter question goes beyond the scope of the present article; for the answer to the former, reference may be made to later passages in the judgment. As already noted,[594] so far as concerns the Court's rejection of the provisional equidistance line as the first step in the delimitation process on the basis of a foreseeable *ex post facto* lack of equitableness due to shifting geographical features, this does not seem consistent with the nature of the equitable *result* required to be achieved. As to the lack of basepoints on the parties' respective coasts, whether agreed or unilaterally asserted,[595] if the parties had specifically asked the Court for a delimitation by an equidistance line,[596] it would, it is suggested, have been part of the Court's duty to decide for itself what should be the appropriate basepoints.

---

[593] On this, see the earlier articles in this series: (1989) *BYIL* 1, 77–84; (2005) *BYIL* 1, 43–52.

[594] Chapter II, section 1(2).

[595] [2007] ICJ Rep, para 278 of the Judgment.

[596] In the *Continental Shelf (Tunisia/Libya)* case, the parties were in agreement in *not* favouring an equidistance line, and the Court observed that it 'must take this firmly expressed view of the Parties into account': [1982] ICJ Rep 79, para 110.

CHAPTER III: OTHER QUESTIONS OF THE LAW OF THE SEA

1. THE HIGH SEAS

The *Fisheries Jurisdiction* case between Spain and Canada arose out of an incident in an area which both parties recognized formed part of the high seas: the arrest by the Canadian authorities of a Spanish fishing vessel on the basis of Canadian legislation authorising measures of conservation and management of fisheries in an area beyond Canadian EEZ or fishery jurisdiction. As a result of the grounds on which the Court decided that it had no jurisdiction, it did not have to make any findings as to the law of the high seas, nor did it do so by way of *dicta*. Judge *ad hoc* Torres Bernárdez, in the course of an extremely long dissenting opinion, made a number of observations on the subject; in themselves, these are non-controversial, and would have been accepted by the other Members of the Court: it was the reasoning that Judge Torres Bernárdez built on them that was not accepted by his colleagues, and left him in the position of a dissenter. The decision in the case turned on whether or not the dispute did or did not fall within the terms of a reservation attached by Canada to its acceptance of optional clause jurisdiction, which excluded 'disputes arising out of or concerning conservation and management measures taken by Canada with respect to vessels fishing in' a defined area, and this depended on how the dispute between the parties was to be defined.

In simple terms, the majority of the Court saw the dispute as concerning a particular incident involving the exercise by Canada of the powers of 'conservation and management' which it claimed over the area; for Spain, and for the dissenting judges, in particular Judge Torres Bernárdez, it was a dispute over Canada's entitlement to act in this way in an area of the high seas.[597] It is possible that if Spain had disputed Canada's right to take 'conservation and management' measures in the abstract, and had brought proceedings simply asking for a declaration, the reservation would have been held inapplicable. In the present context, what are of interest are the efforts made by Judge Torres Bernárdez to derive the Spanish conception of the nature of the dispute from the general law of the high seas.

It was contended by Spain that the dispute 'seriously affect[ed] the very integrity of the *mare liberum* of the high seas and the freedoms thereof', and this was, as explained by Judge Torres Bernárdez, because the Canadian fisheries legislation 'cannot constitute a title in international law in relations between the two States, irrespective of the

---

[597] There were other issues involved, such as the validity of the reservation itself, a question having nothing to do with the law of the sea, and the legal meaning of 'conservation and management'.

position under Canadian domestic law...',[598] and '[i]n order to be able to exercise jurisdiction over an area of the sea, States must be in possession of a title'.[599] This is surely correct, even if it is an unusual way of expressing the point. The purpose was to demonstrate that 'title as a legal category of the law of the sea can on its own provide a sufficient cause of action to support proceedings before the Court'.[600] Again, this can hardly be denied; but the question before the Court was whether this *was* the cause of action relied on, and if so whether or not it was excluded by the Canadian reservation.[601] The unusual feature of Judge Torres Bernárdez's analysis is that the 'title' to exercise a particular jurisdiction over a maritime area is usually viewed on the basis of a legal classification of relationships between States and areas, each relationship entailing a particular bundle of rights: sovereignty over the territorial sea, sovereign rights of exploration and exploitation over the continental shelf, and so on; over the high seas there is no question of title, all States having the same freedoms over it as *res communis*.

Judge *ad hoc* Torres Bernárdez returned to the question of the regime of the high seas when examining the question whether the measures taken by Canada were truly measures of 'conservation and management' so as to fall within the scope of the reservation to Canada's declaration. Essentially Spain's thesis, endorsed by the Judge, was that 'conservation and management' meant *legal* measures of conservation and management, and since no State was entitled to carry out measures of this kind in areas of the high seas, Canada's measures were illegal, and thus not genuinely measures of 'conservation and management'. As a matter of interpretation of the reservation, this would encounter the difficulty that it would mean that the reservation did not achieve the precise purpose that Canada had had in mind when presenting it;[602] but that is not here the question.

2. PROBLEMS OF PASSAGE

In the case of *Maritime Delimitation and Territorial Questions between Qatar and Bahrain*, Bahrain claimed, as 'a multiple-island State,' to be entitled to draw straight baselines 'connecting its outermost islands and such low-tide elevations as lie within their territorial waters.'[603] The Court

---

[598] [1998] ICJ Rep 606–607, para 68.

[599] Ibid, 609. para 75.   [600] Ibid, 610, para 78.

[601] Judge Torres Bernárdez argued that Spain had a 'procedural right' entitling it to bring before the Court a dispute over Canada's title or lack of title; but such a 'procedural right' is meaningless in the absence of jurisdiction. If, as the Court found, the Canadian reservation excluded from its jurisdiction the dispute actually brought before it, that was the end of the matter.

[602] A somewhat similar fate did however befall the reservation made by Yugoslavia to the optional clause declaration it made preparatory to bringing proceedings against the member States of NATO in the case of the *Legality of the Use of Force*: see, for example, [1999] ICJ Rep 551–553, paras. 24–30.

[603] [2001] ICJ Rep 103, para 210.

however found that the necessary conditions prescribed by international law for such a system to be permissible were not met; and that while Bahrain might be in effect a *de facto* archipelagic State, it had not declared itself to be such under Part IV of the 1982 Law of the Sea Convention.[604] Such a declaration, if recognized as valid, would have enabled Bahrain to draw straight baselines round the islands making up the archipelago. At an earlier stage in the judgment, the Court had however considered a claim by Bahrain that it was entitled to the status of archipelagic State even though it had not made the required declaration under the Convention; since Bahrain had not made the claim one of its formal submissions, the Court found that 'it is not requested to take a position on this issue'.[605]

The delimitation line drawn by the Court between the Qatar peninsula and the islands, appertaining to Bahrain, nearest to that peninsular (the Hawar Islands and dependencies) ran through a channel that, as the Court found, was 'narrow and shallow, and little suited to navigation.'[606] Further to the north and the south, the waters separating the two States were wider and deeper, and Qatar was thus entitled to maritime zones which were only connected, on Qatar's side of the delimitation line (or more precisely, in the area through which the delimitation line ran), by the narrow channel just referred to. The Court noted these facts, and continued:

The Court therefore emphasizes that, as Bahrain is not entitled to apply the method of straight baselines..., the waters lying between the Hawar Islands and the other Bahraini islands are not internal waters of Bahrain, but the territorial sea of that State. Consequently, Qatari vessels, like those of all other States, shall enjoy in these waters the right of innocent passage accorded by customary international law. In the same way, Bahraini vessels, like those of all other States, enjoy this right of innocent passage in the territorial sea of Qatar.[607]

The use of the word 'emphasizes' (rather than 'finds' or 'declares') seems intended to indicate that this passage is included simply *ex abundanti cautela*, and that the narrowness and inconvenience of the channel is not the reason why Qatar vessels should be able to pass between the Bahraini islands, but merely the reason why the Court considers the point, established *aliunde*, worth mentioning.

It appears to follow that if the Court, instead of leaving open the claim of Bahrain to be a *de facto* archipelagic State, had upheld that claim, so that the waters between the islands were to be treated as archipelagic waters, this would not have affected its decision on the delimitation (so that its decision to leave the archipelagic claim open was not affected by its finding on the narrowness and inconvenience of the channel). Archipelagic waters under Part IV of the Convention are of course not closed to the vessels of other States, which in principle enjoy the same

---

[604] Ibid, para 214.
[606] Ibid, 110, para 223.
[605] Ibid, 97, para 183.
[607] Ibid.

right of innocent passage as in territorial waters, though subject to suspension, as well as to the right of archipelagic sea lane passage.[608]

Nevertheless, the thinking expressed in the Court's *ex abundanti cautela* declaration is interesting in the context of the overall system of the modern law of the sea established by the Convention. The reference to the inconvenience of the narrow channel recalls the provisions in the Convention concerning straits used for international navigation, and in particular Article 36 and Article 38, paragraph 1, excluding the regime of transit passage where it is rendered effectively unnecessary by the existence of an alternative route 'of similar convenience with respect to navigational and hydrographical characteristics'.

3. IS THE CONTINENTAL SHELF 'TERRITORY'?

In the *Oil Platforms* case, the question before the Court was whether the United States, by attacking and destroying Iranian oil-drilling platforms in the Gulf, had committed a breach of the Treaty between the two States guaranteeing freedom of commerce 'between the territories' of the two contracting parties. One of the less impressive arguments advanced by the United States was to question 'whether the platforms could be said to be on the 'territory' of Iran, inasmuch as they are outside Iran's territorial sea, though upon its continental shelf, and within its exclusive economic zone'. The Court did not consider that this was a valid objection:

The Court does not however consider tenable an interpretation of the 1955 Treaty that would have differentiated, for the purposes of "freedom of commerce", between oil produced on the land territory or the territorial sea of Iran, and oil produced on its continental shelf, in the exercise of its sovereign rights of exploration and exploitation of the shelf, and parallel rights over the exclusive economic zone.[609]

This may be called a common-sense interpretation of the Treaty, on the basis of the presumed common intention of the parties; it enabled the Court to avoid the question whether, in general law and outside the context of a specific treaty, the EEZ or continental shelf forms part of the 'territory' of the State. The answer would seem to be clearly in the negative, on the basis of an *a contrario* interpretation of the term, and concept, 'territorial sea', and the limited nature of the rights enjoyed by the coastal State under Articles 56 and 77 of the Law of the Sea Convention. Were the United States' attacks therefore a use of force against the 'territorial integrity' of Iran, contrary to Article 2, paragraph 4, of the Charter? They were not pleaded as such because of the limited scope of the jurisdictional title invoked, the 1955 Treaty. The

---

[608] Articles 52–53 of the Convention.   [609] [2003] ICJ Rep 200, para 82.

question may however be academic, since it could hardly be denied that the attacks (unless justified by self-defence, as the Court found that they were not) were 'inconsistent with the Purposes of the United Nations' as contemplated by Article 2, paragraph 4. As the Court noted in *North Sea Continental Shelf*, 'the bed of [the] territorial sea...is under the full sovereignty of [the coastal] State'.[610]

4. HISTORIC RIGHTS[611]

Mention has been made, in a footnote to the previous article on the law of the sea in this series,[612] of the treatment of historic rights in the case of the *Land, Island and Maritime Frontier Dispute*, but at that time the series was regarded as more limited in temporal scope than it has proved to be. The matter was thus left for later treatment, and will be examined in this Section. Although, as the Court observed in the *Tunisia/Libya* case, '[h]istoric titles must enjoy respect and be protected as they have always been by long usage'[613], if such usage has in fact ceased, the historic titles may also have lapsed. Thus in the *Qatar/Bahrain* case, the Court took 'note of the fact that the pearling industry', invoked by Bahrain as a matter of historic right, 'ceased to exist a considerable time ago'.[614]

The problem in the earlier case was that of the status of the Gulf of Fonseca, which is unusual in that it would, were it surrounded by the territory of a single State, rank as a juridical bay, and thus as the internal waters of the coastal State,[615] but in fact three States—El Salvador, Honduras and Nicaragua—front on to the bay. Prior to the independence of the three States, Spain enjoyed sovereignty over the territory on all coasts of the bay, and over its waters as what would now be called internal waters.[616]

---

[610] [1969] ICJ Rep 31, para 43.

[611] It has been pointed out by Rosenne that the question of historic titles in the law of the sea has lost much of its 'acerbity', since a number of issues treated, prior to the United Nations Conference on the Law of the Sea, as matters of historic title, were regulated in the 1982 convention under other headings (archipelagic States, passage through international straits, etc.); Rosenne, 'Historic Waters in the Third United Nations Conference on the Law of the Sea' in *Essays on International Law and Practice*, 510. Even in 1982, before the adoption of the convention, the Court noted in the *Tunisia/ Libya* case that the historic rights claimed by Tunisia were 'more nearly related to the concept of the exclusive economic zone': [1982] ICJ Rep 74, para 100. It is thus to be expected that such issues will arise only infrequently before the Court in future.

[612] (1994) *BYIL* 1, 97, fn 414.

[613] [1982] ICJ Rep 73, para 100.

[614] [2001] ICJ Rep 112, para 236.

[615] [1992] ICJ Rep 588, para 383; 594, para 395. The Court referred in this connection to Article 4 of the 1958 Convention on the Territorial Sea and the Contiguous Zone, and Article 10 of the 1982 Law of the Sea Convention, neither of which were applicable as such, but their provisions 'might be found to express general customary law' (ibid) This cautious wording was probably used because the Chamber was speaking of a hypothetical situation.

[616] There are problems of nomenclature, as the ICJ Chamber explained, since the 1917 Judgment of the Central American Court of Justice concerning the Gulf, discussed *infra*, referred to the waters of the Gulf as *aguas territoriales*, which did not mean the same as 'territorial waters' in modern usage: see [1992] ICJ Rep 592, para 392; 596, fn 1; and 604, para 412.

As the Chamber found, the principle of *uti possidetis* was of no assistance (though applicable in principle), since there was no evidence of the attribution of the waters of the Gulf to any particular Spanish administrative entity.[617] However, there had certainly been a State succession at the time of independence, and as the Chamber observed:

A State succession is one of the ways in which territorial sovereignty passes from one State to another; and there seems no reason in principle why a succession should not create a joint sovereignty where a single and undivided maritime area passes to two or more new States.[618]

Apart from a period (1821–1839) during which the three States were members of the Republic of Central America, they had since independence enjoyed a unique system of rights over the Gulf, as was established by a judgment of the Central American Court of Justice in 1917.[619] Each State possessed a band of waters one marine league (3 nautical miles) wide around its coast as part of its territory, subject to rights of innocent passage of each of the other two States. As the Chamber held, following the Central American Court of Justice, the remainder of the waters of the Gulf were 'historic waters and subject to a joint sovereignty of the three coastal States.'[620]

It was easy to say that in principle the waters were under joint sovereignty, but the Chamber was aware of the complications resulting from the presence of the three coastal States.

For an enclosed pluri-State bay presents the need of ensuring practical rights of access from the ocean for all the coastal States; and especially so where the channels for entering the bay must be available for common user, as in the case of an enclosed sea. It was doubtless this problem of navigational access to the pluri-State bay, that accounts for the view, prevalent, though not unopposed, in the time of the 1917 Judgment and even for some years later, that in such a bay, if it is not historic waters, the territorial sea follows the sinuosities of the Coast

---

[617] Ibid, 589, para 386. The Chamber also noted that a partial maritime delimitation in 1900 between Honduras and Nicaragua 'gives no clue that it was in any way inspired by the application of the *uti possidetis juris* to the waters': ibid, 601–602, para 405.

[618] Ibid, 598, para 399.

[619] One problem with this judgment was that it was given in a dispute between El Salvador and Nicaragua, without Honduras being a party to the proceedings, so that on the principle of *res inter alios acta*, it could not be regarded as binding on Honduras, which had protested against it. The ICJ Chamber found that the judgment 'obviously...could not be *res judicata* between the Parties in the present case': [1992] ICJ rep 600, para 402. It held however that 'the Chamber should take the 1917 Judgement into account as a relevant precedent decision of a competent court, and as, in the words of Article 38 of the Court's Statute, 'a subsidiary means for the determination of rules of law'. In short, the Chamber must make up its own mind on the status of the waters of the Gulf, taking such account of the 1917 decision as it appears to the Chamber to merit': ibid, 601, para 403. It may be objected that Article 38, paragraph 1(d), of the Statute surely contemplates decisions between entities other than the parties to the proceedings before the Court, and in other disputes, but which raise the same questions of law as those the Court has to decide. The approach of the Chamber, though probably defensible in the specific case, would make it possible to turn the flank of the principle of the limited scope of *res judicata*.

[620] [1992] ICJ Rep 601, para 404.

and the remainder of the waters of the bay are part of the high seas. This solution, however, is not possible in the case of the Gulf of Fonseca since it is an historic bay and therefore a "closed sea".

The Chamber considered that the 1917 decision had been correct in finding that there was a condominium or co-ownership of the waters of the Gulf; it was at pains to emphasize the unique nature of this situation.

It seems to the Chamber that the Central American Court was correct, as a matter of international law, in holding that the mere absence of the delimitation of divisions of a maritime territory, cannot be said of itself "always" to entail a joint sovereignty over that area of maritime territory. What matters, however, is not what is "always" true, but what was the position in this particular case, in which the maritime area in question had long been historic waters under a single State's sovereignty, apparently without any demarcated administrative limits, and was in 1821 jointly acquired by the three successor States by reason of the succession. That seems to be the essence of the decision of the Central American Court for this confined maritime area which so intimately concerns all three coastal States. Certainly there is no reason why a joint sovereignty should not exist over maritime territory.[621]

But were the waters of the Gulf therefore 'internal waters', in modern terminology, not of a single State, but of the condominium of the three States? The Chamber's finding on this was as follows:

There are some difficulties in using this term which is apt to a single-State historic bay, but is not free from complications when applied to a pluri-State historic bay. Since the practice of the three coastal States still accepts that there are the littoral maritime belts subject to the single sovereignty of each of the coastal States, but with mutual rights of innocent passage, there must also be rights of passage through the remaining waters of the Gulf, not only for historical reasons but because of the practical necessities of a situation where those narrow Gulf waters comprise the channels used by vessels seeking access to any one of the three coastal States. Accordingly, these rights of passage must be available to vessels of third States seeking access to a port in any one of the three coastal States; such rights of passage being essential in a three-State bay with entrance channels that must be common to all three States. The Gulf waters are therefore, if indeed internal waters, internal waters subject to a special and particular régime, not only of joint sovereignty but of rights of passage. It might, therefore, be sensible, to regard the waters of the Gulf, insofar as they are the subject of the condominium or co-ownership, as *sui generis*. No doubt, if the waters were delimited, they would then become "internal" waters of each of the States; but even so presumably they would need to be subject to the historic and necessary rights of innocent passage, so they would still be internal waters in a qualified sense. Nevertheless, the essential juridical status of these waters is the same as that of internal waters, since they are claimed *à titre de souverain* and, though subject to certain rights of passage, they are not territorial sea.[622]

---

[621] Ibid, 599–600, para 401; as an example of a condominium of the waters of a bay, the Chamber mentioned the Baie du Figuier at the Atlantic boundary between France and Spain.

[622] Ibid, 605, para 412.

What then of the bands of waters around the coasts within the Gulf? If the whole Gulf was, in effect, internal waters, what was the status of these? The Chamber in effect reserved this question until it reached the problem of the status of the waters outside of the closing line of the Gulf, where it became relevant for reasons that will appear. It did however have this to say on the question of passage within the Gulf:

[T]he Gulf being a bay with three coastal States, there is a need for shipping to have access to any of the coastal States through the main channels between the bay and the ocean. That rights of innocent passage are not inconsistent with a régime of historic waters is clear, for that is precisely now the position in archipelagic internal waters and indeed in former high seas enclosed as internal waters by straight baselines. Furthermore, there is another practical point, for since these waters were outside the 3-mile maritime belts of exclusive jurisdiction in which innocent passage was nevertheless recognized in practice, it would have been absurd not to recognize passage rights in these waters, which had to be crossed in order to reach these maritime belts.[623]

A further complication was that there had been a partial delimitation, again between only two of the Gulf States, of the waters of the Gulf, effected by Nicaragua and Honduras in 1900.[624] The Chamber was able to find on the facts that this delimitation, to which El Salvador was not a party, had nevertheless been 'accepted by El Salvador in the terms indicated in the 1917 Judgment.'[625]

The practical problem facing the Chamber was the disagreement between the parties, and involving Nicaragua as intervening State, on the question whether the Chamber should effect a delimitation of the waters within the Gulf. As the Chamber pointed out,[626] there were in fact two questions here, one procedural and one substantive: had the Chamber been given jurisdiction by the Special Agreement to effect a delimitation; and was the nature of the juridical situation of the waters such

---

[623] [1992] ICJ Rep 593, para 393. In respect of the second sentence, see Articles 52 and 8, paragraph 2, of the 1982 Law of the Sea Convention (and cf. also Article 35(a)). Since these provisions of the Convention are not presented as codifying existing customary law, they do not seem of themselves to support the Chamber's conclusion as to a legal situation existing at least since 1917.

[624] Ibid, 590, para 389.

[625] ibid, 606, para 413. There is a slight logical difficulty in the Chamber's reasoning here: it based its conclusion on the fact that El Salvador accepted—indeed, invoked—the 1917 Judgment, and that Judgement had found that the waters of the Gulf were 'undivided and in a state of community between El Salvador and Nicaragua', i.e. the parties to the 1917 proceedings, but 'with the exception of' the part divided in 1900. It is however not at all clear that the Central American Court was making any finding as to the validity or opposability of the Honduras/Nicaragua delimitation; at a later stage in its decision it declared the existence of the condominium over the waters of the Gulf with no other exception than that of the belt of one marine league around the coasts: see the translation in the AJIL used by the Chamber, at 716, quoted at [1992] ICJ Rep 596–597, para 397. Nor was a decision on the validity of the bilateral delimitation necessary to decide the essential question in dispute: the consistency of the Bryan-Chamorro Treaty with the legal situation in the Gulf.

[626] [1992] ICJ Rep 603, para 409. The Chamber had in fact already decided that the Special Agreement had not given it jurisdiction to delimit the waters; but if it had accepted the contention of Honduras it would presumably be bound to make a finding to that effect, leaving the parties then to carry out the delimitation that the law required.

that they could, or should, in law be delimited? Honduras had rejected the 'condominium' that was the basis of the 1917 Judgment, in favour of a similar concept which it termed a 'community of interests', which would 'not merely permit of a delimitation of the waters but necessitates such a delimitation.'[627] The Chamber however preferred the view of El Salvador:

The juridical situation of the Gulf of Fonseca, derived from its particular individual nature, does not permit the dividing up of the waters held in condominium precisely because what was in issue was not the recognition of common ownership of an object which is capable of being divided up but rather the definition of an object which had, for geographical reasons, an indivisible character given its configuration and dimensions.[628]

The Chamber did not however read this as a suggestion that 'the waters subject to joint sovereignty cannot be divided, if there is agreement to do so', and added that 'Condominia can cease to exist given the necessary agreement.'[629] It continued with a passage that seems to be directed to the idea that, exceptionally, what can be done by agreement may not be possible by judicial decision:

Account must be taken of the fact that the geographical situation of the Gulf, which underlies the juridical status of the waters, is such that mere delimitation without agreement on questions of passage and access would leave many practical problems unsolved. It is not easy to conceive of a satisfactory final solution without the participation of all three States together in the creation of a suitable régime, whether or not including delimitation of separate areas of internal waters.[630]

When the Chamber turned to the question of the status of the waters outside the Gulf, it was clear that the vital element was that of the rights of Honduras, the State at the back of the Gulf. Did it have any rights to territorial sea, continental shelf or EEZ outside the closing line of the Gulf; or was it cut off from the high seas by the entitlements within the Gulf of the two States on either side of the opening, El Salvador and Nicaragua? As regards the territorial sea, the first question was whether any territorial sea at all could be claimed outside the closing line. The normal situation, expressed in Article 10 of the 1982 Law of the Sea

---

[627] Ibid, 603, para 408.
[628] Quoted from El Salvador pleadings (no reference given) at [1992] ICJ Rep 603, para 409.
[629] Ibid.
[630] Ibid, 603–604. If there were a joint request by all three States to the Court for a delimitation, would the Court be entitled to lay down provisions for passage and access? To do so would apparently be to legislate, since by definition no such provision yet existed, and there would not seem to be any existing rules applicable. Would the approach of the *Gulf of Maine* chamber to the problem of the absence of State practice as to the single maritime boundary be available, that is to say recourse to a more fundamental norm? Cf. the directive by the Court in the *Qatar/Bahrain* case concerning mutual rights of passage through each other's territorial sea, rendered necessary by the Court's finding on the Bahraini baselines: [2001] ICJ Rep 110, para 223, and comment above, this Chapter, Section 2. This part of the judgment was however avowedly declaratory.

Convention, would be that the waters of a bay would be internal waters, and the breadth of the territorial sea of the coastal State could be calculated from the closing line.[631] But each State within the Gulf already possessed a territorial sea, or something very similar, in the form of the 3 nautical mile belt around its coast. The Chamber was thus driven back to the question of the status of this belt.

That a State cannot have two territorial seas off the same littoral is manifest. The question arises, however, whether the littoral maritime belts of 1 marine league along the coastlines of the Gulf are truly territorial seas in the sense of the modern law of the sea. In the view of the Chamber they are not. For a territorial sea normally has beyond it the continental shelf, and either waters of the high seas (in some cases with a contiguous zone of jurisdiction) or an exclusive economic zone. The maritime belts within the Gulf do not have outside them any of these areas. In fact it is the closing line of the Gulf which constitutes "the coast", in the sense of a territorial sea baseline; and this would seem to be so whether the Gulf waters are regarded as subject to joint sovereignty, or indeed, as Honduras would have it, as waters subject to undelimited separate sovereignties subject to a community of interest. The inner littoral maritime belts are therefore certainly not territorial seas in the sense of the modern law. Those maritime belts within the Gulf may properly be regarded as the internal waters of the coastal State, not being subject to the joint sovereignty, and even though subject, as indeed are all the waters of the Gulf, to rights of innocent passage that owe their origin to the exigencies and resulting history of a three-State but relatively small bay, with its problems of navigational access.[632]

There was perhaps a further reason, not stated, why the 3-mile belts could not treated as territorial waters. If that was their status in 1917, such status would presumably follow the development of the law, and as a result would, according to modern law, be extendable to 12 miles (except where they would meet the territorial seas of one or other of the other two States). As a result of the shape of the bay, this would meant that all waters behind the closing line would be territorial sea of El Salvador or of Nicaragua, thus effectively cutting off Honduras from any claim to areas of the seabed or water-column outside the Gulf.

5. FLAGS AND REGISTRATION OF SHIPS

In the *Oil Platforms* case, the United States responded to the Iranian claim of unlawful attacks on its oil-production platforms by invoking self-defence, as a circumstance excluding responsibility. In addition to invoking a specific missile attack on a US-registered ship in Kuwaiti waters, the United States referred to 'a series of unlawful armed attacks

---

[631] As the Chamber observed, '[t]here can be no serious doubt that the closing line of a historic bay is the baseline of the territorial sea': [1992] ICJ Rep 607, para 417; but does 'serious doubt' suggest that there might be a slight doubt?
[632] [1992] ICJ Rep 607, para 416.

by Iranian forces against the United States, including laying mines in international waters for the purposes of sinking or damaging United States flag ships...'[633] Among the specific incidents enumerated by the United States was 'the mining of the United States-owned *Texaco Caribbean* on 10 August 1987'; the Court however noted that that vessel, 'whatever its ownership, was not flying a United States flag, so that an attack on that vessel is not in itself to be equated with an attack on that State'.[634]

This finding would support a general rule that an armed attack on a vessel flying a flag of convenience can only be construed, for purposes of the law relating to self-defence, as an attack on the flag State, not on the State whose nationals own or operate the ship, or which is itself the owner of it. The reasoning appears to be sound: an armed attack on a State, such as to justify self-defence, is *ex hypothesi* a deliberate act aimed at a specific State, and the target is identified as associated with that State, in the case of a ship, by the national flag, not by its ownership.[635] However, the majority of the flags-of-convenience (FOC) States do not cut such a figure in international affairs that they would be likely to be the targets of armed attack; a deliberate attack on such a vessel would in practice therefore be more likely to have been aimed at the State whose material interests are really involved.[636] In the field of diplomatic protection of ships, the fact that only the FOC State can make a formal claim and institute judicial proceedings, for example, does not seem to cause problems. For example, as Judge Anderson notes, applications have been made to ITLOS for prompt release of detained vessels by States with 'open registers' who do not, in all probability, have any real interest in the fate of the vessel, but are acting at the instance of those who do.[637] The only parallel in the context of armed attack would seem to be a request addressed by the flag State to the State really concerned with a view to the exercise of collective self-defence, which may be politically unrealistic.[638]

---

[633] [2003] ICJ Rep 191, para 62.

[634] Ibid, para 64.

[635] *Cf* also the Court's interpretation of the term 'ship-owning nations' in the *Maritime Safety Committee* case as referring to the States of registration, regardless of actual ownership of the individual vessels: [1960] ICJ Rep 167–168, where certainty was required, so that there should be 'an automatic criterion to determine the point of time at which the Convention comes into force.'

[636] Since the *Texaco Caribbean* struck a mine, an indiscriminate weapon, it would have been difficult to maintain that it was a selected target.

[637] D Anderson, 'Freedoms of the High Seas in the Modern law of the Sea', in D Freestone, R Barnes and D M Ong (eds), *The Law of the Sea: Progress and Prospects* (2006) 327, 336–337. Anderson suggests that a similar procedure might be available to compel compliance with Article 94(6) of ITLOS concerning failure to exercise jurisdiction and control over registered vessels.

[638] Cf. the ruling in the *Military and Paramilitary Activities* case that such a request is a *conditio sine qua non* for the exercise of collective self-defence: [1986] ICJ Rep 105, para 199.

BRITISH ACTS OF STATE IN
ENGLISH COURTS

By Amanda Perreau-Saussine[1]

[1] University Lecturer in Law and Fellow of Queens' College, University of Cambridge. For comments on earlier drafts of this essay, I am much indebted to Dapo Akande, James Crawford, Julian Rivers, Nicholas McBride, Roger O'Keefe, Derek Oulton, Brian Simpson, Michael Singer and David Williams, as also to Adam Tomkins and Geoff McLay for allowing me to see copies of forthcoming work on remedies against the Crown.

Underlying act of state doctrines is the idea that the survival of a community may depend upon treating foreigners, and perhaps citizens, in ways that would usually violate legal or even moral rules. Acts of state are actions such as these, taken in the name and the interests of the state to further the public good: "when the act accuses, the result excuses."[2] This essay offers an account of act of state doctrines as applied by English courts to actions of the British government overseas. It is a study of "domestic" act of state doctrines concerning actions of the British state, as distinct from doctrines concerning the incompetence of English courts to adjudicate on the validity or legality of the acts of foreign states.[3] The subject might seem arcane, but the case law sheds light on enduring questions concerning the nature of English public law and its relationship with public international law, as well as on the question of the availability of remedies against the Crown.

Any study which aims to make sense of English act of state doctrines must grapple with two particular problems. First, it must refer to the rules of English constitutional law on prerogative power, "the residue of discretionary power left at any moment in the hands of the Crown, whether such power be in fact exercised by the King himself or by his Ministers".[4] English constitutional lawyers disagree on what these rules are. They disagree on how far, if at all, the monarch's traditional prerogative powers have been subsumed within a set of legally constrained executive powers of the state. At one extreme, British governmental power is held to be a matter of the prerogative powers and immunities special to the Crown and its agents, accountable politically before Parliament; such powers and immunities are non-justiciable in English

---

[2] Machiavelli *Discourses on Livy* Book I Chapter 9.

[3] The focus is on acts of the British state in *English* courts as historically Scottish courts have taken a "more robust view of the individual's rights against the Crown than did the law of England" (Lord Jauncey in *BMA v Greater Glasgow Health Board* 1989 SC (HL) 65, 94); elements of that distinctive approach endure in contemporary Scots law. See generally Adam Tomkins "The Crown in Scots Law" in A McHarg and T Mullen (eds) *Public law in Scotland* (Avizandum: Edinburgh, 2006) 262–280.

[4] A V Dicey *Introduction to the study of the law of the constitution* (10th edn, 1959) at 424.

courts, whose concern is and should be only with the oversight of administrative action.[5] At the other extreme, every power used in government
is termed executive power, and in the name of either the rule of law or
parliamentary sovereignty or both, government is treated as accountable
to Parliament and in English courts for the way it exercises each and
every one of its executive powers.[6]

Since this study concerns the applicability of English act of state
doctrines to government action overseas, it must also address a second
problematic area of constitutional law, that of the status of rules of
international law: again, British politicians, jurists and judges have long
disagreed on the ways (if any) in which rules of international law form
constraints enforceable in English courts on government action.[7]

Given these conflicting accounts of the extent of the government's
legal accountability before English courts and the relevance or otherwise

---

[5] Such accounts often cite Locke's definition of sovereign prerogative power as "the power of
doing public good without a rule", suggesting that its only and ultimate check is popular revolt:
Second Treatise Chapter 14 "Of Prerogative" ss 168, 166.

For Blackstone "[Prerogative] signifies, in its etymology (from *prae* and *rogo*) something that is
required or demanded before, or in preference to, all others. And hence it follows, that it must be in
its nature singular and eccentrical; that it can only be applied to those rights and capacities which
the king enjoys alone, in contradistinction to others, and not to those which he enjoys in common
with any of his subjects; for if once any one prerogative of the crown could be held in common with
the subject, it would cease to be prerogative any longer." Blackstone *Commentaries on the Laws of
England* (Clarendon: Oxford, 1765–9) Bk I, Chapter 7, at 239. But, like most constitutional lawyers
after him, Blackstone was unclear about how far the feudal prerogative powers of the Crown and
its agents should be treated as executive powers subject to legal constraint: "Ever since Blackstone
wrote his *Commentaries*, British law has been wavering between the discourse of prerogative and the
modern language of executive power" (Denis Baranger "Executive power in France" in Paul Craig
and Adam Tomkins (eds) *The executive and public law: power and accountability in comparative
perspective* (Oxford University Press, 2005) 217–242, 218).

[6] Thus Lord Diplock argues in *Town Investments v Department of the Environment* [1978] AC 359
at 380G–381B that it would be preferable "Where...we are concerned with the legal nature of the
exercise of executive powers of government...instead of speaking of 'the Crown'...to speak of 'the
government'—a term appropriate to embrace both collectively and individually all of the ministers
of the Crown and parliamentary secretaries under whose direction the administrative work of government is carried on by the civil servants employed in the various government departments". See
also his reference to "the Crown, which today personifies the executive government of the country"
in *BBC v Johns* [1965] Ch 32 at 79.

The debate on control of prerogative powers is an ongoing one: see in particular the House of
Commons Public Administration Select Committee's Fourth Report (4 March 2004) championing
full-scale law reform in the form of a "Ministers of the Crown (Executive Powers) Bill" as drafted
by Professor Rodney Brazier (online at www.publications.parliament.uk/pa/cm200304/cmselect/
cmpubadm/422/42202.htm,) and the current, eviscerated Constitutional Reform (Prerogative
Powers and Civil Service etc.) Bill (brought from the House of Lords, 25 July 2006) at http://
www.publications.parliament.uk/pa/pabills/200506/constitutional_reform_prerogative_powers_
and_civil_service_etc.htm, excluding not only personal prerogative powers (as in Brazier's version,
cl 1(3)) but *all* "rights and powers which belong to Her Majesty in right of the Crown..., and
which are necessary to allow Her Majesty to continue to act as The Queen in Council or as Head
of State".

[7] See further Amanda Perreau-Saussine "Foreign views on eating aliens: the roots and implications of recent English decisions on customary international law as a source of common law limits
on executive power" in Colin Warbrick and Stephen Tierney (eds) *Towards an international legal
community? The sovereignty of states and the sovereignty of international law* (British Institute for
International and Comparative Law: London, 2006) 75–129.

of international law in such proceedings, it is unsurprising that accounts of English act of state doctrines vary widely. This essay is structured chronologically; it focuses on rival act of state doctrines at their moments of strongest influence. But although rival accounts have each enjoyed times of particular influence, a study of English case law on acts of state cannot be presented as the history of the emergence of one rule, any more than an historical study of English constitutional law could establish the final victory of Enlightenment notions of legally accountable government or Republican notions of political accountability over feudal notions of Crown immunity.[8] Underlying the historical accounts are three rationales, all of which endure as rival English act of state doctrines.[9] This essay aims to shed light on this area of English constitutional law by using a study of leading cases to trace these three doctrines.

THREE RATIONALES FOR THE ENGLISH ACT OF STATE DOCTRINE

On one account, in rare circumstances it can be both necessary and just for a sovereign to rob foreigners (and perhaps even his own subjects overseas) or to deprive foreigners (and perhaps even subjects) of basic personal liberties. On this first account, any assessment of the justice of

---

[8] For a thought-provoking survey of historical selectivity in twentieth century traditions in English public law see John Allison *The English historical constitution: continuity, change and European effects* (Cambridge University Press, 2007); see also Martin Loughlin *Public law and political theory* (Clarendon: Oxford, 1992) (especially chapters 5, 7 and 9 on what he calls "Normativism", Oxbridge liberal writing—focussing on the work of A.V Dicey, William Wade, Paul Craig and Trevor Allan) and David Dyzenhaus "The Left and the question of law" (2004) 17 *Canadian Journal of Law and Jurisprudence* 7–30 (on public law traditions linked with the London School of Economics, focussing on John Griffiths and recent followers in his tradition—Martin Loughlin, Keith Ewing and Adam Tomkins). For an attempt to present English constitutional history as a victory for political (Parliamentary) accountability, see Jeffrey Goldsworthy *The sovereignty of Parliament* (Clarendon: Oxford, 1999) and the critical review essays by Douglas Edlin ("Rule Britannia" (2002) 52 *University of Toronto Law Journal* 313–329) and Mark Walters ("Common law, reason and sovereign will" (2003) 53 *University of Toronto Law Journal* 65–88).

[9] Holdsworth (*History of English Law* (Methuen: London, 1964) XIV 28–52) runs together the first two doctrines (31–32) and asserts that one clear "modern basis" for acts of state has been "established" (45). He holds that the Crown can certify conclusively as to matters of state, but that the courts can decide if the Crown has acted within this power of certification, as more generally whether it has acted within "its power to perform acts of state"(46): if an act alleged to be an act of state is within the Crown's prerogative powers, "it is a valid act of state and the jurisdiction of the courts is ousted: if it is not within these powers it is not an act of state, and the persons who have done the act are responsible in law to any persons injured thereby, in accordance with the doctrine of ministerial responsibility"(51). Holdsworth's account evades the legal issues at stake in act of state cases. Either courts can determine whether an action of the Crown is such an improper use of power that it cannot be characterised as falling within the lawful boundaries of the relevant power (in which case, acts of state are justiciable and the courts can enter into a minimal "merits" review of their justice: the third doctrine, considered in Section III below) or courts cannot adjudicate on the use of such powers and then acts of state are better characterised as non-justiciable (*pace* Cane, below n 25 and accompanying text).

such actions is a political rather than a legal matter. Judicial scrutiny of such unpleasant if necessary actions should be minimised, either because judges lack the capacity or the political legitimacy to assess the political issues at stake, or to avoid a public scrutiny in court that could lead to revulsion among citizens, and to disorder if citizens assumed a licence to follow suit. On this account, the English act of state doctrine is best understood as rendering acts of state non-justiciable: the act of state doctrine identifies acts of state which fall outside the law, actions which are inherently political, and as such are not, or should not be, subject to legal assessment.

On a second account, there is law applicable to acts of state, but (since acts of state are by definition taken on foreign territory) that applicable law is international law rather than English law. This view raises in turn questions about the appropriate forum for application of the relevant rules of international law. As a matter of English law, this means that English courts exercise only a rare and exceptional jurisdiction over overseas acts of the British state: the English act of state doctrine is best understood as a jurisdictional rule.

On a third and final account, acts of state are legally defensible "acts of governance" because and in so far as they are just. The English act of state doctrine is best understood as a legal defence, one that can be invoked by officials to shift sole responsibility for their actions onto the Crown, and so one that recognises the executive's powers to take actions overseas in the interests of the country that would be unlawful were they private acts of an individual. But on this third account of acts of state, the award of compensation to individuals affected by the Crown's acts overseas is a justiciable issue. An act of state defence can be raised by the Crown only where just compensation has been offered; where it has not, the Crown's actions are legally *ultra vires*.

I begin below by elaborating on these three doctrines, and then turn to a more detailed analysis of each one, focusing on the main cases in which the relevant accounts of the act of state doctrine emerge. The cases fall in clusters: the first rationale emerges in a set of decisions concerning legal challenges relating to the establishment and governance of the British Empire; the second rationale emerges in decisions concerning exercises of prerogative powers in the wake of decolonisation; the third rationale emerges sporadically in cases where English courts focus on the justice or otherwise of the Crown's actions overseas.

(i)   The first doctrine: acts of state as non-justiciable because not regulated by law

On one account, it is for the sovereign (and, in modern versions, Parliament) and not the sovereign's courts to judge whether or not the executive has acted in the state's interests. Acts of state should be treated as non-justiciable and withdrawn from the courts: they raise inherently political questions, questions which as a matter of constitutional history courts have not resolved, and which in democratic constitutional theory courts should not resolve. In the blunt terms attributed to Anthony Eden, rejecting the suggestion that the Foreign Office Legal Adviser should be informed of plans relating to Suez, "The lawyers are always against our doing anything. For God's sake keep them out of it. This is a political affair."[10] Acts of state, on this account, are simply not matters subject to legal regulation at all: they are outside the law, "acts by arbitrary power on behalf of the Crown" and acts for which no attempt is made to offer justification "under colour of legal title". The execution of such "a political measure" is not a matter for "the judgment of a legal tribunal".[11]

On such accounts, acts of state are actions of high policy which fall outside the law and therefore outside the jurisdiction of any court. They are to be judged only in terms of divine law, or of moral and political rules, or of expediency, and not in terms of English law. And judgments about their justice are to be made in the sovereign's conscience, or by the King and his Council, or by Parliament, or by the electorate.

Such an account of the overseas powers of the British government is articulated in the work of the late William Wade, who has had considerable influence on the development of English constitutional and administrative law:

It is not so much a matter of nationality as of geography—that is to say, the Crown enjoys no dispensation for acts done within the jurisdiction, whether the plaintiff be British or foreign; but foreign parts are beyond the pale (in Kipling's words, 'without the law'), and there the Crown has a free hand, whether the plaintiff be foreign or British.[12]

James Fitzjames Stephen offers a similar account of acts of state: "The principle is that the acts of a sovereign State are final, and can be called in question only by war, or by an appeal to the justice of the State itself. They cannot be examined into by the courts of the State which does them."[13] As Stephen notes, "If one British subject puts another to death or destroys his property by the express command of the King, that command is no protection to the person who executes it unless it is in itself

---

[10] Sir Anthony Nutting *No end of a lesson: the story of Suez* (Clarkson N Potter: New York, 1967) 95, quoted in Geoffrey Marston "Armed Intervention in the 1956 Suez Canal Crisis: the legal advice tendered to the British Government" (1988) 37 *ICLQ* 773, 798.

[11] The phrases are those of Lord Kingsdown in *Kamachee* [1859] 13 Moo PC 22 at 77 and 85: see below n59 and accompanying text

[12] Wade *Administrative law* (Clarendon Press, Oxford 1st edn, 1961) at 230; Wade and Forsyth *Administrative law* (Oxford University Press) [hereafter "Wade and Forsyth"] 8th edn, 2000 at 824; 9th edn 2004 at 840. In the first edition, this passage concludes with an additional sentence omitted from the second edition (Clarendon Press: Oxford 1967 at 272) and subsequent editions: "British courts maintain the rule of law at home, but there are limits to their jurisdiction." Wade was sole author of the first six editions of the book, joint editor of the seventh and eighth editions with Christopher Forsyth, and died in 2004 shortly before the ninth edition was published.

[13] James Fitzjames Stephen *A history of the criminal law Vol II* (Macmillan: London, 1883) 64.

lawful, and it is the duty of the proper courts of justice to determine whether it is lawful or not."[14] But "if such acts are done by public authority, or, having been done, are ratified by public authority, they fall outside the sphere of the criminal law": "as between British subjects and foreigners, the orders of the Crown justify what they command so far as British courts of justice are concerned".[15]

Stephen's reference to an "appeal to the justice of the State" raises the question of whether such actions are constrained by international law: accompanying this first act of state doctrine, focussing on non-justiciable matters, is a deep scepticism about the legal character of rules of international law. Writing in the wake of the 1871 *Alabama* settlement, Stephen argues that since nations have no "common superior", the authority of international principles of arbitration depends entirely on the will of the parties.[16] For Stephen, as "the great mass of mankind are and always will be to a greater or lesser extent the avowed enemies of considerable sections of their fellow creatures", the only universal principle or *ratio ultima* of kings and "human society in all its shapes" is "the compulsion of war".[17] War decides "whether nations are to be and what they are to be", "what men shall believe, how they shall live, in what mould their religion, law, morals, and the whole tone of their lives shall be cast", and in estimating the character of a war we should take into account not merely who was on the offensive or who struck the first blow "but much more the question, Which of the conflicting theories of life, which of the opposing principles brought into collision, was the noblest, the truest, the best fitted for the development of the powers of human nature, most in harmony with the facts which surround and constitute human life?"[18] All great wars are "wars of principle and sentiment": the wisdom and nobility of a victor will be an element of his strength, and international law is but a reflection or projection of the principles of the strong, a "branch of State morality".[19] In Posner's summary, Stephen's position is one of "utter willingness to rule other peoples, rooted in supreme confidence in the superiority of one's own civilization."[20] That confidence extends to the mechanisms of political as opposed to legal accountability.

---

[14] Ibid at 65.

[15] Ibid at 63, 65.

[16] James Fitzjames Stephen *Liberty, equality, fraternity* Richard A Posner (ed) (University of Chicago Press, 1991) at 239.

[17] Ibid at 164.

[18] Stephen *Liberty, equality, fraternity* at 166 (*ultima ratio regem* is said to have been inscribed around Fredrick the Great's cannon), 165.

[19] Stephen *Liberty, equality, fraternity* at 165, 51 (*Preface to second edition*). For Stephen, to make love for humanity the basis of ones creed is about as silly as declaring: "The human race is an enormous agglomeration of bubbles which are continuously bursting and ceasing to be. No one made it or knows anything worth knowing about it. Love it dearly, O ye bubbles." (243).

[20] Richard A Posner, "Forward" to *Liberty, equality, fraternity* at 8.

(ii)   The second doctrine (a re-writing of the first): acts of state as purely matters of international law and so outside the jurisdiction of English courts

By contrast with the previous account of acts of state, this second account assumes a robust account of the legal character of rules of international law. According to this second account, one that dominates contemporary writing on acts of state, the government actions at issue are susceptible to legal assessment: it is not that there is no law that applies, nor that judges lack a particular capacity to apply the relevant rules of law. But the applicable law is international law and as such to be applied by states among themselves or by an international tribunal, but rarely (if at all) by English courts.

On this account, as actions taken by the Crown or sovereign overseas, acts of state fall outside the jurisdiction of that same sovereign's own courts of law. Legal assessment of acts of state is normally an exclusively international matter since by definition acts of state involve conflicts between different states' interests. Act of state doctrines are then best understood as jurisdictional rules of English law, ones by which English courts have no jurisdiction over international law disputes unless specifically given it.[21] The central question then concerns the possible sources of that exceptional jurisdiction.

(iii)   The third rationale: acts of state as just and legally defensible as such

On a rival account of responsible rule, one at least as venerable as the Thrasymachean or Machiavellian one, prudent sovereigns have a responsibility to maintain and teach the spirit or reason of the laws, something they should treat as binding upon themselves: "the man who tastes a single piece of human flesh...is fated to become a wolf".[22] Such "rule of law" accounts recognise that government requires prerogative powers unavailable to ordinary citizens, but treat these powers as constrained in that acts of state are lawful when and only in so far as they are just:

Judges ought above all to remember the conclusion of the Roman Twelve Tables; *Salus populi suprema lex*: and to know that laws, except they be in order to that end, are but things captious and oracles not well inspired. Therefore it is a happy thing in a State when Kings and States do often consult with judges; and again when judges do often consult with the King and State...[23]

---

[21] See Dapo Akande, "Non-justiciability and the foreign act of state doctrine in English courts" (forthcoming).

[22] Plato *Republic* Bk VIII 565e.

[23] Bacon "Essay of Judicature" *Works VI*, 509.

On this third account, a governmental plea of act of state operates as a defence. If—but only if—a court can be convinced that an otherwise tortious or criminal action by the executive overseas was likely to be in the British state's interest, this will render lawful what would otherwise be unlawful: "It is, I think, for the courts to determine in any particular case as it comes up whether, as matter of policy—the policy of the law— the defence of act of state should be available."[24]

Crucial to this third doctrine is the question of compensation of victims of acts of state. On the first account of the act of state doctrine, the defensibility or justice of acts of state (including the question of compensation) is exclusively a matter of political rather than legal accountability: acts of state are legally non-justiciable and so in English law the Crown has no legal obligation to rectify the harms it has caused. Instead in law it enjoys the freedom to shift the costs of the defence of the state's interests or concerns overseas onto foreigners and perhaps even British subjects. By contrast, on this third and rival account of the doctrine, acts of state are legally defensible, but raising a defence of act of state does not absolve the Crown from acting justly towards those individuals particularly affected: the defence requires that the Crown act justly towards victims of an act of state. If the Crown's actions cannot be characterised as just under any circumstances, then the Crown cannot assert that they amount to an act of state. To characterise a government action as a genuine act of state is to say that it is one considered necessary for the promotion or protection of the public good, and is not only legally but also morally defensible if just compensation has been paid.

The three sections of this essay below trace the case law from which emerge these three accounts of act of state doctrine. A brief concluding discussion suggests reasons for developing the final one of these three rationales.

I   ACTS OF STATE AS NON-JUSTICIABLE BECAUSE SUBJECT TO POLITICAL RATHER THAN LEGAL CONTROL

For the first two thirds of the twentieth century, and in the name of democratic constitutionalism, English public lawyers commonly treated the executive as answerable only to Parliament for the way it exercised its prerogative powers (powers for the protection and promotion of the public good): the executive was answerable to English courts only when and in so far as Parliament had given the courts this role through legislation. Without clear statutory principles given to them by Parliament, it was argued that the courts lacked legal rules with which to scrutinise executive action. By default, scrutiny was a task requiring political judgment by elected

---

[24] Denning LJ in *Buttes Gas and Oil Co v Hammer* [1975] QB. 557 at 573–4 citing *Buron v Denman* (on which see Section III(iii), below).

politicians. And since prerogative powers are residual, non-statutory powers, their exercise was by definition a non-justiciable matter: questions of compensation were questions of justice, politics or humanity—but not of English law.

Articulating this vision of prerogative powers, Peter Cane, writing in 1980, suggested that the obscurity of English law on acts of state could be removed by interpreting every branch of it as based on the non-justiciability of prerogative powers:

The rules about acts of State represent an attempt to set the bounds of judicial control of the Executive in the area of foreign relations. In this light it will be suggested that elaborate attempts to distinguish between prerogative acts and acts of State are misguided because the most important characteristic of both types of act is that they lie beyond the scope of judicial review.

... (i) As a matter of constitutional history, the exercise of certain powers has been left to the discretion of the Crown, subject only to legislative encroachment and the control of the courts in [setting broad limits within which the Crown may operate as it pleases.]

(ii) As a matter of constitutional theory, the courts are not the proper bodies to decide whether decisions on certain matters of "high policy" were proper; they are neither representative nor responsible.

(iii) Certain activities, such as foreign relations and war, are most unsuitably conducted by judicial methods of decision making.[25]

Cane's general assertion that prerogative acts by definition "lie beyond the scope of judicial review" was questionable as an articulation of a principle of English common law even at the time he wrote. Many constitutional lawyers would have emphasized that the prerogative is a residual category and so not necessarily coherent: they might also have echoed Lord Devlin's insistence in *Chandler* that "[t]he courts will not review the proper exercise of discretionary power but they will intervene to correct excess or abuse."[26] And in the *GCHQ* case, decided after Cane wrote, the House of Lords famously insisted on their general common law jurisdiction to review the use of prerogative powers even in the absence of legislation.[27]

This assertion of a general jurisdiction to review the executive's use of the prerogative was coupled with a list of off-limits powers.[28] The Lords pointed to general common law principles of rationality which they held were available for reviewing exercises of prerogative power: an administrative decision flouting these principles would be *ultra vires* and unlawful. But some exercises of prerogative power remained

---

[25] Cane "Prerogative acts, acts of state and justiciability" (1980) 29 *ICLQ* 680, 680–681.

[26] *Chandler v Director of Public Prosecutions* [1964] AC 763 at 810. See also the influential Divisional Court decision (Lord Parker CJ and Diplock LJ) in *R v Criminal Injuries Compensation Board ex p Lain* [1967] 2 QB 864.

[27] *Council of Civil Service Unions v Minister for the Civil Service* [1985] AC 374, 398.

[28] As such, *GCHQ* adopts the position Cane recommended: "It is more desirable to lay down relatively specific rules as to when the courts may intervene and when they should defer."(ibid at 699)

non-justiciable: "those relating to the making of treaties, the defence of the realm, the prerogative of mercy, the grant of honours, the dissolution of Parliament and the appointment of ministers" all lay beyond the reach of judicial review.[29] This non-exhaustive list of non-justiciable powers signalled that in some cases involving the exercise of prerogative powers the application of the otherwise relevant legal principles was to be suspended. There remained a set of "legal black holes" within the law of the land, a set of situations where there is no law.[30]

Some public lawyers would argue that this is a mis-characterisation of the legal position. Building on the venerable argument that "the King hath no prerogative, but that which the law of the land allows him"[31], it must follow, they insist, that the courts always have jurisdiction to determine whether a particular prerogative exists. And if it does exist, its exercise is by definition lawful: the relevant powers are recognised by law and so lawful, but there is no legal control over their abuse. Thus Cane writes:

provided the power purportedly exercised falls within the limits of the prerogative as recognized by the common law, it is entirely up to the Crown to decide what it will do in pursuance of that power. Any exercise of it will be, in the eyes of the law, valid and legally effective. The position is not that the Crown has legal power to do any act of certain descriptions whether lawful or not—a clearly nonsensical proposition—but that any act of certain descriptions done by the Crown is lawful.[32]

There are two objections to this popular account of non-justiciable acts as nonetheless "lawful". At the level of constitutional law, it assimilates non-justiciability with a defence, suggesting that law plays a role where it does not: as such, it is a potentially dangerous constitutional fiction. In Dyzenhaus's terms, it is to suggest that there are not black but only grey holes in the law: "grey holes are disguised black holes, and if the disguise is left in place governments will claim that they govern in accordance with the rule of law and thus garner the legitimacy that attaches to that claim."[33] But also, and less controversially (since some would treat constitutional fictions as politically expedient), this account of non-justiciable acts fails to reflect the classic leading cases on acts of state which are analysed below. The most widely cited cases where this first rationale is given to the act of state doctrine are part of a series of decisions in which

---

[29] Lord Roskill at 418.

[30] The term "legal black hole" is from David Dyzenhaus *The constitution of law: legality in time of emergency* (Cambridge University Press, 2006) at 3 and 61, building on Lord Phillips', characteristic of the position of detainees in Guantanamo Bay: *R v Secretary of State for Foreign and Commonwealth Affairs ex p Abbasi* [2002] EWCA Civ 1598 para 64.

[31] Edward Coke in *Case of the Proclamations* (1611) 2 Co Rep 74 at 76.

[32] Cane "Prerogative acts, acts of state and justiciability", above n 25, 682.

[33] Dyzenhaus *The constitution of law*, above n 30, at 3 and 231–2, arguing that to the extent that "the prerogative can still be invoked as the basis for an official act, a common law legal order has not yet fully taken [..the step] insisting that no official may act unless there is a warrant in a valid law of that order". See also Adam Tomkins *Our Republican constitution* (Hart Publishing, 2005) 103–9.

Crown action overseas is treated as non-justiciable *because* the imperial expansions involved were acts "of arbitrary power" which were not performed "under colour of legal title". Mann's summary of the position is to be preferred:

Justiciability...depends on whether the act in question is performed under colour of legal title. If it is not, if, in other words, it rests on the exercise of power, whether it is being described as arbitrary, sovereign or executive, it is not justiciable...[34]

The doctrine that acts of state are non-justiciable is best understood as isolating certain actions of the Crown from legal scrutiny, removing them from the jurisdiction of its courts by insisting that on the justice of these actions the executive is answerable to Parliament alone. This, I will argue below, reflects more accurately both the leading cases and their constitutional consequences.

(i) Conflicting cases on imperial acts of state in India as non-justiciable: the Nabob of Arcot's debts

In the pair of cases with which the series opens, the Nabob of Arcot (the capital of the Carnatic) sought from the East India Company an account of his revenues.[35] The Nabob was the first of the "glittering puppets" in the names of whom Lord Clive conducted his campaigns on behalf of the British East India Company against Dupleix and the rival French company.[36] In part to gain for himself public recognition as a legitimate ruler, the Nabob had borrowed large sums of money at high rates of interest (as high as 25%) for projects including the maintenance of troops and the building of a great mosque. The case was in effect between the Nabob's private creditors and the East India Company; in reality, in Edmund Burke's words, it concerned the Nabob and his creditors "combining and confederating, on one side, and the public revenues, and the miserable inhabitants of a ruined country, on the other".[37] Many

---

[34] F A Mann *Foreign affairs in English courts* (Clarendon Press: Oxford, 1986) at 184. See also Lords Pearson and Wilberforce in *AG v Nissan* [1970] AC 179, discussed below, p 209.

[35] *The Nabob of the Carnatic /of Arcot v East India Company* High Court of Chancery 1791: 1 Ves Jun 371; 3 Bro CC 292. Court of Chancery 1793: 2 Ves Jun 56; 4 Bro CC 181.

[36] The phrase is Macauley's in his *Critical and historical essays* (London, 1891) Vol I 310–311 (on Lord Clive). Burke writes similarly: "[T]hese miserable Indian princes are continued in their seats for no other purpose than to render them, in the first instance, objects of every species of extortion, and, in the second, to force them to become, for the sake of a momentary shadow of reduced authority, a sort of subordinate tyrants, the ruin and calamity, not the fathers and cherishers, of their people." Burke's "Speech on the motion made for papers relative to the directions for charging the Nabob of Arcot's private debts to Europeans on the revenues of the Carnatic", February 28th 1785 in *The works of the Right Honourable Edmund Burke* vol III (John Nimmo, London 1887) 1 at 71–72.

[37] Burke "Arcot's debts": ibid at 8. See also C A Bayly *The new Cambridge history of India Vol II.i: Indian society and the making of the British Empire* (Cambridge University Press: Cambridge, 1988) 60, 70: "The Nawab's attempts to husband his remaining resources arose from a pathetic desire to maintain independence and the scarcely concealed Anglophobia of his son Umdat-al-Umara. Yet it was powerfully reinforced by the incessant demands of his European creditors for repayment. Here

of the Nabob's creditors were themselves working for the Company, and included several of its Directors and fourteen members of Parliament:[38]

The cabal of creditors who have been the object of the late bountiful grant from his Majesty's ministers, in order to possess themselves, under the name of creditors and assignees, of every country in India, as fast as it should be conquered, inspired into the mind of the Nabob of Arcot (then a dependant on the Company of the humblest order) a scheme of the most wild and desperate ambition that I believe ever was admitted into the thoughts of a man so situated. First, they persuaded him to consider himself as a principal member in the political system of Europe. In the next place, they held out to him, and he readily imbibed, the idea of the general empire of Hindostan.... On this scheme of their servants, the Company was to appear in the Carnatic in no other light than as a contractor for the provision of armies, and the hire of mercenaries for his use and under his direction.[39]

In 1781 the Nabob had reluctantly agreed with Lord Macartney (the newly arrived Governor of Fort St George and subsequently Governor of Madras) to assign the revenues of the Carnatic to the Company on an understanding that that it would account for them, and set those revenues against his debts to the Company. Those debts to the Company (like most of his debts to private creditors) were incurred primarily to pay the troops the Company had recruited to resist attacks by Haidar Ali from the neighbouring Sultanate of Mysore, the main threat to British power in the South. For Burke it was this debt which was "the pretext under which all the other debts lurk and cover themselves. That debt forms the foul, putrid mucus in which are engendered the whole brood of creeping ascarides, all the endless involutions, the eternal knot, added to a knot of those inexpugnable tape-worms which devour the nutriment and eat up the bowels of India."[40]

---

then the Company's public interest and that of its servants and European associates were directly at odds.... As late as 1776 European private interests, feeding on the wealth of indigenous magnates through the Nawab's debts, could imprison a governor who acted against them." [referring to the imprisonment of Pigot].

[38] C H Philips *The East India Company 1784–1834* (Manchester University Press: Manchester, 1940) 36, 41.

[39] Burke "Arcot's debts", above n36 at 47.

[40] Ibid, 46 (ascarides are round-worms). Mill concludes (more kindly towards the Company) that "Hypocrisy was the cause which produced the difficulties resulting to the English from their connexion with the Nabob. They desired to hold him up to the world, as an independent Prince, their ally, when it was necessary they should act as his lord and master.... If the defence of the country rested with the English; and if they found that to govern it through the agency of the Nabob deprived them of its resources, and above all inflicted the most grievous oppression upon the inhabitants; results, the whole of which might have been easily foreseen, without waiting for the bitter fruits of a long experience; they ought from the beginning, if the real substance, not the false colours of the case, are taken for the ground of our decision, to have made the Nabob in appearance, what he had always been in reality, a pensioner of the Company. What may be said in defence of the Company is, that

The Nabob's private creditors continued to demand "repayment of sums both doubtful in origin and exaggerated in amount": the Nabob deliberately admitted the justice of the creditors' claims to play them off against his large debts to the Company.[41] In 1784, almost as soon as Parliament had decided to institute an inquiry into these debts, the creditors obtained extremely controversial agreements with the Company's Board of Control for full payment of debts accrued up to 1777. It was this decision of the Board of Control (a body created by Pitt's India Act in 1784 to provide ministerial oversight of the Company's activities) to acknowledge the debts as just and to appropriate funds to pay them without inquiry that prompted Burke's celebrated speech on the Nabob's debts:

It is not into secret negotiations for war, peace, or alliance that the House of Commons is forbidden to inquire. It is a matter of account; it is a pecuniary transaction; it is the demand of a suspected steward upon ruined tenants and an embarrassed master that the Commons of Great Britain are commanded not to inspect.[42]

On Macartney's departure in 1785, and under pressure from the creditors, the revenues of the Carnatic were reassigned to the Nabob, although in a later series of agreements more than four fifths of that revenue was to be paid to the Company to discharge the Nabob's debts.

The Nabob's creditors however claimed that new debts of £30,000,000 remained outstanding (only one-twentieth of which was eventually found to be valid[43]) and that the sums being paid annually to the company (pursuant to the agreement with Macartney) were "more than sufficient" to satisfy the debts owed to the EIC. They "prayed an account, and that the defendants might pay any balance that might appear thereon to be due to plaintiff".[44] The matter stated was "a mere account, not relative to matters of state ; and certainly, in matters of trade, the East India Company are amenable to this Court, and if, in that respect, they are amenable, they cannot be considered as a sovereign power"; the Company's empowerment to use military force did not "constitute it a sovereign state; so far from it, it speedily will not exist without some act of the sovereign power of this country to continue its existence. Therefore, the Company is merely to be considered as a corporation, and, of course, amenable here."[45]

parliament scanned their actions with so much ignorance, as to make them often afraid to pursue their own views of utility, and rather take another course, which would save them from the hostile operation of vulgar prejudices." *The history of British India* (4th edn, ed Wilson: London, 1848) Vol V Bk VI ch III at 373–4.

   [41] Philips *The East India Company,* above n 38, 37.

   [42] Burke, above n 36, 4. See also Phillips *The East India Company,* above n 38, 40, concluding that Pitt "had received political support from the Arcot interest in the general election".

   [43] Phillips *The East India Company,* above n 38 at n 640.

   [44] 3 Bro CC 292 at 292–3.

   [45] 3 Bro CC 292 at 296, 298.

To protect their funds from these further claims by the creditors, the Company argued that their agreements with the Nabob were treaties between sovereigns and as such outside the jurisdiction of Chancery courts: the Attorney General, acting for the Company, argued that "an account arising from a federal treaty cannot be a proper subject of municipal jurisdiction."[46] But such a plea, the Lord Chancellor objected, was "perfectly new":

It is stated to be a plea to the jurisdiction of the Court; but it differs from a plea to the jurisdiction in all the particulars by which those pleas have been described; because...it is impossible to plead to the jurisdiction of any particular Court, without giving another remedy to the party in some other court. Now this plea says, expressly, that the *party has no remedy in any court of municipal jurisdiction* whatever.... The plea, therefore, as I take it, is a plea in bar, not a plea to the jurisdiction of a particular court, but of all courts: and a plea to the jurisdiction of all courts, I take to be absurd, and repugnant in terms.[47]

The plea was overruled as "bad in every view" and Lord Thurlow refused a motion for leave to further amend the plea. The 'fact' that treaties were involved in the contraction of the debt was not a fact that barred the plea (in modern terms, rendered the case non-justiciable); no cases had been found to defend the Attorney General's position as a legal doctrine.[48]

At the subsequent Chancery hearing, counsel for the Nabob argued that this earlier determination should be treated as "a great and grave authority because there have been few cases more argued, and in which more pains were taken by the Court."[49] But the Attorney and Solicitor General, for the East India Company, argued first—as before—that the Nabob and the Company were acting as neighbouring sovereigns and that sovereigns could not "sue or be sued in a court of municipal jurisdiction, in matters relative to his sovereignty",[50] and secondly, that since the Board of Control was now statutorily empowered to give secret orders to the Company's servants in India,[51] Parliament had placed the Company in a position whereby it would have to keep secret any grounds it may have for a "reasonable apprehension" that the Nabob's debts to the Company (for provision of troops) would not be paid, grounds which would otherwise entitle them to retain the balance of the revenues.[52]

No full judgment was given in the case: the Court hurriedly—but crucially—dismissed the Nabob's creditors' bill for an account from the

---

[46] 3 Bro CC 292 at 300.

[47] *Nabob of Arcot v East India Company*[1791] 3 Bro CC 292 at 301 [original emphasis]: see also 1 Ves Jun 371 at 388.

[48] 3 Bro CC 292 at 310; 1 Ves Jun 371 at 393.

[49] *Nabob of Arcot v East India Company* [1793] 4 Bro CC 181 at 185.

[50] 4 Bro CC 181 at 190.

[51] In fact the government had been giving secret orders to the Company's servants in India since the late seventeenth century: see Philips *The East India Company*, above n 38, 9–10.

[52] 4 Bro CC 181 at 192.

Company on the ground that the Company had now convinced the Court that the relevant treaty was "not mercantile in its nature, but political; and therefore this decision stands wholly clear of the judgment upon the plea".[53] Despite the disclaimer, the assumption that there are "political" treaties standing above any law was in effect the argument on the plea rejected by Lord Thurlow. The Nabob's creditors appealed to the House of Lords, but on the day of the hearing "the Directors of the East India Company received an account of the death of the Plaintiff; which put an end to the suit".[54]

The stage was set: despite the earlier detailed arguments on the plea and the Lord Chancellor's ruling that a plea to the jurisdiction of all courts was in effect a plea in bar, and one that was "absurd and repugnant in terms", there was now a precedent for the notion that some acts of state were inherently political and as such not matters for a court of law.[55]

(ii) Elphinstone *and matters for military rather than civilian courts*

In *Elphinstone v Bedreechund* (1830), in a five-line opinion the Privy Council reversed a judgment of the Supreme Court of Bombay which had awarded to the estate of a nobleman (Narroba Outia) nearly two million rupees in damages and costs for the seizure of his treasure by an agent of the East India Company. Although understandably often treated as an act of state decision, in legal terms this opinion is best treated as authority for a rule that actions carried out in the course of hostilities in

---

[53] 2 Ves Jun 56 at 60. See also 4 Bro CC 189 at 198: "the whole was a political transaction."

[54] 2 Ves Jun 56 at 60. Just as the Court was about to deliver its opinion, the Company's counsel announced that a new treaty with the Nabob had been agreed which rendered the suit unnecessary; the cause was adjourned for the Nabob's lawyers to confirm this. On the final day of that next term, just before the Court rose, counsel for the Nabob declared that "there was no ground for what had been state by the Defendants concerning a treaty" and prayed judgment. Lord Commissioner Eyre commented that if the Court had been asked even an hour sooner a fully reasoned judgment could have been given. The case was cited in argument in *East India Company v Syed Ally* (1827) 7 Moore Ind App 555; 19 ER 417, in which the Master of the Rolls, Sir John Leach, held that the Supreme Court of Madras had no power to "question an act of Sovereignty exercised on the part of the East India Company"—but also that as sovereignty over the Carnatic was ceded to the Company in 1801, the new terms on which the Company had regranted a 'Jaghire' (for life only) prevailed over a prior hereditary grant by the Nabob.

[55] As the second *Arcot* decision assumes a doctrine of treaty non-justiciability denied by Thurlow, in principle it might have been possible to raise a demurrer in a similar subsequent case. But strikingly, none of the leading Chancery pleading manuals published before the Judicature Rules suggest this as a possibility. The main nineteenth century pleading manuals all state simply that in a plea to the jurisdiction, "it must be shewn what other court has jurisdiction" (*Mitford's Chancery Pleadings* first edn, 1785 at 171; third edn 1814 at 182). Smith's *Chancery Practice* (1844) specifically cites the first *Arcot* case as authority for this point (at 316) as does *Daniell's Chancery Practice* (3rd edn 1857, ed Headlam, at 515). It is not until the 8th edn (1914) of *Daniell's* that after the reference to the first *Arcot* decision appears a statement that "A plea to the jurisdiction need not allege the existence of a competent court abroad, when the plea is really a plea in bar, and where the ground of it is a want of jurisdiction in the courts of this country generally", citing *Companhia de Moçambique v British South Africa Company* [1892] 2 QB 358.

a foreign country were subject to the exclusive jurisdiction of military and not civilian courts.

The Attorney General, Scarlett, argued for Monstuart Elphinstone (the East India Company's representative in Peishwa) that "[w]hen the success of a commander of an army enables him to take military occupation of a country, he may either deliver it up to the ravages of his soldiery, if he is cruelly disposed, or may place commissioners in it to preserve tranquillity", although he does treat war-time actions of the army as constrained by martial law.[56] Denman KC (later the Lord Chief Justice) argued for the respondent that a proclamation issued by Elphinstone early in the war of conquest made any land conquered "part and parcel of the dominions of the Crown of England" and as such *did* give the domestic civil courts jurisdiction:

If King William III, at the time of the Revolution, after he had come over to England had refused to abide by the terms of the proclamation he had published in Holland, if he had said, there are two or three forts still holding out in the Highlands; there are forces still in arms against me; my proclamation is no agreement, it is all on one side; there is nothing in it that can oblige me to give a free government to England until the whole realm is subdued; what would have been thought of his argument or his integrity? We are not indeed left entirely to our imaginations to conjecture what opinion would have been formed of them at that time (20th Jan. 1692); for we well know, that when Bishop Burnet maintained in a pastoral letter, that he had gained the throne by right of conquest, and was not bound by his proclamation, the Consequence was, that his letter was ordered by the House of Commons to be publicly consigned to the flames by a not very dignified person.[57]

But in a six-line judgment, Lord Tenterton agreed that the seizure was made "if not *flagrante,* yet *nondum cessante bello*" and consequently not only that "the Municipal Court had no jurisdiction to adjudge upon the subject" but also that "if anything was done amiss, recourse could only be had to the Government for redress".[58]

(iii) The non-justiciability of acts of state emerges: the case of Kamachee

It is only in a series of Privy Council decisions given after the 1857 revolt that explicit arguments are given for treating imperial actions in India as acts of state non-justiciable in *any* court. The first and key decision

---

[56] *Elphinstone v Bedreechund* [1830] 1 Knapp 316 at 351, 354.

[57] *Elphinstone* at 343–344.

[58] *Elphinstone* at 360–361. Knapp adds at 361 that "the Respondent presented a memorial to the King in Council, claiming the treasure seized as his private property and praying that his claim might be heard, either before a Committee of the Privy Council or some other competent tribunal to be appointed by his Majesty for that purpose." A Committee of the Council was appointed and "Lord Tenterton announced their decision to be 'That they could not advise his Majesty that the Memorialist had made out his claim'."

in this series is *Secretary of State for India v Kamachee Boye Sahaba* (1859),[59] which overturned a decision of Sir Christopher Rawlinson sitting as Chief Justice of the Supreme Court of Madras. Rawlinson CJ had ruled that, although the East India Company did enjoy "certain Sovereign powers delegated to them, such as those of making peace and war, and of making Treaties with certain of the native powers in Asia",[60] powers which extended to seizing the Raj of Tanjore on the death of the Rajah (in the absence of male heirs), those powers did not entitle the company to seize and sell the Rajah's private estate and property. (The company had sealed the palace, and had taken even pony carriages, children's carriages, cows, ponies, "numerous female jewels and trinkets", "all the female apparel, clothes, shawls, silks, laces etc."[61]) Against the Company's argument that the seizure was a non-justiciable act of state, Rawlinson CJ held that letters from the Government of India and of Madras showed that the Company's agent was authorized only to seize State property and not to make "an indiscriminate seizure, both of public and private property". Citing *Coke on Littleton*, Rawlinson CJ held that "even in England the Monarch could take real as well as personal property in his own right"; as such, the Rajah's widow could sue for recovery of that property "as a private individual, and as the subject of a country forming part of the British territories".[62]

Appealing to the Privy Council, the Company reiterated their argument that the Supreme Court of Madras did not have power to "ascertain and declare whether [the authority of the Company's agent, Mr Forbes] in general has been rightly exercised" because Forbes's actions were acts of state and as such not subject to the jurisdiction of that Court.[63] The Attorney General, Sir Richard Bethell (instructed as counsel before his appointment), rashly argued for the Rajah's widow not simply (as had Rawlinson CJ) that the Company exercised only *certain* sovereign powers, but that the East India Company "did not stand in the position of a Sovereign power; they were only a corporation endowed, it is true, with considerable franchises and prerogatives, but by legislative enactments made accountable for their acts". The actions of the Company here "were arbitrary acts" and justiciable in that they "were not done in virtue of Treaties or *jure belli*": as such, they were bound to account for their wrongful seizure of the Rajah's private property.[64]

[59] *Secretary of State v Kamachee Boye Sahaba* (1859) 13 Moore PCC 22 (15 ER 9).

[60] *Kamachee* Rawlinson CJ at 46.

[61] *Kamachee* Rawlinson CJ at 42, citing from East India Company lists of property seized.

[62] *Kamachee* Rawlinson CJ at 49, 43 (Co. Lit. 15b n4), 46.

[63] The Solicitor General, Sir Hugh Cairns QC at 58—appointed to conduct the Appellant's case because the Respondent had consulted Sir Richard Bethell, who had subsequently been appointed Attorney-General.

[64] *Kamachee* Bethell A-G at 63. Bethell became Lord Chancellor and Baron Westbury in 1861. One of his biographers summarises: "He disparaged both the common law and the statute book more than any other modern holder of the post [of Lord Chancellor]. His respect for theory was unrivalled in its intensity, and his political energy could eclipse that of Brougham. His capacity for

Lord Kingsdown, delivering the judgment of the Privy Council, held that the East India Company had been invested with "Sovereign powers" and that "acts done in execution of these Sovereign powers were not subject to the control of the Municipal Courts, either of India or Great Britain".[65] Precisely because the Privy Council was unable to find "any ground of legal right" for a seizure described before them by Bethell as "a most violent and unjustifiable measure", the Company's actions had to be understood as non-justiciable acts of state:

It is clear from Mr Forbes's report to the Madras Government of what took place on the occasion, that though no resistance was offered by the family of the Rajah, or the inhabitants of the fort, to the seizure of the Raj, and of the palace and property of the Rajah, it was regarded on both sides as a mere act of power not resisted because resistance would have been vain. 'Much sorrow', he says, 'was expressed and much grief shown; but all submitted at once to the authority of the Government, and placed themselves in its hands.'[66]

In effect then, the Privy Council was allowing the very kind of plea in bar (one "to the jurisdiction of all courts") that Thurlow LC in the *Nabob of Arcot* case had found both absurd and repugnant. In *Kamachee* the Crown was held to have successfully delegated to the East India Company a non-justiciable, "sovereign" power to act despotically. Unsurprisingly, *Kamachee* is one of the two cases cited by James Fitzjames Stephen as authority for his claim that "as between British subjects and foreigners, the orders of the Crown justify what they command so far as British courts of justice are concerned".[67]

(iv) Later inconsistent Privy Council decisions: colonial acts as constrained by law (Sigcau) or as acts of state outside the law (Cook)

The Privy Council followed its approach in *Kamachee* in subsequent imperial succession cases in India.[68] But on the Crown's powers in other

---

sarcasm had no parallel in Victorian chancellors, and exceeded even that of Lord Birkenhead in the twentieth century. His occasional lack of judgement in debate, and in the exercise of administrative duties, has been rivalled by some lord chancellors but never exceeded in its dramatic effect. Looking back on his career, late Victorians were surely right in seeing him as someone afflicted with both an overwhelming belief in his own intellectual superiority and an emotional *need to prove this ability at every possible point, often at the cost of others.* What made him so striking was the extent to which the quality of his mind often justified his own view of his talents." R C J Cocks, "Bethell, Richard, first Baron Westbury (1800–1873)", *Oxford Dictionary of National Biography*, Oxford University Press, 2004.

[65] *Kamachee* Kingsdown at 77.   [66] *Kamachee* at 78–79 and 82.

[67] Stephen *History of the criminal law*, above n 13, II p 65; *Buron v Denman* is the other case on which Stephen relies, on which section III.iii, below.

[68] *Rajah Salid Ram v Secretary of State for India in Council* (1872) LR IA Supp 119; *Sirdah Bhagwan Singh v Secretary of State for India in Council* (1874) LR 2 IA 38; *Doss v Secretary of State for India in Council* (1875) LR 19 Eq 509; *Secretary of State v Bai Rajbai* (1914–1915) LR 42 IA 229; *Vajesingji Joravarsingji v Secretary of State* (1924) LR 51 IA 357; *Dattatraya Krishna Rao Kane v Secretary of State for India* (1930) LR 57 I. A. 318; *Secretary of State v Sardar Rustam Khan* [1941] AC 356 (by terms of treaty of cession and Foreign Jurisdiction Act 1890

colonies, the Privy Council's approach was less consistent, for example holding in a decision concerning the cession of Lagos that "[a] mere change in sovereignty is *not* to be presumed as meant to disturb rights of private owners; and the general terms of a cession are prima facie to be construed accordingly."[69]

The inconsistency is particularly striking in two Privy Council decisions concerning Sigcau, the chief of Eastern Pondoland in South Africa. In early 1894, Sigcau ceded his territory to the British Crown. In June 1895, Sigcau was arrested and imprisoned (without a trial or hearing) under a proclamation issued for that purpose—a proclamation which did not specify his offence. The Governor claimed to issue the proclamation "in virtue of powers vested in me by law" including the Pondoland Annexation Act 1894 and on the grounds that Sigcau had been obstructive and his presence in Pondoland was a public danger.[70] A commission sitting on Sigcau's case "agreed that, on the whole, he had been an obstruction; but it hastened to add that, thanks largely to his influence, his people had behaved well and that, on the two trifling occasions of which complaint was made, all that could be said was that he had not cordially supported the magistrate and had been too intent on maintaining his dignity—the dignity of a great chief, who would remain chief in the eyes of his people till the day of his death".[71]

In the Supreme Court of the Cape of Good Hope, De Villiers CJ held that the relevant legislation did not confer on the Governor the power to make new laws but only to enact laws in force elsewhere in the colony: the proclamation was *ultra vires* and Sigcau's release was ordered. On appeal to the Privy Council, the appellants argued both that the proclamation was valid and that it was a non-justiciable act of state.

Delivering the judgment of the Privy Council, the Lord Chancellor, Lord Watson, treated the proclamation as "an edict, dealing with matters administrative, judicial, legislative and executive, in terms which are beyond the competency of any authority except an irresponsible sovereign, or a supreme and unfettered legislature, or some person or body to whom their functions have been lawfully delegated".[72] But rather than concluding, as in *Kamachee*, that the Governor exercised sovereign powers which *could* be exercised arbitrarily and outside the law, Watson remarked that the action at issue was "hardly an Act of State, but rather

---

81, no requirement to recognise pre-existing titles). For critical comment on these Indian Privy Council decisions– and their use, after independence, in early jurisprudence of the Indian Supreme Court, see Agrawala "The doctrine of act of state and the law of state succession in India" (1963) 12 *ICLQ* 1399.

[69] *Amodu Tijani v Secretary, Southern Nigeria* [1921] 2 AC 399 at 407 (my emphasis). See also Lord Denning in *Oyekan v Adele* [1957] 2 All ER 785 at 788.

[70] "Rhodes, as Minister for Native Affairs, had merely been exercising that 'oriental despotism' which he had once prescribed for tribal natives. The experiment failed.": E A Walker *Lord de Villiers and his times: South Africa 1842–1914* (Constable: London, 1925), 259.

[71] Ibid, 259.

[72] *Sprigg v Sigcau* [1897] AC 238 at 246.

an Act of Attainder by virtue of a special Act of Parliament."[73] He continued:

It was satisfactory to find that the appellant's counsel did not, in the argument before this Board, venture to trace the power of the Governor to enact such a proclamation to any authority directly derived from Her Majesty; because autocratic legislation of that kind in a Colony having a settled system of criminal law and criminal tribunals would be little calculated to enhance the repute of British justice.[74]

Focussing on the legislative authority delegated to the Governor in the Annexation Act, the Privy Council concluded there was "not a word in the Act to suggest that it was intended to make the Governor a dictator, or even to clothe him with the full legislative powers of the Cape Parliament": the proclamation was "a new and exceptional piece of legislation, differing entirely in character from any of the laws, statutes and ordinances which he is authorized to proclaim".[75] As such, they held that the Supreme Court of the Colony had been right to liberate Sigcau and refuse to effect the proclamation.[76]

Two years later, in *Cook v Sprigg*, a similarly constituted Judicial Committee of the Privy Council held in effect that the same Governor *was* clothed with dictatorial power.[77] The appellants in *Cook* sought to enforce rights that they claimed had been granted to them in concessions made by Sigcau prior to British annexation. The Supreme Court of the Cape had held that they had not acquired a good title under the existing local laws: Sigcau might at any time have repudiated the rights he had granted to them, and no remedy for such a repudiation would have been available. De Villiers CJ endorsed US Chief Justice Marshall's position that a new government "takes the place of that which has passed away", but succession could not improve Cook's position: here "the native customs, such as they are, do not recognise such concessions" and "if the chief had revoked the plaintiff's concessions, there would equally have been no remedy for his breach of contract".[78]

But instead of adopting de Villiers' approach, echoing Chief Justice Marshall and addressing the relevant questions of local and Colonial

---

[73] *Sigcau* at 241.   [74] *Sigcau* at 246–7.

[75] *Sigcau* at 247, 248.

[76] General Smuts drew this case to Lord Shaw's attention when they met at an Imperial Conference in London ("we settled all that long ago in a case in Pondoland") and Shaw was working on his dissent in *Halliday* [1917] AC 260 (on whether Regulation 14B of the Defence of the Realm (Consolidation) Regulations 1914 (empowering detention without trial by Order in Council) fell within the terms of the Defence of the Realm Consolidation Act 1914 s1(1)). Walker *De Villiers*, above n 70, 260 quoting from Shaw's *Letters to Isobel* (Cassell: New York, 1921) at 202. Dyzenhaus uses this as an example of how "the migration of legal ideas does not always go from centre to periphery in the Commonwealth, and that those that go from periphery to centre can bear good fruit." (*The constitution of law*, above n 30, 26)

[77] *Cook v Sprigg* [1899] AC 572. The four most senior of the five judges sitting in *Cook v Sprigg* (Lord Halsbury LC, Lord Watson, Lord Hobhouse, Lord Macnaghten, and Lord Morris) were the same four most senior of the seven sitting in *Sprigg v Sigcau* (the Lord Chancellor, Lord Watson, Lord Hobhouse, Lord Macnaghten, Lord Shand, Lord Davey, and Sir Richard Couch).

[78] *Cook Bros v The Colonial Government* (1895) 12 SC 86 at 95, 96, 97.

property law, the Lord Chancellor (delivering judgment for the Privy Council) relied on *Kamachee*, holding that the "taking possession by Her Majesty, whether by cession or by any other means by which sovereignty can be acquired, was an act of State": as such (quoting Lord Kingsdown in *Kamachee*) the question was not a matter for courts of law, although the Privy Council agreed with de Villiers that the appellants had "strong claims to the favourable consideration of the Government and Parliament of the country".[79]

The decision in *Cook* was subject to sustained academic criticism. In one of the earliest critiques the note-writer of the *Law Quarterly Review* (presumably its editor, Pollock) argues that the earlier Indian cases relied on by the Privy Council in *Cook v Sprigg* were "altogether distinguishable": the Judicial Committee's opinion in *Cook* was "offhand", "uninstructive", "perplexing" and "neither sound nor convenient". The decision puts "all private rights in a newly acquired territory at the mercy of the new executive power": it can be read "only as meant to lay down that on the annexation of territory, even by peaceable cession, there is a total abeyance of justice until the will of the annexing Power is expressly made known; and that, although the will of that Power is commonly to respect existing private rights, there is no rule or presumption to that effect of which any court must or indeed can take notice". This doctrine "is contrary to the law of nations as generally understood, and we know of no warrant for it at common law." "If we are wrong", the writer concludes, "it is in Chief Justice Marshall's company. 'A cession of territory is never understood to be a cession of the property belonging to its inhabitants.' "[80] William Harrison Moore suggested that the right of property of British subjects in *Cook* should have been given the same protection by the courts as the right of personal security of British subjects in *Sigcau*:

It is not easy to see why the right of property in this case was not equally with the right of personal security in the other under the protection of the Courts of

---

[79] *Cook v Sprigg* at 578.

[80] (1900) 16 *LQR* at 1–2. Writing in 1943, Mann similarly points out that questions of state succession are in principle justiciable in domestic courts, like Pollock citing Chief Justice Marshall: "The modern usage of nations which has become law would be violated; that sense of justice and of right which is acknowledged and felt by the whole civilized world would be outraged, if private property should be generally confiscated and private rights annulled. The people change their allegiance; their relationship with their ancient sovereign is dissolved; but their relations to each other and their rights of property remain undisturbed. If this be the modern rule even in cases of conquest, who can doubt its application to the case of an amicable cession of territory." (*United States v Percheman* (1833) 7 Peters 51 at 86). Mann suggests that in the cases at issue here, "the Courts recoiled from the possibility of having to find the Executive guilty of a breach of international law and thus to embarrass its standing in international affairs": F A Mann "Judiciary and executive in foreign affairs" 29 *Transactions of the Grotius Society* (1944) 143 at 148. On an unduly narrow reading of the dictatorial or 'autocratic' line of act of state cases considered in the text (and without reference to the rival if much shorter line of cases discussed below n 99 and n 100 and accompanying text), Mann concluded at 147 that "in the eyes of the common law the King is not subject to international law"; he does address the rival line of cases in his *Foreign affairs in English courts*, cited above n 34, at 81–82.

Law; and it is somewhat startling to find the defence of *act of State* accepted in regard to acts done by a subordinate government in territory incorporated into an old established British colony, after a system of law and government has been provided, and when those acts relate to the property of a British subject.[81]

(v) Sekgome *and the possibility of a statutory power to act despotically*

The spirit of *Cook* (like that of its ancestor, *Kamachee*) prevailed before Indian colonial courts,[82] and it resurfaced in a particularly unhappy decision of the Court of Appeal, *The King v The Earl of Crewe ex parte Sekgome*. In *Sekgome*, with the assistance of the Attorney General, counsel for the Secretary of State for the Colonies, the Earl of Crewe, presented with success the very argument that in *Sigcau* Lord Watson had noted the appellant had not "ventured" to raise: colonial governors were empowered to act and legislate as arbitrary despots, either because their actions were acts of state or because they were statutorily empowered so to act under the Foreign Jurisdiction Act 1890.

The original Foreign Jurisdiction Act 1843 (FJA),[83] amended by the FJA 1865, had declared the Crown's actions in foreign dominions to be "as valid and effectual as though the same had been done according to the local Law then in force within such Country or Place". The Crown's powers in protectorates and protected states were to be treated as identical to those it held in conquered and ceded colonies;[84] under the Colonial Laws Validity Act 1865[85] (CLVA) governing the competence of colonial legislatures, the Crown's powers in colonies were constrained *only* by Imperial legislation and not by English common law. The FJA 1890[86] further specified that Orders in Council authorising "a British court in a foreign country to order the removal or deportation of any person from that country" rendered the removal or deportation "as lawful as if the order of the court were to have effect wholly within that country" (section 8); such Orders in Council would be void if "repugnant" to the provisions of an Act of Parliament or related order, or regulation, but could not be declared invalid on the basis of incompatibility with the common law (section 12).

Most commentators interpret the CLVA as a limited "charter of colonial legislative independence".[87] Under the CLVA, colonies were

---

[81] Moore *Act of state in English law* (John Murray: London, 1906) 79–80.

[82] On which see O'Connell *State succession in municipal law and international law* (Cambridge University Press, 1967) vol I 258–262.

[83] 1843 6 & 7 Vict. c94 s1.

[84] FJA 1843 section 2. In *Sekgome*, the Court of Appeal cites Hall's argument (*Foreign jurisdiction of the British Crown* (Clarendon: Oxford, 1894) at 221) that the Crown's extra-territorial jurisdiction is limited to the Crown's own subjects, concluding that it was "impossible now to adopt" this narrow reading of the FJA given its past application to foreign natives (Vaughan Williams LJ at 596).

[85] 1865 28 & 29 Vict c.63.

[86] 53 &54 Vict. c37.

[87] A V Dicey *The law of the constitution* (Macmillan: London, 8th edn, 1920) at 101.

empowered to develop their own constitutional jurisprudence, constrained only by relevant Imperial legislation: in addressing the validity of colonial legislation, colonial courts could appeal to the terms of relevant Imperial legislation (section 2), and to the letters patent or other instruments authorizing the colonial governor to assent to colonial legislation (section 4), but they could not circumvent the constitution and jurisprudence of their colony by direct appeal to English common law (section 3).[88] The first author of the relevant section of Halsbury, writing shortly before Sekgome, presents the "obvious meaning and purpose" of the CLVA as "to preserve the right of the Imperial Legislature to legislate for a colony, although a local legislature has been given, and to make it impossible, when an Imperial statute has been passed expressly for the purpose of governing that colony, for the colonial legislature to enact anything repugnant to the express law applied to that colony by the Imperial Legislature itself."[89] In Sekgome, the Court of Appeal held the High Commissioner for South Africa was acting within his powers in issuing a proclamation to detain the chief (Sekgome) of a native tribe in the Bechuanaland Protectorate and refusing him habeas corpus.

The Lord Chief Justice had held in the Divisional Court that the courts of Bechuanaland Protectorate had jurisdiction to deal with Sekgome's detention. The Court of Appeal were not convinced that in Bechuanaland there existed a court "having authority to grant and issue a writ of habeas and to ensure the execution thereof in the Protectorate"[90]—but felt it unnecessary to address this question as they held the proclamation to be valid. Section 12 of the FJA was "the only limitation on [the High Commissioner's] power of legislation, and that section must be taken to have superseded the dictum of Lord Mansfield in Campbell v Hall as to the inability of the sovereign to make a change in a conquered country which is 'contrary to fundamental principles'".[91]

As all three members of the Court of Appeal recognised with due discomfort, their ruling left the High Commissioner legally unaccountable. Vaughan Williams LJ explained:

---

[88] Boothby J in Adelaide had taken to declaring South Australian legislation void on the ground that it was repugnant to English law: section 7 of the CLVA specifically emphasised the relevance of the CLVA for South Australian legislation.

[89] Sir Charles Tarring and J S Cotton in the first edition of Halsbury (1909, Vol X, para 915 at 536). The Colonial Laws Validity Bill was introduced in May 1865 in the wake of the Privy Council's controversial decision in Re Colenso, Bishop of Natal, concerning the jurisdiction (or otherwise) of the Bishop of Cape Town over the allegedly heretical Bishop of Natal. The case was argued by luminaries including Fitzjames Stephen and Westlake (for the Bishop of Natal) and Phillimore (for the Bishop of Cape Town); giving judgment, the Lord Chancellor held it "to be clear, on principle, that after the establishment of an independent Legislature in the Settlements of the Cape of Good Hope and Natal" Colonial legislation was needed to "give full effect to a Bishopric": the Crown could not use prerogative powers to establish a Metropolitan See once a colonial legislature was in place. 3 Moore PC NS [1864–65] 115 at 148, 150.

[90] Vaughan Williams LJ at 593.

[91] [1910] 2 KB 576 at 587.

It would be more congenial to our love as a nation of liberty and justice to act on the eloquent words of Lord Watson in *Sprigg v Sigcau*, but the country in that case was an annexed country under the Pondo Annexation Act, and our single duty is to construe the Foreign Jurisdiction Act, 1890, the Orders in Council, and proclamations made thereunder. It is made less difficult if one remembers that the Protectorate is over a country in which a few dominant civilized men have to control a great multitude of the semi-barbarous.[92]

And, he added, if the argument about the statutory powers of the Commissioner was ungrounded, Sekgome's detention "would be justified as an act of State". Kennedy LJ held similarly that the detention was "an act of State, justifying the detention of Sekgome, with which neither this nor any other Court of law in this country is entitled to interfere"[93]: while (citing Cicero), "legislation directed against a particular person... commends itself as little to British legislators as it did to the legislators of ancient Rome, in the best days of the republic", here the court had not "the case of a civilized and orderly State, such as modern England or the Rome of Cicero's time, but the administration of a barbarous or, at least, semi-barbarous community".[94] Farwell LJ added, favouring even more directly the upholding of the heavens over just action, that "if it is necessary for the safety of the State, the freedom and even the life of the individual must be sacrificed".[95]

The two other cases sometimes cited to defend a reading of the FJA or CLVA as conferring unlimited statutory powers of foreign or colonial despotism are the martial law decision in the Jamaican case of *Philips v Eyre*, cited in *Sekgome*, and the Privy Council's much later decision in *Liyange*. *Philips v Eyre* is usually read narrowly, confined to a martial law context.[96] And although occasionally cited as authority for a complete

---

[92] *Sekgome* at 610
[93] *Sekgome* at 609, 624–5.
[94] *Sekgome* at 627–8.
[95] *Sekgome* at 615.
[96] Governor Eyre had declared martial law in Jamaica when suppressing an indigenous rebellion with great brutality; through his chairmanship of the Jamaica Committee, John Stuart Mill spearheaded a campaign to have Eyre held legally accountable, losing in the process the friendship of the counsel to the Committee, Fitzjames Stephen. See Michael Taggart "Ruled by law?" (2006) 69 *MLR* 1006–1025 at 1009 and n 16, and more generally R W Kostal *A jurisprudence of power: Victorian Empire and the rule of law* (Oxford University Press, 2005). Narrow readings of *Philips v Eyre* are offered in all bar the most recent edition of Halsbury. Tarring and Cotton (First edition, 1909, Vol X) treat the case (para 912 p 535 and note t) as authority for a rule that "a confirmed Act of a local legislature lawfully constituted, whether in a settled or a conquered colony, has, as to matters within its competence and within the limits of its jurisdiction, the operation and force of sovereign legislation, though subject to be controlled by Imperial legislation", adding at para 902 p 527 and note h: "A Governor can legally take a benefit under a statute of a colony, e.g. an Act of indemnity, though he is himself a necessary party to it, as in fact he is to all legislation in the colony (*Philips v Eyre*). But he cannot be thus protected from prosecution in England on a criminal charge, such prosecutions being brought under Imperial laws which colonial legislation cannot affect." Stanley de Smith in the third edition (1953, Vol V, para 1247 p 582 and note f) cites the case as authority for indemnifying "action performed during a regime of martial law". In the fourth edition, John Finnis invokes a more radical reading of the case (1973, Vol VI para 1074 p 512 and n 29), citing it along

ousting of review of colonial legislation on the basis of fundamental principles[97], it should be remembered that in *Liyange* the Privy Council's remarks on the CLVA (as ousting a review jurisdiction for violation of fundamental principles) are a prelude to their review of colonial legislation, legislation which they declare invalid for violating a (fundamental) principle of the separation of powers that they implied into the colonial constitution of Ceylon. *Liyange* is best interpreted as reiterating that the CLVA limits the sources of law for colonial courts to those recognised by the colonial constitution.[98]

(vi) Cases turning to Sigcau rather than Sekgome

In two cases from Lagos the Privy Council moved away from their position in *Cook* and back towards *Sigcau*. In *Amodu Tijani v Secretary, Southern Nigeria* Lord Haldane treated cession to the British Crown as "made on the footing that the rights of property of the inhabitants were to be fully respected", a principle which "is a usual one under British policy and law when such occupations take place".[99] And in *Eshugbayi Eleko v Officer Administering the Government of Nigeria*, Lord Atkin emphasised that "as the executive", the imperial Governor could "only act in pursuance of the powers given to him by law. In accordance with British jurisprudence no member of the executive can interfere with the liberty or property of a British subject except on the condition that he can support the legality of his action before a court of justice. And it is the tradition of British justice that judges should not shrink from deciding such issues in the face of the executive." As such, it was "necessary for this Board to decide that it is the duty of the Courts to investigate the whole of the questions raised and come to a judicial decision".[100]

---

with *Liyange* as ruling that a dependent legislature may make laws "which are repugnant...to any principles or rules of natural justice; in the 1991 reissue, this passage is qualified with references to New Zealand and Australian cases (para 1027 p 504 and n 29 p 507) and in the 2003 reissue the 1991 qualification and references are replaced (para 839) with a statement that "constitutional rights recognised by the common law and judicially enforced in the UK do not apply in the interpretation and application of the power to legislate for the peace, order and good government of a British overseas territory (which may nonetheless be subject to some substantive limitation): *R v Secretary of State for Foreign and Commonwealth Affairs ex p Bancoult* [2001] QB 1067."

97 Finnis in Halsbury (ibid); Laws LJ in *Bancoult* at para 43—although invoking *Wednesbury* public law limits to conclude that colonial authority "is not wholly unrestrained...every tapestry has a border." para 55: [2001] QB at 1103.

98 As recognised by both Laws LJ and Sedley LJ in their decisions in *Bancoult,* the wider reading of *Liyange*—as applying whether or not a colonial constitutional system (in the sense of a responsible government and independent courts) is in place—turns the CLVA into an absolute ouster clause where colonial constitutional courts are not in existence.

99 [1921] 2 AC 404 at 407.

100 [1931] AC 662 at 670, 672.

Writing in the light of these later decisions, E C S Wade concluded that the "explanation" of such apparently conflicting decisions as *Cook*'s case and *Amodu Tijani*'s case "may be in the latitude permissible to the Judicial Committee which has enabled it to interpret the exercise of the prerogative powers of the Crown sometimes in the direction of auto-cratic rule, sometimes in accordance with the spirit of articles of cession embodying a policy of pre-cession rights".[101] Wade characterises the first set of decisions as "autocratic" because they treat the Crown as subject neither to international law nor to the common law. Understandably if rather too conveniently ignoring the Court of Appeal's judgment in *Sekgome* on the impact of the FJA 1890, Wade adds that cases like *Cook* are difficult to reconcile with Lord Mansfield's ruling in *Campbell v Hall* that undertakings given by the Crown on cession *can* be enforced by domestic courts: articles of capitulation and of peaceful cession must be treated as "sacred and inviolable" and the Crown may not make new laws "contrary to fundamental principles".[102]

(vii) Subsequent reliance on Kamachee, Cook and Sekgome

In a strikingly contrasting decision, *Sobhuza II v Miller*, delivered between those in *Amodu* and *Eshugbayi*, the Privy Council ruled that native agricultural and grazing rights in Swaziland (recognised in rele-vant treaties between Britain and the Chief of Swaziland in 1894) had been abrogated by later Orders in Council. Viscount Haldane held that

The limitation in the Convention of 1894 on interference with the rights and laws and customs of the natives cannot legally interfere with a subsequent exer-cise of the sovereign powers of the Crown, or invalidate subsequent Orders in Council. [... The High Commissioner's power] was exercised either under the Foreign Jurisdiction Act, or as an act of State which cannot be questioned in a Court of law. The Crown could not, excepting by statute, deprive itself of freedom to make Orders in Council, even when these were inconsistent with previous Orders.[103]

Haldane relied on *Sekgome* for his interpretation of the impact of the Foreign Jurisdiction Act, and referred to *Amodu* but puzzlingly made no attempt to distinguish it.[104]

The decision in *Sobhuza* was in turn relied upon in two of three post-war decisions on acts of state that hinged on arguments made by Lord

---

[101] Wade "Act of state in English law: its relations with international law" (1934) 15 *BYIL* 98 at 107. See also Peter Wesley-Smith, "Acts of state: Lord Diplock's curious inconsistency" (1986) 6 *Legal Studies* 325 at 326–327.

[102] (1774) 1 Cowp 204; 98 ER 1045.

[103] [1926] AC 518 at 528–529.

[104] On the argument that the Order in Council, and proclamations made under it, were "unchal-lengeable" acts of state, Haldane refers to the Privy Council in *Re Southern Rhodesia* [1919] AC 211, although the only reference to acts of state in Lord Sumner's judgment in that case is a denial that a relevant concession could be treated as one.

Diplock. In *Nyali Ld v AG*[105], the Court of Appeal accepted Diplock's arguments as counsel that "[t]he courts rely on the representatives of the Crown to know the limits of its jurisdiction and to keep within it. Once jurisdiction is exercised by the Crown the courts will not permit it to be challenged. Thus, if an Order in Council is made affecting the protectorate, the courts will accept its validity without question."[106] In *Post Office v Estuary Radio Ltd*, a case on the extent of the UK's territorial waters in the context of a licensing offence, Diplock LJ (giving the judgment of the Court of Appeal) held that "[t]he Queen's courts, upon being informed by Order in Council or by the appropriate Minister or Law Officer of the Crown's claim to sovereignty or jurisdiction over any place, must give effect to it and are bound by it."[107] And strikingly, giving a sweeping opinion for the Privy Council in *Winfat Enterprise (HK) v AG*, Lord Diplock dismissed the line of Privy Council decisions running counter to *Cook v Sprigg*, arguing that "[a]lthough there are certain obiter dicta to be found in cases which suggest the propriety of the British Government giving effect as *an act of state* to promises of continued recognition of existing private titles of inhabitants of territory obtained by cession, there is clear long-standing authority by decision of this Board that no municipal court has authority to enforce such an obligation."[108]

As one commentator noted, Lord Diplock's opinion in *Winfat* is inconsistent with his own robust opposition to executive autocracy in other areas of constitutional law, "a curious inconsistency, for high authority might well have justified a different approach, one more in keeping with modern constitutional ideas which Lord Diplock himself has done much to promote".[109] But Diplock's position is at least on the surface very close to that of another extremely influential public lawyer,

---

[105] [1956] 1 QB 1 (The case reached the House of Lords, but not on this issue.)

[106] Denning LJ at 15, citing *Sobhuza;* Morris LJ relies on *Sobhuza* at 23 as does Parker LJ at 33.

[107] [1968] 2 QB 740 at 753–4 (relying on a majority of the Court of Appeal in *The Fagernes* [1927] P 311)

[108] [1985] AC 733 at 746 (citing *Cook v Sprigg* and *Vajesingji Joravarsingji v Secretary of State for India in Council* but not *Sobhuza*).

[109] Wesley-Smith, above n 101, 325. Lord Woolf questioned Diplock's position in *Christian v The Queen (The Pitcairn Islands)* [2006] UKPC 47 (30 October 2006), a case concerning the Crown's criminal jurisdiction over rape, sexual assault and incest committed on Pitcairn Island, Britain's smallest colony and a tiny Pacific island roughly midway between New Zealand and Chile:

> In my view the evidence that Pitcairn is and was at all relevant times a British possession was overwhelming and so I agree with Lord Hoffmann, that for the purposes of determining these appeals, it is not necessary to explore the limits of the act of state doctrine. Where this is not the position, in my view it would be necessary to carefully re-examine the authorities including those cited by Lord Hoffmann which support the contention that an act of state is to be regarded as conclusive on issues as to the status of alleged British possessions overseas. Recent developments, mainly in relation to judicial review have demonstrated a greater willingness on the part of the courts to scrutinise the use by the Crown of prerogative powers and so far the limits, if any, of the courts' power of review have not been clearly determined. [33]

Unlike Lord Hoffmann (who at [10] treats an executive statement as non-justiciable), Lord Woolf here accepts that Pitcairn was British on the basis of "overwhelming evidence"—*not* on the basis of an executive statement. Lord Hope similarly relies at [47] on the "evidence" that Pitcairn is a settled colony as a matter of "long standing practice".

William Wade, who defended a very wide act of state doctrine ostensibly based on the old "autocratic" cases. "There is", argues Wade, "a certain sphere of activity where the state is outside the law, and where actions against the Crown and its servants will not lie. The rule of law demands that this sphere should be as narrow as possible. In British law the only available examples relate in one way or another to foreign affairs."[110] As noted earlier,[111] Wade argues that in English law "foreign parts are beyond the pale (in Kipling's words, 'without the law'), and there the Crown has a free hand, whether the plaintiff be foreign or British." According to Wade, the common law offers neither limits on nor redress for the effects of *any* exercises of executive power overseas—although crucial, as we will see, is what Wade counts as "overseas" for this purpose.[112] To fit with his narrow definition of "overseas", Wade cites neither *Kamachee* nor *Cook*, but instead *Buron v Denman*[113] as exemplifying the "fundamental rule that acts of violence in foreign affairs, including acts of war, if committed abroad, cannot be questioned in English courts", a rule which "also casts a complete immunity over all acts of the Crown done in the course of annexing or administering foreign territory".[114]

John Collier similarly argues that the plea of act of state is best characterised as a plea "by which the Crown can cause the court to declare it has no jurisdiction": "once the courts are satisfied that an act is truly an act of state, they must decline to take jurisdiction over any claim arising out of it", although the court *does* have jurisdiction to inquire into whether a particular action does constitute an act of state.[115] The Crown's plea will succeed, Collier implies,[116] not where the Crown has convinced the courts that it has acted in the public interest nor where the Crown has convinced the courts that it is the proper judge of whether it was acting in the public interest (act of state as a defence) but in *all* cases concerning actions of the executive overseas *because* (consciously echoing Wade): "foreign parts are beyond the pale".[117]

The breadth of Wade's doctrine that "foreign parts are without the law" goes far beyond the cases considered above, some of which as we have seen *did* involve English courts accepting that they had a role in inquiring into the legality of Crown actions overseas. But Wade's and Collier's strikingly broad act of state doctrines have equally striking

---

[110] Wade and Forsyth *Administrative law* (2004) 9th edn p 838.

[111] Above n 12 and accompanying text.

[112] Wade also argues that were rules of customary international law to form part of English law, and so a constraint on extra-territorial executive action, those rules of customary international law would necessarily prevail over English legislation in the way in which he argues European law was revolutionarily held to do in the House of Lords' decisions in *Factortame*: Wade "Sovereignty—Revolution or Evolution?" (1996) 112 *Law Quarterly Review* 568–75. On Wade's position on the common law status of customary international law, see my "Foreign views on eating aliens", cited above n 7.

[113] (1848) 2 Ex 167: see text below at p 220.

[114] Wade and Forsyth *Administrative law* (2004) 9th edn at 838.

[115] Collier "Act of state as a defence against a British subject" (1968) 26 *CLJ* 102 at 117, 119, 118.

[116] Ibid, 105, 109.

[117] Ibid, 129, citing Wade *Administrative law* (2nd edn) at 270–272.

limits in terms of what they are prepared to term "foreign". There is, continues Wade, a common law rule that the common law extends to constrain exercises of executive power within British territory or *protectorates ruled as if colonies*. He invokes the Master of the Rolls' judgment in *Mwenya*,[118] reading the Habeas Corpus Act 1862 as legislation "merely for the purpose of abrogating the jurisdiction of the courts of Westminster in favour of colonial independence".[119] The issue of a writ of habeas corpus depended solely on whether a detainee was "under the subjection of the Crown", and not on a territory's formal status.[120] Collier similarly argues that "act of state should be a defence against all but citizens of the United Kingdom and Colonies"—despite the fact that some of the "autocratic" cases involve Crown action against British colonial subjects.[121]

The early cases (*Nabob of Arcot, Elphinstone, Kamachee*) concerned Crown actions against natives of formally "foreign" Indian territories[122]; *Sekgome, Sobhuza* and *Nyali* concerned actions in protectorates; *Cook* concerned claims of British subjects in a Crown Colony. The apparently vast and legally unprecedented discretion Wade accords to the Crown in "foreign parts" seems to be designed to lull readers into a subsequent acknowledgement of the Crown's *legal* responsibilities to inhabitants of colonies and protectorates, a qualification which undermines all but the earliest of the "autocratic" cases.[123]

Wade's quotation of Kipling's phrase "without the law" is taken from the poem "Recessional", in which Kipling inveighs against lawless power politics:

---

[118] [1906] 1 QB 241 at 302.

[119] In line with the narrow reading of the CLVA and the FJA, see above and n 89 and 96, and accompanying text.

[120] [1906] 1 QB at 295.

[121] Collier, above n 115, 117, endorsing Lord Reid's assertion in *Nissan* that the act of state doctrine cannot be invoked against British citizens; in *Nissan*, Lords Morris, Wilberforce and Pearson all countenance the invocation of the act of state doctrine against British citizens overseas. See Stanley de Smith "Civis Britannicus Sum" (1969) 32 *MLR* 427, 480–481 and text below accompanying n 144.

[122] In *Kamachee*, prior to his death the Rajah of Tanjore was treated as a "native independent Sovereign under the protection of the East India Company"; rather than accepting the Company's argument (invoking Dalhousie's "Doctrine of Lapse" under which an Indian prince could not appoint an heir, so that in the absence of a direct male heir his property lapsed to the Government on his death), the Court simply held the seizure an act of state: see above n 65 and accompanying text. (The "Doctrine of Lapse" was renounced by Canning in 1858.)

[123] See de Smith's "Civis Britannicus Sum", cited above n 121, recognising *Cook* "and one or two other awkward cases in which ostensibly unlawful acts in relation to British subjects immediately after the annexation of a territory were held to be defensible as acts of State" (428, n 8). Wade presumably relies on William Holdsworth's interpretation of *Buron v Denman* because *Buron* involved action on straight-forwardly foreign territory against a foreign citizen. But unlike the imperial "autocratic" cases, *Buron* does not support a stark contrast between rule-constrained exercises of executive power (prerogative powers at home) and unfettered exercises of executive power over foreigners (acts of state overseas): text below, p 228. The only authorities for this approach are the "autocratic" line of cases considered above.

In his *International law opinions* I 111–117, McNair relies explicitly on Wade's textbook account, acknowledging in n 1 p 111 that he is "much indebted to Professor Wade for criticism of this subsection".

If, drunk with sight of power, we loose
Wild tongues that have not Thee in awe,
Such boastings as the Gentiles use,
Or lesser breeds *without the Law*—
Lord God of hosts, be with us yet,
Lest we forget—lest we forget.

For heathen heart that puts her trust
In reeking tube and iron shard,
All valiant dust that builds on dust,
And guarding, calls not Thee to guard,
For frantic boast and foolish word—
Thy mercy on Thy People, Lord!

Commenting on the poem in 1942, George Orwell suggests that the verses of this "good bad poem" show that Kipling "does possess one thing which 'enlightened' people seldom or never possess, and that is a sense of responsibility."[124] But according to Orwell, the text, like the lines from Psalm 127 to which it adverts, cannot make much impression on "the post-Hitler mind". Those who pretend otherwise "are either intellectual cowards, or power-worshippers under a thin disguise, or have simply not caught up with the age they are living in": "We all live by robbing Asiatic coolies, and those of us who are 'enlightened' all maintain that those coolies ought to be set free; but our standard of living, and hence our 'enlightenment', demands that robbery shall continue."[125] So according to Orwell, Kipling's autocratic but responsible government, self-constrained by notions of divine law, can evolve only—with a "post-Hitler" loss of faith—into the unconstrained exploitation of foreigners overseas. The dilemma Orwell sketches is not simply a "post-Hitler" one: it returns us to the oldest question in political philosophy, that of the nature of a sovereign's responsibility—and of how far this is a matter of law.

Commonwealth courts have since come to argue that when the Crown acquired already inhabited land, it held that land *not* on a legally unenforceable moral trust for the inhabitants[126] but on a legally enforceable trust: in Canada and New Zealand, courts have held that the Crown's dominium over land was and remains qualified by aboriginal titles, that treaties of cession can be relied on by the courts in defining the relevant titles, and that in its management of their assets the Crown owes aboriginal peoples a legally enforceable fiduciary duty.[127]

---

[124] "A good bad poem is a graceful monument to the obvious." George Orwell "Rudyard Kipling" in *Collected essays* (Secker & Warburg: London, 1968) Vol II 184 at 195. (First published in Horizon, February 1942.)

[125] Ibid at 187.   [126] *Tito v Waddell (No 2)* [1977] Ch 106.

[127] The leading Canadian cases are *Guerin v The Queen* (1984) 13 DLR (4th) 321; *R v Sparrow* (1990) 70 DLR (4th) 385; and *Delmaguukw v British Columbia* (1997) 153 DLR (4th) 193. The New Zealand Court of Appeal has adopted the same approach, treating the Treaty of Waitangi as "major support for such a duty": *Te Runanga o Wharekauri Rekohu Inc v Attorney-General* [1993] 2 NZLR 301 at 306, building on their earlier decision in *New Zealand Maori Council v Attorney-General* [1987] 1 NZLR 641. Toohey J makes a similar argument on the relationship between Australia and its aboriginal peoples in *Mabo v Queensland (No 2)* (1992) 175 CLR 1 at 199–205 (the other judges

The "autocratic" cases continue to be invoked by English courts. But, "post-Hitler", they are no longer invoked for their original ratio as traced in this section, the idea that imperial actions were non-justiciable *because* they involved sovereign exercises "of arbitrary power" which were not performed "under colour of legal title". Dicta from Kingsdown in *Kamachee* and Halsbury in *Cook* are now usually cited to justify a very different rationale for the act of state doctrine, a rule that acts of state are non-justiciable because they concern matters of international law which as such usually fall outside the jurisdiction of the English courts.[128]

The old rationale endures, in emaciated form, in recent decisions relating to the question of the legality under intenational law of the UK's use of force in Iraq. The account the old cases assume of international law was invoked by Lord Hoffmann: offences should not "creep" into English criminal law "as a result of an international consensus to which only the executive of this country is a party."[129] The new rationale for the act of state doctrine is the subject of the following section.

II ACTS OF STATE AS OUTSIDE THE JURISDICTION OF ENGLISH COURTS BECAUSE INHERENTLY INTERNATIONAL

(i) The rewriting of Cook and Kamachee

On this second account, acts of state "cannot be challenged, controlled, or interfered with by municipal courts" *because* they are matters of

---

leave the issue open). See generally Paul McHugh *Aboriginal Societies and the Common Law: A History of Sovereignty, Status and Self-Determination* (Oxford University Press, 2005).

[128] "Obiter dicta" in that none of the claims considered in the "autocratic" cases was *founded* upon a treaty, and in each case the claim was held to be non-justiciable not because it involved questions of international law but because it involved extra-legal acts of state. See also Mann *Foreign affairs in English courts*, above n 34, 74.

[129] *R v Jones (Margeret) et al* [2006] UKHL 16 at para 62, quoting with approval Scalia J in *Sosa v Alvarez-Machain* (2004) 159 L Ed 2d 718 at 765: "American law—the law made by the people's democratically elected representatives—does not recognize a category of activity that is so universally disapproved by other nations that it is automatically unlawful here."
   The decision in *Jones* suggests that, as a matter of English constitutional law, the prerogative to make war has no limits—that it includes a prerogative to make aggressive, internationally unlawful war, the kind of war waged by Hitler and for which the German war criminals were executed. *Jones* is best regarded as decided *per incuriam* for two reasons. First, both Lord Bingham and Lord Hoffmann wrongly invoke the Treason Act 1351 to suggest that it would be high treason to prevent the Crown's ministers waging an aggressive war. Yet the Statute of Treasons protects only the personal security of the monarch: far from conferring an absolute immunity on government action overseas, there is a (remote but genuine) possibility under the same statute of Parliament (acting judicially with the Lords as judges and the Commons as a grand jury) declaring ministers guilty of high treason in "leading the monarch to misgovern the country"—as Burke led the Commons to attempt to do in impeaching Warren Hastings for his actions in India. (James Fitzjames Stephen *History of the criminal law of England vol II* (1883) 250). Secondly, as the Lords accept, the prohibition on aggression emerged as a rule of customary international law at the latest during the second world war, and long before the English courts' current self-denying ban on the recognition of previously unrecognised common law offences. (The appellants were eventually acquitted on the basis that they believed they were acting to prevent an unlawfully disproportionate use of force.)

international law and as such for international settlement.[130] A particularly influential reinterpretation of the old act of state cases along these lines is found in the work of D P O'Connell on state succession:

This doctrine [the "Act of State" doctrine in English law], which was affirmed in several cases arising out of the acquisition of territory in Africa and India, has been misinterpreted to the effect that the substantive rights themselves have not survived the change. In fact English courts have gone out of their way to repudiate the construction, and it is clear that the Act of State doctrine is no more than a procedural bar to municipal law action, and as such is irrelevant to the question whether in international law change of sovereignty affects acquired rights.[131]

The act of state doctrine, argues O'Connell, "has been misinterpreted in both literature and judicial pronouncement" in treating pre-existing legal rights as extinguished by a change of sovereignty. *Cook* was the case "originally responsible for this interpretation", but it is an interpretation which "would seem to be unfounded and to be beyond the limits established in a long series of cases".[132] O'Connell's "long series" includes the second of the *Arcot* cases, *Elphinstone*, and *Kamachee*, but he offers no argument or analysis to explain why he believes these cases support his reading,[133] focusing instead exclusively on dicta in *Salaman v Secretary of State for India*[134] and on *Amodu*. The "long series", he argues, does not "deny a rule of international law" and it insists that "persons who become British subjects by annexation or cession of territory do not lose their duly acquired rights": the only point of conflict within the case law "is on the question of the extent to which machinery for enforcement of these rights exists in English municipal law."[135]

Although inconsistent with the original ratio of cases like *Kamachee*, since decolonisation, this account of the act of state doctrine has become the dominant one in contemporary English law. Subsequent leading cases go beyond O'Connell in rewriting the old case law on acts of the British state. In *AG v Nissan*, Nissan, a naturalized citizen of the United Kingdom and Colonies, claimed compensation for the damage, looting and destruction of his luxury hotel in Cyprus during its occupation by British troops, initially (from December 1963) under an agreement with the Government of Cyprus and from March until May 1964 as part of the United Nations Peace-Keeping Force in Cyprus. The Attorney General argued (invoking *Wade on Administrative Law* and John Collier's essay on act of state[136]) that the initial occupation was an act of state pursuant to an agreement with an independent sovereign (Cyprus), and the

---

[130] Fletcher Moulton LJ in *Salaman v Secretary of State for India* [1906] 1 KB at 639.
[131] O'Connell, above n 82, 378, citing *Salaman* and *Amodu Tijani*.
[132] Ibid, 258–262.
[133] O'Connell also invokes McNair *Legal effects of war* (3rd edn, 1948) 386 and Moore *Act of state in English law* 157ff): ibid 251 n 3.
[134] [1906] 1 KB 613: Fletcher Moulton LJ was *dissenting* on the point about enduring rights.
[135] O'Connell, above n 82, 253 (cases at n 2 p 253), 255.
[136] [1970] AC 179 at 192F; see further above n 110 and n 115 and accompanying text.

occupation from March to May one for which the United Nations was solely responsible.

All the Law Lords in *Nissan* held that as the United Nations was not a foreign sovereign power, no separate plea relating to acts of a foreign state was available for the March-May occupation. Lord Reid's judgment is considered in the final section of this essay[137]: he concludes that "both on principle and on the balance of authority this act was not of such a character that the courts have no jurisdiction to entertain the present action".[138] The other four Law Lords held that, on the assumed facts of the case, the damage to the hotel could not be characterised as an act of state.[139] But three of those four[140] each accepts that the act of state doctrine could operate as a procedural bar against British subjects attempting to bring claims based on actions of the Crown overseas, and each of those three associates acts of state with matters of international law for international settlement rather than for domestic courts.

Lord Morris treats acts of state as "the category of transactions which by reason of being a part of or in performance of an agreement between states are withdrawn from the jurisdiction of the municipal courts" and cites *Cook* as authority for this principle.[141] Lord Pearson, reserving the question of whether an act outside the realm against a British subject could be an act of state, treats an act of state as "something not cognisable" by "an ordinary court of law (municipal not international)". "In such a case", he expands, "the court does not come to any decision as to the legality or illegality, or the rightness or wrongness, of the act complained of: the decision is that because it was an act of state the court has no jurisdiction to entertain a claim in respect of it."[142] Citing passages from Lord Kingsdown's judgment in *Kamachee* referring to transactions between sovereign states to illustrate the nature of acts of state, he continues:

No doubt the making of the treaty was an act of state, and the performance of it must to some extent involve acts of state. But I think the things that were done by the United Kingdom Government had to some extent the character of acts of state in themselves, apart from the fact that they were done under a treaty. [There] was a military operation, involving the use of armed force, so far as might be necessary to keep the peace. It could not be justified under municipal law: it was outside the sphere of municipal law, being in the sphere of international relations.[143]

---

[137] Below, p 239.

[138] *AG v Nissan* [1970] AC 179 at 213E.

[139] *Nissan* Morris at 216H; *Cf* Collier and de Smith, above n 121 and accompanying text.

[140] Lord Pearce recognizes that it "has long been one of the liberties of the subject that when a wrong is done to him by the executive he cannot be shut out from justice by the faceless plea of an act of state", but since the taking of the hotel did not fall within the category of an act of state, he holds it unnecessary to decide whether the plea of act of state could bar British courts from considering interference by the Crown with a subject's liberties of person or property abroad: *Nissan* at 224F, 227A.

[141] *Nissan* at 217C–D.   [142] *Nissan* at 240D, 237F–G.

[143] *Nissan* at 239H–240A.

Lord Wilberforce adheres to the old terminology of "justiciability" (rather than of "jurisdiction" like his peers) but rewrites the substance of the act of state doctrine, treating the relevant rule as "one of justiciability: it prevents British municipal courts from taking cognisance of certain acts. The class of acts so protected has not been accurately defined: one formulation is 'those acts of the Crown which are done under the prerogative in the sphere of foreign affairs'."[144] On this definition, he wonders "why, if the character of the act is what makes it noncognisable, the quality or nationality of the plaintiff should enter into the matter"; surveying case law and jurists' writings, he concludes that "the preponderance of authority and of practice" allows the plea of act of state to operate as a procedural bar against British subjects, although "the scope of the Crown's prerogative, and the consequent non-justiciability of its acts, is uncertain—as uncertain as such expressions as 'the conduct of foreign relations' or 'in the performance of treaties'."[145]

Similarly in *Buttes Gas & Oil Co v Hammer (No 3)*, counsel for *Buttes* treated *Kamachee* and *Cook* as authorities for the rule that "The English courts will decline to try actions which require the courts to interpret the precise nature of obligations or transactions arising between sovereign states."[146] (Buttes' counsel included Robert Jennings, who in later comments supports a "flexible" jurisdictional account of the act of state doctrine.[147]) Endorsing in his judgment this interpretation of the older case law, Lord Wilberforce adopts as the underlying rule Halsbury's "well-known sentence 'It is a well-established principle of law that the transactions of independent states between each other are governed by other laws than those which municipal courts administer'." The cases, Wilberforce concludes, link "the doctrine of non-justiciability" with "a wider area of transactions in the international field."[148]

Again in *JH Rayner (Mincing Lane) Ltd v Department of Trade and Industry*, counsel for the member states of the [i]nternational Tin Commission invoked *Cook* as an authority for the rule that "[i]ndividuals are not the subjects of international law and thus cannot derive rights from the rules of that law unless such rules have been transformed by some means into domestic law."[149] Lord Griffiths accepts this approach, citing *Kamachee* and *Cook* as authorities for the rule that "municipal courts have not and cannot have the competence to adjudicate upon or to enforce the rights arising out of transactions entered into by independent sovereign states between themselves on the plane of international law."[150]

---

[144] *Nissan* at 231E–F, citing *Wade and Phillips's Constitutional Law* (7th edn, 1956) 263.

[145] *Nissan* at 232C; 235E.

[146] [1982] AC 888 at 895–6.   [147] (1990) 39 *ICLQ* 513 at 524–5.

[148] *Buttes* at 933 citing from *Cook* at 578.

[149] [1990] 2 AC 418 at 463.

[150] [1990] 2 AC 418 at 499. For criticism of this approach in the *ITC* case, see Rosalyn Higgins *Problems and Processes* (Oxford University Press, 1994) 206–213; Lawrence Collins (2002) 51 *ICLQ* 485 at 496–8; Lord Steyn in *In re McKerr* at paras 51 (quoting Collins at 497, and arguing this is "not to say that the actual decision in the *International Tin Council* case was wrong. On the contrary, the

(ii) Two dangers of this second act of state doctrine

Although it involves a rewriting of the earlier case law, the appeal of this second act of state doctrine is evident. Treating the doctrine as a jurisdictional rule allows an English court to avoid conflict with the executive without treating the Crown as an autocrat unconstrained by rules of international law. It also accords with a dominant contemporary account of a sovereign's legal responsibility in international law—and for this reason is a doctrine of acts of state nurtured by international lawyers. But this second doctrine is a constitutionally dangerous one. It returns us to the idea of "grey holes", "disguised black holes" in the rule of law which allow the executive to claim that it governs according to law while removing all scrutiny of its decisions from English courts;[151] as a result, the doctrine can blind English courts to applicable rules of English law while claiming to be applying the law. The rationale is also less conducive to the maintenance and development of international law than its defenders assume.

Since the mid-nineteenth century, in accounting for a sovereign's legal responsibility, most international lawyers have treated international law and domestic constitutional law as operating in separate realms. On this account, whether or not an official's breach of rules of international law gives rise to liability under domestic law is a question for domestic law: international law is applied by domestic courts on domestic law's terms. States are free to decide whether and if so how to deal at the domestic level with the official conduct that constitutes a breach of international law. If the state or its courts decides to hold the officials answerable for their actions in the domestic courts, adopting and enforcing the relevant treaty obligation or rule of customary international law, that adoption will be on the terms of domestic law: as such the relevant rule binds as a rule of domestic rather than international law. If the state or its courts decides to offer only an insufficient remedy, or to offer no remedy, declaring the conduct in question an act of state, this decision is not a threat to international law: domestic rules of law like the act of state doctrine and domestic judicial decisions (or other state practices motivated by domestic constitutional concerns) cannot undermine or affect the relevant rule of international law—unless and until the relevant state believes that it must act in a particular way as a matter of international (as opposed to constitutional) law. If the state or its courts *has* offered only an insufficient remedy, at the international level the state (and, in cases of international crimes, the relevant official) remains responsible for the conduct: doctrines and provisions of domestic law cannot be invoked as a defence. But the international obligation to make reparation does not include

critics would accept the principled analysis of Kerr LJ in the Court of Appeal that the issue of liability of member states under international law is justiciable in the national court, and that under international law the member states were not liable for the debts of the international organisation").

[151] Dyzenhaus, above n 33 and accompanying text.

a specific obligation to bring its domestic law in line with the relevant international rules.[152]

The difficulties with this now popular account emerge in reflecting on its consequences. As a matter of international law, a state has a continuing duty to abide by its international obligations: where its officials have acted internationally wrongfully (in breach of an international obligation), the responsible state is under an international obligation to ensure that that act ceases (if it is continuing), to guarantee non-repetition where relevant, and to make full reparation for any injury caused.[153] In practice, these international obligations of cessation, non-repetition and reparation leave the responsible state with two options. The responsible state can decide to adhere to its international obligations, amending its domestic constitutional practices in so far as they would otherwise permit officials to continue to act in an internationally wrongful way. This constitutional change will be taken to reflect an acknowledgement and strengthening of the existing international rule. Alternatively, the responsible state can deny that its officials' actions were internationally wrongful, denying the existence of the rule allegedly breached. It will argue, in other words, that the relevant domestic constitutional practices attest to the correct *international* position, that there is insufficient evidence for the contrary international rule it is supposed to have violated.[154]

---

[152] On accounts along these lines, see Gerald Fitzmaurice "The general principles of international law considered from the standpoint of the rule of law" (1957) 92 *Hague Recueil* 68–94. (At 68–69 Fitzmaurice claims to avoid the monist/dualist debate, but his account of the two "fields" or "separate independent legal orders" of international and domestic law is a dualist one: see Jennings and Watts *Oppenheim's international law* (9th edn, Longman: London, 1996) 53 n24 and Patrick Capps "Sovereignty and the identity of legal orders" in Colin Warbrick and Stephen Tierney (eds) *Towards an International Legal Community? The Sovereignty of States and the Sovereignty of International Law* (British Institute of International and Comparative Law, 2006) 19–73 at 31–32.)

[153] *Cf* International Law Commission Articles on State Responsibility, articles 30 and 31.

[154] See Michael Lobban "Common law reasoning and the law of nations" in Amanda Perreau-Saussine and James B Murphy (eds) *The nature of customary law: legal, historical and philosophical perspectives* (Cambridge University Press, 2007) 256–278. Lassa Oppenheim went to great lengths to persuade his British contemporaries to adopt a dualist account under which international and British law operated in separate realms. He relied heavily on a decision of the full bench of the Scottish High Court of Justiciary in *Mortensen v Peters* 1906 14 SLT 227 that "Whatever may be the views of any one as to the propriety or expediency of stopping [otter] trawling [in the Moray Firth—in waters which in international law were the high seas], the enactment shews on the face of it that it contemplates such stopping; and it would be most clearly ineffective to debar trawling by the British subject while the subjects of other nations were allowed so to fish."(231). But the Lord Justice General went on to argue that it was unclear that international law *did* prohibit legislation for waters "more or less land-locked or land-embraced", though beyond the three-mile limit": *pace* Oppenheim, the case is not an example of a British court rejecting as binding a rule which they had nonetheless acknowledged as clearly established in international law. (Perreau-Saussine "Three ways of writing a treatise on public international law: nineteenth century British textbooks and the nature of customary international law" in Amanda Perreau-Saussine and James B Murphy (eds) *The nature of customary law* (Cambridge University Press, 2007) 228–255.)

Cf James Crawford (1976) *BYIL* 353, commenting on British case law on the status to be granted to rules of international law: "Probably the *dicta* which have been regarded as embodying the 'doctrine of transformation' have been attempting to convey two distinct propositions, both qualifying rather than displacing the basic principle that international law is part of the law of England. First, attention is drawn to the need for clear and satisfactory evidence that the customary rule is as Zcontended

What is really at stake in the "separate realm" account of the act of state doctrine is a resistance to the latter argument: underlying the (re) interpretation of the act of state doctrine as a jurisdictional rule is an idea that the practices of state officials, however constitutional under domestic law, should not be allowed to undermine existing international rules nor to generate new ones without good reason.[155] Without this last condition, it is feared, international law will lose its claim to be anything more than Fitzjames Stephen's projection of imperial power.[156] On one influential account, the crucial judgments about what counts as a reason sufficiently good to distinguish a rule from a habit are themselves judgments determined by *jurists'* customs.[157] On a rival account, reference to jurists' customs is made not because those customs constitute the relevant reasons for accepting the existence of a binding rule, but because—and only in so far as—they are evidence of objectively good reasons underpinning the relevant practice.[158] Both accounts insist that customary international law is not entirely made or unmade by the practices of state officials, but that jurists' reasoning plays a crucial role.

Whatever the "filtering" role of a requirement for *opinio juris,* in practice rules of customary international law are in very significant part a coalescence of the customary constitutional practices of state officials. Those constitutional rules and practices will themselves change and develop through interpretations offered by domestic courts, interpretations which in turn are influenced by customary rules and practices of international law. And once given, each interpretation and application of a written law itself extends that same set of customs. Official British practices sanctioned by English courts can and do contribute to the development and recreation of rules of international law.[159]

In so far as the act of state doctrine operates to persuade English courts to declare themselves an inappropriate tribunal for the application of rules of international law to the exercise of prerogative powers, this will impoverish the development of international law *except* where deliberate blindness to an international rule contributes to reform of that rule. This exception is the concern of the third rationale for the act of state doctrine

---

for, and that it has according to its terms legal effects as part of the municipal law. (The real point in *Thakrar.*) Secondly, emphasis is placed on the status of any such rule, once incorporated, as a distinct and independent rule of English law, subject to the normal rules of *stare decisis.*"

[155] The phrase *"opinio juris"* seems to have entered the discourse of international lawyers under the influence of Savigny and his followers in the German historical school.

[156] See above n 15 and accompanying text.

[157] See eg James Crawford "Public international law in twentieth-century England" in Jack Beatson and Reinhard Zimmermann (eds) *Jurists uprooted: German speaking emigré lawyers in twentieth century Britain* (Oxford University Press, 2004) 681 at 692, 699, 700–701.

[158] See eg John Tasioulas, "Customary international law and the quest for global justice" in Amanda Perreau-Saussine and James B Murphy (eds) *The nature of customary law* (Cambridge Universtiy Press, 2007) 307–335.

[159] *Abbasi* offers a striking recent example on the inter-relation between the developing rule articulated in article 19 of the ILC Draft Articles on Diplomatic Protection and the Court of Appeal's judgment: see Perreau-Saussine "Foreign views on eating aliens", above n 7.

(addressed in Section III, below), according to which acts of state, where morally defensible, are also defensible in English law.

Prior to the danger of sealing up an important source for the development of international law, the primary danger in treating the English act of state doctrine as a jurisdictional rule is that an exclusive focus on rules of international law can create a "grey hole" that blinds English courts to applicable rules of *English* law. As Stanley de Smith suggests, reflecting on *Nissan*:

> it would be undesirable to endorse the proposition put forward in some of the judgments in Nissan's case that direct interference with the liberty or property of such persons might be justified as acts of State if that interference were authorised by treaty or were necessary for the implementation of a treaty. This type of approach would open the door too wide to abuses of power by the executive; the validity of executive action ought to rest on a more impressive basis.[160]

Both dangers are exemplified in the House of Lords' recent decision in *Al Jedda*. Although it receives no mention in any of the judgments, a version of the jurisdictional act of state doctrine underlies the decision.

(iii) The dangers exemplified: the grey hole of Al Jedda

Al Jedda has close factual parallels with the leading act of state cases on *habeas corpus* considered above, cases like *Sigcau*, *Sekgome* and *Mwenya*. It concerned the internment of a dual British and Iraqi national, Al Jedda, who was resident in the United Kingdom but arrested during a visit with his children to Baghdad (where he had relatives) and flown to a British prison in Basra, on suspicion of involvement with weapons smuggling, explosive attacks, and terrorist recruitment in Iraq. His detention was subject to periodic review and authorisation by senior officers in the British Army; at the time of the House of Lords judgment, he had been detained without charge or trial for over three years.

One might have expected the House of Lords to begin by noting Al Jedda's position as a British citizen resident in the United Kingdom, detained in Iraq by British military officials, and so to determine the applicable system of law. On the basis of *Sigcau* and *Sekgome*, one would have expected the House of Lords to ask whether Iraq had a "settled system of criminal law and criminal tribunals"[161] under which Al Jedda could be appropriately charged and tried; or whether the situation was closer to that in *Sekgome* where "a few dominant civilized men have to control a great multitude of the semi-barbarous"[162]; or whether, since Al Jedda was a British citizen resident in the United Kingdom, the stability or otherwise of the Iraqi legal system was irrelevant. One would also have expected discussion of the availability of a writ of *habeas corpus* on the

---

[160] "Civis Britannicus Sum", above n 121, 431.
[161] Lord Watson in *Sigcau*, above n 74 and accompanying text.
[162] Vaughan Williams LJ in *Sekgome*, above n 92 and accompanying text.

basis of Lord Evershed's judgment in *Mwenya*, treating issue of a writ of habeas corpus as depending solely on whether a territory was "under the subjection of the Crown" and not on a territory's formal status.[163] But the question of applicable law is not addressed in these terms, and the availability of *habeas corpus* is not addressed at all.[164]

The appeal to the House of Lords had asked (echoing *Nissan*) whether Al Jedda's detention was attributable to the United Nations rather than the United Kingdom and as such not within the jurisdiction of British courts; whether United Nations Security Council Resolutions could "qualify or displace" Mr Al Jedda's right to freedom from arbitrary detention (in effect a jurisdictional act of state argument); under the Human Rights Act 1998 and Article 5(1) of the European Convention on Human Rights (ECHR) and only third and finally whether British or Iraqi law applied.

In addressing the question of attribution to the UN, the House of Lords understood themselves to be "called upon to assess how a claim by the appellant, that his international law rights under article 5(1) of the Convention had been violated by the United Kingdom, would fare before the European Court in Strasbourg".[165] The argument was that if the European Court of Human Rights were to treat Al Jedda's detention as attributable to the United Nations Security Council, it would hold itself incompetent to rule on the case: the case would fall outside the Strasbourg Court's jurisdiction since the UN is not a party to the ECHR.[166] Lord Rodger accepted this argument, treating Al Jedda's detention by British officials in Basra as attributable solely to the United Nations Security Council: as such, the ECHR did not apply to his detention and "Mr Al Jedda cannot bring proceedings in the English Courts under the HRA, alleging that his detention was unlawful because it was incompatible with his article 5(1) Convention right".[167] It was for the Security Council, "exerting its ultimate authority and exercising its ultimate right of control", to ensure that Mr Al Jedda was treated in accord with the law of armed conflict.[168] On this account, the Security Council can authorise the exercise of autocratic acts of state, constrained only by its self-understanding of the laws of war. In effect this treats the United Nations Security Council as a foreign sovereign whose acts of

---

[163] [1906] 1 QB at 295: see above n 120 and accompanying text.

[164] Brooke LJ giving judgment in *Al Jedda* in the Court of Appeal ([2006] EWCA Civ 327, [2007] QB 621, at para 100) explains that it was only on appeal that Al Jedda's counsel sought permission to introduce an application for *habeas corpus*: "We considered this inappropriate, not only because *habeas corpus* relief is governed by a different procedural code but also, and more importantly, because the claim for judicial review which was before the Divisional Court would enable us to rule that Mr Al-Jedda's detention was unlawful if we were so persuaded."

[165] *R (Al Jedda) v Secretary of State for Defence (JUSTICE and another intervening)* 2007 UKHL 58, 2008 1 AC 153: Lord Rodger at at 195, para 55.

[166] Lord Rodger at 359, para 64, referring to *Behrami v France* (2007) 45 EHRR SE 85 at para 71.

[167] *Al Jedda*, para 112.

[168] *Al Jedda*, para 113.

state fall outside the jurisdiction of British courts: Lord Rodger's position is the one unanimously rejected by the House of Lords in *Nissan*[169]
(another case not addressed in any of the judgments).

The other four Law Lords reject the argument that Al Jedda's detention by British officials should be attributed to the Security Council,
although on very different grounds from *Nissan*.[170] But although they
each attribute Al Jedda's detention to the UK, all four treat the UK's
obligations as a matter *not* of English law but international law and
(notionally) Iraqi law: without acknowledging the point explicitly, they
treat the UK's detention of Al Jedda as an act of state outside the jurisdiction of English courts.

Lord Bingham treats Security Council Resolution 1546 (8th June
2004) as creating an obligation on the UK to intern in Iraq without
trial "where this was necessary for imperative reasons of security". The
Resolution authorises the multinational force to take "all measures necessary" to maintain security and stability in Iraq, and a letter annexed to
the Resolution from the US Secretary of State (Colin Powell) expressly
includes within a list of measures contemplated "internment where this
is necessary for imperative reasons of security". Bingham concludes that,
given the priority accorded to UN Charter obligations by Article 103 of
the Charter, the obligation to intern "where necessary" prevailed over
Article 5(1) of the UN Charter, although the UK "must ensure that the
detainee's rights under article 5 are not infringed to any greater extent
than is inherent in such detention".[171]

The qualification is worthy of Kafka: here a right to be free from
internment is trumped by an obligation to intern. Lady Hale insists that
the right "is qualified only to the extent required or authorised by the
resolution" and that there would remain in the subsequent proceedings
"room for argument about what precisely is covered by the resolution"[172]
although it is difficult to see what of the right could remain—other than,
as she also notes, the question of whether on the facts of the case internment *was* necessary at all ("given that the problem he presents in Iraq
could be solved by repatriating him to this country and dealing with him
here"[173]), and so whether the Security Council authorisation was trig-
gered in the first place.

---

[169] See above n 137ff and accompanying text.
[170] All four accept that in principle actions of British forces on a UN mission could be attributable
solely to the UN, but were not in this case: see Bingham at paras 22, 24 ("The multinational force
in Iraq was not established at the behest of the UN, was not mandated to operate under UN auspices and was not a subsidiary organ of the UN. There was no delegation of UN power in Iraq.");
Hale at para 124 (adopting the arguments of Bingham and Brown); Carswell at para 131 (adopting
Bingham's arguments); Brown at para 147 (treating the UN's role in Iraq as "an essentially humanitarian and civil aid mission", although deciding in a "Post Script" written after reading Rodger's
judgment to "leave over for another day my final conclusion on this point").
[171] *Al Jedda*, para 34, 39.
[172] *Al Jedda*, para 126, 129.
[173] *Al Jedda*, para 128.

Al Jedda's common law claim was one for damages for false imprisonment, and, as a matter of private international law, this was treated as a
tort governed by the law of Iraq rather than English law. For this argument, all five members of the House of Lords invoke Brooke LJ's earlier
judgment in the case in the Court of Appeal.[174] There Al Jedda's counsel
had argued that it "would be substantially more appropriate to apply
English law" since "it would be strange indeed for the English Court to
apply Iraqi law to a claim by a British citizen against the British government in respect of activities on a base operated according to English
law (and inviolable from Iraqi process) by British troops governed by
English law (and immune from Iraqi law)."[175] But Brooke LJ did "not
consider that these considerations are strong enough to displace the normal rule":

> The emergency for which the powers of internment were required was in Iraq.
> The law of Iraq was adapted to include measures deemed necessary to combat
> the emergency. It was in Iraq that "ambush and mutilation, riots and attacks"
> were occurring and there was the risk of "chaos and the real possibility of civil
> war" if international troops were prematurely withdrawn. And it was in Iraq
> that the Security Council gave the MNF all the authority to take all necessary
> measures to contribute to the maintenance of security and stability, including
> internment where this was necessary for imperative reasons of security. Given
> that the laws of Iraq have been adapted to give the MNF the requisite powers, it
> would be very odd if the legality of Mr Al-Jedda's detention was to be governed
> by the law of England and not the law of Iraq.[176]

On this surprising finding, every one of the English act of state cases
involving torts overseas was wrongly decided as English law should not
have been applied.

Brooke LJ considered that "these proceedings have shown that he
is able to have [his internment] tested in an English court. He is not
being arbitrarily detained in a legal black hole, unlike the detainees in
Guantanamo Bay in the autumn of 2002."[177] Yet the grey hole in which
the Court of Appeal and House of Lords left Al Jedda is constitutionally worse.[178] In effect, both the Court of Appeal and House of Lords
treat acts of state as governed by international law *rather than* English
law[179], hence their uncritical focus on UN Security Council authorisation

---

[174] Lord Bingham at para 43 and Lord Brown (para 154) endorse Brooke LJ's argument in the
Court of Appeal; Lord Rodger (para 119) and Lord Carswell (para 131) endorse Lord Bingham
on the point; Lady Hale does not address the issue explicitly but states her general agreement with
Lords Bingham, Carswell and Brown (para 129).

[175] Brooke LJ's judgment in *Al Jedda* [2006] EWCA Civ 327, [2007] QB 621, at para 100.

[176] *Al Jedda* (Court of Appeal), para 106, internal cross-references omitted.

[177] *Al Jedda* (Court of Appeal), para 108, referring to *R (Abbasi) v Foreign Secretary* [2002]
EWCA Civ 1598 at [64].

[178] On grey holes, see Dyzenhaus, above n 33 and accompanying text.

[179] Strictly the Human Rights Act does not require English courts to follow decisions of the
Strasbourg court, only to consider Strasbourg decisions: see Keith Ewing "The unbalanced constitution" in Campbell, Ewing and Tomkins (eds) *Sceptical essays on human rights* (Oxford University

and their complete neglect of the long series of English act of state cases on habeas corpus. Treating British acts of state as falling outside the jurisdiction of English courts, the House of Lords neglects English common law on the validity of executive action and impoverishes the relevant English case law on acts of state. Had they examined the issues at stake in the English act of state cases, they would have become aware by analogy that their judgment also ignores the question of whether there are limits on acts of the Security Council and whether it is empowered to authorise autocratic acts of state violating fundamental freedoms.[180] In ignoring the question of *ultra vires* Security Council resolutions, it also lost an opportunity to contribute to development of international law on the topic.

III ACTS OF STATE AS LEGALLY DEFENSIBLE BECAUSE JUST

British constitutional lawyers frequently insist that all prerogative power is subject to the common law: the view "that the King could by his prerogative withdraw from the common law courts any matter which he chose to say was a matter of state, and decide it as he pleased, was finally disposed of by the Great Rebellion and the Revolution".[181] Just as in domestic affairs common lawyers have held themselves judges of whether a statutory provision ousting their jurisdiction can truly apply or of whether the executive can properly invoke a prerogative power, so in foreign affairs English courts have *sometimes* held that they have jurisdiction to decide whether or not an act is something the Crown had the legal power to do and as such is a lawful act of state.

The courts have sometimes insisted, in other words, that they are the final arbiter of the lawfulness of all executive action, and so of whether and of when a substantive common law defence of act of state is available to the Crown. On this account, raising a defence of act of state does not absolve the Crown from acting justly towards those individuals particularly affected: the defence requires that the Crown act justly

---

Press, 2001) 103–118; two earlier decisions of the House of Lords had nonetheless held rights under the Human Rights Act to be those under the ECHR: *R (Greenfield) v Secretary of State for the Home Department* [2005] UKHL 14 at para 19 (Lord Bingham) and *R (Quark Fishing Ltd) v Secretary of State for Foreign and Commonwealth Affairs* [2005] UKHL 57.

[180] Article 24(2) of the UN Charter limits the powers of the Security Council to those in accord with the purposes and principles of the UN, which include in Article 1(3) "promoting and encouraging respect for human rights and for fundamental freedoms for all": the argument would be that a Resolution incompatible with Article 1(3) is a nullity and as such not an obligation governed by Article 103. See Judge Morelli in the *Certain Expenses of the United Nations, Advisory Opinion*, ICJ Reports 1962 p 151 at 222; Dapo Akande "International Organisations" in Evans (ed) *International law* (Oxford University Press, 2nd edn, 2006) 277 at 292–3.

[181] Holdsworth "The history of acts of state in English law" (1941) 41 *Columbia Law Review* 1313 at 1314 and Holdsworth *History of English law* (1924) Vol 4 85 et seq.; Vol 5 at 430, 439–40; Vol 6 at 21 et seq.

towards victims of an act of state.[182] If, but only if, the executive can offer its courts reasonable grounds for believing that its otherwise unlawful actions were just actions that protected harm to the nation, then those actions should be treated as legally justified.

Such accounts are rare and they raise fundamental questions concerning the nature and extent of English public law remedies: in stark tension with a classical English account of the rule of law, according to which the Crown must be subject to the ordinary private law of the land, on this account acts of state are not treated in the same way as acts of ordinary citizens. On Albert Venn Dicey's celebrated account, the proper remedy for legal wrongs wrought by British officials, as for *any* legal wrong, was to be sought in private law. The rule of law he contrasted "with every system of government based on the exercise by persons in authority of wide, arbitrary, or discretionary powers of constraint", with "almost every continental community" in which "the executive exercises far wider discretionary authority in the matter of arrest, of temporary imprisonment, of explusion from its territory, and the like, than is either legally claimed or in fact exerted by the government in England".[183] In England, argued Dicey, the rule of law means that "every man, whatever be his rank or condition, is subject to the ordinary law of the realm, and amenable to the jurisdiction of the ordinary tribunals" and that constitutional protections are "with us the result of judicial decisions determining the rights of private persons in particular cases brought before the Courts."[184]

According to Dicey, a doctrine "pervades English law, that no one can plead the command of a superior, were it the order of the Crown itself, in defence of conduct otherwise not justified by law".[185] Although "well-informed foreign critics, and perhaps some Englishmen also, often think that there is in reality no remedy against the Crown [for a breach of contract or] a wrong committed by the Crown, or rather its servants", this idea, insists Dicey, is "in substance erroneous." This error is based on the "technical impossibility" of bringing an action against the Crown, an impossibility "often said to be based on the principle that the Crown can do no wrong." But for breaches of contract, a petition of right will generally lie "which though in form a petition, and requiring the sanction of the Attorney General (which is never refused), is in reality an action". And although, Dicey states, neither an action nor a petition of right "lies against the Crown for a wrong committed by its servants", "no injustice

---

[182] "As Lord Pearce put it very pithily; the prerogative involves 'a right to take and pay'. Perhaps it would be even more accurate to say that it involves the right to take and the duty to pay." Mann "Act of state as cause of action" in his *Foreign affairs in English courts*, above n 34, 188–190 at 189. On this account of the act of state doctrine as compatible with *Buron v Denman*, see the discussion of the availability of petitions of right, below at p 228.

[183] *Law of the constitution*, above n 87, 184.

[184] Ibid, 189, 191, citing at n 2 *Calvin's Case*, *Campbell v Hall*, *Wilkes v Wood* and *Mostyn v Fabregas*.

[185] Ibid, 282, citing Mommsen on "a similar principle in early Roman law" but with no reference to *Buron v Denman*.

results from this" as action can be taken "against the person who has actually done or taken part in doing the wrongful act which has caused damage" and the Crown "usually pays damages awarded against a servant of the State for a wrong done in the course of his service".[186]

The key problem with Dicey's enthusiastic account of the constitutional rule of English private law is the case of *Buron v Denman*, a case to which he does not refer[187] and in which a plea of act of state succeeded as a defence in a tort action brought (exactly as Dicey would advise) against a wrong-doing Crown servant. This section begins by showing how the act of state defence as established in *Buron* operates as a defence for Crown servants, shifting liability onto the Crown; I then move on to consider how and when a plea of act of state can also operate as a defence for the Crown.

(i)   The background to Buron v Denman: naval destruction of slave barracoons

Buron ultimately concerned the legality or otherwise of British actions against foreign slave traders overseas. Under Palmerston and the Whigs, and also under Peel, Aberdeen and the Tories, suppression of the slave trade was official British policy. Britain had long been campaigning for international recognition of a general "right of search" allowing the seizure of ships either carrying slaves or preparing to do so: as Sir James Mackintosh had claimed in Parliamentary debate, "the Right of Search was practical abolition".[188] But there was a suspicion that the British claim to a right of search was motivated by economic rather than philanthropic interest. The American Ambassador in Paris, General Cass, made those suspicions explicit: "Who can doubt that British cruisers stationed upon that distant coast, with an unlimited Right of Search, and discretionary authority to take possession of all vessels frequenting those seas, will seriously interrupt the trade of all other nations, by sending in their vessels for trial, under very slight pretences?"[189] At neither the Congress of Vienna in 1815 nor the conference at Aix-la-Chapelle were other European states prepared to concede to the leading maritime power a role in policing the "freedom of the seas", not least since the claimed policing role was closely linked to Britain's insistence on a war-time right to search neutral ships for enemy supplies and British deserters, an insistence that was a cause of the 1812–1814 war between Britain and the United States.[190]

---

[186] Ibid, 556–7.

[187] On Dicey's approach to case law, see Brian Simpson "The common law and legal theory" in Simpson (ed) *Oxford essays on jurisprudence II* (Oxford University Press, 1977) 77.

[188] Hansard House of Commons 9th February 1818. The account that follows is particularly indebted to Christopher Lloyd *The navy and the slave trade* (Cass: London, 1968): see 45 and more generally 39,60.

[189] H G Soulsby *The right of search and the slave trade in Anglo-American relations* (John Hopkins University, 1933) 47; Lloyd, ibid, 52.

[190] A Declaration annexed to the Final Act of 1815 condemned slave trading but deferred to future negotiations the details of the plan for suppressing it.

But by an 1835 treaty with Spain,[191] the first of a series of similar bilateral treaties between Britain and other states, a crucial "equipment clause" (omitted in earlier treaties) permitted British ships to stop and search Spanish vessels on the high seas when those ships were suspected of slave trading; the British ships were also permitted to seize the ships if they were found to contain any of the specified items of slaving equipment (extra messing equipment, shackles, bolts of handcuffs, or materials for building an extra deck). In the spring of 1840, Commander Denman had been sent to the north-west coast of Africa with instructions to join the ongoing British naval patrol attempting to suppress the slave trade.

Denman's patrol was looking for slaving ships at the mouth of the Gallinas river, a major slave trading base established by Pedro Blanco and since sold on to other Spanish slavers who were trading under authorisation from Prince Manna, the eldest son of the bedridden King Siacca of the Gallinas. That autumn the Governor of Sierra Leone asked Denman to liberate (employing " force as far as may be necessary") two British subjects from Sierra Leone, Fry Norman and her child, who were being held in one of the Spanish island prisons (slave "factories" or "barracoons"[192]). Denman set sail with three ships; the two captives had apparently been returned the day after Denman entered the river[193], but Denman and his crew continued to chase the slave traders (who tried to carry off their remaining slaves in canoes to the mainland), capturing ninety slaves including two British men. He then set guard over the barracoons, and demanded that King Siacca liberate the Normans and undertake by treaty to ban slave trading in the Gallinas. Under threats of violence from Denman, Prince Manna and the chiefs of the Gallinas undertook to banish resident slave traders within the month and "totally to destroy the factories belonging to these white men without delay". Two days later, Denman let loose the slaves. The gunpowder was thrown into the river; the casks of spirits opened and left to drain out on the sand ("it being suggested that they were poisoned"); and the traders' other goods "were claimed by King Siacca, as forfeited in consequence of the owner having acted in defiance of his law, and were delivered up to him"; and the barracoons were burned down.[194] Eight hundred and forty one slaves were carried by Denman to Sierra Leone and emancipated. Denman also carried some of the slave traders who, terrified of native exultation over

[191] 28th June 1835; 6 & 7 Will 4, c 6. See Allain in this volume of *BYIL*.

[192] Described by Commander Forbes as "sheds made of heavy piles, driven deep into the earth, and lashed together with bamboos, thatched with palm leaves. If the barracoon be a large one, there is a centre row of piles; along each line of piles is a chain, and at intervals of about two feet is a large neck-link, in one of which each slave is padlocked. Should this method be deemed insufficient, two, or sometimes in cases of great strength, three, are shackled together the strong man being placed between two others and heavily ironed, after being beaten half to death beforehand to ensure his being quiet." E Forbes *Six months service in the African Blockade* (1849) 113; Lloyd, above n 187, 29–30.

[193] David Eltis *Economic growth and the ending of the transatlantic slave trade* (Oxford University Press, 1987) at 120.

[194] *Buron v Denman* (1848) 2 Ex 167 at 176 (154 ER 450 at 454).

their downfall, begged to be taken to Sierra Leone: one of those rescued and given a free passage was Señor Buron.[195]

Reports were sent by the Governor of Sierra Leone to the Admiralty and to Lord John Russell, principal Secretary of State for the Colonial Department. James Stephen, Russell's Under-Secretary and as venerable a campaigner as Russell and Lord Palmerston in the movement to abolish slavery,[196] forwarded the reports to Lord Palmerston, then Foreign Secretary, explaining Russell's plans "to represent to the Lords Commissioners of the Admiralty, that her Majesty's government entertain a high sense of the very spirited and able conduct of Commander Denman, and its important results to the interests of humanity".[197] Palmerston's reply reiterated this praise of Denman's actions, recommending "that similar operations should be executed against all the piratical slave trade establishments which may be met with on parts of the coast not belonging to any civilised power".[198] James Stephen sent on to the Admiralty the set of letters and reports, which were followed by a letter to the Admiralty from Lord Leveson[199] explaining that if it were not possible in future operations to reach an agreement with "the native chiefs", "the commanders of her Majesty's cruisers would be perfectly justified in considering European slave traders established in the territory of the native chiefs as persons engaged in a piratical undertaking".[200] The correspondence was placed before Parliament, who voted to Denman and his men a bounty of four thousand pounds and another three thousand five hundred pounds towards the suppression of the slave trade on the coast of Africa; the Admiralty promoted Denman to the rank of Captain.

Señor Buron, having reached safety, brought an action in trespass against Commander Denman, claiming damages of one hundred thousand pounds (equivalent in today's money of nearly five and a half million pounds) for the loss of four thousand slaves and goods including cottons, woollens, gunpowder and spirits that had been stocked for exchange for more slaves. "Alien friends" had been allowed to bring most kinds of personal action in English courts since the end of the sixteenth century; primarily to encourage trade. Buron's was a test case: other actions by slave traders against members of the British navy were pending in the Court of the Exchequer.

It was not only foreign slave traders who were opposed to the official British policy of active intervention: opposition was also growing among free trade Members of Parliament, who were far from enthused

---

[195] Lloyd, above n 187, 94–96.

[196] James Stephen was also author of *The slavery of the British West Indies* in 1824.

[197] Downing Street 17th March 1841, part of the plaintiff's evidence, quoted in the case report at 2 Ex 177–178 (154 ER 455).

[198] Russell's reply through his Under-Secretary, John Backhouse Foreign Office 6th April.

[199] The second Foreign Office Under Secretary—what would now be termed the Parliamentary Under Secretary.

[200] 28th July 1841—quoted in case report at 2 Ex 180 (154 ER 456).

at Denman's actions. When other naval officers followed Denman's lead, in particular when one Captain Nurse, in the process of destroying a barracoon north of Sierra Leone on the Pongos river in 1841, destroyed the property of foreigners who claimed they were playing no part in the Slave Trade, the free traders became incensed: "What security had any merchant, British or foreign, that an over-zealous naval officer would not burn his goods on the beaches of Africa?"[201]

(ii) Le Louis, the Aberdeen letter and Dodson's advice: the destruction violated international law

Lord Aberdeen (newly appointed as Foreign Secretary in place of Palmerston) asked the Queen's Advocate, John Dodson, for advice on Buron's case against Denman. Dodson answered that he could not "take it upon himself to advise" that the actions of Commander Denman "are strictly justifiable, or that the instructions of her Majesty's naval officers...are such as can with perfect legality be carried into execution":

The Queen's Advocate is of the opinion, that the blockading rivers, landing and destroying buildings, and carrying of persons held in slavery in countries with which Great Britain is not at war, cannot be considered as sanctioned by the law of nations or by the provision of any existing treaties; and that, however desirable it may be to put an end to the slave trade, a good, however eminent, should not be obtained otherwise than by lawful means.[202]

Parliament had passed a series of statutes prohibiting the slave trade: the Acts of 1807 and 1811 were drafted very broadly and seemed to allow British subjects to prevent slave trading by traders whose states still recognised slave trading as lawful.[203] But in the Admiralty case of Le Louis in 1817, Sir Walter Scott (Lord Stowell) had ruled that since slave trading was permitted by international law, Parliament lacked the power to prohibit slave trading among foreigners. Acts against foreigners designed to further the suppression of foreign slave trading must be expressly sanctioned not by statute but by treaty with the relevant state:

To press forward to a great principle by breaking through every other great principle that stands in the way of its establishment; to force the way to the liberation

---

[201] Lloyd's characterisation of the position taken by the Free Trade group of MPs: above n 187, 97. William Hutt (who for Lloyd is the real villain of the story), Cobden, Bright and the young Gladstone argued that the withdrawal of the squadron would lead to a flourishing of legitimate trade *and* a rapid satiation of demand for imported slaves. On Hutt's arguments see Lloyd at 104–114. Lloyd concludes, against the Free Traders' arguments, that "All colonial history in every part of the world supports Captain Fishbourne's statement that, without a naval police force, "the coast would become a nest of pirates; the number of slaves exported would be enormous; all legitimate trade would cease, and in a very short time we should have to increase the squadron for the protection of what trade remained." (at 114, quoting Fishbourne's statement to the House of Lords Committee P.P. 1850 vol IX question 4346.)

[202] Letter from Lord Aberdeen, then Secretary of State for Foreign Affairs, to Lords of the Admiralty, May 20, 1842: quoted in the report of *Buron* at 2 Ex 181 (154 ER 456)

[203] 47 Geo III, c 36, 51 Geo III, c 23.

of Africa by trampling on the independence of other states in Europe; in short, to procure an eminent good by means that are unlawful, is as little consonant to private morality as to public justice.[204]

And in *Denman*'s case, Dodson advised as Queen's Advocate, the 1835 treaty could not possibly be read to sanction patrolling territorial waters, nor landing and destroying the barracoons, nor carrying off liberated slaves. Palmerston had celebrated Denman's attacking the barracoons (as opposed to waiting for slave trading ships to reach the high sea) as taking the "wasps' nest" rather than chasing after individual wasps.[205] But wasp-chasing, advised Dodson, was all the treaty with Spain permitted.

In *Le Louis*, Scott had held that "The Legislature must be understood to have contemplated all that was within its power, and no more."[206] Acts of Parliament, he held, could not affect "any right or interest of foreigners, unless they are founded upon principles and impose regulations that are consistent with the law of nations". The Admiralty court must treat Parliament's legislative jurisdiction as circumscribed by international law: it was "the only law" which Britain could apply to foreigners, and so "the generality of any terms employed in an Act of Parliament must be narrowed in construction by a religious adherence thereto".[207] The question of the legality or otherwise of slave trading according to the law of nations must be considered "not according to any private moral apprehensions of my own (if I entertained them ever so sincerely), but as *the law* considers it". First, international law allowed a right to search only the ships of belligerents on the high seas: to allow searches of ships "of states of amity upon the high seas" would violate two fundamental principles of international law, that of the equality and independence of states and that protecting an equal right to uninterrupted use of the high seas. Slave trading could not be assimilated to piracy since slave traders, unlike pirates, are not enemies of every country: they confine "their transactions (reprehensible as they may be) to particular countries, without exciting the slightest apprehension in others"—and in legislating to make slave trading a transportable rather than a capital offence, Britain itself recognised a distinction between slave trading and piracy.[208]

Secondly, a new rule of customary international law prohibiting slave trading could not be said to have emerged: personal slavery had been protected "with all the sanctions of law, public and municipal, and without any opposition, except the protests of a few private moralists, little heard and less attended to, in every country, till within these very few years in this particular country." Although a considerable change of opinion was now taking place, the "speculative opinions" condemning slave trading at the 1815 Vienna Congress could not "be admitted

---

[204] *Le Louis* 2 Dod. 210 at 257.
[205] See Lloyd, above n 187, 93–99.
[206] *Le Louis* at 254
[207] *Le Louis* at 239.   [208] *Le Loius* at 247.

to have the force of overruling the established course of the general law of nations": the states represented at Vienna continued to permit slave trading by treaty. And even if the principles of the Vienna Declaration had not been undermined by the witness of these contradictory treaties, were an equivalent Congress to declare "that the right of search in time of war, as exercised on neutrals, was contrary to all reason and justice", Britain "I presume would not attribute any such effect to such opinions".[209]

In places in his judgment, Scott assumes an account of international law that treats its principles as the inherently wise, "publicly just and privately moral" fruits of long practice. But he also insists that certain principles such as the ban for which the USA contended on wartime searches of neutral ships (his judgment does not explicitly refer to the USA) could be excluded from English law on grounds of reason and justice: whether this is because as unjust and unreasonable principles they cannot be principles of international law at all, or whether they can be principles of international but not *English* law is not made clear, although the implication seems to be the latter, making the reason and justice of principles of international law subject to assessment by "this country". Scott denies that his moral and political opinions play a role in stating what "*the law* considers" yet also insists that arguments of reason and justice (and in effect British policy) would justify a refusal to enforce as a rule of international law the ban for which the USA contended. (Britain eventually accepted such a prohibition during the Crimean War in the Declaration of Paris.)

On Dodson's report of the decision in *Le Louis*, Scott's arguments for distinguishing slave trading from piracy were those put to him by Lushington, while his denial of a right of search either under the general law of nations or specific treaties was made by the appellant's second advocate who "laid it down as a primary and fundamental rule of the law of nations, that the right to visit and search foreign ships on the open sea does not exist in time of peace; and this position he proceeded to establish upon the three grounds of reason, authority, and practice."[210] That second advocate was the reporter himself, the later Queen's Advocate, John Dodson.

Scott's decision in *Le Louis* was followed by the common lawyers of the Court of the King's Bench in *Madrazo v Willes* (1820),[211] who also held themselves bound to construe the then-extant anti-slavery legislation as applying only to *British* subjects involved in the slave trade. They accepted Scott's argument that neither a "British Act of Parliament, nor any commission founded on it, can affect the rights or interests of foreigners, unless they are founded upon principles and impose regulations

---

[209] *Le Louis* at 250, 252–3.
[210] *Le Louis* at 225.
[211] (1820) 3 B & Ald 353.

that are consistent with the law of nations. That is the only law that Great Britain can apply to them; and the generality of any terms employed in an Act of Parliament must be narrowed in construction by a religious adherence thereto."[212] The case is cited by one twentieth century writer on English law as the "strongest example of courts restraining the effect of widely expressed statutes" in line with what the court understood to be the relevant rules of international law: the broader reading of the statutes, summarises Sir Carleton Allen, "however morally commendable, would have violated an elementary principle of International Law; and in *Madrazo v Willes* the Court of the King's Bench, with regret but without hesitation, so narrowed the statutes that a Spaniard was enabled to recover very large damages in an English court for interference at Havana with his slave ship and traffic".[213]

Countering Scott's argument (highlighting the divergence between statutory penalties for piracy and for slave trading), with an Act of 1824 Parliament bolstered its anti-slavery legislation by assimilating slave trading to piracy, treating it as punishable by death;[214] another crucial piece of legislation was the Emancipation Act of 1833.[215] But when the papers relating to Denman came before Dodson, he stuck to his guns: he advised the Cabinet that slave trading remained lawful under international law and so that under English law foreign slave traders could be constrained only by treaty.[216]

(iii) Baron Parke's summing-up in Buron v Denman: the nature of the defence of act of state

One historian sees Aberdeen's request for legal advice from Dodson as "a serious error on the part of the Whig Government", one that postponed all hope of successful abolition for many years.[217] Given the position on the suppression of slave trading still shared by the executive and by most members of Parliament, and their endorsement of Denman's actions, the executive was in a difficult position, one which became all the more

---

[212] 2 Dods 239 (ER 1474).

[213] C K Allen *Law in the making* (Clarendon Press: Oxford, 7th edition, 1964) 461.

[214] An Act for the more effectual suppression of the African Slave Trade 1824 (5 Geo IV c 17).

[215] An Act for the abolition of slavery throughout the British colonies, for promoting the industry of the manumitted slaves, and for compensating the persons hitherto entitled to the services of such slaves 1833 (3 & 4 Will IV c 73).

[216] As a result of Dodson's advice, Aberdeen appointed a Committee presided over by Stephen Lushington (now a judge of the Admiralty Court) to draft instructions to guide naval officers "employed in the suppression of the slave trade"; Denman was involved in the work of the Committee, whose instructions, published in 1844, aim to give Commanders a detailed outline of their legal position—directing, *inter alia*, Commanders stationed on the Coast of Africa to collect detailed information both on the slave trade and on the possibilities for legitimate commerce, and to use force only on the orders of a Senior Officer on the station *or* for rescuing British subjects and if so confining that use of force "to the liberation of the persons so detained." General Instructions Section 2nd paras 2, 6. The Committee's report is in P.P. 1844 1 vol 50.

[217] Lloyd, above n 187, 97.

difficult as free trade Parliamentarians began to argue more directly in the mid 1840s that naval attempts to suppress the slave trade, and the naval patrols in particular, should cease.

Denman's actions might have been defended as lawful because the relevant rule of customary international law on which *Le Louis* and *Madrazo* were based had now changed. It might have been argued that Dodson was out of date and ignored what was now a rule of international law treating slave traders as the enemies of humanity and so outside the protection of the general rule preventing searches on the high seas.[218] But Dodson was far from alone in arguing as he did: as the campaigners against forcible abolition emphasised, few British international lawyers accepted that such a new rule of customary international law had yet emerged.

Another defence might have been that Denman's actions were lawful because the Court had erred in *Madrazo* in following *Le Louis*: Scott in the Admiralty Court was applying international law rather than national law, but in the eyes of the common law Parliament had legislative jurisdiction even over foreigners overseas and so in English law could empower Denman to do what he did. But to argue this would have required common lawyers not only to ignore the approach of a judge widely regarded as a great civilian, but also to rule in stark rejection of a clearly established rule of international law in a way no English common law court had done.

Only one defence was possible if Denman himself was not to be left liable for the equivalent of five and a half millions pounds in damages for his valiant actions: Denman's actions would have to be attributed exclusively to the state, so that in so far as Buron could have a successful claim against the Crown, the state would bear the relevant costs. The Admiralty eventually agreed to have the Attorney General defend Denman on behalf of the Crown, and the Attorney General argued that in lauding Denman as it had, the Crown had retrospectively adopted Denman's actions as its own, so exempting Denman from all liability.

Furthermore Buron had no right to bring an action against the Crown because as an alien friend he would have a right of action only where a British subject would: here a British subject would not. Those of the Crown's (Denman's) actions falling within the terms of the Spanish treaty could not be questioned: "no subject has a right to bring an action for anything done in pursuance of that treaty, whether sanctioned by the municipal law or not; for his assent is virtually implied to every act of his own government".[219] Those of the Crown's (Denman's) actions falling outside the terms of the treaty should also be treated as retrospectively adopted acts of state "in respect of which no action can be maintained". To defend this second argument, the Attorney General

---

[218] An approach to precedent not endorsed by a common law court until the Court of Appeal's majority judgment in *Trendtex*.

[219] *Buron v Denman* (1848) 2 Ex 167 at 184 (154 ER 457), citing *Conway v Gray* 10 East 536.

cited *Elphinstone*.[220] As seen above, this controversial opinion was at best authority for a rule that actions carried out in the course of a war were subject to the exclusive jurisdiction of military and not civilian courts. If slave trading did amount to piracy, then slave traders could be treated as enemies of mankind and so in effect in a state of constant war, but this could not be argued without challenging Scott's judgment; since Denman's actions should then be treated as carried out in peace time, *Elphinstone* was hardly a relevant precedent. Unsurprisingly, Baron Parke did not refer to the case in summing up in *Buron v Denman*.

But Parke did hesitantly accept the argument that Denman's actions became an act of state when ratified by the Crown—hesitantly because "there appears to me a considerable distinction between the present case and the ordinary case of ratification by subsequent authority between private individuals" since "if the Crown ratifies an act, the character of the act becomes altered, for the ratification does not give the party injured the double option of bringing his action against the agent who committed the trespass or the principal who ratified it, but a remedy against the Crown only (such as it is), and actually exempts from all liability the person who commits the trespass." Parke concludes:

Whether the remedy against the Crown is to be pursued by petition of right, or whether the injury is an act of state without remedy, except by appeal to the justice of the state which inflicts it, or by application of the individual suffering to the government of his country, to insist upon compensation from the government of this—in either view, the wrong is no longer actionable.[221]

There were then, in Parke's summary, two views of the route now open to Buron.[222] On one view, he could pursue a remedy from the Crown by petition of right. On another—in line with the "autocratic" imperial cases considered above—his only remedy was to ask Spain to take up his cause, exercising diplomatic protection on his behalf—in which case under international law any compensation awarded would be the property of the Spanish state (who would be under no legal obligation to recompense Buron). As Buron's case was settled after Parke's ruling (as were the other pending cases), which of the two views was correct was not determined.

If the first view is correct at common law, *Buron* does not give the executive the "free hand" claimed by Stephen and Wade. Their suggestion that it leaves the executive legally unaccountable for acts of state can be defended only if one assumes firstly that Parke, who was celebrated for his knowledge of legal forms and procedures,[223] was wrong to suggest that Buron could have sought compensation by petition of right,

---

[220] See above n 56 and accompanying text.

[221] *Buron v Denman* at 189–190.

[222] Giving judgment in *Nissan*, Lord Morris recognises this possibility ([1970] AC 220A).

[223] Parke resigned in 1855 on the abolition of the forms of action: "His fault was an almost super-stitious reverence for the dark technicalities of special pleading, and the reforms introduced by the

and secondly that in accepting the plea of act of state the court was not shifting responsibility from Buron to the Crown but was declaring (as in *Elphinstone* and more directly in *Kamachee*) that the case was non-justiciable.

This raises the crucial question of whether or not Buron could have sought compensation from the Crown, that is, whether the plea of act of state operated as a defence *for Denman* shifting liability onto the Crown (through a petition of right), or whether the plea also operated as a defence *for the Crown*. The following and final sections of this article address this question.

(iv) The availability or otherwise of damages for acts of state by petition of right

Over the course of the seventeenth century, an alliance of common law-yers and Parliament had insisted that although in the eyes of his courts the king can do no wrong, a wrong apparently done by the king could be attributed to his servants, and that those servants, however senior, were answerable not solely to the king but also to the courts. Resuscitating and extending the medieval principle of the liability of the king's serv-ants under ordinary law, the common lawyers had argued that ministers of State could be made personally liable like any private person.[224] In principle, then, since "a servant of the Crown is responsible in law for a tortious act done to a fellow subject, though done by the authority of the Crown",[225] the doctrine of ministerial responsibility to the law gave alien friends remedies against the king's servants. But any claim Buron might have tried to bring against Russell or Palmerston would be more than likely to be met with an act of state defence.

As Parke suggests, it *might* have been possible for Buron to seek com-pensation directly from the Queen by petition of right.[226] While the monarch cannot issue a writ against herself, she could be petitioned to grant a remedy to a subject who would have had a remedy had his claim been against a fellow subject rather than against the queen herself: "The petition of right, unlike a petition addressed to the grace or favour of the sovereign," explains Cockburn CJ in 1865, "is founded on the violation

---

Common Law Procedure Acts of 1854 and 1855 occasioned his resignation." Sir James Parke, 15 D.N.B. 226.

[224] For an introductory overview see Holdsworth *A history of English law* Vol VI 101–3, 111, 266–7; Vol IX 98.

[225] Cockburn CJ in *Feather v the Queen* (1865) 6 B & S 257 at 297.

[226] See Holdsworth Vol IX at 30–45 on 18th/19th century developments of the remedy by peti-tion of right. The remedy became increasingly popular over the nineteenth century—Holdsworth attributes this partly to "the fact that the manifold activities of the modern state necessitated some remedy against the crown for breaches of contract and other wrongs committed by its agents; and partly to the fact that the old remedy of suing for a writ of Liberate, or petitioning the barons of the Exchequer, had become obsolete with changes in the fiscal machinery of the state." It was made more generally available in 1860 when the procedure on such a petition was reformed by the Petitions of Right Act (23, 24 Victoria c 34). Vol IX at 39.

of some right in respect of which, but for the immunity from all process with which the law surrounds the person of the Sovereign, a suit at law or equity could be maintained".[227]

At the time of *Buron*, the question whether a petition of right might lie for damages in tort had been argued in only one case, *Viscount Canterbury v A-G* (1843), in which the Speaker of the House of Commons sought compensation from the Crown for property destroyed when his home in the old palace of Westminster (containing £10,000 worth of pictures, plate and furniture) was burned down by spectacularly negligent Crown employees who were supposed to have been disposing of old Exchequer tallies in another room of the palace. Lord Lyndhurst LC, dismissing early authorities to the contrary, held that as the Queen herself could not be liable for personal negligence, a petition of right could not lie for compensation from her for the negligence of her employees:

If the master or servant is answerable on the principle *quia facit per alium, facit per se*, this would not apply to the Sovereign, who can be required to answer for his own personal acts.... If the principle now contended for be correct, the negligence of the seamen in service of the Crown would raise a liability in the Crown to make good the damage, and which might be enforced by petition of right. It would require, I think, some very precise and distinct authority to establish such a liability, and in the absence of any such authority, I cannot venture, for the first time, to lay down a rule which it is obvious would lead to such extensive consequences.[228]

Although *Viscount Canterbury* is widely cited as establishing that petitions of right would not lie in tort,[229] Lyndhurst's justification for Crown immunity in negligence is dubious because so confused. The whole point of petitions of right was that they lay for actions that *if* attributable to a subject (rather than to the Sovereign, who can in law do no wrong) *would* constitute legal wrongs. Lyndhurst's argument inverts this, suggesting that since the Sovereign can do no wrong, neither can she be said to have done wrong through her servants: on this argument, petitions of right could *never* lie.

It was not until 1864 that the courts were directly confronted with the question that would have been raised by Buron had the case not settled: in *Tobin v The Queen*[230] the Tobins, Liverpool ship-owners and merchants, claimed damages from the Crown for the destruction of their boat the *Britannia* off the west coast of Africa by Captain Douglas. Douglas had believed that the spare planks found on the ship (unregistered and flying no national flag) were there to be used to create a second slave deck, and burned the boat as involved in the slave trade (along with the barrels of

---

[227] *Feather* at 295.

[228] (1842–1843) 1 Ph 306 at 321–2 (41 ER 648 at 654)

[229] Holdsworth argues that on the basis of medieval precedents a petition of right "ought" to lie for encroachment on property and nuisance, "though whether it would be held to lie in these cases is highly doubtful." Vol IX at 42–3.

[230] 16 CB (NS) 310. The action was brought by Thomas Tobin's son on behalf of the estate.

palm oil being carried on board) on the ground that it was not fit for a voyage to St Helena for adjudication in the Vice Admiralty courts there. The Tobins insisted that they had just bought the boat for carrying out lawful trade in west Africa, that they had no plans to bring the boat to Britain and so no reason to register it, and that the extra planks were being carried because they were "well adapted for repairing such a vessel" and "not easily procurable".[231]

Presumably fearing an act of state defence were they to sue Captain Douglas, and perhaps also seeking direct recognition of and apology for the Crown's destruction of their boat, the Tobins sought a petition of right under the newly enacted Petitions of Right Act (1860).[232] The Tobins' lawyers (Sir Hugh Cairns with Kemplay and Archibald) argued that the petition lay as the claim was not one in negligence for unliquidated damages (as in *Viscount Canterbury*), but one for compensation for the seizure of goods which could not be restored in kind. As such it was a claim for which (invoking early authorities) a petition of right *would* lie: the Crown had seized the ship as forfeited because involved in the slave trade, and Douglas, not knowing this was not the case and continuing to act in good faith as the Crown's servant, had dealt "with the goods in such a manner that they cannot be restored in specie".[233] The Attorney General for the Crown demurred, invoking *Viscount Canterbury* and arguing that Parke's judgment in *Buron* "does not mean to intimate that the subsequent ratification of Captain Denman's act by the Crown gave a remedy by petition of right".[234]

Earle CJ, delivering the judgment of the Court of Common Pleas, held that the Tobins had no case against the Queen since Douglas was acting not as an agent of the Queen but as an agent of Parliament (since he was claiming to act under statutory powers); that even if he were an agent of the Queen he was acting outside his authority and so the Queen could not be liable for his actions; and finally that even if this were not the case, "a petition of right cannot be maintained to recover unliquidated damages for a trespass"—although it would lie for restitution of chattels "or the value thereof if it had been converted to the King's use" and probably would also lie for the restitution of money.[235] Compensation from the Crown might, then, be available by petition of right to someone in Buron's position whose property had been seized by a Crown employee purporting to act under prerogative powers.[236] But here the only claim possible was against Douglas—although such claims would usually "have the same effect as a petition of right for damages for the tort, since, in a

---

[231] 16 CB (NS) 310 at 313.   [232] 23 & 24 Vict, c. 34.
[233] 16 CB (NS) 310 at 331, 334.
[234] 16 CB (NS) 310 at 330.
[235] 16 CB (NS) 310 at 353, 358, 359.
[236] In the following year in *Feather* at 294, Cockburn CJ echoed these ambiguous dicta, ruling that a petition of right could not be sought for trespass, but suggesting that it *would* lie for damages in lieu of restitution of seized chattels.

proper case, the Crown will defend its officer and become responsible for any damages awarded."[237]

Both Dicey and Clode argue that compensation in such a case *should* not be available from the Crown since that compensation "would in such a case be in the nature of damages for conversion, that is for a tort" and so falls within the decision in *Viscount Canterbury*.[238] But in the words of the leading early twentieth century authority on civil proceedings against the Crown, the point was "never formally considered" and "may well provide matter for argument on a future occasion".[239]

The prelude to such a future occasion came before the courts in *AG v De Keyser's Royal Hotel*,[240] in which the House of Lords held that a petition of right *would* lie to enforce the Crown's duty to compensate a British hotelier for his wartime losses while his hotel on the Thames Embankment had been the headquarters of the Royal Flying Corps. The Crown argued that it had occupied the hotel as a prerogative right: in a wartime emergency "private convenience must yield to public necessity", and requisitions made in exercise of this emergency prerogative carried no legal obligation to pay compensation.[241] The Crown also argued that it was not covered by a statutory duty to compensate, relying on the Court of Appeal's wartime decision in *In re a Petition of Right* which refused compensation to the owners of a Brighton aerodrome being used as a military base: the Court of Appeal had concluded in 1915 that the Defence Act 1842 did not apply (as it concerned procedures for compulsory purchase rather than occupation) and that the prerogative right "cannot be interfered with or taken away except by plain language or necessary implication".[242]

---

[237] George Stuart Robertson *Civil proceedings by and against the Crown* (London, 1908) 351.

[238] Clode *The law and practice of Petition of Right* (London, 1887) 89; Dicey *Parties to an action* (London, 1870) 23–24, reiterating fifty years later (without citations) in an appendix on "Proceedings against the Crown" in his *Law of the constitution* that "Neither an action nor a Petition of Right lies against the Crown for a wrong committed by its servants. The remedy open to a person injured by a servant of the Crown in the course of his service is an action against the person who has actually done or taken part in doing the wrongful act which has caused damage. But, speaking generally, no injustice results from this, for the Crown, ie the Government, usually pays damages awarded against a servant of the State for a wrong done in the course of his service.... It would be an amendment of the law to enact that a Petition of Right should lie against the Crown for torts committed by the servants of the Crown in the course of their service. But the technical immunity of the Crown in respect of such torts is not a subject of public complaint, and in practice works little, if any, injustice.": above n 87, 556–7.

[239] Robertson, above n 236, 336, continuing: "The author inclines to the opinion that the remedy by petition of right should, in strictness, be limited to specific property, though such a limitation would no doubt involve hardship." (There is "no doubt whatever that a petition of right will lie in respect of money.")

[240] [1920] AC 508. For a detailed study of compensation offered to owners whose private property had been requisitioned by the state as part of the war effort waged from 1914, see G R Rubin *Private property, government and requisition and the constitution 1914–1927* (Hambledon Press: London, 1994).

[241] [1920] AC 508 at 514.

[242] [1915] 3 KB 649 at 660 (Lord Cozens-Hardy MR).

In *De Keyser*, the House of Lords held that the Crown was bound by the Defence Act 1842 to pay compensation: accordingly, contemporary administrative lawyers focus on the decision as a leading illustration of statutory provisions (and so the will of Parliament) prevailing over executive claims of unfettered prerogative power. The case is at least as striking for the manner in which a majority of the Court of Appeal evaded their own earlier decision in *In re a petition of right* to reach their decision in favour of the hotelier (a decision with which the House of Lords concurred). The Master of the Rolls argued that the 1842 statute should be read in the light of his requested search of the Public Records, which revealed that "it does not appear that the Crown has ever taken the subject's land for the defence of the country without paying for it".[243] Endorsing his assessment, the House of Lords held that "it does not appear that the Crown has ever taken for [defence] purposes the land of the subject without paying for it," that there was "no trace of the Crown having, even in the times of the Stuarts, exercised or asserted the power or right to do so by virtue of the Royal Prerogative", and that the Crown was bound to pay compensation by the Defence Act 1842 which it was not "free at its pleasure to disregard".[244]

In *De Keyser*, the House of Lords followed a majority of the Court of Appeal in justifying their conclusion by drawing on the resources of a reasonably detailed historical study of the common law and legislation. But what would or could a common law court have done had it faced a claim from a foreigner to compensation for war-time requisitioning under prerogative powers? A majority of the Court of Appeal took this to be the question before them in *Commercial and Estates Company of Egypt v Board of Trade*,[245] an appeal from the War Compensation Court (established after *de Keyser* was decided). The Crown had seized timber bought by an Egyptian company which had chartered a British steamer to ship timber from Finland back to Alexandria: as war broke out soon after the steamer had set off, it had been agreed between the company and the steamer's owners that the wood would stay on board the ship until the end of the war when it would sail on to Alexandria, but in August 1917 the steamer was requisitioned by the British Shipping Controller, and the timber on board was brought (some of it on other requisitioned boats) to England where it was requisitioned by the Controller of Timber Supplies. The Crown argued that "an act of State, whether done in this country or abroad, gives no cause of action against a resident alien". Alternatively, it argued, the timber had been requisitioned either under the Defence of the Realm Regulations (which meant that under

---

[243] Lord Dunedin is implicitly critical of the Court of Appeal's decision in *De Keyser* in not only giving the Lords "the benefit of the opinions they had come to on the merits" but also evading their earlier decision by distinguishing their earlier decision on the basis that it had concerned land required "for the conduct of hostilities" while *de Keyser*'s case concerned the taking of land "for administrative purposes" (Ld Cozens-Hardy MR at 229; Ld Dunedin at 526).

[244] *De Keyser* Ld Atkinson at 539.   [245] [1925] 1 KB 271.

the Indemnity Act 1920 the compensation payable would be limited in accord with those regulations). Or, finally, the Crown argued that if the timber was seized under the internationally recognised right of angary (the right of a belligerent state to seize the property of neutrals found on the territory of or occupied by the belligerent), any obligation to pay the full market value of the timber (at the time of requisition) was recognised only by international law; as such, compensation might be obtained by diplomatic means but not through the English courts.

As section 2(1)(b) of the Indemnity Act 1920 directed that compensation should be in accord with the provisions of any such regulation "purporting to be made under any enactment relating to the defence of the realm", and here the Crown purported to have seized the timber under defence regulations, Scrutton LJ held that the compensation should be assessed in line with the principles laid down within those regulations.[246]

By contrast Bankes and Atkin LJJ held that the timber owners were entitled not to the limited compensation that would be awarded under the defence regulations but to full compensation. Those defence regulations had been so widely worded ("any goods wherever in the world" could have been included) that "some limitation was necessary": Atkin LJ argued that "I cannot think it was within the power of the authority making the regulations under the Defence of the Realm Act to make regulations that affected such neutrals" and considered that the provisions of the Indemnity Act relating to "purported" regulations could not "validate both acts of officials and regulations which would otherwise be ultra vires" but "may well have been introduced to cover questions of defect of form or procedure in the making", although not substantively defective regulations.[247] Atkins LJ suggested that he did not need to decide these points, following the conclusion of earlier litigation which had held that the Crown could not justify the seizure under the regulations but only (as it had suggested as an alternative) under the right of angary. Quoting Dicey's "authoritative" definition of prerogative powers as "the residue of discretionary or arbitrary authority, which at any given time is legally left in the hands of the Crown", Atkin LJ held that the right of angary with the accompanying obligation to compensate was one such prerogative power. Were the right of angary not a prerogative right recognised by the common law, the Board of Trade would have been liable for conversion of the timber: the Crown would not have had the right to seize the property in the first place since it is "only in so far as the rules of international law are recognized as included in the rules of municipal law that they are allowed in the municipal Courts to give rise to rights or obligations". And as it was "well recognized by the conventions

---

[246] [1925] 1 KB 271 at 289–290, adding that "it will take a great deal of argument to persuade me that, apart from action justified by statute, the defence that an act is an act of State is open to the Sovereign or the executive within the realm."

[247] *Commercial and Estates* Atkin LJ at 293.

of civilized nations, which constitute the body of international law" that the right of angary required its exercisor to make "full compensation for the property he so seizes", there was "no reason for holding that our municipal law recognizes the right to seize but rejects the obligation to compensate". To hold that there was no common law obligation to compensate "would be to bring our municipal law into conflict with international usage in a matter where a priori principles of justice seem to support the latter" and to the "remarkable" suggestion, in the light of the decision in *de Keyser*, that "our law granted compensation to subjects who had a direct interest in the defence of the realm and denied it to neutrals whose goods were here against their will". So a majority of the Court of Appeal held that a petition of right would lie to enforce the company's claim to compensation.[248]

While in *de Keyser*, the House of Lords justified making a compensatory award (which following the earlier Court of Appeal decision in *In re a petition of right* would otherwise have been refused) in terms of common law tradition, in *Commercial and Estates* the majority of the Court of Appeal invoked international law and arguments of justice to make a full compensatory award in the face of legislation that came into force after *de Keyser* was decided. Atkin LJ argues that justice required that limitations be placed on the statutory provisions (which he refused to interpret in a way that would effectively render retrospectively lawful substantively *ultra vires* regulations), and that in this case the relevant principles of international law offered a suitably just approach and so could be treated as a consistent part of the common law. The case is a striking example of a common lawyer assuming a natural law understanding of the common law and invoking international law to bolster a common law constraint on legislation.

A petition of right could then have lain against the Crown for a *Buron*-type claim for compensation for seizure of property—so long as that claim was framed in restitutionary terms rather expressly as a tort. The plea of act of state served as a defence for Denman but not (*pace* Stephen, Holdsworth, Wade and Collier) as a defence for the Crown—or at least, not as a defence that freed the Crown from any obligation to compensate the victim of the act of state. Accepting the Crown's *post-facto* ratification transformed Buron's claim against a private individual (Denman) into a claim against the State. And on the basis of the decision in *Commercial and Estates*, a restitutionary claim against the Crown (made through a petition of right) could have had a chance of success.

(v) The availability of damages for acts of state after the Crown Proceedings Act 1947: possibilities building on Burmah Oil and Nissan

In 1947, in order "to prevent the little man from being crushed by the juggernaut of the State", a right of action was made available in most of the

---

[248] *Commercial and Estates* at 295–6, 293, 297.

cases where a petition of right would have lain in the past.[249] The Crown Proceedings Act 1947 makes the Crown "subject to all those liabilities in tort to which, if it were a private person of full age and capacity, it would be subject" in respect of torts by its servants or agents, breaches of its duty as an employer, and breaches of its common law duties attaching "to the ownership, occupation, possession or control of property". The liability in tort was subject to a proviso: no proceedings in tort would lie against the Crown for "in respect of any act or omission of a servant or agent of the Crown unless the act or omission would apart from the provisions of this Act have given rise to a cause of action in tort against that servant or agent or his estate".[250] Glanville Williams comments:

It is thought that this proviso was inserted in order to make it plain that the Crown was to participate in the defence of "act of state" that is open to the servant under the rule in *Buron v Denman*. But if this was the intention, the proviso uses a bludgeon to kill a fly—and the fly was already dead, because where the servant has the defence of "act of state" it cannot be said that he has committed a tort...and thus there is nothing for which the Crown could in any event be liable.[251]

Arguably Williams's bludgeon misses the fly. The very cause of Parke's hesitancy in *Buron* was that accepting the Crown's post-facto ratification left the Crown *alone* as the only party responsible for the damage caused, rather than (as would be usual under the law of agency) making Denman and his principal (the Crown) jointly and severally liable. The decision left the Crown not vicariously liable but solely responsible for an action treated by the courts as an exclusively public or state enterprise, an action for which I have argued above *restitutionary* damages could have been available had the case not settled.

The question of the availability or otherwise of compensation for acts of state brings us to two key post-war cases against the Crown, *Burmah Oil* and *Nissan*. Both involved actions against British subjects overseas, and in neither case did the House of Lords accept a defence of act of state that removed the Crown's obligation to compensate.

In *Burmah Oil Co v Lord Advocate*, a majority of the House of Lords, recognising the paucity of case law, held as in *Commercial and Estates* that a prerogative power under which the state had acted entitled the Crown only to "take and pay".[252] The Burmah Oil Company

---

[249] The Crown Proceedings Act has been held to *limit* rights previously enjoyed under Scots law: *Davidson v Scottish Ministers* 2006 SC (HL) 42 (2006 SLT 110), para 33 (Lord Nicholls).

[250] Viscount Jowett LC, the promoter of the then Crown Proceedings Bill on its second reading in the House of Lords on 4th March 1947; Crown Proceedings Act 1947 ss 1, 40(2), 2(1)(a).

[251] Glanville Williams *Crown Proceedings: an account of civil proceedings by and against the Crown as affected by the Crown Proceedings Act 1947* (London, 1948) at 44.

[252] [1965] AC 75. The paragraphs below are indebted to the discussion of the case (accompanied by strong criticism) in "The Burmah Oil affair" (1966) 79 *Harvard Law Review* 614–634. (Harvard case notes are published anonymously; the author of this note was Charles Whitman.) See also T C Daintith "The case of the demolitions" (1965) 14 ICLQ 1006.

and other owners of Burmese oil refineries and inventories of crude petroleum and gasoline were seeking compensation for destruction of this property in March 1942 by General Sir Harold Alexander and his British troops during the British evacuation of Rangoon in what was then the British colony of Burma. (Burmah Oil's refinery continued burning for twenty-three years.) The destruction happened in the face of oncoming Japanese troops: it was part of a "scorched-earth" plan to demolish all property that might be of use to the victorious enemy, a plan approved in advance by the British War Cabinet. The company's claim was assessed at 17 million pounds by the Carter Committee, a claims commission set up to make non-binding assessments of damage complaints in British far eastern colonies. Before any payments had been made, Burma became independent (in 1948); Burmah Oil was advised by the British Lord Chancellor of the Exchequer to seek compensation from Burma, but the new Burmese government (unlike that in Malaya) was loathe to compensate war claimants. In 1949, the British government recognized their "equitable responsibility" to the Burma claimants, making an *ex gratia* payment of 4.75 million pounds to Burmah Oil; Burmah Oil was not required to sign an "accord and satisfaction" agreement, apparently because the British government did not want to prejudice the company's ongoing proceedings in the Burmese courts, proceedings finally dismissed in 1960. But when they failed to recover further compensation through the Burmese courts, the company brought an action against the British Crown instead. As a company registered in Edinburgh, the Scots limitation period (of twenty years, as against the English six) could be applied: by just four months, in October 1961 the company was in time to bring an action against the Queen's Lord Advocate, claiming over 31 million pounds plus interest.[253]

The Deputy Treasury Solicitor wrote to warn the company that if, contrary to the Government's expectations, the company's claim (wholly unfounded in law) were to succeed, it was not "one which ought to be met by the British taxpayer": as such retrospective legislation would be introduced to indemnify the Crown against the claim.[254] But the company pursued its claim. The Crown pleaded "irrelevancy", arguing that claim was legally ungrounded, but in a lucid and scholarly judgment in the Outer House of the Court of Session, Lord Kilbrandon overruled the Crown's plea. He recognised as inherent in sovereignty a prerogative right to take property for public benefit, a right independent of the tort law defence of necessity, and concluded, crucially, that (outside cases of "battle damage") such acts of state required compensation. On the

---

[253] Under the Crown Suits (Scotland) Act 1857 (20 & 21 Vict, c 44), suits in Scotland against the Crown must be brought against the Lord Advocate personally, who is indemnified against loss by the Crown.

[254] Letter of 13th June 1962, quoted in Lord Kilbrandon's judgment at 436.

relation between necessity in tort and takings under the prerogative, Kilbrandon argues:

I do not have to consider exactly what, under the law of Scotland, a man impelled by necessity may do to protect his own interests although he sacrifice those of his neighbours. I am sure, however, that in February 1942 an ordinary citizen could not, consistently with the law of Scotland, have destroyed property belonging to someone else valued at £30,000,000 and justified his action on the ground that he, the ordinary citizen, was entitled to act upon his private conviction that what he was doing was in prejudice of His Majesty's enemies. In time of war, when strategical measures against world wide enemies are in question, the sovereign is the judge of necessity. . . . [I]t is the sovereign's right when necessity obliges him, to sacrifice the property of the private citizen to the good of the commonwealth, and that that right of eminent domain is properly called a prerogative right.[255]

Kilbrandon invoked the one Scottish case quoted to him as reiterating this doctrine of eminent domain, one which he traced as running "through the works on public law".[256] Those works were Kames's *Principles of Equity*, Mackenzie's *Jus Regium* (1722), and Jason, Grotius, Vattel, Pufendorf and Burlamaqui, a list that in itself brings out the strikingly different status of civilian writing in Scots law. (Pufendorf offers a particularly clear statement: "since there are times in the life of every state when a great necessity does not allow the collection of strict quotas from everyone, or when something belonging to one or a few citizens is required for the necessary uses of the commonwealth, the supreme sovereignty will be able to seize that thing for the necessities of the state, on condition, however, that whatever exceeds the just share of its owners must be refunded by the other citizens".[257])

The obligation to compensate for "denial damage" (deliberate destruction of property to prevent it being of use to the enemy) Kilbrandon traced to the limited Scots case law on the subject but again primarily to Grotius and Vattel:

If Grotius is to be accepted—and I suppose there is no higher authority—the attempt made by the Crown in the first branch of the argument, to distinguish between the nature of an exercise of the prerogative and an exercise of a right arising from necessity seems to fail. Whether you call it by the name of prerogative or whether you do not, compensation is payable when private property is taken for public good.[258]

---

[255] 1963 SC 410 at 423.

[256] Lord Kilbrandon's judgment at 425, referring to *Grieve v Edinburgh and District Water Trustees* 1918 SC 700. On the development of doctrines of expropriation and eminent domain in Anglo-Commonwealth courts, see Michael Taggart "Expropriation, public purpose and the constitution" in C Forsyth and I Hare (eds) *The golden metwand and the crooked cord: essays on public law in honour of Sir William Wade QC* (Clarendon: Oxford, 1998) 91–112, concluding at 112 that the bodies of law from various jurisdictions, contexts and times examined in the essay point "to a constitutional principle that private property should only be taken for public purposes".

[257] Pufendorf *De jure naturae et gentium* Book 8, Ch 5, para 7, quoted in Kilbrandon's judgment at p 428.

[258] Lord Kilbrandon's judgment at 425, referring to *Grieve v Edinburgh and District Water Trustees* 1918 SC 700.

The loss occasioned by a prerogative taking or destruction of property, he concluded from the civilians, the sovereign was "bound to cause...to be shared equally among the beneficiaries, with whom is included the private owner despoiled, so that it falls on the state, and not on an individual."[259]

Turning to English law, there was "no authority one way or the other...on the question of whether land could be taken by the Crown under the prerogative without compensation" (in *De Keyser,* no case had been found of a prerogative taking of land, so no instance of compensation either being paid or refused); the little English case law extant on the use of other prerogatives to take property was "not opposed to the principles of Scots law as I have endeavoured to state them".[260] An apparently contrary majority decision of the United States Supreme Court in *Caltex*[261], a similar case, Kilbrandon distinguished as hinging on the terms of the fifth Amendment: the majority treated the requirement "nor shall private property be taken for public use, without just compensation" as *excluding* what had been a prior right under the common law of the United States to compensation for the destruction (as well as the use) of private property.[262] Importantly, Kilbrandon concluded that on the facts of Burmah Oil's case, any award of compensation would need to examine whether the value of the refineries might well have been nominal at the time of their destruction.

The Crown appealed to the Inner House, which upheld the appeal and dismissed the action. Three of the four Inner House judges (Lords Clyde, Guthrie and Carmont) endorsed Kilbrandon's conclusion that prerogative takings require compensation subject to an exception for "battle damage", but, offering alternative tests for "battle damage", concluded that Burmah Oil's losses fell within this exceptional category. Lord Sorn relied on the necessity argument from private law that had been rejected by Kilbrandon.

Burmah Oil appealed to the House of Lords. Lord Reid's judgment begins by questioning why Scots law had been treated as applicable, but concludes "it does not appear that as regards [the matters involved in this appeal] there is any material difference between the law of Scotland, the law of England and the law applicable in Burma in 1942 [i.e Burmese colonial law]."[263] Reid examines the sparse English case law on the subject, concluding that "on balance the weight of opinion was against there being any general rule that no compensation can be due for loss caused by an exercise of this prerogative"; in Scots law, "there is virtually no native authority. But none of the learned judges who took part in this case had any doubt about the general rule."[264] The work of the continental

---

259 Lord Kilbrandon's judgment at 429.
260 Lord Kilbrandon's judgment at 431, 432.
261 *United States v Caltex (Philippines) Inc* 344 US SC 149.
262 Lord Kilbrandon's judgment at 433, 435.
263 1964 SC (HL) at 120.   264 1964 SC (HL) at 126.

commentators was pertinent because the case concerned the status of the prerogative in the seventeenth and eighteenth centuries, a period when the writings of civilians had great influence in Scots law: "the prerogative, having been virtually dormant or in abeyance, should not, in my view, be regarded as any wider today than it was three centuries ago. If, therefore, I find among these writers a consensus of opinion as to the limits of *dominium eminens* I would regard that as very good evidence of the limits of the prerogative."[265] Reid then follows Kilbrandon's judgment closely; including his approach to *Caltex*, concluding that the company was entitled to compensation although (as Kilbrandon had emphasised) "it will be necessary to consider whether compensation must not be related to their loss in the sense of what difference it would have made to them if their installations had been allowed to fall into the hands of the enemy instead of being destroyed."[266]

Lord Pearce holds that the applicable law is "the common law of England" since Burma was a crown colony, but while "not necessarily similar in all respects on this matter, the laws of England and Scotland have sufficient similarity to make the consideration of Scots law a valuable help in ascertaining what is the law of England."[267] And English law should give weight to the civilian writers "as showing what was the general view of natural justice and the practice and theory of monarchy."[268] He builds on Kilbrandon's arguments for distinguishing the Crown's powers from those of a private citizen in case of necessity: "It is not possible that the war prerogative of the warrior king should dwindle to the right and duty of 'every man in a brown coat' (as Lord Thurlow expressed it) and should come into effect only when things are so desperate that the citizen may use his own initiative in improvising defences and burning stores. It would, indeed, be an odd state of affairs if the Crown had no power to blow up these oil wells...unless and until things had reached a pass at which the man in the street was entitled to blow them up."[269] But neither can these broader public powers of the Crown be linked with "a power to take whatever it needs from the subject without payment in the general emergency of war": such a power "has never been laid down by any authority" and "if it existed, war taxation would be largely unnecessary":

If justice requires that the sacrifice of one person's property for the common good be compensated by the rest, which is the principle found in our law of general average (see *Mouse's Case*) and the other legal systems as early as the *lex Rhodia*, the Crown is better placed than the citizen for collecting contribution from the commonality. The Crown or the state can, but the citizen cannot.[270]

---

[265] 1964 SC (HL) at 127.   [266] 1964 SC (HL) at 131.
[267] 1964 SC (HL) at 159.   [268] 1964 SC (HL) at 161.
[269] 1964 SC (HL) at 157.   [270] 1964 SC (HL) at 158.

It is, argues Lord Pearce, "plainly just and equitable that, when the state takes or destroys a subject's property for the general good of the state, it shall pay him compensation": after considering the "slender" arguments for the converse position, he concludes that where "both custom from early times and equity alike favour compensation, it would be strange if your Lordships should deny it."[271] Following Kilbrandon closely, he concludes that the destruction of oil wells "like various forms of economic warfare, is quite outside the battle damage", although any assessment of compensation for the destroyed property should depend on the "chances of its survival and restoration" had it been left to fall into the hands of the enemy.[272]

Lord Upjohn agreed with Lords Reid and Pearce, finding Kilbrandon's judgment "very compelling".[273] The applicable law was that of England, although it "would be most astonishingly inconvenient" if "the Crown had the right to seize and use the property of its subjects on the suspected approach of the enemy if they landed on the south bank of the Tweed on different terms than if they chose to land on the north bank". The English authorities "such as they are, permit the conclusion that in general the prerogative of the Crown to take the property of the subject in times of necessity for the public good is exercisable only upon payment by the state then or thereafter." And "where authority both of Scotland and of England is so sparse and uncertain...I find the writings of the civilians of peculiar assistance." Those writers were "not purporting, as I read them, to propound a general principle of international law but only to lay down the proper judicial concept of the municipal law of any civilised country; accordingly they are of great persuasive force, particularly the views of Vattel.... In argument before your Lordships it was in the end almost a matter of common consent that the effect of the civilian writers was best set out in the writings of Vattel."[274]

Viscount Radcliffe, dissenting, concludes that whatever system of law was applicable, "it was not Scottish law". He focuses on English common law "subject to any ordinances or regulations then in force in Burma by which it was controlled or affected". Although he adds that he has "not seen any reason for supposing that the law of Scotland is in fact in any relevant way different from the law of England on the issue before us", he rejects the conclusion reached by every Scots judge hearing the case (including Lord Reid) apart from Lord Sorn. Civilian writings, like the American case law before the court, "can, of course, be no more than persuasive in the ascertainment of our common law about the prerogative" and "I am bound to say that I regard the American cases as much the more important."[275] The civilians were writing advice for princes on the principles of "natural right in a civilised polity" but not "describing

---

[271] 1964 SC (HL) at 161.   [272] 1964 SC (HL) at 173.
[273] 1964 SC (HL) at 173.   [274] 1964 SC (HL) at 173–4, 177.
[275] 1964 SC (HL) at 132, 144.

the actual legal situation in any given country".[276] The common law, he concluded, "never has provided and does not now provide any remedy for these actions of the Crown": there simply was "no law on the matter to which we can give effect. That there is something which may, by a permissible transfer of language be called a public law which requires the careful attention of the state to damage thus inflicted and calls upon it to make such provision for compensation as the recognised equity in favour of compensation may demand, I would be glad to agree. But that, I think, is not for us."[277]

Lord Hodson, also dissenting, begins by analysing English case law while noting that "I do not understand it to be contended that there is a difference between the law of England and the law of Scotland so far as the prerogative of the Crown is concerned. Nor would I expect such a contention to be raised, seeing that the Crown, in and out of Parliament, occupies the same position and performs the same duties in the same realm."[278] Lord Kilbrandon, he argues, was mistaken in presenting "the principles derived from the institutional writers as part of the common law of Scotland": these writings could be at best of persuasive authority. The principle that the exercise of the prerogative was "lawful, subject to the equitable obligation to make compensation", "even if sound as a matter of policy, has not been incorporated into our law so as to make it possible for the subject to sue the state for compensation in the courts." Although the general principle of the law of average or Rhodian law was not "novel" to the common law, in this context it was "most desirable that Parliament should, if so advised, lay down not only the extent of compensation but the section of the community which should bear the burden. The common law has not readily available the machinery for this purpose."[279] And even if one accepts with Kilbrandon a general principle that compensation must be payable, the losses here fell within what needed to be a broadly drawn category of "battle damage".[280]

Had the majority been more specific about the measure of restitutionary compensation available here (asking whether just compensation had already been awarded to the Company, and developing their remarks that the value of the refineries was that of ones about to be taken by the Japanese, refineries which may well then as Japanese ones have been destroyed as enemy property without compensation being payable), the case would have reconciled a classical common lawyer's emphasis on rule of law constraints on the exercise of prerogative powers with appropriate recognition of the weakness of the claim to compensation on the facts

[276] 1964 SC (HL) at 144.   [277] 1964 SC (HL) at 150.

[278] 1964 SC (HL) at 153. Compare Joseph Jacob *The Republican Crown* (Dartmouth, 1996) at 306, invoking Presbyterian notions of Republican government with which he argues the Scottish constitution remains imbued to challenge the "persistent belief that there is only one British constitution so that what goes on in England is taken to apply in Scotland. On the contrary, if there is one British constitution, it is more of Scotland than of England."

[279] 1964 SC (HL) at 154, 155.   [280] 1964 SC (HL) at 155–6.

of this case. But as principles governing the extent of the compensation payable were left undetermined– "as if [the] refineries had been located in the Scottish highlands"[281]—the House of Lords left open the possibility of a large judgment against the Crown. And so, despite the riders that were given on the suitable level of compensation in the judgments, the company refused to lower its claims for full compensation at "peacetime" value plus compound interest for twenty years, although they sought a settlement with the Treasury. The Tory government in power began drafting the threatened retrospective legislation, entitling the Crown to apply to a court to have set aside common law proceedings for compensation for war damage; that "War Damage Bill" was introduced by the new Labour government into the Commons in December 1964, becoming law—after extended controversy in both Houses—in 1965.[282]

English courts have sinced moved far from the position lamented by an American commentator on *Burmah Oil*, who concludes that one significant legacy of the case was "doubt about the ability of the British courts to offer creative analysis of new problems."[283] English courts have since given ample reasons to quash this doubt in their development of public law over the past forty years. And under the influence both of the HRA and of European law, English courts have developed significant expertise in assessing just compensation in cases of state liability.[284]

But the House of Lords has yet to confront the question at stake here in the light of these developments in English public law. Constitutionally, an appropriate approach for a contemporary English court considering the legal position of an uncompensated victim of an act of state could be to use the flexible remedy of declaratory relief. Relying on *Burmah Oil*, such a declaration could treat the award of just compensation as a condition for the lawful exercise of the relevant prerogative power; the relevant act would be declared *ultra vires* if just compensation had not been paid.[285] In so doing, the court would need to draw on its experience in assessing state liability to give clear guidance on the relevant principles and measure of what *would* amount to just compensation in the case before them.[286] Decisions also remain sorely needed on the other

---

[281] "The Burmah Oil affair", above n 251, 632.

[282] For an account of the relevant proceedings in Parliament, see ibid, 624–631 and Paul Jackson "War Damage Act, 1965" (1965) *MLR* 574. Section 1, containing a prospective ban on common law compensation for war damage, was repealed by the Statute Law (Repeals) Act 1995 c 44.

[283] "The Burmah Oil affair" above n 251, 634.

[284] For an excellent overview, see the Law Commission's *Remedies against public bodies: a scoping report* (2006) http://www.lawcom.gov.uk/docs/remedies_scoping_report.pdf at paras 2.6–2.18.

[285] For an analogous argument on a "benevolent exercise of power" doctrine, treating the award of appropriate damages as a condition for *intra-vires* action, see Mark Elliott "Legitimate Expectations and Unlawful Representations" [2004] CLJ 261 and his *Beatson, Matthews and Elliott Administrative law: text and materials* (Oxford University Press, 3rd edn, 2005) at 7.2.6.

[286] For a revealing study of the unprincipled approach of the First World War compensation bodies, the Defence of the Realm Losses Commission and the War Compensation Court, see G R Rubin *Private property, government and requisition and the constitution 1914–1927* (Hambledon Press: London, 1994).

conditions under which the defence is available for acts of state overseas: on whether the plea can be raised against a British subject[287], on the wrongs short of homicide that are covered by the plea[288], and on the relation between the plea and Article 1 of the First Protocol of the European Convention on Human Rights.

In leaving any final assessment and award of compensation to the executive, accountable to Parliament, the court would be acknowledging not only the crucial distinction between the exercise of public law powers and that of private rights but also the constitutional role of Parliament in making any final decision on award of compensation in such cases involving the exercise of state power in the public interest. But in offering clear indications of the principles to be taken into account in making such an award, the victim of an uncompensated act of state would not be left in a legal "black" or "grey" hole.

Such an approach would be strengthened by the point that even in the conflicting judgments of the House of Lords in *Nissan*[289] there is unanimity on the key issue: the Crown's actions in Cyprus (occupying the luxury hotel (rented by Nissan) for use as the command headquarters for British troops, causing Nissan substantial and uncompensated losses in income and damage to his property in the hotel) could not be defended as acts of state. No member of the House in *Nissan* was prepared to uphold the Wade-Collier suggestion that overseas the Crown operates "without the law".[290] Lord Reid, going further than his peers,[291] dismissed a version of the second act of state doctrine as presented to him, a claim that the occupation of the hotel was done in furtherance of treaty obligations and as such an act of state outside the jurisdiction of the courts: "If the same act would be actionable if done by the executive *ex proprio motu*, how can it matter that the Government had agreed beforehand with some other Government that it would do that act?"[292] It would "be a strange result if it were found that those who have struggled and fought through the centuries to establish the rights of the subject to be protected from arbitrary acts of the King's servants have been completely successful with regard to acts done within the realm, but completely unsuccessful

---

[287] See nn 120, 121 above and accompanying text.

[288] On deprivation of liberty, cf *Sigcau, Sekgome, Mwenya* and *Al Jedda* (above pp 195, 198, 205, 214). The First World War bodies compensating for interference with property denied compensation for interference with personal liberty—although the trustees of a girls' school in Gravesend requisitioned by the Admiralty as a hospital for the treatment of venereal diseases *were* compensated for the "direct loss" constituted to the moral stigma attached to the premises after derequisitioning: War Compensation Court, *Second Report* (London, 1923), 35–39 (claim of Trustees of Milton Mount College, Gravesend) and Rubin, above n 286, 245–6.

[289] See text below; also Gilmour "British forces abroad and the responsibility for their actions" [1970] *PL* 120 at 149: "One of the justifiable grounds for criticism of this decision of the House of Lords is that while it disposes of Mr Nissan's actual problem it leaves everybody else wondering."

[290] In a brave approach to precedent, Wade and Forsyth have suggested that the House of Lords' decision in *Nissan* should be overlooked in favour the Privy Council's decision in *Cook* (which they read as an example of the Crown successfully pleading act of state against British subjects).

[291] Text below.   [292] [1970] AC 179 at 211D.

in gaining any legal protection for British subjects who have gone beyond the territorial waters of the King's dominions."[293] Lord Reid evacuates *Cook* of its old meaning in treating the case as one where the appellant "only had rights against the former ruler"; *Kamachee* similarly "only deals with the property of the dispossessed sovereign and I cannot accept the view that it affords any justification for the submission that the property of a British subject in conquered territory can be confiscated." None of this line of cases, argues Lord Reid,

> decides that when the Crown annexes territory it is entitled to confiscate the property of British subjects which is in that territory.... A British subject cannot complain if the new sovereign alters the law of the annexed territory to his detriment, but he can, in my view, complain of a confiscation of his property which is not justified by any law.[294]

(vi) Possible claims for damages for acts of state

An adviser to an uncompensated victim of an act of state seeking compensation in the English courts would need to think carefully about how to frame any claim for damages, as well as how to defeat arguments (based on the first two act of state doctrines) that the relevant acts were non-justiciable or that the court lacks jurisdiction.

One approach, following Dicey, would be to advise that, like any other victims, those harmed by acts of state should rely on ordinary tort actions against the relevant wrong-doing officials. Such proceedings would have to be brought in the hope that the Crown will advise the responsible officials against raising a *Buron* defence, on the assurance that the Crown will pay any damages awarded against those officials. A tort-based action against the responsible officials could also take heart from the fact that, in both leading twentieth century cases in which act of state defences were raised by officials, the plea was rejected. In *Walker v Baird*[295], the Privy Council upheld a judgment of the Supreme Court of Newfoundland, ruling that it was not open to the defendant Captain (patrolling the coast of Newfoundland where the French exercised fishing rights under the terms of a treaty with Britain) to claim that his right to close down the British appellant's lobster factory was either an act of state or a necessary concomitant of a peace treaty between France and Britain. Although the Privy Council expressly reserved opinion on whether interference with private rights can be authorised by a peace treaty without incorporating legislation, it held that the suggestion that the defendant's actions "can be justified as acts of State, or that the Court was not competent to inquire into a matter involving the construction of treaties and other

---

[293] [1970] AC 179 at 208B.
[294] [1970] AC 179 at 210, 211.
[295] [1892] AC 491.

acts of State, is wholly untenable."²⁹⁶ And in *Johnstone v Pedlar*²⁹⁷, the House of Lords held that Johnstone, the Chief Commissioner of the Dublin Metropolitan Police, could not plead that his seizure of cash and a cheque from Pedlar (an Irish-American arrested in Ireland—then British territory—for illegal drilling) was an act of state.²⁹⁸ The subject of "a State at peace with His Majesty, while permitted to reside in this country, is under the King's protection and allegiance": "the defence of act of State cannot be made good as to acts in the King's Dominions on a bare averment that the plaintiff is an alien."²⁹⁹

There are three problems with this first approach under which remedies would be sought in tort from the relevant officials. First, in both *Walker* and *Johnstone*, the official's defence of act of state was rejected on the facts at stake in the case: no suggestion is made that a *Buron*-type plea *cannot* be raised by an official in an appropriate case.³⁰⁰ A second set of problems can lie in identifying the relevant officials and establishing English law as the applicable law. And a third and final problem is that casting acts of state as torts can be problematic precisely because the relevant actions involve the exercise of state power overseas, highlighting in their facts alone the contrast between acts of state and ordinary torts: as such, questions of justiciability and jurisdiction will arise of the kinds addressed by the first and second act of state doctrines.

Both the second and third problems with this first approach to damages for acts of state are exemplified in the recent *Chagos Islanders* proceedings in tort for damages to compensate for the effects of the islanders' enforced removal or exclusion from their homeland in the early 1970s to accommodate the United States' request to use Diego Garcia as a military base. Both Ouseley J (striking out the entirety of the claim for damages) and Sedley LJ (refusing permission to appeal) highlight the injustice of the British state's actions towards the Chagos islanders:

---

²⁹⁶ [1892] AC 491 at 497 (Lord Herschell).

²⁹⁷ [1921] 2 AC 262, Viscount Findlay claiming at 271 that Baron Parke's summing up in *Buron* treated Denman's act as "an act of State of which a municipal Court cannot take cognisance" and Lord Sumner at 290 that *Buron* was "a case rather of the inability of the Court than of the disability of the suitor.... What the Crown does to foreigners by its agents without the realm is State action also, and is beyond the scope of domestic jurisdiction."

²⁹⁸ Lord Phillimore explains: "[T]he rules of international law and the common law of England and Ireland which agrees with international law are, I think, well established. To begin with the alien takes his character from his State.... If his State is in amity with ours he is considered an alien ami even though his personal intentions are hostile. His individual hostility does not entitle him to the character of an alien enemy. He can be executed for high treason, and is not entitled to be considered as a prisoner of war. By parity of reason neither does his hostility disentitle him to the rights conferred by law upon an alien ami, once he has entered this realm with permission from the King." [1921] 2 AC 262 at 295–6.

²⁹⁹ [1921] 2 AC 262, 273, 275, Viscount Findlay and Lord Phillimore suggesting that in "another case" a question might arise as to whether act of state *was* available against an alien who "is by overt acts showing that he is in active hostility to the Government" (274, 297–8).

³⁰⁰ An attempt might also be made in this context to re-invigorate the defence of necessity, as envisaged by a small minority of judges in the *Burmah Oil* litigation: above, p 236.

The Chagossians alone were made to pay a personal price for the defence establishment on Diego Garcia, which was regarded by the UK and US Governments as necessary for the defence of the West and its values. Many were given nothing for years but a callous separation from their homes, belongings and way of life and a terrible journey to privation and hardship.[301]

A rival approach, focussing on the special nature of acts of state against individuals, would be to claim damages directly against the relevant department for breaching individuals' human rights contrary to section 6 of the Human Rights Act 1998. The HRA "is not a tort statute"[302]: as the Law Commission highlights in its scoping report, *Remedies against Public Bodies*, damages are "discretionary and modest, allowing the court to tailor the remedies to fit the particular circumstances of the case"[303]. The award of damages under the HRA is a discretionary remedy of "last resort"[304], and must take account of the principles applied by the European Court of Human Rights in awarding compensation under Article 41 of the European Convention on Human Rights[305]: "damages have "to be 'just and appropriate' and 'necessary' to afford 'just satisfaction'. The approach is an equitable one."[306] But a key problem with this second approach in the context of acts of state is that the HRA has been held to apply to the exercise of prerogative powers overseas only to the limited extent that the UK's international obligations under the ECHR would so apply.[307]

A third and final approach, developed in line with the case law considered under the rubric of the third act of state doctrine, would be to treat

---

[301] *Chagos Islanders v Attorney General and British Indian Ocean Territory Commissioner* [2003] EWHC 2222 (QB) Ouseley J at [154] ; cf also [2004] EWCA Civ 997, Sedley LJ at [6]: "[I]t would be wrong of us to move on to the legal issues without acknowledging...the shameful treatment to which the islanders were apparently subjected. The deliberate misinterpretation of the Ilois' history and status, designed to deflect any investigation by the United Nations; the use of legal powers designed for the governance of the islands for the illicit purpose of depopulating them; the uprooting of scores of families from the only way of life and means of subsistence that they knew; the want of anything like adequate provision for their resettlement: all of this and more is now part of the historical record. It is difficult to ignore the parallel with the Highland clearances of the second quarter of the nineteenth century. Defence may have replaced agricultural improvement as the reason, but the pauperisation and expulsion of the weak in the interests of the powerful still gives little to be proud of." Sedley LJ did hold that were the proceedings not time barred, he would have granted permission to appeal on two arguable points. The first was whether "in certain exceptional circumstances, for instance where the defendant, by the very making of the deceitful statement or for some other reason, had assumed liability to the claimant, a cause of action [in deceit] could exist." [36] The second was whether the fundamental rights conferred by the Mauritius Constitution were still enjoyed in the Chagos Islands thanks to a standard provision in the relevant Order in Council (creating the British Indian Ocean Territory) continuing in force the laws in force immediately before the making of the Order: "There is in reality no other way of providing continuity of governance, and the process was used in grants of independence throughout the former Empire." [41].

[302] Lord Bingham, asserting the secondary nature of damages in human rights contexts in *R (Greenfield) v Secretary of State for the Home Department* [2005] UKHL14 at [19].

[303] Above n 284, para 2.13.

[304] *Anufrijeva v London Borough of Southwark* [2003] EWCA Civ 1406 at [56].

[305] HRA s 8(3).   [306] *Anufrijeva* Lord Woolf CJ at [66].

[307] *Al Skeini v Secretary of State for Defence* [2007] UKHL 26.

the payment of just compensation to those affected (usually individuals who are not among the people in the name of whose "public interest" the state has acted) as a prerequisite for the lawful exercise of prerogative powers overseas. Declaratory relief would treat the award of just compensation as a condition for the lawful exercise of the relevant prerogative power; the relevant act would be declared *ultra vires* if just compensation had not been paid. In so doing, the court would need to give clear guidance on the relevant principles and measure of what *would* amount to just compensation in the case before them, while leaving any final assessment to the executive, accountable to Parliament.

Were such an approach to be adopted, English judges would disprove accusations that in the realm of state liability they have been "unduly timorous" out of "terror of being thought to dictate to government"[308]; they would be moving a step closer to the position of French courts on state liability, so beginning to compensate for what Lord Woolf recognizes as a major shortcoming of English courts.[309]

But two generations of English common lawyers had been encouraged to believe with Dicey that public or administrative law was a sinister invention of the French resting on "two leading ideas alien to the conceptions of modern Englishmen."[310] Although the French translators of Dicey's book challenged this account, Dicey continued to maintain that *droit administratif* was incompatible with the English conception of the rule of law.[311]

Challenges to this position began eighty years ago, when in 1928 William Robson published his *Justice and administrative law* which he later explained had aimed "to dispel the illusion held by all the leading

[308] Carol Harlow "Fault liability in French and English public law" (1976) 39 *MLR* 516 at 539–540.

[309] H Woolf "Judicial review: have the judges made a mess of it?" *Law Soc. Gazette* 17th Oct 1991, 18. See also Sedley LJ at n336 below, and more generally John Allison *A continental distinction in the common law* (Oxford University Press, revised edn, 1999) 170–189 and Duncan Fairgrieve *State liability in tort: a comparative study* (Oxford University Press, 2003) esp 102–124.

[310] Dicey *The law of the constitution* (Macmillan, 8th edn, 1920) 332. The first of these alien ideas was that "the government, and every servant of the government, possesses, as a representative of the nation, a whole body of special rights, privileges, or prerogatives as against private citizens". The second was that a constitutional separation of powers "means something different from what we mean in England by the 'independence of the judges,' or the like expressions": as "interpreted by French history, by French legislation, and by the decisions of French tribunals, it means neither more nor less than the maintenance of the principle that while the ordinary judges ought to be irremovable and thus independent of the executive, the government and its officials ought (whilst acting officially) to be independent of and to a great extent free from the jurisdiction of the ordinary Courts." Ibid 332–3.

[311] "This misunderstanding has been revealed, the true position in France explained and the fear shown to be groundless." at 4, 22. Dicey responded to his translators in his essay "Droit administratif in Modern French Law" (1901) 18 *LQR* 302, which he transformed into notes x and xi in his appendix added (p xi) to the sixth edition of *The law of the constitution*. For a detailed study of the consequences for English public law of Dicey's "phantom" theses on *droit administratif* , see Allison *A continental distinction in the common law* (above, n 309).

lawyers, politicians, civil servants and academics who had been brought up on Dicey's *Law of the constitution* that in Britain there was no administrative law."[312] In so far as it levels a direct challenge to Dicey, Professor S A de Smith is justified in presenting his 1959 book *Judicial review of administrative action* as "the first of its kind to have been written by an English author". He acknowledges how "recent studies of the work of the *Conseil d'Etat* have dispelled the grosser misconceptions about its status and jurisdiction" and that "in some respects" the protection it gives "to the interests of the citizen in his conflicts with the Administration is still more effective than in England" although "imitation is precluded by three centuries of tradition and myth."[313]

Wade's *Administrative law*, published two years later in 1961 and aiming "to present administrative law in the form of a general discussion

[312] Robson "Justice and administrative law reconsidered" (1979) 32 *Current Legal Problems* 107. Direct challenges to Dicey's work by scholars of English constitutional law began to multiply in the 1930s. Willis's *The parliamentary powers of English government departments* (published in 1933) challenged Hewart's claim that for lack of legislation contemporary government departments were exercising unfettered, 'despotic' power; Professor Sir Ivor Jennings' *The law and the constitution* (first published in 1933 when Jennings was a Reader at LSE) highlighted the Whig assumptions underpinning Dicey's reasoning; Professor Emlyn Wade, editor of the ninth edition (1939) of Dicey's *Introduction to the Study of the Law of the Constitution*, characterised Dicey's as an account of the constitution which appeared "to one who was a firm adherent to a particular school of political thought then current". Importantly, Emlyn Wade included as an Appendix to his edition of Dicey's *Law of the constitution* an essay by Professor René David on *droit administratif* in France, championing "the liberal character" of the Conseil d'Etat and "the efficiency with which the rights of citizens are protected by it in France against any possible encroachment of the Administration". And it would be from among the next generation of constitutional lawyers, those brought up on this edition of Dicey's *Law of the constitution*, that the first textbook writers on English administrative law emerged.

In their 1952 textbook *Principles of Administrative law*, John Griffith and Harry Street dismiss Dicey's misunderstandings of the French system, but maintain the Diceyan orthodoxy that in England statutory grants of arbitrary power are checked by Parliament and public opinion *rather than* the courts: "The courts will not refuse to enforce a statute because it grants wide discretionary or even arbitrary power; or because it dispossesses a subject without compensation." See also Jenning's "In praise of Dicey" (1935) 8 *Public Administration* 2. *Introduction to the Study of the Law of the Constitution* (9th edn, 1939) xv. *Law of the constitution* (Macmillan: London, 9th edn, 1949). John Griffith and Harry Street *Principles of Administrative law* (1952) 4, 22.

[313] S A de Smith *Judicial review of administrative action* (1959) 6, citing at n 11 David, Hamson, Street, Schwartz and Sieghart. De Smith challenges the "widespread impression" that courts will never examine "the conditions precedent" to the exercise of administrative powers. This impression has been created, he suggests, by a modern practice of judicial restraint behind which "lies a partly concealed policy decision—a decision that ministerial responsibility to Parliament shall be deemed by the courts to be an appropriate safeguard against the erroneous exercise of widely framed statutory powers." De Smith attributes this "excess of caution" to the impact of wartime and emergency cases when "judicial zeal for the protection of the individual by means of restrictive interpretation of executive powers might have proved contrary to the public interest"; to a fear of violating the separation of powers or of being seen to be following the path of the United States Supreme Court in the early 1930s; to a disinclination to consider the scope of judicial review accepted by other jurisdictions; and "possibly" to "a higher degree of judicial confidence in extra-judicial safeguards than is usual in other countries". Ibid, 18–19, referring at 18 to his later discussion of "scattered dicta, to which legal advisers might profitably pay more attention, indicative of [the courts'] willingness to probe more deeply in some contexts". Ibid, 19, citing at fn 30 Devlin's *The common law, public policy, and the executive*.

rather than in the cut-and-dried form of a textbook", emphasises in detail how Dicey's picture of French officials acting as "a law unto themselves" was grossly misled as an image of the judicial functions of the Conseil d'Etat. The English separation or "antagonism" between the executive government and civil servants on one side and the legal profession on the other "exaggerates the cleavage between the legal and administrative worlds, and impedes the great objective—the improvement of administration by transfusion of legal standards of justice", giving a "stiff and formal character to our law of judicial control".[314]

As Wade knew well, the one real difference was the existence or otherwise of a system of administrative courts staffed by judges specialising in public law.[315] In the eighth edition (2000), he reiterates how compared to judges of the French Conseil and its first instance tribunals, an English judge "trained basically in private law and administering a more legalistic control, may feel less free to break new ground where new problems of public law call for new solutions".[316]

Given the creation of a special Administrative Court within the High Court, and the experience British judges have gained in assessing state liability in claims made under EU law and the Human Rights Act, a refusal to develop a doctrine of just compensation for acts of state seems now decreasingly justifiable.[317] Those courts and commentators who shy from "any form of justice as natural", even with the positive EU and HRA jurisprudence to guide them, may follow de Smith's suggestion and "take their choice from among 'substantial justice', 'the essence of justice', 'fundamental justice', 'universal justice', rational justice', 'the

---

[314] Wade 1st edn, 8, 18, 37. The only advantages of the English system, argued Wade, are that "it helps to preserve the fundamentals of the rule of law in as undefiled a form as the facts of modern life permit": a judge's career does not "depend throughout his working life on a minister of justice"; it has produced "a civil service in which much pride is rightly taken"; and "the satisfaction of being able to challenge the legality of the government's acts in the ordinary courts by ordinary procedure is a real one, not to be decried." As a French judge's career depends on the Minister of Justice, so does an English judge's career on the Lord Chancellor, and the French take as much ambivalent pride in the Napoleonic tradition of an administration staffed by Enarques as do the English in their civil service staffed by fledgling Sir Humphries. Ibid, 37–38. See Stephen Sedley "The sound of silence: constitutional law without a constitution" (1994) 110 LQR 271 for a particularly ambivalent view of the civil service.

[315] Wade 2nd edn, v–vi.

[316] Wade 8th edn, 25. On the myth of English private law as the exclusive source of English constitutional law, see Allison A continental distinction in the common law (Oxford University Press, 1996).

[317] Cf Sedley LJ in Chagos Islanders v Attorney General [2004] EWCA Civ 997 (refusing leave to appeal) at para 20: "In a civil law system, the judgment in Bancoult would be enough to entitle the claimants, other things being equal, to an award of damages against the state: see the historic decision of the French Conseil d'Etat in Blanco (TC 8 Feb. 1873) [...]. The unlawful exclusion and removal of the islanders would be regarded in such a system as faute lourde and would be compensable in damages." Bacon seems to have envisaged the development of a domestic "Court of State" in which the Lord Chancellor would apply legal rules modified by reason of State—and so the creation of an English juridiction administrative and contentieux administratif: ("Essay of Judicature" Works VI at 509). See Moore Act of state in English law (John Murray: London, 1906) 14–19 and 30–31.

principles of British justice', or simply 'justice without any epithet,' as phrases which express the same idea."[318]

Such notions of restrained judicial oversight of executive action infuse the third account of the act of state doctrine traced above, a doctrine whose spirit is articulated powerfully by Mann in the closing lines of his 1943 lecture to the Grotius Society on "Judiciary and executive in foreign affairs":

> Deference to the foreign policy of the Executive should be a rule of judicial decision "only in clear cases in which the harm to the public is substantially incontestable and does not depend upon the idiosyncratic inferences of a few judicial minds"; it should rest "on tangible grounds, not on mere generalisations". If the Courts have regard to realities as proved by experience, history and facts rather than imaginary possibilities, if they act upon evidence rather than "horrid suspicions to which high-minded men are sometimes prone', they should find it less perplexing, though by no means easy, to delimitate the boundaries within which the policy of the Executive should be allowed to influence the law. Mere possibility of embarrassment should not be sufficient. It is the empirically proven likelihood of actual harm to the common weal that should be required to impose upon the Court the duty of deciding in conformity with the policy of the Executive.[319]

CONCLUSION

This essay has examined three English act of state doctrines that endure within English case law. Although rival doctrines have enjoyed times of particular influence, this study cannot be presented as the history of the emergence of one rule, any more than an historical study of English constitutional law could establish the final victory of Enlightenment notions of legally accountable government or Republican notions of political accountability over feudal notions of Crown immunity.[320]

On the first account, one that emerged with the expansion of the British Empire, acts of state are simply not matters of law at all: in the words of Lord Kingsdown in *Kamachee*, they are outside the law,

---

[318] Wade *Constitutional fundamentals* at 62, referring to the "refreshing candour" of Lord Denning MR in *Dutton v Bognor Regis UDC* [1977] 1 QB 373 at 391: "In the end, it will be found to be a question of policy, which we, as judges, have to decide."

Wade 8th edn, 114–115—the phrase "spirit of autocratic dilettantism" Wade attributes to Redlich and Hirst *History of local government* vol I 102 (all phrases from common law decisions). In the first edition of *his* book, Wade treats arguments from justice as "a mode not of destroying Acts of Parliament but of fulfilling them": "The instinct for justice must be allowed to infuse the work of executive government, just as it must infuse the work of Parliament and the work of the courts." Wade *Administrative law* 1st edn, 129, 7, 37.

[319] F A Mann "Judiciary and executive in foreign affairs" (1944) 29 *Transactions of the Grotius Society* 143 at 163, quoting from Baron Parke in *Egerton v Brownlow* (1853) 4 HLC1, 123 and Lord Atkin in *Fender v Mildmay* [1938] AC1, 12 and 16. Both cases limit the application of public policy arguments in *private* law.

[320] See above n 8 and accompanying text.

"acts by arbitrary power on behalf of the Crown" and acts for which no attempt is made to offer justification "under colour of legal title". Such political measures are not a matter for the judgment of a legal tribunal: uncompensated victims of such acts are legally in a "black hole" and must pursue any remedy through political channels. Any questions concerning the unjust treatment of such victims are a matter of moral law to be considered, if at all, by Parliament.

Echoes of this first act of state doctrine, that of the old autocratic cases, remain in contemporary English law. Nurtured by the Privy Council in cases like *Kamachee* and *Cook*, it shows signs of enduring life in the House of Lords' recent decisions in *Jones* and *Gentle* relating to the question of the legality under international law of the UK's use of force in Iraq.

But this first, frank act of state doctrine is rarely invoked in later case law and scholarly writing.[321] Most judges and jurists prefer to reinterpret the old case law in one of two ways, both ostensibly in line with the notion of the rule of law over the sovereign. On one re-writing, acts of state are *within* the law: the Crown has prerogative powers to act in ways unlawful for individuals, and the way it exercises those powers is non-justiciable, not a matter for courts of law. On a second re-writing, one dominant in contemporary English case law (the second doctrine traced above), acts of state are governed by international law rather than English law: the act of state doctrine is a jurisdictional rule, making clear that acts of state are usually a matter for international resolution and only exceptionally are English courts an appropriate forum for the application of the relevant rules of international law to resolve claims to compensation.

On both re-writings, uncompensated victims of acts of state are legally in a "grey hole".[322] The powers used against them are declared lawful without scrutiny of claims to just compensation, for which no legal remedy is available unless an exceptional claim can be made to ground the jurisdiction of English courts: otherwise, again, any redress must be sought through political channels. Although the phrase "act of state" is evaded in recent case law, variants of this second "grey hole" act of state doctrine dominate contemporary English law on overseas acts of the executive. The doctrine, and its dangers, are manifest particularly strikingly in the House of Lords' decision in *Al Jedda*.[323]

---

[321] Although see Lord Pearson in *Nissan* at 237: "An act of state is something not cognisable by the court: if a claim is made in respect of it the court will have to ascertain the facts, but if it then appears that the act complained of was an act of state the court must refuse to adjudicate upon the claim. In such a case the court does not come to any decision as to the legality or illegality, or the rightness or wrongness, of the act complained of: the decision is that because it was an act of state the court has no jurisdiction in respect of it."

[322] Dyzenhaus, above n 33.

[323] See above n 163 and accompanying text.

On the third account of the doctrine of act of state considered above, true acts of state *are* lawful and within the jurisdiction of English courts: their legality and justice are questions for the courts, on which the executive *is* expected to offer evidence:

The servants of the Crown, like other men animated by the highest motives, are capable of formulating a policy ad hoc so as to prevent the citizen from doing something that the Crown does not want him to do. It is the duty of the courts to be as alert now as they have always been to prevent abuse of the prerogative.[324]

On this third account, to characterise a government action as a genuine act of state is to say that it is one considered necessary for the promotion or protection of the public good, and as such is not only legally but also morally defensible as appropriate compensation has been paid.

This third doctrine emerges sporadically in case law, recognising the Crown's prerogative powers to take actions overseas in the interests of the country that would be unlawful were they acts of a private British citizen. But unlike on the first account, the act of state doctrine operates as a justiciable defence, one that can be raised only where the Crown has offered just compensation; where it has not, the Crown's actions are neither non-justiciable (the first account) nor lawful (the second account) but unlawful, legally *ultra vires*. Any final assessment of compensation is properly for the executive and Parliament, but it is for the courts to offer specific guidance on the relevant principles: a ludicrously small award of compensation, falling outside those principles, would render the act of state *ultra vires*.

Mann, writing in 1943, points out that there is no reason "why in matters relating to foreign affairs, the Courts should not abide by the rule that nothing they decide will amount to the making of policy and why in matters international they should not guard their independence as jealously as in matters municipal." Yet, as Mann notes, "it is a fact, and a really fascinating one, that in international affairs Anglo-American Courts have been inclined to surrender a good deal of their independence, to be guided by and even to submit to the Executive and to refrain from that judicial freedom which otherwise is so proud a feature of the English legal system."[325]

In the absence of a British *Conseil d'Etat*, it is to be hoped that the English courts will have the courage to combine their growing expertise in administrative law and principles of state liability to develop the

---

[324] Devlin in *Chandler* at 811; see further above n 26 and accompanying text.

[325] Mann continues: "It seems to have been in the early 19th century, i.e. under the shadow of great political turmoil, that the doctrine originated which in 1828 Shadwell J expressed in the following words which, perhaps fortunately for him, Lord Coke did not live to read and which may now make some of us tremble: 'It appears to me that sound policy requires that the Courts of the King should act in unison with the Government of the King.'" *Judiciary and executive in foreign affairs* at 146.

arguments offered in *Burmah Oil* into a constitutionally healthier account of the doctrine of act of state as a justiciable defence for the Crown. If our courts do not expect our statesmen to act as "sovereign over themselves", the thickets of the law could be easily torn down and then who "could stand upright in the winds that would blow?"[326]

---

[326] Plato *Republic* Bk IX 580e; Robert Bolt's paraphrase of Thomas More's position in *A man for all seasons* (Random: New York, 1962) at 38.

AWARDS OF INTEREST BY INTERNATIONAL COURTS AND TRIBUNALS

By PENELOPE NEVILL*

* College Lecturer, Downing College, Fellow, Lauterpacht Centre for International Law, University of Cambridge. I am grateful to the Editors for their comments on earlier drafts.

I. Introduction

Interest has been consistently awarded as an aspect of compensation since the Jay Treaty arbitrations at the end of the 18th century. The predominant form of interest award is interest on damages for loss of the use of the principal sum. Interest has also been awarded as the measure of lost profits, as specific damages for interest charges actually incurred or as the measure of enrichment for monies wrongfully withheld. A recurrent question is how the interest award should be quantified, in terms of rate, method of calculation (compound or simple) and start and finish dates for the period of account. The International Law Commission specifically addressed the award of interest in its work on State responsibility. Article 38 on 'Interest' in the 2001 Articles on State Responsibility is a broadly worded provision recognising the obligation to pay interest when necessary to effect full reparation, at a rate and method of calculation necessary to achieve that result and running from the date the principal falls due until date of payment. Like the other articles on reparation, Article 38 gives considerable discretion to the parties and tribunals to determine the particulars of an award in each case.

Unlike their domestic counterparts, international judges and arbitrators do not, in the absence of agreement between the parties before them or between the States establishing their jurisdiction, have legislation which guides or constrains the selection of the interest rate and the method of its calculation (simple or compound), or established rules or practice on start and finish dates for the period of account. The resulting differences and inconsistencies in the particulars of interest awards have attracted critical comment.[1] This article reviews the jurisprudence of the last 50 years of international courts, tribunals and commissions on pre- and post-award interest, investigating this charge of inconsistency and exploring whether any principled guidelines for rate, method of calculation and period of account can nevertheless be discerned from the jurisprudence and parallel developments in domestic law.[2] A separate but related question is whether there has been any development in the principles underpinning interest awards.

This article concludes that both questions can be answered in the affirmative. The jurisprudence confirms that the principle underpinning

---

[1] C Gray, *Judicial Remedies in International Law* (1987), 29–33; the Third Report on State Responsibility by Special Rapporteur Crawford, 15 June 2000, A/CN.4/507/Add.1, 50–1, para 212, referring to the 'present anarchical state of the decisions and of practice'; the conclusions of Special Rapporteur Arangio-Ruiz in his Second Report on State Responsibility, 1989 YBILC, Vol II, Part 1, 23, para 79 and 28–29, paras 95–97; and concurring and dissenting opinion of Judge Brower in *McCollough & Co Inc v Ministry of Post* (1986) 11 Iran-US CTR 35, where he observed that 'international tribunals...furnish precedents for almost any decision one might wish to make in regard to interest' (at 43).

[2] There are comprehensive surveys of the earlier jurisprudence on interest, notably M Whiteman, *Damages in International Law* (1943), Vol III, 1913–2006; and J Subilia, 'L'Allocation d'interets dans la jurisprudence internationale' (1972, Lausanne), thesis cited in Gray, ibid, 11.

the main form of interest award continues to be damages for loss of use of the principal sum. But it also indicates that the principle appears to be shifting to encompass compensation for loss in the value of the principal sum due to the effect of inflation as well as or even instead of loss of use. The jurisprudence also shows that, in addition to the traditional compensatory interest awards, a new form of interest award designed to restore the *status quo ante* has emerged. In terms of the particulars of interest awards, the majority of cases select the date of breach or loss as the start date for the period of account, although some adopt the date of claim. Interest typically runs until either payment of the award or the date of the award, and in the latter case post-award interest is usually awarded separately at the same rate as the pre-award interest. There has been a marked shift towards the use of interest rate formulas based on central bank base rates or market rates, such as the interbank lending rates between commercial banks,[3] the prevailing rates for State treasury bills or bonds, or government guaranteed commercial investment vehicles. Compound rather than simple methods of calculation are becoming more accepted in the practice of investment arbitration tribunals, but there is less evidence of the use of compound methods of calculation elsewhere in the jurisprudence. However, a consideration of the various arguments for and against compound methods of calculation suggests it is difficult to come up with convincing reasons why interest should not be compounded in all types of claim, unless the costs of its calculation outweigh the benefit of doing so.

These developments are explored in Part III. Part IV concludes with guidelines for the treatment of interest awards that may be drawn from the jurisprudence. First in Part II, the work of the International Law Commission regarding interest in its study of State responsibility and its handling of the jurisprudence on principle, period of account, rate and method of calculation is outlined.

II. The International Law Commission's Approach to Interest

An express provision for interest awards was first introduced into the ILC's work on State responsibility on the recommendation of Special Rapporteur Arangio-Ruiz in his Second Report in 1989.[4] It was directed to awards of interest on damages and not other types of interest award. There were at least two prior attempts to formulate a uniform approach to awards of interest on damages. In 1972 Subilia suggested that the ILC should adopt a conventional rate of interest of about 6%, and that

---

[3] Such as the LIBOR, the London Interbank Offer Rate, a daily reference rate based on the interest rates at which banks offer to lend short term unsecured funds in certain currencies to other London banks on the wholesale interbank market.

[4] Second Report on State Responsibility, above n 1, 23–30, paras 77–105.

the annual lending rate of the International Bank for Reconstruction and Development ('IBRD') be referred to, particularly in cases of damage caused directly to a State.[5] The 1974 draft codification of the law of State responsibility by García-Amador, Sohn and Baxter, which focussed on diplomatic protection claims, proposed that interest should run from the date of injury, or date of notice if the claimant was dilatory in presenting his claim, and that the rate of interest on damages

shall be that prevailing with respect to obligations of analogous amount and duration at the time of the award in the place in which the injured alien was habitually resident at the time of the injury.[6]

The proposed interest rate formula was based on the assumption that the claimant would have had to obtain a financial replacement for the sum representing the damage on the local commercial money market.[7]

The weakness of Subilia's conventional 6% interest rate or the IBRD rate is that a fixed conventional rate will not account for shifts in interest rates and the IBRD rate for lending to developing States will not be the appropriate rate for all States, which will have different credit ratings affecting their borrowing rates. Moreover, as individuals typically pay higher borrowing rates than States, it will not necessarily be appropriate to use the same rate for both.[8] The drawback of the interest formula proposed by García-Amador, Sohn and Baxter is that it may not be an appropriate mandatory starting point for awards of interest in all cases of diplomatic protection or individual-State claims, especially in the face of the complex multinational company structures of many international investment arbitrations and the internationalisation of money markets. It also picks a date for the determination of interest rate which is unlikely to reflect changes of interest rate over the period of account and may not, therefore, be a close approximate of the claimant's loss.

Arangio-Ruiz's 1989 draft, unlike these earlier proposals, left the question of rate open. It selected a start date for the period of account premised on the date of breach or loss. It also expressly addressed compounding, concluding that although the majority of case law on compound interest seemed to be negative, it was not conclusive against it, and so 'compound interest should be awarded whenever it is proved indispensable to ensure full compensation'.[9] The report's draft article 9 thus proposed that:

---

[5] Subilia, cited in Arangio-Ruiz's 1989 Second Report on State Responsibility, above n 1, para 97.

[6] F V García-Amador, L B Sohn and R R Baxter, *Recent Codification of the Law of State Responsibility for Injuries to Aliens* (1974), Article 38(3), 342 (emphasis added), and explanatory note, 344.

[7] Of this proposal, Gray notes that 'however unrealistic an assumption, it at least gives a fairly objective standard of assessment' (above n 1, 33). The explanatory note to the draft states that this is an objectively determined measure, and it is 'not necessary that the alien actually have [sic] been required to borrow funds; interest is paid without regard to his actual conduct' (ibid).

[8] See further below n 232 and accompanying text.

[9] Second Report on State Responsibility, above n 1, para 105.

(1) Where compensation due for loss of profits consists of interest on a sum of money, such interest:
  (a) shall run from the first day not considered, for the purposes of compensation, in the calculation of the amount awarded as principal;
  (b) shall run until the day of effective payment.
(2) Compound interest shall be awarded whenever necessary in order to ensure full compensation, and the interest rate shall be the one most suitable to achieve that result.[10]

In the ILC's subsequent debate on interest in the 1990 session there was no disagreement that interest should be awarded where necessary, but Arangio-Ruiz's draft was rejected because there was no agreement on its formulation.[11] The wording was criticised for suggesting that the award of interest was limited to awards of lost profits and liquidated claims,[12] and there was no agreement on the inclusion of a provision requiring compound interest. While almost none of the members suggested that compound interest was not allowable under international law,[13] the view was expressed by several that the award of compound interest should be exceptional rather than the norm,[14] and one member observed that loss at compound rates could not be presumed.[15] Four members linked the requirement in draft Article 9(2) to award compound interest to the more general concern about the impact of the concept of full reparation on developing countries.[16] Many questioned the wisdom of including detailed rules on compensation—such as a requirement of compound interest—in the articles, and stressed the importance of leaving arbitrators and judges room to manoeuvre to calculate compensation in light of the circumstances of each case.[17] The one point of general agreement was that interest rates and methods of calculation should be left to the discretion of courts and tribunals.[18] In the end the ILC opted for a simpler approach, leaving out the proposed separate provision on interest

---

[10] Ibid, 56, para 191.
[11] *Report of the Commission to the General Assembly on the work of its forty-second session*, 1990 YBILC, Vol II, Part 2, paras 380–7.
[12] Ibid, paras 384, 387, and Crawford, Third Report on State Responsibility, above n 1, para 195.
[13] With the possible exception of Díaz González, who said he did 'not agree with the concept of "compound interest"' underlying Article 9(2), *Summary records of the meetings of the forty-second session, 1 May–20 July 1990*, 1990 YBILC Vol I, 191, para 49.
[14] *Summary records of the meetings of the forty-second session, 1 May–20 July 1990*, ibid, Njenga at 161, paras 30–31; Francis at 173, para 46; Thiam at 182, para 50. Mahiou said he did not think the reference to compound interest essential and it might even lead to unfair results (at 167, para 71).
[15] Thiam, ibid.
[16] Ibid, Shi at 164–5, para 57; Al-Khasawneh at 177, para 6; Díaz González at 191, para 49; Rao at 194–5, para 5.
[17] Ibid, Ogiso at 158, para 10; Mahiou at 166, para 70; Barsegov at 170, para 25; Francis at 173, para 46, Hayes at 175, para 62; Al-Khasawneh at 177, para 11; Roucounas at 187, para 11; McCaffrey at 189, para 23; Rao at 194–5, para 5.
[18] *Report of the Commission to the General Assembly on the work of its forty-second session*, above n 11, para 383, Crawford, Third Report on State Responsibility, above n 1, paras 23–4.

and amending the article on compensation to note that it 'may include interest', without any reference to compound interest or the period of account.[19]

Interest was not discussed again by the ILC until the 2000 session when Special Rapporteur Crawford Reintroduced a separate article on interest in his Third Report on State Responsibility.[20] In his view the ILC's placement of a reference to interest within the article on compensation was not sufficiently emphatic that interest was payable.[21] Although interest was an aspect of compensation, in practice it was treated as a separate element of damages and should be treated accordingly in the articles.[22] In respect of compound interest, he proposed that because it was controversial and international jurisprudence was cautious in its approach towards it, the wording of the article should allow for compound interest without expressly referring to it, and this would be explained in the commentary.[23] He was also concerned that if 'the Commission tried to deal in too great detail with the issue of compound interest in the light of the available authorities on compound interest, there was a risk of losing the entire article'.[24] The Special Rapporteur's proposal for a more detailed provision on interest[25] received general acceptance.[26] Comments were primarily directed to whether the provision belonged within the article on compensation and whether interest should be stated to run on compensation rather than on all principal sums.[27] There was much less comment on the question of compound interest than there had been in 1990, and the few express references to it were either in support of its award or directed to the avoidance of double-recovery.[28]

---

[19] Article 8 (Compensation), provisionally adopted at the 45th session of the ILC, *Report of the Commission to the General Assembly on the work of its forty-fifth session*, 1993 YBILC, Vol II, Part 2, para 202. The draft articles were reordered and numbered prior to the ILC session in 1996 so that Article 8 became Article 44 (1996 YBILC, Vol I, 133). For Article 44, see 134.

[20] Above n 1, Article 45 bis, para 214, and *Report of the Commission to the General Assembly on the work of its fifty-second session*, 2000 YBILC, Vol II, Part 2, paras 221–222.

[21] Crawford, Third Report on State Responsibility, above n 1, para 197.

[22] Ibid, para 213.

[23] *Summary records of the meetings of the fifty-second session, 1 May–9 June and 10 July–18 August 2000*, 2000 YBILC Vol I, 182, paras 23–24.

[24] Ibid, 182, para 24.

[25] Draft Article 45 bis (Third Report on State Responsibility, above n 1, para 214) was as follows: '1. Interest on any principal sum payable under these draft articles shall also be payable when necessary in order to ensure full reparation. The interest rate and mode of calculation shall be those most suitable to achieve that result. 2. Unless otherwise agreed or decided, interest runs from the date when compensation should have been paid until the date the obligation to pay compensation is satisfied.'

[26] *Summary records of the meetings of the fifty-second session, 1 May–9 June and 10 July–18 August 2000*, above n 23, Herdocia Sacasa at 201, para 74; Pellet at 207, para 47, 205, para 32; Pambou-Tchivounda at 211, para 9; He at 212, para 23; Kabatsi at 213, para 35; Rao at 216, para 56.

[27] Ibid, Pellet 205, para 33; Economides at 188, para 6, 209–210, para 79; Hafner at 202–203, para 10.

[28] Ibid, Economides at 188, para 6, 209–10, para 79; Pellet at 205, para 32; Rosenstock at 214, para 38; He at 212, para 23.

The proposed article on interest was adopted with minor amendments and became Article 38 of the Articles on the Responsibility of States for Internationally Wrongful Acts. It provides that:

1. Interest on any principal sum due under this chapter [reparation for injury] shall be payable when necessary in order to ensure full reparation. The interest rate and mode of calculation shall be set so as to achieve that result.
2. Interest runs from the date when the principal sum should have been paid until the date the obligation to pay is fulfilled.

As the wording suggests, there is no automatic entitlement to interest. The ILC's commentary explains that interest is not a 'necessary part of compensation in each case',[29] and that 'an injured State has no automatic entitlement to the payment of interest. The awarding of interest depends on the circumstances of each case, and in particular, on whether an award of interest is necessary to ensure full reparation.'[30] However, as 'a general principle, an injured State is entitled to interest on the principal sum representing its loss, if that sum is quantified at an earlier date than the date of settlement of, or judgment or award concerning, the claim'.[31] As to the question of compound interest, the commentary to Article 38 concluded that in the current state of the law it could not be said there is any entitlement to compound interest in the absence of special circumstances, but rejected the view (traced back to Marjorie Whiteman's statement to that effect in her 1943 treatise on damages in international law[32]) that international law prohibits the award of compound interest.[33] The wording of Article 38, reflecting international arbitral practice, also avoids the potential difficulties attending the award of interest in domestic legal systems, such as limitations on interest in some jurisdictions based on Islamic law,[34] prohibitions on awards of interest against the government in jurisdictions such as the United States[35] and the historical difficulties in the English common law of securing interest in an action for damages

[29] J Crawford, *The International Law Commission's Articles on State Responsibility: Introduction Text and Commentaries* (2002), 235, para (1) of commentary to Article 38. Although interest can be said to be an aspect of compensation, it merited a separate Article because it is always dealt with separately by international tribunals: Third Report on State Responsibility, above n 1, para 213.

[30] Commentary to Article 38, para (7), ibid, 237.

[31] Commentary to Article 38, para (2), ibid, 235.

[32] Above n 2, at 1997.

[33] Commentary to Article 38, para (9), in Crawford, above n 29, 238.

[34] For an outline of the origin of the prohibition on charging interest, see J Mokyr (ed), *Oxford Encyclopaedia of Economic History* (2003), Vol 3, 113. It notes further that '[e]lements of ancient and medieval views survive even in modern economies that, although they normally allow interest rates to allocate financial capital, nonetheless use usury laws to set maximum allowable rates of interest, particularly on consumer loans': at 113.

[35] See, for example, the discussion of US domestic law in *Royal Holland Lloyd v United States* (1931), US Court of Claims, 6 *Ann Digest Pub Int'l Law* 442, 445, (1932) 26 *AJIL* 399, 417–18 and the discussion by Whiteman, above at n 2, 1920–4. The Iran-US Claims Tribunal in *Atomic Energy Organisation of Iran v United States* (1986) 12 Iran-US CTR 25 rejected arguments by the US based on its domestic law which prohibited interest in awards against the government. It noted that '[i] t has been the practice of the Tribunal to award interest, when claimed and due, to compensate for damages suffered due to delay in payment, whether the contract in question provides for it or not and notwithstanding general choice of law provisions': at 28.

or in debt for breach of contract for late payment[36] or where the principal is no longer outstanding.[37]

The principle underpinning Article 38—that it constitutes damages for loss of use of the principal sum due at an earlier date—is made explicit in the decisions cited in support of the Article in the commentary.[38] But the commentary also records the use by human rights courts of awards of interest as a mechanism 'to protect the value of a damages award payable by instalments over time',[39] which might suggest a different rationale than that of compensating for loss of use. As for the particulars of awards of interest on principal sums, Article 38 says that interest starts to run from the date when the principal sum should have been paid. However, as the commentary notes, this is not as straightforward as it appears because different legal traditions, in the absence of agreement between the parties, give different answers to the question as to when a principal sum should have been paid. Civil law systems typically fix the date of obligation to pay as the date of demand or date of filing of legal proceedings, while common law systems typically take the date of breach or loss where that is later.[40] Article 38's formulation specifying the date the principal 'should have been paid' is wide enough to embrace date of breach or loss or date of demand. As to rate and method of calculation, Article 38 specifies that the rate and method of calculation should be that necessary to achieve full reparation.

Article 38 has been criticised for 'unhelpfully' leaving the particulars of an interest award to the discretion of parties and tribunals, rather than attempting to give 'detailed rules or guidelines'.[41] However, the schema of the Articles on State Responsibility does not lend itself to more detailed rules for interest awards. Nor is formulating such rules a simple exercise: the difficulties of drafting even a general provision nearly led to a separate provision on interest being left out of the ILC articles altogether. The wide

---

[36] See generally *McGregor on Damages* (17th ed, 2003), chapter 15, paras 15-001–15-005. This was addressed by providing a discretion to award interest under statute, now section 35A of the Supreme Court Act 1981.

[37] Ibid. In the *Interest on Diplomatic Debt Case*, 1903 Great Britain-Venezuela mixed commission, UNRIAA, Vol IX, 479, the Umpire held that the common law rule in Great Britain and the United States that the entitlement to interest otherwise than as provided for in a contract extinguishes on payment of the principal did not apply in international law (at 483).

[38] Crawford, above n 29, 235 at fn 636: *Lucas claim* (1957) 30 ILR 220; Administrative Decision No III (1923), US-Germany Mixed Claims Commission, (1924) 18 AJIL 603 (for property taken during American neutrality, interest was payable from date of taking as the value of the use of sum equal to the value of the property which should have been paid at time of taking (at 605)); *Illinois Central Railroad Co v Mexico* (1926), US-Mexico General Claims Commission, UNRIAA, Vol IV, 134 (just compensation included not only the sum due as claimed in the memorial, 'but compensation for the loss of the use of that sum during a period within which the payment thereof continues to be withheld' (at 136)).

[39] Commentary to Article 38, para (5), in Crawford, above n 29, 236-7.

[40] Commentary to Article 38, para (10), ibid, 238-9.

[41] D Shelton, in 'Symposium: the ILC's State Responsibility Articles: Righting Wrongs' Reparations in the Articles on State Responsibility' (2002) 96 *AJIL* 833, 853, and Shelton, *Remedies in International Human Rights Law* (2nd ed, 2004), 96.

formulation in Article 38 reflects the general consensus in the ILC that these questions should be left to the discretion of the court or tribunal.[42]

The exercise of this discretion by international courts, tribunals and commissions over the last 50 years when awarding interest on damages is the subject of the rest of this article. It also looks at the jurisprudence on interest awards not covered by Article 38: those which fulfil remedial functions other than compensation for loss of use under Article 38—in particular, the use of interest awards as a restitutionary form of reparation under Article 35 of the Articles to restore the *status quo ante*[43]—and post-award interest.[44] The same questions as to development of principle and the particulars of the award arise where the interest is awarded as restitution under Article 35 or as post-award interest.

III. The Jurisprudence: Principles, Particulars and Policy Underpinning Interest Awards

The review of jurisprudence addresses pre- and post-award interest separately. It looks first at the principles invoked by international courts, tribunals and commissions to underpin their interest awards, and then at the particulars of interest awards—period of account, rate of interest and method of calculation—examining new developments in practice and the questions of principle and policy which they raise. More specifically, it asks: which start date for the period of account (date of breach, loss, claim or judgment) is preferred; which rate of interest is preferred in the absence of a relevant contract or treaty provision; how does the appreciation of inflation and its relationship to interest rates affect interest awards; how are changes in interest rates over the period of account accounted for; and which method of calculation—simple or compound—is preferred or should be preferred? In particular, in light of the recent shift in practice towards compound interest awards in investment treaty arbitrations, is compound interest justified at all and, if so, is this only the case in claims concerning investments? Conversely, can simple interest rates ever be justified? Does the character of the court or tribunal—a standing court or tribunal or an *ad hoc* sole matter tribunal—have an impact on the approach to the treatment of interest awards? Finally, post-award interest is considered.

Decisions by international tribunals which are not governed by international law are not included: for example, those determining a contract

---

[42] Commentary to Article 38, para (10), in Crawford, above n 29, 238–239.

[43] See for example the European Commission's claim in Case C-337/04, *Commission v France*, Official Journal of the European Union, OJ C 239, 25.9.2004, p 9. The claim was brought against France's alleged failure to carry out a decision concerning State aid: see further below n 116ff and accompanying text.

[44] Article 38 does not cover post-award interest, on the ground that this is a matter covered by the procedural rules of the court, tribunal or commission concerned: Commentary to Article 38, para (12), in Crawford, above n 29, 239.

claim governed by national law.[45] The line between decisions by international tribunals reached by applying only national law and those relying only on international law is not always clear. A contract specifying an applicable national law may not address all issues which arise from the claims based on it, and so the tribunal might choose to invoke principles of international law which it is entitled to apply by virtue of its constituent treaty. For instance, tribunals formed under the International Convention for the Settlement of International Disputes ('ICSID') are, in the absence of an agreement between the parties, to apply the law of the State party and applicable rules of international law.[46] The Iran-United States Claims Tribunal, which has jurisdiction over private law claims in debt and contract as well as expropriations governed by international law,[47] has held that it is not bound by the law of the contract as far as the assessment of damages is concerned, being free under the terms of its jurisdiction to apply principles of commercial and international law as it determines are applicable.[48] On the other hand, an arbitration tribunal might consider that the applicable international law requires application of national rules.[49]

A. Pre-Award Interest

1. The Principles Underpinning Pre-Award Interest

(a) Overview of the Jurisprudence

In the mixed commissions and arbitral tribunals of the 19th and the first half of the 20th centuries the rationale most frequently given for the award of interest was that it compensated a successful claimant for the damage suffered by the loss of use of the principal sum during the period for which the payment thereof continued to be withheld.[50] It was also characterised as compensation for 'the profits of which the injured party has been deprived' on an ascertained sum of money,[51] and the indemnity

---

[45] Eg, *Ceskoslovenska (CSOB) v Slovak Republic*, Final Award, 29 December 2004, ICSID Case No ARB/97/4. The tribunal's analysis of interest (paras 338–52) is nevertheless worth noting. Another example is *CDC Group Plc v Republic of the Seychelles*, Award of 17 December 2003, 11 ICSID Reports 206.

[46] Article 42 of the ICSID Convention.

[47] The Iran-US Claims Tribunal's jurisdiction includes interstate claims in respect of (i) the interpretation and application of the Algiers General Declaration (Article 17 of the Declaration, 20 ILM 224 (1981), and Article II(3) Claims Settlement Declaration, at 230 ('CSD')) and (ii) claims arising out of contractual arrangements between them for the 'purchase and sale of goods and services' (Article II(2) CSD) and direct individual-State claims (Article II(1), CSD).

[48] *CMI International Inc v Iran* (1983) 4 Iran-US CTR 263, 267–8, referring to Article V of the Claims Settlement Declaration.

[49] See further below n 167ff and accompanying text.

[50] See for example, *Puerto Cabello and Valencia Railway Company*, 1903 Great Britain-Venezuela Commission (Umpire Duffield), UNRIAA, Vol IX, 510, 526–7; *Christern & Co et Ors*, 1903 Germany-Venezuela Commission, UNRIAA, Vol X, 363, 364–5; *Illinois Central Railroad Co v Mexico* (1926), US-Mexico General Claims Commission, UNRIAA, Vol IV, 134, 136.

[51] *The Christina Case*, 1903 Sweden-Venezuela Commission, UNRIAA, Vol X, 765, 766–7.

for the value of the use of property taken for the period between taking and payment of the claim in cases of wrongful possession and use.[52] Regardless of the precise formulation of the principle, similar results were arrived at: interest was usually awarded to run on the principal damages sums at simple rates which fell between 3% and 7% (for the most part 5% or 6%) and from the date of damage or date of claim or, in some instances, the date of the award. Thus interest on damages was by far the most common category of interest award. However, interest might also be awarded as a proxy measure of loss of profits in the absence of another measure of actual lost profit.[53]

The Permanent Court of International Justice made only one award of interest in the 1923 *Wimbledon* case brought by Great Britain, Japan, Italy and France against Germany for refusing free passage to the English steamship, the *SS Wimbledon*, through the Kiel Canal in breach of its obligations under the Treaty of Versailles. Simple interest of 6% per annum (the amount claimed) was awarded on the principal sum without question or any discussion of principle. This was to run from the date of the judgment, notwithstanding that the damages were valued as at the date of loss in March 1921 because this was the date on which the obligation to pay was established and the sum due was liquidated.[54] In *Chorzów Factory* the PCIJ also held that compensation for a lawful expropriation would include interest on a sum equivalent to the value of the undertaking at the date of taking running from that date until the payment.[55]

International courts, tribunals and commissions of the last 50 years have continued to award pre-award interest on damages for the loss of the use of the principal sum, but the expression of principle underpinning its award has shifted in some courts and tribunals to encompass compensation for the effect of inflation, and new forms of interest award informed by different remedial goals have appeared.[56]

From the beginning of its operations in 1981 the Iran-US Claims Tribunal awarded interest on damages 'on the basis of compensation for damages suffered due to delay in payment'.[57] The Tribunal chamber in

[52] *The Lord Nelson Case*, United States-Great Britain arbitral tribunal, established by Special Agreement of 18 August 1910, UNRIAA, Vol VI, 32, 34.

[53] See below n 110–113 and accompanying text.

[54] 1923, PCIJ Reports, Series A, No 1, p 32.

[55] *Case Concerning the Factory at Chorzów (Merits)*, 1928, PCIJ Reports, Series A, No 17, p 47. The case, however, concerned an unlawful seizure of property which could not be expropriated (at 46). Cf the observations of Judges Finlay and Ehrlich in their dissenting opinions, Judge Finlay, p 70, at 70–2, and Judge Ehrlich, p 75, at 90, that the nature of the taking, lawful or otherwise, could not affect quantum where compensation rather than restitution of the property was sought, as compensation was either the value at the time of taking plus interest, or the loss of profit which would have accrued between the time of taking and judgment.

[56] Cf the ICJ, which has only awarded damages in the *Corfu Channel* case. Although the damages were quantified as of the date when they were suffered (the value of the destroyer at time of loss in 1946), the UK did not claim interest on the damages and it was not awarded: *The Corfu Channel Case (Assessment of the Amount of Compensation Due from the People's Republic of Albania to the United Kingdom of Great Britain and Northern Ireland)*, ICJ Reports, 1949, p 244.

[57] *Sylvania Technical Systems, Inc v Iran* (1985) 8 Iran-US CTR 298, 320.

McCollough, after a review of international arbitral practice, concluded that although no uniform rule of law relating to interest had emerged from the practice in transnational arbitration, under normal circumstances interest was to be allocated on the amounts awarded as damages in order to 'compensate for the delay with which the payment to the successful party is made'.[58] It was not until 1987 that the full Tribunal in *Case A/19* confirmed that it was within the Tribunal's jurisdiction to award interest as an aspect of full compensation for damages suffered and that, contrary to Iran's arguments, the silence as to interest in the Claims Settlement Declaration establishing the Tribunal did not preclude its award.[59] Despite the request of both Iran and the US that the full Tribunal establish uniform rules for the award of interest, it declined to do so, holding that responsibility for the determination of the applicable principles of law and whether it was appropriate to award interest rested with the judges in each case.[60]

The International Tribunal for the Law of the Sea ('ITLOS') has awarded interest in only one case, the *M/V Saiga (No 2)*. The Tribunal stated that it is 'generally fair and reasonable that interest is paid in respect of monetary losses, property damage and other economic losses'.[61]

The United Nations Claims Commission established to determine compensation claims arising out of Iraq's invasion of Kuwait delivered a 'Decision on Interest' in 1992 which provided for general damages-interest at 'a rate sufficient to compensate the claimants for the loss of use of the principal amount of the award'.[62]

Arbitral tribunals applying international law generally award interest on damages unless there is a principled reason not to do so.[63] The rationale underpinning the award of interest on principal sums is infrequently expressed and it is usually awarded without proof of loss. Parties rarely challenge its award in principle, focussing rather on the particulars of the award (rate, method of calculation and start date). Where the principle underpinning an interest award is referred to, it is said to be an aspect of compensation under international law.[64] Compensation for

[58] *McCollough & Co, Inc v Ministry of Post* (1986) 11 Iran-US CTR 3, para 98.

[59] (1987) 16 Iran-US CTR 285, para 12.

[60] Ibid, para 13. See also C N Brower and J D Brueschke, *The Iran-United States Claims Tribunal* (1998), 615–7.

[61] *St Vincent and the Grenadines v Guinea (Admissibility and Merits)* (1999) 120 ILR 143, para 173.

[62] 18 December 1992, S/AC.26/1992/16, para 1. See also UNCC decision E3/14, 29 September 2000, S/AC.26/2000/19.

[63] See below n 122-135 and accompanying text for a discussion of instances where pre-award interest has not been awarded.

[64] *AMCO v Indonesia (Award 1)*, Award of 20 November 1984, 1 ICSID Reports 413, para 281; *Agricultural Products Limited [AAPL] v Sri Lanka*, Award of 27 June 1990, 4 ICSID Reports 245, para 114; *Metalclad v Mexico*, Award of 30 August 2000, 5 ICSID Reports 209 (ICSID arbitration under NAFTA), para 128 (citing AAPL); *Middle East Cement Shipping and Handling Co SA [ME Cement] v Egypt*, Award of 12 April 2002, 7 ICSID Reports 173, an arbitration under the 1993 Greece-Egypt BIT, para 174; *Tecnicas Medioambientales Tecmed S.A. v Mexico*, Award of 29 May 2003, 10 ICSID Reports 130 (ICSID arbitration under the Spanish-Mexico BIT), para 211; *Siemens AG v Argentina*, Award of 17 January 2007, ICSID Case No ARB/02/8, para 396.

what, precisely, is rarely explained. Some tribunals note that interest represents the compensation for delayed payment of the principal compensation sum[65] or for loss of use during period of non-payment.[66] The award of interest on damages is distinguished from cases of the award of interest as specific damages, for example where the claimant can prove that it incurred actual interest charges as a direct result of breach[67] or where the primary claim concerns a loan agreement between the parties.[68]

The approach of the regional human rights courts to pre-judgment interest is less clear. The European Court of Human Rights ('ECHR') may award pre-judgment interest in pecuniary damages claims made under any Convention provision where the requisite connection between the right breached and the damages claimed has been established.[69] However, although the Court has accepted that interest should be paid on compensation sums calculated at a date before judgment,[70] discussion of the principles underpinning interest awards is rare and could be interpreted as turning on the depreciation of the principal sum rather than the value of the loss of use caused by delay in payment. In *Stran Greek Refineries v Greece* the Court upheld a claim for interest on a principal compensation sum in a property rights claim under Protocol I, Article 1 because 'the adequacy of the compensation would be diminished if it were to be paid without reference to various circumstances liable to reduce its value', namely the 10 years elapsed since the principal fell due.[71] More recently in *Scordino v Italy (No 1)*, also a case of breach of Protocol I, Article 1, by failure to pay compensation due for an otherwise

---

[65] *CME Czech Republic BV (Netherlands) v Czech Republic*, Final Award on Damages, 14 March 2003, 9 ICSID Reports 264, para 628 (an UNCITRAL arbitration under the Netherlands-Czech Republic BIT). The applicable law provision in the treaty provided that the tribunal was to reach its decision on the basis of law, taking into account the provisions of any contract, international law and the law of the contracting State concerned; in *Nycomb Synergistics Technology Holding AB (Sweden) v Latvia*, Decision of 16 December 2003 (an arbitration before the Stockholm Chamber of Commerce under the Energy Charter Treaty), interest was included in overall compensation as an aspect of 'the claimant's accumulated losses claimed up to the award' (p 42); in *First Eagle Sogen v Bank for International Settlements*, Decision of 19 September 2003, (2004) 43 ILM 893, the PCA Tribunal noted that 'it is a general rule that interest is owed where payments are made on a specific date are not made' (para 90); in *SwemBalt AB (Sweden) v Latvia*, Award of 21 October 2000 (the Court of Arbitration in Copenhagen, based on UNCITRAL rules under the Swedish-Latvian BIT), the Tribunal said interest is to be paid to provide adequate compensation and to take account of the long period of time which elapsed since property taken illegally and dispute was unresolved (para 45).

[66] *Vivendi v Argentina (Award No 2)*, Award of 20 August 2007 (ICSID Case No ARB/97/3, under the France-Argentina BIT), para 9.2.3.

[67] *Liberian Eastern Timber Corporation [LETCO] v Liberia*, Award of 31 March 1986, 2 ICSID Reports 343, 377–9.

[68] Eg, *Southern Pacific Properties (Middle East) (SPP(ME)) v Egypt*, Award of 20 May 1992, 3 ICSID Reports 189, para 230.

[69] Damages will be rejected where causation is not established, eg, *Dularans v France* (2001) 33 EHRR 45, paras 41, 43; *Tinnelly & Sons v United Kingdom* (1999) 27 EHRR 249, paras 89, 93; *Sigurdsson v Iceland* (2005) 40 EHRR 15, paras 48–51.

[70] See, eg, *Pine Valley Developments v Ireland (Just satisfaction)* (1993) 16 EHRR 379, para 14.

[71] (1995) 19 EHRR 293, paras 82–3.

lawful taking of land, the Grand Chamber held that 'interest will have to be paid...so as to offset, at least in part, the long period for which the applicants have been deprived of the land'.[72] In *Lustig-Prean*, a claim under Article 8 (right to respect for family and private life), the Court said that interest could be claimed from the dates on which each element of past pecuniary damage (loss of salary) accrued.[73] The Court has also awarded interest on the costs awarded in respect of ECHR proceedings on the basis that 'some pecuniary loss must have been occasioned by reason of the period that elapsed between the time when the...costs were incurred and the Court's award'.[74] Although compensation for loss of use of the principal sum is not given expressly as the principle underpinning pre-judgment interest on pecuniary losses, the Grand Chamber in *Scordino* cited the reasoning in *Stran Greek Refinery* as a basis for not only awarding interest, but also indexing the principal compensation sum (the value of the property in 1983) to current value to offset inflation.[75] Interest was to be applied to the capital progressively adjusted to account for inflation,[76] thus compensating both for loss of use by way of interest *and* depreciation due to inflation by way of indexing. However, because the Grand Chamber arrived at a global damages sum well below the amount claimed, it is not clear whether this reasoning actually flowed through into the calculation of the award.[77] In *Beyeler v Italy (No 2)* the Court also factored in inflation, but awarded *either* the Italian statutory interest rate or the annual rate of inflation, whichever was the higher, and capitalised the annual interest/inflation sum.[78]

In the Inter-American Court of Human Rights the award of pre-judgment interest on pecuniary damages—where it is recorded in the judgment—arises only on compensation for death and loss of earnings, and its award is accepted as a matter of principle. In *Neira Alegría* the Court explained that, because compensation calculated at the time of death was to be paid many years later, 'the interest that would have accrued during that time must be added to that sum for the purposes of calculating the proper compensation'.[79] Other references to the principle

---

[72] (2007) 45 EHRR 7, para 258.

[73] *Lustig-Prean & Beckett v United Kingdom (Art 41)* (2001) 29 EHRR 548, paras 28–29 (although a lump sum was awarded inclusive of interest). See also *Smith and Grady v United Kingdom* (2001) 31 EHRR 24, paras 24–5.

[74] *Krone Verlag GMbH & Co KG v Austria* (2006) 42 EHRR 28, paras 46–7. The applicant claimed interest at rates between 5 and 10.75% from the time it commenced proceedings in May 1997: a lump sum of €200 was awarded. See also *Bergens Tidende & Ors v Norway* (2001) 31 EHRR 16, paras 68–70 (awarding an equitable sum in respect of interest), *Hentrich v France (Pecuniary damages under Article 50)* (1996) 21 EHHR 199, para 14, *Pine Valley Developments v Ireland (Just satisfaction)* (1993) 16 EHRR 379, para 19.

[75] *Scordino* (1995) 19 EHRR 293, para 258.

[76] Ibid.   [77] Ibid, paras 256–9.

[78] (2003) 36 EHRR 5, para 23.

[79] Reparations and Costs, 19 September 1996, Series C, No 29, para 46. The amount of compensation at time of death discounts the amount the advance payment of future income would earn if invested at normal rates.

underpinning an interest award are more oblique: in *Acevedo-Jaramillo*, where the amount of compensation for lost wages was to be referred back to domestic authorities, the Court simply directed that the length of time the applicants remained unjustly dismissed was to be taken into account in fixing such compensation.[80] In other judgments the Court does not award interest as such but adjusts the amount of compensation to current value at the date of judgment.[81] This appears, like the reasoning in some decisions of the ECHR, to focus on ensuring compensation for depreciation of sums calculated at an earlier date rather than compensation for loss of use. However, it is not apparent whether the distinction between 'interest that would have accrued' (suggesting a return on money invested) and adjustment to current value (suggesting compensation for depreciation of the principal sum) leads to any difference in result. In the *Street Children* case the Court noted that it had adjusted to current value by using a 6% annual rate of interest.[82] Interest on claims for costs and expenses related to, for example, searches for relatives, medical expenses, funerals or legal fees are rarely recorded as including claims for interest and nor is it awarded.[83] On the one occasion where a claim for interest on expenses was recorded in the judgment it was not awarded, and no explanation was given for not acceding to the claim.[84]

The approach of the European Union courts to pre-judgment interest awards is different again. The principles underpinning an award of pre-judgment interest depend on the nature of the claim. Where actions concern a claim under Article 288(1) of the European Community Treaty for damages against one of the Union institutions for breach of contract, the law of the contract will be applied, leading to an award of interest on damages calculated at the contract rate or the statutory rate of the jurisdiction of the law of the contract.[85] In claims of non-contractual liability against Union institutions under Article 288(2) or the staff regulations,

---

[80] Preliminary Objections, Merits, Reparations and Costs, 7 February 2006, Series C, No 144, paras 304–5.

[81] *Case of the 'Street Children' (Villagrán-Morales et al v Guatemala)*, Reparations and Costs, 26 May 2001, Series C No 77, para 81, *El Caracazo v Venezuela*, Reparations, 29 August 2002, Series C No 95, para 88. See also the Commission's claim in *Case of Juan Humberto Sánchez v Honduras*, Preliminary Objections, Merits, Reparations and Costs, Judgment of 7 June 2003, Series C No 99, para 159(a).

[82] Ibid, para 81, fn 79. See to the same effect *Cantoral-Benavides v Peru*, Reparations and Costs, 3 December 2001, Series C No 88, para 49.

[83] Eg, *Case of the 'Street Children' (Villagrán-Morales et al v Guatemala)*, Reparations and Costs, 26 May 2001, Series C No 77, where interest was claimed on loss of earnings but not consequential pecuniary damage (para 70).

[84] *Bulacio v Argentina*, Merits, Reparations and Costs, 18 September 2003, Series C No 100, paras 82, 87.

[85] See, eg, Case C-416/98 *Commission v Nea Energeiaki Technologia EPE* [2002] ECR I-1759, Case C-156/97 *Commission v Van Balkom Non-Ferro Scheiding BV* [2000] ECR I-1095, Case C-337/96 *Commission v Industrial Refuse and Coal Energy Ltd* [1998] ECR I-7943, concerning claims by the Commission against individuals in breach of contract claims, Case C-42/94 *Heidemji Advies BV v European Parliament* [1995] ECR I-1417, Case T-29/02 *Global Electronic Finance Management SA v Commission* [2005] ECR II-835.

the European Court of Justice ('ECJ') has concluded that a claim for interest is in general admissible.[86] Interest is also recoverable on fines repaid by the Community and held to have been improperly levied.[87] In general, where the principal sum is certain or capable of ascertainment, default interest for delay in payment will be payable running until payment from the date of claim or complaint,[88] from the date the principal fell due,[89] from the date of payment of an improperly levied fine[90] or, where the obligation to make good the damage is not established or the amount is unascertainable until judgment, from the date of judgment.[91]

---

[86] See, eg, Case 238/78 *Ireks-Arkady v Council and Commission* [1979] ECR 2955, paras 19–20, and Case T-134/01 *Fuchs v Commission* [2002] ECR II-3909, paras 56–7. See futher A van Casteren, 'Article 215(2) EC and the Question of Interest', in T Heukels and A McDonnell (eds), *The Action for Damages in Community Law* (1997), 199 at 201.

[87] Case T-171/99 *Corus UK Ltd v Commission* [2001] ECR II-2967 (Article 34, ECSC Treaty), paras 52–61.

[88] Case T-15/93 *Phillippe Vienne v Parliament* [1993] ECR-II 1327, para 42 (back payment of allowances), Case T-215/01 *Calberson GE v Commission* [2004] ECR-II 587, paras 144–5, 163 (an Article 238 claim for breach of contract by the Commission). See also Case 532/79 *Amesz v Commission* [1985] ECR 55, para 14 and Case 737/79 *Battaglia* [1985] ECR 71, para 10, where default interest was awarded on back payments of salary adjustments (paid subsequent to proceedings commencing, so the only claim remaining was for default interest), from the date of complaint or the date payment fell due if later.

[89] Case 110/63 *Willame v Commission of European Atomic Energy Community* [1965] ECR 649 (for material losses only, here arrears of salary), Case 75/82 *Razzouk & Or v Commission* [1984] ECR 1509, para 19, Case T-4/92 *Vardakas v Commission* [1993] ECR-II 357, para 50, Case T-285/94 *Pfloeschner v Commission* [1995] ECR II-3029, IA-291, II-889, paras 55–56, Case 271/87 *Fedeli v Parliament* [1989] ECR 993 (repayment of improperly deducted salary), Case 21/86 *Samara v Commission* [1987] ECR 795 (where the obligation to pay interest from the dates the payments fell due was held to be an aspect of the Commission's obligation to comply with an earlier judgment establishing her proper salary grade (paras 7–9)), Case F-126/05 *Borbély v Commission* [2007] ECR 00 (Civil Service Tribunal) (employment allowances). Cf Case T-17/89 *Brazzelli v Commission* [1992] ECR II-293 which distinguished *Fedeli* from cases where default interest is payable only from the date of judgment because in *Fedeli* the amount was certain and not capable of dispute. In *Brazzelli*, a staff claim concerning back payments of salary adjustments, the Commission did not know how much salary it would have to pay because it did not know the weightings in force for accommodation, living costs, etc, which were to be fixed by the Council and involved an element of discretion on the latter's part. As soon as the Commission did know the amounts due, it started paying arrears, so no fault for delay in payment of arrears could be imputed to it (paras 20–7). It was, however, liable for compensatory interest (see below n 98 ff and accompanying text). The CFI's decision was upheld by the ECJ (Case C-136/92, [1994] ECR-I 1981).

[90] *Corus UK Ltd v Commission* [2001] ECR II-2967, para 61.

[91] *Ireks-Arkady v Council and Commission* [1979] ECR 2955, Case C152/88 *Sofrimport v Commission* [1990] ECR I-2477, para 32, Cases C-104/98 and C-37/90 *Mulder v Council and Commission (No 1)* [1992] ECR I-3061, paras 35–6, setting default interest rates of 8% (7% where claimed) from the date of that judgment to payment and the subsequent quantum award ([2000] ECR I-203), Case T-112/95 *Dethlefs v Council and Commission* [1998] ECR II-3819, para 74, Case T-160/03 *Afcon Management Consultants v Commission* [2005] ECR II-981. Cf *Amesz v Commission* [1985] ECR 55 and *Battaglia* [1985] ECR 71, which like *Brazzelli v Commission* [1992] ECR II-293, concerned a claim for default interest on back payments of salary adjustments based on application of regulations on weighting between living costs in the different countries EC staff resided in; like *Brazzelli*, the back payments had already been paid (between December 1983 and January 1984 after the revised weighting and amounts due had been ascertained by the Commission towards the end of 1983), after the claim was commenced in 1979 and after an initial finding of liability by the court in December 1982. However, unlike *Brazzelli* the court did award default interest from the applicants' date of claim, a date *before* the amounts on which default interest was due would have been ascertainable, because it said the Commission had been excessively slow in discharging its duties, presumably

Proof of damage is not required for an award of default interest, but notice of the claim is.[92] The rationale for the award of default interest is rarely discussed, other than by reference to 'the principles common to the legal systems of the Member States' in Article 288(2) claims.[93] But when further explanation is given the courts have said that the default interest is payable to compensate for the loss or pecuniary harm entailed by a delay in payment.[94] In *Reynolds v Parliament*, a staff regulations case, the Court of First Instance ('CFI') went so far as to say that the harm owing to delay in payment was 'equivalent to a loss of profits corresponding to the remuneration which would have been paid...for investing the sums payable had they been made available...as soon as they became payable'.[95] It has been suggested that default interest entails an element of penalty to sanction the debtor for failing to pay on time,[96] but this is not reflected in the judgments of either the ECJ or the CFI.[97]

In cases of non-contractual liability of the Community where liability is not established until the date of judgment and the default interest only starts to run at that date, but aspects of the principal sum are valued by the court as at a date before judgment, compensatory interest may be

those established by its 1982 judgment. This line of cases seems to be an exception to the rule that the principal amount must be ascertainable before liability for default interest arises, at least insofar as the interest ran from date of claim rather the date the commision should have revised and paid the weightings subsequent to the Court's first judgment in 1982. The cases might better be characterised as compensatory interest cases, but the Court could not take this route because the claim for compensatory interest was held inadmissible because it was not properly pleaded.

In these cases, the sum must be ascertainable at the time of judgment. A sum may not be ascertainable at judgment where, for example, the Court establishes liability and leaves it to the parties to reach agreement on the amount of compensation, as was the case in Case T-260/97 *Camar Srl v Council and Commission* [2005] ECR-II 2741. The applicant had not sought a determination of quantum in the initial proceedings in 2000. The parties were unable to reach agreement and so the matter returned to the CFI. Default interest therefore only ran from the date of the second judgment in 2005 (paras 143–6).

Van Casteren, above n 86, notes that the ECJ's approach 'denies the fact that many Member States do not see the need for a precise evaluation of the principal amount due in cases in which its content should be obvious to the person under the obligation to pay...But in the context of default interest, the Court of Justice is not inclined to choose the side of the person awaiting payment of what is due to him. The "established objective factors" ascertaining the primary obligation— and thereby the starting-point of default interest—seem to be more favourable for the debtor', 211–12.

[92] This is evident from the judgments themselves, but for specific articulation of the point see *Fuchs v Commission* [2002] ECR II-3909, para 56 and *Calberson GE v Commission* [2004] ECR-II 587, para 90.

[93] *Ireks-Arkady v Council and Commission* [1979] ECR 2955, para 20, or, in staff regulation claims, the courts refer to their inherent jurisdiction as the basis of an award of compensation and interest, eg, *Borbély v Commission* [2007] ECR 10 (Civil Service Tribunal), para 71; *Phillippe Vienne v Parliament* [1993] ECR-II 1327, para 42.

[94] *Samara v Commission* [1987] ECR 795, para 9, *Fuchs v Commission* [2002] ECR II-3909, para 56 (Article 288(2) case), *Calberson GE v Commission* [2004] ECR-II 587, para 90, Case T-237/00 *Reynolds v Parliament* [2002] ECR II-163, para 150.

[95] Ibid. The default interest rate awarded was 5.25%, clearly based on the ECB rate formula, although this is not explicit.

[96] Van Casteren, above n 86, 207.

[97] But see the Opinion of AG Lenz in *Brazzelli v Commission* [1992] ECR II-293 where he suggests that default interest is an automatic penalty (para 132).

claimed for financial loss due to the inability to earn return on the principal.[98] Unlike default interest loss, claims for compensatory interest must prove actual loss of a return on the principal sum. In the absence of such proof the rate of inflation will be awarded as compensatory interest on the grounds that full restitution is to be made for the damage suffered and therefore loss caused by the fall in the value of money will be awarded.[99] For example, in *Mulder*, the claimants could not establish that they would not have used the principal sum awarded to meet daily living expenses, so compensatory interest equivalent to the average rate of inflation over the period of account was awarded.[100] In *Brazzelli*, a staff regulation claim, the CFI said that

it would be impossible, except in particular circumstances, to establish how the applicants would have spent the arrears of remuneration which were due to them if the arrears had been paid to them in good time. However, in the present cases it is not a question of seeking evidence of individual losses, but of verifying whether facts exist which can be objectively proved on the basis of precise data which have been made public. By producing relevant statistics, which have not been contested by the defendant, the applicants have thus proved to the requisite legal standard the deterioration in purchasing power which affected their arrears of remuneration during the period in question.[101]

Where national courts of member states hear matters of European Community law, for example claims by nationals against their own governments for breach, they apply their domestic procedures and remedies subject to the requirements that the remedy is equivalent to that available in similar claims under domestic law and provides an effective or adequate remedy for the breach of EC law.[102] In respect of the

---

[98] Case C-308/87 *Grifoni v European Atomic Energy Community* [1994] ECR-I 341, paras 39–40, Cases C-104/98 and C-37/90 *Mulder (No 2)* [2000] ECR I-203, paras 220–1, 352 and *Camar Srl v Council and Commission* [2005] ECR-II 2741, paras 137–42 (although the judgment does not refer to compensatory interest *per se*, it relies on *Grifoni* and *Mulder*), *Brazzelli*, ibid, paras 28–42.

[99] *Mulder (No 2)*, ibid, para 220, Case C-104/89 *Mulder v Commission* (Costs) [2004] ECR-I 1, para 86, *Camar*, ibid. Cf *Afcon Management Consultants v Commission* [2005] ECR II-981, where 'compensatory interest' was awarded in a claim for breach of contract by the Commission at the courts' usual default interest rate (ECB main refinancing rate plus 2%) to run from the first day of the month following the month in which the applicant last took steps prior to commencing proceedings without any discussion of fault on the part of the Commission or proof of loss on the part of the applicant (para 130).

[100] *Mulder (No 2)*, ibid, paras 214–9. Compensatory interest has also been claimed to run from the time the principal payments fell due in cases where default interest is awarded from the date of complaint, but has been rejected as inadmissible because made as a fresh complaint in the course of proceedings contrary to the ECJ's statute and rules of procedure: see, eg, *Amesz v Commission* [1985] ECR 55, paras 14–7, *Battaglia* [1985] ECR 71, paras 7–13; see further above n 88. Compensatory interest will only be awarded where the claimant can establish fault on the EU institution's part, damage and a causal link: Case T-17/89 *Brazzelli v Commission* [1992] ECR II-293, paras 35–9. Cf *Afcon*, discussed above n 99.

[101] *Brazzelli*, ibid, para 40. See also Case T-351/03 *Schneider Electric SA v Commission*, paras 34–3 (account must be taken of the rate of inflation). Cf *Afcon*, discussed above n 99.

[102] The current formulation of the principle of national procedural autonomy can be found in Joined Cases C-397 and 410/98 *Metallgesellschaft Ltd and Others, Hoechst AG and Hoechst (UK) Ltd v Commissioners of Inland Revenue and HM Attorney General* [2001] ECR I-1727, para 86.

application of national rules on pre-judgment interest by national courts, the ECJ held in *Marshall (II)*[103] that full compensation for the loss and damage sustained as a result of breaches of Community law

cannot leave out of account factors, such as the effluxion of time, which may in fact reduce its value. The award of interest, in accordance with the applicable national rules, must therefore be regarded as an essential component of compensation.[104]

This means that while the domestic laws of Member States concerning interest will generally apply, national statutory limits or prohibitions on interest awards in claims for compensation must be disapplied by national courts where their application would lead to ineffective compensation. The ECJ's reasoning in *Marshall (II)* appears to focus on compensating for the reduction in value of the principal compensation sum over time because of changes in the value of money,[105] rather than compensation for the loss of use of it. The paragraph in the judgment following that quoted above refers more generally to an interest award 'to compensate for the loss sustained by the recipient of the compensation as a result of the effluxion of time until the capital sum awarded is actually paid',[106] which might be wide enough to encapsulate loss of use. The focus on 'taking account of effluxions of time' rather than a more specific loss of use is highlighted by the subsequent *Evans* judgment, which held that when providing compensation required by a directive, States could 'choose between awarding interest *or* paying compensation in the form of aggregate sums which take account of the effluxion of time'.[107] This jurisprudence, like that of the human rights courts, suggests that the award of interest is being conceived of as an adjustment of principal sums due and quantified as at an earlier date in order to factor in changes in the value of the money between that date and judgment.[108] It is less clear whether interest on damages should also cover loss of use.

(b) Forms of Interest Award Other than Interest on Damages

While interest on damages is the predominant form of pre-award interest, there are other types of compensatory interest awards, including interest as specific damages where the claimant has incurred actual

---

[103] Case C-271/91 *Marshall v Southampton and South-West Hampshire Area Health Authority* (*'Marshall II'*) [1993] ECR I-4367, paras 30–2.

[104] Ibid, para 31. But cf *R v Sec'y of State for Social Security (ex parte Sutton)* [1997] ECR I-2163, para 35. For a critique of the ECJ's jurisprudence on this point, see M Dougan, 'Cutting Your Losses in the Enforcement Deficit: A Community Right to the Recovery of Unlawfully Levied Charges' [1998] 1 CYEL 233, 259–66.

[105] Ms Marshall's claim dated back to March 1980 when she had been compulsorily retired and the ECJ judgment in *Marshall II* was delivered in 1993.

[106] *Marshall II* above n 103, para 32 (emphasis added).

[107] Case C-63/01, *Evans v Secretary of State for the Environment, Transport and the Regions* [2003] ECR I-14447, para 70 (emphasis added).

[108] See further below n 279ff and accompanying text.

interest charges as a direct result of the respondent's breach,[109] awards of interest as an objective measure of a loss of profits award and awards where interest is the principal compensation sum, rather than ancillary to it. There are also interest awards which are not compensatory in function, being designed to restore the *status quo ante* under a treaty rather than to compensate the claimant for loss.

Both Whiteman and Arangio-Ruiz noted in their reviews of the treatment of interest in the jurisprudence that it has been awarded as an objective measure of profits in international law, as it can be in equity in the common law.[110] The number of this type of interest award is low. The arbitrator in the 1896 *Fabiani* case recognised this ground for an interest award but eventually adopted a different quantification of loss of profits.[111] More recently in *MV Saiga (No 2)*, ITLOS awarded a higher rate of interest on compensation for oil cargo losses than for other material damage in order to include loss of profit, but it did not explain the rationale for an award of interest as a loss of profit.[112] Nor was it discussed by the parties in the oral proceedings.[113]

Occasionally an award of interest will form the principal damages sum rather than being ancillary to it. Although the interest award is still compensatory in nature, in the framework of the Articles on State Responsibility it would fall under Article 36 ('Compensation') rather than Article 38 ('Interest'). For example, in *Pammel v Germany* before the ECHR, interest was awarded to compensate for the damage caused by excessive delay in judicial proceedings in breach of Article 6(1) in respect of the loss of opportunity to claim retrospective rent payments at an earlier date. But, as the rent payments were still recoverable under domestic law, in accordance with Article 41 of the European Convention ('Just satisfaction') only interest on those rent payments was awarded.[114] Essentially this was an interest on damages award, akin to those cases where the principal sum has been paid or set off before judgment, leaving the interest on that sum only to be recovered, as was the case in the ECJ

---

[109] *LETCO*, Award of 31 March 1986, 2 ICSID Reports 343.

[110] Arangio-Ruiz, above n 1, 20, Whiteman, above n 2, 1867–71.

[111] J B Moore, *History and Digest of the Arbitrations to Which the United States Has Been a Party* (1898), Vol 5, 4878, 4913–5.

[112] As discussed above n 61 and accompanying text. See also *AIG v Kazakhstan*, Award of 7 October 2003, 11 ICSID Reports 3 (an ICSID arbitration under the US-Kazakhstan BIT) where the investment tribunal without any explanation awarded higher post-award interest on the lost profits component of the award than on the part of the award made up of compensation for money actually expended and the interest thereon: operative para at 116–7.

[113] Oral pleadings, ITLOS/PV.99/17 19 March 1999 a.m., http://www.itlos.org/start2_en.html. St Vincent and the Grenadines claimed interest on the damages without specification of rate in the oral pleadings, and Guinea did not respond on this point. Neither discussed the interest claim or loss of profits.

[114] *Pammel v Germany* (1998) 26 EHRR 100, paras 77–78. See also *Schuler-Zgraggen v Switzerland (Article 50)* (1996) 21 EHRR 404, paras 14–15, *Pialopoulos & Ors v Greece* (2001) 33 EHRR 39, para 77. Under Article 41 (previously Article 50) the Court will only award reparation if national law does not provide for reparation or only allows partial reparation (see, eg, *Scordino v Italy (No 1)* (2007) 45 EHRR 7, para 247).

decision *Metallgesellschaft*. In that case the claimants had been required to pay advance corporation tax in breach of the EC Treaty. This had later been set off against mainstream corporation tax, and so the outstanding damage was only the loss of use of those funds or the Revenue's unjust enrichment for the periods between the time when the tax was prematurely paid and when it was set off. The claimants sought interest as the measure of the damage flowing from breach. The difficulty was that English law precluded a claim for interest where the principal sum had been paid before the commencement of proceedings. The ECJ upheld the claim to reparation based on the claimants' loss and the respondent's benefit and said that the claim could not be rejected on the basis that it was for interest-only.[115]

A new non-compensatory interest claim has developed in European Community law which can be categorized as falling within Article 35 rather than Article 38 of the Articles on State Responsibility because the objective of the award is to restore the *status quo ante* under the Treaty in the event of breach rather than compensate the claimant. For example, in a claim by the European Commission against France for failing to carry out a decision under Article 88 concerning State aid paid by France to Crédit Mutuel in breach of Community law, the Commission argued that the 'simple interest' method used by the French authorities to calculate interest to be paid on the amount recovered would not result in the neutralization of the economic advantage from which Crédit Mutuel benefited, and that only compound interest would achieve that effect.[116] The purpose of the interest award was not compensatory, but to restore the economic balance in the common market required by the EC Treaty. This follows the standard practice of the Commission when redressing advantages obtained by traders or producers from their Member States contrary to EC rules.[117] The CFI has confirmed that the obligation to pay interest meets the requirement in Article 88 to eliminate a financial advantage which is ancillary to the amount of aid initially granted.[118]

The practice under EC law can be compared with that under the WTO Agreement on Subsidies and Countervailing Measures ('SCM Agreement') regarding the withdrawal and repayment of unlawful

[115] [2001] ECR I-1727, discussed above n 102 and accompanying text. The claimants were UK subsidiary companies of parent companies based in other Member States. They had been unlawfully discriminated against by English tax law because it did not, unlike in the case for UK subsidiaries of parent companies which had their seat in the UK, allow them to make a group income election for dividends paid to the parent company which would have allowed them to avoid paying advance corporation tax on those dividends. The result was that the claimant companies were required to pay tax earlier than the subsidiaries of UK parent companies, thus suffering a comparative disadvantage on the ground of nationality.

[116] Case C-337/04 *Commission v France*, action brought on 2 August 2004, 25.9.2004, OJ of the European Union, C 239, p 9.

[117] See Communication to Member States, OJ C 110 8.5.2003, p 21 and para 14 of the preamble to Commission Regulation (EC) No 794/2004 of 21 April 2004.

[118] Case T-459/93, *Siemens SA v Commission* [1995] ECR II-1675, paras 96–100.

subsidies.[119] The Panel in the *Australian Automotive Leather* decision held that the SCM Agreement did not require the payment of interest on repayment of subsidies, because the remedy provided by the SCM Agreement was not intended 'to fully restore the *status quo ante* by depriving the recipient of the prohibited subsidy of the benefits it may have enjoyed in the past'.[120] Nor was it 'a remedy intended to provide reparation or compensation in any sense. A requirement of interest would go beyond the requirement of repayment encompassed by the term "withdraw the subsidy"'.[121]

(c) Cases Where Interest Has Not Been Awarded

There are several instances where pre-award interest has not been awarded in recent jurisprudence: in non-pecuniary damages claims; where the pecuniary loss is valued as at the date of the award or the remedy is loss of profits; where the applicant's conduct precludes an interest award; and where the settlement fund runs out of money.

Non-pecuniary damages awards for personal or moral injury do not usually attract pre-judgment interest, either in the European Court of Human Rights[122] or the Inter-American Court of Human Rights.[123] The reason for treating non-pecuniary awards differently from pecuniary claims is not discussed by either Court.[124]

On occasion interest has not been awarded in pecuniary claims, because the damage is assessed at current value at the date of judgment or because loss of profits is the measure of damage. An example of the former is the Permanent Court of Arbitration ('PCA') Tribunal's 1956 decision in the *Lighthouses Arbitration* between France and Greece.[125]

---

[119] *Australia—Subsidies Provided to Producers and Exporters of Automotive Leather—Recourse to Article 21.5 of the DSU by the United States*, Report of the Panel, 21 January 2000, WT/DS126/RW, para 6.39.

[120] Ibid, para 6.49.   [121] Ibid.

[122] See, eg, *Lustig-Prean & Beckett v United Kingdom* (2001) 29 EHRR 548, para 12, discussed above n 73 and accompanying text; and Shelton, *Remedies*, above n 41, 351. Interest on non-pecuniary damages claims was claimed to run from the date of application to the Court in *Krastanov v Bulgaria* (2005) 41 EHRR 50, paras 84–6, but none was awarded and the Court did not comment on the claim.

[123] But see *Aloeboetoe v Suriname*, Merits, 4 December 1991, Series C, No 11, para 92. The amount claimed by the Commission as moral damages was indexed to the consumer index and interest was included calculated for 'the period in question', seemingly the period between the date of the Commission's submissions on reparations in 1992 and the date of judgment in 1993.

[124] By comparison English legislation allows for interest on non-pecuniary damages in personal injury cases to account for loss of use. As the sum awarded at judgment is a global measure of past and future losses valued at the date of the judgment, it is unnecessary for the interest award to account for diminishment of the value of the damages up to the date of judgment. The purpose of the interest award is only to compensate for the loss of use of the funds from the date the obligation to pay the damages arose. This has led the English courts to use a rate premised on the deduction of the inflation component from the nominal interest rate (awarded in the case of pecuniary damages which are valued at the date the claim arose) to reach a real rate of interest (see *Wright v British Railways Board* [1983] 2 AC 773 (HL), per Lord Diplock).

[125] Award of 24 July 1956, extracted in 23 ILR, 299 and 659, at 673–6, concerning France's claim in respect of the damages suffered by a French concessionaire company. See also *ADC v Hungary*, Award of 2 October 2006, ICSID Case No ARB/03/16 (under the Cyprus-Hungary BIT), para 520; and *AIG Capital Inc v Kazakstan*, above n 112, 115.

Advocating a case-by-case approach, the Tribunal rejected the claim to interest on the principal (the value of the concession based on a loss of profits analysis as at the date the concession was withdrawn) because the principal damages sums in the original currencies at the dates they fell due were converted into their current value as at the date of the award, and thus took account of currency devaluation.[126] The Tribunal's view was that the refusal to award interest met the terms of the *compromis* as the award corresponded exactly to the damage suffered.[127] This approach to damages did not, however, compensate for the loss of the use of the profits which fell due and were valued as at dates prior to the award. In *Liberian Eastern Timber Corporation [LETCO] v Liberia* no interest damages were awarded because the loss of profits from loss of the concession contract and the expenses incurred as a result of the expropriation were compensated at present value at the date of the award.[128] Similarly in *Société Ouest Africain des Bétons Industriels [SOABI] v Senegal* the Tribunal awarded a sum for SOABI's 'compensable loss of opportunity' which took account of all elements of the loss, and said that there was no need to award pre-judgment interest thereon.[129] Likewise, the Chile-United States International Commission in *Re Letelier and Moffit*, a claim concerning both moral and material damage for wrongful death and personal injury, considered it unnecessary to address the interest argument because compensation had been expressed at present value.[130]

An interest award may also be refused because of the conduct of the claimant, although this is rare.[131] One recent example where the refusal to award interest appears to have been used as a vehicle for sanctioning the conduct of one of the parties is the *Protection of the Rhine* arbitral award. The PCA Tribunal held that the Netherlands was precluded from recovering interest on two sums it had advanced in 1998 to France to reduce pollution in the Rhine, under the Convention on the Protection

---

[126] Ibid, 302–3, 675–6. Current value was achieved by converting the past profits as they fell due into a stable currency, the US dollar, and then reconverting into the currency of payment at the date of judgment.

[127] Ibid, 676.

[128] *[LETCO] v Liberia*, Award of 31 March 1986, 2 ICSID Reports 343, 377–9; see further above n 67. Post award interest was awarded at the annual rate of the LIBOR at three months, but no explanation was given as to the rate selected. The applicable law in accordance with the contract between the parties was Liberian law. Incurred interest costs were awarded.

[129] Award of 25 February 1988, 2 ICSID Reports 190, paras 6.23–37 and 7.19. Rather surprisingly, given that the award for breach of contract was based on lost profits rather than expenditures lost, awards were also made for operating costs and reimbursements of expenditure, and 10% pre-judgment interest was awarded on those items of damage. Possibly this was due to the wording of the relevant Senegalese law, though doubts could be raised as to whether the approach led to overcompensation.

[130] Decision of 11 January 1992, 88 ILR 727, para 24. See also the Separate Concurring Opinion of Professor Orrego Vicuña, 745, who added that interest could not be awarded from an earlier date because the claims by their nature could not be evaluated before judgment.

[131] See, eg, *Owners of the Cargo of the Coquitlam (Great Britain v US)*, UNRIAA, Vol VI, 45 (18 December 1920).

of the Rhine, because it knew that the sums were unnecessary: the agreed treaty targets on pollution reduction had already been achieved. The sums could not have been intended by the Netherlands to provide France with the advances it needed to reduce pollution in the Rhine, but rather to earn the agreed long term investment rate which France would have to reimburse under the agreement. In these circumstances the Tribunal did not consider that the 1998 amounts should bear interest.[132] In *First Eagle* another PCA Tribunal refused pre-judgment interest to one claimant because the delay in payment of the principal sum was due to his failure or refusal to take the necessary steps after the respondent Bank had indicated its willingness to pay. That is, the loss was due to his own conduct, not the Bank's.[133]

A final example of when interest may not be awarded is where a settlement fund falls short. A recent example is the UNCC which, in spite of its initial 1992 decision to award interest on damages,[134] held in 2005 that interest would not in fact be awarded because of the limited amount in the special fund.[135]

(d) Conclusions

A number of points emerge from this survey of judicial and arbitral practice. First most interest awards are compensatory, and most awards of pre-judgment interest in the Iran-US Claims Tribunal, ITLOS, the UNCC, by arbitral tribunals, the human rights courts and default interest in the EU courts are awards for interest on damages as compensation for damage suffered because of a delay in payment or the passage of time from the date the principal sum should have been paid until the date

---

[132] *Case concerning the auditing of accounts between the Kingdom of the Netherlands and the French Republic pursuant to the Additional Protocol of 25 September 1991 to the Convention of 3 December 1976 on the Protection of the Rhine Against Pollution by Chlorides*, Permanent Court of Arbitration 12 March 2004 (unofficial English translation available at http://www.pca-cpa.org/upload/files/ Neth_Fr_award_English.pdf), para 139. No unjust enrichment argument was addressed. Under the Protocol the States Parties had paid annual lump sums in advance to France which was responsible for implementing the initiatives for reducing pollution in the Rhine. The Netherlands sought repayment of principal sums advanced but not expended, plus interest thereon, as provided for by the Protocol, but France disputed the principal amounts claimed as it interpreted the relevant treaty articles to arrive at substantially lower amounts.

[133] Decision of 19 September 2003, (2004) 43 ILM 893, para 99.

[134] See above n 62 and accompanying text.

[135] 'Decision concerning awards of interest', Governing Council of the United Nations Compensation Commission, 144th meeting, 10 March 2005, S/AC.26/Dec.243. The special fund was made up of 30% (from 2000, 25%) of the value of Iraqi oil exports under the food for oil programme: http://www2.unog.ch/uncc/introduc.htm. The UNCC decision follows the practice of the United States Foreign Claims Settlement Commission in the *Lucas Claim* (1957) 30 ILR 220, 223. It held that interest would not be awarded because of a lack of money in the compensation fund allocated to the commission. In a similar vein but using a different method, the British domestic board set up in the early 19th century to distribute the 1794 Jay Treaty settlement funds allocated a lump sum between claimants on a pro-rata basis calculated by reference to the total principal and interest sums awarded to them by the board: J B Moore (ed), *International Adjudications*, Modern Series, (1931), Vol 3, 359 (see 371–2 for the treatment of interest).

when it is paid.[136] Practice in awarding interest on damages is not, however, entirely consistent. For example, there seems to be no reason why the Inter-American Court of Human Rights does not award interest on awards reimbursing claimants' expenses for funerals and medical treatment incurred before judgment.

Second, awards of interest on damages are not subject to the rules for recovery of loss: loss is presumed,[137] and directness (foreseeability or remoteness) is not required to be established by the claimant. As such interest on damages (default interest in the EU courts) is the approximate equivalent of interest on damages in the common law systems[138] and default interest in civil law systems, both of which are governed by legislation.

Third, another characterisation of the damage for which interest is intended to compensate has emerged in the jurisprudence of the human rights courts and the EU courts: namely, the loss incurred because of the fall in value or depreciation of a monetary sum due to inflation. The distinction in characterisation of the damage is important because in theory an award of interest for loss of use will be higher than one which compensates only for devaluation of the principal sum, because nominal interest rates factor in inflation as well as a return on money. It is not altogether clear that this is what was intended by courts and tribunals. If so, it would have the result that the appreciation that inflation causes loss in value of the principal sum has led to the effective removal of an element of compensation which was previously accepted by the mixed commissions and arbitral tribunals of the 19th and first half of the 20th centuries, namely compensation for the loss of use of the principal sum while it was outstanding.

One way of confirming the apparent distinctions in formulation of principle is to look at the particulars of interest awards to see whether they reflect the characterisation of the damage which interest is said to be compensating—that is, whether they award an interest rate including

---

[136] This was also the view taken by Arangio-Ruiz in his Second Report and the majority of the authors he cited therein, above n 1, para 78. García-Amador, Sohn and Baxter also state that the payment of interest addresses the claimant's deprivation and loss of his capital and the fact he may be forced to borrow to cover the losses occasioned by the injury (above n 6, 342).

[137] G Savioli, 'Les Intérêts' in 'Responsabilité des États', Recueil des cours, 1929, Vol 28, dismissed the view that it is required damage to be proved by the claimant State (278, citing Anzilotti, Rivista di diretto internazionale, 1913, 54ff). The obligation to pay interest is to repair the prejudice caused by a sum of money being outstanding for a certain period of time, whether this be a claim for late payment of a debt or a damages claim (278–9).

[138] Eg, section 35A of the UK Supreme Court Act 1981 allows the award of simple pre-judgment interest on damages. Although the award of interest under s 35A is discretionary, in practice interest on damages is requested and awarded without question and without questions of proof of loss or remoteness or foreseeability of damage arising (McGregor on Damages, above n 36, para 15-024). The post-judgment statutory rate is often used for the pre-judgment rate, other than in the commercial courts and in personal injury damages claims (Law Commission, England and Wales, 'Pre-Judgment Interest on Debts and Damages', 2004, Law Com No 287, http://www.lawcom.gov.uk/docs/lc287(1).pdf, paras 3.6–3.8, 315, 3.16).

an element representing a return on money or just the rate of inflation. But this is not altogether clear from the jurisprudence because of the practice of making global awards in the human rights courts and because the interest rates awarded as compensation for depreciation do not always appear to be any different from those awarded for loss of use. Moreover, awards of interest on damages expressly based on loss of use during the period of delay, at least in last 40 years or so, have not always appeared to reflect the principle which underpins their award either, insofar as interest is not set by reference to market rates and methods of calculation for the actual use of money. The question then is whether the principle ought to be reformulated to reflect more closely the particulars of interest awards or whether the quantum of interest awards ought to be brought into line with principle. Commentators usually advocate the latter[139] and, as will be seen below, the balance of the jurisprudence favours a rate of interest which, notionally at least, compensates for loss of use as well as inflation.

Apart from compensating the claimant, two other reasons are given for awards of interest on damages: to prevent the unjust enrichment of the respondent, and to promote efficiency in dispute resolution by discouraging respondents from being tardy in resolving disputes or paying awards.[140] Both could justify different start dates, rates and methods of calculation from an award based on loss of use of the principal sum in question. Unjust enrichment and efficiency are rarely invoked by courts or tribunals in their discussions of principle, although unjust enrichment has recently been relied on in two decisions to support compound interest awards, by the European Union Court of First Instance in *Corus*[141] and the investment arbitration tribunal in *Santa Elena v Costa Rica*.[142] It is particularly clear in the latter case that unjust enrichment was invoked solely to reinforce the award of compound rather than simple interest on damages as presumed loss: there was no enrichment of the State by subtracting, wrongfully or otherwise, a sum or asset from the claimant. The claimant remained in possession of the expropriated property, and in any case the respondent State was held to have been entitled to assert its interests over the claimant's property in the way it did.[143] Nevertheless, appealing to a notional unjust enrichment of a debtor as a justification for allowing market interest rates and methods of calculation for measuring

[139] See further below n 301.

[140] J Y Gotanda, 'Damages in Private International Law' (2007) 326 *Recueil des cours* 73, 192.

[141] *Corus UK Ltd v Commission* [2001] ECR II-2967; see further below nn 344–348 and accompanying text.

[142] *Compañía del Desarrollo de Santa Elena v Costa Rica*, Award of 17 February 2000, 5 ICSID Reports 153, para 104. Unjust enrichment was also invoked as an additional rationale for interest awards in earlier decisions such as the *Puerto Cabello and Valencia Railway Company* case, above n 50, and the *Award of the Tribunal of Arbitration between the United States of America and the Kingdom of Norway under the Special Agreement of June 30, 1921*, 1922 (1923) 17 *AJIL* 362 (Permanent Court of Arbitration), 396.

[143] See further below n 368–374 and accompanying text.

the claimant's loss of use has a long pedigree, at least in common law systems.[144]

As for the second reason for allowing interest on damages—promoting speedy resolution of disputes—García-Amador, Sohn and Baxter cited the inducement of States to make prompt settlement of legitimate claims as one of the considerations for selecting the date of injury as the start date in their 1974 work on State responsibility.[145] International courts and tribunals have not so far invoked the efficiency of dispute resolution as a basis for an 'interest on damages' award, but the investment arbitration tribunal in *SPP(ME) v Egypt* did point to efficacy of dispute resolution as a reason for rejecting the date of filing the claim or the date of the award as a start date, because either date would 'encourage parties who have expropriated property to refuse to pay compensation and to delay the proceedings seeking compensation'.[146] The rationale for allowing the award of compound interest on damages under the UK Arbitration Act 1996 was that 'it was thought that the absence of the power encouraged delay by defendants who would eventually pay in interest less than they would make with the funds, with which they would pay the damages, still in their hands, with an equivalent losing out by the claimant'.[147]

The next question is how the foregoing examination of the principles underpinning pre-award interest compares with the particulars of interest awards—start dates, rate and method of calculation. More specifically, the next section considers how compensation for delay in payment of the principal is measured, exploring further the relationship between interest awards and compensation for depreciation in the value of the

---

[144] The debtor's notional enrichment at the expense of the creditor was invoked by Jeremy Bentham as one of the reasons for doing away with the legal prohibition on compound interest: *Defence of Usury* (1788), 145–8. His reasoning was that the creditor could have relent the money and earned compound interest had the debtor paid it on time, and that failure to compensate accordingly rewarded the recalcitrant debtor and punished the lender. However, although the English legislature was moved to pass laws removing the limits on the interest rates that could be charged and to provide for interest on damages awards in court proceedings, it stuck with simple interest (see the Civil Procedure Act (1833), ss 28 and 29). Bentham was echoed by Lord Denning in *Harbutt's Plasticine Ltd v Wayne Tank and Pump Co Ltd* [1970] 1 QB 447, where he said that the 'basis of an award of interest is that the defendant has kept the plaintiff out of his money; and the defendant has made use of it himself'. Lord Denning was in turn cited by the 1978 UK Law Commission Report in support of statutory awards of interest on damages claims in tort, contract and admiralty: Law Commission Report, 'Report on Interest', Law Com No 88, 3, para 12. However the recent 2004 Law Commission Report on Pre-Judgment Interest in Debt and Damages Claims, above n 138, invokes compensation only: 'Awards of interest are designed to compensate claimants for the cost of being kept out of their money. They should put claimants into the position they would have been in had the debt or damages been paid when they fell due' (para 1.9).

[145] García-Amador, Sohn and Baxter, above n 6, 342. See also Van Casteren, above n 86, at 214.

[146] Award of 20 May 1992, 3 ICSID Reports 189, para 234.

[147] *McGregor on Damages*, above n 36, para 15–020 (s 49(3) Arbitration Act). Indeed, one of the arguments supporting the introduction of interest on damages in English legislation in 1833 was that it would take away an incentive to unjust resistance to paying debts: Recommendation in the Fourth Report made to His Majesty by the Commissioners appointed to inquire into the Practice and Proceedings of the Superior Courts of Common Law 1832, 1831–1832 *Parliamentary Papers*, Vols XXV Pt 1, XXV Pt II.1, 34. The Commission recommended removing the powers of arrest and imprisonment for debt, in line with civil law countries, and providing interest as alternative legal relief.

principal caused by inflation, and whether interest on damages for loss of use should be measured by compound rather than simple interest, notwithstanding that loss and the directness of that loss are presumed rather than required to be established.

2. The Particulars of the Interest Award

(a) The Period of Account—Start Date (*Dies a quo*)

If interest on damages is compensation for the delay in payment of the principal damages sum, a key question is the date on which that payment becomes due. Is it the date of breach, or the date when the loss was incurred, if different? Or does the payment become due on the date the respondent was fixed with knowledge that the principal sum is due, that is, the date of notice, demand or commencement of legal proceedings (hence the notion of default interest—debtors cannot be in default of an obligation to pay unless they know the money is due)? This can be taken even further: can debtors be in default if they do not know how much they owe, as in the case of damages claims where the existence of the claim and the amount of damages are often in dispute and neither is fixed until the date of judgment? Article 38 leaves this question open, stipulating only that interest runs from the date on which the principal falls due.

Where the start date for interest accrual is the date of breach or loss, the claimant will be fully compensated for the period of delay in payment. Where the principal damages sum is valued as at the date of breach or loss and the start date for interest accrual is a later date, some of the burden for delay shifts from the respondent to the claimant. Setting the date of judgment shifts the entire burden for delay onto the claimant. Encouraging creditors to be prompt in pursuing claims and fairness to debtors may, however, justify this shift. Domestic legislatures have adopted different start dates accordingly, for the most part taking the date of breach or loss or the date of notice of the claim, often leaving the judge with a discretion to fix the start date.[148] Any loss incurred during the period between the date of loss and the start date which is not directly compensated for may in any case be offset by a generous default interest provision.[149]

International jurisprudence has been similarly varied, either selecting the date of damage (or a representative date where there is no one date this is not clear) or the date of notice of the claim or initiation of

---

[148] See the review of national jurisprudence by Gotanda in *Recueil*, above n 140, 193–237; of the EU Member States by Van Casteren, above n 86, 206–10; and the discussion of interest on damages in various EU Member State jurisdictions in the 'Study on the conditions of claims for damages in case of infringement of EC competition rules', 31 August 2004, produced by the law firm Ashurst under tender from the European Commission, http://ec.europa.eu/comm/competition/cartels/studies/comparative_report_clean_en.pdf, 85–87.

[149] For example, under the Danish law, interest does not start to run until the date of commencement of proceedings, but the interest rate is double the discount rate (*SwemBalt AB (Sweden) v Latvia*, above n 65, para 47).

proceedings. One difficulty specific to international law is that the rule of exhaustion of local remedies in diplomatic protection claims. This may mean that a debtor State does not become fixed with knowledge of the international law claim by the claimant state until some time after the injured national has suffered the damage which is the subject of the claim, because the national has been pursuing a domestic law claim in local courts. If the loss is measured as at the date of injury but the principal does not become due and interest thereon does not start to run until the State had notice of the international claim, a significant period may be unaccounted for. However, given the variety of start dates selected in the jurisprudence of the 19th and first half of the 20th centuries, it does not seem that this factor was determinative of the outcome.[150]

The move to forums for direct individual-State claims has lessened the consequence of this debate. The Iran-US Claims Tribunal tends to award interest running from the date of breach (or loss, if that is different), or the date claimed by the claimant[151] and the majority of arbitral tribunals take the same approach,[152] although a few choose the date of

[150] Outlined by Arangio-Ruiz in his 1989 Report, above n 1, paras 82–92 and Whiteman, above n 2, 1931–63. Commentators such as Salvioli rejected the notion that the period prior to the inter-State diplomatic protection claim had no juridical value for the purposes of calculation of interest because there is an undeniable connection between the claim of the individual and the international relationship (above n 137, 283–4).

[151] Brower and Brueschke, above n 60, 628–9.

[152] *Aminoil v Kuwait*, Award of 24 March 1982, 66 ILR 519, 613 (date of termination of the concession); *AGIP v Congo*, Award of 30 November 1979, 1 ICSID Reports 306, 328–9 (date sums fell due), *Benvenuti & Bonfant v Congo*, Award of 8 August 1980, 1 ICSID Reports 330, paras 4.97–4.98 (dates claimed by claimant), *SOABI v Senegal* Award of 25 February 1988, 2 ICSID Reports 190 (on operating and capital expenditure, running from end of each annual fiscal period); *SPP(ME) v Egypt*, Award of 20 May 1992, 3 ICSID Reports 189, para 234 (date of dispossession); *AAPL v Sri Lanka*, Award of 27 June 1990, 4 ICSID Reports 245 (date of loss); *Santa Elena*, Award of 17 February 2000, 5 ICSID Reports 153, (date of taking); *Metalclad* (date construction permit denied. The Supreme Court of British Colombia found the tribunal made two findings outside its jurisdiction but by the Tribunal an expropriation under NAFTA Article 1110 was within its jurisdiction. As this act of breach was two years later than the earlier acts of breach found one of the two acts it identified as the SC set aside the award insofar as interest accrued from the earlier dates and moved the start date to the date of breach (5 ICSID Reports 236, paras 134–5)); *Maffezini v Spain*, Award of 13 November 2000, 5 ICSID Reports 419, para 96 (date of taking); *Goetz v Burundi*, Award of 10 February 1999, 6 ICSID Reports 3 (date of expropriation); *Pope & Talbot v Canada* (date sought by claimant after proceedings commenced), Award on Damages of 31 May 2002, 7 ISCID Reports 148 (a NAFTA arbitration under the UNCITRAL rules); *ME Cement v Egypt* Award of 12 April 2002, 7 ICSID Reports 173, para 175 (as the expropriation involved a series of events, the start date was the average time of taking); *Feldman v Mexico* (a case of unlawful discrimination in application of VAT laws—the dates the improperly withheld rebates should have been paid in accordance with Mexican law), Final Award on Damages, 16 December 2002, 7 ICSID Reports 341 (a NAFTA arbitration under ISCID); *TecMed* Award of 29 May 2003, 10 ICSID Reports 130 (date of expropriation); *Autopista v Venezuela*, Decision, 23 September 2003, ICSID Case No ARB/00/5 (in a claim under the umbrella clause of the BIT, from the dates claimed by claimant on pre-termination losses in accordance with contract which also reflected Venezuelan law (interest starts running 30 days after obligation falls due) and on post-termination losses, date of loss); *MTD v Chile*, Award of 25 May 2004, 12 ICSID Reports 6 (breach of fair and equitable treatment obligation–the date of the respondent's act which made it clear that the investment would not go ahead as per the approval given two years earlier); *AIG v Kazakhstan*, Award of 7 October 2003, 11 ICSID Reports 3 (date of taking, and future lost profits from the date of the award); *Nycomb v Latvia*, above n 65 (end dates of relevant income periods for tariffs improperly

request for arbitration[153] or the date of notice of the claim.[154] The date of the award is generally selected only where the damages are valued as of that date and the choice therefore does not entail a shortfall in compensation.[155] The UNCC in Decision 16 selected date of loss as the start date.[156] The ECHR also tends to award pre-judgment interest from the date of breach or loss in claims for pecuniary damages in the rare cases where this particular aspect of an interest award is explicitly discussed.[157] Similarly, the Inter-American Court of Human Rights in its loss-of-earnings calculations awards interest on the sums calculated from the date of death 'from the date of the events'.[158]

As noted above, in the European Union courts the start date for accrual of default interest is the date of notice of the claim, unless the principal sum is not capable of ascertainment at that date.[159] This presents

withheld); *Azurix v Argentina*, Award of 23 June 2006, ICSID Case No ARB/01/12 (date concession terminated); *Bogdanov v Moldova*, Decision of 22 September 2005 (arbitration before the Arbitration Institute of the Swedish Chamber of Commerce under a BIT between Russia and Moldova) (date of breach); *First Eagle Sogen* (where claim that not fairly compensated for forced sale of shares in bank, the date on which the proper compensation payment for the shares should have been paid, unless the withholding of payment was due to the claimant's fault—see above n 133); *Enron v Argentina* and *Sempra v Argentina,* Award of 22 May 2007, ICSID Case No ARB/01/3 and Award of 28 September 2007, ICSID Case No ARB/02/16 (the date after the date the principal damages sum was calculated, being the end of the year in which the final acts of breach of the fair and equitable treatment obligation occurred); *Petrobart v Kyrgyz Republic* Award of 29 March 2005, Arbitration Institute of the Stockholm Chamber of Commerce (date of domestic court judgment awarding payment for delivered goods which was never executed due to the actions of the respondent which constituted breach); *Siemens v Argentina,* see above n 64 (date of expropriation or date losses incurred if later, but because of multiple dates post-breach losses incurred, a representative start date was selected being the date by which most losses had been incurred); *PSEG Global Inc &* *Ors v Turkey*, Award of 1 January 2007, ICSID Case ARB/02/05 (as there was no expropriation or termination of the concession, the start date was the mean date during the seven year period during which the expenses representing the damages awarded were incurred); *CMS Gas v Argentina* and *LG&E Energy Corp & Ors v Argentina*, Award of 12 May 2005, ICSID Case No ARB/01/8 and Award of 25 July 2007, ICSID Case No ARB/02/01, (date the day after the principal damages were calculated as of, being the day before the determinative act of breach); *Vivendi v Argentina (Award No 2)*, above n 66 (date of expropriation or date of subsequent loss where later).

[153] *Atlantic Triton v Guinea* (1986) 3 ICSID Reports 13, 30 *AMCO v Indonesia (Award 2)*, Award of 5 June 1990, 1 ICSID Reports 569, para 257; *SD Myers v Canada*, Second Partial Award on Damages of 21 October 2002, 8 ICSID Reports 124 para 303; *SwemBalt* (in accordance with the Danish law applied to this aspect of the case), above n 65, para 77.

[154] *CME Czech*—in accordance with Czech law, which requires demand for payment before interest begins to run. As the claimant had not produced any evidence of such a demand, the Tribunal took the date of initiation of proceedings (above n 65, paras 630–3); *AMCO (Award I)*—the start date was the date of claim—here the date of presentation of the claim—in accordance with the Indonesian law applied to interest on damages (above n 64).

[155] *ADC v Hungary*, Award of 2 October 2006, ICSID Case No ARB/03/16, *AIG v Kazakhstan* (in respect of damages for future lost profits), above n 112.

[156] Above n 62, para 1.

[157] See eg, *Beyeler v Italy (No 2)*, above n 78, paras 22–5, *Lustig-Prean v United Kingdom*, above n 73. Cf *Hentrich v France* (above n 74) where interest was awarded on the costs and expenses previously awarded in a 1994 judgment, from 3 months of the date of that judgment at statutory rate (respondents are given a 3 month grace period before post-judgment interest runs). Judge Martens in a dissenting judgment said he would have allowed interest on the principal damages sum from the 1994 judgment date which was the valuation date.

[158] See *Neira-Alegría,* Reparations and Costs, above n 79, para 50.

[159] See above nn 88–91 and accompanying text.

problems where the sum claimed is not considered to be ascertainable until judgment but the principal is valued as at an earlier date. As noted above, the ECJ has developed a separate compensatory interest claim to offset the claimant's loss for the intervening period which has different characteristics from default interest (interest on damages). It requires proof of any loss over and above depreciation of the principal sum, and fault on the part of the respondent leading to the delay in ascertainment of the amount due.[160]

Thus the weight of jurisprudence favours the date of breach (or loss, where that is later) as the start date for interest on damages to run, unless the principal loss is valued as of a later date. This is in line with the principle that the obligation to make reparation arises on breach and that reparation should compensate for all losses incurred. It also has the advantage of being relatively straightforward, because there is no need for proof of notice of the claim to be established.[161] And, as observed by the Tribunal in *SPP(ME) v Egypt*, it also promotes efficacy of dispute resolution by the respondent.[162] However, there may be good policy reasons to select the date of the notice of the claim, such as fairness to the respondent and an encouragement for claimants to pursue claims promptly,[163] provided that an unduly formalistic approach is not taken to what constitutes notice. Taking the date of judgment—the approach taken by the PCIJ in the *Wimbledon* case on the ground that it was on that date that the obligation was established and pecuniary losses liquidated—is now generally only applied by human rights courts to awards for non-pecuniary damages awards.[164] Such an approach is open to two criticisms. First, in any case where the obligation to pay and/or the quantum is disputed—the majority of cases—the obligation to pay and the sum due can always be said to be unliquidated or unascertainable until judgment.[165] Second, this approach undercompensates the claimant, running counter to the principles that the obligation to make reparation in international law arises at the time of breach and reparation should cover all loss.[166]

---

[160] See above nn 98–101 and accompanying text.

[161] Tribunals have developed mechanisms for selecting start dates in cases where there is no one date of breach but a series of acts amounting to breach, eg *PSEG Global Inc v Turkey*, above n 152, *MTD v Chile*, above n 152.

[162] See above n 146 and accompanying text.

[163] Especially in the absence of the statutory time limits for filing in domestic law or in treaties establishing tribunals and commissions. Laches for delay in prosecuting claims may also sound in a restricted period of account: Whiteman, above n 2, 1960–3, 1992–4.

[164] See above n 122–123 and accompanying text. But see *LIAMCO v Libya* (1977) 62 ILR 141 where interest was awarded to run from the date of the award, not the mid-date of the expropriatory actions some 3 years before requested by the claimant, as the arbitrator considered that interest could only run from the point at which damages were judicially ascertained and liquidated even though the compensation claimed concerned property taken in 1973–1974 and valued as at that date (at 215).

[165] As Salvioli points out, the judgment is declaratory of the international obligation, not constitutive (above n 137, 281).

[166] I Brownlie, *System of the Law of Nations, State Responsibility* (1983), Vol 1, 228.

(b) Rate

(i) What Rate?

The principle underpinning an interest award ought to inform, at least in theory, the rate and method of calculation, whether for an award of interest on damages under Article 38 of the Articles on State responsibility, interest awarded to restore the *status quo ante* under Article 35, or an award of interest as the measure of the principal sum under Article 36. But principle still leaves the adjudicator with a large measure of discretion to select rate in the absence of a specific applicable rate.

The applicable law is not a reliable indicator of the interest rate that might be adopted. In the international jurisprudence of the last 50 years various grounds are given for the selection of interest rates and methods of calculation. Some decisions rely on public international law to apply principles of private international law leading to a domestic rate,[167] and in others it appears that international law is said to allow the application of a domestic statute rate because international law itself does not fix an interest rate.[168] Some ICSID tribunals rely on Article 42 of the Convention—which provides for the application of the law of the contracting State party and such rules of international law as may be applicable in the absence of agreement on the applicable law by the parties—to apply domestic law.[169] Others rely on the same provision to apply international law.[170] Cases where the interest rate and method of calculation is said to be determined in accordance with public international law have used domestic statutory rates,[171] borrowing rates based

---

[167] Swiss law on interest was selected by the PCA tribunal in *First Eagle Sogen* because it had the closest connection to the dispute: for over 70 years the BIS had been registered and situated in Switzerland in accordance with its constitutive treaty, and had made dividend payments in Swiss francs, and the private shareholders dealt with the BIS in Switzerland. The tribunal therefore awarded the moratory (default) rate provided by the Swiss code of 5% per annum to run from the date the bank paid short compensation for the shares (above n 65, para 91). In *SwemBalt AB (Sweden) v Latvia* Award of 21 October 2000, by the Court of Arbitration in Copenhagen, the Tribunal applied the general principles of private international law, 'which forms part of general international law', considering it could select either the legal interest rate of Latvia as the country where the loss was sustained or the seat of arbitration, Denmark. As it had no information as to the former, it applied Danish law which provided for an interest rate payable from the day of initiation of proceedings for the repayment of debts at the official discount rate plus 6%, unless the court decides otherwise (above n 65, paras 44–7, and paragraph 4 of the operative para of the award).

[168] *SPP(ME) v Egypt*, above n 68.

[169] In *Amco (Award 1)* the tribunal applied the 6% rate specified by Indonesian law as this 'would keep the interest on a moderate basis' (above n 64, para 281). In the second award following annulment of the first, the second tribunal upheld the first award and noted that, in the absence of a specific statement as to whether interest was simple or compound, it should be viewed as simple (above n 153), para 258.

[170] *Wena Hotels v Egypt*, Award of 8 December 2000, 6 ICSID Reports 89 paras 128–9.

[171] In *CME Czech*, above n 65. The Tribunal said its award on interest found its basis in the bilateral investment treaty which incorporated the international law principle that just compensation has to be provided to the party deprived of its investment. As neither the treaty nor international law specified an interest rate, the Tribunal applied Czech law. In *Nycomb* domestic law was applied

on the LIBOR,[172] or investment rates such as the US six-month certificate of deposit rate,[173] or the UNIDROIT Principles of International Commercial Contracts,[174] or occasionally some other interest rate for which little or no explanation is given.[175] Some tribunals do not set a rate by reference to either applicable domestic law or international law, or at least they do not seek to explain their interest rate decisions on these grounds.[176] In some cases the lack of explanation of the particulars of the award appears to be because the interest claimed by the applicant, and awarded by the tribunal, was not the subject of argument by the respondent.[177]

Where a contract or treaty governs the relationship between the parties and specifies an interest or default interest rate it will usually be applied.[178] An agreed contract rate from one part of a transaction may be

on the claimant's request without discussion, even though the applicable law on compensation was agreed to be customary international law. Interest was awarded on the principal compensation sums at the prevailing annual rate in Latvia, a simple rate of 6%, also the legal rate in Latvia (although it is not referred to as such by the Tribunal) (above n 65).

[172] *MTD v Chile*, above n 152.

[173] *Azurix v Argentina*, above n 152.

[174] *Petrobart v Kyrgyz Republic*, above n 152. The Tribunal rejected the Republic's claim that interest should be awarded at the statutory judgment rate in the Republic on the ground that the claim was based on the treaty and was therefore governed by international law. Article 7.4.9(2) of the UNIDROIT Principles provides that the

rate of interest shall be the average bank short-term lending rate to prime borrowers prevailing for the currency of payment at the place of payment, or where no such rate exists at that place, then the same rate in the State of currency of payment. In the absence of such a rate at either place the rate of interest shall be the appropriate rate fixed by the law of the State of the currency of payment.

The Tribunal did not set an actual rate by reference to the formula, but referred to Article 7.4.9 in the operative para leaving it to the parties to determine. The UNIDROIT Principles do not make any reference to compounding or capitalisation of interest.

[175] *Sapphire International Petroleum v National Iranian Oil Company*, Award of 15 March 1963, 35 ILR 136, at 170–6. The applicable law was 'principles generally recognised by civilised nations'. Interest was awarded on the principal sum 'at the usual rate' of 5% per annum running from the date of the first step in the arbitration procedure until payment.

[176] In *Aminoil*, below n 292, although the Tribunal ascertained the applicable law was Kuwaiti law which incorporated public international law, it made no reference to either in setting a general damages interest rate of 7.5% per annum, capitalised annually. It simply said this was 'reasonable'.

[177] Eg, *AAPL*, above n 64, para 112 (10% simple interest); *Tecmed*, above n 64 (6% compounded annually); see also *Nycomb*, discussed above n 171.

[178] The agreed contract rate was awarded by the ICSID tribunals in *SPP(ME) v Egypt*, above n 68, in respect of one aspect of the award only. The loan agreement provided for a compound interest rate. On the rest of the award, made up of compensation for expropriation of concessionary rights, interest was awarded at the simple rate of 5% per annum, the rate for commercial debts under the Egyptian Civil Code; *Goetz v Burundi*, above n 152—the BIT provided for interest at a 'reasonable commercial rate'. After an initial decision on liability the parties agreed on a reparations sum which contained provision for interest at 8% (at 51). In respect of the Iran-US Claims Tribunal, see *Raygo Wagner Equipment Co v Star Line Iran* (1982) 1 Iran-US CTR 411, rental agreement rate of 12%; *Pereira Associates v Iran* (1984) 5 Iran-US CTR 198, 226 (6%); *Howard Needles Tammen and Bergendoff v Iran* (1986) 11 Iran-US CTR 302 (6%, agreed rate of default); *Amman & Whitney v Ministry of Housing* (1986) 12 Iran-US CTR 94, 106 (6%); *McHarg, Roberts, Wallace & Todd v Iran* (1986) 13 Iran-US CTR 286, 308–9 (6%); *Pepsico v Iran* (1986) 13 Iran-US CTR 3, 33–5 (LIBOR rate for three month deposits plus 3%); *Bechtel Inc v Iran* (1987) 14 Iran-US CTR 149, 160–1 (11.75% by reference to interest formula in the contract); *Sedco v Iran* (1987) 15 Iran-US

applied as the rate for interest on all damages. For example, in *Autopista v Venezuela* the concession contract contained penalty interest clauses for late payments which the Tribunal applied to all principal compensation sums awarded.[179] Similarly, in *ADC v Hungary* the Tribunal extended the interest rate agreed in a promissory note to all principal sums awarded, albeit as post-award interest only (the principal sum awarded was said to take account of all losses because it was valued at the date of award).[180] The interest rate may also be specified by reference to the treaty which confers jurisdiction on the tribunal. For example, the investment treaty might require application of local law, as was the case in *Bogdanov v Moldova*.[181] However, interest provisions are rarely this specific as to applicable law, and are unlikely to nominate rate and method of calculation. For example, Article 1135(1) of the North American Free Trade Agreement ('NAFTA') provides only for the award of 'monetary damages and any applicable interest'.

The cases applying NAFTA Article 1135(1) provide one example of the variety of outcomes to which such a provision can lead. In *Metalclad v Mexico* the Tribunal awarded interest on the principal compensation amount at the rate of 6% per annum compounded annually to run from the date of breach until 45 days after the date of the award;[182] in *Pope & Talbot v Canada* the Tribunal awarded a 5% interest rate, the Canadian legal rate suggested by Canada, to be compounded quarterly;[183] and the NAFTA tribunal in *SD Myers v Canada* chose the currency of the award as the basis for selection of the interest rate, fixing it at the Canadian

CTR 23, 152, (12% interest agreed on outstanding invoices. Lump sum of interest calculated on this basis. Non-contractual interest also awarded on all principal sums awarded at the rate of 10% without explanation as to rate (at 184)); *Reading & Bates Drilling Co v Iran* (1988) 18 Iran-US CTR 164, 173–4 (1.5% per month, or 18% simple per annum. A 'fair rate' of 10.5% was set on other principal amounts due where a contract rate could not be established (running from Sept 1979); *International Systems & Controls Corp v NIGC* (1990) 24 Iran-US CTR 47, 83–4; *CBS v Iran* (1990) 25 Iran-US CTR 131, 150, (awarded the contract rate of 14% per annum on the loan up to its intended final repayment date (1 Dec 1979), and thereafter interest of 10% on the ground that the loan was intended to be of short duration and the award of interest requested by the claimant would be unforeseen by the contract and inequitable). Cf *Eastman Kodak Company v Iran* (1991) 27 Iran-US CTR 3, 23, awarding the contract rate of 8%, rejecting the claim of 10%, because 'the contractual rate of interest is as closely linked to the Claimant's expectation and potential for repayment as it would have been to repayment itself'.

[179] Decision, 23 September 2003, ICSID Case No ARB/00/5, noted above n 152; see the detailed discussion at paras 366–402. As the bulk of the judgment was an award for lost profits, the only interest was that on out of pocket expenses (running from dates in 1995 onwards) and post-award interest. The tribunal further noted that to award the contract rate accorded with the Venezuelan Civil Code which provides that contract interest shall be awarded unless limited by special law or if it exceeds by one half the current interest rate at the time of contract (Article 1746).

[180] Above n 155, paras 520, 522.

[181] Above n 152, paras 128, 131.

[182] Above n 64, para 128.

[183] Above n 152. The tribunal concluded the NAFTA provisions were an independent basis for recovery of interest (because otherwise domestic law could preclude its award), together with the applicable rules of international law which applied by virtue of Article 1131(1) of NAFTA (para 89).

prime rate plus 1% on the principal award, to be compounded annually.[184] A slightly more specific treaty provision on interest is Article IV(1) of the Argentina-United States bilateral investment treaty which requires that compensation for expropriation include a 'commercially reasonable rate of interest' from the date of expropriation.[185] However, as tribunals have pointed out, there is no equivalent provision for breaches of other treaty articles such as the fair and equitable treatment standard. As it is often found that expropriations have not taken place where there has been violations of such provisions, the 'expropriation' interest provision could not be directly applied. All the same, central bank or market rates are selected, but different conclusions have been reached on rate and method of calculation for breaches of the same treaty provision.[186]

In the absence of use of a contract or a specific treaty rate, the developing trend is towards using central bank- or market-based interest rate formulas. Initially the Iran-US Claims Tribunal awarded simple rates (10% or 12%, or occasionally 8%), either without explanation or with a brief note that the rate was 'fair', 'reasonable' or 'appropriate'.[187] In 1985 the Chamber in *Sylvania Technical Systems Inc v Iran*[188] adopted a market based approach to selection of the interest rate after a review of the principles underpinning pre-judgment interest on damages.[189] In the absence

---

[184] Above n 153, paras 302–307. The parties agreed that interest should be payable on any principal sums awarded and that the period of account and the rate would be a matter of discretion for the tribunal. The decision gave no reasons for the compounding nor further elaboration on the selection of rate.

[185] Treaty between United States of America and the Argentine Republic Concerning the Reciprocal Encouragement and Protection of Investment, signed November 14, 1991.

[186] There are some notable variations between interest awards by ICSID tribunals operating under the same BIT and based on the same treaty breaches. The *CMS Gas* Tribunal, in a case concerning breach of the fair treatment standard under the Argentina-US bilateral investment treaty, rejected the claim that interest should be set at the average rate applicable to US six month certificates of deposit compounded semi-annually, instead holding that the lower US treasury bills rate was more 'appropriate' in the circumstances and that interest should be simple. No reasoning was given as to why the slightly lower six month treasury bill rate (by up to 0.4% but usually much less: see the historical data published by the US Federal Reserve, http://www.federalreserve.gov/releases/h15/data.htm) was more appropriate than the six month certificate of deposit rate, nor for the rejection of compounding (above n 152). In respect of the breach of the same treaty provision, the *LG&E* Tribunal also awarded the 6 month treasury bill rate but compounded semi-annually, the Tribunal in *Azurix* awarded the US six month certificate of deposit rate compounded semi-annually (requested by the claimant) (above n 152), and, the Tribunals in *Enron v Argentina* (above n 152, para 452) and *Sempra v Argentina* (above n 152, para 486) awarded the 6 month LIBOR plus 2% compounded semi-annually.

[187] A handful of early cases awarded interest incorporated into a global compensation sum: *Economy Forms Corp v Iran* (1983) 3 Iran-US CTR 42, 53; *CMI International Inc v Iran* (1983) 4 Iran-US CTR 263, 271; *Gruen Associates Inc v Iran Housing Co* (1983) 3 Iran-US CTR 97, 107; *Ultrasystems v Iran* (1983) 2 Iran-US CTR 100, 111; *Pomeroy v Iran* (1983) 2 Iran-US CTR 372, p 385; *Pomeroy Corp v Iran* (1983) 2 Iran-US CTR 391, 400.

[188] Above n 57, 320–3.

[189] Judges Mosk and Holtzmann had already repeated in several cases that interest awards should be based on prevailing commercial interest rates or, at the least, be the same rate in decisions taken around the same time. See Judge Mosk's opinions in *Granite State Mining Co v Iran* (1982) 1 Iran-US CTR 442, 450–1; *American International Group v Iran* (1983) 4 Iran-US CTR 96, 120–1, *Pomeroy v Iran* (1983) 2 Iran-US CTR 372, 385, 390, and Judge Holtzmann's opinions in *Sea-Land Service Inc v Iran* (1984) 6 Iran-US CTR 149, 216–7, *Iran v US (case B-53)* (1984)

of an applicable contract rate, the *Sylvania* Chamber said it would derive a rate of interest based approximately on the amount that the successful claimant would have earned if it had had the principal invested in a form of commercial investment in common use in its own country. For US claimants it identified six-month certificates of deposit in the US as meeting this objective.[190] The Chamber did not address compounding, and interest was awarded on a simple basis. About 30% of the decisions in individual-State claims since *Sylvania* have expressly followed it, and roughly another 30% have adopted interest rates which appear to use the *Sylvania* formula.[191] Rates based on the *Sylvania* formula have for the most part moved from 11–12% or so until the mid-late 1980s[192] down to 7% per annum in the most recent awards.[193] For short periods, for example, the three months between 1 September and 10 December 1980, the rate derived from the formula was as high as 15.75%.[194] This reflects the fact that interest rates hit historic highs in the late 1970s and early 1980s, and that there have been significant movements in interest rates over the length of the Tribunal's operations.[195]

The European Union courts apply the default interest rate they consider appropriate rather than rely on the domestic law of Member States,[196] unless provision is made for interest in the applicable EC legislation.[197] Since the introduction of the euro, a central bank-based formula has been adopted for the default interest rate. The default rate is set by reference

---

5 Iran-US CTR 105, 111, *International Schools Services Inc v NICIC* (1985) 9 Iran-US CTR 187, 200, 202.

[190] Widely available from banks and other financial institutions and insured by the government Federal Deposit Insurance Corporation for amounts up to $100,000.

[191] Of the 108 decisions after *Sylvania* reviewed by the author, 30 cite *Sylvania* as the basis of their award, and another 32 either give no explanation for the award or say that the interest award is 'fair', 'reasonable' or 'appropriate' but adopt interest rates based on the *Sylvania* formula.

[192] See the table showing movements in the 6 month certificate of deposit rate at n 284.

[193] Eg, *Riahi v Iran* (2003) 37 Iran-US CTR 11, 154, awarding interest rates between 7.305% and 7.045% on various principals based on start dates between Jun 1979 and 16 July 1980 and an end date (the date of award) of 27 February 2003.

[194] Eg, *General Electric Company v Iran* (15 Mar 1991) 26 Iran-US CTR 148, 182–3. Instead of calculating an average interest rate for each of the five principal amounts awarded from the dates they became due between May 1979 and Jan 1983, an interest rate was set for the first amount of principal based on the average six month deposit rate for the period between when it fell due and the next amount of principal falling due. The interest rate on the new amount of principal would then change to the average of the rates for the period between the second and third amounts of principal falling due, and so on. Thus sequential interest rates based on the *Sylvania* formula varied between a high of 15.75% for a period between 1 September 1981 and 10 December 1981 and a rate of 8.25% for the period commencing 1 January 1983 when the last principal amount fell due through to the date of payment, based on the average rates between 1 January 1983 and the date of the award, 15 March 1991.

[195] N Ferguson, *The Cash Nexus; Money and Power in the Modern World 1700–2000* (2001), 164–5.

[196] Van Casteren, above n 86, 203.

[197] Eg, Council Regulation (EEC) No 2187/93, Article 12, applied by the CFI in *Dethlefs*, above n 91. See also Council Regulation no 2891/77 of 19 December 1977 implementing the Decision of 21 April 1970 on the replacement of financial contributions from Member States by the Communities.

to a formula based on the marginal rate[198] for main refinancing operations of the European Central Bank ('ECB') plus 2%.[199] Before this time, the rate awarded varied: in general 6% per annum in the judgments in the period up to the mid-late 1980s,[200] then 8% in judgments up to the introduction of the euro into financial markets on 1 January 1999.[201] With the shift to the ECB-based rate there was an immediate drop in the interest rates awarded. For example, in *Seisenbacher v Commission* interest was awarded for a period of account beginning in October 1998 at the rate of 8% in accordance with previous practice up to 31 December 1998, the date before introduction of the euro, and thereafter at the ECB rate for capital refinancing operations during the various phases concerned plus 2%, which dropped the default interest rate to 5%.[202] Little reasoning is given for the interest rates selected, other than general references to being the proper or appropriate rate.

Where an additional rationale for the award of interest is unjust enrichment for money received without cause, as in claims for repayment of improperly levied Community fines, the Court may set the rate and method of calculation by reference to the Community's gain rather than the usual default rate.[203] As noted above, in claims for compensatory interest rather than default interest the measure of loss is not the ECB-

---

[198] The 'marginal interest rate' is the 'interest rate at which the total tender allotment is exhausted' for the 'main refinancing operation', which is a 'regular open market operation executed by the Eurosystem (in the form of a reverse transaction) for the purpose of providing the banking system with the amount of liquidity that the former deems to be appropriate. Main refinancing operations are conducted through weekly standard tenders (in which banks can bid for liquidity) and normally have a maturity of one week': Glossary, European Central Bank website, http://www.ecb.int/home/glossary/html/glossa.en.html.

[199] Case T-93/01 *Seisenbacher v Commission* [2003] ECR II-2117, *Calberson*, above n 88, *Fuchs*, above n 86, *Borbély*, above n 89. Usually the court just refers to the formula in the *dispositif*, but occasionally it will specify the interest rate derived by applying the formula: eg *Corus*, above n 87, paras 64–65 (fixed at 5.75%) and Case T-231/97 *New Europe Consulting and MP Brown v Commission* [1999] ECR II-2403 (fixed at 4.5%, in absence of claim by applicants from date of judgment establishing the obligation to make the damage good to payment), *Reynolds*, above n 94 (fixed at 5.25%).

[200] *Ireks-Arkady*, above n 86, paras 19–20 (loss suffered as a result of an invalid act. Interest at 6% was awarded as this was 'proper' to apply), *Battaglia*, above n 88 (arrears of remuneration, running from date of complaint to date of payment), *Amesz*, above n 88, para 14. But see 4.5% awarded in *Willame*, above. 89, although 6% was claimed and 8% awarded in Case 115/76 *Leonardini v Commission* [1978] ECR 735 (because there was a lengthy delay in settlement of the claim),

[201] See, eg *Samara*, above n 89, (arrears of salary upgrades); Case C-90/95P *Henri de Compte v Parliament* [1997] ECR I-1999 (arrears of allowances); *Pfloeschner*, above n 89 (arrears of pension). Cf *Dethlefs*, above n 91 (infringement of regulation and non-contractual liability for failing to pay interest as required by regulation) where 6% was awarded, instead of the 8% as requested by the applicants (para 74). The principal compensation sum in this case was made up of interest at 8% (specified by regulation) for the periods that interest had been withheld in breach of the regulation provision on interest on compensation payments (para 73)).

[202] Above n 199. Since the launch of the euro on 1 January 1999, the main refinancing rate has moved at intervals between 2% and 4.75%. As at 9 July 2008 it was 4.25%: 'Key ECB interest rates', Monthly Bulletin—Euro Area Statistics Online, July 2008.

[203] *Corus*, above n 87, paras 60–63. Interest was calculated based on the Community's earnings on the fine for the period until the date it was repaid, but default interest at the usual ECB rate for capital refinancing operations plus 2% was awarded on that amount from that date (para 64).

based interest rate formula, which would reflect the borrowing rate from a commercial bank for secured borrowing,[204] but is based on government inflation figures from year to year.[205] This is because compensatory interest requires proof of loss of use and in the absence of such proof, only diminution in value of the principal sum will be presumed as a direct consequence of breach.

Arbitral tribunals have also moved towards the use of central bank- or market-based rates for pre-judgment interest on damages. Of the 39 arbitral decisions reviewed which awarded pre-award interest without relying on a contract provision, 17 expressly adopted market rates as the measure of interest on damages,[206] and another three have justified their awards by reference to prevailing financial markets conditions or appear to use a market rate.[207] Market interest rate formulas are also preferred where the nature of the interest award might be characterised as a restitution of unjust enrichment or a gain-based remedy rather than compensation.[208] Market rates provide an objective approximation of the respondent's presumed or actual benefit from having had the principal sum in their possession—that is, the saving from not having had to borrow the same amount, or the return from investing it.

Some tribunals and courts continue to award interest rates which are not based on central bank or market based formulas or to make global lump sum awards including interest which is not particularised. A short time after *Sylvania* another Chamber of the Iran-US Claims Tribunal in *McCollough* adopted an approach to fixing rates which led to the practice of awarding a 10% simple interest rate in the cases which followed. The Chamber emphasised the role of its discretion under international law to fix a rate which was 'fair' and 'reasonable', taking due account of all pertinent circumstances. The list of pertinent circumstances was unlimited, but included the rates in effect in the market concerned, as well as any relevant contract provisions, the rules and principles of law

---

[204] The ECB main refinancing rate is the equivalent to, eg the base rate of the Bank of England or the Federal Funds Rate of the US Reserve Bank. An augmentation of 1–2% on this rate is considered to reflect the rate that commercial banks would lend to secured prime borrowers.

[205] *Mulder (No 2)*, above n 98.

[206] *SD Myers v Canada*, above n 153, *CMS Gas v Argentina*, above n 152, *Azurix v Argentina*, above n 152, *LG&E Energy Corp v Argentina*, above n 152, *Sempra v Argentina*, above n 152, *Enron v Argentina*, above n 152, *AGIP v Congo*, above n 152, *Feldman v Mexico*, above n 152, *MTD v Chile*, above n 152, *AIG v Kazakhstan*, above n 112, *Petrobart v Kyrgyz Republic*, above n 152, *Siemens AG v Argentina*, above n 64, *PSEG Global Inc v Turkey*, above n 152, *Atlantic Triton v Guinea*, above n 153 the Tribunal (unusually) had jurisdiction to make a determination *ex aequo et bono* under Article 42(3). On this basis, and although the applicable law was Guinean, the Tribunal awarded a 9% interest rate because the parties had chosen the US dollar as the currency of the contract and 9% was the basic inter-bank lending rate in the US at the time, to be capitalised annually in accordance with the French law then applicable in Guinea (p 30)), *Maffezini v Spain*, above n 152, *Prevention of Pollution of the Rhine*, above n 132, *Biloune v Ghana*, Award on Damages and Costs, (1990) 95 ILR 211, 230.

[207] *ME Cement v Egypt*, above n 64, paras 174–5, *Vivendi v Argentina (Award No 2)*, above n 66, para 9.2.8, *Santa Elena v Costa Rica*, above n 142, para 104.

[208] *Prevention of Pollution of the Rhine*, above n 132, *Maffezini v Spain*, above n 152.

applicable to the contract, the nature of the facts generating damage, the nature of the level of the compensation awarded, particularly if it extended to the lost profit, the knowledge the defaulting party could have had of the financial consequences of default for the other party, and the rates of inflation.[209] Although, citing *Sylvania*, the Chamber noted the desirability of a higher degree of uniformity unless there were reasons for diversity, it considered that the diversity of cases made it difficult to apply an inflexibly determined interest rate.[210] It then awarded a simple interest rate of 10% per annum, the lowest of the various rates sought by the claimant. It did not offer a particularly convincing explanation for the rate selected: it just said that it was 'fair', given that the case concerned an ordinary commercial contract without an interest provision governed by Iranian law, and that the claimant had not submitted any specific reasons for the higher rates of 12% and 15% claimed.[211] It did not refer to previous cases, although a 10% rate was not uncommon in earlier awards.[212] Of the cases which came after *McCollough*, the majority have followed *Sylvania* and awarded a rate based on US six month certificate of deposit rates for the period of account.[213] Nearly all the decisions which have explicitly followed *McCollough* have awarded the same 10% simple rate in spite of the Chamber's observation about the difficulty of applying the same rate in all cases.[214]

The human rights courts tend not to particularise pre-judgment interest where it is awarded, and when they do, it is difficult to identify a consistent approach towards rate. The ECHR's usual practice as regards rates of interest and methods of calculation is to award a global pecuniary damages sum much less than the amount claimed,[215] sometimes but not usually stated to include interest and principal.[216] Even when judgments record that the claimants have sought a specific rate and method of calculation, that claim is rarely addressed by the court other than by reference to ruling 'on an equitable basis'. On the rare occasions when a specific rate has been set, the rate has been that claimed[217] or the statutory rate of the respondent

---

[209] *McCollough & Co, Inc v Ministry of Post*, above n 58, 29–30.

[210] Ibid, 31.   [211] Ibid.

[212] Of the 26 pre-*Sylvania* decisions reviewed by the author, 11 awarded 10%. A further seven awarded 12%.

[213] See above n 191.

[214] Of the 108 decisions reviewed, 18 explicitly followed *McCollough* and only two of those 18 did not award 10%. 10% has also been awarded in a further 17 decisions where the interest award was either unexplained or said to be 'fair', 'reasonable' or 'appropriate'.

[215] Eg, *Scordino v Italy (No 1)*, above n 72, *Efstathiou v Greece* (2006) 43 EHRR 24, paras 31, 37, *Selistö v Finland* (2006) 42 EHRR 8, paras 72, 74.

[216] See, eg, *Xenides-Arestis v Turkey*, Judgment, Application no. 46347/99, 7 December 2006 paras 38–42, and *Amat-G Ltd & Or v Georgia*, Judgment, Application no 2507/03, 15 February 2006, paras 66–70.

[217] In *Stran Greek Refineries* 6% interest (the amount claimed) was awarded for breach of property rights by way of a legislative annulment of an arbitration award in the claimant's favour, to run from the date of the award to the date of judgment (above n 71, paras 77, 82–3), and in *Wasserman v Russia,* Judgment (Merits and Satisfaction), Application no. 15021/02, 18 November 2004, the statutory rate in Israel, the place of residence of the applicant, was sought and awarded (at para 49).

State,[218] and in *Beyeler* the higher of the annual statutory interest rate or the rate of inflation for each year of the period of account was selected.[219] Unlike any other international court or tribunal, the ECHR has on occasion appeared to oppose the use of commercial market rates as the measure of interest on damages in the absence of proof of loss or directness (remoteness or foreseeability) of loss. In *Pine Valley Developments v Ireland* the Court rejected a claim for interest at commercial rates on the ground that this would be more appropriate to claims based on loss of development profits than, as was the case, to claims of compensation for the loss of value of property when planning permission was annulled.[220] In *Qufaj v Albania*, a case of breach of Article 6 (right to a fair trial) by failing to pay a pecuniary judgment awarded by a national court, the Court rejected a claim for interest at bank rates instead of statutory rates because it could not 'speculate on the profit the applicant company would have made by investing the sum awarded by the domestic court, had it been able to use the money in accordance with its plans and expectations'.[221] In both cases the Court said it preferred the statutory rate of the respondent state, and in any event awarded equitable lump sums.[222] Similarly in *Pammel*, where the Court held that interest itself was the proper measure of the principal damages, it nevertheless awarded an 'equitable sum' on the ground that that loss could not be precisely calculated.[223]

The Inter-American Court rarely specifies interest rates.[224] Lump sums for pecuniary damages in respect of loss of earnings without the

---

[218] In *Nikula v Finland* the applicant was awarded default interest at the Finnish statutory rate on the principal sums awarded (the sums she had been ordered to pay in domestic proceedings which were found to be in breach of Article 10), to run from the date she had paid them until payment of the judgment: (2004) 38 EHRR 45, paras 59, 72. The Court treated this pre-judgment interest as default interest running from start date to payment (normally the term default interest is used by the Court to describe post-judgment interest only) (para 71). Interest was to run at 11%, the Finnish statutory rate prevailing on the date of judgment, on the other sums awarded, from the date of judgment (para 72). However, the 'equitable' lump sum approach was taken to her particularised claim for the costs and interest thereon for the domestic and Convention proceedings. In *Karhuvaara v Finland* (2005) 41 EHRR 51, which also concerned a breach of Article 10 by virtue of a domestic prosecution and order to pay damages, the approach was slightly different again. The applicant sought pecuniary damages made up of fines and damages levied in domestic proceedings, plus Finnish statutory interest on those amounts at 11%, and costs. It appears from the sum awarded for pecuniary damages that it was made up of the principal and interest claimed, but not the costs (paras 57, 59).

[219] Above n 78.

[220] Above n 70, paras 14–5. The applicant argued it would have earned this interest on the compensation sum had it been paid at the date of violation of the Convention (para 13). The Irish statutory interest rate was awarded instead.

[221] (2006) 43 EHRR 28, paras 48, 61–2.

[222] Ibid. In *Scordino* the Grand Chamber rejected the applicant's claim for statutory compound interest and without further explanation held that interest should take the form of statutory simple interest. In any event, it awarded pecuniary damages in a lump sum (above n 72).

[223] Above n 114, para 78. Cf the approach in *Wasserman v Russia*, above n 217, where the Court also awarded interest only because the principal was still recoverable by way of enforcement proceedings in Russian law.

[224] Eg, *Loayza-Tamayo v Peru*, Reparations and Costs, 27 November 1998, Series C No 42, para 129, *El Amparo v Venezuela*, Reparations and Costs, 14 September 1996, Series C No 28, para 28.

precise calculations are the norm,[225] and the Court hardly ever addresses particularised claims directly.[226] Where the interest rate is specified, different rates have been used. There is some suggestion of a preference for market rates: in *Aloeboetoe* interest was added to lost income calculations 'as compensation... in keeping with the rates in effect on the international market',[227] and in *Castillo-Páez* it added 'current interest'.[228] For its part the Commission has sought the respondent State's legal interest rate (a rate specified by code and payable as a matter of law for money lent in the absence of an agreed rate),[229] and interest at compound bank rates prevailing from year to year,[230] but in neither case was interest particularised by the judgment.

In the only ITLOS decision to award interest the Tribunal set three different interest rates for different types of loss, noting that it was 'not necessary to apply a uniform rate of interest in all instances'. On the basis of 'commercial conditions prevailing in the countries where the expenses were incurred or the principal operations of the party being compensated are located' it set a 6% simple interest rate for pecuniary losses to run from the date of loss, making an exception for gas and oil losses in respect of which 8% was awarded to include loss of profit. The Tribunal did not explain this decision, but presumably it was using an interest award as a proxy for the loss of profits assumed to flow from the loss of the oil cargo which were assumed to be more than loss of the use of a sum of money. On non-pecuniary losses 3% was awarded, to start running 3 months from the date of the award.[231] The Tribunal did not elaborate on why the interest award was less in the case of non-pecuniary damage than for pecuniary damage.

(ii) Interstate Claims

If an interest rate is selected by reference to the cost of borrowing or the loss of interest earned on sums invested, the loss of the use of money for a State is in principle less costly than for an individual because of their respective positions in relation to the financial markets. Government central bank rates for short term lending to banks and financial institutions (the base rate in England, the Feds Fund rate in the US, and the ECB marginal lending facility rate) inform commercial rates in the market—prime borrowing rates in the market are therefore usually reflective of the

[225] Eg, *Trujillo-Oroza v Bolivia*, Reparations and Costs, 27 February 2002, Series C No 92, para 73, *Juan Humberto Sánchez v Honduras*, Preliminary Objections, Merits Reparations and Costs, 7 June 2003, Series C No 99, para 163.

[226] Eg, *Miguel Castro-Castro Prison v Peru*, Merits, Reparations and Costs, 25 November 2006, Series C No 160, in which one applicant claimed interest on loans expended (para 411(s)), but a global sum 'in equity' was awarded (para 424).

[227] Above n 123, para 89.

[228] *Castillo-Páez v Peru*, Reparations and Costs, 27 November 1998, Series C No 43, para 75.

[229] *Loayza-Tamayo v Peru*, above n 224, para 125(a).

[230] *Street Children case*, above n 74, fn 70.

[231] *St Vincent and the Grenadines v Guinea (Admissibility and Merits)* (1999) 120 ILR 143, para 173; see further above n 61 and accompanying text.

central bank rate. Government borrowing rates, such as those on bonds
and treasury bills have traditionally been less than commercial rates
because of the lower credit risk.[232] There are, however, few decisions
where interest has been awarded in interstate claims, so it is difficult to
discern any trend in practice.

The Iran-US Claims Tribunal observed in *Atomic Energy Organisation
v United States*, a claim under Article II of the Claims Settlement
Declaration for claims arising out of contract arrangements between
the two States, that 'it would be inappropriate to apply a rate of interest
based on commercial investment rates, particularly in the absence of any
evidence as to fiscal practices of either Government'.[233] The *Sylvania*
formula was therefore rejected.[234] However, the Tribunal did not attempt
to develop by analogy a formula for setting an interest rate for interstate
claims which would reasonably approximate the State's loss. Instead it
awarded a rate of 10%, the rate awarded in many individual-State claims,
on the basis of prior practice in two earlier interstate cases and because it
deemed it 'fair'.[235] This reasoning was criticised by Judge Mostafavi in a
concurring opinion. In his view a more realistic, less arbitrary rate would
have been either the average rate of interest on bank deposits over the
relevant period or else the rate of interest provided in the contract, even
though the contract rate was applicable to default by Iran rather than
the US.[236] Notably neither of the rates he suggested would have been
different from those applicable to a private rather than State claimant.[237]
Following the *Atomic Energy* case, a simple rate of 10% has continued to

[232] The bank rate is the rate at which central banks make short term loans to banks and other
financial institutions, and commercial lending rates are normally an augmentation on the bank rate.
'[A]s early as the sixteenth century a differential had begun to emerge between the rate that a financially well-established state could expect to pay and the rate on commercial bills or bonds': Ferguson,
above n 195, 171. However, where the risk of default is high, a government bond rate may be higher
than the rate accorded to a prime low-risk private borrower.

[233] *Atomic Energy Organisation v United States* (1986) 12 Iran-US CTR 25, 28–9. See also
Brower & Brueschke, above n 60, 626–8.

[234] Ibid, 28–9.

[235] Ibid, 29. The period of account was from the date of Iran's formal claim for reimbursement of the sums advanced, rather than the date of expiry of the contracts which provided that
any sums advanced would be reimbursed. The Tribunal suggested that in principle interest was
payable on the interest running on the principal sum due at the date of the earlier partial award
which found the US liable for reimbursement of the advance payments and interest but reserving
the question of, *inter alia*, interest, but did not pursue this point because Iran failed to claim such
interest (at 29).

[236] Ibid, 30–2. He further observed that although the Tribunal purported to move away from
the arbitrary approach to interest rates of earlier jurisprudence towards setting a criterion for fixing
the interest rate, on the ground of fairness it relied on previous interstate decisions which had them
themselves adopted an arbitrary rate (at 30–2).

[237] Judge Mostafavi's criticism of the Tribunal's approach in *Atomic Energy Commission* is
shared by Judge Brower, in Brower & Brueschke, above n 60, 627–8. Judge Holtzmann also advocated an interest rate in interstate claims approximating the average interest rates prevailing during
the period in issue: *US v Iran (Case B-29)* (1984) 6 Iran-US CTR 12, 19 and concurring opinion in
Department of the Environment of the Islamic Republic of Iran v US (Case B-53) (1984) 5 Iran-US
CTR 105, 111.

be awarded in interstate claims[238] unless there is an applicable contract rate.[239] The Tribunal's reasoning suggests that it considers the interest award as being that appropriate to dealings between commercial trading parties,[240] but it has also awarded the *Sylvania* rate in a non-commercial claim.[241]

By contrast, in the *Protection of the Rhine* arbitration between France and the Netherlands the parties agreed on a rate based on the cost to the French State of medium term borrowing on 10 year bonds. This rate seems to be premised on the French government's interest savings by not having to borrow the amounts paid to it by the Netherlands under the treaty scheme.[242]

(iii) Which Central Bank or Market Rate?

The benefit of a central bank- or market-based formula is that it allows some measure of responsiveness to movements in interest rates and can produce a result which is more specific to the circumstances of the parties and the case. It presents a number of choices: the choice between the central bank or market with a close connection to the applicant and that connected to the respondent; between an investment rate and a

---

[238] *Iran v US (Case B-53)* (1984) 5 Iran-US CTR 105, 111; *US v Iran (Case B-29)* (1984) 6 Iran-US CTR 12, 19, *Iran National Airlines Co v US* (1987) 17 Iran-US CTR 238, 244; *Iran National Airlines v US (Case B-12)* (1987) 17 Iran-US CTR 228, 237; *Iran National Airlines v US (Case B-9)* (1987) 17 Iran-US CTR 214, 227; *Iran National Airlines v US (Case B-51)* (1987) 17 Iran-US CTR 200, 212, *Case B-8*, 17 Iran-US CTR 187 at 199; the US claimant in *Harris International Telecommunications Inc v Iran* was ordered to pay 10% interest on amounts found due under the counterclaim ((1987) 17 Iran-US CTR 31, 87); *Telecommunications Co of Iran v US* (1989) 23 Iran-US CTR 320, 337, where the tribunal refers to its practice in 'official claims' of awarding a interest rate of 10%.

[239] *Case B-36* (1996) 32 Iran-US CTR 162, 181–2, awarding interest at the default interest rate specified in a 1948 contract, 2 and 3/8% per annum, to run until date of payment of the award.

[240] In *Avco Corp v Iran* (1988) 19 Iran-US CTR 200, the applicants' claims and the respondents counterclaims were based on an ongoing trading relationship. The Tribunal held that in the absence of any contractual provisions for payment of interest, all parties were entitled to interest at the simple rate of 10% per annum following *McCollough* (paras 134, 136 and 139). A simple interest rate of 10% per annum was also awarded (without explanation) in Article II(2) GD cases brought by Iranian National Airlines against the United States in respect of outstanding invoices for services rendered to various US agencies for the carriage of goods by air, ie in the case of an ongoing relationship based on accepted industry practice and a contractual relationship for the purposes of Article II(2) (*Case B-9*, 17 Iran-US CTR 214, para 36, 227).

[241] *Iran v US (Case A-27)* (1998) 34 Iran-US CTR 39, a successful claim by Iran invoking US responsibility for the failure of US Federal Courts to enforce an earlier tribunal decision in favour of Iran against a US private party. The Tribunal awarded Iran simple pre-judgment interest at the annual rate of 10% (365 day basis) from the date on which the original award was issued by the Tribunal until the date the US Federal Court erroneously denied enforcement at the same rate as that awarded in the original decision. The Tribunal awarded interest from that date at an annual rate of 5% (365-day basis) until payment of the award. The Tribunal gives no explanation for this aspect of the interest award, which was criticised in the Separate Opinion of Judges Noori and Aghahosseini for being the rate routinely applied by the Tribunal in private law disputes and taking the view that it was 'both inadequate and inappropriate' in the context of an interstate claim (at 65). See also Separate Opinion of Judge Allison criticising the decision on pre-judgment interest for setting 'a rate of 10%, far in excess of market rates for the relevant period' (at 66).

[242] Above n 132.

(usually higher) borrowing rate; and between a short term and a long term rate.

One of the most comprehensive discussions as to whether a borrowing or investment rate should be preferred for an award of interest on damages is that of the Chamber of the Iran-US Claims Tribunal in *Sylvania*. It settled on a short term investment rate for a secure government guaranteed investment vehicle, six month certificates of deposit. It rejected a formula based on the prime borrowing rate in the US on the grounds that in the circumstances of that Tribunal, the desirability of uniformity in treatment in many different cases meant that an investment rate was more appropriate.[243] This was because it was difficult to settle on a uniform borrowing rate which might be applicable to all claimants, given their various credit ratings and the fact that not all the claimants actually borrow to cover delayed payment of the principal. Six month certificate of deposit rates were available to all investors at substantially the same rates, whereas borrowing rates would vary according to the credit rating of the borrower.[244] The interest rate formula also had the advantage that historical interest rate data was available from an authoritative source from which the Tribunal could calculate an average interest rate for the period of account in each case.[245]

The market- or central bank-based formulas adopted by investment arbitration tribunals for interest on damages awards are also short term interest rates selected by reference to the market with the closest connection to the applicant. The formulas vary between an investment rate and a borrowing rate. The investment rates adopted include the US treasury bills rate,[246] the US six month certificate of deposit rate,[247] or the rate for federal treasury certificates or bonds issued by the government of State of the claimant.[248] Some tribunals

---

[243] The claimant made an interest claim (averaging 14.03%) based on the prime rate charged by Citibank for loans on equivalent amounts to substantial borrowers.

[244] Above n 57, 321. See Judge Holtzmann's fn 13, 321. In his view it was reasonable to use the prime rate (the interest rate charged by US banks to their most creditworthy customers) on a uniform basis as it was reasonable to assume most businesses habitually borrow while fewer regularly invest in certificates of deposit. The prime rate was generally representative because the difference between it and other lending rates is relatively small.

[245] Ibid. The average rate applying this formula came out at 12.12% per annum for the five year period in question. The tribunal awarded 12%.

[246] *CMS Gas*, above n 152, paras 115–23. The *Decision of the Ad Hoc Committee on the Application for Annulment of the Argentine Republic*, ICSID Case No ARB/01/8, 25 September 2007 annulled one finding by the tribunal, but did not touch on this aspect of the award (at paras 470–1, fn 231). Using this formula the rate was fixed at 2.51%, corresponding to the annualised annual rate as reported by the Federal Reserve Bank of St Louis for six month treasury bill rates. See also *LG&E*, above n 152, paras 55–6, 103. Where the interest was calculated by the tribunal and awarded as a lump sum together with the principal (at para 109).

[247] *Siemens AG v Argentina*, above n 64, *Azurix v Argentina*, above n 152.

[248] *Feldman v Mexico*, noting the applicable law was NAFTA and customary international law, calculated a total interest sum of the principal amount due on rebates wrongly withheld at a simple rate based on the interest rate paid on federal treasury certificates or bonds issued by the Mexican government with a maturity of 28 days and calculated on a monthly basis. It appeared to select that interest rate because it was the rate under Mexican law in force for tax rebates on the dates the

•

award an interest rate based on investment without specifying a particular investment vehicle.[249] A further possibility is a rate based on the return from investing in bonds issued by the respondent State.[250] However, in *LG&E Energy Corp & Ors v Argentina* the proposal to use the respondent state's borrowing rates was rejected as 'speculative and extemporaneous',[251] and in *PSEG* a claim for an interest rate based on the Turkish bond yield was rejected because the claimants would not have placed funds which were not invested in the project in the Turkish financial market at the time. The 'sovereign risk was not the appropriate measurement for an alternative placement of funds'.[252] The respondent State's borrowing rate may however be appropriate in cases based on restitutionary claims.[253]

The borrowing rates which have been awarded are based on central bank rates for short term lending to commercial banks or short term interbank lending rates between commercial banks, such as the LIBOR, sometimes with a percentage increase to take account of the increment a commercial bank would add to the interbank lending rate to prime borrowers.[254] Thus the rates awarded have been the LIBOR,[255] the LIBOR plus 2%,[256] and the lowest rate that a commercial bank in the place of investment provided loans to corporate clients in foreign currency,[257] or

rebates were lawfully requested but not paid, and also because the Mexican peso was the currency of the award (paras 205, 207).

[249] The tribunal in *Vivendi v Argentina (Award No 2)* rejected a claim for 9.7% compound interest because it was not persuaded that this was what the applicants would have earned had the sums been paid on expropriation. Instead, taking into account the anticipated rate of return from the investment and generally prevailing rates for the period in question, it held that 6% represented 'a reasonable proxy' of the rate of return and, on the facts of the case, it was appropriate to compound the interest annually (above n 66). See also *Santa Elena*, above n 142.

[250] Eg, *Wena Hotels v Egypt*, above n 170. No reasoning was given for the selection of the 9% interest rate or quarterly intervals of compounding, but a footnote cited a report filed by the respondent which recorded that long-term government bonds in Egypt were then yielding 10% (at 932, fn 289). (As in *Santa Elena*, interest exceeded the principal—interest from date of taking to the award amounted to US$11,431,386 on a principal of US$8,497466.) The annulment panel upheld the Tribunal's interest award: Annulment Award of 5 February 2002, 6 ICSID Reports 129.

[251] *LG&E*, above n 152, paras 55–6, 102–3 (breach of the provisions on fair and equitable treatment and non-discrimination and the umbrella clause). The interest was calculated by the Tribunal and awarded as a lump sum together with the principal (at para 109).

[252] *PSEG Global Inc v Turkey*, above n 152, para 346.

[253] See the House of Lords' opinion in *Sempra Metals Limited (formerly Metallgesellschaft Ltd) v Commissioners of Inland Revenue* [2007] UKHL 34, [2007] 3 WLR 354, [2007] 7 All ER 657 (applying EC law). See further below n 358 and accompanying text.

[254] *PSEG Global Inc v Turkey*, above n 152.

[255] The *MTD* Tribunal concluded that as it was an international tribunal assessing damages under a bilateral investment treaty in an internationally traded currency relating to an international transaction, 'it would seem in keeping with the nature of the dispute that the applicable rate of interest be the annual LIBOR' (above n 152). See also *Biloune*, above n 206.

[256] *PSEG Global Inc v Turkey*, above n 152, *Enron*, above n 152, and *Sempra v Argentina*, above n 152.

[257] *AIG v Kazakhstan*, above n 112, at 113–4. On the amount which the claimants had actually invested in the project before its unlawful expropriation, the Tribunal awarded compound interest of 18%, the lowest of the rates that Almaty Merchant Bank provided as loans to corporate clients

the rate based on the interest provision in the UNIDROIT Principles of International Commercial Contracts.[258] Similarly, the European Union courts' pre-judgment default interest rate based on the ECB marginal lending facility is a short term rate.[259] A preference for a borrowing formula over an investment formula is rarely discussed, but in *PSEG Global* the Tribunal rejected the respondent's claim that the US treasury bill rate was appropriate because it did not offer a realistic alternative to investment of funds not placed in Turkey.[260] However, the claimants' actual cost of equity was rejected because it was based on subjective determinations by investors.[261]

The trend in international practice of adopting interest rate formulas based on central bank or market rates reflects that in domestic law. Many domestic jurisdictions have adopted formulas for statutory interest rates based on their central bank rate, although the models adopted vary. For example, the French default rate is fixed each year by decree, and is equal to the average of the 12 last months of the 'taux de rendement actuariel des adjudications de bons du Tresor'.[262] The Moldovan code (relied on in *Bogdanov*) uses the refinancing rate of the National Bank of Moldova.[263] The 2002 Russian Civil Code provision on default interest gives a formula for setting the interest rate based on commercial bank rates.[264] The interest provision of the Principles of European Contract Law sets a default interest rate 'at the average commercial bank short-term lending rate to prime borrowers prevailing for the contractual currency of payment at the place where payment is due.'[265] Some

---

in foreign currency, compounded on a semi-annual basis. The second amount awarded was the projected profit (30%) on the projected investment amount less simple interest on the unexpended amount of the investment which could have been invested elsewhere at 6% simple interest, which rate the Tribunal said was roughly the amount of interest on deposits in the world market at the relevant time. It could be questioned whether the Tribunal's compensation methodology would result in double recovery because the amount on which the 30% projected profits was calculated included the other principal amount awarded, ie., the lesser amount the claimant had actually invested before the expropriation, on which the 18% compound interest was awarded.

[258] See further above n 174 and accompanying text.

[259] See further above n 198 and accompanying text.

[260] *PSEG Global Inc v Turkey*, above n 152, paras 341–8. While the tribunal's reasoning suggested it was considering an investment rate, the LIBOR plus 2% would normally be considered a borrowing rate. The Tribunals in *Sempra v Argentina* and *Enron* also espoused a rate based on investment return but awarded a borrowing rate (see above n 186).

[261] Ibid, para 347.

[262] P Malaurie, L. Aynès, P Stoffel-Munck, *Les Obligations* (2003), 490–491, which lists the rates derived from the formula between 1993 and 2003 as follows: 1993–10.40%, 1994–8.40%, 1995–5.82%, 1996–6.65%, 1997–3.87%, 1998–3.36%, 1999–3.47%, 2000–2.74%, 2001–4.26%, 2002–4.26%, 2003–3.29%.

[263] Above n 152. The Moldovan Civil Code provides in Article 585 that 'Taux de l'intérêt Si, conformément à la loi ou au contrat, l'obligation est porteuse d'intérêt, les intérêts à payer sont égaux au taux de refinancement de la Banque Nationale de Moldova, si la loi ou le contrat ne prévoit pas un autre taux.'

[264] Russian Civil Code, Article 395.

[265] 1999 Principles of European Contract Law, Article 9:508: Delay in Payment of Money. Default interest will be compounded annually, unless the parties have agreed otherwise (Article 17:101).

domestic statutory default interest provisions provide for a significant penalty or inducement to pay element. Thus the 1986 Danish law on interest (relied on in *SwemBalt*) provides for default interest at the official discount rate plus 6%, unless the court decides otherwise.[266] The 2002 amended German Civil Code (BGB) has remodeled provisions on default interest which set it at 5% above the basic interest rate or 8% in cases where the parties are not consumers.[267] The Czech Republic civil code (relied on in *CME*) provides for default interest at twice the prevailing central bank rate.[268] The Law Commission for England and Wales in its 2004 'Report on Pre-Judgment and Post-Judgment Interest' has recommended moving the English statutory pre-judgment and post-judgment rates to a formula based on the Bank of England bank rate plus 1%.[269] This is premised on setting a borrowing rate as a uniform rate, and is the rate commonly applied by the English commercial courts. The uniform rate of interest recommended by the Scottish Law Commission—the Bank of England rate plus 1.5%—was also intended to reflect the 'cost of prudent borrowing' for secured debt that took into account the various standard interest rates charged to typical types of lenders.[270]

(iv) Changes in Interest Rates Over the Period of Account

International courts and tribunals which have adopted central bank- or market-based formulas factor in changes in interest rate over the period of account in one of two ways.[271] The first method is illustrated by the

---

[266] *SwemBalt AB (Sweden) v Latvia*, above n 65.

[267] Section 288 provides:

  (1) Interest is payable on a money debt during the period of default. The rate of default interest is 5% per annum above the basic interest rate.
  (2) In the case of legal transactions to which a consumer is not a party the interest rate for claims for remuneration is 8% above the basic rate.
  (3) The obligee may claim higher interest on a different legal basis.
  (4) The right to claim additional loss is not excluded.

[268] *CME v Czech Republic,* above n 65.

[269] The rate at which the Bank of England offers short term lending to commercial banks and financial institutions, 2004 Law Commission Report, above n 138, paras 3.31, 3.33, 3.43.

[270] Large businesses (1.5% on top of base), small businesses (+3%), secured loans for individuals (+1%), and nothing that individuals pay significantly more on unsecured loans and credit cards: Scottish Law Commission, 'Report on Interest on Debt and Damages', September 2006, SCOT LAW COM No 203, SE/2006/146, http://www.scotlawcom.gov.uk/downloads/rep203.pdf, para 7.13.

[271] An early example is the 1904 *Sentence de la Commission Mixte Italo-Colombienne Dans L'Affaire de M. Vicente Spadafora*, UNRIAA, Vol XI, 9. Because the legal rate of interest in Colombia had varied in the 20 years from the date the claims arose it would be 'en dehors des lois de l'équité' to award the rate prevailing at the date of award.
  Some tribunals and the European Union courts may simply state that interest will accrue at the rates applicable from time to time during the period of account: *SD Myers*, above n 153, paras 306–7, *Sempra v Argentina*, above n 152, para 486. For the EU courts see, eg, *Seisenbacher*, above n 199, 'on the basis of the rate set by the European Central Bank for capital refinancing operations in force during the various phases of the period concerned', para 2 of the operative paragraph, *Calberson*, above n 88, para 145, *Fuchs*, above n 86, para 78, *Borbély*, above n 89, para 73. Cf *Corus,*

Iran-US Claims Tribunal decisions following the *Sylvania* formula. They usually set one annual interest rate for the entire period of account by averaging the six month certificate of deposit rates over the same period.[272] This method had also been adopted by several arbitration tribunals, including in decisions where compound methods of calculation have been adopted.[273]

The other method is that of the Tribunal in *Protection of the Rhine*. It set a separate annual rate for each year of account based on the average of the French 10-year bond rates in that year. A similar approach was taken by the *MTD v Chile* Tribunal which took the annual LIBOR rate as at 5 November for each year of account.[274] This method may be preferable if compound methods of calculation are being adopted, especially for a long period of account over a time of large shifts in interest rates, because it more accurately reflects the investment return or cost of borrowing over that period.

In domestic statutory interest rate formulas the approaches to changes in interest rate over the period of account vary. The Law Commission of England and Wales proposes changing the statutory rate annually,[275] and the German BGB does so semi-annually,[276] but both appear to allow for movements in that rate over the period of account to be factored into calculations.[277] By contrast, the Russian code selects the interest rate prevailing on the date of claim or judgment. The Czech Code, applied in *CME v Czech Republic*, also appears to take the bank rate at the date of judgment: the default rate—double the bank rate at the date of judgment—was applied retrospectively over

where the default interest rate was specified by reference to the ECB rate prevailing at the date the principal (made up of interest on the repayment of fines improperly withheld) should have been paid (above n 87, para 64), and *Reynolds*, above n 94, para 50.

[272] Where there was more than one principal amount an interest rate was set for each principal amount based on the average interest rate for the period of account of that principal. Cf the approach to calculation using the *Sylvania* formula in *Rockwell International Systems v Iran* (1989) 23 Iran-US CTR 150, 210–1. It awarded several different rates over the period of account which ran sequentially on the principal as each part of it fell due, and changing on the dates on which the next amount of principal became due (between 13.5% for a period from 1 Nov 1979 to 30 Jun 1980, to 7.75% from 2 Jan 1985 to date of payment). The final rate running until date of payment was set by reference to an average calculated by reference to the date the last principal amount award became due and the date of the award.

[273] Eg, *Biloune*, above n 206, 290, *Azurix v Argentina*, above n 152, para 440, *CMS Gas*, above n 152, *Siemens AG v Argentina*, above n 64, para 396, *Bogdanov*, above n 152, p 19 (separate rates set for each principal related to average bank rate over period of account).

[274] Above n 152, para 250. See also *Feldman*, above n 152, para 211, *Maffezini v Spain*, above n 152, para 96, *Enron*, above n 152, para 452 (average LIBOR rate plus 2% for each year or proportion thereof), *PSEG Global Inc v Turkey*, above n 152, paras 348 and 354(3),

[275] Law Commission Report, above n 138, para 6.9.

[276] The basic interest rate (section 247) changes twice a year, and is referenced to interest rate for the most recent main refinancing operation of the European Central Bank prior to the first calendar day of the six month period concerned.

[277] The proposal of the Law Commission of England and Wales is that the calculation of interest should be based on tables or a computer programme which take the annual changes in statutory interest rate into account for the period of account, above n 138, para 6.9.

the entire period of account notwithstanding any changes in bank rate during that period.[278]

(v) Interest Rates as a Response to Inflation

One advantage of using interest rate formulas based on central bank or market rates rather than a set statutory or conventional rate is that they respond to shifts in interest rates over time. Interest rates move in response to inflation and, since the 1990s, some central banks have used their base rates to target inflation. This section explores the connections made in the jurisprudence between interest rates and inflation.

While the understanding that the purchasing power of a sum of money could drop is not new,[279] expectations of persistent inflation are relatively recent, dating to the 1970s.[280] The response by lenders was to demand higher nominal rates of interest which factored predicted inflation into account in order to ensure a real return on monies lent.[281] As a result interest rates reached record levels in the late 1970s and early 1980s. *A History of Interest Rates* records, for example, that many types of interest rates in the US 'fluctuated very sluggishly' until the 1960s[282] and '[b]efore the 1970s nominal rates were much more stable than either inflation or real rates'.[283] The extent of the fluctuations in interest rates between 1955 and 2007 is illustrated in the tables below using the UK Bank of England base rate and the US Federal Reserve Funds Rate shown against measures of inflation for the same period. The US six month certificate of deposit rate is also shown.[284]

Thus in principle nominal rates factor in not only the current return attributable to the foregone use of money and the risk of default by the debtor, but also the anticipated inflation, so as not to erode the real return

---

[278] *CME v Czech Republic*, above n 65, paras 630–5.

[279] See, eg, F A Mann, *The Legal Aspect of Money* (4th ed, 1982), 86. See generally chapters IV and V, 80–135.

[280] S Homer and R Sylla, *A History of Interest Rates* (4th ed, 2005), 431.

[281] Ibid, 429–433. 'Short rates in London rose almost steadily from 1965 to the highs in 1974. The bank rate rose from 7% to a high of 13%; the bill rate, from 7% to a high of 15%' (at 453).

[282] Ibid, 58.

[283] Ibid, 431.

[284] Table 1 shows the Bank of England base rate. The period 1955–1975 is the annual average of the Bank of England base rate taken from the historical rates from 1694, available at http://www.bankofengland.co.uk/statistics/rates/baserate.xls. From 1975 onwards is the annual average of the official bank rate, data base reference IUAABEDR, http://www.bankofengland.co.uk/statistics/index.htm. The annual inflation data is based on a 2004 paper 'Consumer Price Inflation Since 1750' (ISSN 0013-0400, Economic Trends No 604, pp 38–46) by J O'Donoghue, L Goulding, and G Allen, which estimates historic British inflation back to 1750.

Table 2 shows the US Federal Reserve annual Federal funds effective rate available at http://www.federalreserve.gov/releases/h15/data.htm. The inflation data is taken from the website Inflation Data, http://inflationdata.com/inflation/Inflation_Rate/HistoricalInflation.aspx?dsInflation_currentPage=4.

Table 1—UK Bank of England base rate ('BoE') and consumer price index ('CPI'), 1955–2007

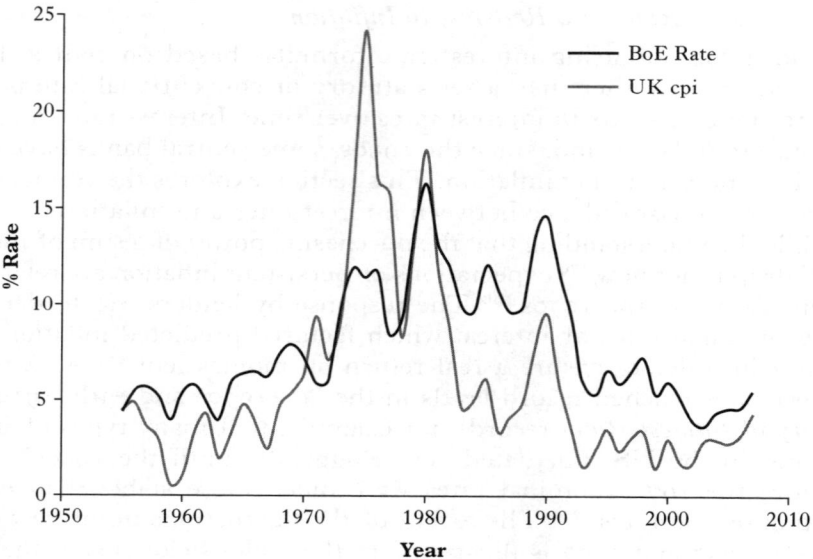

on monies lent.[285] Interest rate formulas in awards which are based on central bank or market rates will therefore account, at least to the extent that inflation is accurately predicted, for changes in value in the principal sum due to inflation over the period of account.

F A Mann emphasised that interest is awarded to compensate for the loss of use of money until payment, not to preserve the value of the principal sum.[286] Nevertheless, the link between compensation for inflation and interest awards has been made by international courts and tribunals in recent awards in three ways. First, claims for compensation for inflation have been rejected on the ground that the payment of interest provides some compensation for it. In *Lithgow v United Kingdom,* before the ECHR, it was argued that national legislation providing for nationalisation of the ship building industry did not properly compensate for rapid inflation during the period in question. The Court rejected the claim on the basis that the compensation paid 'bore interest—at a rate reasonably close to the average Bank of England minimum lending rate—...thus providing some shelter against inflation during the period from then

[285] Homer and Sylla, above n 280, 429–33.
[286] Mann, above n 279, 110, fn 146. See also the German cases discussed by Mann at 99–100.

Table 2—US Federal Reserve Funds rate ('FFR'), CPI and six month certificate of deposit rate ('CD Rate'), 1955–2007

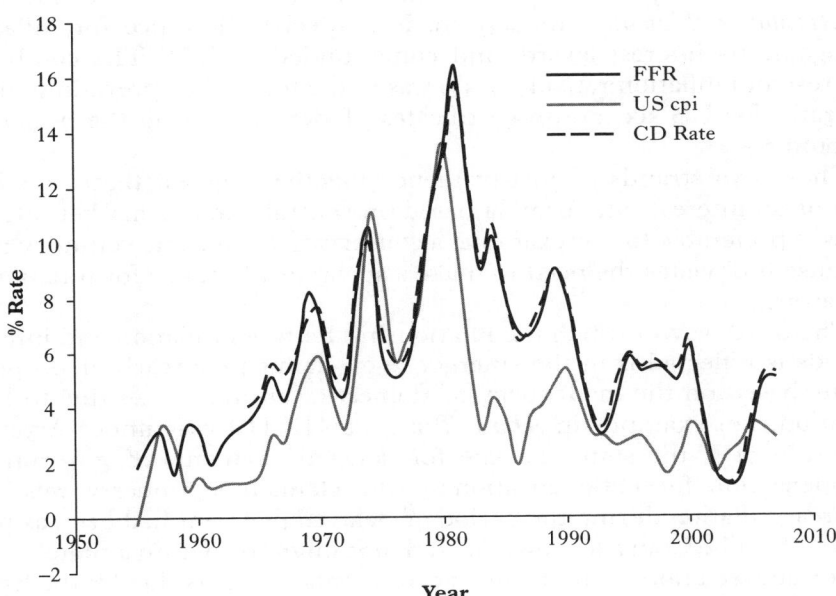

until payment'.[287] The Iran-US Claims Tribunal in *CMI International Inc v Iran* rejected the claimant's argument that it should be compensated for loss caused by inflation in the US because it found 'no legal basis for providing compensation for inflation, *except to the extent that some compensation is provided through the awarding of interest*'.[288] Investment arbitration tribunals have made similar observations.[289] The compensatory interest awards made by the European Union courts awarding only the rate of inflation also suggest that one of the functions of the interest award is compensation for depreciation of the principal sum due to inflation.[290]

Second, where the domestic statutory interest rate has been awarded as interest on damages, tribunals have augmented it because the statutory rate does not account for loss due to inflation. In *SPP(ME) v Egpyt* the Tribunal awarded an additional element of compensation to account for reduction in the value of the principal damages sums due to devaluation

[287] (1986) 8 EHRR 329, para 145. The minimum lending rate is the forerunner to the current Bank of England base rate.

[288] (1983) 4 Iran-US CTR 263, 270 (emphasis added)—although in this case the principal and interest were awarded as a lump sum.

[289] *AMCO* (Award 2), above n 153, para 196, *Bogdanov v Moldova*, above n 152, 19, *Autopista*, above n 152, paras 398–401.

[290] See above n 98–101 and accompanying text.

of the US dollar through inflation, precisely because the Egyptian statutory interest rate it awarded was not a commercial rate, and therefore
did not fully compensate the applicants for those losses.[291] The Tribunal
in *Aminoil v Kuwait* famously made a special allowance for inflation
alongside its interest award, and compounded both.[292] The combined
interest and inflation rate of 17.5% was at the top end of prevailing interest rates for US six month certificates of deposit during the period of
account.[293]

These two strands of jurisprudence together suggest that the adoption of an interest rate formula based on central bank or market interest
rates is preferable to, for example, a conservative domestic statutory rate,
because it obviates the need to make a separate allowance for inflation in
the award.

The third way in which the relationship between inflation and interest
awards is reflected is in the emergence of claims for breach of property
rights based on the inadequacy of domestic statutory rates due to high
inflation. For example, in *Aka v Turkey*, an ECHR case under Article 1
of Protocol I, the statutory rate for delayed payments of government
compensation for nationalisation of the claimant's property was 30%
whereas inflation during the period of delayed payment had been as high
as 70%.[294] The Court acknowledged that it might be within a State's margin of appreciation to limit interest payments on debts due by the State,
but only if that met the requirement of a fair balance between the general interest and the individual's property rights.[295] This balance had not
been met, and the Court awarded pecuniary damages for the difference
between the rate of interest paid under the legislation and the inflation
rate for the periods concerned.[296] In *Estima Jorge v Portugal*, an Article 6
claim for unreasonable delay in domestic enforcement proceedings, the
Court implicitly rejected the respondent's argument that compensation for inflation had already been taken into account by payment of a
small amount of interest.[297] By contrast, as noted above, in *Lithgow v
United Kingdom* the Court held that nationalisation legislation which did
not make special allowance for inflation in compensation entitlements
but paid interest at the Bank of England base rate (then the minimum
lending rate) provided some shelter from inflation, and was within the
State's margin of appreciation.[298]

---

[291] *SPP(ME) v Egpyt*, above n 68, paras 237–9.
[292] *Aminoil v Kuwait*, Award of 24 March 1982, 66 ILR 519, para 174.
[293] According to the monthly data for 6 month certificates of deposit published by the Federal
Reserve, http://www.federalreserve.gov/releases/h15/data/Monthly/H15_CD_M6.txt.
[294] (2001) 33 EHRR 27, para 48.   [295] Ibid, para 47.
[296] Ibid, paras 48, paras 56–7. See also *Akkus v Turkey* (2000) 30 EHRR 365, *Öztürk v Turkey*
(2003) 37 EHRR 5.
[297] *Estima Jorge v Portugal*, Judgment, 21 April 1998, Application No 16/1997/800/1003, paras
48–51.
[298] Above n 287, paras 145–7.

It may be that inflation does not go up or down as anticipated and so a central bank or market rate interest formula may not in fact reflect the true loss.[299] But an interest on damages award predicated on the return on money foregone by not being able to invest it, or the cost of borrowing to replace that money, is the method chosen by legal systems to compensate for delayed payment of principal sums. The simplest measure of this form of compensation is the investment or borrowing rate prevailing in the market relevant to the claimant at the time the breach occurred. To the extent that such rates do not actually provide a return on money, the claimant is in the same position as everyone else in the economy and they would have been in no better position with the principal in hand from the time payment of it fell due. Indeed, in *Lithgow* the ECHR expressly rejected the claim that the UK was obliged to link compensation payments to the retail price index, because to do so would have provided the applicants with an advantage not available to other investors in securities.[300]

(c) Method of Calculation—Simple or Compound?

(i) The Backdrop to the Question

If interest rates are selected using central bank or market based formulas, the question of compounding follows because this is normal financial practice. Investment vehicles such as US six month certificates of deposit pay interest at the end of the six month term which can be reinvested, as do government borrowing vehicles such as bonds or treasury bills. Borrowing, whether by banks and financial institutions from the central bank or on an interbank basis, or by private individuals from banks or financial institutions, involves either the payment of interest at regular intervals or the accrual of interest on a compound basis. Commentators have argued that compound interest should be awarded on this ground.[301]

Whether there is an entitlement to, or prohibition of, the award of compound interest in international law has been a recurrent question. Marjorie Whiteman, in her 1943 treatise on *Damages in International Law*, held that there 'are few rules within the scope of the subject of international law that are better settled than the one that compound interest is not allowable'.[302] This statement is often referred to, notably

---

[299] As can be seen in the UK Table above, in recent years real interest rates have been high because inflation fell faster than had been anticipated in the interest rate.

[300] (1986) 8 EHRR 329, paras 146–7.

[301] See F A Mann, 'Compound Interest in Damages' (1987–88) 21 *UC Davis L Rev* 577, 580, N Affolder, 'Awarding Compound Interest in International Arbitration' (2001) 12 *Am Rev Int'l Arb* 45, J Y Gotanda, 'Awarding Interest in International Arbitration' (1996) 90 *AJIL* 40, 'Compound Interest in International Disputes' (2003) 34 *Law and Policy in International Business* 393, 'Damages in Private International Law' (2007) 326 *Recueil des cours* 73, 259–64.

[302] Above n 2, 1997.

by the Iran-US Claims Tribunal in its decision rejecting compound interest in *RJ Reynolds*.[303] But, as has been observed by others, the decisions cited by Whiteman as authority to support her statement against compound interest do not actually rule out its award.[304] Even Whiteman herself recorded that 'in rare cases compound interest, or its equivalent, has been granted'.[305] In the main, however, claims for compound interest before international commissions and tribunals in the 19th and 20th centuries were rejected on the grounds that there was no agreement between the parties to the underlying claim to allow compound interest (or capitalisation) to accrue, or no express provision in the agreement between the States concerned establishing the tribunal,[306] or no such loss was proved,[307] or because of the lack of supporting precedent.[308] Recently, there has been a shift in practice

---

[303] (1984) 7 Iran-US CTR 181, 191–2.

[304] Gray, above n 1, 32, Affolder, above n 301, 71–3, *Santa Elena*, above n 142, para 99.

[305] Whiteman, above n 2, 1997, citing the 1896 *Fabiani* decision. In fact, although the arbitrator in *Fabiani* considered capitalised interest as a possible measure of the profits lost due to the frustration of the claimant's business, he instead awarded an equitable sum because the amount which would have been achieved by capitalising interest did not provide sufficient redress (Moore's, Vol 5, 4878, 4913–5). The British domestic board set up to distribute the Article VI Jay Treaty settlement sum in its 1803 report allowed capitalisation on the basis of express or implied contract to that effect, but only for the periods of mutual dealing between creditors and debtors interruption by the American war of independence, and not until the Board's determinations. After the interruption interest was allowed at the (simple) rate that would have been recoverable in domestic proceedings in the country of residence of the creditor (Moore, *International Adjudications*, Modern Series, (1931) Vol 3, 385–7). Arangio-Ruiz (above n 1) gave two further examples, *Chemins de Fer Zeltweg-Wolfsburg* (1934) UNRIAA, Vol III, 1795, 1795 et seq, and *Compagnie d'electricité de Varosovie* (Merits) (1936) UNRIAA, Vol III, 1689, 1699.

[306] In *French Claims Against Peru* (1921) 16 AJIL 480. The tribunal rejected a claim for compound interest on the grounds that a right to compound interest can only arise by agreement and the Peruvian government had not agreed to 'assume such an onerous obligation' in the protocol entered with France in 1914 agreeing to submit the outstanding claims of French subjects to an arbitral court up to the sum of 25 million francs. Capitalisation of interest could only result from agreement between the parties or from 'circumstances making clear the consent of the debtor to assume such onerous obligation'. In the *Christern and Co Case*, 1903 Germany-Venezuela Mixed Claims Commission, UNRIAA, Vol X, 423, the umpire rejected the German commissioner's allowance of compound interest on a forced loan to the State of Zulia because it had not been proved that compound interest (at 1% per month or 12% per year, compounded with annual rests) had been agreed between the parties. In the absence of an agreed contract rate the Venezuelan legal rate of 3% simple interest per annum applied (at 424). See to the same effect *Beckman & Co Case*, 1903 Germany-Venezuela Mixed Claims Commission, UNRIAA, Vol X, 436, 437.

[307] As in the *Nautilaa Case (Damages Phase)* (1930) (Portugal and Germany), Special Arbitral Tribunal established under Article 297 of the Treaty of Versailles, decision of 30 June 1930, digested in 5 *Annual Digest Public Int'l Law* 200, reported in *Sentence arbitrale*, 1930, 55–68, which concerned the damage suffered by Portugal's South-West African colony from an unlawful German reprisal in 1914. The Tribunal rejected the claim for loss of profits formulated as a claim to compound interest 'to the amount of 30 per cent.' as the owners could have mitigated their loss by replacing the property in question and thereby earning the lost profits claimed, but simple 5% compensatory interest was awarded.

[308] *Award of the Tribunal of Arbitration between the United States of America and the Kingdom of Norway under the Special Agreement of June 30, 1921, 1922* (1923) 17 *AJIL* 362 (Permanent Court of Arbitration), 395–6, and *Spanish Zone of Morocco Claims* (*Great Britain v Spain*), 'Rapport sur la question des intérêts', 29 November 1924, digested in 2 Annual Digest of Public Int'l Law 214, 215, reported in UNRIAA, Vol II, 615, 650. Neither of these decisions ruled out the award of compound interest if sufficient reasons were established.

towards acceptance of compound interest for awards of interest on damages by some investment arbitration tribunals. Other international courts and tribunals have continued for the most part to award simple interest. The next section reviews this recent practice. The one following asks whether there are any principled reasons for the rejection of the award of compound interest awards in all claims and confining its award to investment arbitrations, drawing on the reasoning in international awards and comparable developments in domestic law, especially in common law jurisdictions.

(ii) Recent Practice

In recent practice most standing courts and tribunals have continued to award simple interest on damages. The 1984 decision of the Iran-US Claims Tribunal in *RJ Reynolds* refusing compound interest is cited by the ILC's commentary to Article 38 of the Articles on State Responsibility as exemplifying that Tribunal's rejection of compound interest in principle.[309] Although the reasoning suggests that the Tribunal would award compound interest on the basis of an express contractual provision,[310] it has never done so. Decisions following the *Sylvania* formula for interest on damages did not respond to the observation by F A Mann that investment in US six-month certificates of deposit involves earning interest on a semi-annual basis which can then be reinvested.[311] Nor have claims for compound interest costs incurred as a direct result of breach (ie, where the claimant had to borrow to cover the loss caused by breach) been successful.[312] The UNCC's general statement on awards

---

[309] (1984) 7 Iran-US CTR 181, and Commentary to Article 38, para (8) in Crawford, above n 29, 237–8.

[310] Ibid, 191–2. See too the discussion in *Anaconda-Iran Inc v Iran* (1986) 13 Iran-US CTR 199, 233–5, where the tribunal also considered that the relevant contract provision (which was more ambiguously worded than that in the *RJ Reynolds* case) did not clearly provide for compound interest, especially in the circumstances of an extended outstanding claim, and therefore it 'must be deemed to be outside the scope of the possible common intent of the Parties' (at 235). The Tribunal listed other factors apart from the ambiguous clause which led to its rejection of compound interest, including the lack of precedent, but ultimately its reasoning turned on what was considered to be the parties' intent. The Tribunal applied the rate provided in the contract (the prime rate being charged by the Chase Manhattan Bank plus 2%) calculated on a simple basis (at 236–7).

[311] Mann, above n 301, 580. A claim for compound interest was rejected without any reasoning by the ICSID tribunal in *CMS Gas,* above n 152, even though the market rate it selected to base its interest award on was the six month US treasury bill rate, a form of investment which builds in a semi-annual compound interest return (principal and interest are paid out at the end of the 6 month period and are thereafter available for reinvestment). The annulment panel in its decision of 25 September 2007, ICSID Case No ARB/01/08 (Annulment Proceeding), although it annulled part of the award, upheld the monetary award against Argentina, which Argentina undertook to pay on its application for a stay pending the annulment decision (at para 160).

[312] An argument for compound interest as special damages was rejected in *Starrett Housing v Iran* (1987) 16 Iran-US CTR 112 with little explanation other than the observation that the tribunal had not made any award of interest on a compound basis, and it was not persuaded by the evidence in *Starrett* to depart from that practice (paras 13, 244, 370). The applicants sought interest on principal sum claimed at the average annual interest rate charged by banks to the applicants on a compound

of interest on damages left open the question of method of calculation,[313] but, as interest on damages was never determined because the fund ran out, compounding was never addressed. It has, however, rejected claims for incurred compound interest costs.[314] The EU courts, subject to one or two exceptions, award default or compensatory interest at simple rates. Similarly, except for two decisions, the ECHR has not awarded compound interest. Where compound interest has been claimed as an aspect of damages—primarily under Article 1, Protocol I claims for interference with property rights—the Court records the claims of the parties and then follows its usual practice of awarding a global compensation sum without particularising the interest award.[315] Whether compound interest is factored in cannot be ascertained, but it seems unlikely as the awards are much less than the amounts claimed. The only judgment in the Inter-American Court to record a claim for compound interest seems to have ignored it.[316]

The big shift towards awarding compound interest is in the practice of investment arbitration tribunals. Capitalised pre-award interest has been awarded on the basis of applicable domestic law[317] or based on a contract or treaty agreement between the parties,[318] but these types of compound interest awards are accepted in both domestic and international law. The key change is in the treatment of interest on damages awards where there is no agreement or guiding legislation, where traditionally only simple interest would be awarded. Now an increasing number of tribunals are awarding compound interest. The decision often cited as signalling this departure in investment arbitration practice is that of the ICSID tribunal in *Santa Elena* in 2000.[319] Before that award there were very few awards of compound interest.[320]

basis over the period of account, arguing they had been forced to borrow at compound rates to cover their losses due to the respondent's actions.

[313] See above n 62. Compound interest is an element of the formula for calculating compensation for death. Report and recommendations made by the Panel of Commissioners concerning part one of the first instalment of individual claims for damages above US $100,000 (Category 'D' claims), S/AC.26/1998/1, Adopted in Governing Council Decision 47 (S/AC.26/Dec.47(1998)), para 215, and Report and recommendations made by the Panel of Commissioners concerning the seventh instalment of individual claims for damages up to US$100,000 (Category 'C' claims), S/AC.26/1999/11, Adopted in Governing Council Decision 70 (S/AC.26/Dec.70 (1999)) para 162.

[314] Because the loss was not caused by the invasion of Kuwait and so it was not recoverable under the Commission's terms: Report and recommendations made by the Panel of Commissioners concerning the first instalment of 'E2' claims, S/AC.26/1998/7, para 220.

[315] See, eg, *Xenides-Arestis v Turkey*, above n 216, paras 41–2, and *Amat-G Ltd & Or v Georgia*, above n 216, paras 66–70.

[316] *Street Children* case, above n 81, para 74, fn 70.

[317] *Atlantic Triton v Guinea*, above n 153, 30–3. Interest was capitalised in accordance with Article 1154 of the French Civil Code in force in Guinea.

[318] *SPP(ME)*, above n 68, paras 229–30, as English law governed the loan contract. However the prohibition on compound interest under Egyptian law applied to the rest of the award for compensation (para 224).

[319] *Santa Elena v Costa Rica,* above n 142.

[320] Other than *Aminoil*, above n 292, *Atlantic Triton v Guinea*, above n 153.

The Tribunal in *Santa Elena*, which concerned an expropriation of property, justified the award of compound interest on the following grounds: the possibility of its award was not excluded by earlier jurisprudence; it had been allowed in some previous decisions such as *Aminoil* and *Fabiani*; the tendency to award simple interest was manifested principally in cases of injury or simple breach of contract and the same considerations did not apply to property rights cases; the Iran-US Claims Tribunal in *Sylvania* had derived a rate based on investment return using an investment vehicle which involved earning compound interest, even though it awarded simple interest; and writers of high authority, such as F A Mann and ILC Special Rapporteur Arangio-Ruiz, had advocated its award to ensure full compensation.[321] Therefore in cases

where an owner of property has at some earlier time lost the value of his asset but has not yet received the monetary equivalent that then became due to him, the amount of compensation should reflect, at least in part, the additional sum that his money would have earned, had it, and the income generated by it, been reinvested each year at generally prevailing rates of interest.[322]

Of the 27 arbitral tribunal decisions after *Santa Elena* which have been reviewed by the author, the majority have awarded full compound interest,[323] and one awarded a mixture of simple and compound interest.[324]

Several central themes emerge in the reasoning in support of awards of compound interest. The first is precedent—regard is had to the previous award of compound interest in *Santa Elena* and the cases which followed it. This has played a key if not decisive role in generating momentum towards a practice of awarding compound rather than simple interest on damages, in much the same way that it appears that precedent played a large role in earlier decisions as a reason for the refusal of compound interest.[325] Several tribunals have said that international law now requires

---

[321] *Santa Elena v Costa Rica*, above n 142, paras 98–103.

[322] Ibid, para 104.

[323] *Maffezini v Spain*, above n 152, *Metalclad*, above n 64, *ME Cement v Egypt*, above n 64, *AIG v Kazakhstan*, above n 112, *MTD v Chile*, above n 152, *Pope & Talbot*, above n 152, *S.D. Myers*, above n 153, *Tecmed*, above n 64, *Azurix v Argentina*, above n 152, *LG&E*, above n 152, *Wena Hotels*, above n 170, *Siemens AG v Argentina*, above n 64, *PSEG Global Inc v Turkey*, above n 152, *Vivendi v Argentina (Award No 2)*, above n 66, *Sempra v Argentina*, above n 152, *Enron*, above n 152. Of the remainder, one awarded a lump sum without explaining whether this included compound interest (*Occidental v Ecuador*, Award of 1 July 2004, 12 ICSID Reports 54, an UNCITRAL arbitration in the LCIA).

[324] *Protection of the Rhine*, above n 132.

[325] Eg, *Wena Hotels* cites *Metalclad*, above n 64; *Tecmed* cites *ME Cement v Egypt*, *Wena Hotels*, *Santa Elena* and *Metalclad*, above n 64, para 196; *AIG v Kazakhstan* cites *Santa Elena*, above n 112, 115; *Pope & Talbot* cites *Aminoil* above n 152, para 89; *MTD* cites *Santa Elena*, above n 152, para 251; *Siemens AG v Argentina* cites *Santa Elena*, *Metalclad* and *Wena Hotels*, above n 64 paras 399–400; *LG&E* cites *Azurix* and *Metalclad*, above n 152, paras 55–8, 103–4; *Vivendi* cites *Santa Elena*, above n 66, paras 9.2.4–9.2.6.

compound interest as an aspect of compensation[326] and that simple interest is no longer the rule.[327]

The second central theme is 'economic reality'. An award of compound as opposed to simple interest is 'generally appropriate in most modern, commercial arbitrations' because almost all financing and investment vehicles involve compound interest which the claimant could have received simply by placing its money in one.[328] The restoration of the claimant to a reasonable approximation of the position in which it would have been if the wrongful act had not taken place therefore requires compound interest.[329]

The third is the connection with loss of property or investment and the inability to invest the principal damages sum where 'an owner of property has at some earlier point lost the value of his asset'.[330]

Practice is not uniform. Several investment arbitration tribunals in the same period have expressly rejected claims for compound interest. The various grounds for its rejection are: lack of provision in the terms of contract;[331] the lack of any rule of international law fixing the interest rate;[332] prohibitions in domestic law;[333] the fact that the claimant did

---

[326] *ME Cement v Egypt* records that 'compound (as opposed to simple) interest is at present deemed the appropriate standard of law in expropriation cases' according to international jurisprudence and literature (above n 64, para 174); see also *Pope & Talbot*, above n 152, para 89; *TecMed* (at least in cases of expropriation), above n 64, para 196.

[327] *Vivendi v Argentina (Award No 2)*, above n 66, paras 9.2.4–9.2.6.

[328] *Wena Hotels*, above n 170, para 129, citing the arguments in favour of compound interest of Gotanda in 'Awarding Interest in International Arbitration' (above n 301, 61), and Mann in 'Compound Interest as an Item of Damage in International Law' (above n 301, 586). Arbitrator Wallace was not persuaded that interest should compounded at quarterly intervals, although he agreed compound interest should be awarded (at 920). Notably compound interest was awarded without the claimant seeking any interest award, compound or otherwise (at para 128).

[329] *Metalclad*, above n 64, para 128; *Wena Hotels*, above n 170, para 129; *MTD v Chile*, above n 152, para 251; *Azurix*, above n 152, para 440; *Siemens AG v Argentina*, above n 64; *LG&E*, above n 152, paras 55–58, 103–104; *Vivendi v Argentina (Award No 2)*, above n 66, paras 9.2.4–9.2.6.

[330] *MTD v Chile*, above n 152, para 251; *LG&E*, above n 152, paras 55–8, 103–4; *Vivendi v Argentina (Award No 2)*, above n 66, paras 9.2.4–9.2.6.

[331] The ICSID Tribunal in *Autopista*, an application under the terms of a concession agreement rather than a bilateral investment treaty, ordered that pre-judgment default interest was not to be compounded because the concession agreement interest clause could not be interpreted to provide for compounding, Venezuelan law precluded the award of compound interest in the absence of express agreement and, following *SPP(ME) v Egypt*, exclusive reliance on domestic law was justified because there was 'no rule of international law that would fix the rate of interest or proscribe the limitations imposed by [domestic] law'. Furthermore, because of its economic implications, an agreement requiring compound interest must be clear and cannot be too easily implied (above n 152, para 386, and see generally paras 383–6). In the Tribunal's view, there was no well-established principle in international law requiring the award of compound interest, as evidenced, it said, by the distinction made in *Santa Elena* and *Wena* between cases of expropriation and those of simple contract (paras 393–6). See also *Protection of the Rhine*, above n 132, para 139.

[332] *SPP(ME) v Egypt*, above n 68, para 222, *Autopista*, ibid.

[333] The ICSID Tribunal in *SPP(ME) v Egypt* rejected a claim for compound interest because it held that the provisions of Egyptian law prohibiting compound interest and requiring that interest not exceed the principal applied, notwithstanding that the compensation award was based on principles of international law and the start date was set by reference to international law, not the Egyptian code provisions on default interest (ibid, paras 183, 222, 234)

not seek compound interest;[334] and the consideration that the applicable domestic law provided effective reparation in the circumstances.[335]

Outside investment treaty arbitration the award of compound interest on damages is much less common, but not unknown. The ECHR has awarded pre-judgment compound interest on damages in at least two cases. In *Beyeler v Italy (No 2)* the applicant sought restitution of a valuable painting compulsorily purchased by the government under a right of pre-emption in 1988 at its 1977 value. As the pre-emption was considered lawful, the Grand Chamber awarded the applicant the difference in value between the price paid by the government in 1988 and its real value,[336] plus compound interest on that amount from 1988 until the date of judgment.[337] Compound pre-judgment interest was also awarded in *Wasserman v Russia* because it was claimed by the applicant and not contested by the respondent State.[338] However, in *Scordino v Italy (No 1)* the Grand Chamber rejected a claim for 'statutory compound interest' on a principal sum due from 1983. It did not give reasons for the rejection.[339] Then again, in the recent decision in *Kirilova v Bulgaria* the First Chamber of the Court accepted that the approach of the applicants to their damages claim—by calculating the loss of rent payments plus compound interest at the prevailing commercial bank rate in Bulgaria for deposits in euros—was reasonable, but rejected the claim on the facts.[340] In terms of State practice under the Convention, two pre-judgment settlement agreements entered by France in satisfaction of a damages award provide for compound interest on the principal amounts agreed in settlement.[341]

The EU courts do not reject compound interest as a matter of principle. In a 1971 case challenging a Commission decision which included a compounding element, the ECJ held that this did not render the decision invalid under Article 230 as claimed by applicant. It observed that 'it does not appear that the legal systems of the Member States include in general a fundamental principle opposed to the charging of compound interest'.[342] In claims by individuals against the Commission the question of compound interest has only been addressed in a handful of

---

[334] *Protection of the Rhine*, above n 132, para 139.

[335] *CME v Czech Republic*, above n 65.

[336] Above n 78. Less depreciation attributed to the claimant because of his conduct (para 23).

[337] Ibid. It based its calculation 'year by year, either on the statutory interest rate or the inflation rate, depending on which was more favourable to the applicant'.

[338] Above n 217. The claimant claimed compound interest at the default Israeli rate of 6% on an unpaid domestic court judgment which Russia had failed to implement.

[339] Above n 72, paras 243, 258.

[340] Judgment (Just Satisfaction) Applications nos. 42908/98, 44038/98, 7319/02, 14 June 2007, paras 29–30.

[341] *Maurice v France*, Judgment (Just Satisfaction and Striking Out), Application No 11810/03, 21 June 2006, Article 2 of paragraph 33 of the judgment. The settlement agreement recorded in *Draon v France*, Judgment (Just Satisfaction and Striking Out), Application No 1513/03, 21 June 2006, contains the same provision.

[342] Case 67/69 *Simet v Commission* [1971] ECR 197 para 15.

decisions and has not resulted in any clear practice. In one case the CFI volunteered that it had not awarded capitalisation of interest in a successful claim by the Commission against an individual under Article 238 for breach of contract because this was not provided for by the contract or by the (English) law of the contract.[343] In *Corus UK Ltd v Commission*, the CFI awarded compound interest in respect of a fine which the Commission had unlawfully levied under the ECSC Treaty and repaid to the applicant five years later without interest.[344] The CFI considered that the payment of interest on the repayment of an amount overpaid was 'an essential component of the Commission's obligation to restore the applicant to his original position following a judgment of annulment'.[345] In addition, a failure to reimburse interest in this case would result in unjust enrichment, contrary to the principles of Community law.[346] It went onto say that while under the national law of Member States generally only simple statutory or judicial rates were applied for the loss of use of money, in this case the Commission had disclosed the amount of compound interest it had earned on the fine between its levy in June 1994 and repayment in April 1999, and it was fair to award this sum.[347] However, for the period after April 1999 until payment only simple interest was awarded on the principal interest amount.[348]

The CFI also awarded compound interest in *AFCon Management Consultants and Ors v Commission*, a damages claim for non-contractual liability under Art 288 as a result of irregularities in an EC tendering procedure.[349] Here the CFI took a rather unusual approach. It said that it had not awarded general compensatory interest at a compound rate (for the period from commencement of proceedings until judgment) because the applicants had not asked for compound interest but had sought the Irish statutory rate of 8% simple interest per annum. Instead the CFI awarded simple interest at the European Central Bank principal refinancing rate plus 2%, amounting to 4.5–4.25% over the period of account. But it awarded post-judgment default interest on a compound basis, running on the principal (excluding costs) from the date of judgment using the same formula of the ECB main refinancing rate plus 2%. It did not explain why it awarded a compound post-judgment rate, and nor has it made a compound post-judgment interest award in other cases.[350] One

---

[343] Case C-337/96 *Commission v Industrial Refuse & Coal Energy Limited* [1998] ECR I-7943, para 58. It awarded the contract rate for interest on reimbursement of funds as the default rate from the date of claim, which was requested by the claimant and not disputed by the respondent.

[344] Above n 141.   [345] Ibid, para 54.

[346] Ibid, para 55. See further para 56.

[347] Ibid, paras 60–2.

[348] Ibid, paras 64–5.

[349] Above n 91. The applicants were awarded their tendering costs and costs of pursuing the claim, to run from the date (in 2003) when they took steps preparatory to commencing proceedings.

[350] Ibid, paras 130–3. The ECJ and CFI do not—apart from this decision—award higher post-judgment than pre-judgment interest and therefore control of procedure does not appear to have been the reasoning behind the post-judgment rate.

inference that could be taken from the judgment is that the CFI considered compound interest more appropriate than simple interest, and would have awarded it as pre-judgment interest had the applicant asked for it. Given the short period of account (two years), the simple Irish statutory rate was perhaps more attractive to the applicants than the ECB rate formula compounded.

Payment of interest at compound rates is also required by the European Commission on the repayment by recipients of state aids paid in breach of Article 88 of the European Community Treaty. The requirement of repayment plus interest is to effect restitution of the *status quo ante* under the Treaty because the unlawful advantage obtained by the recipient includes the financial advantage of having had a sum at its disposal free of charge for a given period.[351] The Commission's power to seek compound interest on recovery of state aids is now set out in regulation.[352]

Where the domestic courts of Member States provide national law remedies for breaches of EC law, subject to the disapplication of national rules where they do not meet the requirements of effectiveness and equivalence, the question is whether effectiveness requires that interest awards be compounded. So far the ECJ and CFI have not had to address this question,[353] but their approach to interest in cases against the institutions suggests that there is no automatic entitlement to or prohibition of compound interest. A recent decision where a domestic court of a Member State has developed its national rules on the award of interest in response to the requirements of effectiveness and equivalence in EC law is the House of Lords opinion in *Sempra Metals Ltd v Commissioners of Inland Revenue*[354] which was based on the ECJ's preliminary ruling

---

[351] See above n 116–118 and accompanying text. *Cf* WTO practice which does not require the payment of any interest at all on the repayment of unlawful subsidies, above n 119–121 and accompanying text.

[352] See n 117. The imposition of compound interest in a Commission decision requiring repayment of a state aid made before the 2004 regulation expressly providing for its recovery has been challenged: Case T-369/00, *Departement du Loiret v Commission* [2007] ECR II-851. The CFI did not reject the compound interest element as such, but annulled the measure because the Commission had failed to properly explain in the decision how the total amount claimed by the Commission, which included compound interest without expressly saying so, resulted in present-day value of the advantage to be eliminated. The decision is under appeal to the ECJ, the Commission arguing that the use of a compound rate was implicit because re-establishing the pre-existing situation meant the interest recovered must necessarily be a compound rate, in order to take account of inflation and of the advantage gained by the recipient of aid with the passage of time (Case C-295/07 P, OJ C 211, 8.9.2007, p 19).

[353] A 2006 reference by the English Court of Appeal to the European Court of Justice explicitly put the question of whether the principles of equivalence and effectiveness require a right to interest on the repayment of sums levied in breach of European law, and if there is such a right, whether this is a *right* to simple or compound interest (Reference for a preliminary ruling from the Court of Appeal (Civil Division) (England and Wales) made on 14/04/2006, *The Queen on the application of British Telecommunications Plc v Commissioners for HM Revenue and Customs*, Case C-185/06, OJ C 154, 01.07.2006, p 9). However, the reference was subsequently withdrawn (Order of the President of the Court, 5 June 2007, OJ C 199, 25.8.2007, p 24).

[354] *Sempra Metals Limited (formerly Metallgesellschaft Ltd) v Commissioners of Inland Revenue* [2007] UKHL 34, [2007] 3 WLR 354, [2007] 7 All ER 657.

in the *Metallgesellschaft* case.[355] The Lords upheld the decisions of the two lower courts that compound interest was the appropriate measure of either a compensation claim for breach of statutory duty or a restitutionary claim based on unjust enrichment for monies paid by mistake, where the claim represented the claimant's loss of use or the Revenue's use of the taxes advanced for the period between their unlawful early levy and subsequent set off against tax liability. While there was some disagreement over the cause of action in restitution, four of the Lords were agreed in regard to the claim for compensation for the breach of EC law, that the English common law allowed compound interest as ancillary damages on claims for non-payment of debts as well as on other claims for breach of contract and tort, subject to ordinary rules for recovery of damages.[356] The reason was that the common law should come into line with economic reality that 'interest payments for the use of money are calculated on a compound basis'.[357] If the alternative restitution action was relied on, the interest measure should be based on the benefit the government received from having the advance payments. Three of the five judges agreed that where the benefit of having the claimant's funds was extremely difficult to quantify, it could be measured on an objective basis by reference to the interest the State paid to borrow funds, and that use of ordinary commercial rates was not an appropriate objective rate.[358] The House of Lords left untouched the Court of Appeal holding that the intervals of compounding should be those related to the commercial interest rate adopted.[359]

Sempra Metals Ltd v Commissioners of Inland Revenue is not only a key development in the common law, but an important discussion of the effectiveness requirement of EC law as it relates to awards of interest. More generally it shows that when domestic judges apply principles of compensation for damage for loss of use of monies wrongfully paid or remedies based in restitution for unjust enrichment to interest awards freed from limitations imposed by common law rules and statutes requiring a simple rate, they accept that market-based rates and methods of calculation follow, subject to the usual rules regarding recovery of damages or gain-based remedies.[360]

---

[355] See n 102 and text at n 115. The obligation to pay compensation measured by interest in these circumstances was held to be an obligation under EC law but the amount so calculated and the basis (or cause of action) for its recovery was a matter for English law (para 81).

[356] Above n 354, Lord Nicholls, paras 89–92, 100. See also Lord Hope, paras 16 and 18, Lord Scott, para 132 and Lord Walker, para 154. Lord Mance's judgment is less clear—see paras 215–6.

[357] Ibid, Lord Nicholls, para 52, Lord Hope, para 16.

[358] Ibid, Lord Nicholls, paras 103, 116–9, 127–8, Lord Hope, paras 48–50, Lord Walker, paras 187–8.

[359] See para 54 of the Court of Appeal decision, [2005] 3 WLR 521.

[360] The *Sempra Metals Ltd* decision in the Court of Appeal also suggests that questions of rate, method of calculation and intervals of compounding ought to be considered together. What is key, the Court of Appeal reasoned, is not the compounding but the overall quantum, whether by reference to simple or compound rates. The rate chosen should dictate compounding and intervals of compounding (ibid). See also Affolder, above n 301, 91.

In conclusion, however, other than in the area of investment arbitration, international courts and tribunals are still cautious about awarding compound interest on damages. The occasional case where the ECHR and ECJ have appeared to support an award of compound interest on damages is barely explained by those courts and cannot be taken as indicative of a decisive change in their practice. The ILC left the question of whether the interest on principal sums should be compounded to the discretion of the court or tribunal.[361]

(iii) Is There a Case for Compound Interest in All Awards?

Investment arbitration tribunals that have awarded compound interest have been criticised for failing properly to justify departures from previous jurisprudence awarding simple interest.[362] Another way of putting this point might be to ask whether there is any justification other than precedent for the continued award of simple rather than compound interest on damages. The reasons for rejecting compound methods of calculation in awards of interest on damages that appear in the jurisprudence are the lack of proof on the part of the applicant of incurring compound interest costs,[363] the lack of causation and the unforeseeability or remoteness of such high damages,[364] the principle that appropriate compensation under international law does not include speculative benefits,[365] the concern that the resulting interest may be out of all proportion to the damages sum,[366] and the view that adequate, effective or fair reparation can represent less than full loss.[367] It might also be argued, based on practice to date, that the nature of the claim or cause of action is determinative—that compound interest awards are restricted to investment cases or those where the respondent has received money from the claimant or has otherwise been unjustly enriched. These arguments are examined below, starting with the relevance of the cause of action.

[361] Commentary to Article 38, para (10), above n 42.

[362] C N Brower & J K Sharpe, 'Awards of Compound Interest in International Arbitration: The Aminoil Non-Precedent' (2006) 3 Transnational Dispute Management 155, 177.

[363] ILC Member Thiam in the 1990 session, above n 13, 182, para 50.

[364] For an early rejection of a compound interest claim of the grounds that such loss was speculative, see the reasoning of the British domestic board set up to distribute Jay treaty funds in its 1803 report, above n 135, 387. See also Judge Brower's concurring and dissenting opinion in McCollough, above n 58, 42–3, and the similar reasoning of the ECHR in Pine Valley rejecting a commercial rate of interest, above n 220.

[365] See the Separate Opinion of Ian Brownlie in CME v Czech Republic, above n 65, for a discussion on the limitation on the award of speculative benefits in the concept of reasonable compensation under the bilateral investment treaty in question and international law, esp paras 66–9, 108, although he considered the interest award in that case was moderate.

[366] International Systems & Controls Corp v NIGC (1990) 24 Iran-US CTR 47, 83–4, rejecting a claim for compound interest on the ground that there was no contractual basis for it. But it also recorded that, citing Anaconda, 'judicial authorities as a general rule avoid awarding interest at compound rates because of the inherent effect of distorting the amount of damages in relation to the real loss compensated' (at 83).

[367] Former King of Greece v Greece (2003) 36 EHRR CD43, para 78, although in Lithgow v United Kingdom, above n 287, para 119, the ECHR said that in a Protocol I, Article 1 claim by a national against their own State the rules of public international law do not apply.

Relevance of the nature of the claim or cause of action: One argument
made by the *Santa Elena* Tribunal in support of its award of compound
interest was that 'the taking State is not entitled unjustly to enrich itself
by reason of the fact that the payment of compensation has been long
delayed'.[368] Is the existence of unjust enrichment therefore decisive in
support of an award of compensatory compound interest on damages?
The facts of *Santa Elena* do not support an affirmative answer to this
question because the respondent was not in fact enriched: Costa Rica did
not end up in possession of the investment property, which remained in
possession of the claimant; nor had Costa Rica actually received money
from the claimant which could have been said to have unjustly enriched
it.[369] Costa Rica benefited from saving the amount of compensation
which it should have paid to Santa Elena on expropriation which (presumably) it would either have had to borrow elsewhere at market rates
or could have invested to generate a return. A distinction is drawn by
common law commentators between claims based on the reversal of
an unjust enrichment and claims for restitutionary remedies where the
defendant has gained a benefit from the commission of a wrong, such
as the interference with property rights in tort[370] or breach of contract
or equitable wrongdoing, even though the benefit was not subtracted
from the claimant.[371] The rationale for restitutionary remedies is not
reversing unjust enrichment, but the award of a gain-based remedy.[372]
It is suggested that this can 'encompass a negative benefit, in the sense
of money saved',[373] as was the case in *Santa Elena*. However, the scope
of application of this restitutionary remedy in the absence of an actual
enrichment is unclear,[374] and it has not been pursued in interest awards
by international tribunals.[375]

In cases of money actually received or property unlawfully taken, there
is a good argument that the award, including any interest award, could be
measured by the respondent's enrichment rather than the claimant's loss.
But then the only difference between the restitutionary and the compensatory approach is whether the interest award is quantified by reference
to the cost of borrowing saved or the return on investment received by
the respondent (restitutionary) or the cost of borrowing or loss of invest-

---

[368] *Santa Elena v Costa Rica*, above n 142, para 101.
[369] G Virgo, *The Principles of the Law of Restitution* (OUP, 2nd ed, 2006), 119.
[370] Ibid, 475.   [371] Ibid, 425–6.
[372] Ibid, 426. The principle is that a defendant should not profit from their own wrongdoing (at 431).
[373] Ibid, 427. See also 437–8.
[374] Not all torts or contract claims give rise to restitutionary remedies. In contract they are only
awarded exceptionally where compensatory remedies are inadequate (ibid, 492). See also *McGregor
on Damages*, above n 36, paras 15-018–15-019. In some civil law jurisdictions only the lower of the
compensatory or restitutionary measure will be awarded: *Azurix v Argentina*, above n 152, para 438
and citations therein.
[375] There are only two arbitration decisions awarding compound interest which concern the actual
taking or withholding of money, *Protection of the Rhine* (for details of the case see above n 132 and
n 242 and accompanying text) and *Maffezini v Spain*, above n 152, in which the respondent had
removed money from a bank account belonging to the claimant.

ment return (compensatory) incurred by the claimant. Both approaches can therefore lead to the award of compound interest, although the quantum may not be the same. Unjust enrichment does not therefore in itself justify an award of compound interest on damages.

The decision in *Santa Elena* also suggests that the primary obligation giving rise to the right interest on damages might affect the method of calculation, because part of its reasoning in support of compound interest was that the same considerations do not apply to cases relating to the valuation of property or property rights as apply to injury and simple contract claims. The Tribunals in *TecMed* and *Middle East Cement*, both cases of expropriation or acts tantamount to expropriation, drew on this distinction to reinforce their awards of compound interest on damages,[376] and the Tribunal in *Autopista*, a case turning on contract obligations, cited the distinction made in *Santa Elena* to confirm a simple interest award.[377] This has led commentators to suggest that the line between simple and compound interest awards in investment treaty arbitration might lie between those cases involving expropriation and those which do not.[378]

This distinction is not, however, made out in practice. Many cases in which compound interest has been awarded do not involve expropriations, whether direct or indirect, but breaches of other obligations such as a treaty obligation of fair and equitable treatment.[379] Moreover, cases where simple interest has been awarded may turn on breaches of an investment treaty rather than contract,[380] and the majority of cases where compound interest on damages is awarded do not justify it by reference to the primary obligation breached, whether they concern unlawful expropriations,[381] failure to compensate for a lawful expropriation,[382] or violations of treaty obligations concerning fair treatment and standards of full protection and security.[383] Nor is there any sense that what is being awarded is a proxy for loss of investment profits: in all cases the award was for the domestic law statutory equivalent of interest *on* damages or default interest rather than interest *as* damages,[384] and the term 'interest

---

[376] *Tecmed*, above n 64, citing to similar effect *ME Cement v Egypt*, above n 64.

[377] Above n 152, paras 394–5.

[378] C McLaughlan, L Shore and M Weiniger, *International Investment Arbitration, Substantive Principles* (OUP, 2007), paras 9.130–9.132.

[379] *SD Myers*, above n 153; *Pope & Talbot*, above n 152; *MTD v Chile*, above n 152; *Enron*, above n 152; *LG&E*, above n 152; *PSEG Global Inc v Turkey*, above n 152. Cf *Azurix* where a province of the state did end up running the concession although there was no expropriation, above n 152.

[380] Eg, *Feldman*, above n 152, *CME*, above n 65.

[381] *Siemens AG v Argentina*, above n 64; *Vivendi v Argentina (Award No 2)*, above n 66; *AIG v Kazakhstan*, above n 112.

[382] *Wena*, above n 170.

[383] *Metalclad*, above n 64; *Azurix v Argentina*, above n 152; *LG&E*, above n 152; *MTD v Chile*, above n 152; *PSEG Global Inc v Turkey*, above n 152; *SD Myers*, above n 153; *Pope & Talbot*, above n 152; *Enron*, above n 152; *Sempra v Argentina*, above n 152.

[384] In *Siemens AG v Argentina* (n 64) the principal compensation—of the value of the investment in the project—did include loans and interest expended, but this is treated separately from the question of interest on that amount.

on' principal or damages is frequently invoked.[385] The award of compound interest on damages in these awards is thus distinct from earlier cases such as *Fabiani* where the arbitrator had considered capitalised interest could be a proxy measure of an award of actual lost profits.[386] The Tribunal in *SD Myers* made it clear that the award of interest on damages is a distinct category of compensation from that of lost profits although they may operate in the alternative.[387]

The balance of the jurisprudence suggests that the nature of the claim or primary obligation breached is not determinative of whether compound interest can be awarded as interest on damages. This is unsurprising. If the purpose of interest on damages is compensation for the loss of use of the principal sum, it is difficult to understand why the nature of the breach (contract or expropriation) which gave rise to the award of the principal sum should make any difference to how the interest on it is calculated.

Causation, proof and directness of loss: The requirement to prove damage, to establish causation between the breach and that damage, and the directness (proximity or foreseeability) of that damage (covered by Article 31 of the Articles on State Responsibility) applies as much to interest awards as to other aspects of reparation.[388] Yet it is never suggested by international tribunals that loss of use of principal sums should not be compensated by a simple interest award as a matter of course without these requirements being established. Interest loss, its causation and directness are presumed, as is generally the case with default interest in civil law systems and interest on damages in common law systems. Questions of proof of loss, causation and directness appear, however, to resurface when interest claims rise above some notional 'reasonable' amount, as when compound interest is claimed. Compound or capitalised interest has traditionally been allowed where there was a clear agreement between the parties or proved trade usage: that is, in those cases where the claimant can show that the loss claimed was direct or foreseeable or not too remote by reference to the express or implied agreement between the parties.

---

[385] Eg, *Pope & Talbot*, above n 152, para 90 ('interest on the principal sum'); *Metalclad*, above n 64, para 128 ('interest payable on the amount of the compensation'); *Azurix v Argentina*, above n 152, para 440 ('interest should be paid on the damages'); *MTD v Chile*, above n 152, para 247 ('interest on the amount of damages'); *Siemens AG v Argentina*, above n 64, para 111(7) ('interest compounded annually on the sums'); *SD Myers*, above n 153, para 302 ('interest should be payable on any sums awarded').

[386] *Fabiani* (1896) reported in Moore, *History and Digest*, above n 111.

[387] *SD Myers*, above n 153, paras 161–2. The applicant's claim for the loss of profits failed because it could not prove the loss to a sufficient standard: in the circumstances of the case, it would be speculative and too remote to allow a return based on what the claimant might have done. Instead the applicant was to be 'compensated for the value of the lost use of money by payment of interest that reflects what the market considered to be the value of money at the time'.

[388] For a comparative discussion of principles which limit recovery of loss, such as remoteness, see Commentary to Article 31 on Reparation, para (10) in Crawford, above n 29, 204.

Questions of directness and proof of loss in respect of an award of interest on damages have been raised in three recent investment arbitration cases. In *PSEG v Turkey* the claimant made a claim for compound interest at 12% and 10.6% based on either the historic and forward-looking cost of equity to finance the expropriated assets or alternatively the Turkish bond yield. Turkey responded that awards of compensation entailed no risk, so only the US treasury bill rate was justified. The difference in the interest rates claimed by both parties would have led to a variation of US$20 million in the award. The Tribunal rejected all arguments: the cost of equity was too subjective—the claimant would not have invested in the Turkish bond market—and US treasury bills were not a realistic alternative for the claimant's investment for funds not placed in Turkey. Instead the Tribunal held that the most appropriate benchmark to adequately compensate an international company was the six month average LIBOR plus 2% compounded semi-annually.[389] Similarly, in *LG&E* the Tribunal rejected the claimant's request for a rate based on Argentina's borrowing rate as this was 'speculative and extemporaneous'.[390] The question of proof of compound interest loss was raised most squarely in *Siemens v Argentina*. Siemens claimed compound interest at 6% per annum based on its average corporate borrowing rate in appraising investments, which it noted was also in line with prior arbitral practice. Argentina responded that this claim might be valid if Siemens had shown it was obliged to make good any financial losses by borrowing money at compound rates. As it had not, the claim was speculative and would result in unjust enrichment. The Tribunal clearly placed some weight on Argentina's argument, as its response was to focus on what the money could have earned—the opportunity cost—not what it would have cost Siemens to borrow the equivalent amount. Accordingly it selected the rate applicable to US six month certificates of deposit compounded semi-annually.[391]

In spite of the questions of proof and directness of loss, in all three cases compound interest losses were presumed and no reference was made to evidence that, for example, the claimant was a net borrower. What this suggests is that tribunals do account for directness (remoteness or foreseeability) of loss by placing a limit on interest awards, but not by refusing compound methods of calculation. They do so by choosing an objective measure of interest by reference to a central bank or market vehicle which either presumes a credit-worthy borrower by, eg using rates available to prime borrowers, or the rate of return from a low-risk secure investment, and by rejecting arguments for interest rate formulas which appear more speculative and would result in higher

---

[389] *PSEG v Turkey*, above n 152, paras 341–8.
[390] *LG&E*, above n 152, para 102. Argentina had supported a rate based on the US six month treasury bill rate.
[391] *Siemens v Argentina*, above n 64, paras 390–401.

interest awards.[392] International arbitration tribunals no longer consider compound interest losses as *per se* too remote or unforeseeable and are prepared to presume such losses in light of economic realities. This is reasonable. The next question is whether this development in international practice is confined to commercial claimants in investment arbitrations, on the ground that it is only in respect of such claimants that compound interest losses can be presumed to be a direct consequence of breach without proof of loss.

There is some support for considering that this might be so: the reasoning invoked in support of the award of compound interest in investment treaty arbitrations often focuses on the applicant as investor or the investment;[393] F A Mann argued that one of the circumstances justifying the award of compound interest is the back-to-back financing obligations of investors;[394] the arbitrator in *Fabiani* observed, in respect of domestic code provisions for capitalisation, that 'La capitalisation d'intérêts est autorisée en matière de comptes-courants et d'opérations analogues, parce que le législateur presume que, dans le commerce, l'argent ne reste pas improductif';[395] and the ECJ in *Mulder* distinguished between principal sums which would have been spent by dairy farmers on daily living expenses and those which might have been put in the bank to justify an award of compensatory interest at a lower rate than prevailing bank and default interest rates. On the other hand, economic realities apply equally to all claimants. Some light is cast on this issue in the treatment of compound interest claims by domestic courts and law commissions.

Domestic courts in common law jurisdictions have increasingly entertained claims for pre-judgment compound interest damages.[396] There are three key decisions, by the Australian High Court, the Canadian Supreme Court and the English House of Lords—the first a claim for

---

[392] The annual LIBOR rate compounded (*MTD v Chile*, above n 152, paras 250–1); the 6 month annual LIBOR plus 2% compounded semi-annually (*PSEG Global Inc v Turkey*, above n 152, para 348; *Enron*, above n 152, para 453; *Sempra v Argentina*, above n 152, para 486), the Canadian prime rate plus 1% compounded annually (*SD Myers*, above n 153, para 306); the US 6 month certificate of deposit rate compounded semi-annually (*Azurix v Argentina*, above n 152, para 442(6)); US 6 month certificates of deposit compounded annually, (*Siemens AG v Argentina*, above n 64, para 403(7)); the US six month treasury bills rate compounded (*LG&E*, above n 156, para 115).

An alternative approach to fixing interest rate formulas for pre-judgment interest is advocated by J M Colón and M S Knoll based on the coerced loan theory which treats the harm caused by the respondent as forced borrowing it. Applying this premise, an interest formula should be adopted using the same interest rate as other unsecured debt of the respondent and taking due account of the risk of default. They see this as a more conceptually correct method of assessing pre-judgment interest which meets other policy goals such as proper compensation of the claimant, avoiding unjust enrichment of the respondent and promoting efficient dispute resolution by removing any incentive for either party to delay proceedings: 'Prejudgment Interest in International Arbitration' (2007) 6 *Transnational Dispute Management* 1. This approach is not reflected in any of the existing cases. It requires acceptance of the underlying premise that the claimant should be compensated for the risk of default on the judgment amount by the respondent. The principle underpinning an award of interest on damages (compensating the claimant's loss of use) would not seem to go so far.

[393] See above n 330 and accompanying text.

[394] Above n 301.   [395] Above n 305, 4914.

[396] As distinguished from default interest/interest on damages.

negligence and breach of contract, the second a claim for breach of contract, and the last a claim for damages for breach of EC law.[397]

In *Hungerfords v Walker* the defendant accountants had been found negligent in their preparation of the claimants' accounts, resulting in the overpayment of tax for several years, which the claimants were statute-barred from recovering from the government.[398] The Australian High Court confirmed the award of compound interest as damages because the defendants' wrong directly led to the paying away of money by the claimants, and so the cost of borrowing money to replace money paid away, or the incurring of opportunity cost in consequence of the defendants' negligence or breach of contract, was foreseeable:

The requirement of foreseeability is no obstacle to the award of damages, calculated by reference to the appropriate interest rates, for loss of the use of money. Opportunity cost, more so than incurred expense, is a plainly foreseeable loss because, according to common understanding, it represents the market price of obtaining money.[399]

In *Bank of America, Canada v Mutual Trust Co* the respondent had agreed by way of assignment to pay monies it was lending to a third party under a mortgage financing scheme directly to the claimant until a loan between the claimant and the third party was paid off.[400] The respondent pulled out of the arrangements, breaching the assignment agreement and causing the third party to default on the loan. The Supreme Court of Canada agreed with the court of first instance that the claimant could recover compound interest damages rather than the simple statutory rate for the breach of contract at the compound rate in the claimant's loan agreement with the third party (the prime rate plus 1% compounded monthly) as this represented the proper measure of expectation damages

---

[397] *Sempra Metals Ltd v Commissioners of Inland Revenue*, above n 354.

[398] *Hungerfords & Ors v Walker* (1990) 171 CLR 125.

[399] Ibid, 143 (per Mason CJ and Wilson J). Furthermore, '[t]he cost of borrowing money to replace money paid away or withheld, in consequence of the defendant's breach of contract or negligence, is directly related to the wrong and is not too remote in the sense in which the common law regarded the loss attributable to late payment of damages as being too remote. We reach this conclusion more readily, knowing that legal and economic thinking about the remoteness of financial and economic loss have developed markedly in recent times' (at 145–6). The judgment further noted that compensation in this case might be ascribed to the second limb in *Hadley v Baxendale*, but they 'would prefer to put it on the footing that it is a foreseeable loss, necessarily within the contemplation of the parties, which is directly related to the defendant's breach of contract or tort' (at 149). See also the concurring judgment of Brennan and Deane JJ, at 152. It was found by the trial judge that if the claimants had had the money they would have used it to pay off their most expensive loans (20% compounding monthly) or, if return on the money would have been greater if put into the business, they would have taken that course (at 150). The total interest award calculated this way was discounted by 20% on a broad brush basis to accommodate the finding of the trial judge that there were insufficient grounds for finding that all the money paid away would have been used to repay loans, and to take account of the possibility that some might have been used for non-business purposes (at 151).

[400] [2002] 211 DLR (4th) 285, esp paras 23–4, 29, 49, 55. The rate of interest and intervals of compounding the Supreme Court considered appropriate were those set out in a contract between the parties.

had the assignment agreement been performed. The Court considered that it could not be said that the costs of delay were not within the contemplation of the parties at the time they entered the assignment agreement concerning payments under the loan agreement. Both parties were in the business of lending, and a loan agreement is an agreement on the cost of borrowing money over a period of time.[401]

In the third decision, already mentioned above in the context of European Community law,[402] *Sempra Metals Ltd v Commissioners of Inland Revenue*, the House of Lords confirmed that compound interest could be awarded as damages for loss of use of money wrongly levied by the respondent (a breach of statutory duty) where it satisfied the usual remoteness tests.[403] In this case, the incurring of compound interest losses was reasonably foreseeable as a direct result of *a sum of money* being improperly levied. The House of Lords went further, making a significant step in the development of the common law regarding interest as damages for breach of contract to pay a debt, by holding that interest as special damages is recoverable where the loss arises according to the ordinary course of things, as well as in cases where it can reasonably be supposed in the circumstances to have been within the contemplation of the parties when they made the contract as a probable consequence of breach. This appears to make compound interest much easier to recover because the reasoning turns on the 'economic reality' that interest payments for the use of money are calculated on a compound basis in the ordinary course of things, so that remoteness is no longer a hurdle to recovery in breach of contract claims for losses actually sustained as a result of late payment of debt. The requirement of proof of loss was met, as it had been established in the trial court below that the claimant was in a net borrowing position. The interest loss was measured on an objective ('conventional') basis according to an ordinary commercial rate for a typical claimant borrowing at the intervals of compounding related to that rate, rather than on the claimant's actual interest losses.[404]

The decisions above each predicated their findings on the basis that the compound interest loss for loss of use of the principal is direct and not too remote or unforeseeable given modern economic realities. The reasoning employed by the courts would extend to non-commercial claimants. The Canadian Supreme Court observed that

[c]ompound interest is now commonplace. Mortgages are calculated using compound interest, as are most other loans, including such worthy endeavours as

---

[401] Ibid, para 49.

[402] See above n 354–360 and accompanying text.

[403] *Sempra Metals Ltd v Commissioners of Inland Revenue*, above n 354.

[404] Ibid, paras 126–7 (per Lord Nicholls), para 50 of the Court of Appeal judgment [2006] QB 37, and paras 18–23 of the High Court judgment, [2004] EWHC 2387 (Ch). The Revenue accepted the choice of a conventional measure based on borrowing rates rather than a case specific interest measure because this was a test case for between 50–70 other cases. This point was not appealed.

student loans. The growth of a company or a country's gross domestic product over a period of years is often stated in terms of an annually compounded rate. The bank rate, which garners much attention as an indicator of the health and direction of the economy, is a compound interest rate. It is for reasons such as these that the common law now incorporates the economic reality of compound interest. The restrictions of the past should not be used today to separate the legal system from the world at large.[405]

In a similar vein, Lord Nicholls in the House of Lords said

[w]e live in a world where interest payments for the use of money are calculated on a compound basis. Money is not available commercially on simple interest terms. This is the daily experience of everyone, whether borrowing money on overdrafts or credit cards or mortgages or shopping around for the best rates when depositing savings with banks or building societies. If the law is to achieve a fair and just outcome when assessing financial loss it must recognise and give effect to this reality.[406]

It could be said, however, that in spite of these widely applicable observations on economic realities, the decisions awarding compound interest thus far are limited to claims where money itself is the subject of the action (damages for breach of contract relating to a loan agreement and loss of use of money the defendant has directly caused to be paid away by the claimant or withheld from the claimant), and might not extend to cases concerning late payment of a damages sum which arises in a claim which does not directly concern money, eg, pecuniary damages for trespass or battery in tort. But however cautious domestic courts in these jurisdictions have been in their application of the decisions, the reasoning is wide enough to apply to any money due, no matter the source of the obligation.

A second point is that the claimants still needed to prove that they incurred compound interest losses or lost the opportunity to invest at compound rates. If the interest losses are not proved, statutory interest at simple rates on damages or debt would prevail. If such loss was presumed, the reasoning on remoteness would allow recovery of compound interest. Lord Nicholls accepted that the 'common law's unwillingness to *presume* interest losses where payment [of a debt] is delayed is...unrealistic,...especially so at times when inflation abounds and prevailing interest rates are high' and that requiring proof of loss in each case might seem 'unduly formalistic'.[407] The common law, he reasoned, could live with that because if the claimant chose not to prove its loss, a remedy lay in statutory provisions on interest.[408] Likewise, the Canadian Supreme Court observed in respect of statutory interest that '[a]lthough not historically available, compound interest is well suited to compensate

[405] *Bank of America, Canada v Mutual Trust Co*, above n 400, para 44.
[406] *Sempra Metals Ltd v Commissioners of Inland Revenue*, above n 354, para 52.
[407] Ibid, para 97.
[408] Ibid. See also Lord Hope, para 17.

a plaintiff for the interval between when damages initially arise and when they are finally paid'.[409]

Recent reviews of statutory provisions on pre-judgment interest on damages and debts by the Law Commissions for England and Wales and Scotland have arrived at similar conclusions. The Law Commission of England and Wales said the award of interest was designed to compensate claimants for the cost of being kept out of their money and it should put the claimants in the position in which they would have been had the debt or damages been paid when they fell due.[410] Compound interest should be awarded because it represents commercial reality, as the claimant has missed an opportunity to invest or had to borrow to cover the loss, in either case at compound interest.[411] It concluded that the only objections to awarding compound rather than simple statutory interest were the difficulties of calculation and associated costs. In the Commission's view, in light of technological advances in computer software and ready access to interest rate data, this was no longer a decisive factor against compound interest in all cases for all claimants. Likewise the Scottish Law Commission consultation paper on pre-judgment interest proposed a statutory compound rate based on the cost of borrowing which would apply to all claimants. In its subsequent report, although it 'remain[ed] of the opinion that compounded interest is the most accurate way to calculate the value of loss of use of money', it decided against recommending compound statutory interest because it would make little difference to the outcome in most cases, and it was still 'viewed with suspicion as a statutory entitlement'.[412] That is, compound interest was not rejected because its loss could not be presumed or because it was too indirect (remote or unforeseeable) or a speculative estimation of loss, and it was not rejected because of any distinction between commercial and non-commercial claimants.

The conclusion which could be drawn from the judicial discussion and the work of the law commissions is that, but for the simple statutory interest provisions, there is no reason why interest on damages in all claims for all types of claimant should not be compound interest to reflect the economic reality of the cost of loss of use of money. International law has no equivalent to the rule on simple statutory interest which applies

---

[409] *Bank of America, Canada v Mutual Trust Co*, above n 400, para 38.
[410] Above n 138, para 1.9.   [411] Ibid, para 4.2.
[412] Above n 270, para 7.39. See generally paras 7.32–7.39. Similarly, the reason the UK Law Commission gave in 1978 in its Report on Interest, 1978 (LAW COM. No 88) for recommending that statutory pre-judgment interest on debts and damages remain simple was not because compound interest is too remote, but because compounding regularly to reflect ordinary practice would mean that the cost of calculation for small debts would be 'out of all proportion to the sum involved'. Setting a threshold sum for compound interest to meet this problem would be arbitrary, so 'whatever attempts are made at streamlining it, a system for compounding statutory interest is bound to be too crude to be fair in all cases or too intricate to be practicable' (at 85, paras 84–5). Nevertheless it recommended a rate based on the rate for the ordinary creditor borrowing money, the minimum lending rate of the Bank of England plus 1% for all claims (at 27, paras 86–7).

in many domestic systems and, therefore, there is nothing preventing international courts and tribunals from taking the step domestic courts cannot. Moreover, the application of simple rates—typically unquestioned by those who criticise compound rates—as well as leading to the possibility of undercompensation, can equally in some instances overcompensate claimants, as identified by the Law Commission for England and Wales. For example, the English statutory discretion to award pre-judgment interest on damages and debts is often exercised by awarding the post-judgment interest rate of 8% under the Judgments Act 1838, and this has remained the same during a period when base rates have fluctuated between 7.5% and 3.5%.[413] The move to central bank-based simple interest rates by the CFI and ECJ saw the interest rates awarded immediately drop by 2%.[414] The UNCITRAL Tribunal in *CME v Czech Republic* refused the request for compound interest on the basis that it was not required to "fully" compensate the damage sustained...having regard to the generous interest provision of the Czech Statute' which provided for double the central bank discount rate prevailing at the time the principal became due.[415]

It has been acknowledged that the application of statutory simple rates which are higher than base rates might to some extent be used to offset the lack of compounding.[416] But if this leads to overcompensation, it abrogates the compensatory principle behind the award of interest on damages. It might also be questioned whether very high simple statutory default interest rates which contain a deterrent or penalty element, such as that in the German BGB (5–8% above base) or the Czech code (twice the central bank discount rate), or the EC Directive on Combating Late Payment in Commercial Transactions (8% above national bank base rate), are appropriate in international law where the principle behind pre-award interest is compensation for loss of use of the principal sums and not the achievement of other policy objectives such as penalising behaviour which damages the market.[417] Thus the difficulty of relying on simple rates based on uncontroversial domestic provisions in the absence of some explicit contract or treaty basis for doing so is that it may well not meet the international law requirements on reparations. On the other hand, it has been said that the 'practical advantages of greater certainty and intuitive fairness of turning to the law of the respondent state might outweigh this problem'.[418] But certainty can be achieved by other means and it is not intuitively fair to automatically turn to the law of the respondent state in all international claims: it must be established it is fair and reasonable to do so. In any case, the trend in international

---

[413] Section 35A(5) Supreme Court Act (UK), Law Commission Report, above n 138, paras 3.9, 3.21.
[414] See above n 198–202 and accompanying text.
[415] Above n 65, paras 642–3.
[416] Law Commission Report, above n 138, para 1.6.
[417] Ibid, para 2.42.
[418] Gray, above n 1, 9.

practice is to focus on where the loss might sound, and not to rely on domestic statutory rates.

In summary, the work of domestic courts and law commissions suggests that there is no reason why compound interest cannot be awarded in all types of claim entailing pecuniary damage and to all types of claimant, and that loss of use at compound interest rates can be presumed without proof and is not too indirect or unforeseeable. Thus the award of compound interest in international law need not be confined to investment arbitrations. Indeed, the award of simple interest may not necessarily result in an award which is less onerous on the respondent given the generosity of some simple statutory interest rates. The final arguments discussed here against the award of compound interest, both applicable to all claimants, are that the award would be out of all proportion to the principal damages sum and that fair reparation need not represent the full loss in international law.

The amount awarded in interest would be out of proportion to the principal damages sum: The Iran-US Claims Tribunal has suggested that this may be a reason for refusing compound interest.[419] This contention is easily dismissed. F A Mann strongly criticised the Tribunal for what he said was the misconceived revival of a peculiar and obsolete Roman law doctrine, because the respondent had 'enjoyed the fruits of the money withheld' during the period of delay in payment and any delay caused by the claimant could be dealt with accordingly.[420] Moreover, the concern that a compound interest award might exceed the principal awarded has not concerned investment arbitration tribunals which have made awards which do just that.[421]

Fair reparation need not represent full loss: Some decisions have referred to the proposition that reparation should not necessarily compensate for all losses which are a direct result of the breach.[422] Even if this was to be accepted, which is doubted in the absence of clear reasons for departing from the principle of full compensation,[423] it is not apparent why this should sound specifically in a rejection of an award of compound methods of calculating interest in favour of simple.

The criticism of compound interest awards appears to be caught up in a larger concern about excessive damages awards, how damages should be quantified, and whether questions of proof, causation and foreseeability

---

[419] *International Systems & Controls Corp v NIGC*, above n 366.

[420] Above n 301, 585–586.

[421] Eg, *Santa Elena*, above n 142, and *Wena Hotels*, above n 170.

[422] Eg, by the ECHR in *The Former King of Greece* case, above n 367, para 78. The Court set out some of the circumstances in which less than full recovery might be justified—measures of economic reform, or measures designed to achieve greater social justice or change in the country's constitutional system from a monarchy to a republic. As the Court itself noted, whether the individual concerned is a national of the state or a foreign investor might—but not necessarily—raises different considerations as to whether the individual should bear any burden in a public interest calculus.

[423] Eg, those outlined by the ECHR in the *Former King of Greece*, ibid, or the limited settlement funds of the UNCC (see n 135 above).

or remoteness of loss are properly addressed. Perhaps the award of simple interest on grounds of precedent and without discussion is one way of keeping damages 'fair', 'equitable' or 'appropriate' without engaging in the larger debate over whether full reparation should be awarded and without engaging in more detail in difficult questions of quantification, evidence of loss and directness. But the problem with this approach is that if interest on damages or default interest is to compensate for loss of use—and the balance of recent practice affirms this principle—and if it is accepted by domestic and international courts, tribunals and law commissions that compound interest reflects economic realities, and therefore that loss at compound rates is a direct (foreseeable and not too remote) result of failing to pay the principal when it became due, then an award of simple interest may not seem fair, appropriate or equitable, especially where it under- or over- compensates the claimant.

To conclude, the reasons given for refusing awards of compound interest can be challenged on the basis of principle and practice, which indicates that the answer to the question of whether there is a case for compound interest in all awards of interest on damages is 'yes'. If the case for interest on damages awards at compound rates is compelling, a separate but related question is whether an award at simple rates is ever justified.

(iv) Is the Award of Simple Interest Justifiable?

The award of simple rather than compound interest may be justified in certain circumstances. The main reason given by domestic law commissions for awarding simple instead of compound statutory pre-judgment interest is that the practical difficulties and costs associated with calculation may outweigh the benefits of a more accurate measure of loss by compound calculations, especially in the case of small claims and claims that have been outstanding for a short time. For this reason the Law Commission of England and Wales recommended a presumption that interest should be simple for all awards of less than £15,000 and for awards over £15,000 which have been outstanding for less than a year,[424] because awards below £15,000 are too small to justify the cost of calculation, cases below that amount are normally dealt with quickly and the costs of calculation should not be disproportionate to the amount at stake.[425] Judge Brower in the Iran-US Claims Tribunal has also observed that the 'the evidentiary complexity of substantiating "interest damages"... may render the effort involved, for litigants and judges alike, disproportionate to the result. In short, the game may not be worth the candle'.[426] The difficulties of calculation have been, however, considerably reduced by new technology and the ready availability of historical data on interest rates now going back over several decades.

---

[424] Above n 138, paras 6.23–4.   [425] Ibid, para 5.30.
[426] Concurring and dissenting opinion, *McCollough*, above n 58, 43.

(d) Differences Between Established Tribunals and Courts and Sole Matter Arbitration Tribunals

A final aspect of the examination of the jurisprudence in respect of the particulars of interest awards is from the perspective of the nature of the court or tribunal, ie whether it is a standing court or tribunal or an *ad hoc* tribunal established for one matter. Established courts and tribunals are more likely to adopt standardised approaches to the award of interest than tribunals established for a particular case. The mixed commissions of the 19th and early 20th centuries tended towards a more uniform approach within tribunals,[427] but as today there were variances between tribunals. The fact a tribunal is standing rather than *ad hoc* does have implications for its treatment of interest awards. The Iran-US Claims Tribunal held in the *Sylvania* decision that it was 'in the interest of justice and fairness to develop and apply a consistent approach to the awarding of interest in cases before it'.[428] The EU courts have established approaches to interest which are applied in a uniform manner between claimants, although there are some slight variations in treatment of pre-judgment interest other than in EU staff claims. The ECHR and Inter-American Court of Human Rights do not appear to have an entirely consistent approach to pre-judgment interest, although the prevalent practice of lump sum awards makes this difficult to ascertain. Both have settled post-judgment interest approaches. The Iran-US Claims Tribunal also has reasonably consistent jurisprudence in that one of the two precedents as to interest awards—a rate based on the US six month certificate of deposit rate over the period of account in *Sylvania* or the 10% rate of the *McCollough* Case—is usually followed.[429]

There are some important policy reasons which support a uniform approach within a court or tribunal or domestic jurisdiction, even if it

---

[427] Early commissions often addressed the question of interest on awards separately or in a key decision which was then generally followed subsequently, for example: the 1839 US-Mexican Claims Commission settled on a practice of awarding 5% in the absence of an applicable contract rate (as reported in Moore, *History and Digest* (1898) Vol 2, 1243); the 1903 German-Venezuelan commission gave a general opinion on interest in *Christern & Co, Becker & Co, Max Fischbach, Richard Friedericy, Otto Kummerow and A Dauman Cases*, UNRIAA, Vol X, 363 (the Commission said that 'on account of the importance and gravity of the question, [it] called for a special argument thereon' (at 366)); Judge Huber set out the general approach to interest of the British Claims in the Spanish Zone of Morocco in *The rapport sur la question des intérêts*, UNRIAA, Vol II, 650; the 1923 US-Mexico Commission set down a uniform treatment of interest in *Illinois Central Railroad Co v Mexico*, 6 December 1926, UNRIAA, Vol IV, 134. However, the General Claims Commission took a different approach (at 310–1). After a number of inconsistent awards, it settled on payment of 6% interest on cases involving contractual claims and forced loans running from the date of the breach until the date of the Commission's last award; and the French-Mexican Commission set out its general approach in *Georges Pinson*, 1928, UNRIAA, Vol V, 327, esp 448–53 (This approach prevailed until the reorganisation of the Commission, after which time interest was not awarded in any cases) (see further A H Feller, *The Mexican Claims Commissions, 1923–1934; A study in the law and procedure of international tribunals* (1935), 312); the 1923 US-Germany Mixed Claims Commission set out its approach in Administrative Decision No III, (1923) 2 *Annual Digest of Pub Int'l Law* 211.

[428] Above n 57, 320.

[429] See above n 188–194, 209–214 and accompanying text.

means an interest award is more or less than an individual claimant actually lost. Uniformity builds perceptions of fairness and equal treatment where there are large numbers of litigants based in the same regions and/or with claims arising out of the same events, and is administratively efficient and more cost effective. These considerations may be factored into an interest rate formula, leading to one based on an investment rate on low-risk government securities, such as the *Sylvania* precedent in the Iran-US Claims Tribunal, or a borrowing rate which reflects secured lending to private individuals on mortgages as well as large commercial borrowers, as proposed by the Law Commissions of England and Wales and Scotland.[430] Considerations of administrative efficiencies and fairness or equality of treatment between all claimants before the same tribunal do not have the same force, as is evident in the variety of rates and methods of calculation adopted by these *ad hoc* tribunals.

Where claims are large and/or long standing, the balance shifts from the cost efficiencies in calculation supporting a uniformly applied objective rate towards assessing loss of use subjectively, based on the facts in the case. This may well be reflected in the parties' conduct of the case.[431] Choosing the interest rate and method of calculation based on the circumstances of the case and the successful claimant (net creditor or debtor), rather than on the application of a uniform interest rate and method of calculation adopted by previous tribunal practice, may well be more appropriate. This is the case in investment treaty arbitrations which are heard by *ad hoc* tribunals established for the purpose of hearing individual claims. Some conformity in approach or principled distinctions between cases is still, however, desirable if interest on damages is awarded on the basis of presumed loss and measured by an objective or conventional measure of loss, especially in cases which arise under the same treaty and in respect of the same events for similar claimants, such as the ICSID cases against Argentina arising out of its 1999–2002 economic crisis.[432]

---

[430] Above n 138, paras 3.35–3.37 (Law Commission for England and Wales) and above n 270, paras 7.11–13 (Scottish Law Commission). As noted above, in *Sempra Metals Ltd v Commissioners of Inland Revenue,* the respondent preferred one rate to be set for all 50–70 cases, regardless of whether each claimant was a net investor or borrower, and an ordinary commercial borrowing rate was ordered on this basis (above n 358).

[431] If the parties do not bother to make arguments on the correct interest rate and method of calculation they implicitly confer a greater discretion on the arbitrators. As the ICSID annulment panel in *Wena Hotels,* above n 170, explained: 'extended practice shows international tribunals and arbitration panels usually dispose of a large margin of discretion when fixing interest. It is normal, therefore, that very limited reasons are given for a decision which is left almost entirely to the discretion of the tribunal ... The requirement to state the reasons supporting the allocation of interest appears particularly weak when, like in these proceedings ... both Parties were not more determinative than referring to the allocation of appropriate interest, thus conferring to the Tribunal a wide discretionary power to assess interest' (paras 96–7).

[432] *CMS Gas,* above n 152, *Azurix v Argentina,* above n 152, *Sempra v Argentina,* above n 152, *Enron,* above n 152, *LG&E,* above n 152. All claimants were US nationals making claims under the same Argentina-US BIT. The rates, method of calculation and, if compound, intervals of compounding in those cases varied considerably, even though the interest rate was set objectively in each.

B. Post-Award Interest

1. Review of Practice

In general post-award interest has been awarded by international courts and tribunals of the last 50 years, although they do not always make a distinction between the award of pre-award interest and post-award interest.[433] An express conferral of power to award post-award interest is rare,[434] but very few tribunals have considered that they do not have jurisdiction to award it, and these decisions are found only in the earlier jurisprudence of mixed commissions or arbitral tribunals.[435] Post-award interest was either refused or the end dates for interest accrual fixed at a date earlier than the date of payment of the award only where tribunals concluded that the jurisdiction conferred on them by the States parties did not confer jurisdiction to order damages running indefinitely until payment.[436]

International courts and tribunals do not usually explain their reasons for awarding post-award interest and the treatment of such interest, ie start date, rate and method of calculation, is not uniform. Standing courts and tribunals, while they differ in approach from one another, tend on the whole to maintain internal consistency in approach; but there is little consistency between arbitration tribunal awards. In a recent decision, an arbitration tribunal even refused to award post-award interest

---

[433] The commentaries to Article 38 of the Articles on State Responsibility state that it does not apply to moratory or post-award interest (see above n 44 and accompanying text), but Article 38 stipulates that interest is to run until date of payment which is, in adjudicated cases, after the award.

[434] Examples treaties excluding post-award interest: Article IV of the Special Agreement of 30 June 1921 for the *Norwegian Ship Owners* arbitration provided for post-award interest of 6% per annum, running from the date of decision to date of payment (UNRIAA, Vol I, 309, 311, (1923) 17 AJIL 362, 395–6), Article XII of the 1921 Protocol for Arbitration of the Landreau Claim against Peru (UNRIAA, Vol I, 349).

[435] Examples of the exclusion of post-award interest: the 1910 Special Agreement of 8 August 1910 establishing the third US-British arbitral tribunal (UNRIAA, Vol VI, 9) and the 1948 settlement treaty between the US and Yugoslavia (recorded in the *Senser Claim* before the United States International Claims Commission in respect of the claims of US nationals against a settlement fund established by the treaty, report published in 1955, 20 ILR 240, 241–2).

[436] *Motion for allowance of interest on awards from the date until their payment*, 1903 Britain-Venezuela Commission, UNRIAA, Vol IX, 470, 470–1. The 1903 German-Venezuelan Commission also refused post-award interest because it had not been agreed by the States parties in the Protocol in circumstances where the parties had included very specific provisions for payment as between them, *Christern & Co, Becker & Co, Max Fischbach, Richard Friedericy, Otto Kummerow and A Dauman Cases*, UNRIAA, Vol X, 363. The genesis of the commission as a body set up to resolve a dispute between States was very much at the forefront of the reasoning in both decisions: 'It is material to remember, in considering this question, that while the amounts are for the ultimate benefit of the claimants, they are to be included in an aggregate sum of money to be paid by the Government of Venezuela to the Government of Germany' (at 368). See for example the decisions of the 1903 Italian-Venezuelan Claims Commission, *Cervetti*, UNRIAA, Vol X, 492, the Protocol of 13 February 1903, Article V, (at 498) and the *Postal Treaty* claim (at 499), where the umpire said that it was 'to be borne in mind that claimants presenting themselves before this Commission appear before a body of limited powers, and are to be regarded as accepting its drawbacks in consideration of anticipated benefits. One possible drawback is the loss of interest after the termination of the Commission.' The 1923 US-Mexico General Claims Commission in *Illinois Central Railroad Co v Mexico* refused interest running beyond the date of termination of its labours because, even though its constituent treaty was silent on the point, an earlier treaty between the US and Great Britain which did address post-award interest had excluded it.

because the applicant had failed to ask for it in accordance with the procedural requirements.[437]

The range of practice can be loosely grouped into three general categories:

(1) pre-judgment interest continues to run on the principal damages sum(s) only until date of payment and not on the total amount of the award including costs and expenses. That is, the award is not treated as replacing the original obligation with a new obligation to comply with the award, but the original obligation is merely confirmed and liquidated by the award;

(2) post-judgment interest is treated separately from pre-judgment interest, and only begins to run on the total amount of judgment (ie damages including any interest awarded, plus costs and expenses) after a grace period for compliance has passed until payment;

(3) post-judgment interest is treated separately from any pre-judgment interest and runs on the total award as in (2), but runs from date of judgment until payment without any grace period for payment.

Category (1) includes the practice of the Iran-US Claims Tribunal. It allows interest to accrue from date of breach, or the date when payment otherwise becomes due, to the date when payment is effected, and does not include any post-judgment interest on other elements of the award such as costs and expenses.[438] This might be because the Tribunal considers that it can only award interest under its compensatory jurisdiction or because of the security of the payment arrangements under which the Iran-US Claims Tribunal operates. The same approach has been adopted by a number of arbitration tribunals[439] and some judgments of the EU courts.[440]

The practice of the European Court of Human Rights and, more recently, the Inter-American Court of Human Rights falls into category (2). Both now award post-judgment interest as a matter of course.[441] They make a clear distinction between interest in the award (pre-judg-

---

[437] *Sempra v Argentina*, above n 152, paras 484–5. The tribunal in *Enron*, above n 152, cited by the tribunal in *Sempra v Argentina*, did not award post-award interest either, but gave no reasons for not doing so. Nor was post-award interest discussed or awarded in *Aminoil*, above n 292, para 178, although the arbitration agreement included a wide power to award interest (Article III(1)(iv)) and the provision on execution of the award was silent as to interest (Article V) (532–5).

[438] See, eg, *Development and Resources Corp v Iran* (1990) 25 Iran-US CTR 20, *General Electric Company v Iran* (1991) 26 Iran-US CTR 148 and *Levitt v Iran* (1991) 14 Iran-US CTR 145.

[439] *AAPL v Sri Lanka*, above n 64, *CME v Czech Republic*, above n 65, *Tecmed*, above n 64, para 201 (each party to bear their own costs and expenses), *Feldman*, above n 152, *Pope & Talbot*, above n 152, *PSEG Global Inc v Turkey*, above n 152. In *PSEG Global Inc v Turkey* the Tribunal said the interest was to run until payment of the award so no separate treatment of post-award interest was necessary (at para 351).

[440] See cases cited at above n 88–89 where default interest is payable from date of claim or complaint, or date payment fell due if later.

[441] The European Court of Human Rights has awarded post-judgment default interest automatically since 1996 (Shelton, *Remedies*, above n 41, p 351), For an example where post-judgment default interest was not awarded, see *Pine Valley Developments*, above n 70, paras 20–1.

ment) and default interest on the award (post-judgment). The ECHR's Court Rules contain specific provision for post-judgment interest, treating it as an element of just satisfaction.[442] Current practice is to provide for default interest on the entire judgment sum, ie the aggregate of compensation, including any interest, costs and expenses,[443] to run from the date 3 months from the date of judgment until payment, calculated at the European Central Bank marginal lending rate plus 3%. The Grand Chamber explained that the move to an interest rate based on the euro for post-judgment interest in *Meftah and Others v France* occurred because 'default interest rate should reflect the choice of the euro as the reference currency.'[444] The choice of the marginal lending rate as the base rate and a 3% increment was not explained. By moving beyond the respondent State's statutory rate to a rate based on the euro, the court effectively arrived at its own interest rate formula. The ECHR sets a 2% higher post-judgment default interest rate than the ECJ and CFI: the ECB's marginal lending rate is 1% higher than the rate for main refinancing operations used as the base rate by the ECJ and CFI, and the ECJ and CFI set the percentage increase at 2% as compared with the ECHR's 3% increase.[445]

The Inter-American Court of Human Rights Rules do not make any provision for post-judgment interest, but a regular practice appears to have developed whereby default interest is awarded on the total award (ie, pecuniary compensation plus non-pecuniary compensation, costs and expenses) if the award is not complied with within one year from the date of the judgment, at the bank rate for arrears in the respondent state.[446] Many arbitration tribunals have adopted the same approach, with grace periods for payment ranging between 30 and 90 days and usually adopting the same rate for pre- and post-award interest.[447]

---

[442] Rule 75(3), as amended 13 December 2004.

[443] See, eg, the operative provisions of the judgments discussed above at n 71–78.

[444] Judgment, Application nos. 32911/96, 35237/97 and 34595/97), 26 July 2002, para 61. Before the introduction of the euro in 1999, the ECHR applied the relevant statutory rate of the respondent State, eg, *Beyeler v Italy (No 2)*, above n 78.

[445] See, eg, the discussion of default interest rates awarded by the EU courts above at n 198 to 202. The 'marginal lending rate' used by the ECHR is interest rate on the Eurosystem's marginal lending facility which banks may use for overnight credit from a national central bank that is part of the Eurosystem: Glossary, European Central Bank website, http://www.ecb.int/home/glossary/html/glossa.en.html. For a definition of the main refinancing rate, see n 198 above.

[446] Eg, *Maritza Urrutia v Guatemala*, 27 November 2003, Series C No 103, para 192; *Myrna Mack Chang v Guatemala*, 25 November 2003, Series C No 101, para 299; *Bulacio v Argentina*, 18 September 2003, Series C No 100 para 159, *La Cantuta v Peru*, 29 November 2006, Series C No 162, para 252.

[447] *AMT v Zaire* (1997) 5 ICSID Reports 11, 60 days; *ME Cement v Egypt*, above n 64, 30 days; *Occidental*, above n 323, 30 days, *Libyan Arab Foreign Investment Company (LAFICO) and the Republic of Burundi*, Arbitral Tribunal (1991) 96 ILR 279, para 80, 332; *Siemens AG v Argentina*, above n 64, para 403, 30 days; *Azurix v Argentina*, above n 152, paras 339–40, 60 days; *ADC*, above n 155, para 543, 30 days; *Wena*, above n 170, 30 days, *SPP(ME)*, above n 68, 248, 30 days.

As for category (3)—treating post-judgment interest separately and running on all sums awarded, including any interest, without allowing a grace period for payment—some of the practice of the CFI follows this pattern,[448] as have several arbitration tribunals, although there are far fewer arbitration awards of this type than in categories (1) and (2).[449]

There are two kinds of decisions which do not award pre-award interest but award interest from the date of the award: first, those that do so because the loss is valued at the date of award at current value[450] and, second, those where the tribunal considers that interest on damages as an aspect of compensation can run only from the date of its award specifying or liquidating the amount to be paid, even if the damages are pecuniary in nature and arose and are valued at an earlier date.[451] While the first kind of decision is unproblematic, as noted above in the discussion of start date, the second approach can be criticised for resulting in under-compensation.[452] In any event, it is quite rare and not preferred practice.

There are some one-off solutions which fall outside the three categories described above. In *Santa Elena* post-award interest was awarded to run from the date of the award until payment, but only if the award was not paid within 21 days.[453] A variation on this approach was taken in *Metalclad*:[454] the pre-award rate was to continue running until 45 days after the date of the award on the total sum awarded, at which time it would increase by shortening the intervals of compounding from annual to monthly intervals. The award in *CMS Gas* was to similar effect, the simple pre-judgment rate running until 60 days after the award and then increasing by the introduction of compounding. The approach of ITLOS in the *MV Saiga (No 2)* is also unusual. In respect of pecuniary losses, interest was set to run from the date of loss to the date of payment, making no distinction between pre- and post-judgment interest. But in respect of non-pecuniary losses it awarded interest at a lower rate, to start running after a 3 month grace period from the date of award.[455] The lower interest rate suggests that no conceptual distinction was being made between pre- and post-judgment interest, in that interest was not running on the entire award sum but on the principal damages sum for non-pecuniary damage after its liquidation. But if that is the case, the grace period is difficult to explain.

---

[448] *AfCon*, above n 91; *Camar*, above n 91.

[449] *Nycomb*, above n 65; *Biloune*, above n 206; *SD Myers*, above n 153, paras 50–2; *LG&E*, above n 152, para 115.

[450] Eg, *The Lighthouses Arbitration*, above n 125. See also *LETCO*, above n 67; *ADC*, above n 125; and *AIG v Kazakhstan*, above n 112.

[451] Eg, *The Wimbledon*, above n 54. Interest was claimed on the losses incurred by the French charterer from 21 March 1921, the date 'The Wimbledon' had been refused passage. The PCIJ rejected this start date on the basis that interest could not run until the date of judgment, 'the moment when the amount of the sum due has been fixed and the obligation to pay established' (ibid).

[452] See above n 164 to 166 and accompanying text.

[453] Above n 142.   [454] Above n 64.

[455] Above n 61, para 175.

One practice, unique to the Inter-American Court, is to make provision for paid but uncollected compensation awards. If the recipient is unable to claim the award, it is to be held on trust for them for a period of 10 years in a banking institution in the respondent State in US dollars and if unclaimed it is to be repaid to the State with accrued interest.[456]

2. Compound Post-Award Interest

Several arbitration tribunal decisions and one CFI judgment have awarded compound post-award interest. Investment arbitration tribunals which have awarded pre-award compound interest usually award compound post-award interest at the same rate.[457] The only discussion of post-award compound interest is in *ADC v Hungary*. The referred to the trend in investor-State arbitration to award compound interest because this reflected economic reality and said compound interest was 'a mechanism to ensure that the compensation awarded the Claimant is appropriate in the circumstances'.[458]

Some tribunals have awarded pre-award interest at a compound rate and post-award interest at a simple rate, and *vice versa*. In *Santa Elena*, notable for awarding compound interest as part of the principal sum of compensation, post-award interest was only awarded at a simple interest rate of 6% per annum.[459] The Tribunal in *CMS Gas*, by contrast, moved from pre-award simple interest at the 6 month US Treasury Bill rate to semi-annual compounding to start 60 days from the award.[460] Neither Tribunal explained its decision on post-award interest. The reason why the CFI awarded compound post-judgment interest in *AfCon*, the only EU court decision to award compound post-judgment interest, may be inferred from its explanation as to why it awarded pre-judgment simple interest—because the claimant had not asked for it. This suggests the CFI might have awarded pre-judgment compound interest had it asked and so the case is not indicative of a different approach to post-judgment interest.[461]

3. Conclusions

The award of post-award interest is the norm. The main difference between the three main trends in practice identified above concerns the

---

[456] See, eg, *Miguel Castro*, above n 226, para 466.

[457] See the awards cited at nn 323–324. The exceptions are *Santa Elena, AIG v Kazakhstan* and *Vivendi v Argentina (Award No 2)*. In *Vivendi (Award No 2)* compound interest was awarded on the principal damages sums to run from date due until payment, but simple post-award interest was awarded on the costs award (para 11.1(v)–(vi)). In *Enron* and *Sempra v Argentina* no post-award interest was awarded because it was not claimed.

[458] Above n 125, paras 521–2.

[459] Above n 142, para 111(3) (the *dispositif*). See also *AIG v Kazakhstan*, above n 112, where simple post-award interest was awarded on both principal damages sums, including the amount on which pre-judgment compound interest had been awarded, and no interest was awarded on costs and expenses (at 116–8).

[460] Above n 152, para 4 of the *dispostif*.

[461] *AFCon*, above n 91, paras 131–3.

amount on which post-award interest runs—whether interest continues to run on the principal compensation sum, or on the total amount awarded including pre-award interest and any costs and expenses. The former reflects the principle that interest on damages runs from the date it falls due until payment and avoids any appearance of an award of interest upon interest where this might be problematic, but the latter is justified by the change in character of the claim when judgment is given—it then becomes enforcement of the award—and the fact that costs and expenses awarded become due as of the judgment date.[462] The practicalities of administration have also been given as a reason for merging all aspects of the award into one judgment sum on which interest runs.[463]

While there are differences in post-award practice concerning the amount on which post-award interest runs and the start date, the interest rate awarded is usually the same as for pre-award interest.[464] This makes sense as the primary reason for awarding pre- and post-award interest is the same, namely the obligation to compensate for loss of the use of a monetary sum.[465] García-Amador, Sohn and Baxter also cite the need to induce prompt compliance with an award as a justification for the requirement to pay interest on the award.[466] Thus, on the rare occasions where the post-award rate is higher than the pre-award rate (because of the imposition of compounding or an increase in the frequency of the intervals of compounding), the answer may lie in control of procedure by increasing the incentive for prompt payment of the award sum.[467] While this approach appears to be justified in principle, traditionally international courts and tribunals have been reluctant to treat states in the same category as defaulting debtors in respect of post-judgment interest.[468]

Higher post-award interest also has ramifications where stays of execution are granted pending annulment decisions, as was the case in *CMS*

---

[462] Although the respondent may not be penalised for default in the obligation to pay the judgment sum until any grace period given has expired.

[463] See Scottish Law Commission Report, above n 270, para 7.41.

[464] A similar approach is taken in some domestic jurisdictions, eg in 1985 Article 1153-I was added to the French Civil Code making separate provision for post-judgment interest at the same statutory rate as pre-judgment interest under Article 1153. Common law systems typically make separate legal provision for pre-judgment interest and judgment interest, and the latter, unlike pre-judgment interest, is set at a specific rate. However in practice claimants often ask for and are awarded the judgment rate as pre-judgment interest: Law Commission Report, above n 138, paras 3.16, 3.21.

[465] J Y Gotanda, *Supplemental Damages in Private International Law* (Kluwer, 1998), 3; *Bank of America* (Supreme Court of Canada), above n 400, para 50.

[466] Above n 6, 343–4.

[467] Gotanda, above n 465, Opinion of Advocate General Van Gerven, *Marshall v Southampton and South West Hampshire Area Health Authority* [1993] ECR I-4381, 4397–8. Salvioli notes that post-award rates may be higher: above n 137, at 281, 284.

[468] The International Court of Justice in the 1923 *Wimbledon* case refused to fix a higher interest rate in the event of the judgment not being complied with by the expiry of the 3 month period (fixed by the Court) for compliance on the grounds that the 'Court neither can nor should contemplate such a contingency' (above n 54, at 32). See also *Libyan Arab Foreign Investment Company (LAFICO) and the Republic of Burundi*, Arbitral Tribunal (1991) 96 ILR 279, 332, para 80; *First Eagle Sogen*, above n 65.

Gas where higher post-award interest was awarded. Provided it is not a frivolous claim, seeking an annulment is, even if unsuccessful, a legitimate reason for the postponement of the execution of an award. In this circumstance, the rationale for a higher post-award rate may no longer apply, at least for the period until the annulment request is refused.[469]

There is only one case, *Santa Elena*, where the post-award rate is lower than the pre-award rate. The Tribunal gave no reason for this. It may be because of its distinction between interest awards in cases of injury and simple breach of contract, in which the tendency to award simple interest had been 'principally manifested', and those relating to the valuation of property or property rights,[470] or because of a distinction between interest in respect of losses of property rights and loss of the use of the judgment sum. But, as pointed out above, these distinctions can be called into question: if interest is said to be compensation for the loss of use of the principal monetary sum, there is no reason to distinguish between the source of the right giving rise to the principal sum when fixing the interest rate. Similarly, where the principal award sum is based on restitution for unjust enrichment rather than compensation, the enrichment continues at the same rate until date of payment.[471]

IV. CONCLUSION

The practice of international courts, tribunals and commissions, as well as domestic law, confirms that the principle underpinning awards of interest on principal sums contemplated by Article 38 of the Articles on State Responsibility is compensation for loss of use of the principal sum during the period of delay in payment, otherwise known as interest on damages or default interest. This is the most common form of interest award. It has certain key features: the loss being compensated by interest on damages is presumed as a result of breach (proof of loss is not required), and it is presumed that such loss is a direct (proximate and foreseeable) result of the delay. The awards also suggest that the rationale underpinning interest on damages awards may be shifting to encompass depreciation due to inflation, acknowledging the relationship between interest rates and inflation. Inflation rates may even be an alternative

---

[469] ICSID Case No ARB/01/08 (Annulment Proceeding), Decision on the Request for a Continued Stay of Enforcement of the Award, 1 September 2006. Neither the decision nor an undertaking given by the Argentine government to comply with the award if ultimately unsuccessful dealt with the question of the higher post-award interest formula. It did hold that any losses CMS incurred by reason of the stay should the annulment be ultimately unsuccessful would be dealt with by interest. This aspect of the stay was not addressed by the Annulment Committee in its Partial Annulment decision of 25 September 2007, ICSID Case No ARB/01/8 (Annulment Proceeding).

[470] *Santa Elena v Costa Rica*, above n 142, para 97.

[471] See for example, *Bank of America*, above n 400, para 51, *Sempra Metals Ltd v Commissioners of Inland Revenue*, above n 354, para 129 (per Lord Nicholls).

measure of the delay in payment of the principal sum where the damages are valued at an earlier date.

Interest on the principal sum for the loss of its use for the period of delay in payment is not the only form of interest award. Interest may also be awarded as specific damages where interest losses have actually been incurred and are not too remote or unforeseeable ('interest as damages'), or as the measure of the principal damages sum under Article 36. Legislative regimes established by regional legal systems such as the European Union or *sui generis* remedial regimes such as that in the World Trade Organisation may call for tailored monetary remedies which depart from the general compensatory principles articulated in *Chorzów Factory*.[472] New categories of interest award have developed which do not have the objective of compensating for loss of use of a principal damages sum, but rather restoration of the *status quo ante* under Article 35.

Regardless of the form of interest award, in the absence of an applicable statute, treaty or contract, the principle which underpins it should guide the particulars of the award, ie rate, method of calculation and period of account. The breach in question might therefore suggest an interest award measured by reference to the respondent's gain rather than the claimant's loss. The principle underpinning an interest award does not, however, give any further guidance as to what rate, method of calculation or period of account should be applied, by necessity leaving a wide discretion to the adjudicator.

Because of the varied expressions of this discretion, there are different approaches to rate, method of calculation and period of account in awards. This is not necessarily problematic. It reflects the different jurisdictions of international courts, tribunals and commissions and the variety of claims now dealt with by international law. But international jurisprudence is still open to the charge of inconsistency, particularly in respect of interest on damages awards. There are some differences in outcome which are difficult to explain, and even within the same international tribunal or court outcomes can be unpredictable: for example, the apparently one-off approach of the CFI in *Afcon*, the approach of the ECHR in *Scordino* as compared with that in *Beyeler*, the two strands of jurisprudence in the Iran-US Claims Tribunal, and the different interest awards made against Argentina for breaches of the same provisions under the US-Argentina bilateral investment treaty.

Nevertheless, there is developing practice, both domestic and international, which provides principled guidelines for the treatment of interest awards (rate, method of calculation and period of account) in the absence of a treaty provisions or an agreement between the parties or a requirement to apply domestic law. The basic consensus can be summarized as follows:

---

[472] *Case Concerning the Factory at Chorzów (Merits)*, 1928, PCIJ Reports, Series A, No 17, p 47.

- the start date of the period of account—'the date the principal falls due'—may be date of breach or loss or a representative date where the breach occurs over a period of time (eg, as in a creeping expropriation), although date of notice of the claim may be preferred;
- interest rates set by formulas based on central bank or market rates are preferred;
- where central bank and market-based interest rates are used the calculation method adopted should factor in movements in the rate over the period of account, rather than fixing the rate by reference to the rate prevailing at the date of decision or the date the principal fell due;
- concerns that compound but not simple interest losses are not sufficiently direct (ie, too remote or unforeseeable) are increasingly considered to be no longer tenable because of modern financial realities. The recent changes in the treatment of interest awards by international and domestic courts and tribunals and law commissions appear to be underpinned by increasing social acceptance of compound interest and recognition of the economic realities of everyday life. Technology now provides tools to make the calculations of compound interest quickly and accurately, and there are interest rate vehicles which have existed for a number of decades in more or less current form which give a steady stream of historical data;
- simple interest can be justified where the benefit of a more accurate compound measure of loss is not justified when compared with the disadvantages in administration and costs, eg, for sums outstanding for a short period or for small awards where it would not make any meaningful difference to the amount of the award;
- where the claimant claims 'interest on damages' without more, ie without establishing directness or loss (the equivalent of statutory interest on damages or default interest) it seems that at least the loss of return on a low-risk investment can be presumed and it is therefore appropriate to award interest measured on an objective basis by reference to an interest rate based on a return on a low-risk investment, such as government securities or government guaranteed investments, compounding at the intervals dictated by the rate chosen;
- where the claimant seeks 'interest on damages' and shows that it is a net borrower, then an objective, representative measure of that loss based on central bank or market rates for lending to prime or low-risk borrowers, compounding at the intervals dictated by the rate chosen may be appropriate. This will usually be a vehicle chosen by reference to the claimant's home State, but may refer to an international measure such as the LIBOR in the currency of the award;
- where the claimant actually proves it has incurred interest losses and claims 'interest as damages' it is appropriate to either apply the interest actually paid or lost by the investor (a 'subjective measure');

• standing tribunals can justify applying the same interest award formula, whether based on borrowing rates or investment rates, to all claimants before them, even if this results in under- or over-compensation for some claimants;
• restitutionary remedies or unjust enrichment claims are based on the respondent's gain, not the claimant's loss and can be measured either subjectively by reference to the respondent's actual gain or objectively by reference to presumed gain, and the function of the interest award should be reflected in the rate and method of calculation adopted;
• similar considerations as to rate and method of calculation apply to post- award interest and to pre-award interest, and it is appropriate to apply the same interest rate formula for the rate.

THE NINETEENTH CENTURY LAW OF THE SEA AND THE BRITISH ABOLITION OF THE SLAVE TRADE

By JEAN ALLAIN*

It would be difficult to underestimate the relevance of the issue of the slave trade in nineteenth-century international relations. The move by Great Britain to suppress the slave trade was *the* issue with global implications during most of that century, as little else required the collective coordination of European States, newly-independent American States and other emerging "civilized nations". However, the process of establishing an international regime which sought to outlaw the slave trade reflected an international system lacking the tools of modern statecraft. In effect Great Britain was left to its own devices in seeking to achieve the suppression of the slave trade at sea. The limited contact between States meant that the establishment of law regarding the slave trade was a slow and awkward process which, though agreed to in principle at the Congress of Vienna in 1815, only emerged as a binding universal instrument at the Brussels Conference of 1890, and ultimately led to the suppression of both the slave trade and slavery with the League of Nations Convention to Suppress the Slave Trade and Slavery of 1926.[1]

The lack of a developed multilateral system during the nineteenth century, however, was not the determining factor in the slow pace by which the slave trade on the seas was outlawed. At the heart of the matter was States' understanding of the nature of the high seas. The challenge was not the slave trade *per se* but rather the conflict between the Grotian notion of freedom of the seas and the right to visit ships suspected of involvement in the slave trade. Over a period of eighty years, Great Britain proposed various understandings of the "right to visit"; first seeking to assimilate slavery to piracy, then arguing for the extension of the French notion of *droit de visite*, an indirect right to visit but not to *search* a ship as a way to suppress the slave trade. Other maritime Powers were originally unwilling to concede *any* right of visit in peace time and baulked at these innovative notions put forward by Great Britain. Yet, a diplomatic compromise was reached in 1890 that accepted the concept of a "right to visit", while limiting its application to a specific maritime zone

---

* School of Law, Queen's University of Belfast.
[1] Slavery Convention, Geneva, 25 September 1926, 60 *LNTS* 255.

and to the type of ship used in the late nineteenth-century slave trade. For most of the century, then, the battle lines were drawn between Great Britain, which put forward an abolitionist agenda primed on the use of its superior naval forces and on the other hand, lesser maritime Powers including Brazil, France, Portugal and the United States of America, that sought to maintain freedom of commerce for their merchant fleets.

THE SLAVE TRADE DURING THE NINETEENTH CENTURY

The legal history of the suppression of the slave trade in the nineteenth century revolves around the "Atlantic Slave Trade," where the most significant legal issues regarding the right to visit and the freedom of the seas manifested themselves. But the century started—and ended—with a focus on other slave trades. In 1815 the United States equipped and sent its first ever naval squadron to liberate American merchant seamen held for ransom by Algiers on the Barbary Coast. Previously, international agreements had existed requiring annual tributes from foreign States to ensure their nationals were not taken at sea, enslaved, and held for payment by pirates under the protection of North African States.[2] The expedition ended the practice by the Barbary States (Algiers, Tunis and Tripoli) of "white slavery" against United States sailors. The decisive blow to this enslavement of Europeans was delivered in 1816 by Great Britain which bombarded Algiers and destroyed its navy. The Royal Navy, assisted by a Dutch squadron, demanded and received a treaty which mandated "the abolition for ever of Christian Slavery".[3] Likewise, the British Commander-in-chief in the Mediterranean "extracted a promise from the Beys of Tunis and Tripoli that they would not, for the future, make slaves of prisoners of war, but would conform to the practice of European Nations".[4] Thus ended this type of enslavement in North Africa.

During the nineteenth century, Great Britain focused primarily on the Atlantic Slave Trade.[5] Although slavery had persisted for more than a thousand years as a continuous oriental trade; the Atlantic Slave Trade emerged as a new "species of slavery".[6] During the sixteenth century,

---

[2] For American actions see F Leiner, *The End of Barbary Terror: America's 1815 War against the Pirates of North Africa* (OUP, 2006).

[3] R Phillimore, *Commentaries upon International Law* (Butterworths, London, 1879), 320.

[4] Ibid, 319.

[5] Over the past thirty years, the Atlantic Slave Trade has been the subject of extensive study by historians. Since the 1960s the "academic study of slavery has, in effect, shifted from the margins of scholarly interest (even of respectability) to become the focus of innovative and imaginative work at the very core of modern historical scholarship" (J Walvin, *Questioning Slavery* (Routledge, London, 1997), vii). Further, "[w]hile the last three decades have seen a reinvigorated interest in almost all aspects of the transatlantic slave trade, legal historians have completely neglected it" (H Kern, "Strategies of Legal Change: Great Britain, International Law, and the Abolition of the Transatlantic Slave Trade" (2004) 6 *Journal of History of International Law* 223).

[6] R Blackburn, *The Overthrow of Colonial Slavery 1776–1848* (Verso, London, 1988), 7.

Portugal and Spain introduced plantations on vast tracts of land in the Americas and manned them with indentured Europeans and enslaved Native Americans.[7] However, for numerous reasons, including rapid economic growth in Europe and the introduction of alien diseases to the New World, African slaves "became the most desired labour force for Europeans to develop their American export industries",[8] which were based on labour-intensive plantations producing commodities such as sugar, coffee, rum, and tobacco.[9]

The Papal Bulls of Donation (specifically, the *Inter caetera* of 1493) and the Treaty of Tordesillas of 1494 established that Portugal and Spain had exclusive right to the undiscovered world, with a line drawn vertically through the Atlantic Ocean from the Arctic to the Antarctic, one thousand miles west of the Azores and Cape Verde Islands. While the Treaty gave Portugal its Brazilian foothold in South America, it excluded Spain from the African coast and direct access to slaves. As a result, Spain turned to granting *Assientos*—trade monopoly licences—to furnish slaves to its colonies.[10] The slave-trade *Assientos* were ultimately amalgamated into one *Assiento* and, by 1701 began to be granted to foreign States by way of treaty. The *Assiento* first went to France. As a result of the Treaty of Utrecht (1713), it was passed to Great Britain, and then, by way of the treaties of Aix-la-Chapelle (1748) and Madrid (1750) reverted back to Spain. However, by this time the *Assiento* was of limited relevance, as Spain and Portugal's maritime rivals had broken the monopolies on both sides of the line; colonies and forts had been established by "interlopers" (including the British, Brandenburgs, Danes, Dutch, French, Norwegians and Swedes) in the New World and in Africa. The ideology of "empire" had shifted and was now commerce-based.[11] It was within this new imperial paradigm that the Atlantic Slave Trade developed and flourished.

The Atlantic Slave Trade, which spanned from 1519 until 1867, formed part of a well-established international market connecting Africa, the Americas, Asia, and Europe.[12] In contrast to common perceptions that

---

[7] See P Manning, *Slavery and African Life: Occidental, Oriental, and African Slave Trades* (CUP, 1990), 30. Such plantations—primarily sugar estates—had previously proven successful in Spanish possessions off the African West Coast.

[8] Ibid, 21.

[9] See R Fogel, *Without Consent or Contract: The Rise and Fall of American Slavery* (Norton, New York, 1994), 17–29; J Thornton, *Africa and Africans in the Making of the Atlantic World, 1400–1800* (CUP, 1999), 152–182. Of these commodities, sugar was by far the most relevant to issues of enslavement: "It is worth recalling, for instance, that some 70 per cent of *all* Africans imported into the Americas were destined, in the short term at least, to work in sugar". Walvin, above n 5, 32. Emphasis in the original.

[10] See G Scelle, "The Slave-Trade in the Spanish Colonies of America: The *Assiento*" (1910) 4 *AJIL* 617; G Scelle, *La traite négrière aux Indes de Castilles, contrats et traités d'assiento, étude de droit public et d'histoire diplomatique puisée aux sources originales et accompagnée de plusieurs documents inédits*,(Larose et Tenin, Paris, 1906).

[11] A Pagden, *Peoples and Empires* (Weidenfeld & Nicolson, London, 2001), 94.

[12] For the dates quoted see D Eltis, "The Volume and Structures of the Transatlantic Slave Trade: A Reassessment" (2001) 58 *William and Mary Quarterly* 17. With regard to the global market, see H Klein, *The Atlantic Slave Trade* (CUP, 1999), 101–102.

Europeans raided the African coast to gain slaves, early European traders actually tapped into a market which already existed. However, they
facilitated the expansion of the slave trade by creating an ever-growing
demand and by supporting the commercial and political ambitions of
African elites. These ambitions were manifested through warfare which,
while producing territorial gains,[13] created the main source of slaves
for the Atlantic trade. Captured enemies were often forced to walk to
the west coast of Africa. Survivors of the journey were offered for sale
in places such as St. Louis (modern day Senegal), Elmina and Cape
Coast (Ghana), most notoriously on the so-called "Slave Coast," in
Ouidah (Benin), and, in greater numbers still, further south in Luanda
(Angola).[14]

A decade-long project started in the late 1980s, conducted under the
auspices of the W. E. B. Du Bois Institute of Harvard University, has
gathered data on "perhaps 70 percent of all slaving voyages", providing
much insight into the various elements of the trade.[15] During the period
in which the Atlantic Slave Trade persisted, more than eleven million
men, women, and children were forcefully enslaved and taken from
Africa. Of these, approximately one and a half million did not reach the
Americas, having died at sea during the so-called "Middle Passage".[16]
Eltis notes that Great Britain and Portugal accounted for more than sev-
enty percent of the Atlantic trade: "the Portuguese dominated before
1640 and after 1807, with the British displacing them in the intervening
period".[17] In the New World, with the exception of "the meteoric rise
and fall of St. Domingue,[18] the primary receiving regions were Brazil,
the British Caribbean and, briefly, in the nineteenth century, Cuba".[19]
Finally, Eltis notes that between "1660 and 1807, when the slave trade
was at its height, the British and their dependencies carried every second
slave that arrived in the Americas, a dominance that would no doubt
have continued but for the politically inspired decision to abolish the
trade".[20]

---

[13] E.g. the creation of the Ashanti and Dahomey Kingdoms in West Africa.

[14] See Thornton, above n 9, 125. Eltis notes that on "the African coast, West Central Africa
[Angola] was an even more important source of slaves than the recent literature credits": Eltis, above
n 12, 41. West Central Africa accounts for 44.2% of departures of all known slaves from Africa heading to the New World (4,887,500 individuals). See Eltis, Table II, 44.

[15] D Davis & R Forbes, "Foreword" (2001) 58 *William and Mary Quarterly* 7.

[16] See Eltis, above n 12. The dataset is found in D Eltis et al (eds) *The Trans-Atlantic Slave
Trade: A Database on CD-ROM* (CUP, 1999).

[17] Eltis, above n 12, 20. Great Britain was responsible for 28.1% of the trade which amounts
to 3,112,300 Africans transported (Portugal being responsible for 45.9%). See Eltis, above n 12,
Table I, 43.

[18] *Viz*, modern-day Haïti, which gained its independence in 1804 as a result of a slave revolt.
Davis writes: "The Haitian Revolution impinged in one way or another on the entire emancipation
debate from the British parliamentary move in 1792 to outlaw the African slave trade to Brazil's
final abolition of slavery ninety-six years later". D Davis, *Inhuman Bondage: The Rise and Fall of
Slavery in the New World* (OUP, 2006), 158. For a consideration of the revolt in St. Domingue and
the emergence of an independent Haïti, see C L R James, *The Black Jacobins* (Secker and Warburg,
London, 1938).

[19] See Eltis, above n 12, 41.   [20] Ibid.

The move by Great Britain to abolish the slave trade was inspired by economic, philanthropic, and populist considerations. Heuman notes that until "the 1940s there was a general consensus among historians about the abolition of slavery in the Empire" where it was "maintained that the British abolished slavery largely because of the strength of religious feelings and humanitarianism".[21] This view, however, is challenged by Eric Williams' 1944 *Capitalism and Slavery*, in which he asserts that slavery was abolished because it had become unprofitable, not because it had become morally wrong and unpalatable to the British. While this perspective has been largely rejected, it has not been completely displaced.[22] More recently, greater emphasis has been placed on the public pressure which moved Great Britain towards abolition of the slave trade, with the anti-slavery movement described by Walvin as "*the* most popular political issue in these years [1789–1838]".[23] Finally, the resistance of slaves themselves increased the costs of participating in the trade and placed New World European settlers in a heightened state of anxiety over their safety, especially after the slave revolt and revolution in St. Domingue.[24]

Although individuals had called for the end of slavery and the slave trade during the eighteenth century, these calls came primarily from individual intellectuals and minority religious sects (principally the Society of Friends) and were easily dismissed.[25] However, as the abolitionist movement grew in popularity, spurred on by the ideas of the American and French revolutions and the increases in literacy and leisure time brought about by the Industrial Revolution, it became a major factor in domestic politics. This was not due to the virtue of the cause *per se*, but because it "reflected the needs and values of the emerging capitalist order,"[26] and impelled successive British governments to make abolition a key part of their foreign policy. This policy permitted British administrations to maintain the moral high ground as against those States which continued to allow their ships to be involved in the slave trade. Great Britain, having lost its greatest colonial asset in 1783 as a result of the American Revolution, no longer needed to support the New

---

[21] G Heuman, "Slavery, The Slave Trade, and Abolition" in R Winks (ed) *Oxford History of the British Empire*, Vol 5 (Historiography) (OUP, 1999), 322.

[22] Ibid. Eric Williams would later become the Prime Minister of Trinidad and Tobago.

[23] Heuman, above n 21, 324. Emphasis in the original. See also C Brown, *Moral Capital: Foundations of British Abolitionism* (University of North Carolina Press, Chapel Hill, 2006).

[24] See D Richardson, "Shipboard Revolts, African Authority, and the Atlantic Slave Trade" (2001) 58 *William and Mary Quarterly* 69–92; in the British context, see M Craton, *Testing the Chains: Resistance to Slavery in the British West Indies* (Cornell University Press, London, 1982) and R Hart, *Slaves Who Abolished Slavery* (University of the West Indies, Mona, 2002).

[25] See, e.g., Ch 10 "Religious Sources of Antislavery Thought: Quakers and the Sectarian Tradition" in D Davis, *The Problem of Slavery in Western Culture* (Cornell University Press, New York, 1966), 291–332.

[26] See Heuman, putting forward David Brion Davis' view (above n 21), 324. For a similar co-opting by States of popular sentiment, consider the evolution of dispute settlement and the peace movements which transpired at the turn of the twentieth century: see J Allain, *A Century of International Adjudication: The Rule of Law and its Limits* (T M C Asser Press, The Hague, 2000), 6–35.

World's slave-based economy. Likewise the mercantile economy, which had been in existence since the late fifteenth century, was being replaced by a capitalist order, wherein Great Britain was best placed to prosper (and dominate) through the advocacy of free trade and supremacy of its Royal Navy.[27] Thus, Great Britain went from being the main slaving nation from 1640 to outlawing the trade in 1807 and becoming the leading proponent of its international abolition.

As Great Britain's campaign for the universal suppression of the slave trade at sea moved towards successful completion at the end of the nineteenth century, it brought in its wake the end of the Atlantic Slave Trade. The last recorded slave ship made its way across the Atlantic to Cuba in 1867; however, another slave trade, the "Oriental Slave Trade," persisted "virtually unnoticed" in east Africa.[28] This oriental trade was an older, more ingrained slave trade which existed for more than a millennium before it was suppressed in the late nineteenth and early twentieth century. The Oriental Slave Trade (as opposed to the western-oriented, capitalist-driven trade) generally enslaved two women for every man, for the purpose of work as domestic servants or concubines in north Africa and western Asia. This trade, like that of the Atlantic, focused on the enslavement of inhabitants of sub-Saharan Africa. The main means of transportation was not ocean-going caravels, but camel caravans crossing the North African desert and small dhows sailing the Indian Ocean, the Persian Gulf, and the Red Sea. It is estimated that this trade involved seven million slaves, of which three million were transported during the nineteenth century.[29]

The suppression of this trade was a rather low priority for Great Britain during the first half of the nineteenth century as, for instance, only two ships could be spared for east coast patrols during Napoleon's stay on St. Helena (1815–1821), and as late as 1854, the Royal Navy "had only three vessels to deploy between Delagoa Bay to Zanzibar, over 1300 miles of coastline".[30] It was only when the Atlantic Slave Trade ended and European States undertook to conquer the whole of the African continent that Great Britain showed any great zeal in promoting the suppression of the Oriental Slave Trade. However, by this time, the legal issues relating to the British wish to establish a right to visit to

[27] See D Davis, *The Problem of Slavery in the Age of Revolution 1770–1823* (Cornell University Press, New York, 1975), 351. See also C Lloyd, *The Navy and the Slave Trade: Suppression of African Slave Trade in the Nineteenth Century* (Cass, London, 1968), xi: "Throughout the nineteenth century the Navy was the chief instrument of preserving the *Pax Britannica*".

[28] J Walvin, *Black Ivory: Slavery in the British Empire* (Blackwell Publishers, Oxford, 2001), 267. Note that the Oriental Slave Trade is also referred to in the literature as the "Arab Trade" the "Islamic Trade" or "Sahara Trade".

[29] Ibid. See also R Austen, "The Mediterranean Islamic Slave Trade out of Africa: A Tentative Census" in P Manning (ed), *Slave Trades, 1500–1800; Globalization of Forced Labour* (Variorum, Aldershot, 1996), 1–36.

[30] See R Beachy, *The Slave Trade of Eastern Africa* (Collings, London, 1976), 20 where he continues: "and this number was reduced to none, when the *Dee* was laid up for refit, and the *Crecian* and *Dart* were recalled to the Cape".

suppress the slave trade at sea had been settled. The end of the Oriental Slave Trade then was a matter for the British squadrons, the 1890 Final Act of the Brussels Conference, and the International Maritime Bureau. The British naval presence on the east coast of Africa was limited by the means at its disposal until the 1870s. Further, with the abolition of the trade on the Barbary Coast and in Egypt, over the nineteenth century the Oriental Slave Trade had been funnelled into one primary outlet on the east coast of Africa, the island of Zanzibar (which, embarrassingly, was under British protection). The Sultan of Zanzibar had, in 1843, negotiated a treaty with Great Britain that allowed for the free passage of Arab dhows along the African and Arabian coast to Oman, thus excluding this traffic from visits to suppress the slave trade. It was only when dhows ventured outside the prescribed zone that they were susceptible to capture.[31]

In 1873, the "provisions of the existing Treaties having proved ineffectual for preventing the export of slaves from the territories of the Sultan of Zanzibar, Her Majesty the Queen and His Highness the Sultan above-named, agreed that from this date the export of slaves from the coast of the mainland of Africa, whether destined for transport from one part of the Sultan's dominions to another [re: Oman] or for conveyance to foreign parts, shall entirely cease". The 1873 Treaty further stipulated that "any vessel engaged in the transport or conveyance of slaves after this date shall be liable to seizure and condemnation" by the British Navy.[32] In all likelihood, the Treaty itself would not have been concluded but for the fact that the East African Squadron had blockaded Kilwa, the transit port to Zanzibar on mainland Africa, in early 1873. While Lloyd states that by 1883 the wholesale trade had ended, the issue of slave trading in the Indian Ocean, the Red Sea, and the Persian Gulf did persist, although on a much more limited scale and often under French flag.

COMMON LAW ATTEMPTS TO OUTLAW THE SLAVE TRADE

Great Britain emerged from the Napoleonic Wars as an unrivalled maritime power. As a means of suppressing the slave trade, it sought to establish a right during peacetime from which all maritime States benefited in war: the right to visit foreign ships. While a belligerent right to visit ships was well established by the end of the Napoleonic Wars, it was limited to visiting neutral ships to ascertain whether they were in fact neutrals

---

[31] See Lloyd, above n 27, 234. An Arab dhow has been described by Captain, later Commander, Phillip Colomb as follows: "If a pear be sharpened at the thin end, and then cut in half longitudinally, two models will have been made resembling in all essential respects the ordinary slave dhow". See Beachy, above n 30, 68.

[32] Article 1, Treaty between Great Britain and Zanzibar for the Suppression of the Slave Trade, 5 June 1873, 63 BFSP 174.

or simply flying flags of convenience; and searching to ensure that no contraband material was on board.[33]

During the early nineteenth century a number of cases in Great Britain and the United States considered whether there existed a right to visit foreign ships on the high seas in times of peace so as to suppress the slave trade. While late-Napoleonic municipal judgments on both sides of the Atlantic were willing to admit a right to visit based largely on domestic law elevated to the international level by way of natural law,[34] by 1825 such pronouncements had been reversed by decisions which conformed to a growing trend of positivism as a means of interpreting international law.[35] The decisions of the British High Court of Admiralty and the United States Supreme Court highlighted the need to gain the consent of a sovereign State for foreign warships to visit its vessels in times of peace on the high seas, no matter the jurisdiction. Great Britain then turned to international relations to seek to develop a right to visit in peacetime.

International Jurisprudence admits no Common Law Right to Visit

During the Napoleonic Wars, the British Admiralty courts were willing, on the basis of a "natural law" right to visit, to condemn ships involved in the slave trade. Such judgments not only violated the rights of neutrals, they were at variance with general international law in seeking to detain foreign ships not in violation of international obligations but merely in breach of the flag ship's own municipal law. In *The Amedie* case of 1810, an American ship carrying one hundred and five slaves from Bonny (on the coast of modern-day Nigeria) to Matanzas in Cuba was condemned by the Vice-Admiralty Court of Tortola (British Virgin Islands) for having engaged in illegal trade. The Claimants failed on appeal. The Lords of Appeal in Prize Causes noted that, ordinarily, they could not be called upon to consider or apply a foreign State's municipal law.

But by the alteration which has since taken places in our law, the question stands now upon very different grounds. We do now, and did at the time of this capture, take an interest in preventing that traffic in which this ship was engaged. The slave trade has since been totally abolished in this country, and our Legislature has declared the African slave trade is contrary to the principles of justice and humanity....

[We] are now entitled to act according to our law and to hold that *prima facie* the trade is altogether illegal, and thus to throw on a claimant the whole burden of proof in order to shew that by the particular law of his own country he is entitled to carry on this traffic. As the case now stands, we think that no claimant can be heard in an application to a court of prize for the restoration of the

---

[33] See L-B Hautefeuille, *Des droits et devoirs des Nations neutres en temps de guerre maritime* (3 volumes) (Guillaume et Compagnie, Libraries, Paris, 1858).

[34] See A Rubin, *Ethics and Authority in International Law* (CUP, 1997).

[35] See A Nussbaum, *A Concise History of the Law of Nations* (Macmillan, New York, 1961), 232–234.

human beings he carried unjustly to another country for the purpose of disposing of them as slaves.[36]

Similarly, in *The Fortuna* in 1811, the High Court of Admiralty considered the case of an American ship which had been re-flagged as Portuguese and, having set out from the Spanish Atlantic island of Madeira, was shortly thereafter captured as prize by the Royal Navy. Lord Stowell noted the principle which had emerged from *The Amedie*:

that any trade contrary to the general law of nations, although not tending to or accompanied with any infraction of the belligerent rights of that country, whose tribunals are called upon to consider it, may subject the vessel employed in that [the slave] trade to confiscation.[37]

Lord Stowell then turned to consider the nature of the ship to see whether it was, in fact, involved in the slave trade:

The construction and furniture of the ship had all the accommodations necessary for the conduct of that trade, and of that trade only. She had platforms ready constructed; she had timbers fit for the construction of more; she had iron shackles and bolts, and running chains and collars—all adapted for the purposes of conveying slaves—and the quantity and species of provision and medicine which such purposes require.[38]

He condemned the foreign ship and its cargo as prize, not on the basis of an established treaty between Great Britain and Portugal but as being, in part, "repugnant to the law of nations, to justice and humanity".[39]

By 1813 however, Lord Stowell acknowledged that the Vice-Admiralty Court at Sierra Leone had gone too far in condemning the *Diana*, a Swedish ship carrying one hundred and twenty slaves from Cape Mount, Liberia, to St. Bartholomew (part of the Lesser Antilles) which had been seized by His Majesty's ship the *Crocodile* and taken to Sierra Leone. While the High Court of Admiralty was willing to award prize for ships involved in the slave trade where the flag-State had outlawed such activity in its municipal law, Lord Stowell was unwilling to do so where it was clear that the State had yet to outlaw the trade:

The ... sentence affirms, "that the slave trade, from motives of humanity, hath been abolished by most civilised nations, and is not at the present time legally authorised by any." This appears to me to be an assertion by no means sustainable. This Court is disposed to go as far in discountenancing this odious traffic as the law of nations and the principles recognised by English tribunals will warrant it in doing, but beyond these principles it does not feel itself at

---

[36] *The Amedie* (1810) 1 *Acton's Admiralty Reports* 240, 250–252. Note that Kern writes: "Yet the reasoning that British rights under international law could depend on the domestic legislation of other countries was hardly consistent with traditional interpretations of international law": see above n 5, 236.

[37] *The Fortuna* (1811) 1 *Dodson's Admiralty Reports* 81, 84. For a general discussion of these case and their relevance in international law to the issue of the slave trade, see W Lawrence, *Wheaton's Elements of International Law* (Stevens & Sons, Limited, London, 1857) and Phillimore, above n 3.

[38] *The Fortuna*, ibid, 90.   [39] Ibid, 85.

liberty to travel: it cannot proceed on a sweeping anathema of this kind against property belonging to the subjects of foreign independent states. The position laid down in the sentence of the [Vice-Admiralty Court of Sierra Leone] that the slave trade is not authorised by any civilised state, is unfortunately by no means correct, the contrary being notoriously the fact, that it is tolerated by some of them.

This trade was at one time, we know, universally allowed by the different nations of Europe, and carried on by them to a greater or less extent, according to their respective necessities. Sweden, having but small colonial possessions, did not engage very deeply in the traffic, but she entered into it so far as her convenience required for the supply of her own colonies. The trade, which was generally allowed, has been since abolished by some particular countries; but I am yet to learn that Sweden has prohibited its subjects from engaging in the traffic, or that she has abstained from it either in act or declaration. Our own country, it is true, has taken a more correct view of the subject, and has decreed the abolition of the slave trade, as far as British subjects are concerned; but it claims no right of enforcing its prohibition against the subjects of those states which have not adopted the same opinion with respect to the injustice and immorality of the trade.[40]

The Diana, however, failed to address the fundamental issue raised in The Amedie and The Fortuna: the right to visit and capture foreign vessels suspected of involvement in the slave trade where no international treaty existed. These decisions were superseded by The Le Louis in 1817. In that case, a French ship was returning from Africa to Martinique when the Royal Navy attempted to board it on suspicion of involvement in the slave trade. The crew resisted and twelve British and three French sailors were killed. The ship was taken and brought to Sierra Leone where it was adjudged as prize for being outfitted for the slave trade. On appeal before the High Court of Admiralty, Lord Stowell considered whether there existed a right to visit foreign ships in times of peace—if not, the resistance by the crew would be lawful:

Upon the... question, whether the right of search exists in time of peace, I have to observe, that two principles of public law are generally recognised as fundamental. One is the perfect equality and entire independence of all distinct states. Relative magnitude creates no distinction of right; relative imbecility, whether permanent or casual, gives no additional right to the more powerful neighbour; and any advantage seized upon, that ground is mere usurpation. This is the great foundation of public law, which it mainly concerns the peace of mankind, both in their politic and private capacities, to preserve inviolate. The second is, that nations being equal, all have an equal right to the uninterrupted use of the un-appropriated parts of the ocean for their navigation. In places where no local authority exists, where the subjects of all states meet upon a footing of ... equality and independence, no one state, or any of its subjects has a right to assume or exercise authority over the subjects of another. I can find no authority that gives the right of interruption to the navigation of states in amity upon the high

40 The Diana (1813) 1 Dodson's Admiralty Reports 95, 97–98.

seas, excepting that which the rights of war give to both belligerents against neutrals.

. . .

But at present, under the law, as now generally understood and practised, no nation can exercise a right of visitation and search upon the common and un-appropriated parts of the sea, save only on the belligerent claim.[41]

Lord Stowell held that although the aims of the British Navy were commendable, they were unlawful. If Great Britain wanted to continue with the suppression of the slave trade it would have to do so within the confines of international law:

To press forward to a great principle by breaking through every other great principle that stands in the way of its establishment; to force the way to the liberation of Africa by trampling on the independence of other states in Europe; in short, to procure an eminent good by means that are unlawful; is as little consonant to private morality as to public justice. Obtain the concurrence of other nations, if you can, by application, by remonstrance, by example, by every peaceable instrument which man can employ to attract the consent of man. But a nation is not justified in assuming rights that do not belong to her merely because she means to apply them to a laudable purpose; nor in setting out upon a moral crusade of converting other nations by acts of unlawful force. Nor is it to be argued, that because other nations approve the ultimate purpose, they must therefore submit to every measure which any one state or its subjects may inconsiderately adopt for its attainment.[42]

In 1817 the British admiralty courts settled that the suppression of the slave trade did not allow for a right to visit foreign ships on the high seas during time of peace, but it took a further eight years for this principle to emerge in the United States. Although the Federal Circuit Court of Massachusetts, in *The Jeune Eugenie* in 1822, relied heavily on domestic law to find the slave trade was "prohibited by universal law,"[43] this

[41] *The Le Louis* (1817) 2 *Dodson's Admiralty Reports* 210, 244–245.

[42] Ibid, 258–259. Despite having found that the British had illegally seized the *Le Louis*, Lord Stowell was unwilling to award damages, see 264.

[43] *The United States v. La Jeune Eugenie* (1822) 26 *Federal Case Reports* 832, 851. Although the Court held that it could indeed confiscate, it handed over the cargo to the French Consul so that it might be "dealt with according to his own sense of duty and right". The following passage emphasises the natural law approach of Justice Story and also vividly portrays the reality of the slave trade:

> It would be unbecoming in me here to assert, that the state of slavery cannot have a legitimate existence, or that it stands condemned by the unequivocal testimony of the law of nations. But this concession carries us but a very short distance towards the decision of this cause. It is not, as the learned counsel for the government have justly stated, on account of the simple fact, that the traffic necessarily involves the enslavement of human beings, that it stands reprehended by the present sense of nations; but that it necessarily carries with it a breach of all the moral duties, of all the maxims of justice, mercy and humanity, and of the admitted rights, which independent Christian nations now hold sacred in their intercourse with each other. What is the fact as to the ordinary, nay, necessary course, of this trade? It begins in corruption, and plunder, and kidnapping. It creates and stimulates unholy wars for the purpose of making captives. It desolates whole villages and provinces for the purpose of seizing the young, the feeble, the defenceless, and the innocent. It breaks down all the ties of parent, and children, and family, and country. It shuts up all sympathy for human suffering and sorrows. It manacles the inoffensive females and the starving infants. It forces the brave to untimely death in defence of their humble homes and firesides, or drives them to despair and self-immolation. It stirs up

decision was followed by the United States Supreme Court in 1825. *The Antelope* case involved the capture of a vessel on suspicion of involvement in piracy as it had been hovering off the coast of Florida for some time. When seized, it was discovered that the *Antelope* had been captured by Spanish privateers off the coast of Africa and was carrying more than two hundred and eighty slaves to be sold in Surinam. The case was brought by the Vice-Consuls of Portugal and Spain who sought restitution for the property they considered had been improperly seized by the American Government. Chief Justice Marshall took a decidedly positivist approach to interpreting the law regarding the slave trade and the notion of visitation:

Whatever might be the answer of a moralist to this question, a jurist must search for its legal solution, in those principles of action which are sanctioned by the usages, the national acts, and the general assent, of that portion of the world of which he considers himself as a part, and to whose law the appeal is made. If we resort to this standard as the test of international law, the question, as has already been observed, is decided in favour of the legality of the trade. Both Europe and America embarked in it; and for nearly two centuries, it was carried on without opposition, and without censure. A jurist could not say, that a practice thus supported was illegal, and that those engaged in it might be punished, either personally, or by deprivation of property.

In this commerce, thus sanctioned by universal assent, every nation has an equal right to engage. How is this right to be lost? Each may renounce it for its own people; but can this renunciation affect others?

No principle of general law is more universally acknowledged, than the perfect equality of nations. Russia and Geneva have equal rights. It results from this equality, that no one can rightfully impose a rule on another. Each legislates for itself, but its legislation can operate on itself alone. A right, then, which is vested in all by the consent of all, can be divested only by consent; and this trade, in which all have participated, must remain lawful to those who cannot be induced to relinquish it. As no nation can prescribe a rule for others, none can make a

---

the worst passions of the human soul, darkening the spirit of revenge, sharpening the greediness of avarice, brutalizing the selfish, envenoming the cruel, famishing the weak, and crushing to death the broken-hearted. This is but the beginning of the evils. Before the unhappy captives arrive at the destined market, where the traffic ends, one quarter part at least in the ordinary course of events perish in cold blood under the inhuman, or thoughtless treatment of their oppressors. Strong as these expressions may seem, and dark as is the colouring of this statement, it is short of the real calamities inflicted by this traffic. All the wars, that have desolated Africa for the last three centuries, have had their origin in the slave trade. The blood of thousands of her miserable children has stained her shores, or quenched the dying embers of her desolated towns, to glut the appetite of slave dealers. The ocean has received in its deep and silent bosom thousands more, who have perished from disease and want during their passage from their native homes to the foreign colonies. I speak not from vague rumours, or idle tales, but from authentic documents, and the known historical details of the traffic,—a traffic, that carries away at least 50,000 persons annually from their homes and their families, and breaks the hearts, and buries the hopes, and extinguishes the happiness of more than double that number. [...] "There is," as one of the greatest of modern statesmen has declared, "something of horror in it, that surpasses all the bounds of imagination." Mr. Pitt's speech on the slave trade, in 1792. It is of this traffic, thus carried on, and necessarily carried on, beginning in lawless wars, and rapine, and kidnapping, and ending in disease, and death, and slavery—it is of this traffic in the aggregate of its accumulated wrongs, that I would ask, if it be consistent with the law of nations?

ibid, 845–6.

law of nations; and this traffic remains lawful to those whose governments have not forbidden it.

...

If it be... repugnant to the law of nations... it is almost superfluous to say in this Court, that the right of bringing in for adjudication in time of peace, even where the vessel belongs to a nation which has prohibited the trade, cannot exist. The Courts of no country execute the penal laws of another; and the course of the American government on the subject of visitation and search, would decide any case in which that right had been exercised by an American cruiser, on the vessel of a foreign nation, not violating our municipal laws, against the captors.

It follows, that a foreign vessel engaged in the African slave trade, captured on the high seas in time of peace, by an American cruiser, and brought in for adjudication, would be restored.[44]

By 1825, therefore, international jurisprudence—at least of an Anglo-American variety—was settled. The principles which emerged were rooted in positive international law, where State consent was required to establish jurisdiction over its flagged ships. Early common law decisions sought to assert a natural law emphasis on the repugnance of the slave trade which, outlawed for the most part at the municipal level, granted States the *right* to suppress the trade in accordance with a flagged State's domestic laws.[45] From *The Le Louis* onwards, Great Britain could no longer use its own common law to justify suppressing the slave trade; this case made plain that visiting ships on the high seas for that purpose was against international law. Instead the British largely followed Lord Stowell's advice and sought: "the concurrence of other nations... by application, by remonstrance, by example, by every peaceable instrument which man can employ to attract the consent of man". When this failed, Great Britain, as we shall see, was not above using force and coercive means to achieve its ultimate objective of suppressing the slave trade through the establishment of a right to visit.

Early Attempts at Outlawing the Slave Trade

Following *The Le Louis*, it was clear that Great Britain was unable to rely on a common law prerogative to develop the means of suppressing the slave trade. Yet it had also been active at the international level prior to this judgment and had sought, as early as the settlement of the Napoleonic Wars, to establish a universal instrument which would allow for the suppression of the slave trade and provide for a reciprocal right of visit to ensure the end of the trade at sea. While Great Britain maintained this strategic foreign policy objective for seventy-five years, for tactical reasons it spent most of the intervening period establishing a web of

---

[44] *The Antelope* (1825), 23 *United States Supreme Court Reports* 66, 121–123.
[45] Rubin, above n 34, 110.

bilateral arrangements which were ultimately subsumed into the General Act of the 1890 Brussels Conference. Gradually Britain locked a growing number of States into its web of bilateral treaties and isolated those outside the system, moving closer towards its original goal: the universal outlawing of the slave trade.

In the lead up to the Congress of Vienna of 1814 the British Foreign Minister, Lord Castlereagh, gained the formal support of a defeated France for the end of the slave trade and for his endeavours to internationalise the issue at Vienna.[46] At the Congress itself, Great Britain proposed that the trade should be outlawed within a three-year period; that a permanent institution be established to supervise adherence to the treaty obligations; and that a reciprocal right of visit be established.[47] Yet French support was not forthcoming at Vienna where capitulation was no longer the order of the day. France and the Iberian States opposed the proposal, and Castlereagh was ultimately unable to gain a binding commitment regarding the abolition of the slave trade beyond a Declaration by the Powers which expressed the wish to "bring to an end a scourge which has for a long time desolated Africa, degraded Europe, and afflicted humanity". The Powers declared that they:

consider the universal abolition of the trade in Negroes to be particularly worthy of their attention, being in conformity with the spirit of the times, and the general principles of our august Sovereigns, who are animated in their sincere desire to work towards the quickest and most effective of measures, by all means at their disposal, and to act, in the use of those means with all zealousness and perseverance which is required of such a grand and beautiful cause.[48]

This pious statement was qualified by a recognition that the Declaration would not prejudice the time it might take any State to conclude its involvement in the trade and that a "determination as to time when this commerce is to universally come to an end would be the object of negotiation as between the Powers".[49]

In the wake of the Congress of Vienna, Great Britain instituted a "formal and permanent conference" in London comprising ambassadors of the Great Powers. With a permanent secretariat, it was intended to represent "both a centre of information and a centre of action". However, although it held sixteen formal meetings between 1816 and 1819, it achieved very little beyond information gathering, as the other Powers remained suspicious of British attempts to promote its abolitionist agenda

[46] M T Barclay, "Le droit de visite, le traffic des esclaves et la Conférence antiesclavagiste de Bruxelles" (1890) 22 *Revue de droit international et de legislation comparé* 319–320.

[47] S Miers, *Britain and the Ending of the Slave Trade*, (Longman, London, 1975), 10–11.

[48] *Declaration des 8 Cours, relative à l'Abolition Universelle de la Traite des Nègres*, Vienna, 8 February 1815, 3 *BFSP* 972. The eight Powers were Austria, Britain, France, Prussia, Russia, Portugal, Spain and Sweden.

[49] Ibid.

at the expense of their right to freedom of the seas.[50] The recognition in the Vienna Declaration that the end of the slave trade would have to result from negotiations was picked up by Castlereagh at Aix-la-Chapelle in 1818 at the first meeting of the Concert of Europe.[51] The British Foreign Minister sought the creation of a right to visit and detain slave ships solely in the Atlantic Ocean north of the equator and the establishment of mixed commissions with the power to adjudicate claims; yet his appeals fell on deaf ears, as the other Powers were unwilling to curtail their freedom of the seas.[52]

At the Congress of Verona of 1822, Great Britain once again sought to achieve an international agreement. By the 1820s, all maritime Powers had abolished the trade domestically and a distinct possibility for success existed. However, the British grand design for a universal treaty outlawing the trade was again thwarted, not because of the principle, but because of a lack of consensus on the modalities to be used. At Verona, the new Foreign Minister, the Duke of Wellington, put forward a proposal to the Powers that included the renewal of the Declaration of Vienna of 1815 and the assimilation of slave trading with piracy.[53] The continental Powers were unwilling to agree to the regime proposed, and what emerged from Verona was not a mechanism to enforce the suppression of the slave trade, but a diplomatic willingness to move beyond the Declaration of 1815 by making the following "Resolution":

That they invariably persisted in their principles and sentiments which these Sovereigns manifested in their Declaration of 8 February 1815—That they have never ceased, and will never cease, to consider the commerce in Negroes—"a scourge which has for a long time desolated Africa, degraded Europe, and afflicted humanity", and that they are ready to contribute to everything which could assure and accelerate the complete and definite abolition of this commerce.[54]

This Resolution was the end product of earlier attempts by Great Britain to establish a universal instrument prohibiting the slave trade at the expense of the freedom of the seas. Yet the failure at Vienna in 1815, more than any other, resulted in a change of tactics by Great Britain in pursuing the creation of a universal instrument which allowed for a right to visit on the high seas. It is to this tactical adjustment which this study now turns.

---

[50] C K Webster, *The Foreign Policy of Castlereagh 1815–1822: Britain and the European Alliance* (G Bell, London, 1925), 457–459. For the Protocols of the London conferences see 6 *BFSP* 23, 25, 50–52.

[51] The Concert system was intended to allow European Powers to consider international issues, at intervals, during peacetime, as opposed to their former practice of solely meeting to settle the peace after war (eg Congress of Vienna). Four meetings took place in this manner: Aix-la-Chapelle (1818), Troppau (1820), Laibach (1821), and Verona (1822).

[52] Memorandum of the British Government, 27 October 1818, Castlereagh, 6 *BFSP* 59.

[53] Memorandum of the Duke of Wellington, 10 November 1822, 10 *BFSP* 95. The Five Powers in attendance at Verona were: Austria, Britain, France, Prussia, Russia.

[54] *Résolution relatives à l'Abolition de la Traite des Nègres*, Vienna, 28 November 1822, 10 *BFSP* 109–110.

The Bilateral Outlawing of the Slave Trade

Thwarted in its multilateral attempts to outlaw the slave trade and in the face of the determination by its domestic courts that visitation of foreign ships on the high seas in peacetime had to be a consensual right, Great Britain turned to the establishment of bilateral treaties to outlaw the slave trade. The building of such a bilateral network, however, would prove ineffective if any maritime power remained outside the system. As noted abolitionist, the parliamentarian Thomas Fowell Buxton stated in 1837: "it will avail us little that ninety-nine doors are closed, if one remains open. To that outlet the whole slave trade of Africa will rush".[55] Great Britain persisted in building its network, and through an increasing number of bilateral treaties was able to isolate the few States outside the system, increasing the momentum towards a universally accepted *right* to visit. That it took until 1890 for a universal treaty to be established speaks to the opposition of a number of States, not to the slave trade *per se*, but to granting to Britain the right to visit their merchant ships.

France and the United States were most obstinate in their call to respect the absolute right (in peacetime) to free commerce upon the high seas. While Brazil, France, Portugal, and the United States each had distinct reasons for opposing the British initiative, they all saw in the British wish to suppress the slave trade an attempt to appropriate the policing of the seas and control maritime commerce. While Brazil and Portugal were persuaded by coercive means to join the system, France and the United States remained adamant in supporting freedom of the seas. Ultimately, France and the United States acceded to the British wish to suppress the slave trade, and Great Britain accepted a *limited* right to visit merchant ships of these two States.

Unable to forge a consensus to establish a universal treaty outlawing the slave trade during the Concert of Europe era, Great Britain ultimately entered into treaties with thirty-one States to suppress the slave trade at sea.[56] There was only one instance in which two States, neither of which was Great Britain, entered into an agreement to suppress the slave trade.[57] Bilateral agreements, as we shall see, evolved over time and were generally of two types: those that provided for a right to visit and those which contained "mutual obligation to maintain squadrons on the coast of Africa".[58]

---

[55] See W Mathieson, *Great Britain and the Slave Trade (1839–1865)* (Longman, Greens & Co, London, 1929) 38–39.

[56] These thirty-one States included, in chronological order of signature: Portugal, Denmark, France, Spain, Netherlands, Sweden, Buenos Aires, Colombia, Brazil, Mexico, Confederation of Peru, Bolivia, Hanseatic Cities, Tuscany, the two Sicilies, Chili, Venezuela, Uruguay, Haiti, Texas, Austria, Prussia, Russia, The United States of America, The Kings and Chiefs of Cape Mount (Africa), Equator, Muscat, Arabs of the Gulf, New Granada, Zanzibar, Egypt. See Phillimore, above n 3, 420–421. This does not include agreements with African leaders who were not considered "civilized nations".

[57] *Convention entre la France et la Suède*, Stockholm, 21 May 1836, 24 *BFSP* 556.

[58] Phillimore, above n 3, 422.

At the beginning of the eighteenth century Great Britain began to solicit agreements whereby other States renounced the slave trade. As early as 1810, Portugal bound itself to such a treaty of principle. Likewise in 1813, in exchange for the island of Guadeloupe, Sweden renounced the introduction of slaves into its colonies and prohibited Swedes from participating in the trade.[59] However, Great Britain realised that it was vital not only to seek agreement with all maritime powers, but that such agreements needed to include enforcement provisions to have any effect on the suppression of the trade. In other words, the right to visit was vital.

In 1817 and 1818, Great Britain concluded treaties with the Netherlands, Portugal, and Spain which went beyond declaratory statements outlawing the slave trade, introducing mechanisms which became the essence of these bilateral agreements over the next half-century. The 1818 Dutch treaty, in which Great Britain and the Netherlands confirmed a "mutual desire to adopt the most effectual measure for putting a stop to the carrying on of the Slave-trade by their respective Subjects, and for preventing their respective Flags from being made use of as a protection to this nefarious traffic,"[60] is exemplary. These early agreements permitted the navies of the contracting parties, under special instruction, to visit merchant ships of the other contracting party suspected of slave trading. If slaves were found on board, the ship was to be brought before mixed commissions to determine whether the ship and cargo were forfeited.[61]

Within a five year period, it was discovered these reciprocal visitation treaties were lacking: ships which did not have slaves on board could not be detained, yet there was a recognition that vessels "employed in the illegal Traffic, have unshipped their Slaves immediately prior to their being visited . . . [having] thus found means to evade forfeiture, and have been enabled to pursue their unlawful course with impunity, contrary to the true object and spirit of the Treaty".[62] As a result, a so-called "equipment clause" was introduced into subsequent treaties, which provided that a ship outfitted with certain materiel would be "considered as *primâ facie* evidence of her actual employment in the Slave Trade." Such equipment included open gratings on hatches, spare planks for the creation of a slave-deck, possession of "shackles, bolts or handcuffs," or an

---

[59] 3 *BFSP* 886.

[60] Treaty between His Britannic Majesty and His Majesty the King of The Netherlands, for preventing their Subjects from engaging in any Traffic in Slavery, The Hague, 4 May 1818, 5 *BFSP* 125.

[61] These treaties, as others that would follow, excluded the right to visit from European waters as well as the Mediterranean. The 1817 Portuguese treaty also excluded the right to visit south of the equator. See Article 2, Additional Convention between Great Britain and Portugal, for the prevention of the Slave Trade, London, 28 July 1817, 10 *BFSP* 88.

[62] See Article 1, Explanatory and Additional Articles to the 4th May, 1818, Treaty between Great Britain and The Netherlands, for the Prevention of the Traffic in Slaves, 31 December 1822, Brussels, 10 *BFSP* 132.

overabundance of water and food for needs of the crew on the planned voyage.[63]

Part of the bilateral regime established by Great Britain to suppress the slave trade was the establishment, between 1817 and 1871, of mixed commissions to adjudicate claims arising from the capture of ships suspected of involvement in the slave trade. These adjudicative organs consisted of judges appointed by the two parties: with no third-party involvement. Instead these mixed courts or more properly "mixed or joint commissions" consisted—at least in theory—of a judge and a commissioner of arbitration from each State party. The judges considered the legality of the capture and, failing agreement, lots were drawn to decide which commissioner would settle the case. As Bethell writes in his historical study of the mixed commissions: "[judges] usually—although by no means always—agreed with their senior partners on the commission, with the result that many ships captured without slaves on board were condemned or acquitted literally on the toss of a coin". He continued:

In December 1841, for instance, two Brazilian vessels, the *Ermelinda* and the *Galianna*, almost identical cases in terms of their fittings, came before the Anglo-Brazilian commission in Sierra Leone, where the judges were unable to agree upon a verdict. In the first case the English arbitrator won the toss and the *Galianna* was condemned; in the second the Brazilian was successful and the *Ermelinda* was released.[64]

The early bilateral treaties allowed for the establishment of two mixed commissions, ordinarily one in West Africa, in the British Crown colony of Sierra Leone, the other in the New World. Thus, for instance, an Anglo-Portuguese mixed commission sat in Rio de Janeiro (later in Spanish Town, Jamaica); an Anglo-Spanish commission in Havana; an Anglo-Dutch commission in Surinam; an Anglo-American commission in New York; and an Anglo-Brazilian mixed commission in the newly independent capital of Brazil, Rio de Janeiro.[65]

The British were at an advantage with respect to these mixed commissions, as their naval squadrons effectively had a monopoly on captures and worked primarily off the coast of Africa.[66] As a result, most captures

---

[63] Further Additional Article to the 4th May, 1818, Treaty between Great Britain and The Netherlands, for the Prevention of the Traffic in Slaves , 25 January 1823, Brussels, 10 *BFSP* 559.

[64] L Bethell, "The Mixed Commissions for the Suppression of the Transatlantic Slave Trade in the Nineteenth Century" (1966) 7 *Journal of African History* 79, 87 [footnote omitted].

[65] Note that although Chile (1839), the Argentine Confederation (1839), Uruguay (1839), Bolivia (1840) and Ecuador (1841) ratified bilateral treaties with Great Britain allowing for mixed commissions, they "waived the right to establish mixed commissions in their own territory", instead allowing the mixed court in Sierra Leone—to which they did not appoint Commissioners—to adjudge captures: ibid, 83.

[66] Bethell notes that 95 percent of all vessels captured under the anti-slave treaties Britain had secured from Portugal, Spain, the Netherlands and Brazil were taken by ships of the Royal British Navy: ibid, 83. Bethell also gives a breakdown of the cases that were heard between 1819 and 1845: at Sierra Leone, 528; Havana, 50; Rio de Janeiro, 44; and Surinam, 1. As for cases dealt with in

were adjudicated in Freetown, Sierra Leone, where Great Britain already had a Vice-Admiralty Court whose officials also sat on the various Commissions. While the Brazilian, Dutch, Portuguese and Spanish Commissioners sat in waiting for one of their own nations' ships to be brought in by the British Royal Navy, the British representatives could handle cases involving slavers from the flagship of any State which had agreed to jurisdiction under a bilateral treaty. Sierra Leone was "a notorious white man's grave," and non-British parties which had agreed to mixed commissions in Freetown had difficulty staffing them. The Anglo-Dutch Mixed Commission is a case in point. In line with the Treaty of 1818, the Netherlands appointed a judge and commissioner in 1819. When the judge left in 1820, he was never replaced; the commissioner remained until 1828, acting sometimes as judge sometimes as commissioner. From 1828 onwards "the Anglo-Dutch mixed courts functioned without a Dutch representative until the court was dissolved in 1871".[67]

It is estimated that the various mixed commissions involved in suppressing the slave trade were "responsible for the condemnation of over 620 slave vessels and the liberation of nearly 80000 slaves". 528 vessels appeared before the Freetown commissions, of which 501 "were condemned and nearly 65000 slaves liberated".[68] However as a result of a change in British policy in 1845, only a further seven cases were heard in Sierra Leone before the mixed commissions finally closed in 1871. The Palmerston Act, enacted in 1839, mandated, inter alia, that ships "not entitled to claim the protection of the flag of any state" be brought before Vice-Admiralty courts. Cases were henceforth increasingly brought, not before what were, in effect, the exclusively British manned "mixed" commissions, but instead to the British Vice-Admiralty Courts of Sierra Leone, St Helena, or Cape Town. Likewise in South Africa, after 1845, only eight cases were brought before the Cape Town mixed commissions, and only three resulted in condemnation.[69] As a result, where slave traders were in actuality in command of a flag ship of a State which sought to take action, not only against the ship, but also against the captain and crew, it was wise for the sailors to quickly "lose" their papers and flag,

Freetown, the Anglo-Spanish Commission heard 241, the Anglo-Portuguese Commission: 155, Anglo-Brazilian Commission: 111, and the Anglo-Netherlands Commission: 21: ibid, 84.

[67] P Emmer, *The Dutch in the Atlantic Economy, 1580–1880: Trade, Slavery and Emancipation* (Ashgate, Aldershot, 1998), 181. According to Bethell: "British officials in the so-called 'mixed' commissions frequently found themselves sitting alone. Each of the three [Dutch, Portuguese, Spanish] commissions at Sierra Leone started out in 1819 with a full complement of officials, but during the next few years all foreign commissioners left, not to return." Bethell, ibid, 87.

[68] J P van Niekerk, "British, Portuguese, and American judges in Adderley Street; the international legal background to, and some judicial aspects of, the Cape Town Mixed Commissions for the Suppression of the Transatlantic Slave Trade in the Nineteenth Century (Part 2)" (2004) 37(2) *The Comparative and International Journal of Southern Africa* 200.

[69] J P van Niekerk, "British, Portuguese, and American judges in Adderley Street; the international legal background to, and some judicial aspects of, the Cape Town Mixed Commissions for the Suppression of the Transatlantic Slave Trade in the Nineteenth Century (Part 3)", (2004) 37(3) *The Comparative and International Journal of Southern Africa* 405.

and thus take command of a "stateless" ship; when captured, they fell under the jurisdiction of the Vice-Admiralty courts where only the vessels and cargo faced judicial sanction.[70]

While eighty thousand slaves were liberated as a result of the pronouncements of the mixed commissions, these numbers paled in the face of the continuing trade which, during the first half of the nineteenth century, resulted in the transportation of more than three million slaves to the New World. Yet, the British bilateral regime did have a deterrent effect on the Atlantic Slave Trade as the number of known slaves transported to the Western Hemisphere dropped by one-fifth in comparison to the latter half of the eighteenth century.[71] Eltis, having considered supply and demand, estimates that as a result of the actions of the British Navy, two hundred and thirteen thousand Africans were spared enslavement after 1830.[72] Despite this reduction in the number of slaves transported, the weaknesses in the bilateral system persisted. The total abolishment of the slave trade required that all maritime States join the British system, as slave traders used false flags and forged papers to avoid visit and capture. Slave ships were not above "acquiring" a new nationality at sea:

During the chase the captain of the *La Fortunée* had been standing on the bow of his ship with two tin boxes in his hand. As soon as the man-of-war had shown the Union Jack, the captain had dropped one of these boxes into the sea. The ship was captured and the remaining box contained only French papers.[73]

In an attempt to complete its bilateral system, during the late 1830s early 1840s, Britain signed a number of such agreements with newly independent Latin American States.[74] However, this did not complete the system, as four States held out, limiting the effectiveness of the British bilateral system for the suppression of the slave trade.

The Recalcitrant States: Completing the Bilateral Regime

For diverse reasons Brazil, France, Portugal, and the United States of America were unwilling to involve themselves in the bilateral treaty regime constructed by Great Britain to suppress the slave trade.[75] While Brazil and Portugal simply needed some "nudging" by the British Navy to join the existing system, France and the United States were not so

---

[70] J P van Niekerk, "British, Portuguese, and American judges in Adderley Street; the international legal background to, and some judicial aspects of, the Cape Town Mixed Commissions for the Suppression of the Transatlantic Slave Trade in the Nineteenth Century (Part 1)" (2004) 37(1) *The Comparative and International Journal of Southern Africa* 35.

[71] Eltis, above n 12, Table 1, 43.

[72] Davis, *Inhuman Bondage,* above n 18, 244.

[73] Emmer, above n 67, 182.

[74] Buenos Ayres (1839), Chile (1839), Venezuela (1839), Uruguay (1840), Bolivia (1840), Texas (1840), Equador (1841), Mexico (1841), and later, New Grenada (re: Colombia; 1851).

[75] Lloyd, above n 27, x.

easily moved. With international law on their side and as "Powers" in their own right, they remained adamant that the freedom of the seas should be respected and that, in the absence of a conventional agreement, a legal right of visitation only existed in times of war. It was only when the domestic situation in both States began to favour abolition that they were willing to seriously discuss the suppression of the slave trade. While France conceded a right to visit for a period of time, it reverted to its former position and ultimately accepted a bilateral arrangement whereby joint naval squadrons patrolled the African Coast. For the United States, a war-time measure by the Northern Union during the American Civil War ultimately allowed it to become party to a bilateral treaty similar to the Anglo-French treaty. Thus, one by one, these four States became part of the web of bilateral treaties which Great Britain had been establishing since 1817. Only then, when all maritime powers had agreed to effective means to suppress the slave trade at sea was it possible to look to developing a universal instrument.

(1) France

British abolitionist tendencies were viewed in France with great suspicion. As Daget noted, it was thought the "envied rival was using ostensibly humanitarian means to further its ambitions for political, commercial and indeed military hegemony".[76] France was hesitant to join the British bilateral system, instead dispatching warships to the West African coast where, from 1817 to 1831, they seized 65 suspected slavers and condemned 51 of a known total of 482 French slavers.[77] Great Britain simply bided its time, witnessing the rise and fall of the Bourbon Dynasty, and in the aftermath of the 1830 July Revolution found a French government with abolitionist leanings willing to sign a visitation treaty. Yet the treaties of 1831 and 1833 were very restrictive and detailed in laying down procedures for visit. They were to apply in specific maritime zones off West Africa and surrounding the islands of Cuba, Madagascar and Puerto Rico and mandated that jurisdiction over seized ships fell to the flag State's judiciary; thus no mixed commissions were attached to these agreements.[78] Further, these treaties were opened to accession, an option which was later taken up by Denmark, Haïti, the Hanseatic League (i.e.: Bremen, Gdansk, Hamburg, and Rostock), Sardinia, the Kingdom of the Two Sicilies, and Tuscany. While the acceding States would remain bound by their agreements with Great Britain, France would not.

---

[76] S Daget, "France, Suppression of the Illegal Trade, and England, 1817–1850" in D Eltis and J Walvin (eds), *The Abolition of the Atlantic Slave Trade: Origins and Effects in Europe, Africa, and the Americas* (University of Wisconsin Press, London, 1981), 194.

[77] Ibid, 200.

[78] For the Treaty of 1831, see *Convention between Great Britain and France, for the more effective suppression of the Traffic in Slaves*, Paris, 30 November 1831, 18 *BFSP* 641; for the Treaty of 1833, see *Supplementary Convention between His Majesty and the King of the French, for the more effectual Suppression of the Traffic in Slaves*, Paris, 22 March 1833, 20 *BFSP* 286.

The mutual right of visitation agreed to by France in the 1831 and 1833 Treaties proved to be contentious, and its application became embroiled in the traditional British-French rivalry which was so much a part of that era. The seizing of two French ships by the Royal Navy in particular—the *Sénégambie* and the *Marabout*—was a rallying point for anti-British sentiment in France.[79] Thus, when Great Britain gained the European Powers' agreement on a multilateral convention, succeeding where it had failed in Vienna in 1815, France acted as the spoiler. In 1841, Austria, France, Great Britain, Prussia, and Russia signed a treaty which assimilated the slave trade at sea with piracy. The United States was the first to make this connection, equating slaving to piracy in its domestic legislation in 1820. Great Britain had also managed to include such a provision as early as 1826 in an agreement with Brazil. The appearance of this provision in the multilateral convention among the European Powers indicated that Great Britain was very close to achieving its foreign policy objective of an established right to visit in international law. The assimilation of slaving to piracy meant that ships involved in the trade would have no right to avail themselves of the protection of any State's flag and as such, could be visited by ships of all States; to use modern terminology, universal jurisdiction was established.[80] The 1841 Convention required domestic courts to assume jurisdiction over seizures; it also provided a right to visit in an expanded rectangular maritime zone which included the east coast of the New World from modern day Florida westward to India, extending southward to a parallel line established just south of Buenos Aires and extending east into the India Ocean.[81] Yet the signing of the 1841 Quintuple Treaty "stirred up a veritable hornets nest in France",[82] in part, for practical reasons—Austria, Prussia, and Russia being land Powers, the provisions only truly applied to France, for geopolitical reasons as Great Britain had recently imposed its will in Egypt and Syria at the expense of France, and also as a result of the actions of the American Ambassador in Paris. The Ambassador, General Lewis Cass, fearing that the United States would be isolated and forced to give up its freedom of the seas, produced an anonymous pamphlet, which "excited violent agitation against" the Treaty.[83] In the end, the 1841 Treaty was not ratified by France, though it did come into

---

[79] S Daget, *La répression de lat traite des Noirs au XIXe sicècle: L'action des croisières français sur les côtes occidentales de l'Afrique (1817–1850)* (Éditions Karthala, Paris,1997), 472–475 and 481–486. Daget also considers the historic rivalry as a means of explaining the lack of cooperation proffered by France: "On ne collabore pas avec des Anglais. Parce que cela offre le plaisir de leur compliquer la vie", 599.

[80] See "'Quasi-Piracy': The Fight Against the Slave Trade" in W Grewe, *The Epochs of International Law* (Walter de Gruyter & Co, New York, 2000), 554–569; Rubin, above n 34, 82–137.

[81] Article 2, *Treaty between Great Britain, Austria, France, Prussia, and Russia, for the suppression of the African Slave Trade*, London, 20 December 1841, 30 *BFSP* 273. For a pictorial representation of the zone, see Grewe, ibid, 559.

[82] Miers, above n 47, 17. See also H de Montardy, *La Traite et le Droit International* (V. Giard & E. Brière Paris, 1899), 87–88.

[83] Mathieson, above n 55, 67. See also Lawrence, above n 37, 188.

force for the other four parties, and was later acceded to by Belgium (1848) and Germany (1879).[84]

In 1845, France and Great Britain concluded a ten-year treaty which suspended the treaties of 1831 and 1833 (as between the two parties only), and ended the mutual right to visit to suppress the slave trade. Instead the parties agreed that, in order that their flags "may not, contrary to the law of nations and the laws in force in the 2 countries, be usurped, to cover the Slave Trade, and in order to provide for a more effectual suppression of that traffic", each would station a twenty-six ship naval squadron off the west coast of Africa.[85] These squadrons were to work in concert, within a specific maritime zone, to suppress the trade "jointly or separately, as may be deemed most expedient" but could only visit ships to ascertain if they had a right to fly the *Tricolore* or the Red Ensign on the basis of Instructions which each had communicated to the other party.[86] While these Instructions were modified over time, the original Instructions for the Senior Officers of Her Majesty's Ships and Vessels of 1845 made plain that "[y]ou are not to capture, visit, or in any way interfere with vessels of France," but at the same time "Great Britain, will not allow vessels of other nations to escape visit and examination by merely hoisting a French flag".[87] Thus, the British Instructions continued:

Accordingly, when from intelligence, which the officer commanding Her Majesty's cruiser may have received, or from the manoeuvres of the vessels, or other sufficient cause, he may have reason to believe that the vessel does not belong to the nation indicated by her colours, he is, if the state of the weather will admit of it, to go a-head of the suspected vessel, after communicating his intention by hailing, and to drop a boat on board of her to ascertain her nationality, without causing her detention.

In seeking to determine the nationality of a ship,

the officer who boards the stranger is to be instructed merely in the first instance to satisfy himself by the vessel's papers, or other proof, of her nationality; and if she proved really to be a vessel of the nation designated by her colours, and one which he is not authorized to search, he is to lose no time in quitting her, offering to note on the papers of the vessel the cause of his having suspected her nationality, as well as the number of minutes the vessel was detained.

If the ship proved to be flying fraudulent colours the commander of the man-of-war was to "deal with her as he would have been authorized and required to do had she not hoisted a false flag".[88] That is, either as a stateless ship, or on the basis of one of the bilateral treaties which Great Britain had negotiated.

[84] Miers, above n 47, 17.

[85] Article 1, Convention between Great Britain and France, for the Suppression of the Traffic in Slaves, London, 29 May 1845, 33 *BFSP* 4.

[86] Ibid, Article 7.   [87] Ibid, "Annex referred to in Article VII", 14.

[88] Ibid, 14.

The Instructions of 1845 were replaced in 1859. These new Instructions, of which the French and British were mirror versions (like all such Instructions), were much more thorough. The Instructions first set down the principle that by "virtue of the immunity of national flags, no merchant-vessel navigating the high seas is subject to any foreign jurisdiction. A vessel of war cannot therefore visit, detain, arrest, or seize (except under Treaty) any merchant-vessel not recognized as belonging to her own nation." The Instructions went on to state that if a ship failed to hoist its flag, that a "first warning may be given her by firing a blank gun, and should this have no result, a second gun warning may be given her by means of a shotted gun, to be levelled in such a manner as not to [strike] her".[89] If a ship did hoist its flag, it was to be understood that the "man-of-war has no right to exercise the least control over her", unless the nationality could be "seriously called into question". On this basis, after hailing the ship and declaring its intentions, a cruiser could send an officer aboard with the understanding that only an examination of papers would be undertaken: "All inquiry into the nature of the cargo; or the commercial operations of the said ships; in a word, on any other subject save that of their nationality; all search, all visit, are absolutely forbidden".[90] In other words, the right to visit had been narrowed, and separated from the right to *search*.

The final set of modified Instructions, issued in 1867, mirrored the above provisions of the 1859 Instructions, but were more focused, allowing an officer to request only specified papers on board a ship suspected of flying a fraudulent flag. If a ship was deemed to be flying such a flag, the warship then escorted it to the nearest port where a representative of the flag State could determine whether it had a right to fly the flag in question.[91] The 1859 Instructions were crucial to the relationship between France and Great Britain where the suppression of slave trade at sea was concerned, as these Instructions remained in force beyond the nineteenth century, as we shall see.

(2) Portugal and Brazil

As previously noted, Portugal entered into agreements with Great Britain to end the slave trade in principle in 1810 and also to establish the means of doing so (ie creation of a right to visit and the mixed commissions) in 1817. The Convention of 1817 included a Separate Article which later caused much friction between the parties. As an afterthought to the 1817 Convention, a time limit of fifteen years was imposed; establishing that, short of a further agreement, in 1832 Portugal would effectively opt-out

[89] Instructions issued to Commanders of French Ships of War in the "Correspondence respecting the Visit of American Vessels by British Cruisers", *British Sessional Papers*, Vol 34, 1857–1858, 427.
[90] Ibid, 428.
[91] "Instructions as to Vessels under the French Flag", *Documents relatives à la Répression de la Traite des Esclaves publiés en execution des Articles LXXXI et suivants de l'Act Général de Bruxelles*, 1892, 272–274.

of the bilateral system Great Britain was building.[92] Under the terms of the 1817 Convention, in conjunction with an earlier 1815 Treaty, Portugal was allowed to carry on with its slave trade south of the equator provided the traffic was destined for the "actual Dominions of the Crown of Portugal".[93] With the independence of Brazil in 1825, Great Britain considered that the Portuguese trade would come to an end but, because of internal strife in Lisbon, it was not until 1834 that a stable government emerged which could negotiate a new agreement. However, even a government with abolitionist leanings in Lisbon could not concede the end of the trade for fear of losing Angola and Mozambique which benefited from the trade. As Miers writes: "With a weak navy and an empty treasury Portugal was in no position to force the issue. [Palmerston, the Foreign Secretary] tried in vain to negotiate a new treaty and finally took the radical step of having Britain simply assume by Act of Parliament the right to arrest and try Portuguese slavers. ... Portugal deeply resented this gross infringement of her sovereignty."[94]

The 1839 Palmerston Act created the legal fiction that Portuguese ships involved in the slave trade should be treated as though they were British, and thus susceptible to capture and trial by British courts.[95] Disregarding the advice proffered by Lord Stowell in *The Le Louis* regarding use of force and acting against international law in seeking an end to the slave trade, Great Britain declared it open season on Portuguese maritime commerce in an attempt to end the Portuguese slave trade. In the leading British international law text of the latter half of the nineteenth century, Phillimore did not truly engage with the issue, stating: "This Act has been vehemently attacked as a violation of International Law; it must of course be considered with reference to the previous Treaties, upon which its authority is found."[96] Indeed, Lord Palmerston sought to justify his actions in Parliament on the grounds that Portugal had not faithfully carried out its previous treaty obligations and was unwilling to come to an agreement on a new treaty. "The conclusion", Palmerston said "which Great Britain draws from hence, is, that she is entitled and compelled to have recourse to her own means, in order to accomplish results which she has a right to obtain."[97] Wilson, acknowledging that Great Britain "contended that her action was distinctly authorized by the terms of existing engagements," declared, having considered the

---

[92] *Article Separe*, Additional Convention between Great Britain and Portugal, for the prevention of Slave Trade, London, 11 September 1817, 4 *BFSP* 115–116.

[93] Article 2, Treaty between Great Britain and Portugal, for the restriction of the Portuguese Slave-Trade; and for the annulment of the Convention of Loan of 1809; and Treaty of Alliance of 1810, Vienna, 22 January 1815, 2 *BFSP* 352.

[94] Miers, above n 47, 24.

[95] Act for the Suppression of the Slave Trade, 24 August 1839 (2 & 3 Vict. c. 73), 27 *BFSP* 849.

[96] Phillimore, above n 3, 413.

[97] Enclosure to a Letter from Viscount Palmerston to Lord Howard de Walden, 20 April 1839, 27 *BFSP* 565.

evidence presented by the Foreign Secretary, that "[h]is case at least manifested a care for legality."[98]

Despite the challenge the Palmerston Act posed to established international law, in its quest to abolish the slave trade, in 1845 Great Britain introduced the so-called "Aberdeen Act" aimed at the Brazilian trade. Great Britain's willingness to recognise the independence of Brazil was predicated on a number of conditions, including signature of a treaty which mirrored the Anglo-Portuguese agreement of 1817. In 1845, Brazil invoked the termination of that Treaty of 1826 "without making any alternative suggestions", and Lord Aberdeen then successfully advocated an "Act authorizing the Government to take action against suspected vessels sailing under Brazilian flag on the basis of the 1826 treaty".[99] Aberdeen contended that, as the Treaty of 1826 had assimilated the slave trade with piracy and had established the complete abolition of the Brazilian trade within three years; it granted jurisdiction to British admiralty courts over any vessels engaged in the Brazilian slave-trade.[100] In 1850 Palmerston, who had regained his position as Foreign Secretary, on the basis of the Aberdeen Act, ordered the Royal Navy into the territorial waters and ports of Brazil, where it captured, burned, and sank a number of slave traders.[101]

The Palmerston and Aberdeen Acts, it must be said, had their intended effects. For its part, Portugal agreed to a new treaty with Great Britain in 1842.[102] Brazil by contrast was forced to accept the British interpretation of the 1826 Treaty, which ultimately moved Brazil to put an end to its slave trade through domestic legislation and patrolling its waters. Lord Palmerston was delighted with the Brazilian outcome, noting that "naval operations on the Brazilian coast . . . had apparently accomplished in a few weeks what diplomatic notes and treaty negotiations had failed to achieve over a period of many years".[103]

Great Britain through gunboat diplomacy was able to achieve the near completion of its bilateral web of treaties aimed at universal suppression of the slave trade. However, there remained one maritime Power outside the bilateral regime. As William Law Mathieson explained in considering the effects of the 1839 and 1845 Acts on slave traders: when they were challenged, they "either hoisted American colours or threw overboard both flag and papers".[104]

[98] H Wilson, "Some Principal Aspects of British Efforts to Crush The African Slave Trade, 1807–1929", (1950) 44 *AJIL* 505, 513–514.

[99] J H W Verzijl, *International Law in Historical Perspective: Nationality and Other Matters Relating to Individuals*, Part V (A Sijthoff, Leyden, 1972), 257.

[100] L Bethell, *The Abolition of the Brazilian Slave Trade: Britain, Brazil and the Slave Trade Question 1807–1869*, (CUP, 1970) 263–65. See also An Act of the British Parliament to amend an Act, intitled as an Act to carry into execution a Convention between His Majesty and the Emperor of Brazil, for the Regulation and final Abolition of the African Slave Trade, 8 August 1845 (8 & 9 Vict. c. 122), 34 *BFSP* 1216.

[101] Bethell, ibid, 329–30, 355.

[102] Treaty Between Great Britain and Portugal, for the Suppression of the Traffic in Slaves, Lisbon, 3 July 1842, 30 *BFSP* 527.

[103] Bethell, above n 100, 344.   [104] Mathieson, above n 55, 74.

(3) United States of America

Just as the three recalcitrant States before it, the United States of America saw ulterior motives in British attempts to abolish the slave trade. In 1895, US Ambassador Eugene Schuyler, a career diplomat, wrote that "the real reason" for attempting to end the slave trade "was fairly well concealed under the mask of philanthropy". The Americans further objected to British attempts to gain the right to visit which they consider had been abused during the Napoleonic Wars. Schuyler points to calls by the colonial agent of Trinidad in the British House of Commons in 1810 for the "effectual" as opposed to "nominal" abolition of the slave trade to counter the advantage of the continued flow of slaves to Spanish possessions which "in its effects [was] ruinous to the British colonies.... He appealed to the British Parliament on the part of our own planters, and trusted that effectual steps would yet be taken for remedying so serious an evil" (i.e. unfair trade; not the slave trade).[105] The second reason which Schuyler gives, while also relating to commerce, deals with British attempts at hegemony over the oceans:

British statesmen soon began to see that, through the right of visitation and search which had been accorded by the treaties with several powers, it might be easy, under the pretext of putting down the slave-trade, to obtain the police of the sea, which once having been granted and made the rule of international law, it would be difficult to take away from them; and this would secure the preponderance of the British navy.[106]

The United States had a further reason for not wanting to cooperate with British attempts to suppress the trade at sea: impressment. As Soulsby wrote in his study focusing on the right to visit and the slave trade in Anglo-American relations:

Great Britain was the traditional upholder of belligerent rights at sea; she had emerged from the wars the greatest naval power in the world, and in any concerted measures against the slave trade her navy would inevitably take a leading part. Hence it was not remarkable that her European neighbors were not enthusiastic over proposals which promised to strengthen her existing maritime supremacy. Still more serious was the opposition of the United States, which had protested in the war of 1812 against an abuse, as it was considered, of the belligerent right of search—the impressment of seamen....[107]

For the United States, after the War of 1812, the issue of visitation became visceral. It had gone to war against Britain in part because the Royal Navy,

---

[105] E Schuyler, *American Diplomacy and the Furtherance of Commerce* (Charles Scribner's Sons, New York, 1895), 236–37; H Soulsby, "The Right of Search and the Slave Trade in Anglo-American Relations 1814–1862", *John Hopkins University Studies in Historical and Political Science Collection*, Series 51(2), 1933, 121 at 134.

[106] Schuyler, ibid, 239. See also W Beach Lawrence, *Visitation and Search; or, An Historical Sketch of the British Claim to Exercise a Maritime Police over the Vessels of All Nations, in Peace as well as War, with An Inquiry into the Expediency of Terminating the Eight Article of the Ashburton Treaty* (Little, Brown & Co, Boston, 1858), 16. Lawrence was the editor of *Wheaton's Elements of International Law*, the leading American international law text of the era.

[107] Soulsby, above n 105, 8.

during the Napoleonic Wars, had impressed sailors who were American citizens under the pretext of a belligerent right to visit neutral ships to check for contraband.[108] Although, the United States President, James Madison, cited Great Britain's support of a new Indian War and the use of "a secret agent to subvert the Union," his main reason for war was the conduct of the British Navy. The United States took issue with the violation of its territorial waters by the Royal Navy, the establishment of "illegal blockades," and importantly, in the eyes of the general public, the impressing of American seamen which, during the period of 1803–1812, was estimated to be in the range of six thousand American citizens.[109] To what extent this issue touched a raw nerve with the United States is made plain by the conversation in the early 1820s between Stratford Canning, the British Ambassador in Washington and John Quincy Adams, the US Secretary of State: "Canning had inquired if he could conceive of a more atrocious evil than the slave trade, to which Adams replied; 'Yes; admitting the right of search by foreign officers of our vessels upon the sea in time of peace; for that would be making slaves of ourselves'."[110] Although Article 10 of the Treaty of Ghent, which settled the War of 1812, made the following declaration, it made no mention regarding either the issues of visitation or impressment:

Whereas the Traffic in Slaves is irreconcilable with the principles of humanity and Justice, and whereas both His Majesty and the United States are desirous of continuing their efforts to promote its entire abolition, it is hereby agreed that both the contracting parties shall use their best endeavours to accomplish so desirable an object.[111]

In 1818 John Quincy Adams laid out the United States' objections to allowing British ships the right to visit American merchant vessels in time of peace as being directly related to its wartime abuse of its status as a neutral during the Napoleonic Wars:

The United States have never disputed the belligerent right of search as required and universally practised conformably to the laws of nations. They have disputed the right of belligerents under *color* of the right of search for contraband, to seize and carry away *men*, at the discretion of the boarding officers, without trial and without appeal; men, not as contraband of war, or belonging to the enemy, but as the subjects, real or pretended, of the belligerent himself, and to

---

[108] In 1821, US Secretary of State John Quincy Adams noted that "the United States had very recently issued from a war with Great Britain, principally waged in resistance to a practice of searching neutral merchant vessels for men in time of war, exercised by Great Britain, as the United States deem, in violation of the law of nations". See J Bassett Moore, *A Digest of International Law*, Vol. 2 (Govt Print Office, Washington, 1906), 919.

[109] D Hickey, *The War of 1812: A Forgotten Conflict* (University of Illinois, Urbana, 1989), 18–24. More specifically, see J Fulton Zimmerman, *Impressment of American Seamen* (Columbia University Press, New York, 1925).

[110] Soulsby, above n 105, 18.

[111] Article 10, Treaty of Peace and Amity between His Britannic Majesty and the United States of America, 4 December 1814, 24 December 1814, Ghent, 2 *BFSP* 364.

be used by him against the enemy. It is the fundamental abuse of the right of search, for the purpose never recognised or admitted by the laws of nations, purposes in their practical operation of the greatest oppression and most crying injustice, that them against assenting to the extension in time of peace of a right of search which experience has shown to be liable to such gross perversion in time of war.[112]

Adams made it plain, in instructions to his Ambassador in London, that the possibility of entering into a treaty regarding the suppression of the slave trade with Great Britain was, for the foreseeable future, impossible:

That the admission of a right in the officers of foreign ships-of-war to enter and search the vessels of the United States in time of peace, under any circumstances whatever, would meet with universal repugnance in the public opinion of this country; that there would be no prospect of a ratification, by advice and consent of the Senate, to any stipulations of that nature; that the search by foreign officers, even in time of war is so obnoxious to the feelings and recollections of this country, that nothing could reconcile them to the extension of it, however qualified or restricted, to a time of peace.[113]

However, by 1821, Adams proposed a course to Stratford Canning which ultimately broke the impasse between the two States and led to the signing of a treaty in 1824:

The expedient proposal on the part of the United States of keeping cruisers of their own constantly upon the coast where the traffic is carried on, with instructions to cooperate by good offices and by the mutual communications of information with the cruisers of other powers stationed and instructed to the attainment of the same end, appears in its own nature as well as to experience so far as it has abided that test, better adapted to the suppression of the traffic than that of the British Government, which makes the officers of one nation the executors of the laws of another.[114]

In 1820, the United States House of Representatives declared that trading in African slaves by American citizens should be assimilated to the concept of piracy and made punishable by death. Although the slave trade was never accepted as piracy in international law, this link found its way into the proposed 1824 Anglo-American Treaty.[115] The draft Convention allowed the cruisers of each States to visit and search each other's vessels "on the coasts of Africa, of America, and of West Indies".[116] It stipulated that the captain and crew were to proceed against seized vessels and crews "as Pirates involved in the African Slave Trade" and try them

---

[112] Soulsby, above n 105. Emphasis in the original.
[113] Ibid.   [114] Moore, above n 108, 921.
[115] Moore writes that the declaration was meant "to enable the United States to join in the movement then on foot to assimilate the slave trade to piracy, both in the measure of its punishment and the method of its repression. This movement, however, did not succeed, owing to the opposition to opening the way to the establishment of the practice of visitation and search in time of peace". ibid, 922.
[116] Article 1, Convention with Great Britain, 12 BFSP 839.

in the courts of either State.[117] The Convention, however, did not come into force as the United States Congress, while accepting the Convention in general terms, sought to amend it by inserting a provision allowing for denunciation of the treaty on six months notice, and by deleting the word "America" from the above noted phrase. The latter provision was "deemed insuperable" to Great Britain which then declared that it was unable to ratify the Convention as modified by the United States.[118] In 1834, the same stumbling block appeared as Great Britain sought to convince the United States to accede to the French treaties of 1831 and 1833. The United States President declined to bring the question before the legislature, as the British Ambassador in Washington had made plain "that the right of search would be extended to the coasts of the United States".[119]

Although the American Ambassador to Paris was successful in preventing France from consenting to the 1841 Quintuple Treaty, the United States, by this time, found itself isolated by the growing number of British bilateral treaties. As a means of deflecting this mounting pressure, the United States agreed, in the 1842 Webster-Ashburton Treaty, to maintain a naval presence of the coast of Africa to suppress the trade, it being understood that "the said squadrons [are] to be independent of each other".[120] United States President John Tyler noted that the provisions removed "all pretext on the part of others for violating the immunities of the American flag upon the seas, as they exist and are defined by the law of nations".[121] Great Britain, having abandoned its attempt to assimilate the slave trade with piracy, changed tack and sought to emphasise the innovation developed in the Quintuple Treaty: the separation of the right to visit from the right to search foreign ships on the high seas, in peacetime, to suppress the slave trade. Great Britain sought to advocate that while there did not exist a right to search ships on the high seas, there did exist a right to approach and visit a ship to inquire, through an inspection of its papers, whether a ship's nationality corresponded to the flag it flew. As the United States and France remained the only two States not party to the British bilateral treaty regime, it was logical that slave ships would gravitate towards flying their flags to avoid capture. By advocating this new understanding of the concept of the "right to visit", Great Britain hoped to close the loophole and include all States in its bilateral treaty regime. Thus, the British Foreign Secretary took issue with the United States President's address and noted that the right to visit had not been part of the discussion leading to the Webster-Ashburton Treaty, nor had

---

[117] Article 7, ibid, 842.   [118] Moore, above n 108, 926.
[119] Ibid, 927.
[120] Article 8, Treaty between Great Britain and The United States, to settle and define the Boundaries between the Territories of the United States and the Possessions of Her Britannic Majesty in North America, for the final Suppression of the African Slave Trade; and for the giving up of Criminals, fugitive from Justice, in certain Cases, Washington, 9 August 1842, 30 *BFSP* 365.
[121] Moore, above n 108, 931.

any concession on the issue been made by Great Britain. Aberdeen went on to say:

The President may be assured, that Great Britain will always respect the just claims of The United States. We make no pretension to interfere in any manner whatever, either by detention, visit, or search, with vessels of The United States, known or believed to be such. But we still maintain, and will exercise, when necessary, our right to ascertain the genuineness of any flag which a suspected vessel may bear.[122]

Sir Robert Phillimore, "one of the most ardent champions" of this new right of visit advocated by Great Britain[123] noted that:

The question of the *Right to Visit* has been a matter of sore contention between Great Britain and the North American United States; the latter refuse to distinguish it from the *Right to Search*, which, they justly say, is an exclusively *belligerent* Right. The British Government, on the other hand, denies the identity of the two Rights, and claims merely to ascertain the nationality of ships hosting, under suspicious circumstances, the flag of the United States, alleging that when once that nationality is ascertained to be that of the United States, they immediately release whatever be her cargo or destination, the vessel; and that it is manifest, that if the mere hoisting of a particular ensign is to supersede all inquiry, the Slave Trade may be carried out with impunity.[124]

The Secretary of State Daniel Webster addressed the issue in a letter to the British Ambassador in Washington, stating that the Government of the United States:

maintains that there is no such well-known and acknowledged, or indeed, any broad and genuine difference between what has been usually called visit, and what has been usually called search; that the right to visit, to be effectual, must come in the end to include search; and thus to exercise, in peace an authority which the law of nations only allows in time of war. If such a well-known distinction exists, where are the proofs of it? What writers of authority on the public law, what adjudications in Courts of Admiralty, what public Treaties recognize it? No such recognition has presented itself to the Government of The United States; but, on the contrary, it understands that public writers, courts of law, and solemn treaties have for 2 centuries, used the word, 'visit' and 'search' in the same manner.[125]

The Secretary of State questioned the approach of the British, noting that the Foreign Secretary had indicated that in exercising its right, if errors were committed, prompt reparations would be forthcoming. Webster indicates the apparent flaw in such an argument as the "general rule of law certainly is, that in the proper and prudent exercise of our

---

[122] The Earl of Aberdeen to Mr. Fox [United States Ambassador to the Court of St. James], 18 January 1843, 32 *BFSP* 444.

[123] L Gessner, *Le Droit des Neutres sur mer* (Stilke et van Muyden, Berlin, 1865), 287.

[124] R Phillimore, *Commentaries upon International Law* (W Benning, London, 1854), 326. Emphasis in the original.

[125] Mr Webster to Mr Evertt, 28 March 1843, 32 *BFSP* 466.

own rights, no one is answerable for undersigned injuries." As such, the British approach to the right to visit "implies, at least in its general interpretation, the commission of some wrongful act."[126] Webster concluded by noting:

On the whole, the Government of The United States, while it has not conceded a mutual right to visit or search, as has been done by the parties to the Quintuple Treaty of December 1841, does not admit that by the law and practice of nations, there is any such thing as a right to visit, distinguished, by well known rules and definition, for the right of search.[127]

Although the United States dispatched a squadron to the African coast in 1843, the British Instructions to its Naval Officers issued in 1844 were almost verbatim those cited earlier with reference to France, that is: "it is no part of their duty to capture or visit, or in any way interfere with vessels of the United States, whether those vessels shall have Slaves on board or not". But, that, "most, assuredly, Great Britain, never will allow vessels of other nations to escape visit and examination by merely hoisting an United States' Flag".[128] In essence a stalemate ensued and the United States was left to challenge by diplomatic means the continuing visits by British warships to inquire whether ships flying the Stars and Stripes were authorised to do so. This diplomatic impasse became acute in 1858, the year following the appointment of General Lewis Cass—who it will be recalled caused France to decline to ratify the 1841 Quintuple Treaty—as United States Secretary of State; and as a result of the Royal Navy's actions off the coast of Cuba, where the slave trade persisted. As Schuyler wrote, noting that Cass had brought to the attention of the United States legislature incidents of British boarding of American ships in the Caribbean which, in turn, had prompted the United States Congress to approve the dispatch of a naval force to protect its maritime commerce in the region: "This looked very much like war."[129] Secretary of State Cass, despite his apparent belligerence, opened a diplomatic window to allow for a compromise: if Great Britain renounced the notion of a *right* to visit to ascertain the propriety of hoisted American flags, the United States would admit that Great Britain could, in suspicious circumstances, visit ships flying American colours to ascertain their right to do so:

The immunity of their merchant-vessels depends upon the rights of The United States, as one of the independent Powers of the world, and not upon

---

[126] Ibid, 467.   [127] Ibid, 470.

[128] British Instructions for the Senior Officers of Her Majesty's Ships and Vessels on the West Coast of Africa, with respect to the Treaty with the United States of America, signed at Washington, 9 August, 1842, *Instructions for the Guidance of Her Majesty's Naval Officers employed in the Suppression of the Slave Trade*, 1844, 16–17. In 1858, the British Commodore of the African Squadron pointed to the fact that the American flag was being used to harbour slave ships, as he "complained to the Admiralty of 'the shameful prostitution of the American flag, for under that ensign alone is the Slave Trade now conducted'". See Lloyd, above n 27, 56.

[129] Schuyler, above n 105, 261.

the purposes or motives of the foreign officers by whom it is violated. A merchant-vessel upon the high seas is protected by her national character. He who forcibly enters her, does so upon his own responsibility. Undoubtedly, if a vessel assumes a national character to which she is not entitled, and is sailing under false colours, she cannot be protected by the assumption of a nationality to which she has not claimed. As the identity of a person must be determined by the officer bearing a process of his arrest, and determined at the risk of such officer, so must the national identity of a vessel be determined, at a like hazard to him who, doubting the flag she displays, search her to ascertain her true character. There, no doubt, may be circumstances which would go far to modify the complaints a nation would have a right to make for such a violation of its sovereignty.

Cass then provided his diplomatic concession:

If the boarding office had just grounds for suspicion, and deported himself with propriety in the performance of his task, doing no injury and peaceably retiring when satisfied of his error, no nation would make such an act the subject of serious reclamation. It is one thing to do a deed avowedly illegal, and excuse it by the attending circumstances; and it is another and quite different thing to claim a right of action and the right also of determining when, and how, and to what extent, it shall be exercised. And this is no barren distinction, so far as the interest of this country is involved, but it is closely connected with an object dear to the American people—the freedom of their citizens upon the great highway of the world.[130]

In response the British Foreign Secretary, the Earl of Malmesbury, made known through his Ambassador in Washington that Great Britain was willing to concede the point: "Her Majesty's Government recognize as sound those principles of international law which have been laid down by General Cass in his note." The Foreign Secretary stated that "Her Majesty's Government agree entirely in this view of the case, and the question therefore becomes one solely of discretion on the part of acting officers". As a result, it was proposed that as the burden of the question fell to each officer's discretion which "is one extremely dangerous to entrust, and onerous to bear...,"[131] the parties should negotiate suitable instruction to be give to their naval commanders. In the meantime, however, Great Britain,

anxious to remove all possible repetition of the acts which appear to have caused so much excitement in the United States, and which might, if repeated at this moment be detriment to the good relations of the two countries, have set further orders to the officers commanding the Cuban squadron to discontinue the search of any vessels of the United States until some agreement, in the sense I have pointed out shall be made.[132]

---

[130] General Cass to Lord Napier, 10 April 1858, 50 *BFSP* 715. Also see General Cass to Mr Dallas, 23 February 1859, 49 *BFSP* 1121.
[131] Earl of Malmesbury to Lord Napier, 11 June 1858, 50 *BFSP* 738 and 739.
[132] Ibid, 740.

The American Ambassador in London was informed that the "President desires you would express to Lord Malmesbury his gratification at this satisfactory termination of the controversy which has given so much trouble to our respective Governments, concerning the claim of a right in behalf of a British cruiser in time of peace to search or visit American merchant vessels upon the ocean."[133] Having settled its differences with the United States, Great Britain sought to close the loophole which allowed slave ships to avoid British capture by hoisting either the American or French flag. The negotiation of Instructions with France, which might then be adopted by the United States, would ensure that no ship, in suspicious situations, could avoid being visited to ascertain the propriety of the flag flown. These negotiations, started in February 1859, were concluded successfully in May of that same year.[134]

The United States, in the throes of a civil war that centred on slavery, shifted policy. In 1863, the United States of America (i.e: the Northern Union of States) concluded a bilateral treaty with Great Britain to suppress the slave trade to gain British support for its conflict with the Southern Confederacy.[135] The attempted equation of the slave trade with piracy, at the core of the 1824 draft Convention, was dropped from the 1863 agreement. Much like the 1845 Anglo-French Convention, the 1863 Anglo-American Treaty required each State to dispatch a naval squadron to the West African coast. However, unlike France, the United States agreed to patrol a differently demarcated maritime zone, one which ran contiguous to the African coast to a distance of two hundred miles. The United States further agreed to the establishment of mixed commissions, though these never heard a case and were superseded by a 1870 agreement that transferred jurisdiction to each State's respective domestic courts.[136]

By negotiation and coercion Great Britain had, by the mid-1860s, created bilaterally what it had failed to achieve multilaterally during the early eighteen hundreds. The four recalcitrant States had, one by one, been integrated into the British regime of slave trade suppression. By the time the United States had agreed to a bilateral treaty however, the tide had clearly shifted in favour of abolition. According to Klein, the 1860s was a turning point as "the pressure that led to the abolition of the trade now shifted to attacking the institution of slavery itself".[137] The forced migration of enslaved African labours was supplanted throughout the Western Hemisphere in the late nineteenth century by European free labour in what was to be the "great age of immigration,"[138] and more

---

[133] General Cass to Mr Dallas, 30 June 1858, 50 *BFSP* 747 and 748.
[134] General Cass to Count de Sartiges, 12 May 1859, 50 *BFSP* 796.
[135] Soulsby, above n 105, 174.
[136] Treaty between Great Britain and the United States, for the Suppression of the African Slave Trade, 7 April 1862, Washington, 52 *BFSP* 50.
[137] Klein, above n 12, 202.
[138] Ibid. David Brion Davis goes further, pointing out that "there can be no doubt that black slave labour was essential in creating and developing the 'original' New World that began by the 1840s to attract so many millions of European immigrants". See *Inhuman Bondage* (above n 18), 80.

importantly, by large numbers of indentured labourers from Asia—primarily from China and India—who took up employment side by side with newly freed slaves.

In essence, therefore, Great Britain had achieved the primary element of its objective by the 1870s: it had managed to totally abolish the Atlantic Slave Trade. For all the fears expressed by the four recalcitrant States, Great Britain had persisted in moving forward its abolitionist agenda when British hegemony over maritime commerce was no longer at issue, when the policing of the seas had become a concern of the past and when New World slave products no longer challenged British goods. While, throughout the nineteenth century, the suppression of the slave trade remained aligned with Britain's strategic imperial interests, it remained true that within Britain, there persisted popular and philanthropic support for the ending of slavery and the slave trade. This required, for much of the nineteenth century, the British Foreign Office to continuously push for completion of its bilateral network of treaties to suppress the slave trade.

While Great Britain had managed to end the Atlantic Slave Trade, its attention now shifted to the east coast of Africa where the Oriental Slave Trade came into play. As a result of the persistence in fighting the slave trade and slavery, Great Britain finally gained in 1890 what it had failed to achieved nearly eighty years previously: a universal right, established by treaty and accepted as international law, to visit ships on the high seas to suppress the slave trade.

THE UNIVERSAL OUTLAWING OF THE SLAVE TRADE

In their quest for what historians termed the "Second European Empires", the ideology used to justify usurpation of land shifted once more.[139] Having colonised the New World, European Powers embarked on a civilizing mission. That mission would descend into an all-out "scramble" for Africa by the 1880s. While much of the colonization of the New World had taken place under the banner of "Gold, Glory and God", the British missionary, David Livingstone, made it known throughout Europe that in Africa "slave raiding and trading were devastating large areas, and his appeal to bring Christianity, commerce, and civilization to the heart of the continent" did not fall on deaf ears.[140] A recurring theme throughout much of this period was the European demand to end the slave trade, not only at sea, but on land on the African Continent. Thus, in the latter part of the nineteenth century, as Africa was opened to the pursuit of Empire, European States concluded treaties with local African elite mandating the

[139] For 'Second European Empires' see A Pagden, *Lords of all the World; Ideologies of Empire in Spain, Britain and France c.1500–c.1800* (Yale University Press, New Haven, 1995), 2.
[140] S Miers, *Slavery in the Twentieth Century: The Evolution of a Global Problem* (Altiamira Press, Walnut Creek, 2003), 20.

suppression of the slave trade. Great Britain became party to more than a hundred such agreements "which eventually covered the whole coast from which slaves were exported".[141] During this period, it was clear that the suppression of slavery and the slave trade had become part of the discourse of international relations and, though it had been championed by Great Britain, other States with holdings in Africa—France, Germany, Italy, and Portugal (and the private Congolese State awarded to King Leopold of Belgium in 1885)—were agreeable to its inclusion on the agenda of international conferences and in international instruments.

When a dispute arose over an Anglo-Portuguese treaty regarding control of the mouth of the Congo River in 1884, the German Chancellor, Otto von Bismarck, proposed an international conference to settle the question. The Berlin Conference, which ultimately provided for the free navigation of the Congo and, more generally, a framework for the effective occupation of the African coast, also found on its agenda a British proposal which called for universal jurisdiction to be established over the slave trade.[142] The proposal was in the form of a declaration that the slave trade was "a crime against the Law of Nations". The draft Declaration read in part that: "The Slave Trade is henceforth a crime prohibited by the Law of Nations, and cognizable by the tribunals of all civilized nations whatever the nationality of the accused."[143] This proposal, however, did not find favour with the fifteen States gathering in Berlin as they were unwilling to commit to a pronouncement which they considered to raise unforeseeable consequences. Instead they accepted a general declaration that the slave trade was indeed prohibited by international law. The Declaration Relative to the Slave Trade, which emerged from the 1885 General Act of the Conference of Berlin, reads:

Seeing the trading in slaves is forbidden in conformity with the principles of international law as recognized by the Signatory Powers, and seeing also that the operations, which, by sea or land, furnish slaves to trade, ought likewise to be regarded as forbidden, the Powers which do or shall exercise sovereign rights

[141] Miers, above n 47, 46. Treaties were concluded by Great Britain with the following regions of Africa up to the 1889–1890 Brussels Conference: *Central Africa*: Gando, Sokoto; *East Africa*: Brava (Somalia), Comoro, Eesa Somal, Habr-Awal, Habr-Gerhajis, Habr-Toljaala, Mohilla, Soomalees (*sic*), Tajowra, Warsangali, Zaila; but primarily from *West Africa*: Abbeokuta, Abo-den-Arfo, Aboh, Acassa, Adaffie, Adinnar Cooma, Afflowhoo, Aghwey, Angiana, Badagry, Baddiboo, Bagroo River, Batanga, Bereira, Biafra, Bimbia, Biombo, Blockouse, Bonney, Boom River, Bulola, Bussama, Cabenda, Cagnabac, Calabar, Cameroons, Camma, Cantalicunda, Cape Lopez, Cape Mount, Cartabar, Chacoonda, Congo, Cumbo, Dahomey, Dalu Mahdoo, Dobacconda, Drewin, Egarra, Epe, Fouricaria, Gallinas, Garraway River, Goom Corkway, Grand Bereby, Grand Lahou, Grand Popoe, Grand Sesters, Ivroy Bay, Joboo, Jack Jaques, Joug River, Kambia, Kinsembo, Kittam, Lagos, Little Booton, Little Popoe, Lucalla, Macbatee, Malghea, Malimba, Manna, Monney, Maricaryah, Naloes, New Calabar, New Cestos, Nyanibantang, Okeodan, Old Town (Old Calabar), Omitska, Otanda, Pocrah, Porto Novo, Qua Plantations, Nio Nunez, Pongas, Ro-Woolah, St. Andrew, St. Antonio, Samo, Samoah, Sherbro, Small Scarcies River, Sugury, Soombia, Zanga Tanga. See *British and Foreign State Papers*, General Index, Volumes 64 and 80.

[142] See H Wesseling, *Divide and Rule: The Partition of Africa 1880–1914* (Praeger, Westport, 1996), 113–119.

[143] Miers, above n 47, 171–72.

or influence in the territories forming the Conventional basin of the Congo declare that these territories may not serve as a market or means of transit for the trade in slaves, or whatever race they may be. Each of the Powers binds itself to employ all the means at its disposal for putting an end to this trade and for punishing those who engage in it.[144]

Great Britain was satisfied with the outcome of the Berlin Conference and saw little reason to push States further with regard to the suppression of the slave trade, though the trade on the east coast of Africa, in places such as Zanzibar and Pemba, was starting to raise difficulties with other European Powers. It was at this point, shortly after the end of Berlin Conference, that an ally to the anti-slavery cause emerged from the most unlikely of sources, in the Roman Catholic Archbishop of Algiers, Cardinal Lavigerie. In what can only be termed a "one-man crusade", Lavigerie gained the support of the Pope, and moved to establish a number of anti-slavery societies throughout Europe and aroused public sentiment by describing the horrors of the slave trade on the African continent. The long established British and Foreign Anti-Slavery Society noted that in the "Summer of 1888 the eloquent orations of Cardinal Lavigerie created an extraordinary impression on the Continent". Likewise his visit to London "aroused some of the dormant enthusiasm of the people of England, and a Resolution, unanimously passed at the meeting was forwarded to the Foreign Minister which suggested that a Conference of the Powers might be convened".[145] Such a conference, Miers notes, was "infinitely more practical and less hazardous" than Lavigerie's other proposal, which was to establish a religio-military order modelled on the Templers or the Knights of Malta to take the battle to Africa in a crusade to suppress the trade.[146]

Lord Salisbury, the then British Foreign Minister, saw the suggested conference as a means of addressing the awkward situation which had developed as a result of slave trading emanating from Zanzibar, a sultanate under the protection of Great Britain. At the request of Germany, Great Britain, along with Italy, had agreed to blockade Zanzibar to "restore the Sultan's authority and prevent the export of slaves and the import of arms [used by slave raiders]".[147] While the blockade was effective, it "highlighted the need for an international treaty against the slave

---

[144] Article 9, *General Act of the Conference of Berlin, relative to the Development of Trade and Civilization in Africa; the free navigation of the River Congo, Niger, etc.; the Suppression of the Slave Trade by Sea and Land; the occupation of Territory on the African Coast, etc.* 26 February 1885. Sir E Hertslet, *The Map of Africa by Treaty*, Vol. 2 (Routledge, London, 1967), 474.

[145] British and Foreign Anti-Slavery Society, *The Slave-Trade Conference at Brussels and the British and Foreign Anti-Slavery Society*, 1890, 6.

[146] "Sur les anciens ordres religieux-militaires et la possibilité d'une association du même gendre pour l'abolition de l'esclavage, dans les contrées Barbares de l'Afrique" in Cardinal Lavigerie, *Documents sur la Foundation de l'oeuvre Antiesclavagiste* (Belin et fils, St Cloud, 1889), 712–15.

[147] Miers, above n 47, 211.

trade".[148] Thus, using the momentum created by Lavigerie, Salisbury requested his ambassador in Brussels, Lord Vivian, to sound out the possibility that King Leopold host an international conference to deal with the slave trade. On 18 November 1889, the seventeen invited States met in Belgium to inaugurate the Brussels Conference to discuss the end of the slave trade by land and sea.[149]

The 1889–1890 Brussels Conference

While the General Act of the Brussels Conference dealt with the suppression of the African slave trade on land in countries of destination, it also established an arms agreement and restricted the traffic in spirits. However, the suppression of the slave trade at sea, it was said, was the "most awaited and most delicate point"[150] to be considered; it was, in fact, the point upon which the Conference hinged.[151] Vivian, having been named plenipotentiary, spelled out the British position on the second day of the Conference:

The Congresses of Vienna and Verona had established the general principles; the Berlin Conference recognized and applied these principles to the territory forming the conventional basin of the Congo. The Powers, therefore, had formally accepted these principles, and the object of this Conference, such as Her Majesty's Government understands it, is to establish efficient measures to put into practice these principles and to substitute individual action for collective action.

Vivian then turned to the suppression of the slave trade at sea, calling for a universal instrument to encompass the established bilateral regime for the suppression of the slave trade:

It is the opinion of Her Majesty's Government that the suppression of the maritime trade is the object upon which the efforts of this Conference should be primarily focused.... It may be possible, perhaps, to come to a unanimous international understanding, which, while respecting the right and interests of the Powers not yet linked by the Treaties, to incorporate and even amplify the provisions of the existing Treaties, which it might well be substituted for.[152]

The British delegation took the initiative and presented a proposal which called for the creation of a *cordon sanitaire* around "the most dreadful

---

[148] Ibid, 219.

[149] The following States attended the 1889–1890 Brussels Conference: Austria, Belgium, Congo Free State, Denmark, France, Germany, Great Britain, Italy, The Netherlands, Persia, Portugal, Russia, Spain, Sweden and Norway, Turkey, the United States of America, and Zanzibar.

[150] de Montardy, above n 82, 141.

[151] H Queneuil, *La Conférence de Bruxelles et ses Résultats* (Larose et Tenin, Paris, 1907), 132.

[152] Protocol 2, Protocoles de Séances Plénieres de la Conférence de Bruxelles, 19 November 1889, *Actes de la Conférence de Bruxelles (1889–1890)*, (Hayez, Brussels, 1890), 21 and 22. All direct quotations which have been taken from French language sources have been translated by the Author.

pest which has ever gnawed on humanity".[153] Within this zone, which would extend south from Port Suez on both coasts of the Red Sea and into the Persian Gulf and follow the African coast southwards, extending to the far extremities of Mozambique, the British proposal called for the right to detain "vessels directly or indirectly suspected of trafficking in Slaves" both in internal and international waters with a view toward bringing them to be judged before mixed tribunals.[154] Yet, as the British and Foreign Anti-Slavery Society related to its readers, where the right to visitation was at issue, the "French have more or less taken the place of the Americans in this curious controversy".[155] The age-old Anglo-French rivalry was once again rearing its head, this time directly linked to the African colonial ambitions of the Powers; anti-British sentiment in France remained high—and *vice versa*—throughout this period (from 1881 and the 'Easter Question' to Fashoda in 1891).[156] The Anti-Slavery Society of France foreshadowed French resistance to the right to visit at Brussels, (and later in Paris) in 1888, stating that "we believe it is utterly impossible to obtain the consent of Parliamentary and public opinion in France, to the right for English cruisers to search French boats sailing under the national flag".[157] In a Declaration made on 20 December 1889, the French representatives in Brussels stated categorically that if the right to visit was placed on the agenda, they were not authorized to participate in such discussions. Acknowledging that the British proposal had not mentioned a right to visit *per se*, the French plenipotentiaries indicated they were willing to discuss the issue of the suppression of the slave trade at sea and put forward a general sketch of a forthcoming proposal, with the understanding that they would produce a more substantial version in the new year. This French diplomatic declaration pointed to the 1867 Anglo-French Instructions and noted that it would submit a proposal which would provide, *inter alia*, for the verification of the nationality of a boat sailing in the zone "contaminated by the exercising of the trade".[158]

The French counter-proposal was made on 20 January 1890. It provided for a zone enlarged to include the west coast of Africa, and laid down the principle that ships in the zone could only be searched by their own navies, with an exception where the right to fly a flag was in question. The counter-proposal, having laid down the manner in which a ship could be visited, then explained that fraudulent ships would be brought to a port where an international tribunal would be located.

---

[153] Annex 2, Protocol 10, "Project présenté par les Plénipotentiaries de la Grande-Bretagne", 28 November 1889, *Actes de la Conférence de Bruxelles (1889–1890)* (Hayez, Brussels, 1890), 149.

[154] Ibid, p. 150.

[155] British and Foreign Anti-Slavery Society, *The Slave-Trade Conference at Brussels and the British and Foreign Anti-Slavery Society*, 1890, 27.

[156] See, generally, Wesseling, above n 142.

[157] British and Foreign Anti-Slavery Society, above n 155, 20.

[158] Annex 3, Protocol 10, "Déclaration des Plénipotentiaires de France", 20 December 1889, *Actes de la Conférence de Bruxelles (1889–1890)* (Hayez, Brussels, 1890), 153.

The supposed flag state's Consul would then undertake an investigation. If there was a difference of opinion between the Captain of the cruiser and the Consul, the international tribunal would consider the case. While the status of the seized ship would be considered by this mixed tribunal, its Captain and crew were to be tried by their respective municipal systems. Finally, the French counter-proposal called for the creation of an international bureau which would act as a registry for ships in the zone.[159]

On 6 February 1890, the British Delegation responded to the French counter-proposal in a positive manner, saying that it "merited serious attention" and "could probably serve as the basis for effective preventative measures which would receive general applicability in the zone where the trade is taking place".[160] However, it noted with regret that the French Government would not accept "under any circumstances, the reciprocal right to monitor sailing ships in the trade zone". For its part the British Delegation refused to discuss "proposals which derogated, in any way, from the treaties to which the Queen is party, or the rights which flow from them". The Declaration said that Her Majesty's Government wanted to go as far as possible to reach an understanding with all Powers, and thus was willing to concede that the "right to visit established in the existing treaties be limited to the zone determined [during the Conference], and to limit the exercise of this right to ships of less than 500 tons [ie tantamount to 'native' African vessels], as long as this final condition, related to the dimensions of vessels, be submitted to revision if experience shows that a change was necessary." The Declaration went on to say that Great Britain "could not make these great concessions if the Conference, for its part, did not consent to adopt the strict regulations suggested in the French Counter-proposal, with a look to preventing, within the limits of the zone, the usurpation or abuse of flags of all the signatory States".[161] The British Declaration conceded that it probably made sense to drop the idea of an international tribunal as its bilateral network already had an established network of mixed commissions attached to it. Finally, the Declaration expressed itself in favour of an international bureau as proposed by France.

The Parties having made plain their positions, it was left to eminent international lawyer, Fyodor de Martens—best known today for penning the so-called "Martens Clause"—to step into the breach, though hesitantly, to mediate a solution. Martens benefited from the fact that, as a Russian plenipotentiary, he was seen as a disinterested party where

---

[159] Annex 4, Protocol 10, "Project de Traité et projet de Règlement présentés par les Pléinpotentiaires de France" *Actes de la Conférence de Bruxelles (1889–1890)* (Hayez, Brussels, 1890), 154.

[160] Annex 5, Protocol 10, "Déclaration des Plénipotentiaires de la Grande-Bretagne", 6 February 1890, *Actes de la Conférence de Bruxelles (1889–1890)* (Hayez, Brussels, 1890), 159.

[161] Ibid, 160.

issues of slavery in Africa and the slave trade at sea were concerned.[162] Martens prepared a report and draft articles which later were "entered into the General Act without major modification".[163] In his Report, Martens stated that the more he studied the British and French proposals, the "more I became convinced that there did not exist between them any fundamental contradictions."[164] He acknowledged Great Britain's century worth of experience in suppressing the slave trade at sea; but believed that the conditions in which the trade persisted had changed. The trade was now exclusively taking place in East Africa, by means of indigenous boats, in a region where nearly the entirety of the coast was either under the sovereignty or the protection of European Powers. There was a real possibility for the Powers to work collectively on land and at sea to end the slave trade. With this in mind, Martens laid out draft articles that would become part of the General Act, which took into consideration the various components of the British and French proposals.[165] A contemporary French jurist, Henry Queneuil, wrote of Martens' mediation work: "thus the different principles found themselves reconciled without having compromised the efficacy of the repression of the slave trade by sea. At the same time, a latent and disquieting conflict between France and Great Britain which had existed for fifty years was put to rest".[166]

The provisions regarding the Repression of the Slave Trade at Sea are contained in Chapter III of the General Act of the Brussels Conference relative to the African Slave Trade, signed on 2 July 1890.

The General Act defined a maritime zone which centred on the high seas contiguous to the East Coast of Africa and included both the Red Sea and the Persian Gulf. It acknowledged a right to visit, search, and detain, in established treaties and that these treaties remained in force "in so far as they are not modified by the present General Act".[167] The two major British concessions were also included, namely that the States agreed that all such rights to visit could only transpire in the newly established maritime zone, and only with respect to "vessels of less than 500 tons burthen."[168]

[162] For consideration of the 'Martens Clause' see Antonio Cassese, "Martens Clause Half a Loaf or Simply Pie in the Sky?" (2000) 11 *European Journal of International Law* 187–216.

[163] Queneuil, above n 151, 136.

[164] Annex 7, Protocol 10, "Rapport de M. de Martens, second Plénipotentiaire de Russie, sur les projets précédents", 17 February 1890, *Actes de la Conférence de Bruxelles (1889–1890)* (Hayez, Brussels, 1890), 169.

[165] See Annex 6, Protocol 10, "Projet de Traité et project de Règlement codifiant les projets précédents et préséntés par les Plénipotentiaires de Russie", 17 February 1890, *Actes de la Conférence de Bruxelles (1889–1890)* (Hayez, Brussels, 1890), 169.

[166] Queneuil, above n 151, 148.

[167] Article 24, General Act of the Brussels Conference relative to the African Slave Trade, 2 July 1890; Hertslet, above n 144, 499.

[168] Ibid, Articles 21–23.

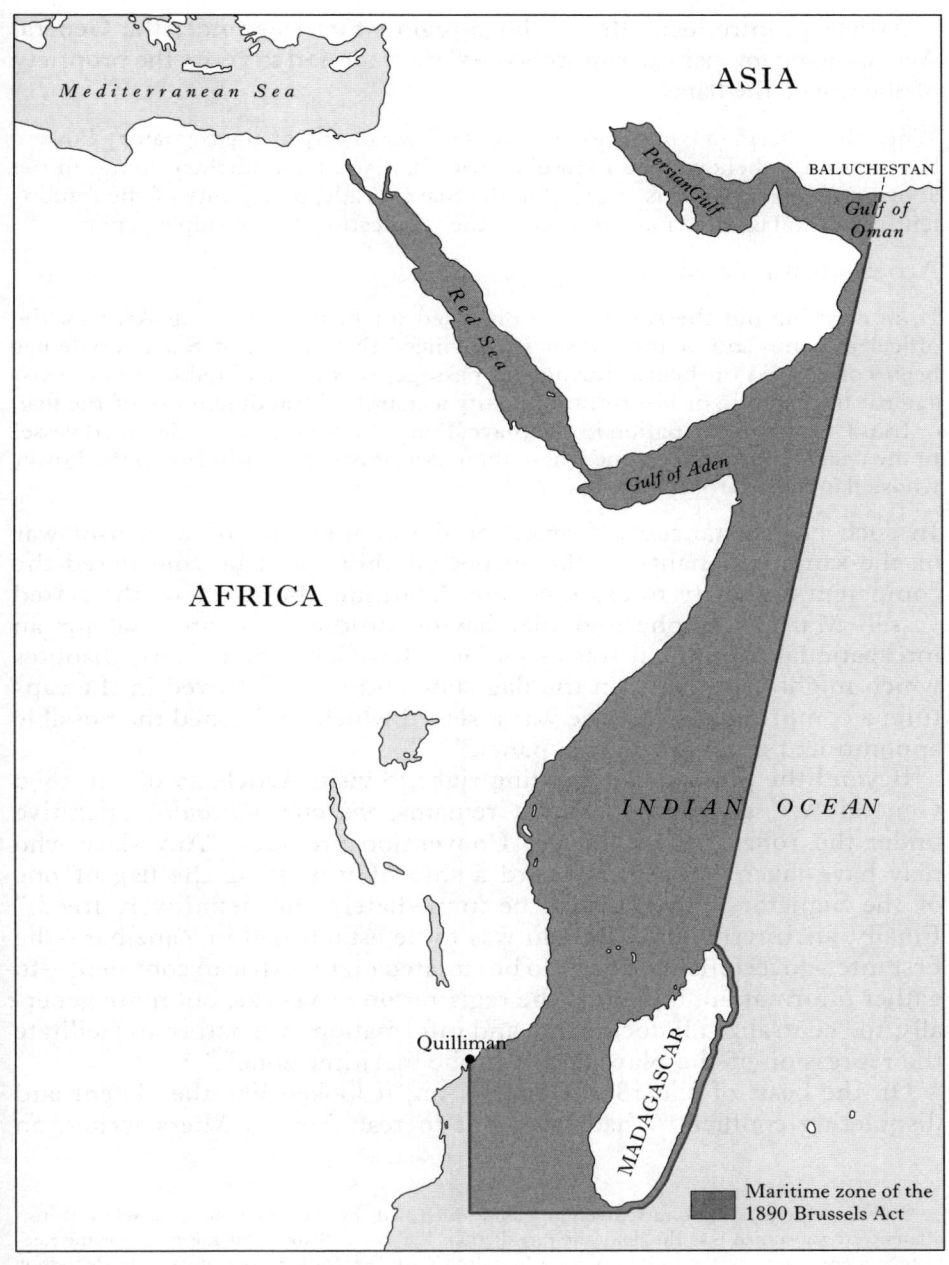

Maritime zone of the
1890 Brussels Act

Article 42 introduced the modified regime for visits under the General Act, allowing for visits to suppress the slave trade and to verify the propriety of the use of the flag:

When the officers in command of vessels of war of any of the Signatory Powers have reason to believe that a vessel of less than 500 tons burthen, found in the above-mentioned zone, is engaged in the Slave Trade, or is guilty of the fraudulent use of a flag, they may proceed to the verification of the ship's papers.

Article 46 stipulated:

If, in carrying out the supervision provided for in the preceding Articles, the officer in command of the cruiser is convinced that an Act of Slave Trade has been committed on board during the passage, or that irrefutable proofs exist against the captain, or fitter-out, to justify a charge of fraudulent use of the flag, or fraud, or the participation in the Slave Trade, he shall take the detained vessel to the nearest port of the zone where there is a competent authority to the Power whose flag has been used.

In such circumstances, a Consul or the commander of a man-of-war of the same nationality as the suspected ship could be considered the competent authority to examine and determine the status of the seized vessel. Martens emphasised that having dropped the proposal for an international tribunal, it was essential to have a means to settle disputes which might arise between the flag state and these involved in the capture: a compromissory clause was inserted which envisioned the possible appointment of an arbitration panel.[169]

Beyond the provisions regarding right to visit, Article 27 of the 1890 General Act, a provision which remains, *mutatis mutandis*, operative under the 1982 Law of the Sea Convention provides: "Any slave who may have taken refugee on board a ship of war flying the flag of one of the Signatory Powers, shall be immediately and definitively freed." Finally, an International Bureau was to be established in Zanzibar—the first inter-governmental entity to be situated on the African continent—to gather information, including the registration of vessels, but more generally, to "centralize all documents and information of a nature to facilitate the repression of the Slave Trade in the maritime zone".[170]

On the basis of the 1890 General Act, it looked like the "latent and disquieting conflict"[171] had been put to rest. Yet, as Miers writes, an

---

[169] Ibid, Article 54. The mixed commissions which had, by the 1870s, become solely British affairs were subsumed into the domestic jurisdiction. For Great Britain this meant either the relevant Supreme Court of the Colony or an Admiralty Court. See *Documents relatives à la Répression de la Traite des Esclaves publiés en execution des Articles LXXXI et suivants de l'Act Général de Bruxelles*; 1892, 260.

[170] Ibid, Article 77. For the work of the International Bureau in Zanzibar see: *Documents relatives à la Répression de la Traite des Esclaves publiés en execution des Articles LXXXI et suivants de l'Act Général de Bruxelles*; from 1892 to 1913 under the heading "*Bureau international maritime de Zanzibar*".

[171] See Queneuil, above n 151, 148.

"unforeseen and serious difficulty"[172] arose as the French Ambassador in Brussels wrote to the Belgian Foreign Minister:

I have the honour to confirm to your Excellency the information which I gave *viva voce* yesterday to Baron Lambermont [the President of the Conference]; after a prolonged discussion occupying the sitting of the 24th and 25th of last month, the French Chamber of Deputies decided to suspend the authorization to ratify the General Act [. . .]. His Majesty's Government must be aware of the part which the Cabinet had taken in this grave debate, and it was certainly been from no want of effort on their part that the conclusion was not entirely different. Your Excellency is further aware that the consideration which weighed with the Chamber were derived from the nature of the measures to be taken for the repression of the traffic at sea.[173]

The Institute of International Law came on side in 1891 declaring that the General Act did not reinstitute an expansive right to visit and that the Act addressed the concerns of France; expressing its hope that all States which had been present in Brussels would ratify the Act.[174] The issue of French ratification remained unresolved until 2 January 1892 when France deposited its instrument of ratification, with the following reservation:

His Excellency [the French ambassador to Belgian] declared that the President of the Republic, in his ratification of the General Act of Brussels, has provisionally reserved, for an ulterior understanding, Articles XXI, XXII, and XXIII, and Articles XLII to LXI.[175]

In essence, France agreed to the General Act but excluded the application of the provisions relating to visitation. The content of Articles 21, 22, and 23 was discussed above. Articles 42 to 61 set out the modalities of the regime of visitation within the General Act. The phrase "provisionally reserved, for an ulterior understanding" was interesting, as the French legislature had determined France would be "governed by the stipulations and arrangements now in force", that is to say, the 1867 Naval Instructions. France further modified its reservation when Belgium, as depositor of the General Act, noted that obligations stemming from Articles 30 to 41, regarding the authorisation of native vessels to fly a State's flag, were only applicable in the zone established by Articles 21 to which France had entered a reservation. France declared that its east coast possessions would form part of that regime, noting that it "will be spontaneously applied by the Government of the Republic

---

[172] Miers, above n 47, 293.

[173] See "France", Protocol of a Meeting held at the Foreign Office at Brussels, respecting the Ratification of the General Act of the Brussels Conference, 2 July 1891, Hertslet, above n 144, 521–22.

[174] Institut de Droit International, "Voeu motive de l'Institut tendant à la ratification intégrale de l'Act general de Bruxelles", *Annuaire de l'Institut de Droit International*, Vol. 11, 1889–1892, 269.

[175] See "France", Protocol of a Meeting held at Brussels, in the Foreign Office, respecting the Exchange of Ratification of the General Act of the Brussels Conference, 2 January 1892, Hertslet, above n 144, 524–25.

in the territory of Obock [Djibouti], and, according to necessity in the Island of Madagascar and the Comoros."[176] The French reservation was accepted by the other Parties and the General Act came into force on 2 April 1892.[177]

Miers, writing about the French reservation, stated that the "solution was unusual in diplomatic history and left France in a privileged position".[178] In reality, as De Montardy noted, it left France disadvantaged: "Only France refused to cooperate with the rest of Europe in its *oeuvre* of civilisation and humanity; and only it was to undertake the policing of ships flying its own colours, while the other State Parties provided mutual assistance: a regrettable situation, as the slavers would tend to cover their operations with the French flag which was less energetically policed".[179] Miers concluded that little had been lost because the French "government agreed to abide by the regulations of 1867 and to put into operation the new rules for the issue of French colours".[180] Queneuil also echoed these sentiments, stating that the differences between the General Act and the 1867 Instructions were not great.[181] However, the limited French acceptance of the 1890 General Act provided at least one means by which slave traders could avoid visits by hoisting the French flag; although that practice was effectively ceased by the Permanent Court of Arbitration in the *Muscat Dhows* case (1905).

In that case, the panel considered whether the status of subjects of the Sultan of Muscat who had been granted the status of *protégé* by France in 1844, and thus benefited from the protection of France and, on the seas, the French flag, was limited by the obligations undertaken by France as a result of the 1890 Brussels Act. The issuance of papers authorising dhows to fly French flags had meant that those "native vessels" had been "commonly employed in the slave trade".[182] In the Award, the arbitrators pointed to Article 32 of the 1890 General Act which set out the conditions under which native vessels were granted authority to fly a flag. This included owners or outfitters "furnishing proof that they enjoy a good reputation, and especially that they have never been condemned for acts of slave trade".[183] The Court determined that after France had ratified the Brussels Act (1892), it was not permitted to "authorize vessels belonging to subjects of His Highness the Sultan of Muscat to fly

---

[176] Ibid.

[177] Beyond the parties which negotiated in Brussels (see n 147 and accompanying text), all of which ratified the General Act, the following States acceded to the instrument: Ethiopia, Liberia, Persia and the Orange Free State. See Hertslet, above n 144, 488.

[178] Miers, above n 47, 293.

[179] Montardy, above n 82, 159–160.

[180] Miers, above n 47, 293. For the 1867 Instructions see *Documents relatives à la Répression de la Traite* (n 91 above).

[181] Queneuil, above n 151, 189.

[182] Syllabus, "The Muscat Dhows Case between France and Great Britain", James Brown Scott (ed), *The Hague Court Reports*, 1916, 93.

[183] Article 32, General Act of the Brussels Conference relative to the African Slave Trade, 2 July 1890, Hertslet, above n 144, 500.

the French flag, except on conditions that their owners or fitters-out had established that they had been considered and treated by France as her *protégés* before the year 1863. It further determined, with regard to another question, that the "authorization to fly the French flag can not be transmitted or transferred to any other person or other dhow, even if belonging to the same owner".[184] Subjects of Muscat might well benefit from the protection of the French flag, but only during their lifetime or that of their precious dhow. Considering the life expectancy in early twentieth century Muscat and that of "native vessels", the Permanent Court of Arbitration had, at the behest of Great Britain, sounded the death-knell of the slave trade at sea.

CONCLUSION

While debate concerning the motives of Great Britain in its attempt to suppress the slave trade remains lively today, it cannot be disputed that Great Britain did, in fact, lead and shoulder most of the responsibility in ending the slave trade and slavery itself. Over the past thirty years, historians have busied themselves uncovering the means and modalities of the Atlantic trade which persisted for nearly three and a half centuries. We know much more today about the slave trade and the manner in which it was undertaken and historians can in no way dispute the centrality of Great Britain to its abolition. Abolition was a lengthy process which required Britain to persist with its foreign policy objective for seventy-five years. When it became evident suppression of the trade could not be achieved through common law pronouncements or agreement on a universal instrument during the era of the Concert of Europe, British foreign policy took a tactical shift towards building a bilateral regime of instruments outlawing the slave trade. Brazil and Portugal were unable to resist muscular interventions by the Royal Navy and joined the burgeoning web of bilateral treaties; France and the United States could not be cajoled so easily.

Despite French reservations regarding visitation under the 1890 General Act, the slave trade was, by this time, clearly in its last throes. Through its bilateral network, Great Britain had managed to abolish the Atlantic Slave Trade by 1867. The limited possessions of France in the zone where the slave trade persisted and its lack of willingness to ascribe to the right to visit established by the Brussels Act slowed the momentum towards complete suppression of the slave trade at sea. As the *Muscat Dhows* case indicates, loopholes persisted in which slavers could find protection of a flag to carry on the trade. However, such instances were very limited in nature and scope. In essence, the bilateral web of treaties

---

[184] *The Muscat Dhows*, Award of 8 August 1905, James Brown Scott (ed), *The Hague Court Reports*, 1916, 99–100.

created by Great Britain in the first half of the nineteenth century had not only ended the Atlantic Slave Trade, but also made it near impossible, legally and politically, for any State to allow its citizens—or for that matter, those under its protection—to continue with the slave trade. It was only in 1890 that Britain finally achieved a right to visit to suppress the slave trade. British ambition to establish a right to visit, despite its overwhelming dominance of the seas during much of the nineteenth century, was ultimately limited for nearly seven decades, not by the moral lassitude of other States, but by the international law imperative to respect the Grotian notion of the freedom of the seas.

THE ROLE AND RELEVANCE OF THE UN CONVENTION ON THE LAW OF THE NON-NAVIGATIONAL USES OF INTERNATIONAL WATERCOURSES TO THE EU AND ITS MEMBER STATES

By DR ALISTAIR S RIEU-CLARKE*

INTRODUCTION

Following over 50 years of development, the UN Convention on the Law of the Non-Navigational Uses of International Watercourses (1997 UN Watercourses Convention) was adopted on 21 May 1997.[1] To date there are only 16 contracting states to the Convention (Finland, Germany, Hungary, Iraq, Jordan, Lebanon, Libya, Namibia, Norway, Portugal, Qatar, South Africa, Sweden, Syria and Uzbekistan), 19 short of the number needed for the Convention to enter into force.[2] Despite the low number of contracting State parties, this framework Convention has proved influential on regional, basin specific and bilateral agreements. For example, the member countries of the Southern African Development Community, revised their 1995 Protocol on Shared Watercourses Systems in 2000 largely to ensure that its provisions reflected those of the 1997 UN Watercourses Convention.[3] Other examples include the 2002 Framework Agreement on the Sava River Basin,[4] the 2003 Protocol for the Sustainable Development of Lake Victoria,[5] and the 2004 Agreement on the Establishment of the Zambezi

---

* Lecturer, Centre for Water Law, Policy and Science University of Dundee.

[1] Convention on the Law of Non-Navigational Uses of International Watercourses, May 21, 1997 (not yet in force), reprinted in (1997) 36 *ILM* 700 (hereinafter 1997 UN Watercourses Convention).

[2] See Status of Multilateral Agreements deposited with the Secretary General, <http://untreaty.un.org/ENGLISH/bible/englishinternetbible/partI/chapterXXVII/treaty43.asp>, (visited Sep. 28, 2007). Article 36(1) of the Convention, ibid, provides that, "[t]he present Convention shall enter into force on the ninetieth day following the date of deposit of the thirty-fifth instrument of ratification, acceptance, approval or accession with the Secretary-General of the United Nations."

[3] SADC Revised Protocol on Shared International Watercourses, Aug. 7, 2000 (not yet in force), reprinted in (2001) 40 *ILM* 321.

[4] Framework Agreement on the Sava River Basin, Dec. 3, 2002, available at http://faolex.fao.org/faolex/index.htm.

[5] Protocol on the Sustainable Development of the Lake Victoria Basin, Nov. 29, 2003, available at http://faolex.fao.org/faolex/index.htm.

Watercourse Commission.[6] Key provisions of the Convention have also been endorsed by the International Court of Justice as providing an accurate reflection of customary international law.[7]

Whilst the 1997 UN Watercourses Convention has therefore proved influential in the development of international law, the purpose of this article is to consider the more specific issue of the role and relevance of the Convention vis-à-vis the EU and its Member States. In so doing, the article will also consider whether there is a case for persuading more EU member states to become contracting states.

Given that the focus of the 1997 UN Watercourses is on transboundary waters, the study will start with an overview of transboundary waters in Europe. The overview will outline the amount of transboundary waters within Europe, and also the importance of such waters to EU Member States. In addition, a synopsis of conflicts and cooperative events concerning Europe's transboundary waters will be offered.

The study will then go on to analyse regional transboundary water law, namely the Directive Establishing a Framework for Community Action in the Field of Water Policy (2000 EU Water Framework Directive)[8] and the Convention on the Protection and Use of Transboundary Watercourses and International Lakes (1992 UN ECE Helsinki Convention).[9] The main aim of this analysis will be to identify similarities and differences between the regional instruments and the 1997 UN Watercourses Convention. An analytical framework will be adopted for this part of the study. The analytical framework essentially identifies the main aspects of a legal regime for the management of transboundary waters through a number of core elements—namely scope, substantive rules and principles, implementation instruments and dispute settlement mechanisms.

Having conducted a comparative analysis of the 1997 UN Watercourses Convention and regional transboundary water law, the study goes on to consider the practice of EU Member States during the development of the Convention in the International Law Commission, the negotiation of the text within the 6th Committee of the General Assembly, and following its adoption. In addition, this section will also look at the parties to the Convention from within the EU, and the reasons behind their participation. The main aim of this section will be to identify which EU Member States appear to be strong supporters of the 1997 UN

---

[6] Agreement on the Establishment of the Zambezi Watercourse Agreement, Jul. 13, 2004, http://www.zacpro.org/downloads/ZAMCOM%20AGREEMENT.pdf.

[7] See for example *Case Concerning the Gabčíkovo-Nagymaros Project* (Hungary v. Slovakia) *ICJ Rep 1997* p 7.

[8] Council and Parliament Directive 2000/60/EC, Establishing a Framework for Community Action in the Field of Water Policy, 2000 O.J. (L 327) (hereinafter 2000 EU Water Framework Directive).

[9] Convention on the Protection and Use of Transboundary Watercourses and International Lakes, Mar. 17, 1992 (entered into force Oct. 6, 1996), reprinted in (1992) 31 *ILM* 1312 (hereinafter 1992 UN ECE Helsinki Convention).

Watercourses Convention, and the possible reasons why other States may or may not wish to become a party to the Convention.

Finally the article will assess the EU's external relations policy, both in terms of its development agenda, and its participation within multilateral environmental agreements. In so doing, the study seeks to judge the possibility of the EU, as a regional economic integration organisation, becoming party to the 1997 UN Watercourses Convention.

1. TRANSBOUNDARY WATERS IN THE EU

1.1 Overview

The International River Basin Register identifies 69 international river basins in Europe.[10] Of the 69 river basins, 28 basins lie solely within the borders of the EU, and a further 29 are shared between EU and non-EU States. In addition, there are around 89 aquifers throughout Europe.[11] A wide range of transboundary waters exist from the Danube basin which is shared between 17 States, to 39 river basins that are shared between only 2 States. In terms of size, basins vary from the Flurry between the UK and Ireland at 60 km², to the Danube, which has a total area of 790,100 km2. Most EU countries are heavily reliant on water resources flowing from outside their territory. In 16 countries, more than 90 per cent of the country is located within an international river basin.[12] An example is Hungary, which relies on its neighbouring countries for as much as 95 per cent of its water resources.[13]

Numerous qualitative and quantitative issues affect transboundary water throughout Europe. In terms of water quantity, Europe enjoys relatively abundant water resources. On average up to 3,300m³ of water is available annually for every European inhabitant and only 600m3 is actually abstracted.[14] However, water is distributed unevenly; with parts of Spain receiving less than 25mm.[15] Droughts can be a major problem in the semi-arid regions of Europe leading to competing claims over scarce transboundary water resources. In Spain and Portugal, for instance, almost one-third of land is at risk of desertification.[16] In addition, droughts are now becoming an increasing problem in other parts

---

[10] International River Basin Register (updated 2002), http://www.transboundarywaters.orst.edu/publications/register/tables/IRB_europe.html; Aaron T Wolf, et al., 'International River Basins of the World' (1999) 15 International Journal of Water Resources Development 387.

[11] G E Arnold & Z Buzás, 'Economic Commission for Europe Inventory of Ground Water in Europe' (2005) 43 Ground Water 669.

[12] International River Basin Register: see above n 10.

[13] Ibid.

[14] European Environment Agency, Europe's Environment: the Third Assessment (2003).

[15] Ibid.

[16] United Nations Environment Programme, Freshwater in Europe—Facts, Figures and Maps (2004), http://www.grid.unep.ch.

of Europe.[17] Floods are also a major problem throughout Europe calling for increased cooperation between States that share rivers. Furthermore, issues of water quality require greater cooperation and coordination between European States in order to reduce the amount of sewage and industrial waste, and the excessive use of pesticides and fertilisers.[18]

1.2 Conflict and cooperation

A long tradition of cooperation over transboundary waters exists throughout Europe. As far back as the 19th century, agreement was reached on the freedom of navigation and equal treatment of riparian States.[19] Treaties signed in the early 20th century also included uses such as fisheries and irrigation.[20] Several early treaties further included provision for the establishment of joint commissions.[21]

In recent decades, there has been a discernable shift in European treaty practice from single purpose agreements, towards the joint management of international waters and their multiple uses. In some cases joint "single issue" commissions have evolved into institutions dealing with a wide range of activities relating to integrated water resources management. An example of such a commission is the Finnish-Norwegian Commission, which was established pursuant to a treaty concluded between the states in 1980 with rather modest powers.[22] Subsequently, the Commission has taken a leading role in developing integrated water resources management plans for the transboundary waters between Finland and Norway.

While there has therefore been extensive State practice throughout Europe relating to cooperation over transboundary waters, conflicts have from time to time arisen. In the early 20th century, Belgium and the Netherlands contested the enlargement of certain canals and the construction of works in the River Meuse, the dispute eventually having to be settled by the Permanent Court of International Justice.[23] The Permanent Court of International Justice was also asked to resolve a dispute concerning the River Oder between Germany, Denmark, France,

[17] Ibid.

[18] S C Nixon et al, Sustainable Use of Europe's Water? State, Prospects and Issues (2000); see also W Krinner et al, Sustainable Water Use in Europe (2000); United Nations Environment Programme, Global Environment Outlook 3: Past, Present and Future Perspectives (2002), 164–166.

[19] See Report of the Secretary-General on the Legal Problems Relating to the Utilisation of International Rivers, U.N. Doc. A/5409 (Apr. 15, 1963); The 1814 Treaty of Paris, the 1815 Final Act of Congress of Vienna, the 1831 Convention of Mainz, the 1856 Treaty of Paris, the 1857 Navigation of the Danube Act, the 1878 Treaty of Berlin and the 1883 Treaty of London, all sought to promote the freedom of navigation throughout Europe's transboundary waters.

[20] See S McCaffrey, 'The Evolution of the Law of International Watercourses' (1993) 45 Austrian Journal of Public International Law 87; Teclaff, The River Basin in History and Law (1967).

[21] Ibid.

[22] Agreement between Finland and Norway on a Finnish-Norwegian Transboundary Water Commission, 5 Nov. 1980 (entered into force 1 May 1981), http://www.ymparisto.fi/default. asp?contentid=187225&lan=en. See generally M Fitzmaurice and O Elias, Watercourse Co-operation in Northern Europe (2004).

[23] Diversion of Water from the Meuse (Neth. v. Belg.) (Merits) [1937] P.C.I.J. (ser A/B), No. 70.

Great Britain, Sweden, Czechoslovakia and Poland.[24] The early 20th Century further witnessed a dispute between France and Spain over Lake Lanoux and the Carol River in the Ebro Basin. France proposed certain works for the utilisation of the waters of Carol River which the Spanish Government feared would adversely affect their rights and interests, contrary to the Treaty of Bayonne concluded by the parties in 1866. Eventually, the dispute was resolved by an international arbitral tribunal.[25]

More recently, the 1990s witnessed Portuguese concern over the Spanish water plans for the diversion of a number of shared transboundary waters—the Minho, Douro, Tagus and Guadiana—for hydropower generation; concern that was aggravated by serious droughts within the Iberian peninsula during the early 1990s.[26] A history of conflicts also exists between Greece and Bulgaria on the Nestos Basin.[27] Despite, the adoption of a basin-wide agreement in 1995, cross-border pollution problems persist.[28] In recent years, Greek citizens have repeatedly complained to Bulgarian authorities about industrial and domestic waste that has been dumped upstream, at the cost of downstream uses of the basin.[29] Both countries have agreed to closer cooperation to stop the pollution of the Nestos Basin, especially given Bulgaria's accession to the EU and its obligation to meet the environmental obligations of EU law.

The Danube has been a source of conflict between several of its basin states. The Gabčíkovo-Nagymaros Dam system, for example, remains a major issue between Hungary and the Slovak Republic. Following a decision of the International Court of Justice decision in 1997, the States were requested to reach a compromise solution based on the Court's findings.[30] However, despite patchy talks, no mutually agreeable decision has yet to be reached, and the case is back on the docket of the International Court of Justice.[31] Various other construction projects have caused controversy within the Danube basin in recent years. Following environmental protests from 10,000 Croats and 5,000 Hungarians in November 2004, Croatian plans to build a Hydroelectric Plant on the Drava River

[24] *Territorial Jurisdiction of the International Commission of the River Oder (U.K., Czech., Den., Fr., Ger., Swed. v. Pol.)* (judgment) [1929] P.C.I.J. (ser A), No. 23. Interestingly, in reaching its opinion the Court recognised, pursuant to the "general principles of international river law", the "community of interests" of riparian States in navigable rivers.

[25] *Lake Lanoux Arbitration (Fr. v. Spain)* (1957) 24 *International Law Reports* 101.

[26] Oregon State University, International Water Event Database, http://www.transboundarywaters. orst.edu.

[27] Athens News Agency, 'Greek-Bulgarian Meeting on Reducing Pollution of the Nestos River' (6 December 2004).

[28] Athens News Agency, 'Greek-Bulgarian Meeting in Drama for the Protection of the Nestos River' (19 March 2005).

[29] Ibid.

[30] *Case Concerning the Gabčíkovo-Nagymaros Project* (Hungary v. Slovakia) *ICJ Rep 1997* p 7.

[31] See International Court of Justice, 'Pending cases', http://www.icj-cij.org/docket/index. php?p1=3&p2=1. See also Budapest Business Journal, 'Hungary/Slovakia Delegations Meet on Dam Dispute, Agreement Still Far' (20 December 2006) http://www.bbj.hu.

have reportedly been put on hold.[32] Similarly, plans by Ukraine to build the Bystroe navigation canal have sparked tension due to Romania's claims that the canal would have serious environmental consequences on the Danube delta's ecosystem.[33] Such claims were substantiated by a UN ECE Inquiry Commission, under the auspices of the Convention on Environmental Impact Assessment in a Transboundary Context.[34]

The abovementioned examples of cooperation and conflict over transboundary waters illustrate the importance such waters are afforded within the EU States. The adoption of two regional instruments, the 2000 EU Water Framework Directive and the 1992 UN ECE Helsinki Convention, dealing with the management of water resources within the EU further attests to the significance that States place on the need to cooperate over transboundary waters. The next section is therefore dedicated to an analysis the two regional instruments.

2. RELATIONSHIP BETWEEN THE 1997 UN WATERCOURSES CONVENTION, THE 2000 EU WATER FRAMEWORK DIRECTIVE AND THE 1992 UN ECE HELSINKI CONVENTION

2.1 Regional Water Law in Context

EU water law and policy dates back over thirty years.[35] Earlier policy adopted a sectoral approach, mainly focussing on setting water quality objectives for particular water uses, or limiting the discharge of certain pollutants.[36] However a piecemeal approach to the adoption of EU

---

[32] Hungarian News Agency, 'Croatian Plans for Hydroelectric Plant on Hold' (8 February 2005).

[33] BBC Monitoring International Reports, 'Ukraine has No EU Approval for Danube Canal—Romanian Minister' (2 March 2005).

[34] Convention on Environmental Impact Assessment in a Transboundary Context, 1991 (entered into force 10 September 1997), reprinted in (1991) 30 *ILM* 800 (1991). See UN ECE, 'UNECE Inquiry Commission concludes that Danube Canal will have "significant adverse transboundary effects" on the environment', http://www.unece.org/press/pr2006/06env_p05e.htm. See also Espoo Inquiry Commission, 'Report on the Likely Significant Adverse Transboundary Impacts of the Danube—Black Sea Navigation Route at the Border of Romania and the Ukraine' July 2006, http:// www.unece.org/env/eia/documents/inquiry/Final%20Report%2010%20July%202006.pdf.

[35] See generally L Krämer, *EC Environmental Law* (5th ed, 2003), 243–262.

[36] Council Directive 75/440/EEC, 1975 O.J. (L 194) 26 (Surface Water Directive)—the Directive established certain quality parameters for the abstraction of drinking water; Council Directive 76/160/EEC, 1976 O.J. (L 31) 1 (Bathing Water Directive)—the Directive requires Member States to ensure that all necessary measures are taken in order that the quality of bathing water complies with certain limit values; Council Directive 78/659/EEC, 1978 O.J. (L. 22) 1 (Fish Water Directive)—the Directive obliges Member States to establish programmes to reduce pollution and ensure that freshwaters capable of supporting fish comply with certain limit values; Council Directive 79/923/ EEC, 1979 O.J. (L 281) 47 (Shellfish Directive)—the Directive obliges Member States to establish programmes to reduce pollution in designated areas in accordance with limit values for the protection of shellfish; Council Directive 80/778/EEC, 1980 O.J. (L 129) 23 (Dangerous Substances Directive);- the Directive requires Member States to take measures intended to ultimately eliminate pollution of water by certain substances and reduce creation other substances; Council Directive 80/68/EEC, 1980 O.J. (L 20) 43 (Groundwater Directive)—the Directive requires Member States to

water law and policy meant that by the mid-nineties there was a lack of coherence and coordination.[37] In 1992 the European Council therefore requested that the European Commission propose a new policy to promote the integrated management of water resources throughout Europe.[38] After considerable negotiation amongst the Member States and other interested parties, the EU Water Framework Directive was adopted on 23 October 2000, and entered into force for all Member States on 22 December 2000.[39]

In addition to EU legislation, many states throughout Europe are also subject to water related laws of the UN Economic Commission for Europe (UN ECE). The UN ECE was established in 1947 by the UN Economic and Social Council, as one of the five regional commissions of the UN.[40] The overarching goal of the UN ECE is to foster greater economic cooperation amongst its Member States.[41] Under the above goal the UN ECE is involved in issues relating to economic analysis, environment and human settlements, statistics, sustainable energy, trade, industry and enterprise development, timber and transport.[42] Activities of the UN ECE include policy analysis, development of conventions, regulations and standards, and technical assistance. There are 55 Member States of the UN ECE, covering Europe, Central Asia, North America and Israel.

The UN ECE first started looking at water issues in the late 1960s.[43] A number of non-binding policy documents relating to various aspects of water were developed by the UN ECE from the 1970s to the 1990s.[44]

---

take measures necessary to prevent the discharge into groundwater of certain substances and limit the discharge into groundwater of other water substances.

[37] A second wave of legislation took place in the early 90s, including Council Directive 91/271/EEC, 1991 O.J. (L 135) 40 (Urban Waste Water Treatment Directive)—the Directive requires Member States to ensure that all agglomerations are provided with collecting systems that satisfy basic requirements; Council Directive 91/676/EEC, 1991 O.J. (L 375) 1 (Nitrates Directive)—the Directive obliges Member States to designate water which might be affected, or could be affected by nitrate pollution, and establish a code or codes of good agricultural practice; Council Directive 96/61/EC, 1996 O.J. (L 257) 26 (Integrated Pollution Prevention and Control Directive)—the Directive sets out an authorisation system whereby a permit lays down limit values for emissions to air, land and water.

[38] The decision was taken at the European Council in Edinburgh, see (1992) 12 *Bulletin of the European Communities,* at 18. The request resulted in the *Communication from the Commission on the European Community Water Policy,* COM (1996) 59, (Feb. 21, 1996).

[39] See above n 8.

[40] *See* http://www.unece.org/about/about.htm.

[41] Ibid.   [42] Ibid.

[43] See P K Wouters, and S V Vinogradov, 'Analysing the ECE Water Convention: What Lessons for the Regional Management of Transboundary Resources?' (2003/4) *Yearbook of International Co-operation on Environment and Development* 55.

[44] *See for example* Charter on Groundwater Management, UN Doc. ECE/ENVWA/12 (1989); Recommendations to ECE Governments on Rational Use of Water in Industrial Processes, UN Doc. ECE/ENVWA/2, (1987); Recommendations to ECE Governments on Water-management Systems, UN Doc. ECE/ENVWA/2 (1987); ECE Declaration of Policy on the Rational Use of Water, UN Doc. ECE/ENVWA/2 (1984); Recommendations to ECE Governments on Drinking Water Supply and Effluent Disposal System, UN Doc. ECE/ENVWA/2 (1982); Recommendations to ECE Governments on Water Pollution from Animal Production, UN Doc. ECE/ENVWA/2 (1981); Recommendations to ECE Governments on Economic Instruments for Rational Utilization

Then in 1992 the UN ECE Convention on the Protection and Use of Transboundary Watercourses and International Lakes was adopted, and entered into force in 1996.[45] As a framework agreement the 1992 UN ECE Helsinki Convention has been strengthened by the development of supplementary protocols, such as the 1999 Protocol on Water and Health,[46] and the 2003 Protocol on Civil Liability and Compensation for Damage Caused by the Transboundary Effects of Industrial Accidents on Transboundary Waters.[47] Numerous policy documents have also been adopted in support of the implementation of the 1992 UN ECE Helsinki Convention.[48] The Convention is further supported by a wider environmental programme of the UN ECE which has seen the adoption of the 1991 Convention on Environmental Impact Assessment in a Transboundary Context,[49] the 1992 Convention on the Transboundary

of Water Resources, UN Doc. ECE/ENVWA/2 (1980); Recommendations to ECE Governments on Rational Utilization of Water, UN Doc. ECE/ENVWA/2 (1979); Recommendations to ECE Governments on Selected Water Problems in Islands and Coastal Areas with special regard to Desalination and Ground Water, UN Doc. ECE/ENVWA/2 (1978); Recommendations to ECE Governments on Long-term Planning of Water Management, UN Doc. ECE/ENVWA/2 (1976).

[45] See above n 9.

[46] Protocol on Water and Health to the Convention on the Protection and Use of Transboundary Watercourses and International Lakes, Jun. 17, 1999 (Aug. 4, 2005), http://http://www.unece.org/env/water/text/text_protocol.htm.

[47] Protocol on Civil Liability and Compensation for Damage Caused by the Transboundary Effects of Industrial Accidents on Transboundary Waters, May 21, 2003 (not yet in force), http://www.unece.org/env/civil-liability/protocol.html.

[48] See 1992 UN ECE Helsinki Convention and Guidelines on Monitoring and Assessment of Transboundary and International Lakes: UNECE Working Group on Monitoring and Assessment; UNECE Task Force on Monitoring and Assessment; Guidelines on Monitoring and Assessment of Transboundary Rivers; UNECE Task Force on Monitoring and Assessment: Guidelines on Monitoring and Assessment of Transboundary Groundwater, 2000; Guidelines on Sustainable Flood Prevention, 2000; Water management: Guidance on public participation and compliance with agreements, 2000; Recommendations to ECE Governments on waste-water treatment, 1988 (ECE/CEP/10); Recommendations to ECE Governments on the protection of soil and aquifers against non-point source pollution, 1988 (ECE/CEP/10); Recommendations to ECE Governments on dam safety with particular emphasis on small dams, UN Doc. ECE/CEP/10 (1989); Recommendations to ECE Governments on waste-water management, UN Doc. ECE/CEP/10 (1991); Recommendations to ECE Governments on the protection of inland waters against eutrophication, UN Doc. ECE/CEP/10 (1992); Recommendations to ECE Governments on ecosystems-based water management, UN Doc. ECE/CEP/10 (1992); Recommendations to ECE Governments on ecosystems-based water management, UN Doc. ECE/CEP/10 (1992); Recommendations to ECE Governments on the five R policies—Reduction, replacement, recovery, recycling and reutilization of industrial products, residues or wastes, UN Doc. ECE/CEP/10 (1992); Recommendations to ECE Governments on the prevention of water pollution from hazardous substances, UN Doc. ECE/CEP/10 (1994); Guidelines on licensing waste-water discharges from point sources into transboundary waters, UN Doc. ECE/CEP/11 (1996); Recommendations to ECE Governments on specific measures to prevent, control and reduce groundwater pollution from chemical storage facilities and waste-disposal sites, UN Doc. ECE/CEP/11 (1996); Guidelines on water-quality monitoring and assessment of transboundary rivers, UN Doc. ECE/CEP/11 (1996); Guidelines for ECE Governments on the prevention and control of water pollution from fertilizers and pesticides in agriculture, UN Doc. ECE/CEP/10 (1995); Guidelines on the ecosystem approach in water management, UN Doc. ECE/ENVWA/31 (1993); Code of Conduct on Accidental Pollution of Transboundary Inland Waters, UN Doc. ECE/ENVWA/16 (1990).Code of Conduct on Accidental Pollution of Transboundary Inland Waters, UN Doc. ECE/ENVWA/16 (1990).

[49] Convention on Environmental Impact Assessment in a Transboundary Context, Feb. 25, 1991 (entered into force Sep. 10, 1997), reprinted in (1991) 30 *ILM* 800.

Effects of Industrial Accidents,[50] and the 1998 Convention on Access to Information, Public Participation in Decision-Making and Access to Justice in Environmental Matters.[51]

The 1992 UN ECE Helsinki Convention has been highly influential in developing several bilateral or multilateral agreements, including the Danube,[52] Rhine,[53] Meuse and Scheldt,[54] Lake Peipsi,[55] the shared waters between Russia and Kazakhstan,[56] and Russia and the Ukraine.[57]

In 2003, a proposed amendment to the 1992 UN ECE Helsinki Convention was adopted to allow non-UN ECE parties to become parties.[58] However, the Meeting of the Parties will not consider any request for accession by States outside the UNECE until the amendment has entered into force for all States and organisations that were party to the Convention when the amendment was adopted.[59] To date, there has only been 6 ratifications to the amendment.[60]

The two abovementioned regional instruments clearly play a significant role in managing transboundary waters throughout Europe; the purpose of the following sections will therefore be to consider the relationship between the latter instruments and the 1997 UN Watercourses Convention. In conducting such an analysis, the article will focus on the issues of scope, substantive norms, implementation instruments and dispute settlement mechanisms.

2.2 Scope

In terms of geographical scope, the 2000 EU Water Framework Directive adopts the broadest approach of the three instruments in that it covers

---

[50] Convention on the Transboundary Effects of Industrial Accidents, Mar. 17, 1992 (entered into force Apr. 19, 2000), http://www.unece.org/env.teia/text.htm.

[51] Convention on Access to Information, Public Participation in Decision-Making and Access to Justice in Environmental Matters, Jun. 25, 1998 (entered into force Oct. 30, 2001), reprinted in (1999) 38 *ILM* 517.

[52] Convention on the Cooperation for the Protection and Sustainable use of the Danube River, 29 Jun. 1994 (entered into force 22 Oct. 1988), reprinted in 19 *Int'l Env't Rep.* (BNA) 997 (Oct. 30, 1996).

[53] Convention on the Protection of the Rhine, Apr. 12, 1999 (entered into force Jan. 1, 2003), http://www.iksr.org/index.php?id=327.

[54] Agreements on the Protection of the Rivers Scheldt and Meuse, Apr. 26, 1994, reprinted in (1995) 34 *ILM* 851 (1995). See A Gosseries, 'The 1994 Agreements Concerning the Protection of the Scheldt and Meuse Rivers' (1995) 4 *European Environmental Law Review* 9 (1995).

[55] Agreement between the Government of the Republic of Estonia and the Government of the Russian Federation on Cooperation in the field of Protection and Sustainable Use of Transboundary Watercourses, Aug. 20, 1997, http://www.envir.ee/58744.

[56] Agreement between Russia and Kazakhstan Concerning the Use and Protection of Transboundary Waters, Aug. 27, 1992, http:// www.transboundarywaters.orst.edu.

[57] Agreement between Ukraine and the Russian Federation on transboundary waters, Nov. 22, 1992, http://www.unece.org/env/water/cwc/legal.htm.

[58] See Amendment to Arts 25 and 26 of the Convention, UN Doc. ECE/MP.WAT/14, Jan. 12, 2004.

[59] See Status of Ratification of the Amendments to the Convention, http://www.unece.org/env/water/status/amend.htm.

[60] Ibid.

all EU waters, including inland surface waters,[61] transitional waters,[62] coastal waters,[63] and groundwater.[64] Not only are international watercourses therefore covered by the Directive but also national waters. In contrast, both the 1997 UN Watercourses Convention and the 1992 UN ECE Helsinki Convention focus entirely on rivers, lakes and connected groundwaters shared between two or more states.[65] The only significant difference between the 1997 UN Watercourses Convention and the 1992 UN ECE Helsinki Convention in terms of the applicable waters is the recognition in the former instrument that international watercourses do not always flow into a common terminus, or for that matter directly into the sea.[66]

A potentially more significant difference between the three instruments relates to the extent to which land use practices are covered. Pursuant to the 2000 EU Water Framework Directive, "river basin districts" must be established throughout the entire EU.[67] Article 2(15) of the 2000 EU Water Framework Directive defines a "river basin district" as being "the area of land and sea, made up of one or more neighbouring river basins together with their associated groundwaters and coastal waters, which is identified under Article 3(1) as the main unit for management of river

---

[61] "Inland waters" are defined in Art 2(3) of the 2000 EU Water Framework Directive as "all standing or flowing water on the surface of the land, and all groundwater on the landward side of the baseline from which the breadth of territorial waters is measures".

[62] "Transitional waters" are defined in Art 2(6) of the 2000 EU Water Framework Directive as "bodies of surface water in the vicinity of river mouths which are partly saline in character as a result of their proximity to coastal waters but which are substantially influenced by freshwater flows".

[63] "Coastal waters" are defined in Art 2(7) of the 2000 EU Water Framework Directive as "surface water on the landward side of a line, every point of which is at a distance of one nautical mile on the seaward side from the nearest point of the baseline from which the breadth of territorial waters is measured, extending where appropriate up to the outer limit of transitional waters".

[64] "Groundwater" is defined in Art 2(2) of the 2000 EU Water Framework Directive as "all water which is below the surface of the ground in the saturation zone and in direct contact with the ground or subsoil."

[65] Article 1(1) of the 1997 UN Watercourses Convention provides that, "[t]he present Convention applies to uses of international watercourses and of their waters....". A "watercourse" is defined under Art 2(a) as "a system of surface waters and groundwaters constituting by virtue of their physical relationship a unitary whole and normally flowing into a common terminus." While confined groundwaters are therefore outside the scope of the 1997 UN Watercourses Convention, the International Law Commission on adopting the 1994 Draft Articles on the Law of the non-navigational uses of international watercourse commended States "to be guided by the principles contained in the draft articles on the law of non-navigational uses of international watercourses, where appropriate, in regulating transboundary groundwater" ('Resolution on Transboundary Confined Groundwater', [1994] 2(2) *Yearbook of the International Law Commission* 135). Subsequently, the International Law Commission has taken up the study of transboundary groundwater, and adopted 19 draft articles on the law of transboundary aquifers (See C Yamada, 'Third report on shared natural resources: transboundary groundwaters', UN Doc. A/CN.4/551, 11 Feb. 2005).

[66] See Art 1(1) of the 1997 UN Watercourses Convention. Article 1(1) the 1992 UN ECE Helsinki Convention defines "transboundary waters", as "any surface or ground waters which mark, cross or are located on boundaries between two or more States; wherever transboundary waters flow directly into the sea, these transboundary waters end at a straight line across their respective mouths between points on the low-water line of their banks."

[67] Article 3 of the 2000 EU Water Framework Directive.

basins".[68] Under the 1997 UN Watercourses Convention and the 1992 UN ECE Helsinki Convention there is no explicit mention of anything similar to the EU Water Framework Directive's "river basin districts".

When the ILC first initiated its study on the law of the non-navigational uses of international watercourse it solicited the opinion of States on whether the geographical concept of an "international drainage basin" should be the appropriate basis for their study, but the term "international watercourse" was preferred as it was considered by some states to be more restrictive.[69] However, while at first glance the 1997 UN Watercourses Convention and the 1992 UN ECE Helsinki Convention might therefore appear to be quite restrictive in terms of the potentially wider basin approach offered by the 2000 EU Water Framework Directive, closer scrutiny of the 1997 UN Watercourses Convention and 1992 UN ECE Helsinki Convention would permit a wider interpretation.[70] Article 1(1) of the 1997 UN Watercourses Convention, for example, provides that: "The present Convention applies to uses of international watercourses and of their waters for purposes other than navigation and to measures of protection, preservation and management related to the uses of those watercourses and their waters."[71] Land-based activities taking place within the river basin, which might affect the protection, management or preservation of the watercourse would therefore be covered.[72] A "river basin approach" is further supported by the substantive norms of the 1997 UN Watercourses Convention, which will be discussed in the next section. Such rules and principles arguably provide that any activities within the river basin that impact on the quantity or quality of the international watercourse, or perhaps event the aquatic ecosystem, would fall under the scope of the Convention.

In a similar approach it could also be argued that the scope of the 1992 UN ECE Helsinki Convention's provisions are not limited to transboundary waters *per se*, but rather cover all activities that may influence

---

[68] Ibid. Article 3(1) provides, inter alia, that "Member States shall identify the individual river basins lying within their national territory and, for the purposes of this Directive, shall assign them to individual river basin districts". "River Basin" is defined in Art 2(13) as the area of land from which all surface run-off flows through a sequence of streams, rivers, and possibly, lakes into the sea at a single river mouth, estuary or delta."

[69] 'Replies of Governments to the Commission's Questionnaire' [1976] 2 *Yearbook of the International Law Commission* 147, U.N. Doc. A/CN.4/294 and Add. 1. The term "international drainage basin" was considered to be in keeping with the International Law Association's Helsinki Rules, Art II of which reads, "an international drainage basin is a geographical area extending over two or more States determined by the watershed limits of the system of waters, including surface and underground waters flowing to a common terminus", S Bogdanović, *International Law of Water Resources* (2001), 100.

[70] See for example, A Tanzi, 'The Relationship between the 1992 UNECE Convention on the Protection and Use of Transboundary Watercourses and International Lakes and the 1997 UN Convention on the Law of the Non-Navigational Uses of International Watercourses', Geneva, February 2000, http://www.unece.org, at 8.

[71] While navigational uses are excluded under Art 1(1), Art 1(2) provides an exception where, "other uses affect navigation or are affected by navigation".

[72] See S McCaffrey, *The Law of International Watercourses* (2001), 34–50.

the conditions of those waters. The latter conclusion is supported by a number of the provisions of the 1992 UN ECE Helsinki Convention. For example, Article 2(1) of the 1992 UN ECE Helsinki Convention requires contracting parties, to "take all appropriate measures to prevent, control and reduce *any* transboundary impact [emphasis added]".[73] "Transboundary impact" is defined broadly as meaning,

"any significant adverse effect on the environment resulting from a change in the conditions of transboundary waters caused by a human activity, the physical origin of which is situated wholly or in part within an area under the jurisdiction of a Party, within an area under the jurisdiction of another Party. Such effects of the environment include effects on human health and safety, flora, fauna, soil, air, water, climate, landscape and historical monuments or other physical structures or the interaction among these factors; they also include effects on the cultural heritage or socio-economic conditions resulting from alterations to those factors."[74]

In addition, an ecosystem approach is supported in that the 1992 UN ECE Helsinki Convention requires the parties to take all appropriate measures to ensure that transboundary waters are used with the aim of ecological sound and rational water management, and that the conservation and, where necessary, restoration of ecosystems is secured.[75]

Ultimately, it could therefore be argued that while the scope of the 2000 EU Water Framework Directive can be said to be wider than the other two instruments in that it covers national and international watercourses, as well as unconnected groundwater, all three instruments support a basin approach to the management of international watercourses.

2.3 Substantive Norms

Under the 2000 EU Water Framework Directive the primary substantive norm is contained under Article 4, which requires Member States to implement the necessary measures to achieve "good water status" in all EU waters by 2015. The criteria for determining what constitutes "good" water status is assessed on the basis of detailed qualitative and quantitative factors, such as abundance of aquatic flora and fauna, the level of salinity, the quantity and dynamics of water flow, nutrient concentrations, and so on.[76] Certain exceptions to the requirements to reach good water status are included in Article 4(4) to Article 4(8). In accordance with the obligation to achieve good water status in all EU waters, Member States are required to adopt more specific measures in relation to pollution and waters used for the abstraction of drinking water. For drinking water Member States must ensure that such water meets the standards

---

[73] 1992 UN ECE Helsinki Convention.
[74] Ibid.   [75] Ibid, Art 2(2).
[76] 2000 EU Water Framework Directive, Annex V.

set out in Directive 80/778/EEC, as amended by Directive 98/83/EC.[77] In relation to pollution a combined approach is to be adopted, whereby Member States must establish and/or implement emission controls based on best available techniques, or the relevant emission limit values, or in the case of diffuse impact the controls including, as appropriate, best environmental practices.[78] Such controls, values and practices are set out in various EU Directives.[79]

The substantive norms contained within the 1997 UN Watercourses Convention centre around the principle of equitable and reasonable utilisation and participation.[80] Inherent in the notion of equitable and reasonable utilisation is the allocation of competing uses between water users. As noted in by the ILC in its commentary to the 1994 ILC Draft Articles:

"In many cases, the quality and quantity of water in an international watercourse will be sufficient to satisfy the needs of all watercourse States. But where the quantity or quality of the water is such that all the reasonable and beneficial uses of all watercourse States cannot be realised, a "conflict of uses" results. In such case, international practice recognises that some adjustments or accommodations are required in order to preserve each watercourse State's equality of right. These adjustments or accommodations are to be arrived at on the basis of equity, and can best be achieved on the basis of specific watercourse agreement."[81]

Article 6 provides a non-exhaustive list of factors that should be taken into account when determining what is equitable and reasonable.[82]

There is therefore a differing focus between the substantive rules and principles of the 2000 EU Water Framework Directive and the 1997 UN Watercourses Convention, in that the latter instrument focuses more on

---

[77] See article 4 of Directive 98/83/EC.

[78] 2000 EU Water Framework Directive, Art 10.

[79] Such instruments include Council Directive 96/61/EC concerning integrated pollution prevention and control, Council Directive 91/271/EEC concerning urban waste-water treatment, Council Directive 91/676/EEC concerning the protection of water against pollution caused by nitrates from agricultural sources. In addition, specific measures to prevent and control groundwater pollution are to be adopted.

[80] Article 5(1) of the 1997 UN Watercourses Convention provides that, "Watercourse States shall in their respective territories utilise an international watercourse in an equitable and reasonable manner."

[81] Draft Articles on the Law of the Non-navigational Uses of International Watercourses (with Commentaries), G.A. Res. 49/52, U.N. Doc. A/RES/49/52 (Dec. 9, 1994), at 98.

[82] 1997 UN Watercourses Convention, Art 6(1), sets out the following factors "(a) Geographic, hydrographic, hydrological, climatic, ecological and other factors of a natural charter; (b) The social and economic needs of the watercourse States concerned; (c)The population dependent on the watercourse in each watercourse State; (d) The effects of the use or uses of the watercourses in one watercourse State on other watercourse States; (e) Existing and potential uses of the watercourse; (f) Conservation, protection, development and economy of use of the water resources of the watercourse and the cost of measures taken to that effect; (g) The availability of alternatives, of comparable value, to a particular planned or existing use." Article 6(3) provides that "the weight to be given to each factor is to be determined by its importance in comparison with that of other relevant factors. In determining what is a reasonable and equitable use, all relevant factors are to be considered together and a conclusion reached on the basis of the whole."

reconciling the competing interests between States, whereas the former focuses more on the protection of the aquatic environment as a whole.

However, while the reconciliation of conflicting uses is at the heart of the 1997 UN Watercourses Convention, environmental protection is still afforded considerable attention. In reconciling conflicting uses, watercourse States should use and develop an international watercourse, "with a view to attaining optimal and sustainable utilisation thereof and benefits therefrom, taking into account the interests of the watercourse States concerned, consistent with adequate protection of the watercourses".[83] This obligation to protect is reinforced in Article 5(2), which stipulates that, "Watercourse States shall *participate* in the use, development and protection of an international watercourse in an equitable and reasonable manner [emphasis]." In accordance with this provision, States therefore not only have a right of use, but an obligation to protect the international watercourse. A further obligation is provided for under Article 7, which stipulates that—when consistent with the principle of equitable and reasonable utilisation—States must to take all appropriate measures to prevent the causing of significant harm to other watercourse States.[84]

Perhaps the most significant provision of the 1997 UN Watercourses Convention in relation to "environmental objectives" is Article 20, which provides that, "Watercourse States shall, individually and, where appropriate, jointly, protect and preserve the ecosystems of international watercourses."[85] Article 20 is complemented by Articles 21–23, which relate to pollution, alien species and the marine environment. From a legal standpoint, it is interesting to note that this obligation does not require significant harm to be caused to another watercourse State. McCaffrey justifies that approach by stating:

"While not linking the obligation to a transboundary impact might seem at first blush to go rather far, there are good reasons...a state's failure to protect the ecosystem of an international watercourse may affect the ecosystems in ways that are not readily perceived, yet whose transboundary effects may become apparent too late to remedy the problem. Species may be lost, flooding may ensue, fish stocks may plummet. This kind of problem can be particularly acute when the watercourse is shared by a number of states, several of which allow activities that modify its ecosystems. Even if these individual modifications are small, they may lead to cumulative impacts that none of the states foresaw individually."[86]

---

[83] Ibid, Art 5(1).

[84] Ibid, Art 7, provides: "(1) Watercourse States shall, in utilizing an international watercourse in their territories, take all appropriate measures to prevent the causing of significant harm to other watercourse States. (2) Where significant harm nevertheless is caused to another watercourse State, the States whose use causes such harm shall, in the absence of agreement to such use, take all appropriate measures, having due regard for the provisions of articles 5 and 6, in consultation with the affected State, to eliminate or mitigate such harm and, where appropriate, to discuss the question of compensation."

[85] Ibid, Art 20.   [86] McCaffrey, above n 72, at 394.

It could therefore be argued that while the 1997 UN Watercourses Convention is not so "environmentally" focussed as the 2000 EU Water Framework Directive—and does not provide specific criteria to determine ecological status—it does support the need to protect ecosystems and as such is consistent with an ecosystem approach.[87] Such an approach is substantiated by the ILC in its commentary to Article 20. Firstly, the ILC links Article 20 to the principle of equitable and reasonableness, noting that, "the obligation to 'protect' the ecosystems of international watercourses is a specific application of the requirement contained in article 5 that watercourse States are to use and develop an international watercourse in a manner that is consistent with adequate protection thereof."[88] In a similar approach, Tanzi and Acari note that, "under the Convention, ecosystem protection is conceived as inherent in the idea of equitable use."[89] Secondly, the ILC notes that the obligation to protect and preserve aquatic ecosystems is needed, "to ensure their continued viability as life support systems, thus providing an essential basis for sustainable development".[90]

Under the 1992 UN ECE Helsinki Convention, the main substantive obligation is that the parties must, "take all appropriate measures to prevent, control and reduce any transboundary impact".[91] Article 2(2) goes on to provide that, in particular, the Parties must take all appropriate measures:

"(a) To prevent, control and reduce pollution of waters causing or likely to cause transboundary impact;
 (b) To ensure that transboundary waters are used with the aim of ecologically sound and rational water management, conservation of water resources and environmental protection;
 (c) To ensure that transboundary waters are used in a reasonable and equitable way, taking into particular account their transboundary character, in the case of activities which cause or are likely to cause transboundary impact;
 (d) To ensure conservation and, where necessary, restoration of ecosystems."[92]

In taking the appropriate measures the parties should be guided by the precautionary principle, the polluter-pays principle and should manage their water resources in a way that meets the needs of the present generation without compromising the ability of future generations to meet their own needs.[93]

There are therefore some parallels between Article 2 of the 1992 UN ECE Helsinki Convention and Article 7 of the 1997 UN Watercourses Convention, which calls upon states to, "take all appropriate measures to

---

[87] O McIntyre, 'The Emergence of an "Ecosystem Approach" to the Protection of International Watercourses under International Law' (2004) 13 *RECIEL* 1.
[88] Draft Articles on the Law of the Non-navigational Uses of International Watercourses, above n 81, at 117.
[89] A Tanzi and M Arcari, *The United Nations Convention on the Law of International Watercourses* (2001) 245.
[90] Ibid.   [91] 1992 UN ECE Helsinki Convention.
[92] Ibid.   [93] Ibid, Art 2(5).

prevent the causing of significant harm to other watercourse States."[94] However, the threshold of harm of "significant harm"[95] under the 1997 UN Watercourses Convention is higher that that of "transboundary impact" under the 1992 UN ECE Helsinki Convention. In line with Article 5 of the 1997 UN Watercourses Convention, the 1992 UN ECE Helsinki Convention also makes specific reference to utilising waters in a "reasonable and equitable way".

The 1992 UN ECE Helsinki Convention is more specific than the 1997 Watercourses Convention in detailing the measures that are considered "appropriate". Accordingly, Article 3 of the 1992 UN ECE Helsinki Convention identifies the relevant legal, administrative, economic, financial and technical measures appropriate to prevent, control and reduce transboundary impact.[96] The 1992 UN ECE Helsinki Convention might therefore provide a useful guide to the 1997 UN Watercourses Convention in assisting both EU and non-EU States in determining what might be considered "appropriate measures" under Article 7 of the latter Convention.

2.4 Implementation Instruments

Institutional Arrangements

Under the 2000 EU Water Framework Directive, Member States must establish competent authorities with responsibility for the implementation

---

[94] 1997 UN Watercourses Convention, Art 7, above n 84.

[95] The commentary to the 'Draft Articles on Prevention of Transboundary Harm from Hazardous Activities, in Report of the International Law Commission on the Work of its Fifty-third Session', U.N GAOR Supp. (No. 10), U.N. Doc. A/56/10, provides that: "It is understood that 'significant' is something more than 'detectable' but need not be at the level of 'serious' or 'substantial'. The harm must lead to a real detrimental effect on matters such as, for example, human health, industry, property, environment or agriculture in other States. Such detrimental effects must be susceptible of being measured by factual and objective standards."

[96] Article 3 of the 1992 UN ECE Helsinki Convention provides that the Parties shall "develop, adopt, implement and, as far as possible, render compatible relevant legal, administrative, economic, financial and technical measures, in order to ensure, inter alia, that: (a) The emission of pollutants is prevented, controlled and reduced at source through the application of, inter alia, low- and non-waste technology; (b) Transboundary waters are protected against pollution from point sources through the prior licensing of waste-water discharges by the competent national authorities, and that the authorized discharges are monitored and controlled; (c) Limits for waste-water discharges stated in permits are based on the best available technology for discharges of hazardous substances; (d) Stricter requirements, even leading to prohibition in individual cases, are imposed when the quality of the receiving water or the ecosystem so requires; (e) At least biological treatment or equivalent processes are applied to municipal waste water, where necessary in a step-by-step approach; (f) Appropriate measures are taken, such as the application of the best available technology, in order to reduce nutrient inputs from industrial and municipal sources; (g) Appropriate measures and best environmental practices are developed and implemented for the reduction of inputs of nutrients and hazardous substances from diffuse sources, especially where the main sources are from agriculture (guidelines for developing best environmental practices are given in annex II to this Convention); (h) Environmental impact assessment and other means of assessment are applied; (i) Sustainable water-resources management, including the application of the ecosystems approach, is promoted; (j) Contingency planning is developed; (k) Additional specific measures are taken to prevent the pollution of groundwaters; (l) The risk of accidental pollution is minimized." Article 3(2) provides for emission limits and the total or partial prohibition of the production or use of certain substances, and states that information from international conventions or regulations "which are applicable in the area covered by this Convention, shall be taken into account."

of EU water legislation within each river basin district. Where a river basin district lies solely within the territory of one Member State it must be assigned to a "competent authority", responsible for applying EU legislation throughout the entire river basin.[97] In the case of river basins shared by Member States there is no obligation to establish a joint competent authority for the entire river basin, but each Member State is obliged to ensure that EU water legislation is coordinated throughout the entire basin.[98] Member States may use existing arrangements for such co-ordination.[99] Where river basin districts extend beyond the borders of the EU there is no obligation to adopt a river basin approach, although coordination with non-Member States is encouraged.[100]

The 1997 UN Watercourses Convention provides that "watercourse State may consider the establishment of joint mechanisms or commissions, as deemed necessary by them, to facilitate cooperation on relevant measures and procedures".[101] In addition the Convention stipulates that, "Watercourse States shall, at the request of any of them, enter into consultations concerning the management of an international watercourse, which may include the establishment of a joint management mechanism".[102]

Both the 2000 EU Water Framework Directive and the 1997 UN Watercourses Convention therefore fall short of obliging Watercourse states to establish joint basin institutions for the management of international watercourses, although the EU Directive arguably goes further than the UN Watercourses Convention in at least requiring some administrative structure to be established at the national level, and coordinated at the international level.[103]

---

[97] 2000 EU Water Framework Directive, Art 3(1).

[98] Ibid, Art 3(3).

[99] Ibid, Art 3(3). See S Nilsson, S Langaas & F Hannerz, 'International River Basin Districts under the EU Water Framework Directive: Identification and Planned Cooperation' *European Water Management Online* (EFIA, 2004).

[100] Ibid, Art 3(5). In the case of international watercourses Member States are obliged to "ensure coordination with the aim of producing a single international river basin management plan". Where such a plan is not produced, Member States must at least produce a river basin management covering the parts of the international watercourse falling within their territory. The River Basin Management Plans must contain various details of the river basin including, a general description of the characteristics of the river basin district, a review of the environmental impact of human activity and an economic analysis of water us a list of environmental objectives adopted pursuant to the WFD, and a summary of the programme or programme of measures adopted. Article 5, 11 and the Annexes to the EU WFD provide considerable detail as to what should be included within the River Basin Management Plan.

[101] 1997 UN Watercourses Convention, Art 3.

[102] Ibid, Art 24(2), which provides that "For the purposes of this article, "management" refers, in particular, to: (a) Planning the sustainable development of an international watercourse and providing for the implementation of any plans adopted; and (b) otherwise promoting the rational and optimal utilisation, protection and control of the watercourse." In addition, Art 8(2) provides that, "In determining the manner of such cooperation, watercourse States may consider the establishment of joint mechanisms or commissions, as deemed necessary by them, to facilitate cooperation on relevant measures and procedures in the light of experience gained through cooperation in existing joint mechanisms and commission in various regions."

[103] An interesting point to note, however, is that in certain circumstances the establishment of joint commissions may be the only effective way in which the substantive provisions of a Convention

A different approach is adopted by the 1992 UN ECE Helsinki Convention in that riparian parties are obligated to establish joint bodies for transboundary waters within their jurisdiction.[104] The tasks of the joint bodies are set out as being, *inter alia*:

"(a) To collect, compile and evaluate data in order to identify pollution sources likely to cause transboundary impact;

(b) To elaborate joint monitoring programmes concerning water quality and quantity;

(c) To draw up inventories and exchange information on the pollution sources...;

(d) To elaborate emission limits for waste water and evaluate the effectiveness of control programmes;

(e) To elaborate joint water-quality objectives and criteria..., and to propose relevant measures for maintaining and, where necessary, improving the existing water quality;

(f) To develop concerted action programmes for the reduction of pollution loads from both point sources (e.g. municipal and industrial sources) and diffuse sources (particularly from agriculture);

(g) To establish warning and alarm procedures;

(h) To serve as a forum for the exchange of information on existing and planned uses of water and related installations that are likely to cause transboundary impact;

(i) To promote cooperation and exchange of information on the best available technology in accordance with the provisions of article 13 of this Convention, as well as to encourage cooperation in scientific research programmes;

(j) To participate in the implementation of environmental impact assessments relating to transboundary waters, in accordance with appropriate international regulations."[105]

In relation to amending or concluding basin agreements, the 1997 UN Watercourses Convention also falls short of the obligation contained in the 1992 UN ECE Helsinki Convention. Article 3 of the 1997 UN Watercourses Convention, provides that:

for the management of international watercourses can be implement. McCaffrey noted that the "management of international watercourse systems through joint institutions is not only an increasingly common phenomenon, but also a form of co-operation between watercourse States that is almost indispensable if anything approaching optimum utilisation and protection of the system of waters is to be attained", S McCaffrey, 'Sixth Report on the Law of the Non-navigational Uses of International Watercourses' [1990] 2(2) *Yearbook of the International Law Commission*, pt. 2, at 41, UN Doc. A/CN.4/427, at para. 7. A similar sentiment was voiced by the International Law Association's Water Resources Committee in 1976, when it stated that "Analysis of Convention Law, State practice, and of the opinion of most qualified publicists does not seem to provide evidence of the formation of a general international custom obliging States interested in the conservation and development of an international drainage basin to set up joint management agencies. However, the need for an institutionalised co-ordination of competitive and concurrent needs and interests is deeply felt by the international community and is evidenced by the considerable number of agreements concluded in this respect" (ILA Report of the fifty-seventh Conference, Madrid, 1976, reprinted in S Bogdanovic, *International Law of Water Resources—Contribution of the International Law Association (1954–2000)*, 245 (Kluwer Law International, London, 2001), at 19.

[104] 1992 UN ECE Helsinki Convention, Art 9(2).

[105] Ibid.

"(1) In the absence of an agreement to the contrary, *nothing in the present Convention* shall affect the rights or obligations of a watercourse State arising from agreements in force for it on the date on which it became a party to the present Convention.

(2) Notwithstanding the provisions of paragraph 1, parties to agreements referred to in paragraph 1 *may,* where necessary, consider harmonizing such agreements with the basic principles of the present Convention.

(3) Watercourse States *may* enter into one or more agreements... which apply and adjust the provisions of the present Convention to the characteristics and uses of a particular international watercourse or part thereof [emphasis added]."[106]

Conversely, the 1992 UN ECE Helsinki Convention stipulates that the riparian parties, "*shall*... enter into bilateral or multilateral agreements or other arrangements, where these do not yet exist, or adapt existing ones, where necessary to eliminate the contradictions with the basic principles of this Convention [emphasis added]."[107]

Also in contrast to the 1997 UN Watercourses Convention, the 1992 UN ECE Helsinki Convention provides for an institutional framework to implement and develop the principles contained within the agreement. A Meeting of the Parties is responsible for defining and reviewing activities and policies under the Convention as well as sharing information on experience gained in negotiating, and implementing bilateral and multilateral agreements concerning transboundary waters.[108] The Meeting of the Parties is held every three years, wherein the parties set their programme of work for the next three or more years. So far there have been four Meetings of the Parties.[109]

The meeting of the Parties is supported by a number of other bodies. There are three working groups charged with developing and implementing new policies, strategies and methodologies to protect transboundary waters, as well as organising workshops and conferences, training and capacity building events. The Working Groups have developed policy guidelines on sustainable flood management, inter-state water distribution, guidelines for the monitoring and assessment of transboundary waters, and public participation in water management.[110] In September 2000, the International Water Assessment Centre was also established under the auspices of the Convention to assist implementation efforts, along with a legal board and advisory service. Lastly, a Secretariat has been established in order to coordinate the activities undertaken pursuant to the Convention.[111]

---

[106] 1997 UN Watercourses Convention, Art 3.

[107] 1992 UN ECE Helsinki Convention, Art 9(1).

[108] Ibid, Art 17; see also Art 18 (right to vote).

[109] The 1st Meeting of the Parties took place in Helsinki in 1997, followed by the Hague in 2000, Madrid in 2003 and Bonn in 2006. The work programme for the next three years is available at, http://www.unece.org/env/water/cooperation/area.htm.

[110] See above n 48.

[111] 1992 UN ECE Helsinki Convention, Art 19.

Monitoring and Assessment

Article 8 of the 2000 EU Water Framework Directive obliges Member States to establish programmes for monitoring the water status, "in order to establish a coherent and comprehensive overview of water status within each river basin district."[112] Further details relating to monitoring the water status are provided in Annex V of the 2000 EU Water Framework Directive. EU Member States, in addition to the requirements of the 2000 EU Water Framework Directive, must comply with EU legislation relating to environmental assessments, including the 1985 Environmental Impact Assessment Directive[113] and the 2001 Strategic Environmental Impact Assessment Directive.[114] The 1985 EIA Directive requires that "projects likely to have significant effects on the environment by virtue, *inter alia*, of their nature, size or location" be subject to environmental assessment.[115] If a project falls under the Directive, the developer is required to provide information on its environmental effects, and the public must be consulted.[116] Transboundary participation is provided for within the Directive.[117] The 2001 SEA Directive requires assessment of all plans and programmes in particular sectors that set the framework for projects either subject to Environmental Impact Assessment or assessment under the Habitats Directive, and also includes a procedure for consultation on plans or programs with transboundary impacts.[118]

In contrast to the 2000 EU Water Framework Directive, the 1997 UN Watercourses Convention does not provide any specific provision on the monitoring of international watercourses. Pursuant to a general obligation to cooperate contained in Article 8, States are obliged to exchange, "readily available data and information on the condition of the watercourse, in particular that of a hydrological, meteorological, hydrogeological and ecological nature and related to the water quality as well

---

[112] 2000 EU Water Framework Directive, Art 8.

[113] Council Directive 85/337/EEC, 1985 O.J. (L 175) 40. Council Directive 85/337/EEC was amended in 1997 by Council Directive 97/11/EC, 1997 (O.J. (L 73) 5 (EIA Directive).

[114] Council Directive 2001/42/EC, 2001 O.J. (L 197) 30 (SEA Directive).

[115] Above n 113, Art 2.

[116] Ibid, Art 5.

[117] Ibid, Art 7. Article 7(1) provides that "Where a Member State is aware that a project is likely to have significant effects on the environment in another Member State or where a Member State likely to be significantly affected so requests, the Member State in whose territory the project is intended to be carried out shall send to the affected Member State as soon as possible and no later than when informing its own public" a range of information, including information on "its possible transboundary impact". The remainder of the Article sets out scope for other Member States' authorities and public to participate in the EIA procedure.

[118] SEA Directive, above n 114, Art 7. Article 7 provides that "1. Where a Member State considers that the implementation of a plan or programme being prepared in relation to its territory is likely to have significant effects on the environment in another Member State, or where a Member State likely to be significantly affected so requests, the Member State in whose territory the plan or programme is being prepared shall, before its adoption or submission to the legislative procedure, forward a copy of the draft plan or programme and the relevant environmental report to the other Member State." Article 7(2) and (3) contain further provisions relating to consultation with Member States' authorities and public.

as related forecasts".[119] If data or information is not readily available, States are under a *best efforts* obligation to comply with the request, but "may condition...compliance upon payment by the requesting State of the reasonable costs of collecting and, where appropriate, processing data or information".[120] In relation to planned measures, State parties to the 1997 UN Watercourses Convention are also obliged to, "exchange information and consult each other and, if necessary, negotiate on the possible effects of planned measures on the condition of an international watercourse".[121] Furthermore, where a Watercourse State,

"...implements or permits the implementation of planned measures which may have a significant adverse effect upon other watercourse States, it shall provide those States with timely notification thereof. Such notification shall be accompanied by available technical data and information, including the results of any environmental impact assessment, in order to enable the notified States to evaluate the possible effects of the planned measures."[122]

The provisions of the 1997 UN Watercourses Convention relating to the regular exchange of data and information, and the notification of planned measures, therefore fall well short of the detailed provisions contained in EU legislation relating to the joint monitoring and assessment of waters.

In terms of monitoring and assessment, the 1992 UN ECE Helsinki Convention obliges riparian parties to, "establish and implement joint programmes for monitoring the conditions of transboundary waters, including floods and ice drifts, as well as transboundary impact."[123] Additionally, the riparian parties are to agree on pollution parameters and pollutants whose discharges and concentrations in transboundary waters are to be regularly monitored."[124] Riparian States are also obliged to exchange "reasonably available data", on environmental conditions of transboundary waters; experience gained in the application and operation of best available technology and results of research and development; emission and monitoring data; measures taken and planned to be taken to prevent, control and reduce transboundary impact; and permits or regulations for waste-water discharges issued by the competent authority or appropriate body.[125]

Both Conventions oblige States to notify other potentially affected States of any emergency situation, such as "flood or ice conditions, water-borne diseases, siltation, erosion, salt-water intrusion, drought or desertification."[126] However, whereas the 1997 UN Watercourses Convention merely obliges watercourse States to "jointly develop contingency plans", the 1992 UN

---

[119] 1997 UN Watercourses Convention, Art 8.
[120] Ibid, Art 9(2). Article 9(3) further provides that, "Watercourse States shall employ their best efforts to collect and, where appropriate, to process data and information in a manner which facilitates its utilisation by the other watercourse States to which it is communicated."
[121] Ibid, Art 11.   [122] Ibid, Art 12.
[123] Article 11(1) of the 1992 UN ECE Helsinki Convention.
[124] Ibid, Art 11(2).   [125] Ibid, Art 13.
[126] Article 27 and 28 of the UN Watercourses Convention.

ECE Helsinki Convention requires the States, where appropriate, "to set up and operate coordinated or joint communication, warning and alarm systems".[127]

Compliance and Enforcement

A number of mechanisms are in place to ensure compliance and enforcement of the 2000 EU Water Framework Directive. The abovementioned obligations relating to impact assessment, public information and consultation will enhance compliance. In addition, Member States are under a number of reporting requirements including sending the river basin management plans and regular updates to the EU commission.[128] The EU Commission must also report on the implementation of the Directive before 2015.

Under the 1997 UN Watercourses Convention no similar provisions exist relating to compliance and enforcement. In contrast, a number of provisions in the 1992 UN ECE Helsinki Convention seek to address compliance and enforcement issues. In addition to the monitoring and assessment requirements, and institutional framework set out above, the parties are also obliged to, "cooperate in the conduct of research into and development of effective techniques for the prevention, control and reduction of transboundary impact".[129] Moreover, under the 1998 Protocol on Water and Health, the UN ECE has drafted a compliance review mechanism.[130] The mechanism proposes that a Compliance Committee, made up of 9 independent experts, meets annually. The function of the committee will be to review submissions of non-compliance from States, the public or the Secretariat. Where a case of non-compliance is identified, various powers will be available to the committee, including providing financial and technical assistance, issuing cautions and declarations of non-compliance, publishing cases of non-compliance, and suspending special rights and privileges accorded to contracting parties under the Protocol.

Public Participation

Article 14(1) of the 2000 EU Water Framework Directive provides that Member States shall, "...encourage the active involvement of all interested parties in the implementation of this Directive, in particular in the production, review and updating of the river basin management plans". Pursuant to the latter obligation, Member States must

---

[127] Article 14 of the 1992 UN ECE Helsinki Convention. In addition, the parties to the Helsinki Convention have developed Model Provisions on Transboundary Flood Management, which were adopted at the 4th Meeting of the Parties, see http://www.unece.org/env/water/meetings/documents.htm#31.

[128] 2000 EU Water Framework Directive, Art 15.

[129] 1992 UN ECE Helsinki Convention, Art 5 and 12.

[130] UN ECE/WHO, *Establishing a Compliance Procedure under the Protocol on Water and Health*, UN Doc. MP.WAT/WG.4/2004/7, 6 Oct. 2004, http://www.unece.org/env/documents/2004/wat/wg.4/mp.wat.wg.4.2004.7.e.pdf.

"... ensure that, for each river basin district, they publish and make available for comments to the public, including users:

    (a) a timetable and work programme for the production of the plan, including a statement of the consultation measures to be taken, at least three years before the beginning of the period to which the plan refers;

    (b) an interim overview of the significant water management issues identified in the river basin, at least two years before the beginning of the period to which the plan refers;

    (c) draft copies of the river basin management plan, at least one year before the beginning of the period to which the plan refers.

On request, access shall be given to background documents and information used for the development of the draft river basin management plan."[131]

Member States must allow at least six months for interested parties to comment on the above documents.[132] The provisions of the 2000 EU Water Framework Directive are complemented by other legislation relating to public participation within the EU. The EU for example is a party to the 1998 Aarhus Convention.[133] Subsequently, the EU has adopted a number of instruments to support the implementation of the 1988 Aarhus Convention within its territory.[134]

Under the 1992 UN ECE Helsinki Convention riparian parties must ensure that "information concerning the conditions of the transboundary waters, measures taken or planned to be taken to prevent, control and reduce transboundary impact, and the effectiveness of those measures, is made available to the public".[135] Further to the latter provision, the UN ECE has developed a guidance document on public participation.[136]

No similar provisions relating to public participation are contained in the 1997 UN Watercourses Convention. The closest is Article 32 relating to non-discrimination, which provides that,

"Unless the watercourse States concerned have agreed otherwise for the protection of the interests of persons, natural or juridical, who have suffered or are under a serious threat of suffering significant transboundary harm as a result of activities related to an international watercourse, a watercourse State shall not

---

[131] 2000 EU Water Framework Directive, Art 14(1).

[132] Ibid, Art 14(2).

[133] Above n 51. The Decision on conclusion of the Aarhus Convention by the EC was adopted on 17 February 2005, see Council Decision 2005/370/EC, 2005 O.J. (L 124) 1.

[134] Council and Parliament Directive 2003/4/EC, O.J. (L 41) 26 on public access to environmental information; Council and Parliament Directive 2003/35/EC, O.J. (L 156) 17 on public participation in respect of the drawing up of certain plans and programmes relating to the environment; Council and Parliament Regulation 1367/2006, OJ (L 264) 13 on the application of the provisions of the Aarhus Convention on Access to Information, Public Participation in Decision-making and Access to Justice in Environmental Matters to Community Institutions and Bodies. The Commission have also proposed a Council and Parliament Direction on Access to Justice in Environmental Matters, COM(2003)624 final (Oct 24, 2003).

[135] Article 16(1) of the 1992 UN ECE Convention.

[136] UN ECE/UNEP Network of Experts on Public Participation and Compliance, Water Management: Guidance on Public Participation and Compliance with Agreements, March 2000, available at http://www.unece.org/env/ water/publications/documents/guidance.pdf.

discriminate on the basis of nationality or residence or place where the injury occurred, in granting to such persons, in accordance with its legal system, access to judicial or other procedures, or a right to claim compensation or other relief in respect of significant harm caused by such activities carried on its territory."[137]

Clearly this obligation falls well short of the provisions for public participation contained under EU and UN ECE instruments.

2.5 Dispute Settlement Mechanisms

There are no specific dispute settlement mechanisms contained within the provisions of the 2000 EU Water Framework Directive, however disputes between the Member States are subject to the general framework set out in the EU.[138] The Commission has general powers and responsibilities to ensure that EU law is implemented. As noted above, Member States are under certain reporting obligations, but the Commission may also undertake its own assessments, or investigate complaints raised by EU citizens or the European Parliament. If the Commission reaches the decision that there has been a breach of EU legislation it may issue infringement proceedings against a Member State.[139] There are several phases of infringement proceedings. Firstly, the Commission will issue the Member State concerned with a formal letter, requesting the Member to submit its observations within 2 months. Where there is a failure to respond or the response is deemed inadequate, the Commission will then issue a reasoned opinion. If the Member State fails to comply with the reasoned opinion within 2 months of its issuance, the Commission can refer the case to the European Court of Justice. If the Court finds the Member State in breach of Community Law, it can order that a State comply with the Judgement of the Court. Certain powers are available to the Court, including imposing fines on Member States, and the form of lump sum or penalty payment.

Similar provisions relating to dispute settlement are found in both the 1997 UN Watercourses Convention and the 1992 UN ECE Helsinki Convention. States are obliged to settle their disputes by a number of peaceful means, and may agree to submit their dispute to Arbitration

---

[137] Article 32, 1997 UN Watercourses Convention.

[138] See Krämer, above n 35, 372–394.

[139] Article 226 of the EC Treaty stipulates that "If the Commission considers that a Member State has failed to fulfil an obligation under this Treaty, it shall deliver a reasoned opinion on the matter after giving the State concerned the opportunity to submit its observations. If the State concerned does not comply with the opinion within the period laid down by the Commission, the latter may bring the matter before the Court of Justice" (Consolidated Version of the Treaty Establishing the European Community, Dec. 24, 2002, 1997 O.J. (C 340) 3). See also European Commission, 'Communication on Better Monitoring of the Application of Community Law', 11 Dec. 2002, COM(2002)725 final. Three categories of breaches of Community Law exist: (i) non-communication, where a Member State has failed to adopt and communicate to the Commission national legislation implementing a directive, after the deadline for implementation has passed; (ii) non-conformity, where the Member State has failed to implement a directive correctly; and (iii) bad application, where a Member State is failing correctly to apply Community law in practice in a particular case.

or the International Court of Justice.[140] Both Conventions provides Annexes relating to the procedural aspects of Arbitration.

One significant difference between the Conventions is that, pursuant to the 1997 UN Watercourses Convention, if within six months the parties have not reached agreement then one or both of the parties may submit the dispute to a third-party fact finding commission, composed of a member nominated by each Party, and third person who shall be nominated by mutual consent of the parties.[141] The role of the Commission is to examine the facts under dispute, and submit a report to the Parties setting out its findings and recommendations for the peaceful resolution of the dispute, which the parties must consider in good faith.[142] This is perhaps one area where the 1997 UN Watercourses Convention provides more detail than the 1992 UN ECE Helsinki Convention, which does not contain any similar provision.

2.6 Conclusions

A comparative analysis of the 1997 UN Watercourses Convention, the 1992 UN ECE Helsinki Convention and the 2000 EU Water Framework Directive shows that there are no major conflicts between the instruments. However, differences do exist, both in the scope of each instrument, and the extent of the obligations placed upon the parties.

In relation to scope, the 2000 EU Water Framework Directive clearly has a wider remit covering *all* EU waters, both national and international; whereas the 1997 UN Watercourses Convention and the 1992 UN ECE Helsinki Convention deal exclusively with international watercourses. In terms of the extent of the substantive obligations contained within the instruments, there is a marked difference in that—while all three instruments are "framework" instruments—the level of provision contained in the 2000 EU Water Framework Directive and the 1992 UN ECE Helsinki Convention is far more detailed and precise compared to the 1997 UN Watercourses Convention. It could also be argued that the two European instruments take a more "ecosystemic" approach to the management of transboundary waters. The latter two instruments are also far more detailed in terms of the implementation instruments in place, and the institutional mechanisms by which to ensure compliance and enforcement. Such a level of detail is most likely to be due to the fact that both regional instruments evolved out of a long tradition of legislative development within the EU and UN ECE.

---

[140] 1997 UN Watercourses Convention, Article 33. Under Art 33(1), States are required to settle disputes in a peaceful manner. In addition, "if the parties cannot reach agreement by negotiation, they may jointly seek the good offices of, or request mediation or conciliation by, a third party, or make use, as appropriate , of any joint watercourse institutions that may have been established by them or agree to submit the dispute to arbitration or to the International Court of Justice."

[141] Ibid, Art 33(2). Pursuant to Art 33(5), if the parties cannot agree on the third person, either may request the UN Secretary-General to appoint that person.

[142] Ibid, Art 33(7) and (8).

Given that there are no major conflicts between the "framework" instruments, the existence of two relatively detailed and evolved instruments at the regional level is arguably of tremendous benefit for the 1997 UN Watercourses Convention. As a global framework instrument, the provisions of the 1997 UN Watercourses Convention are in the large couched in general terms, and require specific interpretation depending on the given context. The 2000 EU Water Framework Directive and the 1992 UN ECE Helsinki Convention both therefore provide a useful guide on how such general norms might be applied at the regional and basin levels.

Having concluded at this stage that there are no significant conflicts between the three instruments, and that the two regional instruments could provide a useful guide on the implementation of the more general global instrument, the next section will consider the attitude of EU states towards the 1997 UN Watercourses Convention.

3. EU State Opinion Towards the 1997 UN Watercourses Convention

3.1 Comments and Observations of States to the ILC Draft Articles

In 1959 the UN General Assembly decided to "initiate preliminary studies on the legal problems relating to the utilisation and use of international rivers with a view to determining whether the subject is appropriate for codification".[143] Following a preliminary study by the UN Secretary-General,[144] the General Assembly, in 1973, recommended that, "the International Law Commission should at its twenty-sixth session commence its work on the law of non-navigational uses of international watercourses".[145] Pursuant to that recommendation, the Commission at its 26th session, set up a sub-Committee on the topic and appointed Mr Richard Kearney as Special Rapporteur. The sub-committee delivered a report that contained a number of questions intended to elicit the views of States on certain aspects of the subject.[146] Quite a large number of

---

[143] G.A. Res. 1401(XIV), (Nov. 21, 1959).
[144] U.N. Doc. A/5409, above n 19.
[145] G.A. Res. 3071(XXVIII), U.N. Doc. A/9334 (Nov. 30, 1973).
[146] The questions posed were the following:

   – Question A. What would be the appropriate scope of the definition of an international watercourse, in a study of the legal aspects of fresh water uses on the one hand and of fresh water pollution on the other hand?
   – Question B. Is the geographical concept of an international drainage basin the appropriate basis for a study of the legal aspects of non-navigational uses of international watercourses?
   – Question C. Is the geographical concept of an international drainage basin the appropriate basis for a study of the legal aspects of the pollution of international watercourses?
   – Question D. Should the Commission adopt the following outline for fresh water uses as the basis of its study: (a) Agricultural uses: 1. Irrigation; 2. Drainage; 3. Waste disposal; 4.

EU Member States submitted comments and observations to the ILC, including Austria, Finland, France, Germany, Hungary, the Netherlands, Poland, Spain and Sweden.[147] These initial comments and observations focused on the scope of the work to be carried out by the ILC, and on the whole the Member States were supportive of the need to codify international law in the field.

In 1991, the ILC provisionally adopted upon first reading a set of draft articles on the law of the non-navigational uses of international watercourses.[148] These draft articles were, through the Secretary-General, transmitted to Governments for comments and observations. Again, several EU Member States submitted comments and observations, including Denmark, Finland, Germany, Greece, Hungary, Netherlands, Poland, Spain, Sweden and the United Kingdom.[149] The EU Member States were largely supportive of the Draft Articles. Germany, for instance, noted that it,

"...welcomes the provisional adoption by the Commission of draft articles on the law of the non-navigational uses of international watercourses. Germany attaches particular importance to the subject dealt with in this draft, not only because of its geographical situation in the centre of Europe, but especially in view of the fact that it shares several major international watercourses. It is of the opinion that the draft articles also meet a global need for regulation in this matter, owing to the fact that since the Second World War the general use of watercourses has been the focus of attention, pushing navigational needs into the background."[150]

Similarly, the Nordic countries welcomed the draft articles, recognizing, "the importance of legal problems relating to the use of international

Aquatic food production; (b) Economic and commercial uses: 1. Energy production (hydroelectric, nuclear and mechanical); 2. Manufacturing; 3. Construction; 4. Transport other than navigation; 5. Timber floating; 6. Waste disposal; 7. Extractive (mining, oil production etc.); (c) Domestic and social: 1. Consumptive (drinking, cooking, washing, laundry, etc.); 2. Waste disposal; 3. Recreational (swimming, sport, fishing, boating, etc.)?
– Question E. Are there any other uses that should be included?
– Question F. Should the Commission include flood control and erosion problems in its study?
– Question G. Should the Commission take account in its study of the interaction between use for navigation and other uses?
– Question H. Are you in favour of the Commission taking up the problem of pollution of international watercourses as the initial stage of its study?
– Question I. Should special arrangements be made for ensuring that the Commission is provided with the technical, scientific and economic advice which will be required through such means as the establishment of a Committee of Experts?

[147] 'Replies of Governments to the Commission's Questionnaire' [1976] 2 *Yearbook of the International Law Commission* 147, (U.N. Doc. A/CN.4/294 and Add. 1); 253 (U.N. Doc. A/CN.4/314); and 178 (U.N. Doc. A/CN.4/324).

[148] 'Text of the draft articles provisionally adopted by the Commission on first reading', in *Report of the International Commission to the General Assembly on the work of its forty-third session*, U.N. GAOR Supp. (No. 10), 1, U.N. Doc. A/46/10, reprinted in [1991] 2 *Yearbook of the International Law Commission* 1 (U.N. Doc. A/CN.4/SER.A/1991/Add.1 (Part 2)), at 66.

[149] 'Comments and Observations from Governments',[1993] 2 *Yearbook of the International Law Commission* 145 (U.N. Doc. A/CN.4/447 and Add.1–3).

[150] Ibid, 151.

watercourses and the need to coordinate work carried out by many international organs".[151] The United Kingdom also noted that, while it was not a major international watercourse State, it welcomed the draft articles as, "a valuable contribution to the international protection of the environment".[152]

Pursuant to the comments and observations of States to the Draft Articles adopted at first reading, the ILC adopted on second reading revised draft articles on the law of non-navigational uses of international watercourses and a resolution on confined transboundary groundwater; and recommended the elaboration of a convention by the General Assembly or international conference of plenipotentiaries on the basis of the draft articles.[153] The General Assembly, taking note of the ILC's recommendation, invited States to submit comments and observations on the draft articles. Of the EU Member States, comments and observations were received from Finland, Hungary, Portugal and Spain. The comments and observations were on the whole positive. Finland reiterated its belief that the draft articles, "would contribute considerably to the development of international law concerning the non-navigational uses of international watercourses".[154] Two common observations were also made by the EU Member States. Finland, Hungary and Portugal all pointed to the need to harmonise the provisions of the 1994 Draft Articles with those of the 1992 UN ECE Helsinki Convention, and the 1991 Convention on Environmental Impact Assessment in a Transboundary Context.[155] In addition, Finland and Portugal noted the need to ensure that the Draft Articles adequately reflected the principles of sustainable development, the polluter-pays and precaution.[156]

3.2 Negotiating Positions within 6th Committee of the UN General Assembly

In its Resolution 49/52 of 1994 the General Assembly also took the decision that at the beginning of its 51st session, the Sixth Committee (Legal) should convene as a Working Group of the Whole open to State Members of the United Nations or members of specialised agencies, for three weeks from 7 to 25 October 1996 to elaborate a framework convention on the topic on the basis of the ILC's draft articles and in light of the comments and observations submitted by States.[157] The Working Group

---

[151] Ibid, 164.   [152] Ibid, 168.

[153] 'Report of the International Law Commission to the General Assembly on the work of its forty-sixth session', U.N. GAOR, Supp. (No. 10), ¶ 210–222, U.N. Doc. A/49/10, reprinted in [1994] 2 *Yearbook of the International Law Commission* 1, U.N. Doc. A/CN.4/SER.A/1994/Add.1 (Part 2).

[154] 'Comments and Observations Received From States, in Report of the Secretary-General on Draft Articles on the Law of the Non-Navigational Uses of International Watercourses', U.N. Doc. A/51/275, at 17.

[155] Ibid. at 10, 13 & 14.   [156] Ibid at 11 & 14.

[157] G.A. Res. 49/52, U.N. Doc. A/RES/49/52 (Dec. 9, 1994). For the procedure of the Working Group and its drafting committee, see Annex to GA Res. 49/52.

met in two sessions, in 1996 and 1997, and generated considerable debate between the States on various aspects of the topic in question.[158]

While all UN Member States were entitled to contribute to the work of the 6th Committee, statements from only 54 delegations were recorded in the official Summary Records of the negotiations. Of the EU Member States, the following lodged statements, Austria, Belgium, Czech Republic, France, Finland, Germany, Greece, Hungary, Italy, Netherlands, Slovakia, Spain and United Kingdom.

During the negotiations three groups of States were discernable. The most active EU States, that is the Czech Republic, France, Slovakia and Spain, belonged to the "upstream" group; Greece, Hungary, the Netherlands and Portugal were part of the "downstream group; while Finland and Germany joined the "mixed-motive" group.[159] The "upstream" group can be categorised as the least cooperative group, and are likely to attempt to prevent the adoption of the Convention or weaken the obligation contained therein.[160] In contrast, the downstream states are more interested in cooperation and reaching agreement.[161] The mixed-motive group tend to push forward the process and are likely to come out in favour of more environmental protection.[162]

3.3 Voting Record of the UN General Assembly

It was proposed by the Chairman that the working group adopt the text of the convention article by article. Most of the articles were adopted with little or not discussion, apart from Article 3, 5–7, and 33 and its annex.

France, who had requested a vote on Article 3, maintained that it was necessary because "it determined the nature of the convention, the manner of its implementation and its potential effects on existing or future agreements".[163] France went on to state that the Article "constituted a limitation on the freedom of States to enter into future watercourse agreements and the common interpretation given to it was insufficient to remove the ambiguity on that point".[164] 36 States voted in favour of the Article, while only 3 States voted against, and 20 States abstained. Of the EU States, Belgium, Denmark, Finland, Germany, Greece, Hungary, Italy, Netherlands, Spain and the United Kingdom all voted in favour; France voted against; and Austria, Czech Republic, Portugal, Slovakia abstained.

---

[158] See P Wouters 'The Legal Response to Water Conflicts: The UN Watercourses Convention and Beyond' (1999) 42 *German Year Book of International Law* 293, at 304–319; Tanzi and Arcari, above n 89, at 35–45.

[159] E Schroeder-Wildberg, 'The 1997 UN Watercourses Convention—Background and Negotiations', Working Paper on Management in Environmental Planning 04/202, http://hydroaid.tinext.net/FTP/Data_Research/E.%20Schroeder-Wildberg-The%201997%20Int%20Watercourse%20Convention.pdf.

[160] Ibid.   [161] Ibid.

[162] Ibid.

[163] U.N. GAOR, 51st Sess., 62nd mtg., UN Doc. A/C.6/51/SR.62 (Apr. 4, 1997) para 43.

[164] Ibid.

In relation to the substantive norms contained in Articles 5–7, the package was adopted with 38 in favour; 23 abstentions; and 4 against. Austria, Belgium, Denmark, Finland, Germany, Hungary, Italy, Netherlands, Portugal and the United Kingdom all voted in favour; while France was one of the States voting against; and the Czech Republic, Greece, Slovakia and Spain abstained. In voting against, the representative of France stated that "his delegation would prefer to ensure at all costs that disputed articles were not adopted, as their adoption could have adverse repercussions for the future of the convention".[165] He went on to explain the reason behind France's objection to Articles 5–7 as being that they "provided the beginnings of a regime of responsibility without defining either its terms or its scope, which was unlikely to resolve possible disputes between riparian States and could even complicate them".[166]

China requested a vote on Article 33 relating to dispute settlement and its annex.[167] 33 countries voted in favour of the text, while there were 5 votes against, and 25 abstentions.[168] Austria, Belgium, Czech Republic, Denmark, Finland, Germany, Greece, Hungary, Italy, Netherlands, Portugal, Spain and the United Kingdom all voted in favour of the text, while France voted against, and Slovakia abstained. France voted against the text because it believed that it was at variance to the purpose of a framework convention.[169]

Finally, a recorded vote was taken on the draft convention as a whole, which resulted in 42 states voting in favour, 3 voting against, and 19 abstentions. France was the only EU State to vote against the text as a whole, and Slovakia and Spain were the only EU States to abstain.[170] Austria, Belgium, Czech Republic, Denmark, Finland, Germany, Greece, Hungary, Italy, Netherlands, Portugal, and the United Kingdom all voted in favour of the text.[171] In its opposition to the text, France made a clear statement of its objection, providing that it had voted against because "the point of order it had raised had been ignored; speakers had been denied the opportunity to explain their vote before the voting; and the Convention had been adopted without the two-thirds majority specified in the rules of procedure".[172] The French delegation stated that it had also voted against it "because of the manner in which the work had been carried out, the procedure used to negotiate the adoption of the draft Convention and the ambiguities of some of its basic provisions, particularly those relating to the scope of the draft".[173] In the opinion of the

---

[165] Ibid, para 14.   [166] Ibid.
[167] Ibid, para 86.   [168] Ibid.
[169] Ibid.
[170] U.N. GAOR, 51st Sess., 62nd mtg, UN Doc. A/C.6/51/SR.62/Add.1 (Apr. 4, 1997), para 3.
[171] Ibid, para 2.
[172] Ibid, para 20. On the point of order, which related to the distribution of the convention in official languages, see UN Doc. A/C.6/51/SR.62, above n 163, para 106. Mr Yamada, the Chairman of the Working Group, responded that the rule to which France had referred was "usually waived when negotiations were prolonged and there was a deadline for the conclusion of the discussion": UN Doc. A/C.6/51/SR.62/Add.1, above n 170, para 1.
[173] Ibid, para 20.

French delegation, "there were also a number of articles which had given rise to numerous reservations, indicating that the Sixth Committee could not consider that it had completed its work; therefore, it could not submit a report on the question to the General Assembly".[174] The French delegation also noted that "the number of votes in favour of adopting the draft Convention was barely over the minimum of 35 States required for its entry into force; that would impede its general acceptance and its contribution to the development of international law and to the strengthening of international peace and security".[175] In oral statements, Spain, the Czech Republic, Hungary and Slovakia all noted that they had reservations with the Convention, and in particular Articles 5–7. However, despite such reservations Portugal noted that the Convention

"represented a milestone in the process of the codification and progressive development of international law relating to the uses of international watercourses and to the uses of water in general, as well as to cooperation in that field, bearing in mind in particular the limitations, both quantitative and qualitative, to which waters and their ecosystem were subject."[176]

The above sentiment was endorsed by the statements from the Czech Republic, Hungary, and the Netherlands.[177]

The 1997 UN Watercourses Convention was ultimately adopted by the General Assembly on 21 May 1997. When the resolution containing the Convention came before the General Assembly, Turkey requested a recorded vote. The vote found 103 States in favour; 27 abstentions; and 3 against. 23 EU States voted in favour of the Convention: Austria, Cyprus, Czech Republic, Denmark, Estonia, Finland, Germany, Greece, Hungary, Ireland, Italy, Latvia, Lithuania, Luxembourg, Malta, Netherlands, Poland, Portugal, Romania, Slovakia, Slovenia, Sweden, and the United Kingdom. No EU States voted against the Convention; and only 3 EU States abstained—Belgium, France and Spain.[178] However, the Belgium delegation subsequently informed the Secretariat that it had intended to vote in favour of the Convention.[179]

Spain mentioned the need for a more effective balance between Articles 5 and 6, and Article 7 as the reason for its abstention.[180] France claimed that, "the haste in negotiations had created serious procedural discrepancies which affected the credibility of resulting text".[181] Both Slovakia and the Czech Republic also made comments in the General Assembly, which, while noting that the text was not perfect, recognised that the Convention was an important step in the codification and progressive development of international law in the field.[182]

---

[174] Ibid. [175] Ibid.
[176] Ibid, para 29. [177] Ibid, paras 23, 30 & 37, respectively.
[178] Press Release, General Assembly, General Assembly Adopts Convention on the Law of Non-Navigational Uses of International Watercourses, U.N. Doc. GA/9248 (May 21, 1997).
[179] 99th plenary meeting, U.N. Doc. A/51/PV.99 (May 21, 1997).
[180] Ibid. [181] Ibid.
[182] Ibid.

3.4 Ratification and subsequent state positions

The 1997 UN Watercourses Convention provides that "the present Convention shall enter into force on the ninetieth day following the date of deposit of the thirty-fifth instrument of ratification, acceptance, approval or accession with the Secretary-General of the United Nations".[183] At present, there are 16 signatories to the Convention and 15 State parties.[184] Within the EU, Finland, Germany, Hungary, Luxembourg, and the Netherlands are signatories; and Germany, Hungary, the Netherlands, Portugal and Sweden are party to the Convention.

In becoming a party Finland cited two key reasons. Firstly, Finland had played an active role in the development of the Convention through the ILC, and the negotiations within the sixth committee.[185] Secondly, Finland pointed to the fact that the 1997 UN Watercourses Convention is consistent with the 1992 UN ECE Helsinki Convention and its bilateral agreements with Norway, Russia and Sweden. Ratification did not therefore require any additional legislation. Given recent developments within the EU region, such as the adoption of both the 1992 UN ECE Helsinki Convention and the EU Water Framework Directive, the Finnish justifications for becoming party to the Convention would appear to hold true for many EU Member States.

4. EU EXTERNAL RELATIONS AND THE 1997 UN WATERCOURSES CONVENTION

4.1 EU and Development Policy

Background

The EU accounts for 55 per cent of the total development aid, making it the world's foremost donor. Title XX of the EC Treaty deals with Development Cooperation.[186] Pursuant to Article 177, Community policy in the sphere of development cooperation, must foster, "the sustainable economic and social development of the developing countries, and more particularly the most disadvantaged among them", "the smooth and gradual integration of the developing countries into the world economy"

---

[183] 1997 UN Watercourses Convention, Article 35.

[184] 'Multilateral Treaties Deposited with the Secretary-General', http://untreaty.un.org/ ENGLISH/bible/englishinternetbible/partI/chapterXXVII/treaty42.asp. The signatories to the Convention are, Côte d'Ivoire, Finland, Germany, Hungary, Jordan, Luxembourg, Namibia, Netherlands, Norway, Paraguay, Portugal, South Africa, Syrian Arab Republic, Tunisia, Venezuela and Yemen; the parties to the Convention are, Finland, Germany, Hungary, Iraq, Jordan, Lebanon, Libyan Arab Jamahiriya, Namibia, Netherlands, Norway, Portugal, Qatar, South Africa, Sweden and Syrian Arab Republic.

[185] See Ulkoasianministeriö, 'Yleissopimus Kansainälisten Vesistöjen Muuhun Kuin Likennekäyttöön Sovellettavista Säännöistä Allekirjoittaminen', (Oct. 9, 1997) (on file with author); Ulkoasianministeriö, 'Yleissopimus Kansainvälisten Vesistöjen Muuhun Kuin Liikennekäyttöön Sovellettavista Säännöistä, Hyväksyminen', (Jan. 9, 1998) (on file with author).

[186] EC Treaty, above n 139.

and "the campaign against poverty in the developing countries".[187] In December 2005, the EU signed a new statement on EU development policy, known as the "European Consensus".[188] The consensus defines the framework for common principles within which the EU and its Member States will implement their development policies. The main objective of the Consensus and EU development policy is to reduce poverty worldwide in the context of sustainable development. In so doing, the EU is committed to meeting the stated aim of the Millennium Development Goals, that is, to halve world poverty by 2015. The purpose of this section is to analyse EU development policy with a view to ascertaining whether ratification of the 1997 UN Watercourses Convention by EU Member States would help achieve its key objectives.

Communication on Water Management in Developing Countries

The EU's 2002 Communication on Water Management in Developing Countries was adopted in order to contribute to the goal of ensuring that "adequate supplies of safe water be accessible to everyone in the world today, while preserving the quantity and quality of the resource to sustain essential ecosystem functions and ensure supplies for future generations".[189] The Communication signifies a shift away from the traditional technically-based solutions of former EU water development policies, to a programme approach with greater emphasis on social and environmental concerns, as well as the improvement of water resources management strategies at the national and international levels.

The Communication recognises water's central role in development issues, and securing the targets set out in the Millennium Development Goals (MDGs).[190] Specific water-related targets are identified as essential to contributing to the overall development target of reducing by at least one half those living in extreme poverty by 2015.[191] In relation to water resources management, the EU endorses the concept of reducing unsustainable exploitation of water resources by developing water management strategies at regional, national and local levels. More specifically, the Communication reiterates the need to develop comprehensive integrated water resources management policies (IRWM) at the national and international levels.[192]

---

[187] Ibid, Article 177.

[188] European Parliament, Council & Commission, Joint Statement by the Council and the Representatives of the Member States meeting with the Council, the European Parliament and the Common on European Policy: 'The European Consensus', 2006 O.J. (C 46) 1.

[189] Communication from the Commission to the Council and the European Parliament, 'Water Management in Developing Countries—Policy and Priorities for EU Development Cooperation', COM(2002) 132 final (Mar. 12, 2002), (searchable at http://eur-lex.europa.eu/ see http://eur-lex.europa.eu/LexUriServ/LexUriServ.do?uri=COM:2002:0132:FIN:EN:PDF). The Communication maintains that water is a cross-sectoral issue to be mainstreamed within development policies associated with poverty reduction.

[190] Ibid, 3.　　[191] Ibid, 6.

[192] Ibid, 7.

In the context of transboundary waters, the Communication emphasises the integration of upstream and downstream areas within river basins, as being central to the application of the core principles of sustainable, equitable and participatory human and social development.[193] The Communication notes that,

"Transboundary cooperation over water resources is becoming increasingly important in many developing regions, where growing population and changing consumption patterns create tensions on both water availability and quality among upstream and downstream users. The challenge in sharing waters is to avoid conflict and promote peaceful co-operation between different interests, both within countries and between them."[194]

The Communication goes on to recognise that a higher profile for water is required on the European Community's development cooperation agenda, and singles out transboundary cooperation as a priority area.

The Communication on Water Management in Developing Countries is complemented by the Communication on Conflict Prevention, which recommends support, "where a clear commitment to regional collaboration exists, to regional actions aiming at a fair management of shared water resources".[195] The Communication on Conflict Prevention goes on to state that, "in the short-term, measures must be built around mechanisms which ensure respect for those national and international agreements on which water-sharing rights are generally based".[196]

The 1997 UN Watercourses Convention, in providing a framework for transboundary IWRM, can potentially play a key role in meeting the above-stated objective of the "fair management of shared water resources". Such a role for the 1997 UN Watercourses Convention is also in line with the Communication's call that Donors should focus, *inter alia*, on supporting mechanisms for the improvement of regional cooperation. Broad based ratification of the 1997 UN Watercourses Convention could support the improved collaboration between bilateral and multilateral donors and international organisations, which as the Communication points out, "is particularly essential in the context of management of transboundary waters".[197]

---

[193] The Communication notes, "Water resources must be managed in an integrated manner taking account of all the legitimate uses and demands, including environmental objectives. Integrated management requires that water resources within a given river basin or lake catchment area are managed in an holistic manner balancing the water needs of the aquatic environment and the different water uses. An integrated approach also requires that all waters including groundwater and coastal waters are taken into account. This applies particularly to rivers which cross national boundaries and to lakes bordered by several different countries. Integrated Water Resources Management and River Basin Management are central principles of EU policy", ibid, 7.

[194] Ibid, 9.

[195] Communication from the Commission on Conflict Prevention, 1.04.2001 COM(2001) 211 final (Apr. 11, 2001), http://ec.europa.eu/comm/external_relations/cfsp/news/com2001_211_en.pdf, 18.

[196] Ibid.

[197] Communication, Water Management in Developing Countries, above n 189, 18.

EU Guidelines for Water Resources Development Cooperation

The EU Guidelines for Water Resources Development Cooperation were published by the EC in 1998.[198] The Guidelines lay down a strategic approach for the equitable, efficient and sustainable management of water resources. All those involved in EU development cooperation in water management, including both public and private sectors, are the intended audience.

The Guidelines provide guiding principles, target areas and priority themes for action. The principles are categorised into six headings: institutional and management aspects; social aspects; economic and financial aspects; environmental aspects; information, education and communication; and technological aspects. The target areas are: evaluation and planning of water resources; water supply and purification services; municipal water and purification services; and management and use of water in agriculture. The priority themes for action, include: institutional development and capacity-building; devising participatory structures to ensure equality of the sexes; natural resources management; expanding the water management knowledge base; demand management and pricing; and awareness-building and communications.

The 1997 UN Watercourses Convention supports the guidelines in a variety of aspects, in particularly, the guidelines urge governments to, "work towards providing a sound legal and policy framework for water resources management".[199] The 1997 UN Watercourses Convention is also mentioned in the Guidelines, as providing "a basis for establishing common rights in transboundary rivers and a framework for the management of international river systems".[200]

EU Water Facility

The EU Water Facility was established in 2004 as a mechanism for implementing EU water development policy, primarily as set out in the 2002 Communication on Water Management in Developing Countries, and the EU Guidelines for Water Resources Development Cooperation.[201] Accordingly, the EU Water Facility is designed to "contribute to the achievement of the Millennium Development Goals for drinking and sanitation".[202] Consistent with EU water development policy, IWRM is placed at the heart of the facility:

"Water resources management needs to be addressed at all levels, including the natural river, lake or groundwater basin. Integrated water resources management with strong stakeholder participation, a pro-poor emphasis, and gender

---

[198] European Commission, *Guidelines for Water Resources Development Cooperation—Towards Sustainable Water Resources Management* (1998) (see http://ec.europa.eu/development/icenter/publication/descript/pubarch85_en.cfm).

[199] Ibid, 12.   [200] Ibid, 36.

[201] Commission 'Communication on the future development of the EU Water Initiative and the modalities of the Water Facility for ACP countries', COM(2004) 43 final (Jan. 26, 2004).

[202] Ibid.

sensitivity is a key approach to ensure the integration of water services within an overall water management framework. Integrated water resource management also provides a framework to promote peace and security in transboundary water basins. As such the EU also confirms its support for initiatives that promote regional co-operation and economic development in transboundary water courses."[203]

The widespread ratification of the 1997 UN Watercourses Convention would support a number of key elements of the EU Water Facility, including reinforcing political commitment to actions and raising the profile of water and sanitation issues in the context of poverty reduction efforts; promoting better water governance arrangements; improving co-ordination and co-operation in the way that water-related interventions are developed and implemented; and encouraging regional and sub-regional co-operation on water management issues, using the integrated management approach.[204]

Member States and Water Development

A number of Member States are active in development cooperation directed towards water issues. For other Member States water may be an integral part of country cooperation, such as in the case of Portuguese development cooperation towards Mozambique.[205] Austria, Denmark, France, Germany, Ireland, the Netherlands, Sweden and United Kingdom adopt their own strategy relating to water issues.[206] Amongst the latter strategies, there has been a shift from technical solutions to a management focus with emphasis on equity and sustainability.[207] Most countries pay particular attention to the need for IWRM and emphasise the transboundary component.

4.2 EU and Multilateral Environmental Agreements (MEAs)

Legal Basis for EU participation in MEAs

Given the strong commitment to transboundary IWRM within EU water development policy, a question worth considering is whether the EU can become party to the 1997 UN Watercourses Convention. The Convention provides that it is open for signature by regional economic integration organisation, of which the EU is clearly one.[208]

The EC has taken an active part in the negotiation, ratification and implementation of numerous international agreements. From a legal standpoint, the Council, acting upon a proposal by the Commission and in consultation with the Parliament, has the power to enter into an

---

[203] Ibid.   [204] Ibid.
[205] Stockholm International Water Institute, *Water Management in Developing Countries—Policy and Priorities for EU Development* Cooperation, (2001), at 19.
[206] Ibid.   [207] Ibid.
[208] 1997 UN Watercourses Convention, Art 35.

agreement on behalf of the EU where the Treaty so permits.[209] In relation to environmental matters, Article 174 of the EU Treaty provides
that "arrangements for Community cooperation may be the subject of
agreements between the Community and the third parties concerned".[210]
In theory, the 1997 UN Watercourses Convention is therefore a "mixed
agreement", in that competence is shared between the EC and Member
States.[211] In such circumstances, common practice is that the EC normally only ratifies an agreement after the Member States concerned.[212]

EU and water-related Agreements

The EU has entered into a number of agreements relating directly and
indirectly to international waters. At the basin level, the EU is party to
both the 2000 Convention for the Protection of the Rhine,[213] and the
1994 Danube Convention.[214] At the regional level the EU is party to the
1992 UN ECE Helsinki Convention. In justifying its participation in the
1992 UN ECE Helsinki Convention, the EU noted that it is the EU's
responsibility to enter into commitments in matters relating to the protection and use of transboundary watercourses and international lakes;
and "community policy on the environment aims at strengthening international cooperation in order to achieve a high level of protection".[215]
The EU also noted that becoming party to the Convention would help
achieve the objectives set out in Article 130r of the EC Treaty.[216]

In addition, to the agreements focussed on freshwater, the EU has
also entered into agreements relating to regional seas, such as the 1992
Convention for the Protection of the Marine Environment of the

---

[209] EC Treaty, above n 139, Article 300.

[210] Ibid, Art 174(4). The 6th Action Programme contains also a specific provision on international action, which recalls the objective of aiming for swift ratification, effective compliance and
enforcement of all international conventions and agreements relating to the environment where the
Community is a Party (Communication from the Commission on the Sixth Environment Action
Programme of the European Community "Environment 2010: Our future, our choice", COM(2001)
31 final (Jan. 24, 2001)).

[211] d McGoldrick, *International Relations Law of the European Union* (1997).

[212] It should be noted that pursuant to the 1997 Watercourses Convention, Article 36(3), ratification, acceptance, approval or accession by the EU would not be counted as an additional instrument
in terms of the 35 instruments needed for the Convention to enter into force.

[213] Convention on the Protection of the Rhine, above n 53; Council Decision 2000/706/EC,
concerning the conclusion, on behalf of the Community, of the Convention for the Protection
of the Rhine, 2000 O.J. (L 289) 30, http://eur-lex.europa.eu/LexUriServ/site/en/oj/2000/l_289/
l_28920001116en00300030.pdf.

[214] Convention on the Co-operation for the Protection and Sustainable Use of the Danube River,
above n 52; Council Decision 97/825/EC, concerning the conclusion of the Convention on cooperation for the protection and sustainable use of the river Danube, 1997 O.J. (L 342) 18, http://eur-lex.
europa.eu/LexUriServ/LexUriServ.do?uri=CELEX:31997D0825:EN:HTML; see also Commission
Communication on Environmental Cooperation in the Danube-Black Sea Region, COM(2001) 615
final, (Oct. 30, 2001).

[215] Council Decision 95/308/EC, on the conclusion, on behalf of the Community, of the
Convention on the protection and use of transboundary watercourses and international lakes, 1995
O.J. (L 186) 42.

[216] Ibid.

North-East Atlantic,[217] the 1992 Convention on the Protection of the Marine Environment of the Baltic Sea Area,[218] the 1983 Agreement for Cooperation in Dealing with Pollution of the North Sea by Oil and other Harmful Substances,[219] and the 1976 Convention for the Protection of the Mediterranean Sea against Pollution.[220]

The EC has also entered into a number of environment-related agreements at the regional and global levels covering such topics at transboundary air pollution,[221] biotechnology,[222] chemicals,[223] industrial accidents,[224] climate change[225] and ozone depletion,[226] public participation,[227] environmental impact assessment,[228] biodiversity and nature conservation,[229] desertification[230] and waste.[231]

CONCLUSION

As this article has shown, a long tradition of cooperation over transboundary waters exists within Europe. Such cooperation has seen the evolution of two relatively sophisticated instruments related to transboundary waters

---

[217] Convention for the Protection of the Marine Environment of the North East Atlantic, Sep. 22, 1992 (entered into force Mar. 25, 1998), reprinted in (1993) 32 *ILM* 1069.

[218] Convention for the Protection of the Marine Environment of the Baltic Sea Area, Apr. 9, 1992 (entered into force Jan. 17, 2000), reprinted at http://fletcher.tufts.edu/multi/texts/ 22los.txt.

[219] Agreement for cooperation in dealing with pollution of the North Sea by oil and other harmful substances, Sep. 13, 1983, http://www.bonnagreement.org/eng/html/welcome.html.

[220] Convention for the Protection of the Marine Environment and the Coastal Region of the Mediterranean, Feb. 16, 1976 (entered into force Feb. 12, 1978), reprinted at http://www.unep.ch/seas/main/hconlist.html.

[221] Convention on Long-range Transboundary Air Pollution, Nov. 13, 1979 (entered into force Mar. 16, 1983), reprinted in (1980) 17 *ILM* 1488.

[222] Protocol on Biosafety to the Biodiversity Convention, Jan. 29, 2000, (entered into force Sep. 11, 2003), reprinted in (2000) 39 *ILM* 1027.

[223] Convention on the Prior Informed Consent (PIC) Procedure for Certain Hazardous Chemicals and Pesticides in International Trade, Sep. 10, 1998 (Feb. 24, 2004), reprinted at http://www.pic.int.

[224] Convention on the Transboundary Effects of Industrial Accidents, Mar. 17, 1992 (entered into force Apr. 19, 2000), reprinted at http://www.unece.org/env/teia/text.htm.

[225] U.N. Framework Convention on Climate Change, May 9, 2002 (entered into force Mar. 24, 1994), reprinted in (1992) 31 *ILM* 849 (1992); Protocol to the U.N. Framework Convention on Climate Change, Dec. 11, 1997 (entered into force Feb. 16, 2005), reprinted in (1998) 37 *ILM* 22.

[226] Convention on the Protection of the Ozone Layer, Mar. 22, 1985 (entered into force Sep. 22, 1988), reprinted in (1987) 26 *ILM* 1529; Montreal Protocol on Substances that Deplete the Ozone Layer, Sep. 16, 1987 (entered into force Jan. 1, 1989), (1987) 1522 *UNTS* 3.

[227] Convention on Access to Information, Public Participation in Decision-Making and Access to Justice in Environmental Matters, above n 51.

[228] Convention on Environmental Impact Assessment in a Transboundary Context, above n 34.

[229] U.N. Convention on Biological Diversity, Jun. 5, 1992 (entered into force Dec. 29, 1992), reprinted in (1992) 31 *ILM* 622.

[230] Convention to Combat Desertification in those Countries Experiencing Serious Drought and/or Desertification, Particularly in Africa, Oct. 14, 1994 (entered into force Oct. 14, 1994) (1994) 1954 *UNTS* 3.

[231] Convention on Transboundary Movements of Hazardous Wastes and their Disposal, Mar. 22, 1989 (entered into force May, 1992), 1973 *UNTS* 57. For a comprehensive list of Multilateral Environmental Agreements to which the EC is party, *see* http://ec.europa.eu/environment/international_issues/pdf/agreements_en.pdf.

at the regional level. Both the 2000 EU Water Framework Directive and the 1992 UN ECE Helsinki Convention lay down comparatively detailed rules for the management of transboundary waters, and as such play an important role in strengthening cooperation and preventing conflict throughout Europe's transboundary waters. In addition, the institutional structure supporting both of these instruments ensures that they are constantly adapted to address gaps or weakness, while also possessing the ability to react to future challenges.

A comparative analysis of both instruments and the 1997 UN Watercourses Convention shows that there is little conflict between the latter and the two regional instruments. One important difference, however, is in the degree of detail contained within the European instruments as opposed to the 1997 UN Watercourses Convention. Such a difference is important to note for two reasons. Firstly, it shows that in terms of strengthening the legal framework for transboundary waters *within* the EU, there is very little advantage in EU Member States becoming party to the 1997 UN Watercourses Convention. Secondly, the difference means that the experiences in the implementation of the European instruments might be useful in providing guidance on how best to implement some of the more general provisions of the 1997 UN Watercourses Convention in other parts of the world. In this regard, an important point to note is the amendment of the 1992 UN ECE Helsinki Convention to allow any UN Member State to become party to the Convention. While many developing countries might not feel that they are in a position to adopt the more onerous obligations contained in the 1992 UN Helsinki Convention, becoming party to the 1997 UN Watercourses Convention could be seen as a stepping stone towards meeting the more detailed commitments contained in the 1992 UN ECE Helsinki Convention.

While it was noted above that EU Member States might not see any value added in becoming a party to the 1997 UN Watercourses Convention in terms of strengthening their own legal frameworks for managing transboundary waters, there may be other justifications for becoming a party to the Convention. The analysis of EU State opinion during the negotiation and adoption of the 1997 UN Watercourses Convention showed that most States were supportive of the exercise. Many States recognised the role the 1997 UN Watercourses Convention could play in supporting the *global* need to strengthen legal framework for the management of transboundary waters, and the need to coordinate work carried out by international organisations. The only significant opposition came from France and Spain. The French opposition was more focused on points of procedure, while the Spanish—arguably adopting an upstream stance—pointed to the need for a more effective balance between Articles 5 and 6, and 7. However, it might now be argued that Spain's State practice in recent years has shown a less "upstream" stance, especially given the fact that it has become a party to the 1992 UN ECE Helsinki Convention, and has concluded a bilateral agreement with Portugal that enshrines many of the principles contained both with the 1992 UN ECE Helsinki Convention and the 1997 UN Watercourses Convention.[232]

It can therefore be concluded that there is no major opposition from EU Member States to the 1997 UN Watercourses Convention. Moreover, while it might be maintained that there is little "internal" gain for EU Member States in becoming party to the 1997 UN Watercourses Convention, there may be other reasons why EU Member States should consider becoming party to the Convention.

EU Development policy already makes a clear connection between alleviating poverty and ensuring that water is managed in an equitable and sustainable manner. The Communication on Water Management in Developing Countries also recognised that a major challenge in implementing equitable and sustainable management of water resources is at that transboundary level. What has not been so clearly articulated, but is evident from an analysis of the 1997 UN Watercourses Convention, is that the latter instrument—while not perfect—provides a widely accepted framework for facilitating *transboundary* integrated water resources management.

If both the EU and its Member States become party to the Convention it would send a clear message of the importance of the Convention in strengthening the management of transboundary waters throughout the world and improving collaboration between bilateral and multilateral donors and international organisations; a message that was highlighted by several EU Member States during the negotiation of the 1997 UN Watercourses Convention. The 1997 UN Watercourses Convention could also act as a catalyst for sharing the knowledge and experiences of EU Member States in implementing the EU Water Framework Directive and the 1992 UN ECE Helsinki Convention. This knowledge and experience has been gained through 10 years of implementing the 1992 UN ECE Helsinki Convention and 30 years of implementing EU water law and policy.

In addition, as noted in the case of Finland, becoming party to the 1997 Watercourses Convention would likely require little in the way of national legislative reform for EU Member States, given that they must implement the EU Water Framework Directive, and the majority of States with transboundary waters are already party to the 1992 UN ECE Helsinki Convention.

---

[232] Agreement on Cooperation for the Protection and Sustainable use of Waters of the Spanish-Portuguese Hydrographic Basins, 30 November 1998, available at http://faolex.fao.org/faolex/index.htm.

Justice-As-Sovereignty:
David Hume and the Origins of
International Law

By John Martin Gillroy*

Introduction

This article argues for a revitalization of international legal thought and suggests a new path for a fuller philosophical understanding of the origin and evolution of the international legal system.

In Part I, I prepare the way for the Humean argument by defining 'Philosophical-Policy.' In Part II, I address the question: why Hume? Can his specific approach to the evolution of social norms, their inherent presuppositions and dialectic relations, and the methodology he employs, lend themselves to the analysis and understanding of an integrated theory/practice for international law? Next, I apply Hume's philosophical system to international law in terms of his fundamental presuppositions about individual agents and the circumstances of justice (Part III), the collective evolution of the unconscious conventions of Justice-As-Sovereignty (Part IV) and the conscious role of global political-legal governance in the persistence of social cooperation through *contract-by-convention* (Part V).

In Part III, the need for global society and the reality of conflict create the circumstances in which conventional practice evolves to provide stability of property. In Part IV, social convention focuses on the creation of the process-norm of *Justice-As-Sovereignty* buttressing peace and order as global society gains refinement and complexity. In Part V, I move to the creation of conscious legal rules and governance institutions from the norm of Justice-As-Sovereignty and Humean "contract-by-convention", which further reinforces social convention and provides for its persistence as "process" in the face of both the evolving normative complexity of the international system and the propensity for nations to discount the future and free-ride on the cooperation of others. Throughout, I will explain how the synthesis argument for the elevation of *process*, or means as an end-in-itself, over *principle*, or ends of moral value trumping process, evolves from the inherent logic of Hume's Philosophical-Policy.

* Professor of International Law and Comparative Environmental Policy, Lehigh University and Visiting Fellow, Lauterpacht Center for International Law and Wolfson College, University of Cambridge. I want to thank Philip Allott, James Crawford, Jennifer Davis, and Roger O'Keefe for their continuing help and support of my Hume project, of which this essay is a first component. I also wish to thank two anonymous reviewers from the British Year Book of International Law and especially Vaughan Lowe for his comments and editing suggestions.

Finally, in Part VI, I indicate six preliminary insights that result from the systematic application of Hume's Philosophical-Policy to the origins of the international legal system.

PART I: PHILOSOPHICAL-POLICY

David Hume (1711–1776) is not the first philosopher an international lawyer would identify as important to his or her work. One may know Immanuel Kant's *Perpetual Peace*, or Jeremy Bentham's *Morals and Legislation*, but David Hume's *Treatise of Human Nature* (1739–1740), as well as his *Enquiries Concerning Human Understanding* (1748) and *Principles of Morals* (1751), are not required reading for scholars or practitioners in the field. The point of this essay is to argue that David Hume, or rather the structure and logic of his philosophical argument applied to international public policy and law, provides unique insights and an important alternative line of reasoning for the origin and evolution of the international legal system.

David Hume was a stalwart of the 18th Century Scottish Enlightenment. His aim was to comprehend the origin and refinement of social coordination and he wrote his philosophical system at a time when positivists had not segregated the empirical from the normative and claimed him as exclusively one of their own. In contrast to the *David Hume* created by positivists in the nineteenth century, Hume actually wrote within an intellectual context where dialectic argument transcended eristic, when philosophical method was considered distinct from scientific, and when philosophers were trying to create an integrated reading of theory, practice, moral values and observable behavior.

Given the current state of international legal practice, where legal positivism confronts dilemmas like that between sovereignty and intervention as eristic dichotomies rather than as inherently dialectic interdependencies, or where *scientific* legal method struggles to properly consider the *non-scientific* social and philosophical dimensions of Constitutionalization, venue proliferation, or international common law, it may be time to take Hume's pre-positivist approach off of the bookshelf and use it to re-conceptualize international law. My purpose is to begin this process by bringing an integrated, if unfamiliar, philosophical perspective to bear on a familiar context, to increase our understanding of the genesis of the international legal system not as it is traditionally assumed to be—an anarchy of individual sovereign states jockeying for power—but as Hume's system of thought describes it, as a form of human social coordination where states, as social constructions, utilize social convention, the process-norm of Justice-As-Sovereignty, and various forms of governance, to stabilize property and make the human need for society secure.

Duncan Forbes described the philosophy of David Hume as an applied philosophy, a *"Philosophical-Politics"*.[1] I propose to take Hume's

---

[1] Duncan Forbes, *Hume's Philosophical Politics* (1975).

philosophical system as a point of departure, and apply it to the evolutionary course of human agency and collective action which has produced contemporary international law. My concern is to understand the nexus of philosophy, policy and law, in the application of Philosophical Method[2] to the design of law through public policy, transcending positivism and dependence on empirical or scientific method alone.[3] I begin with the acknowledgement that dialectic relations exist between policy argument, process, and the codification of law, that create and re-create the rule of law over time. This policy design or refinement process is essential to a better understanding of the core conceptual questions in international politics and law, such as the roots of globalization, or the relationship between intervention and sovereignty.[4] I then contend that an application of Hume's system of thought to international law can give unique insight into this evolutionary process. Since this is a much more comprehensive and applied use of Hume than Forbes suggested, I have altered his terminology better to reflect the integration of philosophy and its application to public policy argument and legal practice. Here the term *Philosophical-Policy* builds on Forbes' concept but better fits my objectives.

This term is intended to describe the integrated application of any philosophical system to the context of politics, policy or the law, with the objective of transcending its prevailing intellectual environment so as to see it anew. *Philosophical-Policy* aims at a comprehensive understanding of theory and practice. It begins with the exegesis of a whole philosophical system (as in this case that of David Hume); but this system is deciphered in order to apply it to various contextual public issues and better understand the policy framework within which the concept of law is being refined (in this case, International Law). It is more than the study of a philosophical system for its own sake or the use of philosophical concepts in a practice- or context-driven analysis. It is an application of philosophical paradigms to collective experience in order to integrate questions of what *ought* to be with questions of what *is*.

There are several ways in which one can write or think about a philosopher's ethical, legal, or political thought. For example, one can reconstruct it from the philosopher's published and unpublished writings, or see how it is understood by contemporary thinkers and deployed in their work. One can also focus upon the body of subsequent scholarship that is inspired by the philosopher's work but which may not necessarily conform to the logic of that philosopher's exegesis.

---

[2] As described in R G Collingwood, *An Essay on Philosophical Method* (1933).

[3] Collingwood argues that scientific and social/philosophical phenomena require different methodological considerations, and with this as a point of departure, I seek pre-nineteenth century philosophical systems for their distinct pre-positivist context. Specifically, David Hume's idea of science is distinct for including a dialectic with philosophical method that, for example, considers both the normative and positive dimension of the law as interdependent.

[4] Cynthia Weber, *Simulating Sovereignty: Intervention, The State and Symbolic Exchange* (1995) 126–7 is a post-modern effort to recast the dialectic in terms of "a logic of simulation".

In integrating these approaches, Philosophical-Policy employs a two-stage process of study. In stage one, the work of the philosopher in question is considered as a logical whole, prior to and independent of any application to practice. Because one begins not with selected bits and pieces of a philosopher's exegesis but with his or her ideas considered as a logically and dialectically interconnected whole, one is approaching that philosophy with more integrity than if one extricates selected components of the philosopher's thought to justify an isolated idea within the context of one's otherwise non-philosophical argument. The emphasis in this stage is to apply the terminology and logic of Philosophical Method (deciphering any existing *dialectic* relations and understanding the systems *metaphysics*), considering the philosopher's work independently, primarily in its own terms but also as it has been understood by others, before applying it to any specific context.

The second stage of Philosophical-Policy applies the philosophical paradigm to a context-driven problem. Because the first stage requires the philosophy to set the standards of evaluation as the point of departure for analysis, in the second stage one can employ modern analytic tools, such as game theory or statistical methods, to gain insight into the internal logic and implications of the system under study. Because these tools, as well as the context of application, are interpreted *ex post* through the logical and structural requirements of the philosophical paradigm itself, and not the other way around, they can only be legitimately used if they bring illumination to the inherent logic of the philosopher's exegesis rather than prejudice or corrupt it.

Philosophical-Policy, stage one, gives us an integrated reading of a view of the world and an account of essential presuppositions concerning the nature and logical dialectic of the concepts involved and their potential philosophical refinement. Stage two gives the concepts a strategic and legal context in the assessment of contemporary practice. Thus, the overall use of Philosophical-Policy generates insights that may be more consistent with both the spirit and the letter of the philosopher's original exegesis. For example, what do Hume's philosophical presuppositions, applied to law and policy, suggest for a better understanding of the evolution of the international rule of law?

With the application of Hume's Philosophical-Policy, the parameters of his philosophical argument are not compromised by a primary concern for context, practice, or the tools of modern analysis. It is the application of these modern tools that is subject to examination by Hume's independent and logically intact philosophical argument that, in this way, renders insights not accessible to modern theory alone. While the long-term exposition of a complete philosophical examination of the international rule of law may take the application of more than one Philosophical-Policy, we need to start somewhere, and the contention of this essay is that the Philosophical-Policy of David Hume provides a fruitful perspective from which to consider the *origins* of international law.

PART II: HUME'S "MORAL-SCIENCE" OF INTERNATIONAL LAW

Hume has both a unique argument about the evolution and refinement of human social relations which has not been fully explored in relation to international law, and an apt methodology that combines a practical empiricism with a clearer focus on the origin and persistence of legal norms than classical legal positivism. Hume's Philosophical-Policy is a dialectic that contains a dynamic interrelationship between the empirical and the normative, and between positive and natural law, and which offers, in the end, an integration of justice and order.[5]

Hume's argument about the origin and persistence of law begins with a theory of the individual human being and his predispositions that could be called an enlightened realism, synthesizing the human tendency toward self-interest and the predisposition toward sympathy into a predilection for limited generosity. He builds an integrated theory of collective action upon this idea of the person, in order to posit a constructivist approach to the importance of society in creating and being created by legal and political norms. Hume argues that justice is refined from the material produced by the unconscious evolution of social conventions which lay the groundwork for the subsequent conscious creation of policy.

With the background of social convention, the possibility arises for contract and promise-keeping as well as for governance institutions, policy processes, and the codification of a rule of law. This contract as conscious policy design is dependant on the pre-existence of convention and is therefore best described as "contract-by-convention".[6] We might speak of Hume's political-legal institutions becoming representatives of society and as being the guardians of a pre-existing process of social cooperation. The institutional role of the state and its legal rules then becomes influential in the continued evolution of the society that creates and affects the behavior of individuals and the maintenance of collective action over time.

Hume's philosophical methodology derives from an empiricism meant to create a "science of man"[7] which, he argues, lies at the generic or "natural" base of all that humanity creates, including its moral, social, and legal systems.

There is no question of importance, whose decision is not compriz'd in the science of man; and there is none, which can be decided with any certainty, before we become acquainted with that science.[8]

---

5 Rosemary Foot et al, *Order and Justice in International Relations* (2003).

6 Russell Hardin, *Collective Action* (1982) 155–172.

7 Christian von Wolff, *The Law of Nations Treated According to a Scientific Method* [1749]. For a purely positivist account of human "science" see J H Burns and H L A Hart (eds) *Jeremy Bentham, An Introduction to the Principles of Morals and Legislation* (1970).

8 David Hume, *A Treatise of Human Nature* [1740] reprinted in L A Selby Bigge (ed) (1975) xvi.

Hume's complex project is better called a socio-moral "science". It tries to describe the dialectical evolution of human propensities as they are made manifest in the physical world though the social regularization of choice and behavior. It is not normative in the sense that it prescribes an ideal toward which we should strive in our moral and social lives, or an *a priori* "ought".[9] Rather, Hume tries to apply scientific observation to the "conjunction" of human "impressions" and "ideas" with "experience" and the resultant "expectations" that create first ethical conventions, then social rules, and then legal institutions.[10] Observation allows Hume to create a set of norms, or standards of behavior, from experience even as that experience creates and refines itself in the innate, unconscious, natural, and joint behavior of persons, free from what he would consider the fiction of any conscious, prior, reasoned or independent moral principles. Hume offers a descriptive moral philosophy that adapts Newton's scientific method in an effort to move toward a social-humanities "science" of human collective action on all levels of political and legal organization—local, national and international.

Hume's Newtonianism, then, consists chiefly in his adherence to two principle elements of the experimental method—the search for simple general causes, and the determination to found all doctrines on fact and observation. He aims, through the practice of this method, to develop a moral science with the same levels of accuracy as, but with much greater utility than, the philosophy of nature. This moral science would be founded on the science of human nature, because human nature is 'the capital or center of these sciences'.[11]

Hume's "empiricism" is distinct from traditional arguments within legal positivism that dismiss or devalue the normative element in human relations to distinguish the "valid" law from the "invalid".[12] Hume, like Hart and Austin[13], describes legal validity in terms of its reference to basic social facts and their observation. Hume differs, however, from Austin's focus on "command",[14] because he considers that no single relational element in human interaction creates valid law. Law is the overlapping sum of all relational elements in a given context as these create material expectations worked out through the dialectic of social cooperation over time. The transition from human predispositions to social convention to state institutions creates valid law in a collective context of human philosophical values and their exchange. Law, for Hume, is not initially a social contract, built upon the whim or conscious will or specific acts of particular individuals or groups. For Hume, the social processes and their overlap and refinement as a set of philosophical presuppositions, are what count in creating the empirical-normative reality of human legal

---

[9] Unlike Immanuel Kant's, *Critique of Practical Reason* [1788]; *Theory and Practice* [1792]; *Perpetual Peace* [1795].

[10] Hume, *A Treatise of Human Nature*, above n 8, at bk I.

[11] Stephen Buckle, *Natural Law and the Theory of Property: Grotius to Hume* (1991) 239.

[12] H L A Hart, *The Concept of Law* (1961) 77–96.

[13] John Austin, *The Province of Jurisprudence Determined* [1832] 1–16.   [14] Ibid, 1.

relations. An evolving society secures itself, first unconsciously and then by design, so that social, moral, and then legal relations become stabilized by a system of positive law based on the norms of justice. Justice is variable and a direct product of social convention, not a command or a specific and principled end that must be pursued.

Similarly, Hume's institutional focus, created from this process of actor cooperation over time, produces what H L A Hart might describe as specific "rules of recognition"[15] speaking to the validity of law. But unlike Hart,[16] Hume's rules for the origin and persistence of social cooperation are not separate from the power of *morality* to obligate the person within this collective interchange. For Hume, norms of coordination evolve within the process of cooperating itself and are essential to the "fact" of human society. These *normative facts* are not independent of or prior to humanity but are artifacts of human interaction and the philosophical foundation upon which all social, political, moral, and legal institutions and laws are built. Therefore, Hume espouses an empiricism that embodies a factual *ought* which causes validity and moral obligation to be interdependent *truths* recorded by the "science of man" as each evolving human community creates substantive law for its particular context and its own persistence over time.

Hume's approach is like Hans Kelsen's because each evolving human community is traced back to a *Grundnorm*, that is, a social fact, convention, or metaphysical presupposition that creates the community's particular legal structure, defines its institutions, and gives value and character to its unique solution to the problems of maintaining collective action or coordination over time. Unlike Kelsen, who does not definitively describe, define, or justify the origin or maintenance of a *Grundnorm*,[17] Hume argues that each community creates this basic norm through social convention from within its own cooperative processes as it defines justice, stabilizes property relations, and creates order out of flux.

A major part of Hume's philosophy is dedicated to the generic description of the interactive processes by which basic norms are created and justified within evolving social conventions. It is his absolute presupposition of humanity's inherent social nature, the use of convention to sustain that social nature in varying contexts, and the creation of institutions to assure the persistence of these conventions over time, that provides the common logic for all of his moral and political-legal arguments. This science of evolving norms underlies his theory of human understanding as well as his theory of social ethics.[18] Where Kelsen argues that meaning "... appears as such in the content of legal norms only in essential

---

[15] Hart, above n 12, 92.   [16] Ibid, 206.

[17] Koskenniemi argues that Kelsen's various definitions render an axiomatic premise (akin to an absolute presupposition) that one must believe the *Grudnorm* exists to posit the existence of the legal system. See Martti Koskenniemi, *The Gentle Civilizer of Nations; The Rise and Fall of International Law 1870–1960* (2001) 241.

[18] Hume, *A Treatise of Human Nature,* above n 8, 465–487 and 512–518; David Hume, *Enquiries Concerning Human Understanding and the Principles of Morals* [1777] 37–41, also reprinted in Selby Bigge's 1975 edition.

connection with human behavior, as its condition or consequence",[19] Hume creates a moral science of human social relations on the norma- tive standards generated by this "behavior". He describes the nature of normative social relations as self-reflective and foundationally empirical in that they are created by an interactive process, in which they simultan- eously guide human action and are refined by observation and analysis.

Hume might agree with Kelsen that norms are "facts" of social life, but for Hume these facts are value-laden and set the boundaries within which legal and political relations evolve. For Hume, legal or social prac- tice is distinct from moral norms only by not being prior, universal, and timeless "imperatives"[20] necessary to all human activity, but consequent and artificial "hypothetical judgements"[21] of human interaction. Law is both *generic*, in that all legal systems are created through the evolution of social convention as a philosophical presupposition, and *particular*, in that each moral system provides the particular value-content for what will be its unique system of positive law (what Kant calls "Gerechtigkeit").[22] Kelsen might agree:

...a norm belongs to a certain system... simply from the fact that the validity of the norm can be traced back to the basic norm constituting this system... the highest principle of validity in the system.[23]

For Hume the "morality" of the system is generic and universal in that all societies evolve the conventions of justice and only then develop conscious legal rules and institutions by which to codify these conventions and assure social persistence. Hume's legal theory proffers a specific and uni- versal process without specific or principled content, which can be applied to the social construction of any level of socio-political organization, as well as explain the way each of these levels generates dispositive rulings.

Morality, under this unusual definition, is not connected to a spe- cific principle or end[24] such as freedom, fairness, or equality, but can be based on any or all of these depending on how convention solves the problem of the need for particular collective action in a specific social context. It is the particular social context that gives the universal pro- cess its *natural* content in the unique way in which a people seek order, stability, and security. Hume promotes *process over principle*, not as a prior normative standard or as the key to a utopian dream but because

---

[19] Hans Kelsen, *Introduction to the Problems of Legal Theory* [1934] translated and reprinted in Bonnie Litschewski Paulson and Stanley L Paulson (eds) (2001).
[20] Immanuel Kant, *Metaphysics of Morals: Principles of Justice* [1797] 222–223 (Academy page numbers used in all Kant references).
[21] Kelsen, above n 19, 23.   [22] Ibid and Kant, above n 20, 297.   [23] Ibid, 55.
[24] Hume's argument is that convention as the unconscious evolution of Justice-As-Sovereignty predates the conditions where reason may trigger critical reflection and the generation of substan- tive principle to, for example, correct for the infringement of social convention on an essential good like individual autonomy. Within Hume's philosophical system, reason is discounted and the use of substantive principle (if possible) is relegated to the conscious political process where contract- by-convention can use either a convention-based process-norm such as sovereignty or a substantive principle such as autonomy to create law.

that is how he observes humans empirically organizing themselves and creating their social lives. Hume's philosophy is, in this way, a detailed scientific or descriptive exercise, aiming to understand both the *is* and *ought* of human society as essential processes, as synthetic phenomena. The necessities of context and the uniqueness of circumstance fill in the blanks; but the process of norms evolving out of social interaction and expectation provides the essential normative sub-structure for a peoples' legal practice.

In the same way that human understanding and morals within the family or within any specific nation can be derived from Hume's "science of man," so might our international laws and relations. Hume devotes only a few pages to the international system at the end of his Treatise.[25] He defines global relations as the next step or stratum of human social interaction, observable through the same fundamental "science of man."

When men have found by experience, that 'tis' impossible to subsist without society, and that 'tis impossible to maintain society, while they give free course to their appetites; so urgent an interest quickly restrains their actions, and imposes an obligation to observe those rules, which we call *the laws of justice*... The same *natural* obligation of interest takes place among independent kingdoms, and gives rise to the same *morality*...[26]

So Hume argues that his Newtonian "science of man" discovers the "same natural obligation" as the foundation for all human morality at all levels of social interaction. If this is so, even though he did not make an exhaustive application of his philosophy to the international legal system, we ought to be able to utilize his Philosophical-Policy as a systemic dialectic that transcends the positivist dichotomy between normative and empirical and discerns the parallels between evolving international law and evolving human social cooperation as Hume describes it. This is our purpose: to discover whether a "moral-science" of international law, in a Humean sense, exists and, if it does, how it might help us to understand the origin of the international rule of law.

PART III: THE INDIVIDUAL AGENT AND THE CIRCUMSTANCES OF JUSTICE

According to Thomas Hobbes, nothing exists before the "covenant" but war and disorder. Our natural right to self-preservation[27] and natural law which dictates that reason should seek peace[28] determines the shape of the covenant where law at the collective level defines and determines values at an individual level. Charles Beitz, as well as most other scholars of the

[25] Hume, *A Treatise of Human Nature,* above n 8, 567–9.
[26] Ibid, 568.
[27] Thomas Hobbes, *Leviathan* [1651] 189 reprinted in C B Macpherson (ed) 1968.
[28] Ibid, 190.

international system,[29] have used this Hobbesian description of anarchy, the stark self-interest of states, and the international "state of nature" to describe the assumed background conditions in which international law arose.[30]

By contrast, Hume's state of nature is not a war "of all against all" but an inconvenient social condition of significant instability where individual agents seek community in order to find a process of interaction that yields greater social order and coordination. Hume claims this is our essential predisposition, what we might call the absolute presupposition for the generic essence of social convention.

In all creatures, ... there appears a remarkable desire of company, which associates them together ... This is still more conspicuous in man, as being the creature of the universe, who has the most ardent desire of society, and is fitted for it by the most advantages. We can form no wish, which has not a reference to society. A perfect solitude is, perhaps, the greatest punishment we can suffer.[31]

This need for fellowship comes directly from the psychological makeup of all persons whose "passions" move them to act on "sensations" that invoke "sympathy",[32] which synthesized with a natural self-interest produces a limited "generosity"[33] for others. Unlike Hobbes, Hume's society is not a desperate solution to chaos but a natural extension of one's propensity for community to ever-greater levels of socio-political complexity.

So far from thinking that men have no affection for any thing beyond themselves, I am of opinion, that tho' it be rare to meet with one, who loves any single person better than himself; yet 'tis as rare to meet with one, in whom all the kind affections, taken together do not over-balance all the selfish.[34]

In seeking ever more complex socio-political relations, however, these agents confront the reality of the empirical world and find that while society becomes increasingly important to them it also makes their lives less secure.

Hume argues that there are three "different species of goods, which we are possess'd of; the internal satisfaction of our mind, the external advantages of our body, and the enjoyment of ... possessions".[35] He acknowledges that the first two species are secure because they are internal and safe from the designs of others. However, the third species of goods, our possessions, are not protected from others and are therefore unstable. The scarcity of possessions and their easy transfer between individuals combined with humanity's tendency to want more than the limited nature of

---

[29] Alexander Wendt, *Social Theory of International Relations* (1999); Scott Burchill et al, *Theories of International Relations* (2nd edn, 1996); Gabriele Wight and Brian Porter (eds) *Martin Wight, Four Seminal Thinkers in International Theory: Machiavelli, Grotius, Kant and Mazzini* (2005) and Hedley Bull, *The Anarchical Society* (1977) 4.

[30] See Charles R Beitz, *Political Theory and International Relations* (1979) and Jack Donnelly, *Realism and International Relations* (2000).

[31] Hume, *A Treatise of Human Nature*, above n 8, 363.

[32] Ibid, 103.   [33] Ibid, 488.   [34] Ibid, 487.   [35] Ibid.

unclaimed property will allow, causes a competition for possessions that works against the social fabric which is so inherently important to each and all.[36] In addition, humans are relatively equal in their normative capacity to secure additional property or interfere with its acquisition on the part of others, both as individuals and in concert with one another. This rough equality further adds to the instability of social relations.

Equality and *scarcity*, as social realities, in combination with the *limited generosity* that is a dialectical product of self-interest and sympathy, combine to establish what Hume calls the *"circumstances of justice"*.[37] These circumstances are necessary for justice to be a concern of humans who only seek more coordination than their state of natural equality grants them, when the juxtaposition of all three circumstances works against the coordination necessary to maintain fundamental social stability. The instability of property or possessions, created by the circumstances of justice, is a threat to the social intercourse which everyone needs as a socio-political creature. This threat requires that humanity evolve a social "convention" to set expectations, generate rules, and insure coordination of behavior, countering the positive circumstances with an ethical sense of justice. Since individual tendencies can conflict with the collective interest, Hume contends that we must create artificial virtue to circumvent our human nature and secure our collective ends. In this way "convention" is created unconsciously from overlapping ideas and actions, over time, to stabilize property and correct for the facts of equality, scarcity, and limited generosity, within the process of human interaction.

'Tis certain, that no affection of the human mind has both a sufficient force, and a proper direction to counter-balance the love of gain, and render men fit members of society, by making them abstain from the possessions of others.[38]

From all this it follows, that we have naturally no real motive for observing the laws of equity, but the very equity and merit of that observance; and as no action can be equitable or meritorious, where it cannot arise from some separate motive... we must allow, that the sense of justice and injustice is not deriv'd from nature but arises artificially, tho necessarily from education, and human convention.[39]

Nations or states are formed in this way; and from these predispositions, as humanity begins to look outside their own nations and toward others, the roots of international law are thus created in social convention. The origins of *ius gentium* are sometimes traced to war and chaos in a Hobbesian world, but from a Humean point of view the origins of pre-legal relations lie in the natural propensity of human beings to seek more and higher levels of social order and coordination, thereby creating law to counter the circumstances of justice on an ever-larger scale of complexity.

Applying Hume's Philosophical-Policy we would expect that having experienced *inter-national* instability of possession and scarcity during the

[36] Ibid, 484.   [37] Ibid, 487–8.   [38] Ibid, 492.   [39] Ibid, 483.

Reformation and the wars that followed, humanity, first by instinct and then upon reflection, would have rediscovered the patterns of interaction that had stabilized smaller social constructions, and would have sought better ways of coordinating national and regional behavior to protect property and establish reciprocity at a more general level of social organization. For Hume, humanity approaches all extensions of social feeling in the same way, and would therefore approach inter-national cooperation as it had approached intra-national cooperation: through the evolution of social convention. From a Humean perspective, international society, both in the choice of states as convenient institutional structures and in the coordination of these states toward more *global* stability of property, is the product of the circumstances of justice and the evolution of convention. Thus international rules of behavior (ie law) originate in scarcity, the rough equality of states and a diplomacy of limited generosity, all in reaction to social instability and by the imperative need of society-states to require convention as that artificial virtue necessary for order and the coordination of their actions in international relations.

The circumstances of justice prevail in terms of the limited generosity of the agents (ie states), who seek order and stability for their territory and internal possessions in the face of scarcity, and the roughly equal capacity and ability of others to threaten these possessions by themselves or through the formation of alliances and the disruption of international commerce.[40] To counter these threats the prime directive becomes the coordination of one's collective choices with the collective choices of others so that, in the long-run, one's social need finds strength in unity with others, cooperating in the stability, ownership, and transfer of possessions between sovereign states.

This is the origin of Humean convention within international law. It is set up by habit and practice between states and creates, unconsciously, a set of choices, behaviors, and expectations that establish the limited generosity of "diplomacy" as that set of initially informal rules and norms by which nations coordinate themselves. At first, the "dignity"[41] of each agent and the "approbation"[42] of other such roughly equal "civilized" agents are the only tools of enforcement.[43] But these minimal sanctions soon need to be supplemented, as human propensities for ever more complex social organization place increasing stress on convention as it tries to

---

[40] The capacities or capabilities of the individual, especially as essential prerequisites of their agency independent of their affect on social coordination, is a subject not treated by Hume. For a focused treatment of capabilities see Martha Nussbaum, *Women and Human Development: The Capabilities Approach* (2000) and her *Frontiers of Justice: Disability, Nationality, Species Membership* (2006). For a Kantian argument about capacity, moral agency, and the law see John Martin Gillroy, *Kantian Philosophy, Environmental Policy and The Law* (2000).

[41] Hume, *Enquiries Concerning Human Understanding and the Principles of Morals*, above n 18, 80–6.

[42] Hume, *A Treatise of Human Nature*, above n 8, 501–2.

[43] Statute of the International Court of Justice, June 26, 1945, art. 38(1)(c), 59 Stat. 1055; see also Hume, ibid, 489.

coordinate larger and more heterogeneous groups of actors. The answer is to coordinate on a specific convention that is a norm fit to the persistence of the process of coordination itself. A *process-norm* is required to maintain that social order which is now threatened by increasing complexity. This process-norm defines *justice* for, in this case, the society of states, and more narrowly delimits the collective sense of morality. What evolves is a more formal and fundamental coordination convention to represent the process of securing that social cooperation already achieved.

..., tis impossible for men to consult their interests in so effectual a manner, as by an universal and inflexible observance of the rules of justice, by which alone they can preserve society, and keep themselves from falling into that wretched and savage condition, which is commonly represented as the *state of nature*.[44]

PART IV: THE EVOLUTION OF JUSTICE-AS-SOVEREIGNTY

Hume's main concern is to explain the evolution of moral obligation from empirical behavior and to demonstrate that convention comes about through the interactions of humanity and creates allegiance to those normative standards that work to facilitate collective action over the long term. In effect, coordination is progressing up a scale of forms from the genesis of small-scale family relations to state and inter-state levels of organization. As humans proceed up this ladder of complexity, overlapping legal, political, and moral concepts are refined and redesigned given the context, so that the dialectical dynamics of ideas produce synthesis solutions for changing coordination dilemmas.

Game theory[45] has been used by contemporary scholars to understand the strategic interactions that turn individual choice into collective outcomes. However, there has been disagreement about the precise nature of Hume's approach, and the evolution of convention as collective action has been characterized in terms of both a prisoner's dilemma and a coordination game.[46] Although our purposes here are not served by the details of this debate, we shall see that by applying Hume's Philosophical-Policy as a prior paradigm to the origins of the international legal system, we gain perspective that finds both of these strategic realities coming into play.

In a nutshell, the argument is that Hume seems to be describing the standard game for the creation and distribution of public or collective goods: the prisoner's dilemma. Because the outcome that is best for

---

[44] Hume, ibid, 534.

[45] For a very good overview of the uses of game theory for legal subjects see, Robert H Gertner and Randal C Picker, *Game Theory and the Law* (1994).

[46] Hardin, above n 6, and 90–100, attempts to evolve convention from within a prisoner's dilemma format in order to reconcile convention and the prisoner's dilemma. For the coordination game and convention, see David Lewis, *Convention: A Philosophical Study* (1969), and for the claim that Hume is not using convention at all to solve collective action problems, see Michael Taylor, *Anarchy and Cooperation* (1976).

each individual player is non-optimal for society[47] within a prisoner's dilemma, the participants, playing out their self-interest, and facing the possibility both of exploiting the cooperation of others and being exploited in the act of unilateral cooperation, prefer to be the last into a cooperative equilibrium and the first out. This is unlike the standard evolution of, for example, language conventions which are based upon the solution to coordination games, where multiple equilibria are possible and where individual behavior and unconscious choice find and maintain coordination that is optimal for both the individual and the society, simultaneously. Paradoxically, if Hume is truly talking about convention then he should be describing a coordination game; but he seems to be describing a prisoner's dilemma in the stabilization of property, so the claim is that normative standards are either not from convention or do not describe cooperative behavior toward collective goods. The usual solution to this supposed paradox is to argue[48] that since there is no doubt Hume is using convention, then the prisoner's dilemma must be capable of producing them; but this solution still replaces the coordination game and its strategic context with the non-cooperative environment of the prisoner's dilemma, which creates a distinct type of convention raised on conflictual foundations, needing a different package of assumptions and expectations.[49]

The trouble is that those involved in this debate do not take the refinement of concepts within Hume's philosophical method seriously. Nor have they examined the particular complexity of the international level of organization as a distinct strategic reality, separate from the context of municipal law which characterizes its component parts. If they did, they would see that, as in the definition of dialectical argument, both sides of this debate are simultaneously correct at different levels of systemic organization. What Hume is describing is a global coordination game creating standard convention built upon hundreds of solved municipal prisoner's dilemmas that have generated the more coercive political–legal solutions demanded by that *non-cooperative* strategic reality. But before we explain this complexity, we need to understand the context of the coordination game.

Lewis'[50] coordination game describes a cooperative strategic interaction where the two self-interested players (Row and Column) prefer joint decision-making to the independent variety. The motivation of the players is to conform to the predominant pattern of behavior, which may arise without conscious choice. Here, knowledge that all other players will choose a specific strategy to cooperate is enough incentive for any other player to choose an identical strategy: all a new player needs to know is on what equilibria—around what latent norm—the cooperation is taking place.

---

[47] Gertner and Picker, above n 45.   [48] Lewis, above n 46.
[49] At least on an international level of organization; see Hume's second "insight" in Part VI of this essay.
[50] Lewis, above n 46.

	C1	C2
R1	1,1	0,0
R2	0,0	1,1

Figure 1: A Lewis Coordination Game

Both players do best if they each choose the same solution by choosing the same strategy as illustrated in Figure 1. In this matrix, the points of equilibria are (R1,C1) and (R2,C2). A point of equilibrium is defined as that combination of payoffs where no one agent could have produced more utility for himself by acting differently. As one can see from Figure 1, it is to the advantage of both Row and Column to cooperate on either of the two points of equilibria. With these strategy pairs each player gains a payoff of 1. There is no incentive for either to fail to coordinate, for this would result in a payoff of 0. Consequently, the actors seek to coordinate themselves on one of the two (1,1) solutions.

These two *coordination equilibria* are said to be indifferent to the players and represent stronger than normal points of equilibrium.[51] When one player has chosen a strategy, neither player's situation can be improved by making any other choice or by defecting from cooperation with the other player.[52] In order for a game to be a Lewis coordination game it must have at least two equal points of equilibrium between which the players are, at least initially, indifferent. These multiple indifferent equilibria dictate that the game has no dominant strategy for either player.[53] There is no clear choice between R1 and R2 for Row or C1 and C2 for Column, no matter what the other player chooses. Each player's strategy is dependent on the choice of the other player in order for a preferred outcome to be achieved. The players' choices are therefore interdependent.

The logic of this game is based on the expectations of the players, from which the solution will also emerge. The pure coordination game is best described as a game of dialectical evolution or iteration, where players gradually build expectations of each other's choices based on the repeated trial and error of synthesis solutions. Each player is eventually better able to anticipate the other and achieve coordination. The establishment of a coordination equilibrium defines a manifestation of social sympathy and self-interest (ie limited generosity) that integrates the utility of the individual with that of the collective.

---

[51] These are strict Nash equilibria meaning not only that no other equilibrium makes anyone better off, but that any other equilibrium makes them worse off.

[52] Lewis, above n 46, 8–14.

[53] A dominant strategy is a choice option (to cooperate or defect from cooperation) that is better for one player no matter what choice the other player makes.

Lewis relates his pure coordination game to the evolution of social convention. He defines a convention in the following way:[54]

A regularity R in the behavior of members of a population P when they are agents in a recurrent situation S is a convention if and only if it is true that, and it is common knowledge in P that, in almost any instance of S among members of P,

1. Almost everyone conforms to R;
2. Almost everyone expects almost everyone else to conform to R;
3. Almost everyone has approximately the same preferences regarding all combinations of actions;
4. Almost everyone prefers that one more conform to R, on condition that almost everyone conform to R;
5. Almost everyone would prefer that any one more conform to R, on the condition that almost everyone conform to R.

Convention is a solution to an iterated pure coordination game where a system of concordant mutual expectations is established over time. This solution is inherently self-enforcing.

Once the process gets started, we have a measurable self-perpetuating system of preferences, expectations, and actions capable of persisting indefinitely. As long as uniform conformity is a coordination equilibrium, so that each wants to conform conditionally upon conformity by the others, conforming action produces expectations of conforming action and expectations of conforming action produces conforming action.[55]

Lewis maintains that Hume's concept of convention fits within his model[56] and I agree. However, at the international level of organization that convention is produced by the coordination game, while at the municipal level players apply the "prisoner's dilemma" to reach their optimal solutions and stabilize property. The critical distinction is that at the municipal level the player's motivation to cooperate is different. The tendency of each player is to take advantage of the conventions of property and to free-ride on the cooperation of others in order to protect himself or improve his own lot. Here, it takes more than the knowledge that everyone else is cooperating for any particular actor to look past his limited generosity and cooperate in collective goods provision without legal background institutions as a security net. In order for Hume's individual to cooperate and maintain society, additional incentives, in the form of coercive institutions, must be evolved.[57]

---

[54] Lewis, above n 46, 78.
[55] Ibid, 42.   [56] Ibid, at 3, 6, and 48.
[57] On the municipal level, Hume's convention is said to violate condition (4) of Lewis's definition of convention: see Hardin, above n 6, 170–172. Also, although there is a wealth of literature that claims that iterated prisoner's dilemma can generate coordination on the optimal collective payoff without government, this is true only in very constricted instances and where defection from cooperation is an ever present threat. See Hardin, above n 6, 90–100 and Taylor, above n 46 and Robert Axelrod, *The Evolution of Cooperation* (1984) *passim*. In addition, there is Elinor Ostrom's argument

But in a pure coordination convention, such as driving on a specific side of the road, it is not in one's interest unilaterally to ignore the convention and drive against traffic. One need only know which side of the road, or which set of property rules, the convention pertains to and it becomes in one's interest to coordinate one's behavior with other players. Lewis' coordination game does not require a strong central government, as all any individual needs to know in order to coordinate himself is where the coordination point, the equilibrium, lies.

However, there is a type of free-riding within Hume's coordination game aimed not at the cooperation itself but at the perceived indifference between the solutions. Once coordination is established, it is possible for an individual player to discount both the utility of their cooperation and the comparative justice of any specific equilibrium, which, by the definition of justice as an artificial virtue, can in any specific instance be unjust and not to one's interest, as the international equilibrium that was the European colonial system may not have been as advantageous to the colonies as to the parent states. To maintain coordination, Hume argues that even though any single act of justice may or may not be advantageous to an individual player, each needs to focus on the overall interplay of all acts of justice, which are cumulatively to everyone's advantage.

A single act of justice is frequently contrary to *public interest*; and were it to stand alone, without being follow'd by other acts, may, in itself, be very prejudicial to society. When a man of merit, of a beneficent disposition, restores a great fortune to a miser, or a seditious bigot, he has acted justly and laudably, but the public is a real sufferer. Nor is every single act of justice, consider'd apart, more conducive to private interest, than to public... But however single acts of justice may be contrary, either to public or private interest, 'tis certain, that the whole plan or scheme is highly conducive, or indeed absolutely requisite, both to the support of society, and the well-being of every individual... Property must be stable, and must be fix'd by general rules. Tho' in one instance the public be a sufferer, this momentary ill is amply compensated by the steady prosecution of the rule, and by the peace and order, which it establishes in society. And every individual person must find himself a gainer, on balancing the account; since, without justice, society must immediately dissolve...[58]

in *Governing the Commons: The Evolution of Institutions for Collective Action* (1990) that "common pool resources" can be self-regulated by the principle cooperators involved, but her argument not only runs into the same size and complexity problems as Hardin's and Axelrod's, but requires that eight background conditions or "design principles" be present including defined boundaries, authoritative monitors, and rules for adjudication and change that suggest prerequisite governance institutions external to the cooperative context itself. Hume's argument suggests that these *circumstances* are, indeed, evidence of political society, or governance with stronger sanctions than either mutual approbation or an informal justice norm can provide. See Hume's use of the "meadow" as a type of "common pool resource" quoted ahead in this argument or at Hume, above n 8, 538. In the end, Hobbes' solution to what we now call a prisoner's dilemma, that is, government and coercive sovereignty with enforcement, may be the only long-term remedy for this strategic context. See David P Gauthier, *The Logic of Leviathan: The Moral and Political Theory of Thomas Hobbes* (1979) 88–89.

[58] Hume, *A Treatise of Human Nature*, above n 8, 497.

Discounting and seeking other, seemingly more advantageous, points of coordination or alternative equilibria, must be discouraged, and so a conventional concept of justice may need to be backed not only by the disapprobation of one's peers but by the further sanctions of some form of decentralized governance, to guarantee the origin or persistence of social order once a particular equilibrium has been conventionally settled upon.[59]

One of the most important differences between the rise of convention on an intra-state level and its evolution between actors internationally, is that the international strategic situation has multiple, solved, prisoner's dilemmas at the municipal level to build upon. This makes the rise of convention through coordination at the international level more stable and more authentically conventional, while it simultaneously acknowledges that, when no established legal systems pre-exist, the evolution or first stabilization of property would be more akin to a non-cooperative prisoner's dilemma solved by a stronger and more sanction-oriented type of contract rather than by convention. But at the international level, built upon the stability of many established constituent legal systems each with its own operational and codified conventions, the coordination game that originates the convention of international justice and generates international law provides a more secure atmosphere in which the states seek only one among the multiple, equally optimal, equilibria upon which they can coordinate themselves. This represents justice, or the process-norm that insures the persistence of one agreed point of social cooperation. This one point of coordination is a socially and philosophically refined convention that builds on the experience of its constituent actors with past success in creating and maintaining social order. It obligates present choice while insuring the long-term integrity of the system.

The coordination game stands as a reasonable model for the strategic reality in which the international system was formed and stabilized. Individual states preexisted, having recently solved their municipal prisoner's dilemmas in the wake of the Thirty-Years War. The treaties of Westphalia created a point of normative focus, or moral equilibrium, for the further development and spread of conventions supporting states and their interrelationship as means to the ends of order and coordination of inter-national behavior. This was done by creating the rules of membership in the society of states and by forming a definition of the state, its power, and how much control each had in domestic and international

---

[59] It is important to note that Lewis equilibria are indifferent for the players only until one is chosen. At that point the parties have a stake in this equilibrium and will no longer be indifferent to change but strongly favor where they are. This asymmetry between loss of an established good and cooperation toward change is sometimes called *hysteresis,* see Hardin, above n 6, 82–83. Sweden changed convention from one side of the road to the other to improve efficiency, but it took a great deal of coercion and government assistance; language conventions, as they evolve, require grammar, rules, and great struggle over new vocabulary and styles of speech in order to move with its society into the future.

affairs. In other words, a formal operationalization of pre-existing convention in *Justice-As-Sovereignty*.[60]

Once the *Westphalian Equilibrium* is established as the solution to the coordination game, it represents a set of shared values that then come to dominate a refined definition of joint decision-making made necessary by growing systemic interdependence and the need to stabilize property at the international level. The motivation to conform to the requirements of this equilibrium spreads beyond the original membership and universal standards come to support and spread the predominant conventional pattern. It is not that the Westphalian Equilibrium is particularly valued (*viz*, there were other alternatives), but that it is the original and predominant point of coordination, which makes it valuable and eventually obligatory for all new states.

When solving a coordination problem, the search is for a set of synthesis norms that the actors can coordinate around to form a consensus. As a solution begets order and stabilizes property, this gives it a sense of permanence, and a prerogative over other competing points of equilibrium as it soon becomes obvious that any national society wishing to participate in international affairs has to accept, for example, the Westphalian Equilibrium, to gain entrance to the "club." Like driving on the left or the right-hand side of the road, once the pattern is established no single actor, or group for that matter, has a strong incentive to fight the predominant pattern of convention and drive against traffic. If you want to get anywhere, you join the established flow.

This also creates a newly refined definition of prudence, not as "self-help"[61] but in terms of attention to mutual coordination in acknowledgement of the interdependence of one's sense of order and purpose with others in the developing international system. With the advent of international law one is moving to a definition of self-help that is tantamount to mutual-aid and evolving reciprocity. An up-and-coming state succeeds only by recognizing that it can achieve more for itself by cooperating with the established conventions that stabilize international property, rather than by fighting the pattern or trying to invent new standards.

Once the coordination convention is established, we could paraphrase Lewis' requirements for a definition of convention in the following way:

A regularity (R = Westphalian Equilibrium) in the behavior of states in international relations (P) when they are agents in a recurrent situation S is a convention if and only if it is true that, and it is common knowledge in P that, in almost any instance of S among members of P,

---

[60] These are also the core criteria for a definition of legitimate constitutional authority, see Daniel Philpott, *Revolutions in Sovereignty* (2001) 15–16. For an examination of the treaties of Westphalia as a paradigm shift see, Stephane Beaulac, "The Westphalian Legal Orthodoxy—Myth or Reality?" (2000) 2 *Journal of the History of International Law* 148.

[61] Kenneth N Waltz, *Theory of International Politics* (1979) 107 *passim*.

1. Almost every state conforms to the Westphalian Equilibrium;
2. Almost every state expects almost every other state to conform to the Westphalian Equilibrium;
3. Almost every state has approximately the same preferences regarding all combinations of actions that allow the Westphalian Equilibrium to persist;
4. Almost every state prefers that one more state conform to the Westphalian Equilibrium, on condition that almost every state conforms to the Westphalian Equilibrium;
5. Almost every state would prefer that any one more state conform to an alternative[62] to the Westphalian Equilibrium on the condition that almost every state conforms to the same alternative to the Westphalian Equilibrium.

It is not only the strategic setting that is important here, however, as the collective action problem, applying Hume's Philosophical-Policy, could not establish the Westphalian Equilibrium as a long-term and stable coordination convention unless it tied it to the concept of justice.

In the end, the search for convention, in Hume's Philosophical-Policy, is the search for a definition of justice and here too *justice* has a unique meaning for the creation of international law. For Hume, there is no natural law in terms of *a priori* or independent principles of justice. Justice, for Hume, is the virtue of respecting other's property;[63] it is the result of a social *process* through which humans unconsciously coordinate themselves, and set mutual expectations, creating the stability they seek in the society they crave. In this innate passion,[64] already Hume's absolute presupposition, one finds the point of origin for a new and distinct concept of the *laws of nature*, one based on the socialization of individuals and the natural evolution of patterns of behavior and expectation that create social convention.

In a little time, custom and habit operating on the tender minds of children, makes them sensible of the advantages which they may reap from society, as well as fashions them by degrees for it, rubbing off those rough corners and untoward affections, which prevent their coalition.[65]

To extend humanity's natural but limited generosity to include an ever larger group of agents on a global scale requires the establishment of a more formal sense of justice in a specific social convention. Our dialectical refinement of the concept of convention is not a departure from the

---

[62] Is it reasonable to analyze specific "revolutions in sovereignty" (Philpott, above n 60), as new or reinforcing alternative coordination equilibria?

[63] This is Hume's definition of justice. "The origin of justice explains that of property." Hume, *Enquiries Concerning Human Understanding and the Principles of Morals,* above n 18, 491. "In fact, Hume takes the very concepts (or 'ideas') of 'property'... to emerge only in the establishment of the rules of justice.": James Baillie, *Hume on Morality* (2000) 171.

[64] The "passions" are not the usual basis for the Laws of Nature, as these were traditionally considered to come from either revelation through god, see *St Thomas Aquinas, Treatise on Law,* or reason through human will, see Hobbes, above n 27 or Kant, above n 20.

[65] Hume, *A Treatise of Human Nature,* above n 8, 486.

agent's limited generosity but, rather, a reflection of its long-term security within a greater and growing social order.

Instead of departing from our own interests, or from that of our nearest friends, by abstaining from the possessions of others, we cannot better consult both these interests than by such a convention; because it is by that means we maintain society, which is so necessary to their well-being and subsistence, as well as to our own.[66]

Social convention is at first derived from unconscious action that creates mutual expectations, and then from habitual acts that produce more fixed and conscious expectations that become enforceable through rules as *proper* and *expected* behavior. In the same way that the origin of diplomacy was not in explicit contracts or covenants in Hobbes' conception of the term, but lay rather in tacit agreements that were voluntary and enforced through a system of mutual restraint and approbation, the rules of the international system, from a Humean point of view, have their beginnings in the social context, or trial and error, of interaction between states as social constructions that create first expectations and then patterns of acceptable behavior that are anointed as the established procedures of "civilized nations".[67] This conventional standard then sets the expectations upon which treaties, and other, more conscious, international legal acts become possible.

These natural or unconscious patterns of behavior and reciprocity eventually create a recognizable system of practice on the level of international society. A core convention of justice arises with its success in correcting for the rough equality, limited generosity and scarcity of property that Hume argues creates the need for justice in the first place. Justice-as-convention gathers customary behavior at a point of coordination that advances and more permanently corrects for these "circumstances of justice". It is the "artificial virtue" of justice as a manifestation of the coordination equilibrium and a shorthand for it, that represents legal practice for a particular social order, allowing it to persist, and granting it normative weight.

There is no passion, therefore, capable of controlling the interested affections but the very affection itself, by an alteration of its direction...[68]

Globally, for Hume, justice is not any specific principle, virtue, or value but the normative product of a refinement or evolutionary process. It is a *conventional process-norm*, an unconscious normative standard, evolved from the dialectic between action and expectation and with which agents can create and maintain coordination for their mutual benefit, that is, for the stability of the property of each and all and to execute collective action free of disruption.

[66] Ibid, 489.
[67] Statute of the International Court of Justice above n 43. See also Gerrit Gong, *The Standard of "Civilization" in International Society* (1984).
[68] Hume, *A Treatise of Human Nature,* above n 8, 492.

This convention is not of the nature of a promise: For even promises themselves, . . . arise from human convention. It is only a general sense of common
interest; which sense all the members of the society express to one another and
which induces them to regulate their conduct by certain rules. I observe, that
it will be for my interest to leave another in possession of his goods, provided
he will act in the same manner with regard to me. He is sensible of a like interest in the regulation of his conduct. When this common sense of interest is
mutually express'd, and is known to both, it produces a suitable resolution and
behavior. And this may properly enough be call'd a convention or agreement
betwixt us tho' without the interposition of a promise . . . Two men who pull the
oars of a boat, do it by an agreement or convention, tho' they have never given
promises to each other. Nor is the rule concerning the stability of possession the
less deriv'd from human convention, that it arises gradually, and acquires force
by slow progression, and by our repeated experience of the inconveniences of
transgressing it. On the contrary, this experience assures us still more, that the
sense of interest has become common to all our fellows and gives us confidence
of the future regularity of their confidence . . . [69]

International society, from a Humean standpoint, evolves generic norms
of obligation, promise, treaty, and transference by consent, as well as
the distinction between a law of peace and a law of war,[70] only with the
establishment of the conventions of justice. These norms are particular
to context and the circumstances of justice, which are, for Hume, both
universal and local. The circumstances of justice are universal in that the
same three conditions (ie equality, limited generosity, and scarcity) always
create the circumstances of justice but local in that the substance of, or
material circumstances of, these conditions will be contextual and create
distinct substantive conventions because of this. Given the circumstances
of our international legal system, order grows out of the Westphalian
Equilibrium and the evolution of the process-norm of *sovereignty* as that
core normative convention anchors custom and experience in practice,
and then law. The norm of sovereignty is a process-norm because it holds
no substantive definition of the right or the good but evolved in order to
maintain the process of coordination, which for Hume is the end-in-itself.
Sovereignty, or the equality and separateness of states, is that definition
of justice which best compensates for the international circumstances
of justice both universally and locally. Sovereignty is the process-based
and context-driven foundational or 'Grundnorm' of our international
system and it simplifies the terms of coordination by segregating the
essential element of cooperation and locating itself as the imperative
within the system for the later conscious codification of social convention
in law. For our international society, *Justice-As-Sovereignty* becomes the

---

[69] Ibid, 490.

[70] One could argue here that Humean convention, on the international level, would focus on the
law of war first, as this was the most prominent point that lacked coordination, making the law of
war distinct and prior to the law of peace. In any case, convention seeks to coordinate these two
distinct areas of collective action.

basis for stability, coordination, and coexistence through reciprocity,[71] representing the Westphalian Equilibrium while it reinforces approbation toward diplomacy as another layer of sanction redirecting those who might free-ride on the cooperation of others.[72]

But why sovereignty? Because the imperative of a Humean convention is to find consensus in how to stabilize property, which, in this context, means giving each actor in the international system sovereignty over its own affairs. A nation's resources, whatever they wish to do with them, can best be stabilized through Justice-As-Sovereignty. In the same way that convention on a national level solidifies the interdependence of persons within social community through rules relating to property that separate each person's possessions and make each the master of that which belongs to him as long as he restrains himself from interference with the possessions of others, Justice-As-Sovereignty, within the international system, creates the same order on a global level. It does this by separating the possessions of every nation and granting each dominion over its own territory and wealth, as long as it restrains itself from interference in the domestic affairs[73] of other "civilized" nations,[74] that is, other agents who share the circumstances of justice, and acknowledge an obligation to the established Westphalian equilibrium, as a solution to the coordination game based upon this convention of justice.

The artificial virtue of Justice-As-Sovereignty, however, does not exist in a static environment. States are presented with real challenges when applying justice within a dynamic, open[75] and ever-changing international system. As we have already seen, the nature of justice as an artificial virtue is such that while the *sovereign* coordination equilibrium is generally in every nation's interest, it may act against a single actor's interest in any specific instance.[76] In the process of defining the rules of Justice-As-Sovereignty, those who see their self-interest infringed in specific cases will have an ever-greater motivation to discount the *status quo* convention of justice and, subsequently, work against the particular coordination equilibrium

---

[71] Hume, *Enquiries Concerning Human Understanding and the Principles of Morals,* above n 18, 310. Hume, when he is describing the evolution of convention, is not concerned with how particular objects are assigned to particular people, but with the allocation and distribution of property (meaning all material rights and goods) by convention, to establish general coordination.

[72] Hardin, above n 6 and Gillroy, above n 40 at 200–229 for a comparison of the collective action problems of Hobbes, Hume, and Kant.

[73] Charter of the United Nations, June 26, 1945, art. 2(7), 59 Stat. 1031.

[74] This stricture does not hold for "uncivilized" nations, as the circumstances of justice which created the value set at the core of convention, and "society" itself, are not shared with them. Hume places Native Americans in this category in terms of their relationship to "civilized Europeans". Specifically, he argues "we...should not, properly speaking, lie under any restraint of justice with regard to them, nor could they possess any right to property...[as] our intercourse with them could not be called society..." Hume, *Enquiries Concerning Human Understanding and the Principles of Morals,* above n 18, 190–191. For a more contemporary counter-argument to this claim see Edward Keene, *Beyond the Anarchical Society: Grotius, Colonialism and Order in Word Politics* (2002).

[75] See James Crawford, *International Law As An Open System* (2002) 17–38.

[76] Hume, *A Treatise of Human Nature,* 497, as quoted above n 58.

that disadvantages them, and for an alternative. The problem of discontent is increased with the growing complexity of global society as more and more nations evolve as states with aspirations to be granted Justice-As-Sovereignty and become part of the established international system. With many heterogeneous potential cooperators, the individual nation also loses touch with the direct effect of its behavior on collective action. In a larger and more complex international society, it is not as evident that individual actions against sovereignty undermine global society, or coordination as a whole, even if such agency has a higher probability of actually disrupting coordination at the Westphalian Equilibrium.[77] Hume's contention that international society can and does establish itself without government is based upon the premise that a society of nations remains small, homogeneous, and the purview of but a few "civilized" nations with shared values and circumstances, who are like one-another and have common expectations formed by Justice-As-Sovereignty and easily controlled by their own mutual sense of moral approbation and justice.

Although a "free-ride", in this context, does not mean the solution to the coordination game is threatened by these complexities, a specific equilibrium and its particular definition of convention may be threatened by alternative equilibria that arise and are argued to be more efficient or effective in maintaining coordination as times change. As global society grows in complexity the moral approbation or disapprobation of civilized nations may no longer be enough to maintain a particular coordination equilibrium. At this point the acknowledgement and further codification of convention becomes necessary to support the emergent norms. Consequently, the Westphalian Equilibrium, as well as its emergent process-norm of Justice-As-Sovereignty need to be institutionalized in a governance structure that further protects them against the growing complexity that empowers the disruptive quality of the circumstances of justice. To secure the normative prerogative of the *status quo* convention, defining as it does, the point of coordination for the international system, conscious rule-generation becomes necessary toward the formation of an international society under law. Viewing the international system as a coordination game, there is always more than one equilibria that may act as an alternative to the *status quo* stabilization of property. It is against the challenge from alternative norms, like efficient trade or collective defense, that Justice-As-Sovereignty and the Westphalian Equilibrium must be empowered. Moral, legal, and political value must be tightly ascribed to the support of that particular global public interest as seen through the eyes of *sovereign* states.

But tho' it be possible for men to maintain a small uncultivated society without government, 'tis impossible they shou'd maintain a society of any kind without

---

[77] For a Humean argument that "...*particular breaches* of the laws of nations do much more harm than particular breaches of the rules of private justice..." see Jonathan Harrison, *Hume's Theory of Justice* (1981) 231.

justice and the observance [of the]...fundamental laws concerning the stability of possessions...These are, therefore, antecedent to government, and are...to impose an obligation before the duty to civil magistrates has once been thought of...Government upon its first establishment,...derive(s) its obligation from those laws of nature...[78]

In this way the advent of blackletter international law comes with a pre-defined normative base of convention: *Justice-As-Sovereignty*. Hume contends that we have a natural obligation to observe this conventional standard, and he notes its power to coordinate behavior and set expectations even before the advent of codified rules, law, or government. This natural obligation to convention, Hume's sense of *natural law*, provides international society, through the circumstances of justice and the limited generosity of states, with a moral obligation to joint decision-making and to the pre-existing coordination equilibrium based upon sympathy, which contributes to the increased security and longevity of collective social action.

Thus self-interest is the original motive to the establishment of justice: but a sympathy with public interest is the source of the moral approbation which attends that virtue.[79]

But when both approbation and the conventions of justice are insufficient to correct the tendency of human nature to work against settled social patterns of behavior, Hume supports a further refinement of the idea of convention with a stronger force for the redefinition of human nature: law and governance institutions.

PART V: LEGAL INSTITUTIONS, GOVERNANCE AND THE CODIFICATION OF JUSTICE-AS-SOVEREIGNTY

Hume's Philosophical-Policy considers the origins of the rule of law, first, in terms of the evolution of unconscious convention. However, with the advent of justice and the process-norm of sovereignty, the legal system reacted to growing complexity by narrowing practice to a single conventional idea. Now, as social complexity continues to create demands on convention, Philosophical-Policy requires a move to the first conscious stage of policy-making. Here political negotiation and legal contract, based upon convention, creates voluntary and codified law enshrining the pre-existing practices, expectations, and traditions of the conventionally-based international system within a positive law created around the process-norm of Justice-As-Sovereignty. The sovereignty standard thus becomes institutionalized, and provides an assurance that the rules of ethical life will be honored as the complexity of global society grows in the continued persistence of that process equilibria by which social convention was created and is being maintained.

[78] Ibid, 541.   [79] Ibid, 499–500.

The institutionalization of Justice-As-Sovereignty also encourages the creation of nation-states, as we soon realize that convention demands a unit of organization that can operationalize sovereign dominion over territory, and stabilize possession globally, so that all can share equally in the advantages of social construction granted by the conventional solution to the inter-state coordination game. Here, the origin of the state follows municipal social convention, just as the origin of international structure to codify Justice-As-Sovereignty follows the first practices of those states in relation to one-another. This is in contrast to Hobbes' sovereign, who as the result of individual covenants, remains the sole source of justice within *Leviathan*, and is the conscious product of a two-stage contract that creates the legal basis for his legitimacy before sovereignty is itself created.[80] Unlike Hobbes, who saw the origin of society, justice, and law in the authorization of sovereignty, Hume describes each as a separate developmental stage in the philosophical refinement of convention on a scale of evolving forms where Justice-As-Sovereignty is antecedent to institutional law and politics but has itself evolved from the moral approbation of custom that creates Justice-As-Sovereignty as a process-norm prior to the policy contract that forms political and legal structures.

Hume's contract is logically based upon pre-existing convention,[81] and is therefore a *contract-by-convention*, internal to a sociological process based on an established idea of Justice-As-Sovereignty that makes convention manifest and persistent in social relations. Here law is an extension of Justice-As-Sovereignty which adds another layer of sanctions to those conventions already established to maintain stability within the international system. Convention, for Hume, is not an independent principle giving imperative force to the achievement of an end that can be either materially produced (ie a national park) or is non-producible (ie an autonomous moral agent),[82] but a process-norm where the means is an end-in-itself, not remaining static but evolving through different stages of dialectical complexity. This is unlike Hobbes' concept of social covenant, which is a one-shot agreement based upon specific *prior* principles from laws of nature common to humanity as a whole.[83]

Before international law and institutions are established, a combination of enlightened self-interest (limited generosity), moral approbation, and social utility foster social convention and define Justice-As-Sovereignty. But, in the same way that nested municipal systems give added incentive to the creation and solution of the international coordination game, the application of Hume's Philosophical-Policy allows one to argue that they

---

[80] Hobbes, above n 27, 227–229.

[81] Hume, *A Treatise of Human Nature*, above n 8, 490. Also Hardin, above n 6, at 155–172.

[82] For the differences between "producible" ends of instrumental value and "non-producible" ends as things-in-themselves see Kant, *Critique of Practical Reason* above n 9 and Alan Donagan, *The Theory of Morality* (1977) 224–232.

[83] Hobbes, above n 27, at 228.

also tend to give states a less pressing allegiance to the resulting equilibrium than to their municipal obligations. Specifically, Hume claims that "...tho' the morality of princes has the same extent, yet it has not the same force as that of private persons, and may lawfully be transgress'd from a more trivial motive".[84]

As humanity's social framework becomes more complex, the human tendency to discount the long-term public interest and prefer the immediate satisfaction of desires, which works against established convention, gains power, requiring more conscious institutional regulation for the equilibrium to persist. Especially on an inter-state level of organization, "...the natural obligation to justice, among different states, is not so strong as among individuals, the moral obligation, which arises from it, must partake of its weakness".[85] Taking the less secure status of international moral obligation into consideration, the evolution or refinement of sanctions must keep pace with the growing size and heterogeneity of international society which make *discounting* Justice-As-Sovereignty more probable without tighter global institutionalization and codification.

Now as every thing, that is contiguous to us, either in space or time, strikes upon us with such an idea, it has a proportional effect on the will and passions, and commonly operates with more force than any object, that lies in a more distant and obscure light... This is the reason why men so often act in contradiction to their known interests; and in particular why they prefer the trivial advantage, that is, present, to the maintenance of order in society, which so much depends on the observance of justice.[86]

Unlike the realists,[87] Hume describes selfishness and self-interest as dysfunctional tendencies which overtake our wider and more foundational sympathy and work against social stability. Contract-by-convention is necessary because Justice-As-Sovereignty is limited by the extent to which it can compensate for this "limited generosity" on the part of individual agents. Humanity needs society at multiple levels of organization and society requires the provision of collective goods for its persistence. The origin of international legal institutions through contract-by-convention builds on approbation and Justice-As-Sovereignty to maintain this provision over time, space, and the increasing complexity of social organization.

Two neighbors may agree to drain a meadow, which they possess in common; because 'tis easy for them to know each others mind; and each must perceive, that the immediate consequences of his failing in his part, is the abandoning the whole project. But 'tis very difficult, and indeed impossible, that a thousand persons sho'd agree in any such action; it being difficult for them to concert so complicated a design, and still more difficult for them to execute it; while each seeks

---

[84] Hume, *A Treatise of Human Nature,* above n 8, 568.
[85] Ibid, 569.   [86] Ibid, 535.
[87] For an overview of the positivist/realist approach see Donnelly, above n 30, at 6–42 and Anthony Clark Arend, *Legal Rules and International Society* (1999) 111–164.

a pretext to free himself of the trouble and expense, and wou'd lay the whole burden on others. Political society easily remedies both these inconveniences.[88]

For the global "meadow," the task of coordinating a diversity of nations toward a recognition of, and adherence to, the universal public interest becomes harder as size encourages any one state to abdicate its global social responsibility and "free-ride" on the participation of the others.[89] This definition of free-rider, however, is not the realist definition where, with size and heterogeneity, independent self-help actors are encouraged to abandon the socially-optimal equilibrium in order to indulge their national self-interest and exploit others.[90] Here we have a coordination game, where a system of international cooperation and a specific, Westphalian, equilibrium is agreed as in the interest of all but where this might change or evolve between indifferent equilibria without destroying international coordination itself. The free-riding here is in the form of seeking a new, more socially-optimal, coordination equilibrium which is indifferent to the players in terms of payoffs (ie stability and order) but which might achieve a *more just* and preferred process with other than a sovereignty norm. Defection is an act of state intended to substitute process-norms that are seen as more beneficial to the community, given the flux of evolving international social history.

In a society of two, the fact that limited generosity may tend to be influenced more by one's self-interest than by sympathy does not detract from the general understanding of the coordination equilibria which represent the common interest and what is needed to secure them. The limited population and common values make general cooperation both expected and sanctioned. In a grand alliance, for example, a small set of like-minded states protecting the sovereignty of all would not defect

---

[88] Hume, *A Treatise of Human Nature,* above n 8, 538.

[89] It may very well be that once an equilibrium is chosen in a global coordination game the nested quality of the game expands so that the interaction between the municipal prisoner's dilemma and the global coordination game create periodic strategic realities akin to a stag hunt model, where the status-quo equilibrium is the *hare* and the new alternative the *stag*. In the stag-hunt the two possible equilibria are separated by one being collective (ie stag) and the other achievable by the individual (ie hare) but where the former outcome is better for all involved. Under these conditions the game becomes reliant on the assurance of all the players to one-another that they will cooperate in hunting the stag. Overall, the dynamic here may be converging toward varieties of assurance games, but my argument on this and the analysis will have to await further work and a distinct venue. For my view of dynamic nested games see Gillroy, above n 40, 218–225; for an argument that Hume is describing multiple games of coordination and assurance see, William C Charron, "Convention, Games of Strategy, and Hume's Philosophy of Law and Government" (1980) 17 *American Philosophical Quarterly* 327, and for the stag hunt as a particular strategic model see Brian Skyrms, *The Stag Hunt and the Evolution of Social Structure* (2004).

[90] Although this assumption can be traced back to the beginnings of realism, see E H Carr, , *The Twenty Years' Crisis* (1939), it is also the most basic assumption in contemporary international theory, see Hans Morgenthau, *Politics Among Nations* (1948) and Waltz, above n 61. The assumptions of the realist position within international relations have also been very influential on positivists within the field of international law, see Koskenniemi, above n 17, 413–509, and Bull, above n 29. They also continue to provide a baseline of theory for the study of international legal practice, see Sean D Murphy, *Principles of International law* (2006) 12–16. For a specific argument that Hume is doing something beyond self-help see Charron, ibid, 329.

casually from the established definition of the common good that brought them together.

However, in a more populous or complex context, the natural tendency toward limiting one's field of concern and taking international obligations less seriously is intensified by the fact that global-social ends become more removed from the perception of the individual nation-state and further discounted. From the point of view of each agent, the immediate gain from satisfying desire in a new equilibrium that seems more advantageous to those disadvantaged in the present, is all the more tempting as the present equilibrium seems less exclusive.

In addition, discounting is exacerbated by the feeling that unanimous participation in any one coordination equilibrium is no longer necessary to produce global collective goods. With so many sovereign states and only a sub-set of them necessary to produce the collective good, a state might think: "why need we be one of the contributors to this particular definition of justice, when an alternative may create more order at less cost for us?" With a population of two, each state must contribute to the alliance or no good will be provided; but for two hundred states, free-riding on the participation of others is possible, and not directly detrimental to any specific global good. Each state will have a stronger inclination to consider that a transgression on its part will entail no immediate collective repercussions. Under these conditions, global society, the Westphalian Equilibrium, and the established convention of Justice-As-Sovereignty are in danger of erosion, to be replaced by another process-norm, point of equilibrium, and definition of justice. That is, unless the established equilibrium is empowered and understood anew.

Considering that society is still of paramount importance to humanity, and that the conventional equilibrium has proven effective in maintaining it, a further adjustment or philosophical refinement of the *status quo* idea of social convention must be made, in order to reinforce Justice-As-Sovereignty and the integrity of global collective action. The conscious creation of political-legal rules from the process-norm of Justice-As-Sovereignty, as well as the international governance institutions to operationalize and enforce them, reaffirm international utility in the collective interest of this particular solution to the global coordination game.

It is evident that, if government were totally useless, it never could have place, and that the sole foundation of the duty of allegiance is the advantage which it produces to society by preserving peace and order among mankind.[91]

When men have once perceiv'd the necessity of government to maintain peace, and execute justice, they wou'd naturally assemble together, wou'd chuse magistrates, determine their power, and promise them obedience.[92]

As justice moves limited generosity to compensate for the tendencies of self-interest that undermine society, legal institutions and actors add needed sanctions and organization to the convention of Justice-As-Sovereignty

---

[91] Hume, *A Treatise of Human Nature*, above n 8, 205.   [92] Ibid, 541.

already established. With the application of Hume's Philosophical-Policy, what previously had only the process-norm of Justice-As-Sovereignty, backed by approbation to insure performance, now has definitive legal sanction (ie rules and rights) to back it up, making the growth and progressive codification of international law a necessary component of the evolving normative complexity of the international legal system. It is possible, through "[p]olitical society",[93] for ever-greater and more diverse international societies to coordinate themselves using Justice-As-Sovereignty to create an ever-wider civilized world.

Tho' there was no such thing as a promise in the world, government wou'd still be necessary in all large and civiliz'd societies; and if promises had only their own proper obligation, without the separate sanction of government, they wou'd have but little efficacy in such societies.[94]

Originally, a social convention dealing with Justice-As-Sovereignty commands a moral obligation from the enlightened self-interest of states. However, the pre-institutional obligation to fulfill diplomatic expectations is predominantly dependent on the value that each state places on its reputation (ie moral character) as a state upholding Justice-As-Sovereignty.

There is nothing, which touches us more nearly than our reputation, and nothing on which our reputation more depends than our conduct, with relation to the property of others.[95]

However, reputation alone will not ensure that every nation develops a proper *sense of justice*,[96] especially if the community of nations becomes more heterogeneously cultural. Hume's introduction of the "Knave" at the end of the second *Enquiry* acknowledges these limitations.

Hume considers "a sensible knave [who] in particular incidents, may think that an act of iniquity or infidelity will make a considerable addition to his fortune, without causing any considerable breach in the social union...." (*viz* any considerable disruption of the overall stability of the coordination equilibrium). This defection from a particular definition of social cooperation is condemned by moral sensibilities, convention, and justice, showing that such actors "themselves are, in the end, the greatest dupes, and have sacrificed the invaluable enjoyment of a character, with themselves at least, for the acquisition of worthless toys and gewgaws" .[97] International actors commonly known as "rogue states" that "free-ride" on established coordination conventions may be described by Hume's Philosophical-Policy as having "lost a considerable motive to virtue"[98] that leaves them beyond social, or might we say, international, protection.

In order to ensure that global society survives despite those who continue to discount the collective interest or search for alternative

---

[93] Ibid, 538.   [94] Ibid, 546.   [95] Ibid, 501.   [96] Ibid, 483.
[97] Hume, *Enquiries Concerning Human Understanding and the Principles of Morals*, above n 18, 282–3.
[98] Ibid, 283.

process-norms, Hume adds the "artifice of politicians" to justice and the desire for reputation as supports for coordination conventions.[99] Specifically, global politics and international legal rules and institutions employ people whose limited generosity is said to be informed by the global public interest rather than their own narrower interests. These individuals are charged with imposing sanctions upon Knave-like anti-social behavior, publicly rewarding participation in and punishing defection from the conventional coordination equilibria. Within Hume's Philosophical-Policy, international lawyers and policy-makers can be said to have a vested interest in global society and are better able to recognize, define, and keep tabs on the health of nations.[100]

Education, and the artifice of politicians, concur in bestowing a farther morality on loyalty, and branding all rebellion with a greater degree of guilt and infamy. Nor is it a wonder, that politicians shou'd be very industrious in inculcating such notions, where their interest is so particularly concern'd.[101]

With lawyers and policy-makers running supra-national governance institutions built upon Justice-As-Sovereignty, the cumulative effect of convention on the cooperation of individual nations is at its most powerful. One builds upon the other, with more complex sanctions to regulate more complex social relations. The social stability of the global society remains both the fundamental presupposition and the moral imperative for the process-norm of Justice-As-Sovereignty.[102]

PART VI: SIX HUMEAN INSIGHTS CONCERNING THE ORIGINS OF THE INTERNATIONAL LEGAL SYSTEM

• *Hume's Philosophical-Policy gives us a new definition of the state as a social construction, bounded by the circumstances of justice and utilizing its limited generosity to stabilize property on an international level.*

The first conclusion one draws from an application of Hume's Philosophical-Policy to the international legal system is that the fundamental imperative of international action is not state interest or personal interests but the search for social cohesion. The fundamental metaphysical presupposition of the Humean agent, whether individual or state, is to seek and coordinate an ever wider society of actors who are assumed to be practically incomplete without one another. It is human society and the state as a social construction, out of which the Westphalian Equilibrium and the process of evolving social convention emerges, that give us the process-norm of Justice-As-Sovereignty and then a positive international law created from it. Within this basically sociological account of the origin of world order, as a coordination game containing actors with limited generosity, the basic motivational assumption is one based not upon

---

[99] Hume, *A Treatise of Human Nature*, above n 8, 500.
[100] Ibid, 538–9.   [101] Ibid, 546.   [102] Ibid, 543.

narrow self-interest but rather upon the dialectical product of a more balanced or limited generosity. States are assumed to be reacting to the circumstances of justice by overcoming scarcity and limited sympathy to reinforce the stability of the collective whole through creation and definition of the legal rules of *de jure* possession.

Here, the state is not an individual,[103] but a social construction. Nor is the state a strictly empirical phenomenon, but rather a social entity created by the conventions of human interaction and for the purposes, not of the expression and maximization of power, but of the stabilization of property within and between states. Justice-As-Sovereignty arises not from the will of a person or government, nor to hold men "in awe,"[104] but from the joint expression of natural, initially unconscious, behavior and the expectations of all states regarding the settlement of their agency on one of a number of possible coordination equilibria. This coordination equilibrium is protected by a refined sense of sympathy which is a philosophical concept which has been adapted, first, to local interaction in family or tribe, then to a wider social context, and finally to the creation of governance institutions to make sympathy and its normative sentiments continually real in an ever more complex world. This process of refinement through convention makes increasing levels of sanctions necessary to maintain the integrity of the process as its constituent members grow and become more diverse. Here, the fundamental presupposition of an inherent sociability or sympathy with the interest of the whole in the stabilization of property makes the imperative for each cooperator not isolation and "self-help"[105] but prudential aid and participation in creating the conditions in which an international society can be established that caters to limited generosity and the collective interest simultaneously, as is the function of a coordination equilibria.

Hume's Philosophical-Policy takes, as its core axiom, the idea of human creatures struggling between their individual need and their sympathy for others, between their interest in the stability and security of their own lives and their consciousness of the role others play in making this security a reality. Hume understands that the *collective* is more than an aggregate of individuals; it is a distinct level of analysis, one that is the product of convention and that builds from the individual to the global level through various strategic situations adapting solutions to fit the empirical contexts it finds. Given the pre-existence of municipal government, international law develops with the assumption that the convention operating at the wider international level is seeking a coordination equilibrium that will allow the various distinct municipal regimes, with their different solutions to their particular collective action problems, to find consensus and cooperate on an international level. This encourages

---

[103] The most basic realist/positivist assumption. See above n 90 and Hobbes, above n 27.
[104] Hobbes, ibid, 185.
[105] Waltz, above n 61.

the rise of conventional process-norms in general and the creation of the convention of Justice-As-Sovereignty in particular. As process-norms are focused on procedure, and are neutral as to specific cultural values, Justice-As-Sovereignty protects all municipal coordination equilibria without discrimination by simultaneously providing at the international level its own coordination equilibrium which is generally agreeable to, and in the interest of, all participants.

- *Hume's Philosophical-Policy gives us a new definition of the international system as an unstable but not anarchic coordination game, laid on a foundation of solved prisoner's dilemma games on the municipal plane, and evolving the convention of Justice-As-Sovereignty to maintain order.*

From the standpoint of Hume's Philosophical-Policy the evolution of Justice-As-Sovereignty on the international level is the solution not to a prisoner's dilemma but to a coordination game, having within it nested prisoner's dilemmas solved by municipal systems of law before they are recognized as part of the international system (ie at the international coordination equilibrium). The existence of a series of stable governments at a lower (municipal) level of organization creates the background condition for the strategic framework of the coordination game and supports its solution through Justice-As-Sovereignty as the normative vehicle of the Westphalian Equilibrium. Agents need to achieve coordination in order to provide social cohesion, and to understand that it is only through the adoption of the coordination equilibrium, and the standards that will inform and protect it, that this integration is possible. International order is critical because without it not only is social cohesion at the inter-state level impossible, but the municipal level of solved games is threatened with disruption from uncoordinated international interaction that breeds its own sanctions, including war. The Westphalian Equilibrium, as an expression of Justice-As-Sovereignty, lessens this threat.

Here it is critical to remember that the Humean perspective does not characterize the international system before law and full governance as a state of "anarchy".[106] Anarchy is that state-of-affairs that threatens individual nations with an existence that is "solitary, poore, nasty, brutish and short"[107] should they defect, in any way, from the established collective equilibrium. The Humean "state of nature" is less a violent condition than an inconvenient or inefficient set of circumstances in which humanity is faced with questions of justice which it has presented before: that is, it is a condition of instability of property that will be lessened by the evolution of convention. It may be that states, with the experience of solving the municipal collective action problem behind them, are more conscious of the coordination game facing them at the international level. But nevertheless,

---

[106] Hobbes, above n 27, at 186, and for an argument that Hobbes' assumption is core to the general understanding of the international system assumed by scholars see Charles Covell, *Hobbes, Realism and the Tradition of International Law* (2004) 86–87.

[107] Hobbes, above n 27, 186.

the solution lies in the establishment of the Westphalian Equilibrium and the evolution of Justice-As-Sovereignty, in the recognition and operation-alization of practice in a world that will be collectively better off for the general adherence to this conventional standard of cooperation.

This is a dramatically different world from what is often thought of as the Hobbesian anarchy of the positivist/realist world system. First, from a Humean standpoint, there is not a desperate motivation to leave the state of nature. The incentive to create international convention is a move prompted by the circumstances of justice that juxtapose the need for wider social relations against the limited generosity of individual state actors. It is a move for efficiency, convenience, and a more stable muni-cipal and international world order. It is a prudent and inherently rea-sonable evolution or philosophical refinement of human social relations. However, it is also a move from a condition characterized by solved pris-oner's dilemma games at the municipal level, to a pending international coordination game which has a distinct strategic set-up and set of expec-tations for the actors. Specifically, the multiple coordination equilibria are competitive but the idea of coordination is in everyone's interest regardless of which equilibria is chosen. This requires less incentive from the state of nature and sets expectations so that it is in everyone's interest to live by the accepted conventions.

The choice of equilibrium is indifferent between the players and will arise, first, by convention and then, with the advent of contract-by-convention and its governance institutions and policy process, by the codification of specific law to address specific social coordination dilem-mas. This will form a system of dispositive rules that, being plainly more efficient and effective, will be what Schelling calls a prominent or "focal point" solution to the coordination situation.[108] This type of solution is more stable in terms of the loss of coordination because the process of coordinating itself is the core value; that is, where the moral quality of the system itself is found. The option for those cooperating is not chaos or cooperation but different process-norms all aimed at the coordination of the system by conventional means, be it at alternative equilibria.

Hume's Philosophical-Policy supposes a state of nature for the inter-national system that is uncoordinated and inefficient but not anarchic, not the threat of death in disorder but the instability of property on a global level that needs attention and solidification over time as more states are created and seek Justice-As-Sovereignty for the sake of the international society as a whole.

• *Hume's Philosophical-Policy gives us a new definition of governance as that level and complexity of international law which is necessary to insure the process of cooperation itself. Specifically, that is the amount of central-ization needed to seek the persistence of convention and secure the chosen*

---

[108] Thomas Schelling, *The Strategy of Conflict* (1960) 57–58.

equilibrium of Justice-As-Sovereignty against a growing, more complex, and heterogeneous world system.

Another concern in the positivist model of the Hobbesian world is the existence and validity of international law itself. When you have an international system with an anarchic foundation and a global prisoner's dilemma to solve, the only governance that will be successful is governance that comes from an integrated and centralized institutional structure with binding enforcement capability. This is Hobbes' argument that government is what "holds men in awe" and creates a central, top-down sovereignty. Without this central government, governance does not exist. This makes what we now call international law suspect both in terms of its status as law and its necessity.[109]

To find a property stabilization equilibrium for Hume's international coordination game does not require a centralized enforcement regime: it can utilize voluntary rules and dispute settlement compliance at a more decentralized level of complexity. The Westphalian Equilibrium already has its growing set of constituent municipal governments which supply enough "awe" for a more decentralized system of international law to work. Seeking a coordination convention or equilibrium is consciously in the interests of all, so when a new state is granted its sovereignty, it recognizes that its interest lies in not alienating itself from this coordinated system but working within it, and cooperating with Justice-As-Sovereignty and the conventions of the prominent solution, even if it finds this, at times, burdensome.[110]

Overall, the idea of governance, from the standpoint of Hume's Philosophical-Policy, has a number of philosophical definitions and levels of possible complexity, depending on which of the multi-equilibria is conventionally chosen to represent justice for the international system. International law needs only to stabilize property and insure coordination. Within the framework of Justice-As-Sovereignty and the Westphalian Equilibrium, this means coordinating the many municipal government models with legal rules, policy institutions, and social organization that encourage social, commercial, and political interaction while honoring the sovereign equality of each and all.

Hume's Philosophical-Policy may, however, require that any international governance system set basic policy or rules for the occupation, prescription, accession and succession of property between states.[111] It might prescribe that good faith and promise-keeping act as core precepts and encourage any and all contact that increases reciprocity without

---

[109] For the latest incarnation of this argument see Jack L Goldsmith and Eric A Posner, *The Limits of International Law* (2005).
[110] Even nations, such as the United States, which may be disobeying international law still feel the necessity to justify their actions in terms of international law. See John F Murphy, *The United States and the Rule of Law in International Affairs* (2004) 4–6 and *passim*.
[111] Hume, *A Treatise of Human Nature*, above n 8, 505.

invading the sovereign space of any state. Because the particular goals pursued through coordination will be different given the context, they cannot be, for Hume, themselves the normative end. The process of maintaining order, whatever the substantive ends are, that is the normative focus of Hume's moral argument. Humean diplomacy, therefore, expecting the circumstances of justice to apply, will work to coordinate that order, without which no substantive ends are possible; that is, diplomacy mindful that justice is sovereignty and that space between international actors is critical to the maintenance of the system, where the process of coordination is, what we might call, the normative end-in-itself.

The process as an end-in-itself is very important because it demotes principles that focus on ends that might trump process and elevates the sanctity of the process over any ideals or regulative moral precepts taken as ends. For example, the conscious consent of states would be an important element of Hume's system of international governance, not as an end-in-itself, but only as a surrogate for the "order" and social stability that is Justice-As-Sovereignty. The coordination convention and its equilibrium as an ordered process is where the normative value lies. It must persist; its governance institutions, a product of contract-by-convention, exist primarily, if not exclusively, to assure the survival of that process.

Under these conditions, governance can be more decentralized and compliance more dependent upon moral approbation, Justice-As-Sovereignty, and the "artifice" of international politicians and lawyers, because the focus of the system is not upon power but upon the stabilization of territory as property. Unlike power, which is a zero-sum good where one person's gain is another's loss, property stabilization is a synthesis solution that is in everyone's interest. Whatever one possesses is more valuable to them for being theirs by convention, rules, and the law. In effect, Humean governance is about states with limited generosity, seeking coordination to stabilize territory and possessions given the circumstances of justice. It is not about self-interested states seeking power and trying to replace an anarchic state of nature with a centralized civil state in one risky all-or-nothing act.

Whatever the level of centralization or complexity the international governance structure may have, Hume's Philosophical-Policy draws a firm distinction between the conventional point of origin for the law and any conscious or rationalist ideas, whether based upon convention or *prior* principle, created through contract-by-convention. Specifically, as we will explain in the next section, within Hume's philosophical framework law originates with contract-by-convention (ie governance institutions). Although legal norms may have roots in conventions or in regulative moral principles, it is with the advent of contract-by-convention that these informal rules and rights are provided the institutional opportunity for realization through the legal governance structures set up to codify them.

This is especially crucial for principles and how they inform the law. Because they require not only the evolution of convention, but of contract-by-convention with its accompanying institutional structures, in order to

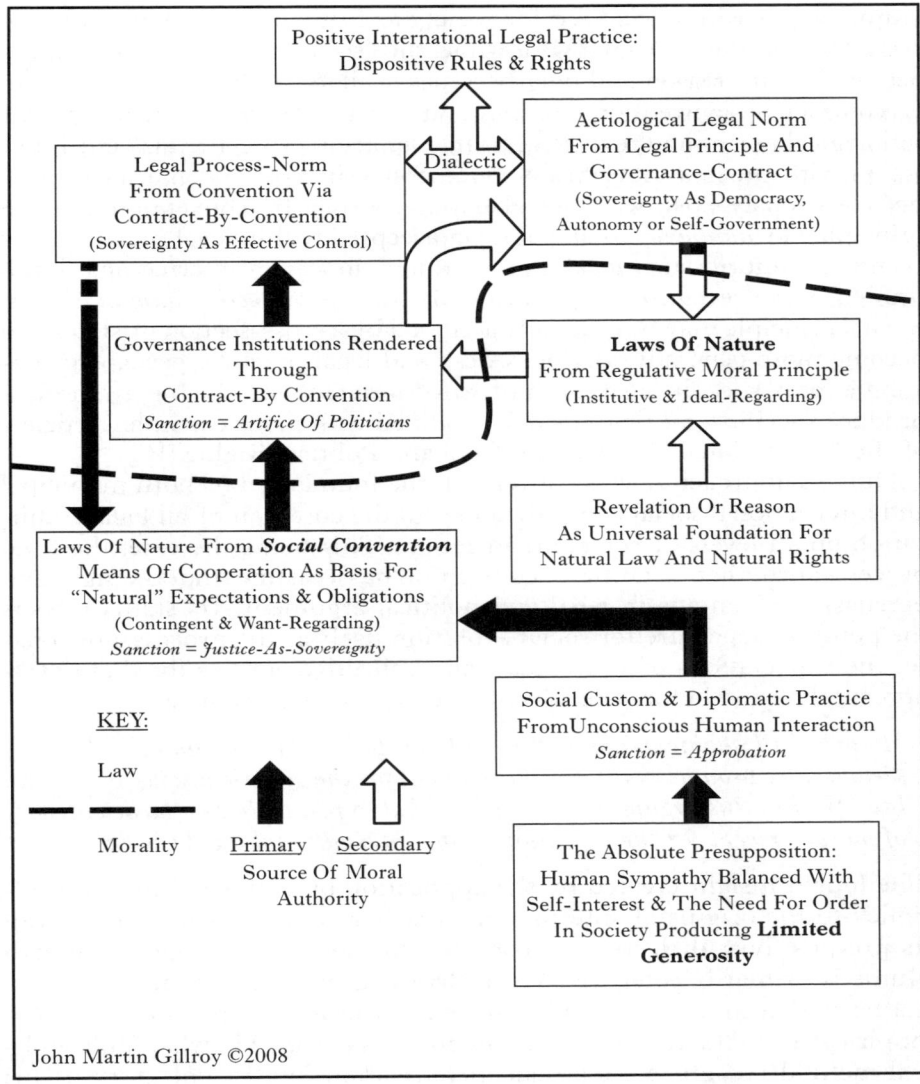

Figure 2: Hume's Evolution Of Law From *Process & Principle*

affect policy argument and the codification of law, our use of principle in law must await the evolution of all three layers of sanctions to stabilize the fundamental social predispositions of humanity. With approbation, justice, and the artifice of politicians established, natural law as regulative moral principle can begin its evolution within legal practice and institutions, moving from the status of moral principle to legal principle, then legal norm, and then legal right or rule dispositive in explicit cases. This can be seen in Figure 2 as the two distinct tracks for the realization of norms in practice are revealed. With the dotted line indicating the boundary between moral argument and legal practice, the "primary" path for

Hume begins with one's need for society and utilizes social convention to eventually produce the law. Meanwhile, the "secondary" path begins independently with reason and only becomes available to law with the advent of contract-by-convention. At this point in the development of the law aetiological norms and regulative principles act in critical or dialectic interaction with process. Specifically, once policy institutions and legal practice consciously exist, with the advent of contract-by-convention, a moral principle like *autonomy,* that is not yet accepted within legal practice, may eventually inform such legal argument and appear in international jurisprudence as a recognized legal principle such as *protecting human dignity.* Such a principle may be gradually accepted by a cross-section of states and become more generally part of widespread legal practice, perhaps generating a more specific legal norm of *self-determination,* which may, in turn, produce specific *legal rights* or *rules,* codified within, for example, Article 1 of the International Covenant on Civil and Political Rights.[112]

Hume's approach makes convention the foundation of both municipal and international social constructions and the core unit of all legal codification on all levels of social organization. This being the case, the legal process-norm that instantiates convention has a distinct moral weight and persuasive advantage in legal and political argument. Its status reflects the point of departure for social evolution itself as the process-norm has set the expectations of individuals and collective entities for that developmental period before the advent of conscious governance.

- *Hume's Philosophical-Policy takes Philosophical Method and the dialectic seriously by producing a refined argument for the generic essence of natural law. Within this argument process is added to principle as a basic category of moral precept for the evolution of the international legal system.*

The fourth insight created by the application of Hume's Philosophical-Policy to the origins of international law is a result of what we can call its pre-positivist dialectic approach to philosophical method. Although Hume is primarily categorized as a British Empiricist,[113] the fact of the matter is that in his writings he treated, for example, the normative and empirical as interactive dynamic components engaged in what philosophical method recognizes as a dialectical relationship.[114] The story of his philosophy is the development of morality, justice, and politics out of the behavior of human beings.[115] As I stated at the beginning of this essay, Hume's Science is a Moral-Science, one that defines the natural in terms

---

[112] John Martin Gillroy, "Adjudication Norms, Dispute Settlement Regimes and International Tribunals: The Status of 'Environmental Sustainability' in International Jurisprudence" (2006) 42 *Stanford Journal of International Law* 8.

[113] Jonathan Bennett, *Locke, Berkeley, Hume: Central Themes* (1971).

[114] Baillie, above n 63, 10–11; Buckle, above n 11, 244 and Knud Haakonssen, *The Science of a Legislator: The Natural Jurisprudence of David Hume and Adam Smith* (1981) 4, 7–8.

[115] *Hume's Law* notwithstanding. The absolute dichotomy between normative and empirical said to be the core of Hume's logic here can be argued to be an invention of 19th century positivism. See Buckle, ibid, 282 note 275 and Gillroy, above n 40, 131.

of the matter to which individuals apply their unconscious passions and how other humans respond to these choices, interacting, setting expectations, and evolving ethical, political, and legal conventions in support of the absolute presupposition of the human need for society and social order on all levels of organization.

This process combines the normative with the empirical as two ever-present halves of the same social reality. Even though, in the end, Hume may fall on the empirical side of the current (and artificial) divide between positive and normative, his philosophy is a combination of the two and applying his Philosophical-Policy suggests how current study of the international system might further redefine its world of norms and in this way expand our understanding.

For example, Hume's Philosophical-Policy makes a distinction, not fully articulated within contemporary international law, between a reasoned principle (prior end), a process-based norm (justice), and a legally-valid rule (positive law), where they appear as distinct answers to the growing needs of social cooperation as society becomes more complex and approbation is aided in maintaining coordination by justice and then governance institutions under contract-by-convention. In making this distinction, however, he shuns the importance of *a priori* principle as a starting point and describes norms as evolving directly from a *process* of human social interaction that produces convention (in this case Justice-As-Sovereignty). Here he anticipates Kelsen, making his methodology empirical, sociological, and constructivist in nature. But unlike Kelsen, Hume maintains the interdependence of normative and positive, with justice and order, so that they integrate or synthesize the solution to the coordination game out of a dialectic dynamic. Specifically, as we seek order at the international level and as Justice-As-Sovereignty is adopted as a core process value in the developing system, Hume is creating new levels of social organization where the normative quality of Justice-As-Sovereignty is *integrated*, first, into the concerns of justice to stabilize property, and then into the creation of governance institutions that use public policy and law to empower convention. Now the philosophical concern for justice integrates with the physical concern for order as positive practice merges with a normative obligation to cooperate and *order* becomes the natural end of both *justice* and the *positive law*.

Hume's *Sovereignty* is, for this reason, not an *a priori* principle but a process-norm, a product of social cooperation, a means (albeit a necessary means) to the goal of convention and one that marks the achievement of membership or statehood, but is not a prerequisite to it. If *legal sovereignty* is but the product of a process that creates social convention, then it may have no *a priori* or necessary moral status within international law as a principle focused on an end (producible or non-producible). While necessary for the emergence of a convention, at least at its origin, legal sovereignty can be overtaken after the advent of contract-by-convention, not just by other competing process-norms, but also by the creation of

legal and political institutions that are built upon and therefore bring
into the global debate "*a priori*" regulative principles which conflict more
substantively with process-norms as they define substantive ends that are
meant to trump means when in conflict with them. For example, economic efficiency in trade can be categorized as a process-norm competing
with sovereignty, as it is focused on the order of the international trading
system rather than any substantive end. The international system would
change were it to switch its equilibrium to efficiency, but not as much as
it would change moving its collective equilibrium to a regulative principle like the human right against genocide. With a focus on substantial
rights, the new equilibrium would have to sacrifice international order for
principle, means for ends, sovereignty for intervention, which more seriously compromises the stability of the international system as it is. Both
of these possibilities challenge the order and stability of the Westphalian
Equilibrium, but to different degrees.

   If sovereignty is a norm whose dialectical integration is found not in
principle but in process, how does that effect its status in the modern
international legal system? What happens when an institutional regime
based upon Justice-As-Sovereignty, protecting the cooperative process
as an end-in-itself, is confronted by a legal regime created from an *a priori* principle such as human autonomy which is meant to make means
bend to ends (eg the law of armed conflict, to the extent that it is based
upon sovereignty, versus the law of human rights, to the extent that it is
based upon intervention to uphold the principle of human dignity)? If
the Humean system is logically intact, then process-norms, which evolve
without substance but in order to protect coordination equilibria from
disruption, will fight off those substantive principles that will, by their
nature, cause disruption in established order. Process-norms will down-
play the legitimacy of *prior* principle within the international legal system
in an effort not to have to drastically adjust established and cooperative
means to any particular end. We might also expect that Justice-As-
Sovereignty will be less defensive against other process-norms (eg economic efficiency), suggesting alternative but effective or indifferent
coordination equilibria, which could replace Justice-As-Sovereignty
without the disruption of moving from a moral focus on means to a
moral focus on ends. This may be an explanation for why intervention
in domestic affairs for the purposes of an efficient and stable world trading system[116] (ie replacing one process-norm with another) seems more
acceptable to the international community than intervention against
genocide (ie replacing a process-norm with a principle), for example, in
Rwanda.

---

[116] As when the World Trade Organization struck down municipal endangered species law in
the United States. *United States—Importation Prohibition of Certain Shrimp and Shrimp Products*
WTO Panel Report, 15 May 1998 as modified by WTO Appellate Body Report adopted November
6 1998. Both reported in Cairo A R Robb et al (eds) *International Environmental Law Reports*
(Volume 2) 270.

This gives Hume's Philosophical-Policy a unique definition of "Natural Law" that further helps to integrate the dialectic between normative and positive. In the same way that the dialectic between justice and order integrates into a definition of justice as sovereign order, Hume's sense of natural law integrates the idea of core precepts and universal application with the idea of positive convention, observable behavior, and the coordination of elective agency.

Because of Hume's transcendence of traditional positivism, his philosophy takes both essential normative arguments and positive methodology seriously. Although Hume's sense of natural law puts not reason, but the passions, substantially in charge, application of his Philosophical-Policy makes the process-norm of Justice-As-Sovereignty both the "is" and "ought" of international coordination and the international law that this coordination requires.

For Hume's Philosophical-Policy, "natural law evolves and is learned by experience",[117] as individuals interact and create process-norms in order to coordinate their behavior and secure its order. Convention, based upon sympathy and the human need for society, which are its basic presuppositions, is the core of this solution to the problem of collective action and creates a normative character for itself from the morality of natural human interactions. Although Hume's concept of natural law may contain more than the norms of sympathy and the need for society which grows out of it,[118] these are the core moral presuppositions, arising from human interaction, without which other norms, and society itself, are impossible.

Conventions of property, coordination and reciprocity are natural laws as they are not conscious but evolve spontaneously out of repeated interactions and diverse interests.[119]

The obligation to follow a convention also arises naturally from the setting of human expectations and the need for enforcement of these conventions by approbation (the first stage of social sanction). As the coordination game clearly indicates, it is in our individual interest to follow a convention once it is established and in our collective interest to establish them in order to coordinate ourselves toward political/legal stabilization. The laws of nature, as convention, create from their inherent evolution and existence expectations of what we, and others, ought to do.

Around these conventions a system of morality grows up; we come to recognize a moral obligation to play our part in cooperative arrangements and learn to condemn those who try to take free rides on other people's efforts.[120]

Hume integrates a sense of evolving universal morality into his natural law, but it is one which can be methodologically assessed by the empirical logic of process rather than independent moral principle. It is moral

---

[117] Robert Sugden, *The Economics of Rights, Cooperation and Welfare* (1986) 162.
[118] Ibid. As sentiments are the normative product of sympathy, which is an empirical fact.
[119] Ibid, 146.   [120] Ibid, 161.

in that "we believe that we ought to keep the Laws of Nature"[121] and it is empirical in that it is not some *a priori* principle that provides the imperative to moral choice but process-norms and their "[c]onventions [that] ought to be kept."[122]

Overall for international law (see the flow of the two paths in Figure 2), the foundations, or metaphysics of justice, applying Hume's Philosophical-Policy, have been sorted out so that (1) the human need for society sits as the absolute presupposition of the argument for convention, (2) process-norms are made distinct from substantive principles, (3) convention is made distinct from contract in a Hobbesian sense and (4) process and convention are made prior to principles and contracts (or in Hume's case contract-by-convention).

• *Hume's Philosophical-Policy creates a unique argument for the process-norm of sovereignty as, dialectically, both a top-down and a bottom-up idea, built on a hierarchy of sanctions and natural law presuppositions which also redefines a particular story about the role and development of the sources of international law.*

Hume's Philosophical-Policy contains the dialectic nature of the concept of sovereignty and its contemporary applications. Sovereignty is more than just a contested concept, it has its origin in the social construction of convention for the stabilization of property and is inherently dialectical not only externally, in terms of other concepts such as intervention[123], but internally, in terms of its own normative content and empirical application. In effect, Sovereignty has a scale of definitional refinement that can be deciphered through philosophical examination and which redefines it as our understanding of its essence grows.

Within international law, sovereignty finds its traditional imperative in that top-down process that ensures *Effective Control* over territory, coordination at the Westphalian Equilibrium, and the equal status of any state to have its internal affairs under its own aegis. In contemporary international legal scholarship, however, there have been arguments that sovereignty must also represent such bottom-up developmental and empowering ideas as self-determination, human rights, and autonomy.[124] This presents us with a conundrum. Can sovereignty, especially that idea connected to the state and its function, dialectically provide for both top-down and bottom-up ideals at the same time? Faced with a sovereignty connected to the state that defines territory and a sovereignty not connected to the state which focuses on bottom-up moral and development

---

[121] Ibid, 143.   [122] Ibid, 155.   [123] Weber, above n 4.
[124] Hoffman, *Sovereignty* (1998) 18–20. If sovereignty is a process-norm, then it cannot simultaneously be a principle, as it cannot define both means and ends as trump cards. Even assuming that principle and process have a dialectic relation, the resulting snapshot or policy representing sovereignty at any one time must either emphasize its role as a process-norm, as Hume would have it, or as a principle that trumps the cooperative stability of the international system for the independence of states as an end-in-itself.

concerns, a natural course might be to solve the conundrum by separating sovereignty from the state and making it an independent, stand-alone principle.[125]

However, from a legal vantage point, this presents a further problem, as the state is traditionally the primary possessor of sovereignty and subject of law in the world system. Although Hume's Philosophical-Policy does not require the existence of the state *per se*, as long as the coordination equilibria has been chosen at the Westphalian point, and the coordination convention is Justice-As-Sovereignty, stability requires that the institutional structure carrying the convention be supported. There is also a problem here with the argument that sovereignty is, or ought to be, a free-standing principle, because Hume's Philosophical-Policy, within his definition of natural law, makes a distinction between principle as an aetiological norm[126] and convention as a process-norm, classifying Justice-As-Sovereignty exclusively in the latter category.

Hume's approach to state sovereignty solves the conundrum through philosophical method without dropping the context of the state or denying the importance of bottom-up moral content. First, sovereignty is essentially a normative, rather than an empirical, concept for Hume. It is not just the observable practice of states that matters but also the underlying metaphysics or presuppositions built upon humanity's predisposition for society. The resulting logical system of moral conventions and regulative moral principles that form the foundation of legal norms and entail human obligation to conform to them,[127] come about to protect and foster social interaction, which is the imperative of his moral argument. Second, sovereignty is essentially dialectic in that its formation comes from a bottom-up process of creating and forming obligations to follow conventions, while its persistence is a creature of the top-down solidification and institutionalization of sovereignty within the state. Third, Hume essentially argues that legal norms have both a *primary* and a *secondary* source of moral authority which must be reconciled in order to establish a stable international legal system. The primary source lies in the fact of social convention and diplomatic practice; and the secondary source lies in the obligations inferred by reason or revelation as part of natural law (see the delineation of primary and secondary sources of moral authority in Figure 2). Although he argues that the former is more basic than the latter, more exclusive and also more elemental, it is in the reconciliation of the dialectic between them that one finds the complete story of the concept of sovereignty. But how is this reconciliation accomplished for Hume?

---

[125] Ibid, 19 and 96–107.

[126] I use the English rendering of "aetiological" rather than the American (etiology) because it is closer to the Greek root of the word "aitia" meaning causal and "logia" meaning logic. I use this term to signify the causal logic of the underlying principle that gives this norm its ideal-regarding and regulative moral value as an end.

[127] Gillroy, above n 112, 45.

Hume's primary source of moral or normative authority for law is the process-norm of social convention which is not based upon *a priori* moral principle but is produced by the bottom-up, iterated, and unconscious desire for social cohesion, breeding sets of expectations and social order out of the extrapolation of habitual behavior. As we know, convention has three layers of sanction, moral approbation, Justice-As-Sovereignty, and contract-by-convention, each reinforcing the previous one and buttressing the terms of property ownership, transfer, and stability as systems become larger and more heterogeneous.

The secondary source of moral or normative authority in a Humean international legal system are the aetiological norms that are ideal-regarding,[128] self-referential[129] and based upon inherent or self-reflective principle which is not conventional but conscious and based on the ability of practical reason to morally sanction a producible or non-producible end as an imperative of human agency and policy-choice. For Hume's Philosophical-Policy, moral as well as legal principle is not *prior* but *posterior* to the existence of not only convention but also the governance institutions created through contract-by-convention in the third level of sanctions. With the aid of these legal institutions, regulative moral principles become legal principles and then legal norms through their persuasive success within the legal governance structure. Since principle, for Hume, presupposes the existence of a conscious Hobbesian social contract which is a product of political discourse and policy decision-making, it also presumes that the development of convention and contract-by-convention has preceded it and that the basic governance structure of the legal system has been created to process moral principles and sort them as to their potential for status as legal principles, norms, and then dispositive rights and rules in law (see Figure 2).

The secondary route to law is, by definition, supplemental for Hume while the metaphysical foundation of convention in social cooperation is essential. It is in the latter that he refines the dialectic in the process of the evolution of convention and its layers of sanction. Specifically, the evolution of the convention of Justice-As-Sovereignty is a bottom-up process of social construction where individuals preserve their social predispositions and solve collective action problems (eg collective goods, war), progressively compensating for practices such as discounting and free-riding as the social milieu becomes more complex. In the process of creating the layers of sanctions for convention, Justice-As-Sovereignty

---

[128] Brian Barry, *Political Argument* (1965) 39–40.

[129] The idea of a meta-policy or meta-law is one which assumes that a policy or law is more than an open concept that is widely adaptable given its context. Majone argues that in contrast, a meta-policy has a self-contained and self-referential evaluative principle that defines its character and is vital to its inherent value as a concept. The meta-policy of environmental pollution control, for example, might have the principle of Kaldor Efficiency as its evaluative core giving it its character as a policy and acting as a standard by which to evaluate the law meant to implement it. Giandomenico Majone, *Evidence, Argument and the Policy Process* (1989) 146–147.

becomes the foundation of governance and a top-down solution to the persistence of convention and justice. No matter how decentralized or voluntary international law may be, the coordination of states at the Westphalian Equilibrium requires territory to be stabilized and general cooperation to be maintained, and this becomes a top-down exercise of sanctions, but one contained within a bottom-up process of convention formation, creating an integrated synthesis solution to the dialectic. Sovereignty is then, simultaneously, both a top-down and a bottom-up concept from within Hume's Philosophical-Policy.

Does Hume's solution work? In effect it does, if convention remains the primary source of social-norms and it is enough to build sovereignty out of the process of social convention as the sole place for bottom-up moral concerns, leaving persistence to governance institutions. But what if it is the case that moral concerns, like autonomy and self-determination, are bottom-up, but not satisfied by convention? What if they affect sovereignty and the obligation to conform to it after the evolution of governance? If bottom-up ideas cannot be limited to pre-governance convention, then Hume's logic may fall short.

But it can be argued that Hume does address the problem of sovereignty adapting to changes in the world system, taking account of new bottom-up pressures on international governance. Hume's Philosophical-Policy treats this concern through his argument for principle as a secondary route to moral authority.

Although Justice-As-Sovereignty is predominantly a top-down concept, it inherently provides for bottom-up moral ideals in two ways. *Ex ante*, it begins the dialectic of agency and obligation with the evolution of convention, before top-down institutions are created. *Ex post*, it provides a secondary route for ideal moral principle to become law through contract-by-convention. From the perspective of Justice-As-Sovereignty, it has both its roots (process-norm) and its secondary moral authority (principle) in bottom-up moral precepts, and in this way Hume not only finds a solution to the dialectic but to a changing international system which may require that future law consider sovereignty in light of a set of non-conventional moral concepts "which denote empowerment and development—a concept which embraces democracy, autonomy and self-government."[130]

Moral principle remains as a source of law for Hume, but a secondary one that should not trump process or be a threat to the established coordination equilibrium which is protected by governance institutions. Principle is placed within the context of pre-evolved convention and the requirement that contract-by-convention exists before principle is integrated into the international legal system. It is here that governance institutions, by creating law and the policy apparatus behind it, allow regulative, aetiological, moral principle to become part of dynamic policy and legal discourse. With the institutions of contract-by-convention,

---

[130] Hoffman, above n 124, 20.

a regulative moral principle can become argument, persuade others and seek acknowledgement in court cases as a legal principle, then become a generally accepted legal norm, and eventually function as the normative core of dispositive rules and codified rights (see Figure 2).

However, because Hume argues that convention and process precede contract and principle and are primary and foundational, sovereignty's core connotation is within Justice-As-Sovereignty as a process-norm. Sovereignty is not a stand-alone principle, a moral imperative to which one might sacrifice process,[131] but the process-norm itself. If those who champion the bottom-up connotations of sovereignty agree that process and order are where the primary moral value is, then Hume's solution to the dialectic may be enough. However, if they insist that self-determination, autonomy, or democratic values are regulative aetiological principles that should trump process when inhibited by it, then Hume has only a secondary place for this connotation of sovereignty within his argument.

For Hume there is no confusion. Justice-As-Sovereignty is a process-norm and to the degree that process cannot integrate human autonomy, self-determination or democratic responsiveness, these values will not be advanced as primary concerns. If Justice-As-Sovereignty is to maintain the process of cooperation that stabilizes property and ensures the persistence of the human desire for society on the international level, its normative character will remain tied to the state as the vehicle of conventional justice. Its priority will also remain with top-down governance as the third level of sanction dialectically integrating the concept of coordination or order with the ideal of justice—unless another process-norm with different institutions and a more effective way to protect the need for social interaction comes along.

- *Finally, Hume's Philosophical-Policy tells a particular story about the role and development of the sources of international law.*

As the evolution of convention and the three levels of sanctions affect the definition of sovereignty, they also play a role in the practical evolution of the sources of international law. Applying Hume's Philosophical-Policy creates a three-stage process of achieving global society where local social groupings first evolve through approbation regarding unconscious behavior. The refinement of the idea of justice then establishes a pattern that is repeated on the national level to create states, and then on the inter-national level to create diplomacy (approbation), then sovereignty as a process-norm (justice), and then, finally, multi- or supra-national law and institutions all to protect order and coordination through Justice-As-Sovereignty (governance).

---

[131] One might argue that the civil rights movement in the United States is a good example of aetiological principle (autonomy and integrity of the individual) confronting conventional process-norms (separate but equal). Hume's moral theory recognizes a core dialectical question in human social relations: is a particular principle so important that we are willing to disrupt established social practice to change the law? Constitutional issues in the United States, like civil rights, frequently furnish an affirmative answer to this question.

Hume's refinement of sanctions should also be present in the evolution of the sources of international law and the story of how each influences the resulting pattern of international legal practice. Let us take *custom* as a point of departure, specifically, *opinio juris et necessatis*, or the consent/acknowledgement dimension of custom. We should expect that if *opinio juris* is a creature of the third, or governance stage, produced through contract-by-convention, it will have no foundational or conventional priority, and be independent from, an afterthought of, and not necessary to the origin, but only the persistence, of international customary law. Under these conditions, to say that it is an equal and fundamental component of customary international law may need amendment.

The history of general or customary international law, from the standpoint of Hume's Philosophical-Policy, begins with the solid dominance of evolving conventional practice as that observable dimension of Justice-As-Sovereignty that sets expectations and can be depended upon to protect the interests of constituent states in maintaining the Westphalian Equilibrium. This foundation of practice would police itself through approbation until it required more definitive defense against the growing numbers of distinct conventional solutions to municipal collective action problems and the increasing challenge, in a growing world system, provided by alternate points of coordination.

With the advent of the idea of Justice-As-Sovereignty to further stabilize international property, sovereign coordination may be protected by the tacit rule that any behavior not specifically prohibited by international constraints would be permissible.[132] This, in turn, would be the core norm for any future governance institutions created through contract-by-convention at the next level in the refinement of sanctions.

For *opinio juris* as a component of customary law, Hume's philosophical analysis suggests that social convention and therefore the original legitimacy of international custom would cause obligation to be generated out of iterated practice where the sanction of approbation is enough to secure cooperation. Hume's *social* convention becomes established as a *legal* convention by interaction and the "mutual" acceptance of that behavior through the systematic coordination of actors at the Westphalian Equilibrium. Here consent is neither tacit or real but simply inferred from the fact that states are acting in concert within a coordination game. In this way consensus is secured through the operation of Justice-As-Sovereignty.

This definition of custom without *opinio juris* can justify itself until contract-by-convention and governance institutions are built to further shore-up Justice-As-Sovereignty. To reconfirm collective action through the shorthand of sovereignty, legal institutions may coordinate on an additional layer of sanction for international custom to insure that it discourages discounting and free-riding on the established or conventional

---

[132] *Lotus* (PCIJ Rep.Series A No 10, 1927 at 18) maintains this exact precept.

coordination equilibrium. With the need for governance structures and law, applying Hume's Philosophical-Policy may require states to submit customary law (not heretofore subject to actual consent beyond mere participation), more openly to the strictures of conscious contract-by-convention through some form of real assent to the obligations of customary law. The imperative is to support the conventions of the system; and the additional level of sanction will reinforce Justice-As-Sovereignty by adding to the *acceptance* of practice, the idea that states need to consciously know and demonstrate what amounts to a further obligation to custom through *opinio juris*.[133]

This same hierarchy of sanctions combines sovereignty and governance in terms of the evolution of *treaty* law. Here we should expect the origins in terms of real consent to negotiate, first through arbitration conventions and eventually more formal agreements on specific topics. The voluntary actions of states, in the approbation stage of convention, is policed in a trial-and-error method as part of the "civilized" or diplomatic behavior of states. With the advent of Justice-As-Sovereignty, and then contract-by-convention, there would eventually be created a treaty for treaties.[134] Throughout this evolution of more sophisticated treaty recognition, as a basis for the coordination of states around the conventions of inter-state negotiation, there may come the evolution of more and more concrete rules for arbitration[135] and the more conventional use of multi-lateral treaties evolving from the experience with two party coordination.

Many conventions that cover substantial groups or populations are built up out of dyadic or very small number interactions.... Most of the conventions Hume and Lewis discuss...are built out of dyadic and small-number interactions.[136]

During this evolution, the practice of states, backed by Justice-As-Sovereignty, will emphasize voluntary consent, but from Hume's perspective, not for its own sake. Although many international lawyers would characterize the pertinent dialectic as that between consent and justice,[137] applying Hume's Philosophical-Policy, consent is a surrogate for the order and property stabilization protecting human social propensities and protected by Justice-As-Sovereignty and its governance institutions. This is especially true in terms of real consent as an idea within promise-keeping (ie *pacta sunt servanda*) which is a core element of Hume's philosophy that he contends requires the pre-existence of convention but is nonetheless necessary, not for its own sake, but for the persistence of order in support of convention as it faces an ever more complex world.[138]

---

[133] The International Court of Justice has affirmed this idea in a number of cases. See *North Sea Continental Shelf Cases* ICJ Rep 1969 p 3; *Nicaragua* ICJ Rep 1986 p 14; *Asylum* ICJ Rep 1950 p 3.
[134] The Vienna Convention On The Law Of Treaties, May 23, 1969, reprinted in (1969) 63 *American Journal of International Law* 875.
[135] J G Merrills, *International Dispute Settlement* (4th ed, 2005) 91–126.
[136] Hardin, above n 6, 196.
[137] Martti Koskenniemi, *From Apology to Utopia* (rev, 2005) §5.1.1.
[138] Hume, *A Treatise of Human Nature*, above n 8, 516 and Baillie, above n 63, 180–185.

One might also expect that treaties, being interpreted in terms of Justice-As-Sovereignty, would emphasize *in dubio mitius* or that interpretation of the treaty most favorable to the process-norm of Justice-As-Sovereignty. It would also be protective of Justice-As-Sovereignty and its coordination equilibrium, if, at the origins of treaty law a liberal system of reservations was adopted.[139] Hume's Philosophical-Policy might prescribe that wide subscription to a treaty, or a point of *process* equilibrium, not be sacrificed for a smaller number of signatories with more immediate and *principled* dedication to the conventions of the international system and its established stabilization point. This system of liberal reservations, which encourages participation in coordination that could grow more complete over time, may even be codified,[140] in the contract-by-convention phase of legal evolution, and remain fast until challenged by alternative regulative principles or competitive process-norms.

The Humean perspective might also allow us to anticipate expectations about the third and last source of international law: the role and acceptance of regulative *principles* such as human dignity and environmental integrity, within an international legal governance system based upon a process-norm of Justice-As-Sovereignty.[141] Since aetiological principles represent the secondary route to moral authority and are constructive of ends assumed to challenge the established status and order created by our core process-norm, they may be unconsciously assumed to be disruptive to the established coordination equilibrium. For example, one may argue that civil rights were anticipated to threaten (by design) the peace and order of the Jim Crow South and its *separate-but-equal* doctrine. Alternatively, the introduction of the idea of *jus cogens* principles might have been thought to threaten sovereignty by encouraging intervention on the pretext of rights that to be affective need to trump the peaceful order of the *Westphalian* system. Aetiological principle is here devalued within the system to the advantage of process-norms like Justice-As-Sovereignty.

The origin of international law in the Westphalian Equilibrium, was, by this reading, a direct reaction of diplomatic convention to the instability of property caused by thirty years of *principled* religious war, which was itself caused by the breakdown of the previous international coordination equilibrium created by the *universal* church and Papal rule before the reformation.[142] Accordingly, the negotiators of the Treaties of Westphalia could not help but see ideal principles aimed at *prior* ends as inherently disruptive of the greater social order. Applying Hume's argument, we should expect that this evolutionary pattern would seize upon a

---

[139] As when the Latin American approach to multi-lateral treaties (that was willing to accept reservations to gain parties to a treaty) became conventional in practice instead of the European approach (that chose unreserved participation over number of parties).

[140] Vienna Convention, above n 134, at Art. 19, 20 and 21.

[141] These may be the principles that are a source of international law through Art 38(1)(c), see Statute of the International Court of Justice, above n 43.

[142] Harold J Berman, *Law and Revolution* (1983) 95.

point of coordination based on something akin to Justice-As-Sovereignty, which insured the liberty of individual states to oversee their own particular internal conventions by finding a point of coordination and a neutral process-norm that avoided having principle trump the reintroduction of orderly social process.

Even in the contract-by-convention stage, when aetiological principle is codified as a legitimate, yet secondary, source of international law,[143] Hume's Philosophical-Policy will protect Justice-As-Sovereignty from any substantive regulatory principle that threatens it. This protection may take the form of demoting all moral discourse, and the principles it renders, to the status of *soft* rather than *hard* law, allowing only those principles and rights that are inherently consistent with sovereignty and the process-norm of convention to be considered as valid international law. In any case, all regulative moral principles that compete for the status of international law will have to be actively integrated into pre-existing social convention and become part of the shared values instituted and supported by Justice-As-Sovereignty, in order to become valid law.[144] Within Hume's Philosophical-Policy, principle must yield to the process of insuring the persistence of human social cooperation.

In the end, it is the continued persistence of the established coordination equilibrium and Justice-As-Sovereignty that matters to questions of Humean justice and it requires that any conscious recognition of principle be filtered, conditioned, or devalued by the system for the sake of the pre-existing order.[145]

Conclusion

With an application of Hume's Philosophical-Policy, the law of nations arises from the absolute presupposition that humanity seeks society and social order on all levels of organization. It creates a metaphysics of presuppositions where convention arises from custom with levels of sanctions that protect the human need for society as the absolute presupposition of local, municipal, and international cooperation. The concepts of limited generosity, sympathy and self-interest integrate to generate an imperative to discover a coordination equilibrium that can take states from an inefficient state of nature to a more collectively optimal international system. Convention in Justice-As-Sovereignty is a process of

---

[143] Statute of the International Court of Justice, above n 43.
[144] Ibid. Limiting acceptable principles to those recognized by "civilized nations."
[145] Moral principle and any consideration of ends as ideals would not be granted the status of full law but only soft law; and if they are eventually given such full status, as peremptory norms (*jus cogens*) or universal obligations (*erga omnes*), Hume's Philosophical-Policy would expect that they are granted full status only to the degree that they do not disrupt the established equilibrium and the conventions of Justice-As-Sovereignty. The other option is for them to become the core of a new international coordination equilibrium.

stabilizing territory and creating, in the fullness of time, that system of international law and those governance institutions that are needed to progressively adapt human coordination to a dynamic, open, and ever more complex world system.

Justice-as-Sovereignty is the refined philosophical solution to the dialectic between justice and order, as it creates justice out of the imperative for cooperative social behavior. It solves the larger dialectic between normative and positive law by creating a definition of natural law that regards moral obligation[146] as evolving from the experience of finding and stabilizing a coordination equilibrium within the positive actions, expectations, and interactions of humans in the natural course of their agency. It also attempts to handle both bottom-up and top-down definitions of sovereignty and creates two routes for the moral authority of such essential legal concepts.

Overall, Hume's "Moral-Science of Man" can be expanded to include international law and offers a provocative argument about the origin and persistence of global society which seems to fit with the actual evolution of practice to date. It also provides a cogent explanation of the current resistance of the international community to matters of morals, rights, and aetiological principles in the law. Against current trends in support of non-consequentialist moral precepts[147] trumping sovereign concerns, Hume's Philosophical-Policy offers a theoretical defense and justification in support of the idea that process is a distinct and primary source of international legal norms which ought to be considered essential and obligatory, prior to any content-driven matter of making regulative principles real in a global context.

Hume's Philosophical-Policy also has more to say about the history of law, the evolution of international society, the moral foundations of the international rule of law, and the future of economic globalization, but these must await a distinct and more lengthy venue.

---

[146] Hart, above n 12, 80–81 states the distinction between "having" and "being under" an obligation, both of which, according to Hume, are matters of social convention where the evolving levels of sanction first create the former, and then the latter, with the advent of political institutions and positive law.

[147] For example, human rights interventions, international criminal law prosecutions or international environmental regulation of a nation's domestic pollution or species preservation law. For a WTO rejection of any attempt to force other sovereign nations to accept international environmental regulation that interfere with trade see *United States—Importation Prohibition of Certain Shrimp and Shrimp Products,* above n 116.

REVIEWS OF BOOKS

Peremptory Norms in International Law. By ALEXANDER ORAKHELASHVILI. Oxford: Oxford University Press, 2006. xxxv+622 pp. £60.

'The aim is to provide a comprehensive study of peremptory norms, something which is lacking in international legal doctrine' (p. 1). The aim is a worthwhile one given the impression that the concept of *jus cogens* is seemingly pervasive in the literature and yet is of limited impact in an international legal order that is still theoretically based on consent. Though the *Lotus* doctrine has been diluted by the advent of organizations and the vast expansion of the international community of States, the transactional basis of international law has not been replaced or indeed adequately reconciled with a constitutional model. In a sense, the author shows us a way through this debate by both his understanding of *jus cogens* and a very thorough explanation of its application within the international legal order.

Part I, in which the author discusses the concept and identification of peremptory norms, is crucial to the book, which then goes on to consider the impact of *jus cogens* in the international and national legal orders. While there is a certain intuitive feel for what *jus cogens* is, there are very few convincing and thorough analyses of the conceptual underpinnings of such fundamental norms. The first five chapters are dedicated to this issue in which the nature of peremptory norms is carefully unveiled with copious references to the relevant literature and jurisprudence. *Jus cogens* is an aspect of the hierarchy of norms, prevailing over lesser norms 'not because the States involved have so decided but because they are intrinsically superior and cannot be dispensed with through standard inter-State transactions' (p. 8). It is controversial in many ways for the author to make the argument that *jus cogens* is somehow inherent in the international legal system, rather than the common perception that they emerge as some form of superior custom. He states that *jus cogens* is 'similar to natural law in that they are not the product of the will of States and hence not comprehensible through a strict positivist approach' (p. 38). Further, the author declares that 'while customary norms are built through practice, peremptory norms follow directly from a judgment as to the moral or social values predominant for the international community' (p. 114).

But as with all international laws, that judgment must be made by the international community. How then is it possible to distinguish *jus cogens* from custom? The author states that there is a problem of behaviour that is contrary to a peremptory norm, which might call into question its customary status. He states that 'custom, unlike *jus cogens*, can be corrupted by contrary practice or persistent objection' (p. 114). Having said this he then admits that peremptory norms can be modified, though he envisages this process as being an expansion of the scope of the norms, which does not help those advocating that the peremptory rules on the use of force have been (or have to be) modified to allow for some forum of humanitarian intervention. Whether such arguments are accepted or not, it must be possible to change the peremptory norms.

In truth the author struggles in trying to pin down the source of peremptory norms, though his explanation that 'peremptory norms operate as a public order protecting the legal system from incompatible laws, acts and transactions' (p. 10), contains a great deal of interesting analysis. *Jus cogens* then protects international law from 'certain norms and transactions which are fundamentally repugnant to it (p. 10). This sort of justification conjures up Hart's picture of the minimum content of natural law that is inherent in any society as opposed to a suicide club. In the international order this would necessitate certain fundamental rules limiting significant acts of violence (aggression, genocide, crimes against humanity), and protecting the integrity and independence of the main actors through norms of non-intervention and self-determination, but would it lead to the much larger body of *jus cogens* argued for by the author? He argues that the rules on the use of force (and not just the prohibition of aggression) are *jus cogens,* as is the principle of self-determination, fundamental human rights (not just the accepted prohibitions of torture and slavery, but also as an example, the principle of *non-refoulement* in refugee law), some humanitarian laws, and certain norms of environmental law such as the principle of harm prevention (pp. 50–66). Insufficient space is dedicated to establishing these norms as peremptory, though for the author it is not so much a question of proof, but of logical deduction of what are essential community norms, as opposed to ordinary transactional norms.

Peremptory norms, 'dictated by transcendent community interest' (p. 70) are absolute while other rules are relative. The author categorises areas like diplomatic immunities, trade, or expropriation of property as *jus dispositivum* but, for this reviewer at least, it remains unclear why established central international norms such as that requiring the inviolability of diplomatic premises are different from peremptory norms. Certainly if the underlying values of the international community change, then the peremptory rules must also reflect those changes, so that new norms, such as the principle of free trade, can emerge. Some more explanation on the distinction between *jus cogens* and *jus dispositivum* would have been welcome.

Intrigued, and in no less measure challenged by the discussion in the first part, the reader is then exposed to a very detailed exposition of the effects of peremptory norms in general international law in Part II. Here the author deals comprehensively with the effects of *jus cogens,* for example on the law of treaties in Chapter 6, which contains useful analyses of chosen treaties such as the Treaty of Guarantee on Cyprus of 1960 (p. 157); and on the validity of actions of States (Chapter 7). The discussion of remedies for breaches of *jus cogens* brings together the doctrine and practice, but in so doing, reveals the weaknesses within the international legal order when attempting to enforce community norms (see for example discussion on third party countermeasures at pp. 270–2).

Less well-trodden ground is dealt with in Part III, where the author considers the effect of peremptory norms on the powers of international organisations. The author sees the issue not really from the perspective of those who would argue that organisations are created, in part, to uphold and, if possible, enforce fundamental norms, but as an issue of accountability. This is made clear when he states that 'international organizations violate peremptory norms quite often in the field such as the *jus ad bellium,* self-determination of peoples, or human rights and humanitarian law' (p. 414). The analysis of the nature and scope of *jus cogens* limitations on the powers of the Security Council in Chapter 12, its core being the opinion of Judge *ad hoc* Lauterpacht in the *Bosnia* case, is followed by an equally compelling analysis of the legal consequences of a conflict of a Security Council resolution with *jus cogens* in Chapter 14, though the lack of real judicial review in the UN legal order has prevented any effective application (pp. 480–84). The role of international tribunals in the recognition and application of *jus cogens* is discussed in the final part of the book, and in a way this brings us back full circle to the conflict between the consensual nature of international law, reflected in the jurisdictional limitations of international courts (embodied in the *East Timor* case), and the demands that peremptory norms bring.

While there is no doubt about the high level of scholarship the author brings to bear on the issue, it is still difficult to fully agree with his conclusion that '*jus cogens* has emerged in international law as a body of superior rules controlling bilateral and multilateral transactions of every kind' (p. 576). While we may judge laws and decisions by such standards, the author recognizes that the 'translation and implementation' of the effects of *jus cogens* in 'the areas where the compliance rates with the relevant norms and principles is less than satisfactory' (p. 577). Even after having read the book, it still seems debatable whether the gap between *jus cogens* and its impact on the international legal order means that the concept operates at an aspirational rather than normative level (but see p. 580). Nevertheless, there is no doubt at all that this is a very powerful, well-argued piece of work, which will become a major point of reference for all international lawyers.

N D WHITE

Sovereignty and Interpretation of International Norms. By C FERNANDEZ DE CASADEVANTE ROMANI. Berlin Heidelberg: Springer-Verlag, 2007. XI + 302 + bibliography. £92.50.

The interpretation of international norms has always received particular interest from scholars, but with the multiplication of actors, norms and adjudicators in international law the topic is receiving increasingly more attention. This volume is an example of various attempts to discern whether the established principles of interpretation of international law still apply in light of these institutional and normative developments. The author takes a comprehensive approach to interpretation and examines the interpretation of different types of sources of international law and by various types of actors. The most important contribution of this volume is the part devoted to the impact of the institutionalization of international law on principles of interpretation and interpretive techniques of international courts and tribunals.

The volume looks at interpretation in its broadest sense: interpretation by States, international organizations, and third party dispute settlement, interpretation of general, abstract, customary and conventional norms, and interpretations that are authentic, unilateral, collective, executive or institutional in scope. Although this multitude of categories might not always be necessary for the purpose of analysis, this classification nevertheless shows how there are more actors and more norms to interpret. Part One elaborates on this classification and clarifies some of the basic assumptions of the author. The first assumption is that the institutionalization of the international community, if one exists, has affected law-making and the use of language in international law. More precisely, language is used to capture more diverse interests because, as it becomes more difficult to find an agreement among the multitude of actors involved in law-making in international law, it is necessary to use more general language. The second assumption is that rules or principles of interpretation necessarily constitute a constraint for any interpreter. Unfortunately, this assumption is not further developed and there is no discussion of the character of these rules or principles. Thirdly, the author assumes that, at least for the interpretation of treaties, Articles 31 to 33 of the Vienna Convention on the Law of Treaties ('VCLT') contain a closed list of rules of interpretation. He considers codification as an attempt to restrict a process that is very dependent on the autonomy of the will of States.

In the discussion of Articles 31 to 33 VCLT, the author introduces a distinction between ordinary, vulgar or non-legal and special interpretations. This is another classification that possibly obscures the analysis in the relevant sections of the volume. Articles 31 to 33 VCLT are described as if they were intended to provide 'solutions' to problems of treaty interpretation. Apart from treaties, the author also focuses on the interpretation of institutional norms and customary international law. The example of UN General Assembly resolutions is used to illustrate the heterogeneous character of the sources of international law and the impact on their interpretation of the tension between the individual consent of States and the consensus among a plurality of States. The author finds that the criteria used in interpreting institutional norms are not different from the criteria prescribed by Articles 31 to 33 VCLT, but in addition it is necessary to take account of the process of the formation of institutional norms, at least more than in the case of treaties. The interpretation of customary international law is more complex and cannot entirely be divorced from the establishment of the customary norm in question. In interpreting customary norms, the 'interpreter' simultaneously creates law. A similar conclusion is reached with respect to the interpretation of unilateral declarations.

Part Two focuses on the practice of treaty interpretation by the International Court of Justice ('ICJ') and arbitral tribunals, though a considerable amount of practice has been discussed in Part One. This Part is less detailed and is confined to organizing a selection of cases under the rubrics of the natural and ordinary meaning, context, object and purpose, subsequent practice, preparatory work, multiple authentic interpretations, the intention of parties, the role of practical effect, the spirit of the treaty, equity and inter-temporal law. Some of these classifications are superficial or confusing. For example, the rubric of the 'spirit of the treaty' is taken literally from an ICJ case but there is no discussion of whether, and how, this might have been merely another articulation of the object and purpose of the treaty as mentioned in Article 31(1) VCLT. The author briefly contrasts the interpretive practices of arbitral tribunals with those of the ICJ and concludes that arbitral tribunals have generally followed the rules in Articles 31 to 33 VCLT more closely than the ICJ. More of the practice of the ICJ is analysed in Part Three, which is essentially devoted to the interpretation of selected substantive norms and procedural rules, but organized on the basis of the types of sources in which the norms or rules are articulated. The ICJ as a third party resolving disputes has a considerable amount of autonomy in interpreting different types of norms, depending on its jurisdiction in a particular case. The author is critical of the manner in which the ICJ has exercised this autonomy and in particular of how it has given context, subsequent practice and the object and purpose a supplementary role. In other words, the point is made that the ICJ has correctly applied Article 32 VCLT, but misapplied Article 31 VCLT.

Finally, a few comments on the style and language used by the author are appropriate. The book is a translation from the original Spanish and it remains unclear whether some precision and fluency in style and language were lost in translation. The analysis is often confusing and the reasoning difficult to follow, but this is mostly a matter of structure and organization of ideas.

This volume is a welcome contribution to the discussion of whether the practice and general understanding of treaty interpretation also applies to other instruments of international law, such as decisions of international organizations. This question is currently being tested in different fora of dispute settlement and more thought is needed on the matter. If this volume had concentrated merely on this question, it would have been sufficient. But the author tries to achieve more; he tries to also answer questions relating to the relationship between State sovereignty and the competencies of international organizations and international courts and tribunals, the interpretation of a catalogue of norms in international law, the negotiation of norms and their interpretation in a diplomatic context, and the range of interpretive techniques embodied in certain principles of treaty interpretation. Although the volume does not lack ambition, sometimes this comes at the cost of precision, consistency and clarity of analysis.

ISABELLE VAN DAMME

Délimitation maritime sur la côte Atlantique africaine. By MAURICE K
KAMGA. Brussels: Bruylant, 2006. xviii +317 pp. £55.

Arguably studies on the law of maritime delimitation may be divided into two categories.
The first is studies analysing State practice and the case law relating to maritime delimitations in a global context with a view to establishing a general theory of the law in this
field. The second focuses on maritime delimitations in a particular region. The book under
review further enriches the regional studies in this field by thoroughly examining African
State practice in the Atlantic region. Since a systematic analysis of maritime delimitations
in this region has long been needed, this study is to be warmly welcomed. It has two distinct parts, and contains four annexes which include documents and illustrations.

This book commences with an introduction to historical, geographical and socio-
economical situations of African States along the Atlantic coasts. The opening chapter is
then devoted to a general consideration of the development of the law of maritime delimitation. After those preliminary considerations, Part One, which constitutes the heart of
this book, carefully examines existing maritime boundaries between African States in the
Atlantic region. Specifically, this part addresses maritime delimitations between the following States: Morocco and Mauritania, Mauritania and Cape Verde, Mauritania and Senegal,
Senegal and Gambia, Senegal and Cape Verde, Senegal and Guinea-Bissau, Guinea-Bissau
and Guinea, Nigeria and Cameroon, Nigeria and Equatorial Guinea, Nigeria and São Tomé
and Príncipe, São Tomé and Príncipe and Equatorial Guinea, São Tomé and Príncipe and
Gabon, Congo and Angola, Namibia and Angola, and Namibia and South Africa.

Chapter 1 addresses the means of maritime delimitations in the Atlantic region of
Africa. Not surprisingly, it concludes that maritime delimitations in this region have been
effected mainly by the diplomatic method, and the intervention of third States has been
rare (p. 88). Furthermore, chapter 2 analyses the methods of maritime delimitation in this
region. This reveals that the equidistance method is the most frequently used method
(p. 100). At the same time, it is suggested that other methods of delimitation—such as
the use of astronomical lines, the prolongation of terrestrial boundary, the line perpendicular to general direction of the coast, and the establishment of the joint exploitation
zones—have also been adopted in some instances (pp. 111–132). Chapter 3 contains an
examination of the spatial and temporal scope of maritime delimitations. In this respect,
the author notes that there is a trend that delimitations in this region have been effected
in a comprehensive manner by drawing single maritime boundaries for the exclusive economic zone and the continental shelf (pp. 134–135). Chapter 3 also addresses the application of the principle of *uti possidetis* to maritime delimitations, as well as the stability
of maritime boundaries (pp. 145–152). The thorough analysis of State practice in Part
One is undoubtedly a valuable contribution to the ever increasing literature in this field.
The results of the analysis appear to show that African State practice reflects in essence
a general trend in the law of maritime delimitation.

Part Two presents a perspective on maritime delimitations which remains unresolved
along the Atlantic coasts of Africa. To this end, chapter 4 considers future maritime
delimitations in North-West Africa, including delimitations between Morocco, on the
one hand, and Spain and Portugal on the other; delimitations between Morocco and
Madeira Islands (Portugal), as well as the Canary Islands (Spain) and; delimitations
between the hypothetical State of West Sahara, on the one hand, and Morocco and
Mauritania on the other. Furthermore, this chapter contains discussion with respect to
future maritime delimitations in West Africa, including maritime delimitations between
Cape Verde and Gambia, between Sierra Leone and Guinea, between Sierra Leone and
Liberia, as well as maritime delimitations among Ivory Coast, Ghana, Togo and Benin.
Chapter 6 follows with a discussion on possible maritime boundaries in the Gulf of
Guinea, that is to say, maritime boundaries between Cameroon and Equatorial Guinea,

between Gabon and the Equatorial Guinea, and between Gabon and Congo (Brazzaville). Finally, chapter 7 addresses maritime delimitations in South-West Africa, which relate to maritime delimitations between Angola and the Democratic Republic of Congo, as well as between Namibia and South Africa.

For each unresolved boundary it would seem that the author is attempting to propose an equitable solution. Part Two is certainly a valuable feature, not always found in similar studies. On the other hand, it would appear that proposed solutions rely mainly on geographical factors, and little reference is made to non-geographical elements. Furthermore, some arguments in this Part are based on assumptions, such as the independence of West Sahara. Hence, it must be pointed out that the author's proposals represent only one of the possible solutions and that the validity of his perspective awaits the test of subsequent State practice.

YOSHIFUMI TANAKA

Whaling Diplomacy. By ALEXANDER GILLESPIE. Cheltenham: Edward Elgar, 2005. 509 pp. £95.

The tragedy of the International Whaling Commission (IWC) and the debate on whaling lies in its degeneration into a dialogue of the deaf between two extremes, in which there is no sign of the willingness to compromise that is usually the hallmark of the diplomacy in the title of Professor Gillespie's book. Instead of engaging in a serious search for the middle ground, the pro- and anti-whaling camps take rhetorical pot-shots not so much at each other's arguments, but at caricatures of them. One of the virtues of Professor Gillespie's book is that, although he is clearly *parti pris* in this debate, he does attempt to present an objective view of both sides, and for the most part succeeds. Thus, while he refers to a "general overall perception of failure to act in good faith" (p. 125) in relation to scientific whaling and at one point accuses of Japan of having "continually sought to obstruct the objectives of the sanctuaries" by conducting such whaling in them (p. 126) without citing evidence of such an intent,[1] elsewhere he concedes that Japan and other States sceptical of the IWC's competence to entertain "humane killing" arguments have nonetheless cooperated in discussions in good faith on this subject (p. 161).

The book itself is a comprehensive survey of the whole field of the politics and law of international whaling, and, at some cost to its tightness of focus, of much else besides. Professor Gillespie's fruitful main method is to burrow deep into the meeting reports of the IWC and it generally serves him well. Part I consists of four chapters of which the first two are an historical introduction; he first traces the history of the IWC's management of its stocks from the blue-whale unit to the revised management scheme, and then moves to a diachronic overview of the numbers of various cetacean species. His history of the IWC's failure to take the necessary conservation measures in the early decades is competent, although the account of the gradual fall in catch limits in the 1960s and 1970s is at times difficult to follow and the story has been more lucidly told by one of the first-hand participants, Sidney Holt.[2]

[1] Might it not equally be the case that Japan is conducting a whaling equivalent of the United States Freedom of Navigation program, asserting its rights for their own sake lest it be deemed to have lost them? It may of course be argued that it would be better if the scientific whaling exception were subordinated to the sanctuaries rather than the other way round, but this is not what the legal position is under the Whaling Convention.

[2] S.J. Holt, "Sharing the Catches of Whales in the Southern Hemisphere," in R. Shotton, ed., *Case studies on the allocation of transferable quota rights in fisheries* (FAO Technical Paper 411) (Rome: FAO, 2001), 322 at 335–362.

The loss of focus begins with the next chapter, on environmental threats to whales, particularly persistent organic pollutants, and is only partly regained by the following chapter, on the question of bycatch. Since IWC Member States have wider interests in the minimisation of marine pollution beyond avoiding harm to cetaceans, it seems reasonable to surmise that those interests are more efficiently pursued through international organisations directly concerned with such questions, and Professor Gillespie admits as much, though he is not confident that they will succeed (pp. 45 and 50). The former assumes rather a lot of prior knowledge on the part of the reader, for example in not explaining the pollutants' "semi-volatility" and "ability to bioaccumulate" (p. 47). In the latter, while his definition of "bycatch" by reference to non-target species is standard (p. 85), much of the ensuing discussion appears to reduce it to a general problem of insufficient selectivity in captures, proceeding on the basis that it also includes individuals of the target species which happen to be of the wrong sex or size. The larger doubt, however, is about the purpose of these chapters, which is not easy to discern. While a certain amount of tangential comment is warranted because of the many related issues whaling raises, Professor Gillespie gets easily sidetracked in a way that leaves a number of unsatisfying loose ends; for example, along the way to some sensible suggestions for reducing bycatch (pp. 97–98) he does not explain why he regards the *Shrimp-Turtle* case as a "débâcle" (p. 91) and does not consider the subsequent unsuccessful challenge to the second set of US measures—but equally one might ask why in a book about whales it is necessary to devote as much space as he does to incidental catch of turtles and seabirds.

Part II then turns to broad philosophical questions surrounding whaling, with chapters on scientific whaling, humane killing, non-lethal utilisation (essentially whale-watching) and Aboriginal subsistence whaling. The last of these is soundly enough argued from a largely sceptical viewpoint, but in the other three the trench warfare in which Professor Gillespie engages has led him to dig down to a level from which he has lost sight of the overall lie of the land: the wider context of the management of the living resources of the oceans. Chapter 5 on scientific whaling is as commendably even-handed as one could reasonably expect. On the difficult predator-prey issue, however (in essence, whether culling of seals in order to hasten the recovery of depleted fish stocks ought to be permitted), he oversimplifies in deploring "attempts to blame seals for a collapse in fish stocks" (p. 131). It is one thing to deny that they actually caused the collapse, but quite another to dismiss any possibility that their continued predation might in some instances be sufficient to prevent a recovery. Here Professor Gillespie is perhaps a little too keen to take refuge in the current state of play, in which he says "there is no concrete evidence that cetaceans harm fisheries". The more interesting question on which it would have been beneficial to have his view is the so far hypothetical one of whether or not it is legitimate to try to restore a damaged ecosystem to its prior state if sufficiently compelling such evidence were to emerge, and who—the IWC or the relevant fisheries commission—should decide.

In the same vein, he overargues the case on humane killing in Chapter 6. Training his sights on the objection that this issue has no place in the IWC because it is culturally relativistic and invisible to international law, he sets out to demolish not just the conclusion but also, quite unnecessarily, the premises. Whatever the proponents' motives, the implied incidental powers that any international organisation has are surely ample to give the IWC the cover it needs. The loss of perspective comes to the fore here in the way that Professor Gillespie tends to pile example upon example, seemingly without pausing to consider whether each actually supports the argument he is making. Thus at p. 150 he properly defends the notion of minimum pain as objective, but seems not to notice that the Compact Oxford English Dictionary's definition of "humane" that he cites is itself very subjective. Similarly, when it comes to his excursus into national hunting laws, intent on proving the wood, he misses the exotic nature some of the trees, such as why a Norwegian law on requiring hunting and trapping to be pursued in a way that does not expose wildlife to unnecessary suffering should contain a prohibition on hunting at Christmas and Easter (p. 152), or whether Malaysia's ban on killing of young (p. 154) owes anything at all to humaneness as opposed to conservation.

Much the same can be said of Chapter 7 on non-lethal utilisation. Professor Gillespie rightly betrays a certain sympathy for the Irish compromise proposal, at least in its original form (p. 180). Those who opposed it from either side of the divide both accused each other of refusal to compromise—and both, he invites us to infer, were right. He takes issue with the stance of those States that argue they have the right to exploit the living resources of their EEZs, but aims at the wrong (easy) target: the opposing argument he refutes instead is that they have the *obligation* to do so ("the assumption that whales must be exploited if it will not cause their endangerment"—p. 183)—clearly incorrect in view of Article 65 of UNCLOS—which does not take him as far as he would like to go. He recognises the inconsistency between advocating preservation of whales but not other mammals commonly eaten in the West, but the reviewer will not hold his breath waiting for governments to adopt his suggested solution in an endnote (p. 192) to the anomalous position of whales under the moratorium, which is to extend the present treatment of whales to all mammals rather than *vice versa*.

This also makes unconvincing his denial that "the so-called anti-whaling countries are not telling the pro-whaling countries what to do in their sovereign territories. Rather, the anti-whaling countries are asserting that decisions about how to manage whales are as much theirs as they are those of countries who want to hunt whales, because although whales may migrate through some territorial seas, in essence they exist in the oceanic commons and belong to no nation" (p. 183). Professor Gillespie's view that the IWC's measures prevail over those of the coastal State in its EEZ is correct in so far as this is what the International Convention on the Regulation of Whaling (ICRW), an instrument predating the emergence of the EEZ, dictates. He seems unaware, however, that the argument that whales do not belong to the coastal State while they are in its EEZ is the exact opposite of the position of coastal States interested in protecting their fisheries for straddling and highly migratory stocks from damage by high-seas fishing unrestrained or insufficiently restrained by ineffective fisheries commissions. Such an argument would be risky in the extreme if the moratorium on commercial whaling is lifted. True, the modern legal order concerning marine living resources, in which Article 7 of the United Nations Fish Stocks Agreement (UNFSA) gives coastal States a slight upper hand on the implicit assumption that they are likely to take a more conservationist approach to the living resources of their EEZs than distant-water fishing States are to those of the high seas, could be expected sooner or later to reassert itself. But because UNFSA does not actually apply to whales, this outcome is likely to take much longer to emerge than it otherwise would.

There are eight chapters in Part III, on sanctuaries, small cetaceans, the IWC's relationship with other international organisations, compliance, reservations to the ICRW, transparency, vote-buying and the finances of the IWC. Chapter 9, on sanctuaries, is doubly worrying. First, while it is possible to agree with Professor Gillespie's conclusion that the sanctuaries are lawful—the attacks on them by Burke have always seemed rather overblown to this reviewer—he all but admits the validity of Burke's criticism that the advocates of the view that the purpose of the ICRW has evolved from conservation of whales against overexploitation to preserving them from all exploitation "turn upside down and defeat the major purpose of the original agreement" (p. 262). Commenting that "the interpretation of the ICRW, and its subsequent designated purpose, may not be as immovable as the Sanctuary's opponents suggest", he continues: "The reality is far from the implicit assertion that there is only one correct way to interpret the ICRW." While one may readily concede that it is possible for parties to a treaty to interpret its provisions differently, if the practical consequences of their differences become so acute that they give rise to a dispute needing to be settled by recourse to a third party, that third party will have to prefer one interpretation to the other, or possibly substitute a third. A degree of ambiguity on a peripheral point does no harm when its resolution can be postponed indefinitely, allowing parties to cooperate on more central matters. But diversity of opinion on such a crucial element of a treaty regime as its very purpose is not something to be celebrated; the longer it persists, the more likely the regime is to collapse under the strain.

At pp. 260–265 Professor Gillespie spends much space arguing that "optimum utilisation" in Article V of the ICRW does not require and is not limited to lethal utilisation. This much may be admitted in so far as it is perfectly acceptable for coastal States that have developed a whale-watching industry to bring that interest to the table under this rubric, but it does not follow that non-lethal has come to supplant and now exclude lethal utilisation, as he appears to argue on the basis of Articles 31–33 of the Vienna Convention on the Law of Treaties (VCLT). While it is an accepted technique of interpretation to allow words to change in meaning over time, it is a far greater step to turn the meaning on its head in a context where a significant minority of the parties to the treaty is opposed to this. Taken to its logical conclusion—and it is not clear where or why he would stop short of that—Professor Gillespie's approach would introduce a dangerous indeterminacy into all treaty texts, which cannot be conducive to stable and peaceful international relations. To achieve what he favours would—and should—take a formal amendment. Although reinterpretation can sometimes take the place of treaty amendment, Edeson has recently cautioned against the overuse of this technique[3] and where it is a substitute for an amendment that would have failed if put forward as such, as this one inevitably would have, governments will rightly be wary of adopting many of Professor Gillespie's arguments for fear of the destabilising precedent they would set.

Secondly, apart from scientific whaling, sanctuaries are the next most fraught subject on which scientists do battle and it is very difficult for non-scientists to know whom to believe. One way out of this dilemma is to argue as Professor Gillespie does (p. 255, and see also the endnote on p. 422) that it is naïve to expect that science alone should guide decisions, since "science and the interpretation of scientific material is not value free, and policy makers may choose to accept or reject such material for a multitude of ethical, social and/or political reasons". He does not deny "the importance of scientific guidance", but writes that "it must always be hemmed in by greater philosophical considerations which only the elected and representative should decide." This might not be a problem if the scientists were asked to advise on the relative risks of differing harvesting strategies, sheeting home to policymakers the responsibility for choosing the level of risk they are running, but that is not presently an option in circumstances where the debate is about whether harvesting of admittedly abundant species should be allowed at all. Moreover, if it is acceptable to underharvest for ethical, social or political reasons, then overharvesting for some of the same reasons becomes equally excusable. In retrospect, this may well explain Professor Gillespie's otherwise curious reluctance in Chapter 1 to reprove the IWC for continually ignoring scientific advice in its early years to the undoubted detriment of the stocks—but note once more how in the wider marine living resources context this reasoning has proved, and is still proving, disastrous for fish stocks.

As to whether the ICRW covers small cetaceans, in Chapter 10 (pp. 278ff) Professor Gillespie disposes persuasively of the argument that the nomenclature annexed to the 1946

---

[3] As blurring the distinction between amendment and subsequent practice, allowing practice to depart too far from the terms of the instrument and possibly also circumventing national processes of parliamentary scrutiny where these are required for treaty actions: W Edeson, "Some Future Directions for Fishing Entities in Certain Regional Fisheries Management Bodies" (2006) 37 *Ocean Development and International Law* 245 at 246.

text is exhaustive, but is on much less firm ground in contending that all small cetaceans are (as opposed to ought to be) within the IWC's remit. To achieve this he asserts that "whales, dolphins and porpoises are known collectively as whales"—but, having dismissed one tendentious interpretation based on taxonomy, it is ironic that he himself resorts to another. What is needed, but at present is sadly unachievable, is a clear dividing line—but even in the absence of one it is stretching credulity to imagine that dolphins and porpoises are encompassed in the ordinary meaning of "whales" to which Article 31 of the VCLT directs us. Indeed at p. 279 he cites a report from an IWC subcommittee on small cetaceans advocating the amendment of the ICRW to cover all cetaceans, which would not be necessary if this were the case.

In another contorted argument, Professor Gillespie denies (p. 276) that coastal States have "near absolute competence over them based on their location in those States' territorial seas and EEZs" because of the "mistaken" view that "UNCLOS...accord[s] to coastal States a complete sovereignty". He argues that the sovereignty is "limited in the sense that nations can waive their rights...and freely consent as nations have historically done, to the authority of overlapping international organizations such as the IWC." This is, to put it mildly, a very odd view of what constitutes a limitation on sovereignty. The reviewer is not aware of any statement from any governmental source that sovereign rights in the EEZ, let alone sovereignty in the territorial sea, somehow preclude cooperation. This amounts to the obviously absurd proposition that a right is not really a right unless it is inalienable.

In keeping with his propensity to puncture the bad arguments of his opponents but leave the more plausible ones standing, his attempt (pp. 299–300) to bring down Russia's argument that small cetaceans are outside the IWC's competence by a *reductio ad absurdum* is unsuccessful. If Russia is right, his reasoning runs, then the appropriate management body would be CCAMLR—but that body has deferred to the IWC: "This deference was carefully spelt out in the 1980 Convention on the Conservation of Antarctic Marine Living Resources", Article VI of which states that "Nothing in this Convention shall derogate from the rights and obligations of Contracting Parties under the [ICRW]". But if Russia is right, then CCAMLR's deference under Article VI cannot extend to small cetaceans. Far from Russia's argument being circular, as Professor Gillespie implies, it continues to turn on the same central point of whether all cetaceans are whales, and he is here himself assuming what is to be proved, i.e. begging the question.

It is on the relationship between the IWC and other bodies that may have a concurrent incidental competence over whaling (Chapter 11) that Professor Gillespie's arguments are weakest. At times he seems to regard the IWC's competence as absolute and exclusive. Yet, since international law is not a hierarchical system, it will often be the case that two or more fora are concurrently dealing with the same question, or different aspects of it. This is seen most starkly in the controversy over proposals to downlist various species from Appendix I to Appendix II to the Convention on International Trade in Endangered Species of Wild Fauna and Flora (CITES). The obligation of the Secretariat under Article XV of CITES, cited on p. 343, is one of consultation with the relevant "inter-governmental bodies having a function in relation to those species...with a view to ensuring coordination with any conservation measures enforced by such bodies". This is manifestly inadequate as a basis for asserting that CITES could be acting "in contravention of its own constitution and the established principles of international law, as laid down by the VCLT" (presumably he means the parties to CITES acting in contravention of its text) if it were to downlist those species. It might, from one point of view, be cooperating less effectively with the IWC in so doing, but the consequences of an Appendix II listing are no less compatible with the current moratorium than those of the Appendix I listing, and would not amount to a modification of it. Because nothing that CITES parties *qua* parties do can affect the moratorium—except possibly influence

IWC members' views on whether or not it should be retained, though that is surely legitimate—it is difficult to agree with Professor Gillespie's description of this as "forum shopping" (p. 345). And it smacks of desperation to argue that the procedural requirement for the proponent State of a downlisting to provide "an assessment of the effectiveness" of the instruments under which the species is currently governed "in ensuring the protection and/or wise management of the species" means that the assessment would automatically become that of CITES parties as a whole should they adopt the proposal. States can have many reasons for how they vote on an issue, and since there are only three possibilities—for, against, or abstain—only very seldom can inferences be drawn about what reasons led a given State to vote a certain way. He would presumably not claim—or would he?—that CITES parties should allow other international organisations that manage living resources to dictate the listing in the appendices, and changes to listings, of the species concerned. And if the deference argument is not to be selectively applied, then the IWC would have had no business making its calls in 1980 and the 1990s call for its members to prevent marine pollution generally (pp. 45–46).

In Chapter 13, on reservations to the ICRW, Professor Gillespie's treatment of the general undesirability of reservations and the trend away from them in resource management treaties is thoughtfully presented. He highlights (pp. 386–389) some of the more farcical elements of Iceland's re-entry into the IWC, but in preferring the first, short-lived outcome (Iceland's reservation to the moratorium provision in the Schedule, and hence its IWC membership, rejected as contrary to the object and purpose of the ICRW) to the second (Iceland's reservation and membership accepted), concedes that the central legal point is not that one of them must be right and the other wrong, but that the applicable law left the decision in the hands of the IWC itself, suggesting that either conclusion is in principle supportable. Thus the rapid reversal is simply yet another manifestation of the trouble caused by the almost even division of views within the IWC, leaving any decision vulnerable to shifting majorities. The historical overview of the reservations to the ICRW itself is persuasive, and, other things being equal, the present reviewer would share Professor Gillespie's conclusion. But they are not equal; the fatal omission is that he does not discuss at all the objection procedure; whatever the other merits of his reasoning, the reviewer does not see how any reservation to a treaty can be contrary to its object and purpose if, under an objection procedure within that treaty itself, any party could have exempted itself from the relevant provision at the time of its adoption. (Characteristically, Professor Gillespie defends the objection procedure as respecting the sovereignty of the IWC's members, seemingly oblivious to the damage it has done in fisheries commissions such as NAFO and ICCAT where it has undermined conservative fisheries management to the point where serious consideration is being given to putting disciplines on its invocation.)

There is a good if overly rhetorical critique of proposals for secret voting as contrary to the principle of transparency (pp. 418–419) in the brief chapter on the subject, but the purpose of the last two substantive chapters is unclear. There is a wealth of detail on official development assistance flows and budgeting within international organisations, but their relevance to the IWC, except on the debate about how the budget costs should be divided among its members, is not obvious. It is not necessary to defend the practice of vote-buying to note that States indifferent to whaling may well be acting quite rationally and maximising the benefits to their citizens by in effect treating not just their right to utilise the living resources of the high seas, but also their votes within relevant international organisations that they are eligible to join, as assets to be leased a year at a time. Since the rules of the game do not forbid them, it is the secrecy surrounding such transactions, more than the transactions themselves, that ought to be assailed. Of course, if the States involved are not prepared to admit they have engaged in them, it is reasonable to draw adverse conclusions about how acceptable they really are, or should be.

Professor Gillespie writes for the general reader rather than the legal specialist, and his terminology is therefore at times rather loose—for example, he has evidently thought it best to spare his readers the nuances of the law of treaties, consistently referring to parties to treaties as "signatories" and succumbing to the lamentable but ever more prevalent trend to misspell depositary as "depository" (e.g. several instances on pp. 388–390). Yet most of the numerous inaccuracies, major and minor, scattered throughout the text are less excusable because wholly avoidable, notably that on p. 296, where the astonishing assertion is made that in the *Southern Bluefin Tuna* case ITLOS "found that" Japan had breached its obligations under Articles 64 and 116–119 of UNCLOS, and the discussion of the blue whale unit on pp. 4–7 is marred by frequent confusion in use of that term between the actual catch limit and the unit in which it was expressed. A similar confusion between the international organisation and the treaty establishing it is evident in the decidedly odd formulation of a reservation "at the IWC" (p. 395, a subheading all the more puzzling for being within the chapter bearing the orthodox title "Reservations to the ICRW").

To some extent he may have been let down in this respect by his editors, for anachronisms too abound: e.g. he places a threat of trade sanctions from President Clinton in the context of a response to a Japanese announcement in 2002 (p. 121); only by recourse to the endnotes does one discover that the threat was made in 2000 when he still held that office. He gives the 1958 UN Conference on the Law of the Sea as the "Second" (p. 160), and a decade would need to be halved in length for his statement that it is "five decades since the moratorium on commercial whaling was agreed" (p. 357) to be true. More broadly, to judge by the endnote in which, several years out of date, UNFSA is still as described as "not yet in force" (p. 313), the references as a whole might have benefited from a thorough updating before publication. The problems are not confined to time but extend also to space: as the place is 1000km or more from the nearest open water, the references at p. 299 to the "marine environment of the South Pole" and of a "cetacean species which often resides at the South Pole" are especially jarring.

What, then, to make of Professor Gillespie's heroic but flawed book? Seeing wider problems though the prism of a single issue, in this case whaling, inevitably distorts the picture. Politically controversial questions are a game anyone can play, but lawyers are frequently bad at it because all too often they forget that most bad ideas are not illegal, and fall into the trap of setting themselves the impossible task of trying to show that their preferred position is not merely permitted by the law, but actually required to the exclusion of all others. Since the book is at its strongest when the opposing arguments are at their weakest, it is unlikely to persuade many waverers to his side, so that its main use seems destined to remain in preaching to the converted. If preservation of whales is accorded an importance beyond any other question of public policy, then perhaps it does not much matter what arguments are used to support this position. But those concerned for the fate of the world's hard-pressed fish stocks, to say nothing of the rule of law in international affairs, should approach this book with great caution. For the foreseeable future, the main task of whaling diplomacy must be to avoid a head-on collision between these desiderata. But the diplomatic element is a commodity that will remain in short supply for as long as normally level-headed and circumspect Ministers allow themselves to indulge in the sort of invective against those of a different persuasion that in any other international relations context would be unacceptable. Ultimately, though, even if for these reasons Professor Gillespie's book does not convince, its mostly measured tone will perhaps contribute to a return to civilised discourse which is the only way in which the IWC's members, pro- and anti-whaling alike, can extricate themselves from their self-imposed predicament.

ANDREW SERDY

Constitutionalism, Multilateral Trade Governance and Social Regulation.
Edited by C JOERGES and E U PETERSMANN. Oxford and Portland,
Oregon: Hart Publishing, 2006. 554 pp. £75.

The work under review is a collection of papers that have been revised and updated since
first presented at the conference on *Legal Patterns of Transnational Social Regulation
and International* held at the European University Institute (EUI) in September 2004.
The intention was to help develop the debate surrounding the complexity of the legal
networks of economic governance by way of a collection of cross-sectoral and interdis-
ciplinary analyses. Of particular interest to the editors was the question of how law can
help develop the legitimacy of governance beyond the State, and what different legal
sectors and disciplines see as significant in terms of economic governance. Accordingly,
a wide range of related issues are addressed by the contributors, who represent a mix
of political scientists and lawyers with a range of private, public, European, and international focuses. Most of the contributors are connected with the University of Bremen
and/or the EUI.

Although the approaches taken are diverse, the editors found sufficient commonalty
in subject matter to split the eighteen chapters into four sections. This helps to make
the large volume of material more manageable and also sheds light on the meaning of a
broad title. Section I, eight chapters, concentrates on constitutionalisation and judiciali-
sation within the World Trade Organisation (WTO), particularly what evidence there is
of such processes and their significance in terms of legitimacy and effectiveness of the
governance features. Section II, five chapters, addresses the emergence of transnational
governance arrangements for product safety; a prominent concern in this respect is the
achievement of a balance between protection of health and economic freedom. The third
section, three chapters, looks at the overlap between economic and environmental governance, and the practical difficulties that this can cause. The fourth section, a single chapter
by Joerges, suggests how a conflict of laws approach is a useful means of co-ordinating a
plurality of regimes when exact relationships are still being worked out.

It is unsurprising that the WTO, as the focal point of economic governance beyond
the State, is a prominent feature for analysis in the majority of contributions. There are
some contributions that focus on the WTO in isolation, such as Helmedach and Zangl's
chapter, which empirically compares dispute settlement under GATT and WTO. Most,
however, take a broader contextual approach and relate analysis of an aspect of the WTO
to regional arrangements and/or the growing significance of NGOs for economic governance, as well as social regulation in other sectors such as the environment or protection of
human health. This is in accordance with the broad title of the work.

A chapter that clearly indicates the impact of the WTO beyond matters of trade and
the legal complexities that can arise as a result is Gerstetter's. This chapter is about the
reasoning process of the WTO Appellate Body when faced with a regulatory measure in
a different sector. Analysis is centred on the reasoning in the well-known *Shrimp-Turtle
case.* In this case the substantive interests at stake were unrestricted trade and the protection of endangered species. Gerstetter believes that, depending on the judicial context,
and as a means of showing fidelity to the letter of the law and doing justice in a particular case, one can expect a varying degree of judicial balancing between strict textual
interpretation and a more policy-orientated approach in the decision. By analysis of the
reasoning, Gerstetter shows that balancing does occur, but that the Appellate Body is
careful, through subtle interpretation, to present it as a duty for the WTO members
themselves, in this case the US, to perform the balancing act when regulating in different
sectors which might affect trade. Gerstetter suggests that this subtle approach to balancing is a result of the Appellate Body needing to stay within the limits set by the WTO

members, who are the law making masters of the WTO, while at the same time taking account of the wider impact of the WTO beyond matters of trade. Gerstetter offers a useful insight into the decision making process. One can infer from Gerstetter's chapter that the dispute settlement process of the WTO can play a useful role in working out the intricacies of the developing legal system. However, it appears that there are inherent limits in the nature of the WTO judicial bodies, so any systemic coherence they can help build is likely to be subtle and a long term project.

In light of the inference above, it is appropriate that many other chapters seek to help resolve some of the complexities that define the state of flux which economic governance beyond the State finds itself in. Two dominant themes in this respect are analysis of the points of linkage between international trade law and other social regulation, and assessment of the legitimacy of the sources of this increasingly dense normative web. Particularly interesting in both respects is the status of the body of international standards that have grown up alongside the globalisation of trade but tend not to be considered as legally binding.

The WTO Technical Barriers to Trade Agreement relies upon international standards as the basis for judging whether national regulations are a barrier to trade. Those in accordance enjoy a rebuttable presumption of not being a barrier to trade. Schepel and Howse, in their respective chapters, address different aspects of how the TBT agreement deals with the interaction of international standards and international trade law.

Schepel offers an overview of the role of standards in international trade law; he concentrates on the loose manner in which the TBT agreement defines international standards. Schepel explains how, by not defining the category of relevant international standards by reference to a specific organisation, and not being sufficiently specific about the characteristics of a valid international standard, 'we are now left with a trade agreement obliging members to "use as a basis" normative material upon which the agreement sets no institutional, representational or procedural requirements.'(p. 409) The significance of this lacuna is increased when one reads Howse's account of how the TBT agreement, with the help of WTO dispute settlement interpretation, turns international standards into international law. The essential point is that the key clause in relation to the use that national regulators should make of international standards is susceptible to different interpretation. So far the Panel and the Appellate Body have offered indications that international standards are to be treated not as things that must be shown to have been taken into consideration, but as the law governing the situation. Thus standards not intended to have legal force appear to be transformed by the TBT agreement into international law.

The situation with the TBT agreement and international standards is another sign of a system that is still very much finding its feet. In a period of flux, when intricate relationships are still being worked out, an initial degree of flexibility in key agreements could be seen as appropriate, because, for example, it might enable judicial bodies to take new contexts which arise as a market develops into account. However, in this instance, Schepel suggests that the looseness in definition is a result of not wanting to specify the obvious body to provide the relevant standards 'as the body' because of the status of the International Standards Organisation (ISO) as a private organisation. As such, the benefits of any flexibility are replaced by confusion and uncertainty as to what characteristics are required of an international standard for it to be a valid one in this process. One can only hope that analyses such as those of Schepel and Howse will help the Appellate Body, when it next gets an opportunity, to better clarify the situation.

This is a large collection of generally well-written and thought provoking chapters, which collectively cover most of the major issues in the debate. The work as a whole would have benefited from a chapter setting out the meaning of key concepts. More specifically, the tendency in a number of chapters for developments to be described as 'constitutional' without there always being an adequate explanation of what is meant by this term is a potential source of confusion. Indeed, in a period of flux it may be a good idea to avoid conceptualising developments as constitutional because, certainly without explanation, the concept implies a sense of absoluteness and order much in contrast with the evolving condition that economic governance beyond the State finds itself in, as this work testifies.

MATTHEW W SAUL

Reclaiming Development in the World Trading System. By Y-S LEE. Cambridge: Cambridge University Press, 2006. xvi + 168 pp + bibliography + index. £40.

The issue of development in international trade law is not a new one. Nevertheless, it remains both contentious and pivotal in equal measure. The initiation of the Doha Development round of trade negotiations, as part of the ongoing evolution of the World Trade Organization, in 2001 was explicitly based upon the realisation that '[i]nternational trade can play a major role in the promotion of economic development and the alleviation of poverty....The majority of WTO members are developing countries. We seek to place their needs and interests at the heart of the Work Programme adopted in this Declaration' (para. 2).

But the rhetoric remains just that; the Doha round of trade talks quickly lost its way—old divisions resurfaced, with much of the debate centring on US-EU arguments over agriculture, though increasingly the debate has also become much more splintered. In any event, the high—if unrealistic—hopes of an early and principled settlement, in which developing countries would finally 'secure a share in the growth of world trade commensurate with the needs of their economic development' remains a distant objective.

Development, of course, cannot be achieved by trade alone; issues as far-ranging as monetary stability and sovereign debt, on the one hand, and good governance and human rights, on the other, indicate the complex nature of the topic. As the 1986 UN General Assembly Declaration on the Right to Development reminds us, '[t]he right to development is an inalienable human right by virtue of which every human person and all peoples are entitled to participate in, contribute to, and enjoy economic, social, cultural and political development, in which all human rights and fundamental freedoms can be fully realized'. Development is thus very much an all-encompassing process; some may dislike the notion of third-generation rights, but the language of the 1986 text nevertheless gets across very well the comprehensive nature of the issue.

And what a situation it is; poverty is not simply a socio-economic or political concept, it is a reality for a significant proportion of the global population. That is why the attempt to establish the New International Economic Order in the 1970s was so important to developing countries. True, it was unduly partisan at points, but for its proponents, it was a life-and-death attempt to reorder a system that was perpetually and unfairly biased against the poor majority—'life-and-death' because the poverty that results from lack of development was not (nor continues to be) an abstract issue.

It is into this context that one should read this short monograph. Though some may consider it almost passé to criticise the WTO and point out its failings, Lee's comments are not vague and impressionistic, but rather he provides a direct and incisive critique to highlight a very specific—and as the Epilogue shows—a very personal concern.

The purpose of Lee's work is two-fold; to highlight the inequities within the current regulatory system and to propose solutions thereto. Undoubtedly, many will disagree with his recommendations, on which I say something below. I would suggest, however, that even those who dislike his ideas will find it difficult to disagree as vehemently with his analysis of the current situation; thus, on that basis, this work has much to commend it. In particular, his discussion of present difficulties in the structure and operation of such issues as anti-dumping and safeguards highlights his deep knowledge both of the legal situation, as well as the wider economic context to which it relates.

But out of all the issues, Lee's principal concern is the adoption of WTO disciplines inhibiting policy flexibility and sovereign autonomy and the corresponding difficulties and restrictions these present for developing and least-developed countries. On this issue, he relies heavily upon the work of economist Ha-Joon Chang and the idea that developed countries today have removed the advantages which they themselves had. As Lee says, 'Chang notes that almost every developed country today, including those strongly advocating liberal market economies and open trade, employed state-led industrial promotion policies during their own development process, which often included trade protection. Yet after achieving economic development, they have been "kicking away the ladder" and preventing developing countries from adopting effective development policies by imposing regulations of international trade and policy recommendations against these development policies'. Lee, as a national of South Korea who has experienced the astonishing exponential growth in his own country, perhaps unsurprisingly seeks to expound internationally some of the ideas which that particular Asian Tiger has used to particularly useful effect.

In particular, Lee seeks—in his own words—to 'put back the ladder'; which he argues would be best achieved not only through reform of various current disciplines and a strengthening of the 'developmental' provisions of the WTO, but specifically through the adoption of two new mechanisms, a development-facilitation subsidy (DFS) and development-facilitation tariff. As he notes, '[w]e can provide a more development-friendly regulatory environment for trade by carefully calibrating preferential treatment to developing countries without altering the current regulatory framework for open trade in a fundamental way. To facilitate development, I have introduced the concept of the "sliding scale" in the DFT and DFS that would allow differentiated treatment to developing countries according to their respective development stages gauged by income levels' (p. 156).

This short book has much to recommend it, as well as giving policy-makers and commentators in this field much to think about (as well as argue over). If there is a substantive criticism, it is that Lee does not seem to place his ideas within the wider political economy or current political realities, at least as sufficiently clearly as he might. Noting that these suggestions would be good for developed countries' long-term security and prosperity is, I would suggest, neither particularly astute nor controversial. Nevertheless, as a challenge to the current situation, this book is an important part of a much wider debate.

D FRENCH

Defining Terrorism in International Law. By BEN SAUL. Oxford: Oxford University Press, 2006. xxxiii + 373 pp. £60.

Since the 1920s, the international community has grappled, unsuccessfully, to achieve a universal definition of terrorism and its associated terminology such as 'terror', 'terrorize' and 'terrorist', including in international law. This is despite international consensus on condemning the phenomenon of terrorism. Whilst a definition has been achievable at the domestic and even regional levels, this has not been possible yet at the international level where only partial definitions exist in relation to specified criminal acts, such as in United Nations sectoral anti-terrorism conventions and under international humanitarian law. However, as Saul notes, even here there is a significant disparity between the meaning of terrorism in the non-armed conflict context of the sectoral conventions, and the armed conflict context under international humanitarian law (p. 9).

The debate as to why and how terrorism should be defined has generated much discourse and many publications, including among lawyers and those engaged in international relations. Saul also seeks to address why terrorism should be defined, and more specifically why and how it may be criminalized (chapter 1), including the availability of possible defences and justifications for terrorist violence (chapter 2). Throughout, the author is concerned that the term 'terrorism' is too readily applied in both the national and international contexts, when it should in fact be reserved for the most serious of political offences which are not already criminalized under, for example, international humanitarian law. He is equally concerned that the Security Council will more readily utilise its Chapter VII powers, and that Member States will seek to extend the right of self-defence, in the absence of a clearly defined international crime. Any such actions have the potential for abuse, and are likely to erode established norms. However, the thrust and uniqueness of this book is its comprehensive survey of established and developing international norms on defining terrorism. Specifically, he considers in meticulous detail international and regional treaty law (chapter 3), customary international law (chapter 4) and international humanitarian law (chapter 5). This includes a most comprehensive survey of relevant State and institutional practice, as well as judicial decisions.

Saul's approach is primarily one of international criminal law, starting from the premise in chapter 1 of the desirability of creating an international crime of terrorism, which requires a clear, agreed definition. Certainly, it is a fundamental requirement of any criminal law that the legal elements are clearly identifiable, including the *actus reus* and *mens rea*. In addition to the legal certainty that a definition of terrorism would bring here, Saul refers to some of the practical and policy justifications. As far as the former is concerned, he argues that 'it is not possible coherently or systematically to describe, analyse, understand or ultimately counter the threat posed by terrorism unless there is basic agreement on what constitutes it' (p. 320). Clearly, this is of significance beyond an international criminal response to terrorism, including that it impacts upon the ability of the United Nations, and the Security Council in particular, to respond effectively and consistently to threats to international peace and security (pp. 45–57). Certainly this was one of the conclusions of the United Nations' High-Level Panel Report in 2005, which stated that the 'United Nations' ability to develop a comprehensive strategy has been constrained by the inability of Member States to agree on an anti-terrorism convention including a definition of terrorism'(See UN Doc. A/59/565, para 157). As far as policy considerations are concerned, Saul argues that' 'criminalization is a powerful symbolic mechanism for delineating internationally unacceptable behaviour, even if deterrence of ideologically motivated offenders is unlikely' (pp. 67–8). Certainly the characterization of some criminal acts as being 'terrorist' affords a certain degree of emotional and political stigmatization of particular importance to its victims, and places terrorist offences on a par with war crimes and crimes against humanity. However, it is here that much of the current international debate and impasse is concentrated, including on the political and other ideological motivations of any 'terrorist' acts.

Chapter 2 examines one key aspect of this policy debate, namely whether activities that some classify as 'terrorist violence' can ever be justified in law, or even be morally excusable, whether within or outwith the context of an armed conflict. On the former, Saul's examination includes the *jus ad bellium* and *jus in bello* aspects of self-determination struggles, which are key to the current impasse on Article 18 of the United Nations' draft comprehensive convention on international terrorism. Saul first concludes that recourse to force by those engaged in self-determination struggles is permitted when this right is forcibly denied by a repressive regime; to interpret otherwise would be to deny this fundamental human right. As far as *jus in bello* is concerned, Saul argues that this is sufficiently covered by the existing framework of international humanitarian law. He does advocate, though, a wide rather than narrow application of this framework, ensuring that those engaged in any form of legitimate liberation violence against a repressive regime are classified as lawful combatants rather than as terrorists. To do otherwise would be to deny such movements fundamental human rights. Saul argues that such an approach would also depoliticize the current definitional impasse. However, in addition to affording these actors protections available under existing international law, this would also ensure that they are bound by the associated obligations. In particular, under Article 51(2) Additional Protocol I 1977, 'acts of violence, the primary purpose of which is to spread terror among the civilian population' are specifically prohibited. Outside the armed conflict context, thought-provoking consideration is given to whether defences might be available to otherwise 'terrorist violence' under criminal law defences of self-defence, duress and necessity. This includes identification of legal or normative gaps, such as the absence of a defence for group actors accused of terrorism (p. 106).

The remainder of the book includes a most succinct, yet comprehensive, analysis of relevant state and institutional (regional and United Nations) practice in the development of hard and soft law terrorism norms towards achieving a universal definition. Whilst fully acknowledging and engaging current scholarship, the author concentrates on, and engages in much needed fresh critical analysis of, primary sources. Specifically, in Chapter 3, the normative development of defining terrorism is considered within international and regional treaty law. The author traces the drafting history of United Nations anti-terrorism conventions in order to highlight the normative developments towards, and the obstacles against, achieving a universal definition. One particularly difficult issue addressed is that of terrorist activities by state actors, currently part of the negotiations impasse on Article 18 of the draft comprehensive convention. Saul contends that there is a legitimate case to be made for criminalizing acts committed by state officials that amount to terrorism, especially when committed outside of an armed conflict context and beneath the threshold of crimes against humanity. Not only would this ensure that such acts would not fall into a moral and legal vacuum, but it would also ensure a moral symmetry with the criminalization of corresponding acts by non-state actors (p. 318).

Chapter 4 gives a thorough account of the creation of customary international law on terrorism, especially by tracing its normative development within the General Assembly and the Security Council. In addition to highlighting important normative differences between these two organs, the detailed analysis of the practice of the Security Council on terrorism prior to the terrorist attacks of 11 September 2001 is particularly noteworthy, especially as it has attracted little prior scrutiny yet reveals a significant change in practice pre and post 11 September 2001. Prior to that date, Security Council resolutions did not define terrorism, but rather designated specific incidents and types of violence by and against various actors as being terrorism in an inconsistent manner. However, following the 11 September 2001 terrorist attack, the Security Council practice changed significantly to imposing binding, quasi-legislative measures against terrorism in general, unconnected to specific incidents and unlimited in time, as illustrated by Security Council Resolution 1373. This has been coupled with a greater readiness to classify any act of terrorism as constituting a threat to international peace and security, regardless of its severity or international consequences. The author concludes that detailed analysis of customary international law reveals that, despite repeated condemnation and the presence of 'moral norms', no generic international crime nor distinct legal concept of terrorism exist currently (p. 90).

Finally, terrorism is considered in the context of international humanitarian law in Chapter 5. Firstly, historic developments which establish discrete concepts of terrorism in international humanitarian law are considered, including little-known prohibitions on terrorism. There is then a detailed examination of current developments and interpretations, including within the International Criminal Tribunal for the former Yugoslavia. It is concluded that the meaning of terrorism in international humanitarian law is both distinct from and narrower than its meaning outside. In particular, it is concerned with the literal instillation of fear rather than any politically motivated coercion of governments or international organisations.

Overall, Saul provides the reader with a most comprehensive review of existing legal norms, including innovative suggestions as to how current definitional difficulties may be minimized if not overcome. However, the weakness of the definitional approach, in terms of actual implementation, is that it is dependent upon the political will of States, which is not currently evident. As to the future, the inability of the international community to agree a universally accepted definition of terrorism in the wake of 11 September 2001 terrorist attacks, a time of unusual international consensus and momentum, does not bode well. Certainly it is difficult to see how the current impasse might be overcome, including agreeing a distinction between terrorism and legitimate national liberation and self-determination, and criminalizing state terrorism, as advocated by *inter alia* the Organisation of Islamic Conference, whose central cause is the Palestinian struggle for an independent state. The current *realpolitik* is such that it is most unlikely that the political will for a universal definition will exist, if ever, until current national liberation and self-determination struggles, including in Palestine, Lebanon, Syrian Golan, Kashmir and Jammu, have been justly and finally resolved. Nor is it likely that Israel and the US, nor their allies, would ever agree to defining and criminalizing the terrorist activities of States, including as the most frequently accused perpetrators of such acts.

In the meantime, general State and institutional practice does not suggest that States and international organisations feel impeded in their current counter-terrorism efforts in the absence of a universal definition. Rather, even despite the potentially *ultra vires* legislative nature of Security Council Resolution 1373 (2001), many States have ratified existing United Nations anti-terrorism sectoral conventions, and most States have complied at least in part with its national legislative and Counter Terrorism Committee reporting requirements. This may be reflective of a growing trend, whereby grounds of international legitimacy can be as influential and persuasive as international legality for international community action. This is to be expected in an arena such as international terrorism which is primarily concerned with issues of international peace and security, of which international criminal law is currently only one small part. This is not to say that a universal definition would not be beneficial—not least in ensuring more consistent domestic legislation and the non-violation of other existing norms including those of international human rights law—nor that the robust yet fair treatment of those engaged in international terrorist activities is not important; rather, it is to say that the achievement of such a definition is most unlikely in the current political climate.

In conclusion, whether or not the political will exists in the future to implement at least some of Saul's innovative and well-argued suggestions towards achieving a universal definition of terrorism, this excellent and thoroughly researched book will undoubtedly serve as an important source of reference to both practitioners and academics engaged on matters of terrorism. Both are likely to benefit especially from the parallel consideration of treaty, customary international and international humanitarian law which highlights areas of tension and inconsistency; the thorough and concise review of relevant State and institutional practice; and the progressive nature of Saul's arguments. It is also envisaged that the work will provide a most useful legal framework for further analysis, including for comparative studies of individual State and regional organisational norms with corresponding international norms.

KATJA L H SAMUEL

The UN International Criminal Tribunals; The Former Yugoslavia, Rwanda and Sierra Leone. By WILLIAM SCHABAS. Cambridge: Cambridge University Press, 2006. liii + 711 pp. £85hb, £43 pb.

This is another masterful book by William Schabas. Neither the title nor the sub-title tell us more than that this book is about these particular tribunals. In the preface, however, Schabas explains that 'with the three *ad hoc* tribunals organising their activities so as to complete their work by the end of the decade, this seemed a good point to attempt a stock-taking. Hopefully, the lessons and observations are of more than academic interest, and will guide the International Criminal Court as it develops its own judicial personality.'

Schabas selects the Special Court for Sierra Leone (and not the other 'hybrid' tribunals) for inclusion in his study because it, unlike those others, is 'a creature of international law, not domestic law,' (p. 6). Not all will see this distinction in such clear terms but, at the present time and given the contribution to international law made by the Special Court, an analysis of it alongside the ICTY and the ICTR is likely to be particularly useful to scholars and practitioners alike.

In Part 1 Schabas discusses the establishment of the tribunals, including their legitimacy and legality along with the sources of the applicable law. In Part II he considers their jurisdiction along with the crimes which may be charged. Part III is concerned with the substantive and procedural aspects of prosecution, whilst Part IV deals with the structure and administration of the tribunals. Within each part very detailed reference is made to judgments of the various tribunals and to other source material. There is, however, much more than this. Schabas uses his 'tribunal-watching' experience over the years to considerable effect when he addresses, amongst other issues, how each of the tribunals deals with difficulties in the execution of their respective orders. He concludes that in this 'the differences between the two types of tribunals based on the nature of their creation may be more theoretical than real...since the [Security] Council has never responded to any specific request from the [ICTY or the ICTR]... [and] there is nothing to prevent the Special Court from appealing to the Security Council to assist it' (pp. 58–59).

It is perhaps, surprising to see only three pages devoted to the 'legacy of the tribunals' (pp. 44–46) in a work of this size. In reality, however, the whole book is a statement of their legacy (which Schabas recognises at p. 44) since the International Criminal Court is not a completely different form of trial process, but one which owes much to the groundwork prepared by its predecessors both in terms of development of the crimes (along with ancillary issues) and in the process of trial.

Chapter 12 deals with the issue of evidence before the tribunals. Whilst this must, of necessity, be based upon the particular form of the rules of procedure and evidence for the individual tribunals, Schabas draws out some common issues. In all cases the test of admissibility is either that the evidence should be 'relevant' (Special Court) or 'probative' (ICTY and ICTR), see p. 453. There is, in reality, little difference in substance between these tests, since in determining admissibility the judges will be required to assess how relevant or how probable a piece of evidence is to prove a particular event or state of mind, assuming it is not inherently unreliable. An item of hearsay evidence may possess a degree of relevancy or probative value to make it admissible. Once it is admitted into evidence its weight can be assessed by those same judges, but acting now as deciders of fact. Schabas explains the admissibility of hearsay evidence (or more correctly, the absence of a rule of exclusion for this type of evidence) on the basis that 'judges are supposed to be able to make the relevant distinctions, and to appreciate when hearsay evidence may deserve some degree of weight,' (p. 479). Whilst this may be true, the real safeguard against the admissibility of hearsay evidence (which has troubled common law systems) is that the judges, unlike juries, give their conclusions on fact in the form of a reasoned judgment drawn from weighing the evidence available to them. These reasons and conclusions can then be assessed objectively by the Appeals Chamber.

Scholars and practitioners will have cause to be grateful to William Schabas for compiling such an authoritative and detailed work on the three tribunals. Such a work is likely to be supplemented by further accounts written by the judges themselves. See, for example, the story behind the composition of the Trial Chamber of the ICTY in *Prosecutor v Tadic* recounted by President Antonio Cassese in T. McCormack and C. Saunders (eds.), *Sir Ninian Stephen, a Tribute* (Melbourne, the Miegunyah Press, 2007) p. 191. Hopefully, William Schabas will produce a second edition of the present volume in due course to sweep up important decisions (and significant comment made by their former judges) before the work of these tribunals becomes merely part of the history of 'war crimes' tribunals.

PETER ROWE

International Human Rights and Humanitarian Law: Treaties, Cases, and Analysis. Edited By F F MARTIN, S SCHNABLY, R WILSON, J SIMON & M TUSHNET. Cambridge: Cambridge University Press, 2006. xxxii + 990 pp. £55.

This book, which is designed primarily for an American (student) audience, is published under the auspices of Rights International, The Center for International Human Rights Law, Inc. Rights International is a non-profit making organisation devoted to protecting and furthering the rights recognised in the Universal Declaration of Human Rights and other human rights and humanitarian instruments.

The book takes as its starting point an integrationist view of the fields of international human rights law and international humanitarian law. The authors argue that historically these fields may have developed in a somewhat "disjointed fashion", but hope to show that these areas have become increasingly integrated and "rely on each other for their own respective coherence". The authors claim that the integrationist approach adopted by them is supported by the texts of international human rights and international humanitarian treaties; they exemplify the fact that human rights treaties deal with issues of rights protections during armed conflicts (the subject that humanitarian law customarily covers) and humanitarian treaties often explicitly prohibit certain acts (such as genocide and crimes against humanity) that occur outside of armed conflict situations, the customary period of international human rights law application.

The book is divided into six chapters. The first chapter introduces an "Overview of International Human Rights and Humanitarian Law Development and their Protection Mechanisms". It includes material on the historical and conceptual origins of the two streams of protection and then examines the history and organisation of international protection mechanisms. Treaty-based and Charter-based procedures are highlighted. The treaty-based systems that are covered include: the International Criminal Court, the Human Rights Committee, the Committee on Elimination of Racial Discrimination, the Committee Against Torture, the Committee on Elimination of Discrimination Against Women and the Committee on Economic, Social and Cultural Rights, but strangely no mention is made of the Committee on the Rights of the Child and the Committee on the Protection of the Rights of All Migrant Workers and Members of their Families. The Charter-based systems covered include: the International Court of Justice, the International Criminal Courts for the Former Yugoslavia and Rwanda, the UN High Commissioner for Human Rights, the UN High Commissioner for Refugees, the International Labour Organisation (but not UNESCO), the ECOSOC 1235 and 1503

Procedures, Thematic and Country-based mechanisms (but nothing on the former Human Rights Commission or the new Human Rights Council). Regional human rights tribunals, including the European Court of Human Rights, the Inter-American Commission and Court of Human Rights, the African Commission and Court of Human and Peoples' Rights and (interestingly) the Caribbean Court of Justice are covered, as are certain other specialist tribunals such as: the Human Rights Commission for Bosnia and Herzegovina, the East Timor Tribunal, the Special Court for Sierra Leone and the Extraordinary Chambers in the Court of Cambodia.

The second chapter deals with "Formal Sources and Principles of International Human Rights and Humanitarian Law". This chapter consists of a number of sections on: formal sources (with sub-sections on treaties, custom and *jus cogens*), principles of treaty interpretation, principles of liability (with sub-sections on State liability, individual liability, conspiracy and corporate responsibility and defences). Each of these sections follows a pattern of exposition, relevant extracts (primary materials, case law and academic commentary) and analysis by way of "questions & comments".

The third chapter is directed principally at a U.S. law student audience and deals with "Incorporation of International Human Rights Law and Humanitarian Law in U.S. Law". This chapter consists of three sections on: construction rules, conflict rules and the self-execution doctrine; each of these sections has several pertinent sub-sections; the familiar pattern of primary materials, case law and academic commentary, supported by "questions & comments" is adopted.

The fourth chapter deals with "International Human Rights Tribunal Procedure and Remedies". This chapter consists of four sections on: jurisdiction, standing, exhaustion of domestic remedies and remedies and State compliance. Within the familiar structure, there are also extracts from the jurisprudence of the Inter-American Court of Human Rights, the European Court of Human Rights and the Human Rights Committee.

Chapter 5 (which is over 600 pages in length) covers "Substantive International Human Rights and Humanitarian Law Protections". The chapter includes substantial material on the whole range of civil and political rights, genocide, crimes against humanity and war crimes. Economic, social and cultural rights are given much more perfunctory treatment with sub-sections on: instruments, employment and property. The pattern of the previous chapters is adopted and each sub-section concludes with "questions & comments".

The final chapter is entitled "Critique and Theory" and contains seven extracted academic commentaries together with "questions & comments", intended to expose the student to more abstract and critical analysis.

The book contains also two Tables: one on "Selected International Instrument Citations" and the other on "Selected Cases, General comments, & Advisory Opinions".

This treaties, cases and analysis book is aimed unashamedly at the U.S. (particularly student) market; this is highlighted repeatedly by the authors. Thus, one of the justifications for chapter three (on incorporation of international law norms in U.S. law), is stated to be that: "[t]he comparative analysis with U.S. law may offer a small contribution to demystifying and clarifying to a U.S. audience the ramifications of a full commitment to human rights and humanitarian law". So too, the selection of particular issues in chapter 5 (such as abortion, the death penalty, torture, gay rights, war crimes, genocide, discrimination, free speech and economic, social and cultural rights) is justified on the ground that: "[w]e believe that a U.S. law student audience would find [them] especially interesting and timely". No doubt this book will be well received by U.S. students, but whether it will be as successful here is somewhat open to doubt: the treatment given to the topics is very broad brush, with insufficient attention to detail; while regard is paid to academic literature with excerpted articles, the attention given to the serious academic literature in the footnotes is not substantial, and nor is there any sort of bibliography. The procedure of international human rights tribunals is given very limited treatment. It is also somewhat surprising to find no reference to the landmark decision of the Constitutional Court of South Africa in the *Treatment Action Campaign* case in the context of economic, social and cultural rights.

SANDY GHANDHI

Democracy, Minorities and International Law. By STEVEN WHEATLEY. Cambridge: Cambridge University Press, 2005. 201 pp. £50.

This book seeks to examine a controversial topic which is rarely far from the news and looks set to challenge the international agenda for the foreseeable future. A logical approach is taken to the topic in three principal chapters, starting with the rights of minorities (from the League of Nations onwards), continuing with the right to self-determination and then considering the right to democracy. The overall objective is to consider cultural minorities under international law and the accommodation of diversity in democratic States. As that overview suggests, the book has a structured argument, clearly expressed and eminently readable.

Although noting that the United Nations instituted a system of respect for individual human rights rather than minority rights (p. 10), Wheatley proceeds to outline the present international human rights regime, extracting provisions which impact on 'minorities' then focussing on Article 27 of the International Covenant on Civil and Political Rights, with the necessary discussion of the applicable definition and scope of 'minorities' (p. 17 et seq). As the author concludes '[e]thno-cultural groups are imagined communities' of whom it is not possible to provide a typography (p. 62). This is unproblematic in the present text as, pointedly, the author notes that '[t]he recognition of "minority rights" does not work to eliminate difference, but to maintain (cultural) difference' (p. 22). All too frequently this is overlooked in the area of minority rights and, especially, with indigenous peoples, where assimilationist overtones permeated earlier instruments (eg ILO Convention No. 107,1957). A range of standard cases on minorities before the Human Rights Committee and other bodies is referenced, as is a wide range of academic commentary to support consideration of treaty provisions and soft law, concluded under the auspices of the United Nations and regional (European) organisations.

Discussion on the right to cultural security (pp. 34 et seq) is particularly interesting and relevant, one of a range of rights which may require 'positive measures' on the part of States. Indeed, the right to cultural security forms the central tenet of the thesis expounded in the text: 'decentralisation of power to local communities increases the possibilities that minority groups may effectively participate in decision-making' (p. 64). This kind of internal self-determination, or partial autonomy, whereby the State retains authority over matters such as foreign policy but the group enjoys independence of decision on, for example, education, is the main thrust of this second chapter.

For self-determination, a distinction is drawn between minorities and national minorities, who seek cultural security, and indigenous and other peoples seeking 'classic' self-determination. Given the focus of the book, attention is given to self-determination as a conflict resolution tool for addressing conflict caused by breaches of cultural rights and practices. The right of peoples to self-determination, in the book's context, is stated as requiring representative government (p. 142), a controversial contention but one with clear benefits for States seeking to avoid the spectre of separatism.

The final chapter moves the text away from conventional discussions of minority rights and self-determination, positing a solution in the democratic rights contained in the International Covenant on Civil and Political Rights. Drawing on political science, democratic theories are analysed in an international law framework. It is in this chapter that the innovative features of the argument are most apparent (although the preceding chapters methodically, and usefully, provide the groundwork). The right to democracy is meticulously analysed, drawing on a range of primarily civil and political rights. Rights to self-determination and democratic government are linked (with corroboration sought from the work of the Human Rights Committee) (p. 136) which then leads to a discussion on equal rights to political participation, linking to the preceding chapter. The thorny issue of parliamentary representation raises many issues for States with a plurality of identities. Given the continuing discussion concerning gender equality, such 'cultural equality' is clearly a goal not yet achieved. Interesting links can be drawn to subsidiarity (evinced in the EU) and devolution (eg in the UK), both mechanisms by which the organisation/State can ensure greater political participation of a range of peoples in an organisation/State. Consociational societies and governance is considered as a goal, with an analysis of the arrangement pertaining in deeply divided States such as Bosnia-Herzegovina.

Overall, the emphasis is on creating democratic societies in accordance with models conducive to the co-existence of a multiplicity of cultural identities within the State. According to Wheatley's argument, diverse democratic models can ensure that the State does not adversely impact on cultural identity (eg separation of religion and State) and/or that minorities and other peoples are adequately represented within democratic decision-making mechanisms thereby dissipating any tension. 'Cultural conflicts in a democratic State should be resolved in a way that is either acceptable or defensible and defeasible to all citizens, including persons belonging to ethno-cultural minorities' (p. 198). An admirable sentiment to conclude an enjoyable book, but like so much of international law and human rights, it remains to be seen whether the rhetoric can be matched by reality. In the interim, this book is a useful contribution to legal literature and political and legal discussions on democracy, minorities and international law.

RHONA SMITH

International Criminal Accountability and the Rights of Children. Edited By KARIN ARTS and VESSELIN POPOVSKI. The Hague: The Hague Academic Press, 2006. 191 pp. £38.

This is a very interesting book, collecting together essays from a number of distinguished contributors, surrounding the issue of children and armed conflict. Its raison d'etre is neatly summed up in a quotation, found on the opening page, from a UNICEF Report, *Humanitarian Action Report 2005,* where it is stated:

'During emergencies, children are especially vulnerable to disease, malnutrition and violence. In the last decade, more than 2 million children have died as a direct result of armed conflict, and more than three times that number have been permanently disabled or seriously injured. An estimated 20 million children have been forced to flee their homes, and more than 1 million have been orphaned or separated from their families. Some 300,000 child soldiers—boys and girls under the age of 18—are involved in more than 30 conflicts worldwide'.[1]

It is divided into three main sections. Part I deals with international law, criminal accountability and the rights of the child. Part II discusses the criminal responsibility of minors and Part III covers the unfolding practice in international courts. The book

---

[1] New York, UNICEF 2005, p.VII.

is more descriptive of matters throughout, rather than presenting a very detailed analytical critique although, of course, there is critical analysis, and is unique in the way that it focuses on different accountability mechanisms for serious violations of the rights of children. It provides an excellent launch pad for anyone interested in the rights of children in international law and who wishes to have an overview.

Chapter One, written by Karin Arts, provides a general introduction. She clearly defines both the scope and the limits of the book. She points out that the focus is mainly on war crimes, crimes against humanity and genocide. Thus she acknowledges this leaves many areas of crimes against and injustice towards children uncovered, but there is, of course, a limit to what can be considered. She stresses the importance of the United Nations Convention on the Rights of the Child (CRC) and its three general principles concerning children, the best interests of the child, non-discrimination and participation. The best interests principle is particularly important in relation to the prosecution of child perpetrators and she argues that holding children accountable does not necessarily require criminal proceedings, a large range of other options exist. Impunity for children may not be the sensible option as it might encourage those recruiting and forcing children to participate as child soldiers to assign them the 'dirtiest' tasks. In other chapters in the book some of the examples given of crimes committed not just on, but also by, children are indeed truly stomach churning.

William Schabas considers the rights of the child and customary international law in Chapter Two via the two important decisions of *Roper v Simmons*[2] and the Sam Hinga Norman case.[3] In *Roper v Simmons* the US Supreme Court ruled the imposition of the death penalty for crimes committed while under the age of eighteen to be unconstitutional, finding it in breach of the Eighth Amendment which forbids 'cruel and unusual punshment'. Schabas argues this has important consequences well beyond the United States of America. Sam Hinga Norman was indicted, amongst other things, in the Special Court for Sierra Leone (SCSL) for conscripting or enlisting children under 15 into armed forces. Schabas provides an interesting analysis of the reasoning of the decision and concludes that there is doubtful justification for the eventual outcome'.

Chapter 3 by Vesselin Popovski provides a clear description of the law and practice of the UN regarding children's rights in situations of armed conflict and contains useful cross-references and allusions to issues arising in some of the other chapters . This is followed in Chapter 4 by a discussion of child participation at the Sierra Leone Truth and Reconciliation Commission, written by Sandamini Siegrist, whilst An Michels discusses the support given to especially vulnerable witnesses at the Commission in Chapter 10. Siegrist warns that although actively involving children can assist in providing accountability, special measures need to be put in place in order to ensure that children are not exposed to further harm. Michels develops this theme further, pointing out the divided loyalties that many children face and the difficulties that child ex-combatants and victims of sexual abuse may face in reintegrating into their communities. Michels provides two very thought provoking final paragraphs on the issue of compensation for victims and whether or not they should acquire 'party' status in such proceedings.

Chapters 5 and 6 by Matthew Happold and Claire McDiarmid concentrate on the criminal responsibility of children. Happold considers their responsibility at international level and the difficulty raised by the fact that it is unclear what the minimum age of criminal responsibility is in respect of international crimes. McDiarmid looks at four possible models for the age of criminal responsibility in national legal systems: an irrebuttable presumption of lack of criminal capacity; age as a gateway into the adult system;

---

[2] 543 US 551 (2005).
[3] *Prosecutor v Norman* Case No. SCSL-2004–14-AR72(E), Decision on Preliminary Motion Based on Lack ofturisdiction (Child Recruitment) 31 May 2004.

age as conferring immunity from prosecution; and finally absolute incapability followed by a rebuttable presumption of incapability. She follows this with a consideration of issues required to establish whether a child should bear responsibility.

Angela Veale in Chapter 7 considers psychological matters arising from the criminal responsibility of former child soldiers. She raises a lot of questions but provides no easy answers and in particular concludes that there are so many influential variables that any judgment on the developmental and psychological capability to participate in a restorative justice initiative would probably need to be considered on a case-by-case basis.

Luis Moreno-Ocampo provides a brief introduction to the rights of children and the International Criminal Court (ICC) in Chapter 8, followed by David Crane's brief history of the conflict leading up to the establishment of the SCSL in Chapter 9. The mandate of the Court is to try those who bear the greatest responsibility for serious violations of international humanitarian law and Crane lays out the challenges faced by the court and himself as prosecutor, in laying charges against those using children in a conflict. David Tolbert is similarly a prosecutor, this time at the International Tribunal for the Former Yugoslavia (ICTY), the work of which he discusses in Chapter 11. This chapter is especially stimulating in raising and discussing a number of difficult issues surrounding the use of child witnesses and whether and to what extent children who testify should be treated differently from other witnesses. His presentation is particularly interesting and thoughtful.

In Chapter 12 Jenny Kuper considers military training regarding children and the international accountability of military personnel for violations against children. The international courts pay particular attention to crimes committed against children and thus in aiming to deter such violations the prosecution of military personnel should be highlighted. She selects cases from both Yugoslavia and Rwanda to illustrate this point. Finally, before the concluding chapter, Nuala Mole, in Chapter 13, looks at the work of the European Court of Human Rights (ECHR). She looks at the only three cases so far to reach the court which have directly concerned children and conflict, *Aydin* v *Turkey*[4] *Isayeva* v *Russian Federation*[5] and *Behrami* v *France*.[6] The cases involved sexual violence in *Aydin* and indiscriminate attacks on civilians in *Isayeva,* and in which breaches of Article 2, the right to life and Article 3, the prohibition on torture and ill-treatment, were found. *Behrami* was different as it involved a failure to act by the French military. She also considers two UK cases, *Osman* v *United Kingdom*[7] and *Z and Others* v *United Kingdom*[8], which were purely national decisions but which had implications on the failure to protect the life of a child in *Osman* and the failure to protect from inhuman or degrading treatment in *Z and Others*. Mole goes on to consider further purely national decisions, the conjoined decisions of *T* v *United Kingdom* and *V* v *United Kingdom*,[9] *Hussain* v *United Kingdom*[10] and *Singh* v *United Kingdom*[11] all of which were cases involving children accused of murder. In all four cases the UK was found wanting and from all four it is clear that the young age of the defendants and their potential to develop and change were taken into account in deciding whether there had been any breach of the Convention. Because of this all of them have ramifications for the international prosecution of children.

The book concludes with a Chapter by Hans van Ginkel with some summarising observations. He highlights that the book contributes towards the bridging of two concepts—the development of international criminal justice and the protection of the rights of children. He comments that there is an emerging consensus that children should be free from prosecution in international courts, but should only be held accountable in

[4] No. 23178/94, 28 June 1997, 25 EHRR251 (1998).
[5] No. 57947,48 and 49/00, 24 February 2005.   [6] No. 71412/01.
[7] No. 23452/94, 28 February 1998, 29 EHRR 245 (2000).   [8] No. 29392/10 May 2001.
[9] Nos. 24724/94 and 24888/94, 30 EHRR 121 (2000).   [10] No. 21928/93, 21 February 1996.
[11] No. 23389/94, 21 February 1996.

domestic courts if appropriate. Furthermore, on the issue of accountability, all mechanisms should be child oriented and child friendly. There are many subjects for further discussion and research and van Ginkel concludes by raising some of the issues that are still to be explored and developed.

Overall this is a thoroughly useful and interesting collection of essays, which should be of interest to a wide readership. Anyone with an interest in the rights of children, criminal law, human rights law and international law would certainly find this a helpful addition to their collection.

CATHERINE WILLIAMS

Sexual Orientation Discrimination in the European Union: Nationality Laws and the Employment Directive. By C WAALDIJK and M BONINI-BARALDI. The Hague: TMC Asser Press, 2006. 256 pp. £48.

Waaldijk and Bonini-Baraldi have written an analytic account of how the Directive 2000/78/EC establishing a general framework for equal treatment in employment and occupation (in force 2 December 2003) has been transposed into the laws of the current 27 Member States of the European Union, insofar as the Directive covers lesbians, gays and bisexuals ('LGB people'). It was not until 1999 that the institutions of the European Community gained the competence to issue directives on matters such as discrimination against homosexuals in employment and the Council acted promptly in respect of religion or belief, disability, age and sexual orientation. It should be noted that this Directive goes under several names e.g. the 'Framework Directive'; this book calls it the 'Employment Equality Directive' which has the merit of demonstrating that the Directive applies to employment, read broadly, and not, for example, to schools and goods and services (cf. the Directive 2000/43 implementing the principle of equal treatment between persons irrespective of racial or ethnic origins, the 'Race' Directive).

Chapters are written by the individual author and a good deal of the book is based on the work of the European Group of Experts on Combating Sexual Orientation Discrimination, established by the Commission in 2002 to report on the implementation of the Directive in respect of LGB people in the then 15 Member States. The Report, published in 2003 and updated in 2004, was edited by this book's authors and was entitled *Combating Sexual Orientation Discrimination in Employment: Legislation in Fifteen EU Member States—Report of the European Group of Experts on Combating Sexual Orientation Discrimination, About the Implementation up to April 2004 of Directive 2000/78/EC establishing a General Framework for Equal Treatment in Employment and Occupation,* 2004, Universiteit Leiden, Leiden. The Report, which is available at www.emmeiiers.nl/experts as well as on the European Commission's website (in English and French), is divided into chapters dealing with each of the then Member States and is well worth reading in its own right. For example, the chapters on Ireland and the United Kingdom by Mark Bell and Robert Wintemute respectively may be singled out as of interest to readers who wish for a very good introduction to present law on sexual orientation discrimination in the British Isles.

The book under review is a synoptic overview of the Report together with material provided by lawyers on the ten Member States which have recently acceded and the two states, Bulgaria and Romania, which were about to become members at the time of the writing of the text, together with the work of the European Network of Legal Experts in the Non-Discrimination Field, particularly the country reports in *Report on Measures to Combat Discrimination* (Utrecht/Brussels, Human Consultancy & Migration Policy Group, 2004 and 2005). The chapter division reflects this distinction and the core of the book is chapters 4 and 5 entitled 'Comparative analysis of legislation implementing the Directive in the fifteen old member states' and 'Implementation of the Directive in the ten new Member States and in the two acceding states'. It should be noted that of the 'old' 15 Member States Germany, Greece and Luxembourg had not enacted legislation to transpose the directive into national law and that accordingly they are omitted from the analysis. Other chapters focus on how the Directive came about (including a study of the European Convention on Human Rights' application to LGB people and the European Court of Justice's refusal to apply Article 141, previously 119, on equal pay between men and women to LGB people while extending its protection to transgendered people), on pre-existing national protection for LGB people (Table 5 on pp. 73–5 is particularly helpful in this regard), on the interpretation of the Directive (e.g. the Directive applies to sexual orientation but does it apply to sexual behaviour?) and on comparing Member States' implementation of the Directive. The Directive itself appears in an Annex. There is a bibliography, tables of cases and legislation and an index.

The book suffers from the defects of highly analytical accounts in that other material is simply not there. There are surveys found in tables on pp. 62–3 on whether 'straight' people would not like homosexuals to live next to them and whether homosexuality is ever justified: the figures are to say the least varied across the EU. There is also the table on p. 83 detailing the decriminalisation of sexual acts between adult males and the recognition of same-sex partnerships. However, these examples going beyond the implementation of the Directive are rare in the book and there is for instance, no discussion on whether the Directive has increased the acceptance of homosexuality (e.g. has homosexual harassment declined in the workplace?). There are some cryptic remarks such as (p. 48) whether negative statements about homosexuality may constitute harassment (an issue 'requiring a sensitive balancing act on the part of those responsible for enforcing the rules of the Directive') but discussing the width of the Directive's concepts is not the primary focus of the book, though there are some pointed comments in the final chapter about the vague wording of the Directive. The discussion of the interaction between homosexuality and religions (pp. 50–1 and 126–8) is particularly compressed and unhelpful to those engaged in determining the boundaries between religion or belief legislation and the sexual orientation legislation under review: the reviewer looked for Catholicism and Islam in the index but the relevant passages in the book are found in the index under 'Churches', 'Religion or belief' and 'Religious employment'. It is accepted that this book is not about empirical matters and that it may still be too early to grapple with such issues, but the book has to be read with other material to understand not just the state of the law but the efficacy of that law. The book came out before there were any decisions of the ECJ interpreting the Directive. As may be expected in an analytical approach there is a degree of repetition e.g. the restriction of French law to protection of LGB people themselves with the result that it does not apply to *perceived* sexual orientation is mentioned at several different points.

The reviewer was impressed by the tables, particularly Table 8 on p. 148, 'Major shortcomings in the implementation of the Directive' but the print is very small and colour would have been helpful. It is also not immediately evident how the legislation in each individual Member State falls short of all of the Directive's provisions. For example, a reader from one of the Member States may wish for a subchapter dealing with all the deficiencies in that State's provisions but one has to go through the authors' relevant chapter to understand that State's partial (or total) non-implementation of the Directive, though the diagram on p. 148, mentioned above, is helpful in this respect. On the basis of that table of the then 15 Member States (but excluding Greece, Germany and Luxembourg for the reason stated above) France, Italy, Portugal and the UK appear to be the worst offenders. The reviewer would especially point to the discussion of indirect discrimination (pp. 100–2) as demonstrating the principal areas in which current UK law falls short of the Directive's requirements, but the whole of the Chapter repays careful study.

The book is extremely well-produced and is well-written (though the sub-heading 'A certain implementation of the Directive' on p. 209 is strange to Anglo-Saxon ears); orthographical errors are vanishingly small. The phrase 'chaotic and fragmented' is used on p. 217 to describe the multi-level character of discrimination law across geographic Europe, but could also be used of the failures to transpose the directive across the now 27 Member States of the European Union. In sum, the book is a splendid addition to the bookshelves of any discrimination lawyer, whether in the EU or beyond.

M JEFFERSON

European Union Law: Text and Materials. Edited By DAMIAN CHALMERS, CHRISTOS HADJIEMMANUIL, GIORGIO MONTI & ADAM TOMKINS. Cambridge: Cambridge University Press, 2006. 1235 pp. £35 pb.

A new book on European law combining text, cases and materials over more than 1,200 pages will inevitably be compared to its main competitor in the market for European legal literature, the "bible" on European law: Craig and de Burca's *EU Law* available in the 4th edition from autumn 2007.

The book under review comprehensively covers the institutional and substantive law of the European Union, including the history of European integration, the different aspects of European constitutionalism, the EU's institutions, law making powers and administrative law, as well as the internal market with the four freedoms, competition law and policy, anti-discrimination law and financial services. When published in 2006 it had one major advantage: within its range of comprehensiveness it was the only book available that was up-to-date, stating the law as at 30 September 2005 and taking into account the, by then rejected, draft Constitutional Treaty as a reference point and possible point of departure for the future development of EU law. Naturally, over time this advantage will evaporate. Others, however, will remain. The book is elegantly written which makes it very readable and highly accessible, in particular to a student audience. The re-printed materials are very well chosen and edited. Even notoriously difficult writers, like Jürgen Habermas and Jacques Derrida, become easily accessible and the reader can fully engage with the thoughts of a wide range of important legal, political, social and philosophical thinkers, such as Joseph Weiler, Neil Walker, Fritz Scharpf, Neil MacCormick and Mario Monti to name but a few.

The authors themselves try to keep a balance between an in general positive view of the European project and a sceptical analysis of European law and its working in practice. At points the book is very critical, in particular in respect of the ECJ's case law. One example in the context of EU fundamental rights protection may suffice here (at p. 241): "It would seem that Community law has reached a position where it recognises a very wide variety of rights as fundamental. Yet the reasons for recognising these rights in this way have been left undetermined. This has led to a great deal of uncertainty about effectiveness and meaning of these rights, as well as to confusion about their relationship to each other. As there is no clear underpinning logic, the circumstances when one will be preferred to the other are completely unclear." Overall the authors get the balance right, however. And even the sharpest critique is never polemical or off-putting, but always thought provoking and productive.

On the downside, the book seems on some topics to somewhat lag behind Craig and de Búrca's in terms of the detail provided. One example is the different aspects of vertical and horizontal direct and indirect effect of EC law and of directives in particular;

another, the issues surrounding the Cilfit-doctrine in the context of the preliminary ruling procedure. One can, however, ask whether in fact one needs to know more than the book under review provides; and those readers who want to dive deeper into a specific subject matter can easily do so by consulting the very up-to-date recommended reading that accompanies each chapter. Overall, it is probably fair to say that the accessibility and readability of the book by far outweigh any limitation on the information provided that there might be.

European Union Law, therefore, has to be welcomed as enrichment to the market for European legal literature. Its readability makes it particularly well suited for students both at undergraduate and postgraduate level. Practitioners too might find the sections on substantive law and competition law particularly useful. For researchers on European law the book will be able to provide an important starting point for further inquiry. Consequently, the book can be highly recommended and should not be missing in any European and international law library.

M SCHILLIG

The Constitution for Europe: A Legal Analysis. By JEAN-CLAUDE PIRIS. Cambridge: Cambridge University Press, 2006. xxiii + 267 pp. £50 hb, £22.99 pb.

On 29 May and 1 June 2005 respectively the draft Treaty on a Constitution for Europe was rejected by public referendum in two founding Member States: France and The Netherlands. Subsequently, the heads of State of the EU Member States decided to extend the ratification process until 2007 and to enter a "period of reflection" on the future of the draft Constitutional Treaty and the EU as a whole. Whilst in some Member States compulsory or promised public referendums were put on hold, other Member States went ahead. At the time of writing, 18 Member States have ratified the draft Treaty. At the same time the enlargment process continues with Bulgaria and Romania having joined in January 2007 resulting in a total of 27 Member States. This makes the reform of the EU institutions and procedures with the aim of increased democracy and efficiency ever more pressing. As a result, the German presidency of the Council has put the re-vitalisation of the constitutional process high on its agenda for the first half of 2007. Whatever the outcome of these efforts may be, it seems likely that any future considerations of institutional and procedural reform within the EU will take the draft Constitutional Treaty as its starting point. In order to have an informed opinion in these future discussions, detailed knowledge of the existing draft Treaty appears indispensable.

This book is a clear and concise study of the main aspects and characteristics of the draft Constitutional Treaty. After a brief introduction summarising the history of European integration, The book opens with a question: "Is the Constitution for Europe 'dead and buried'?". This first chapter contains a careful analysis of the two 'No' votes in France and The Netherlands together with a look back at the earlier occurrences of negative referendums in Denmark on the Maastricht Treaty in 1992 and in Ireland on the Treaty of Nice in 2001. The author concludes that a better economic and social situation, greater popularity of the national governments and better information on the EU and the content of the Constitution would have led to a different result, given that a majority of French and Dutch people wish their countries to continue to participate in the integration process (p. 23). Since the ratification process at least officially continues it is, according to Piris too soon to pronounce the Constitution or its content 'dead and buried' (p. 30). However, at some point the French and Dutch governments will have to decide whether to hold a second referendum. If they decide against it, the problem of institutional reform will remain. One way forward offered by the author could be to take the present text as a starting point to negotiate a new, simplified and shortenes Treaty; another would be to cut the Constitution into pieces and adopt it bit by bit. Both options seem to be politically difficult. In any event, according to the author any future European integration seems inconceivable as long as France appears to have said 'No'. Therefore a second referendum in France may be unavoidable. The basis could be the present text with added declarations or protocols addressing concrete issues of concern to the French people, as was done in Denmark and Ireland. The author calls upon the EU institutions to put an end to the lack of knowledge on the part of the citizens by developing a "proactive communication strategy". "The aim should not be self-congratulation on each and every EU initiative, but to obtain increased media attention, so as to stimulate a public debate and a political discussion.... This implies, rather than hiding disputes and difficulties, the EU decision making process should make them more apparent, in order to better attract the attention of the media." (p. 35).

The second Chapter deals with the political background and process that led to the Constitutional Treaty. The author identifies the "pressure of the coming enlargements" as the driving force behind the constitutional process (p. 40). Interestingly, the work of the "Convention of the Future of Europe" as convened by the European Council in the "Laeken Declaration" of 2001 was carried out without the presence of any Legal Advisers or Legal Service. Consequently, "from a legal and drafting point of view, the text of the Constitution as drafted by the Convention was not very good" (p. 50). "For instance, if the text as drafted by the Convention had been kept unchanged, the Commission would have legally 'disappeared' upon entry into force of the Constitution, due to the absence of proper transitional provisions." (p. 53). In order to be adopted by the IGC, the final text had to be revised by a "Working Party of Legal Experts" which was chaired by the author. As Legal Adviser and Head of Secretariat of the IGC, he is best placed to give an insightful account into the procedures and deliberations which led to the final text.

In Chapter III on the "Changes in structures and procedures", we learn that the draft Constitutional Treaty, despite its often criticised length, actually reduces the number of pages of primary law considerably from 2,800 pages to 560 pages (p. 58) and leads to a considerable simplification of the EU structure and procedures. The author also highlights the fact that by codifying existing categories of comptences and long standing principles of law in Part I the constitution makes these principles more tranparent without any change in substance.

Chapter IV deals with the institutional changes introduced by the draft Constitution. The main focus of the book in this part is on the two most contentious issues: (i) qualified majority voting (QMV) in the Council; and (ii) the structure of the Commission. The author does not just give a comprehensive account of the rules laid down by the Constitution, but also describes in detail the debate during the Convention and the IGC which led to the respective provisions. In relation to QMV, he writes that the compromises reached "caused further collateral damage to the supposed simplicity of the new QMV system, thus undermining one of the main arguments which were used to support the introduction of this system. One could even see the new system as less simple and less transparent than the classic weighted voting system ... " (p. 105).

At the beginning of Chapter V on the changes in substance, the author makes it absolutely clear that the Constitution does not confer on the EU substantive new areas of competences and that in this respect the text is "far from being revolutionary" (p. 132). One of the most visible changes however, is the incorporation in full of the EU Charter of Fundamental Rights as Part II of the Constitution. According to the author, this is not just a symbolic change but also one of substance (p. 134). Given that human rights are already protected under the jurisprudence of the European Court of Justice the explanation for this change in substance remains somewhat lacking. It is here that he could have been more critical. He highlights, however, the fact that, as a symbol, the "bill of rights" could easily backfire. The list does not just contain enforceable rights but also principles which merely have to be respected by the legislature and Member States are only addressees when they are implementing EU law. Therefore the ordinary citizen could easily be disappointed when relying on the "fundamental rights" in Part II of the Constitution. "The symbol is powerful, but it could possibly over-simplify the real situation." (p. 142). Further substantive improvements mainly concern the areas of Common Foreign and Defence Policy (CFSP) and Justice and Home Affairs (JHA). In respect of each, the author provides a short history of the development of the respective area within the EU, followed by a detailed analysis of the innovations brought about by the Constitution and their critical evaluation.

In Chapter VI the author offers a general assessment of the text based on two premises: does the Constitution fulfill the agendas set by the 2000 Nice Declaration and by the 2001 Laeken Declaration and what are its legal, social and economic implications? (p. 179). As for the former, according to the author, the Constitution, although far from being perfect, would lead to more clarity, tranparency, democracy and efficiency, bearing in mind that the special multi-layered character of the Union sets natural limits to any attempts at simplification and reduction (p. 180). Legally the Constitution is not a revolution and changes neither the nature of the EU nor the nature of the EU's relations with its Member States (p. 187). In respect of the socio-economic implications, the Constitution is neither more "liberal" nor more "socialist" than the present Treaties (p. 188). From a political point of view, the author sees the Constitution as "a very important symbolic step" (p. 190). "It is true that the political step taken to baptise the Treaties as a 'Constitution' does not match the content of the modifications actually made to the Treaties. It may however be seen as the culmination of a slow and successful evolution." (p. 191).

Just as it starts the book finishes with a question: "What will the final form of the Union be?" According to the author, it is and will remain in the foreseeable future a "Partially Federal Union" (p. 192) with the purpose of finding "the right balance between, on the one hand, respect for the national identities of its Member States, their cultures, traditions and diversities and, on the other hand, the necessity to develop an efficient democratic, transparent, central system of decision-making and to ensure the uniform application of the law this system will make. That is what is needed for Europe to be able to respond effectively to the economic, social, environmental and security challenges of the present century, challenges which none of the Member States, whatever its size and importance, is able to deal with on its own." (p. 195).

The book under review offers a concise, comprehensive and authoritative guide to the draft Constitutional Treaty. The evaluation and assessment of the constitutional provisions as well as suggestions for the way forward are often thought-provoking and inspiring. Despite his involvement in the drafting process, the author's analysis is overall very balanced and does not spare criticism where criticism is due. The book is clearly and elegantly written and highly accessible. Consequently, it is to be recommended not just to the scholar, practioner or student but also to every interested citizen who wants to partake in an informed debate about the future of the draft Constitutional Treaty and the future of the European project.

M SCHILLIG

The European Union and its Court of Justice. By ANTHONY ARNULL. Oxford: Oxford University Press, 2006. Second edition. lxxx + 699 pp inc index. £95.

Professor Arnull worked at the European Court of Justice for three years, and has held a Chair in European Union law for some 15 years. He is therefore ideally situated 'to examine the contribution the European Court of Justice has made to shaping the legal framework within which the European Union operates' (p. ix, p. 5). There has been considerable comment on the Court, much of which is rather generalised. By contrast, Arnull's book, in both its first and second editions, is grounded in meticulously careful, detailed exposition of the decisions made by the Court, within their respective legal contexts.

The book opens with a section on 'The Court and its jurisdiction'. In chapter 1, there is more extended treatment of the composition of the Court, and the practicalities of how it works, than is found in the standard texts. Greater integration of the material in the substantive chapters that follow, giving examples, or at least some cross-referencing, would have been beneficial here. For instance, Arnull cites Judge David Edward as describing the Court's collegial decision-making process as occasionally producing the proverbial 'camel', that is, 'a horse designed by a committee'. Which, in Arnull's view, of the substantive judgments discussed later in the book, might be considered to be 'camels'? Chapter 3 on the 'judicial architecture of the EU', which includes discussion of the judicial panels, and the relationship between the Court and the Court of First Instance, also takes the book beyond the standard texts. Its discussion in chapter 2 of the main heads of the Court's jurisdiction makes the book a useful reference text for pertinent details. Referencing is meticulous throughout. By contrast, however, the indexing is not as robust as one might have liked. For instance, enlargement arguably is the single most significant event for the EU in recent years. The Court has nearly doubled in size, receiving new judges, many from former communist states. Concerns have been expressed about their training, experience, background and even their intellectual capabilities ('how do we know they won't appoint the Minister of Justice's brother-in-law?'), as well as the effect of such a considerable expansion of the Court's size on a hitherto collegial institution. According to the index, the book includes only one reference to enlargement (p. 153). Nevertheless there is some exposition of Arnull's considered views on these questions, elsewhere in the book (e.g. pp. 7–9; p. 23; 117), which did not make it to the index.

The detailed content of Arnull's balanced analysis in the main body of the book covers both the 'constitutional' law of the EU (including judicial review of the acts of the institutions (chapter 2), the preliminary reference procedure (chapter 2), supremacy and direct effect of EU law (chapters 6 and 7), the power to determine the scope of EU law (chapter 8), the relationship between EU law rights and national remedies (chapter 9) and fundamental rights in EU law (chapter 10)), and selected elements of its substantive law (principally the law of the internal market (chapters 11 on goods, 12 on workers, 13 on establishment and services, 14 on citizenship of the EU), but also the law on equal treatment of men and women (chapter 15)). Although Arnull does concentrate on describing EU law through the lens of the decisions of the Court, these are set in context by some fairly extended passages on relevant legislative rules, as well as the provisions of the EC Treaty and Treaty on European Union.

The bottom line of what is, in each case, too detailed an argument to do justice in a review, is that Arnull is a supporter of the Court's overall approach. The vast majority of the judgments he discusses are assessed positively. For example, *ERTA* is 'a masterpiece of balanced creativity' (p. 57); the excessive deficit procedure case is 'aptly described as Solomonic' (p. 59); *Les Verts* and *Chernobyl* are not activist judgments in a pejorative sense (pp. 67–68); the cases discussed in chapter 9 on supremacy, remedies for EU law rights and *Francovich* damages are 'bold and creative' but not 'conjured out of thin air' (p. 98); *CILFIT* departs from the Treaty text, but doesn't extend the Court's jurisdiction, so the Court has got it about right (pp. 122–4); the trend in cases on justice and home affairs has been 'broadly in the right direction' (p. 136); *Van Gend* is a 'highly persuasive ruling' (p. 168); the Court's approach is *Costa* is 'the only one consistent with the spirit of the Treaty' (p. 180); *Omega Spielhallen* and *Schmidberger* provide a 'constructive negotiation over constitutional conflicts' (quoting Neil MacCormick) (p. 261,

363); the remedies case law, including *Francovich* strikes an 'acceptable balance' (p. 329); development of general principles of EU law is 'inspired' (p. 335); the case law on equal treatment in pensions 'strikes a skilful balance' (p. 558); that on positive action 'balances fairness to individuals with the need to tackle group-based disadvantage' (p. 600). Occasionally, Arnull is more critical of the Court. For instance, the Court's jurisprudence on *locus standi* is a 'matter for regret' (p. 91); *Faccini Dori* is deficient in its reasoning given the strength of the arguments for extending horizontal direct effect of directives (pp. 226–8); *Akrich* is obscure and poorly reasoned (p. 459); the Court should adopt a *de minimis* test for the free movement of goods (pp. 440–441); the citizenship case law is based on a 'romantic idea of solidarity', which 'risks proving counterproductive' (p. 532). So, the implication is that mostly the Court gets it right, and those who criticise the Court for being inappropriately 'activist' (seminally Hjalte Rasmussen), without the detailed analysis that Arnull provides, are wrong, or at least provide inadequate reasoned evidence to support their views.

One of the strengths of the book is the level of detail with which Arnull engages in the debate. But this can also be a weakness. It can be difficult for a reader to discern Arnull's overall message—to see the wood for the trees. Chapter 16 identifies the most important of the methods used by the Court to determine the meaning and effect of the texts of EU law that it must apply. The Court's approach is to have recourse not only to the literal words of the text, but also to the objectives of the provision concerned and its broader context. The Court cannot always treat the wording of a particular provision as decisive, because of the multilingual nature of EU law, and the ways in which provisions of EU law are drafted. If different language texts suggest different meanings, the Court is obliged to 'treat the objective of the provision and its legal context as decisive' (p. 610). The Court's judicial style, covered in chapter 17, is a modified version of that of French civil courts (p. 632). The Court would improve the quality of its style by becoming less 'bureaucratic' (the French model) and more of an advocate (the English model). An explicit pinning of each section of the substantive chapters to the book's overall narrative, as set out in these two chapters, and a deeper exploration of the observations Arnull makes, might make the argument easier to follow. How would Arnull describe the Court's approach in more general terms? What does he mean by 'creative' (an adjective used to describe many of the Court's judgments): creative of what? What about 'balanced'? What is 'the right direction'? And, indeed, 'the spirit of the Treaty'?

The final chapter 18, tantalizingly entitled 'Judging Europe's Judges', distracts from the overall narrative. In this chapter, Arnull seeks to put the *evolution* of the Court's case law centre stage, and to sent in its wider context. This promises to be Amull's take on well-known scholarly analyses of the Court (all of which are of course cited), such as Joseph Weiler's 'The Transformation of Europe' 100 *Yale Law Journal* (1991) 2403 and 'Journey to an Unknown Destination: A Retrospective and Prospective of the European Court of Justice in the Arena of Political Integration' 31 *Journal of Common Market Studies* (1993) 418, or Martin Shapiro's 'The European Court of Justice' in Craig and Burca, eds, *The Evolution of EU Law* (1999), or Grainne de Burca's 'The European Court of Justice and the evolution of EU law' in Borzel and Chichowski, eds, *The State of the European Union* (2003). But we are not explicitly told in this chapter the extent to which Amull's account takes us beyond the existing literature, either by confirming or refuting its central findings. Arnull sees three stages, with a possible fourth stage emerging post-Nice. During the first stage, up to the early 1980s, the Court's contribution was to make the system work (e.g. *ERTA,* but also *Plaumann)* and to protect rights in EU law, so as to make the Member States comply with their obligations under the Treaty (*Van Gend en Loos* and so on). In the second phase, qualified majority voting in Council and the Single Market programme heralded a reduced role for the Court, but with some areas of keeping the momentum going (equal treatment for men and women), making up for lost time in completing the internal market, and protecting the new institutional balance brought about by the Single European Act. During phase three following the Treaty on European Union, the Court was more ambivalent still, and in many ways adopted a more restrained approach.

If Arnull had taken chapter 18 (currently 28 of the book's 667 pages) as the guiding narrative for the whole, it would be quite a different book. The substantive material would have been rearranged, in order to show that there have been distinct historical phases in the Court's approach, and to what extent, and how, these are related to broader events in the history of the European Union. Now that the single market is more or less complete, has the Court's approach changed, for instance to reflect the EU's widening, rather than deepening, agenda? How does the detailed analysis of the constitutional and substantive case law of the Court tell a story of 'increasing sophistication' of the way the Court deals with its case law (p. 632), or of a move from a civil to a common law model (p. 638), in the Court's approach? Arnull mentions the debate on the EU's financial perspective 2007–13 in the last few paragraphs of the book. What about other budgetary events in the life of the EU? What about new methods of governance, such as the open method of coordination? More significantly, how would Amull substantiate the underlying assumption of the historical narrative that the Court is at least a key, if not the key, driver of the integration process?

TAMARA HERVEY

DECISIONS OF BRITISH COURTS DURING 2007 INVOLVING QUESTIONS OF PUBLIC OR PRIVATE INTERNATIONAL LAW

A. Public International Law[1]

Statutory construction—statute enacted to give effect to obligation under European Council framework decision—European Council Framework Decision on the European arrest warrant—Extradition Act 2003, Part 1—whether certificate referred to in Extradition Act, section 64(2) need be in addition to European arrest warrant

Case No. I. Dabas v High Court of Justice in Madrid, Spain, 28 February 2007, [2007] UKHL 6, [2007] 2 AC 31, [2007] 2 WLR 254, [2007] 2 All ER 641 (HL).

There is a divergence between Part 1 of the Extradition Act 2003, which deals with 'extradition' from the UK to so-called 'category 1 territories',[2] and the European Council Framework Decision of 13 June 2002 on the European arrest warrant and the surrender procedures between Member States,[3] to which Part 1 of the Act is designed to give effect. Section 64 of the Extradition Act defines what constitutes an extradition offence for the purposes of Part 1 in relation to persons not sentenced for an offence. Paragraph 2 of section 64 deals with conduct included within the European framework list,[4] in respect of which, in accordance with article 2(2) of the Framework Decision, section 64(2) embodies no requirement of double criminality. Section 64(2) does, on the other hand, require a certificate issued by an appropriate authority of the category 1 territory showing that the conduct falls within the European framework list (subparagraph b) and is punishable under the law of that territory with imprisonment or another form of detention for a period of 3 years or a greater punishment (subparagraph c). The Framework Decision requires no such certificate.

The case came on appeal from the decision of a District Judge (Magistrates' Court) that the appellant be extradited to Spain pursuant to a European arrest warrant issued by the Central Court for Committal

---

[1] © Dr Roger O'Keefe, 2008.

[2] These are territories designated for the purposes of Part 1 of the Act by order made by the Secretary of State: Extradition Act, s. 1(1).

[3] Decision 2002/584/JHA, OJ 2002 L 190, 18/07/2002, 1. Although, as made clear in recital 5 of its preamble, the Framework Decision's effect is to abolish extradition between member States and to replace it with a system of surrender between judicial authorities on the basis of the European arrest warrant, Part 1 of the Extradition Act 2003 persists in referring to the procedure as 'extradition'. As explained by Lord Hope in *Office of the King's Prosecutor, Brussels v Cando Armas* [2006] AC 1, 16, para. 22, (2005) 76 *BYIL* 603–14 (HL), the regime provided for in Part 1 'is really just a system of backing of warrants'.

[4] The list is reproduced in Schedule 2 to the Extradition Act.

Proceedings No. 6 of the High Court of Justice in Madrid, where the appellant was wanted in connection with the Madrid bombings of 11 March 2004. In accordance with the formal requirements of the European arrest warrant as adopted by way of annex to the Framework Decision, the nature and legal classification of the offence and the applicable statutory provision were listed ('collaboration with Islamist terrorist organisation foreseen in article 576 of Penal Code'); the framework offence for which surrender was requested was indicated in box (e) of the warrant by a tick against 'terrorism'; and the sentence by which the offence was punishable (five to ten years) was indicated in box (c) of the warrant. The appellant argued, however, that although the warrant satisfied the formal requirements of the Framework Decision, it did not satisfy Part 1 of the Extradition Act, in that it was not accompanied by a certificate as required by section 64(2)(b) and (c).

The House of Lords dismissed the appeal. The certificate referred to in section 64(2)(b) and (c) need not be a separate document but could comprise the European arrest warrant itself where the latter contained, as here, all the information needed for it to constitute a Part 1 warrant. It was true that, on its face, section 64(2) of the Extradition Act suggested that a separate certificate was required, an inference strengthened by the reference in section 142(3), not found in section 64(2), to an arrest warrant 'which contains' a certificate.[5] But section 64(2) had to be read in the light of the Framework Decision,[6] the aim of which was to simplify and expedite the surrender, as between EU member States, of persons accused of crimes in another member State (or to be sentenced or to serve sentences for such crimes) through the uniform acceptability of a common arrest warrant.[7] Although leaving to national authorities the choice of form and methods, European Council framework decisions were binding on member States as to the result to be achieved, in accordance with article 34(2)(b) of the Treaty on European Union. A national authority which, in its choice of form and methods, sought to frustrate or impede achievement of the purpose of the Framework Decision would infringe the general duty of co-operation binding on member States under article 10 of the EC Treaty. In this light, while a national court could not interpret its law *contra legem*, it was obliged to interpret that law as far as possible in the light of the wording and purpose of the Framework Decision in order to obtain the result which the latter pursues and thereby to comply with article 34(2)(b) of the Treaty of European Union. This was made clear by the European Court of Justice in *Criminal proceedings against*

---

[5] [2007] 2 AC 31, 39, para. 3 (Lord Bingham) and 59, para. 74 (Lord Brown).

[6] [2007] 2 AC 31, 39–41, paras 4–8 (Lord Bingham), 48–51, paras 38–43 (Lord Hope) and 59–60, paras 75–8 (Lord Brown). Lord Mance agreed with the reasoning and conclusions of all three: [2007] 2 AC 31, 61, para. 81.

[7] [2007] 2 AC 31, 39–40, para. 4 and 40–41, para. 8 (Lord Bingham), 43, para. 18 and 50, para. 42 (Lord Hope) and 60, para. 78 (Lord Brown).

Pupino (Case C-105/03),[8] where it was held that the obligation to interpret national law in conformity with Community law applied as much to framework decisions as to directives. 'And that [obligation] in turn, as Lord Steyn explained in *Ghaidan v Godin-Mendoza* [2004] 2 AC 557, para 45, is essentially the same strong interpretative obligation which section 3 of the Human Rights Act 1998 imposes... to avoid breaches of the European Convention on Human Rights: the requirement "so far as it is possible to do so" to read and give effect to legislation in a way which is compatible with Convention rights.'[9] Since the purpose of the Framework Decision on the European arrest warrant, namely 'to remove the complexity and potential for delay that was inherent in the existing extradition procedures'[10] and to replace it with a mechanism providing for 'swift, speedy surrender',[11] would be frustrated by the insistence on a separate certificate[12] without doing anything to protect the rights of the appellant,[13] section 64(2) of the Extradition Act was to be read 'as permitting the basic assertions in the warrant itself to constitute the necessary certificate'.[14] Such a construction was, in the words of Lord Brown, 'well within the court's power':[15]

[It] would not be regarded as exceeding the permissible bounds of the court's interpretative power under section 3 of the Human Rights Act; it would not, to use Lord Steyn's phrase, cross the Rubicon. No more is it to be regarded as a construction 'contra legem', forbidden by the Luxembourg case law.[16]

Lord Scott, while agreeing with the other Lords on the outcome of the case, dissented on the point. What he considered to be section 64(2)'s requirement of a separate certificate was not inconsistent with the Framework Decision.[17] Moreover, there was, his Lordship asserted, 'good reason to suppose' that a straightforward construction of section 64(2) reflected Parliament's intention:[18]

The implementation of the Framework Directive by the 2003 Act raised a good deal of concern in both Houses of Parliament. The imprecision of the framework list categories coupled with the removal of the requirement of double criminality was the basis of much of that concern.... The presence in section 64 of the requirement of a 'certificate' by a judicial authority... is consistent

---

[8] [2006] QB 83.   [9] [2007] 2 AC 31, 61, para. 79 (Lord Brown).

[10] [2007] 2 AC 31, 43, para. 18 (Lord Hope).

[11] [2007] 2 AC 31, 50, para. 42 (Lord Hope).

[12] [2007] 2 AC 31, 40–41, para. 8 (Lord Bingham), 50–1, para. 43 (Lord Hope) and 60, para. 76 (Lord Brown).

[13] [2007] 2 AC 31, 41, para. 8 (Lord Bingham). This assessment is implicit in the conclusion of Lord Hope, given that his Lordship had earlier stated that the inclusion of the certificate requirement in section 64(2) 'cannot be dismissed as unimportant' but 'must be taken to have been included... as an additional safeguard': [2007] 2 AC 31, 47, para. 33.

[14] [2007] 2 AC 31, 60, para. 76 (Lord Brown).

[15] [2007] 2 AC 31, 60, para. 76.

[16] [2007] 2 AC 31, 60, para. 76 (Lord Brown).

[17] [2007] 2 AC 31, 57–58, paras 68–9.

[18] [2007] 2 AC 31, 57, para. 66.

with a Parliamentary intention to alleviate that concern. The requirement of the certificate would, at least, make certain that in every case where double criminality was not a requisite a judicial mind had been brought to bear on the two points and that the judge was prepared to certify accordingly.[19]

It was not, in his Lordship's opinion, 'for the judiciary to remove from the Act provision that Parliament thought it right to include for the greater protection of those who are for the time being in this country and therefore entitled to the protection of our laws'.[20]

The judgment raises the question of the impact of the ECJ's judgment in *Pupino* and, more generally, whether there is any real contrast in terms of their use in statutory construction between the UK's general treaty obligations, on the one hand, and its obligations in relation to European directives and framework decisions and—by virtue of section 3(1) of the HRA—the ECHR, on the other. When the interpretation of the European Council Framework Decision on the European arrest warrant last, and first, came before the House in *Office of the King's Prosecutor, Brussels v Cando Armas*, the judgment in *Pupino* had not been rendered, and their Lordships treated framework decisions as equivalent for all intents and purposes to multilateral treaties. Using the familiar canon of statutory construction seen in cases such as *Salomon*[21] (where the statute is intended specifically to implement the treaty) and *Garland*,[22] *Brind*[23] and *Lyons*[24] (where it is not), Lord Bingham, with whose reasoning and conclusions the other Lords agreed, approached the question before the House on the assumption 'that Parliament did not intend the provisions of Part 1 [of the Extradition Act] to be inconsistent with the Framework Decision'.[25] While the case turned on a different point, one issue arising in *Cando Armas* was not dissimilar from that at stake here. 'Extradition' under Part 1 of the 2003 Act is initiated by the receipt from a category 1 territory of a 'Part 1 warrant', which in accordance with the definition contained in section 2(2) must, in the case of a person yet to be prosecuted and in the words of section 2(3), contain a statement both that the person in respect of whom the Part 1 warrant is issued is accused in the category 1 territory of an offence specified in the warrant and that the warrant was issued with a view to his arrest and extradition to the territory for the purpose of being prosecuted for the offence. No such statement is required by article 8 of the Framework Decision, which sets out the form and contents of the European arrest warrant; the warrant issued

---

[19] [2007] 2 AC 31, 57, para. 66.

[20] [2007] 2 AC 31, 58, para. 70.

[21] *Salomon v Commissioners of Customs and Excise* [1967] 2 QB 116, 143 (Diplock LJ), (1967) 42 *BYIL* 291–3 (CA).

[22] *Garland v British Railway Engineering Ltd* [1983] 2 AC 751, 771 (Lord Diplock), (1982) 53 *BYIL* 291–3 (HL).

[23] *R v Secretary of State for the Home Department, Ex parte Brind* [1991] 1 AC 696, 747–8 (Lord Bridge) and 760–1 (Lord Ackner), (1991) 62 *BYIL* 437–40 (HL).

[24] *R v Lyons* [2003] 1 AC 976, 992, paras 27–8 (Lord Hoffmann), (2002) 73 *BYIL* 428–34 (HL).

[25] [2006] AC 1, 10, para. 8.

by the Belgian authorities in the case did not include one; and the question was whether this rendered the warrant void, as not being a Part 1 warrant as defined in section 2(2). While their Lordships reserved their respective opinions on the matter, none of them except (as here) Lord Scott ruled out reading section 2(2) down to permit the requisite statement to be inferred from other material available to the District Judge. Lord Hope, whose views were in line with Lord Bingham's,[26] stated:

[T]he court should be slow to construe those words in a way that would make it impossible to give effect to a warrant which is in the terms which the Framework Decision has laid down. The purpose of the statute is to facilitate extradition, not to put obstacles in the way of the process which serve no useful purpose but are based on technicalities.[27]

The dictum could have come from the present case. But this says more about the Lords' skewed application in *Cando Armas* of the traditional canon of statutory construction that Parliament does not intend to legislate contrary to the UK's treaty obligations than it does about the lack of practical difference between this and what Lord Brown (who did not sit in *Cando Armas*) calls the 'strong interpretative obligation'[28] at issue here. And there is a difference—indeed, there are three of them. First, the traditional canon of statutory construction, which applies as much to customary international law as it does to treaties,[29] can be brought to bear only where the relevant statutory provision is ambiguous (and it is very hard to see how section 2(2) of the Extradition Act, at issue in *Cando Armas*, or section 64(2) of the Act, at issue in the present case, could be considered ambiguous, either in isolation or in the light of the Act as a whole). On the other hand, the obligation to read the relevant statutory provision in conformity with the international instrument in question, as laid down in *Pupino* (European Council framework decisions), *Marleasing*[30] (EC directives) and section 3(1) of the HRA (the ECHR), is not dependent on the provision's ambiguity.[31] In other words, the 'strong interpretative obligation' obliges the court to bring the statute into line with the international obligation even at the expense of Parliament's apparent intention (although a contrary parliamentary

---

[26] See [2006] AC 1, 15, para. 18.

[27] [2006] AC 1, 23, para. 44.

[28] See his Lordship's use of the same terminology in *R (Hurst) v London Northern District Coroner* [2007] AC 189, 216, para. 52, *infra*, pp. 520–7 (HL).

[29] See *eg Salomon v Commissioners of Customs and Excise* [1967] 2 QB 116, 143 (Diplock LJ).

[30] *Marleasing SA v La Comercial Internacional de Alimentación SA (Case C-106/89)* [1990] ECR I-4135.

[31] As regards section 3(1) of the HRA, see *R (Hurst) v London Northern District Coroner* [2007] AC 189, 215, para. 50, where Lord Brown stated that '[s]ection 3 is only invoked where, to achieve compliance with the Convention, the court must depart from the unambiguous meaning the legislation would otherwise bear'. But *cf R v F* [2007] QB 960, 970, para. 26, where the Court of Appeal demanded 'absurdity or ambiguity', having at 969–70, paras 23–4 treated as one and the same thing the 'strong interpretative presumption' laid down in section 3 of the HRA and the principle recognized by Diplock LJ in *Salomon v Commissioners of Customs and Excise* [1967] 2 QB 116, 143.

intention clearly manifest in the statute's provisions will still prevail). Secondly, at least as far as European framework decisions and directives are concerned,[32] the obligation, in the words of *Pupino*, is to read the statute as far as possible in the light of not only the wording but also the purpose of the international instrument so as to obtain the result pursued by the latter.[33] Finally, the traditional canon of statutory constuction can be brought to bear only on statutes which post-date the UK's entry into the treaty,[34] since, as a matter of logic, Parliament cannot be presumed to intend to legislate consistently with international obligations whose content is unknown. As made clear by Lord Brown (with whom Lords Bingham, Rodger and Mance agreed on point) one month after the present case in *R (Hurst) v London Northern District Coroner*, the same logic similarly rules out recourse for the purpose of statutory construction to any international judicial decision on the interpretation and application of a treaty obligation undertaken prior to the statute in circumstances where the effect of the decision is radically to transform the content of the obligation undertaken by the UK.[35] The 'strong interpretative obligation', by contrast, applies even in relation to statutes which predate the UK's obligation. Advocate General Kokott explicitly stated in *Pupino* that the interpretative tenet enunciated in that case applies 'regardless of whether [the relevant] laws were adopted before or after the framework decision',[36] a statement quoted by Lord Hope in the present case.[37] This is a function of article 34(2)(b) of the Treaty on European Union and of article 10 of the EC Treaty. For its part, section 3(2)(a) of the HRA expressly provides that the interpretative obligation laid down in section 3(1) applies to primary and subordinate legislation 'whenever enacted'. Leaving aside Lord Scott, who was right in *Cando Armas* but probably wrong here, the similarity of their Lordships musings in *Cando Armas* with their reasoning and conclusions in the present case leads one to wonder whether, at least as regards the first and second of the differences outlined above, the canon of statutory construction classically applied to the UK's treaty obligations risks being muscled out in practice by its younger, stronger cousin. Perhaps not if Lord Brown has anything to do with it.

Relationship between treaty and English law—unincorporated treaty— administrative decision-making—statutory construction—European Convention on Human Rights, article 2 (right to life)—obligation to investigate death of next-of-kin through alleged omission by State—Human Rights Act 1998,

---

[32] In relation to the ECHR, section 3(1) of the HRA states simply that, so far as it is possible to do so, primary and subordinate legislation must be read and given effect in a way which is compatible with Convention rights.

[33] [2006] QB 83, 109, para. 43 of the judgment of the Court.

[34] See eg *Garland v British Railway Engineering Ltd* [1983] 2 AC 751, 771 (Lord Diplock).

[35] [2007] AC 189, 215, para. 50.

[36] [2006] QB 83, 93, para. 36 of the Advocate General's opinion.

[37] [2007] 2 AC 31, 49, para. 39.

sections 3 and 6—non-retroactivity of HRA—Coroners Act 1988, sections 11(5)(b)(ii) and 16(3)—whether persons seeking resumption of adjourned inquest into death occurring prior to entry into force of HRA entitled under English law to benefit of ECHR, article 2

Case No. 2. R (Hurst) v London Northern District Coroner, 28 March 2007, [2007] UKHL 13, [2007] AC 189, [2007] 2 WLR 726 (HL).

Section 11(5)(b)(ii) of the Coroners Act 1988 provides that a coroner's inquisition (that is, the report on the findings of the inquest) shall set out, as far as such particulars have been proved, 'how, when and where the deceased came by his death'. This was interpreted narrowly by the Court of Appeal in the 1995 case of *R v Coroner for North Humberside and Scunthorpe, Ex parte Jamieson*[38] to mean that an inquest is to determine 'by what means' (for example, natural causes, homicide, suicide), as opposed to 'in what broad circumstances', the deceased came by his death—a decision affirmed as correct as a matter of pre-HRA English coronial law by the House of Lords in the 2004 case of *R (Middleton) v West Somerset Coroner.*[39] But *Middleton* also held that since the coming into force of section 6 of the HRA on 2 October 2000, the word 'how' in section 11(5)(b)(ii) of the Coroners Act was to be interpreted to extend to the possibility that omissions by a UK public authority had contributed to the deceased's death, since as a matter of article 2 of the ECHR, as interpreted by the European Court of Human Rights in *McCann*[40] and *Osman*,[41] the UK was obliged to hold an investigation in the event of this possibility. The question for determination by the Lords in the present case was whether persons seeking—by means of a coroner's discretion, pursuant to section 16(3) of the Coroners Act, to resume an adjourned inquest after the conclusion of related criminal proceedings—an investigation into a death occurring prior to the coming into force of the HRA were entitled under English law to the benefit of article 2 of the ECHR, despite the fact that in *In re McKerr*[42] their Lordships had held that the so-called 'procedural' obligation to hold an investigation as required by article 2 did not extend to deaths occurring before the HRA's entry into force. The Court of Appeal[43] had held that they were, on grounds not before the House in *McKerr*, which in turn had been decided on the basis of the interaction between article 2 of the ECHR and section 6 of the HRA: first, the Court of Appeal reasoned, the interpretative obligation imposed on courts by section 3 of the HRA was an obligation to give effect to legislation in a manner compatible with rights under the ECHR itself, and not merely with rights under the HRA; secondly, the administrative-law requirement that decisions be rational compelled a

---

[38] [1995] QB 1.   [39] [2004] 2 AC 182.
[40] *McCann v United Kingdom* (1996) 21 EHRR 97.
[41] *Osman v United Kingdom* (2000) 29 EHRR 245.
[42] [2004] 1 WLR 807, (2004) 75 *BYIL* 411–19 (HL).
[43] *R (Hurst) v London Northern District Coroner* [2005] 1 WLR 3896.

coroner, when exercising the discretion to resume an inquest into a pre-HRA death, to act in accordance with article 2 of the ECHR.

The House of Lords (Baroness Hale and Lord Mance dissenting on a different point) upheld the appeal from the Court of Appeal's judgment. Lord Brown gave the leading opinion, with which Lords Bingham and Rodger agreed and from which, on the points discussed here, Baroness Hale's opinion did not differ. Lord Mance agreed with the first and second of these points but not the last.[44]

Lord Brown acknowledged that *McKerr* was based on section 6 of the HRA and thus said nothing as to the interpretative obligation under section 3.[45] But to the argument that the two sections of the HRA produced different results, his Lordship responded:

For my part I have the greatest difficulty with this approach which necessarily involves construing the words 'the Convention rights' where they appear in section 3 differently from their meaning in section 6 ('a Convention right'). But why should they be construed differently? The plain object of section 3 is to avoid where possible action by a public authority which would otherwise be unlawful under section 6. It applies only where there would otherwise be a breach of a Convention right under domestic law. In the present case, as *McKerr* established, it would not be unlawful under domestic law for no further investigation to be carried out into [the deceased]'s death. The scheme of the 1998 Act and the link between sections 3 and 6 are to my mind plain. This is perhaps most clearly demonstrated by the language of section 6(2)(b), language which expressly mirrors that of section 3 ... [46]

In *Pearson v Inner London North Coroner*,[47] a case involving precisely the issue before the House, the Divisional Court had explicitly rejected an argument based on section 3, concluding that the 'logic of *McKerr* [was] inexorable', namely that '[i]f the positive obligation did not arise in domestic law prior to 2 October 2000, the consequential, secondary, ancillary or adjectival obligation cannot now give rise to a domestic obligation because it is consequential upon and secondary, ancillary and adjectival to the substantive obligation to protect life'.[48] The Divisional Court's judgment in *Pearson* was compelling. It could not be supposed

---

[44] The judgment in the present case was delivered on the same day as the Lords' judgment in *Jordan v Lord Chancellor* [2007] 2 AC 226, a case (in fact, two cases) from Northern Ireland implicating the same general questions, to which the judgment in *Hurst* was considered to provide the answers: see [2007] 2 AC 226, 256, para. 35 (Lord Bingham).

[45] [2007] AC 189, 212, paras 42–3.

[46] [2007] AC 189, 213, para. 44. HRA, s. 3(1) reads: 'So far as it is possible to do so, primary legislation and subordinate legislation must be read and given effect in a way which is compatible with the Convention rights.' HRA, s. 6(1) states that '[i]t is unlawful for a public authority to act in a way which is incompatible with a Convention right'; and s. 6(2)(b) provides that s. 6(1) does not apply to an act if 'in the case of one or more provisions of, or made under, primary legislation which cannot be read or given effect in a way which is compatible with the Convention rights, the authority was acting so as to give effect to or enforce those provisions'.

[47] [2005] EWHC 833 (Admin).

[48] [2007] AC 189, 213, para. 45, quoting [2005] EWHC 833 (Admin), para. 9 (Maurice Kay LJ, with whom Moses J agreed).

that their Lordships' decision in *McKerr* would have been any different had the case proceeded under section 3.[49]

Lord Brown also dismissed an argument by the respondent that the decision in *Jamieson*, accepted by the Lords in *Middleton* as an accurate pre-HRA construction of section 11(5)(b)(ii) of the Coroners Act, was now to be reinterpreted in the light of the UK's international legal obligations under article 2, as interpreted after *Jamieson* by the European Court of Human Rights in *McCann*. For a start, the argument flew in the face of the conclusion already reached as to the effect of *McKerr*; and 'if *McKerr* necessarily preclude[d] the use of section 3 to achieve the contended for result, so too surely it must preclude the achievement of the same result by the back door route now suggested'.[50] But there were other objections:

49...[A]ny contention for the re-interpretation of section 11(5)(b)(ii) [of the Coroners Act] requires first that it contains a relevant ambiguity, i.e. that it is capable, within the ordinary canons of construction, of bearing one or other of two possible meanings. Again, however, that seems to me irreconcilable with the House's opinion in *Middleton* which, in widening the meaning of 'how', expressly relied on section 3. Section 3 is only invoked where, to achieve compliance with the Convention, the court must depart from the unambiguous meaning the legislation would otherwise bear....

50 Even, moreover, were the respondent's argument to satisfy the threshold condition of ambiguity, she would still have to show that it would be appropriate to resolve that ambiguity by reference to the presumption 'that Parliament intended to legislate in conformity with the Convention, not in conflict with it' (Lord Bridge of Harwich's formulation of this principle of construction in *R v Secretary of State for the Home Department, Ex parte Brind* [1991] 1 AC 696, 747–748). That too, however, presents the respondent with real difficulties. The meaning of the word 'how' in this legislation was...first established in *Ex p Rubenstein* in 1982. Not only was the 1988 Act (in which the present provision appears) itself a consolidating Act (and concerned, therefore, to enshrine the existing law) but it was enacted at a time when Parliament can have had no thought that one day the United Kingdom might be under a procedural obligation to inquire into deaths pursuant to article 2 of the Convention. As already observed, it was not until 1995 that the European Court of Human Rights in *McCann* itself identified any such Convention duty. And, as the [appellant] points out, even had Parliament been aware of this duty, it might well have thought it sufficiently or better discharged by other means: criminal proceedings, a judicial inquiry or some different process. It can hardly be supposed that Parliament would have wanted the wider *Middleton* approach to be adopted for all future inquests.[51]

The allied submission, 'plainly contrary to what the House in *Middleton* intended',[52] that *Middleton* was now the binding authority on the meaning

---

[49] [2007] AC 189, 214, para. 46. See also [2007] AC 189, 204, para. 10 (Lord Rodger), 205–6, para. 17 (Baroness Hale) and 222, para. 71 (Lord Mance).

[50] [2007] AC 189, 214, para. 49.   [51] [2007] AC 189, 214–15.

[52] [2007] AC 189, 216, para. 52.

of section 11(5)(b)(ii) of the Coroners Act in all circumstances, post- and pre-HRA, was equally flawed:

The answer to it in my judgment is to be found…in the analogous field of European Community law where, pursuant to *Marleasing SA v La Comercial Internacional de Alimentación SA (Case C-106/89)* [1990] ECR I-4135, a similarly strong interpretive obligation is imposed on member states to construe domestic legislation whenever possible so as to produce compatibility with European Community law. The closeness of this analogy has been recognised by the House in *Ghaidan v Godin-Mendoza* [2004] 2 AC 557: see particularly Lord Steyn's opinion, at para 45. Where the *Marleasing* approach applies, the interpretative effect it produces upon domestic legislation is strictly confined to those cases where, on their particular facts, the application of the domestic legislation in its ordinary meaning would produce a result incompatible with the relevant European Community legislation. In cases where no European Community rights would be infringed, the domestic legislation is to be construed and applied in the ordinary way. Thus in *R v Secretary of State for Transport, Ex parte Factortame Ltd* [1990] 2 AC 85, Part II of the Merchant Shipping Act 1988 was to be disapplied in those cases where its operation would infringe directly effective European Community rights; but not otherwise. Similarly in *Imperial Chemical Industries plc v Colmer (No 2)* [1999] 1 WLR 2035 the House, following a reference to the Court of Justice of the European Communities (*Imperial Chemical Industries plc v Colmer* [1999] 1 WLR 108), held that ICI remained bound by domestic legislation upon its ordinary meaning notwithstanding that in certain circumstances such a construction would be incompatible with European Community rights. This principle was again applied by the Court of Appeal in *Gingi v Secretary of State for Work and Pensions* [2002] 1 CMLR 587 where Arden LJ expressly approved the following passage from *Bennion, Statutory Interpretation*, 4th ed. (2002), p. 1117:

'It is legitimate for the national court, in relation to a particular enactment of the national law, to give it a meaning in cases covered by the Community law which is inconsistent with the meaning it has in cases not covered by the Community law. While it is at first sight odd that the same words should have a different meaning in different cases, we are dealing with a situation which is odd in juristic terms.'

Buxton LJ, who gave the leading judgment in *Gingi*, recognised the relevance of the principle to the present case and…rejected this limb of the respondent's argument….[53]

This rejection was, in his Lordship's view, correct.[54]

Lord Brown then turned to the second of the two submissions accepted by the Court of Appeal in the present case, namely that the interpretative obligation imposed on courts by section 3 of the HRA was an obligation to give effect to legislation in a manner compatible with rights under the ECHR itself, and not merely with rights under the HRA. His Lordship noted 'many dicta of high authority supporting the proposition that it is

---

[53] [2007] AC 189, 216, para. 52.
[54] [2007] AC 189, 216, para. 52. See also [2007] AC 189, 204–5, paras 11–14 (Lord Rodger) and 222, para. 72 (Lord Mance).

lawful to have regard to unincorporated treaty obligations in the exercise of a discretion', pointing by way of example to the words of Lord Bingham in *R v Lyons*.[55] But it was another thing 'to say that the decision-maker is *bound* to have regard to such obligations and, moreover, ... bound to give effect to them unless there is good reason not to'.[56] Such a contention ran 'flatly counter' to the decision in *R v Secretary of State for the Home Department, Ex parte Brind*, where the House of Lords 'roundly rejected'[57] the submission that decision-makers are under an obligation to exercise discretionary powers conferred on them by English law so as to comply with unincorporated treaty obligations.[58] Lord Brown explained that there were some considerations that were required to be taken into account by decision-makers, others that were required not to be, and others still that the decision-maker 'may choose for himself whether or not to take into account'.[59] Quoting a passage from Cooke J in the New Zealand case of *CREEDNZ Inc v Governor General*,[60] approved by Lord Scarman (with whom the other Lords agreed) in *In re Findlay* as 'a correct statement of principle',[61] his Lordship stressed that if a decision-maker chose not to take into account a consideration in circumstances where he or she was so free to choose, it was no ground for impugning the decision as irrational that the consideration 'is one that may properly be taken into account, nor even that it is one which many people, including the court itself, would have taken into account if they had to make the decision'.[62] He added, however, again in the words of Cooke J as approved by Lord Scarman, that 'there will be some matters so obviously material to a decision on a particular project that anything short of direct consideration of them by the ministers ... would not be in accordance with the intention of the Act'.[63] Applying these principles to the instant case, Lord Brown found it 'quite impossible to say that the unincorporated international obligation on the United Kingdom here was "so obviously material" to the coroner's decision ... that he was required to give it "direct consideration" '.[64] For her part, Baroness Hale thought that '[i]t may be that [the coroner] would have been justified in ignoring [the Convention] altogether', although she treated as significant the fact that he did not.[65]

---

[55] [2007] AC 189, 217, para. 55, quoting [2003] 1 AC 976, para. 13, (2002) 73 *BYIL* 428–34 (HL), where Lord Bingham stated that '[e]ven before the Human Rights Act 1998 the Convention exerted a persuasive and pervasive influence on judicial decision-making in this country, affecting the interpretation of ambiguous statutory provisions, *guiding the exercise of discretions,* bearing on the development of the common law' (Lord Brown's emphasis). See also [2007] AC 189, 224, para. 78 (Lord Mance).

[56] [2007] AC 189, 217, para. 56.   [57] [2007] AC 189, 218, para. 58.

[58] [2007] AC 189, 217–18, para. 56, citing and quoting from [1991] 1 AC 696, (1991) 62 *BYIL* 437–40 (HL). See also [2007] AC 189, 206, para. 18 (Baroness Hale), not citing *Brind* but refusing 'to incorporate the Convention into domestic law by the back door', and 224, para. 78 (Lord Mance).

[59] [2007] AC 189, 218, para. 57.   [60] [1981] 1 NZLR 172, 183.

[61] [1985] 3 AC 318, 334.   [62] [2007] AC 189, 218, para. 57.

[63] [2007] AC 189, 218, para. 57.   [64] [2007] AC 189, 218, para. 58.

[65] [2007] AC 189, 206, para. 18. Although her Ladyship did not make the link explicit, the fact that the coroner purported to take into account article 2 of the ECHR would seem to bring into play

On this last point, Lord Mance sought to differ, 'find[ing] unattractive the proposition that it is entirely a matter for a discretionary decision-maker whether or not the values engaged by this country's international obligations, however fundamental they may be, have any relevance or operate as any sort of guide (the term used by Lord Bingham in *R v Lyons* at para 13)'.[66] His Lordship, alluding to the words of Cooke J quoted by Lord Brown that 'there will be some matters so obviously material to a decision on a particular project that anything short of direct consideration of them by the ministers...would not be in accordance with the intention of the Act', took the view that '[t]his country's international obligations in relation to a death potentially involving state responsibility appear...to merit equivalent recognition at least as a relevant factor, even if the decision-maker were in the event to regard them as outweighed by other considerations'.[67]

On the arguments considered here, Lord Brown's opinion is an excellent one. In its response to the respondent's submissions on the second point, it usefully highlights the difference in principle between the permissible use of treaties in general for the purpose of statutory construction and the 'strong interpretative obligation' mandated in respect of the ECHR by section 3(1) of the HRA. It also indicates that the distinction continues to have practical consequences at least in respect of unincorporated treaties.[68] It is worth noting in this regard that Lord Brown did not sit in *Cando Armas*, where the House, Lord Scott dissenting on the particular point, seemed to ignore the need for ambiguity in the statute.[69]

R v Secretary of State for the Home Department, Ex parte Launder [1997] 1 WLR 839, (1996) 67 *BYIL* 548–51 (HL) and *R v Director of Public Prosecutions, Ex parte Kebilene* [2000] 2 AC 326.

[66] [2007] AC 189, 224, para. 78.

[67] [2007] AC 189, 224, para. 79. His Lordship found support for this approach in the Court of Appeal's reasoning in both *Rantzen v Mirror Group Newpapers (1986) Ltd* [1994] QB 670, 692 and *R v Lord Saville of Newdigate, Ex parte A* [2000] 1 WLR 1855, para 37. See also [2007] AC 189, 223, para. 75 (Lord Mance), accepting the Court of Appeal's ruling that the coroner, even absent the HRA, should have taken the UK's international obligations under article 2 of the ECHR into account in deciding whether there was sufficient cause to resume the inquest.

[68] There is no indication in the leading authorities that any distinction is to be drawn, when it comes to applying the canon of construction that Parliament does not intend to legislate in a manner contrary to the UK's treaty obligations, between cases where the statute in question was enacted to give effect to the relevant treaty obligation and cases where it merely regulates a sphere of domestic activity which is also, perhaps coincidentally, within the material scope of the treaty. See, on the one hand, *Salomon v Commissioners of Customs and Excise* [1967] 2 QB 116, 143 (Diplock LJ), (1967) 42 *BYIL* 291–3 (CA) and, on the other, *Garland v British Railway Engineering Ltd* [1983] 2 AC 751, 771 (Lord Diplock), (1982) 53 *BYIL* 291–3 (HL); *R v Secretary of State for the Home Department, Ex parte Brind* [1991] 1 AC 696, 747–8 (Lord Bridge) and 760–1 (Lord Ackner); and *R v Lyons* [2003] 1 AC 976, 992, paras 27–8 (Lord Hoffmann). But *cf* the view of Lord Neuberger in *Boake Allen Ltd v Revenue and Customs Commissioners* [2007] 3 All ER 605, 619, para. 51 that '[t]his principle is of less weight in a case such as the present where there is no question, as in *Salomon*, of the legislative provision in issue...having been enacted to give effect to a specific treaty obligation', a dictum picked up and applied by the Court of Appeal in *Abdirahman v Secretary of State for Work and Pensions* [2007] EWCA Civ 657, paras 36 (Lloyd LJ) and 66 (Moses LJ), with both of whom Sir Andrew Morritt C agreed.

[69] See *Office of the King's Prosecutor, Brussels v Cando Armas* [2006] AC 1, (2005) 76 *BYIL* 603–14. See also *Dabas v High Court of Justice in Madrid, Spain* [2007] 2 AC 31, *supra*, pp. 515–520 (HL).

While it is hard not to sympathize with Lord Mance's view on the final point, especially as his Lordship so persuasively puts it, legally it is open to question. For a start, it is a mistake or sleight of hand to characterize it as an application of Cooke J's words in *CREEDNZ* as adopted by the Lords in *Findlay*. What is the relevant Act? The HRA, an Act of strictly prospective effect intended to incorporate the previously unincorporated obligations of the ECHR? The Coroners Act, passed seven years before the European Court's decision in *McCann*? Moreover, and more fundamentally, Lord Mance's position probably amounts in the end to a rejection of *Brind*. To say that the UK's unincorporated treaty obligations are a relevant factor to be directly considered when exercising an administrative discretion would seem to suggest that, in the complete absence of countervailing considerations, the decision-maker's refusal to act in accordance with this sole relevant consideration would be perverse—that is, irrational, hence liable to be overturned on *Wednesbury* grounds. In short, it appears effectively to say, as the Lords rejected out of hand in *Brind*, that an unincorporated treaty can, at least in some circumstances, compel a decision-maker to act in accordance with its obligations. Indeed, the submission in *Brind* itself, conveniently summarised as a submission to the effect that a decision-maker's failure to act in accordance with an unincorporated treaty obligation would be irrational, was more subtle, as Lord Ackner explained:

[Counsel] claims [not only] that the Secretary of State before issuing his directives should have considered...the Convention (it is accepted that he in fact did so) but that he should have properly construed it and correctly taken it into consideration. It was therefore a relevant, indeed a vital, factor to which he was obliged to have proper regard pursuant to the *Wednesbury* doctrine, with the result that his failure to do so rendered his decision unlawful.[70]

Presumably, on Lord Mance's view, where an unincorporated treaty obligation is the only relevant consideration, a decision-maker would be obliged to have 'proper' regard to it, to take it 'correctly' into consideration. But this is precisely what Lord Ackner, with whom the other Lords agreed, rejected as a 'fallacy'—as 'incorporating the Convention into English domestic law by the back door',[71] in the words echoed by Baroness Hale in the present case.[72] Whether this is an accurate way of characterizing the matter is another question.

Non-justiciability of foreign sovereign acts—foreign act of State doctrine— 'Buttes' non-justiciability—public policy exception—whether English court barred from examining at foreign State's request payments authorized by its Parliament in alleged pursuance of conspiracy by State officials to defraud State

Case No. 3. Attorney General of Zambia (for and on behalf of the Republic of Zambia) v Meer Care & Desai (A Firm) and others, 4 May 2007,

---

[70] [1991] 1 AC 696, 761.   [71] [1991] 1 AC 696, 761–2.   [72] [2007] AC 189, 206, para. 18.

[2007] EWHC 952 (Ch) (Chancery Division, Peter Smith J, sitting as Special Examiner at the High Court, Lusaka).

The Attorney General of Zambia, for and on behalf of the Republic of Zambia, sought to recover sums totalling over US$72,000,000 from various defendants, including the former President of Zambia, Frederick Chiluba, several former State officials and two London law firms. The sums had been transferred by the Zambian Ministry of Finance between 1995 and 2001 ostensibly in order to pay debts owed by Zambia. It was alleged that these monies had been diverted by the defendants to private ends by means of three separate conspiracies to defraud the Republic. The defendants sought to prevent the court from investigating the payments by arguing that, since the transfers had been budgeted for and approved in relevant Appropriations Acts by the Zambian Parliament, an English court was barred from calling them into question effectively by both the foreign act of State doctrine proper and the doctrine of judicial abstention coined by Lord Wilberforce in *Buttes Gas and Oil Co. v Hammer (No 3)*.[73] In short, it was submitted that the question whether the payments were an aspect of the alleged conspiracies to defraud was non-justiciable.

Peter Smith J in the Chancery Division, sitting as Special Examiner at the High Court, Lusaka, rejected the defendants' argument. After recalling the words of Lord Wilberforce in *Buttes* and the judgments of the Court of Appeal and the House of Lords in *Kuwait Airways*, as well as two more obscure and irrelevant cases cited by the defendants,[74] his Lordship continued:

[193] I do not regard these decisions as being authority for an application [of a] principle of non-interference as contended for by the Defendants in this case. I am not being asked to reconsider the decision of Parliament to approve the budget. I am not being asked to consider the effectiveness of internal procedures of the High Court or Parliament or whether any of those procedures were effectively followed. I am not being asked to strike down any law of Zambia. . . . I simply do not see that the claims brought by [the Attorney General] that authorisation was obtained from Parliament for the budget which included matters where the officers of the then Government fraudulently concealed within the budget monies which were subsequently to be stolen by them involves a challenge to the supremacy of the laws of Zambia or the procedure of the Zambian Parliament.

---

[73] As is frustratingly common, counsel and the court elided these two distinct doctrines—the first the rule whereby an English court will not enquire into the legality of the acts of a foreign State within its own territory, as per *Duke of Brunswick v King of Hanover* (1848) 2 HL Cas 1, the second so-called '*Buttes*' non-justiciability, a broader and territorially unlimited rule according to which an English court will not question the legality of the 'transactions of foreign sovereign states' or 'acts done abroad by virtue of sovereign authority', in the words of Lord Wilberforce in *Buttes Gas and Oil Co. v Hammer (No 3)* [1982] AC 888, 931 (1982) 53 BYIL 259–68 (HL). For a lucid account of the distinction, see *Kuwait Airways Corpn v Iraqi Airways Company* [2001] 3 WLR 1117, (2000) 71 BYIL 408–12 (CA). But see also *Kuwait Airways Corpn v Iraqi Airways Company (Nos 4 and 5)* [2002] AC 883, (2002) 73 BYIL 400–4 (HL), effectively effacing the distinction.

[74] These were *Hoani Te Heuheu Tukino v Aotea District Maori Land Board* [1941] AC 308 (PC) and *Pickin v British Railways Board* [1974] AC 756 (HL).

[194] In the context of the principles as set out in the *Buttes* and *Kuwait* cases it would be absurd in my view if the courts could not adjudicate in the present claim because the budget was approved by Parliament in ignorance of the fact that the President and the Head of Security were to use this obtaining of funds for a dishonest purpose. The major difference between the cases cited to me is the fact that by [the Attorney General] the Government in question is a party to the proceedings. No case has been cited to me (and I am told Counsel could not find one) where this principle was applied to preclude a sovereign state which was bringing a claim. Given the principles as to why the rule occurs I can well understand that to be the case. There can be no problem of diplomacy or international sovereign embarrassment when the sovereign state whose law is in question is actually a party to the court proceedings in question and accepts the court can investigate it.

[195] If I am wrong in that then as the *Kuwait* case shows (see the judgment of Lord Hope especially) there are public policy exceptions. The list is not confined to the actual case adjudicated upon in the *Kuwait* case. It is a question in each case as to whether or not public policy would prevent the rigid application of this rule operating. [The Attorney General]'s case is that its principal officers at the time have defrauded the Republic. Part of that defrauding operation was their presentation of false budgets to Parliament and the procurement of the approval without Parliament discovering that fraud....

[196] I do not believe that when the sovereign state wishes to impugn the legislative acts (if that is the case) that public policy which is designed to prevent the courts 'embarrassing it' would be used against that sovereign state. I can see no reason why this case calls for 'judicial restraint' and overwhelming reasons why I should investigate these matters. This is plainly a public policy exception. Any other decision would be absurd.

With that his Lordship held the question justiciable.

Apart from its conflation of the foreign act of State doctrine proper and *Buttes* non-justiciability, along with their distinct rationales, a conflation to which the House of Lords in *Kuwait Airways* has lent respectability, this passage of Peter Smith J's judgment is convincing. The defendants' argument was spurious in every way.

'Jurisdiction' within meaning of European Convention on Human Rights, article 1—extraterritorial application of ECHR—Human Rights Act 1998—extraterritorial application of HRA—statutory construction—whether ECHR and HRA applicable to certain conduct of UK armed forces in belligerent occupation of southern Iraq

Case No. 4. R (Al-Skeini and others) v Secretary of State for Defence, 13 June 2007, [2007] UKHL 26, [2008] 1 AC 153, [2007] 3 WLR 33 (HL).

The facts of the case, arising out the conduct of UK forces in belligerent occupation of parts of southern Iraq, have been outlined previously.[75] What was sought by the claimants at this stage was an independent official inquiry into the deaths and, in one case, the alleged ill-treatment

---

[75] See (2004) 75 *BYIL* 513–18 (QBD (DC)); (2005) 76 *BYIL* 634–40 (CA).

prior to death of their next-of-kin, in accordance with articles 2 and 3 respectively of the ECHR, as given effect in English law by section 6 of the HRA. The five unsuccessful claimants before the Court of Appeal appealed its ruling that neither the ECHR nor the HRA applied to their deceased relatives, four of them shot by British troops and one of them possibly so. The Secretary of State cross-appealed the Court of Appeal's ruling that the HRA applied to the sixth claim, brought in respect of the alleged severe ill-treatment and death of an individual in a British-controlled prison in Basra. The Secretary of State accepted that the ECHR applied to this last claim.

The House of Lords unanimously dismissed the five appeals and, Lord Bingham dissenting, the Secretary of State's cross-appeal. The HRA applied extraterritorially to those situations in which the UK enjoyed 'jurisdiction' within the meaning of article 1 of the ECHR, and in the present case this meant only the sixth claim.[76]

Lord Bingham, the senior law lord, although dissenting on the point,[77] outlined the uncontroversial fundamentals of the approach to be taken when seeking to answer the first question before the House, that of the possible extraterritorial application of the HRA:

8 The HRA is a statute enacted by Parliament. Where an issue arises as to its meaning, it must be construed. This is a task which only a UK court can perform. The court in Strasbourg is the ultimate authority on interpretation of the European Convention, but it cannot rule on the interpretation of a domestic statute. That is the task which the House is now called upon to perform.

9 In carrying out that task the House must employ the familiar tools of statutory interpretation. The starting point is the language of the Act, from which the court seeks to derive the meaning of what Parliament has enacted. Significance may be attached not only to what Parliament has said but also, on occasion, to what it has not said. Attention may be paid to presumptions applicable to the drafting of statutes, since these are rules which expert professional draftsmen may ordinarily be expected to follow in the absence of reason to conclude that they may not have done so or an indication in the statute that they have not done so. While the express terms of a statute are always crucial, the courts will eschew an overly literal construction, taking account of the purpose of the statute, the mischief sought to be remedied and other circumstances relevant to interpretation. It is of course very relevant that the HRA is directed to the protection of human rights, with particular reference to the European Convention, which the UK ratified on 8 March 1951 and which came into force on 3 September 1953...[78]

His Lordship recalled that, although the object of the HRA had been to give domestic legal effect to the international obligations embodied in the ECHR, 'there [was] a distinction between (1) rights arising under the Convention and (2) rights created by the 1998 Act by reference to the

---

[76] Given factual developments since the Divisional Court's original order, their Lordships remitted the sixth claim to the Divisional Court.

[77] See below.   [78] [2008] 1 AC 153, 178.

Convention', as made clear by Lords Nicholls and Hoffmann in *McKerr* and by Lord Hoffmann in *Lyons*.[79]

Turning to details, Lord Rodger, giving the leading opinion on the first question, drew a distinction between the extent of an Act and its possible application to matters and persons outside the UK.[80] The HRA was effectively[81] stated in section 22(6) to extend to the UK as a whole, and, in accordance with the accepted canon of construction, this was taken to mean that it did not extent to any territory outside the UK. But what this indicated was simply that the HRA formed part of the law of the UK and did not form part of the law of any other territory for which Parliament could have legislated,[82] such as the Channel Islands or the Isle of Man.[83] An Act which extended to the UK alone—that is, which formed part of the law of the UK alone—could nonetheless contain provisions with express extraterritorial application.[84] So the fact that the HRA was stated to extend to the UK alone was 'neutral'.[85] When it came to application, there was a general presumption that statutes did not apply to matters or persons beyond the territory to which they were stated to extend.[86] But the cases showed 'that the concept of the territoriality of legislation [was] quite subtle' or, in the words of Lord Nicholls in *Quark*, 'slippery':[87]

Behind the various rules of construction, a number of different policies can be seen at work. For example, every statute is interpreted, 'so far as its language permits, so as not to be inconsistent with the comity of nations or the established rules of international law': *Maxwell on the Interpretation of Statutes*, 12th ed. (1969), p. 183. It would usually be both objectionable in terms of international comity and futile in practice for Parliament to assert its authority over the subjects of another sovereign who are not within the United Kingdom. So, in the absence of any indication to the contrary, a court will interpret legislation as not being intended to affect such people.[88]

---

[79] [2008] 1 AC 153, 178–9, para. 10, considering *In re McKerr* [2004] 1 WLR 807, para. 25 (Lord Nicholls) and paras 62–5 (Lord Hoffmann), (2004) 75 *BYIL* 411–19 (HL) and *R v Lyons* [2003] 1 AC 976, para. 27 (Lord Hoffmann), (2002) 73 *BYIL* 428–34 (HL). See also [2008] 1 AC 153, 216, para. 134 (Lord Brown).

[80] See also [2008] 1 AC 153, 203, para. 86 (Baroness Hale).

[81] '[I]n accordance with the usual, slightly puzzling, practice, section 22(6) provides specifically that [the HRA] extends to Northern Ireland. On the accepted rule of interpretation which Bennion states in this passage, the Act therefore extends to the United Kingdom as a whole': [2008] 1 AC 153, 191, para. 38 (Lord Rodger), citing Bennion, *Statutory Interpretation* (4th ed., 2002), 282. See also [2008] 1 AC 153, 182, para. 15 (Lord Bingham).

[82] [2008] 1 AC 153, 191, para. 38, citing *Lawson v Serco Ltd* [2006] ICR 250, 253, para. 1 (Lord Hoffmann). See also [2008] 1 AC 153, 203, para. 86 (Baroness Hale).

[83] See [2008] 1 AC 153, 191, para. 41.

[84] [2008] 1 AC 153, 191, para. 42.

[85] [2008] 1 AC 153, 192, para. 42. See also [2008] 1 AC 153, 203–4, para. 87 (Baroness Hale).

[86] [2008] 1 AC 153, 192, para. 44, citing Bennion, *Statutory Interpretation* (4th ed., 2002), 306.

[87] [2008] 1 AC 153, 192, para. 44, quoting *R (Quark Fishing Ltd) v Secretary of State for Foreign and Commonwealth Affairs* [2006] 1 AC 529, 545, para. 32, (2005) 76 *BYIL* 589–93 (HL).

[88] [2008] 1 AC 153, 192, para. 45, considering *Clark v Oceanic Contractors Inc* [1983] 2 AC 130, 152 (Lord Wilberforce) and *Ex parte Blain; In re Sawyers* (1879) 12 Ch D 522, 526 (James LJ). See also [2008] 1 AC 153, 217, para. 141 (Lord Brown), considering *Lawson v Serco Ltd* [2006] ICR

In this light, 'there [could] be no doubt that, despite the lack of any qualifying words, section 6(1) of the 1998 Act applie[d] only to United Kingdom public authorities and not to the public authorities of any other state'.[89] His Lordship continued:

46 Subjects of the Crown, British citizens, are in a different boat. International law does not prevent a state from exercising jurisdiction over its nationals travelling or residing abroad, since they remain under its personal authority: *Oppenheim's International Law*, 9th ed. (1992), vol. 1, Pt I, para. 138. So there can be no objection in principle to Parliament legislating for British citizens outside the United Kingdom, provided that the particular legislation does not offend against the sovereignty of other states....

47 The cases indicate...that British individuals or firms or companies or other organisations readily fall within the legislative grasp of statutes passed by Parliament. So far as they are concerned, the question is whether, on a fair interpretation, the statute in question is intended to apply to them only in the United Kingdom or also, to some extent at least, beyond the territorial limits of the United Kingdom. Here, there is no doubt that section 6 applies to public authorities such as the armed forces within the United Kingdom: the only question is whether, on a fair interpretation, it is confined to the United Kingdom.[90]

Even then, '[i]n the absence of an intention clearly expressed or to be inferred either from its language, or from the object or subject-matter or history of the enactment, the presumption is that Parliament does not design its statutes to operate on its subjects beyond the territorial limits of the United Kingdom'.[91] This canon of construction again had to be seen against the background of international law:

One state is bound to respect the territorial sovereignty of another state. So, usually, Parliament will not mean to interfere by legislating to regulate the conduct of its citizens in another state. Such legislation would usually be unnecessary and would often be, in any event, ineffective. But sometimes Parliament has a legitimate interest in regulating their conduct and so does indeed intend its legislation to affect the position of British citizens in other states.... [I]f the words of a statute are open to more than one interpretation, whether or not it binds British citizens abroad 'seems to depend...entirely on the nature of the statute': *Maxwell on the Interpretation of Statutes*, p. 169.[92]

250, 254 (Lord Hoffmann), in turn considering *Clark v Oceanic Contractors Inc* [1983] 2 AC 130, 152 (Lord Wilberforce).

[89] [2008] 1 AC 153, 193, para. 45. See also [2008] 1 AC 153, 182, para. 15 (Lord Bingham), 204, para. 88 (Baroness Hale) and 217, para. 139 (Lord Brown).

[90] [2008] 1 AC 153, 193, considering *Ex parte Blain; In re Sawyers* (1879) 12 Ch D 522, 531-2 (Cotton LJ) and *Clark v Oceanic Contractors Inc* [1983] 2 AC 130, 145 (Lord Scarman). See also [2008] 1 AC 153, 204, para. 88 (Baroness Hale).

[91] [2008] 1 AC 153, 193-4, para. 48, quoting *Maxwell on the Interpretation of Statutes* (12th ed., 1969), 171 and discussing *Tomalin v S Pearson & Son Ltd* [1909] 2 KB 61, 64 (Cozens-Hardy MR). See also [2008] 1 AC 153, 179-80, para. 11 (Lord Bingham) and 216-17, para. 137 (Lord Brown).

[92] [2008] 1 AC 153, 194, para. 49.

When considering the territorial scope of the HRA, it was necessary, as the case-law indicated,[93] to have regard to the Act's 'overall nature and purpose':[94]

53 In the first place, the burden of the legislation falls on public authorities, rather than on private individuals or companies. Most of the functions of United Kingdom public authorities relate to this country and will therefore be carried out here. Moreover, exercising their functions abroad would often mean that the public authorities were encroaching on the sovereignty of another state. Nevertheless, where a public authority has power to operate outside of the United Kingdom and does so legitimately—for example, with the consent of the other state—in the absence of any indication to the contrary, when construing any relevant legislation, it would only be sensible to treat the public authority, so far as possible, in the same way as when it operates at home.

54 The purpose of the 1998 Act is to provide remedies in our domestic law to those whose human rights are violated by a United Kingdom public authority. Making such remedies available for acts of a United Kingdom authority on the territory of another state would not be offensive to the sovereignty of the other state. There is therefore nothing in the wider context of international law which points to the need to confine sections 6 and 7 of the 1998 Act to the territory of the United Kingdom.

55 One possible reason for confining their application in that way would, however, be if their scope would otherwise be unlimited and they would, potentially at least, confer rights on people all over the world with little or no real connexion with the United Kingdom. There is, however, no such danger in this case since the 1998 Act has a built-in limitation. By section 7(1) and (7), only those who would be victims for the purposes of article 34 of the Convention in proceedings in the Strasbourg court can take proceedings under the 1998 Act. Before they could sue, claimants would therefore have to be 'within the jurisdiction' of the United Kingdom in terms of article 1 of the Convention. Whatever the precise boundaries of that limitation, it blunts the objection that a narrow construction of the territorial application of the Act is the only way to prevent it having extravagant effects which could never have been intended. The requirement for a claimant to be within the jurisdiction of the United Kingdom is a further assurance that, if the Act were interpreted and applied in that way, the courts in this country would not be interfering with the sovereignty or integrity of another state.[95]

'By this somewhat circuitous route', Lord Rodger came to what he considered 'surely the crucial argument in favour of the wider interpretation of section 6'.[96] He noted the Secretary of State's acceptance 'that "the central purpose" of Parliament in enacting sections 6 and 7 was "to provide a remedial structure in domestic law for the rights guaranteed by

---

[93] See [2008] 1 AC 153, 194–5, paras 50–2, considering *Howgate v Bagnell* [1951] 1 KB 265, especially at 274.
[94] [2008] 1 AC 153, 195, para. 52.
[95] [2008] 1 AC 153, 195–6. See also, as regards the purpose of the HRA, [2008] 1 AC 153, 204, para. 88 (Baroness Hale) and 217, paras 138 and 140 (Lord Brown).
[96] [2008] 1 AC 153, 196, para. 56.

the Convention"': that is, 'claimants were to be able to obtain remedies in United Kingdom courts, rather than having to go to Strasbourg'.[97] His Lordship further noted the Secretary of State's agreement that, while the 'jurisdiction' of Contracting States for the purposes of article 1 of the ECHR was essentially territorial, there were exceptional cases in which conduct performed by the State, or producing effects, outside its territory could constitute an exercise of jurisdiction by it within the meaning of article 1.[98] He continued:

56... Nevertheless, the Secretary of State says that sections 6 and 7 are to be interpreted in such a way that, in these exceptional cases, a victim is left remedi-less in the British courts. Contrary to the central policy of the Act, the victim must resort to Strasbourg.

57 My Lords, I am unable to accept that submission. It involves reading into sections 6 and 7 a qualification which the words do not contain and which runs counter to the central purpose of the Act. That would be to offend against the most elementary canons of statutory construction which indicate that, in case of doubt, the Act should be read so as to promote, not so as to defeat or impair, its central purpose. If anything, this approach is even more desirable in interpreting human rights legislation. As Lord Brown of Eaton-under-Heywood points out, this interpretation also ensures that, in these exceptional cases, the United Kingdom is not in breach of its article 13 obligation to afford an effective remedy before its courts to anyone whose human rights have been violated within its jurisdiction.[99]

The speech of Lord Nicholls in *Quark*—which confirmed that, in interpreting the rights contained in the Schedule to the HRA, courts were to take account of the territorial scope of the relevant right under the ECHR—lent 'powerful support' to the approach suggested by his Lordship.[100] Lord Rodger concluded:

58... In the present case, that means having regard to those exceptional situations where article 2 would apply outside the territory of the United Kingdom. In other words, on a fair interpretation, article 2 Schedule to the Act must be read as applying wherever the United Kingdom has jurisdiction in terms of article 1 of the Convention. The corollary is that section 6 must also be interpreted as applying in the same circumstances.

59 For these reasons, section 6 should be interpreted as applying not only when a public authority acts within the United Kingdom but also when it acts

[97] [2008] 1 AC 153, 196, para. 56, quoting *Aston Cantlow with Wilmcote and Billesley Parochial Church Council v Wallbank* [2004] 1 AC 546, 564, para. 44 (Lord Hope).

[98] [2008] 1 AC 153, 196, para. 56, quoting *Bankovic v Belgium* (2001) 11 BHRC 435, 450, para. 67.

[99] [2008] 1 AC 153, 196.

[100] [2008] 1 AC 153, 196–7, para. 58, considering [2006] 1 AC 529, 546, para. 34. See also [2008] 1 AC 153, 218, para. 143 (Lord Brown). On the same general point, see too [2008] 1 AC 153, 206, para. 98 (Lord Carswell), speaking of Parliament's 'general intention', manifest in statements inside and outside the chamber, 'to equate the scope of the Act with the scope of the Convention'; and [2008] 1 AC 153, 218, para. 144 (Lord Brown), considering *R (B) v Secretary of State for the Foreign and Commonwealth Office* [2005] QB 643, para. 79, (2004) 75 *BYIL* 483–9 (CA).

within the jurisdiction of the United Kingdom for purposes of article 1 of the Convention, but outside the territory of the United Kingdom.[101]

The Secretary of State's cross-appeal had therefore to be dismissed.

The argument based on article 13 of the ECHR advanced by Lord Brown, as alluded to by Lord Rodger, took as its starting point Diplock LJ's dictum in *Salomon* in which his Lordship referred to 'a prima facie presumption that Parliament does not intend to act in breach of international law, including therein specific treaty obligations'.[102] Lord Brown acknowledged, as had the European Court on many occasions, that the UK had undertaken no specific treaty obligation to incorporate the ECHR into domestic law.[103] But he recalled that article 13 imposed on the UK an international obligation to afford everyone whose rights and freedoms under the ECHR were violated an effective remedy before a national authority. The Strasbourg court had elaborated on article 13 in *James v United Kingdom*, explaining that, while the ECHR contained no obligation of incorporation, article 1 provided that 'the substance of the rights and freedoms set forth must be secured under the domestic legal order, in some form or another, to everyone within the jurisdiction of the contracting states', with the result that article 13 'guarantee[d] the availability within the national legal order of an effective remedy to enforce the Convention rights and freedoms in whatever form they may happen to be secured'.[104] In *Smith and Grady v United Kingdom*, the Court had found the UK to be in violation of article 13 where domestic law had effectively excluded any consideration by the domestic courts of the substance of the claim.[105] So too, his Lordship concluded, would article 13 be held to have been violated in the present case if the HRA were held not to apply to the sixth claim, since '[the claimant's] complaints could not then be considered on their merits under domestic law'.[106] 'If, therefore, it were necessary to resort to a countervailing presumption to justify construing the Act so as to apply extraterritorially to the limited extent necessary to correspond with the Strasbourg case law on the reach of article 1', his Lordship would have concluded, contrary to the view expressed by Lord Bingham,[107] 'that the *Salomon* presumption [was] indeed available to the appellants here'.[108]

Lord Bingham, dissenting on the question of the extraterritorial application of the HRA, noted by way of preface that 'while a claim cannot succeed under the Act unless it falls within the scope of the Convention

---

[101] [2008] 1 AC 153, 197. See also [2008] 1 AC 153, 206, para. 96 (Lord Carswell).
[102] [2008] 1 AC 153, 219, para. 147, quoting *Salomon v Commissioners of Customs and Excise* [1967] 2 QB 116, 143 (Diplock LJ), (1967) 42 *BYIL* 291–3 (CA).
[103] [2008] 1 AC 153, 219, para. 147. See also [2008] 1 AC 153, 180–1, para. 12 (Lord Bingham), holding as a result that the *Salomon* presumption gave the claimants 'little if any help'.
[104] [2008] 1 AC 153, 219, para. 147, quoting (1996) 8 EHRR 123, 158–9.
[105] [2008] 1 AC 153, 219, para. 148, considering (1999) 29 EHRR 493, para. 138.
[106] [2008] 1 AC 153, 219, para. 148, considering (1999) 29 EHRR 493, para. 138.
[107] See [2008] 1 AC 153, 180–1.   [108] [2008] 1 AC 153, 219, para. 149.

the converse is not true: a claim may in some circumstances fall within the scope of the Convention but not within the scope of the Act'.[109] Turning to construe the HRA, his Lordship found force in the Secretary of State's submission regarding the absence from the Act of any of the forms of words usually used where Parliament intends a provision to have extraterritorial application: while he acknowledged that a clear inference of extraterritorial application could otherwise be drawn from the terms of a statute, it could not be doubted 'that, if Parliament had intended the Act to have extra-territorial application, words could very readily have been found to express that intention'.[110] Similarly, although the absence of article 1 of the ECHR from the Act was readily explicable as unnecessary in a domestic statute, '[h]ad article 1 been included in section 1 and the Schedule, this would have assisted the claimants, since by 1997–1998 the Strasbourg jurisprudence had recognised some limited exceptions to the territorial focus of the Convention, and it could have been said that Parliament intended the territorial scope of the Act to be subject to the same limited exceptions'.[111] As it was, the omission of any reference to article 1 was 'of some negative assistance to the Secretary of State'.[112] His Lordship also considered a variety of other alleged textual indications said by each side to support its case,[113] not finding them very compelling in favour of one or the other, although they did lend 'some slight support' to the Secretary of State's contention.[114] But '[m]ore compelling in his favour [was] the absence of any clear pointer in the claimants' favour, for it is on the Act itself that they must primarily rely to rebut the presumption of territoriality'.[115] As for case-law, the judgment of the Court of Appeal in *R (B) v Secretary of State for the Foreign and Commonwealth Office*, in which the HRA was held to apply to the actions of UK consular staff in Melbourne, was 'plainly very helpful to the claimants'.[116] But the Court of Appeal had reached its conclusion by means of heavy reliance on the obligation in section 3 of the HRA to interpret legislation as far as possible in a manner compatible with Convention rights, a provision which was not, in his Lordship's view, 'a tool which can be used to determine the extent of the rights which are protected by the Act',[117] as he had made clear earlier in his opinion, as follows:

Section 3 provides an important tool to be used where it is necessary and possible to modify domestic legislation to avoid incompatibility with the Convention

---

[109] [2008] 1 AC 153, 176, para. 4.
[110] [2008] 1 AC 153, 181, para. 13.   [111] [2008] 1 AC 153, 182, para. 14.
[112] [2008] 1 AC 153, 182, para. 14.   [113] See [2008] 1 AC 153, 182–3, para. 15.
[114] [2008] 1 AC 153, 183, para. 16. See also [2008] 1 AC 153, 216, para. 135 (Lord Brown), not suggesting, however, that these textual details even slightly assisted the respondent.
[115] [2008] 1 AC 153, 183, para. 16.
[116] [2008] 1 AC 153, 184, para. 17, citing [2005] QB 643.
[117] [2008] 1 AC 153, 184, para. 17. See also [2008] 1 AC 153, 219, para. 147 (Lord Brown).

rights protected by the Act, but it cannot be used to determine the content or extent of the rights which are to be protected. It is in my view plain that section 3 was not intended to be used in construing the Act itself.[118]

Nor could the statement by Lord Nicholls in *Quark* 'be treated as reliable authority on the [present] point', as it was not directed to it, was seemingly contradicted by a later passage from his Lordship's speech and did not clearly claim majority support.[119] Coming to his conclusion, Lord Bingham stated:

In the course of its careful consideration of this question the Divisional Court observed, in para. 304: 'It is intuitively difficult to think that Parliament intended to legislate for foreign lands.' In similar vein, Brooke LJ in the Court of Appeal said, at para. 3:

'It may seem surprising that an Act of the UK Parliament and a European Convention on Human Rights can arguably be said to confer rights upon citizens of Iraq which are enforceable against a UK governmental authority in the courts of England and Wales.'

I do not think this sense of surprise, which I share, is irrelevant to the court's task of interpretation. It cannot of course be supposed that in 1997–1998 Parliament foresaw the prospect of British forces being engaged in peacekeeping duties in Iraq. But there can be relatively few, if any, years between 1953 and 1997 in which British forces were not engaged in hostilities or peacekeeping activities in some part of the world, and it must have been appreciated that such involvement would recur. This makes it the more unlikely, in my opinion, that Parliament could, without any express provision to that effect, have intended to rebut the presumption of territorial application so as to authorise the bringing of claims, under the Act, based on the conduct of British forces outside the UK and outside any other contracting state. Differing from the courts below, I regard the statutory presumption of territorial application as a strong one, which has not been rebutted.[120]

His Lordship added a few words on the reasoning of the Divisional Court and of Brooke LJ in the Court of Appeal (reasoning taken up by Lords Rodger, Carswell and Brown in the present case):[121]

The Divisional Court based its finding of extra-territorial application in part on its understanding of the modest extent to which the Strasbourg court had

---

[118] [2008] 1 AC 153, 182, para. 15.

[119] [2008] 1 AC 153, 185, para. 20, having considered [2006] 1 AC 529, paras 34 and 36 (Lord Nicholls), para. 25 (Lord Bingham himself) and para. 57 (Lord Hoffmann). See also [2008] 1 AC 153, 186, para. 22 (Lord Bingham) and 216, para. 136 (Lord Brown); but *cf*, contradicting the spirit if not letter of his earlier statement, [2008] 1 AC 153, 218, para. 143 (Lord Brown). Similarly unhelpful, in Lord Bingham's view, were the decisions in *R (European Roma Rights Centre) v Immigration Officer at Prague Airport* [2006] 1 AC 173, [2004] 75 *BYIL* 504–12 (HL) and *R (Carson) v Secretary of State for Work and Pensions* [2006] 1 AC 173. See also [2008] 1 AC 153, 216, para. 136 (Lord Brown).

[120] [2008] 1 AC 153, 186–7, para. 24.

[121] See [2008] 1 AC 153, 195, para. 55 (Lord Rodger), 206, para. 98 (Lord Carswell) and 220, para. 150 (Lord Brown).

recognised the Convention itself as having extra-territorial application. In para. 301 it said:

> 'Whatever may have been the position if our conclusion, or Strasbourg jurisprudence, had been that article 1 of the Convention was founded on some form of broad personal jurisdiction, nevertheless where on the contrary, for the reasons which we have described above, article 1 should be and has been given an essentially territorial effect, it is counter-intuitive to expect to find a parliamentary intention that there should be gaps between the scope of the Convention and an Act which was designed to bring rights home, that is to say as we understand that metaphor to enable at any rate domestic or British claimants to sue in the domestic courts rather than in Strasbourg.'

Thus the Divisional Court found the Act to have extra-territorial application (para. 306) to 'allow of the narrow exception which we have framed and applied in the case of the sixth claimant'. Brooke LJ similarly confined the extra-territorial effect of the Act by limiting it, at para. 147, to cases 'where a public authority is found to have exercised extraterritorial jurisdiction on the application of [state agent authority] principles'. I think, with respect, that there is a certain danger in this line of reasoning. It is one thing to say (if there is ground for doing so) that Parliament intended the Act to have the same extra-territorial effect as the Convention. It is another to base that conclusion on the finding that the exceptions to the territoriality principle recognised by Strasbourg were minor, unless it could be assumed that the Strasbourg court would recognise no other or wider exceptions in future.... [122]

Lord Bingham accordingly held that the HRA had no extraterritorial application, so that a claim under the Act would not lie against the Secretary of State based on acts or omissions of British forces outside the UK.[123]

On the extraterritorial scope of the ECHR, five of their Lordships were in agreement, Lord Brown delivering the leading speech on point. (Lord Bingham, having ruled the five appeals out on the HRA question, thought it 'not only unnecessary but unwise' to express an opinion on the second question.[124]) Lord Brown first outlined the basic approach to be taken to the question:

105 The ultimate decision upon this question, of course, must necessarily be for the European Court of Human Rights. As Lord Bingham of Cornhill observed in *R (Ullah) v Special Adjudicator* [2004] 2 AC 323, 350 (para. 20), 'the Convention is an international instrument, the correct interpretation of which can be authoritatively expounded only by the Strasbourg court.' In the same paragraph Lord Bingham made two further points: first, that a national court 'should not without strong reason dilute or weaken the effect of the Strasbourg case law'; secondly that, whilst member states can of course legislate so as to provide for rights more generous than those guaranteed by the Convention, national courts should not interpret the Convention to achieve this: the Convention must bear the same meaning for all states party to it. Para. 20 ends: 'The duty of

---

[122] [2008] 1 AC 153, 187, para. 25.   [123] [2008] 1 AC 153, 187, para. 26.
[124] [2008] 1 AC 153, 188, para. 27.

national courts is to keep pace with the Strasbourg jurisprudence as it evolves over time: no more, but certainly no less.'

106 I would respectfully suggest that last sentence could as well have ended: 'no less, but certainly no more.' There seems to me, indeed, a greater danger in the national court construing the Convention too generously in favour of an applicant than in construing it too narrowly. In the former event the mistake will necessarily stand: the member state cannot itself go to Strasbourg to have it corrected; in the latter event, however, where Convention rights have been denied by too narrow a construction, the aggrieved individual *can* have the decision corrected in Strasbourg. *Ullah*, of course, was concerned with the particular scope of individual Convention rights, there article 9, in the context of removing non-nationals from a member state. Lord Bingham's cautionary words must surely apply with greater force still to a case like the present. As the Grand Chamber observed in *Bankovic v Belgium* (2001) 11 BHRC 435, 449, para. 65:

'the scope of article 1 . . . is determinative of the very scope of the contracting parties' positive obligations and, as such, of the scope and reach of the entire Convention system of human rights' protection.'

107 Your Lordships accordingly ought not to construe article 1 as reaching any further than the existing Strasbourg jurisprudence clearly shows it to reach. . . . [125]

In this light, the starting point for the present analysis was the judgment of a Grand Chamber of the European Court of Human Rights in *Bankovic v Belgium*,[126] rightly described by the Divisional Court as 'a watershed authority in the light of which the Strasbourg jurisprudence as a whole has to be re-evaluated'.[127] *Bankovic* emphasized that article 1 of the ECHR reflected an 'essentially territorial notion of jurisdiction', 'other bases of jurisdiction being exceptional and requiring special justification in the particular circumstances of each case'; and that the ECHR operated, subject to article 56, 'in an essentially regional context and notably in the legal space (*espace juridique*) of the contracting states' (that is, within the area of the Council of Europe's member States).[128] In those rare cases where the European Court had held the ECHR to apply to conduct outside the territory of the respondent State, this had been 'to avoid a "vacuum in human rights' protection" when the territory "would normally be covered by the Convention" . . . (ie in a Council of Europe country) where otherwise (as in Northern Cyprus) the inhabitants 'would have found themselves excluded from the benefits of the Convention safeguards and system which they had previously enjoyed'.[129] *Bankovic* also stated that

---

[125] [2008] 1 AC 153, 195, 207–8, original emphasis. See also [2008] 1 AC 153, 188, para. 28 (Lord Bingham), 198, para. 66 (Lord Brown) and 204–5, paras 90–1 (Baroness Hale).

[126] (2001) 11 BHRC 435.

[127] [2008] 1 AC 153, 208, para. 108, quoting [2005] 2 WLR 1041, para. 268. See, similarly, [2008] 1 AC 153, 198, para. 68 (Lord Rodger).

[128] [2008] 1 AC 153, 209, para. 109, quoting (2001) 11 BHRC 435, paras 61 and 80. See also [2008] 1 AC 153, 198, para. 69 (Lord Rodger) and 204, para. 91 (Baroness Hale).

[129] [2008] 1 AC 153, 209, para. 109, quoting (2001) 11 BHRC 435, para. 80. See also [2008] 1 AC 153, 201, para. 77 (Lord Rodger).

the rights and freedoms defined in the ECHR could not be 'divided and tailored'.[130] As for what the exceptions to the otherwise strictly territorial scope of the Convention were, the first recognised in *Bankovic* was where the respondent State, ' "through the effective control of the relevant territory and its inhabitants abroad as a consequence of military occupation or through the consent, invitation or acquiescence of the government of that territory, exercises all or some of the public powers normally to be exercised by [the government of that territory]" (*ie* when otherwise there would be a vacuum within a Council of Europe country, the government of that country itself being unable "to fulfil the obligations it had undertaken under the Convention"...(as in Northern Cyprus))'.[131] The second situation in which the ECHR had been held to apply to conduct outside the territory of the respondent State involved the activities of that State's diplomatic or consular agents abroad or activities on board craft and vessels registered in, or flying the flag of, that State, where 'customary international law and treaty provisions have recognised the extraterritorial exercise of jurisdiction'.[132] There was also a third category of exceptional case cited by the Court where a State's jurisdiction under article 1 'could, in principle, be engaged because of acts...which produced effects or were performed outside their own territory', although the only such case referred to by the Court in *Bankovic* was *Drozd and Janousek v France and Spain*, the facts of which were highly particular.[133] '[O]n the face of it', then, his Lordship found 'nothing in *Bankovic* which [gave] the least support to the appellants' arguments',[134] based as they were on an expansive reading of the 'effective control' exception. Reference to article 56, in accordance with which a Contracting State could extend the application of the ECHR to one of its dependent territories, further undermined these arguments. Lord Brown first recalled that when a State chose to extend the Convention to a dependent territory, which was by definition not within the Council of Europe area, the rights and freedom secured therein were applied 'with due regard...to local requirements'.[135] He further recalled that the ECHR could not apply to dependent territories except by way of a declaration under article 56, and, in particular, that the 'effective control' principle did not apply to them.[136] In this light, his Lordship continued:

113 How then could [the 'effective control'] principle logically apply to any other territory outside the area of the Council of Europe? As the respondent

---

[130] [2008] 1 AC 153, 209, para. 109, quoting (2001) 11 BHRC 435, para. 75. See also [2008] 1 AC 153, 198–9, para. 69 (Lord Rodger).

[131] [2008] 1 AC 153, 209, para. 109, quoting (2001) 11 BHRC 435, paras 71 and 80.

[132] [2008] 1 AC 153, 209, para. 109, quoting (2001) 11 BHRC 435, para. 73.

[133] [2008] 1 AC 153, 209, para. 109, quoting (2001) 11 BHRC 435, para. 69 and citing (1992) 14 EHRR 745.

[134] [2008] 1 AC 153, 209, para. 109.

[135] [2008] 1 AC 153, 210, para. 111, quoting *Py v France* (2005) 42 EHRR 548.

[136] [2008] 1 AC 153, 210, para. 112, citing *Quark v United Kingdom* (2006) 44 EHRR SE 70.

submits, it would be a remarkable thing if, by the exercise of effective control, for however short a time, over non-Council of Europe territory, a state could be fixed with the article 1 obligation to secure within that territory, without regard to local requirements, all Convention rights and freedoms whereas, despite its exercise of effective control over a dependent territory, perhaps for centuries past, the state will not be obliged to secure any Convention rights there unless it has made an article 56 declaration and even then it would be able to rely on local requirements.

114...The logic...[is] clear: subject only to a few narrow exceptions the Convention applies solely within the Council of Europe area and must then apply in full measure. The same point was more recently made in *Ilaşcu v Moldova and Russia (Admissibility)* (Application No. 48787/99) (unreported) 4 July 2001 where the Court, rejecting Moldova's assertion that the Convention did not extend to Transdniestria, expressly distinguished a state's right not to extend the Convention to non-Council of Europe territories under article 56.[137]

The four Grand Chamber decisions on the scope of article 1 since *Bankovic* had expressly followed the latter's analysis, one of them by reference to a line of exceptional cases contemplated in that case.[138] Nor did the *Drozd*-style or embassy and consulate exceptions assist the appellants.[139] His Lordship then turned to 'the high watermark of the appellants' case',[140] namely paragraph 71 of *Issa v Turkey*,[141] a decision that he noted by way of preface was not a Grand Chamber decision, did not ultimately succeed and was found admissible in a decision pre-dating *Bankovic* in which, as noted in *Bankovic* itself, no issue of jurisdiction had been raised.[142] His Lordship found *Issa* 'unconvincing':[143]

If and in so far as *Issa* is said to support the altogether wider notions of article 1 jurisdiction contended for by the appellants on this appeal, I cannot accept it. In the first place, the statements relied upon must be regarded as obiter dicta. Secondly, as just explained, such wider assertions of jurisdiction are not supported by the authorities cited (at any rate, those authorities accepted as relevant by the Grand Chamber in *Bankovic*). Thirdly, such wider view of jurisdiction would clearly be inconsistent both with the reasoning in *Bankovic* and, indeed,

---

[137] [2008] 1 AC 153, 210.
[138] See [2008] 1 AC 153, 210–12, paras 115–20, considering *Assanidze v Georgia* (2004) 39 EHRR 653, *Ilaşcu v Moldova and Russia* (2004) 40 EHRR 1030, *Bosphorus Hava Yollari Turizm ve Ticaret Anonim Sirketi v Ireland* (2005) 42 EHRR 1 and *Öcalan v Turkey* (2005) 41 EHRR 985, the last citing *Sánchez Ramirez v France* (1996) 86-A DR 155 and *Freda v Italy* (1980) 21 DR 250.
[139] See [2008] 1 AC 153, 212, paras 121–3, citing, in the first category, *X and Y v Switzerland* (1977) 9 DR 57 and *Gentilhomme, Schaff-Benhadji and Zerouki v France*, Application Nos 48205/99, 48207/99 and 48209/99, unreported, 14 May 2002 and, in the second category, *X v Federal Republic of Germany* (1965) 8 Yearbook of the European Convention on Human Rights 158, *X v United Kingdom* (1977) 12 DR 73, *M v Denmark* (1992) 73 DR 193 and the English Court of Appeal case of *R (B) v Secretary of State for the Foreign and Commonwealth Office* [2005] QB 643.
[140] [2008] 1 AC 153, 213, para. 126.
[141] (2004) 41 EHRR 567.
[142] [2008] 1 AC 153, 212, para. 124, citing Application No. 31821/96, unreported, 30 May 2000. On the fact that *Issa* was an unsuccessful claim, see also [2008] 1 AC 153, 200, para. 73 (Lord Rodger).
[143] [2008] 1 AC 153, 213, para. 126.

with its result. Either it would extend the effective control principle beyond the Council of Europe area (where alone it had previously been applied, as has been seen, to Northern Cyprus, to the Ajarian Autonomous Republic in Georgia and to Transdniestria) to Iraq, an area (like the FRY considered in *Bankovic*) outside the Council of Europe—and, indeed, would do so contrary to the inescapable logic of the court's case law on article 56. Alternatively it would stretch to breaking point the concept of jurisdiction extending extraterritorially to those subject to a state's 'authority and control'. It is one thing to recognise as exceptional the specific narrow categories of cases I have sought to summarise above; it would be quite another to accept that whenever a contracting state acts (militarily or otherwise) through its agents abroad, those affected by such activities fall within its article 1 jurisdiction. Such a contention would prove altogether too much. It would make a nonsense of much that was said in *Bankovic*, not least as to the Convention being 'a constitutional instrument of European public order', operating 'in an essentially regional context', 'not designed to be applied throughout the world, even in respect of the conduct of contracting states' (para 80). It would, indeed, make redundant the principle of effective control of an area: what need for that if jurisdiction arises in any event under a general principle of 'authority and control' irrespective of whether the area is (a) effectively controlled or (b) within the Council of Europe?[144]

A further objection to the appellants' argument was the 'indivisible nature' of jurisdiction within the meaning of article 1 of the ECHR: in the words of *Bankovic*, the rights under the Convention could not be 'divided and tailored'.[145] Moreover, the Convention operated as a 'living instrument', so that in *Öcalan*, for example, the European Court had considered article 2 to have been modified by the fact that the Council of Europe had become a zone free of capital punishment.[146] His Lordship also drew attention to the rigour with which the Court applied the Convention, 'well exemplified by the series of cases from the conflict zone of south eastern Turkey in which, the state's difficulties notwithstanding, no dilution has been permitted of the investigative obligations arising under articles 2 and 3'.[147] In this light, he reasoned:

The point is this: except where a state really does have effective control of territory, it cannot hope to secure Convention rights within that territory and, unless it is within the area of the Council of Europe, it is unlikely in any event to find certain of the Convention rights it is bound to secure reconcilable with the customs of the resident population. Indeed it goes further than that. During the period in question here it is common ground that the UK was an occupying power in Southern Iraq and bound as such by Geneva IV and by the Hague Regulations. Article 43 of the Hague Regulations provides that the occupant 'shall take all the measures in his power to restore and ensure, as far as possible,

---

[144] [2008] 1 AC 153, 214, para. 127. See also [2008] 1 AC 153, 210, paras 75–7 (Lord Rodger).

[145] [2008] 1 AC 153, 214, para. 128, going on to quote (2001) 11 BHRC 435, para. 40. See also [2008] 1 AC 153, 202, para. 79 (Lord Rodger): 'In other words, the whole package of rights applies and must be secured where a contracting state has jurisdiction.'

[146] [2008] 1 AC 153, 214, para. 128, considering (2005) 41 EHRR 985, para. 195. See also [2008] 1 AC 153, 201–2, para. 78 (Lord Rodger).

[147] [2008] 1 AC 153, 214–15, para. 128.

public order and safety, while respecting, unless absolutely prevented, the laws in force in the country'. The appellants argue that occupation within the meaning of the Hague Regulations necessarily involves the occupant having effective control of the area and so being responsible for securing there all Convention rights and freedoms. So far as this being the case, however, the occupants' obligation is to respect 'the laws in force', not to introduce laws and the means to enforce them (for example, courts and a justice system) such as to satisfy the requirements of the Convention. Often (for example where Sharia law is in force) Convention rights would clearly be incompatible with the laws of the territory occupied.[148]

Thus, in Lord Brown's view, *Issa* 'should not be read as detracting in any way from the clear—and clearly restrictive—approach to article 1 jurisdiction adopted in *Bankovic*'.[149] Taken as a whole, and according particular weight to Grand Chamber judgments, subsequent Strasbourg case-law, rather than weakening the principles laid down in *Bankovic*, reinforced them. 'Certainly, whatever else [could] be said of the Strasbourg jurisprudence', it could not be said to establish clearly that any of the five appellants came within the UK's jurisdiction within the meaning of article 1 of the Convention.[150]

Lord Brown was alone in considering not only whether the five appellants' cases should be considered covered by the Convention but also on what basis the sixth claim, conceded by the Secretary of State, should be, the latter being an issue on which the Divisional Court and the Court of Appeal had differed. He recognised the UK's jurisdiction over the deceased 'only on the narrow basis found established by the Divisional Court, essentially by analogy with the extraterritorial exception made for embassies (an analogy recognised too in *Hess v United Kingdom* (1975) 2 DR 72, a Commission decision in the context of a foreign prison which had itself referred to the embassy [case of] *X v Federal Republic of Germany)*'.[151]

The first question before the House, that of the territorial scope of the HRA, could have been answered plausibly either way. The majority decision, while drawing support from one or two unreliable sources and strained arguments, is eminently defensible, even if Lord Bingham's is probably the more right: given the almost complete want of evidence, either textual or circumstantial, of Parliament's intent as to the HRA's

---

[148] [2008] 1 AC 153, 215, para. 129. See also [2008] 1 AC 153, 202, paras 78–9 (Lord Rodger).

[149] [2008] 1 AC 153, 215, para. 131. His Lordship acknowledged that the subsequent cases of *Isaak v Turkey*, Application No. 44587, unreported, 28 September 2006 and *Ben El Mahi v Denmark*, Application No. 5853/06, unreported, 11 December 2006 had repeated the substance of paragraph 71 of *Issa*; but he noted that in neither case did there appear to have been any relevant argument on the scope of article 1. See also [2008] 1 AC 153, 198, paras 67–8 and 202, paras 80–1 (Lord Rodger) and 204, para. 91 (Baroness Hale).

[150] [2008] 1 AC 153, 215–16, para. 132. Lord Rodger, agreeing with the conclusion of Brooke and Richards LJJ in the Court of Appeal, adds that, even if the *Issa* approach were to be applied, the first five deceased could not be said in any real sense to have been under the control of the British soldiers who were, or may have been, responsible for their deaths: [2008] 1 AC 153, 202–3, paras 82–3. See, similarly, [2008] 1 AC 153, 206, para. 97 (Lord Carswell).

[151] [2008] 1 AC 153, 216, para. 132.

scope of application *ratione loci*, it is difficult to conclude that the presumption against extraterritorial application has been rebutted. In the final analysis, however, the difference between the majority and Lord Bingham appears to lie chiefly in the weight to be attached to this presumption— that is, in the evidentiary muscle required to budge it.[152] That said, there may also be a related, unstated and perhaps unwitting dynamic at play in at least some of the majority opinions. Although Lord Brown agrees with Lord Bingham, and rightly so, that the 'strong interpretative obligation' imposed by section 3 of the HRA[153] does not apply to the interpretation of the HRA itself, one cannot help but feel that the majority makes more effort to harmonise the Act and the Convention—and, conversely, places less genuine emphasis on parliamentary intent—than is justified by the standard canons of construction, including that enunciated by Diplock LJ in *Salomon*.[154] Lord Rodger's argument that making remedies available for acts of a UK authority on the territory of another State 'would not be offensive to the sovereignty of the other state', and that therefore there is 'nothing in the wider context of international law which points to the need to confine sections 6 and 7 of the 1998 Act to the territory of the United Kingdom',[155] is boot-strapping, policy-based stuff which owes little to a consideration of what Parliament may or may not have thought. The same goes for his Lordship's contorted reasoning in the following paragraph that the need for the claimants to be within the 'jurisdiction' of the UK within the meaning of article 1 of the ECHR 'blunts the objection that a narrow construction of the territorial application of the Act is the only way to prevent it having extravagant effects which could never have been intended'.[156] Lords Carswell and Brown also deploy this second argument, in which parliamentary intent is no more than a fig leaf. Lord Carswell reasons that '[t]he stringency of the test for establishing jurisdiction makes it the more likely that Parliament intended the Human Rights Act to operate extraterritorially within the jurisdiction of the United Kingdom'.[157] Lord Brown states, even more transparently:

I, like the Divisional Court, am readier to conclude that Parliament intended the Act to operate extraterritorially in a case where article 1 jurisdiction falls within

---

[152] Lord Bingham refers to the presumption of territorial application as a strong one, pointedly contrasting his view with those of the courts below: [2008] 1 AC 153, 187, para. 24. He earlier describes the presumption as 'hav[ing] become stronger over the years': [2008] 1 AC 153, 180, para. 11.

[153] See *eg R (Hurst) v London Northern District Coroner* [2007] AC 189, *supra*, pp. 520–7 (HL). Consider also *Dabas v High Court of Justice in Madrid, Spain* [2007] 2 AC 31, *supra*, pp. 515–20 (HL).

[154] See *Salomon v Commissioners of Customs and Excise* [1967] 2 QB 116, 143–4.

[155] [2008] 1 AC 153, 195, para. 54.

[156] [2008] 1 AC 153, 195, para. 55. Recall that his Lordship rounds off his argument with the following sentence, in which Parliament's intent plays even less of a part: 'The requirement for a claimant to be within the jurisdiction of the United Kingdom is a further assurance that, if the Act were interpreted and applied in that way, the courts in this country would not be interfering with the sovereignty or integrity of another state.'

[157] [2008] 1 AC 153, 206, para. 98.

one of the narrow categories of exception established under the Strasbourg case law (as in the sixth appellant's case), than I might be were Strasbourg to construe the reach of the Convention substantially more widely.[158]

In addition, Lord Rodger and, *malgré lui*, Lord Brown's uncritical reliance on the much-trumpeted dictum by Lord Nicholls in *Quark*,[159] patently referable to a different point, completely at odds with a later dictum in his Lordship's same speech and citing no evidence to support its assertion as to the intended identity in territorial scope between the HRA and ECHR, suggests a conclusion casting about for authority.

Lord Brown's argument as to article 13 of the ECHR—that if the HRA did not apply to the sixth claimant's case, it would amount to a violation of article 13 of the ECHR, since it would prevent the domestic courts from considering the claim on its merits—overlooks several possible alternative avenues of redress, not the least of them being the tort of battery (as in *Bici v Ministry of Defence*[160]) and the war crimes provided for in the International Criminal Court Act, both mentioned by Lord Bingham.[161] It is true that neither of these would grant the sixth claimant the independent official inquiry he was seeking in the present case, as also acknowledged by Lord Bingham[162] (even if a judicial examination of the facts would of necessity take place in the course of an action in tort or prosecution). But if this alone were to constitute a violation of article 13, then article 13 would amount to a *de facto* obligation on Contracting States to incorporate the ECHR into domestic law—an obligation the European Court accepted did not exist in *James*, the *Observer* case and *McCann*.[163] The blame, however, lies more with Strasbourg than with Lord Brown: the conflation of the primary obligation to secure the right to life and the secondary obligation to afford satisfaction is a further ground for questioning the 'procedural' or 'adjectival' obligation[164] to conduct an inquiry into a death at the hands of the State held by the Court in *McCann* to be an aspect of article 2.[165]

Their Lordships' answer to the second question, that of the territorial scope of the ECHR, is for the most part compelling. In the words of Lord Rodger, '[t]he problem which the House ha[d] to face, quite squarely, [was] that the judgments and decisions of the European court

---

[158] [2008] 1 AC 153, 220, para. 150.
[159] See [2008] 1 AC 153, 196–7, para. 58 (Lord Rodger) and 218, para. 143 (Lord Brown). But contrast [2008] 1 AC 153, 216, para. 136 (Lord Brown).
[160] [2004] EWHC 786, (2004) 75 *BYIL* 422 (QBD, Elias J).
[161] [2008] 1 AC 153, 187–8, para. 26.
[162] [2008] 1 AC 153, 188, para. 26.
[163] See *James v United Kingdom* (1986) 8 EHRR 123, para. 84; *The Observer and The Guardian v United Kingdom* (1991) 14 EHRR 153, para. 76; *McCann v United Kingdom* (1995) 21 EHRR 97, para. 153.
[164] [2008] 1 AC 153, 190, para. 36 (Lord Rodger), citing *In re McKerr* [2004] 1 WLR 807.
[165] For criticism on a different ground, see (2004) 75 *BYIL* 418.

do not speak with one voice'.[166] The Lords were quite right to dismiss the value of *Issa*: Turkey clearly missed a trick in failing to challenge the claim's admissibility, and the dictum of the European Court at paragraph 71, if taken at face value, is flatly inconsistent with the Grand Chamber's judgment in *Bankovic*. The Court should admit this, at least in private, and afford the case a discreet burial. Instead, as Lord Brown notes (albeit more diplomatically), the offending dictum has twice been parroted since, 'as so commonly occurs in Strasbourg judgments'.[167]

Inviolability of a foreign head of State—State Immunity Act 1978, section 20(1)(a)—Diplomatic Privileges Act 1964—Vienna Convention on Diplomatic Relations 1961, article 29—whether article 29 of Vienna Convention on Diplomatic Relations requiring redaction of court judgments to remove material by which foreign head of State could be identified

Case No. 5. Aziz v Aziz and others, 11 July 2007, [2007] EWCA Civ 712 (CA (Civ Div)).

The claimant, a former wife of the Sultan of Brunei, had successfully sued the tenth and main defendant, an Iraqi-born Israeli fortune-teller, for the return of payments totalling over £2,000,000 and for compensation for gifts, in a bizarre case involving a fraudulently fictitious text-and-telephone gentleman caller and two audio cassettes sent by the claimant to the defendant containing confidential material allegedly relating to the former's marital life with the Asian monarch. An order had been made early on anonymising the proceedings, and interlocutory orders were then made prohibiting the defendant from disclosing the information on the cassettes. The claimant subsequently applied to have the defendant committed for contempt, alleging that the latter had breached the court's orders by disclosing to a representative of the Sultan information likely to lead to the identification of the claimant as a party to the action and by divulging to him the nature of the recorded material. It was also claimed that the defendant had pressured the Sultan's representative to arrange for the proceedings to be withdrawn by threatening to reveal confidential information about the claimant's marriage to the Sultan. The Sultan sought directions preventing the publication, in connection with the proceedings, of his name and of anything by which he could be identified. He relied on article 29 of the Vienna Convention on Diplomatic Relations 1961,[168] applicable to him by virtue of section 20(1)(a) of the State Immunity Act 1978.[169] Incorporating the 'necessary modifications' referred to in section 20(1)(a) of the SIA, article 29 of the VCDR

---

[166] [2008] 1 AC 153, 198, para. 67.   [167] [2008] 1 AC 153, 215, para. 131.

[168] Vienna, 18 April 1961, 500 UNTS 95.

[169] SIA, s. 20(1)(a) provides that the Diplomatic Privileges Act 1964 shall, subject to the necessary modifications, apply to a sovereign or other head of State as it applies to the head of a diplomatic mission. In turn, the Diplomatic Privileges Act incorporates into English law, by way of schedule, the Vienna Convention on Diplomatic Relations.

provides that the receiving State shall treat a foreign head of State with due respect 'and shall take all appropriate steps to prevent any attack on his... dignity'. Gray J, in the Queen's Bench Division, denied the Sultan the relief sought, holding that the protection afforded by article 29 of the VCDR was not available to him in his personal capacity, and proceeded to make a suspended committal order against the defendant. The trial judge, Underhill J, gave judgment for the claimant,[170] and committed the defendant to prison following further acts of contempt. The Sultan appealed Gray J's denial of relief, and sought redactions to Gray and Underhill JJ's respective judgments in order to remove any material which could lead to his identification.[171]

The Court of Appeal (Civil Division) unanimously dismissed the Sultan's appeal, Lawrence Collins LJ giving the leading judgment which Sedley LJ and Sir Anthony Clark MR agreed.

Lawrence Collins LJ first accepted, contrary to Gray J's ruling, that the protection of article 29 of the VCDR was indeed available to the Sultan in his personal capacity.[172] The privileges and immunities of a head of State under international law were accorded *ratione personae*, in other words regardless of the character of the acts in question, as made clear in the English courts in *Mighell v Sultan of Johore*[173] and as acknowledged over a hundred years later in article 3(2) of the United Nations Convention on Jurisdictional Immunities of States and Their Property.[174] Moreover, the application of article 29 of the VCDR to a foreign head of State in his personal capacity had been assumed in *Harb v King Fahd Abdul Aziz*,[175] a case relating to divorce proceedings in the English courts against the King of Saudi Arabia. As for the suggestion that article 29 related only to cases where the offensive conduct would prevent the head of State from carrying out his or her functions, his Lordship considered this an 'inappropriate test'.[176]

Turning to the content of the obligation in article 29 of the VCDR and especially to the concept of the 'dignity' of a foreign head of State, Lawrence Collins LJ noted the agreement of counsel that authority on point was 'very scant'.[177] After surveying the material put to the court,[178] his Lordship summarised the position:

[88] What then is the present state of international law on the right to dignity of a head of state? There is no doubt that a State is obliged to take steps to prevent physical attacks on, or physical interference with, a foreign head of state who

---

[170] See *A v Aziz* [2007] EWHC 91 (QB).
[171] In the Court of Appeal, Lawrence Collins LJ accepted that the Sultan was entitled to make an application for the redaction of the judgments without waiving his immunity for any other purpose: see [2007] EWCA Civ 712, para. 124.   [172] [2007] EWCA Civ 712, paras 55–7.
[173] [1894] 1 QB 149, 159 (Lord Esher MR).
[174] A/RES/59/38, Annex, 2 December 2004 (not yet in force).
[175] EWCA Civ 632, (2005) 76 *BYIL* 571–5 (CA).
[176] [2007] EWCA Civ 712, para. 61.   [177] [2007] EWCA Civ 712, para. 62.
[178] See [2007] EWCA Civ 712, paras 63–87.

is in this country. This would be so equally under customary international law, and the combination of s. 20 of the 1978 Act and art. 29 [of the VCDR]. Nor would I doubt that the duty would apply to acts in this country preparatory to, or directed at, some form of physical attack against a head of state who is in his or her own country or in a third country.

[89] But, outside physical attack or interference, the material in relation to the prevention of offensive conduct supports the view that to the extent there is any uniform practice (which is doubtful) it amounts to no more than courtesy or comity. That view is in substance suggested by what Sir Arthur Watts QC (co-editor of *Oppenheim's International Law*, and a former Legal Adviser to the Foreign and Commonwealth Office), said in his Hague lectures *The Legal Position in International Law of Heads of State, Heads of Government and Foreign Ministers*, in Hague Academy of International Law, *Recueil des Cours*, Volume 247 (1994-III), pp. 35 to 48, to which I have already referred. Sir Arthur draws a distinction between offensive conduct by an official representative of the State, and conduct by a private party. As regards the latter, Sir Arthur says that it is uncertain to what extent international law imposes a positive obligation on States to prevent offensive conduct by private individuals directed against foreign heads of state, or requires them to punish such conduct if it occurs. His view is that it is not clear in State practice whether it is a matter of diplomatic courtesy rather than a recognition of legal responsibility.

Recalling that the establishment of a rule of customary international law required settled state practice allied to a belief that the practice was rendered obligatory by the existence of a rule of law requiring it, his Lordship declared himself 'far from convinced' by the material before the court that there existed a rule of customary international law imposing 'an obligation on a state to take appropriate steps to prevent conduct by individuals which is simply offensive or insulting to a foreign head of state abroad'.[179] If it had been necessary to do so, he would have decided that there was insufficient material to support such a rule.[180]

But it was not necessary to do so, as Lawrence Collins LJ was satisfied that there had been no relevant attack on the Sultan's dignity and that, in any case, all appropriate steps had been taken to prevent any such attack.[181] His Lordship rejected the proposition that an attack on the dignity of a head of State connoted any deliberate act intended to lower the head of State in others' estimation or to injure his or her honour or that of his or her office: such a reading of article 29 of the VCDR 'would be a wholly impermissible invasion of the principle of free speech'.[182] He recalled, as the Law Officers had advised in the nineteenth century, that heads of State subject to false vilification in England and Wales could avail themselves of the law of defamation.[183] In sum, he found it 'extremely difficult, if not impossible, to envisage any situation in which speech, otherwise permitted

---

[179] [2007] EWCA Civ 712, para. 91, citing Jennings & Watts (eds), *Oppenheim's International Law. Volume I: Peace* (9th ed., 1992), p. 28, itself quoting *North Sea Continental Shelf Cases (FRG/ Denmark; FRG/Netherlands)*, ICJ Rep 1969, p. 3 at p. 44. See also [2007] EWCA Civ 712, para. 93.
[180] [2007] EWCA Civ 712, para. 93.   [181] [2007] EWCA Civ 712, para. 93.
[182] [2007] EWCA Civ 712, para. 94.   [183] [2007] EWCA Civ 712, para. 95.

under English law, could be prohibited on the ground that it was an attack on the dignity of a foreign head of state'.[184] In this light, whatever the content of the UK's duty to take appropriate steps to prevent an attack on the dignity of a foreign head of State, there was 'not the slightest trace' of any conduct in the instant case which, even in accordance with the most extensive interpretation of an 'attack on dignity', could have amounted to such an attack.[185] The references in Gray and Underhill JJ's judgments to the identity of the claimant's ex-husband could not possibly constitute an 'attack'. Nor could the fact that the committal judgments were the consequence of the defendant's conduct in meetings with the Sultan's representative which was calculated to embarrass the Sultan comprise an attack or complicity in such an attack.[186] Equally, there was no interference with the 'dignity' of the Sultan: to identify him as the former husband of a defrauded claimant or as the employer of an official through whom the defendant had tried to pressure the claimant to withdraw the proceedings did not, in his Lordship's judgment, affect the Sultan's dignity in the sense used in the international legal authorities.[187]

As for the remedies sought by the Sultan, English common law, CPR 39.2(1) and article 6(1) of the ECHR all laid down a general rule, subject to certain exceptions, that a hearing was to be in public.[188] Lawrence Collins LJ also accepted that the case of *Colombani v France*, in which the European Court of Human Rights held that a law making it an offence publicly to insult a foreign head of State infringed the guarantee of freedom of speech embodied in article 10 of the ECHR, 'strongly suggest[ed] that the court would not lightly accept that greater protection should be given to the dignity of a head of State than to ordinary members of the public'.[189] Moreover, the duty of a judge to give reasons was 'a function of due process and therefore justice', both at common law and under article 6 of the ECHR.[190] At the same time, judges were normally sensitive to the interest of parties and non-parties, especially to the need to avoid making findings of fact adverse to persons who had not had an opportunity to be heard.[191] In the instant case, Gray and Underhill JJ had dealt sensitively with the confidential and personal information before them, and had made appropriate orders: they had ordered privacy in relation to the committal applications and to the trial to the extent necessary; there was no suggestion that any confidential information would be disclosed, since this was already covered by an order made by Gray J; and the judgments of both judges had been redacted to remove confidential or potentially embarrassing

---

[184] [2007] EWCA Civ 712, para. 96.
[185] [2007] EWCA Civ 712, para. 97.
[186] [2007] EWCA Civ 712, para. 97.
[187] [2007] EWCA Civ 712, para. 98.
[188] [2007] EWCA Civ 712, paras 102–15.
[189] [2007] EWCA Civ 712, para. 121.
[190] [2007] EWCA Civ 712, para. 123.
[191] [2007] EWCA Civ 712, para. 124. See, similarly, [2007] EWCA Civ 712, para. 131 (Sedley LJ).

material.[192] Mention of the Sultan was not irrelevant to the findings.[193] Furthermore, nothing discreditable was said about him in the judgments, no finding was made against or about him, and neither judgment contained confidential information relating to him. His Lordship was prepared to accept 'that the court, in exercising its discretion to make part of a judgment private, may take into account the fact that the Applicant is a foreign head of State, and may also take into account the international obligations of the United Kingdom to the foreign State of which he is head'.[194] But he could see 'no basis for the proposition that the identification of the Sultan in the judgments could be a breach of the international obligations of the United Kingdom'; nor could he see any other reason why the Sultan should not be identified.[195] There was no reason to order further redaction of the judgments.

The decision and Lawrence Collins LJ's judgment are unimpeachable.

Convention relating to the Status of Refugees 1951, articles 1F, 32 and 33—definition of 'refugee'—exclusion clauses—acts contrary to the purposes and principles of the United Nations—terrorism—non-refoulement—treaty interpretation—Vienna Convention on the Law of Treaties, article 31—whether exclusion from refugee status possible for acts contrary to purposes and principles of United Nations committed after admission as refugee

Case No. 6. MT (Algeria) v Secretary of State for the Home Department, 30 July 2007, [2007] EWCA Civ 808, [2008] 2 WLR 159 (CA (Civ Div)).

The Secretary of State served notice of deportation back to Algeria on the claimant, an Algerian national granted refugee status in the UK in 2001 and subsequently tried and acquitted of terrorism offences in relation to his alleged role in a UK-based plot in 2004 to disperse the nerve agent ricin. The Secretary of State argued that the claimant's deportation was in the interests of national security. The claimant argued before the Special Immigration Appeals Commission (SIAC) that, in accordance with the obligation of *non-refoulement* imposed on Contracting States by article 33(1) of the Refugee Convention,[196] as incorporated into domestic law by section 2 of the Asylum and Immigration Appeals Act 1993,[197] the Secretary of State was prohibited from expelling or returning him in any manner whatsoever to the frontiers of territories where his life or freedom would be threatened on account of his race, religion, nationality, membership of a particular group or political opinion. SIAC upheld the Secretary of State's decision, accepting that the claimant was a danger to national

---

[192] [2007] EWCA Civ 712, para. 125. See also [2007] EWCA Civ 712, para. 131 (Sedley LJ).

[193] [2007] EWCA Civ 712, para. 128.   [194] [2007] EWCA Civ 712, para. 124.

[195] [2007] EWCA Civ 712, para. 130.

[196] Convention relating to the Status of Refugees, Geneva, 28 July 1951, 189 UNTS 2545.

[197] See *R (European Roma Rights Centre) v Immigration Officer at Prague Airport* [2005] 2 AC 1, 44, para. 42 (Lord Steyn), (2004) 75 *BYIL* 504–12 (HL). Section 2 of the Asylum and Immigration Appeals Act provides that nothing in the Immigration Rules enacted under the Immigration Act 1971 shall lay down any practice which would be contrary to the Refugee Convention.

security and that he could no longer be considered a refugee on account of article 1F(c) of the Refugee Convention. Article 1F as a whole reads:

The provisions of this Convention shall not apply to any person with respect to whom there are serious reasons for considering that:

(a) he has committed a crime against peace, a war crime, or a crime against humanity, as defined in the international instruments drawn up to make provision in respect of such crimes;

(b) he has committed a serious non-political crime outside the country of refuge prior to his admission to that country as a refugee;

(c) he has been guilty of acts contrary to the purposes and principles of the United Nations...

The terrorist acts of which the claimant had been accused were considered contrary to the purposes and principles of the United Nations. The claimant appealed the decision, arguing that SIAC had erred in concluding that article 1F(c) of the Refugee Convention extended to acts committed after the claimant's recognition as a refugee: article 33(2) of the Convention governed such acts, serving to deny a recognised refugee article 33(1)'s protection against *refoulement*, whereas article 1F related only to acts committed by applicants prior to recognition of their status as refugees. (Article 33(2) provides that the benefit of article 33(1) may not be claimed 'by a refugee whom there are reasonable grounds for regarding as a danger to the security of the country in which he is, or who, having been convicted by a final judgment of a particularly serious crime, constitutes a danger to the community of that country'.)

The Court of Appeal (Civil Division) dismissed the appeal, holding that SIAC had not erred in relying on article 1F(c) of the Refugee Convention to permit the claimant's deportation. Sir Andrew Clarke MR delivered the judgment of the Court.

As per article 31(1) of the Vienna Convention on the Law of Treaties, which the Court considered to have codified pre-existing customary international law, article 1F(c) was to be construed in accordance with the ordinary meaning to be given to the terms in their context and in the light of the Refugee Convention's object and purpose.[198] In response to the claimant's submission that article 1F applied only to acts committed prior to recognition of refugee status, the Court of Appeal stated:

80 There is no support for that conclusion in the language of article 1F. A comparison between the language of article 1F(c) with that of article 1F(b) suggests the contrary. Article 1F(b) is limited to a person who has committed a serious non-political crime outside the country of refuge 'prior to his admission to that country as a refugee'. Article 1F(c) contains no limitation of time. It seems reasonable to suppose that, if the draftsman had intended a temporal limitation, he would have provided for one.

81 On the other hand we accept that differences of language do not resolve all questions. For example, article 1C expressly provides for circumstances in which

the Convention 'shall cease to apply' whereas articles 1D, 1E and 1F simply provide for circumstances in which the Convention 'shall not apply'. It might be argued that only cases within article 1C apply post-recognition. However, it is correctly accepted that there is no significance in that difference in language because it is plain that article 1E applies post-recognition. In our view, if article 1E applies post-recognition, there is no reason why article 1F(c) should not equally apply post-recognition.

82 As to policy, [the claimant] submits that the object and purpose of the article 1F was to deny access to refugee status at the point of application. He submits that that is true of article 1F(b) and that the explanation for the restriction in article 1F(b) is that it introduces a geographical limitation as well as a temporal limitation. This does not seem to us to be convincing.... [199]

The claimant had further argued that the general purpose of article 1F was not to protect the host State from dangerous refugees, this being the purpose of article 33(2).[200] In support of his submission, he quoted Bastarache J for the majority of the Supreme Court of Canada in *Pushpanathan v Canada (Minister of Citizenship and Immigration)*:

The purpose of article 1 [of the Refugee Convention] is to define who is a refugee. Article 1F then establishes categories of persons who are specifically excluded from that definition. The purpose of article 33 of the Convention, by contrast, is not to define who is and who is not a refugee, but rather to allow for the *refoulement* of a bona fide refugee to his or her native country where he or she poses a danger to the security of the country of refuge, or to the safety of the community.... Thus, the general purpose of article 1F is not the protection of the society of refuge from dangerous refugees, whether because of acts committed before or after the presentation of a refugee claim; that purpose is served by article 33 of the Convention. Rather, it is to exclude ab initio those who are not bona fide refugees at the time of their claim for refugee status. Although all of the acts described in article 1F could presumably fall within the grounds for *refoulement* described in article 33, the two are distinct.[201]

The Court of Appeal acknowledged that this passage 'undoubtedly afford[ed] [the claimant]'s argument some support'.[202] But *Pushpanathan* was not addressing the issue before the Court here; and, had it been, the Supreme Court 'would no doubt have considered the difference in language between paragraphs (b) and (c)' of article 1F, although it could not be said what conclusion it would have reached.[203] For its part, SIAC had preferred to *Pushpanathan* the reasoning of the Immigration Appeal Tribunal in *KK v Secretary of State for the Home Department*,[204] where the Tribunal had emphasized the contrasting wording of articles 1F(b) and 1F(c) of the Refugee Convention, a difference it saw 'no reason at all to suppose...[was] accidental', since '[a]cts which merit the condemnation of the whole international community must lead to exclusion from the benefits of the Refugee Convention whenever they occur'.[205] The

[199] [2008] 2 WLR 159, 189.   [200] See [2008] 2 WLR 159, 189, para. 82.
[201] [2008] 2 WLR 159, 189–90, para. 83, quoting [1999] 1 SCR 982, para. 58.
[202] [2008] 2 WLR 159, 190, para. 84.   [203] [2008] 2 WLR 159, 190, para. 84.
[204] [2004] UKIAT 00101.   [205] [2008] 2 WLR 159, 190, para. 86.

Court of Appeal agreed with this logic, and, insofar as there was a difference, preferred it to the reasoning in *Pushpanathan*.[206] It continued:

87 In any event, we accept [the Secretary of State]'s submission that it is or may be significant that... in Pushpanathan's case Bastarache J refers to the 'general purpose' of article 1F as not being the protection of the country of refuge from dangerous individuals. We agree with [the Secretary of State] that this is not inconsistent with the possibility of a further purpose, which is to ensure that if an individual successfully claims the benefit of refugee status and then, while enjoying the surrogate international protection of his human rights afforded by the country of refuge, commits acts which show that he no longer deserves the benefit of that status, that status can be removed from him, just as he would never have qualified for that status if he had committed those acts before making a claim for refugee status.

88 We agree with the conclusion of SIAC... that being or becoming a 'refugee' as defined in the Refugee Convention does not require or start with a formal state act of recognition of status. A person simply is or is not a refugee within article 1A. He may lose the status of refugee in a number of circumstances as provided in articles 1C, D, E or F. We can see no reason to distinguish in terms of status between a person who, to take [the Secretary of State]'s example, becomes a mercenary in a war and commits war crimes before or after he is (or would but for the war crimes be) recognised as a refugee.

89 As SIAC held,... article 1 is concerned with the definition, not recognition of the status, of refugees. There is nothing in article 1F to indicate that it was intended that its provisions should only apply to those who had not hitherto been accorded the status of refugees.... [207]

The Court finally turned to the question of article 33(2), characterized by the claimant as the sole power by reference to which a refugee could lawfully be removed after the recognition of his or her status. In this regard, it agreed with the following conclusions of SIAC:

Article 33(2) permits someone to be removed notwithstanding that he would be persecuted on return, in circumstances which may overlap with those in article 1F(c). But they are not expressed in the same way and may not cover the same facts in any particular case. Nor is the possibility of removing someone who is a refugee on that basis the same as the obligatory exclusion of someone from being a refugee, formally recognised or not. True it is that almost all of the Convention is about the position of those who are refugees but that does not mean that their position cannot change or that the exclusion provisions cannot apply to exclude someone from being a refugee before or after formal state recognition as such. The focus remains on acts in the past rather than on future risk.[208]

In the light of all of the above, the Court of Appeal concluded that SIAC had been correct to hold that article 1F(c) of the Refugee Convention applied both before and after recognition as a refugee.[209]

---

[206] [2008] 2 WLR 159, 190, para. 86.   [207] [2008] 2 WLR 159, 191.
[208] [2008] 2 WLR 159, 191–2, para. 89.   [209] [2008] 2 WLR 159, 192, para. 90.

The point of treaty interpretation raised by the case is a very tricky one on which reasonable people can differ; and although no reference is made in the judgment to crucial recent evidence (set out below), the Court of Appeal's decision appears to be the way the wind is blowing. But it is hard to say if this makes it a correct reading of the Convention as things stand.

There is no doubting that the contrast between the wording of article 1F(b), with its phrase 'prior to his admission to that country as a refugee', and that of articles IF(c) and 1F(a) is striking; and there is a presumption against an interpretation of article 1F(c) that would render the words in article 1F(b) redundant. But, given the countervailing arguments, the Court may not have been justified in according the point quite the weight it does. Conversely, it arguably places insufficient emphasis on another significant contextual element, alluded to by the Supreme Court of Canada in *Pushpanathan*: given article 32, entitled 'Expulsion', and article 33, entitled 'Prohibition of expulsion or return ("refoulement")', it is unlikely that article 1, entitled 'Definition of the term "refugee"', can also be brought to bear on the expulsion of refugees, since this too would create a degree of textual redundancy. That said, the rejoinder might be as follows: articles 32 and 33 deal with the expulsion of persons satisfying article 1's definition of a refugee; as universally recognized, refugee status attaches to a person by virtue of his or her satisfaction of article 1, whether or not a formal determination has been made to this effect by the state of refuge;[210] conversely, a person who does not satisfy article 1's definition is not a refugee, regardless of whether the state of refuge has previously recognized him or her as one, with the result that article 1 and articles 32 and 33 in no way overlap. The riposte might be that the rejoinder is premised on the assumption that someone who was once a refugee, whether recognized or not, can no longer be one if he or she commits, while a refugee, an act contrary to the purposes and principles of the United Nations—which poses precisely the question we are trying to answer. And so back to the beginning.

Either way, one of the Court's central arguments, namely that the contrast between the wording of article 1C ('shall cease to apply') and the wording of articles 1D, 1E and 1F ('shall not apply') is insignificant because 'it is plain that article 1E applies post-recognition', is mistaken, although the mistake is more counsel's for apparently accepting this in argument. Counsel and the Court read article 1E—which states that the Refugee Convention 'shall not apply to a person who is recognised by the competent authorities of the country in which he has taken residence

---

[210] See *eg* UNHCR, *Handbook on Procedures and Criteria for Determining Refugee Status under the 1951 Convention and the 1967 Protocol relating to the Status of Refugees* (Geneva: UNHCR, 1979, re-edited 1992), UN Doc. HCR/IP/4/Eng/REV.1, para. 28: 'A person is a refugee within the meaning of the 1951 Convention as soon as he fulfils the criteria contained in the definition. This would necessarily occur prior to the time at which his refugee status is formally determined. Recognition of his refugee status does not therefore make him a refugee but declares him to be one. He does not become a refugee because of recognition, but is recognized because he is a refugee.'

as having the rights and obligations which are attached to the possession of the nationality of that country'—as referring to the situation where a refugee, after a period of residence in the State of refuge and the fulfilment of any other requisite criteria, qualifies for naturalization and opts for it. But article 1E refers to a different situation altogether, as made clear in the UNHCR *Handbook*,[211] namely that of persons who, at time of admission to the territory of the State of refuge, already qualify for that State's nationality, for example Jews entering Israel in the exercise of their right of return, *Aussiedler* (sometimes referred to as *Volksdeutsche*) entering Germany pursuant to the equivalent provision codified in article 116 of the German constitution, or, in the past, citizens of the British Commonwealth/British subjects entering the UK.[212] The situation envisaged by counsel and the Court is actually covered by article 1(C)(3), which provides that the Convention 'shall cease to apply to any person falling under the terms of section A if ... he has acquired a new nationality, and enjoys the protection of the country of his new nationality', a provision applicable to the nationality of the State of refuge as much as it is to third-State nationality, as indicated in the UNHCR *Handbook*.[213] In short, the words 'shall not apply' in article 1E apply only to qualities possessed by the relevant individual prior to recognition as a refugee. In this light, the contrast between article 1C's 'shall cease to apply' and the phrase 'shall not apply' as found in articles 1D, 1E and, crucially for present purposes, 1F becomes more telling; and it is not for nothing that the UNHCR *Handbook* refers to the provisions of article 1C as the 'cessation clauses' and to those of articles 1D, 1E and 1F as the 'exclusion clauses'.[214] Moreover, as regards the former, the UNHCR *Handbook* states that the cessation clauses 'are exhaustively enumerated ... and no other reasons may be adduced ... to justify the withdrawal of refugee status'.[215]

---

[211] See UNHCR *Handbook*, para. 144: 'This provision relates to persons who might otherwise qualify for refugee status and who have been received in a country where they have been granted most of the rights normally enjoyed by nationals, but not formal citizenship. (They are frequently referred to as "national refugees".) The country that has received them is frequently one where the population is of the same ethnic origin as themselves.' The older literature refers to such persons as 'con-nationals': see *eg* Grahl-Madsen, *The Status of Refugees in International Law. Volume I: Refugee Character* (Leyden: Sijtoff, 1966), 265–70.

[212] A footnote to the UNHCR *Handbook*, para. 144 reads: 'In elaborating this exclusion clause, the drafters of the Convention had principally in mind refugees of German extraction having arrived in the Federal Republic of Germany who were recognized as possessing the rights and obligations attaching to German nationality.' See also Grahl-Madsen, *idem*, 266–9; Hathaway, *The Law of Refugee Status* (Toronto; Butterworths, 1991), 211–12; Goodwin-Gill & McAdam, *The Refugee in International Law* (3rd ed.) (Oxford: Oxford University Press, 2007), 161–2.

[213] UNHCR *Handbook*, para. 130. Indeed, as para. 130 states, '[t]he nationality that the refugee acquires is usually that of the country of his residence'. See, similarly, Grahl-Madsen, *idem*, 395: '... normally, but not necessarily, the country where he has found refuge'; Hathaway, *idem*, 209: '[T]he Convention provides for the cessation of [refugee] status when the refugee becomes a citizen of her asylum state or of some other country which is able effectively to protect her.'

[214] See UNHCR *Handbook*, chapters III and IV respectively.

[215] UNHCR *Handbook*, para. 116. See also Grahl-Madsen, *supra*, 369: 'In other words, once a person has become a refugee as defined in Article I of the Convention ..., he continues to be a refugee until he falls under any of the cessation clauses.'

The subsequent judicial practice of the parties in the interpretation and application of article 1F(c) is of little help. As the *Handbook* states, 'there are hardly any precedents on record for the application of this clause',[216] and what readily available case-law there is is not on point.

The *travaux préparatoires*, in which the discussion is all of exclusion on entry, do not address the specific point at issue here, perhaps because the application of article 1F to pre-entry acts alone was taken as read. Highly relevant, however, is that the *travaux* provide an explanation for the words 'prior to his admission to that country as a refugee' in article 1F(b). These were inserted for the avoidance of doubt, in order to make abundantly clear that article 1F(b)—and seemingly, as a consequence, article 1F in its entirety—could not be used 'to revoke the refugee status...of one who committed a crime after entry, in circumstances in which the exceptional limitations on *non-refoulement* did not apply'.[217] In other words, the most likely reason for the contrast in wording on which SIAC and the Court of Appeal stake their respective decisions serves to undermine them.

In all of this, it is puzzling that the Court makes no mention of the UNHCR *Handbook*, re-edited in 1992, to which the House of Lords has attached 'high persuasive authority'.[218] As regards the temporal element of article 1F, the *Handbook* states:

Normally it will be during the process of determining a person's refugee status that the facts leading to exclusion under these clauses will emerge. It may, however, also happen that facts justifying exclusion will become known only after a person has been recognized as a refugee. In such cases, the exclusion clause will call for a cancellation of the decision previously taken.[219]

In other words, the *Handbook* envisages only one situation in which refugee status is to be cancelled pursuant to article 1F, and this relates to conduct prior to entry. Scholarly opinion, no trace of which is to be found in the Court of Appeal's judgment either, has also previously supported the view that article 1F applies only to pre-entry acts. Hathaway states that article 1F 'applies only to persons believed to have committed serious, pre-entry crimes'.[220] Gilbert elaborates on the distinction between article 1F and article 33(2):

In other parts of Europe [excepting Germany], rather than use Article 33(2), with its higher demands, States would prefer to use Article 1F where a refugee commits terrorist acts in the country of refuge...[This] is clearly a case specifically within Article 33(2) and ought to be decided with respect to that provision's requirements.... It should also be noted...that the grounds listed in Article 1F

---

[216] UNHCR *Handbook*, para. 141.   [217] Goodwin-Gill & McAdam, *supra*, 172–3.

[218] *R v Secretary of State for the Home Department, Ex parte Adan* [2001] 2 AC 477, 520 (Lord Steyn), (2000) 71 *BYIL* 422–6 (HL). See also the weight accorded the *Handbook* by Lord Hutton in the same case: [2001] 2 AC 477, 525. See too *Horvath v Secretary of State for the Home Department* [2001] 1 AC 489, 498–9 (Lord Hope), 503 (Lord Lloyd) and 515 (Lord Clyde), (2000) 71 *BYIL* 418–22 (HL); and *Januzi v Secretary of State for the Home Department* [2006] 2 AC 426, 440, para. 7 (Lord Bingham), (2006) 77 *BYIL* 458–64 (HL).

[219] UNHCR *Handbook*, para. 141.   [220] Hathaway, *supra*, 225.

are not grounds for cessation under Article 1C. Article 33(2) is the proper route where a refugee commits a particularly serious crime in the country of refuge and constitutes a danger to the community of that country, although even in this situation refugee status does not cease, only the protection of *non-refoulement*.[221]

He states flatly that article 1F 'only applies to pre-entry acts by the applicant'.[222]

But in an apparent reflection of States' changing attitudes since 11 September 2001, UNHCR's position on the question seems to have changed dramatically since the 1992 edition of its *Handbook* and the publication of those academic views in line with it. In 2003, UNHCR published new 'Guidelines on International Protection. Application of the Exclusion Clauses: Article 1F of the 1951 Convention relating to the Status of Refugees',[223] superseding its 1995 Guidelines and 1997 Note on the topic. The preface to the new Guidelines explains that they 'result, *inter alia*, from the Second Track of the Global Consultations on International Protection process which examined this subject at its expert meeting in Lisbon, Portugal, in May 2001'. It adds that updating the old Guidelines 'was also deemed necessary in light of contemporary developments in international law', although there is no indication whether this statement pertains to the present question. The new Guidelines state in relevant part:

C. Temporal scope

5. Articles 1F(a) and 1F(c) are concerned with crimes whenever and wherever they are committed. By contrast, the scope of Article 1F(b) is explicitly limited to crimes committed outside the country of refuge prior to admission to that country as a refugee.

D. Cancellation or revocation on the basis of exclusion

6. Where facts which would have led to exclusion only come to light after the grant of refugee status, this would justify **cancellation** of refugee status on the grounds of exclusion.... Where a refugee engages in conduct falling within Article 1F(a) or 1F(c), this would trigger the application of the exclusion clauses and the **revocation** of refugee status, provided all the criteria for the application of these clauses are met.[224]

---

[221] Gilbert, 'Current issues in the application of the exclusion clauses', in Feller, Türk & Nicholson (eds), *Refugee Protection in International Law. UNHCR's Global Consultations on International Protection* (Cambridge: Cambridge University Press, 2003), 458–9, references omitted.

[222] Gilbert, *idem*, 428.

[223] UNHCR Doc. HCR/GIP/03/05, 4 September 2003.

[224] 2003 Guidelines, p. 7. Paragraph 81 of the superseded 1995 Guidelines stated: 'Whereas Article 1F(b) specifies that the crime in question is one committed prior to admission, the other exclusion clauses contain no temporal references. In general, the exclusion clauses are applicable to acts committed prior to entry: the Convention makes provision for the handling of crimes committed by the refugee following admission. A refugee committing a crime in the country of refuge is subject to due process of law in that country. Therefore, in the event that a recognized refugee were to commit such crimes, the principle generally applicable is that of the obligation of the host country to bring to trial, or to extradite the individual, subject to the *non-refoulement* principle.' Paragraph 82

The 2003 Guidelines are a summary of UNHCR's 'Background Note on the Application of the Exclusion Clauses: Article 1F of the 1951 Convention relating to the Status of Refugees',[225] which, according to the Guidelines' preface, 'forms an integral part of UNHCR's position on this issue'. The Background Note states in relevant part:

E. Temporal scope

11. Whereas Article 1F(b) specifies that the crime in question must have been committed 'outside the country of refuge prior to [the individual's] admission to that country as a refugee', the other exclusion clauses contain no temporal or territorial references. Given the serious nature of the crimes concerned, Articles 1F(a) and 1F(c) are therefore applicable at any time, whether the act in question took place in the country of refuge, country of origin or in a third country. Once such crimes are committed, the individual is excluded from refugee status. If the individual has already been recognised as a refugee, his or her status would need to be revoked.

[...]

G. Revocation of refugee status (*ex nunc*)

17. In principle, refugees, including those recognised on a *prima facie* basis, must conform to the laws and regulations of the country of asylum as set out in Article 2 of the 1951 Convention and if they commit crimes are liable to criminal prosecution. The 1951 Convention foresees that such refugees can be subject to expulsion proceedings in accordance with Article 32 and, in exceptional cases, to removal under Article 33(2). Neither action *per se* involves revocation of refugee status. Where, however, a refugee engages in conduct coming within the scope of Article 1F(a) or 1F(c), for instance, through involvement in armed activities in the country of asylum, this would trigger the application of the exclusion clauses. In such cases, revocation of refugee status (from now or *ex nunc*) is appropriate, provided of course that all the criteria for the application of Article 1F(a) or 1F(c) are met.

Neither the new or old Guidelines are cited by the Court of Appeal.

The new position embodied in the UNHCR's 2003 Guidelines is mirrored in, and was doubtless informed by the emergence of, the approach recently adopted by the European Union. Whereas the EU's previous position was true to that of the now-seemingly-outdated UNHCR *Handbook*,[226] article 14(3)(a) of Council Directive 2004/83/EC of

---

continued that '[f]acts which would have justified exclusion may, however, become known only subsequently', before reproducing para. 141 of the *Handbook*.

[225] 4 September 2003.

[226] See para. 13 ('Article 1F of the Geneva Convention') of the Joint Position of the Council of the European Union of 4 March 1996 on the harmonized application of the definition of the term 'refugee' in Article 1 of the Geneva Convention of 28 July 1951 relating to the status of refugees, 96/196/JHA, OJ L 063, 13/03/1996, 2–7. See, similarly, the note on Article 1F of the Refugee Convention presented by the Secretary of State for Justice of the Netherlands to the Dutch parliament on 19 November 1997, reproduced in van Krieken, *Refugee Law in Context: The Exclusion Clauses* (The Hague: TMC Asser Press, 1999), 300, 303.

29 April 2004[227] provides that 'Member States shall revoke, end or refuse to renew the refugee status of a third country national or a stateless person, if, after he or she has been granted refugee status, it is established by the Member State concerned that...he or she should have been *or is excluded from being* a refugee in accordance with Article 12'.[228] Article 12(2) reproduces, with some tinkering, article 1F of the Refugee Convention. It is unclear whether the EU's position, and UNHCR's in its 2003 Guidelines, is yet representative of the practice of all the Contracting Parties to the Refugee Convention. But there can be little doubt that it will come to be.

It is also interesting to note article 14(4) of the 2004 EU Directive:

Member States may revoke, end or refuse to renew the status granted to a refugee by a governmental, administrative, judicial or quasi-judicial body, when:

(a) there are reasonable grounds for regarding him or her as a danger to the security of the Member State in which he or she is present;

(b) he or she, having been convicted by a final judgment of a particularly serious crime, constitutes a danger to the community of that Member State.

Subparagraphs (a) and (b) reproduce article 33(2) of the Refugee Convention. Crucially, however, the chapeau does not. Rather than just permitting *refoulement* in the circumstances specified in article 33(2), as article 33(2) itself does, the Directive allows Member States to revoke, end or refuse to renew refugee status. It was seemingly pursuant to article 14(4) of the Directive that the Secretary of State chose to act in the present case, as the terms of the notification served on the claimant (although not the judgment of the Court) indicate. But since article 14(4) of the Directive, and hence the Secretary of State's order, cannot be justified as a matter of public international law by reference to article 33 of the Refugee Convention, the Secretary of State was forced to argued by reference to article 1F(c).

There is perhaps a collateral reason for the Secretary of State's strategy in the present case. Another basis on which the claimant resisted return to Algeria was that he would be exposed there to treatment contrary to article 3 of the ECHR. By pursuing and winning the Refugee Convention argument on the basis of article 1F(c), rather than article 33(2), the Secretary of State stood to gain even if ultimately he was prevented by the ECHR from deporting the claimant, who, while safe for the time being from *refoulement*, would no longer be entitled to the refugee regime's many additional benefits.[229]

---

[227] Council Directive 2004/83/EC of 29 April 2004 on minimum standards for the qualification and status of third country nationals or stateless persons as refugees or as persons who otherwise need international protection and the content of the protection granted, OJ L 304, 30/09/2004, 12–23.

[228] Emphasis added.

[229] In *K v Secretary of State for the Home Department*, Lords Hope and Brown both emphasized the range of entitlements beyond mere *non-refoulement* afforded by the Refugee Convention: see

Finally, despite past debate, there can now be no doubt that terrorism falls within the scope of article 1F(c) of the Refugee Convention. The Declaration on Measures to Eliminate International Terrorism annexed to UN General Assembly resolution 49/60 of 9 December 1994 states that '[a]cts, methods and practices of terrorism constitute a grave violation of the purposes and principles of the United Nations'.[230] This was reaffirmed in the Declaration to Supplement the 1994 Declaration on Measures to Eliminate International Terrorism annexed to General Assembly resolution 51/210 of 17 December 1996.[231] Going further, the declaration on the global effort to combat terrorism annexed to Security Council resolution 1377 (2001) of 12 November 2001 '[s]tresses that acts of international terrorism are contrary to the purposes and principles of the Charter of the United Nations, and that the financing, planning and preparation of as well as any other form of support for acts of international terrorism are similarly contrary to the purposes and principles of the Charter of the United Nations'.[232] It does not come clearer than this.

Convention relating to the Status of Refugees 1951—internal relocation alternative—whether internal relocation unreasonable only where conditions in proposed safe haven liable to infringe article 3 of European Convention on Human Rights or equivalent—whether comparison between conditions in place of persecution and those in proposed safe haven to be given priority

Case No. 7. AH and others (Sudan) v Secretary of State for the Home Department, 14 November 2007, [2007] UKHL 49, [2007] 3 WLR 832 (HL).

The three claimants, who had all fled the Darfur region of Sudan to the capital Khartoum before arriving in the UK, had appealed the decision of the Asylum and Immigration Tribunal (AIT) that they were not entitled to refugee status within the meaning of article 1(A)(2) of the Refugee Convention,[233] as incorporated into domestic law by section 2 of the Asylum and Immigration Appeals Act 1993,[234] since Khartoum was a safe 'internal relocation' option—that is, they would not be persecuted there and, in accordance with the test laid down by the Lords in *Januzi v Secretary of State for the Home Department*,[235] it was reasonable, in the sense of not unduly harsh, to expect them to move there. The Court of

---

[2006] 3 WLR 733, 753, para. 35 (Lord Hope) and 780, para. 121 (Lord Brown), (2006) 77 *BYIL* 534–43 (HL).

[230] UN Doc. A/RES/49/60, 9 December 1994, para. 2.

[231] UN Doc. A/RES/51/210, 17 December 1996, para. 2.

[232] UN Doc. S/RES/1377, 12 November 2001.

[233] Convention relating to the Status of Refugees, Geneva, 28 July 1951, 189 UNTS 2545.

[234] See *R (European Roma Rights Centre) v Immigration Officer at Prague Airport* [2005] 2 AC 1, 44, para. 42 (Lord Steyn), (2004) 75 *BYIL* 504–12 (HL). Section 2 of the Asylum and Immigration Appeals Act provides that nothing in the Immigration Rules enacted under the Immigration Act 1971 shall lay down any practice which would be contrary to the Refugee Convention.

[235] [2006] 2 AC 426, (2006) 77 *BYIL* 458–64.

Appeal overturned the decision on the grounds, first, that the AIT had set the standard of reasonableness or undue harshness too high by requiring treatment so serious as to meet the threshold of ill-treatment under article 3 of the ECHR or its equivalent; and, secondly, that the AIT had compared the conditions in the country as a whole with the conditions prevailing in the place of proposed relocation, instead of comparing the conditions in the applicant's place of habitual residence, the starting point of the analysis, with those in the place of relocation. The Secretary of State now appealed the decision of the Court of Appeal.

The House of Lords, Lord Bingham delivering the leading opinion (with the reasoning and conclusions of which the other Lords agreed), allowed the appeal. The AIT had not founded its decision on the article 3 reasoning imputed to it by the Court of Appeal, and the Court of Appeal was wrong to consider a comparison with the conditions in the applicant's habitual place of relevance as the crucial determinant.

Lord Bingham stated that if the AIT had, in fact, considered that internal relocation could not be unreasonable or unduly harsh unless conditions in the place of intended relocation were liable to infringe an applicant's rights under article 3 of the ECHR or its equivalent, it would plainly have been wrong, since nothing in *Januzi* suggested such a test.[236] 'To the extent that reference was made to article 3 in *Januzi* it was to make clear, as might be thought obvious, that a claimant for asylum could not reasonably or without undue hardship be expected to return to a place where his rights under article 3 or its equivalent might be infringed.'[237] As for whether the correct comparator was the conditions in the applicant's home country as a whole or the conditions in his or her habitual place of residence, 'there was no contest between the two bases in *Januzi* and nothing was said to suggest that one basis is to be preferred, or is to be the starting point'.[238] Both were relevant, and the weight to be given to each was a matter to be judged by the decision-maker in relation to a particular applicant in a particular case.[239] The test propounded in *Januzi* 'was one of great generality, excluding from consideration very little':[240]

[T]he inquiry must be directed to the situation of the particular applicant, whose age, gender, experience, health, skills and family ties may all be very relevant. There is no warrant for excluding, or giving priority to, consideration of the applicant's way of life in the place of persecution. There is no warrant for excluding, or giving priority to, consideration of conditions generally prevailing in the home country.[241]

Lord Brown agreed that 'the speeches in *Januzi* are really quite irreconcilable with the respondents' submission...that the comparison between

---

[236] [2007] 3 WLR 832, 838, para. 9. See also [2007] 3 WLR 832, 843, para. 26 (Baroness Hale).
[237] [2007] 3 WLR 832, 838, para. 9. See also [2007] 3 WLR 832, 841–2, para. 22 (Baroness Hale).
[238] [2007] 3 WLR 832, 839, para. 13.   [239] [2007] 3 WLR 832, 839, para. 13.
[240] [2007] 3 WLR 832, 839, para. 13. See also [2007] 3 WLR 832, 845, para. 36 (Lord Brown).
[241] [2007] 3 WLR 832, 836, para. 5. See also [2007] 3 WLR 832, 840–1, para. 20 (Baroness Hale).

conditions in the place of persecution and those in the safe haven is the all important one':²⁴²

The ultimate decision to be made is, as stated, whether it is on the one hand 'reasonable' or on the other hand 'unduly harsh' to require the claimant to relocate. Clearly the conditions and circumstances of his previous way of life may inform that decision, bearing for example upon his ability to adapt to whatever changes and challenges are involved in relocation. But it is wrong to suggest, as the Court of Appeal do, that the critical contrast to be struck is between the circumstances in which the claimant lived when persecuted and those he would face in the proposed safe haven—so that if, for example, he had been rich and lived well but now, if relocated, would face comparative poverty, he would for that reason be entitled to asylum.²⁴³

But in seeming contrast to Lord Bingham, Lord Brown gave priority to conditions generally in the country of origin, citing in support UNHCR's Guidelines on International Protection of 23 July 2003, as well as statements by Lord Hope and Lord Bingham himself in *Januzi* to the effect that '[i]f the claimant can live a relatively normal life [in the proposed safe haven] judged by the standards that prevail in his country of nationality generally ... it will not be unreasonable to expect him to move there'.²⁴⁴ As to the approach taken by the AIT in comparing the standards generally prevailing in Sudan with those prevailing in Khartoum, the proposed safe haven, Lord Brown took issue with the respondents, who had been 'fiercely critical'²⁴⁵ of the Tribunal:

To my mind, ... this criticism is misplaced. It is not necessary to establish that a *majority* of the population live at subsistence level for that to be regarded as a 'relatively normal' existence in the country as a whole. If a significant minority suffer equivalent hardship to that likely to be suffered by a claimant on relocation and if the claimant is as well able to bear it as most, it may well be appropriate to refuse him international protection. Hard-hearted as this may sound, and sympathetic although inevitably one feels towards those who have suffered as have these respondents (and the tens of thousands like them), the Refugee Convention ... is really intended only to protect those threatened with specific forms of persecution. It is not a general humanitarian measure. For these respondents, persecution is no longer a risk. Given that they can now safely be returned home, only proof that their lives on return would be quite simply intolerable compared even to the problems and deprivations of so many of their fellow countrymen would entitle them to refugee status. Compassion alone cannot justify the grant of asylum.²⁴⁶

Baroness Hale, however, sounded a note of caution, which Lord Brown thought 'valuably illuminate[d] the correct approach to the question of undue harshness':²⁴⁷

²⁴² [2007] 3 WLR 832, 846, para. 39.   ²⁴³ [2007] 3 WLR 832, 845–6, para. 37.
²⁴⁴ [2007] 3 WLR 832, 846–7, paras 39–40, quoting [2006] 2 AC 426, 457, para. 47 (Lord Hope).
²⁴⁵ [2007] 3 WLR 832, 847, para. 42.   ²⁴⁶ [2007] 3 WLR 832, 847–8, para. 42.
²⁴⁷ [2007] 3 WLR 832, 848, para. 43.

27 We know that the lives [the applicants] led before the persecution are a relevant factor but not, as the Court of Appeal thought, the starting point. We know that the lives they will face on return have to be considered in the context of 'standards prevailing generally in the country of nationality': Lord Bingham in *Januzi* [2006] 2 AC 426, para. 20. If people can return to live a life which is normal in that context, and free from the well-founded fear of persecution, they cannot take advantage of past persecution to achieve a better life in the country to which they have fled: see Lord Bingham in para. 5 of his opinion [in the present case]. But this does not mean that the holistic consideration of all the relevant factors, looked at cumulatively, can be replaced by a consideration of whether their circumstances will be worse than the circumstances of *anyone else* in that country.

28 Yet the tribunal concluded that because the conditions faced by returning Darfuris, however appalling, would be no worse than those faced by other Sudanese [internally displaced persons] it would not be not 'unduly harsh' to expect them to return. The standard of comparison was, not with their lives in Darfur before their persecution, not with the general run of ordinary lives in Sudan, not even with the lives of poor people in Sudan, but with the lives of the poorest of the poor, internally displaced victims of the civil war in the south, living in camps or squatter slums, and 'subject from time to time to relocations, sometimes involving force and human rights violations' (para. 244). They too had been subsistence farmers, ill-equipped to survive in the city slums (para. 239); they too had suffered the psychological horrors of civil war (para. 238), if not of government-backed genocide; the Darfuris would be no worse off, unless particular individuals attracted the adverse interest of the authorities (para. 242). With respect, this is not the individualised, holistic assessment which the question requires.

29 My concern...is that, although the [tribunal's] determination does refer to many relevant considerations, it effectively...subordinates all considerations to a comparison with the very worst lives led by other Sudanese; and rejects any claim unless there is reason to believe that the individual will be targeted for special attention by the authorities...[248]

Her Ladyship did not disagree with the other Lords on the outcome of the case; rather, she raised her concerns 'in the hope that similar concerns will not arise in such cases in the future'.[249]

Their Lordships' judgment, which is largely a good one, goes some way to clarifying their inconsistent, contradictory and vague attempts in *Januzi* to describe the situations where internal relocation would not be reasonable and *refoulement* from the UK therefore precluded by the Refugee Convention. It exhibits, it has to be said, a rather selective memory of *Januzi*, according to which it was only a single statement in the case by Lord Hope that could have been misconstrued,[250] it otherwise being 'not easy to see', in the words of Lord Bingham, how the rule

---

[248] [2007] 3 WLR 832, 843.

[249] [2007] 3 WLR 832, 844, para. 40.

[250] See [2007] 3 WLR 832, 839, para. 10 (Lord Bingham) and 841, para. 22 (Baroness Hale), both citing [2006] 2 AC 426, 459–60, para. 54 (Lord Hope).

could be more simply or clearly expressed'.[251] Yet it was Lord Bingham himself in *Januzi* who, in describing the circumstances in which internal relocation would not be reasonable, cited the UNHCR Guidelines on International Protection to refer to places where 'basic human rights standards' are not met, 'including in particular' those relating to non-derogable rights.[252] In this light, the present judgment is unlikely to be the last to employ redactive amnesia. Similarly forgetful, given what he said to the apparent contrary in *Januzi* as recalled by Lord Brown here, is Lord Bingham's careless and confounding statement that '[t]here is no warrant for... giving priority to... consideration of conditions generally prevailing in the home country'.[253] While its faithful repetition of the structure of the previous sentence (about the conditions prevailing in the applicant's place of residence) is rhetorically attractive, further reflection might have led his Lordship to resist the temptations of style in the interests of substance.

European Convention on Human Rights 1950, article 5 (right to liberty)— Human Rights Act 1998—United Nations Security Council resolutions 1511 (2003) and 1546 (2004)—attribution of conduct to international organizations—International Law Commission's Draft articles on responsibility of international organizations, article 5—United Nations Charter, articles 25 and 103—Vienna Convention on the Law of Treaties, article 31(3)(b) and (c)—whether detention without trial in British-run facility in Iraq compatible with HRA

Case No. 8. R *(Al-Jedda)* v Secretary of State for Defence, 12 December 2007, [2007] UKHL 58, [2008] 2 WLR 31 (HL).

The facts of the case have been recounted previously.[254] On appeal to the House of Lords, the claimant did not pursue his previous argument as to the putative difference between his rights under the ECHR and his rights under the HRA, submitting solely that the effect of paragraph 10 of United Nations Security Council resolution 1546 (2004)[255] was not to override the protection secured to him, via section 6 of the HRA, by the right not to be arbitrarily detained embodied in article 5(1) of the ECHR. The Secretary of State, however, with leave of the House granted on account of a development in ECHR case-law since the Court of Appeal decision of March 2006, introduced an additional line of argument, in the alternative to its contention that the combined effect of resolution 1546 (2004) and article 103 of the UN Charter was lawfully to override the claimant's rights under ECHR, article 5(1). In the case(s) of *Behrami*

[251] [2007] 3 WLR 836, para. 5, endorsed at 845, para. 36 (Lord Brown).
[252] [2006] 2 AC 426, 448, para. 20   [253] [2007] 3 WLR 832, 836, para. 5.
[254] See R *(Al-Jedda)* v Secretary of State for Defence [2005] EWHC 1809 (Admin), (2005) 76 BYIL 578–85 (QBD (Div Ct)). See also R *(Al-Jedda)* v Secretary of State for Defence [2007] QB 621, (2006) 77 BYIL 481–5 (CA).
[255] S/RES/2004/1546, 8 June 2004.

and Behrami v France & Saramati v France, Germany and Norway[256] of May 2007, a Grand Chamber of the European Court of Human Rights had held the second application inadmissible on the ground that the impugned action by NATO forces in Kosovo—operating under unified command and control as part of KFOR,[257] alongside UNMIK,[258] pursuant to Security Council resolution 1244 (1999)[259]—was attributable to the UN and not to the respondent States, the Security Council having delegated only operational command to NATO while retaining ultimate authority and control over the deployment; and that as operations pursuant to Security Council resolutions under Chapter VII of the Charter were fundamental to the UN's mission of securing international peace and security and relied for their efficacy on member States, the ECHR could not be interpreted in such a manner as to subject to the Court's scrutiny acts and omissions of Contracting Parties covered by such resolutions and occurring prior to or in the course of such operations. The Court was thus incompetent *ratione personae* to adjudicate the matter. In the present case, the Secretary of State submitted, in the light of *Behrami*, that the claimant's detention by UK forces in Iraq—operating under unified command and control as part of the MNF,[260] in support of *inter alia* UNAMI,[261] pursuant to Security Council resolutions 1511 (2003)[262] and 1546 (2004)[263]—was attributable to the UN, not the UK, and was thus outside the scope of the ECHR.[264]

The House of Lords unanimously dismissed the claimant's appeal, holding (Lord Rodger dissenting on the first point and Lord Brown in two minds) that although the impugned conduct was attributable to the UK, not the UN, the combined effect of Security Council resolution 1546 (2004) and article 103 of the UN Charter was to override the claimant's rights under article 5(1) of the ECHR. Lord Bingham gave the leading opinion.

---

[256] Application Nᵒˢ 71412/01 and 78166/01, Decision as to admissibility, European Court of Human Rights (Grand Chamber), 2 May 2007, especially at 16, para. 43 and 37–44, paras 128–53.

[257] 'Kosovo Force'.

[258] 'The United Nations Mission in Kosovo'.

[259] S/RES/1999/1244, 10 June 1999.

[260] 'Multinational Force'.

[261] 'The United Nations Assistance Mission for Iraq'.

[262] S/RES/2003/1511, 16 October 2003.

[263] Two further Security Council resolutions, namely 1637 (2005) and 1723 (2006), renewed the authorization in SC res. 1546 (2004): see S/RES/2005/1637, 8 November 2005 and S/RES/1723, 28 November 2006.

[264] Note that the issue did not arise in the earlier Iraq case of *R (Al-Skeini and others) v Secretary of State for Defence* [2008] 1 AC 153, *supra*, pp. 529–546 (HL), since there the impugned conduct was alleged to have occurred prior to the handover of power to the Iraqi Interim Government by the US and UK on 28 June 2004 and the concomitant applicability of SC res. 1546 (2004). Note too that *Al-Skeini* resolved the issue of the extraterritorial application of the ECHR and HRA to the actions of British forces in Iraq, with the consequence that the claimant in the present case, held as he was in a British-run detention facility in Iraq, was considered to enjoy the protection of both instruments: see [2008] 2 WLR 31, 53, para. 48 and 56, para. 64 (Lord Rodger).

On the attribution point, it was agreed that the governing principle was that laid down in article 5 (as fleshed out by the commentary thereto) of the International Law Commission's Draft articles on responsibility of international organizations,[265] cited by the Grand Chamber in *Behrami*, in which the test of attribution to an international organization of the conduct of State organs or agents placed at its disposal was whether the organization exercised effective control over that conduct.[266] After outlining the factual and legal circumstances relevant to the MNF's mandate in Iraq (including the invasion of Iraq by the US, UK and Australia in March 2003 and the exercise prior to resolution 1546 (2004) of the powers of belligerent occupants by the US and UK through the CPA[267]), and having recalled the crucial passages and determinative issues in *Behrami*, Lord Bingham continued:

22 Against the factual background described above a number of questions must be asked in the present case. Were UK forces placed at the disposal of the UN? Did the UN exercise effective control over the conduct of UK forces? Is the specific conduct of the UK forces in detaining the appellant to be attributed to the UN rather than the UK? Did the UN have effective command and control over the conduct of UK forces when they detained the appellant? Were the UK forces part of a UN peacekeeping force in Iraq? In my opinion the answer to all these questions is in the negative.

23 The UN did not dispatch the coalition forces to Iraq. The CPA was established by the coalition states, notably the US, not the UN. When the coalition states became occupying powers in Iraq they had no UN mandate. Thus when the case of Mr Mousa reached the House as one of those considered in *R (Al-Skeini) v Secretary of State for Defence* [2007] 3 WLR 33, the Secretary of State accepted that the UK was liable under the European Convention for any ill-treatment Mr Mousa suffered, while unsuccessfully denying liability under the Human Rights Act 1998. It has not, to my knowledge, been suggested that the treatment of detainees at Abu Ghraib was attributable to the UN rather than the US. Following UNSCR 1483 in May 2003 the role of the UN was a limited one focused on humanitarian relief and reconstruction, a role strengthened but not fundamentally altered by UNSCR 1511 in October 2003. By UNSCR 1511, and again by UNSCR 1546 in June 2004, the UN gave the multi-national force express authority to take steps to promote security and stability in Iraq, but (adopting the distinction formulated by the European court in para. 43 of its

---

[265] Draft articles on responsibility of international organizations provisionally adopted so far by the Commission, article 5 and commentary, *Report of the International Law Commission. Fifty-sixth session (3 May–4 June and 5 July–6 August 2004)*, UN Doc. A/59/10, 109–15.

[266] [2008] 2 WLR 31, 35, para. 5 (Lord Bingham), citing *Behrami*, para. 30. See also [2008] 2 WLR 31, 57, para. 54 (Lord Rodger), although mistakenly referring to draft article 3. Lord Bingham, at [2008] 2 WLR 31, 35–8, para. 6, further quoted the following documents, none of them cited in *Behrami* but all iterating the 'effective control' or 'effective command and control' test: 'Responsibility of international organizations: Comments and observations received from international organizations', UN Doc. A/CN.4/545, 25 June 2004, 17–18; 'Report of the Secretary-General', UN Doc. A/51/389, 20 September 1996, 6, paras 17–19; 'Responsibility of international organizations: Comments and observations received from Governments and international organizations', UN Doc. A/CN.4/556, 12 May 2005, 4 (note 3) and 46.

[267] 'Coalition Provisional Authority'.

judgment in *Behrami and Saramati*) the Security Council was not delegating its power by empowering the UK to exercise its function but was authorising the UK to carry out functions it could not perform itself. At no time did the US or the UK disclaim responsibility for the conduct of their forces or the UN accept it. It cannot realistically be said that US and UK forces were under the effective command and control of the UN, or that UK forces were under such command and control when they detained the appellant.

24 The analogy with the situation in Kosovo breaks down, in my opinion, at almost every point. The international security and civil presences in Kosovo were established at the express behest of the UN and operated under its auspices, with UNMIK a subsidiary organ of the UN. The multi-national force in Iraq was not established at the behest of the UN, was not mandated to operate under UN auspices and was not a subsidiary organ of the UN. There was no delegation of UN power in Iraq. It is quite true that duties to report were imposed in Iraq as in Kosovo. But the UN's proper concern for the protection of human rights and observance of humanitarian law called for no less, and it is one thing to receive reports, another to exercise effective command and control. It does not seem to me significant that in each case the UN reserved power to revoke its authority, since it could clearly do so whether or not it reserved power to do so.[268]

In this light, the Secretary of State's submission based on *Behrami* was to be rejected. Baroness Hale[269] and Lord Carswell[270] agreed with this reasoning and conclusion.

Lord Rodger took the opposing view. His Lordship first took issue with some of the points considered determinative by Lord Bingham, Baroness Hale and Lord Carswell:

61 It respectfully appears to me that the mere fact that Resolution 1244 was adopted before the forces making up KFOR entered Kosovo was legally irrelevant to the issue in *Behrami*. What mattered was that Resolution 1244 had been adopted before the French members of KFOR detained Mr Saramati. So the resolution regulated the legal position at the time of his detention. Equally, in the present case, the fact that the British and other coalition forces were in Iraq long before Resolution 1546 was adopted is legally irrelevant for present purposes. What matters is that Resolution 1546 was adopted before the British forces detained the appellant and so it regulated the legal position at that time. As renewed, the provisions of that resolution have continued to do so ever since.

[...]

63 Another factual difference between the situations in Kosovo and Iraq is, in my view, equally irrelevant to the legal position of the members of the military forces. In Kosovo the United Nations itself was in charge of the civil administration of the country through the United Nations Interim Administration Mission in Kosovo (UNMIK). In Iraq, after the end of June 2004, the civil

---

[268] [2008] 2 WLR 31, 45–6.
[269] See [2008] 2 WLR 31, 72, para. 124, adding that it seemed 'unlikely in the extreme that the United Nations would accept that the acts of the MNF were in any way attributable to the UN'.
[270] See [2008] 2 WLR 31, 74, para. 131.

government of the country was in the hands of the Iraqi Interim Government and the United Nations Assistance Mission for Iraq (UNAMI) was there simply to provide humanitarian and other assistance. The fact that the civilian administration in Kosovo was in the hands of UNMIK played no part in the European court's decision that the actions of members of KFOR were attributable to the United Nations. Similarly, the fact that the civil government of Iraq was in the hands of the Iraqi Interim Government at the relevant time must be irrelevant for purposes of deciding whether the actions of members of the MNF in detaining the appellant were attributable to the United Nations.[271]

His Lordship highlighted that the key question posed by the Grand Chamber in *Behrami* was whether, in resolution 1244 (1999), the Security Council had delegated some of its own powers to KFOR, in which case KFOR's acts would be attributable to the UN, or whether it had merely authorized KFOR to take action, in which case conduct performed in the exercise of that mandate remained attributable to the States in question.[272] In this regard, the ultimate consideration was, in the words of the European Court, 'whether the UNSC retained ultimate authority and control so that operational command only was delegated', a question the Court answered in the affirmative.[273] What therefore fell to be considered in the present case was whether, in resolution 1546 (2004), the Council was delegating to the MNF its powers to take the necessary military measures to maintain peace and security in Iraq.[274] In this light, Lord Rodger first compared resolution 1244 (1999) with resolution 1511 (2003), the latter the legal basis for the MNF's deployment in Iraq:

87 If one compares the terms of Resolution 1244 and Resolution 1511, for present purposes there appears to be no relevant legal difference between the two forces. Of course, in the case of Kosovo, there was no civil administration and there were no bodies of troops already assembled in Kosovo whom the Security Council could authorise to assume the necessary responsibilities. In Resolution 1244 the Security Council accordingly decided 'on the deployment in Kosovo, under United Nations auspices, of international civil and security presences'. Because there were no suitable troops on the ground, in Resolution 1244 the council had actually to authorise the establishing of the international security presence and then to authorise it to carry out various responsibilities.

88 By contrast, in October 2003, in Iraq there were already forces in place, especially American and British forces, whom the Security Council could authorise to assume the necessary responsibilities. So it did not need to authorise the establishment of the MNF. In para. 13 the council simply authorised 'a multi-national force under unified command to take all necessary measures to contribute to the maintenance of security and stability in Iraq'—thereby proceeding on the basis that there would indeed be a multi-national force under unified command. In para. 14 the council urged member states to contribute forces to the MNF. Absolutely crucially, however, in para. 13 it spelled out the mandate which it was giving to the MNF. By 'authorising' the MNF to take the

---

[271] [2008] 2 WLR 31, 55–6.   [272] [2008] 2 WLR 31, 60–1, paras 79–81.
[273] [2008] 2 WLR 31, 62, para. 84.   [274] [2008] 2 WLR 31, 61, para. 82.

measures required to fulfil its 'mandate', the council was asserting and exercising control over the MNF and was prescribing the mission that it was to carry out. The authorisation and mandate were to apply to all members of the MNF—the British and American, of course, but also those from member states who responded to the council's call to contribute forces to the MNF. The intention must have been that all would be in the same legal position. This confirms that—as I have already held—the fact that the British forces were in Iraq before Resolution 1511 was adopted is irrelevant to their legal position under that resolution and, indeed, under Resolution 1546.

89 Allowing for the different situations on the ground, the terms of that mandate to the MNF are comparable with the terms of the mandate given to KFOR in Resolution 1244. The terms of the mandate to the MNF were, of course, subsequently altered by Resolution 1546 in June 2004, but the changes had the effect of making the mandate more specific. Just as Resolution 1244 defined the responsibilities which KFOR was to carry out in terms of its mandate from the Security Council, so, equally, Resolution 1546 defined the tasks which the MNF was to carry out in terms of its mandate from the Security Council. The two resolutions were essentially similar in these respects.[275]

It was true that the words 'under United Nations auspices' appeared in resolution 1244 (1999) and not in resolutions 1511 (2003) and 1546 (2004), but in his Lordship's view there was nothing in *Behrami* to suggest that the inclusion of these words in resolution 1244 (1999) played any part in the Strasbourg court's reasoning.[276] He concluded that 'when the Security Council, acting under Chapter VII, authorised the MNF to carry out its various tasks in terms of Resolution 1546, it was purporting to delegate these functions to the MNF, just as it had delegated functions to KFOR in Resolution 1244', and he saw no reason why Strasbourg would hold otherwise.[277] Lord Rodger then turned to compare resolutions 1244 (1999) and 1546 (2004) in more detail, in the light of the elements of the former treated as relevant in *Behrami*. First, the Grand Chamber had recalled, and the same was the case here, that the Charter permitted the Security Council to delegate powers to member States and relevant international organizations and that the power in question was one it was permitted to delegate.[278] Next, the Court had considered the delegation in resolution 1244 (1999) to be 'prior and explicit' (even though, in fact, the power to detain was not spelled out in the resolution); and in resolution 1546 (2004), the Council, by annexing and referring to Secretary of State Powell's letter,[279] had expressly and in advance authorized the MNF to resort to internment where this was necessary for imperative reasons of security.[280] Furthermore, resolution 1546 (2004), just like resolution 1244 (1999) as discussed in *Behrami*, 'put sufficiently defined limits on the delegation by fixing the mandate with adequate precision', even if, as with resolution 1244, 'the relatively broad nature of

[275] [2008] 2 WLR 31, 63–4.
[276] [2008] 2 WLR 31, 64, para. 90.
[277] [2008] 2 WLR 31, 64, para. 90.
[278] [2008] 2 WLR 31, 65, para. 93.
[279] See (2005) 76 BYIL 580–1.
[280] [2008] 2 WLR 31, 65, para. 94.

the [provisions] could not be avoided since the purpose of the resolution was to fix broad objectives and goals and not to describe, or interfere in the detail of, operational implementation and choices'.[281] The respective reporting requirements were also more than comparable:

96...[T]he court noted that Resolution 1244 required the leadership of KFOR to report to the Security Council so as to allow the council to exercise its overall authority and control. In fact,...that resolution requested the Secretary General to report to the council at regular intervals on the implementation of the resolution, 'including reports from the leaderships of the international civil and security presences, the first reports to be submitted within 30 days of the adoption of this resolution'.

97 Resolution 1546 was different but, if anything, the difference was designed to give the council more, not less, control of the MNF....[T]he Security Council requested the United States, on behalf of the MNF, to report within three months from the date of the resolution on the efforts and progress of the force, and on a quarterly basis thereafter. This was a tightening of the system of six-monthly reports under Resolution 1511 and must represent the considered view of the council as to the frequency and type of reporting which were necessary to allow it to maintain its ultimate authority and control over the MNF. So, unlike in Resolution 1244, there was provision for the United States, the member state with the lead in the MNF, to report directly to the Security Council within three months and on a quarterly basis after that....[282]

The Council's control over the period of the respective mandates was also germane:

98...[T]he court noted that Resolution 1244 provided that the mandate was for an initial period of 12 months and was to continue thereafter, 'unless the Security Council decides otherwise'. Adverting to the familiar problem of the possibility of a veto by a permanent member preventing the council from deciding to terminate the delegation, the Grand Chamber did not consider that this factor alone was sufficient for it to conclude that the Security Council did not retain ultimate authority and control.

99 Again, the provision in Resolution 1546 is different and must have been tailored to the realities of the situation in Iraq. It provided for the mandate of the MNF to be reviewed after 12 months or at the request of the Government of Iraq. So the Security Council could terminate the mandate after 12 months or alter it if experience showed that this was desirable. This is a further element which is designed to ensure that the council retains ultimate control of the MNF. In addition, the mandate was to expire on the completion of the political process for the development of democratic civil government in Iraq set out in...the resolution. So there was no question of the MNF having an indefinite open-ended mandate. Moreover, the Security Council declared that it would terminate the mandate earlier if requested by the Government of Iraq. This provision, too, is designed to make sure that the forces whose actions are authorised by the mandate cannot stay on beyond the time when their presence and assistance are required.

100 Arguably, in this respect also, Resolution 1546 gave more control to the Security Council than Resolution 1244. Under Resolution 1244, the mandate

---

[281] [2008] 2 WLR 31, 65, para. 95.   [282] [2008] 2 WLR 31, 65–6.

to KFOR was to continue, unless the Security Council decided otherwise. The risk, identified by the Grand Chamber, was that by using its veto, a permanent member could prevent the council from deciding to bring the mandate to an end. By contrast, under Resolution 1546, the mandate to the MNF was to terminate automatically on the completion of the political process described... This meant that a permanent member could not prolong the MNF's mandate by using its veto. Admittedly, the veto could be used against any proposal to alter the terms of the mandate after a review. But, if the provision in Resolution 1244 was not sufficient for the Grand Chamber to conclude that the Security Council did not retain ultimate authority and control over the actions of the members of KFOR, I can see no reason why the court would decide differently in respect of Resolution 1546.[283]

Finally, as had the European Court in relation to KFOR, his Lordship closely examined the MNF's chain of command, coming to the conclusion that there was 'no material difference between the chain of command in the present case and the chain of command for KFOR which the Grand Chamber was considering in *Behrami*'.[284] In the light of all of these factors, Lord Rodger concluded:

Just as the members of KFOR were exercising powers of the Security Council lawfully delegated to them by the Council, so also the members of the MNF were exercising powers of the Security Council lawfully delegated to them by the council under Resolution 1546. That being so, the court would hold, first, that the council retained ultimate authority and control and so remained responsible in law for the exercise of those powers and, secondly, that the action of the British troops, as members of the MNF, in detaining Mr Al-Jedda was in principle attributable to the United Nations in terms of article [5] of the draft articles on the Responsibility of International Organizations.[285]

It was not necessary for his Lordship to go on to consider in detail, as the European Court had done, whether the latter would be competent to review the acts of Contracting States carried out on behalf of the United Nations, 'since the Court would plainly adopt the same approach in any case where it had concluded that the actions of the respondent state in question had been carried out on behalf of the United Nations'.[286] He recalled as well that the Court had distinguished the situation in *Behrami* from that in *Bosphorus*, in which it had subjected to review the actions of a Contracting State performed pursuant to a Security Council resolution adopted under Chapter VII, and he stated that the reasoning in *Behrami* would apply to the present case.[287] Lord Rodger concluded:

111 I am accordingly satisfied that, since the detention of the appellant by British forces taking part in the MNF was an action which was covered by Security Council Resolution 1546 and occurred in the course of the mission of the MNF, the European court would hold that the Convention could not be

---

[283] [2008] 2 WLR 31, 66. [284] [2008] 2 WLR 31, 67, para. 101.
[285] [2008] 2 WLR 31, 68, para. 105. [286] [2008] 2 WLR 31, 68, para. 107.
[287] [2008] 2 WLR 31, 69, para. 109, citing *Bosphorus Hava Yollari Turizm ve Ticaret Anonim Sirketi v Ireland* (2005) 42 EHRR 1.

interpreted in a manner that would subject that action to its scrutiny. A complaint by Mr Al-Jedda, based on the same allegations of a violation of article 5(1) as in the present case, would accordingly be held to be incompatible *ratione personae* with the provisions of the Convention. In consequence, the court would hold an application based on that complaint to be inadmissible.

[...]

113 In my view, the result is accordingly that, like Mr Saramati, following the decision of the Grand Chamber in *Behrami*, 2 May 2007, Mr Al-Jedda must find his protection from arbitrary detention in the commitment, given by Mr Powell to the Security Council, that members of the MNF would at all times act consistently with their obligations under the law of armed conflict, including the Geneva Conventions....[288]

'It [was] for the Security Council, exerting its ultimate authority and exercising its ultimate right of control, to ensure that this commitment [was] fulfilled.'[289]

Lord Brown found the question of attribution 'altogether the most difficult' of the issues before the House,[290] and he wished he 'found it so easy' so conclude, as did Lord Bingham, that the analogy with Kosovo broke down at almost every point.[291] He took issue first with Lord Bingham's view that, in contrast to the position in respect of Kosovo, there was no delegation of UN power in Iraq, since it seemed to him that the two legal situations were the same.[292] His Lordship then considered the five factors relevant to the Grand Chamber's determination in *Behrami* that the UN had retained ultimate authority and control over KFOR, coming to essentially the same conclusions as Lord Rodger on all of them[293] bar the circumstances in which the MNF came to be authorized and mandated in the first place. In this last regard, his Lordship drew attention to what was, to his mind, the material distinction between *Behrami* and the present case:

145... Resolution 1244 decided... 'on the deployment in Kosovo, under United Nations auspices, of international civil and security presences'—the civil presence being UNMIK, recognised by the court in *Behrami*... as 'a subsidiary organ of the UN'; the security presence being KFOR. KFOR was, therefore, expressly formed under UN auspices. Paragraph 7 of the resolution '[a]uthorise[d] member states and relevant international organisations to establish the international security presence in Kosovo as set out in point 4 of Annex 2...

146 Resolution 1511 (2003), by contrast, was adopted on 16 October 2003 during the USA's and UK's post-combat occupation of Iraq and in effect gave

---

[288] [2008] 2 WLR 31, 69–70. [289] [2008] 2 WLR 31, 70.
[290] [2008] 2 WLR 31, 77, para. 141. [291] [2008] 2 WLR 31, 77, para. 143.
[292] [2008] 2 WLR 31, 77, para. 143.
[293] [2008] 2 WLR 31, 78, para. 144. In one point of difference from Lord Rodger, Lord Brown characterized the requirement in resolution 1244 (1999)'s that KFOR's reports be presented by the Secretary-General as an 'additional safeguard', albeit one the absence of which was 'counterbalanced by the fact that the MNF's mandate cease[d] unless renewed by the UNSC whereas KFOR's mandate was to continue until the UNSC decided otherwise (a decision which, at least theoretically, a permanent member could have vetoed)'.

recognition to those occupying forces as an existing security presence. Para. 13 of the resolution is instructive:

'Determines that the provision of security and stability is essential to the successful completion of the political process as outlined in para. 7 above and to the ability of the United Nations to contribute effectively to that process and the implementation of Resolution 1483 (2003), and authorises a multi-national force under unified command to take all necessary measures to contribute to the maintenance of security and stability in Iraq, including for the purpose of ensuring necessary conditions for the implementation of the timetable and programme as well as to contribute to the security of the United Nations Assistance Mission for Iraq ["UNAMI"], the Governing Council of Iraq and other institutions of the Iraqi interim administration, and key humanitarian and economic infrastructure.'

147 By Resolution 1483, adopted on 22 May 2003, the UNSC had 'resolved that the United Nations should play a vital role in humanitarian relief, for reconstruction of Iraq, and the restoration and establishment of national and local institutions for representative governance' and, pursuant to it, the Secretary General had established UNAMI, an essentially humanitarian and civil aid mission. As Resolution 1511 indicated, it was that mission which was the UN's contribution to the situation in Iraq. The MNF under unified command which para. 13 was authorising was to contribute to the security of, amongst others, UNAMI. Unlike KFOR, however, it was not itself being deployed 'under UN auspices'. UNAMI alone represented the UN's presence in Iraq.[294]

Nor did the position change with the adoption of resolution 1546 (2004):

Nothing either in the resolution itself or in the letters annexed suggested for a moment that the MNF had been under or was now being transferred to United Nations authority and control. True, the UNSC was acting throughout under Chapter VII of the Charter. But it does not follow that the UN is therefore to be regarded as having assumed ultimate authority or control over the force. The precise meaning of the term 'ultimate authority and control' I have found somewhat elusive. But it cannot automatically vest or remain in the UN every time there is an authorisation of UN powers under Chapter VII, else much of the analysis in *Behrami* would be mere surplusage.[295]

It was 'essentially on this basis' that his Lordship regarded the present case 'as materially different from *Behrami*' and concluded that the claimant's internment was attributable not to the UN, acting through the MNF, but to the UK.[296] But at the end of Lord Brown's opinion is to be found an extraordinary paragraph headed 'Postscript':

Since writing this judgment I have had the advantage of reading in draft the speech to be delivered by my noble and learned friend, Lord Rodger of

---

[294] [2008] 2 WLR 31, 78–9. See also [2008] 2 WLR 31, 72, para. 124 (Baroness Hale). Point 4 of Annex 2 to Security Council resolution 1244 (1999) provides: 'The international security presence with substantial NATO participation must be deployed under unified command and control and authorised to establish a safe environment for all people in Kosovo and to facilitate the safe return to their homes of all displaced persons and refugees.'

[295] [2008] 2 WLR 31, 79, para. 148.   [296] [2008] 2 WLR 31, 79, para. 149.

Earlsferry. I confess to having found it sufficiently persuasive to cause me to doubt the correctness of my own conclusion on the difficult issue of attribution. Given, however, that a majority of your Lordships are for the appellant on this issue and that in any event, having regard to the unanimity of view on issue two, it cannot decide the outcome of this appeal, I prefer to leave over for another day my final conclusion on the point. I just wish to indicate that I may change my mind.[297]

As a consequence, his Lordship is referred to in the law reports as 'dubitante'.[298]

It was on an affirmative answer to the second question before the House, namely whether the combined effect of Security Council resolution 1546 (2004) and article 103 of the UN Charter overrode the claimant's rights under article 5(1) of the ECHR, that the Divisional Court and Court of Appeal had found in favour the Secretary of State. On this issue the Lords were all in agreement.[299] The first question was whether resolution 1546 (2004) imposed in effect an obligation on the UK, within the meaning of article 103 of the Charter, to detain the claimant or whether the resolution at most authorized the UK to do so. Lord Bingham acknowledged the 'obvious attraction' of the claimant's argument, given that resolution 1546 (2004) used the language of authorization, not obligation.[300] But his Lordship cited three main reasons for rejecting the claimant's submission. To begin with, article 43 of the 1907 Hague Rules[301] provided that an occupying Power—the status of which the UK enjoyed in Iraq prior to the transfer of power to the Iraqi Interim Government on 28 June 2004 and the concomitant applicability of resolution 1546 (2004)—'shall take all the measures in his power to restore, and ensure, as far as possible, public order and safety'; and 'if the occupying power considers it necessary to detain a person who is judged to be a serious threat to the safety of the public or the occupying power there must be an obligation to detain such person', as suggested by the International Court of Justice in *Armed Activities on the Territory of the Congo*.[302] Although the claimant was not detained during the period of belligerent occupation, 'both the evidence and the language of UNSCR 1546 (2004) and the later resolutions strongly suggest[ed] that the intention

---

[297] [2008] 2 WLR 31, 81, para. 156.   [298] [2008] 2 WLR 31, 32.

[299] See, agreeing with Lord Bingham, [2008] 2 WLR 31, 70, para. 114 (Lord Rodger), 74, para. 129 (Baroness Hale), 74, para. 131 (Lord Carswell) and 80, para. 152 (Lord Brown).

[300] [2008] 2 WLR 31, 47, para. 31. See also [2008] 2 WLR 31, 75, para. 135 (Lord Carswell).

[301] Regulations concerning the Laws and Customs of War on Land, annexed to the Convention concerning the Laws and Customs of War on Land, The Hague, 18 October 1907, UKTS No. 9 (1910), Cd 5030.

[302] [2008] 2 WLR 31, 48, para. 32, citing *Armed Activities on the Territory of the Congo (Democratic Republic of the Congo v Uganda), Judgment*, 19 December 2005, para. 178, where the ICJ states that article 43 of the Hague Rules involves an obligation to protect the inhabitants of the occupied territory against acts of violence. The customary character of the stipulations embodied in the 1907 Hague Rules was acknowledged by the ICJ in *Construction of a Wall in the Occupied Palestinian Territory, Advisory Opinion*, ICJ Rep 2004, 136, 172, para. 89 and *Armed Activities*, para. 217.

was to continue the pre-existing security regime and not to change it'.[303] Next, while the Security Council was capable of adopting resolutions in mandatory terms,

language of this kind cannot be used in relation to military or security operations overseas, since the UN and the Security Council have no standing forces at their own disposal and have concluded no agreements under article 43 of the Charter which entitle them to call on member states to provide them. Thus in practice the Security Council can do little more than give its authorisation to member states which are willing to conduct such tasks, and this is what (as I understand) it has done for some years past.... There is, however, a strong and to my mind persuasive body of academic opinion which would treat article 103 as applicable where conduct is authorised by the Security Council as where it is required...This approach seems to me to give a purposive interpretation to article 103 of the Charter, in the context of its other provisions, and to reflect the practice of the UN and member states as it has developed over the past 60 years.[304]

Lastly, in a situation such as the present one, the word 'obligations' in article 103 of the Charter was not in any event to be given a narrow meaning. The importance of maintaining peace and security in the world could not be exaggerated. This was the UN's mission and the end to which its involvement in Iraq was directed. States that contributed to the multinational force became bound by article 25 of the Charter to carry out the decisions of the Security Council so as to achieve the latter's lawful objectives. It was true that the UK did not become specifically bound to detain the claimant in particular, but it was bound to exercise its power of detention where this was necessary for imperative reasons of security. 'It could not be said to be giving effect to the decisions of the Security Council if, in such a situation, it neglected to take steps which were open to it.'[305] Although the special character of the ECHR as a human rights instrument had often been emphasized, the reference in article 103 to 'any other international agreement' left no room for exceptions, a position supported by 'the consensus of learned opinion'.[306] His Lordship did not think that the Strasbourg court, if the present claim under article 5(1) were before it, would ignore the significance of article 103 of the Charter, since it had 'on repeated occasions taken account of provisions of international law, invoking the interpretative principle laid down in article

---

[303] [2008] 2 WLR 31, 48, para. 32.

[304] [2008] 2 WLR 31, 48–9, para. 33, citing Goodrich, Hambro & Simons (eds), *Charter of the United Nations: Commentary and Documents* (3rd ed., 1969), 615–16; *Yearbook of the International Law Commission 1979*, Vol. II, Pt One, para. 14; Sarooshi, *The United Nations and the Development of Collective Security* (1999), 150–1; and quoting Frowein & Krisch, 'Chapter VII. Action with respect to Threats to the Peace, Breaches of the Peace, and Acts of Aggression', in Simma (ed.), *The Charter of the United Nations: A Commentary* (2nd ed., 2002), 701, 729. See also [2008] 2 WLR 31, 70, para. 115 (Lord Rodger) and 75–6, para. 135 (Lord Carswell).

[305] [2008] 2 WLR 31, 49–50, para. 34. See, similarly, [2008] 2 WLR 31, 80, paras 151–2 (Lord Brown).

[306] [2008] 2 WLR 31, 50, para. 35, citing Bernhardt, 'Article 103', in Simma (ed.), *supra*, 1292, 1299–1300.

31(3)(c) of the Vienna Convention on the Law of Treaties, acknowledging that the Convention cannot be interpreted and applied in a vacuum and recognising that the responsibility of states must be determined in conformity and harmony with the governing principles of international law'; and, indeed, this had been stated in *Behrami*.[307] As to the argument that 'it would be anomalous and offensive to principle that the authority of the UN should itself serve as a defence of human rights abuses', given that the promotion of the respect for human rights ranked with the maintenance of international peace and security as one of the Organization's purposes, the dilemma was acute in cases such as the present one, where it was 'difficult to see how any exercise of the power to detain, however necessary for imperative reasons of security, and however strong the safeguards afforded to the detainee, could do otherwise than breach the detainee's rights under article 5(1)'.[308] One suggested solution was for parties to the ECHR to invoke article 15 of the Convention to derogate from their obligations under article 5(1). But his Lordship was not convinced:

[S]uch power may only be exercised in time of war or other public emergency threatening the life of the nation seeking to derogate, and only then to the extent strictly required by the exigencies of the situation and provided that the measures taken are not inconsistent with the state's other obligations under international law. It is hard to think that these conditions could ever be met when a state had chosen to conduct an overseas peacekeeping operation, however dangerous the conditions, from which it could withdraw. The Secretary of State does not contend that the UK could exercise its power to derogate in Iraq (although he does not accept that it could not). It has not been the practice of states to derogate in such situations, and since subsequent practice in the application of a treaty may (under article 31(3)(b) of the Vienna Convention) be taken into account in interpreting the treaty it seems proper to regard article 15 as inapplicable.[309]

Lord Bingham continued:

Thus there is a clash between on the one hand a power or duty to detain exercisable on the express authority of the Security Council and, on the other, a fundamental human right which the UK has undertaken to secure to those (like the appellant) within its jurisdiction. How are these to be reconciled? There is in my opinion only one way in which they can be reconciled: by ruling that the UK may lawfully, where it is necessary for imperative reasons of security, exercise the power to detain authorised by UNSCR 1546 and successive resolutions, but must ensure that the detainee's rights under article 5 are not infringed to any greater extent than is inherent in such detention.[310]

---

[307] [2008] 2 WLR 31, 50, para. 36, citing *Loizidou v Turkey* (1996) 23 EHRR 513, paras 42–3 and 52; *Bankovic v Belgium* (2001) 11 BHRC 435, para. 57; *Fogarty v United Kingdom* (2001) 34 EHRR 302, para. 34; *Al-Adsani v United Kingdom* (2001) 34 EHRR 273, paras 54–5; *Behrami and Saramati*, 2 May 2007, paras 122 and 149. See also [2008] 2 WLR 31, 70–1, paras 115–18 (Lord Rodger).

[308] [2008] 2 WLR 31, 51, para. 37.

[309] [2008] 2 WLR 31, 51, para. 38. See also [2008] 2 WLR 31, 74–5, para. 132 (Lord Carswell) and 80, para. 150 (Lord Brown).

[310] [2008] 2 WLR 31, 51, para. 38. See also [2008] 2 WLR 31, 73, para. 125 (Baroness Hale) and 76, para. 136 (Lord Carswell).

Baroness Hale, who agreed, added nonetheless a word of caution:

The right is qualified but not displaced. This is an important distinction, insufficiently explored in the all or nothing arguments with which we were presented. We can go no further than the UN has implicitly required us to go in restoring peace and security to a troubled land. The right is qualified only to the extent required or authorised by the resolution. What remains of it thereafter must be observed. This may have both substantive and procedural consequences.[311]

It was not clear how far Security Council resolution 1546 (2004) went:[312] there still had to be 'room for argument about what precisely is covered by the resolution and whether it applies on the facts of this case'.[313]

Their Lordships' respective views on the attribution point raise intriguing questions. It is hard not to think that Lord Bingham's analysis, concurred in by Baroness Hale and Lord Carswell, is overly brisk and assertive, even glib, taking as given findings that needed to be argued towards. Nor, as Lord Rodger points out, is all of it focused on the central legal issue, namely whether the UN exercised effective control over the MNF—or to put it in the words of *Behrami* (and there is arguably a significant difference), whether the UN retained 'ultimate authority and control'[314] over the MNF. Moreover, one could be forgiven, when reading the majority opinions, for thinking that KFOR was the disinterested initiative of a united Security Council involving forces assembled from scratch to do its bidding, rather than the US-, UK- and French-driven exercise in chutzpah that it was—an operation mostly by NATO forces already massed on Kosovo's borders with Albania and Macedonia in preparation for an illegal invasion after an illegal bombing campaign, tolerated by a co-opted Russia, based on an agreement with Yugoslavia that fell just this side of coerced and ratified by the Council strictly *faute de mieux*. Conversely, the majority view underestimates the scandalous extent to which, to its knowledge and chagrin, the Council was played for a sucker over Iraq by the Coalition, who had the brass to call in the UN to clean up after them, an offer they knew the Council, eager to re-establish its influence over international peace and security, could not refuse. As for the argument in relation to the MNF in Iraq that '[a]t no time did the US or the UK disclaim responsibility for the conduct of their forces or the UN accept it',[315] the contrast with Kosovo is not as great as his Lordship supposes. In the pre-*Behrami* case in the English courts of *Bici v Ministry of Defence* (referred to in the present case in a different context[316]), the MoD conceded its vicarious liability for any wrongs committed by UK soldiers operating in Kosovo as part of KFOR, on the ground

---

[311] [2008] 2 WLR 31, 73, para. 126. [312] [2008] 2 WLR 31, 73, para. 127.
[313] [2008] 2 WLR 31, 74, para. 129. [314] *Behrami*, paras 133–5 and 140.
[315] [2008] 2 WLR 31, 46, para. 23 (Lord Bingham).
[316] See *eg* [2008] 2 WLR 31, 80–1, para. 154 (Lord Brown).

that the UK had retained operational command over its contingent.[317] For its part, nowhere did the UN, in the course of its submissions to the European Court in *Behrami*, accept responsibility for the acts of KFOR in relation to the second application.[318]

In contrast to Lord Bingham *et al*, Lord Rodger's detailed forensic examination is a model of conscientious judging, and for the most part persuasive, especially in its attentive application (insofar as the judgment permits) of the reasoning in *Behrami*. Equally attractive is Lord Brown's opinion, at least before his Lordship's attack of the Hamlets. His close reading of the terms of establishment of KFOR and the MNF respectively is impressive, although again one must wonder whether it is sufficiently tied to *Behrami*.

The real question in all of this—the one that was, realistically, never going to be put to the Lords so soon after Strasbourg's judgment—is whether *Behrami* itself is correct. It certainly came as a surprise. One might reasonably ask, first, whether 'ultimate authority and control'[319] or, as referred to once in the judgment, 'overall authority and control'[320] is really sufficient to attribute KFOR's conduct to the UN. Article 5 of the ILC's Draft articles on responsibility of international organizations speaks of 'effective' control, and it is by no means self-evident that this is the same thing: 'effective' rather suggests that operational control or, synonymously, operational command, precisely what the Court in *Behrami* found NATO to enjoy in Kosovo,[321] is the index of attribution. Indeed, in a telling formulation, the Court in *Behrami* speaks at one point of NATO's '*effective* command of the relevant operational matters'.[322] As for the ILC's commentary to draft article 5, this states that '[t]he criterion for attribution of conduct either to the contributing State…or to the receiving organization is based according to article 5 on the factual control that is exercised over the specific conduct taken by the organ or agent placed at the receiving organization's disposal';[323] and, later, that 'when an organ or agent is placed at the disposal of an international organization,

---

[317] See [2004] EWHC 786, (2004) 75 *BYIL* 422–8 (QBD, Elias J). The MoD also disavowed reliance on the British act of State doctrine previously invoked in cases such as *Nissan v Attorney-General* [1970] AC 179, 231, (1968–69) 43 *BYIL* 217–26 (HL). In the event, the court held the MoD liable in tort for death and personal injury caused when UK troops serving as part of KFOR opened fire on a group of Kosovars, a decision the MoD did not appeal. It should be added, however, that vicarious liability under English law and responsibility under international law are distinct concepts, and are thus not necessarily coextensive. As a consequence, it is perhaps possible as a matter of logic—and as a formal legal matter it is clearly possible—for the MoD to concede its vicarious liability under English law for acts of its soldiers performed in the course of their employment while maintaining that international responsibility lies with the UN. But one would then expect the UK to seek an indemnity from the Organization, something that does not appear to have happened in the wake of *Bici*.

[318] See *Behrami*, paras 118–20.   [319] *Behrami*, paras 133–5 and 140.

[320] *Behrami*, para. 134.

[321] *Behrami*, paras 133, 135–6 and 139 ('operational command') and para 139 ('operational control').

[322] *Behrami*, para. 140, emphasis added.

[323] *Report of the International Law Commission. Fifty-sixth session*, 111, para. (3).

the decisive question in relation to attribution of a given conduct appears to be who has effective control over the conduct in question'.[324] More revealingly, paragraph (8) of the commentary quotes the following statement of the UN Secretary-General, reproduced by Lord Bingham in the present case:

In joint operations, international responsibility for the conduct of the troops lies where operational command and control is vested according to the arrangements establishing the modalities of cooperation between the state or states providing the troops and the United Nations. In the absence of formal arrangements between the United Nations and the state or states providing troops, responsibility would be determined in each and every case according to the degree of effective control exercised by either party in the conduct of the operation.[325]

Similarly, in a written comment to the ILC in relation to its work on the responsibility of international organizations, the UN Secretariat, as also quoted by Lord Bingham, wrote:

The principle of attribution of the conduct of a peacekeeping force to the United Nations is premised on the assumption that the operation in question is conducted under United Nations command and control, and thus has the legal status of a United Nations subsidiary organ. In authorized chapter VII operations conducted under national command and control, the conduct of the operation is imputable to the state or states conducting the operation. In joint operations, namely, those conducted by a United Nations peacekeeping operation and an operation conducted under national or regional command and control, international responsibility lies where effective command and control is vested and practically exercised...[326]

Most compelling is a further written comment by the UN Secretariat to the ILC, as quoted once more by Lord Bingham:

In the practice of the organization,...a measure of accountability was...introduced in the relationship between the Security Council and member states conducting an operation under Security Council authorization, in the form of periodic reports to the council on the conduct of the operation. While the submission of these reports provides the council with an important 'oversight tool', the Council itself or the United Nations as a whole cannot be held responsible for an unlawful act by the state conducting the operation, for the ultimate test of responsibility remains 'effective command and control'.[327]

It might also be asked, even if the two situations are not wholly analogous, how the criterion of 'ultimate' or 'overall' authority and control applied by the Court in *Behrami* in the context of a State organ placed at the disposal of an international organization sits with the International Court

---

[324] *Report of the International Law Commission. Fifty-sixth session*, 113, para. (7), quoted at [2008] 2 WLR 31, 36, para. 5 (Lord Bingham).
[325] *Report of the International Law Commission. Fifty-sixth session*, 114, para. (8), quoting UN Doc. A/51/389, 6, para. 18, as quoted in turn at [2008] 2 WLR 31, 37, para. 6.
[326] UN Doc. A/CN.4/545, 18, quoted at [2008] 2 WLR 31, 37, para. 6.
[327] UN Doc. A/CN.4/556, 46, quoted at [2008] 2 WLR 31, 38, para. 6.

of Justice's explicit rejection in *Application of the Genocide Convention* of 'overall control' as the test for attribution to a State of the conduct of private persons under article 8 of the Articles on Responsibility of States for Internationally Wrongful Acts.[328] With respect to the latter situation, the ICJ, having held (affirming what it said in *Nicaragua*[329]) that a State could be found responsible for the acts of private persons 'where it exercised effective control over the action during which the wrong was committed', observed that, '[i]n this regard the "overall control" test is unsuitable, for it stretches too far, almost to breaking point, the connection which must exist between the conduct of a State's organs and its international responsibility'.[330] Rather, the Court held, it must be shown 'that this "effective control" was exercised . . . in respect of each operation in which the alleged violations occurred, not generally in respect of the overall actions taken by the persons or groups of persons having committed the violations'.[331] The same could be said, *mutatis mutandis*, of the responsibility of an international organization, in accordance with the 'effective control' test posited by article 5 of the ILC's Draft articles, for the conduct of a State organ placed at its disposal.

Their Lordships' decision on the article 103 point is relatively uncontroversial, at least in the specific circumstances of the present case where Lord Bingham's argument based on (the customary equivalent of) article 43 of the Hague Rules, as implicitly kept on foot by paragraph 10 of Security Council resolution 1546 (2004), is persuasive. On the broader question of obligations versus authorizations, there is an argument for saying that, for the purposes of article 103, the distinction between mandatory and permissive Chapter VII resolutions is illusory. What member States of the UN agree in article 25 to accept and carry out are not the 'obligations' imposed by the Security Council—a circular proposition, since article 25 is itself the source of such obligations—but rather the 'decisions' of the Security Council. That is, a decision of the Security Council, in and of itself, creates an obligation for member States in that it must be accepted and carried out. If, therefore, the Council uses the word 'decides' in the relevant paragraph of the resolution in question, as it did in paragraph 10 of resolution 1546 (2004) when it decided that the MNF shall have the authority to take all necessary measures to contribute to the maintenance of security and stability in Iraq in accordance with the letters annexed to the resolution, this can be taken, for the purposes of article 103, to represent an obligation on member States under

---

[328] See *Application of the Genocide Convention (Bosnia and Herzegovina v Serbia and Montenegro), Judgment*, International Court of Justice, 26 February 2007, paras 402–7.

[329] *Application of the Genocide Convention*, para. 399, quoting *Military and Paramilitary Activities in and Against Nicaragua (Nicaragua v United States of America), Merits, Judgment*, ICJ Reports 1986, 14, 65, para. 115 ('For this conduct to give rise to legal responsibility of the United States, it would in principle have to be proved that that State had effective control of the military or paramilitary operations in the course of which the alleged violations were committed.')

[330] *Application of the Genocide Convention*, para. 406.

[331] *Application of the Genocide Convention*, para. 400.

the Charter, which therefore trumps all other treaty obligations owed by those member States. This is so regardless of whether the specific decision in question obliges or merely authorizes a given course of action. But even if one were not to accept this formalist, hermeneutical argument, *Namibia* establishes that subsequent practice in purported application of a Charter provision, even if seemingly contrary to the ordinary meaning of a term, can effectively modify the provision.332 Here, while at first blush an obligation and an authorization are not the same thing, they could be treated as such for the purposes of article 103—in the same way that an abstention in the Security Council is, for the purposes of article 27, the functional equivalent of an affirmative vote—if member States actually did consistently treat them as such. The only problem in the present case is that it is not obvious of what the supposed 60 years of relevant State practice referred to by Lord Bingham consists. Bernhardt's account of the application of article 103 (which opens with the statement 'For more than 40 years, Art. 103 did not play any significant role in the practice of the [UN] Organisation and international co-operation in general'333), although cited by Lord Bingham in support of his argument,334 makes no mention whatsoever of the authorization versus obligation issue. Frowein and Krisch's account, also cited by his Lordship,335 states that a literal reading of the word 'obligations' in article 103 'would not seem to correspond with State practice at least as regards authorizations of military action', which 'have not been opposed on the ground of conflicting treaty obligations'; but the authors refer to no concrete instances, and it is hard to discern what treaty obligations could have been *prima facie* violated by those member States which have taken part to date in uses of armed force authorized under article 42.336

Finally, it is disappointing that the claimant did not appeal the Court of Appeal's ruling on the possible continuing application of the HRA in spite of the overriding of article 5 of the ECHR. The Court of Appeal's decision on this point—which focuses on the fact that, through the combined effect of sections 1(1)(a) and 21(1) of the HRA, 'Convention rights' within the meaning of the Act are the rights set out in the Convention 'as it has effect for the time being in relation to the United Kingdom'337— therefore stands, as made clear in the present case by Lord Rodger.338 In

---

332 See *Legal Consequences for States of the Continued Presence of South Africa in Namibia (South West Africa) notwithstanding Security Council Resolution 276 (1970)*, Advisory Opinion, ICJ Rep 1971, 16, 22, paras 21–2.

333 Bernhardt, *supra*, 1299.

334 See [2008] 2 WLR 31, 50, para. 35, citing Bernhardt, *supra*, 1299–1300.

335 [2008] 2 WLR 31, 48–9, para. 33, citing Frowein & Krisch, *supra*, 729.

336 The other passages from academic works cited by Lord Bingham at [2008] 2 WLR 31, 48–9, para. 33 do not purport to rely on State practice.

337 [2006] 3 WLR 954, 983, para. 93, citing *R (Quark Fishing Ltd) v Secretary of State for Foreign and Commonwealth Affairs* [2006] 1 AC 529, 544, para. 25 (Lord Bingham), 545–6, para. 32 (Lord Nicholls), 551, para. 56 (Lord Hoffmann), 559, para. 87 (Lord Hope) and 562–3, para. 97 (Baroness Hale), (2005) 76 *BYIL* 589–93.

338 [2008] 2 WLR 31, 53, paras 52–3 and 69, para. 112.

short, what the Court of Appeal says is that if the ECHR does not apply, the HRA does not either. But if this were the case, there would have been no need for the system of designated derogations and designated reservations provided for in articles 14 and 15 of the Act, in relation to which article 2 specifies that the 'Convention rights' enumerated in article 1(1) are to have effect for the purposes of the Act 'subject to any designated derogation or reservation'. Derogations from and reservations to the ECHR entered by the UK would, on the Court of Appeal's reasoning, have had direct effect in domestic law without these provisions, rendering the latter redundant.

State immunity—indirect impleading—separate entity—central bank— 'commercial transaction' exception—State Immunity Act 1978, sections 3 and 14(2)—United Nations Convention on Jurisdictional Immunities of States and Their Property 2004, article 6(2)(b)—whether commercial bank in which central bank of Mongolia holding unallocated account entitled to rely on state immunity in proceedings for third-party discovery

Case No. 9. Koo Golden East Mongolia v Bank of Nova Scotia and others, 19 December 2007, [2007] EWCA Civ 1443 (CA (Civ Div)).

The claimant was a gold mining company based in Mongolia. Under Mongolian banking law, the right to hold deposits of gold is limited to the central bank of Mongolia, known as 'MongolBank', and other banks authorised by MongolBank. It is the practice for gold mining companies operating in Mongolia to place their mined gold with MongolBank for safekeeping in accordance with a safe custody agreement, which is really a complicated sale and purchase agreement governed by Mongolian law, usually releasing it for sale at a later date.

In July 2006, the claimant entered into such an agreement with MongolBank, any dispute in relation to which was to be resolved by negotiation on the basis of Mongolian law and, failing this, was to be adjudicated in the Mongolian courts pursuant to procedures established by Mongolian law. The relevant terms of the agreement were as follows: the claimant would deliver to MongolBank, during a set 'sale and delivery' period, not less than one million grams of gold bullion bars for safekeeping, and subsequently sell to MongolBank not less than one million grams of the metal on a date no later than 25 December 2007 to be specified by the claimant by means of a 'metal sale letter'; the price paid by MongolBank would be the metal price per ounce as set by MongolBank on the date the metal sale letter was delivered; MongolBank was obliged to ensure the security of the metal delivered for safe custody from the moment of the acceptance of the metal into its depository until its sale by the claimant; risk was to pass to MongolBank on deposit of the gold, but title was to remain with the claimant until its issue of the metal sale letter; MongolBank had the right to accept metal in an amount greater than the minimum specified by the agreement; and MongolBank would pay 85% of the value of the metal deposited into safe custody on the date of delivery, this sum being deducted from the actual purchase price, the balance to be payable to or by the claimant. It was accepted that the claimant had an arguable case under Mongolian law that it was not obliged to sell to MongolBank the whole of the amount deposited and that it could—subject to the repayment of the 85% of the value of the gold delivered or, after sale to MongolBank, of the price prevailing on the date of the metal sale letter—withdraw the whole amount deposited or the whole amount less one million grams, which it could retain for itself, transfer out of Mongolia and sell on the world market. Pursuant to the agreement, the claimant deposited 3,299,184.13 grams of unrefined gold bars with MongolBank between 21 July 2006 and 19 January 2007, but it was yet to send the metal sale letter. In November 2006, the claimant was assessed by the Mongolian tax authorities for windfall profit tax and royalties on about one million grams of gold out of the two million delivered by that point to MongolBank for safe custody.

By letter of early November 2006, MongolBank informed the claimant that, given the gold price fluctuations in the international market, 'a certain portion' of the gold had been exported for refining. In response to claims in the media by the claimant that the gold had disappeared, MongolBank issued a press statement dated 24 August 2007, which included the following paragraphs:

MongolBank, implementing the Law on Central Bank (MongolBank) and the Law on Precious Metals and Stones Fund and with the purposes of increasing the country's currency reserves, purchases from gold producing business entities and individuals unrefined gold at the market price, published as of a certain date. According to the standards, accepted in the international financial markets, refined gold is placed on the most favourable terms. As of today Mongolia's hard currency reserves amount to US$1 million.

This gold, which according to the agreement made with KOO Golden East—Mongolia, will be definitely purchased by MongolBank, has been refined and placed abroad.

In a letter to the claimant dated 19 November 2007, MongolBank further stated:

With the purpose of increasing the state currency reserves MongolBank when purchasing from business entities purified gold produced by them would calculate its pure weight according to common practice of the international financial markets and would make settlements for the value of the gold based on the market price of the gold as of a particular day.

Given that MongolBank has an obligation to refine the purified gold purchased into the state currency reserves and place the same in the international financial markets pursuant to the most favourable arrangements, MongolBank refined 3.1 tons of your gold, being in possession of MongolBank in accordance with the law.

With this please be informed that as of 16 November 2007 out of the total amount of gold delivered by your company under the agreement, 190.8kg are kept in custody of MongolBank as 43 unrefined gold bullion bars, whereas 3.109kg of 999.9 fineness are held in our metal account in London.

This metal account was supposedly held with the first defendant, the Bank of Nova Scotia. In fact, what was held with the first defendant was an unallocated account, containing merely credit derived from the sale by a gold clearing bank of the refined gold, which may have become commingled with other refined gold.

The claimant sought and was granted at first instance in the High Court a *Norwich Pharmacal* order[339] mandating full disclosure by the first defendant of any information likely to enable the claimant to recover the gold by identifying and claiming in conversion against any wrongdoer, such as the gold clearing bank or the refiner. On appeal, the first defendant raised a procedural defence of State immunity, arguing that, as MongolBank's agent in London, it was entitled to benefit from the immunity that MongolBank would enjoy were the order sought against it instead.

The Court of Appeal (Civil Division) upheld the appeal, holding that the first defendant was entitled to State immunity. Sir Andrew Clarke MR gave the leading judgment, with which Smith and Pumfrey LJJ agreed.

After reproducing the relevant provisions of the State Immunity Act 1978, Sir Andrew Clarke MR turned to the facts of the case:

It is not in dispute that MongolBank is the central bank of Mongolia or that it is a state entity within the meaning of the 1978 Act. If these were proceedings against MongolBank, MongolBank would have state immunity if these were proceedings relating to a transaction or activity of a commercial, financial or other similar character into which MongolBank had entered in the exercise of sovereign authority. MongolBank entered into a contract with the bank [*ie* the first defendant] which was of a commercial, financial or similar character. If these proceedings were against the bank [*sic*, the intended reference presumably being to MongolBank] they would relate to such a transaction. It follows that the question is whether MongolBank entered into the contract in the exercise of sovereign authority. In my judgment it did.[340]

The sovereign character of the transaction or activity was manifest, in his Lordship's view, in MongolBank's press statement of 24 August 2007.[341] It was also seen in MongolBank's letter to the claimant of 19 November 2007:

That evidence shows that the purpose of the transactions including the refining of the gold and the placing of a quantity of refined gold on the unallocated account at the bank was for the purposes of increasing Mongolia's currency

---

[339] See *Norwich Pharmacal v Customs and Excise Commissioners* [1974] AC 133, 175 (Lord Reid): '[I]f through no fault of his own a person gets mixed up in the tortious acts of others so as to facilitate their wrong-doing he may incur no personal liability but he comes under a duty to assist the person who has been wronged by giving him full information and disclosing the identity of the wrongdoers.'

[340] [2007] EWCA Civ 1443, para. 40.   [341] [2007] EWCA Civ 1443, para. 41.

reserves. In my judgment that was an exercise of sovereign authority within the meaning of the 1978 Act. That conclusion seems to be entirely consistent with that of Aikens J in the slightly different context in *AIG Capital Partners Inc v Kazakhstan* [2005] EWHC 2239 (Comm), [2006] 1 All ER 284, [2006] 1 WLR 1420 at para. 58.[342]

His Lordship took counsel for the claimant to accept this analysis.[343] What counsel for the claimant had submitted, however, was that the present application was not being brought against MongolBank but against the first defendant, an ordinary commercial entity, in order to discover either the physical whereabouts of the gold or the name of the refiners who arguably committed a tort actionable at the suit of the claimant. In response, counsel for the first defendant had argued that, while this was no doubt true, the application was for an order for the disclosure of information that was confidential as between the first respondent and its client, a central bank, and that in the circumstances the information was held in a real sense on behalf of MongolBank as the central bank of Mongolia. To require the bank to disclose this information would amount to the claimant's obtaining relief against the agent of a central bank in circumstances in which it would not be able to obtain relief against the central bank itself, something foreclosed by *Twycross v Dreyfus*,[344] where it was not permitted to obtain relief against the agents of a foreign state and where the facts were 'not so dissimilar from those in the instant case'.[345] Moreover, in *Jones v Saudi Arabia*, 'in a very different context', Lord Bingham had stated that '[t]he foreign state's right to immunity cannot be circumvented by suing its servants or agents'.[346] It was true that the first defendant was not MongolBank's agent 'in the narrow sense', but the narrow sense was not the one intended in *Twycross v Dreyfus*.[347] In addition, article 6(2)(b) of the United Nations Convention on Jurisdictional Immunities of States and Their Property 2004[348] said that '[a] proceeding before a court of a State shall be considered to have been instituted against another State if that other State...is not named as a party to the proceeding but the proceeding in effect seeks to affect the property, rights, interests or activities of that other State'. While the Convention was not part of English law, it provided 'valuable guidance on the extent of state immunity', and had been looked to in this light by Aikens J in *AIG Capital Partners v Kazakhstan*.[349] In sum, since the first defendant was, on the facts of the case, an agent of MongolBank for the purpose of the rule in *Twycross v Dreyfus*, and given section 1(2) of the

---

[342] [2007] EWCA Civ 1443, para. 42. [343] [2007] EWCA Civ 1443, para. 43.

[344] (1877) 5 Ch D 605. [345] [2007] EWCA Civ 1443, para. 45.

[346] [2007] EWCA Civ 1443, para. 45, quoting [2007] 1 AC 270, 281, para. 10, (2006) 77 *BYIL* 499–520 (HL).

[347] [2007] EWCA Civ 1443, para. 46.

[348] A/RES/59/38, Annex, 2 December 2004 (not yet in force).

[349] [2007] EWCA Civ 1443, para. 47, citing [2006] 1 All ER 284, (2005) 76 *BYIL* 593–601 (QBD (Comm Ct), Aikens J).

SIA ('A court shall give effect to the immunity conferred by this section even though the State does not appear in the proceedings in question.'), his Lordship declined, on the ground of State immunity, to make the order sought by the claimant.[350]

State immunity cases such as the present one can present diabolical difficulties even for full-time public international lawyers, framed as they are around what might charitably be described as a user-unfriendly piece of legislation, and dependent as the outcome often is on highly nuanced, case-specific legal characterizations of fact. Matters were made trickier still in this case by the urgency of the appeal:[351] non-specialist counsel were required to prepare their respective cases (in which State immunity was only one of three issues to be aired) within a week and to argue them in a day, and the Court of Appeal had only one full day after oral argument to write the judgment. The upshot is a problematic decision with some shaky reasoning.

One might first ask if this was really an example of indirectly impleading the State, or in this case a separate entity of that State. Leaving aside the question whether the first defendant could rightly be considered MongolBank's agent, the action here was for *Norwich Pharmacal* relief, a form of discovery available only as against third parties. This was not an action that could possibly have been brought against MongolBank, even if the latter had not been immune. Furthermore, it is hard to see how an application for an order against the first defendant for disclosure of information relevant to the fate of the gold could in any real sense be considered a proceeding which 'in effect seeks to affect the...rights, interests or activities' of MongolBank, in the words of article 6(2)(b) of the UN Convention on Jurisdictional Immunities of States and Their Property—a claim in conversion against the gold clearing bank or refiner, quite possibly (although the more compelling procedural bar would be the foreign act of State doctrine); but an action at one remove for discovery against the first defendant, this must be doubtful. The penumbra of State immunity is unlikely to be cast that wide. But it is a tricky question.

More obviously unsatisfactory is Sir Andrew Clarke MR's treatment of the question whether MongolBank would have been immune had it been the defendant to the action. To begin with, his Lordship cites the requirement in section 14(2)(a) of the SIA that the proceedings relate to anything done by the separate entity in the exercise of sovereign authority, but never so much as alludes to section 14(2)(b), with its further requirement that the circumstances are such that a State would have been immune—in other words, that none of the exceptions to State immunity

[350] [2007] EWCA Civ 1443, para. 47.

[351] The deadline by which the claimant was required by the agreement to send the metal sale letter to MongolBank, failing which title was deemed to pass to the latter, was 25 December 2007. The requested *Norwich Pharmacal* order was issued by the High Court on 10 December. The appeal was heard on 17 December, and the Court of Appeal delivered its judgment on 19 December.

in sections 2 to 11 of the Act would have applied. At the same time, he frames the question in terms of whether the proceedings related 'to a transaction or activity of a commercial, financial or other similar character into which MongolBank had entered in the exercise of sovereign authority', thereby paraphrasing the exception to State immunity provided for, via the 'commercial transaction' exception in section 3(1)(a) of the SIA, by the definition of 'commercial transaction' in section 3(3)(c). But be that as it may. More significantly, his Lordship makes no mention whatsoever of the English jurisprudence on what an exercise of sovereign authority is; and if *I° Congreso del Partido*,[352] *Littrell*,[353] *Holland v Lampen-Wolfe*[354] and *Kuwait Airways (No. 1)*[355] make one thing clear, it is that the purpose of a transaction or activity is not the sole criterion of its sovereign character. Thirdly, and more seriously still, his Lordship, despite having recalled it, in the event overlooks section 3(3)(a) of the SIA, which alternatively defines 'commercial transaction' within the meaning of section 3(1)(a) to mean 'any contract for the supply of goods or services', the word 'any' being critical: a State is not immune in respect of proceedings relating to a contract for the supply of goods or services whatever the purpose of that contract. Lastly, and crucially, his Lordship focuses on the wrong transaction or activity. It is not to MongolBank's contract with the first defendant that the proceedings would have related had they been brought against MongolBank, but rather to MongolBank's contract with the claimant—that is, the agreement pursuant to which MongolBank assumed safe custody over the gold. And this agreement, being a contract for the supply of services by MongolBank and for the supply of goods by the claimant, was, in accordance with section 3(3)(a) of the SIA, a commercial transaction within the meaning of the exception to State immunity provided for in section 3(1)(a).

---

[352] [1983] AC 244, (1981) 52 *BYIL* 314–19 (HL).
[353] *Littrell v United States of America (No. 2)* [1994] 4 All ER 203, (1994) 65 *BYIL* 491–6 (CA).
[354] [2000] 1 WLR 1573, (2000) 71 *BYIL* 405–7 (HL).
[355] *Kuwait Airways Corporation v Iraqi Airways Company* [1995] 1 WLR 1147, (1995) 66 *BYIL* 496–501 (HL).

DECISIONS OF BRITISH COURTS IN 2007

B. PRIVATE INTERNATIONAL LAW*

1. The scope and validity of an arbitration agreement: Premium Nafta Products Ltd v Fili Shipping Co Ltd.[1]

Really, the issues could hardly have been more straightforward. Acting through their agents, certain vessel owners had entered into various charters which had been negotiated with them. The charters provided that dispute resolution was to take place in London, by judicial adjudication but subject to the right to elect arbitration. When problems arose, the charterers instituted arbitration in accordance with the terms of the agreement. The owners, evidently now reading the terms of the charters for the first time, claimed to have discovered that their content was so commercially disadvantageous that it could be explained, as they surmised, only as the result of bribery by the charterers. They therefore purported to rescind the contract, and all of it, and commenced proceedings in the High Court for a declaration that they were no longer bound by the contract which they had disavowed. In a piece of exemplary contract law analysis, Morison J upheld the owners' contention: rescission of a contract served to rescind all of it, as English law[2] does not acknowledge the possibility of partial rescission. The Court of Appeal reversed him in a piece of exemplary arbitration law analysis, holding that the separation of the substantive contract from the agreement for arbitration meant that complaint about and rescission of the substantive contract left the arbitration agreement untouched. The House of Lords held that the Court of Appeal had been quite right, and save for a few observations of its own, simply approved the reasoning below. All this makes the case extremely difficult, for as all the judgments handed down made perfect legal sense, the choice between them has to be made in terms of axiomatic legal policy rather than superiority of legal analysis. And the view which will be tentatively advanced here is that the House of Lords may have asked itself the wrong question in coming to the right answer.

First, however, it is necessary to address the question of what the arbitration agreement actually meant. It defined its material scope as extending

---

* © Adrian Briggs.

[1] [2007] UKHL 40, [2007] Bus LR 1719: Lord Hoffmann, Lord Hope of Craighead, Lord Scott of Foscote, Lord Walker of Gestingthorpe and Lord Brown of Eaton-under-Heywood, dismissing the appeal from *Fiona Trust & Holding Corp v Privalov* [2007] EWCA Civ 20, [2007] Bus LR 686 (Tuckey, Arden and Longmore LJJ), which had reversed Morison J: [2006] EWHC 2583 (Comm), and whose decision was noted in this Year Book (2006) 77 *BYIL* 591-2. It is probable that most law reports and other sources will report and refer to the decision of the House of Lords as *Fiona Trust & Holding Corp v Privalov*, but the title to the House of Lords report is used in this Note.

[2] There was no doubt that all relevant contracts were governed by English law.

to 'any dispute arising under this charter'. The owners' opening gambit was to say, reasonably enough, that a dispute about whether they were bound by a charter which their agent had agreed to in return for a bribe, was not a dispute *under* the charter, but one which, if these prepositions meant anything, arose *outside* it. In support of this submission it was able to cite a long list of pretty horrible authorities which had written at length, and not always consistently, on the meaning of various prepositional terms which parties had used to define the relationship between a dispute and a court or tribunal. There were three areas of difficulty. First, prepositional expressions referred to claims arising 'under', 'from', 'in connection with', 'relating to', a contract. This raised the possibility that a particular dispute fell outside this form of relationship. Then there was the idea of a 'contract': how did such an expression deal with those claims which asserted the original or subsequent invalidity of the contract and which sought their relief on the footing that the contract was invalid or had been invalidated or unwound as a source of voluntary legal obligation? Finally there was the problem which arises when a claimant, seeking to evade an agreement on jurisdiction or choice of law or both, claimed to disregard the contract but to formulate a cause of action under a parallel legal relationship, most commonly in the law of tort. It takes little imagination, and not much more reading,[3] to obtain a flavour of the really perplexing nature of the problem. It would be all very well if the contract had been drafted by those trained in the precise arts of grammar and syntax, but few Englishmen and fewer non-native speakers have such skills. For a court to interpret the words of a dispute-resolution provision in contract as though they had been weighed and chosen with such insight was to denature the agreement actually made. Reacting against this, the Court of Appeal and House of Lords demanded that there be a halt: they preferred the approach that where there was a plausible connection between the dispute and the court or tribunal designated to deal with disputes of which this may be one, the words of the contractual agreement on dispute resolution would be taken to embrace it unless there were very clear grounds for holding otherwise. It is a very rough science; indeed, it may not be a science at all; but for the courts, the ends justified the means. By the time the case was before the House of Lords it was possible for the court to notice and approve the decision of the Full Court of the Federal Court of Australia in *Comandate Marine Corp v Pan Australia Shipping Pty Ltd*,[4] in which Allsop J had delivered an extremely detailed judgment refuting the linguistic science of preposition as a means to the interpretation of contracts. Certainly the tide was running strongly; and the House of Lords was happy to be swept along by it.

The trouble is that once one moves away from the proposition that contractual words have a precise meaning, and interprets them instead as

---

[3] Anyone who wishes to should see the analysis of the case-law in the judgment of the Court of Appeal. The House of Lords did not enter into it at all.

[4] (2006) 157 FCR 45.

signposts rather than boundary marks, there is no reliable way of telling what the scope of an agreement on the resolution of disputes actually is. Assuming that these contract terms do have a scope, there has to be a way to define and determine it. It is not clear that the House of Lords actually came up with an answer to this particular question. Instead, the judgments seem designed to intimidate those who would contend that the words of a dispute-resolution agreement do not extend to the dispute in question, out of advancing the argument. This cannot be right; for if contracts are written, the writing defines the terms of the promises made. A commercially-realistic interpretation is all very well, but it is still an interpretation of the words used in the written contract, and these still have meanings. Unless one takes the view that a dispute-resolution clause means what it would have said if it had been drafted by someone with Lord Hoffmann's linguistic dexterity, there is no way to avoid asking the patiently insistent question of what the words do actually mean. For we appear to be very close to holding that a contract for dispute resolution does not mean what it says, but what it ought to have said, and that would be very dangerous.

Even if one accepts, as we now must, that the wording used was expressed in terms wide enough to cover the dispute in question, the owners had discovered, as they claimed, that the contracts had been procured by the bribery of their officers, and that as a result they were entitled to repudiate the contracts, so freeing themselves of the substantive charters just as much as the agreement for the resolution of disputes arising in connection with them. The immediate answer of the Court of Appeal and the House of Lords[5] was that such a pleading was bad: that the separability of the agreement for the resolution of disputes from the substantive obligations of the contract meant that though the latter may have been rescinded, the former had not been. So far as the charterers' application for a stay of the owners' judicial proceedings concerned an arbitration agreement,[6] such an outcome was motivated by Arbitration Act 1996, section 7. It also seemed to be justified by the pragmatic reflection that, if contracting parties were to have been asked whether they intended their choice of tribunal to have jurisdiction to deal with a plea that the contract had been rescinded, they would be most likely to say yes. All this comes naturally enough in the law of arbitration, where the inclination of arbitrators and those who practice it is to regard arbitration as an objective good, and judicial control (except for the purpose of preventing judicial proceedings from cutting across the arbitration) as an occasionally necessary evil. Though the justification, and the statutory underpinning for it, does not extend to cases involving a jurisdiction agreement, it seems certain that the House of Lords intended the outcome to be just the same

---

[5] Morison J, on the other hand, had accepted it.

[6] There is no analogous statutory rule for jurisdiction agreements; these must take their effect according to the authority of the common law.

where a challenge is made by one party to the enforceability of a jurisdiction agreement. But however one looks at it, a contract procured by
bribery or fraud is, as a matter of English law, a contract which is liable
to be rescinded. The law of misrepresentation provides that where a lie
induces a contract, in the sense that unless the very same contract would
still have been entered into if the lie had not been told (the burden of
proving which falls on the liar), the victim is entitled to rescind. There
is no requirement that the lie be the sole motivation for the one party to
have entered into the contract, neither that the victim actually believed
the truth of the representation. The right to rescind exists unless the liar
can show that his lie had no effect whatever. The law on bribery proceeds,
mutatis mutandis, along parallel analytical lines.

The owners therefore said that they had rescinded the contract because
of the fault of the charterers. This pleading should have put the charterers on the spot: if they were to say that they would have entered into the
same contract if the agent had not been bribed, it was for them to prove it.
Faced with so powerful, and orthodox, a pleading, but needing to defeat
it, the House of Lords took refuge in the principle that the alleged fault
in the negotiation of the contract was irrelevant unless it could be shown
to have been aimed at the dispute resolution agreement specifically, as
distinct from being aimed at the validity of the contract in general. This,
with respect, simply will not do. A party induced by his counterparty's
wrongdoing to enter into a contract does not generally lose his right to
rescind because the wrongdoing induced more contracts than one. Why
should the law be any different if the wrongdoing induces a combination
of contracts, or a contract which may be separated into two parts? Let
it be supposed that the owners had been asked: 'if the charterers bribe
your agent to make a contract which provides for the hire, on disadvantageous terms, of your vessel and for the mechanism for the resolution of
disputes, would you still agree to be bound by the arbitration agreement
though rescinding the contract of hire?'. Now the answer would, in all
probability, be that the owners would disavow the whole of the contract,
or contracts, negotiated by the corruption of their agent. A different
answer is possible, one must admit, but it does not seem very likely. The
House of Lords therefore ruled that the question was inadmissible.

The proposition that the contract to arbitrate disputes survives the
rescission of the contract has therefore been elevated to a matter of
dogma. It is treated in the same way as the termination of a contract
which, ever since *Heyman v Darwins Ltd*,[7] has been regarded as excluding from the termination those terms which are ancillary to the substantive contract. This always made, and still makes, sense: only when a
contract is terminated, or broken, will a provision for the resolution of
disputes come into its own. In the general run of cases, the dispute will
not arise, and the provision for the resolution of disputes will have no

---

7 [1942] AC 356.

meaning, until there is a termination or a purported termination of the contract. Contract doctrine is therefore entirely familiar with the proposition that certain terms survive the termination of the contract, or continue after the discharge by breach of the primary obligations of the contract; but unlike rescission, termination for breach does not impugn the original validity of the contract. Unless the ordinary contract law doctrines of misrepresentation, duress, bribery, and so forth, do not apply to dispute-resolution agreements (and if they are excluded from these, is there anything else from which they are excluded?), there is no easy theoretical justification for the proposition that the misconduct on the part of the charterer and the agent does not permit rescission by the agent's principal of the contract resulting from such misbehaviour, and that the agent negotiated two separable contracts, rather than one entire contract, is of arithmetical, but not legal, significance.

It would, one has to admit, be more than irksome if a dispute resolution agreement could be routinely deprived of effect by the calculated expedient, possibly simple and convenient, of denying that the provision for the resolution of disputes had actually been agreed to. The whole of the justification offered by the Court of Appeal and House of Lords was, in effect, that such agreements should be respected and enforced, and protected by those who set about undermining the clear public good which they do. In the particular case of arbitration, the whole point of the clause is to keep the parties well clear of the courts; and the single greatest disincentive to parties to agree upon London for commercial arbitration of their disputes will be, as it seems, the prospect that the English courts will meddle in the process of arbitration at the first invitation. Setting out English law to discourage such invitation from being made therefore betrays the real agenda, in much the same way as the inclination of Lord Hoffmann, at least, to cite German rather than English judicial authority for the conclusions he considered it to be correct to reach.[8] It is still a funny old way to make the law; and a university student, looking at the arbitration agreement and asking why this contract is different from all other contracts will receive an answer which is grounded in faith and not in science.

Where there is no good answer to a question, it sometimes means that the question was not well chosen in the first place. It is useful to observe that *Premium Nafta* was not, despite appearances to the contrary, concerned to answer the question whether the dispute resolution agreement was invalidated by the discovery of the bribery which was said to have induced it. Rather, the question was whether this decision should be taken by a court, at the behest of the party seeking to impugn the alleged agreement, or by the tribunal itself, at the behest of the party seeking to uphold the agreement to arbitrate. The House of Lords has held, in effect, that

---

[8] See at [14], citing the unnamed decision of the German Federal Supreme Court of 27 February 1970.

this question should be determined by the tribunal: one must suppose that the owners will renew their objection to the arbitration to the arbitrators themselves who, in accordance with the theory now generally taken to be sound, have jurisdiction to rule on a challenge to their jurisdiction.[9] If this is all the decision really amounted to, what was the reason for it? There are two possibilities. One is that because there was an arguable case that there was a valid agreement to arbitrate, the first examination of the validity of the agreement to arbitrate should have been given by the tribunal. This would suppose that where there may be an arbitration agreement, the claims of judicial abstention outweigh those of judicial supervision. The trouble with this is, as Professor Schlosser has already pointed out and as cannot be gainsaid, that where one party to the alleged agreement to arbitrate wishes to obtain a ruling that he is not so bound, it is absurd for him to have to constitute a tribunal for the purpose of obtaining a ruling that he had no need to constitute a tribunal, *et cetera*. It is not clear that a rule which would give preference to the tribunal where there is a good arguable case, or something of the sort, is really up to the task of serving as a rule of decision. The alternative is to allow a rule for prior seisin: to allow the court to go first if the procedure before the tribunal has not yet been invoked; to allow the tribunal to go first where its procedure has been invoked before the contradictory court procedure has.[10] One lesson to be learned from the Brussels Convention and the Brussels I Regulation,[11] as well as from the common law authority of the High Court of Australia,[12] is that a rule of first seisin is decently neutral as between the contentions of those who assert that there is a valid and binding agreement and those who say—for whatever reason—that there is not. The traditional English preference, in the context of agreements on jurisdiction, has been to favour the primary decision-taking role of the court allegedly chosen, which will frequently be the English court.[13] But freedom to make a contract, and the judicial instinct to uphold and defend it, is surely something which has to be counterbalanced by recognition of the freedom *not* to make a contract, or not to be contractually bound in

[9] We have the authority of Professor Schlosser for the insight that this idea, rendered in many contexts as *Kompetenz-Kompetenz*, is a German pun: Einhorn & Siehr (eds), *Intercontinental Cooperation Through Private International Law: Essays in Memory of Peter E Nygh* (2004) 305, 321.

[10] For an illustration of the complexity which may be developed from competitive seisin, see *Albon v Naza Motor Trading Sdn Bhd (No 3)* [2007] EWHC 665 (Ch), [2007] 2 Lloyd's Rep 1 (Lightman J): the judge decided that the English court should decide whether there was a valid arbitration agreement for Malaysian arbitration, it being alleged that the documents were forgeries. This may distinguish the case from *Premium Nafta*, in which there was no doubt about the making (as distinct from the validity) of the agreement to arbitrate; but the English judicial proceedings were instituted before the Malaysian arbitration, and so on the view advanced here, it was appropriate for the English court to take the first decision about the validity of the disputed agreement to arbitrate.

[11] Regulation (EC) 44/2001, [2001] OJ L12/1.

[12] *Henry v Henry* (1996) 185 CLR 571; *CSR Ltd v Cigna Insurance Australia Ltd* (1997) 189 CLR 345.

[13] See, for example, *Continental Bank NA v Aeakos Compania Naviera SA* [1994] 1 WLR 588.

certain circumstances; and the judicial instinct should be just as prepared to defend this distinct aspect of contractual autonomy. For freedom to agree is also freedom not to become bound to an agreement. Although English courts stood on what they considered to be the higher ground when they reinforced agreements on jurisdiction and arbitration with anti-suit injunctions,[14] they were in effect asserting the superiority of the proposition that there was a valid and binding contract over the contrary proposition. It was not clear that they were always right to do so, for 'I did not agree to be bound in these circumstances' is not a disreputable plea, but is a principled assertion of contractual autonomy. Whether they were consciously taking this position or not, the decision of the Court of Appeal and House of Lords had the effect of allowing the tribunal, and the courts of the seat of the tribunal, to rule on whether the parties had made a binding agreement to arbitrate their disputes, even in circumstances in which the applicant wishes to ascertain that he is not bound to arbitrate. However, Professor Schlosser has observed that to require a party, who believes that he is not bound to arbitrate but is free to litigate, to constitute an arbitral tribunal for the sole purpose of obtaining his non-arbitration ruling from it, 'is not based on coherent reflections'.[15]

If, however, one opts for a first-seised rule, this will allow the court to avoid taking a view, even provisionally, in favour of one side or the other, and it will leave the procedural question of where the decision is to be taken to the body—court or tribunal—which is first seised with the issue. If the decision is coupled with an effective costs jurisdiction, so as to discourage frivolous or vexatious applications, so much the better. It will mean that the court (if it is first seised) or tribunal (if it is first seised) will determine the validity of the jurisdiction or arbitration agreement; and the party who brings proceedings before a court or tribunal which should not have been seised will be made to pay for it.

Seen from this perspective, *Premium Nafta* makes sense. The London arbitration was commenced a month before the judicial proceedings before the English court got underway, and in those circumstances it was entirely defensible to allow the arbitrators to decide whether there was a valid agreement to arbitrate, and to prevent the court from helping itself to jurisdiction to derail an arbitration. In an area of the law where the substantive analysis is beset by circularity and contradiction, a well chosen procedural question may yet offer the best way ahead.

One should finally note the additional comments which Lord Hope added to his agreement with the views of Lord Hoffmann. He said, sensibly enough, that a contractual provision for jurisdiction/arbitration and for governing law was an important part of any commercial contract, and that the parties would expect a court to give effect to it rather than to indulge a party who saw some advantage in protracted litigation about it. No-one would disagree with a syllable of this, but it leads to the surprising conclusion that a contractual provision for governing law is

---

[14] See, for example, ibid.   [15] Schlosser, above n 9, 323.

to be treated in the same general way as one for the arbitration or adjudication of disputes. And that is to say, it should be given an ample construction, and should be applied to all disputes which fall within its verbal scope. So a provision which stipulated that 'all disputes shall be determined in accordance with English law' will mean that all disputes, in the broad sense of that expression favoured by Lord Hoffmann in particular and the House of Lords in general, will be determined by the application of the law chosen in the agreement. This will be so where the dispute concerns the enforcement of the contract, the validity of the contract, or the right to avoid or rescind the contract. It will also apply to claims framed as claims in tort which are brought between the parties to the contract, likewise to those formulated by reference to the principle which prohibits unjust enrichment. If Lord Hope is taken at his word, no technical question of choice of law interposes itself between the term of the contract and the selection of governing law by the court. If he is right about this—and in the present submission it would be very welcome if he were right—it would mean that an express choice of law would make the chapters in Dicey, Morris & Collins[16] quite unnecessary. One would not enquire whether the express choice of law was validated by (for example) the Private International Law (Miscellaneous Provisions) Act 1995 where the claim is one in tort, or by Dicey's Rule 230 where the claim alleges an unjust enrichment. One would simply apply the law which the parties appeared to have chosen. Though one may come up with all sorts of objection to doing so, the by-passing of the choice of law rules, which stand between the parties' choice and effect being given to that choice by a judge, is certainly attractive. It has been suggested elsewhere that to give effect to an expressed choice of law, and to reserve traditional learning on choice of law (at least in commercial areas of the subject) to the control of those cases in which the parties have not expressed a choice of law, makes much sense. The observations of Lord Hope, and the effortless, almost casual, way in which he expressed himself, suggest that this development may arrive rather sooner than one may have anticipated.[17]

2. The promises made in an arbitration agreement: *A v B*,[18] *A v B (No 2)*,[19] *C v D*.[20]

The previous Note in this Survey looked at the issue of how an English court should deal with disputes as to the scope and validity of an agreement to arbitrate, but a distinct question arises in close connection: when

---

[16] *The Conflict of Laws* (14th edn, 2006).
[17] For a fuller analysis of this issue, see Briggs, *Agreements on Jurisdiction and Choice of Law* (2008), and [2008] LMCLQ 1.
[18] [2006] EWHC 2006 (Comm), [2007] 1 Lloyd's Rep 237 (Colman J).
[19] [2007] EWHC 54 (Comm), [2007] 1 Lloyd's Rep 358 (Colman J).
[20] [2007] EWCA Civ 1282, [2008] Bus LR 843 (Sir Anthony Clarke MR, Longmore and Jacob LJJ), affirming Cooke J: [2007] EWHC 1541 (Comm), [2007] 2 All ER (Comm) 557. Longmore LJ delivered the only reasoned judgment.

parties make an agreement to arbitrate, but one of them brings judicial proceedings outside the courts of the seat of the arbitration, what should be the attitude of the English court if complaint is made of doing so? According to these three cases, it is a breach of the arbitration agreement to maintain such arguments outside the courts of the seat of the arbitration, with the result that the party doing so may be ordered to exercise self-restraint and, if this has not been demonstrated, to indemnify the other. On the face of it, this is sensible in cases where there is no doubt that the parties have made an agreement to arbitrate and that it has been broken. But where one of them claims to have rescinded the agreement to arbitrate, it is much harder to see that it is a breach of the agreement for a party to bring proceedings which seek to determine the validity of the agreement to arbitrate outside the courts of the seat. And where a party against whom an award has been made brings proceedings before a court in the place where enforcement of the award may be sought, it is just as hard to see that there is anything wrong. Yet that is the effect of these decisions; and though they are not plainly wrong, they do illustrate just how far the courts are now willing to go to discourage genuine arguments outside the framework of tribunal and courts of the seat. The previous Note suggested that this may be part of the international competition between arbitration *fora* and, regrettable though it would be if this were correct, it may be that something of this sort is happening.

In the bitter litigation reported as *A v B*, one of the parties to an agreement to arbitrate considered that he had grounds to rescind the agreement to arbitrate. His doing so did not trespass into the territory mapped by *Premium Nafta*, as the agreement to arbitrate was self-contained, and was not part of a larger substantive agreement: it had been entered into in order to resolve a long-running, and probably deeply distressing, family-commercial dispute. The agreement, which provided for arbitration with a Swiss seat, had been made between two brothers (whom it is convenient to refer to as the good and the bad brother, but on the clear understanding that no finding of goodness or badness has ever been made) and the arbitrator: the good brother complained that he had been duped into making the arbitration agreement by fraud and duress practised by the bad brother and the arbitrator. Considering that he was entitled to rescind the agreement to arbitrate, and to bring claims for substantive relief in the English courts, the good brother sought his relief in London. The conclusion of Colman J was that the English proceedings should be stayed: against the bad brother, under Arbitration Act 1996 s 9, and against the arbitrator under the inherent jurisdiction of the court.[21] There being no doubt that, as a matter of fact, the agreement to arbitrate in Switzerland had been made, all challenges to its validity were thereafter to be brought before the Swiss arbitrator[22] and, if anyone were so advised, before the

---

[21] Section 9 did not apply to proceedings against the arbitrator.
[22] The fact the arbitrator was in fact a London solicitor being nothing to the point.

Swiss courts as supervisory court of the seat of the arbitration. The judge's conclusion can be accepted without great difficulty. The good brother did not deny that he had entered into the arbitration agreement, only that he was still bound by it; and the arbitration had been running for some months before the English courts were seised with the good brother's application. If one takes the view that either of these facts tilted the balance against the involvement of the English courts, then the decision is one which need not be criticised. Even so, it meant that the good brother, believing that he had been the victim of serious wrongdoing, had to pursue the remedies which might put this right before the arbitrator about which he made his complaint. Even if the result can be defended, it cannot be denied that it looks more than a little odd.

Odder by far was the judge's approach to the issue of costs. In the second-reported judgment, he ordered that costs be paid on the indemnity basis, a measure which is used to signify the court's particular disapproval of the manner in which the losing party has behaved in or in relation to the litigation. This is much more difficult to understand. The judge started from the premise that what had been done, by the good brother bringing proceedings in England, was to be seen as though it was a breach of contract. When proceedings have been brought before English courts, the costs recovered may leave the successful party out of pocket, but it is not permitted to bring an action for damages to recover such additional sum as is needed to top up the costs order to the level of a down-to-the-last-penny indemnity.[23] The judge seems to have regarded this as a most unfortunate limitation on his power to do justice as he saw it, and he responded as best he could, by making an award of costs on the indemnity basis. This was as close as he could get to awarding the bad brother and the arbitrator damages for the good brother's breach of the contractual promise to arbitrate.[24]

But was it right to see the claim of the good brother as being akin to a breach of contract? This must be doubtful. A party who considers that he is entitled to rescind a contract may act at his peril when he refuses to perform, and if in due course it is held that he was bound by the contract and was not entitled to refuse to perform, he may be liable in damages and for costs. But this is not what was going on in *A v B*.

---

[23] *Quartz Hill Consolidated Gold Mining Co v Eyre* (1883) 11 QBD 674 (CA).

[24] There is no need to mention them in any greater detail, but in two cases decided in 2007, the courts applied the principle that where foreign proceedings were brought in breach of an English jurisdiction agreement, damages for breach of contract were recoverable from the English courts. The proposition was accepted by the Court of Appeal as simple and well established in *Sunrock Aircraft Corp v SAS Denmark-Norway-Sweden* [2007] EWCA Civ 882, [2007] 2 Lloyd's Rep 612. In *National Westminster Bank plc v Rabobank Nederland* [2007] EWHC 1056 (Comm), Colman J held that a claim for damages was well founded even though the foreign court had made a limited award of damages in dismissing the proceedings brought before it; in *National Westminster Bank plc v Rabobank Nederland* [2007] EWHC 1742 (Comm), [2008] 1 Lloyd's Rep 16, the judge assessed the damages as the equivalent of his having ordered costs on the (English) indemnity basis. This followed from his earlier decision that the loss resulting from the breach of jurisdiction agreement was the 'costs' of defending the Californian proceedings which the defendant had promised not to bring.

The good brother's contention that he was entitled to rescind the contract was not adjudicated by the English court, still less rejected by it. Instead, the decision was that the good brother had to take his chance before the arbitrator and the Swiss courts. To see this as a case in which he had broken his contract is, at first sight, to anticipate the outcome of the Swiss proceedings, which cannot possibly be right. At second sight, the approach of Colman J is to see the agreement to arbitrate, even where it is disputed, as containing a contractual promise to have recourse only to the tribunal and the courts of the seat for the purpose of obtaining a ruling that the agreement is ineffective. It is not only Professor Schlosser who would regard this as incoherent.[25] The decision in *A v B (No 2)* takes hostility to those who dare to challenge an agreement to arbitrate to a new and preposterous level. Those who seek to challenge an arbitration agreement cannot be said to have breached their contractual promises unless and until it be found, finally, that the agreement—here the agreement to arbitrate in Switzerland—was valid and binding. Colman J was in no position to make such a finding. His conclusion that he should, nevertheless, treat the good brother as though in breach of contract in having the temerity to make his application was not one which was called for by the facts of the case.

In *C v D*, an arbitral tribunal sitting in London had rendered a final award. The unsuccessful party considered that there were serious problems with the award made against it, but took the view (which seems to have been perfectly realistic) that the grounds allowed by Arbitration Act 1996 for a challenge to the award were unlikely to bring it any joy. But it was an American entity, and on the footing that enforcement against it in America might have been on the cards, it commenced proceedings before the American courts for such relief, by way of review of the award, as American law permitted. This infuriated the successful party, which applied for and obtained an injunction to restrain the unsuccessful party from proceeding in the United States at all. On the face of it, this is plainly wrong, but below the surface appearance it may be importantly right.

When parties agree to arbitrate—and in *C v D* there was no challenge to the proposition that they had made such an agreement—they are taken to buy into the totality of law and procedures available to parties under the law of the place where the arbitration has its seat. As the parties had agreed upon arbitration in London, it was entirely correct that they had subscribed to an agreement, which comprised the reference itself and the law and procedure of the Arbitration Act 1996. It followed that they had agreed that post-hoc challenges to the award would be brought within the limited scope of the Arbitration Act 1996 itself. But they had not agreed that enforcement of any award was to be restricted to enforcement in England, no doubt because such a limitation would be daft. It followed that each of the parties had, when making the reference

---

[25] See above n 15.

to arbitration, preserved its freedom to enforce in any country in which enforcement seemed possible and sensible, and its freedom to oppose enforcement in any such country on such ground as the local law permitted to be advanced. The Court of Appeal, following the lead of Cooke J, saw matters differently. Its decision was that the proceedings, brought by the losing party before the American courts, were a breach of contract, a breach of the broad agreement to arbitrate in London; and as such were liable to be restrained by injunction. In its opinion, a choice of the seat for arbitration was also a choice about, and limiting, the arguments which could subsequently be made to attack the award. This, according to the court, appeared to extend to prevent arguments admissible as part of the enforcement law of a court other than that of the seat.[26]

This is difficult. Neither side had made any promise about the place of enforcement of the award, and neither side had made any promise about the arguments which would or would not, could or could not, be taken to resist enforcement. It is not clear that any such agreement, had it been made, would have been one which an American court would have respected, but the issue of which points may be taken in an enforcement was surely one for them. It might have been possible to justify the injunction on the ground that the successful party had made no move to suggest that it planned to enforce the London award in America, and that the proceedings brought by the losing party, being justifiable only as a defence to an application to enforce the award, should have been seen as premature and therefore restrained as vexatious. But the court appeared to think that for the losing party to plead US law on the enforceability of arbitration awards before a US court was to treat the agreement to arbitrate with such disrespect that it should be restrained as though it were a breach of contract. It is hard to see that this should be correct.

But on closer inspection, it may be just that. Let it be supposed that the parties had made an express promise that 'points of US arbitration law which may be applicable to resist the enforcement of an arbitral award under the law of the US shall not be taken'. As said above, whether such a promise could be given effect in American judicial proceedings would be for an American court, and only for an American court, to decide. But as a promise made by the parties, it may be mutually binding on them *in personam*, so that even if it did not serve to tie the hands of the American judge, it would still be a breach of contract for it to be advanced, no matter the reception it might receive. The rule in *Penn v Lord Baltimore*,[27] given an outing most recently in *Pattni v Ali*,[28] serves to explain how the mutual promise not binding on the judge is still effective to tie the hands of the parties in personam. If it be correct to interpret the reference to arbitration as one by which the parties promised to take as objections to the award only those points which the Arbitration Act 1996 would have

---

[26] At [17].   [27] (1750) 1 Ves Sen 444.
[28] [2006] UKPC 51, [2007] 2 AC 85 (noted in (2006) 77 *BYIL* 575).

permitted to be taken in an English court, then it was a breach of contract for the unsuccessful party to raise before the American court arguments which, on this analysis of the reference, it had agreed not to take
anywhere at all. The injunction was therefore justified as the remedial
response to a breach of contract. The judgment is therefore well supported by reason and authority.

It is finally to be noted that the Court of Appeal rejected the submission, but which Cooke J had accepted, that the unsuccessful party should
be ordered to pay costs on the indemnity basis. In this the Court of
Appeal was absolutely right. The attitude that no-one should ever dare
challenge the agreement to arbitrate, or the award, for fear of a punitive
costs order is at risk of running out of control. In the adult world, where
commercial parties incur costs in dispute resolution, there is no reason to
depart from the ordinary view that indemnity costs are for very special
cases. Challenging an agreement or an award is not, in this sense, so very
special.

3. Attitudes to service out of the jurisdiction: *Tasarruf Mevduati
Sigorta Fonu v Demirel;*[29] *City & Country Properties Ltd v Kamali;*[30]
ED & F Man (Sugar) Ltd v Lendoudis.[31]

Attitudes to service out of the jurisdiction with leave of the court are
rarely in need of examination. It is hornbook law that the grounds on
which permission to serve may be sought are to be interpreted conservatively, for fear that an exorbitant jurisdiction will be made wider than it
already is. Those who mess up their application for permission, or who
do not apply when application was demanded, have a harder task than
usual to persuade the judge to regard what has gone wrong as a curable
error of procedure.[32] And the requirement that England be the proper
place to bring the claim[33] serves as an overall mechanism of control. The
year produced three cases which showed that there was, perhaps, more
life in the law than had been supposed.

Tasarruf Mevduati Sigorta Fonu v Demirel was easy enough. A Turkish
court had given judgment for the claimant, and the claimant wished to
prepare the ground for the enforcement of its judgment in England. As
Demirel was not present within the jurisdiction, but enforcement had to
be by action on the judgment, TMSF applied for permission to serve
him out of the jurisdiction, relying on CPR r 6.20(9). This allows the
court to authorise service to be made if 'the claim is made to enforce any

---

[29] [2007] EWCA Civ 799, [2007] 1 WLR 2508: Sir Anthony Clarke MR; Arden and Hooper LJJ,
affirming Lawrence Collins J: [2006] EWHC 3354 (Ch).

[30] [2006] EWCA Civ 1879, [2007] 1 WLR 1219: May, Neuberger and Wilson LJJ.

[31] [2007] EWHC 2268 (Comm), [2007] 2 Lloyd's Rep 579: Christopher Clarke J.

[32] *Leal v Dunlop Bio-Processes International* [1984] 1 WLR 874; for errors of procedure, see
CPR r 3.10.

[33] CPR r 6.21(2A), which is the statutory formulation of the rule in *Spiliada Maritime Corp v
Cansulex Ltd* [1987] AC 460.

judgment or arbitral award'. The claim plainly was just that; but Demirel resisted the application on the ground that he had, as he said, no assets in England. That, he said, meant that the court should exercise its discretion against granting the order applied for. The Court of Appeal was unimpressed. The material question was whether England was plainly the natural forum for litigation about whether the Turkish judgment might be enforced in England; and the answer was obvious. In answer to the contention of Demirel that the absence of assets meant that leave should not be given, the Court of Appeal gave the eminently sensible response that (1) if the judgment creditor wanted to spend its money on getting an order which might not do it much practical good, that was, by and large, the judgment creditor's business, and (2) if Demirel were to obtain the relief applied for, the order of the judge below were to be set aside, and Demirel were then to move his assets to London, a fresh application would have to be made, which would be irresistible. The Court could see no reason for so asinine an outcome, and it confirmed that the order granting leave to serve out had been properly made.

There is only one place in which the enforceability of a judgment in England can be resolved: in England. In such a case, there is little or no chance of resisting an order granting permission to serve out. It must be possible to imagine, in an extreme case, that the permission may be opposed on the ground that it is fanciful to suppose that enforcement will ever take place within the six years permitted for it,[34] but no case so holds. CPR r 6.20(9) is unique among the cases listed in the Rule. All the others refer to proceedings which could, in principle, be prosecuted in England or elsewhere; but the enforcement of a judgment or award in England could take place only in England. In this case alone, the requirement that England also be the natural forum will add nothing to the law. The judgment called for nothing original or profound, just for a straightforward application of orthodox principle.

So did *City & Country Properties Ltd v Kamali*, but this time things seemed to go awry. A tenant, Mr Kamali, had absconded leaving a modest unmet rent obligation of some £6000-odd behind him. The claim form was posted to his business address in England. The claim form was not responded to, and within four weeks of the issue of the claim form, the landlord entered judgment in default of acknowledgment of service. Six months later[35] the tenant applied to have the judgment set aside on the ground that he had not been properly served. This, he said, was because he had been, and had been known by the landlord to have been, out of the jurisdiction when the claim form was served. He had not been served: not in England, because he had not been there to be served, and not out of the jurisdiction, for the procedure for service on a defendant out of the jurisdiction had not been followed and the claim form had not

---

[34] Limitation Act 1980.
[35] It being unclear just when the claim and judgment had come to the actual notice of the tenant.

been served outside England. There having been no service of the claim form, judgment in default should be set aside. But the Court of Appeal rejected the tenant's analysis. He had been served within the jurisdiction, and there was no more to be said about it. The fact that he had been physically outside the jurisdiction for the whole of the period during which the claim form was valid for service did not mean that he could be served only outside the jurisdiction. The contrary view, which had been expressed by Lawrence Collins J in *Chellaram v Chellaram (No 2)*,[36] was repudiated in surprisingly sharp language.

If the decision in *Kamali* is taken to have been correctly reasoned, it will circumvent a very substantial part of the law on service out of the jurisdiction with leave of the court. If it is taken that service out of the jurisdiction invokes a jurisdiction properly regarded as exorbitant, it is most unwelcome to discover that it can be outflanked by a form of service within the jurisdiction on someone who was not there. In other contexts this procedure, or one similar to it, is described as 'pretend service',[37] and there is no reason to jib at the designation. The proposition that the tenant had been served within the jurisdiction was indeed a pretence, and it was extraordinary that the court considered service to have been effectively made thereby. No doubt it was aware that if permission to serve out had been sought it would certainly have been granted, for the claim concerned the rent of commercial premises in Middlesex; and to set aside the judgment and service would have been an empty formality. Perhaps it was also aware that in other countries, and not only civilian ones where they understand the law rather differently, service which is to be made out of the jurisdiction does not require the prior permission of a judge.[38] Perhaps also it took the view that the tenant was taking a point which was devoid of substantial merit: he had not paid his rent, and what else was there to argue about? May LJ in particular seemed almost cross that the point had been given the time and attention which it had.[39] But the case holds that service out of the jurisdiction may not be necessary even though the defendant is out of the jurisdiction for the whole of the period from the issue of the claim form to the date on which its validity for service expires.

For all anyone knew, the tenant was telling the truth: he had left the country, albeit with the rent arrears unpaid, and did not return until after the claim form had ceased to be valid for service. The court seemed to be suspicious that defendants in the position of the tenant may be lying

---

[36] [2002] EWHC 632 (Ch), [2002] 3 All ER 17.

[37] This expression is encountered in connection with the practice in certain countries in which a foreign defendant may be 'served' by making service on a court officer who is supposed to transmit the writ, or on a diplomatic representative of the defendant's national state. But it is not service on the defendant; it is a pretence at such service.

[38] In many Australian states, service is made and the claimant will sometimes be required to apply for leave to continue the action; in many other countries service out requires no permission at all.

[39] At [1].

when they made such assertions, and incredulous that the manner of service might have to depend on where the defendant was on the day of service.[40] If, however, a claimant sees fit to obtain a judgment without making service out of the jurisdiction, he runs the risk that such other form of service as he has made will be irregular. The case is, therefore, really about the circumstances in which service may be, and will be deemed to have been, made within the jurisdiction, as opposed to service out of the jurisdiction. But its significance is very great.

As hinted above, the appeal was treated as though it were in substance against the reasoning of Lawrence Collins J in *Chellaram*. There, it had been contended that service of a writ on a defendant who was physically out of the jurisdiction at the time of service, or at any time which could have been regarded as a time of service, had to be made under the rules for service out. The judge had been pressed with the argument that, on a plain reading of it, CPR r 6.5 appeared to allow service to be within the jurisdiction by leaving the claim form at the last-known place of business of the defendant, and did not appear to restrict itself to cases in which the defendant was physically within the jurisdiction (if not at this place of business); he had rejected it for orthodox private international law reasons. But for those whose experience was gained in the county courts, things stood rather differently. Service of county court process was for many years permitted to be made by post to the last address of the defendant, even though he was out of the jurisdiction at the time. In *Rolph v Zolan*,[41] the defendant had emigrated to Spain, but service by posting the claim form to his last known residence in England was held to be good service. May LJ simply took the view that the CPR rules for service of High Court process were, pretty much, the old county court rules,[42] and that as a result, there was no need for the defendant to be present within the jurisdiction when the claim form was served by post to or delivery at an address within the jurisdiction. Service by post was the normal form of service, and it made no difference whether the defendant was home or away when the postman called. The only reason why May LJ did not see this as overthrowing an established principle was that he considered the principle—that personal service requires the person physically to be where service is actually made—to have been overthrown by the rule which permitted service by post. The proposition, accepted by almost everyone who had thought about it, that service by post was a mechanism for making personal service without the bother of the process-server having to attend in person, but was not otherwise substantially significant, was simply rejected.

---

[40] See esp Wilson LJ at [35]. One is drawn to think that he had not previously had cause to open Dicey and see what it was all about. If the defendant acknowledges service and does not challenge jurisdiction, any irregularity is cured in any event.

[41] [1993] 1 WLR 1305 (CA).

[42] Surprisingly, he deduced this from the fact that High Court process may now be served by post by the court, in the fashion of the old county court rules.

Though there is nothing in Wilson LJ's single paragraph to suggest that he was at all sympathetic to the approach which had been taken in *Chellaram*, Neuberger LJ was notably more polite, though his conclusion was not markedly different from that of May LJ: the rules had changed, and the decision in *Rolph v Zolan* was effectively binding on the court. All he observed was that the requirement to enquire into the defendant's movements, in order to discover whether an address within the jurisdiction really was his last known place of residence or business (as the case may be) may reveal that the defendant was overseas, with the consequence that he may not be served in England.[43] But the illogic of this is plain enough. It is also true, as Neuberger LJ observed, that to make the manner of service depend crucially on whether the defendant is in or out of the jurisdiction when service is made may seem wrong, and may seem worse where service is made by the court on a date not known to or under the control of the claimant. For all that, service made on a defendant who is out of the jurisdiction has never been understood to be properly made by pretending to serve within England. *Rolph v Zolan* notwithstanding, the decision in *Kamali* is bound to produce uncertainty and trouble.

We have seen before that English courts are troubled by the defendant who, fearing that he is about to be served, absconds with a view to evading service. Almost a century ago it arose in connection with the question whether an order for substituted service could be made for service on a defendant who had managed to flee the jurisdiction before service on him had been made. In *Porter v Freudenberg*,[44] the Court of Appeal made an order for substituted service within the jurisdiction on a defendant who had fled the jurisdiction to avoid service of a writ. This bad decision was criticised, as was only to be expected, by the High Court of Australia in *Laurie v Carroll*,[45] and was effectively not followed by the Court of Appeal in *Myerson v Martin*.[46] The rules on substituted service were held to operate subject to the rules for service on defendants out of the jurisdiction; these required a claimant to make the proper application and obtain permission to serve—the 'where' rules—before any question of the method of service might be made—the 'how' rules—would arise. That was sound law, and it is a great pity that the Court of Appeal in *Kamali*, clearing its desk before the long vacation, thought otherwise.

A much preferable approach may be seen in the judgment of Christopher Clarke J in *ED & F Man (Sugar) Ltd v Lendoudis*. The successful party to a London arbitration award, made in 1994, sought to enforce it in Greece. He obtained permission from the Greek court of first instance in 1995; and though it may have taken six years to come about, the final appeal was dismissed in 2001: the decision that award was entitled to be enforced in Greece was confirmed. At this point, sleep seems to have descended. In 2007, very nearly six years after the final appeal in Greece,

---

[43] At [26]–[27].   [44] [1915] 1 KB 857 (CA).   [45] (1958) 98 CLR 310.
[46] [1979] 1 WLR 1390 (CA).

an application was made to enforce the 1994 award in England as a judgment pursuant to Arbitration Act 1950, and to register the Greek judgment under Brussels I Regulation. This terrible procedural muddle got past David Steel J, who made the orders applied for; but the truth was exposed before Christopher Clarke J. The application under Arbitration Act 1950 was barred by lapse of time; and the Brussels Regulation did not apply to 'judgments' which decreed enforcement of arbitral awards. The applicant therefore changed tack, and claimed to be entitled to enforce the 1995 Greek judgment under the common law rules for the enforcement of foreign judgments. There were several troubles with this. First, it was not clear that the Greek judgment was a judgment capable of enforcement, as distinct from an order declaring that the English award could be executed in Greece. Second, the order of the Greek court of first instance, which was eventually upheld on appeal, was more than six years old, and the Limitation Act 1980 prescribes a six year period for bringing an action on a foreign judgment. It was altogether unclear whether this could be circumvented by bringing an action on the Greek judgment of 2001 upholding the Greek judgment of 1995 as to the enforceability of the award, and measuring the six years from 2001, but if the claimant were to be allowed to amend, his argument would face trouble ahead.[47] And third, the documents which had been served on the defendant in Greece did not assert that the claim was to enforce a foreign judgment by action at common law, and no application had been made to obtain permission to serve out under CPR r 6.20(9). The judge was asked to authorise all manner of amendments to 'cure the irregularity', but he refused, and quite rightly too. The rules governing service out of the jurisdiction have been construed strictly, conservatively, for a very long time. To allow the documents which were served to be amended to make a claim which had not been made, and to grant permission for service out which had never been applied for, would make a mockery of the law. That is not the business of the Commercial Court, and the judge was quite right to refuse to accede to the various applications, even where, as in this case, the claimant would be out of time to make a fresh application.

Service in general, and service out in particular, is a corner of the law in which the arguments are almost wholly technical and may allow a defendant with no merit to fall back on them to derail the attempt to invoke the processes of the court. It is not surprising that, from time to time, a court appears to allow its sense that a defendant should not be allowed to get away with it to get the better of it. That appears to be what happened in *City & Country Properties Ltd v Kamali*, but it is always unsatisfactory when it happens; the approach in *ED & F Man (Sugar) Ltd v Lendoudis* is much more satisfactory. After all, the rules for service out may be pernickety, but they are not inherently puzzling;

---

[47] See at [49]–[54].

and some formality to the start of litigation is inevitable. But however it is approached, there is something wrong with the judgment in *Kamali*'s case. Unless on making enquiries the claimant is unable to ascertain that an address within the jurisdiction has ceased to be an address of the defendant, for example by his discovering where the defendant is now living outside the jurisdiction, he may 'serve the defendant' by posting the claim form to, or by leaving it at, an address in England.[48] In cases in which the defendant is out of the jurisdiction at the time, that way of going about things does not appear to be the story which the cases on service out of the jurisdiction actually tell.

4. Disputes as to seisin under the Brussels regime: *Bentinck v Bentinck;*[49] *Moore v Moore;*[50] *Kolden Holdings Ltd v Rodette Commerce Ltd;*[51] *WPP Holdings Italy srl v Benatti.*[52]

Though the law has been improved by Article 30 of the Brussels I Regulation, which provides a reasonably effective and clear statement of when a court is to be regarded as seised (on issue or on service, according to which comes first in time in the particular court's procedure), and though this appears to be likely to be reproduced in Regulations modelled on Brussels I, and in the amended Lugano Convention, there is still room for argument in slightly complex cases about the date on which a court was seised. The textbooks had predicted that there were still issues to resolve, and had suggested answers. In four cases decided in 2007 the English courts had to apply the 'first seised' rule in circumstances in which the answer to the 'when seised?' question was not free of all doubt. Three of the decisions seem to have got the answer spot on; the fourth was more complex, and the result is less convincing, though this is not to say that it is wrong.

Bentinck v Bentinck was, however, a case decided under the Lugano Convention,[53] into which the new law in Article 30 of the Brussels I Regulation has not yet been copied.[54] Accordingly it was necessary for the English court to decide whether it or the Swiss court was seised

---

[48] Neuberger LJ at [26], citing *Cranfield v Bridgegrove Ltd* [2003] EWCA Civ 565, [2003] 1 WLR 2441; *Collier v Williams* [2006] EWCA Civ 20, [2006] 1 WLR 1945. It is not certain that this obiter dictum is completely accurate, though; and it introduces needless uncertainty into the issue whether service may be made in England. This is bad; it is worse when one observes that the enforcement of English judgments overseas will often require the receiving court to determine whether service was duly made.

[49] [2007] EWCA Civ 175, [2007] 2 FCR 267: Thorpe, Wall and Lawrence Collins LJJ.

[50] [2007] EWCA Civ 361, [2007] 2 FCR 353: Thorpe, Lawrence Collins LJJ; Munby J.

[51] [2007] EWHC 1597 (Comm), [2007] 2 All ER (Comm) 723: Aikens J. The Court of Appeal dismissed on appeal: [2008] EWCA Civ 10, [2008] 1 Lloyd's Rep 434.

[52] [2007] EWCA Civ 263, [2007] 1 WLR 2316: Sir Anthony Clarke MR; Buxton and Toulson LJJ.

[53] Civil Jurisdiction & Judgments Act 1982 Sch 3A.

[54] It is, however, anticipated that this development will take place in 2008, as the final text of the amended Lugano Convention was signed on 30 October 2007. Its final enactment will be only a matter of time.

first, in the old fashioned sense of asking when the proceedings satisfied the criterion of being 'definitively pending' before each of the courts in question. Carol, Baron Bentinck, was Swiss-Dutch; his wife Lisa (nee Hogan), was Irish. When they married, which they did in Klosters, their pre-nuptial agreement was expressed to be governed by Swiss law. When they fell out, the baron issued matrimonial proceedings in the Swiss courts. These took the form of a request for conciliation, as was required by cantonal procedural law, and proposed orders for maintenance pending suit. Several months later the baroness petitioned for divorce and for maintenance in London, and applied to have the papers served through official channels. This was immediately accompanied by irregular attempts to serve process, described by Thorpe LJ[55] with evident justification, as 'bizarre'. The baroness refused to participate in the Swiss conciliation proceedings, and challenged the jurisdiction of the Swiss court. In due course, the Swiss court transferred the proceedings to the competent divorce court for matters to take their course. The baron in his turn applied to have the irregular service of English process set aside; and when eventually served through official channels, he applied to have the court declare that it had no jurisdiction over the maintenance claim, on the ground that the Swiss court was seised first. The Lugano Convention applies to maintenance, though not to divorce.

Though the English proceedings got into a fearful muddle, with all sorts of strange procedural decisions being hurried, when the dust cleared the question was whether the English or Swiss court was first seised of the maintenance claim. To the baron's contention that the Swiss court had been seised first, the baroness responded with the argument that it was not until the conciliation proceedings had been brought to an end (by her refusal to participate in them) and the subsequent transfer of the matter to the divorce court, that the claim for maintenance was definitively pending before the Swiss court. By that date, as she asserted, the English claim for maintenance had been served and the English court seised. By the time the case came before the Court of Appeal, the Swiss courts were about to rule on the date on which they were seised; the contention of the baroness was that, despite this, the English court should press ahead, taking expert evidence from Swiss lawyers who would have been selected to support each side's case, and decide that issue of Swiss law for itself. Little which would have been more procedurally daft could have been imagined, and Thorpe LJ refused to entertain it. He took the view that the English court should wait to see what the Swiss court said about the date of Swiss seisin,[56] rather than add to the third of a million pounds which the lawyers had managed to run up in costs to date. How right

---

[55] At [8] and [9].

[56] By the date of the hearing in the Court of Appeal, the Swiss court had heard argument and had reserved judgment. The Court of Appeal, on this point, was also following *Chorley v Chorley* [2005] EWCA Civ 68, [2005] 1 WLR 1469. The decision of the Swiss court was that it had been seised at the date of the conciliation application, not the later date of transfer to the divorce court.

he was: even if the structure of the Lugano Convention encourages this unseemly scrambling to get ahead, the idea that an English court should make a non-binding decision about a rule of Swiss procedural law, about to be conclusively elucidated by a Swiss appellate tribunal, had nothing to commend it. A procedural stay was the only sensible possibility; and the court ordered it.

Moore v Moore was another divorce and big money case. The parties had married in England, but soon after their move to Spain, scheming thereby to avoid UK taxes, they fell out and wasted their money instead on lawyers' fees, which is oddly satisfying: the court was told that costs had consumed £1.5 million so far, but there was evidently still quite a lot left. The legal issue was simply one of jurisdiction. The husband had got the ball rolling by petitioning for divorce in Marbella, but did not invoke the maintenance jurisdiction of that court.[57] That opened the way for the wife to petition in London for divorce and maintenance. Her divorce petition was stayed pursuant to the Brussels II Regulation,[58] as the Spanish court was unquestionably seised first. The Spanish proceedings made their way ahead, the wife not asking for a financial order from the Spanish court, presumably as she preferred to pursue this before an English court. Though there was apparently some evidence that the parties had negotiated a financial settlement, the Spanish judge refused to make any financial order, as neither side had formally applied for one in their pleadings. In due course the husband sought to invoke the jurisdiction of the Spanish court to order a financial settlement, but the Spanish court ruled that it was now too late for this to be done. The wife then made a claim for financial relief in England; and the husband tried again to get the financial relief claim before the Spanish judge by means of a further pleading. This was rejected by the Spanish court, which then changed its mind and allowed the claim for financial relief, then changed its mind again. A still further appeal by the husband against this most recent Spanish decision was pending when the matter came before the Court of Appeal. On any view the entire process had been a shambles from its start to the finish which was nowhere in sight.[59]

So far as concerned the financial claim, the question whether it was pending before the Spanish court before it was pending in the English court appeared to be more complex than it actually was. As the Spanish judicial system had changed its mind about allowing the husband's maintenance claim from time to time, the wife had been able to argue that at the point at which the Spanish court had ruled that it had no jurisdiction over the financial relief claim, the English court was alone, and therefore was first, seised. This made no sense, as the prospect that the Spanish

---

[57] This has all the outward appearances of being a terrible mistake.

[58] Regulation (EC) 1347/2000, now superseded by Regulation (EC) 2001/2003, known as Brussels II*bis*.

[59] See the judgment at [6] and [7] where the 'lamentable and grotesque waste of family resources', seemingly without any rational purpose or end in sight, was pointed out.

court would reverse the judgment below was always present. One text-book had indicated that the rational answer was that the court first seised was first seised until the final determination of any appeal, and that this was unaffected by the decision to allow or to dismiss an appeal along the way.[60] The Court took the same view, though neglecting to cite the signpost which had pointed to the right answer.[61] It was certainly right to approve this approach: the court first seised must be regarded as still-first seised until the final determination of any challenge to its jurisdiction. But there were two reasons why the court did not actually need to apply this principle. The first was that the claim for financial relief was, when introduced in Spain, not part of the divorce proceedings which had been unquestionably started in Spain first, but separate and distinct. That fatally weakened the contention that the Spanish court was seised first. The second was that the Spanish claim was for an adjustment of property, as distinct from maintenance. Unlike maintenance, the judicial adjustment of property rights on divorce still lies outside the material scope of the Brussels Regulations,[62] and the rule of prior seisin is, there-fore, inapplicable to it. The sole question was therefore whether the judge should have permitted the wife to make a claim under the Matrimonial and Family Proceedings Act 1984; and on that point the court refused to upset the judgment of the judge below who had held that she could.

The decision is helpful for its confirmation that proceedings remain pending before a court even though a decision has been taken to dismiss them on jurisdictional grounds if that decision is under appeal, or still capable of being appealed. It is the only sensible answer. The case also highlights the problems which arise when proceedings before a national court contain matters which fall both inside and outside the Brussels jur-isdictional regime, and the larger problems which arise when applications are made to join into pending proceedings distinct matters which could have been raised at the time, but which were not. Beyond that, it is diffi-cult to see that one can do much more than join the court in its amazement at the money which had been spent on this utterly pointless dispute. As it appeared common ground that the Spanish court, even if it finally con-cluded that it had jurisdiction, would apply English law to the financial or property claim, it was unsurprising that the court's question as to what was the point of the husband's determination to have this aspect of the matter dealt with in Spain, was one his counsel was unable to answer.[63]

The issue of seisin and amendment also arose in *Kolden Holdings Ltd v Rodette Commerce Ltd* which, by happy contrast, was a purely commer-cial case. Proceedings had been brought in England by three companies against two Cypriot companies. Some time after the proceedings had

---

[60] Briggs & Rees, *Civil Jurisdiction and Judgments* (4th edn, 2005), para 2.205, fn 1139.
[61] At [103], which cites the textbook for the problem, but ignores the footnote with the proposed answer.
[62] Article 1 of each.   [63] At [6].

been started, a corporate reorganisation on the claimants' side vested all the assets, including the causes of action, in K. K's lawyers wrote to the Cypriot companies to inform them that they had applied for permission to amend the English proceedings but the Cypriot companies, seeing their chance, instantly seised the Cypriot court with a claim against K as defendant, seeking a declaration that they owed no liability to K. And on the footing that the Cypriot court was seised days before the application to amend the title to the English action, the Cypriot companies argued that the English court was now seised second, and was therefore required to stay its proceedings (if the jurisdiction of the Cypriot court was being challenged, as it was), and to dismiss them if the Cypriot court were to dismiss the challenge to its jurisdiction. Aikens J had to apply the provisions of the Brussels I Regulation to determine whether the proceedings in his court had an earlier date of seisin than the competing proceedings before the Cypriot court, just as, if in mirror image, did the Cypriot court. Aikens J had little trouble in concluding that as the original English action had become pending first of all, and as there had been an assignment of the original cause of action to K, K stepped into the shoes of the assignor-claimants, and was to be regarded as having been claimant to the proceedings from the beginning. That being so, the Cypriot court was seised second, not first, and there was therefore nothing in the Brussels I Regulation to require the English court to sustain the challenge to its jurisdiction.

It is true that where pending proceedings are amended to add a new party or a new claim, it is very difficult to say that the court has been seised of the added matter from the date of the original claim form. Even if national procedural law backdates the date from which the (new) claim was made, for example for the purposes of national law on limitation of actions, it cannot be said with any accuracy that the proceedings were pending until the date on which the amendment was made (or, conceivably, on which the order was applied for).[64] But amendment to record and reflect the fact that a pending cause of action has been assigned from assignors to an assignee raises a different issue: the substantive claim which was pending before the court to begin with is exactly the same (if perhaps subject to set-offs[65]) as after the amendment. This was the view of Aikens J, and it appears to be consistent with the view of the Regional Court of Appeal at Cologne.[66] It was not necessary to bend the law to frustrate the manoeuvring of the Cypriot entity, but it was nevertheless satisfying that the result could be reached as it was.

The decision was justifiable on these grounds without reference to more. But insofar as authority was needed, it supported the view of common sense. In essence the question was whether the assignee and

---

[64] See *Molins plc v GD SpA* [2000] 1 WLR 1741 (CA).
[65] Which will not count for these purposes: Case C-111/01 *Gantner Electronic GmbH v Basch Exploitatie Maatschappij BV* [2003] ECR I-4207.
[66] 16 U 110/02, Sept 8th 2003 (OLG Köln); 2004 IPrax 521.

assignors counted as the 'same parties' for the purposes of Article 27 of the Regulation. If they were, the English action would always have been between the same parties as the Cypriot action, both before and after the assignment. The question was to be answered by reference to the judgment in *Drouot Assurances SA v Consolidated Metallurgical Industries*,[67] where the European Court had established the test that if the interests of A are 'identical to and indissociable from' those of B, A and B may be regarded as the same party for the purpose of Article 27 of the Regulation. In *Drouot*, that test allowed it to be concluded that the owner of a vessel and the insurer of its hull were not the same person; but in *Kolden*'s case, the test led to the decision that as assignors and assignee had exactly the same interest in the claim against the Cypriot defendants, the assignors and assignee were the same party. That meant that the English court was seised first, and that no question of a stay of proceedings arose. It also makes it plain that there will be other instances of and causes for amendment, and that the analysis of these may be different.

The fourth decision concerns the approach to be taken to irregularities in service, and the effect that these may have on the decision whether (and if so, when) proceedings were definitively pending before a national court. It underlines the importance of getting service right, and the substantial expense, in terms of legal costs if nothing else, if this is got wrong. In *WPP Holdings Italy srl v Benatti*, B, an Italian businessman, was retained by an Italian company to provide professional services to it. The parent company of the WPP group was based in London, and B's service agreement was expressed to be governed by English law and subject to the jurisdiction of the English courts. In these circumstances, one may think, the fact that B was struggling so hard to escape the jurisdiction of the English courts deserved to be looked at with little sympathy.

When B's contract was terminated by WPP, he received a letter reminding him of his post-contractual obligations owed to the WPP companies.[68] Two days later proceedings against him were commenced in London by one only of the WPP companies; several days later B instituted proceedings in Italy against a number of WPP companies, claiming relief due to him as an employee unlawfully dismissed. The Italian writ was served in London, but without a translation into English. It was only a couple of months later that the Italian writ was re-lodged and re-served with a translation, by which time a considerable muddle of writs, translations, notices of service and so on, had been generated. At their heart lay two factual difficulties. First, service of the Italian writ without

---

[67] Case C-351/96, [1998] ECR I-3075.

[68] There was a point about whether WPP companies associated with the WPP company which made the contract with B could claim that their reliance on B's contractual promises was in a matter relating to a contract for the purposes of Article 5(1). The conclusion that it was, and that where the Contracts (Rights of Third Parties) Act 1999 gave a claimant a statutory right to enforce the contract, then the claim was one relating to a contract for the purposes of the Regulation, was plainly correct: see Toulson LJ at [54], approving Briggs & Rees, *Civil Jurisdiction and Judgments* (4th edn, 2005), 2.216.

a translation into English could be seen to invalidate the service made on the defendants when regard was had to the requirements of Article 14 of the Service Regulation.[69] Second, the Italian writ had mis-stated the name of one of the parties against whom the action was brought: possibly from unforced unilateral error, but possibly as a result of a corporate reconstruction in the WPP group. But if either of these was fatal to the attempt to seise the Italian court, any temporal priority which the Italian proceedings might have had was liable to have been lost, for the English writ had been amended in the meantime to add the missing WPP companies to the list of those claiming against B.

The decision of the Court of Appeal was that neither shortcoming prevented the Italian court being seised as on the day it would have been seised if neither error had been made: it regarded errors in service as irrelevant to the date of seisin, and to the extent that the proceedings otherwise satisfied Article 27 of the Regulation, the Italian courts were seised first. Toulson LJ got there by interpreting Article 30 of the Regulation as requiring B to deliver the Italian writ to the Italian entity charged with making service of it. According to Toulson LJ, the fact that the process-server may not have served in strict accordance with Italian law, which included the Service Regulation, did not allow the defendant to say that B had failed to take the steps necessary to have the document served. This may be defensible if one takes the view that any error in service was not attributable to B, so that any error could not fairly be laid at the door of B. It followed that even if there was a sustainable objection to service—Toulson LJ was distinctly cool about the nature of the shortcomings which could be alleged[70]—it did not prevent the Italian court being seised when the first writ was lodged with the court for service.

On the other hand, the failure to provide the defendants with a translation of the writ (as well as any mis-naming of the party to be sued) was hardly the fault of the service agency: it served what it had been given by B to serve; and it had served an Italian writ without translation on which the wrong entities were addressed. That was, as Buxton LJ saw, and correctly, nobody's error but B's. Had things stood there, Buxton LJ would have held, again surely correctly, that if B had managed to arrange it so that service would not comply with the Service Regulation, it did not lie in his mouth to aver that service had been good, or that if it was not, the Italian court was still seised on the date the writ was lodged. But Buxton LJ was able to persuade himself that when a correctly-translated writ was re-lodged with the Italian court, this had the effect under Italian law of validating the seisin of the court from the date of the first lodging of the writ. If this is what Italian law actually said, it reduces the scope for taking issue with the judgment. Certainly, the decision of the European

<hr>

[69] Regulation (EC) 1348/2000. This will be replaced by Regulation (EC) 1393/2007 with effect from 13th November 2008.
[70] At [68].

Court in *Leffler v Berlin Chemie AG*[71] lends support to the view that, for the purpose of the Service Regulation, the absence of a translation is not fatal to the claim to have made good service. Even so, the proposition that the Italian court was not seised when there was lodged with it a writ which was not fit for service under the Service Regulation, but was seised from that date once a revised and corrected version of the writ was re-lodged, is unattractive. Both Buxton and Toulson LJJ seem to have been highly unsympathetic with the points taken on service; but judicial impatience is no substitute for reasoned analysis.[72] Consider what would have happened if the English proceedings had managed to get themselves definitively pending after the service of the untranslated writ, but before the supply of a correction. The eventual conclusion that it did not actually matter which date was chosen for the seisin of the Italian court would not have been the consolation which Sir Anthony Clarke MR found it to be. The conclusion which appears to follow from Buxton LJ's analysis would be that the English court would have had jurisdiction, only to have lost it again once a corrective step had been taken in Italy: a conclusion pretty much at odds with the three cases discussed earlier in this Note, and contrary to the general authority of the European Court.[73]

More than this probably need not be said, for a version of the same issue—how to treat the case in which incomplete documentation is served, and by the time a corrected set of papers is served, the party upon whom they were served has started foreign proceedings of his own, was before the Court of Appeal in *Phillips v Symes*,[74] in which a further appeal was argued before the House of Lords late in 2007. The message of the Court of Appeal in that case was that it was not open to a party who had messed-up service[75] to 'jump the seisin queue', by re-serving a set of papers purged of the flaw and pretending to have rewritten history as a result. Though the issues were not completely identical, and though the Lugano Convention which governed in *Phillips v Symes* is worded differently from the Brussels I Regulation, the basic orientations of the two decisions of the Court of Appeal are plainly in conflict. Either one takes irregularity in the service of documents seriously, or one does not. There is a fair argument to make on either side, but the choice remains to be made. Averting the eyes, or pretending that there is no need to make a choice after all, does not seem to be such a good idea.

It is necessary to say something about the other points which arose in the judgment in *Benatti*'s case. There was disagreement about whether B

---

[71] Case C-433/03, [2005] ECR I-9611.

[72] Sir Anthony Clarke MR preferred the views of Toulson LJ to those of Buxton LJ.

[73] Case C-111/01 *Gantner Electronic GmbH v Basch Exploitatie Maatschappij BV* [2003] ECR I-4207.

[74] [2006] EWCA Civ 654, [2006] 1 WLR 2598 (noted (2006) 77 *BYIL* 595).

[75] In that case, by arranging for what was an incomplete set of papers (the incompleteness being contributed to by the actions of a court official in the Swiss canton of Aargan, who removed a vital document from the package which he was serving on behalf of the claimant and at the request of the English court).

was an employee or a provider of services to the WPP companies. This was critical, for the jurisdiction agreement in B's contract which gave jurisdiction to the English courts was not liable to be given effect if B were an employee. The distinction between employment and self-employment is not easy to draw: every first year undergraduate student finds this out in the law of tort, and it gets no easier when one comes across it in other contexts as one grows older and the taxman starts nosing around. The judge below had concluded that B was a consultant rather than an employee; and in various places the Court of Appeal suggested that this was a matter in which his judgment would not be disturbed unless it was very wrong.[76] This treats the judgment as though it involved a discretion, and it does not look right: a jurisdictional rule is just that, and errors of law are not to be waved away on the footing that making them was within the judge's authority. Even so, in the light of the evidence as to the terms and nature of B's relationship with WPP, the conclusion that B was a consultant rather than an employee seemed right. But as there was dispute about it, what was the standard of certainty which was required to be met on the point? The answer is found by starting from the proposition that what is required is a good arguable case on the point for decision. If (as to which there is more to be said) the English court would not have had jurisdiction apart from the agreement on jurisdiction, the current sense of the law would be to require a good arguable case that B was not an employee: this would be sufficient to prevent Section 5 of Chapter II of the Regulation invalidating the jurisdiction agreement for the English courts.[77] This would normally be taken to mean that WPP would need to have much the better of the argument on the point.[78] But Toulson LJ, in a very puzzling passage,[79] appeared to deny that the 'much the better of the argument' test was applicable in this context. In his opinion, jurisdiction might still be established even if neither side had the better of the argument. This gratuitous and now heretical observation was immediately followed by his saying that he was unwilling to decide the point which was not in any event necessary for the decision. None of this adds clarity to our understanding of the law.

Whether the contract of B was to be assessed as employment or consultancy may have depended on the approach taken to answering the question. Toulson LJ preferred to look at the terms of the agreement, and at the way the duties of the contract were in fact performed as time went by: this led him to agree with the judge's conclusion that B was a consultant. Buxton LJ preferred the view that, as the contract was governed by English law, one should use an English-law interpretation to

---

[76] At [45] (Toulson LJ) and [75] (Buxton LJ).

[77] See generally *Konkola Copper Mines plc v Coromin Ltd* [2006] EWCA Civ 5, [2006] 1 Lloyd's Rep 410.

[78] *Canada Trust Co v Stolzenberg (No 2)* [2002] 1 AC 1; *Bols Distilleries BV v Superior Yacht Services Ltd* [2007] 1 WLR 12 (PC Gib).

[79] At [42]–[44].

decide whether it was employment or not: this would have precluded any reference to events taking place after the conclusion of the contract.[80] Sir Anthony Clarke MR did not choose between them, noting only that the European Court had given no useful guidance on the particular question of how to interpret the facts, but not ruling out that Buxton LJ's approach may be correct. The answer, surely, will be held to be that one is not restricted to facts and matters which were in existence at the date the contract was made. The European Court has tended to take a pretty broad view of the matters which may be looked at to determine the place of performance of the employee's duties, and has refused to limit itself to facts and matters known at the date of the making of the contract.[81] It is certainly not the same question, but it is unlikely that an analysis of the contract, to understand whether it sets out the duties of an employee or the duties of a consultant, will be subjected to a radically different methodology.

5. The Brussels Regulation and the right to an anti-suit injunction: *Samengo-Turner v Marsh & McLennan (Services) Ltd*[82]

We have come to understand that the Brussels I Regulation does not accept, any more than the Brussels Convention did, that an English court may order an anti-suit injunction to require the respondent to cease proceedings before the courts of another Member State.[83] The European Court did not explain, and maybe did not even pause to wonder, whether this was because the Brussels Regulation, establishing the rules of the club of Member States, precluded it, or because the rules themselves were more correctly understood as rules of public law which gave rise to no enforceable private law rights. But the issue arose acutely in *Samengo-Turner v Marsh & McLennan (Services) Ltd*; and the Court of Appeal, sad to say, did not make a good job of it. Indeed, its decision was quite extraordinary and, one assumes, driven by unsound submissions. The answers, and almost all the authority for those answers, were all in the books. It seems that nobody looked for them.

S and two colleagues worked in the finance industry, employed by a company in the MM group. As people like S tend to be loyal to greed rather than to any employer, MM arranged for another company in the group, this time a Delaware entity, to enter into an incentive contract with the employees, which provided benefits to be paid as long as the employees remained in their employment. No doubt the whole thing was arranged to reduce the charge to legitimate UK taxes. S and his colleagues, having taken substantial sums under this arrangement, then

---

[80] *Whitworth Street Estates (Manchester) Ltd v James Miller & Partners Ltd* [1970] AC 583.
[81] Case C-37/00 *Weber v Universal Ogden Services Ltd* [2002] ECR I-2013.
[82] [2007] EWCA Civ 723, [2008] ICR 18: Tuckey, Longmore and Lloyd LJJ.
[83] Case C-159/02 *Turner v Grovit* [2004] ECR I-3565.

decided to resign and, so far as one can tell, join a rival which would pay them even more. The Delaware entity, taking the view that such rotten behaviour was conduct which entitled it under the incentive contract to recover the sums it had paid out, brought proceedings in New York for repayment. A challenge to the jurisdiction of the New York court was dismissed, for the incentive contract contained New York law and exclusive jurisdiction clauses. Faced with the brisk management of the proceedings in New York, the employees applied in England for an anti-suit injunction. And, bizarrely, they succeeded. The result was that proceedings in New York to enforce the terms of a New York law contract, in the agreed contractual forum, and in circumstances in which there appeared to be no defence to the claim, were restrained by the Court of Appeal. And the reasoning which was offered in justification is as painfully wrong as is the result of its application to the facts.

The basis on which the court was induced to make its lamentable order was that the employees had a statutory right[84] to be sued in England. As the court in New York was unable[85] to give effect to that right, it fell to the English court to enforce it. What nonsense that was. For from its being true that the New York court was unable to enforce the employees' 'right to be sued in England', the New York court took the view that there was no such right and nothing to enforce. For the English court to assert its personal power to make decrees was not for it to do something which the New York court could not do, but was to contradict and override the substantive law of New York and the contents of the contract. This will, of course, occasionally happen: it is why we have a conflict of laws, after all. But where was this right which the employees were entitled to ask the court to enforce?

According to the court, it was a right, conferred by the Brussels Regulation, to be sued in England. Given that there was an express contractual promise to accept the exclusive jurisdiction of the New York court, asserting the existence of this right was something of a surprise. But according to the employees, (i) their relationship with the Delaware company was that of employment; (ii) a jurisdiction agreement in a contract of employment was invalidated by Section 5 of Chapter II of the Regulation; (iii) it made no difference that the jurisdiction agreement was for the courts of a non-Member State, (iv) once that jurisdiction agreement was removed from the picture, the employees were entitled to be sued where they were domiciled, and (v) an injunction could and should be ordered to enforce that right. Wrong, wrong, wrong, wrong, and wrong.

As to point (i), the relationship was not one of employment: the employees had such a relationship with the English company, but not with the Delaware incentive-provider: it was more than a little rich for parties to a scheme which was deliberately structured so as to separate the incentive from the employment to turn round and claim that it was an

---

[84] At [38], [43].   [85] At [43].

employment relationship after all. Nor could it be said that the employee and the Delaware company were 'the same person': the test for this, put forward by the European Court in *Drouot Assurance SA v Consolidated Metallurgical Industries*,[86] required it to be said that the interests of each of the two entities were 'identical to and indissociable from' those of the other. In *Samengo-Turner*, the contractual and other interests of the various MM entities were related, coordinated even, but were plainly not identical. By contrast, the court appealed to 'the reality of the situation'[87] in coming to the conclusion that the incentive provider was an employer of the applicants. But it was not and everyone had been at pains to ensure that it was not.

But even if this were correct, it did not follow that Section 5 of Chapter II of the Regulation invalidated the jurisdiction agreement for New York. So far as point (ii) was concerned, the Regulation protects an employee from certain jurisdiction agreements, in order to allow employees the benefit of being sued in a court with which they are familiar, or in which they will be afforded protection by employment laws to which they are entitled to look. That would have prevented the employment contract in the present case being subjected to a jurisdiction agreement for, for example, the Irish courts. It would have prevented the Irish courts exercising jurisdiction over the employees, a proposition which makes perfect sense if the Regulation is understood as an instrument by which the Member States define—by conferring and restricting—the jurisdiction of their courts. This has nothing to do with the courts outside the Member States, which can neither be given judicial jurisdiction by the Regulation, nor prevented from exercising such jurisdiction as their law gives them. It should have followed that the New York jurisdiction agreement was untouched by Section 5 of Chapter II of the Regulation, as it was not an agreement which purported to confer jurisdiction on the courts of a Member State.

As to point (iii), the European Court had recently made it clear that the effectiveness of a jurisdiction agreement for the courts of a non-Member State was a matter for the private international law of the court seised: *Coreck Maritime GmbH v Handelsveem BV*[88] had been clear and explicit to this effect in following the opinion of Professor Schlosser. How could it have been otherwise? The Regulation lacks a mechanism by which to force non-Member States to give effect to jurisdiction agreements, and as a result cannot extend its complex of jurisdictional rules into such cases. Unless the European Court is prepared to say that a jurisdiction agreement for a non-Member State is null and void—a conclusion to which some commentators seem to be drawn but which is even dafter than

---

[86] See above n 67.
[87] At [33]. This aspect of the decision was followed in *Duarte v Black & Decker Corp* [2007] EWHC 2720 (QB), [2008] 1 All ER (Comm) 401.
[88] Case C-387/98, [2000] ECR I-9337.

most wrong ideas—it is bound to say that the effect to be given to these agreements is, until there is EU legislation on the point, a matter for the national law of the court seised.[89] As a matter of the national law of the court seised, the jurisdiction clause for New York was valid and binding. No argument existed for refusing it effect, not least because the constant position of the common law is that jurisdiction agreements are meant to be observed.

The argument to the contrary proceeds from two points. The first involves an interpretation of *Owusu v Jackson*[90] as though it said that a jurisdiction agreement for a non-Member State is without effect, as its validity is not provided for by the Regulation. *Owusu* said no such thing, and the reason that it did not was that it would have made no legal sense to do so. If nothing else, the argument that the Regulation should be interpreted to promote legal certainty—a good aim, to be sure—means that agreements on jurisdiction should be given effect. The second involves a mis-reading of the Opinion by which the Court declared that competence to settle the terms of a new Lugano Convention was vested in the European Union.[91] The Opinion makes the obvious point that, unless there is EU-wide legislation to give effect to non-Member State jurisdiction clauses, jurisdiction agreements for Lugano States will not be subject to uniform rules of application. This is precisely correct, and it provides an orthodox justification for legislation to secure uniformity of treatment of agreements undertaken by international Convention. How one gets from there to the proposition that, as things currently stand, non-Member State clauses are ineffective is a mystery which is not worth exploring. The current state of the law is one of fractured effectiveness, not of uniform ineffectiveness. This had been painstakingly set out in print in various places;[92] it does not appear that the Court of Appeal was referred to any of the writing. Its conclusion that a jurisdiction agreement for New York could be treated as indistinguishable from one for Dublin was simply unsustainable.

As to point (iv), if there had been, as the court proceeded to suppose, no jurisdiction agreement for New York, there were still proceedings in New York. There was no evident legal wrong committed by the party who had invoked the jurisdiction of the New York courts, but the Court of Appeal was persuaded to find that the employees had a right to be

---

[89] This is the reason for the European Union to enter into a Convention with the non-Member States who are party to the Lugano Convention, to produce a uniform EU rule on the enforcement of jurisdiction agreements with Lugano States which would otherwise be legally impossible: Opinion C-1/03, [2006] ECR I-1145, at [153]. The suggestion that the Court was there saying that a national court currently has no power to give effect to a non-Member State jurisdiction clause (see Knight (2007) 66 *CLJ* 288; Hartley, *The Modern Approach to Private International Law: International Litigation and Transactions from a Common-Law Perspective* (Hague Recueil, Vol 319, 2006) at 137) is wrong.

[90] Case C-281/02, [2005] ECR I-1383.

[91] Opinion C-1/03, [2006] ECR I-1145.

[92] [2005] LMCLQ 363, 378; and Dicey, Morris & Collins, para 12-021, 12-022.

sued in England. This right, not found in any contract, was traced to
Article 2 of the Brussels Regulation, as reinforced by the special rules
on cases of individual employment in Section 5 of Chapter II. This is
hopeless, for if it is correct, it means that any person with a domicile in a
Member State[93] will be entitled to assert a right to be sued in a Member
State, to assert as corollary that he has a right not to be sued anywhere
else, from China to Peru, and to seek a remedy to enforce this right so
lone as he can hale his opposite party before the English court. That
ascribes an effect to the Judgments Regulation which, it seems safe to
say, would have startled Mr Droz at the time the Brussels Convention
was born, and everyone else who has been involved with it since. If any
principle can be said to explain the recent jurisprudence of the European
Court, it is that the Regulation does not give rise to private rights, does
not operate at the level of private law. Instead, it stipulates the jurisdiction of courts in Member States so that, when a court in a Member State
has to decide whether it has or has not jurisdiction, it looks to this code
alone. It may not look at this set of rules to deal with a submission that
the courts of another Member State do not have jurisdiction;[94] it may
not look at this code to ascertain whether the courts in another Member
State may be prevented from exercising any jurisdiction they may (think
they) have.[95] The proposition that it is consistent with this to use the
Regulation as the legal source of a right not to be sued in a non-Member
State is ludicrous.

Potter J, as he then was, saw the point as long ago as 1995.[96] Since then
the law has become only clearer, that what is now the Regulation does not
confer private law rights; and especially not a private law right 'to have
the Regulation applied properly'. It was a surprise to see this rational
view upset by the Court of Appeal, and a shame that it was invited to do
so without, apparently, any reference to the decision of Potter J. But now
instead of a good decision at first instance, we have a bad one from the
Court of Appeal which, unless it is shown to the next Court of Appeal
to have been decided *per incuriam*—which, in the present submission, it
was—will bind until someone pays for the law to be restored.

As to point (v), injunctions give effect to legal rights or to equitable
rights: this is true of anti-suit injunctions because they are injunctions.
Even if there are other areas in which such orders may be made, none
was relevant here. The Court of Appeal ordered the injunction on the
basis that there was a legal right not to be sued in New York. This is,
on any view of the matter, nonsense. There was a legally-binding agreement to accept the jurisdiction of the New York court, which the New

---

[93] And some who do not have such a domicile, for some of the rules of the Regulation apply without regard to the domicile of the defendant.

[94] Case C-116/02 *Erich Gasser GmbH v Misat srl* [2003] ECR I-14693.

[95] Case C-159/02 *Turner v Grovit* [2004] ECR I-3565.

[96] The *Eras EIL Actions* [1995] 1 Lloyd's Rep 64; see Briggs & Rees, (above n 60) para 5.39
fn 235, where the point is discussed.

York court had found to be valid and binding. The contract of which it had been a part was not impugned: indeed, the employees had cheerfully pocketed substantial sums from the Delaware company, relying on the very contract which they were now breaching. For make no mistake about it: what the employees were up to was a shameless breach of the obligations to which they had subscribed. They had no right not to be sued in New York; they had accepted a duty to turn up and defend there: that is what their contract said they would do. And if this were not enough, it is ancient law that equity follows the law; that he who comes to equity must come with clean hands; and that he who seeks equity must do equity. As to these: equity followed the law in regarding this contract as unimpeachable; the employees were in flagrant breach of its terms, and whether this fact, or the money previously taken, dirtied their hands, the dirt was thick on them; and they were seeking the assistance of equity to stop the other, blameless, party from enforcing the contractual promises which the employees had made: they were doing inequity. On any view of the matter they had no equity, and nothing to enforce. Their application should have been dismissed, with costs in the indemnity measure, for the application to the English courts was, by any measure, a flagrant breach of contract to sue in New York.

These things happen, but it is rare, and when they do they need to be put right, fast. It is understood that no application was made for permission to appeal to the House of Lords, which only means that there will be no opportunity for a court, with more time to consider what it is being asked to do,[97] to point out how terribly wrong this judgment is, and how unsatisfactory must have been the procedure which led the Court to this calamitous conclusion. That burden falls on those who comment from the sidelines.

6. The arbitration exclusion from the Brussels Regulation: *West Tankers Inc v Riunione Adriatica di Sicurta.*[98]

It is necessary only to note briefly the decision of the House of Lords to refer to the European Court a question concerning the exclusion of 'arbitration' from the Brussels I Regulation.[99] The case was one in which the English courts considered the parties to be bound to an agreement to arbitrate their disputes in London, but the other (an insurer, which had been subrogated to the rights of its insured) claimed that the agreement to arbitrate, which was contained in a charterparty, was not binding on it.

---

[97] It is plain from the judgment of the Court of Appeal that the procedure was very hurried. It is to the credit of the Court that it can offer this service, but it places a much heavier burden on the lawyers to make the submissions which the Court needs to hear, and to cite the authorities which touch on the issues arising for decision.

[98] [2007] UKHL 4, [2007] 1 Lloyd's Rep 391: Lord Nicholls of Birkenhead, Lord Steyn, Lord Hoffmann, Lord Rodger of Earlsferry and Lord Mance.

[99] Article 1(2)(d).

The insurer, with a good claim for damages against the wrongdoer, therefore commenced civil proceedings before the court at Syracuse. Colman J ordered an injunction to restrain the party in breach of the arbitration agreement and, leap-frogging the Court of Appeal,[100] the appeal went straight to the House of Lords, which referred to the European Court a question designed to ascertain whether Colman J had been right to do as he had done. The decision may take a while to come back from Luxembourg, but when it does it will settle some issues and, in all probability, open up others.

It appears to be the general view among commentators, and especially German ones who can barely contain themselves, that the European Court will hold that the injunction to restrain the insurer from proceeding before the Italian court is incompatible with the Brussels Regulation, and that this conclusion is unaffected by the fact that the subject matter of the dispute before the English courts is arbitration. There is a view, which ought to be disreputable but which still has been advanced by many German writers[101] who probably know no better, that there is a hidden agenda: that the English courts are seeking to encourage arbitration business to London, by making available supportive remedies of a kind which other centres do not have.[102] Such considerations are pathetically beside the point. From an English perspective—and the charterparty and the agreement to arbitrate were expressed to be governed by English law—the defiance of the arbitration agreement was a breach of contract; breaches of contract are susceptible to restraint by injunction, and the rest is an irrelevance. It is really that easy. Of course, different legal systems may diverge on the issue of what law governs a contract, but it is improbable that the Italian court would have disagreed with the conclusion that the charterparty was governed by English law: there was an express choice of law in a contract between commercial actors. As soon as that step has been taken, the question of whether the insurer is bound by the arbitration agreement is a matter of English law as *lex contractus*: it was.[103] The insurer was therefore in breach, and the rights and remedies which follow from that breach were a matter for English law to decide. From this perspective, the ordering of an injunction should have been no surprise, as it was the ordinary incident of a contract expressed to be governed by English law. Whether this makes London arbitration more

---

[100] On account of the decision of the Court of Appeal in *Through Transport Mutual Insurance Association (Eurasia) Ltd v New India Assurance Co Ltd* [2004] EWCA Civ 1598, [2005] 1 Lloyd's Rep 67.

[101] A balanced account, which gives access to more unbalanced German writing, is Steinbrück (2007) 26 *CJQ* 358; a much more unbalanced one is by Illmer & Naumann (2007) 10 *Int Arb LR* 147.

[102] This impression is, one has to say, contributed to by the extraordinary manner in which Lord Hoffmann and Lord Mance referred almost exclusively to non-English authority and writing in giving judgment to justify the making of the reference.

[103] This followed from the analysis in *Through Transport Mutual Insurance Association (Eurasia) Ltd v New India Assurance Co Ltd* [2004] EWCA Civ 1598, [2005] 1 Lloyd's Rep 67.

or less attractive than arbitration overseas is a silly question to which no answer need be given. It is simply the way English law works.

The injunction would, however, interfere with the proceedings before the judge in Syracuse, and that fact remains true, whatever else may be said about the proceedings in the English courts: that the injunction is an order made against the party in breach does not in any way contradict the assertion that it will interfere with the procedure in Syracuse. As far as the Italian judge was concerned, the proceedings in his court were in a civil or commercial matter (there is, after all, no other way to look at marine insurance); and in civil or commercial matters the courts of one Member State have no power to grant injunctions to restrain the bringing of proceedings before the courts of another Member State.[104] That, from an Italian perspective, was the very thing the English court was doing.

Not quite so, would be the English response. Article 1(2)(d) of the Regulation carves out from the scope of civil or commercial matters 'arbitration'; and whatever the scope of arbitration may be, an injunction ordered as a measure to reinforce the parties' agreement to arbitrate has arbitration as its subject matter. That it may also have other subject matter, and that these subject matters may overlap or coexist, is nothing to the point. The injunction did no more than to rule on the submission that there was an agreement to arbitrate (there was), which bound the applicant to the respondent (it did), which was being broken (it was), and which breach an injunction could restrain (it could). The injunction was therefore ordered; that was all that the judge was asked to rule on, and that was all that he did.

It will be apparent that there can be no right answer to the puzzle posed by this case which is not just as obviously wrong: every answer provokes a perfectly convincing contradiction. The matter is civil or commercial, but it is also about arbitration. It is true that the subject matter of the issue before Colman J was the enforcement of an agreement to arbitrate,[105] and it is true that in an earlier judgment, the European Court had explained that 'arbitration', as excluded from the Brussels Convention, had a wide meaning which exempted arbitration in its entirety.[106] On the other hand, the Court has also developed what one may regard as an 'umbrella' principle, which points to the opposite conclusion. According to this, if the whole of the subject matter of a claim is outside the Regulation, the fact that an issue arising within it, tried separately, might appear to be within the material scope of the Regulation, is legally irrelevant. This principle explained why a dispute about whether a commercial judgment had been obtained by documentary forgery and oral perjury was not within the material scope of the Brussels Convention.[107] The issue

---

[104] Case C-159/02 *Turner v Grovit* [2004] ECR I-3565.

[105] Though this is not how the claim was presented to the Italian judge, a point which is just as important.

[106] Case C-190/89 *Marc Rich & Co AG v Soc Italiana Impianti PA* [1991] ECR I-3855.

[107] Case C-129/92 *Owens Bank Ltd v Bracco* [1994] ECR I-117.

had arisen in the broader context of proceedings designed to determine whether a judgment from the courts of St Vincent and the Grenadines could be recognised as *res judicata* in Italy and in England.[108] That subject matter, the Court held, was entirely outside the material scope of the Brussels Convention; and as a consequence, issues and applications arising and made within the scope of those proceedings were also outside the Convention. If that principle applies in reverse, the fact that an issue between the shipowner and the insurer concerns arbitration would not take it outside the material scope of the Regulation if the broader context— the claim by the insurer for damages; the claim by the shipowner to be free of liability—is within the material scope of the Regulation.

A tolerable answer has been hinted at above.[109] The judicial proceedings in Syracuse were instituted in 2003; it was not until fifteen months later that the shipowners instituted the arbitration proceedings in London. A rational way out might be to hold that the Italian court, rather than the English tribunal-and-supervising-court, should be allowed to rule on the validity and effect of the arbitration agreement. If there is genuine disagreement as to the parties' obligations in relation to the dispute, the court seised first has a rational and non-partisan claim to go first. It may be irksome to the shipowners that this court is in Syracuse, where probably nothing happens fast, but that is simply the consequence of their ship colliding with a jetty in the south of Sicily. It can hardly have come as a surprise to the shipowner that it became involved in litigation in the place where its vessel did its damage over which the dispute arose. There is a principled basis for allowing the decision to be taken by the Italian court, and nothing shocking in its doing so.

Even so, the consequence of a decision that the English court may not enforce the arbitration agreement by injunction is not one to be taken lightly. The judicial proceedings in Italy will proceed, probably very slowly. The London arbitration will proceed, probably faster. There will be a judgment and an award, and these may well conflict. The Italian judgment will be entitled to recognition under Chapter III of the Brussels Regulation; the London award will be liable to enforcement under the New York Convention in a rather larger number of states. Enforcement of the judgment under the Brussels Regulation will be the enforcement of a judgment in a civil or commercial matter. If the arbitration exception is inapplicable, there will no apparent basis for a contention that the Regulation permits the English court to refuse recognition of the Italian judgment. Even if the Italian judgment is contradicted by an English arbitration award, Article 34(3) of the Regulation will be inapplicable. For even if an English judgment is obtained in terms of the award, for a judgment decreeing enforcement of an arbitration award is not a judgment for the purposes of the Regulation.[110] If the answer is

---

[108] In England, [1992] 2 AC 443.   [109] See above n 9 and accompanying text.
[110] Case C-190/89 *Marc Rich & Co AG v Soc Italiana Impianti PA* [1991] ECR I-3855.

that the Italian judgment can be refused recognition, on the ground that to recognise it would be to contradict the English law of arbitration—the *Hoffmann v Krieg*[111] argument, which is wholly sound and which the Court has never questioned—it leads ineluctably to the conclusion that the English proceedings were excluded from the Regulation in the first place. It will all be a frightful mess for which no statute provides the answer. There is much that might be written about the consequences to be foreseen as flowing from any answer which the European Court may give, but these are best left for another day.

7. Choosing non-national laws to govern a contract: *Halpern v Halpern;*[112] *Musawi v RE International (UK) Ltd.*[113]

There are a number of reasons why parties to a contract may wish to have a contract governed by something other than a system of municipal law. They may belong to some religious community or sect which has its own code of behaviour, by which the members profess to be bound. Jews and muslims in particular, or at least those who consider themselves to be current adherents, may take the view that a contractual (or perhaps a non-contractual) relationship should be governed by jewish 'law' or by muslim 'law'. After all, if the teachings and traditions of these systems are taken by its adherents to govern their family law and certain questions of property, it is not surprising that they may wish to have the same system govern contractual relations. It may also be that where two contracting parties hail from different countries,[114] the choice of a religious 'law' which they have in common may be something on which they can agree, whereas the national law of either may be objected to. So insofar as the choice of a system of superstition can ever be seen as rational, the choice of a religious 'law' may be understood.

It is equally clear that, in the common law and in Western Europe, such things are not accommodated. As a matter of common law, a choice of religious 'law' could not be made: though it is only recently that this has been made clear, *Musawi v RE International (UK) Ltd* does it. The Rome Convention is more specific about it: its several references to the law of a country eliminate any role for the choice of a non-national 'law': this was always understood, but *Halpern v Halpern* has recently supplied judicial authority for what we always knew. The parties can no more choose the muslim sharia or the jewish equivalent than the Book of Mormon or the writings of L Ron Hubbard[115] to govern a contract. And, many will think, that is just as it should be.

---

[111] Case C-145/86, [1988] ECR 645.
[112] [2007] EWCA Civ 291, [2008] QB 195: Waller, Sedley and Carnwath LJJ.
[113] [2007] EWHC 2891 (Ch), [2008] 1 All ER (Comm) 607: David Richards J.
[114] In *Musawi*'s case, Iraq and Iran.
[115] The founder, in some sense, of the cult of scientology.

The facts of the cases are relatively unimportant. *Halpern v Halpern* concerned a bitter post-inheritance dispute between members of a family who more or less devoutly considered themselves to be jewish. A compromise agreement had been made following an arbitration before a jewish religious tribunal in Zürich, and this was said to be governed by jewish religious 'law'. If this were so certain rights would be available to the party who, as he alleged, had been victimised by duress into making the agreement. Whether such a claim could have been sustained in fact or law was not relevant because, as the court clearly saw, the Rome Convention confined the list of possible governing laws to the laws of countries. As the law of a country had not been chosen, the law of the country with which the contract had its closest connection was applicable. That made it impossible to find that jewish 'law' governed the contract; and the clear further conclusion is that a choice of jewish 'law' would have been irrelevant to the identification of the governing law. But this did not preclude the governing law finding that the some of the terms of the contract were defined by reference to jewish 'law': a contractual obligation to behave in a certain way could be defined by reference to any social, moral, other code susceptible of proof, and jewish 'law' was certainly capable of meeting that standard. But this did not displace the conclusion that English law, not jewish 'law', governed the contract. In this the Court confirmed the correctness of *Shamil Bank of Bahrein EC v Beximco Pharmaceuticals Ltd*,[116] and distinguished[117] *Al Midani v Al Midani*.[118] The consequences of that conclusion were to be dealt with in separate proceedings, but on the issue of choice of law under the Rome Convention, the decision is entirely orthodox.

Musawi's case concerned a disputed development of land in Wembley, the dispute being between an Iraqi and an Iranian who both considered themselves to be muslims of shia orientation. The claim was based on an arbitration award which had been made, in accordance with the intentions of the parties and the Arbitration Act 1996, section 46, by appointing an ayatollah as arbitrator and requiring him to apply islamic 'law'. The judge found that the common law rules for choice of law[119] allowed only a selection (by parties or by court) of the law of a country, and that the contract in question was governed by English law. But the agreement to arbitrate was governed by English law; English law, as contained in the Arbitration Act s 46 allowed the parties to direct the arbitrator to apply sharia principles as though they were law; and there

---

[116] [2004] EWCA Civ 19, [2004] 1 WLR 1784.

[117] But saying, in effect, that Rix J had been wrong in that case to find that the law governing a contract was 'either sharia law, or such law as modified by Saudi law'. The case concerned choice of law under the rules of the common law, but even there, it was generally understood, and was confirmed in *Musawi v RE International (UK) Ltd*, that the laws available as *lex contractus* were national laws only.

[118] [1999] 1 Lloyd's Rep 923.

[119] The relevant contract pre-dated the coming into force of the Rome Convention.

was no basis for challenging the arbitrator's award. The entire judgment is entirely sound.

Apart from the healthy secular tradition of the common law and civil law, there are two probable reasons for the law to exclude the possibility of a non-national 'law' to govern a contract. The first is that though choice of law in contract now places primary focus on whether the parties have chosen and expressed the choice of law, it developed from an approach which enquired into the law with which the contract had its closest and most real connection, and further back in time, from the law of the place where the contract was made. These antecedent rules for choice of law cannot possibly have allowed for a religious law. Take the 'closest and most real connection' test, and the example of *Halpern v Halpern*. A contract made between two jews may well be most closely connected to the law of England so far as a country is concerned, and with jewish 'law' so far as non-national 'law' is concerned, but how could one conclude that it was more closely connected to English law than to jewish 'law'? A contract made between two individuals who consider themselves to be muslims, as in *Musawi v RE International (UK) Ltd*, to develop land in London, may be most closely connected to English law, and also to sharia 'law': but how could one pretend to find it was more closely connected to one than to the other? It cannot be done; and if choice of law in contract is seen as a subject in which the menu of available laws is the same whether the parties make a choice or not, there is no room for religious 'laws' on the list.

Likewise, though a judge may be trained in his own law, and able to apply foreign law proved to him as a matter of fact, he or she will generally be at home in applying national law, and adrift if called upon to apply something else. The position is worse in civilian systems, which evidently start from the improbable premise that the judge knows the law, taking this to indicate the law of any and every country which choice of law rules might call to be applied. It is quite a fiction as it is, but it would be still odder if it included the teachings of these belief systems as well. If the parties want an adjudication by reference to these systems of rules, it is theirs to have, but they need to do it in the form of arbitration. That way, they will be able to arrange for a tribunal of priests or professors, who will be mystically or professionally able to apply the system of rules which the parties have, in all seriousness of purpose, chosen.

There is no reason to depart from any of this. But it may just be that there is no need to be so rigid about it. For it is clear that a significant part of the commercial world is willing, and maybe increasingly willing, to choose the principles of the sharia, whatever they are, to govern the commercial relationship established by a contract. As banks become sensitive to the need to offer forms of business with which all of their customers are comfortable, so too might the courts think that their services should be reviewed in the same way. And if the parties choose the law of a country which has enacted the sharia to govern in particular circumstances, a choice of the law of that country will bring the choice of the sharia with it. This cannot be objected to as an example of renvoi, which would be forbidden by Article 15 of the Rome Convention, as it does not involve reference to the law of another country, as distinct from reference to a particular code of internal laws (of which the Vienna Convention on the International Sale of Goods, or even the Sale of Goods Act, would be an example). If the parties can by such means select the 'law' of a religious tradition, it becomes a little harder to see why they may not do so by direct means.

Of course, this could only be allowed within the parties' express choice of law. For reasons set out above, it is impossible to ascertain the *lex contractus* by reference to the test of closest connection when the laws available for identification are secular and religious. But there is some reason to suppose that the rules for choice of law should be reconsidered, with a view to drawing distinct lists of laws which may be chosen by the parties, on the one hand, and chosen by the courts on the other. One indication came with the current and continuing negotiation of a Rome I Regulation[120] on choice of law for contractual obligations, and with the suggestion that systems of rules which were not the law of a country might, in some circumstances, be chosen to govern a contract. Though the line was drawn at sets of rules such as the Vienna Convention on the International Sale of Goods, the UNIDROIT Principles of 1994, and the Principles of European Contract Law, and was intended to exclude religious 'laws' and the *lex mercatoria*, presumably on the basis of uncertainty of content, the idea will not now go away. Another indication may be found in the scholarly view that if a choice of law is in fact a choice of the rules to be applied in dispute resolution, a choice of religious 'law' does not appear to be invalid if arbitration is also chosen, but is invalid if arbitration is not. It may be thought that the judicial system is robust enough to apply the rules which are proved to its satisfaction,[121] whether these are national laws of the traditional kind, or non-national laws. They are, when all is said and done, all rules. And if they are not English, then they are all, as Rix J observed in *Al Midani*,[122] alien, and if they are all alien they can, in principle, all be proved or not, according to the parties. Though it may shock a judge to have to apply religious laws, if these are proved, and especially where they embody what the parties chose, freely and deliberately, it is a little hard to accept that the judge should not even try to enforce this aspect of the parties' agreement.

[120] Which will supplant the Rome Convention.
[121] This may be a significant problem, for there is reason to think that there is not a single and clear statement of the content of these religious laws. After all, a choice of 'christian law' could not be made to work, and a choice of 'common law' would be challenging unless it were to identify which country's common law was intended.
[122] [1999] 1 Lloyd's Rep 923.

8. The law which determines title to tangible moveable property:
Islamic Republic of Iran v Berend;[123] *Islamic Republic of*
Iran v Barakat Galleries Ltd.[124]

Two cases, resulting from attempts made by the Iranian government to recover cultural artefacts which it considered to be part of its cultural heritage, raised questions of the law which determined title to moveable property in English private international law. It is good to see the principles of common law choice of law debated in the courts; and in one of the two cases it was good to see the conclusion to which these led. Let us start with the other one.

In *Iran v Berend*, a sculpture had been removed from Iran, sold at auction in New York in 1974, and delivered to the purchaser in France soon thereafter. In 2005 she sent it to Christies in London to be sold at auction; Iran discovered this, and obtained an injunction to restrain the sale. In due course it claimed the return (as it saw it) of the sculpture, and in due course the matter came on before Eady J. Though it is not clear from the judgment, it seems that the allegation was that Berend and/or the auction house had converted the sculpture by acts done in London, and that the claim for delivery up was in form an allegation of conversion. It was clear enough that any such claim would first require Iran to establish that it had title to the sculpture, though it did not follow that establishing its title under Iranian law would necessarily result in an order being made for delivery up. Even so, it was common ground that the property had vested in the Iranian state while it was still in Iran, with the consequence that the issue turned on the effect of the delivery to Berend after she had bought it at auction. This raised a question of French law; the more difficult question was what 'French law' actually meant. As a matter of French domestic law, delivery to a purchaser who had bought in good faith would vest a clean title in the purchaser, and would override and destroy the prior title of Iran. But it was argued for Iran that a French judge would in such a case apply Iranian law to the issue.

The immediate problem for Iran was the absence of French authority to bolster this submission,[125] and the evidence of French private international law was therefore rather insubstantial. The preference of the judge, however, was to decline to take notice of it: he saw no reason to apply the principle of renvoi to the question of title to moveable property, and, therefore, was unimpressed by what a French judge, seised of the question, might have said about whether the purchaser obtained

---

[123] [2007] EWHC 132 (QB), [2007] 2 All ER (Comm) 132: Eady J.

[124] [2007] EWCA Civ 1374, [2008] 1 All ER 1177: Lord Phillips CJ; Wall and Lawrence Collins LJJ.

[125] English authority was equally sparse: see *Glencore International AG v Metro Trading International Inc* [2001] 1 Lloyd's Rep 284; Dicey, Morris & Collins, para 4-025. Eady J preferred to follow what he took to be the guidance of Millett J in *Macmillan Inc v Bishopsgate Investment Trust plc (No 3)* [1995] 1 WLR 978, 1008, a case on title to registered shares, and in which the analysis of renvoi was not raised before the Court of Appeal. That makes it an authority, but of a rather weak and remote kind.

title when the thing was delivered to her in France.[126] As the judge took English judicial authority to stop short of allowing renvoi to operate in the consideration of title to moveable property, he saw no reason why he should, as he saw it, extend it. In this he was misguided. The case for renvoi only arises where evidence of foreign law is sufficient to sustain it, so we must assume that the judge would have been satisfied that, as a matter of French private international law, whether Ms Berend acquired title would have been determined by the law of Iran. If that is the view of French law, the single question is whether the *lex situs* rule, which English private international law seeks to apply, is more faithfully given effect by referring to French domestic law (which is not the answer a French court would have given to the material question) or French private international law. The answer, as today's students are inclined to say, is a no-brainer, but the judgment fell short. Eady J's conclusion, that the only justification for making reference to French private international law was because French law had 'control' of the asset, which he correctly regarded as specious, was unconvincing.

The judge admitted that he found it difficult to see that anything might be said in support of the principle of renvoi.[127] Perhaps he did. But he observed that the defendant had taken delivery of the sculpture in Paris in 1974, and that it had sat in her salon for thirty years.[128] If at any point during those three decades the Iranian government had discovered the sculpture, it would have sued Berend for its return before a French court, and the French judge would have applied rules of French private international law to determine the claim. Yet it was not until the thing surfaced at Christies that Iran had any idea where it was. The state therefore sued in the place where the thing had come to light and could be detained, which was where an effective order for its return could be made, and which seems rational enough. But the defendant was Berend, not Christies. The question whether Berend had acquired title by taking delivery and detaining the thing in France was determined not as a French court would have determined it at any point in the history of that acquisition and detention, but by the private international law rules of the place where it was sent for auction, simply because it surfaced at an auction. If the judge sees nothing to say the proposition that the claim against Berend should have been determined as a French court would

---

[126] To be fair to the judge, he did go on to consider the evidence of French private international law which was before him, as the second question set for him to answer was formulated on the footing that the court would apply French private international law. The judge found on the evidence of French law that he could not decide whether a French court would or would not have applied the law of Iran, and did not pursue the second question to its final conclusion. It is unclear whether this conclusion was arrived at wholly independently of his decision on the application of renvoi as a matter of English private international law, but it is undeniable that, on the evidence before him, the judge did have a difficult question to answer.

[127] At [23]. In the only other comment, by Knight [2007] Conv 564, it appears that the writer could not see anything either, on which further comment is unnecessary.

[128] At [60].

have determined it, that is a matter for him. It does not mean that there is nothing to say. It is not a question which asks which law or court had 'control' of the moveable thing which, unlike land and as anyone can see, did what it said on the label and moved. It is a question which enquires after the most appropriate approach to the choice of law issues which inevitably arose for decision. But for the accident that the defendant consigned the sculpture to Christies, her title to it would have been determined (within Europe, at least[129]) by rules of French private international law. That seems to amount to something which may be said for the application of the law which the judge rejected.

The High Court of Australia has shown the correct methodology by which to map these trackless areas of private international law. When interpreting the *lex loci delicti* rule for choice of law in tort the court, in *Neilson v Overseas Projects Corp of Victoria*[130] asked whether the policy which the choice of law rule sought to promote was better served by understanding the rule as making a reference to Chinese domestic law or to the law which a Chinese judge would apply if hearing the case in China. The majority preferred the latter. Whatever one thinks of it,[131] the methodology was instructive. It did not, however, instruct Eady J. He preferred the view, all too frequent in those who are intimidated by private international law, that the subject is hard enough to begin with, and that renvoi is the cause of horrid complexity; and refused to countenance its application to title to moveable property. One cannot pretend that the judge went against the weight of much direct authority, for there was very little. But it would still have been encouraging to see the task being approached with the insight and reflection demonstrated by the High Court of Australia. For this, however, we must wait for another day. As for the case, the decision resulted in judgment for the purchaser who, as the judge found, had the only title to the property which English private international law would acknowledge.

In *Iran v Barakat*, the artefacts in question probably came from Iran, but the Barakat Gallery claimed to have acquired good title to them by virtue of sales to it which had taken place in France, Germany, and Switzerland. The claim appears to have been one for delivery up, though the cause of action pleaded against the gallery was that, by refusing to return the artefacts, it was converting the property of Iran, and doing it in London. This justified seeing the case through the lens of the English tort of conversion, and in order for its claim in conversion to succeed, Iran needed to show that it had an immediate right to possession of the artefacts in question. Iran asserted that Iranian law gave it title to the artefacts, and would in due course assert that it had not lost that title and was entitled to assert it. Reversing Gray J, the court held that as a matter

---

[129] Jurisdiction over the defendant would have been confined to the courts of France, to the exclusion of any other Member State.

[130] [2005] HCA 54, (2005) 233 CLR 331.

[131] The writer thinks it was a brilliantly perceptive judgment: [2006] LMCLQ 1.

of Iranian law, Iran had title to the artefacts when they were in Iran and were removed from there, and that it was not prevented by English private international law from asserting its title by a principle against the enforcement of foreign penal, revenue, or other public laws.

The first part of the judgment concerned a detailed analysis of the mass of Iranian statute law which touched on the ownership of antiquities discovered and not discovered in the territory of the Iranian state. This need not concern us, but the judgment of the Court of Appeal makes it plain that it was no disgrace that the judge below had come to what was held to be a wrong conclusion about it. It came to the conclusion that the law of Iran, patchy and confusing as it was, had vested ownership of these artefacts in the Iranian state, unearthed and undiscovered as they were at the date of the material legislative act which brought about the result. The court accordingly moved to consider whether the Iranian law in question was a penal, revenue, or other public law, and what would follow if it were. It recited a number of orthodoxies, which included the truth that a law is assessed as to its form and by reference to English criteria of assessment in order to decide whether it is a penal law. Unhelpfully, it did not offer a definition of 'penal', as opposed to a description of the methodology which was to be used to identify a law as penal. But it did offer the important insight that though several provisions of a piece of legislation may be penal by any measure, that was insufficient to characterise every article of that law as penal. This is correct, even though the application of the law to the facts may be problematic. In the case of the Iranian legislation which was held to vest title to antiquities in the state, though much of it imposed penalties for exporting without the permission of the state, the provision which vested title to unearthed and previously-unowned antiquities in the state could not be so seen. The legislation did not override the title of any person who had previously acquired title, nor did it otherwise operate retrospectively. It was not penal, and in this sense it probably did not matter than a comprehensive definition of 'penal law' was not given in the judgment.

The proposition that the Iranian state was seeking to enforce an 'other public law' was harder to deal with, not least because of the persistent doubts in the authorities as to what this category might mean. It is now too late to question its very existence, but it is still hard to see precisely what it covers. Two categories of laws should be examined. First, there are those which are close in character to penal or revenue laws, such as those which control the movement of foreign exchange. But second are those which involve or which underpin the claim by a state to invoke rules of private law in the service of interests which are unique and specific to governments. When the government of Equatorial Guinea claimed to recover the costs it had incurred in putting down an invasion and insurrection, some of which could have been pled by an ordinary claimant,[132] and when the United Kingdom claimed relief against a blabbermouth

---

[132] *Mbasogo v Logo Ltd* [2006] EWCA Civ 1370, [2007] QB 846 (noted (2006) 77 *BYIL* 554.)

spy who had showed disloyalty in every way, some of which looked to be pure private law,[133] the Court of Appeal and the High Court of Australia, respectively, disallowed the claims. The answer, which seems pretty certain to emerge as a final statement of English private international law (though it has not quite arrived there yet) is that a claim which seeks to give effect to a purely (foreign) governmental interest is one which may not be brought in the English courts, and that this will operate alongside an exclusionary rule for other public laws. An attempt to define the categories as congruent seems bound to fail, as the judgment accepts,[134] though it may be that the category of 'other public laws' is in fact a subset of claims which enforce a governmental interest.[135] Claims which are legally indistinguishable from those which a private citizen may bring are not to be excluded as being based on 'other public laws'. What may exclude them from the jurisdiction of the English courts may be the conclusion that they still be giving effect to governmental interests if the claim is, or is also, one which only a state could bring. This cannot avoid looking a little untidy, for an employer may recover against a disloyal employee, and the only thing to distinguish Wright from an employee was the fact that he was a spy. But what if the Royal Mail sues a postman? Until English law changes, the Royal Mail has a statutory and state monopoly in the operation of mail services. A claim against a postman who has broken the obligations of his employment and status is, in the end, one which only the state may bring, and in this respect, the claim against the tittle-tattling spy was much the same: he was employed by the state in a relationship which only the state can have with its servants. When it comes, therefore, the 'claims which give effect to governmental claims', definition of those claims which are treated as though they were based on other public laws will not be without its difficulties. By the time this Note is published, the House of Lords may have committed the law to this path: next year we shall examine where it leads.

But it was not a problem for Iran. Iran said, in effect: 'we own this thing, which was excavated and unlawfully taken away; and we claim as owners of it to secure its recovery. No special laws are required for that; no relationship unique to states is relevant to our recovery of our things'. Subject to one point, this is true. The one point is that only a state can do something to vest in itself all the things, known and unknown, buried in the sand and soil of the state; and for the state to recover such a thing was for it to vindicate a claim which, in the actual circumstances, only a state could ever have brought. Though it was not an action to enforce an 'other public law', the claim was still one which, in the circumstances, was unique to a state. The Court of Appeal denied that the claim was one to give effect to the governmental interest of Iran. It distinguished the case where the state had come into its ownership by seizure from another: in

[133] *Att-Gen (UK) v Heinemann Publishers (Australia) Pty Ltd* (1988) 165 CLR 30.
[134] At [123].   [135] At [126].

such an instance, its law would be a public law and its interest governmental, and if it required the assistance of the English courts to complete the process, this would be withheld. This explained the relevance of the plea that the state had or had not yet had possession; but as the Iranian state had become owner according to its own law, and did not require the assistance of the English courts to complete the acquisition of ownership, there was no more to be said about it: Iran had ownership in the same way as an individual citizen had ownership. This, it must be said, is not completely convincing. Iran had ownership based simply on legislative fiat, and that method of acquiring an original title is not open to other individuals, who have to rely on *occupatio, accessio, specificatio,* and *thesauri inventio.* By the test which it appeared to lay down, the Iranian claim was one which only a state could have brought. True, it was also a claim by an owner, but the ownership was one of a character which was unique to a state. According to the question which the court appeared to ask—is this a claim which only a state could make?—the answer was yes, and the claim fell outside the jurisdiction of the English court. But if one asked a different question: whether the state was claiming as owner, and not as an owner who had torn up the title of the previous owner, the answer was that Iran claimed as owner, and there was no more to be pleaded or proved to sustain its claim. The judgment seems to have selected very carefully the question to which it needed an answer; and having asked it, the answer was Iran, as owner of the property as a matter of English private international law, was bringing a claim which any other owner could have brought.

The result was that the requirement that the state have reduced the property into its possession[136] while the property was within the territory of the foreign seizing state was confined to cases in which the acquisition of title by the state had been by confiscation or nationalisation of another's property. Such acts are uniquely governmental, which entails the consequence that all the steps necessary to complete a good possessory title must be completed before the claim comes before the English court. But where the acquisition is not originally hostile to the title of a previous lawful owner, possession need not be taken, and a claim based on that ownership which carries with it an immediate right to possession may be enforced in an English court. It is a plausible line of distinction: the more invasive the actions of the foreign state, the more they need to be prosecuted to perfection while the property is within the territory of the foreign state: see *Luther Co v James Sagor & Co,*[137] and *Princess Paley Olga v Weisz.*[138] The only lingering doubt is whether a workable, predictable, and comprehensive rule may be derived from the principle that if the state is bringing a claim which only a state may bring, this disqualifies it from being brought in an English court.

---

[136] A principle identified by Lord Denning MR in *Brokaw v Seatrain (UK) Ltd* [1971] 2 QB 476 (CA) and in *A-G (NZ) v Ortiz* [1984] AC 1 (CA).
[137] [1921] 3 KB 532 (CA).   [138] [1929] 1 KB 718 (CA).

United Kingdom Materials on International Law 2007

Compiled by Kaiyan Kaikobad,[1] Jacques Hartmann,[2] Sangeeta Shah[3] and Colin Warbrick.[4]

1. This selection of UK materials on international law is made from published sources. It does not purport to include everything that could be of interest to an international lawyer but it is not wholly restricted to materials that could be called "state practice" in the strictest sense: some context is provided.

We have to make very considerable exclusions of material that we know would be of interest to some international lawyers. We bear in mind first, the need to avoid the purely ephemeral, and second, to exclude materials that are concerned mainly with the UK's implementation of the international law of co-operation, particularly at the general level. We are very sparing with matters of EU law, though we report some EU positions on questions of international law with which the UK is associated.

There is only limited material on UK treaties because the texts and explanatory memoranda are readily available on the web: **www.fco.gov. uk/treaties**.

Extracts are generally reproduced in their original form, which leads to inconsistencies, eg in spelling ("judgement"/"judgment") or capitalisation "UN charter" or designation ("Chapter Seven"/"Chapter VII"/ "Chapter 7").

Introductory material is printed thus:

"The Foreign Secretary wrote to the FAC..."

Material from documentary sources is printed thus:

"We have signed a Memorandum of Understanding..."

We have inserted a small amount of editorial material in the form "[...Ed.]" where it appears to be helpful to do so.

Cross-references to previous editions of UKMIL are written, "See **UKMIL [2006] 16/1**".

2. Hansard references are to the Web version. There may be minor discrepancies between the column references in the Web edition and the bound volumes.

[1] Brunel Law School
[2] Jesus College Cambridge
[3] School of Law, University of Nottingham
[4] The Birmingham Law School

References to Hansard are given in the following forms:

Commons—HC Deb 13 November 2001 Vol 374 c345 or c134W or c101WH or c1WS, where W, WH and WS stand for Written Answers, Westminster Hall and Written Statements;

Lords—HL Deb 8 October 2002 Vol 639 c222 or 16 October 2003 Vol 653 cWA125, where WA stands for Written Answer or HL Deb 29 January 2003 Vol 643 cGC170, where GC stands for Grand Committee.

3. Some sources are given as **www.fco.gov.uk.** These are references to Press Releases or Speeches on the FCO website. The appropriate link should be followed to the date given for the item in the text.

4. From its start in 1978 and up to and including 1996, the materials in UKMIL were classified on the basis of the *Model Plan for the Classification of Documents concerning State Practice in the Field of Public International Law* adopted by the Committee of Ministers of the Council of Europe in its Resolution (68) 17 of 28 June 1968. The Committee of Ministers considered that developments in public international law since 1968 made it necessary to amend the Model Plan. Accordingly, by Recommendation (97) 11 of 12 June 1997, it adopted an Amended Model Plan as a contribution by the Council of Europe towards implementing General Assembly Resolution 2099 (XX) on technical assistance to promote the teaching, study, dissemination and wider understanding of international law. The present issue of UKMIL is based on the 1997 Amended Model Plan.

5. We are glad to acknowledge the assistance of Joanna Foakes, Jonathan Drakeford and their colleagues in the Legal Adviser's Department of the Foreign & Commonwealth Office.

6. We are grateful for financial assistance in the preparation of UKMIL to the Whittuck Trust.

INDEX

E. Consequences of invalidity, termination or suspension of operation

V.   State succession in respect of treaties (see Part Five)
VI. Depositaries, notifications, corrections and registration
VII. Arrangements other than treaties

PART FOUR: RELATIONSHIP BETWEEN INTERNATIONAL LAW AND INTERNAL LAW   664

I.   In general
II.   Application and implementation of international law in internal law
III. Remedies under internal law for violations of international law

PART FIVE: SUBJECTS OF INTERNATIONAL LAW   665

I. States
  A. Status and Powers
    1. Personality
    2. Sovereignty and independence
    3. Non-intervention
    4. Domestic jurisdiction
    5. Equality of States
    6. State immunity
    7. Other powers, including treaty-making powers
  B. Recognition
    1. Recognition of States
    2. Recognition of Governments
    3. Types of recognition
       (a) de facto/de jure
       (b) conditional/ unconditional
    4. Acts of recognition
       (a) implied/express
       (b) collective/unilateral
    5. Effects of recognition
    6. Non-recognition and its effects
    7. Withdrawal of recognition
  C. Types of States
    1. Unitary States, federal States and confederations
    2. Personal and real unions
    3. Protected States
  D. Formation, continuity, extinction and succession of States
    1. Conditions for statehood
    2. Formation
    3. Identity and continuity

Part One: International Law in General

Part One: I.A. *International Law in General: Nature, basis, purpose: In general*

1/1

In his speech at the Lord Mayor's Banquet on 12 November 2007, the Prime Minister said:

Tonight, I want to speak about Britain's unique place in the new world. And where, as a result, our responsibilities lie; how our national interest can be best advanced; and what we can achieve by working together internationally and by contributing to building the strongest and broadest sense of common purpose.

The new context

. . .

Our international institutions built for just 50 sheltered economies in what became a bipolar world are not fit for purpose in an interdependent world of 200 states where global flows of commerce, people and ideas defy borders. With such transformative change comes a clear obligation, but also a great opportunity, to write a new chapter—to set down for a new era a better 21st century way of delivering peace and prosperity.

Of course the first duty of Government—our abiding obligation—is and will always be the safety of the British people, the protection of the British national interest... Yet the timeless values that underpin our policies at home—our belief in the liberty of all, in security and justice for all, in economic opportunity and environmental protection shared by all—are also ideals that I believe that it is in our national interest to promote abroad. But we do so in a changing world where six new global forces unique to our generation are demonstrating our growing interdependence and pressing the international community to discover common purpose.

First, few expected when the adamantine certainties of the Cold War came to an end, we would have to address the constantly changing uncertainties of violence and instability from failed states and rogue states. The spread of terrorism has destroyed the old assumption that states alone could access destructive weapons. As dramatic in a different way is a third force for change: global flows of capital and global sourcing of goods and services have brought the biggest shift of economic power since the industrial revolution—the rapid emergence of India and China as global powers with legitimate global aspirations. The new frontier is that there is no frontier.

The unprecedented impact of climate change transforms the very purpose of government. Once quality of life meant the pursuit of two objectives: economic growth and social cohesion. Now there is a trinity of aims: prosperity, fairness and environmental care. And as energy supplies are under pressure there is a new global competition for natural resources. New global forces at work—from pandemics to worldwide migration—make the task of overcoming the great social evils of hunger, illiteracy, disease, squalor and poverty even more challenging. And if, as Tom Friedman has written, the defining image of the 20th century was a wall representing division, the defining image of the 21st is a web championing connections—a world where we can rightly now talk not just of the wealth of nations but the wealth of networks. The web cannot be controlled in the end by any single force or any single leader. And what happens within it cannot be predicted from day to day.

...And because our world is now so connected and so interdependent it is possible in this century, for the first time in human history, to contemplate and create a global society that empowers people.

Why do I believe this is not only possible but essential? Because we cannot any longer escape the consequences of our interdependence. The old distinction between 'over there' and 'over here' does not make sense of this interdependent world. For there is no longer an 'over there' of terrorism, failed states, poverty, forced migration and environmental degradation and an 'over here' that is insulated or immune. Today a nation's self interest today will be found not in isolation but in cooperation to overcome shared challenges. And so the underlying issue for our country—indeed for every country—is how together in this new interdependent world we renew and strengthen our international rules, institutions and networks. My approach is hard-headed internationalism:—internationalist because global challenges need global solutions and nations must cooperate across borders—often with hard-headed intervention—to give expression to our shared interests and shared values;—hard-headed because we will not shirk from the difficult long term decisions and because only through reform of our international rules and institutions will we achieve concrete, on-the-ground results.

Building a global society means agreeing that the great interests we share in common are more powerful than the issues that sometimes divide us. It means articulating and acting upon the enduring values that define our common humanity and transcending ideologies of hatred that seek to drive us apart. And critically—and this is the main theme of my remarks this evening—we must bring to life these shared interests and shared values by practical proposals to create the architecture of a new global society.

...I believe that Europe and America have the best chance for many decades to achieve historic progress ----

• working ever more closely together on the project of building a global society;

• and helping bring in all continents, including countries today outside the G8 and the UN Security Council, to give new purpose and direction to our international institutions.

...

A new framework for security and reconstruction

Today, there is still a gaping hole in our ability to address the illegitimate threats and use of force against innocent peoples. It is to the shame of the whole world that the international community failed to act to prevent genocide in Rwanda. We now rightly recognise our responsibility to protect behind borders where there are crimes against humanity.

But if we are to honour that responsibility to protect we urgently need a new framework to assist reconstruction. With the systematic use of earlier Security Council action, proper funding of peacekeepers, targeted sanctions—and their ratcheting up to include the real threat of international criminal court actions—we must now set in place the first internationally agreed procedures to prevent breakdowns of states and societies.

...

There are many steps the international community can assist with on the ladder from insecurity and conflict to stability and prosperity. So I propose that, in future, Security Council peacekeeping resolutions and UN Envoys should make stabilisation, reconstruction and development an equal priority; that the international community should be ready to act with a standby civilian force including police and judiciary who can be deployed to rebuild civic societies; and that to repair damaged economies we sponsor local economic development agencies ---- in each area the international community able to offer a practical route map from failure to stability.

...

(www.number-10.gov.uk/output/Page13736.asp)

Part Two: Sources and Codification of International Law

Part Two: I.A. *Sources and Codification of International Law—Sources of international law—Treaties*

2/1

In answer to a question about global warming, the Environment Secretary said:

It is only through the UN and United Nations Framework Convention that we can have legally binding treaty obligations. All the work that is being done through the European Union, the Group of Eight and the Gleneagles dialogue is vital preparatory work, but in the end it must be in the UN forum that we make progress.

(HC Deb 8 March 2007 Vol 457 c1662)

Part Two: II: *Source and Codification of International Law—Codification and progressive development of international law*

2/2

The FCO Legal Adviser made the following statement to the UNGA Sixth Committee on 30 October 2007:

It is of course important that all States take the opportunity to engage with the Commission, and to assist the Commission with its work. The conduct of States is the pivot around which the work of the Commission operates, whether it is codification or progressive development.

... it is of course also important that the Commission reflects the contribution of States, not in the sense of adopting the views of any one State, but in the sense of seeking the views of States and of addressing those views in its work. While the Commission is usually attentive to this responsibility, and does seek the contribution of States, this has not always been the case. On occasion, even under the current work programme, it is not always clear, on every topic, that the Commission is addressing the comments of States. We can of course appreciate the desire of Special Rapporteurs and of the Commission more generally to make progress with its work. It is important, however, that the Commission proceeds in step with the community to which it is speaking. In this regard, the working methods of the Commission will also stand as an exemplar for the practice of other bodies that are engaged in similar endeavours, even in different areas, such as the International Committee of the Red Cross, which engages actively in the codification and progressive development of international humanitarian law...

(Text supplied by FCO)

2/3

(See also **6/21**)
The FCO Legal Adviser made the following statement to the UNGA Sixth Committee on 30 October 2007:

Turning finally to chapter VI of the ILC Report [Fifty-ninth session, A/62/10, Ed.], on the topic of expulsion of aliens. We thank the Special Rapporteur, Mr Maurice Kamto, for his Third Report. This is a difficult and complex subject, and one with which many countries, including the United Kingdom, are having to grapple on a daily basis.

As the Commission's work on this topic progresses, it is becoming increasingly clear to the United Kingdom that this is a problematic issue for the Commission to address at the present time. Indeed, we have come to the view that this is not yet a suitable topic for codification. The United Kingdom does not believe that the law on this topic—in its present form—can be consolidated or codified, given the numerous political and legal sensitivities and difficulties which surround these issues. We note that several members of the Commission have also expressed this view, and have observed that it is more suited to political negotiation than codification by an expert body.

The United Kingdom also agrees with the comment made by some members of the Commission during the debates on this topic that the issue of expulsion of aliens is mainly governed by national laws, subject, of course, to respect for the relevant rules of international law. Another of the inherent difficulties with this topic is that different States have different international obligations concerning the expulsion of aliens.

The United Kingdom also notes that the issue of expulsion of aliens is one which is being discussed in various regional fora. The many political and legal difficulties in this topic are increasingly plain from these discussions. Whether a solution to these difficulties can be found which could form the basis of wider international work remains to be seen. For the moment, the United Kingdom can only emphasise its strong doubts about whether now is the right time for an effort to codify and consolidate the law in this area.

The United Kingdom considers that one way in which to proceed would be for the Commission's work on this topic to take the form of a study of State practice on the issue of expulsion of aliens, without attempting to codify that practice.

(Text supplied by FCO)

2/4
(See also 5/45)
The UK representative made the following statement to the UNGA Sixth Committee on 23 October 2007:

The Sixth Committee and the General Assembly have considered the future of the Articles [on State Responsibility] on two occasions. In 2001, at its fifty-sixth session, the General Assembly welcomed the Articles in Resolution 56/83, the text of which was annexed to the resolution, and 'commend[ed] them to the attention of Governments without prejudice to the question of their future adoption or other appropriate action'. Three years later, at its fifty-ninth session in 2004, in Resolution 59/35, the General Assembly postponed further consideration of the final form of the Articles until the sixty-second session of the General Assembly in 2007.

The United Kingdom is of the view that the action of the General Assembly in 2001 in commending the Articles to the attention of Governments was the right course of action to adopt, and that no further action was necessary or desirable. The United Kingdom is also of the view that the General Assembly's action in 2004 to commend them to the attention of Governments, without prejudice to the question of their future adoption, was the right course. For the reasons set out in our written comment to the Secretary-General in January this year [see below], and which are reproduced in UN Doc A/62/63 dated 9 March 2007, this remains our firmly held opinion. It suffices to summarise the reasons for the United Kingdom's view.

First, reaching agreement on the text of the Articles was not easy, and required intense negotiation and compromise. Consequently, the text of the Articles in its entirety is not wholly satisfactory to any State. Nevertheless, States generally have accepted the Articles in their current form. At present, many of the Articles reflect an authoritative statement of international law and have been referred to by international courts and tribunals, writers and, more recently, domestic courts. As is evidenced by the Report by the Secretary-General dated 1 February 2007 containing the Compilation of Decisions of International Courts, Tribunals and Other Bodies (UN Doc A/62/62), and also a more recent study undertaken by the British Institute of International and Comparative Law, which is available on the British Institute's website, the Articles have gained widespread recognition and approval. Many States, including the United Kingdom, regularly turn to the Articles and the commentaries as guidance on issues of State responsibility that arise in day-to-day practice.

Second, it is difficult to see what would be gained by the adoption of a convention. Resolution 56/83 provided the Articles with a firmer standing than if they had not been annexed, and Resolution 59/35 enhanced this standing. The Articles are already proving their worth and are entering the fabric of international law through State practice, decisions of courts and tribunals, and the writings of publicists. They are referred to consistently in the work of foreign ministries and other government departments. The impact of the Articles on international law is likely only to increase with time, as is demonstrated by the growing number of references to the Articles in recent years.

Finally, the United Kingdom considers that there is a real risk that in moving toward the adoption of a convention based on the Articles, old issues may be reopened. Our view remains that any move at this point towards the crystallisation of the Articles in a treaty text would raise a significant risk of undermining the carefully constructed balance represented by the scope and content of the Articles. The danger is therefore that if the negotiation of a treaty is forced at this stage, any text emerging is unlikely to enjoy the wide support currently accorded to the Articles. If few States were to ratify a convention, that instrument would have less legal force than the Articles as they now stand, and may stifle the process of development and consolidation of the law that the Articles in their current form have set in train. In fact, there is a significant risk that a convention with a small number of participants may serve to undermine the current status the Articles have achieved, and may be a 'limping' convention, with little or no practical effect.

Accordingly, the United Kingdom considers that it would be sensible and appropriate to take no further action on the Articles, leaving them to exert a growing influence through state practice and jurisprudence.

The written comments referred to above:

3. The United Kingdom is of the view that the action of the General Assembly in 2001 in commending the draft articles to the attention of Governments was the right course of action to adopt, and that no further action was necessary or desirable. For the reasons set out below, this remains our firmly held opinion. We understand that other States share this view.

4. Reaching agreement on the text of the draft articles was not easy, and required intense negotiation and compromise. Consequently, the text of the draft articles in its entirety is not wholly satisfactory to any State. It is well known within the Sixth Committee that the United Kingdom has some concerns regarding certain provisions of the draft articles. Of course, some aspects of the draft articles are more controversial than others.

5. Despite this, States generally have accepted the draft articles in their current form. At present, the draft articles reflect an authoritative statement of international law and have been referred to by international courts and tribunals, writers and, more recently, domestic courts. As is evidenced by the table set out in section III of the present document, since 2001 the draft articles have gained widespread recognition and approval. Many States, including the United Kingdom, regularly turn to the draft articles and the commentaries as guidance on issues of State responsibility that arise in day-to-day practice. Interestingly, reliance on the draft articles is not restricted to generally accepted provisions.

As is seen in section III, reference has also been made to more controversial articles, including those concerning countermeasures and violation of peremptory norms.

6. It is difficult to see what would be gained by the adoption of a convention. Resolution 56/83 provided the draft articles with a firmer standing than if the draft articles had not been annexed, and resolution 59/35 enhanced this standing. The draft articles are already proving their worth and are entering the fabric of international law through State practice, decisions of courts and tribunals and writings. They are referred to consistently in the work of foreign ministries and other Government departments. The impact of the draft articles on international law will only increase with time, as is demonstrated by the growing number of references to the draft articles in recent years.

7. This achievement should not be put at risk lightly. The United Kingdom considers that there is a real risk that in moving towards the adoption of a convention based on the draft articles old issues may be reopened. This would result in a series of fruitless debates that may unravel the text of the draft articles and weaken the current consensus. It may well be that the international community is left with nothing. Our view remains that any move at this point towards the crystallization of the draft articles in a treaty text would raise a significant risk of undermining the currently held broad consensus on the scope and content of the draft articles. Accordingly, we consider that it would be sensible and appropriate to take no further action on the draft articles at this point.

8. Even were a text to be agreed, it is unlikely that the text would enjoy the wide support currently accorded to the draft articles. The Commission's work on State responsibility differs from the more discrete and specific subject matter of other topics, in that the draft articles are a common thread running through all State practice and will have implications for a vast number of international legal issues. This is already evident in the wide range of areas in which references to the draft articles are occurring, from traditional areas of international law such as the use of force, to human rights and international trade law. For many States, including the United Kingdom, there is a difference between noting and utilizing the work of the Commission, even though there may be some concern as to certain elements, and signing up to a convention that would be binding upon the State in all aspects. If few States were to ratify a convention, that instrument would have less legal force than the draft articles as they now stand, and may stifle the development of the law in an area traditionally characterized by State practice and case law. In fact, there is a significant risk that a convention with a small number of participants may have a de-codifying effect, may serve to undermine the current status of the draft articles and may be a "limping" convention, with little or no practical effect.

9. The preferable course of action is to take no further action on the draft articles, leaving the draft articles to exert a growing influence through State practice and jurisprudence. The United Kingdom is aware, however, that other States do not share this view, favouring instead the adoption of a convention based on the draft articles. Given the risks, we would urge those States to reconsider, having regard to the possible consequences of moving towards a convention.

(UN Doc A/62/63, 9 March 2007)

2/5
(See also **6/4**)
The UK representative made the following statement to the UNGA Sixth Committee on 19 October 2007:

As is evident from the commentaries to the draft articles [Report of the ILC's fifty-eighth session, 2006, A/61/10, pp. 22–100, Ed.] diplomatic protection is a long established area of international law and there exists a large body of State practice on much of the subject-matter covered by the draft articles. The topic has remained largely uncodified, with development achieved through State practice and the decisions of international courts and tribunals.

The United Kingdom notes the recommendation of the Commission that Governments move toward the adoption of a convention based on the text of the draft articles. However, the United Kingdom would prefer, for various reasons, that member States pause for a period of reflection before making any decision about the negotiation of such a convention.

First, the Commission's draft articles are still relatively new. They and their commentaries were only recently made available to Governments, and it remains the case that we have not had sufficient time to go through the necessary process of extensive study and consultation within Government on the text and the commentaries. Further, as the United Kingdom has noted on a number of occasions, there are also important elements of the draft articles that constitute proposals for the development of new law, for example, article 8 on the diplomatic protection of stateless persons and refugees. While the United Kingdom may be willing to accept some of these elements as a desirable direction for the development of customary international law, we are not so comfortable with other aspects. Among the latter aspects, we are concerned with the inclusion of the new article 19, entitled 'recommended practice'. It is the view of the United Kingdom that the inclusion of this article risks undermining well-established rules of customary international law. For these reasons that the United Kingdom considers that further time is needed for Governments to become familiar with the draft articles before deciding on any future action.

Second, the United Kingdom notes the comment of the International Law Commission's Special Rapporteur, John Dugard, who observed in his Seventh Report on Diplomatic Protection that the fate of the draft articles is closely bound up with that of the ILC's Articles on State Responsibility. The United Kingdom concurs in that assessment, and considers that so long as no decision is made about elaborating a convention on State responsibility, any decision to do so for the draft articles on diplomatic protection would be also premature.

Third, and finally, the relative novelty of these draft articles means that we have not had the opportunity to put the articles to the test of practical application in State practice or in the decisions of international courts and tribunals. The United Kingdom considers that postponing any decision on the future of the draft articles would permit them to be consolidated and refined through their application in State practice and by international courts and tribunals.

(Text supplied by FCO)

2/6

The UK representative made the following statement to the UNGA Sixth Committee on 22 October 2007 on the matter of international liability in case of loss from transboundary harm arising out of hazardous activities:

As the United Kingdom has previously stated, it is generally satisfied with the overall direction of the work of the Commission and the Special Rapporteurs on this topic (UN Doc A/CN.4/516 of 3 April 2001). With regard to the Commission's work on the first part of this topic, the United Kingdom welcomes the draft articles on 'Prevention of Transboundary Harm from Hazardous Activities' (UN Doc A/CN.4/L.601 of 3 May 2001). At this stage, the United Kingdom sees little need for the conclusion of a convention in this respect, as in our view there are a number of sectoral and regional instruments governing issues of harm from hazardous activities by which we are already bound. However, if other States are firmly convinced of the added value of a convention based on the Commission's work, we are prepared to consider the matter with an open mind. As for the second part of the Commission's work on this topic, the United Kingdom also agrees with the Commission's approach in concluding that the outcome of its work should be adopted as non-binding draft principles (UN Doc A/CN.4/562/Add.1 of 12 April 2006).

(See also **UKMIL [2006] 13/1**)

(Text supplied by FCO)

Part Three: The Law of Treaties

Part Three: I.B. *The law of treaties—definition, conclusion, and entry into force—conclusion, including signature, ratification, and accession*

3/1 Text of Explanatory Memorandum for Treaty of Amity and Co-operation in South East Asia (01/07/07) Cm 7196

Subject Matter

The Treaty of Amity and Co-operation in Southeast Asia (TAC) binds together the 10 countries of the Association of Southeast Asian Nations (ASEAN) (Burma, Brunei Darussalam, Cambodia, Indonesia, Laos, Malaysia, Philippines, Singapore, Thailand and Vietnam).

The original Member States of ASEAN signed the Treaty on 24 February 1976 and it entered into force on 21 June 1976. Its purpose is to promote peace, stability and co-operation in Southeast Asia. The TAC contains provisions to enhance co-operation in economic, trade, social and scientific matters. The TAC also contains the principle of non-interference in the internal affairs of one another as well as the mutual respect for sovereignty, territorial integrity and national identity of all nations. The TAC is essentially a political declaration of intent in these areas in a treaty format, however the UK would not be required to change any existing laws or practices.

While the TAC was originally designed to apply only to States within the Southeast Asian region, it was amended in 1987 to allow for States outside the region to accede to it. States outside the region that have acceded to the TAC are: Papua New Guinea, China; India; Japan; Pakistan; Republic of Korea; the Russian Federation; Mongolia; New Zealand; Australia; East Timor; France.

In July 2006 EU Member States agreed to initiate proceedings towards the accession of the EU and the European Community to the TAC. However the TAC will first need to be amended further to allow for the accession of non-states. It is therefore unlikely that EU and EC accession will take place before the end of the year. As stated above, France has already acceded to the TAC bilaterally.

...

(3) Reservations and Declarations

On accession to the TAC, the UK will write to the Chair of ASEAN formally recording our understanding of the TAC. This ensures that UK accession to the TAC will not affect the UK's rights and obligations under other bilateral or multilateral agreements, that the TAC is to be interpreted in conformity with the principles of the UN Charter and that the TAC will not apply to, nor affect the UK's relationship with States outside Southeast Asia.

Consultations

Relevant UK government departments were consulted regarding UK accession to the TAC, no objections were raised. ASEAN Member States were consulted through the Philippines as Chair of the ASEAN Standing Committee who has extended a formal invitation for the UK to accede to the TAC.

Presented to Parliament July 2007

(Treaty Series No. 34 (2006) Fourth Supplementary List of Ratifications, Accessions, Withdrawals, etc., for 2006 Cm 7159)

Part Three: I.C. *The law of treaties—definition, conclusion, and entry into force—reservations, declarations, and objections*

3/2

The Attorney-General was asked by the Constitutional Affairs Committee about his decision to terminate a corruption investigation on grounds of national security. He said:

My view in relation to that is very clear. I do not believe that the OECD Convention prevents any country which has signed up from having regard to something so fundamental as national security. I do not believe we would have signed up to this Convention if we believed that we could not have regard to national security. Put on one side commercial considerations, ordinary diplomatic relations, I do not believe we would have signed up to it. I would be astonished if any country would have signed up to it on that basis and there is absolutely nothing in the Convention which says, certainly explicitly, that you cannot. So I do not believe that national security is something you cannot take into consideration at all. [Q.26]

He was then asked:

The problem with that is that a definition of national security which is that broad would undermine the international relations part of the Treaty itself?

He said:

I do not know, if I may say so, why you regard it as so broad. The details...why Saudi Arabian cooperation in the counter-terrorism field is regarded by those who understand it as so important. That is not a broad definition of national security, that is really quite a narrow definition of national security, recognising security to citizens in this country and to others within our shores. [Q.27]

He went on:

I absolutely stand where I am in relation to this and where the Director is. The Convention took a very important step, which we entirely support, that countries should not have regard to commercial considerations in determining investigation or prosecution and what I would term "general relations" with another state. It is no use saying just, "Well, if we prosecute in this case they will get upset with us," in a sort of very general sense, but I do not accept that we would have signed up to that Convention if the effect was that there is a case in which national security would be put at jeopardy—the way, for example, the Prime Minister has spoken about it—and that is something that we simply cannot regard. We have to say, "We have signed up to put our citizens' lives at risk," particularly against an uncertain, or in my view a case which would never have gone ahead. [Q.31]

(Constitutional Affairs Committee, The Constitutional Role of the Attorney-General, Evidence 7 February 2007, HC 306-i))

3/3

The representative of the UK made the following statement to the UNGA Sixth Committee on 2 November 2007:

I will turn first to chapter IV of [the ILC Report, Fifty-ninth session, A/62/10, Ed.], on reservations to treaties...

The United Kingdom notes that the Commission considered and provisionally adopted nine draft guidelines during its session for 2007. The first of the draft guidelines, guideline 3.1.5, states that: 'A reservation is incompatible with the object and purpose of the treaty if it affects an essential element of the treaty that is necessary to its general thrust, in such a way that the reservation impairs the raison d'être of the treaty.' Draft guideline 3.1.6 goes on to give guidance on the determination of the object and purpose of the treaty. The United Kingdom has previously expressed its scepticism about the exercise of defining the concept of the 'object and purpose' of the treaty in an abstract way, and has wondered whether the search for object and purpose is necessarily identical in different contexts. The Commission's commentary to draft guideline 3.1.5 highlights that the phrase 'object and purpose' is used in no less than eight different provisions of the Vienna Convention on the Law of Treaties, none of which provide any particular 'clues' as to the meaning of the concept. We note that the Commission has indicated that this draft guideline indicates a 'direction' rather than establishing a clear criterion that can be directly applied in all cases. We would agree with the Commission's view that identifying the object and purpose is a question of interpretation, and we commend the Commission for having adopted the flexible approach encapsulated in draft guidelines 3.1.5 and 3.1.6.

The United Kingdom has also previously expressed doubts about draft guidelines 3.1.7 to 3.1.13. Having now had a further opportunity to review these, together with the commentaries, we agree with draft guideline 3.1.7, on vague or general reservations. As for draft guideline 3.1.8, on reservations to a provision reflecting a customary norm, we are not convinced by the first paragraph, which provides that the fact that a treaty provision reflects a customary norm is a pertinent factor in assessing the validity of a reservation. As we said in our observations on the Human Rights Committee's General Comment No 24, 'there is a clear distinction between choosing not to enter into treaty obligations, and trying to opt out of customary international law.' We do, however, agree with the second paragraph of that draft guideline, which states that such a reservation does not affect the binding nature of the relevant customary norm, which shall continue to apply.

With respect to draft guideline 3.1.12, the United Kingdom does not agree that human rights treaties should be treated any differently than other international agreements. As we said in our comments to the Sixth Committee last year, and also in the previous year, it is the United Kingdom's firmly held view that reservations to normative treaties, including human rights treaties, should be subject to the same rules as reservations to other types of treaties. We see no legal or policy reasons for treating human rights treaties differently. Any suggestion that special rules on reservations may apply to treaties in different fields, such as human rights, would not be helpful. It should not be forgotten that the law on reservations to treaties owes its origin to the Advisory Opinion of the International Court of Justice of 28 May 1951 on Reservations to the Genocide Convention.

As regards draft guideline 3.1.13, on 'Reservations to treaty provisions concerning dispute settlement or the monitoring of the implementation of a treaty', the United Kingdom observes that this draft guideline may be redundant. This is because it merely confirms that such reservations are to be assessed in accordance with their compatibility with the object and purpose of the treaty in question, which should already be apparent from the content of draft guidelines 3.1.5 and 3.1.6.

(Text supplied by FCO)

3/4
International Convention for the Suppression of the Financing of Terrorism Adopted New York 09 Dec,. 1999 028/2002 Cm 5550

Note-

On 03 August 2006, the Secretary–General of the United Nations, as depositary, received from the government of the United Kingdom, an Objection to the declaration made by Bangladesh upon accession 1, as follows:

"The Government of the United Kingdom of Great Britain and Northern Ireland have examined the understanding of the International Convention for the Suppression of the Financing of Terrorism made by the Government of the People's Republic of Bangladesh at the time of its accession to the Convention. The Government of the United Kingdom consider the understanding made by Bangladesh to be a reservation that seeks to limit the scope of the Convention on a unilateral basis.

The Government of the United Kingdom objects to the aforesaid reservation."

[Bangladesh's Understanding reads as follows:

"[The] Government of the People's Republic of Bangladesh understands that its accession to this Convention shall not be deemed to be inconsistent with its international obligations under the Constitution of the country.", Ed.]

(Treaty Series No. 34 (2006) Fourth Supplementary List of Ratifications, Accessions, Withdrawals, etc., for 2006 Cm 7159)

3/5

On 28 February 2007, the Secretary-General of the United Nations, as depositary, received an objection from the government of United Kingdom, as follows;

"The Government of the United Kingdom have examined the reservations made by the Government of the Sultanate of Oman to the Convention on the Elimination of all Forms of Discrimination Against Women (New York, 18 December 1979).

In the view of the Government of the United Kingdom a reservation should clearly define for the other States Parties to the Convention the extent to which the reserving State has accepted the obligations of the Convention. A reservation which consists of a general reference to a system of law without specifying its contents does not do so. The Government of the United Kingdom therefore object to the Sultanate of Oman's reservation from all provisions of the Convention not in accordance with the provisions of the Islamic Sharia and legislation in force in the Sultanate of Oman.

The Government of the United Kingdom further object to the Sultanate of Oman's reservations from Article 15, paragraph 4 and Article 16 of the Convention.

These objections shall not preclude the entry into force of the Convention between the United Kingdom of Great Britain and Northern Ireland and Oman."

[Oman has entered the following reservations:

1. All provisions of the Convention not in accordance with the provisions of the Islamic sharia and legislation in force in the Sultanate of Oman;

2. Article 9, paragraph 2, which provides that States Parties shall grant women equal rights with men with respect to the nationality of their children;

3. Article 15, paragraph 4, which provides that States Parties shall accord to men and women the same rights with regard to the law relating to the movement of persons and the freedom to choose their residence and domicile;

4. Article 16, regarding the equality of men and women, and in particular sub-paragraphs (a), (c), and (f) (regarding adoption).

5. The Sultanate is not bound by article 29, paragraph 1, regarding arbitration and the referral to the International Court of Justice of any dispute between two or more States which is not settled by negotiation, Ed.]

(First Supplementary List of Ratifications, Accessions, Withdrawals, etc., for 2007 Cm 7258)

Part Three: I.D. *The law of treaties—definition, conclusion, and entry into force—provisional application, and entry into force*

3/6
(See also **19/29**)
Extradition Treaty between the Government of the United Kingdom of Great Britain and Northern Ireland and the Government of the United States of America with Exchange of Notes, Washington, 31 March 2003

EXCHANGE OF NOTES

No. 1

The Home Office to the Embassy of the United States of America in London

Your Excellency
I have the honour to refer to the Extradition Treaty between the Government of the United Kingdom of Great Britain and Northern Ireland and the Government of the United States of America signed at Washington on 31 March 2003 hereinafter "the 2003 Treaty"). The United Kingdom has completed the steps necessary under its law to implement the 2003 Treaty in the United Kingdom, and in Jersey, but not in Guernsey or the Isle of Man.

In order to permit entry into force of the 2003 Treaty without further delay, I have the honour to propose that the United Kingdom and the United States proceed with an early exchange of instruments of ratification. Having regard however to the need to complete the necessary steps in both Guernsey and the Isle of Man, the Government of the United Kingdom is not yet able to apply the 2003 Treaty in respect of those Dependencies. I therefore have the honour to propose that the 2003 Treaty be suspended in its application to Guernsey and the Isle of Man until the Government of the United Kingdom should notify the Government of the United States of America by Diplomatic Note that the steps necessary for its implementation in respect of Guernsey and the Isle of Man have been completed.

Notwithstanding any provision to the contrary in the 2003 Treaty, the Extradition Treaty between the Government of the United Kingdom of Great Britain and Northern Ireland and the Government of the United States of America signed at London on 8 June 1972 and the Supplementary Treaty signed at Washington on 25 June 1985, as amended by an Exchange of Notes signed at Washington on 19 and 20 August 1986, will continue to apply to Guernsey and the Isle of Man until such time as the 2003 Treaty is no longer suspended with respect to those Dependencies.

If the forgoing proposals are acceptable to the Government of the United States of America, I have the honour to propose that this Note and Your Excellency's reply in that sense shall constitute an agreement between the two Governments concerning the 2003 Treaty.

No.2

The Embassy of the United States of America in London to the Home Office

Your Excellency

I have the honour to acknowledge receipt of your Note dated 26 April 2007 Referring to the Extradition Treaty between the Government of the United Kingdom of Great Britain and Northern Ireland and the Government of the United States of America signed at Washington on 31 March 2003. Your Note reads as follows:

[As in No.1]

I am pleased to confirm that your proposals are acceptable to the Government of the United States of America and that your Note and this reply shall constitute an agreement between the two Governments concerning the 2003 Treaty and that this agreement shall enter into force today.

(Treaty Series No. 34 (2006) Fourth Supplementary List of Ratifications, Accessions, Withdrawals, etc., for 2006 Cm 7159 [Instruments of Ratification were exchanged on 26 April 2007 and the Treaty entered into force on 26 April 2007])

3/8
International Convention for the Suppression of Terrorist Bombings, New York, 15 December 1997

Note

On 03 August 2006, Secretary-General of the United Nations, as depositary, received from the government of United Kingdom, the following objection to a declaration made by Arab Republic of Egypt upon ratification, as follows;

"The Government of the United Kingdom of Great Britain and Northern Ireland have examined the declaration, described as a reservation, relating to article 19, paragraph 2 of the International Convention for the Suppression of Terrorist Bombings made by the Government of the Arab Republic of Egypt at the time of its ratification of the Convention.

The declaration appears to purport to extend the scope of application of the Convention to include the armed forces of a State to the extent that they fail to meet the test that they do not violate the rules and principles of international law. Such activities would otherwise be excluded from the application of the Convention by virtue of article 19, paragraph 2. It is the opinion of the United Kingdom that the Government of Egypt is entitled to make such a declaration only insofar as the declaration constitutes a unilateral declaration by the Government of Egypt that Egypt will apply the terms of the Convention in circumstances going beyond those required by the Convention to their own armed forces on a unilateral basis. The United Kingdom consider this to be the effect of the declaration made by Egypt.

However, in the view of the United Kingdom, Egypt cannot by a unilateral declaration extend the obligations of the United Kingdom under the Convention beyond those set out in the Convention without the express consent of the United Kingdom. For the avoidance of any doubt, the United Kingdom wish to make clear that it does not so consent. Moreover, the United Kingdom do not consider the declaration made by the Government of Egypt to have any effect in respect of the obligations of the United Kingdom under the Convention or in respect of the application of the Convention to the armed forces of the United Kingdom.

The United Kingdom thus regard the Convention as entering into force between the United Kingdom and Egypt subject to a unilateral declaration made by the Government of Egypt, which applies only to the obligations of Egypt under the Convention and only in respect of the armed forces of Egypt."

[Egypt has entered the following reservation to Article 19(2):

"The Government of the Arab Republic of Egypt declares that it is bound by Article 19, paragraph 2, of the Convention insofar as the military forces of the State, in the exercise of their duties do not violate the rules and principles of international law."]

(Treaty Series No. 33 (2006) Third Supplementary List of Ratifications, Accessions, Withdrawals, etc., for 2006, Cm 7045)

3/9
Note-
On 03 August 2006, Secretary–General of the United Nations, as depositary, received from the government of the United Kingdom, the following objection to a declaration made by the Arab Republic of Egypt upon ratification, as follows;

"The Government of the United Kingdom of Great Britain and Northern Ireland have examined the explanatory declaration relating to article 2, paragraph I (b) of the International Convention for the Suppression of the Financing of Terrorism made by the Government of the Arab Republic of Egypt at the time of its ratification of the Convention. The Government of the United Kingdom consider the declaration made by Egypt to be a reservation that seeks to limit the scope of the Convention on a unilateral basis.

The Government of the United Kingdom objects to the aforesaid reservation."

[Egypt's reservations and declaration:

1. Under article 2, paragraph 2 (a), of the Convention, the Government of the Arab Republic of Egypt considers that, in the application of the Convention, conventions to which it is not a party are deemed not included in the annex.

2. Under article 24, paragraph 2, of the Convention, the Government of the Arab Republic of Egypt does not consider itself bound by the provisions of paragraph 1 of that article.

Explanatory declaration:

Without prejudice to the principles and norms of general international law and the relevant United Nations resolutions, the Arab Republic of Egypt does not consider acts of national resistance in all its forms, including armed resistance against foreign occupation and aggression with a view to liberation and self-determination, as terrorist acts within the meaning of article 2, paragraph 1, subparagraph (b), of the Convention, Ed.]

(Treaty Series No. 33 (2006) Third Supplementary List of Ratifications, Accessions, Withdrawals, etc., for 2006, Cm 7045)

Part Three: IV.C. *The law of treaties—invalidity, termination and suspension of operation—termination and suspension of operation, denunciation, and withdrawal*

3/10
Agreement establishing an International Foot and Mouth Disease Vaccine Bank London 26 June, 1985 043/1985 Cmnd 9602

In a depositary note dated 20 March 2007, the Government of the United Kingdom of Great Britain and Northern Ireland, proposing to terminate the Agreement unless in 90 days... , no such objection was raised by participating states indicating their objection to the depository in writing. Terminated 19 June 2007.

(Treaty Series No. 29 (2007) Second Supplementary List of Ratifications, Accessions, Withdrawals, etc., for 2007 Cm 7267)

3/11
Convention on the Reduction of Cases of Multiple Nationality and Military Obligations in Cases of Multiple Nationality

On 01 May 2007, the Secretary-General of the Council of Europe, as depositary, received a declaration, from the government of Belgium, as follows;

In accordance with the Agreement on the interpretation of Article 12, paragraph 2, of the Convention, accepted by the Parties to the Convention and signed by the Secretary General on 2 April 2007, the Kingdom of Belgium denounces Chapter I of the Convention.

On 05 April 2007, the Secretary-General of the Council of Europe, as depositary, issued, the following;

Certificate of the Secretary General of the Council of Europe containing the agreement on the interpretation of Article 12, paragraph 2, of the Convention on the Reduction of Cases of Multiple Nationality and Military Obligations in Cases of Multiple Nationality (ETS n° 43)

Considering that Austria, Belgium, Denmark, France, Ireland, Italy, Luxembourg, the Netherlands, Norway, Spain, Sweden and the United Kingdom are Parties to the Convention of 6 May 1963 on the Reduction of Cases of Multiple Nationality and Military Obligations in Cases of Multiple Nationality (ETS 43), which entered into force on 28 March 1968 and was supplemented by two protocols;

Considering that Article 12, paragraph 2, of the Convention provides that any Contracting Party may, in so far as it is concerned, denounce this Convention by means of a notification addressed to the Secretary General of the Council of Europe;

Considering that some of the States Parties have declared that they no longer wish to be bound by Chapter I of the Convention concerning the reduction of cases of multiple nationality;

Considering that the Committee of Experts on Nationality (CJNA), after having consulted the Committee of Legal Advisers on Public International Law (CAHDI), recommended the twelve States Parties to the Convention to reach an agreement, through written procedure, on the interpretation of Article 12, paragraph 2, of the Convention allowing the partial denunciation of the Convention;

Considering that the Chair of the Rapporteur Group on Legal Co-operation informed orally the Committee of Ministers about this question at the 829th meeting of the Ministers' Deputies, on 26 February 2003;

Considering that, by letter dated 5 March 2003, the Secretary General proposed to the twelve States Parties to the Convention the following agreement:

1. Any Contracting Party may at any time, in so far as it is concerned, denounce Chapter I of this Convention by means of a notification addressed to the Secretary General of the Council of Europe.

2. Such denunciation shall take effect one year after the date of receipt by the Secretary General of such notification.

3. The provisions of Article 7, paragraph 2, of the Convention shall apply as amended by the 1977 Protocol.

Considering that the twelve States Parties to the Convention have notified to the Secretary General their acceptance of the agreement;

The Secretary General of the Council of Europe hereby certifies as follows:

The following text constitutes the agreement on the interpretation of Article 12, paragraph 2, of the Convention on the Reduction of Cases of Multiple Nationality and Military Obligations in Cases of Multiple Nationality (ETS 43), of 6 May 1963.

AGREEMENT ON THE INTERPRETATION OF ARTICLE 12, PARAGRAPH 2, OF THE CONVENTION ON THE REDUCTION OF CASES OF MULTIPLE NATIONALITY AND MILITARY OBLIGATIONS IN CASES OF MULTIPLE NATIONALITY (ETS 43)

1. Any Contracting Party may at any time, in so far as it is concerned, denounce Chapter I of this Convention by means of a notification addressed to the Secretary General of the Council of Europe.

2. Such denunciation shall take effect one year after the date of receipt by the Secretary General of such notification.

3. The provisions of Article 7, paragraph 2, of the Convention shall apply as amended by the 1977 Protocol.

Done at Strasbourg, on 2 April 2007.

(Treaty Series No. 29 (2007) Second Supplementary List of Ratifications, Accessions, Withdrawals, etc., for 2007 Cm 7267)

3/12
In a statement to Parliament, the Foreign Secretary said:

The Government regret the unilateral decision by the Russian Federation to cease compliance with its obligations under the Conventional Forces in Europe Treaty (CPE) [sic] from 12 December. Russia has sought to explain this decision principally on the grounds that members of the North Atlantic Treaty Organisation (NATO) have not ratified the adapted version of the CFE treaty. Together with our NATO allies, the United Kingdom has made a public statement (http://www.nato.int/docu/pr/2007/p07-139e.html).

This Russian decision is unjustified. The United Kingdom, along with NATO allies, has made clear our commitment to ratify as quickly as possible the adaptation of the CFE treaty, which would provide the basis for addressing most of Russia's concerns about the current CFE regime. But it remains right that Russia should in parallel honour its own commitments, made at the 1999 Organisation for Security and Co-operation in Europe summit in Istanbul, to regularise the status of its forces and equipment in Georgia and Moldova. The principle that host nation consent is required for the stationing of foreign forces is central to effective security and stability in Europe. NATO has engaged intensively with the Russian Federation to seek ways of overcoming differences over how to ensure both these sets of commitments are delivered.

The Government also consider that the Russian Federation's "suspension" of their obligations cannot be justified either under the provisions of the CFE

Treaty or on the grounds set out in the Vienna Convention on the Law of Treaties. Accordingly, on 11 December, we sent a Note Verbale, via the Treaty Depository, to all CFE States Parties, making this clear.

We judge, however, that European security is not fundamentally or immediately threatened by this Russian action. In the short term, we understand Russia will stop exchanging data or sending notifications on the whereabouts and composition of its conventional forces, and will refuse to allow verification inspections. However, if Russia were to persist in this course of action, in the longer-term that would erode the transparency and predictability which the CFE regime contributes to overall stability in Europe.

To help maintain that stability, the United Kingdom will until further notice, along with its NATO allies, continue to honour all our obligations under the CFE Treaty, including towards the Russian Federation. We will assess the impact of any non-compliance by the Russian Federation, and consult with NATO allies on a further joint response. With NATO allies, we will also continue to promote engagement with the Russian Federation with a view to reaching an agreed way forward.

(HC Deb 13 December 2007 Vol 469 c57WS–58WS)

Part Four: Relationship between International Law and Internal Law

Part Four: I. *Relationship between international law and internal law—In general*

4/1

The Foreign Secretary was asked if she would extend the Ponsonby Rule to apply to all international treaties; and if she would bring forward proposals for the referral by the House of all such treaties to the relevant select committee for scrutiny and report where appropriate. An FCO Minister wrote:

Most treaties that are signed by the Government and which are subject to ratification, accession, acceptance or approval, or the mutual notification of completion of procedures, are subject to the Ponsonby Rule. Such treaties must therefore be laid before both Houses as a published Command Paper for a minimum of 21 sitting days, and be accompanied by an explanatory memorandum, prior to ratification, accession, acceptance or approval. Only bilateral double taxation agreements, which are scheduled to the relevant Order in Council which implements the agreement, and treaties that enter into force on signature are exempt from this requirement. There are no plans to extend the Ponsonby Rule to such agreements.

All treaties that are subject to the Ponsonby Rule are copied to the relevant departmental select committee when they are laid, in accordance with an undertaking given by the Government in response to a report by the Procedure Committee in October 2000. Additionally, all treaties that raise significant human rights issues are copied to the Joint Committee on Human Rights.

(HC Deb 27 February 2007 Vol 457 c1186W)

Part Four: II. *Relationship between international law and internal law—Application and implementation of international law in internal law*

4/2
The Foreign Secretary was asked if she would meet the Cabinet Secretary for Justice in the Scottish Government at an early date to discuss the implications of the recently signed memorandum of understanding between the UK and Libya. [The MoU apparently dealt with the repatriation of prisoners. There was a strong Scottish interest in the position of Ali Mohmed al-Megrah, who was imprisoned in Scotland for his part in the Lockerbie bombing, Ed.] An FCO Minister wrote:

Officials in Government Departments are consulting with their counterparts in the Scottish Executive, according to the principles set out in the memorandum of understanding with the devolved administrations of 2001. It sets out how the Government and the devolved administrations should interact in the conduct of international relations.

(HC Deb 14 June 2007 Vol 461 c1217W)

4/3
An FCO Minister wrote:

The UK was not in a position to sign the Council of Europe Convention on the Protection of Children against Sexual Abuse and Exploitation at the Conference of European Ministers of Justice in Lanzarote. Before we sign any convention we must be satisfied that we will be in a position to implement the obligations contained in the convention. We are in the process of formally confirming with relevant departments and the devolved administrations that we are in position to sign and hope to be able to do so shortly.

(HL Deb 4 December 2007 Vol 969 cWA173)

Part Five: Subjects of International law

Part Five: I.A.1. *Subjects of international law—states—status and powers—personality*

5/1
The representative of the UK made the following statement in the Security Council following the adoption of Resolution 1762 on 29 June 2007 on the termination of the mandate for UNMOVIC:

The United Kingdom would like to draw the attention of the Security Council to the report of the Special Advisor to the Director of the CIA. This catalogued the state of Iraq's disarmament and the residual stocks of WMD material. UNMOVIC has previously reported to the Security Council on Chemical Weapons finds made by coalition forces.

The United Kingdom welcomes the commitment made by the Government of Iraq to respect and apply existing international commitments and obligations to non-proliferation of nuclear, chemical and biological weapons.

In particular, we welcome the Government of Iraq's full constitutional commitment to taking disarmament forward. This includes: preparations to accede to the Chemical Weapons Convention; its intention to agree an Additional Protocol to its Safeguards Agreement with the International Atomic Energy Agency; and the establishment of a National Monitoring Directorate to oversee and control the movement of dual use items.

We are not closing the file on WMD in Iraq. But we are changing the approach. We look forward to the Government of Iraq's report to the Security Council on its progress in adhering to all applicable treaties and international agreements; in harmonising Iraqi export legislation with international standards; and on progress made by the National Monitoring Directorate in its work.

It is the United Kingdom's assessment that for some time neither UNMOVIC nor the IAEA's Iraq Nuclear Verification Office have been in a position to carry out their functions in a way which serves the aims of disarmament and non-proliferation. Instead, we should now move forward and focus on ensuring that Iraq itself continues to take steps to support the international non-proliferation regime and itself adheres to disarmament and non-proliferation treaties and related international agreements. The UK will continue to help Iraq do that, both as a friend of Iraq and as a partner within the Multinational Force.

We also encourage Iraq's neighbours and the international community to co-operate with and assist Iraq in implementing its non-proliferation obligations and building capacity in the relevant areas.

(UN Doc S/PV.5710, 29 June 2007)

Part Five: I. A.2. *Subjects of international law—states—status and powers—sovereignty and independence*

5/2 (See also **5/5–6, 5/23–25,**)
Somalia
An FCO Minister wrote:

We have urged all of Somalia's neighbours to respect its sovereignty and to play a constructive role in bringing peace and stability to Somalia. We believe that the deployment of a regional force along the lines of United Nations Security Council Resolution 1725 will help to create the conditions for sustainable security in Somalia.

We have continually made it clear to all parties that we do not believe there can be an exclusively military solution to the situation in Somalia. Consequently we have consistently called for discussions to create a broad and representative government.

(HC Deb 15 January 2007 Vol 455 c830W)

5/3

The Foreign Secretary was asked what reports she had received of the role of Somalia's clans and tribal groups in the peace process; [and] what assessment she had made of whether political consensus can be achieved across the different clans and tribal groups. She wrote:

A broad base of support within Somalia's complex clan structure is crucial to a lasting peace in Somalia. Therefore, it is vital that the Transitional Federal Government (TFG) reaches out to all the clans and lends a fully inclusive political process. We are stressing this in our contacts with the TFG, for example when the Under-Secretary of State for Foreign and Commonwealth Affairs met President Yusuf in London on 22 February. We are urging the TFG to convene as soon as possible the National Reconciliation Congress, to involve all clans. We are encouraging other members of the international community to do likewise and we strongly endorse the Communiqué of 3 April from the International Contact Group on Somalia, of which the UK is member. The Communiqué emphasises the paramount importance of establishing an inclusive and genuine political process reaching out to all parts of Somali society.

(HC Deb 10 May 2007 Vol 460 c398W)

5/4
Cyprus
An FCO Minister wrote:

The Government are not able to prevent property development in northern Cyprus. We believe that the difficult and complex issue of property is only likely to be fully resolved in the context of a comprehensive settlement. In our contacts with the Turkish Cypriot leadership, we recognise the Turkish Cypriots' need for economic development in support of reunification. But we urge them to ensure that any property development that does take place does so in a manner that is both environmentally sustainable and does not complicate an eventual solution.

Similarly, we call on the Turkish Cypriot administration to show sensitivity to Greek Cypriot churches and cemeteries in the north. Our high commissioner in Nicosia visited the Karpas region on 22 June and raised such issues with his Turkish Cypriot interlocutors.

The 8 July 2006 agreement between the leaders of the two communities presented an opportunity to make progress towards a resumption of full settlement negotiations. Despite attempts since by the UN to implement this agreement no real progress has been made. We continue to urge both sides to show the political will and flexibility required to bridge the gap between words and deeds, and engage constructively with the efforts of the UN. Negotiations on a final political solution have been at an impasse for too long.

We consider that confidence-building measures, such as the opening of Ledra Street, and other crossing points, would help bring the two communities closer together. This message was reinforced in the resolution adopted by the UN Security Council on Cyprus on 15 June [Resolution 1758, Ed.]. The Security

Council's resolution also expressed concern about the diminishing opportunities for bicommunal activity within Cyprus. As such, we hope that the announcement by the Republic of Cyprus of a package of measures to address this will promote reconciliation between the communities.

(HC Deb 25 June 2007 Vol 462 c209W)

Part Five: I.A.3. *Subjects of international law—states—status and powers—domestic jurisdiction*

5/5
Somalia
The Foreign Secretary was asked what assessment she had made of the extent of the presence of al-Qaeda in Somalia. An FCO Minister wrote:

Al-Qaeda seeks to exploit ungoverned space to advance its terrorist agenda. Therefore, we are working with the international community to re-build the Somali State, through the establishment of Transitional Federal Institutions, in order to bring peace and stability to the country. This will make it more difficult for al-Qaeda to operate in Somalia.

In the meantime, we continue to work with the Transitional Federal Government of Somalia, and our international allies, in tackling the threat posed by al-Qaeda from Somalia.

(HC Deb 16 April 2007 Vol 459 c48W)

5/6
The Foreign Secretary was asked what steps she was taking to seek a ceasefire by Islamic insurgents in Somalia. An FCO Minister wrote:

The UK does not have contact with the Islamist insurgents in Somalia, but we have called for an immediate end to all fighting and publicly urged all parties to commit to a truce and agree a lasting ceasefire.

We have repeatedly made clear that all parties in Somalia need to reject violence and allow the Transitional Federal Government (TFG) to do their job. Any differences that some groups in Mogadishu might have with the TFG should be pursued through the National Reconciliation Congress and dialogue with the TFG rather than by resorting to violence. We condemn any attacks on the TFG, which is the only legitimate route through which governance, peace and stability can be restored to Somalia. At the same time, we have repeatedly made clear to the TFG that they must make genuine attempts to reach out to all groups in Somalia that credibly reject violence.

(HC Deb 2 May 2007 Vol 459 c1717W)

5/7

Democracy

(See also **6/47**)

The Foreign Secretary was asked what (a) her Department's and (b) EU policy was on funding non-governmental organisations in other democratic countries which campaign actively against those countries' Governments' policies. An FCO Minister wrote:

The Foreign and Commonwealth Office (FCO) is committed to promoting democratic values and principles, including a vibrant civil society.

We recognise the vital role civil society plays in promoting human rights, democracy and good governance. We value the expertise which many non-governmental organisations (NGOs) working to implement human rights possess and therefore work with them to encourage governments, including democratic ones, to meet international human rights standards.

The FCO has a range of programme funds which aim to support its work on human rights. The merits of all funding requests are considered on a case by case basis. Further information can be found on the FCO website at:

www.fco.gov.uk/servlet/Front?pagename=OpenMarket/Xcelerate/ShowPage&c =Page&cid=1007029394988.

The EU has a human rights and democracy programme, the European Instrument for Democracy and Human Rights (EIDHR). NGOs are eligible to bid for project funding. Information on the activities and actions of EIDHR is accessible at: http://ec.europa.eu/europeaid/projects/eidhr/index_en.htm.

(HC Deb 16 May 2007 Vol 460 c779W)

Part Five: I.A.4. *Subjects of international law—states—status and powers—non-intervention in domestic jurisdiction*

5/8

Northern Ireland

The Secretary of State for Northern Ireland made the following Ministerial Statement:

Following the successful restoration of devolution in Northern Ireland, I am pleased to enter into an intergovernmental agreement with Ireland.

This treaty reaffirms both Governments' commitment to protect, support and where appropriate implement the provisions of the Belfast agreement, subject to the alterations to the operation of the institutions agreed at St. Andrews. The conditions laid out in legislation for the restoration of the devolved institutions in Northern Ireland have now been met. In this historic context, it is fitting that these commitments are formalised promptly with the Irish Government and the

Government welcome this opportunity to provide a shared understanding of these arrangements across these islands.

This agreement was laid before Parliament as a Command Paper (Cm 7078) on Wednesday 18 April. The tenets of this agreement have been considered by Parliament during the passage of the Northern Ireland (St. Andrews Agreement) Act 2006 and, following the successful restoration of devolution to Northern Ireland on 8 May, the Government consider it appropriate to truncate the standard 21-day laying period under the Ponsonby rule to ensure the agreement can be brought into force as soon as possible. This will provide swift formal clarity to the agreed alterations to the arrangements and institutions established by the Belfast agreement of 1998.

(HC Deb 9 May 2007 Vol 460 c14WS)

5/9
Estonia
(See also **7/4**)
The Foreign Secretary was asked what reports she had received of Russia's action in relation to Estonia since the relocation of the Russian war memorial statue; and what representation she had made to the Russian authorities on this subject. An FCO Minister wrote:

The Government recognise the right of the Estonian Government to relocate war memorials and war graves and see this as an internal matter for Estonia. The Foreign Secretary was briefed on Estonian-Russian relations by Estonian Foreign Minister Urmas Paet at the EU General Affairs and External Relations Council on 14 May. Russian-Estonian relations were discussed at the EU-Russia Summit on 18 May.

The Government support the remarks made by the President of the EU Commission, Jose Manuel Barroso, at the EU-Russia summit that the EU is based on principles of solidarity and difficulties for one member state constitute a difficulty for the entire EU. We are fully supportive of both the EU presidency statement of 2 May and the NATO statement of 3 May, which both expressed grave concern over the safety of the Estonian Embassy and its staff in Russia and urged Russia to address the dispute through dialogue.

(HC Deb 24 May 2007 Vol 460 c1488W)

5/10
The EU had earlier issued the following statement:

The Presidency of the European Union is gravely concerned about current developments in relations between Estonia, a Member State of the European Union, and the Russian Federation. At the present time the situation of the Estonian Embassy in Moscow gives cause for concern. The Presidency of the European Union strongly urges the Russian Federation to comply with its international obligations under the Vienna Convention on Diplomatic Relations and protect the staff and premises of the Estonian mission and ensure unimpeded access to it.

In talks with all parties the Presidency is endeavouring to help de-escalate the situation.

Given the emotionally charged atmosphere surrounding the Soviet war graves in Estonia, it would be advisable to have a dispassionate dialogue on the matter. The Presidency of the European Union strongly urges that the problems that have arisen should be addressed in a spirit of understanding and mutual respect.

(CFSP Statements, 2 May 2007, www.eu2007.de)

5/11
[NATO had earlier issued the following statement:

NATO is deeply concerned by threats to the physical safety of Estonian diplomatic staff, including the Ambassador, in Moscow, as well as intimidation at the Estonian Embassy. These actions are unacceptable, and must be stopped immediately; tensions over the Soviet war memorial and graves in Estonia must be resolved diplomatically between the two countries. NATO urges the Russian authorities to implement their obligations under the Vienna Convention on diplomatic relations.

(Press release (2007)044, 3 May 2007, www.nato.int), Ed]

Part Five: I.B.1. *Subjects of international law—states—recognition of States*

5/12
Bosnia and Herzegovina
An FCO Minister said:

The UK recognised Bosnia and Herzegovina (BiH) as an independent state in 1992. BiH's constitutional arrangements and internal boundaries are those set out in the Dayton Accords which were concluded in Paris on 14 December 1995.

We remain firm in our support for the Dayton Accords: they are the basis of the peace and stability that BiH now enjoys. We regularly make this clear, both bilaterally and in multilateral fora. If the people of BiH wish to revisit their constitutional arrangements, this must be through a consensual process in accordance with constitutional procedures.

(HC Deb 18 July 2007 Vol 694 cWA24)

5/13 (See also **5/27–28**)
Cyprus
The Government were asked whether the United Kingdom was meeting its obligations as a signatory of the 1960 Treaty of Guarantee about Cyprus. An FCO Minister wrote:

As a guarantor power, an EU partner, and UN Security Council member, the UK continues to work for progress towards a comprehensive settlement in

Cyprus which would be of benefit to all Cypriots. We continue to support the EU initiatives aimed at ending the isolation described in the reply I gave to the noble Lord on 4 December 2006 (Official Report, cols. WA92–93). Our efforts in support of a settlement and those in pursuit of lifting the isolation of the Turkish Cypriots are mutually reinforcing.

(HL Deb 31 January 2007 Vol 689 c49WA)

5/14
An FCO Minister wrote:

The economic situation of ordinary Turkish Cypriots has improved significantly over the past five years. However, as the World Bank report on north Cyprus recognises, the economy of north Cyprus remains underdeveloped, with only very limited opportunities to trade with the outside world. This lack of legitimate economic outlets encourages an unhealthy focus on uncontrolled construction, much of it on Greek Cypriot property, and closer integration with the Turkish economy. We therefore support the German presidency's efforts with all concerned to enable preferential trade between north Cyprus and the EU. This will facilitate a settlement by promoting convergence of living standards on the island and by bringing the Turkish Cypriots closer to the EU

(HL Deb 31 January 2007 Vol 689 c50WA)

5/15
An FCO Minister wrote:

The UK recognises the Republic of Cyprus as the sole state foreseen in the 1960 constitution. The "Turkish Republic of Northern Cyprus" (TRNC), established by a "unilateral declaration of independence" in 1983, is not recognised by the UK (or by any other state apart from Turkey). Following the "unilateral declaration of independence" the then Foreign Secretary... made the following statement in another place: "Her Majesty's Government deplore this action by the Turkish Cypriot community, which amounts to a declaration of secession. We have issued a statement which makes it clear that this is incompatible with the 1960 treaties. Our position has always been that we recognise only one Republic of Cyprus. That remains the position today". The UK policy on recognition of the TRNC has remained unaltered since 1983.

The Government continue to support the EU initiatives aimed at ending the isolation of the Turkish Cypriots... In particular, the Government support efforts to bring the Turkish Cypriot community closer to Europe through, for example, financial aid and trade liberalisation.

The continued division of Cyprus has an impact on the ability of Cypriots from both communities to enjoy the full range of freedoms and rights. The recent United Nations report from the Office of the High Commissioner for Human Rights on the question of human rights in Cyprus (available at: www.ohchr.orb/english/countries/cy) highlights a number of ongoing concerns. However, as that report concludes, the situation of human rights in Cyprus would be greatly improved by the achievement of a comprehensive settlement to the Cyprus problem. It is on this that the UK will continue to focus its efforts.

(HL Deb 25 July 2007 Vol 694 cWA90)

5/16
Serbia, Montenegro
The FCO issued the following Note:

INFORMATION NOTE ON THE STATUS OF SERBIA AND MONTENEGRO

DECLARATION OF INDEPENDENCE
AND UK RECOGNITION

On 3 June 2006 the Republic of Montenegro formally declared independence from the State Union of Serbia and Montenegro. This followed a referendum on the 21 May 2006. The UK has formally recognised Montenegro as an independent sovereign state on 13 June 2006, and proposed the establishment of diplomatic relations between the UK and Montenegro.

On 5 June 2006 the Serbian National Assembly decreed that Serbia is the continuing international personality of the State Union of Serbia and Montenegro and fully succeeds to its legal status. The UK accepts this. Serbia will thus remain a party to international agreements to which Serbia & Montenegro was a party and a member of international organisations of which Serbia & Montenegro was a member.

The two new independent republics will be known as:

The Republic of Serbia

The Republic of Montenegro

LEGAL OBLIGATIONS OF MONTENEGRO

In a letter from the Montenegrin Foreign Minister to the Foreign Secretary on 4 June, the Government of Montenegro stated that it would remain faithful to all international obligations formerly incumbent on the State Union of Serbia and Montenegro. Letters from Prime Minister Blair to Prime Minister Djukanovic and President Vujanovic of Montenegro confirmed that the UK regards treaties and agreements in force to which the UK and the State Union of Serbia and Montenegro were parties as remaining in force between the UK and the Republic of Montenegro. In slower time we aim to confirm exactly which treaties continue to be applicable and reach a mutually agreed schedule of treaties in force between the UK and Republic of Montenegro. We will circulate a list of existing treaties to Government Departments, who may wish to consult their legal advisers to decide if treaties relevant to them should remain in force. This list of treaties will then need to be verified by the Government of Montenegro, before a formal exchange can take place.

(Supplied by FCO)

5/17
(See also **5/18–20**)
Kosovo
In a debate, an FCO Minister was asked if the position of the UK Government was exactly the same in relation to the timing of any new UN resolution coming forward or not. The Minister said:

Yes. We want to see a UN resolution come forward, and we want to see it sooner rather than later...We are determined that the time has come for the Security Council to make this decision and we will discuss that with Russia, which is an extremely important player...

We can either bring the process to completion or consign it to the "too difficult" tray...it would be a very risky move. It would remind me too much of the mistakes that were made early on, when Yugoslavia broke up. The latter course carries real risks for the stability of the region. The situation will not stand still. The lesson from the 1990s in the Balkans is that drift leads to instability. The choice is to tackle Kosovo in a smooth and orderly way on the basis of a UN process endorsed by the Security Council, or to find ourselves reacting to future events in a way that could involve far greater challenges.

What of Serbia in all this? It is important to say something about it. I want to be clear that bringing the Kosovo status process through to completion is not and should not be seen as punishing Serbia. We understand the strong emotions that this issue can arouse, but this process is about putting in place the right outcome—the only realistic outcome from our point of view—for Kosovo. I want to see both countries and both Kosovo Serb and Kosovo Albanian communities prospering and moving forward towards EU and NATO membership, if that is what they want.

There has been some progress by Serbia in recent weeks. The chief prosecutor for the International Criminal Tribunal for the former Yugoslavia told the UN Security Council on 18 June that the Serb authorities had

"expressed a clear commitment to provide all necessary assistance to locate and arrest the remaining fugitives".

That has started to deliver results, with the arrest of two fugitive indictees in recent weeks...

[The debate was terminated, Ed.]
(HC Deb 27 June 2007 Vol 462 cs448–452)

5/18
An FCO Minister was asked by the FAC about the recognition of an independent Kosovo. He said:

Your general point that it is not for the UN initially to recognise is, of course, accurate...The issue of recognition is a matter for other sovereign states, as is their approach to any potential declaration by Kosovo. (Q.143)

I have to make it clear to the Committee that in our view Kosovo is destined to be an independent sovereign state. (Q.144)

But, it was put to him:

Resolution 1244 also gives the mandate to the police and the soldiers. It has either to be rescinded or it will endure...It either has to be repealed or altered by resolution of the Security Council. If it does not, it goes on.

The Minister said:

What is clear is that whatever scenario we end up with, in terms of Kosovan independence, there needs to be international authorities on the ground with legal cover. [Q.149]

And, asked about other contested situations in Europe and the impact of the Helsinki Final Act on their resolution, the Minister said:

In terms of precedent, I know that this Committee has looked at these important issues of the frozen conflicts, not least Transnistria, Abkhazia and others, and will rightly continue to do so. However, we do not believe that the process in which we are now engaged in Kosovo establishes a precedent in the way that you are alluding to, in the way that the Russians have said publicly. We do not believe that. [Qs.150, 151]

(FAC Second Report, Global Security: Russia, HC 51(2007))

5/19
The Foreign Secretary wrote:

On 7 December, representatives of the Contact Group submitted to the UN Secretary-General the report by the EU-Russia-US troika on their work aimed at achieving a negotiated settlement for Kosovo's future status.

The troika correctly set themselves the objective of "leaving no stone unturned" in the search for an outcome mutually acceptable to both Belgrade and Pristina. During the four months of their mandate, the troika undertook an intense schedule of meetings with the parties. Over ten rounds of negotiations—including six sets of direct talks, one of them in extended conference format—the parties considered options covering the spectrum from independence, autonomy, confederation, partition and a status-neutral approach. One or other of the parties rejected all these options.

The troika have therefore reported that the parties have been unable to reach an agreement on Kosovo's status.

I pay tribute to the troika's work. They have worked tirelessly and imaginatively. Although they did not secure an agreement between the parties, their work generated sustained and intensive high-level dialogue between Belgrade and Pristina. The troika have also been able to extract important commitments from the parties, including pledges to refrain from actions that might jeopardise the security situation in Kosovo or elsewhere and not to use violence, threats or intimidation. These are important commitments to which we shall expect both sides to adhere strictly in the period ahead.

The troika's efforts followed those of UN Special Envoy Ahtisaari who laboured heroically for 14 months to reach agreement between the parties before concluding that this was out of reach. He therefore drew up his own proposal for how to move forward based around the concept of supervised independence. That recommendation was supported by the EU, US and UN Secretary-General. It was rejected by Serbia and Russia.

It is hard to argue now that there is any value in further negotiations or that serious options have yet to be fully explored. The failure to reach agreement is not because of lack of time, energy or imagination on the part of the international community. It is because the positions of the parties are irreconcilable. Kosovo insists on independence. Serbia insists on a settlement that locks the door on any prospect of independence. The UK shares the firm view of the EU representative on the troika, Ambassador Wolfgang Ischinger, that the parties would not be capable of reaching agreement on this issue if negotiations were to be continued, whether in the troika format, or in some other form.

The Kosovo status process has now reached a decisive moment, presenting the international community with difficult but important decisions.

One point on which almost all in the international community are agreed is that the status quo is unsustainable. This was stated in clear terms by the UN Secretary-General when he addressed the Contact Group Ministerial meeting in September in New York. The Contact Group, including Russia, subsequently expressed their agreement in a joint Ministerial statement.

The international community cannot therefore allow the status process to grind to a halt or to be shuffled off into a siding by convening further fruitless negotiations. We learned to our cost in the 1990s the heavy human and political price attached to an indecisive international response to looming problems in the Western Balkans. The stability and security of part of Europe is at stake. It is essential that we respond in a decisive and far-sighted manner.

The UK's preference would be for a settlement to be supported by the passage of a resolution of the UN Security Council. We believe there should be further rapid consultations in New York to this end before the end of 2007. However in the absence of agreement between the parties, we need to be realistic about the slim prospects of securing the necessary level of consensus in the Security Council.

Against this background it is important that the EU demonstrates its readiness to meet its responsibilities and objectives in respect of stability and security in Europe. Securing a viable and sustainable future for Kosovo is a major responsibility for the EU. The effectiveness and cohesiveness of the EU's common foreign and security policy will be judged against our ability to deliver on this responsibility. The EU must demonstrate firm resolve to bring the status process through to completion and play a leading role subsequently in implementing a settlement. I welcome the fact that the EU is already intensively engaged in the necessary preparations to meet these responsibilities.

In moving towards a Kosovo settlement, it will be necessary for the EU and others to take a strategic approach answering to a series of key challenges. There will be a need to ensure Kosovo's security. The North Atlantic Treaty Organisation is already deployed in strength in Kosovo to maintain a safe and secure environment. The EU has indicated a readiness to provide a European Security and Defence Policy policing/rule of law mission. The EU should deliver on this commitment.

There will be a need to ensure good governance in Kosovo. The proposal of the UN Special Envoy provides a good basis for this. The provisions it set out for the internal governance of Kosovo, and the allocation of responsibilities it contains, must be the foundation for how we deliver security and help Kosovo improve its ability to meet European standards. The EU should be ready to play a major part in settlement implementation including through the appointment of an EU Special Representative and through contributing to an International Civilian Office in Kosovo.

There will be a need to achieve certainty and permanence in respect of Kosovo's future status. Again, the UK believes that the proposal of the UN Special Envoy for supervised independence provides a good basis.

There will be a need to look beyond the immediate challenge of resolving Kosovo's future status. Following a settlement, Kosovo will face formidable economic and state-building challenges. The international community—with the EU to the fore—will need to be ready to meet this challenge, including through the swift convening of a donors' conference.

Finally, there will be a need to address the regional dimension. The UK recognises that moving through this phase will be difficult for Serbia, as well as for other countries in the region. The EU must be clear and far-sighted in its commitment to helping them meet European standards and so move farther towards eventual accession. There is a compelling strategic case for enlargement to the Western Balkans so that this troubled region can share in the security, stability and prosperity that the EU offers. The EU needs to take forward this agenda vigorously in the months ahead.

(HC Deb Vol 467 c28WS–30WS)

5/20

The Foreign Secretary was asked by the FAC:

Are you confident that there is an adequate legal basis for implementation of the Ahtisaari plan [for Kosovo] within Security Council resolution 1244 without a new successor resolution?

He said:

In short, yes, but as I said in my written ministerial statement yesterday [(above)] we want to go to the UN. The last four months of dialogue and mediation have taken place in good faith. We have urged all sides—I have done so personally when meeting them-to engage properly to try to bridge the gap between the sides, but as Ahtisaari found, the troika team have also found it impossible to bridge the gap. We think that it is right to go back to the UN, but we think that there is a full force in resolution 1244—NATO Foreign Ministers agreed that last Friday, so NATO forces will stay there—and I think that it provides a sound legal base for the future. [Q.605]

He was asked further:

Would that include the European Union civilian presence there with regard to assistance to the judicial and police authorities? Can that continue without a Security Council resolution?

He said:

There is a Security Council resolution-1244. It provides the foundation for the European Security and Defence Policy mission as well as the KFOR mission. [Q.606]

He was asked:

Will that view be shared by all your fellow [EU, Ed.] Foreign Ministers at the discussions tomorrow?

He said:

Strikingly large numbers of EU Foreign Ministers have looked carefully at the legal text, and it is much less of an issue between us than before. I do not want to say "all", but a vast majority now accept 1244 as a sound legal basis. [Q.607]

And then he was asked:

... it is still possible, is it not, that several EU countries will decide for their own domestic or other reasons that they will not support the implementation of an Ahtisaari plan without the Security Council resolution?

He replied:

There are two issues. One is going along with an Ahtisaari plan, and the second is recognising a newly independent country. Different European countries take different views on those two issues. I am not sure whether any European countries will hold out against the use of 1244 as the basis for European action...

I think that there will be some that do not recognise an independent Kosovo in the first wave; I do not know whether there are countries that will say that they will never do so. [Qs.608, 609]

He was then asked:

... as we know, the writ of the Kosovo Government does not run in the Serbian northern area of the country. In effect, to recognise Kosovo as an independent state on its present boundaries is basically to endorse a Cyprus-type situation. Do you rule out the possibility of partition as a solution?

He said:

Yes. Partition has floated around in discussions during the past two years. It certainly does not have our support, and it has very few supporters elsewhere. People often ask whether an independent Kosovo can make a go of it as a viable country. If that question is asked of Kosovo, it applies in spades to the north of the country around Mitrovica. I do not think that partition offers a way forward. The truth is that the Ahtisaari plan has significant devolved authority for that northern part of Kosovo, rightly, and it is important that the minority rights there are respected, although, as I said in the House yesterday, there are Serb minorities elsewhere in Kosovo and not just in the north. [Q.610]

The Foreign Secretary was asked:

What is your present assessment as to what the repercussions would be in Kosovo at the moment, and indeed in Serbia, if there is effectively a unilateral declaration of independence by the Kosovan Government?

He replied:

I think that the best answer is that it depends. If it was unilateral in the sense of being chaotic and unconnected to the international community's response, I think that there would be dangers. If it is carefully done, in a way that recognises and lives by the guarantees that have been made by the Kosovan Government and the Serbian Government to the international authorities with regard to preventing violence, and if it also respects the Ahtisaari plan with regard to minorities, there is a reasonable chance of moving forward, not in a way that everyone would like, but in a way that would preserve the basics of a respect for life and security on all sides. [Q.611]

He was asked about holding out to Serbia the prospect of membership of the EU. He said:

...the more that we can all keep making the point, within our different contexts, that this process is not about punishing Serbia but about finding a sustainable way for Serbia to live in the wider region, with its "European vocation", which the Serbian Foreign Minister often talks about, the better. [Q.612]

It was put to the Foreign Secretary that Serbia

...will [not] contemplate anything that takes the Kosovo province away from them... They now believe that, legally and properly, Kosovo is part of Serbia. I think that there is absolutely no chance of the Russians ever agreeing to anything that the Serbians do not want. What I seek from you today, Foreign Secretary, is a commitment that Britain will not join again with America and invade, taking part in something that may have nothing to do with us at all, unless there is a clear, concise, agreed mandate from the UN and that the "enforcement" of the separation of Kosovo from Serbia would be different from anything troops already there were intended to do. [Qs.613, 614]

He said:

The "enforcement" is a separate issue. It is up to individual countries to recognise other countries. It will be for every country to make a decision about whether or not it wants to recognise a putative Kosovan state. I think that resolution 1244 set out a political process that did not circumscribe the outcome. It did not prescribe one outcome or another; it left the outcome open. But it did create a political process.

I do not know if you will agree, but I think that it is important that the UN Secretary-General came to a Contact Group meeting in New York that I chaired in September. He started off by saying that the status quo is unsustainable. That is a very, very important point. It is unsustainable politically, because you have a UN protectorate within a sovereign country; it is unsustainable economically, because no one is investing in Kosovo because they do not know the political status, and it is unsustainable socially, because you have this limbo. You may be right that it is a situation that none of us would have chosen to be in, and certainly no one wanted the tragedies of the 1990s to happen, but we have to deal with the situation as it now.

Just so that we are clear, the mandate of the NATO forces is to prevent violence against people. That is what they are there for. They are there to protect human life. [Qs.613–615]

(FAC, Foreign Policy Aspects of the Lisbon Treaty, HC120-I (2007))

Part Five: I.B.2. *Subjects of international law—states—recognition of governments*

5/21
Fiji
An FCO Minister wrote:

On 5 December 2006 we issued a press statement condemning the military coup in Fiji and calling for a return to democracy as quickly as possible. A full copy of the statement can be found on the Foreign and Commonwealth Office website at:
www.fco.gov.uk/servlet/Front?pagename=OpenMarket/Xcelerate/ShowPage&c=Page&cid=1007029391638&a=KArticle&aid=1163678514483

On 29 December 2006 we issued a further statement following reports of human rights abuses committed by the Republic of Fiji Military Forces (RFMF), urging the RFMF to respect their citizens' human rights and reiterating a call for a return to democracy.

We have made no representations for elections to be held, but have urged the military, and the interim government, to return to democracy as quickly as possible.

We continue to discuss the situation in Fiji with our high commissions in Suva, Canberra and Wellington on a regular basis. We are also liaising closely with our EU partners and the Governments of Australia, New Zealand and the US in support of efforts to bring about a restoration of democracy and constitutional government in Fiji.

(HC Deb 15 January 2007 Vol 455 c824W)

5/22
Palestine
In its reply to the FAC Report, Global Security: the Middle East, The Government wrote:

17. The Government viewed the issue of a National Unity Government as an internal matter for the Palestinian people. But we, along with our international partners, made clear—starting from 30 January 2006—that we would be ready to engage with any new government that was based on the Quartet principles.

(Eighth Report of the Foreign Affairs Committee Session 2006–7 Global Security: The Middle East Response of the Secretary of State for Foreign and Commonwealth Affairs Cm 7212)

5/23
Somalia
An FCO Minister wrote:

We are concerned about the conflict in Somalia. With our international partners we are working actively to promote a peaceful resolution to Somalia's difficulties on the basis of a sustainable peace process.

We have frequent bilateral contacts with the Transitional Federal Government of Somalia and countries in the region including Ethiopia. We are working closely with EU partners and in the UN Security Council to achieve peace and stability in Somalia.

We urge rapid implementation of the UN Security Council Resolution 1725, adopted unanimously on 6 December 2006, which authorises the Intergovernmental Authority on Development and the African Union to establish a protection and training mission in Somalia. In this regard, we look forward to Ethiopia withdrawing its troops from Somalia as quickly as it can, as it has stated it wants to.

We are also encouraging all parties inside and outside Somalia to use the current opportunity to embed a political process across Somalia as envisaged in the Transitional Federal Charter. We will support the Transitional Federal Institutions and Transitional Federal Government in pursuing this.

(HC Deb 8 January 2007 Vol 455 c361W)

5/24
The Foreign Secretary was asked what recent assessment she had made of the (a) political and (b) security situation in Somalia. She wrote:

After years of lawlessness and little effective government, a historic opportunity now exists for a sustainable political solution to Somalia's difficulties. We fully support the Transitional Federal Institutions in their efforts to find a lasting and inclusive political settlement and to become an effective governing authority. The Transitional Federal Charter sets out a roadmap for constitutional process and transition to a democratically elected Government. This is the framework within which the Transitional Government should pursue a political process in Mogadishu.

The security situation is still confused and volatile. At the moment no British officials can travel to Somalia. But we hope the Transitional Federal Government and the Transitional Federal Institutions will be able to move from Baidoa to Mogadishu shortly. We are working with Somalia's Transitional Federal Institutions, and our international partners, to help stabilise Somalia through the early deployment of a regional security force, restore governance through an inclusive political process, and rebuild Somalia through increased international assistance.

(HC Deb 18 January 2007 Vol 455 c1334W)

5/25
The Foreign Secretary was asked if she would make a statement on the visit of the President of the Transitional Federal Republic of Somalia to the UK on 21 to 22 February. She wrote:

President Yusuf of the Transitional Federal Republic of Somalia visited the UK as a guest of the Government. His programme included calls on the Secretary of State for International Development and the Parliamentary Under-Secretary of State for Foreign and Commonwealth Affairs. He also called on the Foreign Affairs Committee and spoke at Chatham House.

Asked further what discussions the Minister for Africa had had on the independence of Somaliland from Somalia when she met the President of the Transitional Federal Republic of Somalia on 22 February, she wrote:

The independence of Somaliland was not discussed in any detail when President Yusuf of the Transitional Federal Republic of Somalia met the Parliamentary Under-Secretary of State for Foreign and Commonwealth Affairs on 22 February. We continue to encourage the Transitional Federal Government and institutions to discuss with the Somaliland authorities all issues of mutual interest.

(HC Deb 7 March 2007 Vol 459 c2002W)

Part Five: I.B.4(a). *Subjects of international law—states—recognition— acts of recognition—implied/express*

5/26
Diplomatic relations with Transnistria area
The Government were asked:

Does the FCO have any diplomatic relations with the area known as Transnistria near to Moldova? And if so what level of communication does the FCO have with the authorities in Transnistria and since the 1st of January 2005 how many times have FCO staff travelled to Transnistria and for what purposes.

An FCO representative said:

Her Majesty's Government does not have any diplomatic relations with Transnistria. Staff from our Embassy in Chisinau do visit the Transnistrian region. However, our Embassy does not keep a record of these visits.

Our Embassy does have very limited contact with the so-called Transnistrian authorities. This contact is part of wider EU efforts to contribute to a peaceful settlement of the Transnistria conflict. In his capacity as local EU Presidency, our Ambassador in Chisinau has accompanied the EU's Special Representative (EUSR) for Moldova to two meetings with the so-called 'Transnistrian Foreign Ministry' this year (in April and July). These meetings were part of the EUSR's efforts to establish and maintain contacts with the relevant actors in the Transnistrian settlement process, in accordance with his mandate. Our Ambassador also travelled to Transnistria on 23 September, this time accompanying the EUSR's political adviser.

He was then asked what was the current FCO policy towards Transnistria on arms exports and arms control measures.

He said:

The FCO does not have specific arms export or arms control measures for Transnistria. However, we do have security concerns about alleged trafficking of arms from the region. For this reason the FCO fully supports the EU's decision to respond positively to the joint Moldovan-Ukrainian request for assistance in enhancing the effectiveness of border and customs control and border surveillance activities on the Moldova-Ukraine border, in particular the Transnistria segment.

(Text supplied by FCO)

Part Five: I.B.6 *Subjects of international law—states—recognition—acts of recognition—non-recognition and its effects*

5/27
Northern Cyprus
(See also **5/13–15**)
A note by the FCO to the FAC said:

So far as entry to the UK is concerned, Official Home Office guidance states that "The "Turkish Republic of Northern Cyprus" (TRNC) is not recognised as a state by the United Kingdom Government and its passports must not, therefore, be endorsed by immigration officers. Holders of such documents should not be refused entry. Leave to enter, if granted, should be endorsed on another document, eg. a Declaration of Identity for Visa Purposes (also known as a GV3). If the person otherwise qualifies for entry, leave to enter should be given by endorsing that document.

(FAC Report, Visit to Turkey and Cyprus, HC 473 (2007), p.16 fn3)

5/28

The Government were asked what were the legal obstacles to direct flights to the Turkish Republic of Northern Cyprus that cannot be overcome without the co-operation of the Greek Cypriot Administration in the south of the island; what was the legal authority for this opinion; and whether the human rights of Turkish Cypriots had been considered. An FCO Minister wrote:

The simplest way of enabling direct flights would be a decision by the Republic of Cyprus to designate Ercan as an international airport under the terms of the Chicago Convention on International Civil Aviation. In the absence of such a decision there are legal obstacles. The Government do not intend to pursue a policy which would be in contravention of international law. An application for a licence is under consideration by the Department for Transport and it would be inappropriate to comment further at this stage.

The UK and its EU partners remain committed to lifting the economic isolation of the Turkish Cypriots through targeted financial aid and trade liberalisation.

And further, whether there were any embargos between other nations or traditions in the European Union comparable to that of the Turkish Republic of Northern Cyprus and the Greek Cypriot Administration on direct flights to the former.

The Minister wrote further:

The status of the divided island of Cyprus is unique within the EU and as such creates an unparalleled situation with regard to direct flights. There are no direct flights between Northern Cyprus and any EU member states. The Government fully support the work of the EU towards lifting the isolation of the Turkish Cypriots. We welcome the ongoing implementation of the financial aid regulation and support further progress on trade liberalisation. However, a full solution to the difficulties faced by the Turkish Cypriots can be achieved only through a comprehensive settlement facilitated by the UN. We would echo the call of the UN Secretary-General in his latest report to the Security Council, as well as the statement of the Finnish EU presidency on 11 December, in urging the two communities to engage in discussions under UN auspices to achieve a resumption of negotiations for a comprehensive settlement as early as possible in 2007.

(HL Deb 8 January 2007 Vol 688 cWA18)

5/29

Taiwan

An FCO Minister wrote:

The UK does not recognise Taiwan as a state or country, nor its authorities as a government.

(HC Deb 24 July 2007 Vol 463 c1060W)

Part Five: I.D.5(a)(iii). *Subjects of international law—states—formation, continuity, extinction and succession of states—succession—situations of state succession—separation*

5/30

Montenegro

Note-

In a letter addressed to the Foreign Secretary, dated 04 June 2006, the Minister of Foreign Affairs of the Republic of Montenegro wrote:

The Republic of Montenegro shall observe all principles of international law and all treaties and provisions of international agreements signed by the state union of Serbia and Montenegro.

In a letter addressed to the Montenegrin Foreign Minister Mr Vlahovic dated 13 June 2006, the Foreign Secretary wrote:

I note that the Government of Montenegro has stated that it will remain faithful to all international obligations formerly incumbent on the State Union of Serbia and Montenegro, and I can confirm that we regard treaties and agreements in force to which the United Kingdom and the State Union of Serbia and Montenegro were parties as remaining in force between the United Kingdom and the Republic of Montenegro.

(i) Convention for the Amelioration of the Condition of the Wounded and Sick in Armed Forces in the Field Geneva 12 Aug., 1949 039/1958 Cmnd 550

(ii) Convention for the Amelioration of the Condition of Wounded, Sick and Shipwrecked Members of Armed Forces at Sea Geneva 12 Aug., 1949 039/1958 Cmnd 550

(iii) Geneva Convention Relative to the Treatment of Prisoners of War Geneva 12 Aug., 1949 039/1958 Cmnd 550

(iv) Convention relative to the Protection of Civilians in Time of War Geneva 12 Aug., 1949 039/1958 Cmnd 550

(v) Protocol Additional to the Geneva Conventions of 12 Aug., 1949, and relating to the Protection of Victims of International Armed Conflicts (Protocol I) Geneva 08 June, 1977 029/1999 Cm 4338

(vi) Protocol Additional to the Geneva Conventions of 12 Aug., 1949, and relating to the Protection of Victims of Non-International Armed Conflicts (Protocol II) Geneva 08 June, 1977 030/1999 Cm 4339.

(Treaty Series No. 34 (2006) Fourth Supplementary List of Ratifications, Accessions, Withdrawals, etc., for 2006 Cm 7159)

5/31

The Treasury was asked what continuing financial commitments the UK has towards countries which gained independence from the British Empire. A Minister wrote:

Upon independence from the UK, financial (and all other) responsibility passed to the independent country's government.

(HC Deb 9 July 2007 Vol 462 c1226W)

Part Five: I.E. *Subjects of international law—states—self-determination*

5/32
Papua
An FCO Minister said:

[I] must start with a clear statement that the UK does not support independence for Papua. Like the vast majority of other international players, we respect Indonesia's territorial integrity and have never supported Papuan independence...

The best way to resolve the complex issues in Papua is through promoting peaceful dialogue between Papuan groups and the Indonesian Government. Meaningful dialogue with the Government of Indonesia cannot take place on the basis of preconditions of Papuan independence. President Yudhoyono has said that he is committed to a just, comprehensive and dignified solution, including through consistent implementation of special autonomy. We welcome this important objective, and encourage him to press ahead with it. The special autonomy legislation is enshrined in Indonesian law, and was supported by Papuan groups and the international community. Full implementation of the legislation will lay the groundwork for a sustainable resolution to the internal differences and the long-term stability of the province. The UK is of course also committed to improving the well-being and political participation of Papuan people, as well as encouraging freedom of expression throughout Indonesia...

[P]rogress [on autonomy] is being made; for example, the establishment of the Papuan People's Council and the election of a provincial governor. Legislation has been, or is in the process of being, approved on the use of Papuan symbols—essentially the flag and certain anthems—the special autonomy budget, forestry issues, protection of customary rights, health and education...

I return to the Act of Free Choice [This was the referendum in Papua conducted by Indonesia in 1969 and later noted by the UN, which, the Indonesian government said, produced a unanimous result against independence, Ed.].. Although we recognise that it was extremely flawed, the UK has no plans to support a review of that Act. We believe that is a matter for the Netherlands and the UN. As the 1962 New York agreement was between the Dutch and Indonesian Governments, and the UN oversaw the 1969 Act, we have little locus to question the legality of either. The 2001 special autonomy law allows the establishment of a truth and reconciliation committee to look at the incorporation of Papua into Indonesia in the 1960s, which we believe indicates that the Indonesian Government recognise the need to address the long-standing problems in Papua...

In respect of human rights, we do indeed have an interest...We believe that the human rights situation in Papua too is improving. There is little credible information to suggest that major systematic abuses of human rights are currently taking place... The major concerns are chronic low-level harassment, freedom of expression and association, and social and economic rights—as in other areas of eastern Indonesia. Of course, we will continue to take reports of human rights violations seriously; we raise these with the Indonesian Government, together with our European partners and as part of our bilateral dialogue... Several Jakarta-based correspondents, including representatives of the BBC and the Washington Post, received permission to visit Papua in 2006, including sensitive areas in the central highlands. We welcome this increased access for journalists. We regularly encourage the Indonesian Government to permit journalists to visit Papua to promote better international understanding of conditions within the provinces.

[The cases of] Filep Karma and Yusak Pakage who were shamefully imprisoned in 2005 for flying a flag identified with the separatist struggle [were raised]. The Indonesian Government have obligations under the International Covenant on Civil and Political Rights and their own constitution to guarantee freedom of expression throughout Indonesia. We encourage the Indonesian Government to implement those obligations...

Papua is one of the wealthiest provinces in Indonesia in fiscal terms. However, most Papuans do not see the benefits of that wealth. Papua is the province with the highest level of poverty—40 per cent of Papuans live below the poverty line—and health, education and infrastructure are consistently below the national average. Much of that discrepancy can be put down to corruption, which is serious and endemic at the local government level. The UK's projects to build local government capacity, which I described earlier, aim to improve that. We welcome the fact that, at the urging of the new governor, Papua's provincial budget is now being scrutinised by the national anti-corruption commission.

...we will do everything that we can to support the implementation of the special autonomy law and the dialogue between the representatives of the Papuan people and the Indonesian Government. In the mean time, we are working to improve the economic and political situation for ordinary Papuans through targeted development assistance, the encouragement of dialogue between the Government and their representatives, and project-funding to improve human rights and local government accountability.

(HL Deb 8 January 2007 Vol 688 c101–106)

5/33
Western Sahara

A Minister said:

The UK regards the status of Western Sahara as undetermined, pending UN efforts to find a solution. To this end, the UK fully supports the efforts of the UN Secretary-General and his Personal Envoy to the Western Sahara, Peter Van Walsum, to assist the parties to achieve a just, lasting and mutually acceptable political solution, which will provide for the self-determination of the people of Western Sahara.

On 30 April the UN Security Council, chaired by the UK, adopted UN Security Council Resolution 1754, which took note of Morocco's proposal presented to the UN Secretary-General on 11 April, and called for both sides to enter into negotiations without preconditions.

The UK welcomes the first round of these talks between Morocco, the Polisario, and their neighbours, hosted by the UN on 18–19 June and the agreement by all parties to take part in a further round in August.

(HC Deb 25 June 2007 Vol 462 c222W)

5/34
Kurds
An FCO Minister said:

[the Government] have no plans to assist the development of regional autonomy for Kurds in eastern Turkey and western Iran. We respect the territorial integrity of Turkey and Iran.

...it is absolutely proper that the rights of ethnic minorities—or large ethnic minorities—should be respected. However, autonomy and self-determination are, and must be, a matter for sovereign Governments.

(HL Deb 3 July 2007 Vol 693 c899)

Part Five: II.A.1(b). *Subjects of international law—international organisations—general—status and powers—privileges and immunities of the organisation*

5/35
The Foreign Secretary was asked what reports she had received on the arrest and detention of Marios Matsakis MEP in Akrotiri Sovereign base area, Cyprus. An FCO Minister wrote:

Having already failed to attend the Sovereign base area court following two previous summonses relating to alleged acts of criminal damage on property belonging to the Ministry of Defence in the Sovereign base areas, warrants were issued for the arrest of Dr. Matsakis. He was therefore arrested at the direction of the Court on 12 April, while making a visit to the Sovereign base areas. Although he was offered the opportunity of making a modest bail payment pending court appearance, Dr. Matsakis refused and declined an offer by a colleague to pay on his behalf. He was therefore remanded in police custody. Following concern for his health Dr. Matsakis was transferred to medical facilities in the Republic of Cyprus. This resulted in his leaving the jurisdiction of the Sovereign base areas and therefore his release from custody.

(HC Deb 14 May 2007 Vol 460 c498W)

5/36
A Treasury Minister wrote:

Under UK tax law there is no such person as an "international civil servant". However, officials of the United Nations are sometimes referred to as international civil servants. There is no requirement for visiting officials to notify HM Revenue and Customs of their presence in the UK. Those who are present in the UK for a sufficient length of time to become resident in the UK will be dealt with locally. Information is not collated centrally.

The UK tax position of employees of the United Nations is set out in the United Nations and International Court of Justice (Immunities and Privileges) Order 1974. This provides immunities and privileges that are normal for international organisations. It includes among other things that officials of the UN shall be exempt from income tax on remuneration received by them from the UN. UN Officials are however subject to a form of internal tax operated by the UN, which is referred to as the Staff Assessment.

(HC Deb 17 October 2007 Vol 464 c1142W)

Part Five: II.A.2(a) *Subjects of international law—international organisations—general—participation of states and international organisations in international organisations and in their activities—admission*

5/37
The Foreign Secretary was asked if she had made an assessment of whether Scotland would automatically assume membership of the EU should it become an independent state. An FCO Minister wrote:

By virtue of the United Kingdom's EU membership, Scotland is part of the EU. If Scotland were to leave the UK, it would not automatically assume membership of the EU. The terms under which an independent Scotland might become a member of the EU would have to be negotiated.

(HC Deb 16 January 2007 Vol 455 c1003W)

Part Five: II.A.2(b) *Subjects of international law—international organisations—general—participation of states and international organisations in international organisations and in their activities—suspension, withdrawal, expulsion and deportation*

5/38
NATO
The Government were asked whether there was any procedure whereby NATO members could be expelled or suspended from the organisation

in light of their inability or unwillingness to provide troops to take part in the organisation's operation in Afghanistan. An FCO Minister wrote:

There is no mechanism for expelling or suspending a NATO member. All allies contribute troops to the NATO operation in Afghanistan and at the recent Riga summit reaffirmed their commitment to the operation's success.

(HL Deb 8 January 2007 Vol 688 cWA5)

5/39
EU
An FCO Minister wrote:

Parliament may amend or repeal any existing Act of Parliament, including the European Communities Act 1972. There is no formal procedure for withdrawal in the EU treaties, nor are there any provisions in the treaties or any other international obligations which affect the ultimate ability of the UK to withdraw from the EU. However, given that the UK has been a member of the EU for more than 25 years, and its laws and economy are intricately bound up with those of the EU, the Government would in practice have to negotiate the terms of any departure over a lengthy period.

(HL Deb 8 February 2007 Vol 689 cWA155)

5/40
Council of Europe
The Foreign Secretary was asked if she would suspend the UK's financial contribution to the Council of Europe pending review of the appropriateness of Serbia taking the Presidency of the Committee of Ministers of the Council of Europe. An FCO Minister wrote:

The Government do not believe it would be in the United Kingdom's interest to suspend its financial contribution to the Council of Europe. To do so would be in breach of our obligations under Article 39 of the Statute. Failure to fulfil our financial obligations could result in the suspension of the UK's right of representation on the Committee of Ministers and Parliamentary Assembly. A suspension in contributions would also damage the vital work of the Council of Europe in promoting and protecting human rights, democracy and the rule of law in Europe.

Serbia still has much work to do to meet its Council of Europe accession commitments, as well as other international obligations, in particular full co-operation with the International Criminal Tribunal for the former Yugoslavia (ICTY). However, we hope that their Chairmanship of the Committee of Ministers will provide encouragement for Serbia to demonstrate its commitment to Council of Europe core objectives of human rights, democracy and the rule of law as well as other international obligations, in particular full co-operation with the ICTY.

(HC Deb 14 May 2007 Vol 460 c501W)

5/41
Commonwealth

It was put to the Foreign Secretary that the ground rules for membership of the Commonwealth that are enshrined in the Harare declaration mean that a dictatorship cannot be a member of the Commonwealth—or at least, that such a state must be suspended from it. He was asked:

...at what point will the British Foreign Secretary deem that the line has been crossed so that we must consider suspension of a state from the Commonwealth?

He replied:

Clear rules were set out, ironically, in Harare. In 2002, we showed that suspension is a tool to be used, and Zimbabwe was expelled from the Commonwealth. We have to judge each case against the criteria as it comes up...matters will be properly dealt with.

(HC Deb 12 November 2007 Vol 467 c400)

Part Five: II.A.3. *Subjects of international law—international organisations—general—legal effect of the acts of international organisations*

5/42
An FCO Minister wrote:

As a longstanding, committed and active member of the UN, the UK takes seriously all resolutions which are adopted by UN bodies. While the majority of these resolutions do not give rise to binding obligations, they are important expressions of the international community's opinion on an issue. Only the UN Security Council can adopt binding resolutions. The Government considers that it is acting in compliance with all such legally-binding resolutions applicable to the UK.

(HC Deb 8 March 2007 Vol 457 c2152W)

5/43 (See also 14/7)
The UK representative gave the following explanation of his vote in a Security Council debate on the situation in Lebanon about the establishment of the Special Tribunal for Lebanon:

The United Kingdom welcomes the adoption of resolution 1757 (2007). The proposed Tribunal is vital for Lebanon, for justice and for the region. The establishment of the Tribunal through Lebanese internal procedures had been thwarted. The Council, for its part, has been asked to adopt a binding decision to create the Tribunal. This is not a capricious intervention or interference in the domestic political affairs of a sovereign State. It is a considered response by the Council, properly taken, to a request from the Government of Lebanon for

action to overcome a continued impasse in Lebanon's internal procedures, despite long and serious efforts to find a solution within Lebanon. It is a long-held
United Kingdom view that, to make this decision binding, it was necessary for
such a resolution, inter alia, to be taken under Chapter VII. The use of Chapter
VII carries no connotation other than that it makes this resolution binding. That
is why the United Kingdom supported this resolution. We hope that all parties
in Lebanon will now be able to move forward together to take the necessary decisions to build upon this formal establishment of the Tribunal.

(UN Doc S/PV.5685, 30 May 2007)

Part Five: II.A.5. *Subjects of international law—international organisations—general—responsibility of international organisations (see Part Thirteen:
II.A.2 (a)., below)*

5/44
The FCO Legal Adviser made the following statement to the UNGA
Sixth Committee on 30 October 2007:

Turning to chapter VIII of the ILC's Report [Fifty-ninth session, A/62/10,
Ed.], on the responsibility of international organisations...

In the past, the United Kingdom has expressed hesitation about how closely
the Commission's work on this topic has been following the Commission's
Articles on State Responsibility. We have also cautioned against the wholesale
application of the Articles on State Responsibility to international organisations
without giving due consideration to the differences between States and international organisations, or allowing for the diversity in the types of international
organisations and their functions. I reiterate those comments today. The United
Kingdom would encourage the Commission to explore the practice of international organisations, and to give further thought to the issues raised by extending the principles of State responsibility to international organisations. In this
regard, we take note of the Special Rapporteur's comments in his Fifth Report,
where he explains that the Commission's draft articles are expressed at a level
of generality, which means that it is not appropriate that they be tailored to suit
certain entities. We agree, but remain nonetheless uncertain as to how some of
the draft articles might ever apply to an international organisation. Accordingly,
we welcome the suggestion of the Special Rapporteur to consider including a
draft article which would incorporate the *lex specialis* rule, and also his proposal
to revisit some of the issues raised in the comments of States and international
organisations before the end of the first reading.

The United Kingdom is aware that difficulties may be posed by the relative lack
of practice concerning the responsibility of international organisations, to which
the Commission has referred on numerous occasions in its Report, such as at
paragraphs 331 and 337, and also within the commentaries to the draft articles
themselves. We would encourage the Commission to seek further responses from
international organisations and States in order to fill in the practical background.

The United Kingdom would also like to comment on certain specific provisions
that have been adopted at this year's session. First, draft article 35 sets out a

general principle that an international organisation cannot invoke its own rules in order to justify a failure to comply with obligations under international law which are entailed by the commission of an internationally wrongful act. The commentary clarifies that this provision has been drafted with reference to article 32 of the Commission's Articles on State Responsibility. The United Kingdom considers that these two situations are not identical. States have full sovereignty under international law, and as such, have the full range of powers to fulfil their international obligations. The powers of international organisations, however, are limited. They can only exercise those powers which are conferred on them, either expressly or impliedly, in their constitutive instruments. In this regard, article 27, paragraph 2, of the Vienna Convention on the Law of Treaties between States and International Organisations does not represent a complete parallel for draft article 35. If an international organisation has accepted a treaty obligation, it must be assumed to have the powers to carry out that obligation. But this is not necessarily the case for all the international obligations that an international organisation may have, such as those which arise under customary international law. The lack of relevant practice makes this provision difficult to assess, but we consider that more consideration is needed of the wording of this draft article.

The United Kingdom also notes the content of draft article 43, and the commentary to this provision, where it is recorded that the majority of the Commission considered that States which are members of an international organisation are not under any general obligation to take all appropriate measures to provide the organisation with the means for making reparation. The United Kingdom agrees with this view, and observes that this was also the conclusion of the English courts in the litigation concerning the International Tin Council. However, we do not consider that the compromise provision, as drafted, accurately reflects that view. The key point is that this is an issue which is determined by the rules of the international organisation in question. The draft article, as it presently stands, provides that the member States have to take 'appropriate measures' in accordance with those rules, but whether this obligation is only owed to other member States, as an internal institutional rule, or to non-members as well, is not clear. The way that the provision is presently drafted might even be interpreted as supporting the existence of the general obligation, which the majority of the Commission rejected. We would therefore recommend that the wording of this draft article be given further consideration.

(Text supplied by FCO)

Part Five: II.B.2. *Subjects of international law—international organisations—particular types of organisation—regional organisations*

5/45
The Foreign Secretary was asked what articles of the EU treaties require membership of the European Court of Human Rights. An FCO Minister wrote:

There is no requirement in the EU treaties for member states to accede to the European Convention on Human Rights (ECHR). However, all EU member states are members of the Council of Europe and signatures of [parties to, Ed.] the ECHR. There is no provision in the treaty establishing the European Community which either requires or empowers the European Community to accede to the ECHR. Article 6 of the treaty on EU, which requires the EU to respect fundamental rights, refers to the ECHR as an instrument containing such rights, but does not require the EU as an organisation to accede to the ECHR.

(HC Deb 27 February 2007 Vol 457 c1187W)

Part Five: IV.B. *Subjects of international law—international organisations—entities and groups other than states and international organisations—dependencies*

5/46 (See also 11/4)
Gibraltar

The Foreign Secretary was asked a number of questions about Gibraltar:

1. What status the tripartite agreement gave to British aircraft travelling to Gibraltar when in Spanish airspace.

An FCO Minister wrote:

The tripartite agreement has no effect on the status of British aircraft flying in Spanish airspace. The rights of an airline of one country to traverse the airspace of another country are enshrined in the International Convention on Civil Aviation, signed at Chicago in 1944.

2. What effect the tripartite agreement had had on claims by the Spanish Government over sovereign British territorial waters surrounding Gibraltar.

The Minister wrote:

The tripartite agreement has had no effect on the United Kingdom and Spain's respective positions on the waters surrounding Gibraltar.

3. What were the UK's claims to territorial water surrounding Gibraltar.

The Minister replied:

Under international law, coastal states are entitled, but not required, to claim territorial sea up to a maximum breadth of 12 nautical miles. Where the coasts of two states are opposite or adjacent, neither is entitled, unless they agree otherwise, to extend its territorial sea beyond the median line. The Government consider that a limit of three nautical miles is sufficient in the case of Gibraltar.

4. Whether there were plans to discuss claims to increase British territorial water surrounding Gibraltar with the Spanish Government.

The Minister wrote:

There are no such plans.

5. What restrictions exist on vessels travelling from Gibraltar to Spanish ports.

The Minister wrote:

Spanish restrictions require military vessels travelling from Gibraltar to travel to another non-Spanish port before entering a Spanish port. This restriction is not applied to cargo vessels, cruise ships or other passenger boats.

6. What the customs procedures are for Gibraltarian citizens who cross the border from Spain to Gibraltar.

The Minister replied:

Gibraltarian citizens who cross the border from Spain to Gibraltar are not in practice subject to customs checks by the Spanish customs authorities before they can exit Spain. They are subject to a customs check by Gibraltarian customs upon entering into Gibraltar.

(HC Deb 2 March 2007 Vol 457 c1611W)

5/47
(See also 12/2)
The FCO wrote to the FAC on 9 November 2006 about the Cordoba Trilateral agreements.

The committee will be aware that the recent Cordoba agreements on the enhanced use of RAF Gibraltar relate only to commercial aircraft, and that Spanish restrictions on the use of their airspace by British Military aircraft flying to and from Gibraltar have not yet been lifted. The Committee's recollection is correct that it remains the UK Government's objective to lift these restrictions and we continue to lobby the Spanish Government to reconsider its position on this. With respect to the Gibraltar/Spain direct military communication link, we understand that the UK MoD is reassessing the requirement for this capability. Based on this reassessment, which we expect to be complete in early 2007, the decision can be made as to whether or not we continue to lobby the Spanish on this issue.

With regard to your second question, the UK and Spain have made a number of attempts to resolve the blocked ratification of the 1996 Hague Convention on the International Protection of Children. As the Committee may be aware it was most recently discussed as part of the trilateral process and while we were unable to reach an agreement ahead of 18 September, the UK and Spain are both committed to finding a solution. Negotiations are consequently at an advanced stage and we hope that a final agreement will be reached within the next few weeks. Indeed, this is the position that the British and Spanish delegations jointly presented to delegates at the recent Hague Conference's Special Commission on child protection issues.

Finally, you ask about the settlement on pensions. The Cordoba settlement does not directly address Community Care's Household Cost Allowance. However, both the UK and Spanish Governments view the Cordoba settlement as a satis-factory and equitable outcome for all involved and a full and final resolution of the longstanding pensions issue. The wider effect of the Cordoba arrangements is that they will facilitate the unfreezing of Gibraltar Social Insurance Fund (GSIF) pensions for pensioners remaining in the GSIF. To this end, the Chief Minister has already announced that the Government of Gibraltar will uprate the pensions of all those in the GSIF from April 2007 (i.e. from the same date that the UK starts to make uprated payments to Spanish pensioners who have opted to leave the GSIF).

(FAC Report Developments in the European Union (Written Evidence) HC 166-iv) (10 October 2007))

5/48
Diego Garcia
An FCO Minister wrote:

Under the 1966 Exchange of Notes between the US and UK [about Diego Garcia], non-US and non-UK nationals who are not serving members of the US military cannot be detained without notification to the Government.

There is no US facility for foreign detainees on Diego Garcia. The only civilian detention centre is at the small UK-run police station.

The US authorities have repeatedly given us assurances that no detainees, prisoners of war or any other persons in this category are being held on Diego Garcia, or have at any time passed in transit through Diego Garcia or its territorial waters or airspace. This was most recently confirmed during the 2007 US/UK Political Military Talks held in Washington on 11 and 13 September.

The Government co-operated fully with the Council of Europe's inquiry last year, together with an inquiry on similar issues by the European Parliament. At that time the Government explained that we had carried out extensive searches of official records and found no evidence of detainees being rendered through the UK, or Overseas Territories, since 1997, where there were substantial grounds to believe there was a real risk of torture.

(HC Deb 11 October 2007 Vol 464 c703W)

5/49
The Minister of Defence wrote:

The 1966 UK/US Exchange of Notes [on Diego Garcia] requires the US to seek prior approval at the highest political level for any offensive action by the US from their base at Diego Garcia. It is a matter of record that the UK approved US offensive action from Diego Garcia in support of operations in Afghanistan in 2001 and Iraq in 2003. However, I am withholding a full list of the occasions when the US has sought such approval as the release of such information would, or would be likely to, prejudice our international relations.

(HC Deb 17 October 2007 Vol 464 c1117W)

5/50
Overseas Territories
Speech by an FCO Minister to Cayman Islands Chamber of Commerce

Good governance in the Overseas Territories is one of the UK's key priorities. We will ensure the highest standards of governance with transparency and accountability at all levels of government. I commend the recent enactment of a Freedom of Information Law.

We will also ensure that our Overseas Territories meet international norms, whether a Caribbean Financial Action Task Force evaluation or a UN convention. For example, at our meeting last week, we agreed to extend conventions on Child Labour, Discrimination against Women, and Corruption to the Overseas Territories.

I look forward to constitutional talks. The desire for greater autonomy is a natural one, and we will consider any proposals carefully. But the British government must retain certain powers relating to good governance and law and order. Any new constitution has to give due weight to human rights. The challenge for us all now is to find the right balance.

(www.fco.gov.uk/news, 12 December 2007)

Part Five: IV.C. *Subjects of international law—international organisations—entities and groups other than states and international organisations—special regimes*

5/51 (see also 5/32)
An FCO Minister said:

We do not plan to raise Papua in the United Nations Security Council. We respect Indonesia's territorial integrity and do not support Papuan independence. We believe that full implementation of existing special autonomy legislation is the best way to proceed towards a sustainable resolution to the internal differences and the long-term stability of Papua. The best way to resolve the complex issues in Papua is through promoting peaceful dialogue between Papuan groups and the Indonesian Government.

(HL Deb 13 November 2007 Vol 969 c446)

Part Six: The Position of the Individual (including the Corporation) in International Law

Part Six: I. *The individual (including the corporation) in international law—nationality*

6/1
In the written observation of the UK in C-300/04 *M.G. Eman and O.B. Sevinger v College van burgemeester en wethouders van Den Haag*), it was argued on behalf of HMG:

"The grant of nationality is recognised in international law as an essential attribute of State sovereignty. If Member States were not free to confer their nationality on persons resident in the OCTs (Overseas Countries and Territories):

The British Overseas Territories Act 2002 (and, it is believed, the equivalent provisions of the other Member States with Annex II territories) would have to be repealed and replaced.

The basis for the relationship between the Member States and the people of their Annex II territories would be transformed, and could even be jeopardised.

Some residents of the OCTs could be left stateless, since in many cases it is far from clear where their citizenship would come from if not from the associated Member State".

At the hearing, counsel for HMG said:

"The grant of nationality is recognised in international law as an essential attribute of state sovereignty. It is also recognised in Community law as a matter entirely for the Member States."

(Text supplied by FCO)

6/2

The FCO wrote to the FAC about changes in British citizenship law brought about as a result of changes in the laws of India and Nepal:

Ethnic Citizenship (EMC) Applications—British Nationality Act (Hong Kong) 1997

Recent clarification of Indian citizenship law means that British nationals of Indian descent who were previously thought not to meet the criteria for registration as British citizens under the British Nationality (Hong Kong) Act 1997 (BNA (HK) 1997), may now qualify. In addition, the Nepalese community in Hong Kong have recently become aware of their potential eligibility for registration as British citizens under the Hong Kong Act.

* * *

Applicants of Indian Descent

The Indian authorities had previously indicated that minors of Indian descent would continue to be considered Indian nationals even if they had been registered as British Dependent Territory Citizens (BTDC) or British Nationals (Overseas) [BN{O}]. They would therefore not meet the criteria to be solely British and were considered ineligible for registration under the Hong Kong Act. Around 600 applications were refused for this reason. The Indian authorities have now provided further clarification of their citizenship laws and have stated that any minor who was registered as a BDTC or BN(O) would have lost Indian citizenship upon registration and therefore could have met registration requirements (children who were BDTCs by birth retain Indian citizenship until they reach 18).

The Home Office has decided to reassess these cases on request. New applications are also expected from those who did not previously apply on the basis that they believed they did not meet the "solely British" criteria.

Handling

The most commonly affected provision of the British Nationality Act is Section 1(1) of the BNA (HK) 1997 available to individuals who were and continue to be ordinarily resident in Hong Kong.

The majority of the requests for reassessment of Indian cases and new applications for both Nepalese and Indian cases will be in Hong Kong. Guidance for both Nepalese and Indian cases is posted on the Hong Kong website and the IND page of the Home Office website. Reassessment of Indian cases which have been previously refused will be done remotely. Applicants will be asked to post or fax written details of their initial application, including Home Office reference numbers, to their nearest British mission. These requests should be sent to the Home office for reassessment. The Home Office have given a definitive time scale of five weeks for completing reassessments, effective from April 2006.

(Letter from FCO to FAC, 13 February 2007)

6/3

During evidence on 13 December 2006 for the Developments in the EU Inquiry, [a member] asked about overseas territories citizens and visa requirements for travel in Europe (Q95–99). The Foreign Secretary undertook to provide further details on the visa requirements of certain categories of British Nationals who wished to travel within the Schengen area. The FAC was concerned that there might be an alteration to the Schengen Common Visa List (CVL) that would require British overseas territories citizens (BOTCs) from Bermuda and the five British overseas territories in the Caribbean to have visas in order to visit the Schengen area of Europe. In order to provide a full and comprehensive answer I will set out the background and context of the amendment to the CVL and its implications for British Nationals.

Categories of British Nationals and the requirements for their entry into the UK

BOTCs come from any of 14 British overseas territories scattered across the globe. The great majority of BOTCs have a right of abode in the UK as in 2002 the British Overseas Territories Act made all existing BOTCs, except those whose BOTC status derived solely from a connection with the Cyprus Sovereign Base Areas (CSBA), automatically become British citizens. As British citizens, these BOTCs are not subject to immigration control for entry into the UK.

There are a small number of BOTCs who are not also British citizens and who therefore do not have the right of abode in the UK. These are persons who were registered or naturalised as BOTCs after 2002 and who have not subsequent y been registered as British citizens, and those whose BOTC status derives solely from a connection with the CSBA. People who became BOTCs after 2002 can apply for British citizenship unless their BOTC status derives from a connection with the CSBA, or unless they have previously held, but given up, British citizenship. The application will then be considered at the Home Secretary's discretion, and in practice all applications are granted except for when an applicant is suspected of acquiring BOTC status improperly.

BOTCs who are not also British citizens, British Overseas citizens (BOCs), certain categories of British subjects (BSs)—primarily those who have a connection with India and Pakistan rather than with Southern Ireland -- and British protected persons (BPPs) do not have automatic returnability to their country of residence or any right of abode in the UK. These categories of British nationals must satisfy an immigration officer that they qualify for entry into the UK in accordance with the Immigration Rules. These nationals also need a visa in certain situations, e.g., when seeking entry for a period exceeding six months or for a purpose for which prior entry clearance is required under the Immigration Rules.

There is one important exception to this. All BOTCs who derive their BOTC status through a connection with Gibraltar are EU Citizens. As EU Citizens they benefit from free movement rights within the EU.

All British citizens have the right of abode in the UK, i.e. they are entirely free from UK immigration controls.

Negotiations on the CVL

The United Kingdom does not participate in the CVL, and therefore does not have a vote on matters pertaining to it. Nevertheless, the Commission agreed to take our views into account as long as our position was clear and unambiguous, and no immigration risk was perceived by other Member States.

In their initial proposal the Commission suggested that the 3.4 million British Nationals Overseas (BN(O)s) should be exempt from visa requirements to enter the Schengen area. The Commission considered that they would not constitute a migratory risk or a risk in terms of public policy, as they are re-admissible to Hong Kong and the passports that British offices issue exclusively to them have highly reliable security features. Most BN(O)s also hold Hong Kong Special Administrative Region passports, which allow visa-free travel to EU Member States.

This change was agreed by Member States BN(O)s do not have the right of abode in the UK. They do not need a visa to come to the UK, unless seeking entry for a period exceeding 6 months or for a purpose for which prior entry clearance is required, but they must satisfy an immigration office that they qualify for entry in accordance with the Immigration Rules.

The Commission's initial proposal also stated that all BOTCs and BSs should be subject to the Schengen visa regime. However, at the Visa Working Group meetings of 26 October 2006 and 14 November 2006 the Commission agreed — in view of a UK intervention and ECJ case law—to allow those BSs and BOTCs with a right to abode in the UK visa free access into the Schengen area. The Commission felt that re-admissability to the country of origin was less certain for those BOTCs and BSs without the right of abode in the UK than for the BN(O)s, and was therefore unwilling to grant visa exemptions to them.

This proposal was accepted by the Strategic Committee on Immigration, Frontiers and Asylum (SCIFA)/Mixed Committee of 9 November 2006 and the Permanent Representatives Committee (COREPER) of 23 November 2006 where agreement was reached on the text of the then draft Regulation. The amendments to the CVL mean that Schengen immigration control requirements for the relevant British nationals are now more in alignment with the UK's immigration control. The FCO was consulted about how to conduct the above negotiations, and was content with the strategy that was used.

Proving a right of abode in the UK

BOTCs have a right of abode in the UK if they simultaneously possess British citizenship. As British citizens, they additionally enjoy the rights of free movement and establishment conferred by or under the EC Treaty and, therefore, visa free access to the Schengen area. The majority can prove their status at border controls by producing one of two documents; a British citizen passport or a BOTC passport containing a certificate of entitlement to the right of abode in the UK. A BOTC passport without this certificate will not suffice. The only exception to this is for BOTCs who derive their status from a connection with Gibraltar, as their passports are in an EU format and are evidence of the holders free movement rights within the EU. All BOTCs who are also British citizens would be granted a British citizen Passport and/or a certificate of entitlement to the right of abode in the UK (to put in their BOTC passport) upon application and payment of the requisite fee.

BS passports are endorsed on issue either to show that the holder has right of abode (generally speaking, those whose BS status derives from birth in Ireland) or that the holder has right of re-admission to the UK.

As mentioned above, BOTCs who derive their BOTC status from a connection with Gibraltar have no need to prove a right of abode in the UK. Spain recognised Gibraltarian ID cards as valid travel documents to establish the holders right of free movement within the EU in 2000. Free movement rights are governed by the Free Movement Directive 2004/38/EC that entered into force on 30 April 2006, which also supports that Gibraltarian ID cards establish the holders right of free movement within the EU. All BOTC(Gib) EU format passports arc [sic] also evidence of the holders free movement rights. We are writing separately to the Commission on this point.

Conclusion

BOTCs from Bermuda and the British overseas territories in the Caribbean who possess British citizenship, and hence have the right of abode in the UK, have visa free access to the Schengen area. The great majority of these BOTCs possess British citizenship, and most of those who do not possess British citizenship can register as British citizens if they wish and also obtain the right of abode.

To pass Schengen border controls without a visa, a BOTC with simultaneous British citizenship may need to show either a British citizen passport or a BOTC passport which contains a certificate of entitlement to a right of abode in the UK. Those who do not already possess either one of these documents can apply for them by virtue of their British citizenship. The certificate of entitlement to a right of abode in the UK is applied for separately from the BOTC passport, but they must be displayed together.

Background

Beside British citizens there are, as a legacy of empire, a number of other categories of British passport holders: British Nationals (Overseas) (BN(O)s), British overseas territories citizens (BOTCs), British subjects (BSs), British Overseas citizens (BOCs) and British protected persons (BPPs). EU Member States previously imposed national visa requirements on certain British nationals resulting in a variegated system to the latters' detriment. (For example, a BOC needed a visa to enter France but not Malta.) It has long been our policy to seek the removal of EU visa requirements on British nationals, particularly the 3.4 million BN(O)s.

Schengen, of which the UK is not a member for the purpose of border control, operates a Common Visa List (CVL). The amendment to the Schengen CVL (Regulation 539/2001) for the first time introduced a common EU visa policy for British nationals. Because of our approach to Schengen border provisions, we are not allowed to participate or vote on legislation in this area. However, we engage in debate and have been able to persuade the Commission and other Member States to act in our interest. Regulation (EC) 1932/2006 amending Regulation (EC) 539/2001 entered into force on 19 January 2007.

Below is a table on the different categories of British National, and how the amendment to the CVL has affected them. We cannot guarantee the exact location of all British nationals, so I include our best approximation.

Category of British Passport

Category of British Passport	Location (approx)	Previous Visa situation	New Visa situation
BOTC (200,000)	Across the globe in British Overseas Territories	No visa required if using a British citizen passport, a BOTC passport from Gibraltar, or a Gibraltarian ID card. If using a BOTC passport from other territories then visa requirements varied.	No visa required if using either a British citizen Passport, a BOTC passport from Gibraltar, or a BOTC passport from another territory which contains a certificate of entitlement to a right of abode in the UK.
BOC (1,500,000)	Mostly Malaysia or East Africa	Visa required (except in Estonia, Malta, Greece, Lithuania, Slovenia, Benelux)	Visas required— situation regularised

BPP (10,000)	Mostly East Africa	Visa required (except in Estonia, Malta, Greece, Lithuania, Slovenia, Benelux)	Visas required—situation regularised.
BN(O) (3,400,000)	Mostly Hong Kong	Visa required except Estonia, Malta, Greece, Lithuania, Slovenia, Benelux, Denmark, Iceland, Italy, Greece, Luxembourg, Netherlands and Sweden	No visa required
British Subjects (200,000)	Mostly Indian sub-continent and East Africa	Visas for all (except in Estonia, Malta, Greece, Lithuania, Slovenia, Benelux)	No visa required except for those subject to UK immigration control

(www.publications.parliament.uk/pa/cm200607/cmselect/cmfaff/memo/166/uceu2502.htm)

Part Six: II. *The individual (including the corporation) in international law—diplomatic and consular protection (see also Part Thirteen II.A.1 (c), below)*

6/4
(See also **2/5**)
The Government's reply to the EU Commission's Green Paper on Diplomatic and Consular Protection (28304, 6192/07, COM(06) 712) was annexed to a report of the European Scrutiny Committee:

1. Introduction

1.1 The UK welcomes the Commission's Green Paper on Diplomatic and Consular Protection of Union citizens in third countries. Our commitment to providing high quality consular assistance is reflected in the UK Government's current strategic international priorities, the ninth of which reads:

"Delivering high-quality support for British nationals abroad, in normal times and in crises".

1.2 The UK takes seriously Member States' obligation not to discriminate against other unrepresented EU nationals in delivering consular assistance. We are acutely aware that, in some parts of the world, delivering consular assistance to British nationals is only possible through the consular and diplomatic networks of our EU Partners. And while providing assistance at times of crisis is only one element of the broad range of activities which make up consular assistance, co-ordination amongst Member States is integral to planning and providing effective responses to crises when they do occur.

1.3 The UK shares the Commission's objectives of ensuring unrepresented Member States' nationals know they can seek consular assistance from other Member States' missions, and of ensuring any assistance provided to them is efficient, effective and non-discriminatory. We are pleased co-ordination amongst Member States has improved in recent years and grateful to the Commission for its consideration of how it might be improved still further.

1.4 Member States provide their consular assistance in a variety of international and domestic legal frameworks. Consequently, it would be useful to set out the basis on which the UK provides consular assistance.

1.5 Firstly, the UK differentiates between consular assistance, passport issuance, notarial services and visa applications. Although these four activities are often performed by the same personnel, they have different legal and policy foundations. The Green Paper is concerned primarily with consular assistance: the provision of assistance by consular officials or diplomatic authorities to nationals in difficulty overseas. The list of activities under Article 5 of Decision 95/553/EC serves as good illustration. Article 20 TEC, to which Decision 95/553/EC and this Green Paper respond, is also concerned with consular assistance.

1.6 Secondly, it is important to recognise diplomatic protection as a distinct legal concept from consular assistance. Consular assistance can be easily confused with diplomatic protection. This may be because consular assistance is often referred to as consular protection, or because it is frequently provided by staff who have both consular and diplomatic functions. Diplomatic protection is formally a state-to-state process by which a state may bring a claim against another state in the name of a national who has suffered an internationally wrongful act at the hands of that other state. Under international law, states may exercise diplomatic protection only on behalf of their own nationals, and not on behalf of nationals of other states. Conversely, consular assistance is the provision of support and assistance by a state to its nationals, or those nationals to whom it has agreed to provide assistance, who are in distress overseas. The vast majority of such cases do not involve an internationally wrongful act.

1.7 Thirdly, British nationals do not have a legal right to consular assistance overseas. The UK Government is under no general obligation under domestic or international law to provide consular assistance (or exercise diplomatic protection). Consular assistance is provided as a matter of policy, which is set out in the public guide, "Support for British Nationals Abroad: A Guide". Other Member States provide consular assistance on a range of bases, some of which recognise a right to consular assistance under national law, and some of which do not.

1.8 In relation to EU law, Article 20 TEC sets out an obligation of non-discrimination. It requires Member States to treat requests for consular assistance by unrepresented nationals of Member States on the same basis as requests by their own nationals. In compliance with this, the UK provides consular assistance to significant numbers of unrepresented Member States' nationals. But Article 20 TEC, does not create any right to assistance beyond this. Decisions 95/553/EC and 96/409/CFSP do not affect this position or broaden the basic legal principle set out in Article 20.

1.9 In relation to EU law, Article 20 TEC sets out an obligation of non-discrimination. It requires Member States to treat requests for consular assistance by unrepresented nationals of Member States on the same basis as requests by their own nationals. In compliance with this, the UK provides consular assistance to significant numbers of unrepresented Member States' nationals. But Article 20 TEC, does not create any right to assistance beyond this. Decisions 95/553/EC and 96/409/CFSP do not affect this position or broaden the basic legal principle set out in Article 20.

2. Information for citizens

2.1 The UK agrees with the Commission that Member States' nationals should be better informed about Article 20 and their opportunity, where unrepresented by their own State, to seek consular assistance from other Member States. To this end, we welcomed the General Secretariat's recent brochure on Decision 95/553/EC. We would encourage the Commission to co-ordinate with the Council to ensure the public is aware of further action pursuant to Article 20...

2.10 Individual Member States are in the best position to advise their nationals on the risks they face and how to mitigate them. Different EU nationalities do not necessarily face the same risks in third countries or benefit from the same advice. These differences can only be captured by the provision of separate travel information.

2.11 Fundamentally, it is to their own Member State that nationals will turn for information and assistance and it is their own Member State to whom they may make further requests or complaints if the information or assistance provided is thought to be inaccurate or unhelpful. We believe the current arrangements for keeping Member States informed of changes to one another's travel information are the best means to allow Member States to benefit from one another's knowledge.

3. The scope of protection for citizens

3.1 The UK does not believe the consolidation of consular assistance between Member States is either necessary or desirable. There is no evidence that Member States' nationals are inconvenienced by the varying levels of consular assistance offered. The only comparison they are likely to make is with the consular assistance they expect to receive from their own Member State. In any event, given the necessary complexity of consular policy and procedures, and their widely varying legal contexts, the task of agreeing and implementing a common standard of consular assistance would be disproportionate to the benefits achieved.

3.2 As a general matter of policy, the UK does not normally provide consular assistance to non-nationals, including family members of British nationals. UK consular assistance is funded exclusively through passport fees. UK residents make 65 million trips overseas a year and 13.6 million potential British passport holders resident overseas; a significant proportion are related to third country nationals. Extending consular assistance to third country nationals could not be covered by current resources and would not justify a rise in current passport fees.

3.3 There are also legal obstacles to providing such assistance. As discussed in paragraph 5.1 below, a sending state may not normally exercise consular functions in the receiving state on behalf of a third state unless the receiving state has been notified and been given an opportunity to object. In any event, Article 20 only requires non-discriminatory treatment of Member States' nationals, not their family members.

3.4 The UK applies a different, more flexible policy in responding to crises. In a crisis, the UK offers the same level of consular crisis assistance to the third country dependants of British nationals as we do our own nationals, particularly during evacuations, where it is our policy to avoid splitting families. In doing so, we are acting in accordance with the 'Lead State' framework, recently agreed in COCON. Where the UK offers to assist an unrepresented Member State, we aim to apply the same policy to their unrepresented national and their third country dependants as we do our own. Of course, this may be impossible where we are unable to evacuate third country nationals because they do not have the right visa status for the destination country.

3.5 Many Member States operate similar policies, with some variations. However, for the reasons stated in paragraph 3.1 above, we do not believe that harmonising this policy across all Member States is necessary or desirable. Instead, we should work together within the Lead State framework to ensure third country dependants of Member States' nationals are provided sufficient consular assistance at times of crisis...

4. Structures and resources

4.1 We share the Commission's objective of ensuring consular assistance for unrepresented Member States' nationals is provided in as efficient a manner as possible. Member States have made significant progress in the co-ordination of their consular services. The recently reviewed guidelines for co-ordinating consular assistance in third countries, agreed by COCON in 2006, are a good example of this. Some Member States' consular operations are already co-located. The UK co-locates in Almaty, Ashgabat, Dar es Salaam, Pyongyang, Quito, Reykjavik, Minsk and Chisinau. Co-location can drive down costs and improves co-ordination amongst Member States. Similarly, Member States' consulates—fully aware of their Article 20 obligations—should allocate unrepresented nationals amongst themselves on the basis of resources, language, and so on. Such agreements are best agreed, monitored and adjusted by consulates locally. They are in the best position to assess the needs of unrepresented nationals and identify those best placed to assist them. It is they that can best react to changing circumstances and demand. As part of its efforts to promote Article 20 amongst Member States' nationals, the Commission might consider maintaining a central record of these arrangements for public enquiry.

4.2 The concept of "common offices" for EU consular work in third countries is not clearly defined in the Green Paper. For example, it is not clear on what basis the level of consular assistance being provided would be set. Would it depend on the nationality of the applicant, the consular officer or a common policy? And would all Member States' nationals seek assistance from these "common offices", or just those that are unrepresented? The benefits of such "common offices" are also unclear. They would not, for example, provide any resources savings over co-location. And experience shows that Member States' nationals will continue to expect consular assistance from consular staff of their own nationality, wherever possible. This is certainly the case for British nationals.

4.3 We would like to note that consular assistance, with which this Green Paper is primarily concerned, should be distinguished from providing visa and passport services. Member States are under no obligation to provide these services to unrepresented nationals on a non-discriminatory basis.

. . .

4.8 However, we are concerned by the suggestion that, in the longer term, the EU should provide consular assistance through Commission delegations. The Commission has no experience in providing consular assistance and we do not believe that EU nationals would receive better consular assistance from the Commission than can be achieved by cooperation among the Member States. Additionally, it is not clear to the UK that there is a legal basis for the Commission to exercise consular functions. The rules and principles established by the Vienna Convention on Consular Relations and customary international law provide for the provision of consular assistance by states, not international or intergovernmental organisations. Although the UK accepts and welcomes the role of the Commission in facilitating co-operation and ensuring non-discrimination in the provision of consular assistance, the Commission has no competence under the EU Treaties to provide consular assistance.

5. The consent of the third country authorities

5.1 The UK understands the importance of obtaining the consent or acquiescence of the receiving state in providing consular assistance to Member States' unrepresented nationals. However, whether this requires Member States to negotiate bilateral agreements with third states depends on the agreements and arrangements already in place with the receiving states. For example, Article 8 of the Vienna Convention on Consular Relations allows consular assistance to be provided to non-nationals where the receiving state has been notified and been given an opportunity to object. In our experience, receiving states are generally content for assistance to be provided by other Member States. Consequently, the need for consent clauses in bilateral agreements is unproven in many circumstances.

5.2 However, the UK recognises the value of these provisions in facilitating such assistance. Consequently, we would welcome discussing the possibility of "consular provisions" in the context of any consultations held with the Commission pursuant to Decision 88/384/EC. Of course, it would be inappropriate for any Member State to commit in advance to the inclusion of such provisions. The negotiation of agreements with third states is complex and difficult. Whilst the inclusion of a "consular provision" may be uncontroversial in some instances, its benefits are unlikely to justify efforts to negotiate it in many others. Moreover, any such provision would be without prejudice to the division of responsibility amongst Member States' missions for unrepresented nationals.

(European Scrutiny Committee, Sixteenth Report, Documents considered by the Committee on 28 March 2007, including:... Diplomatic and Consular Protection of Union Citizens in Third Countries, HC 41-xvi (2007))

6/5

These are extracts from "Support for British Nationals Abroad: a Guide", an FCO Publication.

WHO WE CAN HELP

We can provide the support detailed in this guide to people outside the UK who are:

British nationals (whether or not they normally live in the UK—but see [below]);

in certain limited circumstances,

British nationals with another nationality—'dual nationals'—see [below]; and

European Union or Commonwealth nationals whose country does not have a local mission, in circumstances where we have agreed to help their nationals.

We cannot provide this support to other countries' nationals, even if they may have been lawfully living in the UK.

WHAT KIND OF HELP WE CAN PROVIDE

We offer help which is appropriate to the individual circumstances of each case, including:

• issuing replacement passports;

• providing information about transferring funds;

• providing appropriate help if you have suffered rape or serious assault, are a victim of other crime, or are in hospital;

• helping people with mental illness;

• providing details of local lawyers, interpreters, doctors and funeral directors;

• doing all we properly can to contact you within 24 hours of being told that you have been detained;

• offering support and help in a range of other cases, such as child abductions, death of relatives overseas, missing people and kidnapping;

• contacting family or friends for you if you want; and

• making special arrangements in cases of terrorism, civil disturbances or natural disasters.

WE CANNOT:

• get you out of prison, prevent the local authorities from deporting you after your prison sentence, or interfere in criminal or civil court proceedings;

• help you enter a country, for example, if you do not have a visa or your passport is not valid, as we cannot interfere in another country's immigration policy or procedures;

• give you legal advice, investigate crimes or carry out searches for missing people, although we can give you details of people who may be able to help you in these cases, such as English-speaking lawyers;

• get you better treatment in hospital or prison than is given to local people;

• pay any bills or give you money (in very exceptional circumstances we may lend you some money, from public funds, which you will have to pay back);

• make travel arrangements for you, or find you work or accommodation; or

• make business arrangements on your behalf.

BRITISH NATIONALS ABROAD: A GUIDE

SUMMARY

We can help you if you are either travelling or living abroad and are a British national.

You are a British national if you are one of the following:

• A British citizen

• A British Overseas Territories citizen (see note 1 below)

• A British overseas citizen

• A British national (overseas) (see note 2 below)

• A British subject

• A British protected person

We cannot help non-British nationals, no matter how long they have lived in the UK and what their connections are to the UK. The only exception to this rule is where a specific agreement exists with another state, for example, the agreement between European Union member states to help those EU nationals without a local embassy or consulate. We may also help Commonwealth nationals in non-Commonwealth countries where they do not have any diplomatic or consular representation, depending on the circumstances of the case.

Note 1:

Because the British Overseas Territories are 'Crown possessions' under British sovereignty, British nationals should contact the local authorities if they are in difficulty in these Territories. We provide the same help to British Overseas Territories citizens living or travelling outside the Overseas Territory as we do to any other British national in difficulty.

Note 2:

We cannot help British nationals (overseas) of Chinese ethnic origin in China, Hong Kong and the Macao Special Administrative Regions. The Chinese authorities consider British nationals (overseas) of Chinese ethnic origin as Chinese nationals, and we have no power to get involved if they are held in mainland China. However, we provide the same help to all British nationals (overseas) living or travelling outside China, Hong Kong and Macao as we do to any other British national in difficulty.

WHAT ABOUT DUAL NATIONALS?

If you have some connection with a foreign or Commonwealth state, for example, by birth, by descent through either parent, by marriage or by residence, you may be a national of that state as well as being a British national. You should check with the authorities of any other state which you are connected with. You may have certain responsibilities with that state, such as compulsory military service. Becoming a British national may not cause you to lose your original nationality.

If you are a dual national travelling on your British passport in a third state (that is, a country of which you are not a national), we will offer you our full support. If you are travelling on the passport of your other nationality, we will normally direct you to that state's local Embassy, High Commission or Consulate. So, for example, if you are a dual US-British national travelling in France and you used your US passport when you entered France, then we would normally direct you to the nearest US Embassy or Consulate for help. We may make an exception to this rule if, having looked at the circumstances of the case, we consider that there is a special humanitarian reason to do so.

If you are a dual British national in the state of your other nationality (for example, a dual US-British national in the US), we would not normally offer you support or get involved in dealings between you and the authorities of that state. We may make an exception to this rule if, having looked at the circumstances of the case, we consider that there is a special humanitarian reason to do so. Such circumstances might include cases involving minors, forced marriages or an offence which carries the death penalty. However, the help we can provide will depend on the circumstances and the state of your other nationality must agree.

If you need help in a country where there is no British diplomatic or consular mission, you can receive help from the diplomatic or consular mission of another member of the European Union. There are also informal arrangements with some other countries, including New Zealand and Australia, to help British nationals in some countries. If other countries provide help on our behalf, you should receive the same level of help as they would give to their own nationals.

BRITISH NATIONALS IN DETENTION
OR PRISON OVERSEAS

• If you are arrested or held in custody or prison in a country overseas, the authorities in that country should ask you whether you want them to contact the British Embassy, High Commission or Consulate. However, you can also ask for this to be done, and should do so particularly if you are charged with a serious offence.

• We will aim to contact you, depending on local procedures, within 24 hours of being told about your arrest or detention. If you want us to, we will then aim to visit you as soon as possible.

• Our staff are there to support you and to take an interest in your welfare. We aim to be sensitive and non-judgemental. We also aim to treat all prisoners the same no matter what crime they are being held for, or whether they are on remand or have been sentenced. You should stay in touch with our staff and ask for their help as they have experience in dealing with many of the problems you may face.

• But, we cannot get you out of prison or detention, nor can we get special treatment for you because you are British.

• If you want us to, we can tell your family or friends that you have been arrested. If you are thinking about not telling your family, please consider the distress it may cause them if they are not told where you are. It can also be a disadvantage to you if you need money for anything in prison or fall ill. Once we have told your family and friends, we can pass messages between you in places where phone or postal services are not available.

• Although we cannot give legal advice, start legal proceedings or investigate a crime, we can offer basic information about the local legal system, including whether a legal-aid scheme is available. We can give you a list of local interpreters and local lawyers if you want, although we cannot pay for either. It is important to consider carefully whether you want to have legal representation and to discuss all the costs involved beforehand.

• We can offer you information about the local prison or remand system, including visiting arrangements, mail and censorship, privileges, work possibilities, and social and welfare services. We can also explain where there are different regulations for remand prisoners and sentenced prisoners. For example, in some countries, prisoners are allowed to send more mail when they are on remand.

• Where appropriate, we will consider approaching the local authorities if you are not treated in line with internationally-accepted standards. This may include where your trial does not follow internationally-recognised standards for a fair trial or is unreasonably delayed compared to local cases.

• With your permission, we can take up any justified complaint about ill treatment, personal safety, or discrimination with the police or prison authorities. Again, with your permission, we can make sure that any medical or dental problems you might have are brought to the attention of any police or prison doctor.

• If you are in prison in a European Union country, or in Iceland, Liechtenstein, Norway, Switzerland, Canada, the USA, Australia or New Zealand, we aim to visit you once after sentencing and then after that only if there is a real need. In other countries, while you are in prison we aim to visit you at least once a year, although we may visit you more often if necessary.

• We may be able to give you information about any local procedures for a prisoner's early release in exceptional circumstances. These procedures are generally known as pardon or clemency. We will only consider supporting pardon or clemency pleas:

- in compelling compassionate circumstances, such as where a prisoner or close family member is chronically ill or dying;

- in cases of minors imprisoned overseas; or

- as a last resort, in cases where we have evidence that seems to point to a miscarriage of justice.

• We can explain to you how you may be able to apply to transfer to a prison in the UK if you are in a country from which prison transfers are possible.

• The local authorities may have a policy of deporting foreign nationals after they have completed a prison sentence and we cannot prevent them from applying it to you, even if you had previously lived in the country before your prison sentence.
(www.fco.gov.uk/travel)

6/6

An FCO official submitted the following witness statement in *Mechan v FCO* [2007] EWHC 1689 (QB):

3. I can state that the applicable FCC leaflet concerning consular assistance offered to British nationals imprisoned abroad during the period 2000 until 2006 is the first document appended to my statement. This leaflet sets out what the FCO's consular staff could and could not do, during the period for which the leaflet was valid, in respect of assisting British nationals detained in foreign States. This leaflet has since been superseded by an updated version (2006), a copy of which is also appended to this statement (6/5).

4. It is apparent from the FCO's files that various forms of assistance and support were provided to Mr. Mechan at each stage of the proceedings in his case, in accordance with the guidelines set out in the FCO's leaflet in use at the time. This included assisting him with obtaining legal representation, providing him with information about the conditions of his detention, and ensuring that he had contact with his family. By way of illustration, I append to my statement various letters concerning Mr. Mechan's case from the FCC's files, in the following order

Memo of 11th January 2000 from an Embassy officer in Bahrain to Consular Division, London;

Memo of 12th January 2000 from the Vice Consul in Bahrain to Consular Division, London;

Letter of 12th January 2000 from the Consular Division, London, to Mr. Terry Mechan, the Claimant's father;

Memo of 15th January 2000 from the Vice Consul in Bahrain to Consular Division, London;

Letter of 16th January 2000 from the Vice Consul in Bahrain to Mr. Mechan;

Letter of 17th January 2000 from the Vice Consul in Bahrain to Consular Division, London; and,

Letter of 26th January 2000 from the Vice Consul in Bahrain to Mr. Mechan.

5. From the files it is evident that the Vice Consul in Bahrain paid weekly visits to Mr. Mechan before his trial and maintained contact with him during his trial when Mr. Mechan had legal representation. The Vice Consul and others 2 facilitated all contact between Mr. Mechan and his family and took care of many administrative and other matters on his behalf. My view, based on my reading of the papers relating to his case, and my knowledge and experience of dealing with consular assistance cases involving British nationals imprisoned overseas, is that consular staff handled the case in an exemplary manner.

6. After the trial the FCO assisted Mr. Mechan during his appeal. He was visited by FCO staff in detention. When he failed to meet a deadline for filing an appeal, the FCO prevailed on the Bahrain authorities to permit the appeal to proceed.

7. After Mr. Mechan's appeal, much work on the part of the FCO was put into considering and supporting Mr. Mechan's early release from prison. This culminated in the Foreign Secretary writing to the Government of Bahrain on 3rd June 2003 requesting that Mr. Mechan be released on compassionate grounds. A copy of this letter is appended to my statement. Mr. Mechan was released shortly thereafter in July 2003.

8. I have found in the FCO's files a copy of an e-mail from Mr. Mechan's father, dated 3rd August 2003, after his release, which thanks the Embassy for all that had been done to assist Mr. Mechan. A copy is appended to my statement.

9. From these records, it is apparent that the FCO took all appropriate steps to assist Mr. Mechan thoroughly, diligently and in line with EGO consular assistance policy while he was detained in Bahrain, and to support his case for an early release from prison.

(Supplied by FCO)

6/7

A Minister said in response to a suggestion that consular assistance be put on a statutory footing:

...it will be recognised that putting consular assistance on a statutory basis is a profound legal proposition...it raises substantial issues for the Government.

Once it was in statute, it would mean that all the consular service's actions in respect of incidents abroad would potentially become subject to litigation. We are all too well aware that consulates do their best and work constructively under enormous difficulties and in a vast range of circumstances. The House will recognise how significant it would be if such actions were potentially subject to litigation in this country about their effectiveness.

(HL Deb 20 April 2007 Vol 691 c461)

6/8

An FCO Minister wrote:

Under the Vienna Convention on Consular Relations, states are under an obligation, when requested to do so by a foreign national arrested or detained, to notify their consular representatives and that consular representatives shall be free to communicate with nationals of the sending state and to have access to them.

The Foreign and Commonwealth Office does not keep a central record of those states which may have breached this obligation. But we take very seriously any complaint that signatories to the Convention have not fulfilled this obligation, and we will continue to make representations with host Governments on a case by case basis. We also work with host Governments to promote greater awareness of their obligation with regard to British nationals among their law enforcement authorities, for example poster campaigns where posters are displayed in local police stations.

(HC Deb 18 June 2007 Vol 461 c1477W)

6/9

The Foreign Secretary was asked what further steps she planned to take on the case of joint UK/Chinese citizen Mr. Yu Lam Chan, imprisoned in China. An FCO Minister wrote:

The Chinese authorities continue to deny UK officials consular access to Mr. Yu Lam Chan as they consider him to be a Chinese national in China. The Director for Consular Services in the Foreign and Commonwealth Office raised this case with his Chinese counterpart on 5 June and we will continue to raise our concerns over Mr. Yu Lam Chan's health and welfare with the Chinese authorities at every appropriate opportunity...

Consular officials do not have first hand knowledge of Mr. Yu Lam Chan's medical conditions, as they are not permitted access to him. However, officials do maintain contact with family members and we have made clear our concerns to the Chinese authorities regarding Mr. Yu Lam Chan's health and welfare. The Chinese authorities assure us that he is receiving appropriate treatment for his illnesses.

(HC Deb 25 June 2007 Vol 462 c222W)

6/10

The Minister of Defence was asked if he would remove Zimbabwe from the list of countries given Commonwealth status for army recruits. A Defence Minister wrote:

The list to which you refer is in Schedule 3 of the British Nationality Act 1981 whose citizens have Commonwealth status by virtue of section 37 of that Act. Despite Zimbabwe voluntarily withdrawing from the Commonwealth in July 2003, following their suspension from the Council of the Commonwealth earlier that year, the status of their citizens is not affected in UK law, and they remain eligible to join the British armed forces. To change this situation would require an Order in Council amending the British Nationality Act 1981 and currently there are no plans to make such an Order in respect of Zimbabwe.

(HC Deb 27 February 2007 Vol 457 c1148W)

6/11

A Minister said:

I thank New Zealand for taking on consular responsibility [in the Pacific area] in countries in which the UK is not represented. We reciprocate that assistance in countries in which New Zealand is not represented.

(HC Deb 30 January 2007 Vol 456 c211)

Part Six: VI. *The individual (including the corporation) in international law—refugees*

6/12

The Foreign Secretary was asked what estimate she had made of the number of refugees leaving Somalia; what discussions she has had with her (a) Kenyan and (b) Ethiopian counterparts about the treatment of refugees from Somalia; [and] what the outcome was of those discussions. She wrote:

We are very concerned about the plight of Somali refugees and internally displaced persons in Kenya and on the Kenya/Somalia border...

We understand that the Kenyan border remains closed to Somalis seeking to leave the country. Our high commissioner in Nairobi has raised the issue with the Kenyan Foreign Minister, emphasising the need to allow humanitarian access across the border, while recognising Kenya's legitimate security concerns. We are maintaining close contact with the Kenyan Government and with the United Nations and other international agencies in Kenya on this issue.

We are not aware of significant numbers of Somali refugees in Ethiopia and therefore have not raised this issue with the Ethiopian Government.

(HC Deb 10 May 2007 Vol 460 c400W)

6/13
A Home Office Minister wrote:

The Waleed camp is inside Iraq. As such the Iraqis in Waleed are internally displaced persons (IDPs) and cannot be recognised as refugees within the 1951 UN Convention relating to the Status of Refugees. Individuals can be referred for resettlement only if they are already outside of their country of origin and have been recognised as a refugee within the 1951 UN Convention by UNHCR. The UK cannot resettle any of the IDPs within Waleed.

The UK has not made representations to the Government of the United States about the situation of people in Waleed and Al-Tanf. The USA operates a large scale resettlement operation in the region and discusses directly with UNHCR which people it can assist.

(HL Deb 25 October 2007 Vol 695 cWA130)

Part Six: VII.B *The individual (including the corporation) in international law—immigration and emigration, extradition, expulsion, asylum—extradition*

6/14
(See also **6/56** and **12/3, 4**)

Extraordinary Rendition
An FCO Minister was asked if the FCO had given full co-operation to the Committee of the European Parliament which was inquiring into irregular rendition. He said:

Yes. We have not only co-operated fully with it, but by co-operation we have arranged meetings with the delegation on a range of other matters, including ministerial involvement. At the end, for all the huffing and puffing—if I can put it that way—about non-co-operation, the truth of the matter is that when it went through all the evidence, it could find no new evidence whatever in respect of the United Kingdom. That was the bottom line when it came to it. I am certain that with the resources of the European Parliament and the co-operation between ourselves and other states, if there was any evidence it would have produced it. [Q.68]

(FAC Report on Human Rights Report 2006, HC269 (2007)

6/15
The Intelligence and Security Committee reported on Rendition. It provided definitions of the way it would use various terms:

6. The term "rendition" is used to mean different things by different people.[2] It encompasses numerous variations of extra-judicial transfer such as: to countries

---

[2] The Committee has taken the term "Rendition" as not applying to transfers of individuals by methods such as extradition, deportation, removal or exclusion, although others do include such transfers in their definitions of the term.

where the person is wanted for trial; to countries where the individual can be adequately interrogated; transfer for the purposes of prolonged detention; and military transfer of battlefield detainees.

7. In order to provide clarity, the Committee has used the following terms throughout this Report:[3]

"Rendition": Encompasses any extra-judicial transfer of persons from one jurisdiction or State to another.

"Rendition to Justice": The extra-judicial transfer of persons from one jurisdiction or State to another, for the purposes of standing trial within an established and recognised legal and judicial system.

"Military Rendition": The extra-judicial transfer of persons (detained in, or related to, a theatre of military operations) from one State to another, for the purposes of military detention in a military facility.

"Rendition to Detention": The extra-judicial transfer of persons from one jurisdiction or State to another, for the purposes of detention and interrogation outside the normal legal system.

"Extraordinary Rendition": The extra-judicial transfer of persons from one jurisdiction or State to another, for the purposes of detention and interrogation outside the normal legal system, where there is a real risk of torture or cruel, inhuman or degrading treatment (CIDT).

8. For example, the transfer of battlefield detainees from Afghanistan to Guantánamo Bay would fall into the category of "Military Renditions". The transfer of a detainee unconnected to the conflict in Afghanistan to Guantánamo Bay would be a "Rendition to Detention". A transfer to a secret facility constitutes cruel and inhuman treatment because there is no access to legal or other representation and, on that basis, we would describe this as an "Extraordinary Rendition".

We set out below the legal aspects surrounding rendition.[4]

UK Domestic Law

10. The case of Nicholas Mullen (often referred to as Peter Mullen) provides the basis of the UK's position on renditions. In 1989, the Secret Intelligence Service (SIS) facilitated the transfer of Mr Mullen from Zimbabwe to the UK in order for him to stand trial on charges related to Irish republican terrorism. His transfer falls into the category of what we now call "Rendition to Justice". Mr Mullen's conviction was overturned by the Court of Appeal in February 1999 on the grounds that his deportation represented a "blatant and extremely serious failure to adhere to the rule of law" and involved a clear abuse of process.[5]

---

[3] Quotations from third parties may not necessarily conform to these definitions.

[4] It is worth noting that the Human Rights Act, European Convention on Human Rights and other international conventions were framed without rendition operations in mind and therefore do not address such transfers explicitly.

[5] *R. v. Nicholas Mullen* [1999].

11. This judgment set a legal precedent which meant that the Security Service and SIS did not look to conduct any further renditions to the UK. The Chief of SIS told the Committee: "This outcome made it clear to SIS that rendition for trial in the UK was not viable."[6]

12. As regards torture, or CIDT, under section 6 of the Human Rights Act 1998 it is unlawful for a public authority to commit torture or to inflict inhuman or degrading treatment within UK territorial jurisdiction.

International Law

13. Under Article 3 of the United Nations Convention Against Torture (UNCAT):

No State Party shall expel, return ("refouler") or extradite a person to another State where there are substantial grounds for believing that he would be in danger of being subjected to torture.

The UK therefore has an obligation to ensure that it does not knowingly assist in sending a person to another country, including by any form of rendition operation, where there is a real risk that he may be tortured.[7]

14. Article 3 of the European Convention on Human Rights (ECHR)—incorporated into UK domestic law by the Human Rights Act 1998—provides that:

No one shall be subjected to torture or to inhuman or degrading treatment or punishment.[8]

Article 7 of the 1966 International Covenant on Civil and Political Rights (ICCPR) goes further than this, adding a prohibition on cruel treatment or punishment:

No one shall be subjected to torture or cruel, inhuman or degrading treatment or punishment.

15. The UK interpretation of what constitutes CIDT is based upon definitions outlined by the European Court of Human Rights. Referring to inhuman and degrading treatment, the Court has said:

The acts complained of were such as to arouse in the applicant feelings of fear, anguish and inferiority capable of humiliating and debasing him and possibly breaking his physical and moral resistance.[9]

16. In a 2005 House of Lords ruling, Lord Bingham of Cornhill argued that "the prohibition of torture requires Member States to do more than eschew the practice of torture".[10] He cited the International Criminal Tribunal for the former Yugoslavia as saying:

---

[6] Oral evidence—SIS, 7 November 2006.

[7] "... the risk of torture must be assessed on grounds that go beyond mere theory or suspicion. However, the risk does not have to meet the test of being highly probable." UN Committee Against Torture, General Comment No. 01 to UNCAT.

[8] European Convention on Human Rights (Convention for the Protection of Human Rights and Fundamental Freedoms), 1950.

[9] *Selmouni v. France* [1999].

[10] *A (FC) and Others v. Secretary of State for the Home Department* [2005].

... States must immediately set in motion all those procedures and measures that may make it possible, within their municipal legal system, to forestall any act of torture or expeditiously put an end to any torture that is occurring.[11]

17. The rules governing consular access are laid down in Article 36 of the Vienna Convention on Consular Relations (1963), which is generally accepted as being customary international law. Under the Convention, the UK Government cannot offer consular protection to non-British nationals. In 2005, the then Foreign Secretary said:

... in international law we only have the standing to take up consular matters in respect of British citizens... It means that we cannot make representations on behalf of people, however long they have been resident in the UK, who are not our nationals. More to the point, the U.S. Government, consistent with their obligations under international law, would not accept such representations.[12]

The UK Government may make representations on behalf of non-British nationals in exceptional humanitarian cases, although it is under no obligation to do so. Furthermore, it may make informal non-consular representations in specific cases where it believes there are sufficient grounds, and we have seen that the U.S. may accept such representations in certain circumstances.

18. The legal aspects of the alleged use of UK airspace and airports in relation to possible Central Intelligence Agency (CIA) rendition flights are addressed separately in the "Ghost Flights" section of the Report (pages 57 to 63).

U.S. Interpretations of International Law

19. It is important to highlight the different legal framework under which U.S. agencies such as the CIA operate. UK domestic law and European law, including the ECHR, do not apply to U.S. operations conducted outside the UK/Council of Europe. The ECHR does not impose obligations directly on the United States; however, U.S. nationals acting in the UK are bound by UK law, which conforms to the ECHR.

20. The U.S. has said that it considers itself in a state of war against global terrorism. This has led to a number of executive and military orders authorising actions to counter the threat from terrorism. President Bush said on 29 November 2001:

... non-U.S. citizens who plan and/or commit mass murder are more than criminal suspects. They are unlawful combatants who seek to destroy our country and our way of life... We're an open society. But we're at war. The enemy has declared war on us. And we must not let foreign enemies use the forums of liberty to destroy liberty itself. Foreign terrorists and agents must never again be allowed to use our freedoms against us.[13]

21. In ratifying UNCAT, the U.S. entered an understanding as to their interpretation of "where there are substantial grounds for believing that he would be

---

[11] Ibid., *Prosecutor v. Furundzija* [1998].

[12] Statement by the Foreign Secretary, The Rt. Hon. Jack Straw, MP, 11 January 2005, Hansard Columns 179–180.

[13] Remarks by President Bush to the U.S. Attorneys Conference, 29 November 2001.

in danger of being subjected to torture". The U.S. interprets this to mean "if it is more likely than not that he would be tortured".[14]

22. This "more likely than not" approach differs significantly from that of the UK, which uses the lower "real risk" threshold. Theoretically, this means that an operation could be legal for U.S. agencies under U.S. law (because there is less than a 50% probability of torture or CIDT) but illegal for the UK Agencies to be involved with under UK law (because there is nevertheless still a real risk of torture or CIDT).

23. On 7 December 2005, an official in the Foreign Secretary's Private Office sent a memorandum to the Prime Minister's Office which discussed the limited circumstances in which assistance to other countries' rendition operations might be legal. This document was leaked in the New Statesman in January 2006:

In certain circumstances, [rendition] could be legal, if the process complied with the domestic law of both countries involved, and their international obligations. Normally, these international obligations, eg under... ICCPR would prevent an individual from being arbitrarily detained or expelled outside the normal legal process. Council of Europe countries would also be bound by the ECHR, which has similar obligations in this sense. Against this background, even a Rendition that does not involve the possibility of torture [or CIDT] would be difficult, and likely to be confined to those countries not signed up to eg the ICCPR.[15]

Memorandum entitled "Detainees", sent from the Foreign and Commonwealth Office to the Prime Minister's Office, 7 December 2005. (Report of the Intelligence and Security Committes—Rendition, CM 7171 (2007))

6/16
The Committee presented a "Summary of Conclusions and Recommendations"

A. Our intelligence-sharing relationships, particularly with the United States, are critical to providing the breadth and depth of intelligence coverage required to counter the threat to the UK posed by global terrorism. These relationships have saved lives and must continue.

B. We are concerned that Government departments have had such difficulty in establishing the facts from their own records in relation to requests to conduct renditions through UK airspace. These are matters of fundamental liberties and the Government should ensure that proper searchable records are kept.

C. Prior to 9/11, assistance to the U.S. "Rendition to Justice" programme—whether through the provision of intelligence or approval to use UK airspace—was agreed on the basis that the Americans gave assurances regarding humane treatment and that detainees would be afforded a fair trial. These actions were appropriate and appear to us to have complied with our domestic law and the UK's international obligations.

---

[14] United States Understanding II.(2)—www.ohchr.org/english/countries/ratification/9.htm#reservations

[15] The United States ratification of the ICCPR also includes a reservation: "That the United States considers itself bound by article 7 to the extent that 'cruel, inhuman or degrading treatment or punishment' means the cruel and unusual treatment or punishment prohibited by the Fifth, Eighth, and/or Fourteenth Amendments to the Constitution of the United States."

D. Those operations detailed above, involving UK Agencies' knowledge or involvement, are "Renditions to Justice", "Military Renditions" and "Renditions to Detention". They are not "Extraordinary Renditions", which we define as "the extra-judicial transfer of persons from one jurisdiction or State to another, for the purposes of detention and interrogation outside the normal legal system, where there is a real risk of torture or cruel, inhuman or degrading treatment". We note that in some of the cases we refer to, there are allegations of mistreatment, including whilst individuals were detained at Guantánamo Bay, although we have not found evidence that such mistreatment was foreseen by the Agencies. The Committee has therefore found no evidence that the UK Agencies were complicit in any "Extraordinary Rendition" operations.

E. In the immediate aftermath of the 9/11 attacks, the UK Agencies were authorised to assist U.S. "Rendition to Justice" operations in Afghanistan. This involved assistance to the CIA to capture "unlawful combatants" in Afghanistan. These operations were approved on the basis that detainees would be treated humanely and be afforded a fair trial. In the event, the intelligence necessary to put these authorisations into effect could not be obtained and the operations did not proceed. The Committee has concluded that the Agencies acted properly.

F. SIS was subsequently briefed on new powers which would enable U.S. authorities to arrest and detain suspected terrorists worldwide. In November 2001, these powers were confirmed by the Presidential Military Order. We understand that SIS was sceptical about the supposed new powers, since at the time there was a great deal of "tough talk" being used at many levels of the U.S. Administration, and it was difficult to reach a definitive conclusion regarding the direction of U.S. policy in this area. Nonetheless, the Committee concludes that SIS should have appreciated the significance of these events and reported them to Ministers.

G. The Security Service and SIS were also slow to detect the emerging pattern of "Renditions to Detention" that occurred during 2002. The UK Agencies, when sharing intelligence with the U.S. which might have resulted in the detention of an individual subject to the Presidential Military Order, should always have sought assurances on detainee treatment.

H. The cases of Bisher al-Rawi and Jamil el-Banna and others during 2002 demonstrated that the U.S. was willing to conduct "Rendition to Detention" operations anywhere in the world, including against those unconnected with the conflict in Afghanistan. We note that the Agencies used greater caution in working with the U.S., including withdrawing from some planned operations, following these cases.

I. By mid-2003, following the case of Khaled Sheikh Mohammed and suspicions that the U.S. authorities were operating "black sites", the Agencies had appreciated the potential risk of renditions and possible mistreatment of detainees. From this point, the Agencies correctly sought Ministerial approval and assurances from foreign liaison services whenever there were real risks of rendition operations resulting from their actions.

J. After April 2004—following the revelations of mistreatment at the U.S. military-operated prison at Abu Ghraib—the UK intelligence and security Agencies and the Government were fully aware of the risk of mistreatment associated with any operations that may result in U.S. custody of detainees. Assurances on humane treatment were properly and routinely sought in operations that involved any risk of rendition and/or U.S. custody.

K. The Committee has strong concerns, however, about a potential operation in early 2005 which, had it gone ahead, might have resulted in the ***. The operation was conditionally approved by Ministers, subject to assurances on humane treatment and a time limit on detention. These were not obtained and so the operation was dropped. *** [The asterisks represented redacted material, Ed.]

. . .

Q. The sharing of intelligence with foreign liaison services on suspected extremists is routine. [In two named cases, there] was nothing exceptional in the Security Service notifying the U.S. of the men's arrest and setting out its assessment of them. The telegram was correctly covered by a caveat prohibiting the U.S. authorities from taking action on the basis of the information it contained.

R. In adding the caveat prohibiting action, the Security Service explicitly required that no action (such as arrests) should be taken on the basis of the intelligence contained in the telegrams. We have been told that the Security Service would fully expect such a caveat to be honoured by the U.S. agencies— this is fundamental to their intelligence-sharing relationship. We accept that the Security Service did not intend the men to be arrested.

S. The Security Service and Foreign Office acted properly in seeking access to the detained British nationals, asking questions as to their treatment and, when they learnt of a possible rendition operation, protesting strongly.

T. We note that eventually the British nationals were released, but are concerned that, contrary to the Vienna Convention on Consular Relations, access to the men was initially denied.

U. This is the first case in which the U.S. agencies conducted a "Rendition to Detention" of individuals entirely unrelated to the conflict in Afghanistan. Given that there had been a gradual expansion of the rendition programme during 2002, it could reasonably have been expected that the net would widen still further and that greater care could have been taken. We do, however, note that Agency priorities at the time were—rightly—focused on disrupting attacks rather than scrutinising American policy. We also accept that the Agencies could not have foreseen that the U.S. authorities would disregard the caveats placed on the intelligence, given that they had honoured the caveat system for the past 20 years.

V. This case shows a lack of regard, on the part of the U.S., for UK concerns. Despite the Security Service prohibiting any action being taken as a result of its intelligence, the U.S. nonetheless planned to render the men to Guantánamo Bay. They then ignored the subsequent protests of both the Security Service and the Government. This has serious implications for the working of the relationship between the U.S. and UK intelligence and security agencies...

Y. What the rendition programme has shown is that in what it refers to as "the war on terror" the U.S. will take whatever action it deems necessary, within U.S. law, to protect its national security from those it considers to pose a serious threat. Although the U.S. may take note of UK protests and concerns, this does not appear materially to affect its strategy on rendition.

Z. It is to the credit of our Agencies that they have now managed to adapt their procedures to work round these problems and maintain the exchange of intelligence that is so critical to UK security.

AA. The Committee notes that the UK Agencies now have a policy in place to minimise the risk of their actions inadvertently leading to renditions, torture or cruel, inhuman or degrading treatment (CIDT). Where it is known that the consequences of dealing with a foreign liaison service will include torture or CIDT, the operation will not be authorised.

BB. In the cases we have reviewed, the Agencies have taken action consistent with the policy of minimising the risks of torture or CIDT (and therefore "Extraordinary Rendition") based upon their knowledge and awareness of the CIA rendition programme at that time.

CC. Where, despite the use of caveats and assurances, there remains a real possibility that the actions of the Agencies will result in torture or mistreatment, we note that the current procedure requires that approval is sought from senior management or Ministers. We recommend that Ministerial approval should be sought in all such cases.

DD. The Committee considers that "secret detention", without legal or other representation, is of itself mistreatment. Where there is a real possibility of "Rendition to Detention" to a secret facility, even if it would be for a limited time, then approval must never be given...

FF. The use of UK airspace and airports by CIA-operated aircraft is not in doubt. There have been many allegations related to these flights but there have been no allegations, and we have seen no evidence, that suggest that any of these CIA flights have transferred detainees through UK airspace (other than two "Rendition to Justice" cases in 1998 which were approved by the UK Government following U.S. requests).

GG. It is alleged that, on up to four occasions since 9/11, aircraft that had previously conducted a rendition operation overseas transited UK airspace during their return journeys (without detainees on board). The Committee has not seen any evidence that might contradict the police assessment that there is no evidential basis on which a criminal inquiry into these flights could be launched.

HH. We consider that it would be unreasonable and impractical to check whether every aircraft transiting UK airspace might have been, at some point in the past, and without UK knowledge, involved in a possibly unlawful operation. We are satisfied that, where there is sufficient evidence of unlawful activity on board an aircraft in UK airspace, be it a rendition operation or otherwise, this would be investigated by the UK authorities...

JJ. The alleged use of military airfields in the UK by rendition flights has been investigated in response to our questions to the Prime Minister. We are satisfied that there is no evidence that U.S. rendition flights have used UK airspace (except the two cases in 1998 referred to earlier in this Report) and that there is no evidence of them having landed at UK military airfields.

(Report of the Intelligence and Security Committee—Rendition, Cm7171 (2007))

6/17

The Government published a response to the Report.

The Government accepts that, with hindsight, an emerging pattern of renditions during 2002 can be identified but notes that, as the Committee acknowledges elsewhere in the Report (Conclusion U), at the time the Agencies' priorities were correctly focused on disrupting attacks rather than scrutinising U.S. policy. Moreover, as the Committee has also recognised (Conclusions I and J), once the potential risk of mistreatment arising from renditions became clear, SIS and the Security Service routinely sought approval from Ministers and assurances from foreign liaison services on humane treatment whenever there were real risks of rendition operations arising from their actions. They also took steps to provide more detailed guidance to staff.

The Government accepts that, where the Agencies consider that counter-terrorist work with foreign services raises a real possibility that torture or mistreatment could occur, they should consult Ministers before proceeding. In practice this already happens.

Since before September 2001, we have worked closely with the U.S. on a wide range of counter-terrorism issues to achieve our shared goal of combating terrorism. The UK has had continued dialogue with the U.S. on detainee-related issues, including rendition.

In response to a letter from the then Foreign Secretary, Condoleezza Rice, the U.S. Secretary of State, made a statement on 5 December 2005 in which she stated:

"The United States has respected—and will continue to respect—the sovereignty of other countries. The United States does not transport, and has not transported, detainees from one country to another for the purposes of interrogation using torture."

Dr Rice also confirmed that the U.S. respects the rules of international law, including the UN Convention Against Torture, that the U.S. does not authorise or condone the torture of detainees, and that torture and conspiracy to commit torture are crimes under U.S. law wherever they may occur in the world.

In addition, the U.S. Detainee Treatment Act, enacted on 30 December 2005, provides that no individual in the custody or under the physical control of the U.S. Government, regardless of nationality, shall be subject to cruel, inhuman or degrading treatment or punishment. This legislation makes a matter of statute what President Bush had made clear was already U.S. Government policy.

The Government welcomes these important conclusions, which underline the fact that, as the Committee reflects in paragraph 46 of its Report, the UK's intelligence and security Agencies will not assist or involve themselves in a rendition operation where there are grounds to believe that the person being rendered would face a real risk of torture or CIDT.

The Government notes the Committee's view [conclusion DD]. The UK opposes any form of deprivation of liberty that amounts to placing a detained person outside the protection of the law.

As we have pointed out in response to Conclusions C to E, when we are requested to assist another State in a rendition operation, and our assistance would be lawful, we would decide whether or not to assist taking into account all the circumstances. We would not assist in any case if to do so would put us in breach of UK law or our international obligations, including under the UN Convention Against Torture.

The Government welcomes these clear conclusions, which support the Government's repeated assurance that there is no evidence to suggest that renditions have been conducted through the UK without our permission, or in contravention of our obligations under domestic and international law. The conclusions support our clearly stated position that we have not approved, and will not approve, a policy of facilitating the transfer of individuals through the UK to places where there are substantial grounds to believe they would face a real risk of torture.

The Government agrees that it is not possible to check every flight—instead an intelligence-led approach is and must be employed. If individuals are reasonably suspected of committing criminal offences, or if there are reasonable grounds to suspect that aircraft are being used for unlawful purposes, then action can be taken. The nature of that action would depend on the facts and circumstances of any case.

(Government Response to the Intelligence and Security Committee's Report on Rendition, Cm 7172 (2007))

6/18

The Foreign Secretary was asked what undertakings have been (a) sought and (b) received from the US Administration since January 2001 that the US Administration has not rendered any detainee through UK territory or airspace since May 1997. An FCO Minister wrote:

We are clear that the US would not render a detainee through UK territory or airspace without our permission. In an interview covering these issues alongside the then Foreign Secretary in March 2006 the US Secretary of State said

"the United States respects the sovereignty of our allies and of other countries in the international system".

We have also carried out extensive searches of official records and have found no evidence of detainees being rendered through the UK or overseas territories since 1997 where there were substantial grounds to believe there was a real risk of torture.

There were four cases in 1998 where the US requested permission to render one or more detainees through the UK or overseas territories. Records show the Government refused the US request in two cases and granted the request in the two others. In both these cases, the detainees were subsequently tried and later prosecuted on criminal charges in the US.

(HC Deb 20 June 2007 Vol 461 c1608)

6/19

An FCO Minister said:

There have been persistent allegations that the Government have refused to address rendition fully and openly and that we have somehow sought to evade accountability to Parliament. The debate is an opportunity to set the record straight.

I wish at the outset to tackle two persistent myths about rendition. First... I reiterate that the Government have not approved and will not approve a policy of facilitating the transfer of individuals through the United Kingdom to places where there are substantial grounds to believe that they would face a real risk of torture.

Secondly, I reject totally the allegation that the Government have refused to address the issue fully and openly. In fact, we have done everything we can to keep the House informed and co-operated fully with international inquiries into rendition, including by the Council of Europe and the European Parliament.

I recently wrote to... the all-party extraordinary rendition group... I underlined in my letter that we carried out extensive searches of official records and found no evidence that detainees were rendered through the UK or overseas territories since 1997 if there were substantial grounds to believe that there was a real risk of torture.

...new legislation has been called for to prescribe how any future requests for rendition through the UK should be dealt with. I am not persuaded that new legislation would add practical value, but, given the work that he and the all-party group have done, I have asked my officials to consider the matter further to confirm that assessment...

...the term "rendition" is inexact. However, the Government's policy is clear: the facts of each individual case will determine whether any particular rendition is lawful. [It was not mentioned] that there are many other states that "rendite" people. Some of them are geographically close to us. If we are requested to assist another state and our assistance would be lawful, we will decide whether to assist, taking into account all the circumstances. We would not assist in any case if it would put us in breach of UK law or our international obligations.

In 1998, the US made four requests for permission to render one or more detainees through the UK or overseas territories. Records show that the Government refused two requests and granted two others. In both cases where permission was granted, the detainees were subsequently tried on criminal charges in the US. One pleaded guilty to murder, and the other was charged for his part in the 1998 attack on the US embassy in Nairobi. He was sentenced to life imprisonment...

In its fourth report, "Foreign Policy Aspects of the War against Terrorism", which was published last summer, the Foreign Affairs Committee concluded that although there had been speculation about the complicity of the British Government in unlawful rendition, "there has been no hard evidence of the truth of any of these allegations."

I commend that conclusion...

...I believe that torture is wrong in every respect, and I will fight the corner for not using it or any technique that puts an individual in a position in which, for the sake of getting intelligence or information out of them, their human rights are degraded and they are treated in an abhorrent way...We are completely opposed to such activities. They are a violation of every international treaty that we have signed up to and of British law, and I hope that that is clear.

The Minister was asked if he was seriously suggesting that the overwhelming body of evidence that has been produced in Washington to show that the Americans have been engaged in rendition, a policy that involves cruel, inhumane and degrading treatment that amounts to torture, did not exist or had been made up? The Minister said:

No, it certainly is not a figment of the imagination. Such treatment would not take place in Britain, in British prisons or in prisons that Britain is responsible for administering in any other territory.

I said that we would not allow the kinds of things that we have heard about from Guantanamo Bay to take place in this country.

I would like to make this important point. Since before 11 September 2001, we have worked closely with the US to achieve our shared goal of fighting terrorism. As part of that close co-operation, we have made it clear to the US authorities that we expect them to seek permission to render detainees via UK territory and airspace, and that we will grant permission only if we are satisfied that the rendition would accord with UK law and our international obligations. We have explained our understanding of our obligations under the UN convention against torture and the European convention on human rights. Indeed, it was this country that moved the UN General Assembly resolution—we co-sponsored it last year. It sets out our opposition to any form of deprivation of liberty that amounts to placing a detained person outside the protection of the law.

(HC Deb 26 June 2007 Vol 462 c44–48WH)

6/20

Diplomatic Assurances
An FCO Minister wrote:

We have signed memoranda of understanding concerning the provision of assurances in respect of persons subject to deportation with Jordan, Libya and Lebanon. Arrangements allowing deportations with assurances (DWA) are also in place with Algeria on the basis of an exchange of letters, signed by the former Prime Minister [Tony Blair] and Algerian President Abdelaziz Bouteflika on 11 July 2006 and exchanges of diplomatic Notes Verbale. (See **[2006] UKMIL 6/33**)

To date, eight Algerian terrorist suspects have been deported to Algeria under these arrangements. Individual assurances were also sought in each case, concerning their treatment on return and criminal status in Algeria. A ninth individual holding dual Algerian/French nationality was deported to France outside the framework of the DWA arrangements.

There is no formal monitoring body in Algeria. Individuals deported from the UK under the DWA arrangements may remain in touch with our embassy in Algiers after their return and were invited to provide details of next of kin or an alternative contact point in Algeria. In turn they were provided with a contact point at the embassy and it was explained that they, or their nominated contact point, could maintain contact with the embassy after their return to Algeria. To date, two individuals have taken up this offer. Further to any deportation under these arrangements, UK officials also maintain close contact with the Algerian authorities.

We are in discussion with other countries and will update the House if and when we reach agreement. We draw on experience to date in seeking to negotiate any new agreement.

There are no plans to make reports on monitoring regularly available.

(HC Deb 4 December 2007 Vol 696 cWA181)

Part Six: VII.C *The individual (including the corporation) in international law—immigration and emigration, extradition, expulsion, asylum—expulsion*

6/21
The UK Borders Act 2007 provides, *inter alia*, for the mandatory deportation of certain foreign criminals after they have served their sentences, subject to exceptions:

33 Exceptions

(2) Exception 1 is where removal of the foreign criminal in pursuance of the deportation order would breach–

(a) a person's Convention rights, or

(b) the United Kingdom's obligations under the Refugee Convention.

(4) Exception 3 is where the removal of the foreign criminal from the United Kingdom in pursuance of a deportation order would breach rights of the foreign criminal under the Community treaties.

(5) Exception 4 is where the foreign criminal [is subject to various kinds of extradition proceedings].

(7) The application of an exception–

(a) does not prevent the making of a deportation order;

(b) results in it being assumed neither that deportation of the person concerned is conducive to the public good nor that it is not conducive to the public good;

but section 32(4) [that the deportation of the foreign criminal is conducive to the public good] applies despite the application of Exception 1 or 4.

6/22

It was put to an FCO Minister by the FAC that Manfred Nowak, the UN special rapporteur on torture, had suggested that [the UK's] MOUs with various countries, including Jordan, Libya and Lebanon, might be being used to circumvent international obligations on torture. Quite recently, a Canadian-Syrian had been picked up by US border officials and sent back to Syria, where he was duly tortured. In the past few days, the Canadian Prime Minister had apologised and compensated the victim of that wrongful arrest. The Minister was asked what assurance the FAC could have that our MOUs carry any greater certainty than the Canadian one. The Minister said:

I will deal with this in three parts. First, I have spent a great deal of time with representatives of the Human Rights Council. In addition to speaking to them personally, I have had policy and legal advisers explain to them what we are attempting to do. Our policy is absolutely consistent with our values and our obligations. It not only ensures that we meet our international obligations, it provides a platform for engagement, which is important for capacity-building work on human rights issues. The policy cannot be seen on its own. It is not about watering down our values; it is about trying to ensure the best guarantee of our own security, while at the same time being able to engage with countries about certainty on human rights and values.

Each of these agreements has its own parts... Six men were deported to Algeria between June 2006 and 2007; I cannot supply the names because of court proceedings. No detainees have so far been returned to Libya, Lebanon or Jordan. [Q.65]

The Minister was asked why there should be confidence in the scrutiny arrangements when well-known international non-governmental organisations had refused to take part. He said:

The confidence comes from the fact that we do not go into these lightly. As I said, they are set down on our principles and our values. It is not true to say that every NGO will not get involved in issues concerned with these countries. We have not, to my knowledge, asked those two organisations [Amnesty International and Human Rights Watch, Ed] to participate in that regard. There is a need for work in a range of countries, including those with which we have deportation arrangements, on the wider issues of human rights. It is true that this is best done by building capacity and working with civil society in those countries, as well as with the Governments concerned. In doing that, we need to ensure that the work that is being done in those countries is promoted and is seen through to its logical conclusion. We must try to ensure safety for our own citizens too, so we must get the balance right. The balance must be one where we deport people with assurances, but where the assurances are worth the paper that they are written on. [Q.66]

(FAC Report, Human Rights Report 2006, HC 269 (2007))

6/23
An FCO Minister wrote to the FAC with further information to the evidence he had given orally to the Committee. He wrote:

DEPORTATION WITH ASSURANCES (Q65/66)

I undertook to write to the Committee with fuller details of the arrangements with Algeria, Libya, Jordan and Lebanon. We have already made much of the information that follows available to the Committee in the form of our recent response to the Committee's response to the Annual Human Rights Report... For ease of reference I attach a copy of the arrangements we have concluded with Libya. (See **UKMIL [2005] 6/24**) I hope that this short overview will be of assistance to the Committee in their work.

Libya, Jordan and Lebanon

MOUs were signed with Libya, Jordan and Lebanon in October 2005, August 2005 and December 2005 respectively. The MOUs are bilateral framework agreements which formalise the process of obtaining assurances regarding the future treatment of people we wish to deport from the UK. They contain assurances, agreed by both parties, that we believe will safeguard the rights of individuals being returned. Examples include access to medical treatment, adequate nourishment and accommodation as well as treatment in a humane manner in accordance with internationally accepted standards. Additional, specific assurances may be obtained in individual cases depending on the circumstances of each case.

At the time of signature, the British Government also set out to the governments of Libya, Lebanon and Jordan, its firm opposition to the use of the death penalty in any circumstances and confirmed in writing that the Government would not return an individual if that person were at significant risk of being subjected to such a penalty.

In Libya, Lebanon and Jordan monitoring bodies have been appointed to oversee the implementation of assurances. Monitoring is one element of the wider package (which includes the assurances which I have mentioned above). In selecting and appointing monitoring bodies, the British Government and the government of the receiving State take into consideration eg capacity, independence, access to expertise. Our Embassies are closely involved in the selection process and liaise with monitoring bodies once appointed. The monitoring body in each case must have capacity for the task ie have experts ("Monitors") trained in physical and psychological sign of torture and ill-treatment; have, or have access to, sufficient independent lawyers, doctors, forensic specialists, and specialists on human rights, humanitarian law and prison systems and the police. Where necessary, additional training or capacity building measures can be provided to ensure the monitoring can function effectively.

The monitoring body operates under terms of reference, which are agreed by the British Government, the receiving state and the monitoring body itself. Under the Terms of Reference the monitoring body will undertake a number of tasks, including accompanying deportees from the UK to the receiving state and to their home, or other destination; to ensure that contact details are obtained for the returnee and his/her next of kin. They will make arrangements to maintain contact with an individual whether he/she is in detention or at liberty. The monitoring body should provide frank reports to authorities of both States and should contact the sending State immediately if its observations warrant.

The Qadhafi Development Foundation has been appointed as the monitoring body in Libya, the Adaleh Centre in Jordan and the Institute for Human Rights of the Beirut Bar Association in Lebanon.

Capacity building training is already being provided to the monitoring body in Jordan and will shortly be provided in Libya and Lebanon in the area of international human rights law and also in the detection of signs of torture and ill-treatment. The British Government also supports, and has done so for some time, wider human rights projects in the Middle East and North Africa. For example the British Embassy in Libya run a Prison Management Project with the International Centre for Prison Studies (ICPS) of King's College, and the Libyan Judicial Police. In Jordan the Embassy has funded training courses, capacity building and study visits in the UK for the Jordanian Ministry of Justice and the Jordanian police, as well as a project with the National Centre for Human Rights to disseminate knowledge of human rights in Jordanian schools.

Algeria

There is no MOU with Algeria. Instead the arrangements include an Exchange of Letters, signed by the Prime Minister and Algerian President Bouteflika on 11 July 2006 and an exchange of Note Verbales in each individual case. The Exchange of Letters and assurances in individual cases safeguard the rights of the individuals being returned. In the Exchange of Letters both Governments undertake to abide by fundamental freedoms such as the freedom of movement and right of abode. In particular they undertake to uphold their obligations under national and international law. The British Government set out in the Exchange of Letters its firm opposition to the use of the death penalty in any circumstances and confirmed that the Government would not return an individual to Algeria if that person were at significant risk of being subjected to such a penalty. No monitoring body has been appointed in Algeria.

General remarks

The arrangements with Algeria, Libya, Jordan and Lebanon apply to individuals whom the Government wishes to deport on grounds of national security. An individual who is served with a deportation order in these circumstances has the right to appeal against his deportation. Deportation may not take place if an appeal to the British courts is outstanding.

To date the British courts have considered five appeals against deportation to Algeria, as well as one Jordanian case and one Libyan appeal. The Special Immigration Appeals Commission has published judgments in four cases, the Jordanian and three involving Algerians. In each case the court upheld the deportation order. The Government welcomes these judgments. Judgment in respect of the Libyan case is expected shortly. [*DD & Anor v Secretary of State for the Home Department* [2008] EWCA Civ 28, upholding the SIAC conclusions that the MoU did not reduce the risk to the applicants, Ed.]

During my evidence to the Committee I also undertook to provide further information about the two Algerians who were deported from the United Kingdom in June of last year. The paragraphs below detail this information. I have also included an explanation of the position of a further four individuals, who have also since returned to Algeria.

In my evidence I explained to the Committee that I used initials to refer to the men because of British court proceedings. The same procedure applies here.

Two Algerians, "I" and "V", were deported in June 2006 following withdrawal of their appeals against deportation from the UK. They were detained and interviewed on arrival in Algeria. They were released after five days and six days in detention respectively. On release they were reunited with their families.

Between 20 and 27 January 2007 a further four Algerians were deported to Algeria after either withdrawing or waiving their appeals against deportation. They were known as "K", "H" and "P". The fourth man was formerly known as "Q"; he recently waived his right to anonymity and is now known as Mr Dendani.

Prior to removal, each individual was provided with the contact details of the British Embassy in Algiers and it was explained that they or a representative could maintain contact with the Embassy following their return. British Embassy officials have been in and remain in close contact with the Algerian authorities regarding all four deportees. Only one individual, "H", specifically requested contact arrangements. These were established before "H" left the UK. The British Embassy in Algiers has been in touch with H's family since "H" returned.

The Algerian authorities have told us that "K" was detained on 24 January 2007 and released without charge on 4 February. "P" was detained on 27 January 2007 and released without charge on 30 January. Amnesty International reported on 8 February that "K" had rejoined his family and had not reported being subject to any ill-treatment during his detention. Mr Dendani was detained on 25 January 2007 and subsequently brought before a court. He has been charged with offences under Article 87 of the Algerian Criminal Code, (membership of an armed terrorist group active abroad) and under Article 249 (assumption of the name of a third party).

"H" was detained on 31 January 2007 and brought before a court on 5 February 2007. He has been charged with offences under Article 87 of the Algerian Criminal Code (membership of an armed terrorist group active abroad). He has had contact with his family since being charged and it is the Government's understanding that he is being held in a civilian prison. He has had access to an Algerian lawyer. The British Government will continue to monitor the cases of "Q" and "H" closely.

All four men were either released or charged before the 12 day detention period, provided for in Article 51 of the Algerian Criminal Code, had expired. All were able to contact their families during that initial period of detention.

By way of conclusion I would only add that, as I said when I gave my evidence to the Committee, the United Kingdom is not in any way seeking to evade its international human rights obligations. Indeed it is precisely to uphold these obligations that the Government has sought assurances from Libya, Lebanon, Jordan and Algeria before deporting these individuals.

(FAC Human Rights Annual Report 2006, HC269 (2007)

6/24

The FCO responded to a FAC question, as follows:

3. HOW WELL ARE THE MEMORANDA OF UNDERSTANDING WITH JORDAN, LIBYA AND LEBANON WORKING, AND WHETHER ANY FURTHER SUCH MEMORANDA ARE DUE TO COME INTO FORCE.

Libya

The Memorandum of Understanding (MoU) on deportation with assurances was signed with the Libyan authorities on 18 October 2005. The related agreement to appoint the official monitoring body in Libya, the Qadhafi Development Foundation (QDF), was signed on 8 May 2006. Agreement has also been reached to appoint the National Council to the Independent Monitoring Boards as the UK monitoring body. Since the MoU's first test in a court of law, during the hearing of an appeal against deportation by two Libyans currently held in the UK, concluded only on 10 November, it is too soon to assess fully how well it is working. The Court (the Special Immigration Appeals Commission—SIAC) is now considering its decision.

During the hearing, the detail, advantages and reliability of the MoU and the monitoring bodies were covered in detail by the Government witness, Counsel for the Government and Counsel for the Appellants. Until SIAC's judgment is handed down, we will not know how well the MoU and its assurances were received by the Court, but one aspect of the MoU which has worked particularly well so far is the co-operation the Libyan authorities have given to our requests for additional information and/or assurances in relation to individual deportation cases subject to appeal.

We also believe that the QDF have the ability and capacity to carry out the full range of duties to oversee the implementation of the assurances set out in the MoU. The Government is working, together with the Foundation, to enhance the capabilities of the QDF in preparation for its monitoring role. This includes plans for training in international human rights law and recognising torture.

Jordan

The MoU with Jordan was signed on 10 August 2005. A monitoring body (the Adaleh Centre) was appointed on 13 February 2006. Their terms of reference will allow them to monitor, unrestricted, an individual who is returned to Jordan under the MoU. The first Jordanian MoU case (Abu Qatada) was heard by SIAC in March/April 2006. A judgment is expected shortly. [*Othman (Jordan) v Home Secretary* [2008] EWCA Civ 290, denying removal to Jordan on the basis that the admissibility of evidence obtained by torture in Jordan render a real risk that the applicant would not receive a fair trial, Ed.] Jordanian co-operation during this hearing was excellent. We are most grateful to the Jordanians for their continued assistance and support for the MoU and we believe, strongly, that the Jordanians will adhere to the terms of the MoU as and when any individuals are returned. The Government is working with the monitoring body in Jordan to enhance its capabilities in preparation for its monitoring role. Training has been carried out in international human rights law.

There are two further Jordanian cases being prepared, to be heard by SIAC in the early part of 2007. Jordanian co-operation on both these cases continues and there is good understanding by the Jordanians as to the importance of the MoU to the UK.

Lebanon

The MoU with Lebanon was signed on 23 December 2005. No Lebanese cases have yet come before SIAC and no one has been deported to Lebanon under the terms of the MoU.

As the Committee may be aware, the framework for deportations to Algeria is not an MoU but an Exchange of Letters on deportation between the Prime Minister and President Bouteflika that was concluded during the President's visit to London on 11 July 2006. This high level exchange is supplemented by individual assurances in each case.

The Government judges that based on these arrangements it can deport terrorist suspects to Algeria while remaining consistent with the UK's domestic and international human rights obligations. This judgment is based on the changing circumstances in Algeria—in particular the Algeria Charter for Peace and National Reconciliation, on the rapidly developing relationship between the UK and Algeria and on the assurances given by the Algerian Government on individual deportees.

The Special Immigration Appeals Commission has so far (14 December) heard four Algerian cases. Judgment has been handed down in two of those cases. In both, SIAC found it would be safe to deport the Appellant to Algeria. [*MT and Others (Algeria) v Home Secretary* [2007] EWCA Civ 808—the cases were sent back to the SIAC (but not on the adequacy of the assurarances from Algeria to reduce the risk of ill-treatment), Ed]

(FAC Report, Human Rights Report 2006, HC 269 (2007))

6/25

The Foreign Secretary was asked what (a) investigations she had undertaken into and (b) reports she had received on the detention of the Algerian nationals known as Q and K in Algeria following their deportation from the UK; [and] whether access is permitted to the two men. An FCO Minister wrote:

Four individuals suspected of involvement in terrorist activity were deported to Algeria between 20 and 27 January 2007. Embassy officials in Algiers are in regular contact with senior Algerian Government officials. The Algerian Government have provided information on all four men, including whether they have been detained. The latest information is that all four men were detained for questioning; two were released before the 12 day period of detention authorised under the Algerian Penal Code expired; one man remained in detention as of 6 February (the 12 day period of detention not having expired in his case); and one remained in detention, having been charged with an offence before the 12 day period expired. Article 51(a)(l) of the Algerian Penal Code states that a person held in custody is entitled to communicate with his family and to receive visits, subject to preservation of the secrecy of the investigation. Embassy officials will stay in close touch with the Algerian Government.

(HC Deb 8 February 2007 Vol 456 c1125W)

6/26

She was asked for further information. The Minister wrote:

Embassy officials in Algiers have remained in close contact with the Algerian Government concerning the situation of the four individuals deported from the UK between 20 and 27 January 2007. Algerian Government officials have confirmed that "K" was detained on 24 January and released on 4 February; that "P" was detained on 27 January and released on 30 January; that Reda Dendani ("Q") was detained on 25 January and subsequently brought before a court and charged with membership of an armed terrorist group under Article 87 of the Algerian Criminal Code as well as assumption of the name of a third party under Article 249 of that same Code; and that "H" was detained on 31 January and subsequently brought before a court and charged with membership of an armed terrorist group under Article 87 of the Code. Each individual was either charged or released before the expiration of the 12 day detention period authorised under the Algerian Criminal Procedure Code. Embassy officials continue to stay in touch with Algerian Government officials.

(HC Deb 6 March 2007 Vol 457 c1826W)

6/27
A Home Office Minister wrote:

We put migration at the heart of our bilateral relations. We have good long-standing migration relationships with many countries. We have signed Memoranda of Understanding (MoU) that include arrangements for the return of failed asylum seekers and illegal migrants. We have these arrangements with Afghanistan, Azerbaijan, China, India, Iran, Iraq, Nigeria, Pakistan, Somaliland, United Arab Emirates (Dubai) and Vietnam. We have not been able to implement our MoU with Iran as the arrangements originally negotiated are no longer appropriate or practical. In addition to the European Community Readmission Agreements to which the UK is party, we have bilateral readmission agreements with Albania, Bulgaria, Romania and Switzerland. We have concluded negotiations with Serbia and Montenegro, but texts have not yet been signed with those countries. An agreement has been signed with Algeria and is currently in the process of ratification. The content of MoU negotiations is confidential for operational reasons; however the text of a bilateral readmission agreement becomes publicly available once it has been signed and laid before Parliament. Broadly, MoUs cover the mechanics of arranging returns of immigration offenders between the UK and the relevant country.

(HC Deb 8 March 2007 Vol 457 c132WS)

6/28
The Home Secretary was asked what provisions he had made for the safe reception of the families and children due to be removed by charter flight to the Democratic Republic of Congo in the week beginning 26 February. A Home Office Minister wrote:

All removals are carried out in accordance with our obligations under the 1951 Geneva Convention Relating to the Status of Refugees and its 1967 Protocol (Refugee Convention), the European Convention on Human Rights (ECHR) and in line with international human rights law.

The Home Office do not routinely monitor the treatment of individuals once they are removed from the UK. However, if specific allegations are made that any returnee, to any country, has experienced ill-treatment on return from the UK, then these are followed up through the FCO and the high commission in the returned country as a matter of urgency.

(HC Deb 27 February 2007 Vol 457 c1208W)

Part Six: VII.D *The individual (including the corporation) in international law—immigration and emigration, extradition, expulsion, asylum—asylum*

6/29

The Government were asked whether their current policy and practice regarding the repatriation of children of unsuccessful asylum applicants met all the needs of those children. A Home Office Minister said:

...asylum seekers who have been found by the Home Office and independent appeals process not to be in need of international protection and who therefore have no legal basis to stay in the United Kingdom are expected to return, along with their dependants. There are safeguards in place to ensure that those whom we remove are not at risk of persecution or inhuman treatment. We cannot take responsibility for the welfare of families after their return but, when deciding whether return is practicable and when making arrangements for the return, the welfare of any child involved is, of course, an important consideration.

(HL Deb 21 February 2007 Vol 689, 1063)

Part Six: VIII. *The individual (including the corporation) in international law—human rights and fundamental freedoms*

6/30 (see also **6/49**)

Afghanistan

The Minister of Defence wrote:

The Memorandum of Understanding between the Government of the UK and the Government of Afghanistan on the transfer of detainees was signed on 30 September 2006. Since then, three individuals have been held in detention by UK armed forces. One was subsequently transferred to the Afghan authorities and two were released.

Although there have been some minor procedural problems with the timely notification of the International Committee of the Red Cross and the Afghan Independent Human Rights Commission, both organisations have been informed about these detentions, and all other detentions which took place before the MoU was signed. We are working with both organisations with a view to ensuring that in future all notifications will occur in a timely manner.

(HC Deb 8 January 2007 Vol 455 c77W)

6/31

The Foreign Secretary was asked which NATO members currently involved in ISAF in Afghanistan do not have Memoranda of

Understanding on the transfer of detainees with the Afghan authorities. He wrote:

We are aware of bilateral Memorandum of Understanding (MoU) between the Afghan Government and The Netherlands, Canada, Norway, and Denmark. The UK also has a bilateral MoU.

Our MoU details the arrangements reached between the UK and Afghan Governments and sets out the responsibilities of both parties before and after the transfer to Afghan authorities of persons detained in Afghanistan by British forces.

(HC Deb 27 November 2007 Vol 468 c340W)

6/32

Burma

[This is an example of many similar answers about human rights concerns in individual foreign States. They are not generally reproduced in UKMIL because the details are readily available in the FCO's Human Rights Report—www.fco.gov.uk/resources/en/pdf/human-rights-report-2007, Ed.]

The Foreign Secretary was asked what progress she had made in persuading the Government of Burma to improve their observance of human rights. An FCO Minister wrote:

The Foreign and Commonwealth Office identifies Burma as a country of concern in our 2006 Annual Report on Human Rights. The Government's policy is to promote full respect for human rights in Burma encouraging the rule of law, democracy and good governance, and the freedom of association and speech in accordance with international human rights law.

We have been at the forefront of international efforts over many years to bring pressure to bear on the military regime to re-establish democracy and to respect human rights. We take every opportunity to raise human rights issues with the regime and remind them of their obligations to adhere to international human rights law. Our Embassy in Rangoon also delivers capacity building assistance through our Global Opportunities Fund in support of these objectives.

I have raised the human rights situation regularly with the Burmese regime and other Governments in the region. On 16 June 2006, I called in the Burmese Ambassador and on 5 July 2006 I wrote to the Burmese Foreign Minister, highlighting our many concerns. On 18 September 2006, I raised the serious human rights situation with the Association of South East Asian Nations (ASEAN) Ambassadors, including the Burmese Ambassador, and on 4 December 2006 with the ASEAN Secretary-General. I have also raised Burma with the Governments of China, India, Japan, Thailand, Malaysia and South Korea. I have discussed the human rights abuses taking place in Burma with Juan Mendez, the UN Special Adviser on the Prevention of Genocide. I discussed Burma in detail with Ibrahim Gambari, the UN Under Secretary-

General for Political Affairs, on 15 November 2006, following his visit to the country. Most recently, I raised the human rights situation in Burma in my address to the Human Rights Council in Geneva on 13 March and at the EU/ASEAN Ministerial Meeting in Nuremberg on 15 March, in the presence of the Burmese Deputy Foreign Minister.

In addition, our Ambassador in Rangoon regularly raises human rights with the regime, most recently when he met the Burmese Ministers for Planning and Immigration and the Burmese Deputy Foreign Minister on 5 January.

The UK works closely with the EU and other international partners, including the UN and ASEAN, to promote human rights in Burma, and fully supports the efforts of the UN Special Rapporteur for Human Rights in Burma, Professor Sergio Pinheiro.

We supported the efforts to have Burma added to the UN Security Council agenda in September 2006 and co-sponsored with the US a UN Security Council Resolution on Burma. This was put to the vote on 12 January. Nine members of the Security Council supported the Resolution. However, three States, including two Permanent Members of the Council, voted against and as such the Resolution was not adopted. While the result was disappointing, it is important to note that all Security Council members agreed that there were serious issues of concern in Burma. This, and the positive votes from the majority of Security Council partners, reflected the international community's deep concern over the plight of Burma's people. Burma remains on the UN Security Council agenda.

(HC Deb 19 April 2007 Vol 459 c736W)

6/33

The Foreign Secretary was asked whether Burma will be taking part in negotiations regarding a free trade area between the EU and ASEAN. An FCO Minister wrote:

The European Commission, on behalf of the EU, and the Association of South East Asian Nations (ASEAN) countries as a bloc agreed to enter into negotiations on a Free Trade Agreement (FTA) on 4 May. It is for the ASEAN states to decide how they are to be represented at the negotiations. The mandate to negotiate the FTA was agreed by the EU at the 23 April General Affairs and External Relations Council. The UK and like-minded member states were instrumental in securing language within the council conclusions and the mandate, which will have the effect of excluding Burma from the EU/ASEAN FTA. Burma will not benefit from the proposed EU-ASEAN FTA under its current regime.

(HC Deb 13 June 2007 Vol 461 c1089W)

6/34

An FCO Minister wrote:

There are provisions in the Constitution of the International Labour Organisation (ILO) which allow a state to pursue a complaint that another state has breached an ILO convention; this could ultimately lead to proceedings in the International

Court of Justice. However, the Secretariat of the ILO believe that it would be wrong to start such action now in respect of forced labour in Burma. The ILO want to see the Memorandum of Understanding, that they signed with the Burmese government on 26 February 2007, produce results. The memorandum provides that alleged victims of forced labour in Burma will have full freedom to submit complaints to the ILO Liaison Officer in Rangoon.

We support the actions of the ILO aimed at ensuring that Burma complies with its international obligations on forced labour. We are actively working with our European and international partners, as well as through the UN and ILO, to press the regime to end the appalling human rights violations and to engage in a genuine process of national reconciliation involving all relevant parties and groups in Burma.

(HC Deb 13 November 2007 Vol 467 c107W–108W)

6/35

Convention on the Elimination of All Forms of Discrimination against Women

A Minister wrote:

The United Kingdom entered an immigration reservation when it ratified the Convention on the Elimination of All Forms of Discrimination against Women in 1986, in order to ensure that the Convention would not impede immigration policies and procedures in operation at the time. However, preparatory work for the implementation of the Human Rights Act 1998 subsequently ensured that all policies and practices operated by the then immigration and nationality directorate were non-discriminatory on the grounds of sex. An Interdepartmental Review of International Human Rights Instruments was carried out in 2004 and concluded that the reservation for immigration purposes was no longer appropriate and, therefore, the United Kingdom should withdraw its immigration reservation on this Convention.

(HC Deb 9 July 2007 Vol 462 c1350W)

6/36

An FCO Minister wrote:

The Government are working to encourage the extension of the UK's obligation under the UN Convention on the Elimination of Discrimination against Women to all the UK populated Overseas Territories. With the agreement of the respective territory governments, we have extended this Convention to the British Virgin Islands, the Falkland Islands and the Turks and Caicos Islands.

The Cayman Islands Government have formally requested that the Convention on the Elimination of Discrimination Against Women should be extended to them. Further legislative work is ongoing and will need to be completed before the Convention can be extended. The Governments of Bermuda and Gibraltar have also agreed to draft legislation to enable the Convention on the Elimination of Discrimination Against Women to be extended to them.

We will continue to encourage those UK Overseas Territories that have not yet agreed to the extension of the Convention on the Elimination of Discrimination Against Women to do so.

(HC Deb 10 October 2007 Vol 464 c673W–674W)

6/37
Convention on the Rights of the Child

The Home Secretary was asked if she will consider removing the UK's immigration reservation to Article 22 of the United Nations Convention on the Rights of the Child. A Minister wrote:

The UK supports the work that the United Nations is doing in improving standards of care for children in countries where care arrangements are non-existent or poor. In the UK our domestic laws honour the spirit of the Convention in relation to the standards of care and treatment available to children, including asylum-seeking children. The Government believe the reservation remains justified in order to maintain an effective immigration control. The Convention on the Rights of the Child obliges its signatories to put the 'best interests' of the child first in making decisions and there are a number of instances where this may prevent lawful immigration functions being carried out. The Convention on the Elimination of Discrimination against Women obliges signatories to treat men and women equally which creates less of a concern for carrying out immigration functions.

We provide protection to children subject to immigration control via the Children Act and other domestic legislation that requires the authorities to fulfil duties in relation to children; and also through the Human Rights Act. In addition we are proposing to introduce a code of practice to ensure that in carrying out its functions in the UK the Border and Immigration Agency takes appropriate steps to keep children safe from harm while they are in the UK.

[The reservation reads as follows:

The United Kingdom reserves the right to apply such legislation, in so far as it relates to the entry into, stay in and departure from the United Kingdom of those who do not have the right under the law of the United Kingdom to enter and remain in the United Kingdom, and to the acquisition and possession of citizenship, as it may deem necessary from time to time, Ed.].

(HC Deb 9 July 2007 Vol 462 c1350W–1351W)

6/38
An FCO Minister said:

The Government have no plans to incorporate the Convention on the Rights of the Child into domestic legislation. UK law often goes further than the convention requires. The key articles and general principles are given full effect in the Human Rights Act 1998, which incorporates the articles of the European Convention on Human Rights.

(HL Deb 21 November 2007 Vol 696 c827)

6/39

Death Penalty

An FCO Minister wrote:

Since 1 May 1997 we have made numerous representations about the application of the death penalty. In that period, over 20 countries have abolished the death penalty for all crimes. As stated in the Foreign and Commonwealth Office's 2006 Annual Human Rights Report we and the EU have lobbied in 2005–06, among other countries, Afghanistan, Bangladesh, Belarus, Botswana, Cameroon, China, the Democratic People's Republic of Korea, India, Indonesia, Iran, Iraq, Japan, Kenya, Kuwait, Kyrgyzstan, Libya, Malawi, Papua New Guinea, Pakistan, the Palestinian Authority, the Philippines, Republic of Korea, Rwanda, Saudi Arabia, Sierra Leone, Singapore, Somalia, Sudan, Syria, Taiwan, Tajikistan, Tanzania, Trinidad and Tobago, Uganda, the US, Vietnam and Yemen. Since 1 May 1997, we have lobbied most, if not all, countries which retain the death penalty in law. We have carried this out through multi-lateral and bilateral démarches or dialogues, and through lobbying for co-sponsorship of resolutions in the Commission for Human Rights and at the United Nations General Assembly.

(HC Deb 15 January 2007 Vol 455 c822W)

6/40

Death Penalty—Afghanistan

Statement by the EU Presidency on behalf of all EU Member States and Norway on the execution by the Government of Afghanistan of fifteen Afghan nationals on the 7th October 2007 Kabul, Afghanistan

It is with deep regret that the EU and Norway have learned of the execution of fifteen Afghan Nationals on the 7th October. The European Union and Norway oppose the death penalty in all cases and accordingly seeks its universal abolition, through a global moratorium on the death penalty as the first step.

The European Union Member States and Norway would like to make an urgent appeal to halt any possible further executions and to request the Government of Afghanistan to reconsider establishing a moratorium on the death penalty. Furthermore they would like to request the Government of Afghanistan to consider the accession of Afghanistan to the Second Optional Protocol to the International Covenant on Civil and Political Rights (ICCPR) on the abolition of the death penalty.

The EU and Norway are concerned that the procedural guarantees for a fair trial were not in place given the weak state of the Afghan judicial system.

Furthermore they are concerned about the way the death penalty was carried out in secrecy. Executions under these circumstances are contrary to internationally recognised human rights norms and neglect the dignity and worth of the human person.

The EU and Norway call on the Government of Afghanistan to respect their international obligations, particularly in the field of Human Rights.

(www.fco.gov.uk/news)

6/41
A Minister wrote:

The Government were concerned to hear about the case of Sayed Pawez [a journalist who was convicted on insulting Islam, Ed.]. We are opposed to the death penalty for any crime. We fully support the right to freedom of expression and the right to a fair trial. We are pursuing the matter in Afghanistan through the EU and UN. The office of the UN Special Representative in Afghanistan has already called publicly for a review of the case.

(HC Dec 30 January 2007 Vol 456 c395W)

6/42

Death Penalty—Iran
The FCO sent a memorandum to the FAC:

57. Iran executed more people in 2005 and 2006 than any other country in the world except China (whose population is over 15 times the size). Iran does not issue official figures and reliable data is hard to come by. But, against a worldwide decreasing trend in the use of the death penalty, Amnesty International estimates that at least 94 people were executed in Iran in 2005, and 177 in 2006. Numbers look set to grow again in 2007, as, at time of writing, over 150 people have been executed already this year.

58. The UK has repeatedly called on Iran to abolish the death penalty. In particular we object to the Iranian authorities' failure to respect even the most basic of minimum standards regarding the application of capital punishment. Many death sentences are carried out in public. We have doubts as to whether all death sentences are the result of a fair trial and whether everyone who is sentenced to death in Iran is able to exhaust all avenues of appeal available to them. The hanging of two youths aged 17 and 20 in Khorrambad (Lorestan province) on 13 May 2006 occurred barely a month after their alleged crime.

Juvenile executions

59. Iran is one of the few countries in the world that still imposes the death sentence for crimes committed before the age of 18. It was one of only two

countries in the world known to have executed child offenders in 2006. Reports suggest that between five and eight juvenile executions took place in 2005—more than in any recent year—at least two in 2006, and two so far in 2007. According to Amnesty International, over 60 juvenile offenders (under the age of 18 when their crimes were committed) remain on death row in Iran.

60. This is contrary to Iran's international commitments under the International Covenant on Civil and Political Rights (ICCPR) and the Convention on the Rights of the Child (CRC). The executions also run contrary to Iranian assurances that a moratorium is in place on capital punishments against minors, including the Iranian declaration to the UN Committee on the Rights of the Child in January 2005.

61. In January 2007, the UN Special Rapporteur on Extrajudicial, Summary or Arbitrary Executions criticised Iran over the continued use of the juvenile death penalty in clear violation of its international obligations: "Between August 2004 and March 2006 I sent 12 communications, involving nine boys and six girls who had been sentenced to death in Iran for crimes committed when they were under 18... The information received is clearly credible and there is every reason to believe that the Iranian judiciary is freely ignoring the prohibition on the juvenile death penalty."

62. The UK remains committed to supporting EU action to highlight Iranian death penalty cases that fall short of EU minimum standards (including death sentences handed down for crimes committed before the age of 18). The EU has raised concerns about six juvenile execution cases already this year.

Cruel and inhuman punishment

63. Our concerns about criminal justice in Iran are not limited to the death penalty. Cruel and inhuman punishments (floggings, stoning, amputations) remain on the statute books. It is unclear how frequently such sentences are carried out. However, we have received two reports of public amputations for robbery in the province of Kermanshah in February and May 2007. These are the first confirmed cases of amputation in recent years and contravene the commitment Iran made to the EU in March 2003 to implement a moratorium on amputations. The EU has lobbied the Iranian authorities on these sentences.

64. The Iranian Judiciary confirmed that a man was stoned to death for adultery in Qazvin province on 5 July this year. Stoning sentences are still handed down by judges, but this was the first confirmed report of an execution by stoning since Iran announced a moratorium on stoning in 2002. The EU Presidency issued an immediate statement condemning the sentence and calling on Iran to respect its international and human rights commitments, and Dr Howells (Minister with responsibility for our relations with Iran) called in the Iranian Ambassador to protest. HMG and EU partners continue to lobby on a case-by-case basis, and press Iran to introduce these moratoria into law.

(FAC, Global Security: Iran HC142 (2007)

[See also HC Deb 18 July 2007 Vol 463 c407W and HC Deb 6 December 2007 Vol 468 c1430W, Ed.]

6/43

Death Penalty—Singapore

The Foreign Secretary was asked what assessment she had made of the use of the death penalty in Singapore; and what representations she has made to the Government of Singapore on the use of the death penalty. She wrote:

The UK is opposed to the death penalty in all circumstances. We believe that the abolition of the death penalty is essential for the protection of human rights under Article 3 of the Universal Declaration of Human Rights. The Singapore Government continue to use the death penalty, though the number of executions in recent years has been much lower than in the past. There is little public opposition in Singapore to use of the death penalty.

The Singapore Government are well aware of our views. Our high commissioner in Singapore raised the issue most recently in December 2006 with the Singapore Deputy Prime Minster, who is also Minister for Law.

(HC Deb 18 January 2007 Vol 455 c1333W)

6/44

Death Penalty—United States—Krishna Mahraj

The Foreign Secretary was asked how many times officials from her Department had (a) met and (b) made representations on behalf of Krishna Maharaj. An FCO Minister wrote:

Officials from our consulate in Orlando have met with Mr. Maharaj on several occasions since 2002 when he was re-sentenced to life imprisonment. The most recent of these visits was made by our consul on 19 January. Mr. Maharaj and his wife are in frequent contact with our consular officials in Orlando both by letter and telephone.

Since 2002, we have submitted three amicus curiae briefs to the US courts on a point of international law in Mr. Maharaj's case. Officials from the Foreign and Commonwealth Office both here and overseas are following this case very closely, and representations at official level are made at every appropriate opportunity. We continue to monitor the case in consultation with Mr. Maharaj's legal representatives in the US and UK.

(HC Deb 24 May 2007 Vol 460 c1484W)

6/45

An FCO Minister wrote:

Further to the letter sent by [an FCO Minister] of 22 May to the governor of Florida in support of Krishna Maharaj's clemency petition, our consul in Orlando attended Mr, Maharaj's clemency waiver hearing on 9 August.

The Aides to the Florida Clemency Board granted a waiver which means his clemency case could be heard by the full clemency board, including Governor Crist, as early as December. We welcome this decision and remain in close contact with Mr. Maharaj's legal team about the full consideration of his clemency plea by the Florida Clemency Board.

We continue to offer appropriate consular assistance to Mr. Maharaj and our consul in Orlando last visited him on 24 August.

(HC Deb 10 September 2007 Vol 463 c2007W)

6/46

Death Penalty—Pakistan

The Foreign Secretary was asked if she would raise with the Government of Pakistan the case of Younis Masih, a Christian who has been sentenced to death under section 295C of the Pakistan penal code; and if she would urge the Pakistani authorities to ensure that he is able to access a fair appeals process and proper protection to prevent attacks from extremists while he is appealing the sentence.
An FCO Minister wrote:

We do not usually raise individual cases and have not recently made any representations to the Pakistani authorities concerning Younis Masih. However, we are aware of this case and regularly raise our concerns about the treatment of religious minorities in Pakistan both bilaterally and with our EU partners. We oppose the death penalty in all circumstances as a matter of principle.

Although we do not usually raise individual cases, we regularly raise our concerns over the situation of religious minorities with the Government of Pakistan. Most recently, in May, we again voiced our concerns over the treatment of religious minorities in Pakistan, together with our EU partners.

(HC Deb 14 June 2007 Vol 461 c1220W)

6/47 (See also 5/7)

Democracy

The Secretary of State for International Development was asked what steps his Department was taking to encourage the composition of parliaments in developing countries to reflect the population of those countries in terms of (a) gender, (b) ethnicity, (c) religious belief and (d) sexuality. He wrote:

As part of its commitment to promoting good governance, DFID works to strengthen the parliaments of developing countries. What we do is different in different countries, depending on our assessment of what the priorities are. In some places we will focus more on the legislative function of parliaments, for instance, while in others our efforts will be channelled more towards strengthening oversight of the executive.

Representation is of course a core function of parliaments everywhere, and DFID recognises that a representative parliament has a head start on this.

One of the initiatives DFID has supported recently to improve representativeness is the High Level Committee on Reservations [in Nepal] which has developed recommendations for affirmative action for women and dalits in the political structures of Nepal. Another group we have supported is the Forum des Femmes Rwandaises Parliamentaires (FFRP). The FFRP comprises all the women members of the Rwandan Parliament—and at 48.8 per cent. Rwanda has the highest female representation in the world. Our most recent support to the FFRP funded a conference on 22 and 23 February that celebrated the progress made towards gender equality in Rwanda. It also produced the "Kigali Declaration", that will add vitality to the efforts of other African countries to get more women into Parliament—following Rwanda's example.

(HC Deb 19 March 2007 Vol 458 c616W)

6/48

Detention

In response to a question about Government policy on the treatment of Iranian nationals captured while fighting as insurgents against British troops in (a) Afghanistan and (b) Iraq, the Minister of Defence wrote:

In Afghanistan, the UK policy is that any individual detained by ISAF forces should be transferred to the Afghan authorities at the first opportunity and within 96 hours, or released.

In Iraq, following the detention of any individual by multi-national force Iraq, a decision will be made to either release the individual, transfer him to the Iraqi judicial system (where criminal evidence exists), or to intern him if this is deemed necessary for imperative reasons of security, as permitted under UNSCR 1723. This decision is based on an assessment of the threat posed by the individual and is not related to his nationality.

All new UK internees have their cases reviewed by the Divisional Internment Review Committee no later than 48 hours after they are apprehended, and then every 28 days thereafter. Cases are also reviewed by the Combined Review and Release Board, a joint UK-Iraqi board, every three months. Individuals held for 18 months have their cases referred to the Joint Detention Committee which is co-chaired by Prime Minister Maliki and the Commander Multi-National Force Iraq.

[See **(2006) UKMIL 16/16** and *R (on the application of Al-Jedda) v Secretary of State for Defence* [2007] UKHL 58, Ed.]

(HC Deb 2 March 2007 Vol 457 c1612W)

6/49

The Defence Secretary was asked:

(1) whether the requirement in paragraph 5.1 of the Memorandum of Understanding between the Government of the UK and the Government of Afghanistan on the transfer of detainees for the UK armed forces to notify the International Committee of the Red Cross and the Afghan Independent Human Rights Commission, normally within 24 hours, and if not, as soon as possible after, of when a person has been transferred to Afghan authorities had been complied with fully in respect of all the detainees concerned; and

(2) how many individuals arrested and detained in Afghanistan by UK armed forces had been transferred to the authorities of Afghanistan since the date on which the Memorandum of Understanding between the Government of the UK and the Government of Afghanistan on the transfer of detainees came into effect.

He wrote:

The Memorandum of Understanding between the Government of the UK and the Government of Afghanistan on the transfer of detainees was signed on 30 September 2006. Since then, three individuals have been held in detention by UK armed forces. One was subsequently transferred to the Afghan authorities and two were released.

Although there have been some minor procedural problems with the timely notification of the International Committee of the Red Cross and the Afghan Independent Human Rights Commission, both organisations have been informed about these detentions, and all other detentions which took place before the MoU was signed. We are working with both organisations with a view to ensuring that in future all notifications will occur in a timely manner.

[The MOU is reproduced at *www.publications.parliament.uk/pa/cm200607/cmselect/cmfaff/44/4412.htm*, Ed.]

(HC Deb 8 January 2007, Vol c77W)

6/50

The Foreign Secretary was asked whether the UK Government have entered into any written agreements with (a) US authorities and (b) Iraqi authorities on the conditions on which individuals arrested and detained by UK armed forces in Iraq may be transferred to (i) US authorities and (ii) Iraqi authorities. The Minister of Defence wrote:

The Government signed a Memorandum of Understanding (MOU) with the Governments of the United States and Australia governing the transfer, in accordance with the Third and Fourth Geneva Conventions of prisoners of war, of civilian internees and detainees taken during operations against Iraq in 2003. This MOU is no longer in use.

The UK contingent of the Multinational Force in Iraq signed a MOU with the Iraqi Ministry of Justice and Ministry of Interior in 2004, that governs the transfer of individuals in the custody of UK forces in Iraq to the Iraqi criminal justice system. We will make public the text of this MOU subject to obtaining the consent of the Iraqi Government as the co-signatory.

(HC Deb 21 May 2007 Vol 460 c1051W)

6/51

The Minister of Defence was asked whether any individuals arrested and detained by UK armed forces in Iraq and subsequently transferred to (a) US authorities and (b) Iraqi authorities might be subsequently transferred to the authority of another state, including detention in another country, without the prior written agreement of the UK. He wrote:

No individual arrested and detained by UK forces in Iraq will be transferred to US authorities without prior written agreement governing the terms and conditions of such transfer.

The Memorandum of Understanding between the UK contingent of the Multinational Force in Iraq and the Iraqi Ministries of Justice and Interior governing the transfer of individuals detained in Iraq by UK forces contains no provisions on the possible further transfer of such persons. However, the Constitution of Iraq prevents the Government of Iraq from surrendering any Iraqi national to foreign entities and authorities.

(HC Deb 9 January 2007 Vol 455 c520W)

6/52

The Foreign Secretary wrote:

The UK currently holds 36 detainees at the divisional internment facility at Basra air station, all of whom are Iraqi nationals.

The UK detains individuals in Iraq for imperative reasons of security under the authority of UN Security Council Resolution 1723 (2006). It is a power we use sparingly and we take our responsibilities to our detainees seriously. Where possible, we seek to release individuals or transfer their cases to the Iraqi justice system. The UK has obtained assurances from the government of Iraq to ensure that anyone transferred from UK to Iraqi custody will be treated in accordance with basic international human rights principles.

(HC Deb 15 November 2007 Vol 467 c391W)

6/53

Deportation

The Home Secretary was asked what assessment he had made of the effect of the operation of the Human Rights Act 1998 on the

Government's ability to detain or deport terrorist suspects. A Minister wrote:

The Human Rights Act 1998 does not affect our ability to detain or to deport. The Human Rights Act simply incorporated our pre-existing international obligations into domestic law.

Detention has to be consistent with Articles of the European Convention for the Protection of Human Rights and Fundamental Freedoms (the European Convention on Human Rights). In deporting someone from the United Kingdom, we have to have regard to our obligations under Article 3 of the ECHR as defined in the case law of the European Court of Human Rights.

The Government are seeking to secure a modification of the current case law through its intervention in two cases currently before the Court [*Saadi v. Italy*, ECtHRs [GC] (Judgment of 28 February 2008) Appl. no. 37201/06, upholding *Chahal v. UK* 70/1195/576/662 (1996) ECtHRs and *Ramzy v. The Netherlands*, Appl. No. 25424/05, UK intervening, pending, Ed.]

(HC Deb 20 June 2007 Vol 461 c1968W)

6/54

Enforced Disappearance

An FCO Minister wrote:

The Government support the International Covenant for the Protection of All Persons from Enforced Disappearance. The UK was active throughout the negotiations to draft the convention and we supported its adoption last year at both the UN Human Rights Council and the UN General Assembly. The preliminary work necessary to identify any changes required to UK law in order to ratify the convention necessarily began when the convention was under negotiation, but it has not yet been possible to progress it further to date. Until this work is complete, we will not be able to determine the UK's position towards ratification, including whether we would need to make any reservations. At the adoption of the convention at both the UN General Assembly and the Human Rights Council, the UK made an interpretative statement clarifying our understanding of certain provisions, including what constitutes an enforced disappearance, the application of obligations under international humanitarian law and the procedures applicable to the adoption and placement of children found to have resulted from an enforced disappearance. This statement can be found at: www.fco.gov.uk/ukmisgeneva.

(HL Deb 14 November 2007 Vol 696 cWA20)

6/55

European Charter for Minority Languages

An FCO Minister wrote:

The UK ratified the European Charter for Minority Languages on 27 March 2001 and the Charter entered into force for the UK on 1 July 2001. The UK recognises Welsh, Irish, Scottish-Gaelic, Ulster Scots, Manx Gaelic, Cornish and Scots under the Charter's definition of a regional or minority language.

The Charter's monitoring mechanism requires member states party to the charter to produce, a year after entry into force of the charter for the state and thereafter every three years, a periodical report detailing the policy pursued under Part II of the charter and the measures taken in application of those provisions of Part III of the charter which they have accepted. Since ratification the UK has produced two such periodical reports, the first published on 1 July 2002 and the second on 1 July 2005. The UK's third periodical report is due for publication on 1 July 2008.

The UK's first and second periodical reports can be found on the Council of Europe website at:

www.coe.int/t/e/legal_affairs/local_and_regional_democracy/regional_or_minority_languages/ 2_Monitoring/Monitoring_table.asp#TopOfPage

(HC Deb 12 November 2007 Vol 467 c38W)

6/56
(See also **6/14–19 and UKMIL [2006] 6/13**)

Extraordinary Rendition

The Foreign Secretary wrote:

In his speech of 6 September 2006, President Bush acknowledged the existence of a detention programme operated by the CIA.

Prior to this speech, we were aware of the existence of a secret US detention programme only in general terms.

In 2005 the Intelligence and Security Committee (ISC) reported that the agencies had told them: "Clearly the US is holding some Al Qaida members in detention, other than at Guantanamo, but we do not know the location or terms of their detention and do not have access to them". These comments were published in the ISC's report "The Handling of Detainees by UK Intelligence Personnel in Afghanistan, Guantanamo Bay and Iraq" of March 2005, Cm 5611..

(HC Deb 18 January 2007 Vol 455 c1335)

6/57

General Assembly—Individual States

An FCO Minister wrote:

The Government consider that the UN General Assembly (UNGA) has a responsibility to address situations of human rights violations in particular countries. We believe that the most effective means of improving such situations is through a co-operative relationship between the UN human rights machinery and the Government of the relevant country. However, where the situation is of serious concern and where the Government in question refuses to co-operate or to make use of the support offered to them by the UN human rights mechanisms, it is entirely appropriate for the UNGA or the UN Human Rights Council to express concern over the situation through a resolution, if necessary without the support of the country concerned. The Government worked very actively with European Union and other partners to secure the recent adoption of resolutions by the UNGA Third Committee on the situations in Iran, Burma, Belarus and the Democratic People's Republic of Korea.

(HC Deb 6 December 2007 Vol 468 c1430W)

6/58

Guantanamo Bay

An FCO Minister said:

I need to begin by asking the House to respect the wider context of this debate. Before I enter into the detail of Mr. al-Rawi's case, it is important for us all to remember the circumstances which led to Guantanamo Bay and how they have had a profound effect on the US Government's security policy, and indeed our own, over the past few years. None of us can forget that almost 3,000 people were killed during the horrific terrorist attacks of 11 September 2001...

Let us not think that 9/11 was an isolated incident. The list of major terrorist attacks, preceding and subsequent, is long. They include attacks and hundreds of people killed in East Africa, Yemen, Saudi Arabia, Turkey, Indonesia, Spain, Morocco, Tunisia, Egypt, Syria, Jordan and Pakistan—and of course 52 people were killed in this city in 2005. The casualty figures would have been even higher had any of the numerous planned attacks that have been foiled since 2000 succeeded—in the hundreds, perhaps even thousands. We face a major threat from international terrorism and are likely to do so for many years to come. This is the shocking reality we face, and international co-operation to counter this global threat is of critical importance. We will continue to take steps to protect our citizens: for that I make no apologies.

Let me turn to Guantanamo Bay. The British Government's position is clear. Notwithstanding what I have said about the reasons why the US created Guantanamo Bay in the first place and the continuing threat from terrorism, we believe...as the Prime Minister and other colleagues have said, that Guantanamo should close...

we have interviewed detainees there about the threat to the UK's national security—it would have been irresponsible not to do so. However, we have also worked tirelessly to secure the release of all the UK nationals who were detained there. Five were released in March 2004 and the remaining four in January 2005. That was our understandable priority. Since then, we have pressed the US

Government hard on Guantanamo's future and the broader issues raised by the camp. The hon. Gentleman mentioned some of them this evening.

We welcome the US President's public commitment to close Guantanamo Bay as soon as practicable, and the US Government's progress to that end. I understand that nearly 800 detainees have passed through Guantanamo, of whom approximately 340 have been released, leaving about 435 detainees. Four were recently transferred back to Bahrain, Iran and Pakistan, and I know that the US Government are working hard to reduce the numbers as quickly as possible. That is a complicated task. Careful consideration should—and is—being given to how numbers at the camp can be reduced. The dilemma for the US is maintaining international security while respecting the human rights of detainees when they are released.

Our position on Guantanamo's future is principled and pragmatic, reflecting the need to balance security and liberty. We will continue to follow developments in Guantanamo Bay closely and to discuss conditions there, as well as wider detainee issues, with the US Government...

We are often asked about the circumstances of detainees who were formerly resident in the United Kingdom. It is a long-standing Government policy not to offer consular assistance to non-British nationals, except when a specific agreement to do so exists with another state. A long period of residence in the UK is not a substitute for British nationality. However, in 2005, [an FCO Minister] agreed exceptionally to meet, on a humanitarian basis, the families and representatives of those detainees whom we knew were formerly resident in the UK but were not British nationals, and we passed on the concerns that the families expressed to the US authorities. We continue regularly to raise humanitarian concerns about detentions at the Bay with the USA, including those about detainees who were formerly resident in the UK...

I would like to draw the House's attention to President Bush's speech of 6 September 2006. We welcomed a number of steps announced in this speech—in particular, the stated intention to treat all detainees in accordance with the provisions of the Geneva conventions and to grant the International Committee of the Red Cross access to 14 so-called "high value" detainees. The US intention to prosecute those key detainees is also welcome, not least to the many victims of international terrorism and their families. The Prime Minister, Foreign Secretaries and senior Government officials and lawyers have all been actively involved in Guantanamo-related matters for a long while. It is a picture of considerable and overall productive engagement.

I turn now to deal with the specific subject of this debate: Mr. al-Rawi and what we are doing to achieve his release from Guantanamo. I must begin by responding to the charge...that the British Government were complicit in his constituent's arrest and detention... Mr. al-Rawi travelled to Gambia and was arrested on arrival. I must stress absolutely and categorically that the UK did not request [his] detention...nor did the UK play any role in his transfer to Afghanistan or Guantanamo Bay. To suggest otherwise is, quite simply, not the case.

...the then Foreign Secretary agreed in March 2006 to make representations to the US Government for Mr. al-Rawi's release from Guantanamo Bay and his return to the UK. That decision was based on the particular circumstances in Mr. al-Rawi's case. On 6 April 2006, having taken that decision, [the Foreign Secretary] wrote to the US Secretary of State to ask formally for his release and return. The US State Department replied to the British ambassador in Washington later that month and detailed discussions between our Governments have continued since.

I reiterate that we are committed to securing Mr. al-Rawi's release from Guantanamo Bay and his return to the UK. We believe that our work should be allowed to come to a successful conclusion...

[There were] also raised concerns about Mr. al-Rawi's health and the conditions of his detention. I stress that we continue to raise humanitarian concerns about detentions at Guantanamo Bay with the US authorities. As part of our regular exchanges with the United States, we have raised on a number of occasions issues relating to detainees who were formerly resident in the UK, including Mr. al-Rawi...

Following contact with Mr. al-Rawi's lawyers just before Christmas, we raised specific concerns about his conditions of detention and health with the United States Government...the US Government have confirmed to us that they are looking into them. We are taking full account of Mr. al-Rawi's well-being in our work to secure his release.

(HC Deb 8 January 2007 Vol 455 c123–126)

6/59
The Foreign Secretary was asked what representations she had made to the United States on returning Hambali (Riduan Isamuddin) from Guantanamo Bay to Indonesia to stand trial for the Bali bombing. An FCO Minister wrote:

The Government think that suspected terrorists should be brought to trial whenever possible. The US Government are fully aware of this policy.

British Government officials have conveyed to the US authorities concerns that Hambali has not yet been brought to justice. In his speech of 6 September 2006, President Bush announced the transfer of 14 so-called high-value detainees to Guantanamo Bay, including Hambali. He also said that the International Committee of the Red Cross would be granted access to them, and that they should face justice.

(HC Deb 18 January 2007 Vol 455 c1331W)

6/60
The Foreign Secretary wrote:

The House will be aware that, with the agreement of the Home Secretary, I wrote to US Secretary of State Condoleezza Rice on 7 August to request the release from Guantanamo Bay and return to the UK of five men who, while not UK Nationals, had been legally resident in the UK prior to their detention. These are the only individuals now at Guantanamo who have been identified as having been given leave to enter or remain in the UK under the Immigration Acts.

The Home Secretary and I decided to seek the release of the five in light of work by the US Government to reduce the number of those detained at Guantanamo and our wish to offer practical and concrete support to those efforts. In reaching this decision we gave full consideration to the need to maintain national security and the Government's overriding responsibilities in this regard.

Detailed and constructive discussions have since taken place between the British and US Governments, considering the circumstances of each individual case. The US agreed on 10 December that three of the five men—Mr. Jamil El Banna, Mr. Omar Deghayes and Mr. Abdennour Sameur—will be returned to the UK shortly as soon as the practical arrangements can be made. The Foreign and Commonwealth Office has been in contact with the families and legal representatives of Mr. El Banna, Mr. Deghayes and Mr. Sameur to let them know of this decision.

I should add that the decision to make this request does not constitute a commitment that they may remain permanently in the UK. Their immigration status will be reviewed following their return and the same security considerations will apply to them as would apply to any other foreign national in this country. As always, all appropriate steps will be taken to protect national security.

The US Government has expressed significant additional security concerns in regard to the cases of the other two men covered by the original request—Mr. Shaker Aamer and Mr. Binyam Mohammed. They have so far declined the request for the release and return of Mr. Aamer and we are no longer in active discussions regarding his transfer to the UK. We are still discussing with the US the case of Mr. Mohammed although again the US Government is not inclined to agree to his release and return.

Moving ahead, we will continue to discuss with the US Government how best we can work with them to see the closure of the Guantanamo Bay detention facility. We will continue to encourage our allies to consider taking steps similar to our own to reduce the numbers of those detained at Guantanamo Bay, such as accepting the transfer of eligible detainees, thereby hastening the closure of the detention facility.

(HC Deb 13 December 2007 Vol 469 c56WS–57WS)

6/61

Human Rights Council
(See also **6/72**)

The Foreign Secretary was asked what the UK Government's position was on the candidacy of Belarus for the 17 May elections for the UN Human Rights Council. She wrote:

We continue to have deep concerns at the deteriorating human rights situation in Belarus, including Belarus' failure to co-operate with the UN human rights mechanisms; its failure to conduct free and fair elections, including the detention and arrest of political and civil society activists; and persistent reports of harassment and closure of non-governmental organisations, national minority groups, independent media outlets, religious groups, opposition political parties and independent trade unions.

We do not consider that countries whose human rights situations continue to be of deep concern fulfil the criteria for membership of the UN Human Rights Council (HRC).

The UN General Assembly resolution establishing the HRC in March 2006 sets out clear expectations of the Council's members, including that they "uphold the highest standards in the promotion and protection of human rights". We fully support these expectations of the Council's members. We urge all members of the General Assembly, responsible for electing the HRC membership, to take candidates' performance against these standards fully into account when casting their votes. European Union member states have publicly committed only to support those states who meet these standards, and who contribute to the promotion and protection of human rights.

(HC Deb 15 May 2007 Vol 460 c695W)

6/62

The Foreign Secretary was asked if she would make a statement on proposals to abolish the UN Human Rights Council envoy posts charged with reporting on (a) Belarus, (b) Cuba, (c) North Korea, (d) Burma, (e) Somalia, (f) Sudan and (g) Uzbekistan. An FCO Minister wrote:

When the UN Human Rights Council was established in March 2006, it was tasked with reviewing its tools and mechanisms, including its so-called Special Procedures (for example Special Rapporteurs and Independent Experts dedicated to specific country situations). On 18 June, the Council agreed a package of measures at the conclusion of this review. Throughout the review the UK consistently took a strong position, nationally and with the rest of the EU, in favour of maintaining all the existing country-specific and thematic Special Procedures. There was a great deal of opposition at the Council to the continuation of country-specific Special Procedures. I was profoundly disappointed that, because of this opposition, the mandates of the Special Rapporteurs on the human rights situations in Cuba and Belarus were not renewed. The situations in both those countries continue to be of deep concern and we will continue to monitor the situation in each closely. I was, however, pleased that the mandates of all the other country-specific Special Procedures (including the Special Rapporteurs on the situation of human rights in the Democratic People's Republic of Korea, Burma and Sudan, and the Independent Expert appointed by the UN Secretary-General on the situation of human rights in Somalia) were renewed.

The Council inherited an Independent Expert on the human rights situation in Uzbekistan, created through the confidential complaints procedure under the old UN Commission on Human Rights. At its fourth session (12–30

March) the UN Human Rights Council discontinued consideration of the specific file relating to Uzbekistan under its confidential complaints procedure. The confidential nature of that procedure prevents us from commenting on any details of the cases and on the position taken by the UK. We do, however, emphasise strongly our deep concern over persistent violations of human rights in Uzbekistan.

The Council also agreed on 18 June a new system of universal periodic review, which will look at every state's individual work on human rights implementation, including Cuba's and Uzbekistan's.

(HC Deb 25 June 2007 Vol 462 c222W)

6/63

Indigenous Peoples: ILO Convention

An FCO Minister wrote:

The Government have no plans to sign and ratify the International Labour Organisation (ILO) Indigenous and Tribal Peoples Convention 1989 (ILO 169). The UK takes its international law obligations very seriously and as a general rule will only sign and ratify an instrument when we can ensure our full compliance with it and commit to its implementation. The UK position with regard to ILO 169 was set out in a 1989 Department for Education and Employment White Paper ("Convention on Indigenous and Tribal Peoples in Independent Countries" Command Paper Number: Cm 1078). As the White Paper noted, ILO 169 was essentially an update of the 1957 ILO Convention 107. The White Paper explained that Convention 107 could not be applied to the UK as there are no indigenous, tribal or semi-tribal people there, and so had not been ratified by the UK. The same arguments applied to ILO 169 as it did not alter the scope of Convention 107. This position still stands.

The UK is committed to the promotion and protection of the rights of indigenous peoples. On 13 September 2007, the UK voted in favour of the adoption of the UN Declaration of the Rights of Indigenous Peoples at the UN General Assembly, as we had previously done at the Human Rights Council in June 2006. The adoption of this Declaration marks a significant advance for indigenous peoples around the world.

(HC Deb 20 November 2007 Vol 467 c736W)

6/64

Individual petition

The Government was asked whether it were in the interest of those within the jurisdiction of the United Kingdom to have recourse to the international complaints mechanisms under the United Nations

International Covenant on Civil and Political Rights and Convention on the Elimination of All Forms of Racial Discrimination; and, if it were not, what was the reason. A Minister wrote:

The Government remain to be convinced of the practical value to people in the United Kingdom of rights of individual petition to the United Nations. The United Nations committees that consider petitions are not courts, and they cannot award damages or produce a legal ruling on the meaning of the law, whereas the United Kingdom has strong and effective laws against discrimination under which individuals may seek remedies in the courts or employment tribunals.

(HL Deb 29 November 2007 Vol 696 cWA142)

6/65

An FCO Minister said:

Attention has be drawn to the optional protocols [to UN human rights treaties] on individual petitions. On women's rights, we have, as a matter of experimentation, signed up to the optional protocol to allow women to bring such cases. We have not done so more broadly because these optional protocols are not a judicial process and do not allow the awarding of damages. We believe that we can more effectively address these issues through other arrangements.

(HL Deb 10 December 2007 Vol 697 c10)

6/66

Kashmir

The Foreign Secretary was asked if she would support the appointment of a special rapporteur with an ongoing mandate to publish regular and public reports on the human rights situation in Jammu and Kashmir and Azad Kashmir. An FCO minister wrote:

The UK continues to call for an end to all external support for violence in Kashmir and an improvement in the human rights situation there. But it is not for us to intervene and prescribe a solution. That is for those parties directly involved to determine through dialogue. We hope that the dialogue process between India and Pakistan will build on progress achieved to date and, in due course, lead to the resolution of all outstanding differences between the two countries, including over Kashmir.

Asked further about any representations the Foreign Secretary had received on the prosecution in civilian courts in India of members of the army and other security forces implicated in rights abuses in Jammu and Kashmir, the Minister wrote:

We have not received any such representations. Criminal prosecutions before Indian courts are a domestic matter for the Government of India and the Indian judiciary.

(HC Deb 28 June 2007 Vol 462 c844W)

6/67

Overseas territories

The Foreign Secretary was asked what discussions it had had with the UN Human Rights Commission about the status of those living on Ascension Island. A Minister wrote:

The Foreign and Commonwealth Office has had no discussions with the United Nations Human Rights Commission on the status of those working and living on Ascension Island. The human rights of those currently on Ascension Island are protected by various human rights instruments which have been extended to the island, including the European Convention on Human Rights. Details of these instruments are available on the FCO website at:

www.fco.gov.uk/servlet/Front?pagename=OpenMarket/Xcelerate/ShowPage&;c=Page&cid=1013618138395

(HC Deb 17 July 2007 Vol 463 c247W)

6/68 (See also 1/1, 15/8, 16/69–70)

Responsibility to protect

An International Development Minister wrote:

The "responsibility to protect" concept, endorsed at the 2005 UN World Summit, made clear that individual states hold the primary responsibility to protect their own populations from genocide, war crimes, ethnic cleansing and crimes against humanity. The international community also confirmed its readiness to act, collectively, to prevent and stop such crimes, through the United Nations. Such action includes using appropriate diplomatic, humanitarian and other peaceful means, including sanctions. On a case by case basis, should peaceful means be inadequate and national authorities manifestly fail to protect their populations, the UN Security Council may authorise the use of force.

Since the World Summit, the UN Security Council has adopted resolutions on the Protection of Civilians in Armed Conflict and on Darfur, both of which refer to the World Summit agreement on the responsibility to protect. In addressing the situation in Darfur, we have also used diplomacy and applied political pressure; reminded the Sudanese Government of their own responsibility to the people of Darfur; worked through the Security Council to apply sanctions; referred the situation in Darfur to the International Criminal Court; and are working on UN support to the African Union Mission in Sudan.

Through the Global Conflict Prevention Pool, the UK is also supporting an NGO network to raise the profile of responsibility to protect with national governments and civil society, particularly in Africa.

The Government will continue to advocate appropriate and speedy responses—bilaterally, within the EU and UN, and at the Security Council—to protect vulnerable populations against genocide, war crimes, crimes against humanity and ethnic cleansing.

(HC Deb 8 January 2007 Vol 455 c377W)

6/69
An FCO Minister wrote:

We continue to uphold strongly the value of the concept of the responsibility to protect, to which all UN member states committed themselves during the world summit of 2005. Here, for the first time, world leaders agreed that Governments have the responsibility to protect their populations from genocide, war crimes, ethnic cleansing and crimes against humanity within states. The UK believes it to be a powerful tool in reminding Governments and the international community of their protection responsibilities.

The responsibility to protect is relevant to the entire international community, as all UN member states have signed up to it. In particular, the UK secured specific reference to the concept in Security Council resolutions (SCRs) relating to the situation in Sudan (SCR 1706 and SCR 1755), and in SCR 1674 on the protection of civilians in armed conflict.

The UK will continue to encourage and help states to build capacity to exercise their responsibility to protect; to assist states which are under stress before crises and conflicts break out; and to ensure that the responsibility to protect commitment is translated into a willingness to act, speedily and appropriately, in specific cases.

(HL Deb 8 October 2007 Vol 695 cWA6)

6/70

Sri Lanka—European Convention on Human Rights

A Home Office Minister wrote:

The Government responded to the request from the European Court of Human Rights on 31 October 2007 stating that we do not consider that the current situation in Sri Lanka warrants the suspension of removal directions to all Sri Lankan Tamils but we will continue to suspend removal in individual cases where the European Court has issued a Rule 39 indication.

We continue to carefully assess each case on its individual circumstances taking into account relevant case law and the current situation in Sri Lanka before a decision is made to remove from the United Kingdom. [*NA. v. the United Kingdom*, no. 25904/07—2007 Activities Report www.echr.coe.int/NR/rdonlyres/96443711–4133–4043–8FB6–331AEC510FCA/0/2007_section_activity_reports.pdf, Ed.]

(HL Deb 14 November 2007 Vol 696 cWA26)

6/71

Sri Lanka—Child Soldiers

An FCO Minister wrote:

We have been seriously concerned by reports that have criticised parties to the Sri Lanka conflict including the Liberation Tigers of Tamil Eelam (LTTE) and the Karuna faction for the recruitment and use of child soldiers in violation of applicable international law. We deplore this practice: there can be no excuse for failing to observe such basic human rights. The UK is a member of the UN Security Council Working Group on Children and Armed Conflict. We fully support the Working Group's conclusions of 13 June 2007, which strongly condemned the unlawful recruitment and use of child soldiers and all other violations and abuses committed against children by the LTTE and the Karuna faction and called for an immediate end to these practices. The UK also supports the Working Group's call for further steps to be taken in the coming months if parties to the conflict in Sri Lanka do not heed this call for progress to be made.

(HC Deb 29 October 2007 Vol 464 c825W)

6/72 (See also 6/61)

United Nations—Human Rights Council

The FCO submitted the following written evidence to the FAC:

1. THE FCO'S ASSESSMENT OF HOW THE HUMAN RIGHTS COUNCIL IS WORKING OUT IN PRACTICE.

Since we last updated the FAC on the UN Human Rights Council (HRC), the HRC's first members have been elected (including the UK). It has met in three regular, and four special, sessions....

The General Assembly resolution establishing the Council left much of the detail of its agenda, working practices, and tools to the Council itself to develop. In addition, it provided for a new system of Universal Periodic Review to be created in the Council's first year; and for a review of the old Commission on Human Rights' Special Procedures, expert advice body and complaint procedure, also within one year. The Council therefore continues to be, to some extent, a work in progress.

[An FCO Minister] set the tone for the UK's close engagement in this process during participation at the Council's inaugural session in June 2006. (See **UKMIL [2006] 6/97**) He delivered a speech on behalf of the UK: focusing on the complex human rights challenges we all face; stressing the need for the

Human Rights Council to develop the tools to address them; and emphasising that countries must work together at the Council to find common solutions, rather than fostering divisions. In addition, he held a series of bilateral meetings with Ministerial colleagues from various different regions, in which he set out the UK's vision of the Council and exchanged ideas on how [sic] to develop it...

The HRC has made some promising progress. Unanimous decisions at its first regular sessions provided for the uninterrupted functioning of the Special Procedures, complaints procedure and other reporting mechanisms during its first year of transition and review. The extent and quality of Council dialogue with the Special Procedures has been positive. The Council considered and debated more than 40 Special Procedures' reports across a range of human rights issues at its second regular session. NGO participation was at a higher level than ever achieved at the previous Commission on Human Rights. There has been strong NGO involvement overall in the Council's work. We are also pleased by the close interaction established between the Council and the High Commissioner for Human Rights, who has briefed each regular session.

Although still developing its tools, the Council has taken some positive, concrete steps on substantive human rights issues. It agreed by consensus at its second session to keep under consideration two cases under its confidential complaints procedure (relating to Iran and Uzbekistan). It also agreed consensus resolutions welcoming progress made and encouraging further steps in the protection and promotion of human rights in Nepal and Afghanistan. These resolutions, tabled by Switzerland and the EU respectively, show the Council able to agree texts on specific countries, including with the countries concerned. This begins to put into practice early rhetoric from many delegations favouring co-operative rather than confrontational means of engaging with individual countries.

In the meantime, the Council has made steady progress on its institution-building agenda, ie: review of the mandates of the Special Procedures, expert advice system and complaints procedure; and creation of the new system of Universal Periodic Review, a mechanism to examine every state's human rights record. These are complex tasks, with a wide variety of views to be combined and reconciled. The Council is maintaining momentum on these; consensus is beginning to emerge. As with any multilateral negotiation, the most sensitive decisions will be taken at the end: some of the most difficult discussions are therefore yet to come. In the meantime, [the Minister] has instituted a programme of inviting Special Procedures and other senior UN officials to Parliament to talk about their work and increase the UK's engagement with them...

The Council has been hampered in its early stages by a lack of clarity at its regular sessions over the organisation and direction of the sessions' work. For example, the late tabling in the second session of over 47 individual resolution texts made it impossible for the session to finish its work within the allotted timeframe. To some extent this effect is inevitable, as the Council seeks to move beyond the precedents and practices of its predecessor body.

However, more problematic, and damaging to the Council's early work and credibility, has been the questionable commitment of some of its members to the successful fulfilment of its mandate. After much early talk of the need to "depoliticise" UN human rights work and increase dialogue, some regional blocs have pushed through their own agendas at the expense of others'. This led to a disproportionate and unbalanced focus on the situation in the Middle East in July-August. Three Special Sessions were called on this in four months. It is important for the Council's credibility to discuss these issues. But it must show it can address situations and issues with equal focus across its mandate and across the world. We also want to see those discussions held transparently, constructively, and in a balanced manner.

The situation in Darfur has been a real test of members' willingness to address urgent situations of human rights violation in whatever part of the world they occur. The Council passed a resolution on 28 November expressing concern at the situation and calling for certain steps to be taken to improve it. After long negotiations, this text failed to reflect our and EU partners' wish to see reference to concrete future follow-up by the Council. After trying unsuccessfully to amend the text during the vote, EU members of the Council and 25 others (33 in all) requested the Council's fourth Special Session, to discuss Darfur. This session convened from 12–13 December. The Council agreed a short, operationally-focused decision to dispatch a high-level expert mission to assess the human rights situation in Darfur. The mission will report back to the Council's fourth session in March 2007. We welcome the dispatching of the assessment mission, and will continue to work actively to make sure that the Council follows up its recommendations effectively.

Looking ahead, we will continue to work hard to meet the challenges outlined above. Specifically, we are working with EU partners to increase the effectiveness of our interventions in the Council's debate and work. We will intensify efforts to build partnerships with those countries across the world that, like us, wish to see an effective and credible Human Rights Council. We will continue to promote open and balanced dialogue on all human rights issues, including the most sensitive. Finally, we continue to work closely with the NGO community to promote our shared goals for the Council. [The Minister] has held roundtable discussions with NGO representatives before every regular session of the Council, to discuss priorities and listen to NGOs' ideas on how best to develop the Council. These are consistently constructive exchanges, which he is committed to continuing.

2. WHAT USE THE GOVERNMENT HAS MADE OF UN PROCEDURES TO RAISE HUMAN RIGHTS ISSUES SINCE ITS RESPONSE TO THE COMMITTEE'S PREVIOUS REPORT.

We have continued to raise human rights issues through relevant procedures and at relevant bodies in the UN. The main focus of these efforts has inevitably been on the UN Human Rights Council and the UN General Assembly Third Committee (which deals with human rights and social development). However, human rights issues form an integral part of much of the UN's work, eg on conflict resolution and prevention, and development issues. They have therefore remained a key element in the full range of the UK's work at the UN. This has gone well beyond our activities in the bodies specifically dedicated to human rights. For example, we have also continued to raise human rights issues in the Security Council, the General Assembly plenary, the Economic and Social Council, and in other ad hoc UN fora. Full details of the UK's activities in using

UN procedures to raise human rights issues are contained in the attachment to this letter.

(FAC Report, Human Rights Report 2006, HC 269 (2007))

6/73

Slavery

The International Development Secretary was asked what steps his Department was taking to tackle modern slavery. A Minister wrote:

DFID supports long-term development programmes to tackle the poverty and social exclusion that make people vulnerable to modern slavery.

The UK is also a major supporter of the International Labour Organisation (ILO) and its Special Action Programme on Forced Labour (SAP-FL). We will provide core funding of almost £2 million to SAP-FL over the next three years, in addition to support to individual country programmes.

Last month DFID published a booklet, "Breaking the Chains: Eliminating slavery, ending poverty" [www.dfid.gov.uk/pubs/files/slavery-brochure.pdf, Ed.]. It highlights the link between the fight against slavery and poverty and some of the work the UK is supporting through the ILO and other organisations.

(HC Deb 19 March 2007 Vol 458 c617W)

6/74

Terrorism

A Home Office Minister said:

...when we consider whether new counterterrorism measures are compatible with human rights, we take into account all relevant case law. That includes any decisions of the European Court of Human Rights where these are assessed as appropriate to the measures under consideration. We do not believe that this approach inhibits the introduction in the United Kingdom of counterterrorism measures.

(HL Deb 10 July 2007 Vol 693 c1277)

6/75

Torture

An FCO Minister was asked what the Government's position was about information which it knew had been obtained by torture. He said:

If we received information about a situation in which our civilians could be put at risk, we would have an obligation to take into account the information that had been passed to us. I will be blunt: these are difficult issues. I may or may not be the Minister who has to deal with them, but if I were and I received information from whatever source that led me to a risk assessment that death and injury might result, in this or any other country, I would be extremely irresponsible if I did not act on it; so I would act on it. [Q.67]

(FAC Report, Human Rights Report 2006, HC 269 (2007))

6/76
An FCO Minister wrote:

We take all allegations of mistreatment of British nationals abroad very seriously and unreservedly condemn the use of torture. There are no longer any British nationals detained in Guantanamo Bay. However, we did pursue all credible allegations of abuse regarding those British detainees who were detained there and subsequently released in 2004 and 2005. We pressed the US to examine the allegations. We also raised concerns about issues including isolation, lack of access to daylight and lack of exercise with respect to the British detainees, and secured a number of improvements to their physical conditions of detention.

(HC Deb 2 July 2007 Vol 462 c895W)

6/77
The Minister of Defence was asked what definition of (a) torture and (b) abuse he uses in the context of the activities of British armed forces in Iraq; and what account he took of the advice of the Attorney General in formulating this definition. He wrote:

The definition of torture derives from section 134 of the Criminal Justice Act 1988 which makes it an offence for a public official to commit torture. Article 1 of the United Nations Convention Against Torture outlines what is considered torture for the purposes of the convention. We are also guided by, among other sources, judgments of the European Court of Human Rights and those of our own domestic courts.

(HC Deb 9 July 2007 Vol 462 c1285W)

6/78
The Foreign Secretary wrote:

Torture is one of the most abhorrent violations of human rights and human dignity, and its use is absolutely prohibited under international law. We unreservedly condemn the use of torture and have made it an important part of our foreign policy to pursue its eradication world-wide. Where we are helping other countries to develop their own counter-terrorism capability, we ensure our training or other assistance promotes human rights compliance.

The Government, including the Intelligence and Security Agencies, never use torture for any purpose, nor would we instigate others to do so. Our rejection of the use of torture is well known by our partners and our intelligence agencies routinely seek assurances from foreign liaison services on humane treatment of detainees.

(HC 3 December 2007 Vol 468 c1064W)

6/79

Trafficking

The Home Secretary said:

The Government are committed to tackling all forms of gender-based violence through our national action plans, including those for domestic violence, sexual violence and trafficking. I fully support the multiple aims of the European Convention on Human Trafficking and we participated actively in the negotiations for it. I believe that the signing of the convention and the protection framework it imposes for victims of trafficking remain a primary goal for the Government...

I have wanted to make sure in my considerations that the Convention is absolutely compatible with our enforcement of managed immigration into this country. However, I repeat that I believe that the signing of the convention and the protection framework that it imposes for dealing with victims of trafficking remains a primary goal for the Government.

(HC Deb 15 January 2007 Vol 455 c541)

6/80

The Government were asked how many trafficked children, given leave to remain in the United Kingdom, have been deported on reaching the age of 18 years in each of the past three years; whether efforts were made to ascertain their subsequent well-being; and, if so, with what result.
A Minister wrote:

The Immigration and Nationality Directorate (IND) does not hold central records of the number of trafficked children given leave to remain in the United Kingdom (UK) and who have been repatriated/removed on reaching the age of 18.

However the UK operates a system whereby each case is considered on its own individual merits, and it is recognised that some individuals who may have experienced exploitation at the hands of traffickers will need time to recover and reflect on their position and this is why IND will only take a decision to pursue the repatriation of an individual where it is deemed appropriate to do so. In reaching such a decision consideration will be given to our obligations under the immigration laws and European Convention on Human Rights and the unique circumstances of each case including any outstanding applications or appeals.

(HL Deb 31 January 2007 Vol 689 c56WA)

6/81

Western Sahara

An FCO Minister wrote:

The UK is concerned about the welfare of the people of Western Sahara. We have set out our concerns about human rights and the humanitarian situation in the region in the Foreign and Commonwealth Office's 2006 Annual Human Rights Report, which is available at:

www.fco.gov.uk.

We have raised human rights issues with Morocco. We continue to support ongoing confidence building measures for the region, such as establishing a regular telephone and mail service between Tindouf and the territory, and family visits between the territory and the camps.

The UK remains concerned that the issue of the status of Western Sahara remains unresolved, with consequent problems for the people of the region. The UN Security Council unanimously adopted resolution 1783 on 31 October, which renewed the mandate of the UN Mission for the Referendum in Western Sahara until 30 April 2008. The resolution also calls upon the parties to continue negotiations under the auspices of the UN Secretary-General without preconditions and in good faith. The UK fully supports these negotiations, with a view to achieving a just, lasting and mutually acceptable political solution, which will provide for the self-determination of the people of Western Sahara.

(HC Deb 26 November 2007 Vol 468 c229W)

6/82

Zimbabwe

The Foreign Secretary was asked what recent discussions she had had with the United Nations on democracy in Zimbabwe. An FCO Minister wrote:

The Government's concern relating to human rights abuses, governance and democracy in Zimbabwe were most recently raised this week at the fifth session of the UN Human Rights Council in Geneva. The EU and UK asked a number of questions of the UN special rapporteurs on the rights to food and housing concerning the impact of the denial of both for the human and political rights of ordinary Zimbabweans. In March, 50 UN member states supported a statement at the Human Rights Council by the EU presidency, on behalf of all EU member states, expressing concern at the situation in Zimbabwe. The UK also continues to raise these concerns in dialogue with the UN High Commissioner for

Human Rights, Louise Arbour, and to press for her and other UN rapporteurs to have access to Zimbabwe. Other recent discussions with the UN have taken place with senior officials in the Department for Humanitarian Affairs, following on from the briefing in March to the UN Security Council on the humanitarian situation in Zimbabwe which was given by the Office of the Commissioner for Humanitarian Affairs at the UK's request. Our embassy in Harare is in regular discussion with the UN Development Programme Office regarding human rights, democracy and good governance.

(HC Deb 14 June 2007 Vol 461 c1221W)

Part Six: IX. *The Position of the Individual (Including the Corporation) in International Law—Crimes under international law*

6/83
Text of Protocol between the Crown Prosecution Service (CPS) and the Metropolitan Police

War Crimes and Crimes Against Humanity

The Crimes against Humanity Unit of SO15 in the Metropolitan Police (SO15) and the Counter Terrorism Division of the Crown Prosecution Service (CTD) have agreed the following in relation to allegations of War Crimes and/or Crimes against Humanity.

Other than in urgent cases, SO15 will forward a report and relevant enclosures to CTD who will provide initial advice within 28 days. This advice will address jurisdiction, immunity and any potential offences disclosed. Once initial advice is given, SO15 will decide whether or not to pursue a full investigation. Thereafter CTD will advise in the usual manner.

In some cases, complaints are made to SO15 by individuals, solicitors or organisations, pending the arrival of an individual suspect expected to visit England and Wales. In these urgent referrals, SO15 will request the complainant to provide:

• Details of the individual concerned including his position of authority, if relevant

• Details of when he is arriving into the jurisdiction, and by what means

• Copies of the evidence against that individual.

Provided the above documentation is received in sufficient time for it to receive proper consideration, SO15 will seek the advice of CTD on jurisdiction, immunity and any potential offences disclosed. If there is no jurisdiction or the suspect has immunity, SO15 will inform the complainant. If there are potential justiciable offences, SO15 will decide whether or not to carry out an investigation.

If a decision to investigate is made, the complainant will be informed that SO15 are willing to take over the investigation. It should be made clear that from that point all investigative decisions will be made by SO15. In those circumstances, any decision on prosecution will be made independently by CTD in accordance with the Code for Crown Prosecutors. The decision whether or not to arrest a suspect when he/she arrives in the UK will be one for SO15.

If the decision is not to investigate, SO15 will inform the complainant or his/her solicitor.

If there is insufficient information upon which to make an initial decision on jurisdiction, immunity or any potential offences, SO15 will write and request further information from the complainant. It will be stressed to the complainant that if this information is not provided in sufficient time for it to be given proper consideration before a suspect's arrival in the UK, neither SO15 nor CTD can consider the matter further and the letter at Annex 1 will be sent to the complainant or his/her solicitor.

This letter explains the roles and responsibilities in a private prosecution and what might happen at a later stage if a private prosecutor asks the DPP to exercise his right to take the case over.

(www.cps.gov.uk/publications/agencies/war_crimes.html)

6/84

The Home Secretary was asked:

(1) what discussions she had had with her French and Belgian counterparts on the search for and prosecution of suspected Rwandan genocidaires residing in those countries;

(2) what steps she was taking to encourage other EU Governments to arrest suspected Rwandan genocidaires residing in their countries;

and

(3) what discussions she has had with EU counterparts about procedures for extradition to Rwanda of suspected Rwandan genocidaires residing in Europe.

She wrote:

It is for each member state to determine, in accordance with its own laws, what action might be appropriate in particular cases. Regular discussions, however, are held with EU counterparts, both at ministerial and official level, about a range of judicial cooperation issues including, from time to time, about bringing to justice alleged genocidaires from Rwanda. No one fleeing prosecution in that country should expect to find safe haven or to enjoy impunity within the EU. That is why the Government have entered into special extradition arrangements with Rwanda in respect of four cases currently before the courts.

(See *Brown et al v Governor of Belmarsh Prison et al* [2007] EWHC 498 (Admin)—There is an MOU with respect to each applicant, to which the judgment refers without specifying their details. Ed.]

(HC Deb 9 October 2007 Vol 464 c477W)

6/85 (See also 14/5–6)

Special Court for Sierra Leone

An FCO Minister said on introducing the second reading of the International Tribunals (Sierra Leone) Bill:

Sierra Leone are preparing to go to the polls to elect the leaders who will take the next steps on that path of recovery. The UK is providing support for that process, and we will work closely with those leaders as they face the difficult challenges ahead. However, part of the future of Sierra Leone is in coming to terms with the past, and ensuring that those alleged to have committed the shocking crimes of the country's civil war are held to account. In turn, taking such action sends a message to those who would commit such crimes in future, that if they do so, they will answer for it.

With those aims, the Government of Sierra Leone and the United Nations negotiated an agreement back in 2002 to establish the Special Court for Sierra Leone. The Special Court is an international criminal tribunal of a hybrid nature, in that it combines elements of Sierra Leonean and international law, and draws on the skills of Sierra Leonean and international staff. The United Kingdom has been one of the Special Court's strongest supporters since its inception. That has meant ensuring that the court has the resources that it needs to do its work. To that end, we recently made a further payment of £2 million towards meeting the costs of the court, bringing our total contribution since 2002 to £12 million.

Our support for international justice goes beyond the financial. As my right hon. Friend the Secretary of State for Foreign and Commonwealth Affairs said in June last year, if we want to live in a just world, we must take responsibility for creating and fostering it. In practice, that means that we and other states must provide practical assistance to the different international criminal tribunals as they take forward their important work. We live up to that challenge.

For example, we co-operate in the exchange of information with the international criminal tribunals, we take witnesses into our witness relocation system, and we imprison some of those convicted by the tribunals in the UK prison system. The legislative basis for doing that is the International Criminal Court Act 2001, which provides, among other things, for our entering into sentence enforcement agreements with the International Criminal Court and other international criminal tribunals established by resolution of the UN Security Council, such as those for former Yugoslavia and Rwanda.

The Minister was asked whether or not the issue of arrest warrants by international criminal courts might inhibit political settlements. He said:

I would have to look at that assertion on a case-by-case basis. The hon. Gentleman mentions northern Uganda...I am sure that he would not like anyone in Uganda or its neighbouring countries to sense a degree of impunity regarding the crimes that they have committed and continue to commit. We would have to look into that matter very carefully and on a case-by-case basis, as I said, but I take his point. It can be a very sensitive issue, which has to be considered very carefully.

...we have imprisoned some of those convicted by tribunals in the UK prison system. The legislative basis for doing so is the International Criminal Court Act 2001, which makes provision, among other things, for our entering into sentence enforcement agreements with the International Criminal Court and also with other international criminal tribunals established by resolution of the UN Security Council, such as those for former Yugoslavia and Rwanda.

It was only after the coming into force of the International Criminal Court Act 2001 that the Special Court for Sierra Leone was established. It is because the court was a new model of tribunal—a hybrid, as I mentioned—established with the full agreement and participation of the Government of Sierra Leone, that a UN Security Council resolution was not required to bring it into being. None the less, the Special Court enjoys full support from the international community. Indeed, the UN Security Council indicated its support by passing a resolution that authorised the UN Secretary-General to negotiate the founding agreement with the Government of Sierra Leone. That is not, however, sufficient to provide an adequate basis for our entering into a sentence enforcement agreement under the terms of the ICC legislation as it stands. The short, two-clause Bill before us will therefore extend the International Criminal Court Act's provision on sentence enforcement to the Special Court for Sierra Leone.

Let me briefly explain why we are taking this important step in the case of the Special Court for Sierra Leone. First, we do so because it is another demonstration of the UK's commitment to international justice—the same commitment apparent in our steadfast support of the tribunals for former Yugoslavia and Rwanda, and the same commitment that has since led us to help establish the permanent International Criminal Court and to take a lead as one its strongest supporters, in principle and in practice. I am pleased to note that the ICC is now playing a vital role in breaking down impunity for the shocking crimes taking place in Darfur, in northern Uganda, as we have heard, and elsewhere.

Secondly, we are moving this forward because of the UK's particular commitment to peace, security and development in Sierra Leone. When we made that intervention in May 2000, we also made a commitment to see it through and finish the job. Our support for the Special Court is an important part of that. Through the actions that we are taking, we also safeguard the investment—military, political and financial—that the United Kingdom has made in Sierra Leone.

Thirdly—I come now to the reason for our approaching the Bill in expeditious fashion today—we do so to give effect to the commitment that we gave to imprison former President Taylor if he should be convicted at the trial, which began last week in The Hague. Let me speak for a few moments about that commitment and its role in making the trial possible.

Former President Taylor was transferred to the detention facility of the Special Court for Sierra Leone in Freetown on 29 March last year, having been indicted for alleged crimes against humanity and war crimes. Within a short period of time, considerable security concerns arose about former President Taylor's presence in Freetown. There were fears that his supporters might seek to free him, with terrible consequences for the stability of the region. Owing to those fears, President Kabbah of Sierra Leone and President Johnson-Sirleaf of Liberia proposed that former President Taylor's trial should take place away from the court's headquarters in Freetown.

The Government of the Netherlands agreed to allow the Special Court to sit in The Hague to hear former President Taylor's trial and the International Criminal Court agreed to allow the court to use its facilities for the trial, but the Dutch insisted that, should former President Taylor be convicted, he must serve his sentence in another state. The UN Secretary-General, in the light of the security concerns and on the advice of UN staff operating on the ground, added his call to that of the regional governments and requested that the United Kingdom agree to make the necessary commitment to the Dutch.

I should emphasise that the proposal to transfer the location of former President Taylor's trial was considered long and hard. We and others were and remain instinctively supportive of the principle that, where possible, a trial should be conducted locally, where it is most accessible and most visible to those who have been affected. However, the security threat was significant and the requests from Kofi Annan, from Presidents Kabbah and Johnson-Sirleaf and from the ECOWAS—Economic Community of West African States—grouping of states were impossible to ignore.

On 15 June last year, we announced that my right hon. Friend the Foreign Secretary had agreed that, subject to parliamentary legislative approval, the United Kingdom would allow former President Taylor—if convicted and should the circumstances require it—to enter the UK to serve any sentence imposed by the Special Court for Sierra Leone.

The Minister was asked to confirm that it was the government's intention that only Taylor should serve his sentence in the UK. He said:

Yes, I can put that on the record without any hesitation. It is important to recognise that the other trials, which seem to be proceeding very well in Freetown, are at a rather different level from that of Charles Taylor. In that sense, Charles Taylor is a very special prisoner. That is why he is being tried in The Hague and why he could be imprisoned here. We would certainly never rule out a request from the International Criminal Court or from the Sierra Leone authorities regarding someone else whom we might consider imprisoning, but that would have to be a matter for careful consideration. We certainly do not envisage that happening at this time.

Former President Taylor's transfer to The Hague was subsequently authorised by the President of the Special Court for Sierra Leone and confirmed by United Nations Security Council resolution 1688. Just five days after the announcement of the UK's commitment, former President Taylor was transferred to The Hague. A real threat to peace and security in Sierra Leone and the wider region had been overcome, and the trial which has now begun had been made possible.

Let me stress again that the Bill and any subsequent signing of a sentence enforcement agreement represent a contingency arrangement. Imprisonment in the United Kingdom would take place only if former President Taylor were convicted, if the Special Court requested that the United Kingdom imprison him, and if the United Kingdom agreed to do so. I should also stress that the Bill, and any sentence enforcement agreement signed as a result of its provisions, will not apply specifically to former President Taylor...

The Bill, which comprises only two clauses, simply establishes the legal basis under which the United Kingdom may sign a sentence enforcement agreement with the Special Court. None the less, I can confirm that the request that was made to us and the political undertaking that we have given relate only to imprisoning former President Taylor, should that be necessary. We have not received a request in respect of any other individual on trial before the Special Court for Sierra Leone. Indeed, our expectation is that any other individuals convicted by the court will serve their sentences elsewhere.

...The territorial extent of the Bill is limited to England and Wales...It follows, therefore, that any sentence of imprisonment would be served in a prison in England or Wales.

I cannot say how long the trial of former President Taylor will last. The reality is that the wheels of international justice have so far turned relatively slowly. None the less, it is possible that the trial might come to a speedy conclusion. That is a factor beyond our control, but it could happen. Our objective is to ensure that, if we are called on to honour our commitment, we are ready to do so as soon as that becomes necessary.

The Bill is a further expression of the United Kingdom's commitment to international justice. It is evidence of our determination to finish the job that we started in Sierra Leone, and it is a clear signal to those who would commit the most serious crimes known to humanity that justice will be done. I commend the Bill to the House.

(HC Deb 13 June 2007 Vol 461 c784–788)

6/86
The Minister concluded the debate saying:

I fully expect former President Taylor to receive a fair trial. The Special Court for Sierra Leone has been established in accordance with international norms as they relate to all aspects of trial proceedings...the funding for Taylor's defence is a matter for Taylor, his lawyers and the court. It is of course essential that the defence is adequately resourced to ensure that Taylor is well represented and that the trial is fair and seen to be fair. Ultimately, those are decisions for the court. The United Kingdom is absolutely committed to ensuring that overall the court has the resources to carry out its vital work in accordance with accepted international norms.

[I was] asked an important question about asylum applications subsequent to any release of former President Taylor. Clearly any decision would be made in the light of the circumstances at the time, but if Taylor were convicted by the Special Court, served a sentence in the United Kingdom and was then released, I expect that he would leave the United Kingdom or face removal. Under current immigration law it is open to the Home Secretary to order the deportation of any non-British citizen whose removal from the United Kingdom is deemed to be conducive to the public good. Any asylum claim would be considered in accordance with the refugee convention, which contains provisions to refuse asylum to those involved in genocide, crimes against humanity or war crimes...

Where a convicted criminal is transferred to the UK to serve a sentence, it is Home Office policy to refuse that individual leave to enter, but to grant temporary admission for the duration of the sentence. That ensures that residency rights and benefits do not accrue to the individual as a result of imprisonment in the UK. That point needs making.

[I was] asked about the Cassese report. I remind him that Judge Cassese came in at our instigation and our representation. The UK was represented on the court's management team in New York that commissioned the report by Judge Cassese, the independent expert. We welcome the report and its recommendations. The management committee is supervising the implementation of the recommendations in consultation with the court...the report rightly draws attention to the need for long-term financial security for the court. The recent United Kingdom contribution of £2 million is another step forward. We are pressing management committee partners and other states to make further contributions...the present management committee partners include, but not exclusively, the United States, the United Kingdom, the Dutch, Canada, Sierra Leone, Nigeria and the United Nations Office of Legal Affairs. We are pressing hard to ensure that adequate funding comes forward.

I was asked...about what happens when the Special Court winds up. In the event that the court has ceased to exist in its current form owing to the completion of its trial load, judicial responsibility will pass to a designated successor body. Discussion has already taken place about an international successor body to take on the residual functions of the Yugoslavia, Rwanda and Sierra Leone tribunals once their work is mostly complete

I was asked...whether the trial would be too remote from ordinary Sierra Leoneans. We thought long and hard about that. It is essential that, despite the physical distance, the Special Court's proceedings in The Hague are accessible and relevant to the people of Sierra Leone. After all, it is in their name that justice is being done...

Sierra Leone has been working hard to achieve Kimberley process certification. It remains a fragile region and the UK is working hard with Sierra Leone to ensure that progress is maintained, including in preventing conflict diamonds from entering Sierra Leone from Côte d'Ivoire.

...our attention [was drawn] to the curse of ad hockery...we have to get the structure and system of international law properly organised and funded. The international community must tackle that project with much greater urgency and determination than it has shown until now...that should be one of the centrepieces of the reform of the secretariat and of the operation of the United Nations.

...international law is much the poorer if it does not have a chapter that is effective, robust and able to try international criminals—not in an ad hoc way but in an organised way. I could not agree more.

(HC Deb 13 June 2007 Vol 461 c809–812)
[The Bill Became the International Tribunals (Sierra Leone) Act 2007, Ed.]

6/87

Hissene Habre

The Foreign Secretary was asked what discussions she had had with (a) the Government of Senegal and (b) her EU counterparts on the trial of the former president of Chad, Hissene Habre, and potential EU assistance in that trial. An FCO Minister wrote:

The UK has regular consultations with EU colleagues on the progress of Hissene Habre's trial, most recently in the Africa Working Group on 28 February. We will continue, with the EU, to discuss and review the development of the trial.

Our ambassador in Dakar made representations to the Government of Senegal in October 2006 to urge them to pass the required legislation to enable the trial of Hissene Habre to be held in Senegal with minimum delay. We welcome the passing of the necessary legislation by the Sengalese National Assembly on 31 January 2007 to permit a trial to take place in Senegal and urge the Government of Senegal to expedite the process.

(HC Deb 7 March 2007 Vol 457 c1999W)

6/88

Saddam Hussein

An FCO Minister was asked by the FAC whether it is the view of the British Government that Saddam [Hussein's] trial fulfilled the "accepted norms of justice". The Minister said:

He was prosecuted under the procedures prescribed by Iraqi law. The trial was open and held with independent monitors and the media present. He never once gave that to any citizen of his country. I acknowledge that there are criticisms of the trial process, and they were raised with the Iraqi authorities not just by ourselves, but by others too. It was the Iraqi high tribunal's first case. We should remember that it was carried out in a climate in which senior officials, including judges, were under physical and mortal threat.

In general, I have to say that he was prosecuted properly under the procedures of Iraqi law. I am hoping that in the coming years, the legal system will continue to improve, both in its prosecuting and defence standards and in dealing with outcomes such as jail sentences and other things. In the final analysis, we made it quite clear, when he was given the death penalty, that the Government oppose the death penalty in all circumstances, including for him. We made it clear that

that was the case. We do not support the death penalty even for those found
guilty of crimes against humanity. [Q.71]

(FAC Report, Human Rights Report 2006, HC 269 (2007))

6/89
It was put to the Minister:

After we defeated Germany, we did not let the new German Government
try Hess and the rest of them—an international tribunal was set up. When
we captured war criminals in the Balkans, we did not hand them back even
to the democratically elected Governments for them to be tried. They were
tried in The Hague. As you said earlier, we are seeking to catch two more
war criminals, but they will not be handed back to any kind of democratic
Government. They will be tried by an international tribunal. Would it not
have been better for Saddam and the others to have been tried by an international tribunal?

He replied:

International tribunals hear cases only where local justice is either unwilling or
unable to do so. That was not the case in Iraq. Iraqis were willing to do it and
had a legal system set up and established that fulfilled international norms. They
tried him and he was found guilty of appalling crimes. [Q.72]

(FAC Report, Human Rights Report 2006, HC 269 (2007))

6/90
The FAC put to an FCO Minister a newspaper report which said:

"warlords in the Afghan parliament have granted themselves an amnesty from
human rights charges in a move that has shocked the country's Western back-
ers... The rule states that anyone who fought against the Soviet Army in the
1980s cannot be prosecuted... and anyone who described an MP as a warlord
would risk prosecution."

He was than asked for the Government's position. He said:

It is important that... we redouble our efforts to ensure the agreed strategy for
transitional justice, which is to work up into 2008 and was set out in the national
action plan for peace, reconciliation and justice—that was done in collaboration with the Afghan Government and the United Nations and was adopted in
December 2005—is committed to and seen through.

What we also need to make sure is seen through is the justice process—including
vetting, truth telling, prosecutions and reconciliation processes—to deal with
war crimes and gross human rights violations committed during the conflict in
Afghanistan. None of us is resiling from any of those issues, irrespective of this
decision, which, as I said, is not only extremely unhelpful, but sends the wrong
messages altogether. [Q.74]

(FAC Report, Human Rights Report 2006, HC 269 (2007))

6/91

An FCO Minister wrote:

The International Convention for the Suppression of Acts of Nuclear Terrorism entered into force on 7 July. The UK signed the Convention on 14 September 2005. The legislation required to implement the Convention is now in place in the UK, and the Government are currently preparing the necessary documents to be laid before Parliament prior to ratification. The Convention imposes an obligation on States Parties to report to the UN Secretary-General the final outcome of criminal proceedings undertaken in respect of the offences set out in the Convention. States Parties will also be expected to report to the committees of the UN Security Council that monitor implementation of States' counter-terrorism and non-proliferation obligations, on the implementation of their obligations under the Convention in a more general sense. While the Overseas Territories will not be included at the time of the UK's ratification, there remains the possibility of extending the Convention to the Overseas Territories following consultation with them and the passing of any necessary legislation in each Territory. With our international partners, the UK has strongly encouraged all States to sign and ratify the Convention. Most recently, in a joint statement on counter-terrorism issued at the Heiligendamm Summit on 8 June, the leaders of the G8 called on all States to ratify the Convention. [As of May 2008, the UK had not ratified the Convention, Ed.]

(HC Deb 16 July 2007 Vol 463 c29W)

Part Seven: Organs of the State and Their Status

Part Seven: I. *The state and its organs—heads of state*

7/1

The FCO produced the following summary of its own written submissions, the submissions of the court-appointed advocate in the case and those of the Appellant in *Mrs A v Avia Amir and Others, HM The Sultan of Brunei (intervening)* [2007] EWCA Civ 712—The case involved certain questions of the privileges and immunities of a serving Head of State.

Question A: Is it a matter of discretion or obligation for the Court to give effect to Article 29 [of the Vienna Convention on Diplomatic Relations] in such a case?

FCO Written Submissions

4. The Court is obliged to treat a foreign head of State with "due respect" and to take "all appropriate steps to prevent any attack on his [. . . . . .] dignity."(see paragraph 3 above). It is submitted, however, that the use of the term "appropriate" allows the Court a margin of appreciation in determining what measures may be appropriate in each case. In this connection, the Foreign and Commonwealth Office would refer the Court to the negotiating history of Article 29 as set out in paragraphs 80 and 81 of the Written Submissions of the Advocate. This issue is

addressed in more detail below in considering what steps may be thought to be "appropriate" in terms of Article 29.

Submissions of the Advocate to the Court

The negotiating history shows that the inclusion of the word "appropriate" was deliberate, and intended to qualify the duty on the State... The International Law Commission's draft articles, which were the basic text before the Conference which drew up the Vienna Convention on Diplomatic Relations, referred to "all reasonable steps". A proposal simply to delete the word "reasonable" was adopted, whereupon the British delegate explained that: "removal of the word "reasonable" would give the article unlimited scope, and impose an impossible task on receiving States."

The Conference thereupon decided to introduce the word "appropriate." It is not considered that there is any significant difference between the expressions "all reasonable steps" and "all appropriate steps".

* * *

Question B: Does Article 29 of the Vienna Convention on Diplomatic Relations 1961 (as applied by the Diplomatic Privileges Act 1964 and section 20 of the State Immunity Act 1978) endure for the protection of a serving foreign Head of State *ratione personae*, ie without regard to whether the affected interest touches his personal life or his public functions?

FCO Written Submissions

5. It is submitted that Article 29 applies to a serving foreign Head of State *ratione personae*, that is without any distinction between his or her personal or public acts. Such application is in accordance with well established principles of international law by which the functions of certain categories of State officials are recognised as so important to the proper maintenance of international relations that they require protection and immunity in respect of both official and private acts. Such categories include Heads of State and diplomatic agents. As the Advocate to the Court has indicated, the immunity *ratione personae* of Heads of State under international law is expressly acknowledged in Article 3.2 of the 2004 United Nations Convention on the Jurisdictional Immunities of States and their Property.

Submissions of the Advocate to the Court

8. It is submitted that article 29 of the Vienna Convention on Diplomatic Relations scheduled to the Diplomatic Privileges Act 1964 applies, by virtue of section 20 of the State Immunity Act 1978, to a serving foreign Head of State *ratione personae*, that is, without distinction between his personal or public acts. This is in accordance with the principle that serving heads of State enjoy privileges and immunities *ratione personae* (by contrast with former Heads of State, who are only entitled to immunity *ratione materiae*, i.e. for their official acts). See, for example, article 3.2 of the 2004 United Nations Convention on Jurisdictional Immunities of States and their Property, which provides: "The

present Convention is without prejudice to privileges and immunities accorded under international law to heads of State *ratione personae.*"

* * *

Question C: What modifications (if any) under section 20 of the 1978 Act are necessary or appropriate in the application of the terms of Article 29 to a serving Head of State as opposed to a serving Ambassador?
FCO Written Submissions

6. The Foreign and Commonwealth Office has nothing to add to the submissions of the Advocate to the Court and Counsel for the Appellant on this point.
Submissions of the Advocate to the Court

11. It is submitted that the necessary modifications are, first, that the reference in article 29 to 'a diplomatic agent' should be read as a reference to 'a Head of State'; and second, that the reference to 'the receiving State' should be read as a reference to 'a foreign State', that is any State other than the State of which the person concerned is Head. With these modifications, article 29 would read:

"The person of a Head of State shall be inviolable. He shall not be liable to any form of arrest or detention. A foreign State shall treat him with due respect and shall take all appropriate steps to prevent any attack on his person, freedom and dignity."

12. The first modification needs no explanation. As to the second, the notion of "the receiving State" is not relevant in respect of a Head of State. Unlike a diplomatic agent (Ambassador, etc.), a Head of State is not accredited to a particular State or States. And, as Lord Slynn explained in *R v Bow Street Metropolitan Stipendiary Magistrate ex p. Pinochet (No. 1)* [2000] AC 61 at 72F to 73B, the reference in article 39.1 of the Vienna Convention (the commencement of privileges and immunities) to "the moment he enters the territory of the receiving State on proceeding to take up his post" should be read, in its application to a Head of State, as the time when he becomes Head of State.

Submissions by the Appellant

4. The Appellant is once again content to adopt—so far as they go—the submissions of the Advocate to the Court on this question. The substitution of the reference to 'Head of State' for 'diplomatic agent' is already implicit in the statutory provision itself, and the further substitution of 'foreign State' for 'receiving State' necessarily follows from the generally accepted understanding that (without prejudice to what the precise content of those duties may be) the duties owed under international law and comity to a serving Head of State are not dependent on the physical presence of the Head of State in the territory of another State. That this was Parliament's intention in enacting the State Immunity Act is established by the speeches in *Pinochet (No. 3)*, notably those of Lord Browne-Wilkinson (at p. 203C–D) and Lord Goff of Chievely (at p. 209F–210C).

5. The Appellant submits however in addition that the application of the terms of article 29 (so modified) must take account of the particular status and position of the Head of State, which is not functionally identical to that of his Ambassador (or that of diplomatic agents more generally). The time factor and

space factor aside, a serving Head of State may be entitled to more extensive courtesies and privileges than an Ambassador, those owed to the Ambassador being only the a fortiori minimum (see Sir Arthur Watts, Hague Lectures (Hague Academy, Receuil des Cours, Vol. 247 (1994-III)) at p. 40).

* * *

Question D: What should be understood in the terms of Article 29, by an "attack" on the Head of State's "dignity"?

FCO Written Submissions

8. The Preamble to the Vienna Convention on Diplomatic Relations states that the purpose of privileges and immunities is "not to benefit individuals but to ensure the efficient performance of the functions of diplomatic missions as representing States." In his Skeleton Argument at paragraph 12 and 13, Counsel for the Appellant takes issue with the Advocate to the Court's submissions which seek to limit the specific treatment owed to a Head of State to that strictly necessary for the effective exercise of his functions. The Foreign and Commonwealth Office submit that there is a proper analogy between the "dignity" of a diplomatic mission, as referred to in Article 22 of the Vienna Convention, and the dignity of an individual under Article 29, but, for the reasons advanced by Counsel for the Appellant, would agree that the concept may not be identical in its application in both cases.

Submissions by the Appellant

12. In the second place, the Appellant submits that the analogy with the functional immunity of a diplomatic mission (on which the Advocate to the Court principally relies) is wholly misplaced:-

there is a statutory definition setting out in detail what the functions are of a diplomatic mission (article 3 of the Convention), but none either in the Convention or elsewhere of the 'functions' of a Head of State;

the functions of a diplomatic mission are ex hypothesi designed to be carried out in the territory of a particular foreign State; exactly the converse is true of a Head of State;

nor is there any legitimate analogy between criticism of a government, and specifically of its policies, and insult or injury to a Head of State in his person (see further paragraph 28(a) below);

in actual practice, there is an exceedingly wide variation between the duties and functions conferred on the Head of State by the constitutional dispensations of different States, ranging from virtual dictatorships, through executive Presidencies and constitutional monarchies, to the largely or entirely ceremonial; but even a Head of State who was a mere ceremonial figurehead with no executive duties of any kind would be entitled to claim the same immunities, privileges and other courtesies as any other Head of State.

13. For all of these reasons, the Appellant submits that it makes no logical sense to conceive of the immunities, privileges and courtesies due to a foreign Head of State as having as their essential purpose to protect the 'functioning' of the Head of State in the territory of States other than his own. On the contrary, they

are marks of the respect due to the Head of State simply in virtue of his status as such, in accordance with the principle of 'sovereign equality' (cf. Article 2(1) of the Charter of the United Nations). This is especially true of the Head of State's 'dignity'.

* * *

Question E: In terms of article 29, what steps might be thought to be appropriate to be taken to "prevent" an attack on the dignity of a Third Party Head of State?

FCO Written Submissions

16. State practice and the limited caselaw on this issue support an interpretation of Article 29 which permits a margin of appreciation for States in deciding what steps are "appropriate". In doing so, it is clear that States must strike a balance between the principles governing the protection of diplomats and diplomatic missions and well established rights such as those pertaining to free speech and assembly. (see the *Magno* case referred to in paragraph (10) above) and *Colombani and Others v France*... which is also cited in the Written Submissions of the Advocate to the Court, paragraphs 83–84). In cases involving political demonstrations outside diplomatic missions, the United Kingdom Government takes the view that existing legal powers enable this balance to be struck effectively and have been content to leave the management of such situations to the police. It has stated:

"The police are the best judges in each case of the controls required: how to preserve the peace and dignity of a mission is essentially a matter of sensible policing practices rather than a question of law." (Government Report on Review of the Vienna Convention on Diplomatic Relations and Reply to "The Abuse of Diplomatic Immunities and Privileges", April 1985, Cmnd 9497, p17, paragraph 39(e))

Submissions of the Advocate to the Court

83. In *Colombani and others v France* (Application No. 51279/99, judgment of 25 June 2002)...the European Court of Human Rights held that a French Law of 1881, which made it an offence "publicly to insult a foreign head of State", infringed article 10 of the Convention (freedom of expression). The case was brought by the editor-in-chief of Le Monde and a journalist, who had been convicted under the Law for insulting the King of Morocco. The Court took the view that, at least in the context of article 10 (freedom of expression), special protection for Heads of State cannot be justified under the European Convention. Paragraphs 68 and 69 of the Chamber judgment of 25 September 2002 read as follows:

"68. The Court notes that the effect of a prosecution under section 36 of the Act of 29 July 1881 is to confer a special legal status on heads of State, shielding them from criticism solely on account of their function or status, irrespective of whether the criticism is warranted. That, in its view, amounts to conferring on foreign heads of State a special privilege that cannot be reconciled with modern practice and political conceptions. Whatever the obvious interest which every State has in maintaining friendly relations based on trust with the leaders of other States, such a privilege exceeds what is necessary for that objective to be attained.

69. Accordingly, the offence of insulting a foreign head of State is liable to inhibit freedom of expression without meeting any "pressing social need" capable of justifying such a restriction. It is the special protection afforded foreign heads of State by section 36 that undermines freedom of expression, not their right to use the standard procedure available to everyone to complain if their honour or reputation has been attacked or they are subjected to insulting remarks."

84. The *Colombani* case concerned restrictions on the freedom of expression under article 10, not limits on the right to a public hearing under article 6. There is no reference in the judgment to the special protection due to a foreign Head of State under international law. Nevertheless, the case strongly suggests that the Strasbourg Court would not lightly accept that greater protection should be given to the dignity of a Head of State than to ordinary members of the public, at least where a legal system provides adequate safeguards for the latter. It is submitted that the same principle should be applied in the context of publicity of proceedings under article 6.

(Text supplied by FCO)

Part Seven: IV. *The state and its organs—diplomatic missions and their members*

7/2

The Foreign Secretary was asked what arrangements were in place in Madagascar for the representation of the interests of (a) British exporters and (b) British nationals. An FCO Minister wrote:

UK consular and commercial interests in Madagascar are represented through our High Commission in Port Louis, Mauritius.

We continue to push for swift accreditation from the Government of Madagascar for our High Commissioner in Mauritius to be non-resident ambassador to Madagascar and for our appointed honorary consul in Antananarivo. Until that authority has been granted to our honorary consul in Antananarivo, our high commission in Port Louis is dealing with all consular inquiries. A British honorary consul has been appointed in Toamasina, and has the necessary authority from the Government of Madagascar to act as the first point of contact for British nationals requiring consular assistance in the Toamasina region. The French embassy in Antananarivo has agreed to provide support for British nationals in the event of a serious consular incident in Madagascar.

(HC Deb 8 January 2007 Vol 455 c355W)

7/3

The Foreign Secretary was asked how much income tax or money in lieu of income tax was collected in respect of (a) UK citizens and (b) non-UK citizens who were locally engaged staff in the UK's embassy in Italy in each of the last 10 years for which figures are available; what value of these deductions was (i) remitted to the Italian tax authorities, (ii) remitted to the UK's Inland Revenue, (iii) retained by the UK's embassy in Italy and (iv) remitted to London and retained by her Department in each year. An FCO Minister wrote:

The Italy-UK Double Taxation Agreement 1988 exempts those staff employed on Government service who are British but not Italian from local income tax. Our embassy in Rome remitted to the Italian authorities the amounts shown as follows on behalf of their non-UK local staff from 1999–2006. No figures are available before 1999. Staff without local liability for income tax in the host country, including some UK and third country nationals, have their salaries abated. When salaries are abated no monies are remitted to either Italian or UK authorities, including the Foreign and Commonwealth Office, instead the salaries are determined on a net basis.

(HC Deb 10 May 2007 Vol 460 c396W)

7/4 (See also 5/9–11, 19/21–22)
The Foreign Secretary was asked what assessment she had made of the Russian Government's adherence to the 1961 Vienna Convention on Diplomatic Relations. An FCO Minister wrote:

The Government urge Russia, and all states, to uphold the 1961 Vienna Convention on Diplomatic Relations. We have been deeply concerned about the threat to the Estonian embassy in Moscow following a dispute over the relocation of a war memorial in Tallinn. We therefore fully support the EU presidency statement of 2 May and the NATO statement of 3 May which expressed grave concern over the safety of the Estonian embassy and its staff in Russia, asked Russia to respect the Vienna Convention and urged Russia to address the dispute through dialogue.

(HC Deb 15 May 2007 Vol 460 c700W)

7/5
The Foreign Secretary was asked in which European Union countries the UK did not remit to the local tax authorities income tax, or sums in lieu of income tax, collected in respect of locally engaged British embassy staff; in which EU countries there were different arrangements for those locally engaged staff who were (a) UK citizens, (b) citizens of the host EU country and (c) citizens of a third country; and what the reasons were for such differences. An FCO Minister wrote:

Consistent with global diplomatic practice, Foreign and Commonwealth Office (FCO) policy is that to the extent compatible with local law, local staff should take responsibility for their own income tax arrangements. The differences in arrangements between FCO missions are determined by local tax regulations, which vary from country to country. The following table [not reproduced, Ed.] summarises the current position in FCO missions in the EU.

Staff without income tax liability in the host country, including some UK and third country nationals, have their salaries abated. The aim is that staff with and without liability to pay income tax should receive comparable take home pay.

(HC Deb 10 May 2007 Vol 460 c387W)

7/6
The Foreign Secretary wrote:

There were 5,484 outstanding parking and other minor traffic violation fines incurred by diplomatic missions and international organisations in the United Kingdom recorded during the year 1 January 2006 to 31 December 2006. These totalled £506,475. In April this year the Foreign and Commonwealth Office wrote to all diplomatic missions and international organisations concerned giving them the opportunity either to pay their outstanding fines or appeal against them if they considered that the fines had been issued incorrectly. As a result of subsequent payments totalling £22,713 and formal appeals lodged, there remains a total of 4,859 (£448,965) unpaid fines for 2006(1). The table below details those diplomatic missions and International Organisations that have outstanding fines totalling £1,000 or more.

[There follows a list by mission and amount, Ed.]

The number of outstanding fines incurred by diplomatic missions in the United Kingdom for non-payment of the London congestion charge since its introduction in February 2003 until 3 April 2007 was 74,198. The table below shows the 10 diplomatic missions with the highest value of outstanding fines.

Mission	Number of Outstanding Fines	Value £
1. USA	15150	1,484,765
2. Nigeria	6949	682,370
3. Sudan	5633	545,990
4. Japan	4119	386,150
5. Tanzania	3119	298,940
6. Kenya	3099	292,830
7. South Africa	2773	267,290
8. Sierra Leone	2619	252,310
9. Germany	2515	223,950
10. Zimbabwe	1641	157,430

(HC Deb 20 June 2007 Vol 461 c92–93WS)

7/7
The Foreign Secretary wrote:

The majority of diplomatic missions in the United Kingdom pay the national non-domestic rates requested from them. They are obliged to pay only 6 per cent. of the total national non-domestic rates value, which represents payment for specific services such as street cleaning, lighting, maintenance and fire services. The total amount outstanding from all diplomatic missions is approximately £821,000.00. However, as at 31 March 2007, the missions listed below owed over £10,000 in national non-domestic rates. Twelve additional diplomatic missions, who owe £10,000 or more in respect of national non-domestic rates, have made arrangements with the Valuation Office Agency to clear their outstanding debts and have not been included in this list.

[There then followed a list of States and amounts not paid, Ed.]

(HC Deb 20 June 2007 Vol 461 c94WS)

7/8

The Foreign Secretary wrote:

In 2006, 15 serious offences allegedly committed by people entitled to diplomatic immunity were drawn to the attention of the Foreign and Commonwealth Office. "Serious Offences" are defined as offences that would, in certain circumstances, carry a penalty of 12 months or more imprisonment. Some 24,000 people are entitled to diplomatic immunity in the United Kingdom.

The table below lists those foreign missions whose diplomats allegedly committed serious offences and the type of offence from 2002–2006.

[There follow annual lists by offence and mission, Ed.]

(HC Deb 20 June 2007 Vol 461 c94–97WS)

7/9

The Foreign Secretary was asked how many notifiable offences were committed by foreign diplomats based in London in 2006, broken down by (a) offence and (b) country of diplomatic status. An FCO Minister wrote:

We were notified by the police of 126 alleged criminal offences committed in 2006 by the approximately 24,000 individuals entitled to diplomatic immunity in the UK. 15 of these alleged offences were serious offences that would, in certain circumstances, have carried a penalty of 12 months or more imprisonment...the Foreign Secretary provided details of these alleged serious offences in her written ministerial statement of 20 June 2007, Official Report, columns 94–96WS. The following table lists the other alleged offences not included in the Foreign Secretary's statement:

[There follows a detailed list by offence and by mission, Ed.]

(HC Deb 25 June 2007 Vol 462 cs192–193W)

7/10
The Foreign Secretary was asked what assessment she had made of (a) the extent and nature of the recent harassment of guests to the United Kingdom embassy in Iran and (b) the extent to which the Iranian authorities assisted in minimising the harassment and controlling the demonstrators. An FCO Minister wrote:

There was a large demonstration outside our embassy in Tehran before and during Her Majesty the Queen's Birthday Party reception on 14 June. The demonstrators blocked access to the embassy for some hours and harassed and intimidated guests on their way into the reception. There were some instances of physical violence. Harassment continued as guests left the party and we are aware of a number of instances of guests being questioned and detained on departure.

The Permanent Under-Secretary at the Foreign and Commonwealth Office summoned the Iranian ambassador on 19 June to register our dismay that the authorities had failed to prevent this harassment from taking place. Our embassy in Tehran has done likewise with the Iranian authorities.

(HC Deb 26 June 2007 Vol 462 c664W)

Part Seven: VII. *The state and its organs—trade and information offices, trade delegations etc*

7/11
In a statement, the Foreign Secretary said:

The Russian authorities announced yesterday that they planned to shut down the British Council's offices in St Petersburg and Yekaterinburg on 1 January 2008.

Russia's threatened actions are illegal. The British Council's presence in Russia is entirely consistent with international law, including the Vienna Conventions. Its presence and activities are also specifically sanctioned by a 1994 UK/Russia Agreement on Co-operation in Education, Science and Culture, signed by Russia, and which binds both the UK and Russia. The British Council is the designated agent of the British Government for the implementation of the agreement. For the past nine years, the UK has been keen to conclude a further Cultural Centres Agreement with Russia. Pending such an agreement being reached, the 1994 Agreement remains in force.

For Russia to carry out its threat would therefore constitute a serious attack against the legitimate cultural agent of the British Government would show a disregard for the rule of law and would only damage Russia's reputation around the world.

Damage will also be done to EU-Russia cultural co-operation. We are discussing with partners (including the EU and the G7), the implications of Russia's threat. I am grateful to the European Commission for expressing its concern to Russia about the situation facing the British Council.

Overall, Russia's threats set back bilateral and multilateral efforts to improve cultural links, severely affect large numbers of Russians who benefit from the British Council's presence, and damage Russia's reputation around the world. We are urging the Russian authorities to reconsider. At the same time we are working closely with the British Council to ensure the welfare of their staff.

(HC Deb 13 December 2007 Vol 469 c56WS)

7/12
The Foreign Secretary was asked by the FAC about the Russian decision to order the closure of certain British Council offices in Russia. He said:

Today, a Foreign Ministry spokesman in Moscow announced that Russia has ordered the closure of British Council offices in St. Petersburg and Ekaterinburg from 1 January 2008.

That is a very serious and illegal measure. The 1963 Vienna convention on consular relations and the 1994 UK-Russia agreement on culture confer legal status on the Council's activities throughout Russia.(Q.604)

(FAC, Foreign Policy Aspects of the Lisbon Treaty, HC120-II (2007))

7/13
The Foreign Secretary was asked:

(1) what assessment she had made of the activities of the Russian authorities towards the work of the British Council in Russia.

(2) whether she had raised the treatment of the British Council in Russia with her Russian counterpart.

(3) what assessment she had made of the progress towards the conclusion of a new Cultural Centres Agreement with Russia.

(4) what discussions she has had with her European Union counterparts on the (a) treatment of the British Council in Russia and (b) progress towards the conclusion of a new Cultural Centres Agreement and what the outcome was of those discussions.

An FCO Minister wrote:

The British Council has been present in Russia for many years,, during which it has enjoyed the support of federal ministries, local authorities and officials for activities in the fields of education, language training, scientific co-operation, culture and the arts. Hundreds of thousands of people across Russia have been able to benefit from the activities of the British Council network...

More recently the British Council in Russia has experienced a number of legal. [sic], administrative and practical difficulties. The British Council has sought to comply with the demands of the authorities, for example in respect of taxation and other regulations, despite difficulties caused by the lack of clear legal status, Most recently a series of tax inspections in Moscow and across the network was launched and the British Council are providing information requested by the inspectors.

We have pressed the Russians to resolve uncertainties about the legal status of the British Council in Russia by concluding a new Cultural Centres Agreement, taking the place of a 1994 Agreement on Co-operation in the Fields of Education, Science and Culture. The absence of an updated Agreement is causing difficulties for some regional British Council centres established in co-operation with local partners and authorities. A text was agreed at official level with Russia in 2001. In March 2006, Russia submitted a revised text. Productive negotiations with the Russian Foreign Ministry in January brought the text of a new Cultural Centres Agreement very close to conclusion. However, the Russian authorities have been reluctant to guarantee consent, under the terms of the Agreement, for the British Council to establish centres (which already exist as their current network of offices), outside Moscow. We await the Russian authorities' reply to our outstanding proposals for finalising the text, which we hope can lead to a quick and satisfactory outcome.

These issues are raised frequently with the Russian authorities at both Ministerial and official levels. Our Embassy in Moscow keeps EU colleagues informed of developments in the course of regular meetings in Moscow.

(HC Deb 25 June 2007 Vol 462 cs214W–215W)

Part Eight: Jurisdiction of the State

Part Eight: I.A. *Jurisdiction of the State—bases of jurisdiction—territorial principle See* **19/23**

Part Eight: I.E. *Jurisdiction of the state—bases of jurisdiction—other bases*

8/1

The Foreign Secretary was asked about representations the Government had made to the US authorities on the impact on UK tourists and businesses of the expansion of extra-territorial financial measures against Cuba. An FCO Minister wrote:

The European Commission has responsibility within the European Community for dealing with extraterritorial measures taken by third countries against EU member states. Council regulation EC2271/96 (the 'EU blocking statute') was introduced by the EU in 1996 to offer protection to EU individuals and companies against certain specific extraterritorial legislation, including the US Helms/ Burton Act which applies sanctions against Cuba.

My officials are in discussion with the European Commission in relation to recent cases of US extraterritoriality in the context of UK trade with Cuba, and the Commission is considering how best to take these issues forward.

(HC Deb 2 May 2007 Vol 459 c1666W)

Part Eight: II.C *Jurisdiction of the State—types of jurisdiction—jurisdiction to enforce*

8/2
(See also **19/24**)

On 25 January 2007, the Attorney-General published an agreement with the Attorney-General of the United States about the handling of criminal cases where there was concurrent jurisdiction.

GUIDANCE FOR HANDLING CRIMINAL CASES WITH CONCURRENT JURISDICTION BETWEEN THE UNITED KINGDOM AND THE UNITED STATES OF AMERICA

1. Investigation and prosecution agencies in the United Kingdom and the United States of America are committed to working together to combat crime. It is appreciated that there is a need to enhance the exchange of information in criminal cases involving concurrent jurisdiction. Early contact between prosecutors, after discussing the cases with prosecutors, is intended to enable them to agree on strategies for the handling of criminal investigations and proceedings in particular cases. Such liaison will help to avoid potential difficulties later in the case. In particular, early contact will be valuable in cases which are already subject of proceedings in the other jurisdiction.

2. This document provides guidance for addressing the most serious, sensitive or complex criminal cases where it is apparent to prosecutors that there are issues to be decided that arise from concurrent jurisdiction. In deciding whether contact should be made with the other country regarding such a case, the prosecutor should apply the following test: does it appear that there is a real possibility that a prosecutor in the other country may have an interest in prosecuting the ease? Such a case would usually have significant links with the other country.

3. As a matter of fundamental principle any decision on issues arising from concurrent jurisdiction should be and be seen to be fair and objective. Each case is unique and should be considered on its own facts and merits.

4. This guidance follows a step-by-step approach to determining issues arising in cases with concurrent jurisdiction. Firstly, there should be early sharing of information between prosecutors in the jurisdictions with an interest in the case. Second, prosecutors should consult on cases and the issues arising from concurrent jurisdiction. Third, where prosecutors in the jurisdiction with an interest in the case have been unable to reach agreement en issues arising from concurrent jurisdiction, the offices of their Attorneys General or Lord Advocate, as appropriate, should take the lead with the aim of resolving those issues

Information

5. In the most serious, sensitive or complex cases where issues of concurrent jurisdiction arise, investigators and prosecutors, in the UK and US, should consult closely together from the outset of investigations, consistent with the procedures established by their agencies. Each jurisdiction intends to make its best efforts to ensure that there are arrangements in place requiring investigators, in such cases, to draw issues arising from concurrent jurisdiction to the immediate attention of prosecutors. The aim of such a cooperative approach is to agree to at co-ordinated strategy in relation to the particular case that respects the individual jurisdictions but recognises the benefits of co-operation in these areas.

    . . .

9. In particularly sensitive cases, involving for example classified information, it may be appropriate for the sharing of information and the consultation to take place between the heads of prosecuting divisions in the UK and US or between the offices of the Attorneys General or Lord Advocate as appropriate.

10. Discussions between UK and US prosecutors should take place with the aim of developing a case strategy on issues arising from concurrent jurisdiction. The information shared between the UK and US should include the facts of the case, key evidence, representations on jurisdictional issues, and, as appropriate, any other consideration which will enable the prosecutors to develop a case strategy and resolve issues arising from concurrent jurisdiction.

11. The information shared in accordance with this guidance is provided in order that prosecutors in the UK and US may reach decisions on issues arising from concurrent jurisdiction. The information should not be disclosed to other countries without permission of the originating state.

Consultation

12. The procedure set out in this guidance is intended to preserve and strengthen existing channels of communication between prosecutors in the UK and US. This guidance is intended to enable each country's prosecutors to consult closely together on issues arising from concurrent jurisdiction and ensure, where appropriate that each Attorney General and the Lord Advocate are consulted on such issues.

13. This guidance does not create any rights on the part of a third party to object to or otherwise seek review of a decision by UK or US authorities regarding the investigation or prosecution of a case or issues related thereto.

14. The aim of consultation, having shared the information set out at paragraph 10, will be to enable each country's prosecutors to decide on the issues arising from concurrent jurisdiction through bilateral discussion, including, but not limited to:

    a. where and how investigations may be most effectively pursued:

    b. where and how prosecutions should be initiated, continued or discontinued; or

   c. whether and how aspects of the case should be pursued in the different
      jurisdictions

It is of course for the prosecuting authority, having applied the guidance, to
decide that a case should properly be prosecuted in its country, where that
is in accordance with the law and the public interest.

...

16. The offices of the Attorneys General and Lord Advocate should provide
    such additional domestic guidance to their own agencies and prosecutors as
    may be necessary to ensure that their offices are advised at an early stage of
    serious, sensitive, or complex cases involving issues arising from concurrent
    jurisdiction.

17. Early contact with the offices of the Attorneys General or Lord Advocate,
    as appropriate, is intended to ensure that the Attorneys General, or Lord
    Advocate, can be consulted on these cases before final decisions are taken
    by the prosecutors on Issues arising from concurrent jurisdiction. In such
    cases it may be necessary for the offices of the Attorneys General or Lord
    Advocate to make early contact to discuss issues arising from concurrent
    jurisdiction.

Monitoring

18. The offices of the Attorneys General and Lord Advocate intend to review
    the implementation of this guidance on an annual basis.

The Rt Hon Lord Goldsmith QC   Alberto R. Gonzales

Majesty's Attorney General   Attorney General of the United
                                        States of America

(www.attorneygeneral.gov.uk/)

Part Nine: State Territory

Part Nine: I.A.1. *State territory—territory—elements of territory—land,
international waters, rivers, lakes and land-locked seas (see also parts ten
and eleven)*

9/1

On 27 March 2007, the Secretary-General of the United Nations, as
depositary, received a communication from the government of Argentina,
as follows:

The Argentine Republic objects to the extension of the territorial application to
the Kyoto Protocol to the United Nations Framework Convention on Climate
Change of 11 December 1997 with respect to the Malvinas Islands, which was
notified by the United Kingdom of Great Britain and Northern Ireland to the
Depositary of the Convention on 7 March 2007.

The Argentine Republic reaffirms its sovereignty over the Malvinas Islands, the South Georgia and South Sandwich Islands and the surrounding maritime spaces, which are an integral part of its national territory, and recalls that the General Assembly of the United Nations adopted resolutions 2065 (XX), 3160 (XXVIII), 31/49, 37/9, 38/12, 39/6, 40/21, 41/40, 42/19 and 43/25, which recognise the existence of a dispute over sovereignty and request the Governments of the Argentine Republic and the United Kingdom of Great Britain and Northern Ireland to initiate negotiations with a view to finding the means to resolve peacefully and definitively the pending problems between both countries, including all aspects on the future of the Malvinas Islands, in accordance with the Charter of the United Nations.

[A similar communication was made by Argentina on the same day with respect to the extension of the United Nations Framework Convention on Climate Change Rio de Janeiro 04 June, 1992 -14 June, 1992 (028/1995 Cm 2833) to the Falklands etc and with respect to the United Nations Convention against Transnational Organised Crime of 15 November 2000., Ed.]

(Treaty Series No. 29 (2007) Second Supplementary List of Ratifications, Accessions, Withdrawals, etc., for 2007 Cm 7267)

9/2

Argentina made the following statement with its ratification of the Agreement on the Conservation of Albatrosses and Petrels Canberra 19 June, 2001 TS 038/2004 Cm 6333

Statement [Translation Original: Spanish]

NESTOR KIRCHNER, PRESIDENT OF THE ARGENTINE NATION

WHEREAS:

The AGREEMENT ON THE CONSERVATION OF ALBATROSSES AND PETRELS, done at Canberra—AUSTRALIA—on 19 June 2001 has been approved under Law N° 26017.

ACCORDINGLY:

I ratify, in the name and on behalf of the Argentine Government, the aforementioned Agreement, and make the following STATEMENT:

"The ARGENTINE REPUBLIC rejects the extension of the territorial application of the Agreement on the Conservation of Albatrosses and Petrels, done at Canberra on 19 June 2001 and which entered into force on 01 February 2004, to the Malvinas, South Georgia and South Sandwich Islands, notified by the UNITED KINGDOM OF GREAT BRITAIN AND NORTHERN IRELAND to the Secretariat of the Agreement in ratifying the said instrument on 25 March 2004, reiterating the statement to the same effect made on the occasion of the First Meeting of the Parties to the Agreement (Hobart, Australia, 10 to 12 November 2004).

(Treaty Series No. 34 (2006) FOURTH SUPPLEMENTARY LIST OF RATIFICATIONS, ACCESSIONS, WITHDRAWALS, ETC., FOR 2006 Cm 7159)

9/3

The ARGENTINE REPUBLIC reasserts its sovereignty over the Malvinas, South Georgia and South Sandwich Islands and surrounding maritime spaces as an integral part of its territory and notes that the United Nations General Assembly has adopted Resolutions 2065 (XX), 3160 (XXVIII), 31/49, 37/9, 38/12, 39/6, 40/21, 41/40, 42/19 and 43/25 acknowledging the existence of the sovereignty dispute and calling on the Governments of the ARGENTINE REPUBLIC and the UNITED KINGDOM OF GREAT BRITAIN AND NORTHERN IRELAND to establish negotiations with a view to finding the means to settle peacefully and definitively the outstanding differences between the two countries including all matters relating to the future of the Malvinas Islands in accordance with the United Nations Charter.

The ARGENTINE REPUBLIC, without prejudice to the provisions of Article IV of the Antarctic Treaty, likewise rejects the extension of the Agreement to the so-called "British Antarctic Territory", and reasserts its legitimate rights of sovereignty over the Argentine Antarctic Sector, comprised between the meridians of 25 and 74 degrees west longitude and the parallel of 60 degrees south latitude and the South Pole, which is an integral part of the Argentine national territory."

(Treaty Series No. 34 (2006) FOURTH SUPPLEMENTARY LIST OF RATIFICATIONS, ACCESSIONS, WITHDRAWALS, ETC., FOR 2006 Cm 7159)

9/4

Convention on the Prohibition of the Development, Production, Stockpiling and Use of Chemical Weapons and on their Destruction Paris 13 Jan., 1993 -15 Jan., 1993 045/1997 Cm 3727

On 27 April 2006 the Secretary-General of the United Nations, as depositary, received from the government of the United Kingdom of Great Britain and Northern Ireland a communication, as follows

"In accordance with instructions received from my Government, I have the honour to refer to the communication dated 30 November 2005 from the Government of Argentina to the United Nations relating to the extension of the Convention on the Prohibition of the Development,

Production, Stockpiling and use of Chemical Weapons and their Destruction, to the Falkland Islands, South Georgia and the South Sandwich Islands, and the British Antarctic Territory.

The Government of the United Kingdom of Great Britain and Northern Ireland are fully entitled to extend the Convention on the Prohibition of the Development, Production, Stockpiling and use of Chemical Weapons and on their Destruction to the Falkland Islands, South Georgia and the South Sandwich Islands, and the British Antarctic Territory.

The Government of the United Kingdom of Great Britain and Northern Ireland have no doubts about the sovereignty of the United Kingdom over the Falkland Islands, South Georgia and the South Sandwich Islands, and the

British Antarctic Territory, and their surrounding maritime areas, and reject the claim by the Government of Argentina to sovereignty over those islands and areas and that the Falkland Islands and South Georgia and the South Sandwich Islands are under illegal occupation by the United Kingdom."

(UN Doc A/60/830, 28 April 2006)

9/5

The British Government sent the following note to the Government of Norway about Spitzbergen (Svalbard) concerning the exercise of maritime jurisdiction in the area through Norway's title to Spitzbergen (Svalbard).

Her Britannic Majesty's Embassy present their compliments to The Royal Norwegian Ministry of Foreign Affairs and have the honour to refer to the Treaty concerning the Archipelago of Spitzbergen (Svalbard), done at Paris on 9 February 1920.

In the light of recent activity by the Norwegian authorities in the area north of the northern coastline of Norway, the United Kingdom considers that it is timely to restate its position concerning the application of the Treaty of Paris to the maritime zones designated around Svalbard.

The United Kingdom considers that the Svalbard archipelago, including Bear Island, generates its own maritime zones, separate from those generated by other Norwegian territory, in accordance with the United Nations Convention on the Law of the Sea. It follows therefore that there is a continental shelf and an exclusive economic zone which pertain to Svalbard.

Second, the United Kingdom considers that maritime zones generated by Svalbard are subject to the provisions of the Treaty of Paris, in particular Article 7, which requires that Svalbard should be open on a footing of equality to all parties to the Treaty and Article 8, which inter alia specifies the tax regime which applies to the exploitation of minerals in Svalbard.

The United Kingdom expects that the Norwegian authorities will fully comply with the obligations of Norway under the Treaty of Paris, as set out above.

11 March 2006
(Text supplied by FCO)

Part Ten: International Watercourses

Part Ten: I.C. *International Watercourses—Rivers and lakes—Uses for purposes other than navigation*

10/1

A Minister wrote:

The UK has no immediate plans to accede to the 1997 United Nations (UN) Convention on the Law of Non-Navigational Uses of International

Watercourses. Only 16 countries have ratified the Convention, whereas 35 countries are required for the Convention to enter into force. The Department for International Development (DFID) is currently reviewing the international development benefits of accession, and as part of this is seeking views from foreign Governments, NGOs and academics.

DFID is supporting transboundary water processes in the Middle East, and in Africa through the Nile Basin Initiative. These demonstrate the value of practical approaches to transboundary cooperation on water that yield significant benefits. In neither case is accession to the Convention considered necessary for our support of these processes.

(HC Deb 5 December 2007 Vol 469 c1259W)

10/2
An FCO Minister said:

...the Convention [on the Law of Non-navigational Uses of International Watercourses] seemed extremely important at the time. The UK did not accede to it because of difficulties around the waters of Northern Ireland versus the Republic, which have subsequently been well resolved through EU arrangements. That means that we have no direct waterways of our own to be affected. However, that does not prevent us using the principles of the Convention in parts of the world such as the Nile basin, where we are providing assistance to countries that share common water fronts.

(HL Deb 11 December 2007 Vol 697 c112W)

Part Eleven: Seas and Vessels

Part Eleven: II. *Seas and vessels—territorial sea, including overflight*

11/1
The Foreign Secretary said:

I would like to make a statement about the current situation regarding the 15 British service personnel detained by Iranian forces on Friday of last week, and say that the Government are doing all they can to ensure that they are released immediately

I would like to begin by explaining the facts of what happened last Friday and the actions we have taken since, and to share with the House some of the details about the location of the incident on which the Ministry of Defence briefed this morning. At approximately 0630 GMT on 23 March, 15 British naval personnel from HMS Cornwall were engaged in a routine boarding operation of a merchant vessel in Iraqi territorial waters in support of Security Council resolution 1723 and of the Government of Iraq. They were then seized by Iranian naval vessels.

HMS Cornwall was conducting routine maritime security operations as part of a multinational force coalition taskforce operating under a United Nations mandate at the request of the Iraqi Government. The taskforce's mission was to protect Iraqi oil terminals and to prevent smuggling. The boarding party had completed a successful inspection of a merchant ship 1.7 nautical miles inside Iraqi waters when they and their two boats were surrounded by six Iranian vessels and escorted into Iranian territorial waters.

On hearing this news, I immediately consulted the Prime Minister and the Secretary State for Defence, and asked my permanent under-secretary to summon the Iranian ambassador to the Foreign and Commonwealth Office. We set out our three demands to the ambassador: information on the whereabouts of our people; consular access to them; and to be told the arrangements for their immediate release. Cobra met that afternoon, as it has done every day since. On 24 March my colleague the Parliamentary Under-Secretary of State, Lord Triesman, held a further meeting with the ambassador to repeat our demands. He has had several such meetings since that date.

At that first meeting the Iranian ambassador gave us, on behalf of his Government, the co-ordinates of the site where that Government claimed that our personnel had been detained. They were not, of course, where we believed that the incident took place but we took delivery of them as the statement of events of the Government of Iran. On examination, the co-ordinates supplied by Iran are themselves in Iraqi waters.

On Sunday 25 March, I spoke to Minister Mottaki, the Iranian Foreign Minister, as I did again yesterday. In my first conversation, I pointed out that not only did the co-ordinates for the incident as relayed by HMS Cornwall show that the incident took place 1.7 nautical miles inside Iraqi waters, but that the grid co-ordinates for the incidents that the Iranian authorities had provided to our embassy on Friday 23 March and to Lord Triesman on Saturday 24 March also showed that the incident had taken place in Iraqi waters. I suggested to the Iranian Foreign Minister that it appeared that the whole affair might have been a misunderstanding which could be resolved by immediate release.

In Iran, our ambassador, Geoffrey Adams, has met senior Iranian officials on a daily basis to press for immediate answers to our questions. He has left the Iranian authorities in no doubt that there is no justification for the Iranians to have taken the British Navy personnel into custody. He has provided the grid co-ordinates of the incident which clearly showed that our personnel were in Iraqi waters and made it clear that we expect their immediate and safe return. I should tell the House that we have no doubt either about the facts or about the legitimacy of our requirements.

When our ambassador and my colleague Lord Triesman followed up with the Iranian authorities on Monday 26 March, we were provided with new, and—I quote—"corrected" grid co-ordinates by the Iranian side, which now showed the incident as having taken place in Iranian waters. As I made clear to Foreign Minister Mottaki when I spoke to him yesterday, we find it impossible to believe, given the seriousness of the incident, that the Iranians could have made such a mistake with the original co-ordinates, which, after all, they gave us over several days.

There has inevitably been much international interest in the situation, particularly given our personnel's role in a multinational force operating under a UN mandate. I have spoken to a number of international partners, including the American Secretary of State Rice, the Turkish Prime Minister Erdogan and the Saudi Foreign Minister, Prince Saud. We have also been keeping other key international partners informed, and I am pleased to be able to tell the House that many of them have chosen to lobby the Iranians or to make statements of support. I am particularly grateful to my colleague Hoshyar Zebari, the Iraqi Foreign Minister, who has confirmed publicly that the incident took place in Iraqi waters, and called for the personnel, who are acting in Iraq's interests, to be released.

The Iranians have assured us that all our personnel are being treated well. We will hold them to that commitment and continue to press for immediate release. They have also assured us that there is no linkage between this issue and other issues—bilateral, regional or international—which I welcome. However, I regret to say that the Iranian authorities have so far failed to meet any of our demands or to respond to our desire to resolve this issue quickly and quietly through behind-the-scenes diplomacy.

That is why we have today chosen to respond to parliamentary and public demand for more information about the original incident, and to get on the public record both our and the Iranian accounts, to demonstrate the clarity of our position and the force of the Prime Minister's words on Sunday 25 March when he said:

"there is no doubt at all that these people were taken from a boat in Iraqi waters. It is simply not true that they went into Iranian territorial waters, and I hope the Iranian Government understands how fundamental an issue this is for us. We have certainly sent the message back to them very clearly indeed. They should not be under any doubt at all about how seriously we regard this act, which is unjustified and wrong."

The House might also be aware that, even if the Iranian Government mistakenly believed that our vessels had been in Iranian waters, under international law warships have sovereign immunity in the territorial sea of other states. The very most that Iran would have been entitled to do, if it considered that our boats were breaching the rules on innocent passage, would have been to require the ship to leave its territorial waters immediately.

We will continue to pursue vigorously our diplomatic efforts with the Iranians to press for the immediate release of our personnel and equipment. As Members of the House will appreciate, with sensitive issues such as these...getting the balance right between private, but robust, diplomacy and meeting the House's and the public's justified demand for reliable information is a difficult judgment...

As the Prime Minister indicated yesterday, however, we are now in a new phase of diplomatic activity. That is why the Ministry of Defence has today released details of the incident, and why I have concluded that we need to focus all our bilateral efforts during this phase on the resolution of the issue. We will, therefore, be imposing a freeze on all other official bilateral business with Iran until the situation is resolved. We will keep other aspects of our policy towards Iran under close review and continue to proceed carefully. But no one should be in any doubt about the seriousness with which we regard these events.

(HC Deb 28 March 2007 Vol 458 c1499–1501)

11/2
The FCO submitted the following written evidence to the FAC:

Detention of Royal Navy personnel in Iran: Foreign and Commonwealth Office response

STRATEGY AND ACTIONS

2. As the Foreign Secretary said in her statement of 28 March, we initially pursued a policy of quiet but robust diplomacy...,

4. During the initial period we deliberately kept our public statements low key to give the Iranians room for manoeuvre and give force to our argument that the whole incident was a misunderstanding which could be resolved by immediately releasing the personnel, while aiming to build the diplomatic pressure incrementally.

5. When it became apparent that this strategy was not having the necessary effect on the Iranians, we decided to ratchet up the pressure by going public with the facts, and increasing diplomatic activity through third parties and international institutions. This was done through an MOD-led media brief ... on the morning of 28 March on the facts surrounding the incident, highlighting our evidence that the incident took place in Iraqi waters, that the Iranians had initially provided co-ordinates also placing the incident in Iraqi waters, and that once this was pointed out to them they changed their account of where the incident took place. The Foreign Secretary set out the facts surrounding the seizure in her statement to Parliament that afternoon, [see **11/1** above Ed.] during which she announced a "freeze on all other official bilateral business with Iran until this situation is resolved", which focussed minds in Tehran.

8. In the first indication that the Iranian system had agreed a position the Iranians eventually handed over a note verbale on Thursday 29 March setting out their position. It stated that this was not the first incident of its kind, protested against the UK's "illegal action" in violating Iran's territorial waters, and highlighted the British Government's responsibility for the consequences of this "violation" and demanded "that necessary guarantees should be given that such kinds of action will not be repeated." We responded to this note on 30 March: recalling our explanation of events; reiterating that the personnel involved were operating as part of the Mutli-National Force (Iraq) at the request of the Iraqi government under UN mandate and bore no hostile intent; and proposing discussions with the relevant Iranian authorities for a full resolution of this matter, which would include arrangements for the immediate release of the British personnel, and mechanisms to avoid further repetition. Our note did not contain any admission that the personnel had been in Iranian waters, as the Iranian media subsequently claimed, nor did it include any apology. We then took a decision to moderate our public statements to maximise the prospects for an early diplomatic solution.

9. On Tuesday 3 April the Ministry of Foreign Affairs in Tehran informed our Ambassador in Tehran and the Iranian Ambassador informed Lord Triesman

that President Ahmadinejad would be giving a press conference the following day, which had previously been postponed. They told us that we should say nothing before then, not overreact to what he said and that we would subsequently be granted consular access...

10. President Ahmadinejad held a press conference as expected on 4 April. He promised that the personnel would be released without charge after the conference, as "a gift from the Iranian nation to the British people." They were taken to meet Ahmadinejad at the end of the conference. The Ministry of Foreign Affairs at this stage told the Embassy that it would be given consular access later in the day and informed the Embassy that the personnel would be treated as guests of the Ministry and would be put up in a government guest house overnight. The Ambassador was finally granted consular access late that evening.

11. The detainees were released from Iranian custody on the morning of 5 April at Tehran's Mehrabad Airport, from where they took a BA/BMed flight to Heathrow, accompanied by members of the Embassy, who had arranged the flight with BMed well in advance of the release. On arrival they were taken by air to Chivenor to be debriefed and reunited with their families.

12. Bilateral meetings in London and Tehran throughout the crisis were vital to gauge where the Iranians stood, and to pass our key messages directly into the Iranian system. These were reinforced both by our public messages and through lobbying third parties, which we assess had great impact on the Iranians. At each meeting before President Ahmadinejad announced the release of the detainees on 4 April, the UK side demanded: information on where the personnel were being detained; immediate consular access for British Embassy officials; and the immediate release of the personnel and their equipment. At every meeting the Iranians emphasised that they were making no direct linkage to other specific issues, bilateral, regional or international. We took the same position. As the Prime Minister said afterwards, the release was secured through the dual track of bilateral dialogue and international pressure "without any deals, without any negotiation."

(FAC, Foreign Policy Aspects of the Detention of Naval Personnel by the Islamic Republic of Iran. HC880 (2007))

11/3
In his response to the FAC Report, the Foreign Secretary said:

[The FAC] conclude that there is evidence to suggest that the map of the Shatt al-Arab waterway provided by the Government was less clear than it ought to have been. The Government was fortunate that it was not in Iran's interests to contest the accuracy of the map. We recommend that, in its response to this Report, the Government state why it chose to mark the boundary as a purely 'territorial water boundary' rather than including aspects of the 'land boundary' agreed to in 1975. (Paragraph 32)

He responded:

4. The map was a simplification, designed to clarify a complex situation for presentation to the media and public. The Government believes that the graphic

provided a reasonable depiction of the agreed Algiers 1975 "land" boundary that applies within the Shatt al-Arab, and a median line boundary depicted on UK Admiralty Fleet Charts, as issued to the Royal Navy, in a way that could be used for televisual and similar media purposes. The Government acknowledges that there are differences between the status of the "land" boundary and the maritime territorial limits. The general term "territorial water boundary" was used on the graphic to avoid making the situation more complex for the media. It was not intended to undermine the formal status of the land boundary which applies in this part of the Gulf, nor to imply that there is a de jure maritime boundary. It was unfortunate, however, that this annotation was placed against an area of the Gulf where the land boundary applies. The Government's objective has always been to ensure that the merchant vessel was shown in its correct position in Iraqi waters. The Government notes that the views expressed in the Committee's Report do not challenge this.

[The FAC] conclude that Iran deserves strong censure for its illegal and provocative seizure of a group of lightly armed British personnel who posed no threat to its interests or security. We further conclude that it is a matter of urgency that systems are established to ensure that a repeat situation cannot occur. We recommend that, in its response to this Report, the Government set out what steps have been taken in this regard. (Paragraph 65)

15. The then Foreign Secretary made clear to the Iranian Foreign Minister on 3 May our strong concern about the detention of the 15 Royal Navy personnel. We have also discussed with the Iranian authorities steps to ensure that no further incident of this kind takes place. Our Ambassador in Tehran raised this with the Iranian Ministry of Foreign Affairs on 1 and 9 May.

(Foreign Policy Aspects of the Detention of Naval Personnel by the Islamic Republic of Iran: Response of the Secretary of State for Foreign and Commonwealth Affairs, Cm7211 (2007))

11/4
(See also **5/46–47**)
The FCO wrote to the FAC on 7 September 2007:

Thank you for your letter of 20 July, forwarding a request from the Foreign Affairs Committee into the detention of the Ocean Alert in international waters off Gibraltar in July...

As requested, I attach a memorandum on the Ocean Alert incident, including a full explanation of the application of international law to the waters off Gibraltar; responsibility of the British and/or Gibraltar authorities for the activities of Ocean Alert while it was operating from Gibraltar and for the removal of artefacts recovered from the seabed apparently to the United States by air from Gibraltar; and confirmation of whether the Odyssey vessels had the use of a RN berth or other RN facilities in Gibraltar.

MEMORANDUM ON THE OCEAN ALERT INCIDENT

Application of International Law to the Waters off Gibraltar

The Ocean Alert, a Panamanian-registered vessel belonging to the US company Odyssey Marine Exploration, was detained by Spain's Guardia Civil at a point 3.5 miles south of Gibraltar on 12 July, in waters which the United Kingdom considers to be high seas. Accordingly, in our view, the detention should only have taken place with the consent of the flag State. This was the basis for our protest to the Spanish authorities.

Under the terms of the 1982 United Nations Convention on the Law of the Sea (UNCLOS—ratified by the UK in 1997), coastal States are entitled, but not required, to claim territorial sea up to a maximum breadth of twelve nautical miles. Where the coasts of two States are opposite or adjacent—as is the case around Gibraltar—neither is entitled, unless they agree otherwise, to extend its territorial sea beyond the median line. The British Government considers a limit of three nautical miles to be sufficient in the case of Gibraltar. Under UNCLOS, the nine miles beyond that limit are high seas, and cannot be claimed by another State; it was in this area that the Ocean Alert was detained.

Spain maintains that the Treaty of Utrecht of 1713, which granted sovereignty over Gibraltar to Britain, ceded only the town and castle, together with the Rock's fortifications and its port. Spain therefore disputes our claim that, as a result of later developments in international law, including particularly UNCLOS, Gibraltar generates its own territorial waters.

We categorically reject the Spanish view, and we do not allow Spain's assertion that Gibraltar has no territorial waters to go unchallenged.

This was most recently explained to the House of Commons in an answer to a written Parliamentary Question tabled by the Honourable Member for Romford, Andrew Rosindell, on 2 March (Official Record, Column 1625W). **(5/46)**

A map of our interpretation of the status of the waters is attached. [The map is not attached to the published document, Ed.]

Responsibility of the British and/or Gibraltar authorities for the activities of Ocean Alert while it was operating from Gibraltar and for the removal of artefacts recovered from the seabed apparently to the United States by air from Gibraltar

Odyssey Marine Exploration is a private US company specialising in deep-ocean shipwreck exploration.

Since 2004, they have had a contract with the Disposal Services Agency of the MOD to identify and excavate the possible wreck of The Sussex, a British military ship which sank in a storm off Gibraltar in 1691 with the loss of her crew and valuable cargo. Work on this project has been delayed due to Spanish objections. After nine years of intervention and delay, Spain finally agreed in March this year to allow the project to proceed as long as two Spanish experts were on board Odyssey's vessels. However, there were further delays as the Andalucian Government failed to nominate its two experts.

While waiting in Gibraltar for work on The Sussex to proceed, Odyssey worked on other projects in the Mediterranean and Atlantic. On 10 April and 16 May they sent consignments from a wreck they named Black Swan to the USA via chartered flights from Gibraltar. Odyssey told us that this wreck lay about 180 miles off the coast of Portugal, in the high seas outside Spanish or Gibraltar waters. Both consignments were given export licenses by the Government of Gibraltar, in accordance with Gibraltar law. These consignments, containing gold and silver coins, are now the subject of a court case in Florida between Odyssey and the Spanish Government.

The Spanish Ministry of Foreign Affairs has been particularly critical of the MOD's role. The MOD has no authority regarding Gibraltar Customs procedures, as the Government of Gibraltar is responsible for its own Customs controls. The MOD is obliged to honour its contract with Odyssey unless a legal or operational security issue exists to prevent it from doing so.

Neither the British or Gibraltar authorities were responsible for the activities of Odyssey in relation to the Black Swan.

Confirmation of whether the Odyssey vessels had the use of a RN berth or other RN facilities in Gibraltar.

Odyssey have had a commercial contract with the MOD (Defence Estates, Gibraltar) since December 2005 to use the MOD berths and facilities within the military part of Gibraltar harbour. Such an agreement is not unique.

Two of the company's vessels, the Ocean Alert and the Odyssey Explorer, have operated out of Gibraltar throughout this period.

(FAC, Overseas Territories, HC147 (2007))

11/5
A Defence Minister wrote:

The UN Convention of the Law of the Sea (1982) allows right of innocent passage to all warships through territorial waters provided it is not prejudicial to peace, good order or security of the coastal state. Submarines and other underwater vehicles are required to navigate on the surface and to show their flag. It is normal international practice to seek diplomatic clearance before warships enter or transit territorial waters.

In September the Russian destroyer Severomorsk was invited to enter UK waters to participate in a memorial ceremony. HMS Lancaster hosted Severomorsk while in UK territorial waters.

(HL Deb 15 October 2007 Vol 695 cWA33)

11/6
The Foreign Secretary was asked if he would take steps to ensure that the gold onboard the sunken warship, the *Sussex*, was not claimed by the Spanish government. An FCO Minister wrote:

The wreck in question [found off the coast of Gibraltar] has not yet been confirmed to be that of the Sussex and its cargo has also still to be identified. If the sunken vessel is identified as the Sussex, the Government of Spain has informed us that it will respect international laws of sovereign immunity and lay no claim to the wreck. We also understand that Spain has no intention of investigating the wreck site.

(HC Deb 25 October 2007 Vol 465 c592W)

Part Eleven: VII. *Seas and vessels—continental shelf*

11/8
The Foreign Secretary was asked what recent discussions he had had with countries with a territorial interest in the Arctic on potential claims. An FCO Minister wrote:

[We have] not had any discussions with countries with a territorial interest in the Arctic on the subject of potential claims which they may make in the region. States parties to the UN Convention on the Law of the Sea may be entitled to claim an extended continental shelf beyond their territorial waters, subject to certain geological conditions, as defined in the Convention.

(HC Deb 25 October 2007 Vol 465 c587W)

11/9
The Foreign Secretary was asked to list the maritime areas where the UK has plans to stake territorial claims. An FCO Minister wrote:

The UK has so far made one claim to the UN Commission on the Limits of the Continental Shelf (CLCS) for the extension of the continental shelf under Article 76 of the UN Convention of the Law of the Sea. We are also considering lodging up to four more claims before the right to do so expires in May 2009.

The UK has submitted a claim, jointly with France, Ireland and Spain, for an area of the Bay of Biscay, and this is currently under consideration by the CLCS. The UK is also considering the potential submission of claims for the areas around the Ascension Islands, off the British Antarctic Territory, around the Falkland Islands and South Georgia, and in the Hatton/Rockall area.

(HC Deb 25 October 2007 Vol 465 c587W)

Part Eleven: VIII.D. *Seas and vessels—high seas—piracy*

11/10

The Minister of Defence was asked what assistance the UK was (a) sending and (b) planning to send to aid the United States' efforts to end piracy off the coast of Somalia in the Gulf of Aden and the Indian Ocean. A Defence Minister wrote:

The UK currently has forces deployed as part of the Coalition Naval Task Force which operates in the Arabian sea and Indian ocean, including off the coast of

Somalia. These assets are deployed on a range of maritime security tasks, and could respond to incidents of piracy should they arise.

(HC Deb 20 June 2007 Vol 461 c1808W)

Part Eleven: VIII.E. *Seas and vessels—high seas—conservation of living resources*

(See also 11/17–20)

11/11

The Secretary for the Environment was asked what action his Department was taking with the International Whaling Commission to stop the commercial farming of threatened fin whales in Icelandic waters. A Minister wrote:

In the immediate wake of Iceland's announcement to target fin whales, DEFRA issued a press statement condemning the action and summoned the Icelandic ambassador in London to explain the decision. On 1 November 2006, the UK ambassador to Reykjavik led a diplomatic démarche of 25 countries (including Australia, Germany and the US) together with the European Commission, which called upon the Government of Iceland to reconsider its decision to resume commercial whaling, arguing that the action was unjustified and unnecessary.

It is clear that the strength of opposition to Iceland's actions has surprised the Icelandic Government, and there is a healthy debate in the Icelandic press about the wisdom of the Government's decision. Icelandic companies engaged in significant trade with the UK and other EU countries have suggested that the potential gains from commercial whaling are minimal, compared to the damage that might be done to Icelandic trade in other goods and services.

(HC Deb 27 February 2007 Vol 457 c1176W)

11/12

The Foreign Secretary wrote:

Since the last meeting of the International Whaling Commission (IWC) in June 2006, Foreign and Commonwealth Office (FCO) posts in Bulgaria, Croatia, Cyprus, Estonia, Greece, Latvia, Lithuania, Macedonia, Montenegro and Serbia have made representations to host Governments, encouraging them to join the IWC and vote in favour of maintaining the world-wide moratorium on commercial whaling.

...the Minister for Europe raised the matter with the Foreign Minister of Andorra in October 2006.

The FCO has distributed copies of the Department for Environment, Food and Rural Affairs publication 'Protecting Whales—A Global Responsibility' to 57 countries, including all potential EU candidates.

Croatia and Cyprus have now joined the IWC. Estonia, Greece, Latvia and Romania have committed themselves to joining as soon as domestic legislative procedures allow.

(HC Deb 12 March 2007 Vol 458 c83W)

11/13

The Secretary of State for Environment was asked what the Government's policy was on fish imports from (a) Norway and (b) Iceland; and what account was taken of those countries' policies on whaling in formulating this policy. An Environment Minister wrote:

Fisheries agreements with third countries, including those on imports, are negotiated by the European Commission on behalf of all member sates. Neither the Council of Ministers nor the Commission exercises Community competence over whaling issues and there is no common EU line on whaling matters. Not all EU member states are even members of the International Whaling Commission. As such, negotiations with third countries on fisheries and trade matters are unaffected by those countries' stance on whaling. While the European Commission joined the recent demarche against Iceland over its resumption of commercial whaling, it did so on its own behalf, rather than on behalf of member states.

The Minister went on:

The Foreign Secretary has recently jointly written to a dozen EU and Accession States encouraging them to join the International Whaling Commission. A new publication, 'Protecting Whales —A Global Responsibility' [www.defra.gov.uk/marine/pdf/whales.protecting-whales.pdf, Ed.] endorsed by the Prime Minister and Sir David Attenborough has also been sent to these countries encouraging them to join the effort to protect all cetacean species. UK embassies and Ministers across Government will continue to lobby on this issue in the run-up to the next annual meeting of the IWC in Alaska in May. However, not all of those who are willing to join the IWC will be able to complete the necessary parliamentary processes in time to secure voting rights at the 2007 meeting.

(HC Deb 19 March 2007 Vol 458 c595W)

11/14

An FCO Minister wrote:

The UK plays a prominent role in building and maintaining the coalition of anti-whaling countries within the International Whaling Commission (IWC).

In advance of the 2007 Annual Meeting in Anchorage, the UK and its like-minded allies recruited a further six countries into the IWC with the result that the pro-whaling majority in that organisation was overturned.

In a further response to UK lobbying efforts, several other countries have indicated willingness to support our opposition to Japanese whaling and to join the IWC in time for next year's annual meeting. British embassies and missions will shortly deliver to certain governments an updated version of the Department for Environment, Food and Rural Affairs publication "Protecting Whales—A Global Responsibility" [www.defra.gov.uk/marine/pdf/whales/protecting-whales. pdf, Ed.] as part of a lobbying campaign to encourage more countries to join the IWC, to strengthen further the global opposition to commercial whaling.

(HC Deb 20 November 2007 Vol 467 c740W)

11/15
In answer to a question about "carbon capture", a Minister said:

The United Kingdom has already taken the lead in proposing amendments to the London Convention on the Prevention of Marine Pollution by the Dumping of Waste and other matters. As a result, the London Convention has been amended to allow carbon dioxide to be stored in the sub sea bed, including in the North Sea. The Government have also taken action by setting up a joint taskforce with Norway to establish the underlying principles on which such carbon capture and storage can take place. As I said, we have already instructed engineers to advise us and they are due to report to the Government next month so that we can take forward detailed work in relation to the suggestions about funding...

(HC Deb 27 February 2007 Vol 457 c748)

11/16 (See also 11/23)
In a debate on the MSC Napoli, a Transport Minister said:

[I was] asked about arrangements for compensation...Claims for property and environmental damage caused by the Napoli are governed by the liability provisions set out in the 1995 Act in respect of damage, and the international convention on limitation of liability for maritime claims 1996—commonly known as LLMC—in respect of cost recovery. Section 154 of the 1995 Act provides strict liability on the shipowner for oil pollution damage caused outside the ship by the contamination, for the cost of preventing or minimising the damage, and for any damage caused by the preventive measures taken—for example, the removal of heavy fuel oil from the bunker tanks and preventive measures taken to minimise the threat of pollution. The proper mechanism to recover costs associated with a liability, where one is established, is the LLMC, which entered into force in May 2004. It established a framework of rules and duties on shipowners, including the right of shipowners to limit their liability according to the tonnage of the ship. In the case of the MSC Napoli, the limitation amount will be approximately £14.5 million.

There is no right of direct action against the insurer in the case of the Napoli, so claimants must submit their claims in court. I am led to believe that the owner of the Napoli has agreed to establish a limitation fund in the UK. Claims for damages must be submitted through the courts. Claimants who believe that they have eligible claims may submit such claims for the judgment of the court, but such claims may include those for property damage, as well as for clean-up and cargo. It is for all claimants to determine, after taking appropriate legal advice, whether they have a legitimate claim to pursue, and for the courts to decide whether to accept those claims.

The allocation of money from the limitation fund among the various claimants is a complex legal matter that has occupied the Admiralty court on numerous occasions. As a general rule, claims subject to limitation under article 2 of the International Convention on Limitation of Liability for Maritime Claims do not preclude claims presented by the property owners. However, all claimants will be treated in proportion to their established claims. If the amount of money claimed from the limitation fund were to exceed the amount in the fund, all claims would be paid on a pro rata basis. Ultimately, that is a matter for the administrator of the limitation fund and the courts to determine.

The House might also be interested to know that the UK has ratified the International Convention on Civil Liability for Bunker Oil Pollution Damage 2001. It is expected that the Convention will enter into force some time during 2008. It provides a strict liability and compulsory insurance requirement, including the right of direct action against the insurer. That means that claimants need not prove fault and that eligible claims need not go before the courts before settlement. Another developing International Maritime Organisation instrument pertinent to the Napoli case is the wreck removal convention. The Department is actively engaged in the negotiations on that, which will come to fruition at a diplomatic conference in May this year. The instrument will provide similar compulsory insurance and direct action provisions to those contained in the bunkers convention...

In the wake of such an incident, it is understandable that questions will be asked about the cause from an early stage. There has been much speculation whether the Napoli was seaworthy following her earlier beaching in 2001. Ships are required to undergo periodic surveys of their condition in much the same way as motor cars. Ships are also subject to inspection when calling at UK and other ports. Ships that are found to have major defects can be detained in port until the defects have been rectified. However, it would not be appropriate to speculate on the causes of the Napoli's structural failure at this time. A full investigation will be carried out by the marine accident investigation branch. That investigation will not take the form of a public inquiry. Lengthy and costly formal public hearings are considered an inappropriate way of conducting modern accident investigation.

(HC Deb 28 February 2007 Vol 457 c286–287WH)

Part Eleven: XIV. *Seas and vessels—marine scientific research*

11/17
(See also **11/11**)
The Government was asked what steps it planned to take (a) to reduce and (b) to bring to an end (i) commercial and (ii) scientific whaling. An Environment Minister wrote:

The UK will continue to protest at the highest diplomatic level against Norway and Iceland's commercial whaling activities which, though legal, are not in keeping with the spirit of the International Whaling Commission (IWC). We will continue our efforts, along with other countries, to urge these countries to reconsider their position and end this unjustified and unnecessary practice. Indeed, in November 2006, the UK led a diplomatic demarche of 25 countries together with the European Commission in condemning the Icelandic Government's decision to resume commercial whaling.

The UK Government have regularly criticised Japanese and Icelandic scientific whaling programmes as being of little scientific value and urged both countries to terminate them forthwith. In December last year, the British ambassador to Japan took part in a 27-country demarche to both the Japanese Ministry of Foreign Affairs and the Japanese Fisheries Agency to protest against Japan's programme of lethal special permit ("scientific") whaling in the Southern Ocean.

In order to help recruit more conservation-minded countries to the IWC, we have produced a new publication, "Protecting Whales—A Global Responsibility", endorsed by the Prime Minister and by Sir David Attenborough, which has been sent to 57 countries, both anti and pro-whaling, encouraging them to join the effort to protect all cetacean species.

DEFRA officials ensure that Foreign and Commonwealth Office posts in the relevant capitals are briefed, and engage in discussion with their counterparts on whaling at every appropriate opportunity. This ensures that countries are in no doubt of the importance that the UK attaches to whale conservation. This is particularly important as we approach the next IWC meeting to be held in Anchorage, Alaska in May.

(HC Deb 27 February 2007 Vol 457 c1176W)

11/18
An Environment Minister wrote:

The UK, together with a majority of members of the International Whaling Commission (IWC), has consistently criticised Japan for its lethal whaling operations, authorised under special permits (so called 'scientific' whaling) and urged Japan to desist from these operations forthwith.

Like most IWC members, we do not believe that lethal scientific research can be justified: there are perfectly adequate non-lethal alternatives which could secure the information required by the IWC for stock assessment and management purposes. The whale meat and other products from this so-called 'scientific' whaling are sold domestically in Japanese markets and restaurants. These whaling operations severely hamper international efforts to conserve and protect whales, and clearly demonstrate that these programmes are driven by commercial, rather than scientific considerations.

Japan's proposal to kill 50 humpback whales, a species that remains on the World Conservation Union's (IUCN) List of Threatened Species, is nothing less than outrageous. We will continue to make our opposition to whaling known to Japan at every appropriate opportunity, and argue that Japanese action undermines the credibility of the IWC as an effective organisation for the conservation of whale stocks worldwide.

Whaling is not an issue on which the European Union (EU) exercises competence. As such, it is not generally a subject for discussion at meetings of EU Ministers.

At official level, we do have regular contact with other like-minded countries, including those EU countries who are, like the UK, parties to the International Convention on the Regulation of Whaling and thus members of the IWC.

(HC Deb 22 November 2007 Vol 467 c1060W–1061W)

11/19
An FCO Minister wrote:

The UK believes that any scientific whaling should be confined to non-lethal research, and should be undertaken only if relevant proposals have been approved by the Scientific Committee of the International Whaling Commission (IWC).

The right of member states to issue permits for the killing of whales for scientific purposes is enshrined in article VIII of the 1946 International Convention for the Regulation of Whaling, the IWC's parent treaty. However, 'Scientific purposes' are not defined by the Convention. Furthermore, we doubt that the authors of the Convention anticipated that parties would undertake research on the scale now practised by Japan.

Contrary to Japan's claims, its research programmes have not met with universal support or acclaim from the IWC Scientific Committee. That committee has not endorsed this research and has expressed many reservations.

Japan says its scientific whaling programmes are essential to understand better whale populations and the ecosystems in which they reside. They state that a range of information is needed for the management and conservation of whales, such as population, age structure, growth rates, reproductive rates, feeding—and that this can only be obtained through lethal research.

The UK has consistently voiced its opposition to Japanese scientific whaling. Like most IWC members, the UK does not believe that scientific research can justify the large-scale killing of whales. In our view, Japan's research programmes are deeply flawed.

(HC Deb 3 December 2007 Vol 468 c1066W)

11/20
An FCO Minister wrote:

The UK takes every appropriate opportunity to condemn all lethal whaling operations carried out under the guise of 'scientific' research. Japan carries out this research legally under the International Convention on the Regulation of Whaling (ICRW), the parent treaty of the International Whaling Commission (IWC).

The UK believes the IWC is the internationally recognised body for the management and conservation of whale stocks and any amendment to the ICRW would need to be ratified by all parties. The UK sees no advantage in pressing for the termination or renegotiation of the 1948 International Whaling Convention, as this is the legal instrument by which a general moratorium on commercial whaling has been upheld since 1986. In addition, Japan is unlikely to sign up to a new convention that restricts her current 'scientific' whaling.

(HC Deb 10 December 2007 Vol 469 c165W)

Part Eleven: XVIII.A.1(b) *Seas and vessels—vessels—legal regimes— public vessels other than warships*

11/21

The Minister of Transport was asked a number of questions about the shipping of radioactive material. A Transport Minister replied.

1. What the required response time was in the event of an (a) incident and (b) terrorist attack involving a transport ship carrying plutonium-based MOX fuel in European Union waters.

Reply: Ships carrying MOX fuel are required to have a shipboard emergency plan which would be activated immediately in the event that an incident occurred. Emergency support is available 24 hours a day, 365 days a year.

An immediate response to a terrorist attack would be provided by the onboard escort team, comprising authorised firearms officers of the Civil Nuclear Constabulary.

2. What account was taken of whether a ship in the Nuclear Decommissioning Authority nuclear transport fleet possesses the best available technology when decisions are being taken on which ship will undertake shipments of MOX plutonium-based nuclear fuel in European Union waters.

Reply: Ships used to transport MOX fuel are classified as INF class 2 or 3. These ships are designed and built to the highest standards and are certified according to national and international agreements.

The choice of particular ship is a matter for the operator.

3. What assessment he had made of the merits of requiring an escort for transport ships used to transport plutonium-based MOX fuel in European Union waters.

Reply: All shipments of MOX fuel in UK flagged vessels are escorted by members of the Civil Nuclear Constabulary's (CNC) Marine Escort Group, comprising authorised firearms officers who have been trained to a high standard by the Royal Navy.

Ships flagged to other nations may also transport MOX fuel. Approval of arrangements for such movements are the responsibility of that State's competent authorities.

(HC Deb 17 May 2007 Vol 460 c841W-842W)

Part Eleven: XVIII.A.1(c) *Seas and vessels—vessels—legal regimes—*
warships

11/22
The FCO Legal Advisers provided the following opinion for a case in
Canada about the wrecks of HMS *Fantome* and HMS *Tilbury* which
lie off the coast of Nova Scotia. [*Le Chameau Exploration Ltd v. Nova*
Scotia (Attorney General), 2007 NSSC 386, Ed.]

SOVEREIGN IMMUNITY IN RESPECT OF WARSHIPS

Warships have sovereign immunity whether in the coastal waters of another
State or on the high seas. This is a long established principle of the international
law of the sea.

That this is the case on the high seas and in the exclusive economic zone is evident from Article 96 of the UN Convention on the Law of the Sea.

Warships on the high seas have complete immunity from the jurisdiction of any
other State than the flag State.[1]

That this is the case within territorial waters is evident from Article 32
UNCLOS:

With such exceptions as are contained in subsection A and in articles 30 and 31,
nothing in this Convention affects the immunities of warships and other government ships operated for non-commercial purposes.

Within the territorial sea, therefore, the exceptions to the rule of otherwise complete immunity from the jurisdiction of any other State than the flag State are
as follows[2]:

non-compliance by warships with the laws and regulations of the coastal State
(subsection A and Article 30): the sole remedy for the coastal State is to require a
non-compliant warship to leave its territorial waters immediately responsibility
of the flag State for damage caused by a warship (Article 31)

The practical consequences of sovereign immunity in the domestic sphere have
clearly been set out in the leading textbook on international law.

A warship with all persons and goods on board, remains under the jurisdiction
of her flag-state even during her stay in foreign waters. No legal proceedings can
be taken against her either for recovery of possession, or for damages for collision, or for a salvage reward, or for any other cause [footnotes omitted].[3]

---

[1] By virtue of Article 58(2) UNCLOS, this provision also applies to the exclusive economic zone.
[2] The legal context and applicable regime might be different if a situation of armed conflict
arose.
[3] *Oppenheim's International Law* (9th ed., 1992), Jennings and Watts (eds.), p.1168, §563.

A convenient and authoritative modern definition of "warship" is stated in Article 29 of the UN Convention on the Law of the Sea (UNCLOS):

For the purposes of this Convention, "warship" means a ship belonging to the armed forces of a State bearing the external marks distinguishing such ships of its nationality, under the command of an officer duly commissioned by the government of the State and whose name appears in the appropriate service list or its equivalent, and manned by a crew which is under regular armed forces discipline.

There is no question that active warships enjoy these immunities. But wrecked warships also have the benefit of sovereign immunity unless expressly abandoned.

While there is a multilateral convention which purports to deal with wrecks, the UNESCO Convention on Underwater Cultural Heritage signed at Paris on 2 November 2001, it has not yet entered into force and neither the United Kingdom nor Canada are parties. In any event, nor does that Convention affect the pre-existing customary international law position on sovereign immunity, as made explicit by Article 2(8):

Consistent with state practice and international law, including the United Nations Convention on the Law of the Sea, nothing in this convention shall be interpreted as modifying the rules of international law and state practice pertaining to sovereign immunities, nor any state's rights with respect to its state vessels and aircraft.

The position therefore is governed by customary international law which, as is well known, is made up of State practice (evidence of what States do) and *opinio juris* (evidence of what States think).

In the view of the HM Government, customary international law indicates that sovereign immunity in warships is lost only by:

belligerent conquest (by capture or surrender before sinking during an armed conflict);

international agreement; or

express act of abandonment

In the case of HMS Fantome and HMS Tilbury, there is no question of sovereign immunity lapsing due to belligerent conquest. Neither vessel was lost during hostilities and so no issue of capture or surrender arises.

Obviously, no international agreement has been concluded between the United Kingdom and Canada in respect of either vessel.

There has also been no express act of abandonment by the United Kingdom. It is the position of the United Kingdom that an express act of abandonment is necessary in order for a State to be unable to claim sovereign immunity in respect of a vessel that once enjoyed its benefits. This approach is clearly backed by the United States of America who have made a public explanation of their position.[4] Other States also have indicated their support for this approach and a number of major maritime powers voted against the UNESCO Convention for this reason.[5]

Since the position of the wrecks became known, the United Kingdom has consistently stated that it considers the wreck sites to be subject to sovereign immunity. The Canadian Department of Foreign Affairs and International Trade have kindly transmitted some of these statements to the relevant authorities, in Nova Scotia and elsewhere. In stating this position, the United Kingdom has also indicated that its ultimate purposes in doing so are, firstly, to try to ensure the site is dealt with in accordance with the highest international archaeological and cultural standards, and also to attempt the protection and respect of what, in the case of the HMS Tilbury is a war grave where over one hundred sailors perished at sea.

Further and in the alternative, there has been no tacit or implied act of abandonment by the United Kingdom. As soon as the wreck sites became known, the United Kingdom registered its concerns. Tacit or implied abandonment has to be read as referring to actions in respect of a particular wreck or wrecks. If lapse of time or failure to conduct a search for the wreck is taken as tacit or implied abandonment, then for sovereign immunity to have any meaning the United Kingdom—and other historical maritime powers including Canada—will need to engage in long and expensive searches throughout the globe for their lost warships. No other States does this, and no State thinks it is necessary. So there is no support in State practice or *opinio juris* for such a broad interpretation of tacit abandonment (although the United Kingdom continues to believe that express abandonment is necessary for sovereign immunity to be properly waived). Tacit or implied abandonment can only mean inaction, apathy or demonstrated indifference to a particular wreck or wrecks once the site or sites have been located.

Sovereign immunity applies to the site of a wreck. Although this could be spread over a wide area, unless and until other wrecks in the vicinity are identified and located in the same site, it is reasonable to maintain a presumption that debris found on that site belongs an identified wreck subject to sovereign immunity. Of course, this presumption is rebuttable by evidence, but the United Kingdom holds the view that to permit the gathering of evidence without ensuring the maintenance of the highest archaeological and cultural standards would defeat the purpose of its claim to sovereign immunity in these cases. In other words, there is little point in digging up the wrecks to prove they are subject to sovereign immunity when the goal in such a claim was to protect them in situ—which is what most maritime nations believe to be the appropriate action in this case. The days of asset-strippers and treasure hunters belong to a different era.

Notwithstanding the United Kingdom's maintenance of its legal position in accordance with international law and international rules of comity, the United Kingdom has repeatedly offered to negotiate with both the Nova Scotian authorities (with whom fruitful contact has been established) and also the potential salvors. This would not amount to a waiver of sovereign immunity, but could

---

[4] "Sunken warships and military aircraft", Marine Policy, Vol. 20, No. pp.351–354, 1996, a Note stating official policy of the US Government by Captain J. Ashley Roach.

[5] Among those voting against were Chile, France, Germany, Greece, Hungary, The Netherlands, Sweden and the United Kingdom.

form the basis for discussions based on a common approach to protect the wreck sites in accordance with the highest archaeological and cultural standards so that the historical and cultural significance of these wrecks can be appreciated by all the people of Canada and the United Kingdom. There are too many examples of bilateral agreements concerning the protection of wrecks to helpfully list, but working towards the conclusion of such agreements is the common international practice in this field and the ultimate goal of the United Kingdom.

(Text supplied by FCO)

11/23
The Minister of Defence was asked (1) what the Government's policy is on the wreckage of the *Sussex* lying off the coast of Gibraltar since 1694; (2) what progress has been made in salvaging the wreck of the *Sussex* which sank in 1694 off the coast of Gibraltar. A Defence Minister wrote:

Given that the excavation involves what is believed to be a Royal Navy shipwreck, the Ministry of Defence has retained ownership of the project and is closely monitoring its progress. Some preliminary work has been conducted at the site including a survey of the area. Operations are currently suspended pending the resolution of certain outstanding heritage issues between Odyssey Marine Exploration and the Spanish authorities.

(HC Deb 7 March 2007 Vol 457 c1985W)

Part Eleven: XVIII.A.3 *Seas and vessels vessels—legal regimes—merchant ships*

11/24 (See also **11/6**)
A Transport Minister said about the stranding of the MSC Napoli:

During severe weather conditions on the morning of 18 January, the MSC Napoli, a UK-registered vessel, suffered flooding in her engine room on the French side of the English Channel. The MSC Napoli's master took the decision that the danger to the vessel was sufficient to order the crew to abandon the ship. All the crew were successfully rescued by UK helicopter from royal naval air station Culdrose. The marine accident investigation branch is carrying out a full investigation into the causes of the structural damage.

The English Channel is a zone of joint responsibility between France and the UK as regards maritime pollution incidents. There is an Anglo-French joint maritime contingency plan, which is usually referred to as the Mancheplan. The French and English authorities were faced with a large container ship known to be carrying a cargo that included potentially hazardous materials and to have more than 3,500 tonnes of fuel oil on board. Particular account had to be taken of the strong advice from environmental experts that the ship's cargo and oil would need to be recovered and should not be left to sink in deep water. The effects of sinking in deep water would have been serious long-term environmental damage. In the first instance, there would be the strong possibility of a large release of oil and spreading of the cargo caused by the trauma of the vessel striking the seabed. In any case, the oil would have escaped and found its way on to many beaches on both sides of the English Channel for many years, whereas in shallow waters the hydrocarbons and other pollutants could be recovered as soon as possible.

In line with the Mancheplan, French authorities led the initial response to the incident, liaising closely throughout with the UK Secretary of State's representative for maritime salvage and intervention—commonly known as SOSREP. French tugs arrived on the scene promptly. A French Government intervention team went on board the vessel. Having made an on-scene assessment of its condition, experts concluded that its state was such that it was unlikely to survive prolonged exposure to severe weather conditions. To prevent a serious marine pollution incident, the French and UK authorities decided that the vessel should be towed to a place of refuge where she could be dealt with in a controlled manner. The need for a place of refuge and its location are always driven by the circumstances of an incident, including the weather, the size and condition of the vessel and the potential threat posed by the vessel and its cargo. Taking all those factors into account, the French authorities were unable to identify a suitable place of refuge on the French coast within about 200 miles.

All other options were on the UK south coast from Falmouth to Portland...There was no safe option to enter any south coast port.

An anchorage with good shelter from south-west winds was needed. The most suitable option was Portland because it affords shelter combined with good access to port facilities and, later, the potential for moving the ship into the inner harbour. It also meant that the vessel could be towed in a direction that minimised the stress on its hull. A tow was attached on the evening of 18 January. However, in the early hours of 20 January, the cracks on both sides of the ship worsened and the stern of the ship started settling lower in the water. It became clear that the MSC Napoli would not reach Portland. The priority was to keep the vessel intact, as there was real concern that it might start to break up.

That concern was urgent and a decision had to be taken without delay. In accordance with the UK's national contingency plan, environmental groups and local authorities were consulted. Moreover, through forward planning, which is an integral part of the UK system, SOSREP had the necessary knowledge about the suitability of locations as a place of refuge for this vessel. SOSREP decided that the only viable option was to beach the ship in shallow water, where there was a greater chance of successful salvage, and decided to turn the vessel towards an identified beaching site in the shelter of Lyme bay. SOSREP regularly updated me throughout the incident...

The MSC Napoli was carrying approximately 2,300 containers, of which 157 contained potentially hazardous materials, including perfume, pesticides and batteries. The contents of all containers have now been identified. Altogether, 103 containers were lost overboard, 57 of which were washed ashore, and we are searching for the other 46. Sampling of sediments and marine wildlife in the area began on Tuesday. As of Tuesday, 900 live oiled birds had been handed to the RSPCA, while 700 had been found dead.

Salvors were engaged at a very early stage in the incident. It was necessary for some work vessels and equipment to be brought from Rotterdam and these were despatched at the earliest possible opportunity. Work on removing the Napoli's bunker oil is continuing apace. About 2,600 tonnes of bunker fuel have been removed. The salvors are averaging 20 tonnes per hour and we expect to have removed most of the remaining fuel by the end of Sunday.

The process of removing containers from the MSC Napoli is also underway. As more containers are removed, the stress on the ship's hull decreases, as does the risk of break-up. A crane barge is removing containers and passing them to a container barge that can take them ashore. Every precaution is being taken to ensure safety. It is expected that the removal of all the cargo will take between five to eight months to complete...

SOSREP is continuing to lead the response to the incident. Our thanks are due to that representative and all those working with him to bring the incident to the safest and swiftest conclusion practicable with the minimum possible impact on the environment. SOSREP's decision in respect of a place of refuge and the salvage operation was entirely transparent and thoroughly professional.

It is worth recording that the European Commision's senior maritime official, Fotis Karamitsos, last week endorsed our SOSREP system, which he regards as a model for other EU states. He supported SOSREP's decision to beach the MSC Napoli rather than tow it to port as originally planned, because it

"diminished the risk of catastrophe".

I receive daily reports on the situation from SOSREP. I am reassured that the national contingency plan has enabled us to take prompt and appropriate action. I am pleased to see the co-operation between SOSREP and all the parties concerned, including the French authorities. This incident has once again demonstrated why the UK's SOSREP arrangement is so much admired by our international colleagues.

[The oil and cargo were successfully removed from the Napoli. The damage which it had suffered was such that it was necessary to break it into large parts which were taken to Belfast for disposal in July and August 2007, Ed.]

(HC Deb 1 February 2007 Vol 456 c376–378)

11/25
A Transport Minister wrote:

In accordance with the Anglo-French Joint Maritime Contingency Plan (Mancheplan), HM Coastguard had been monitoring the situation involving the MSC Napoli together with the French search and rescue (SAR) authorities from the outset of the incident. Co-ordination of the incident was passed to the Maritime Rescue Co-ordination Centre at Falmouth from the French co-ordination at CROSS Corsen at approximately 16:10 on 19 January 2007 when the MSC Napoli passed over the UK/French median line. At this point the ship was approximately 60 nautical miles from Portland and Cherbourg. Taking all the environmental and safety factors into account, the French authorities were unable to identify a suitable place of refuge on the French coast within about 200 nautical miles.

A salvage contract was agreed at 14:45 on 19 January 2007, when the ship was still in French waters and approximately 110 nautical miles from Portland and Cherbourg.

(HC Deb 5 February 2007 Vol 456 c 682W)

11/26

The Secretary of State for Transport was asked what assessment she had made of the implications for a ship calling at a port which does not meet the 2004 International Ships and Ports Facility Security Code. A Minister wrote:

The Code requires that a ship's own Security Plan sets out the procedures to be followed when it is calling at a port facility that does not meet the Code. A ship may make provision for its own security or where appropriate a master of a ship may request a "Declaration of Security". This is a standard form that addresses the security requirements that are to be shared between a port facility and a ship and states the responsibility for each. The Code also requires ships to keep records of their last 10 ports of call prior to arrival in a destination, including details of how security was maintained at ports not meeting the Code. If the ship has at all times met the provisions of the Code there should be no significant implications for the ship.

(HC Deb 19 November 2007 Vol 467 c462W)

Part Twelve: Airspace, Outer Space and Antarctica

12/1

Part Twelve: I.A. *Airspace, Outer Space and Antarctica—Airspace— Status*

The Minister of Defence was asked what assessment he had made of the likely impact on military aviation operations by British and US forces of the EU proposal to treat all airspace above 25,000 feet as European airspace. A Defence Minister wrote:

The EC initiative to establish a European upper flight information region encompassing all airspace above 28,500 feet is not expected have any impact on military aviation operations by British and US forces based in the UK.

(HC Deb 18 January 2007 Vol 455 c1260W)

Part Twelve: I.B. *Airspace, Outer Space and Antarctica—Airspace— Uses*

12/2 (See also **5/47**)

The Government were asked what steps they were taking to increase safety at Gibraltar airport, given the increased traffic being created by more airlines flying there. An FCO Minister wrote:

Aviation safety and security relating to civil operations at Gibraltar Airport are governed by the pertinent rules and regulations of the International Civil Aviation Organisation. The safeguarding of the aerodrome is regulated by the Government, with the assistance of Air Safety Support International, which makes regular visits to Gibraltar to ensure that the relevant standards are met. Gibraltar Airport has considerable capacity to expand and the increased traffic that is envisaged will not affect the capacity of the airfield to continue to meet its international obligations.

Additional safety measures are planned following the Cordoba ministerial statement on Gibraltar Airport, including the introduction of new final approach paths to the airport in order to enhance operational safety conditions.

(HL Deb 8 January 2007 Vol 688 cWA10)

12/3

The Minister of Defence was asked whether any special agreements or other arrangements under the provisions of Article 3 of the Convention on International Civil Aviation have been made in relation to overflight through the UK, its overseas territories and bases by US state aircraft. A Defence Minister wrote:

The UK has bilateral arrangements with over 30 countries, including the United States, under which routine flights by military aircraft are cleared to overfly and land in the UK without seeking prior permission. All foreign and Commonwealth military aircraft transporting VIPs or carrying dangerous air cargo need to seek advance clearance.

(HC Deb 1 March 2007 Vol 457 c1531W)

12/4

The Minister of Defence was asked, pursuant to his answer of 1 March 2007...on rendition, whether the bilateral arrangements mentioned apply to state aircraft acting in a civilian capacity. A Defence Minister wrote:

The Department's bilateral arrangements cover routine flights by military aircraft from the relevant countries transiting UK airspace and landing in the UK. They also apply to other state aircraft landing at UK military airfields on routine business. These arrangements do not provide any form of immunity from customs and immigration procedures, national or international law, or regulations covering safe use of UK airspace. Action would be taken by the appropriate authority with MOD support should illegal activity be detected.

(HC Deb 25 April 2007 Vol 459 c1119W)

12/5

An FCO Minister wrote:

On 12 September 2001, the North Atlantic Council invoked article 5 of the Washington Treaty. Following that decision NATO allies agreed to grant blanket overflight clearance to US and other allies' military flights subject to national procedures. This remains the case. Decisions of this type remain in force unless revoked by the North Atlantic Council.

Under UK procedures all flights through UK airspace must comply with UK law. We have also made clear that we expect to be consulted on any request to render a detainee through UK territory or airspace.

(HC Deb 26 July 2007 Vol 463 c1474W)

12/6

The Minister of Defence was asked, pursuant to the answer of 21 May 2007, Official Report, column 1052W, on rendition, on which 14 dates aircraft HZ-124 landed at RAF Brize Norton between 1 July 2006 and 21 May 2007; and what the total amount is of the fees paid by the owner of HZ-124 to his Department for using RAF Brize Norton since 1 July 2006. He said:

It is not the practice of the Government to make public details of travel arrangements by foreign governments. The fees for the use of RAF Brize Norton by aircraft HZ-124 since 1 July 2006 were waived in accordance with the regulations in Chapter 7, Annex F of Joint Service Publication 360, which govern the waiver of charges for the use of military airfields by British and foreign civil and military aircraft.

The hon. Member may also wish to note that my answer of the 21 May 2007, Official Report, column 1053W, was incorrect and should have read:

Since 1 July 2006, aircraft HZ 124 has landed 15 times at RAF Brize Norton. The aircraft operated in accordance with the MOD regulations for civil aircraft use of military airfields. The regulations also cover the applicability and level of landing, housing, parking and insurance fees charges. The regulations have been adhered to for each flight.

[HZ-124 is an airbus belonging to Saudi Arabia, Ed.]
(HC Deb 29 June 2007 Vol 462 c881WA)

Part Twelve: II.B. *Airspace, Outer Space and Antarctica—Outer space and celestial bodies—Uses*

12/7

The Government were asked what diplomatic response they have made to the use by China of a ballistic missile to disable a Chinese satellite. An FCO Minister wrote:

On 18 January officials from our embassy in Beijing made representations to the Chinese Ministry of Foreign Affairs about the missile test, expressing concern about the lack of international consultation before the test was conducted and the possible impact of debris from the test on other objects in space.

The Government have also expressed concern that the development of this technology and the manner in which this test was conducted is inconsistent with the spirit of China's statements to the UN and other bodies on the military use of space. As part of our regular bilateral dialogue on international issues, we will continue to work to encourage China to play a constructive role in the international community.

(HL Deb 31 January 2007 Vol 689 c66WA)

12/8

The Trade and Industry Secretary was asked if he would undertake research into the economic threat to UK companies who use commercial satellites for transacting business of increases in space clutter.
A Minister wrote:

The Government have not directly funded such a study and have no immediate plans to do so. However, the potential risk is increasingly well known and Government and industry are involved in mitigation practices and the development of relevant international standards.

In licensing UK space activities, a safety assessment is carried out for each application and this includes a study of the debris mitigation measures put in place by the applicant for the launch and end of life of the satellite, plus measures taken to minimise debris in the event of an accident to the craft.

BNSC is also developing a database of relevant good practice and standards to support keeping space open for business. This will be used to improve further the safety assessment and be made available to licence applicants.

(HC Deb 2 March 2007 Vol 457 c1589W)

Part Twelve: III.C. *Airspace, Outer Space and Antarctica—Antarctica—Protection of the Environment*

12/9

The Foreign Secretary was asked what steps the Government were taking to assist international conservation efforts with regard to Antarctic krill. An FCO Minister wrote:

The UK, led by the Foreign and Commonwealth Office and supported by scientists from the British Antarctic Survey and Imperial College, plays a leading role in the Commission for the Conservation of Antarctic Marine Living Resources (CCAMLR) which pioneered an ecosystem-based approach to fisheries management. CCAMLR recognises that krill play a central role in the Antarctic food web. It has therefore taken a number of significant steps, including imposing

strict precautionary catch limits to avoid large catches of krill that could compromise the availability of food in key foraging areas of Antarctic fauna

(HC Deb 25 June 2007 Vol 462 c204W)

Part Thirteen: International Responsibility

Part Fourteen: Peaceful Settlement of Disputes

Part Fourteen: II.D. *Peaceful settlement of disputes—means of settlement—
mediation*

14/1
An FCO Minister wrote:

We are in constant contact with [Eritrea and Ethiopia], including at ministerial
level, on this issue. We have urged them to implement UN Security Council
Resolution (UNSCR) 1767 (adopted on 30 July 2007) including to "show maximum restraint and refrain from any threat or use of force against each other"
(paragraph 2 of UNSCR 1640 (2005) reiterated in UNSCR 1767 (2007)).

We continue to urge both Eritrea and Ethiopia to behave in accordance with
international law; specifically, to implement the Eritrea Ethiopia Boundary
Commission's decision and to demarcate their common frontier. We continue to
press Eritrea to lift its restrictions on the UN Mission to Ethiopia and Eritrea to
allow it to fulfil its mandate and to withdraw from the temporary security zone.

I met the Foreign Ministers of both Eritrea and Ethiopia in the margins of the
UN General Assembly in New York in September and urged them to find a
peaceful way forward.

We are also working with the UN, EU, the US and other international partners
in order to prevent any renewal of fighting.

(HL Deb 29 October 2007 Vol 695 cWA147)

Part Fourteen: II.G.2. *Peaceful settlement of disputes—means of settlement—judicial settlement—courts and tribunals other than the International
Court of Justice*

14/2
International Criminal Court
An FCO Minister was asked by the FAC what the Government was
doing about reports that the Government of Uganda was pressing the

ICC to drop the charges against Joseph Kony in return for his agreeing to a peace settlement. He said

We are pretty firm about the role of the International Criminal Court ('ICC') in this matter and I will explain why. You cannot offer impunity to a group of individuals who have carried out mass murder, rape, violence of all sorts and would continue to do so were it not that they knew with some certainty that they would face a court for their crimes against humanity.

A fragile process has been in place in Uganda, supported by the international community, and it has been making progress. Sadly, a few weeks ago out of the blue, those who have been in charge of most of the violence took a decision not to withdraw from the talks but to carry on the talks only if they took place in a different location. But that was a pretext, of course, just to delay the talks and discussions.

There is already in place an amnesty for those who have fought from the bush who are not the authors of the terrible crimes that took place. That offer is there still and it continues to be utilised. Alongside this attempt to get the process back in place, which is ongoing, there is a great deal of humanitarian work and effort, to which we are a serious partner, to deal with those who are in displaced persons camps. At the moment there are still over a million people in displaced persons camps, although at one point it was almost 2 million people. A humanitarian aid programme for those who are in the displaced persons camps is trying, with the local community, to put together a process of stability to allow the local community to have a great deal more freedom in the area without the fear of retribution.

I give you the absolute assurance that we are doing everything that we can to encourage African Union involvement. The role of the UN is important, as is the role of the negotiators. Remember that these cases from Uganda are the first cases ever put before the International Criminal Court and if there was impunity in those cases it would simply send the signal that you can disengage from conflict for a short period, have the cases dropped and return to conflict if you do not get what you want. That is not a signal that anybody should be sending out.

There is not a crisis in the International Criminal Court; it is in its early stages of development. It already has one person facing trial, six arrest warrants have been issued and another three investigations are under way, so we continue to support it. That includes investigations in Darfur; there has been a unprecedented referral passed by the Security Council. In establishing itself well, the ICC has got UK support. It is a central pillar of international justice. [Q.62]

(FAC Report, Human Rights Report 2006, HC 269 (2007))

14/3
An FCO Minister wrote:

The Government support international efforts to develop a peaceful and sustainable democracy in Somaliland. The UK provides around £8 million of assistance to Somaliland, including supporting governance, democratisation, health, education and reconciliation in Somaliland. We also encourage the Somaliland authorities to engage in constructive dialogue with the transitional federal government to agree a mutually acceptable solution regarding their future relationship.

The International Criminal Court (ICC) is an independent, permanent court that tries people accused of genocide, crimes against humanity and war crimes. It is a court of last resort and will not act if a case is investigated by a national judicial system, unless the proceedings are not genuine. As Somalia is not a state party to the Rome Statute of the ICC, cases would have to be referred to the ICC by the UN Security Council.

(HL 11 December 2007 Vol 697 cWA46-WA47)

14/4
An FCO Minister wrote:

Under the terms of the Rome Statute of the International Criminal Court no proposal to amend the Statute may be made until July 2009 at the earliest. If a proposal is made, the Government will give it full consideration in the light of circumstances at the time.

The Government's view, as we continue to state in the Special Working Group, is that any proposal in relation to the crime of aggression must reflect the primary responsibility of the UN Security Council for the maintenance of peace and security as enshrined in the UN Charter.

(HC Deb 10 December 2007 Vol 469 c156W)

14/5
(See also **6/85-87**)

Special Court for Sierra Leone
AGREEMENT WITH SPECIAL COURT FOR SIERRA LEONE (10/07/07)

After signing the sentence enforcement agreement with the Registrar of the Special Court for Sierra Leone, today, Lord Malloch-Brown, Minister for Africa at the Foreign and Commonwealth Office said:

Signing this agreement enables the UK to give effect to our commitment to imprison former Liberian President Charles Taylor if he is convicted by the Special Court and demonstrates again our strong support for the Court.

I pay tribute to the Court's work in bringing to justice those accused of crimes against humanity and war crimes during Sierra Leone's civil war. This is making a major contribution to the cause of international justice and is an essential part of the process of restoring and maintaining stability in Sierra Leone.

We must all continue to make clear that there can be no impunity for those who would commit these most serious crimes. I therefore urge the international community to maintain its support, financial and otherwise, for the Court so that it can continue this important work.

(www.fco.gov.uk/news)

14/5

In a press release issued on the day the agreement was signed, the FCO said:

In response to requests from the SCSL and the Government of Liberia, the Security Council unanimously concurred that the continuing presence of Charles Taylor in Sierra Leone, for trial or imprisonment, was a threat to that country's stability and passed Resolution 1688 that enabled him to be tried by the SCSL in the premises of the International Criminal Court in The Hague. The UK helped to facilitate this by passing the International Tribunals (Sierra Leone) Act into law this year which will enable the Court to sentence Charles Taylor to imprisonment in the UK if he is convicted. The last stage of this process is the signature of the Sentencing Agreement today.

[See also International Tribunals (Sierra Leone) Act 2007, which adds a new section to the International Criminal Court Act 2001 to facilitate the arrangements made under the Agreement in the law of England and Wales, Ed. See also **6/85, 6/86**].

(The Agreement between the Government of the United Kingdom of Great Britain and Northern Ireland and the Special Court for Sierra Leone on the Enforcement of Sentences of the Special Court of Sierra Leone, UKTS No.21, Cm7208, [The Agreement entered into force on 9 August 2007], Ed.)

(www.fco.gov.uk/news)

International Criminal Tribunal for Yugoslavia

14/6

An FCO Minister wrote:

Co-operation with the International Criminal Tribunal for the former Yugoslavia (ICTY) is a legal requirement under UN Security Council Resolutions 1244 and 1534. The International Court of Justice also ruled on 26 February that Serbia had breached its obligation to punish the perpetrators by failing to transfer individuals accused of genocide, including Ratko Mladic, to the ICTY.

The EU has made clear that EU membership is open to all the countries of the western Balkans once they meet the established criteria. In Serbia's case, full co-operation with the ICTY is a key condition. Serbia is currently negotiating a stabilisation and association agreement (SAA) with the EU. This is seen as the first step along the road to EU membership and will cover political dialogue, support for political and economic reform, aid and trade relations. Conclusion of the SAA will require full co-operation with ICTY. The UK regularly raises ICTY co-operation with the Serb authorities. When...the then Minister for Europe visited Belgrade on 7 February he discussed this issue with both President Tadic and Prime Minister Kostunica.

(HL Deb 23 July 2007 Vol 694 cWA68)

14/7 (See also 5/43)

Special Tribunal for Lebanon

In a statement, the Foreign Secretary said:

The UK continues to be deeply concerned by the political instability resulting from the absence of a President in Lebanon. President Lahoud's term of office expired on 23 November. The ongoing political divisions over who should succeed him remain a source of instability. We have been urging all sides to come together in the spirit of compromise to choose a President who can lead the country forward. We support them in their efforts to do so and hope they will be able to resolve the political crisis as rapidly as possible.

Despite the ongoing uncertainty, progress continues towards the establishment of the Special Tribunal for Lebanon. On 30 May 2007, the Security Council adopted Security Council Resolution 1757, establishing the Tribunal. The Tribunal will try those accused of killing the former Lebanese Prime Minister, Rafiq Hariri, who was assassinated on 14 February 2005 along with 21 others in a car bomb in central Beirut. This attack was part of a campaign of targeted political attacks against anti-Syrian MPs and political activists in Lebanon. The most recent of these was the assassination of MP Antoine Ghanem on 19 September. Mr. Ghanem was killed along with two bodyguards and four other civilians in a car bomb explosion in east Beirut which also injured more than 70 other innocent civilians.

The UK has been, and remains, firmly committed to the pursuit of justice for Rafiq Hariri's murder and the sequence of assassinations that followed it. The UK worked closely with UN partners to establish the UN Independent International Investigation Commission (UNIIIC) into Mr Hariri's assassination. We were also co-sponsors of UN Security Council Resolution 1757 establishing the Special Tribunal. As part of our continued commitment, and in response to the UN Secretary-General's call for contributions, I am pleased to announce that the UK will be contributing £500,000 ($1 million) to the Tribunal.

The success of the UN-led investigation process and of the Tribunal remain vital for the stability of Lebanon. It is essential that justice is done to send a clear message that political assassinations will not be tolerated. The UK will continue to offer its strong support to the UN and the Lebanese Government as they take this important work forward.

(HC Deb 10 December 2007 Vol 496 c6WS–7WS)

Part Fourteen: II.H.1. *Peaceful settlement of disputes—means of settlement—settlement within international organisations—United Nations*

14/8

The Foreign Secretary was asked what her estimate was of the outstanding amount of interest accrued by delays in the payment by the UN

Compensation Commission of compensation relating to the detention of UK nationals in Iraq during the first Gulf war. An FCO Minister wrote:

A decision was taken at the 55th session of the UN Compensation Commission (UNCC) Governing Council in March 2005 that interest would not be paid by the UNCC to claimants on top of their principal awards. This decision was made for a variety of reasons, including the fact that assumptions made about the capacity of the Compensation Fund (its revenue generated from Iraqi petroleum export earnings) did not materialise which resulted in inadequate funds being available, and the estimated projection that payment of all principal awards would not be completed until 2045.

The decision was taken against the background of the need for Iraqi oil proceeds to be used towards reconstruction of Iraq. Payment of interest would place an additional and unacceptable financial burden on the Iraqi people.

No outstanding interest therefore accrued in the period between determination and payment of awards.

A letter was sent by the Foreign and Commonwealth Office to all UK claimants in March 2005 explaining the decision taken on the question of interest by the Governing Council.

In answer to a further question asking how many payments to UK nationals from the UN Compensation Commission relating to detention in Iraq during the first Gulf war had been subject to delay; and what the average length of this delay was, the Minister wrote:

Individuals claims had to be filed with the UN Compensation Commission (UNCC) by 1 January 1995; corporate and government claims by 1 January 1996. 5,000 UK claimants duly received awards from the UNCC totalling US$ 428 million.

The Foreign and Commonwealth Office was initially unable to locate 47 of the successful UK claimants on the basis of information provided by the UNCC. However, following renewed efforts in 2006, we subsequently located 26 of the 47 and are currently in the process of finalising the payment of their outstanding awards.

To calculate the average time between the lodging of the 5,000 UK claims and the payments (made in instalments) could not be done without incurring disproportionate cost.

(HC Deb 24 May 2007 Vol 460 c1482W)

14/9

The Foreign Secretary was asked a number of questions about the UN Compensation Commission, to which an FCO Minister replied.

1. What measures does the UN expect to be undertaken to recover monies overpaid to claimants.

Reply: The Governing Council of the UN Compensation Commission has asked that "best efforts" be made by all concerned governments to seek to recover relevant overpayments from affected claimants and for governments to report back before the next Governing Council in June.

2. How much compensation was paid to claimants; and how much was overpayment.

Reply: Nearly 5,000 UK claimants have so far received disbursements of varying amounts totalling US$428 million from the UN Compensation Commission (UNCC) through the Government.

The UNCC has identified the sum of US$391,000 as the total amount of overpayment to UK claimants. To provide the information requested for each claimant would require the permission of each individual company and institution concerned. It is therefore not possible to provide such information without incurring disproportionate cost.

3. What part the UK played in discussions on the consensus in the UN Compensation Commission Governing Council on the best efforts approach.

Reply: The UK, as one of the permanent members of the Governing Council, played a full role in discussions and supported the decisions taken by general consensus in response to the UN Compensation Commission's investigation of duplicate and overpaid claims, including the adoption of a "best efforts" approach for concerned governments to seek the recovery of overpayments from affected claimants.

4. When did the UN Compensation Commission make the decision to request recovery of overpayments; and what representations did the UK make when it was informed of the decision.

Reply: The UN Compensation Commission (UNCC) Governing Council, at its 61st session in November 2006, adopted 22,000 corrections to awards identified during its investigation into duplicate claims and decided to request governments concerned to seek recovery of relevant overpayments from affected claimants. The same "best efforts" approach has been adopted for all corrections adopted by the UNCC in response to its investigation.

As one of the permanent members of the Governing Council the UK supported the general consensus to adopt a "best efforts" approach to the recovery of overpayments.

5. Whether the Government would be responsible for repaying any overpayment not recovered from individuals.

Reply: No. The Government are required to use their best efforts to contact and seek to recoup overpaid amounts totalling US$391,000 from 113 affected UK claimants.

(HC Deb 10 May 2007 Vol 460 c394W–395W)

Part Fifteen: Coercive Measures short of the Use of Force

Part Fifteen: I.A. *Coercive measures short of the use of force—unilateral measures—retorsion*

15/1
Answering questions about sanctions against Zimbabwe, an FCO Minister said:

...the Government expect that targeted measures against Zimbabwe will be renewed in February. Since their rollover last February, the situation in the country has only worsened: peaceful demonstrations have been violently disrupted, the economy continues to be grossly mismanaged and the opposition and independent media remain suppressed. Until democracy, the rule of law and full human rights are restored in Zimbabwe, it is right that Mugabe and his regime should continue to be isolated by the international community.

[It] is absolutely right to say that when talking of sanctions we are talking of a travel ban, not of economic sanctions. We will certainly make that clear to our colleagues in the African Union. Indeed, the travel ban has been strengthened four times since 2002, to include others who have supported the Government of Zimbabwe's efforts to suppress the people...

...it would indeed be irresponsible if the European Union were to renege on its sanctions now. I am confident that it will not, but I am sure that Her Majesty's Government will continue to make the very strong case in favour of sanctions. In respect of aid being given to Zimbabwe, of course we must maintain that aid, but it should be balanced by sanctions, and we must ensure that the people of Zimbabwe are not harmed in any way.

I can ensure that the Government will do their utmost to minimise the loopholes. It is extraordinary that such loopholes exist, but they do. The EU Zimbabwe travel ban contains standard exemptions that enable travel to the EU by banned Zimbabweans in a few, narrowly defined cases. We do our utmost to ensure that they are narrowly defined, because to see people such as Grace Mugabe stomping up and down the streets of the Côte d'Azur is an affront to humanity.

[It] is absolutely right that the sanctions must hit the regime and not the poor people of Zimbabwe, who have to suffer continual atrocities. However, the EU sanctions put real pressure on the regime. They ensure that Mugabe remains isolated—hence his attempts to seek financial lifelines from China and Iran to buy time. It is important to point out that the targeted sanctions have the support of the democratic opposition and the NGO community in Zimbabwe. Mugabe and his regime detest the restrictions on their movement.

(HL Deb 8 January 2007 Vol 688 c7–11)

Part Fifteen: II.A. *Coercive measures short of the use of force—collective measures—United Nations*

15/2
Proscribed Organisations

The Home Secretary was asked to list the UK-based organisations which are listed as proscribed terrorist organisations under international agreements to which the UK is a party. A Home Office Minister wrote:

Both the EU and the UN maintain lists of terrorist organisations. Member states are obliged to apply financial sanctions (such as asset freezes) on the organisations on these lists.

The EU list can be accessed at the following website:

http://ec.europa.eu/comm/external_relations/cfsp/sanctions/list/consol-list.htm

The New Consolidated List of Individuals and Entities Belonging to or Associated with the Taliban and the Al-Quaida Organisation, as established and maintained by the United Nations 1267 committee, can be accessed at the following website:

http://www.un.org/Docs/sc/committees/1267/1267ListEng.htm

(HC Deb 18 January 2007 Vol 455 c1299W)

15/3

In reply to a number of questions about Darfur, an FCO Minister wrote:

We have pressed the Government of Sudan to act on its obligations under UN Security Council Resolution (UNSCR) 1706 (2006). This requires implementation of an effective ceasefire and of the Darfur Peace Agreement, including its provisions for the disarmament of the Janjaweed/armed militias; and a renewed political process between the Government of Sudan and the rebel groups.

The Foreign Secretary condemned the most recent Government of Sudan bombing raids in North Darfur, between 19 and 21 April, which resulted in a number of civilian injuries and deaths.

To maintain pressure on the Government of Sudan to implement their commitments to the international community, we are currently discussing the elements of a new UNSCR with international partners and the UN.

We utterly condemn the recent bombings in North Darfur by the Sudanese Government. They are in direct violation of UN Security Council Resolution 1591 and demonstrate a lack of commitment to the peace process.

The Sudanese Government must commit to an immediate ceasefire. If they do not, we will be forced to press for tougher measures. We are considering all options, including measures to allow better monitoring of the illegal use of aircraft in Darfur.

We are very concerned by reports that the Government of Sudan are operating aircraft with UN markings in Darfur. The Sudanese Government resumed bombing villages in Darfur last week, resulting in a number of civilian injuries and deaths. We condemn these attacks, which show little regard for human life.

We continue to discuss the case for further sanctions in the UN.

We are aware of the steps taken by the US Administration to block transfers by US commercial banks of oil payments to the Government of Sudan. We are keeping the situation in Sudan under close review. If the Sudanese Government do not co-operate with the international community, we are prepared to consider further sanctions. We are discussing the elements of a new UN Security Council Resolution with international partners, which would include further targeted sanctions against individuals engaged in violence or responsible for authorising it; an extension of the arms embargo to cover the whole of Sudan; and, measures to allow better monitoring of the illegal use of aircraft in Darfur.

(HC Deb 2 May 2007 Vol 459 c1717W–1718W)

15/4

The Chancellor of the Exchequer was asked what powers were available to enforce (a) UN and (b) EU sanctions on export of goods with military applications to Sudan; what reports he has received of the export of such goods by (i) Dallex Trade and (ii) Land Rover to Sudan. A Treasury Minister wrote:

HM Revenue and Customs (HMRC) is the enforcement authority for export licensing controls on military goods. An exporter attempting to export military goods from the UK to any destination without a valid export licence is committing an offence under Section 68 of the Customs and Excise Management Act (CEMA) 1979. The provisions of CEMA provide HMRC officers with wide ranging enforcement powers to investigate offences and to seize unlicensed goods. Should an investigation reveal sufficient evidence of an offence then the case will be referred to the Revenue and Customs Prosecutions Office (RCPO). The RCPO will then consider whether to commence criminal proceedings.

EU and UN arms embargoes prohibit the export of military goods to Sudan. Military goods are defined as all goods listed in Part 1 of Schedule 1 to the Export of Goods, Transfer of Technology and Provision of Technical Assistance (Control) Order 2003. Non-military goods which may have a military application are not subject to export licensing controls and therefore HMRC enforcement powers do not apply.

Section 18 of the Commissioners for Revenue and Customs Act 2005 provides that HMRC may not disclose information held in connection with a function of HMRC unless there is lawful authority. HMRC is therefore unable to disclose information in relation to specific campaigns.

(HC Deb 16 May 2007 Vol 460 c757W)

15/5

Iran

The Foreign Secretary was asked what sanctions were in place against Iran in relation to nuclear proliferation. An FCO Minister wrote:

United Nations Security Council Resolution (UNSCR) 1737, adopted unanimously on 23 December 2006, imposes a number of sanctions on Iran under article 41 of chapter VII of the UN Charter. These are proportionate and targeted at Iran's sensitive nuclear and missile activities. All states have a legal obligation to comply. In general terms, the measures include:

a prohibition on supplying certain nuclear and missile related items to Iran and on providing related assistance;

a prohibition on the export from Iran of such items and their procurement from Iran;

monitoring of the travel of certain individuals engaged in or providing support for Iran's proliferation sensitive activities;

limits on International Atomic Energy Agency (IAEA) technical co-operation with Iran;

freezing of the assets of persons and entities designated in the resolution's annex as well as those subsequently identified by the Security Council or the Sanctions Committee; and

a call on states to prevent specialised teaching or training of Iranian nationals, which would contribute to Iran's proliferation sensitive nuclear activities.

The implementation of measures will be suspended if, and for as long as, Iran suspends uranium enrichment related and reprocessing activities, as verified by the IAEA. A copy of the resolution is available on the UN website at:

www.un.org/Docs/sc/unsc_resolutions06.htm.

EU Foreign Ministers discussed the resolution on 22 January and agreed that:

to ensure effective implementation of measures in UNSCR 1737 while remaining consistent with EU policy, and recalling the EU policy not to sell arms to Iran...the EU should prevent the export to and import from Iran of the goods on the NSG (Nuclear Suppliers Group) and MTCR (Missile Technology Control Regime) lists; ban transactions with and freeze the assets of individuals and entities covered by the criteria in UNSCR 1737; ban travel to the EU of the individuals covered by these criteria; and take measures to prevent Iranian nationals from studying proliferation sensitive subjects within the EU.

On 12 February, EU Foreign Ministers gave political endorsement to a Common Position giving effect to this decision; we expect the Common Position and a related EC Regulation to be adopted shortly.

We have also taken steps at a national level to implement UNSCR 1737, including through the adoption of the Iran (Financial Sanctions) Order 2007, which came into force on 9 February. The order is available at:

http://www.opsi.gov.uk/si/si2007/20070281.htm.

On 20 February, the UK submitted a report to the President of the Security Council setting out in detail all the steps we have taken to implement UNSCR 1737.

(HC Deb 2 March 2007 Vol 457 c1613W)

15/6

In a written statement, a Treasury Minister said:

The Government are strongly supportive of international efforts to tackle the proliferation of weapons of mass destruction and to prevent the abuse of financial systems. My written ministerial statement of 7 February 2007, Official Report, column 37WS informed Parliament that the Government were seeking the agreement of the Privy Council for the adoption of an Order in Council concerned with giving effect to the financial sanctions against Iran's nuclear programme as required by UNSCR 1737. The Iran (Financial Sanctions) Order 2007 was laid before Parliament on 8 February and came into force on 9 February.

On 19 April, the European Union adopted EC Regulation No 423/2007. This regulation implements at a Community level the sanctions against Iran agreed under UNSCR 1737. It also establishes an autonomous EU financial sanctions list against entities and individuals associated with Iran's nuclear and ballistic missile programmes. The regulation came into force on 20 April and is directly applicable in the UK. Council decision 2007/242/EC establishing the autonomous EU financial sanctions list came into force on 24 April.

In order to enforce the financial sanctions elements of EC Regulation No 423/2007, the Government are today laying before the Parliament the "Iran (European Community Financial Sanctions) Regulations 2007". These establish prohibitions, offences and penalties with regard to persons who are on the autonomous EU financial sanctions list in relation to Iran. The "Iran (Financial Sanctions) Order 2007" continues to apply with regard to persons who are on the UN financial sanctions list in relation to Iran.

As set out in the explanatory memorandum to the regulations, it is necessary that the regulations come into force as soon as possible in order to minimise the risk of asset flight. For this reason, the Government consider it necessary to waive the usual convention that there should be at least a 21 day period between regulations being laid and coming into force. Accordingly, the regulations will come into force tomorrow.

(HC Deb 3 May 2007 Vol 459 c42WS)

15/7

Kimberley Processs

An FCO Minister wrote:

The UK is fully committed to implementing the Kimberley Process Certification Scheme (KPCS). The body responsible for this, the Government Diamond

Office (GDO), is a department of the Foreign and Commonwealth Office (FCO), and works closely with HM Revenue and Customs, the UK diamond industry and civil society groups to ensure effective implementation of the provisions of the KPCS document.

The UK is supportive of the current European Union Chairmanship of the KPCS, which began on 1 January. The FCO has provided funds for the European Commission to second additional staff for the duration of the Chairmanship. An official from the GDO has taken part in a review visit to Romania and formed part of the recent review mission to Ghana, as part of wider efforts to ensure full compliance of the KPCS among all participants in order to eradicate the trade in conflict diamonds. A GDO official will be taking part in the forthcoming review visit to Bulgaria.

The UK supported the recent lifting of UN sanctions on the diamond trade in Liberia, following an inspection from the Kimberley Process Expert Mission which confirmed that Liberia had the necessary systems in place in order to ensure compliance with the KPCS.

(HC Deb 25 June 2007 Vol 462 c186W)

15/8
(See also 1/1, 6/68–70, 16/13)

Sanctions—General

The Foreign Secretary wrote:

The UK is already playing a leading role alongside international partners in ensuring that the international community can become more effective in preventing the breakdown of states and societies. Effective measures will require international consensus on the challenges and the backing of the international community. That is why the UK is pressing the UN and other bodies to deliver the 2005 World Summit commitment to the creation of a single Early Warning System and to operationalise the concept of Responsibility to Protect also endorsed at that World Summit...the Prime Minister set out the clear challenge to the international community to deliver its commitments by improving procedures to prevent conflict. Specifically, the UN Security Council needs to act earlier, and there needs to be more use of targeted sanctions and international criminal court actions. The UK will continue to work with international partners on specific mechanisms to deliver existing international commitments.

(HC Deb 13 December 2007 Vol 469 c829W)

15/9
An FCO Minister said:

The Government is committed to informing Parliament annually of the sanctions regimes which the United Kingdom implements. Currently the United Kingdom implements United Nations sanctions in relation to al-Qaeda and the

Taliban, Cote d'Ivoire, the Democratic Republic of the Congo, the Democratic Peoples' Republic of Korea, Iran, Iraq, Lebanon, Liberia, Rwanda, Sierra Leone, Somalia, Sudan and terrorism.

The UK also implements sanctions regimes imposed autonomously by the EU in relation to Belarus, Burma, China, the former Federal Republic of Yugoslavia (in connection with individuals indicted by the International Criminal Tribunal for the former Yugoslavia or responsible for certain acts of violence at Mostar), the Republic of Macedonia, Moldova, Uzbekistan and Zimbabwe.

In accordance with a decision of the Organisation for Security and Co-operation in Europe, the United Kingdom implements arms embargoes on Armenia and Azerbaijan. The Government also takes full account of the Economic Community of West African States moratorium on certain exports of small arms and light weapons to Economic Community of West African States members.

A full list of sanctions regimes and restrictive measures implemented by the UK is published on the Foreign and Commonwealth Office website at: www.fco.gov.uk/sanctions

Following a request... this document now includes objectives and lift criteria for each regime.

(HL Deb 18 December 2007 Vol 696 c346)

15/10

Somalia

An FCO Minister wrote:

The Government fully support the UN arms embargo [against Somalia]. The UK sponsored UN Security Council Resolution 1766, adopted unanimously on 23 July 2007, extended the mandate of the Arms Embargo Monitoring Group for a further six months. The Monitoring Group reports to the Security Council on violations of the arms embargo.

Somalia unfortunately has a proliferation of illegal arms, many imported in violation of the embargo. The lack of a functioning government means that arms markets are unregulated. The situation is further exacerbated by the presence of clan militias and insurgents operating in the country. The Government institutions in Somalia do not currently have the capacity to hinder the illegal arms trade. The UK is working with the UN, and wider international community, to encourage the development of Government institutions in Somalia that will enable the authorities to develop its capacity in this area.

(HC Deb 22 November 2007 Vol 467 c1041W)

15/11

Sudan

The International Development Secretary said in answer to a question about sanctions against Sudan because of the situation in Darfur:

It is precisely because parts of the international community have been threatening sanctions that we got both the result in relation to the heavy support package and yesterday's decision by the Government of Sudan on the hybrid (international force). Our position as a Government, as he will be aware, has been extremely clear that the Government of Sudan must honour the commitments that they have entered into, and we need to keep under review what further steps need to be taken, because commitments are not good enough; they must be matched by actions to support the deployment. We should say to the Government of Sudan, "We will continue to watch the steps that you take, and if at any point you fail to honour the agreement that you have given, we will go back to the UN Security Council."...not all members of the Security Council are in the same position as the United Kingdom Government, the United States of America and one or two other countries on the question of further sanctions.

He went on:

As I said in answer to the earlier question, in the end we must judge yesterday's announcement by the actions of the Government of Sudan and nothing else. There are proposals for an oil trust fund, but the question is how that would be established without the agreement of the Government of Sudan.

There is a second issue in relation to disinvestment, which is another matter that we discussed in the debate last week, and the genuine difficulty is that, given that the proceeds of Sudan's oil wealth are shared with the Government of South Sudan—for them, that is an important part of the comprehensive peace agreement—one would need to be careful about taking steps that reduced the money available to that part of Sudan's new Government, because the need for resources, health and education is huge in that part of the country.

I set out in my earlier replies the steps that we are taking to ensure that the Government of Sudan honour those commitments. In the meantime, the best that we can do is to provide support to the African Union mission, which we are doing via the substantial amount of money we have put in, and by getting agreement through the UN to the use of assessed contributions. The Government of Sudan have said that they want an all-African force and I hope very much that Africa will be able to come up with the number of troops. We discussed that in Addis Ababa in November and said that we should look to Africa first, but if the troops cannot all come from Africa, we should look elsewhere. I hope that it will be possible to find those troops.

...a comprehensive peace agreement is the only real solution to the crisis...the statement that was agreed at the G8 in Heiligendamm...shows that we have continued to press to make sure that the G8 gives a very strong lead. We have to get the talks going. That is a responsibility both on the Government of Sudan and on the rebels, because they too are partly responsible for the current banditry and attacks on humanitarian workers. They too have to stop doing that, get round the table and negotiate a peace deal.

(HC Deb 13 June 207 Vol 461 c742–744)

15/12

An FCO Minister wrote:

We believe sanctions have contributed towards containing the crisis in Darfur, for example in the Government of Sudan's acceptance of the UN's Heavy Support Package to the African Union peacekeeping force in Sudan. However, we want a solution to the crisis which may require further sanctions.

We are concerned that sanctions should not impact on those in Sudan who have no responsibility for violence in Darfur, or on the Comprehensive Peace Agreement, thus damaging the south. We are therefore pressing for further targeted sanctions on individuals and an extension of the UN arms embargo from Darfur to all of Sudan, in line with the EU embargo, if the Government of Sudan and the rebel movements fail to honour their commitments.

(HC Deb 14 June 2007 Vol 461 c1220W)

15/13

Terrorism

A Treasury Minister wrote:

In my written ministerial statement of 10 October 2006, I undertook to report to Parliament on a quarterly basis on the operation of the UK's asset freezing regime. This is the first of these reports and covers the period October–December 2006(1).

Asset-freezing framework

The following changes have been made to asset-freezing legislation:

Terrorism (United Nations Measures) Order 2006, made in October; and

al-Qaeda and Taliban (United Nations Measures) Order 2006, made in November

These two Orders updated the previous Orders, as I explained in statements to the House on 10 October and 7 November 2006.

The Treasury has also strengthened the asset-freezing regime by agreeing, on the advice of law enforcement and intelligence agencies, to use closed source evidence in cases where there are strong operational reasons to impose a freeze but insufficient open source evidence available. I notified Parliament of this decision in October.

Asset-freezing Designations

In the quarter October–December 2006, the Treasury made seven domestic designations under the Terrorism Order and the Al-Qaeda and Taliban Order.

Of these, two persons already listed were re-designated under the new Orders.

The Terrorism Order and the Al-Qaeda and Taliban Order provide, where appropriate, for designations to be made confidentially and with restricted circulation of notice. Four persons were listed on this basis.

Two persons were listed on the basis of closed source evidence provided by law enforcement and intelligence agencies.

In addition, the following financial sanctions listings of persons with links to the UK took place:

none at the EU; and

one person at the UN.

No designated persons have been delisted in this quarter.

Designations this quarter make a total of 195 separate accounts and approximately £525,000 of suspected terrorist funds frozen in the UK since 2001.

Litigation

There has been one case of domestic litigation regarding financial sanctions.

The recent High Court judgment of 22 September 2006 in the case of *MA and MM v Her Majesty's Treasury* [2006] EWHC 2328 (Admin) upheld the Treasury's actions regarding benefits payments to the households of designated individuals. The case was heard by the Court of Appeal on 18 December 2006 and we are awaiting the judgement. [*In R (on the application of M, AM and MM) v HM Treasury et al* [2007] EWCA Civ 173, the Court of Appeal upheld the High Court judgment, Ed.]

Reviews

The Treasury keeps domestic asset-freezing cases under review. A number of formal reviews have been initiated in this quarter and the reviews of two cases have been completed. In both cases decisions were taken following the review to maintain the asset freeze.

Licensing policy

In accordance with UN Security Council Resolution 1452 (2002), the Treasury operates a licensing system whereby designated persons and others are able to apply to make or receive payments under specific and, if necessary, monitored conditions. In this quarter, the following licences were issued:

two listed persons were granted basic expenses licences, one of which was for benefits payments

there were no extraordinary expenses licences granted; and

eleven listed persons were granted legal expenses licences.

In addition, the household of one listed person was granted a benefits licence in accordance with the policy I set out in my statement of 3 July 2006 to Parliament.

(1) The detail which can be provided to the House on a quarterly basis is subject to the need to avoid the identification, directly or indirectly, of personal or operationally sensitive information.

(HC Deb 1 March 2007 Vol 457 c93WS)

Part Sixteen: Use of Force

Part Sixteen: II.A. *Use of force—legitimate use of force—self-defence*

16/1

Turkey—Northern Iraq

In its reply to the FAC Report, Global Security: the Middle East, the Government wrote:

102. The Government welcomes the fact that, despite Turkey's legitimate concerns about terrorist groups operating from Iraqi territory, it has shown restraint in its response. We continue to encourage Turkey to maintain its channels of dialogue with the Government of Iraq and to engage with the Kurdish Regional Government. We are urging the Government of Iraq to do more to address Turkey's legitimate security concerns. We have urged the Government of Iraq to proscribe the PKK as a terrorist organisation and to take firm steps to remove its ability to launch attacks against Turkey. We welcome the recent visit by Prime Minister Maliki to Turkey and the Memorandum of Understanding that was signed regarding cooperation between Turkey and Iraq to prevent and suppress terrorism and organised crime.

(Eighth Report of the Foreign Affairs Committee Session 2006–7 Global Security: The Middle East Response of the Secretary of State for Foreign and Commonwealth Affairs Cm 7212)

16/2

Israel

An FCO Minister said:

the Government of Israel have a responsibility to ensure the security of their people. They have a right to self-defence. If they want to build a barrier...they are entitled to do so. But that barrier must be on or behind the green line. Any barrier on occupied land contravenes international law and must come down. We have made that point to the Israeli Government on numerous occasions and we will continue to do so.

(HC Deb 3 July 2007 Vol 693 c987)

16/3

An FCO Minister wrote:

The Government have discussed the continued firing of rockets by Palestinian militants from Gaza into Israel with the Israeli Government on numerous occasions, and most recently during the visit of the Foreign Secretary to Israel and the Occupied Palestinian Territories on 17–19 November.

Over 1,000 Qassam rockets and mortar shells have been fired at Israeli targets since Hamas seized control of Gaza on 14 June 2007, wounding a number of Israelis. It has also caused damage to infrastructure. We continue to call for an immediate halt to these attacks, which target civilians and only escalate an already tense situation. While acknowledging Israel's right to defend itself, we call on Israel to show restraint in the face of these attacks and make clear that any response must be in accordance with international law.

(HC Deb 4 December 2007 Vol 468 c1136W)

Part Sixteen: II.B.1. *Use of force—Legitimate Use of Force—Collective Measures—United Nations*

16/4

Afghanistan

The Government were asked whether they intended United Kingdom military forces deployed in the Helmand province of Afghanistan to target drug traffickers, as distinct from drug growers, operating in the province. A Defence Minister wrote:

Under the terms of NATO's operational plan for the International Security Assistance Force (ISAF), ISAF forces can provide, within means and capabilities, training and operational support to Afghan counter-narcotics efforts. But they are not there to take direct action against the drugs traffickers or to eradicate opium poppies in the fields. That is a job for the Afghan Government.

16/5

Further, the Government were asked how many suspected drug traffickers United Kingdom forces deployed in the Helmand province of Afghanistan had detained and handed over to the Afghan authorities. The Minister wrote:

UK Armed Forces deployed in Helmand province have not detained any drug traffickers.

The UK, as Afghanistan's partner nation on counter-narcotics remains committed to supporting the Afghan Government in implementing their national drug control strategy. The arrest and prosecution of drug traffickers is conducted by Afghan drugs law enforcement agencies, the Counter Narcotics Criminal Justice Task Force and the Government of Afghanistan.

(HL Deb 8 January 2007 Vol 688 cWA3)

16/6

The Government were asked whether the use of force by the European Union, the United Nations or NATO to prevent countries or territories from dividing or amalgamating is permitted under international law. An FCO Minister wrote:

Use of force, whether on behalf of the European Union or the United Nations or by NATO, to prevent countries dividing or amalgamating would be permitted under international law if authorised by a mandatory United Nations Security Council resolution under Chapter VII of the United Nations Charter.

(HL Deb 8 January 2007 Vol 688 cWA25)

16/7

The Foreign Secretary in relation to UK activities in Afghanistan wrote:

The UK took on lead G8 responsibility for counter narcotics following the Bonn Agreement in 2001. In 2006 it was agreed that the concept of 'lead nation' was redundant, as the Afghan Government now had lead responsibility for all aspects of security sector reform. The UK therefore became Afghanistan's 'partner nation' on counter narcotics.

Signed in July 2005, the Joint Declaration of An Enduring Relationship between the UK and Afghanistan is a bilateral agreement between the UK and Afghanistan. The Enduring Relationship Action Plan 2006–07 sets out the commitments between the two Governments under the 2005 Joint Declaration... Under both the Joint Declaration and the Action Plan, the UK agreed to help Afghanistan mobilise and co-ordinate international efforts to end the drugs trade, in support of the four national priorities identified in the Afghan Government's national drug control strategy (NDCS)—targeting the trafficker, strengthening and diversifying legal rural livelihoods, reducing demand and developing state institutions. We are spending £270 million over three years in support of the NDCS.

[The Joint Declaration is at

http://66.102.9.104/search?q=cache:6wRn4oVnIR8J:www.fco.gov.uk/resources/en/pdf/pdf15/fco_ukaghanenduringrelationship+%22joint+declaration+of+an+enduring+relationship%22&hl=en&ct=clnk&cd=1&gl=uk; the Action Plan appears to be available only in Pashto, Ed.]

16/8

Chad

An FCO Minister wrote:

In response to the continuing security and humanitarian crisis in Chad, in September the UK co-sponsored UN Security Council Resolution 1778, which authorises the deployment of an EU force (EUFOR) and a UN multi-dimensional mission (MINURCAT) to Chad. The force aims to contribute to the stabilisation of the regions in eastern Chad and north eastern Central African Republic which border Sudan. Improved security will facilitate the delivery of humanitarian aid and help create the conditions necessary for voluntary, secure and sustainable return of refugees and internally displaced persons. EUFOR and MINURCAT support the larger African Union/UN mission to Darfur, which is mandated to protect civilians and is in the process of being deployed.

Long-term peace and security in the region needs to be underpinned by a lasting political solution. The UK supports the agreement reached between President Deby and Chadian rebel groups on 25 October in Sirte, Libya and urges all parties to implement the ceasefire. The EU is also sponsoring a process of dialogue between President Deby and the political opposition forces in Chad, which should contribute to creating a more stable political environment in which to promote peace. The UK takes every opportunity to call on the governments of Chad and Sudan to fulfil their obligations under the Tripoli agreement, which calls for a ceasefire between Chad and Sudan, and an end to support for armed movements, which destabilise the region.

(HC Deb 3 December 2007 Vol 468 c1043W)

16/9

Iraq

The Prime Minister said:

I entirely agree that British forces are doing a fantastic job in Iraq in circumstances of difficulty and danger, but let us remind ourselves of why they are there. They are there under a United Nations resolution with the full support of the Government of Iraq...in 2003, after the conflict and the invasion of Iraq, there was a United Nations resolution that specifically endorsed the multinational force. We are there with the agreement of the Government of Iraq.

(HC Deb 24 January 2007 Vol 455 c1414)

Part Sixteen: II.B.2. *Use of force—Legitimate Use of Force—Collective Measures—outside the United Nations*

16/10

An FCO Minister wrote:

The Government supports France in their use of warships to protect humanitarian supply ships sailing to Somalia from incidents of piracy.

The UN Security Council unanimously passed resolution 1772 on 20 August 2007, calling for military protection of merchant shipping from such acts, in line with relevant international law.

(HC Deb 22 November 2007 Vol 467 c1042W)

Part Sixteen: II.C. *Use of force—Legitimate Use of Force—Others*

16/11

Non-proliferation

In answer to a question about restricting the proliferation of nuclear weapons States, specifically Iran, an FCO Minister told the FAC:

We have a good record in this country-better than anyone in the world-for reducing our number of warheads and the technologies that we employ for delivering them, and so on. Iran signed up to that co-ordinated reduction, which we have all aimed at and which the non-proliferation treaty is about. We want the Iranians to abide by the rules that they signed up to-nothing more, nothing less. [Q.205]

And later he said:

We have certainly never threatened Iran with any form of military action and we have no intention of doing so. [Q.246]

(FAC, Global Security Iran, HC142 (2007))

16/12

"Rogue" States

The Secretary of State for Defence was asked what his definition of the term "rogue state" as used in his statement on Ballistic Missile Defence of 25 July 2007, Official Report, Vol.463 column 72WS is; whether the term differs from the term "countries of concern"; [and] when the decision was taken to begin using the term "rogue state" in relation to UK involvement in the US Ballistic Missile Defence programme. He wrote:

The terms "rogue state" and "country of concern" both refer to states that operate outside of or near to the boundaries defined by international agreements and accepted norms of behaviour.

(HC Deb 19 November 2007 Vol 467 c485W)

16/13

"Responsibility to Protect"/Humanitarian Intervention

(See also 1/1, 6/68–69 and 15/8)

An FCO Minister in a debate on "Liberal Intervention" said:

It is clear to all of us that within the broad-based concept of liberal intervention is a subset called humanitarian intervention, where... there is a tighter, clearer definition of rules, terms and rationales for intervention. It is around that subset that I express the Government's support for [such an] approach... It was that subset which the Prime Minister had in mind when he talked about hard-headed internationalism, and which the former Prime Minister, Mr Blair, had in mind when, in that important Chicago speech [in 1999], which has been mentioned today, he set out criteria.

There are, of course, long historical antecedents on intervention from Gladstone to Palmerston and Don Pacifico, as was suggested. However, this concept of humanitarian intervention is at its core moving towards a doctrine which is not just an optional one of conscience at the one end or national interest at the other motivating us to intervene, but instead involves a set of criteria in a globalised world where these are not interventions of choice but interventions of necessity, either because of the internal threat posed by mass crimes against humanity to the citizens of the state in which we are considering intervening, or because of an external threat that that state poses to its neighbours and to the world, as Afghanistan did when it harboured Al-Qaeda in 2001.

As regards the internal threat, a lot of work has been done to develop the doctrine of the responsibility to protect, and to intervene where a Government themselves have become the source of mass human rights abuses of their people, or at least are failing to protect their people against that. But that intervention, which is humanitarian in character, is very specifically motivated by the protection of people rather than by the claim of regime change. This is an enormously important distinction that has been brought out today. We are moving towards a world where we understand that there are circumstances involving external or internal threat to people which merit intervention. Mr Blair's conditions have been reviewed very well today. Therefore, I offer a slightly separate but overlapping set of criteria against which one might want to assess such interventions: first, that they are rule-based; secondly, that we are willing to sustain them over many decades; thirdly, that they are adequately burden-shared with others to allow us to sustain them; and, fourthly—this is what I think Mr Blair had in mind—that they are doable and achievable and that we will not end doing more harm than good and causing more loss of life.

I should say a word on each of those. First, obviously the most straightforward rule-based approach is where there is an unequivocal resolution of the UN Security Council to endorse an intervention, but we are all aware that sometimes life is not so simple. The case of Kosovo was raised. I believe that in a Written Answer of 1998 [a Minister] said that a limited use of force was justifiable in support of purposes laid down by the Security Council, but without the council's express authorisation, when that was the only means to avert an immediate and overwhelming humanitarian catastrophe. Such cases would in the nature of things be exceptional and would depend on an objective assessment of the factual circumstances at the time and on the terms of relevant decisions of the Security Council bearing on the situation in question. The argument can be made that Kosovo met those conditions. The intervention, which averted a dramatic loss of life, was followed by a Security Council resolution that endorsed the subsequent military and political arrangements that were put in place.

The second criterion is that any intervention must be sustained. A number of senior British officials have, over recent months, talked of periods of up to 30 years to establish a successful, democratic, freestanding, prosperous and effective state in Afghanistan. Sometimes those statements are little misunderstood as meaning an open-ended military commitment by the UK for that period—which is not what is meant by that and I devoutly hope is not what occurs. Nevertheless, a role in training and a deep role in development and reconstruction support, at a significant cost to the United Kingdom and others, is likely to be the consequence of our intervention in 2001. While I argue that it is utterly justified by the circumstances that led us to make that intervention, perhaps politicians need to be clearer with each other and with electorates about the fact that these commitments and interventions are rarely short, clean and quickly over in the way that is sometimes implied at the start.

Thirdly, any intervention must be burden-shared. That brings us back to the United Nations and to the importance of trying to do it within a broad and, if possible, universal international coalition. It means that the human and financial costs are shared, and that it is easier to sustain the political will because we are all in it together. Fourthly, any intervention must be doable. Sierra Leone was doable. Kosovo was doable. We are going to make sure that Afghanistan is doable. But we are always tempted by that bridge too far to take on operations of such complexity and scale that they do not enjoy the confidence of the military that we ask to take on the task, let alone of public opinion.

In that, I argue that, as has been said today, Darfur posed a situation where the prospect of direct intervention to end the terrible killings that were going on in that region was properly resisted by British and other western politicians. It ultimately was not doable. The prospect of putting a British expeditionary force, with perhaps American and other European allies, into a landlocked region of Sudan the size of France with no obvious logistics and support systems available, against the overt hostility and military opposition of the Government in Khartoum, was not a plausible route to pursue, despite the dreadful things that were happening in Darfur. Instead, we were required to go through the painstakingly difficult, preposterously extended and still not ultimately successful effort to build an international coalition and to secure the support of China for more effective sanctions and pressure on the Government. We continue with that. The level of killing, fortunately, has gone down to a much lower level. We cannot pretend that we are not tempted. How much more difficult this is than the easier pulling the trigger on an intervention might have seemed; but ultimately we will conclude that, for all its difficulties, this is the correct way to proceed.

That brings us to the great gap between soft and hard power. At the hard power end, when it is doable and meets that test, it has all the clarity and cleanness of going in, sorting out the situation and changing the situation on the ground in a dramatic way. Soft power is just that; often just too pliable, too soft, too putty-like in its ability to change the behaviours of Governments in their international relations and in how they behave towards their own people. We will hear increasingly from both sides of the House the discussion about how we develop something between soft and hard power. What range of instruments is available to us which, through international coalitions and having the will of the international community behind us, allows us to pressure Governments more effectively to moderate and change how they behave?

When we make an intervention because we believe that we have answered correctly the questions that we have posed ourselves—even there we move first from the pre-emptive phase where we want to apply soft power or harder forms of it to make an intervention unnecessary—we move to the next phase, which is peacekeeping. The need to strengthen UN and AU peacekeeping capabilities to give them the means to act effectively is an enormous challenge for all of us. Sierra Leone has been mentioned as a success. We should remember the circumstances under which that British intervention took place. The UN force there had not been sufficiently strongly armed to do the job. It had essentially been routed at the time the UK deployed. The UK was brilliantly able to restore order and allow a strengthened UN force to take over again. In East Timor, an Australian expeditionary force under a UN mandate initially established order before UN peacekeepers could take over. UN peacekeepers are lightly armed and are usually unable to undertake much offensive action.

Even when they do take over in the next phase, we are seeing the difficulties of mobilising a force for Darfur and the difficulties of even beginning to plan a force for Somalia. We have huge challenges of training, equipment, cost, mobility, and shaping the kinds of forces that these operations need. At one end, they need highly mobile forces that are able to undertake offensive activity if necessary and, at the other end, given that these wars are in countries' population centres, there is the need for police capabilities, normally of an armed Carabinieri kind, which can keep peace in refugee camps and can keep ethnic groups from each other's throats. Those are skills that often soldiers do not have but police forces do. As we work our way through the mechanics of intervention, we can see that there are a lot of capabilities and issues that we have not adequately addressed if we are to do this on an international basis.

Thinking about moving beyond the intervention, I will quote from the Prime Minister's speech earlier this week [speech at the Lord Mayor's Banquet, 12 November 2007. See above 1/1, Ed.], in which he argued that it is not just a matter of military intervention and peacekeeping but whether afterwards we have sufficient commitment to and vision of a recovery and reconstruction effort, and whether we have sorted out how the UN can be the fulcrum of an international effort to engage in that. He said:

"But where breakdowns occur, the UN—and regional bodies such as the EU and African Union— must now also agree to systematically combine traditional emergency aid and peacekeeping with stabilisation, reconstruction and development.

There are many steps the international community can assist with on the ladder from insecurity and conflict to stability and prosperity. So I propose that, in future, Security Council peacekeeping resolutions and UN envoys should make stabilisation, reconstruction and development an equal priority; that the international community should be ready to act with a standby civilian force including police and judiciary who can be deployed to rebuild civic societies; and that to repair damaged economies we sponsor local economic development agencies—in each area the international community able to offer a practical route map from failure to stability".

So we have our work cut out for us if we are to go beyond the doctrinal conditions for intervention to creating the means, institutions and processes to deliver on stabilisation and nation-building, where we need to do it.

Finally, I look forward to the debate next week on our Armed Forces. I suspect that we will discuss a situation where there is a great fear that too much is being asked of our Armed Forces and that our investment in them and the support we are giving them are insufficient to the growing challenges we are putting their way. I suspect we will hear some voices say that we should, therefore, retrench and pull back from the activities we ask our Armed Forces to undertake. I suspect that from some of those same voices we will hear a caution about nation-building, the long commitment that that takes and the implicit romanticism of the idea that you can stand up other people's nations for them.

Against that, as we grapple with a global society where other people's problems are our own problems, where terrorists can find sanctuary in Afghanistan, where illegal migration from failing and failed societies can cause huge difficulties, where failed societies harbour not just poverty but breakdowns of public health and other issues that impact on all of us, from these Benches you will hear the argument that humanitarian intervention with clear rules built around an internationalised effort to achieve the goals that we mutually set ourselves will become more, not less, important as we seek to build a world of justice and opportunity for all and, equally, a world where those of us living in rich societies believe that our Governments, our armed forces and the institutions we have created, such as the UN, work not just to help the world's poor and those living in weak countries, but to offer protection for a 21st-century global society where no problems can be kept out any more by old-fashioned borders alone.

(HC Deb 15 November 2007 Vol 696 c626–630)

Part Sixteen: III. *Use of force—disarmament and arms control*

16/14

Comprehensive Nuclear Test Ban treaty

An FCO Minister wrote:

China and the US signed the Comprehensive Nuclear Test Ban treaty (CTBT) in 1996 but have not yet ratified it. India has neither signed nor ratified the treaty

The United Kingdom strongly supports the earliest possible entry into force of the CTBT. We continue to take every appropriate opportunity, both bilaterally and through the EU, to urge all states who have not yet done so to sign and/or ratify the CTBT without delay and without condition. We most recently took action with India in April 2007, with the US in September 2007, and agreed EU action with China in November 2007. The UK also continues to support the outreach activities of Ambassador Ramaker, the Special Representative of the ratifiers of the treaty, staff of the Provisional Technical Secretariat and the Executive Secretary of the CTBT. In addition, the UK actively participates in the annual events held under the provisions of article XIV of the treaty to facilitate entry into force.

(HC Deb 27 November 2007 Vol 468 c348W)

16/15

Iran

On Thursday [22 February 2007, Ed.], Dr. Mohammed elBaradei, the director general of the International Atomic Energy Agency...issued another report on Iran's nuclear programme. The report makes it clear that Iran is continuing—and, indeed, expanding—its uranium enrichment activities in defiance of the Security Council. If mastered, those activities would give Iran the know-how to produce fissile material that could be used in nuclear weapons.

President Ahmadinejad claims that bullying western powers are trying to deny Iran its rights. He says that Iran's ambition is simply to generate electricity. For the sake of clarity, it should be put on record...that we have no wish to deny Iran, or any other country, its rights under the nuclear non-proliferation treaty, provided that it meets its obligations. We have not sought to stop Iran building a nuclear power station at Bushehr to generate electricity. We have even offered to help Iran develop a modern nuclear power industry, if it shows that its intentions are peaceful.... That was the offer made by the E3 plus three...the P5 plus Germany. It was one offer among many. Today, I have heard pleas for us to try to engage with Iran in whatever way we can. We have tried endlessly to engage with Iran, and we will continue to do so. The notion that somehow we are not part of an attempt to engage with Iran in rational discussions is probably the most serious slur of all....

Above all, Iran needs to establish that it is not developing nuclear weapons. Iran has to answer some basic questions. If its ambitions are solely peaceful, why did it hide its enrichment programme for so long? Why is the military involved in a supposedly civilian programme? Why does Iran not give a full account of its dealings with AQ Khan's network, which helped North Korea and Libya with their secret nuclear weapons programmes?

The International Atomic Energy Agency board of governors and the UN Security Council have set out the essential steps that Iran needs to take to build confidence, which include the full suspension of enrichment-related and reprocessing activities. The measures required by the Security Council would not affect Iran's pursuit of nuclear energy. Iran does not need to enrich uranium to generate electricity. However, the suspension would help to provide confidence that Iran is not seeking the know-how to make fissile material for weapons...

We remain committed to finding a negotiated solution and our approach has been to make it clear to Iran how it might benefit from meeting its obligations. At the same time, we have made it clear that it will face the risk of greater international isolation if it fails to take the steps required by the Security Council.

In June 2006, Javier Solana—the EU's high representative—presented proposals to Iran on behalf of the so-called E3 plus three—the UK, France, Germany, China, Russia and the US. Those proposals are far-reaching and offer a way forward that would provide confidence that Iran is not developing nuclear weapons. The proposals would also give Iran everything that it needs to develop a modern civil nuclear power industry, plus other political and economic benefits. Despite that, Iran has failed seriously to engage in discussions. The proposals are still on the table and, even at this stage, I hope that Iran will acknowledge the benefits of them and take the steps required by the Security Council so that talks can begin. The current sanctions will be frozen if Iran complies with the proposals and would be lifted in the event of a long-term solution. I welcome the efforts by Javier Solana in the past few weeks to urge the Iranians to take a positive path. I hope that everybody understands the significance of that and that real attempts have been made to engage with the Iranian Government. If the Iranians do not address international concerns, the Security Council will have no choice but to impose further measures.

[On] the effectiveness of financial sanctions, which are incredibly important...[w]e know that such sanctions worry the Iranians most. An indication of that is the 400,000 Iranians who live in Dubai, where they think that they can do their business. They are living there in preparation for what they consider the inevitable imposition of sanctions as a consequence of the intransigence of the Ahmadinejad regime. Iran is not North Korea. It has a great history...and it has a large merchant class—traders, scientists and engineers. The people of Iran want a prosperous country, but they know that that will not happen under the leadership of Ahmadinejad. The people of Iran understand that economic sanctions would be effective and therefore they are taking measures to ensure that, if necessary, they can carry on with their business outside Iran.

Another argument that I have heard from time to time is that sanctions will make Iran more rather than less determined to defy the international community. Security Council resolution 1737, which was adopted on 23 December, imposed a number of sanctions that focused on Iran's sensitive nuclear and missile activities. Those sanctions are a useful political toolkit to counter the activities of greatest concern, and they are also having a political effect. The Security Council's unanimous adoption of the measures has shown that President Ahmadinejad's claim that the international community is disunited and lacking in the will to act is a fantasy. Far from making the Iranian regime and people more united, the measures have...fuelled greater debate inside Iran about the costs of the course on which the regime has set the country.

(HC Deb 27 February 2007 Vol 457 c229–231WH)

16/16

The Foreign Secretary was asked about relations with Iran. He wrote:

The review of relations with Iran is continuing, but the principles underpinning our policy towards Iran have not changed.

Iran has every right to develop its own economy and society. We welcome dialogue and engagement with Iran as it does so, but it must also accept that it has responsibilities to the region and the wider international community. It cannot violate the terms of the Nuclear Non-Proliferation treaty nor undermine regional stability.

(HC Deb 23 July 2007 Vol 463 c707W)

16/17

The Prime Minister said:

It is diplomacy that we want to be the way forward, but we have to face up to the fact that in enriching uranium with no civil nuclear power process at work, the Iranian Government are in breach of the non-proliferation treaty and of all the commitments that they have made to the international community.

(HC Deb 17 December 2007 Vol 469 c606)

16/18

Libya

The Foreign Secretary was asked what support had been given to Libya in relation to its decommissioning of weapons of mass destruction as agreed between Libya, the UK and third parties.
An FCO Minister wrote:

Libya's renunciation of its weapons of mass destruction programmes in December 2003 was a historic decision. The UK has been working closely with Libya and the United States, in particular through the Trilateral Steering and Co-operation Committee, to support Libya through the de-commissioning process.

This has included helping Libya to dismantle its nuclear weapons programme, allowing other international partners to convert its heavy-water nuclear reactor at Tajura into a light-water reactor. This in turn has helped Libya to meet the international standards required for its nuclear reactor to be placed under an Additional Protocol Safeguards Agreement with the International Atomic Energy Agency.

A comprehensive programme of redirection and engagement with Libya's scientific community into more conventional areas is under way. This includes helping Libya to establish a regional nuclear medical centre, which would enable the production of nuclear isotopes for radiological medicine, and assistance and engagement with Libya's life-sciences community, particularly in the fields of human and animal infectious diseases, such as AIDS and Avian Influenza. Libya has also acceded to the Chemical Weapons Convention and will, under the verification regime of that convention, destroy its chemical weapons stockpile by the end of 2010.

The UK is also pursuing wider scientific co-operation with Libya, and signed with Libya a Memorandum of Understanding on Science Co-operation on 27 March.

(HC Deb 14 May 2007 Vol 460 c498W)

16/19

Non-proliferation—UK

The Minister of Defence was asked if he would list the 13 practical steps toward nuclear disarmament referred to on page 13 of the White Paper Cm6994, in respect of which of these steps progress has been made. The Minister wrote:

We continue to support and have made progress on the "13 Practical Steps", agreed at the Nuclear Non-Proliferation Treaty Review Conference in 2000, which are applicable to the UK. These are listed in 2000 Review Conference of the Parties to the Treaty on the Non-Proliferation of Nuclear Weapons, Final Document, a copy of which is available in the Library of the House. The 13 steps are:

1. The early entry into force of the Comprehensive Test Ban Treaty (CTBT).

2. A nuclear testing moratorium pending entry into force of the CTBT.

3. The immediate commencement of negotiations in the Conference on Disarmament on a non-discriminatory, multilateral, and effectively verifiable fissile material cut-off treaty. The negotiations should aim to be concluded within five years.

4. The establishment in the Conference on Disarmament of a subsidiary body to deal with nuclear disarmament.

5. The principle of irreversibility to apply to all nuclear disarmament and reduction measures.

6. An unequivocal undertaking by nuclear-weapon states to eliminate their nuclear arsenals.

7. The early entry into force and implementation of START II, the conclusion of START III, and the preservation and strengthening of the Anti-Ballistic Missile Treaty.

8. The completion and implementation of the Trilateral Initiative between the United States, the Russian Federation, and the International Atomic Energy Agency (IAEA).

9. Steps by all nuclear-weapon states toward disarmament including unilateral nuclear reductions; transparency on weapons capabilities and Article VI-related agreements; reductions in non-strategic nuclear weapons; measures to reduce the operational status of nuclear weapons; a diminishing role for nuclear weapons in security policies; the engagement of nuclear-weapon states as soon as appropriate in a process leading to complete disarmament.

10. The placement of excess military fissile materials under IAEA or other international verification and the disposition of such material for peaceful purposes.

11. Reaffirmation of the objective of general and complete disarmament under effective international control.

12. Regular state reporting in the NPT review process on the implementation of Article VI obligations.

13. The development of verification capabilities necessary to ensuring compliance with nuclear disarmament agreements.

We have signed and ratified the Comprehensive Nuclear Test Ban treaty, continued to observe the moratorium on nuclear weapons testing, continued to press for the negotiation in the Conference on Disarmament, without preconditions, of a fissile material cut-off treaty whilst maintaining our moratorium. We have demonstrated our commitment to the irreversibility of nuclear disarmament. We continue to reiterate our unequivocal undertaking to accomplish the total elimination of our nuclear arsenal leading to nuclear disarmament and have undertaken several unilateral steps towards nuclear disarmament including reductions in warhead numbers, increased transparency by publishing historical accounting records of our defence fissile material holdings and reduced the operational status of our deterrent.

All fissile material no longer required for defence purposes is under international safeguards. We continue to reaffirm our commitment to achieving the general and complete disarmament objectives of Article VI. We report regularly in a number of different formats and fora on the progress we have made under Article VI. We have pursued a widely welcomed programme to develop UK expertise in methods and technologies that could be used to verify nuclear disarmament. Finally, we produced a series of working papers culminating in a presentation at the 2005 NPT—non-proliferation treaty—Review Conference. The Atomic Weapons Establishment continues to undertake research in this area.

(HC Deb 8 January 2007 Vol 455 c97W)

16/20
An FCO Minister wrote:

Article VI [of the Nuclear Non-Proliferation Treaty, Ed.] requires Parties to the Treaty to "pursue negotiations in good faith on effective measures relating to the cessation of the nuclear arms race at an early date...".

While it is not possible to define precisely the timescale implied by the phrase "at an early date", we would note with regard to the cessation of the nuclear arms race that, since the end of the Cold War, the world's major nuclear arsenals have been significantly reduced.

The UK maintains only a minimum nuclear deterrent. Following the implementation of our December 2006 White Paper on the Future of the UK Nuclear Deterrent, we will have reduced our nuclear arsenal to 160 operationally available warheads: a reduction of 75 per cent. since the end of the Cold War. The largest nuclear stockpiles, those of the US and Russia, also continue to reduce significantly, for example under the terms of the Strategic Offensive Reductions Treaty.

(HC Deb 22 February 2007 Vol 457 c1896W)

16/21
An FCO Minister wrote:

Article VI [of the Nuclear Non-Proliferation treaty, Ed.] imposes an obligation on all states to pursue in good faith negotiations on effective measures for cessation of the nuclear arms race at an early date, on nuclear disarmament, and on a treaty on general and complete disarmament. The NPT review conference in 2000 agreed by consensus 13 practical steps towards implementation of article VI. The UK remains committed to those steps and is making progress on them.

We are disarming. The House heard in March of our decision to reduce the UK's stockpile of operationally available warheads by a further 20 per cent. to less than 160. Significant as that is, it is just the latest in a series of dramatic reductions in the UK's nuclear weapons. Since the end of the cold war, the explosive power of UK nuclear weapons will have been reduced by 75 per cent. UK nuclear weapons account for less than 1 per cent. of the global inventory.

We have withdrawn and dismantled our tactical marine and airborne nuclear capabilities and, consequently, have reduced our reliance on nuclear weapons to one system: submarine-based Trident. As hon. Members have said, we are the only nuclear-weapons state to have done that. We have also reduced the readiness of the remaining nuclear force. We now have only one boat on patrol at any one time and it carries no more than 48 warheads. We have not conducted a nuclear test explosion since 1991, and we have signed and ratified the comprehensive nuclear test ban treaty. We have ceased production of fissile material for nuclear weapons. We have also increased transparency of our fissile material holdings, and we have produced historical records of our defence holdings of both plutonium and highly enriched uranium.

Our decision to renew the Trident system did not reverse or undermine any of those positive disarmament steps. The UK is not upgrading the capabilities of the system, and there is no move to produce more useable weapons and no change in our nuclear posture or doctrine. The UK's nuclear weapons are not designed for military use during conflicts. They are a strategic deterrent that we would contemplate using only in extreme circumstances of self-defence. Over the past 50 years, the deterrent has been used only to deter acts of aggression against our vital interests, never to coerce others.

. . .

The simple truth is that the UK is implementing its obligations under the NPT, while those states that are developing illicit nuclear weapons programmes are not.

. . .

First, we will continue to call for significant further reductions in the major Russian and US nuclear arsenals. We hope that the existing bilateral treaties will be succeeded by further clear commitments to significantly lower warhead numbers, including tactical as well as strategic nuclear weapons. We are clear that when it becomes useful to include in any negotiations the 1 per cent. of the world's nuclear weapons that belong to the UK, we will willingly do so.

Secondly, we must press on with the comprehensive test ban treaty and with the fissile material cut-off treaty. Both treaties limit in real and practical ways the ability of states that are party to them to develop new weapons and expand their nuclear capabilities. The treaties play a very powerful symbolic role, too, signalling to the rest of the world that the race for more and bigger weapons is over, and that the direction from now on will be down not up. In other words, they are exactly the sort of

"effective measures relating to cessation of the nuclear arms race"

that article VI requires us to negotiate. That is why we are so keen for those countries that have not yet done so to ratify the comprehensive test ban treaty, and why we continue to work hard for the start of negotiations on a fissile material cut-off treaty in Geneva.

Thirdly, we should begin now to build deeper relationships on disarmament between nuclear weapon states. For the UK's part, we have made it clear that we are ready and willing to engage with other members of the P5 on transparency and confidence-building measures.

Finally, we have also announced a series of unilateral activities that the UK will undertake as a "disarmament laboratory". We will participate in a new project by the International Institute for Strategic Studies on the practical steps required for the elimination of nuclear weapons, and we will undertake further detailed work at the UK's Atomic Weapons Establishment on the nuts and bolts of nuclear disarmament. That work will examine three discrete issues related to the verification of disarmament, the authentication of warheads, chain of custody problems in sensitive nuclear weapons facilities, and monitored storage of dismantled nuclear weapons.

(HC Deb 24 July 2007 Vol 463 c197WH–201WH)

16/22

The Foreign Secretary was asked what were the reasons the UK voted against the resolution Towards a Nuclear-weapon-free World:

Accelerating the Implementation of Nuclear Disarmament Commitments at the UN First Committee on Disarmament and International Security on 17 October 2007 [GA res 62/25: 154–5–14, Ed.] An FCO Minister said:

The United Kingdom abstained on rather than voted against this resolution at the UN General Assembly's First Committee. The resolution contained a great deal that we would have been happy to endorse. However, we remained unable to support the text because it gave no recognition to the significant nuclear disarmament achievements of most nuclear weapons states since the end of the cold war. We made this clear in an oral explanation given at the time of the vote.

(HC Deb 27 November 2007 Vol 468 c348W)

16/23
The Minister of Defence wrote:

The nuclear non-proliferation treaty makes an invaluable and irreplaceable contribution to multilateral nuclear disarmament and is the cornerstone of UK policy in this area. All actions that the UK undertakes on nuclear disarmament are concomitant to our legal obligations under Article VI of that treaty, which are equally applicable to the other recognised nuclear weapons states. The White Paper on The Future of the UK's Nuclear Deterrent (Cm 6994), published in December 2006, set out the UK's record on nuclear disarmament and announced the reduction of operationally available warheads to fewer than 160, which has now been achieved.

The NPT has now achieved near universality and includes states which renounced their nuclear weapons programmes when they joined the NPT as non-nuclear weapons states. We continue to call upon those remaining states outside the NPT to accede as non-nuclear weapons states.

(HC Deb 3 December 2007 Vol 468 c843W)

16/24
An FCO Minister wrote:

The UK is fulfilling all its obligations under the treaty on the non-proliferation of nuclear weapons (NPT), including those on disarmament under article VI of the treaty. We continue to support the relevant disarmament measures contained in the Final Document from the NPT Review Conference in 2000, including the 13 practical steps towards disarmament, and we have a good record on meeting the priorities they set out. Not all the 13 steps are relevant to the UK, such as those relating to bilateral measures between the US and Russia. However, we have made progress on the majority of those that are. The 2006 White Paper on the future of the UK nuclear deterrent committed us to a further 20 per cent. reduction in our stockpile of operationally available warheads and the then Foreign Secretary announced on 25 June, at the Carnegie Institute, further work on the development of expertise in methods and techniques to verify the reduction and elimination of nuclear weapons. We continue to call for the entry into force of the comprehensive test ban treaty as soon as possible and, pending its entry into force, maintain a moratorium on nuclear weapons test explosions and any other nuclear explosions. The UK is also pressing for the immediate commencement of negotiations on a fissile material cut-off treaty, without pre-conditions, at the Conference on Disarmament in Geneva.

(HC Deb 3 December 2007 Vol 468 c1058W)

16/25

Non-Proliferation—India and Pakistan

The FCO wrote in a memorandum to the FAC about India and Pakistan:
WMD Proliferation

63. India and Pakistan have both ratified the Chemical Weapons Convention (CWC) and the Biological and Toxin Weapons Convention (BTWC). India is destroying its stockpile of chemical weapons under the CWC verification regime. The Pakistani Ambassador is President-designate of the five-yearly BTWC Review Conference scheduled for later this year.

64. Neither country has signed the Nuclear Non-Proliferation Treaty (NPT), nor the Comprehensive Nuclear Test Ban Treaty (CTBT). Both India and Pakistan are on the list of countries which must ratify the CTBT before entry into force. For many years their nuclear status was ambiguous: even when India conducted a partially successful nuclear test in 1974, it characterised it as a "peaceful nuclear explosion". But in 1998 India conducted a series of nuclear tests, closely followed by Pakistan, and both countries openly declared them-selves to have nuclear weapons programmes. However, since nuclear-weapon States (NWS) are defined by the NPT as "states which manufactured and exploded a nuclear weapon or other nuclear explosive device prior to 1 January 1967", India and Pakistan have to be regarded as non-nuclear-weapon States (NNWS) for NPT purposes.

65. In the aftermath of the 1998 tests the UN Security Council, on the basis of a P5 Joint Communiqué, unanimously adopted UNSCR 1172. This con-demned the tests and, among other things, called on India and Pakistan to stop their nuclear weapon development programmes and to become parties to the NPT.

66. The UK is a member of the Nuclear Suppliers Group (NSG). The NSG's present Guidelines on nuclear-use-only items prohibit their supply to any NNWS which does not have a safeguards agreement with the IAEA covering all its nuclear material (a so-called "comprehensive safeguards agreement", CSA). For the purposes of the NSG Guidelines India and Pakistan are not nuclear weapons states. There is no prospect of either accepting a CSA, which would require them to put under safeguards materials they intend for their nuclear weapons programmes. Consequently the Guidelines require that NSG members should not supply nuclear use only items to either country.

67. On 15 March 2002, the then Minister of State Ben Bradshaw set out HMG's policy towards nuclear exports to both countries. [HC Deb Vol. 381, c12298W-1299W, Ed] This policy was to deny all exports for items on the NSG Dual-Use List to India and Pakistan and to discourage contacts between UK nuclear scientists and their South Asian counterparts.

68. This policy was revised in August 2005 with respect to India. It now stipulates that we will continue to refuse:

• applications in respect of all NSG Trigger List items; and

• applications in respect of all items on the NSG Dual-Use List, when they are destined for unsafeguarded nuclear fuel cycle or nuclear explosive activities, or when there is an acceptable risk of diversion to such activities.

69. We will now, however, consider on a case-by-case basis licence applications for items on the NSG Dual-Use List destined for other activities. We will also consider all applications to export other items assessed as licensable, including those assessed as licensable under WMD end-use control, on a case-by-case basis, taking into account:

• the risk of use in, or diversion to, unsafeguarded nuclear fuel cycle or nuclear explosive activities, or acts of nuclear terrorism;

• the risk of possible onward transfer of these items to other States for proliferation purposes, including the recipient State's export control performance; and

• the potential utility of the items concerned for, and contribution that they would make to, such activities.

70. We will continue to consider applications for exports which will contribute to the physical protection or security of civil or military nuclear facilities or assets in India. Licences may be issued in exceptional cases, consistent with our obligations and commitments...

72. This announcement followed careful consideration of moves by India to improve its non-proliferation laws and their implementation. Following the revelation of the proliferation network run by AQ Khan, it was concluded that it was inappropriate at that point to make similar changes to our policy towards Pakistan.

(FCO Memorandum to FAC, Global Security: South Asia (2007) www.publications.parliament.uk/pa/cm200607/cmselect/cmfaff/uc55-iv/ucmem102.htm)

16/26

Non-proliferation—Israel

An FCO Minister wrote:

The Government have on a number of occasions called on Israel to accede to the nuclear non-proliferation treaty as a non-nuclear weapon state, and to conclude a full scope safeguards agreement and additional protocol with the International Atomic Energy Agency (IAEA). We continue to take appropriate opportunities to discuss all aspects of non-proliferation with representatives of the Israeli government.

Israel has a site-specific safeguards agreement with the IAEA, which gives the IAEA access to the Soreq nuclear site for monitoring purposes. Details of this can be found on the IAEA website at:www.iaea.ors.

(HC Deb 23 July 2007 Vol 463 c708W)

16/27

An FCO Minister wrote:

The Nuclear Non Proliferation Treaty (NPT) defines a nuclear weapon state as: any state which has manufactured and exploded a nuclear weapon or other nuclear explosive device prior to 1 January 1967. This definition is exclusive to the following states party: the People's Republic of China; the French Republic; the Russian Federation; the United Kingdom of Great Britain and Northern Ireland; and the United States of America.

As the State of Israel has never signed the NPT, it is classed as neither a Nuclear Weapon State, nor a Non-Nuclear Weapon State.

(HC Deb 26 July 2007 Vol 463 c1472W)

16/28

Security Council Resolution 1540

The Foreign Secretary was asked what steps the Government had taken to meet their obligations under Article 2 of UN Security Council Resolution 1540 (2004) on the prevention of non-state actors from financing activities to support the development of nuclear, chemical or biological weapons and their means of delivery. An FCO Minister wrote:

In its national reports to the 1540 Committee, the UK set out the framework of domestic legislation that relates to Article 2 of UN Security Council Resolution (UNSCR) 1540 (2004)... The UK has one of the best records in the world on implementation of UNSCR 1540 and we work constantly to ensure that all aspects of the resolution are fully implemented, including on proliferation finance. In addition, the standards agreed within the Financial Action Task Force (FATF), of which the UK is a member, help to promote the international legal framework necessary to combat illicit finance of all kinds. In February, G7 Ministers called specifically for the FATF to examine the risks involved in weapons of mass destruction proliferation finance.

[For the UK Reports to the Security Council, see www.un.org/Docs/ journal/asp/ws.asp?m=S/AC.44/2004/(02)/3]

(HC Deb 21 May 2007 Vol 460 c1094W)

Part Seventeen: The Law of Armed Conflict and International Humanitarian Law

Part Seventeen: I.B.2. *The Law of Armed Conflict and International Humanitarian Law—International armed conflict—The Law of International Armed Conflict—The commencement of international armed conflict and its effects (for example diplomatic and consular relations, treaties, private property, nationality, trading with the enemy, locus standi personae in judicio)*

17/1

The FCO Legal Adviser made the following statement to the UNGA Sixth Committee on 30 October 2007:

First, I turn to chapter VII of the Report [of the ILC, Fifty-ninth session, A/62/10, Ed.] on the effects of armed conflicts on treaties...

The United Kingdom has made comments on the draft articles at previous meetings of the Sixth Committee. We welcome the decision of the Special Rapporteur to restrict the present study to the effects of armed conflicts on treaties between States. As we have previously stated, expanding the scope of the draft articles to include treaties entered into by international organisations would not take into account the differences between States and international organisations, and also the widely disparate functions of international organisations.

As for the definition of 'armed conflict', the United Kingdom has previously noted that the question of whether to include non-international armed conflicts within the scope of the study is difficult. In considering this issue, it is worth recalling two points. First, the Special Rapporteur noted in his Second Report that it would be inappropriate to seek to provide a definition of 'armed conflict' which would be applicable for all areas of public international law. We agree with this observation, and note that the definition, as presently drafted, is expressed to be 'for the purposes of the present draft articles', a point which was highlighted by the Special Rapporteur in his Third Report. We consider this point to be particularly important. Second, we would also repeat the Special Rapporteur's observation that article 73 of the Vienna Convention on the Law of Treaties, which is the starting point for the present study, refers to the 'outbreak of hostilities between States'.

The United Kingdom has previously stated that it is in favour of including the criterion of 'intention' in draft article 4, and we confirm our view that it is important to include this provision. Any practical difficulties in ascertaining the intention of States can usually be overcome. In any case, this is a task in which both domestic and international tribunals are regularly required to engage.

The United Kingdom does have some outstanding concerns about the indicative list of categories of treaties in draft article 7. We note the Special Rapporteur's explanation in his Third Report that the list simply reflects a series of factors that might lead to the conclusion that a treaty, or some of its provisions, might continue in the event of armed conflict. However, we consider that clarification is needed in the draft articles of the role of international humanitarian law in forming the *lex specialis*. We note that the Special Rapporteur has proposed to revisit the relevant provision, being draft article 6bis, and we look forward to seeing a revised text in due course.

(Text supplied by FCO)

Part Seventeen: I.B.3. *The Law of Armed Conflict and International Humanitarian Law—International armed conflict—The Law of International Armed Conflict—Land warfare*

17/2

In reply to a question about the rules of engagement in response to mortar and rocket attacks on British forces in Afghanistan, the Minister of Defence wrote:

Rules of Engagement detail the levels of permissiveness for the application of force in all environments across a wide range of activities in which our forces may be employed. Profiles do not constrain the inherent right of self-defence, and neither do they provide detailed tactical instructions to commanders.

Our Rules of Engagement entitle our forces to take reasonable and necessary action in self-defence in response to mortar and rocket attack. The commander in situ would use his military judgment to determine what would be the most appropriate means to counter the attack at the time.

In order to safeguard the security of our armed forces on operations, it is MOD policy not to comment on specific operational profiles or the rules therein.

(HC Deb 1 February 2007 Vol 456 c501W)

17/3

The Minister of Defence was asked how many (a) 16-, (b) 17- and (c) 18-year-olds have served in Iraq, broken down by gender. A Defence Minister wrote:

Provisional estimates collated from manual records show that no 16-year-old and fifteen 17-year-old personnel have been deployed to Iraq since the "Optional Protocol to the Convention on the rights of the child on the involvement of children in armed conflict" was ratified on 24 June 2003. None have been deployed since July 2005.

Fewer than five of the 17-year-old personnel deployed were female.

The vast majority of those that were deployed were within one week of their 18th birthdays or were removed from theatre within a week of their arrival.

Fewer than five 17-year-olds were deployed for a period of greater than three weeks.

New administrative guidelines and procedures have been introduced by each of the Services following the ratification of the Optional Protocol to ensure that under 18-year-old personnel are not deployed to areas where hostilities are taking place unless there is a clear operational requirement for them to do so. Unfortunately, these processes are not infallible and the pressures on units prior to deployment have meant that there have been a small number of instances where soldiers have been inadvertently deployed to Iraq before their 18th birthday, as described above.

Figures on those aged 18 could be provided only at disproportionate cost.

All numbers are rounded to the nearest five.

(HC Deb 1 February 2007 Vol 456 c508W)

Part Seventeen: I.B.6. *The Law of Armed Conflict and International Humanitarian Law—International armed conflict—The Law of International Armed Conflict—Distinction between combatants and non-combatants*

17/4
The Solicitor-General was asked what steps had been taken by the Law Officers' Department to ensure the UK's compliance with United Nations Security Council Resolution 1738, on the protection of journalists in armed conflict. He wrote:

The United Kingdom takes seriously its obligations, under international humanitarian law, to protect journalists and other civilians in situations of armed conflict and already has in place the necessary measures to ensure compliance. The Law Officers' departments have not been required to take additional steps following the adoption of United Nations Security Council Resolution 1738 (2006).

(HC Deb 25 June 2007 Vol 462 c4W)

Part Seventeen: I.B.7. *The Law of Armed Conflict and International Humanitarian Law—International armed conflict—The Law of International Armed Conflict—International humanitarian law*

17/5
A Defence Minister wrote:

The Joint Warfare Publication 1–10 was replaced by the Joint Doctrine Publication 1–10 in May 2006 Prisoners of War, Internees and Detainees. Joint Doctrine Publication 1–10 has been separated into three sections—Prisoners of War, Internees and Detainees—reflecting the requirement for differing approaches to the range of categorisation of those captured, interned or detained by UK Armed Forces deployed on operations abroad.

This publication recognises the change from the post-Cold War environment to the UK's more expeditionary approach and peace enforcement operations. It provides clarification on current detention procedures giving guidance on, among other things, the standards of treatment and facilities for prisoners of war, internees and detainees, and the training of UK Armed Forces on the handling of detained personnel.

Joint Doctrine Publication 1–10 remains in line with domestic UK law, international law and the laws of armed conflict, as does our operational practice towards detainees in Afghanistan which reflects Joint Doctrine Publication 1–10 [www.mod.uk/NRrdonlyres/749088E6-E50A-470E-938D-459A74481E88/)/jsp381.pdf, Ed.].

(HL Deb 9 January 2007 Vol 688 cWA58)

17/6

The Foreign Secretary was asked what steps the Government had taken (a) to comply with Article 1, and (b) to prosecute breaches under Article 147, of the Fourth Geneva Convention. An FCO Minister wrote:

The United Kingdom has signed and ratified the Fourth Geneva Convention and complies with its provisions. Every appropriate opportunity is taken in our bilateral relations and through appropriate international bodies to promote respect for the Convention and its articles.

The UK has enacted legislation (Geneva Conventions Act 1957, as amended) to enable prosecutions in respect of the grave breaches set out in article 147 in the UK. Alleged breaches of the convention relevant to the UK that are brought to our attention are investigated by the appropriate authorities. Prosecution decisions are made in accordance with criminal law principles by the appropriate prosecuting authority.

(HC Deb 25 June 2007 Vol 462 c200W)

17/7

An FCO Minister wrote:

The impact of Israel's military operations remains a real concern. Israel has the right to defend itself against terrorism but it must respect international humanitarian law. We regularly raise our concerns about this with the Israeli Government.

(HC 3 July 2007 Vol 462 c998W)

17/8

An FCO Minister wrote:

International forces, including UK forces, seek at all times to avoid loss of civilian life. The targeting process, weapons selection, doctrine, training and rules of engagement are all in line with international humanitarian and human rights law and the law of armed conflict.

The Afghan security forces operate alongside two international forces, the International Security Assistance Force and Operation Enduring Freedom. Co-ordination between these groups is therefore key and has been the subject of further work over recent weeks. We are satisfied that there are sensible, pragmatic command and control relationships between the forces and that these are reassessed regularly.

All reports of civilian casualties are investigated promptly and thoroughly, in co-ordination with the Afghan authorities. Where the UN Assistance Mission in Afghanistan chooses to investigate an incident, it is entirely free to do so.

(HL 5 July 2007 Vol 693 cWA183)

Part Seventeen: I.B.8. *The Law of Armed Conflict and International Humanitarian Law—International armed conflict—The Law of International Armed Conflict—Belligerent occupation*

17/9
In its reply to the FAC Report, Global Security: the Middle East, in October 2007, the Government wrote:

...

37. Although there is no permanent physical Israeli presence in Gaza, Israel maintains a significant degree of control, including control of Gaza's borders, airspace and territorial waters. We consider that Israel's obligations under the Fourth Geneva Convention 1949 continue to apply in respect of Gaza.

47...We have also repeatedly urged Israel to fulfil its Roadmap commitments to remove settlements established since March 2001, and to cease settlement expansion.

48. Since the signing of the Oslo Accords in 1993, the settler population in the West Bank has more than doubled, with profound economic implications. Each settlement requires a range of security measures to protect its inhabitants—one reason why the separation barrier is twice the length of the Green Line. The current barrier route around the major settlement blocks encloses between 8–10 per cent of the West Bank. In addition, the fences, checkpoints, road systems and permit regime associated with the settlements and outposts east of the barrier also have a severe impact on Palestinian freedom of movement, and thereby on the Palestinian economy.

49. We fully support the right of Israel to defend itself. The Government of Israel judges that checkpoints and the barrier are essential to provide that security. We are not in a position to judge the security implications of removing individual checkpoints, but have repeatedly urged Israel to reduce its restrictions on Palestinian movement as far as it can, consistent with its own security. We

believe there are some measures Israel could take without jeopardising its security. We have always accepted Israel's right to build the barrier, but maintain that it should move those parts of the barrier built on Palestinian land to the Israeli side of the Green Line. We have made this clear to the Government of Israel.

(Eighth Report of the Foreign Affairs Committee Session 2006–7 Global Security: The Middle East Response of the Secretary of State for Foreign and Commonwealth Affairs Cm 7212 (2007))

17/10

The Government were asked what specific measures they were taking to ensure that the European Union is implementing its guidelines (Heading III) on (a) compliance with international humanitarian law, and (b) the protection of human rights defenders, in respect of the occupied Palestinian territories. An FCO Minister wrote:

The EU has agreed guidelines in five areas: children and armed conflict, action against torture, death penalty, human rights dialogues and human rights defenders. There are no separate EU guidelines on compliance with international humanitarian law. However, we continue to stress to the Government of Israel and the Palestinian Authority the need to ensure that their actions comply with international law.

We are a strong supporter of the EU human rights defender guidelines, which were last reviewed earlier this year. At the time of the review, the Foreign and Commonwealth Office sent out instructions to all posts, including our Consulate-General in Jerusalem, inviting contributions to this evaluation. Following the conclusion of the review on 7 July 2006, we circulated the evaluation to all posts with instructions to support local EU presidency action as appropriate. Under the Austrian and Finnish presidencies in 2006, the EU has run a campaign on women human rights defenders. This builds on a freedom of expression campaign launched under the UK presidency in 2005.

We continue to take action to tackle human rights issues in Israel and the Occupied Territories. This action includes working with non-governmental organisations and raising our concerns bilaterally. We remain concerned at the restrictions of movement of Palestinians in and between Gaza and the West Bank. We continue to call on both sides to implement the 2005 Agreement on Movement and Access in full. We also call on Israel to route the barrier on or behind the Green Line and freeze all settlement activity and dismantle all outposts built since 2001. The routing of the barrier and the construction of settlements on occupied land is illegal. We continue to raise these issues with the Israeli Government.

(HL Deb 8 January 2007 Vol 688 cWA29)

17/11

The Government was asked whether they would make representations to the Government of Israel on issues concerning permanent family reunification, both within the recognised frontiers of Israel and within the West Bank and Gaza. An FCO Minister wrote:

We are concerned at the effect the Citizenship and. Entry into Israel Law (Temporary Order) 2003. The law prevents the granting of residency status in Israel to most Palestinians from the Occupied Territories. The emergency order on which the current law is based expired on 16 January, but it has been extended for a further two months. In January 2007, an Israeli non-governmental organisation filed a petition to the Israeli High Court against the order. We also understand that the Government of Israel are considering new legislation dealing with this issue. We will continue to monitor events.

We are also concerned at Israeli practices which restrict entry into Israel for Palestinians who live outside Israel and the Occupied Territories and are married to Israeli citizens. We will raise our concerns with the Israeli Government.

(HL Deb 31 January 2007 Vol 689 c53WA)

17/12
An FCO Minister wrote:

We are concerned about the announcement of new housing units in Ma'aleh Adumim. We share the EU's concern noted in the 22 January General Affairs and External Relations Council about Israel's settlement activities in and around east Jerusalem as well as in the Jordan Valley and support the call for Israel to desist from any action that threatens the viability of an agreed two-state solution. The EU will not recognise any changes to the pre-1967 borders other than those agreed by both parties. Settlements are illegal under international law and settlement construction is an obstacle to peace. The road map is clear that Israel should freeze all settlement construction including the "natural growth" of existing settlements and dismantle all outposts built since 2001 ... the Foreign Secretary raised our concerns about settlement activity in the West Bank with Israeli Foreign Minister Livni on 2 January. Our ambassador in Tel Aviv raised our concerns about Ma'aleh Adumim with the Israeli Government on 17 January.

(HL Deb 31 January 2007 Vol 689 c53WA)

17/13
An FCO Minister wrote:

We are concerned at reports that the Israeli government are considering changing the route of the barrier to incorporate two west bank settlements. We fully recognise Israel's right to self-defence, but the barrier's route should be on or behind the green line and not on occupied territory. Construction of the barrier on Palestinian land is illegal. The route is particularly damaging around east Jerusalem, as it risks cutting the city off from the west bank and dividing the west bank in two. Our ambassador in Tel Aviv raised this with Israeli Foreign

Minister Livni's office and the Israeli Ministry of Foreign Affairs legal advisers on 31 January 2007.

(HC Deb 5 February 2007 Vol 456 c672W)

17/14

The Foreign Secretary was asked what steps her Department had taken to ensure that no products emanating from settlements built in occupied territory in breach of the Fourth Geneva Convention are purchased by her Department and its overseas missions. An FCO Minister wrote:

The Foreign and Commonwealth Office (FCO) does not currently have a policy precluding the purchase of goods emanating from the settlements in the Occupied Palestinian Territories. The FCO's policy on the procurement of goods is based on value for money, having due regard to propriety and regularity and ensuring full compliance with the EU consolidated Public Procurement directive, implemented in the UK by the Public Contracts Regulations 2006, where applicable. However, in practice the FCO in London and FCO Posts do not purchase goods from the settlements...

There is no provision in either the EU consolidated Public Procurement directive or the UK Public Contracts Regulations 2006 (SI 2006 No. 5) to instruct the Foreign and Commonwealth Office's overseas missions in this way and I do not therefore intend to do so.

(HC Deb 2 May 2007 Vol 459 c1715W)

17/15

The Foreign Secretary was asked what the UK position was on the legality of (a) marketing in the UK and (b) purchasing from the UK property for sale in settlements in the Occupied Palestinian Territories which are deemed illegal according to international law; and what advice the Government give to British companies and organisations on the legal status of such transactions. An FCO Minister wrote:

We regard all settlements in the Occupied Palestinian Territories as illegal under international law and have repeatedly raised our concerns about settlement activity with the Israeli Government. The Government do not advise or encourage companies and organisations to market or sell property in the settlements, however it is not unlawful to do so under UK law.

(HC Deb 16 April 2007 Vol 459 c 39W)

17/16

An FCO Minister wrote:

Settlements are illegal under international law and settlement activity is an obstacle to peace. The Roadmap is clear that Israel should freeze all settlement construction including the "natural growth" of existing settlements, and dismantle all outposts built since 2001. The EU will not recognise any changes to the pre-1967 borders other than those agreed by both parties. We support this...

Punitive house demolitions—the demolition of the homes of the families of suicide bombers and militants—were suspended on 17 February 2005. However, due to Israeli restrictions on the granting of housing permits to Palestinians in Jerusalem, Palestinians often build houses without obtaining permits. These homes are then demolished and heavy fines imposed. We are concerned about Israel's policy of house demolitions, especially in East Jerusalem, which leaves hundreds of Palestinians homeless each year and threatens to change the nature of some areas of the city. We have repeatedly raised our concerns with the Israeli authorities.

(HC Deb 25 June 2007 Vol 462 c210W)

17/18
The Foreign Secretary was asked whether she had held discussions with the government of Israel... on the (a) labelling and (b) claiming of trade preferences on goods produced in Israeli settlements in the Occupied Palestinian Territories and imported to the EU. An FCO Minister wrote:

Under a technical arrangement adopted by the EU-Israel Customs Co-operation Committee on 12 December 2004 all imports from Israeli Settlements in the Occupied Palestinian Territories and claiming Israeli preferential origin have been required since 1 February 2005 to indicate the place of production and accompanying zip code. The full rate of customs duty is payable on any consignment which is indicated as originating in a settlement.

(HC Deb 25 June 2007 Vol 462 c210W)

17/19
An FCO Minister wrote:

The Government are in regular contact with the US, Palestinian and Israeli Governments on a number of issues concerned with advancing the Middle East peace process, including settlements. Our embassy in Tel Aviv raised the issue of settlements and outposts with the Israeli Ministry of Defence on 29 November. Our consulate-general in Jerusalem discussed the issue of settlements with the Palestinians on 4 December and our embassy in Washington also discussed this issue with the US State Department on 5 December.

Settlements are illegal under international law and settlement construction is an obstacle to peace. The road map is clear that Israel should freeze all settlement construction including the "natural growth" of existing settlements, and dismantle all outposts built since 2001. The EU will not recognise any changes to the pre-1967 borders other than those agreed by both parties. The Government support this.

(HL Deb 12 December 2007 Vol 697 cWA69)

Part Seventeen: I.B.9. *The Law of Armed Conflict and International Humanitarian Law—International armed conflict—The Law of International Armed Conflict—Conventional, nuclear, bacteriological and chemical weapons*

17/20

Biological Weapons

An FCO Minister wrote:

Members will wish to be aware of the outcome of the Sixth Review Conference of States Parties to the Biological and Toxin Weapons Convention held in Geneva from 20 November to 8 December 2006.

On 8 December, States Party agreed a three-part Final Document which included a Final Declaration where States declared their continued commitment to the Convention and their determination to exclude completely the possibility of the use of biological weapons. States Party reviewed the operation of the Convention and expressed their views on all its Articles in some detail. Importantly States Party agreed that the prohibitions in Article I, which defines the scope of the Convention, apply to all scientific and technological developments in the life sciences and in other fields of science relevant to the Convention that have no peaceful purpose.

The Conference also:

endorsed the work done between 2003 and 2005 by States Party on five specific topics relevant to the Convention;

established a three-person implementation support unit based in the UN in Geneva, to perform specific tasks in support of States Party and to serve as a focal point...;

agreed to a concerted effort by States Party to persuade other States to join the Convention;

agreed a further inter-sessional work programme for 2007–2010 to discuss:

in 2007

(a) ways and means to enhance national implementation, including enforcement of national legislation, strengthening of national institutions and co-ordination among national law enforcement institutions; and

(b) regional and sub-regional co-operation on BTWC implementation;

in 2008

(c) national, regional and international measures to improve bio-safety and bio-security, including laboratory safety and security of pathogens and toxins; and

(d) oversight, education, awareness-raising, and adoption and/or development of codes of conduct with the aim to prevent misuse in the context of advances in bio-science and technology research with the potential of use for purposes prohibited by the Convention;

in 2009

(e) with a view to enhancing international co-operation, assistance and exchange in biological sciences and technology for peaceful purposes, promoting capacity in building in the fields of disease surveillance, detection, diagnosis and containment of infectious diseases: (1) for States Parties in need of assistance, identifying requirements and requests for capacity enhancement, and (2) from States Parties in a position to do so, and international organisations, opportunities for providing assistance related to these fields;

and in 2010

(f) provision of assistance and co-ordination with relevant organisations upon request by any State Party in the case of alleged use of biological or toxin weapons, including improving national capabilities for disease surveillance, detection, and diagnosis and public health systems.

The above agreement provides a good basis for future collaboration and co-ordination between States Party to the Convention. The United Kingdom worked closely with European Union partners and with a wide range of other States in the preparatory phase and at the Conference itself to build agreement on the middle ground, which ultimately provided the basis for the final consensus.

(HC Deb 8 January 2007 Vol 455 c3WS–4WS)

17/21
A Defence Minister wrote:

The Chemical, Biological, Radiological and Nuclear (CBRN) defence research being conducted by the Defence Science and Technology Laboratory (DSTL) at Porton Down is directed towards helping the UK achieve its policy aim of maintaining political and military freedom of action, despite the presence, threat or use of CBRN weapons.

The current nature of the biological research is summarised under the headings of Hazard Assessment, Detection and Diagnostics, and Medical Countermeasures in the UK annual Confidence Building Measures returns to the United Nations. These returns are submitted by the UK in accordance with the Biological and Toxin Weapons Convention.

The returns for 2003 to 2005 can be found on the Foreign and Commonwealth Office website at:

www.fco.gov.uk/servlet/Front?pagename=OpenMarket/Xcelerate/ShowPage&c =Page&cid=1065432161527.

The return for 2006 is currently being collated for submission to the UN in April and will be available on the website in due course.

Future directions in CBRN research are set out in the recently published Defence Technology Strategy which can be found on the Ministry of Defence website at:

www.mod.uk/DefenceInternet/DefenceNews/DefencePolicyAndBusiness/ LordDraysonLaunchesDefenceTechnologyStrategy.htm

(HC Deb 1 February 2007 Vol 456 c510W)

17/22

The Government were asked whether Article III of the Biological and Toxin Weapons Convention would prohibit the direct or indirect transfer by states of agents specified in Article I of the Convention to non-state actors. An FCO Minister wrote:

At the Sixth Biological and Toxin Weapons Review Conference, state parties reaffirmed that Article III of the convention is sufficiently comprehensive to cover any recipient whatever at international, national or sub-national levels and called on states parties to ensure that direct and indirect transfers of materials relevant to the Convention are authorised only when the intended use is for purposes not prohibited under the Convention.

[Article I contains the duty not "to develop, produce, stockpile or otherwise acquire or retain" biological agents or weapons based on them; Article III provides a duty not to transfer the prohibited items to "any recipient whatsoever", Ed.]

(HL Deb 8 February 2007 Vol 689 cWA151)

17/23

Cluster Bombs

The Foreign Secretary was asked if she would make a statement on the outcome of the Oslo conference on cluster munitions; and how her Department plans to implement the agreement reached at the conference. She wrote:

The UK is pleased to be able to support the Oslo Declaration, committing us to work towards a new legally binding instrument on cluster munitions that cause unacceptable harm to civilians. The UK's interpretive statement at Oslo explains how this fits with our national policy available on the Foreign and Commonwealth Office website at:

www.britishembassy.gov.uk/servlet/Front?pagename=OpenMarket/Xcelerate/ ShowPage&cid=1163677198241.

We will pursue the aim agreed at Oslo with all the users and producers through the convention on certain conventional weapons and other relevant fora.

Asked further what discussions she has had with her (a) US, (b) Russian, (c) Chinese and (d) Israeli counterparts on the outcome of the Oslo conference on cluster munitions; what the outcome was of those discussions, She wrote:

I have not discussed cluster munitions with my US, Russian, Chinese or Israeli counterparts since the Oslo conference (22–23 February). The UK delegation to the conference on disarmament in Geneva has spoken to the aforementioned countries on the outcome of the Oslo conference and on addressing the issue of cluster munitions within the convention on certain conventional weapons. We continue to remain in close contact with these and other interested Governments on this important issue.

(HC Deb 7 March 2007 Vol 457 c1997W)

17/24
In its Report on Global Security: the Middle East, the FAC had written:

We conclude that the failure rate of 'dumb' cluster bombs could be as high as 30%, much higher than the Government's estimate of 6%. We further conclude that the failure rate of 'smart' cluster bombs could be as high as 10%, again significantly higher than the Government's estimate of 2.3%. We recommend that, in its response to this Report, the Government state whether it is prepared to accept that the failure rate of 'smart' cluster munitions could be as high as 10%, and if so, how it justifies continuing to permit UK armed forces to hold such munitions (Paragraph 106).

In its reply, the Government wrote:

55. The Government's policy on the use of cluster munitions balances military necessity with humanitarian concerns. Following an MoD assessment, the Defence Secretary announced on 20 March this year the immediate withdrawal of the UK's "dumb" cluster munitions, the RBL 755 and the MLRS M26 (these being systems that have neither an autonomous guidance capability, nor a self-destruct mechanism). The UK variant of the M85 submunition, which we retained, has a self-destruct mechanism and therefore does not fall into this category. It has undergone rigorous and comprehensive testing prior to entering service and is subject to regular in-service trials. In September 2005 an in-service safety and performance test carried out at the Hjerkinn Range, Dombass, Norway, concluded the failure rate was 2.3%. As such we do not accept that failure rates of the UK variant of the M85 could be as high as 10%.

56. The Government is concerned by reports of high failure rates of the Israeli M85 sub-munition in Lebanon, but notes that without Israeli firing data the quoted failure rates cannot have a status greater than an estimate. We are awaiting the results of Israel's internal investigation into their system's performance. We continue to call on Israel to make available to the UN full details of cluster munitions strikes from last summer's conflict between Israel and Hizbollah.

57. We share the Committee's concerns about certain types of cluster munitions. That is why the UK has withdrawn its "dumb" cluster munitions and is committed to securing a legally binding international instrument to address the

humanitarian impact of such cluster munitions. The UK is playing a leading role in multilateral discussions with this aim.

The Committee had written:

We accept that Israel has an inalienable right to defend itself from terrorist threats. However, we conclude that elements of Israel's military action in Lebanon were indiscriminate and disproportionate. In particular, the numerous attacks on UN observers and the dropping of over three and a half million cluster bombs (90% of the total) in the 16 hours after the Security Council passed Resolution 1701 were not acceptable. We recommend that, in its response to this Report, the Government explicitly state whether it believes that, in the light of information now available, Israel's use of cluster bombs was proportionate. (Paragraph 108)

The Government replied:

58. As the UK made clear during the conflict last year, we were deeply concerned by the deaths of civilians and damage to infrastructure in both Lebanon and Israel. We consistently urged Israel to act proportionately, to conform to international law, and to do more to avoid civilian death and suffering.

59. The Government recognises the UN statistics that the Committee highlights in its report. It is concerned by the estimate that one million cluster bombs remained unexploded; that 26% of Lebanon's cultivable land had been contaminated; and that 90% of the cluster bombs dropped on Lebanon occurred in the last 72 hours of the conflict. The Government is concerned by the findings of both the UN Commission of Inquiry's investigation into the conflict in Lebanon and Human Rights Watch's September 2007 report, both of which conclude that Israel's use of force was disproportionate and failed to adequately distinguish between military and civilian targets. However, it should be noted that the UN Commission of Inquiry itself recognises in its Report (para. 20) that the Report cannot constitute a full and final accounting of all alleged violations. We also note the US State Department's announcement in January 2007 that "there were likely violations" by Israel with regard to a "use agreement" between the US and Israel on their supply of cluster munitions.

60. We recognise that Israel faced a genuine threat throughout the conflict, and suffered a significant number of civilian casualties as a result of Hizbollah's rocket campaign. However, the large scale use of cluster munitions in the final 72 hours of the conflict following the adoption of UNSCR 1701 caused significant loss of life and injury, and economic hardship, for the population of south Lebanon. We have expressed these concerns to the Israeli Government and will continue to urge the Israelis to provide all relevant information to UN on the location of their cluster munition strikes in south Lebanon.

(Eighth Report of the Foreign Affairs Committee Session 2006–7 Global Security: The Middle East Response of the Secretary of State for Foreign and Commonwealth Affairs Cm 7212 (2007))

17/25
A Defence Minister wrote:

The UK does not carry out post-conflict humanitarian impact assessments after munitions, including cluster munitions, have been used; there is no requirement to do so under International Humanitarian Law. The priority following operations is to clear unexploded ordnance in order to provide freedom of movement for our forces and conduct the highest priority clearance operations that threaten civilian lives.

We recognise that Explosive Remnants of War, caused by unexploded ordnance, including cluster munitions, are a humanitarian problem. That is why the UK has played an active role at the UN in creating a new legally binding protocol containing a number of new legally binding provisions that will provide significant humanitarian benefit to those civilians in areas affected by Explosive Remnants of War. We are urging all states to sign and ratify this protocol as soon as possible. We are in the process of ratifying this and the MOD is in the process of implementing its provisions. The universal implementation of this will drive a significant reduction in the post-conflict effects of Explosive Remnants of War.

We are still waiting for the outcome of the Israeli inquiry into their use of cluster munitions in Lebanon. To date the UK has contributed £2.7 million towards the clearance of unexploded munitions, including cluster munitions, in Lebanon. This is specifically intended to minimise the humanitarian impact of unexploded submunitions and other Explosive Remnants of War.

(HC Deb 25 July 2007 Vol 643 c1078W)

17/26

An FCO Minister wrote:

There is no internationally agreed definition of a cluster munition, or of a distinction between "dumb" and "smart". A definition will be the key element to negotiate in any future instrument, both in the Oslo Process and in the framework of the Convention on Certain Conventional Weapons. We believe the focus should be on banning those cluster munitions that pose the greatest risk to civilians: those without target discrimination or an in-built self-destruct/self-deactivation mechanism.

(HC Deb 4 December 2007 Vol 648 c1131W)

17/27

Non-lethal Weapons

The Minister of Defence was asked (1) in what circumstances military personnel use non-lethal weapons on operations; and (2) what types of non-lethal weapons may be used in current military operations. He wrote:

UK military personnel use non-lethal weapons primarily on public order operations such as crowd control, when the safety of personnel needs to be protected but the use of lethal force would not be appropriate. This role has been fulfilled in Northern Ireland in support of the Police Service of Northern Ireland, and in overseas operations in Iraq, Afghanistan and the Balkans. Depending on circumstances, UK military personnel may use batons, plastic baton rounds and CS smoke.

And further, what the policy reasons are for non-lethal spray type weapons not being routinely carried by British forces during operations.

17/28

A Defence Minister wrote:

Under the Chemical Weapons Convention, non-lethal spray weapons such as CS smoke may only be used for law enforcement, including domestic riot control purposes and are therefore unsuitable for use on many types of operations carried out by British forces.

(HC Deb 9 January 2007 Vol 455 c521W)

17/29

Nuclear Weapons

A Defence Minister said:

So what is our nuclear deterrence policy? Our deterrent is intended to help ensure that nobody seeks to threaten our vital interests, and that nobody seeks to use nuclear weapons to blackmail us or the international community. It is not intended to coerce or threaten others; nor is it intended as a tool for war-fighting or to seek military advantage on the battlefield.

The principles which govern our approach to nuclear deterrence are unchanged, and the White Paper spells them out: our focus is on preventing nuclear attack; we will retain only the minimum deterrent required for our security; we maintain ambiguity about the circumstances in which we might contemplate use of nuclear weapons, although we are very clear that we would consider using them only in extreme circumstances of self-defence, including the defence of our NATO allies; our deterrent supports collective security through NATO; and an independent centre of nuclear decision-making in the UK enhances the overall deterrent effect of allied nuclear forces.

We will continue, as now, to have the flexibility to vary the number of missiles and warheads that might be employed, as well as having the option of a lower yield from our warhead. That flexibility can make our nuclear forces a more credible deterrent against smaller nuclear threats, but we remain clear that any conceivable use of our nuclear weapons—at whatever scale—would necessarily be strategic, both in intent and effect. Indeed, we have deliberately discontinued the use of the term sub-strategic, in the sense that it had been used previously to apply to a possible, limited use of our nuclear weapons.

One concern that has been expressed is that our deterrent is somehow operationally dependent on the United States, or that we can be prevented from employing it. This is simply not the case. Decisions on any use of our nuclear weapons would be sovereign UK decisions, and no other country could prevent their employment. Only the Prime Minister can authorise the use of our nuclear weapons, even if the missiles are to be fired as part of a NATO response. The instruction to fire would be transmitted to the submarine using only UK codes and UK equipment. All the command and control procedures are fully independent, and the missiles do not use the global positioning satellite system: they have an inertial guidance system. Nothing in the planned Trident D5 life extension programme will change that position.

While we have never concealed that we choose to procure certain elements of our system from the United States, I can provide assurance that the system is fully operationally independent of the United States. Successive Governments would not have sustained our nuclear deterrent on these terms were that not the case.

Another charge levelled is that the retention and renewal of our deterrent system is illegal and, in particular, incompatible with our obligations under the nuclear non-proliferation treaty. Again, that is simply not the case. The UK has been, and will continue to be, at the forefront of efforts to reduce the size of existing arsenals and to fight proliferation. We have reduced the explosive power of our nuclear weapons stockpile by over 70 per cent since the end of the Cold War. We have the smallest stockpile of any of the five recognised nuclear powers, and only we have reduced to a single system. We already have less than 1 per cent of the total global stockpile of nuclear weapons.

Following careful assessment of our future deterrent needs, we have now decided to make a further 20 per cent cut, involving the dismantling of about 40 warheads. In future, the maximum number of operationally available warheads will be fewer than 160, down from fewer than 200. That will represent a reduction by about half since 1997, compared to the plans of the previous Government.

(HL Deb 24 January 2007 Vol 688 c1107)

17/30

In a debate on the future maintenance of the UK's strategic nuclear deterrent, the Foreign Secretary said:

Since the non-proliferation treaty came into force in 1970, all nuclear weapons states have taken steps to maintain their deterrents. The decisions on which we are seeking agreement today are no different. But the UK has been more open and transparent than any other state in explaining the basis of our decisions in advance to our people and to the international community.

There are four key issues. I will address each in turn. The first is what are we doing to fulfil our obligations under the nuclear non-proliferation treaty...The NPT created two distinct categories of states. Those that had already conducted nuclear tests—ourselves, the US, the Soviet Union, China and France—were designated nuclear weapons states and could legally possess nuclear weapons. All other states-signatory were designated non-nuclear weapons states. Article VI of the NPT imposes an obligation on all states "to pursue negotiations in good faith on effective measures relating to cessation of the nuclear arms race at an early date and to nuclear disarmament, and on a Treaty on general and complete disarmament".

The NPT review conference held in 2000 agreed, by consensus, 13 practical steps towards nuclear disarmament. The UK remains committed to these steps and is making progress on them.

We have been disarming. Since the cold war ended, we have withdrawn and dismantled our tactical maritime and airborne nuclear capabilities. We have terminated our nuclear capable Lance missiles and artillery. We have the smallest nuclear capability of any recognised nuclear weapon state, accounting for less than 1 per cent. of the global inventory, and we are the only nuclear weapon state that relies on a single nuclear system. The Prime Minister has announced a further unilateral reduction in our nuclear weapons in line with our commitment to maintain only the minimum necessary deterrent. We will reduce the stockpile of operationally available warheads by another 20 per cent., to fewer than 160 warheads during the course of this year. This will involve the eventual dismantlement and disposal of about 40 warheads. The UK will then have cut the explosive power of its nuclear weapons by three quarters since the end of the cold war. That is more than any other nuclear weapon state has yet done...

The latest proposal does not change the trend of disarmament that we have been pursuing. I want clearly to spell out to the House what we are not doing. We are not upgrading the capability of the system. We are not producing more usable weapons. We are not changing our nuclear posture or doctrine—in particular, we do not possess nuclear weapons for "war fighting" or tactical use on the battlefield. And we have not lowered the threshold for the use of nuclear weapons...

We have taken other unilateral actions in line with the 13 steps. We have not conducted a nuclear test since 1991. We ceased production of fissile material for use in nuclear weapons in 1995. And all excess fissile material stocks no longer required for defence purposes have been placed under international safeguards. Those unilateral actions have been complemented by active diplomacy on multilateral nuclear disarmament... We led international efforts on the comprehensive test ban treaty. The UK ratified the treaty in 1998, and our diplomats continue repeatedly to urge other countries to ratify so that it can enter into force. As I said, we have called repeatedly for the immediate start of negotiations in the conference on disarmament in Geneva on a fissile material cut-off treaty...

I share the view of many in the House that it is perhaps time for a fresh push on these measures on the international stage. How successful such a push would be remains to be seen, but there have been a series of bilateral agreements since the end of the cold war, which have greatly reduced the major nuclear arsenals. By the end of this year, the United States will have fewer than half the number of silo-based nuclear missiles that it had in 1990. By 2012, US operationally deployed strategic nuclear warheads will be reduced to about one third of 2001 levels. Under the terms of the strategic offensive reductions treaty, Russia is making parallel cuts, and the French have withdrawn four complete weapons systems.

Britain remains committed to the abolition of nuclear weapons, and we are actively engaged, and encouraging others to be engaged, in a process that will lead to that goal. But progress will be steady and incremental, and only towards the end of that process will it be helpful and useful for us to include our own small fraction of the global stockpile in treaty-based reductions.

So there is no basis to suggest that we have done anything other than fully comply with our obligations under the NPT. Indeed . . . I regard it as dangerous folly to equate our own record, as some have tried to do, with that of countries such as North Korea and Iran, which have stood or stand in clear breach of their obligations as non-nuclear weapon states under the NPT. There is no legal or moral equivalence between their position and ours. I would urge people, whatever other arguments they might use to oppose the motion, not to use that one, because it undermines the very basis of the treaty itself: that those recognised as non-nuclear weapon states should not seek to acquire nuclear weapons. The international non-proliferation regime is not perfect, but it has prevented the wide-scale proliferation of nuclear weapons. I regard it as dangerously irresponsible to use the excuse that the UK is retaining its weapons to justify others seeking to acquire them, and it runs the real risk of increasing the global nuclear threat, not reducing it.

(HC Deb 14 March 2007 Vol 458 c301–303)

17/31
The Minister of Defence wrote:

The Government are strongly committed to the Nuclear Non-Proliferation Treaty (NPT), which is the cornerstone of the nuclear non-proliferation regime. The White Paper on the Future of the United Kingdom's Nuclear Deterrent published on 4 December 2006 (Cm 6994) makes clear that renewing our minimum nuclear deterrent capability is fully consistent with all our international obligations, including those under the NPT . . .

As stated in paragraph 3–4 of the White Paper . . .

"Our focus is on preventing nuclear attack. The UK's nuclear weapons are not designed for use during military conflict but instead to deter and prevent nuclear blackmail and acts of aggression against our vital interests that cannot be countered by other means."

It is a key part of our deterrence posture that we retain ambiguity about precisely when, how and at what scale we could contemplate use of our nuclear deterrent. We would only consider using nuclear weapons in self-defence—including the defence of our NATO allies—and even then only in extreme circumstances. That has been and will remain our policy.

(HC Deb 12 March 2007 Vol 458 c57W–58W)

Part Eighteen: Neutrality and Non-Belligerency

Part Nineteen: Legal Aspects of International Relations and Co-operation in Particular Matters

Part Nineteen: I.A. *Legal Aspects of International Relations and Co-operation in Particular Matters—General economic and financial matters—Trade*

19/1

The International Development Secretary was asked what assessment he had made of the potential impact on access to HIV treatment of the Government of Thailand's issuance of compulsory licences to produce locally or import generic versions of the drugs efavirenz and lopinavir/ritonavir.

A Minister wrote:

The Thai Government only recently announced their intention to issue compulsory licences for a number of patented medicines; therefore the impact of this action on access to HIV treatment is not yet clear.

We support the right of developing countries to implement the WTO Agreement on Trade Related Aspects of Intellectual Property Rights (TRIPS) as is appropriate for their circumstances and in order to ensure access to HIV treatment. We also support the right of developing countries to utilise the flexibilities allowed under TRIPS to ensure affordable access to medicines to meet public health needs, this includes the use of compulsory licensing provisions included in the TRIPS agreement.

(HC Deb 6 March 2007 Vol 457 c1824W)

19/2

A Minister wrote:

The UK Government's 2005 position paper on Economic Partnership Agreements (EPA) (http://www.dfid.gov.uk/aboutdfid/organisation/ukpolicy-epas.pdf, Ed.) states that

"The [European] Commission should be ready to provide an alternative to an EPA at the request of any African, Caribbean or Pacific (ACP) country."

This remains our position. We would be very happy to consider and implement a WTO compatible alternative if put forward by any member of the ACP. However, the ACP have made it clear that they are committed to completing EPA negotiations by the end of this year and the UK Government consider it a priority to work with them towards that goal.

In the event that the deadline is not met in any of the regions, our position is that we would like to see arrangements which are least disruptive to ACP exporters and that do not leave the ACP any worse off than they are under current arrangements.

(HC Deb 10 September 2007 Vol 463 c2031W–2032W)

19/2

The Secretary of State for International Development was asked why there was such urgency about concluding economic partnership agreements between certain ACP countries and the EU. He said:

Straightforwardly, the urgency is not set down by the European Commission per se, but the Cotonou agreement has been deemed World Trade Organisation-incompatible, and the deadline of 31 December is of long standing. Simply rolling forward the Cotonou provisions would be WTO-incompatible, and the deadline has been clear.

(HC Deb 15 November 2007 Vol 467 c875)

19/2

A Minister wrote:

No intellectual property provisions have been included in the Economic Partnership Agreements (EPAs) signed to date.

The UK has always been clear that issues other than trade in goods should only be included in EPAs if the African, Caribbean or Pacific regions wish them to be. If a region wants to negotiate intellectual property rights in their EPA, then the UK policy is that no country should be required to go beyond existing commitments under the World Trade Organisation (WTO) agreement on trade related intellectual property rights (TRIPS). This agreement includes the right for countries to improve their access to cheaper medicines by producing, exporting or importing generic medicines under a compulsory licence. The UK supports this right. The Department for International Development has financed a number of organisations to assist developing countries to make better use of their TRIPS flexibilities, including compulsory licensing.

(HC Deb 13 December 2007 Vol 469 c839W)

19/3

A Minister wrote:

We continue to provide support and advice to build developing countries own ability to meet International Labour Organisation (ILO) and environmental standards, rather than seeking to impose solutions from outside.

The UK has consistently promoted efforts to ensure that international trade takes place on a sustainable basis, the principles of which include respect for the rights of workers and for environmental standards. We support voluntary codes of practice such as the Ethical Trading Initiative and the Fairtrade Foundation. We also support the work of the International Labour Organisation (ILO), which has a three-year, £20 million partnership agreement with DFID. The UK Government are also supporting sustainable development through measures such as the Extractive Industries Transparency Initiative (EITI) and the EU Forest Law Enforcement, Governance and Trade (FLEGT) initiative.

There are no restrictions available to be applied to imported goods which are manufactured for United Kingdom-based retailers by work forces that are either employed under conditions that do not meet International Labour Organisation (ILO) standards, or that operate in factory conditions that breach local environmental pollution regulations. This is because there would be significant practical obstacles to implementing such measures, as well as the fact that it would be difficult to make them compatible with World Trade Organisation (WTO) rules.

(HC Deb 15 October 2007 Vol 464 c757W)

19/4
A Minister wrote:

Internationally, many animals hunted and traded as bush meat are listed in the appendices to the Convention on International Trade in Endangered Species (CITES). Where this is the case, any international trade in these animals, their parts or derivatives is therefore either banned completely or controlled by means of a permitting system.

(HL Deb 30 October 2007 Vol 695 cWA182)

19/5
A Minister wrote:

International commercial trade in ivory has been prohibited under the Convention on International Trade in Endangered Species (CITES) since 1989 and this is actively enforced by HM Revenue and Customs at our borders and the police service internally. The illegal import or export of ivory can result in a large fine and/or several years imprisonment.

The UK fully supports efforts undertaken by the CITES community to improve enforcement activity in source and destination markets as well as working to eradicate illegal trade within the UK itself. The UK financially supports two key CITES programmes related to ivory trade; the Monitoring of the Illegal Killing of Elephants (MIKE) and the Elephant Trade Information System (ETIS) programmes. These enable the international community to monitor poaching and illegal trade levels so resources can be targeted where they are most needed.

(HC Deb 15 November 2007 Vol 467 c341W)

Part Nineteen: I.B. *Legal Aspects of International Relations and Co-operation in Particular Matters—General economic and financial matters—Loans*

19/6
A Minister wrote:

Last autumn, after strong lobbying by the UK, the international community agreed to remove the requirement (known as the Heavily Indebted Poor

Countries (HIPC) sunset clause) that countries must have started a programme of support with the IMF by the end of 2006 to remain eligible for debt relief. All 13 countries that have yet to reach HIPC decision point will therefore still be able to qualify for debt relief.

The UK supports debt relief for all poor countries—not just HIPCs—that would use the savings to progress towards the millennium development goals. We therefore continue to offer debt relief (reimbursements of 10 per cent of debt service payments to IDA and the AfDF) to qualifying low-income countries under the UK Multilateral Debt Relief Initiative. Moldova recently qualified for this assistance, bringing the total number of recipients to seven countries.

The UK is working with the World Bank, IMF, African Development Bank and other development partners to ensure that countries that have benefited from debt relief can access the financing they need to reach the millennium development goals, without re-accumulating unsustainable levels of debt. The joint World Bank/IMF Debt Sustainability Framework (DSF) provides guidance on new borrowing and lending to low-income countries. Countries that may struggle to repay loans receive grants from the World Bank and African Development Bank instead. The UK is also leading efforts among export credit agencies (ECAs) to agree new guidelines on responsible lending to countries that have received debt relief. It is important that borrowers and lenders work together to ensure any new borrowing is appropriately concessional, well targeted and used for productive purposes.

(HL Deb 9 January 2007 Vol 688 cWS6)

19/7
A Minister wrote:

To be eligible for debt relief under the heavily indebted poor countries (HIPC) initiative, as defined by the international system, a country must:

have unsustainable debts (debt-to-export levels above 150 per cent. or debt-to-government revenues above 250 per cent.) after the application of traditional debt relief measures, such as those offered by the Paris Club group of government creditors;

only be eligible for assistance on highly concessional terms from the International Development Association (IDA) at the World Bank, and the International Monetary Fund's (IMF) Poverty Reduction and Growth Facility;

establish a track record of reform and implement a Poverty Reduction Strategy Paper, using the savings from debt relief to reduce poverty;

and have cleared any outstanding arrears to the International Financial Institutions.

Each heavily indebted poor country has to decide whether or not to seek debt cancellation under the HIPC initiative. Those that complete the HIPC process are granted complete cancellation of their debts to the IMF, IDA and African Development Fund under HIPC and the Multilateral Debt Relief Initiative.

(HC Deb 5 July 2007 Vol 462 c1165W)

19/8
A Minister wrote:

DFID has not made its own assessment [of the debt status of Lesotho] as, like other agencies, it relies on the assessments made by the IMF and World Bank, which administer the HIPC initiative.

In June 2005, the International Monetary Fund conducted a Debt Sustainability Analysis and concluded that Lesotho's debt levels were sustainable. This means that Lesotho does not classify as a heavily indebted poor country (HIPC). However, the UK is committed to ensuring debt relief for all IDA—only low income countries that can use the resources effectively for poverty reduction. Lesotho would qualify for DFID's Multilateral Debt Relief Initiative once its public expenditure management systems are effective enough to ensure funds can be spent on the intended purposes of poverty reduction.

(HC Deb 25 July 2007 Vol 463 c1120W)

19/9
A Minister wrote:

The poorest countries are eligible for 100 per cent. debt cancellation on their bilateral debts under the Heavily Indebted Poor Countries (HIPC) Initiative, as well as 100 per cent. debt cancellation on their debts to the World Bank, International Monetary Fund (IMF) and African Development Bank under the Multilateral Debt Relief Initiative (MDRI). The UK is at the forefront of debt cancellation for poor countries and international poverty reduction. We exceed our commitments under the Heavily Indebted Poor Countries (HIPC) and Multilateral Debt Relief Initiatives (MDRI), providing the poorest countries with 100 per cent. cancellation on their bilateral and multilateral debts. The HIPC and MDRI systems have cancelled billions of pounds worth of debt and we continue to believe that they are the most appropriate way to tackle sovereign debt problems. Unpayable debts should not hinder the poorest countries from making progress towards the millennium development goals.

All of our loans are made to internationally recognised governments, are bound by legal contracts and are recognised in international law, we do not therefore consider them to be "illegitimate". We believe that debt relief should be provided on the basis of a country's economic situation rather than their history of poor or corrupt governance. Many countries that have a history of poor governance are now middle-income countries. If we cancelled so-called "illegitimate" debts for such countries, the full cost would have to be met from DFID's aid budget, diverting vital resources away from poorer countries. It is also likely that creditors and investors would take a negative view of the credit worthiness of developing countries in case the loans were later repudiated. This would be damaging for developing countries trying to strengthen their economies and reduce poverty through access to international investment and financing.

(HC Deb 16 October 2007 Vol 464 c985W)

Part Nineteen: III. *Legal Aspects of International Relations and Co-operation in Particular Matters—Environment*

19/10
A Minister said:

The Government are deeply concerned about the reported cruelty during the Canadian seal hunt. They have undertaken a review of policy on this issue and have concluded that the UK should press the European Commission to propose EU-wide measures to ban the import of listed harp and hooded seal products. This would establish a harmonised EU approach.

It is the Government's view that action taken at EU level would be more effective than national measures alone, avoiding distortions in the operation of the single market and allowing for effective enforcement by customs authorities. The UK is committed to pursuing EU action and ensuring that any resulting EU Commission proposal will be effective. We are writing to Commissioner Dimas requesting urgent action.

Meanwhile, the EU proposal for an EU-wide ban on the domestic cat and dog fur trade is under active discussion within the Council of the European Union and European Parliament and we hope to be able to agree this proposal as quickly as possible.

(HC Deb 8 February 2007 Vol 456 cWS43)

19/11
Winding up a debate on illegal logging, an Environment Minister said:

...the $15 billion lost each year by some of the poorest countries in the world through illegal logging is calculable. That is the extent of the problem...Some of the poorest people in the world lose the most. More than that, 20 per cent. of CO_2 emissions into the atmosphere, which contribute to climate change, come from deforestation. That is a measure of the social importance of the issue.

In both procurement and the wider control of wood supplies, sustainability absolutely remains the Government's goal. Verification of legality...is simply the first step and an indicator of sustainability. It is not an alternative to it.

There are some differences between the Government's policy and that being adopted by some member states. In particular, our standard contract requirements exclude reference to the protection and well-being of forest-dependent people...the UK has been challenged on that. We are a signatory to international agreements on sustainable forestry that recognise the importance of protecting forest-dependent peoples' rights and customs, so that challenge is understandable. We are seeking further advice on procurement law, and will change our position to include relevant social criteria if we are confident that it would be appropriate and legal to do so.

...the Governments of Denmark and the Netherlands concluded that that was appropriate and legal. Our previous legal advice is that that would not be appropriate or legal, and we are considering whether to revise that and whether we can press it further.

The development of a discerning market for legal and sustainable timber requires institutional and market processes to work together. The UK has continued to support co-operation with the timber trade, especially in getting messages to the supply chain that legal timber is now required. Much has been achieved... but I am determined that there must be a serious step change in Government procurement and in our actions to address illegal and unsustainable timber production.

(HC Deb 28 February 2007 Vol 457 WH314)

19/12
The Secretary of State for Business wrote:

The Government are also working towards a regulatory regime which will manage the safe and reliable storage of CO_2 and does not conflict with international agreements. We currently expect to consult on UK regulation of CCS in November [2007].

Regulatory work also includes amendments to international conventions and working towards the inclusion of CCS in the EU ETS. The UK has already taken the lead in proposing and securing amendments to the London Convention and OSPAR treaties which legalise CO_2 storage beneath the seabed, a major step towards enabling the implementation of CCS.

With Norway we have established a taskforce to establish the underlying principles for CO_2 storage in the North Sea basin. The work of the taskforce is progressing well and has already produced its first deliverable, a report on a set of common principles for the regulation and management for storing CO_2 in geological formations beneath the seabed.

(HC Deb 5 July 2007 Vol 462 c117W)

19/13
An Environment Minister wrote:

The UK Government works actively through several international organisations to further the protection offered to dolphins and other cetaceans. These include the Agreement on the Conservation of Small Cetaceans of the Baltic, North East Atlantic, Irish and North Seas (ASCOBANS), the Convention for the Protection of the Marine Environment of the North-East Atlantic (the "OSPAR Convention") and the Convention on International Trade in Endangered Species (CITES).

The UK Government have implemented a comprehensive system of by-catch monitoring under the requirements of the EC Habitats Directive and Council Regulation 812/2004. In 2003, the UK was the first member state to publish a response strategy for the monitoring of small cetaceans by-catch. In December 2004, the UK banned pelagic pair trawling for bass by UK vessels within 12 miles off the south-west coast of England. The Sea Mammal Research Unit

(SMRU) regularly reports the results of its research on by-catch monitoring which covers all relevant UK fishery sectors, including the bass pair trawl fishery to the Department, and has recently presented us with their 2006 findings. This report will be submitted to the European Commission and published on DEFRA's website in due course. The Commission evaluate all contributing member states' schemes.

The UK Government have identified the potential benefits of acoustic devices, such as pingers, in reducing bycatch of dolphins and other cetaceans in fixed gear fisheries and argued successfully at an international level for these devices to be required in certain fisheries by EU legislation. Prior to enforcing the use of pingers under Council Regulation EC 8121 2004, the UK Government wants to ensure that those we recommend to be used are safe and cost effective for the industry and offer the maximum protection to porpoises.

We have also provided significant funding for collaborative working with other countries to collect information on the distribution and abundance of cetaceans in European Atlantic offshore waters. Other countries participating in this research study are France, Ireland and Spain. The outputs from this work will provide new information on the distribution, abundance and habitat preferences of a number of cetaceans, which include the bottlenose dolphin and common dolphin. This information will be used to assess the threats to dolphins and inform what mitigation measures may be required.

All dolphins are listed in either Appendix I or II of CITES. Under CITES, commercial trade in wild-taken Appendix I dolphins is only allowed in exceptional circumstances. Appendix II dolphin species are not necessarily threatened with extinction, but may become so unless trade is regulated. The UK supports the listing of dolphins on the appropriate Appendix and, in 2004, supported the up-listing of the Irrawaddy dolphin from Appendix II to I. Under CITES, countries manage trade in listed species to ensure that their conservation is not threatened by trade. Under that management regime, the UK (and EU) takes strict measures in respect of trade, and keeping in captivity, of all dolphins. Trade in wild-taken dolphins would only be allowed in exceptional circumstances, for example scientific, breeding, or educational purposes (where these would bring conservation benefits to the species concerned). Commercial trade in the EU in these species is strictly prohibited. The UK encourages other countries to adopt similar standards.

(HC Deb 21 November 2007 Vol 467 c861W–862W)

Part Nineteen: IV. *Legal Aspects of International Relations and Co-operation in Particular Matters—Natural resources*

19/14
An Environment Minister wrote:

The UK Government are pursuing rainforest protection through a number of measures that include research on improving forest management, banning trade in endangered species and reducing trade in illegally logged timber products.

On reducing the trade in illegal timber from rainforests, and all other forest types, the Government are working to implement the EU Forestry Law Enforcement Governance and Trade (FLEGT) regulation, adopted in 2005. This allows the EU to enter into Voluntary Partnership Agreements with timber producing countries, and will include a licensing system to identify legal timber products for export to the EU.

Collaboration continues with other major consumer countries in the G8 (plus China) and with the private sector. In particular, the UK Government's timber procurement policy, which requires all timber supplied to have derived from legally harvested trees, has become a beacon for other Governments to tackle illegal logging through voluntary consumer action.

Developing countries currently have no obligations to mitigate greenhouse gas (GHG) emissions, although they can contribute to global emission reductions by hosting projects under the Clean Development Mechanism (CDM). The CDM includes afforestation and reforestation projects, but not deforestation, because of concerns that forestry protection projects would displace the deforestation elsewhere, with little or no net gain.

Under the United Nations Framework Convention on Climate Change negotiations, Papua New Guinea and the Coalition of Rainforest Nations (CRN), and subsequently Brazil, have proposed that developing countries might participate in climate change agreements by voluntary targets to reduce deforestation below national (rather than project specific) baselines.

Achievement relative to a national reference level would take account of any displacement of deforestation within a country.

At the launch of the Stern Review in October 2006... the Chancellor of the Exchequer announced that the UK would be working in partnership with a number of partners to explore ways of mobilising international resources to assist developing countries in sustainable forestry management. These partners include Brazil, the CRN, other developing countries, Germany (as Presidency of the G8) the EU and the World Bank. We are currently in talks with Germany and developing countries to establish how best to take this forward.

Furthermore, the UK Government are committed to working with other countries to promote the conservation of the world's wildlife, for example, through our membership of agreements such as the Convention on International Trade in Endangered Species (CITES)...

United Nations Food and Agriculture Organisation (FAO) data shows that about 13 million hectares of the world's forests are lost annually due to deforestation. Brazil (3,103) and Indonesia (1,871) demonstrated the largest net forest loss (1,000 hectares per year) between 2000 and 2005. However, the net rate of loss is slowing down, thanks to new planting and natural expansion of existing forests. A range of initiatives introduced by Brazil are thought to have reduced deforestation rates in the Amazon by an estimated 31 per cent. in 2004–05 and 30 per cent. in 2005–06.

No single action can stop illegal logging. Combating it requires the simultaneous implementation of many policies and measures in and between those countries that produce timber and those that import it. In 2002, the UK signed a Memorandum of Understanding with Indonesia that commits both Governments to work together to tackle illegal logging and the associated trade in timber between the two countries. Forest Law Enforcement, Governance and Trade (FLEGT) legislation was adopted under the UK Presidency of the European Union (EU) in December 2005. This will allow the EU to enter into agreements with developing countries that export timber.

In January 2006, new funding of £24 million over five years to tackle illegal logging and underlying governance problems was announced. This will focus on tropical countries in Africa and Asia.

Action to reduce emissions from deforestation is not currently included under the Kyoto Protocol. This is because of the risk of such projects simply resulting in displacement of deforestation, to no net environmental gain. Proposals recently put forward by Brazil, Papua New Guinea (PNG) and Costa Rica, supported by the Coalition of Rainforest Nations, measure reductions in emissions relative to a national baseline, rather than a project-specific one. This greatly reduces the risk of displacement. The UK welcomes both proposals, and is actively working with the EU and international negotiating partners to secure a successful outcome on reducing emissions from deforestation in developing countries at the UN climate negotiations in Bali, in December 2007.

(HC Deb 24 January 2007 Vol 455 c1800W–1801W)

19/15
A Minister said:

Let me start with international labour standards, which are set out in various international treaties. Perhaps the most quoted are...the ILO Conventions and the European Convention on Human Rights. The UK was one of the founding members of the ILO and was among the first to ratify its key conventions, including the central ones relating to trade union rights—conventions 87 and 98. We therefore take our obligations seriously. During the 1980s, our reputation was diminished internationally by the removal of trade union rights at GCHQ, and hon. Members will recall that one of the first acts of the Labour Government when they came to office in 1997 was to restore trade union rights at GCHQ, which signalled both domestically and internationally where we stood on these issues.

The ILO has mechanisms to monitor member state compliance with international standards, and there is often debate about whether member states are conforming with the spirit and letter of the conventions. Even this country has been part of those debates over the years, and I am pleased to say that it has never been formally reprimanded by the ILO's governing body, although there has been debate about laws in this country and others and the extent to which they comply with the conventions. The conventions often focus on broad principles, which is important, because they need to apply to many different settings around the world, with different labour market conditions, in both developed and developing countries.

Over the years, we have engaged in an ongoing and constructive dialogue with the ILO about the conventions, and I understand that its advisory committees have not interpreted its trade union conventions as requiring companies to recognise trade unions for collective bargaining purposes. That is subject to national legal systems and the negotiation that takes place between unions and companies.

...

When it comes to ILO obligations, the United States is not signed up to every Convention that we are signed up to, and, in any case, virtually every ILO member state faces questions as to whether it is interpreting its obligations fully. These are not clear-cut issues, and different interpretations of treaty obligations are possible. This is not always as simple as saying that because these questions are raised, the basic international standards are not being observed.

It should also be expected that the terms and conditions of work forces around the world will vary, as will even those between work forces in developed countries. That is because labour market conditions, tax and social security systems and so on differ from state to state.

...

We would expect [British companies operating abroad] to comply with the legal systems in which they operate. Some countries have ensured that basic standards are built into their employment law, although that is not the case in others. We would encourage British companies operating around the world voluntarily to apply the basic minimum standards. We cannot compel our companies to operate in that way in foreign jurisdictions, although we have instituted arrangements in our own corporate law and we are party to monitoring arrangements that provide for greater openness and transparency in this area.

(HC Deb 24 July 2007 Vol 463 c226WH–229WH)

19/16

The representative of the UK made the following statement to the UNGA Sixth Committee on 2 November 2007:

I now turn to chapter V [the Report of the ILC, Fifty-ninth session, A/62/10, Ed.] on shared natural resources...

The United Kingdom notes that the Drafting Committee of the Commission adopted, in 2006, 19 draft articles on transboundary aquifers. We have, in past meetings of the Sixth Committee, refrained from making substantive comments on this topic, primarily because we do not consider that we are directly affected by this aspect of the Commission's work. We have, however, followed the Commission's work closely, and recognise the importance of this issue.

The United Kingdom observes that the Special Rapporteur and the Commission have had a lengthy debate on whether or not, and how, the Commission might cover the issue of shared oil and gas resources. We have previously expressed the view in this Committee, as have other delegations, that any study on oil and gas would entail great complexity, and we are also uncertain about the existence of, or need for, any universal rules on this question. Like many other States, we have a lot of experience in dealing with cross-boundary oil and gas fields. In general, bilateral discussions with neighbouring States are guided by pragmatic considerations, based on technical information. Our general approach to these issues is that States should co-operate in order to reach agreement on the division or sharing of such cross-boundary fields.

With this in mind, the United Kingdom is not convinced, at this stage, that there is a pressing need for the Commission to elaborate a set of draft articles or guidelines on shared oil and gas resources.

(Text supplied by FCO)

Part Nineteen: VIII. *Legal Aspects of International Relations and Co-operation in Particular Matters—Legal matters (for example judicial assistance, crime control, etc.)*

Aut dedere aut iudicare

19/17

The representative of the UK made the following statement to the UNGA Sixth Committee on 2 November 2007:

Finally, I will turn to chapter IX of the [International Law] Commission's Report [Fifty-ninth session, A/62/10, Ed.] on the obligation to extradite or prosecute (*aut dedere aut judicare*)...

The United Kingdom has some general comments about the direction of the Commission's work on this topic. Last year, in the Sixth Committee, we urged the Commission to treat the principle of universal criminal jurisdiction with caution, and not to be diverted by a comprehensive study of universal jurisdiction. In this regard, we welcome the Special Rapporteur's decision to draw a clear distinction between the obligation to extradite or prosecute and the principle of universal jurisdiction, and to carry out a careful examination of their mutual relationship.

The United Kingdom also welcomes the Special Rapporteur's confirmation that the Commission's further work on this topic will not examine the so-called 'triple alternative', which refers to the possible obligation to extradite, prosecute, or surrender an individual to an international criminal tribunal. As we stated last year in the Sixth Committee, the surrender of individuals to international criminal courts is governed by a distinct set of treaty arrangements and legal rules.

The United Kingdom has previously expressed the opinion that the obligation to extradite or prosecute only arises as a matter of treaty law, and is not a rule of customary international law. This remains our view. Even if the obligation were said to exist as a matter of customary international law, this would exist only in relation to a very narrow class of crimes.

Finally, with regard to the final form of the Commission's work, the United Kingdom encourages the Commission to remain flexible at this early stage of its consideration of this topic.

(Text supplied by FCO)

19/18

Memorandum of understanding on co-operation between the Office of the Prosecutor General of the Russian Federation and the Crown Prosecution Service of England and Wales, February 2006:

The Office of the Prosecutor General of the Russian Federation and the Crown Prosecution Service of England and Wales, hereinafter referred to as the Participants,

RECOGNIZING the importance of strengthening and further developing mutual co-operation in the enforcement of criminal law,

AWARE OF the need to ensure that co-operation is carried out in the most effective way,

BASED on the principles of equality, respect for sovereignty and universally recognized norms of international law aimed, in particular, at securing protection of human rights and freedoms,

HAVE DECIDED AS FOLLOWS:

Article 1

The Participants will co-operate on the basis of this Memorandum of Understanding within the limits of their competence and in accordance with the law and international obligations of their respective States.

Article 2

The Participants will, upon mutual agreement, hold meetings and consultations in order to exchange their practical experience and discuss the issues of mutual interest, including those discussed at relevant international fora and organizations including the United Nations Organization, the Group of Eight and the Council of Europe.

Article 3

The Participants will co-operate in the sphere of extradition and in other issues of mutual legal assistance. Where appropriate, this shall include consultation and the provision of advice at the stage when such requests are being drafted.

Article 4

The Participants will, upon mutual agreement, co-operate on issues of mutual interest concerning professional training of the staff of both the Office of the Prosecutor General of the Russian Federation and the Crown Prosecution Service of England and Wales.

Article 5

The Participants may, upon request or upon their own initiative, exchange information on the legal systems and national legislation of their respective States.

Article 6

The Participants will, upon mutual agreement, hold joint conferences, workshops and round table discussions.

Article 7

This Memorandum of Understanding shall not prevent the Participants from defining and developing any other mutually acceptable directions and forms of co-operation.

Article 8

1. Within the framework of this Memorandum of Understanding, the Participants may communicate with each other directly.

2. Each Participant will appoint a department and/or officers responsible for maintaining contact with the other Participant and inform the other Participant thereof, specifying the relevant contact details within 30 days from the date of signature of this Memorandum of Understanding.

Article 9

Documents falling within the framework of this Memorandum of Understanding will be forwarded with a translation into the language of the State of the Participant to whom they are addressed unless otherwise agreed.

Article 10

The Participants will each bear their own expenses arising from co-operation on the basis of this Memorandum of Understanding unless otherwise agreed.

Article 11

The Participants will settle any disputes arising from the interpretation and application of this Memorandum of Understanding through consultations on the basis of mutual understanding and respect.

Article 12

1. This Memorandum of Understanding will enter into force upon the date of its signature.

2. This Memorandum of Understanding will remain in force unless and until its denunciation by either Participant by notice in writing to the other Participant. This Memorandum of Understanding shall cease to be in force 60 days after the receipt of such notice by the other Participant.

Done at London on this 15th day of November 2006 in duplicate, in Russian and English, all texts being equally authentic.

(www.cps.gov.uk/publications/agencies/opgrf_cps.html)

19/19

Corruption

The Minister for Trade said:

The International Development Secretary accounted for much of the work in his progress report to the Prime Minister, published on 12 March. I offer a few examples. First, we continue to push the anti-corruption agenda in international forums, such as the G8, the European Union and the UN, particularly the implementation of the UN convention against corruption, whose provisions on improving international co-operation on asset recovery are particularly important.

Secondly, we are implementing the third EU money-laundering directive to make it even harder to move criminal money, including looted assets, through our financial system. Thirdly, thanks to funding of £6 million from DFID over three years, in recognition of the impact of the scourge on developing countries, we have strengthened the UK's law enforcement capacity to investigate allegations of foreign bribery and the laundering of corrupt assets by political elites. On the former, the City of London police are already supporting the Serious Fraud Office in five investigations and made arrests in January. On the latter, the UK has restrained £34.6 million of assets acquired through corruption by foreign political elites.

The Metropolitan police has established a strong operational relationship to bring specific cases to prosecution. The Met's arrest of the former Governor of Bayelsa state had a strong impact in deterring wealthy Nigerians from trying to launder money through London. The Met has also responded to requests from the Nigerian Government relating to a second former state governor. In one case, £1 million was returned and in the other, property bought in London is about to be sold so that the proceeds can be returned to the people of Nigeria from whom they were stolen.

Let me provide other examples. Following an investigation by the Ministry of Defence police, an MOD official, Michael Hale, after taking bribes from a Californian company, was convicted earlier this month on nine counts of corruption. For the OECD, that case does not count, since the conviction was of the bribe taker rather than the bribe giver, but I stress that it shows that the legal framework and the requirement for the Attorney-General's consent worked as they should. It also showed the judge's resolve to punish such crimes with a custodial sentence.

Separately, a UK citizen, Joyce Oyebanjo, was convicted earlier this year of laundering £1.4 million of stolen assets from Nigeria. She was sentenced to three years' imprisonment. The Attorney-General has secured an extra £22 million to fund Serious Fraud Office investigations arising from alleged corruption under the UN oil-for-food programme.

On top of the hundreds of millions of pounds that the Department for International Development has already spent on improving governance in dozens of countries around the world, we recently launched a new £100 million governance and transparency fund to strengthen the ability of civil society, parliamentarians, trade unions and a free media to hold their Governments to account.

As well as boosting the UK's own capacity to investigate international corruption allegations, we have taken an important role in the International Association of Anti-Corruption Authorities, set up by the Chinese to improve co-ordination and sharing of best practice among anti-corruption law enforcement authorities. Both the Director of Public Prosecutions for Northern Ireland and the director of the Serious Fraud Office will help to direct the organisation. The UK's leadership on the extractive industries transparency initiative has allowed it to become widely recognised as the international standard for the management of public revenues from oil, gas and mining.

We were also in at the beginning of the conception of the Kimberley process to boost transparency in the diamond trade and stamp out "conflict" diamonds. That is now so successful that it is estimated that more than 99 per cent. of rough diamonds are certified as conflict-free. We continue to work with partners to address outstanding issues, most recently by representing the EU on a review visit to Ghana in March.

In partnership with the private sector, the UK is now one of only a handful of countries with independent oversight of our national contact point on the OECD guidelines on multinational enterprises. That is an important step towards boosting the credibility of this important complaints procedure. All of these are good examples of the benefits that all parties derive from co-operation between Governments, business and non-governmental organisations.

We have been praised by the OECD, particularly for the work that we have done to train front-line officials and raise awareness in the UK business community—both here in the UK and around the world. One of the ways in which we have done that is by commissioning a DVD. We are one of few Governments in the world training front-line staff to make them aware of the damage that corruption can cause and what their responsibilities are in helping to find it, bring it to court, stamp it out and bring to justice the people who are perpetrating it in the first place.

There are many positive stories about how a strong political will and courageous individuals can make a tangible difference. Several other OECD countries have asked us for more details about our activities to help inform their own efforts. That, I must say to the hon. Member for Twickenham, does not show a laggard, self-interested or irresponsible response to the key issues of the day on these matters. His comments therefore bear no resemblance to reality...

We are supporting the work of the Nigerian Economic and Financial Crimes Commission to tackle money laundering and corruption. That includes collecting financial forensic evidence in line with international standards and tracking suspicious transactions—a general issue that the hon. Gentleman raised. That has helped to secure 150 convictions and the recovery of about

$5 billion since our activities started in 2002. Our work is making a substantial difference...

We can all improve our performance on these matters. This is a difficult and complex area, but I want to make it absolutely clear that the Government are completely committed to doing the best by the British people and the international community. We are at the forefront of tackling corruption. In the last decade, we have made great strides. We are not squeamish about the role of the OECD. I am talking not just about our peer review, but about what happens in all international communities, whether we are thinking of the Human Rights Council or the OECD. We are very committed to peer review—and that includes ourselves. Every time that there is a peer review, there is an example of improving practice. We accept that.

We play an active part in the OECD—with the individuals and the institution. We also fund it and put in the right resources to make sure that we have an effective international legislative framework to expose and root out corruption where it exists and to repatriate the resources that corruption sucks out of states that mostly cannot afford to lose those resources in the first place. That money can then be put into education, health, transport and all the other key things that we take for granted in this country. Sadly, many countries that are victims of corruption lose out significantly in those areas.

(HC Deb 1 May 2007 Vol 459 c1489–1493)   .

Extradition–UAF

19/20
A Home Office Minister wrote:

Before the bilateral extradition treaty between the UK and the UAE was signed on 6 December 2006, there were two formal treaty negotiation meetings between our two countries. There were also informal discussions between officials of both countries.

The treaty will come into force once both Governments have exchanged instruments of ratification and the UAE has been designated as a Category 2 territory under the Extradition Act 2003. Until this time, there are no general extradition relations between the UK and UAE...under section 193 of the Extradition Act 2003, the UK can have extradition relations with non-treaty partners who are party to international conventions that contain extradition provisions and to which the UK is also a party.

The UK is also able to process ad hoc extradition requests from non-treaty partners under section 194 of the 2003 Act.

(HC Deb 15 January 2007 Vol 455 c835W)

[See United Arab Emirates No. 3 (2007) Extradition Treaty between the United Kingdom of Great Britain and Northern Ireland and the United Arab Emirates on Extradition London, 6 December 2006 Cm 7283]

The Explanatory Memorandum of the Extradition Treaty between the UK and the UAE says:

POLICY CONSIDERATIONS

GENERAL

There are currently no formal extradition arrangements between the UK and the UAE; however, there are a number of international conventions that establish arrangements for conduct covered by certain conventions that both countries are party to. This Treaty is one element in a package of crime-fighting measures that were signed on 6 December 2006. The UAE is a key partner for the UK, in particular in work on financial crime—including money laundering, VAT fraud, counter narcotics and counter-terrorism. This package of measures will enhance our ability to work in close co-operation with the UAE on these important issues.

These agreements will provide a sound framework for co-operation between the two states. The introduction of a formal basis for extradition for conduct covered by the Treaty will lead to a more efficient and effective process for extradition between the two countries instead of relying on the ad hoc provisions in domestic extradition law for the many offences which do not fall under an international convention

[(www.fco.gov.uk/treaties), Ed.]

19/21 (See also 7/4)

Extradition—Russia—Litvinenko

An FCO Minister was asked by the FAC what would be the extent of UK co-operation with Russia following the measures taken by the UK as part of the "Litvinenko" affair? The Minister said:

Primarily, in addition to the expulsion of the individuals, it is . . . about visa regulations. We were in the process of discussing improvements in the administration of visas, which would primarily have affected officials initially. That has been put into suspension. We have also put our position in respect of a similar set of arrangements for visas that Moscow already applies to the United Kingdom. Perhaps it would be helpful to say that the UK receives more than 120,000 applications for visas through Moscow, the vast majority of which are successful. However, this suspension of co-operation is not about the regular travellers—the visitors, tourists and business people—but about applications made by Russia's Government authorities. That is the suspension that has been put in place. [Q.95]

He was asked if other areas of co-operation might be affected. Could he assure the Committee that areas of co-operation such as on that on climate change or co-operation on common efforts against terrorism will not be damaged by this response? He said:

The Foreign Secretary said in his statement to the House that this is a precise response to the failure to co-operate on a serious crime. Our response is intended to be measured, and I think that it is largely accepted as being measured. Our European Union partners acknowledge it as such, and it is intended to say to the Russians how seriously we take this matter. I can say additionally that it is not our intention for it to affect the type of issues that you have commented on, which I am sure we will touch on later in our proceedings. However, specifically on counter-terrorism co-operation, we work strategically and operationally with the Russians, and will continue to do so when it is clearly in the UK's national interest and our wider interests. For example, we will continue to work together at the United Nations on the Counter-terrorism Committee, and at the UN on the Sanctions Committee on the Taliban and al-Qaeda. That is very important work, which we will continue. As I say, this is a precise and measured response to a very serious crime and the lack of Russian co-operation and it addresses how seriously we take this issue. [Q.96]

The Minster was asked if the Government was prepared for possible retaliatory non-co-operation by Russia in response. He said:

The proper response from the Russians is the extradition of the individual identified by independent UK authorities as the suspect in this dreadful murder. That is the proper response. [Q.97]

Since the Russians had made it clear that they were not prepared to do that, was the Government prepared for them simply to retaliate in any other way.

The Minister replied:

We still believe that the Russians should extradite. In terms of what the Russians do next, clearly, they have indicated their attitude through spokespersons both in Moscow and in London. It is certainly our intention, through this process, to emphasise that we still see Russia as a strong ally on important issues, and a country with which we have important bilateral and multilateral arrangements. It is our certainly our intention, as we go through this process, to conclude it. That remains the case...we are clear that the action that we have taken is the absolutely appropriate action, and many other member states in the European Union have acknowledged that over the last 24 hours. [Q.98]

The further, he was asked:

You have made it clear what you want the Russians to do and I am sure many would agree with you. But do you want to see disengagement by UK business and UK investors, in respect of investing in Russia, to put further pressure on the Russian authorities? Or are you content simply with putting pressure on Russian officials?

He said:

I do not think that would be helpful at all. The UK's national and strategic interest is served by continued UK investment in Russia and, indeed, Russian investment in the United Kingdom. So it is not in the UK's interests for that to happen. It is not an initiative and not a process that we would seek to initiate at all. [Q.99]

The Minister was asked if the Government would consider a trial in a court outside Russia and the UK.

He said:

No. [Q.101]

And he continued:

We are ruling that out because it does not suit our purposes and does not suit the stated purposes and concerns of the Russians, in terms of their constitutional bar and the extradition. So it does not suit either nation's purposes in terms of the idea of a third country. [Q.102]

The Minister was asked more generally about relations with Russia in this area—"I also mention Berezovsky. Why do we not send him back to Russia? He is calling for the overthrow of the Russian Government. This is a man who should be subject to the new laws we made in the late 1990s to try to prevent that kind of activity. Have we tried a more diplomatic approach, saying, 'Okay, you can have him, if we can have him,' and going down the usual channels. Just what is your end game? What do you want to achieve?" He said:

I do not think it would be helpful for us to get into a process of "You can have him, if we can have him," to use your colloquial expression. The processes are not connected in that way...Without going into the evidence and the nature of the extradition requests from the Crown Prosecution Service to the Russian Government, a substantial amount of detail has been compiled by independent UK authorities, which led them to believe that a Russian national had a case to answer for the murder of a British national in Britain. It is entirely appropriate that the CPS, after coming to that assessment independently, makes that independent application to the Russian authorities. That is what they have done; that is why it is significantly different from the type of scenario that you spoke about. In the case of Berezovsky and others, there is a similar independent process in the UK in which the CPS carries out an assessment of comments or actions of individuals who live in the United Kingdom, under whatever status, as to whether they would legitimately have a case to answer. Sometimes that does not translate directly into the Russian understanding. [Q.114]

The Minister was asked if policy was been conducted consistently. He said:

The end game for us is Russian co-operation with the independent judicial process of the United Kingdom, and the extradition of one individual against whom substantial evidence has been compiled to legitimise the request for extradition. On the matter of the Russian constitution, there is an acknowledgement that other countries have been in a similar situation but have found a way of co-operating on extradition that the Russians have seemed entirely unwilling to seek. That is the important point for us—the Russians have failed to co-operate or to register the severity with which we consider the matter. The Germans, for example, had certain constitutional issues with regard to extradition, but they found a way of co-operating with their independent judicial process. The Russians not only failed to do that but failed to attempt to do so. [Q.115]

(FAC Second Report, Global Security: Russia, HC 51(2007))

19/22

In a written statement, the Solicitor-General said:

Today the Crown Prosecution Service (CPS) has decided, after applying the evidential and public interest tests set out in the Code for Crown Prosecutors, to prosecute Mr Andrey Konstantinovich Lugovoy, a Russian citizen, for the murder of Alexander Valterovich Litvinenko. The CPS decision was reached after they had consulted the Attorney-General, which is the usual practice in serious and complex cases. The CPS have concluded that there is sufficient evidence to prosecute Mr Lugovoy for murder and it is in the public interest to do so.

It is alleged that in London on or about 1 November 2006, Mr Lugovoy poisoned Mr Litvinenko by administering a lethal dose of Polonium 210, a radioactive material. Mr Litvinenko died on 23 November 2006 in a London hospital of an acute radiation injury.

The CPS will now take immediate steps to seek the extradition of Mr Lugovoy from Russia to the United Kingdom so that he can be charged and prosecuted for murder in this country.

The Attorney-General agrees with the CPS decision.

(HC Deb 22 May 2007 Vol 460 c75WS)

19/23
(See also **3/7**)

Extradition—United States

The Home Secretary wrote:

Since 28 June the Home Office has handled 14 pieces of correspondence from hon. Members and members of the public on the subject of UK/US extradition arrangements...

The representations supported inaccurate claims in the press that I was about to introduce an additional statutory bar to extradition called "forum" which could prevent extradition where a case could be tried in the UK.

The Government keep extradition legislation under review, but have no plans to introduce this additional bar, which would apply to all countries with which the UK has extradition relations, including the US. I am satisfied that the Extradition Act 2003 already contains full and effective safeguards for the rights of requested persons. Introducing a ground for refusal of extradition based on forum is not only unnecessary, but would make the Act operate in a manner that is inconsistent with all of the UK's bilateral extradition treaties—including the bilateral treaty between the UK and the US. It would also give rise to real practical difficulties for prosecutors and would risk allowing criminals to evade justice.

Home Office Ministers have consistently made it clear in Parliament and to the press that the new extradition treaty with the United States is not one-sided, and we are satisfied that the provisions ensure that extradition is dealt with under procedures that are as broadly comparable as it is possible to achieve between two different jurisdictions.

The UK/US extradition treaty means that both the UK and the US are under an international obligation to assist with extradition requests to the extent compatible with the law. The key issue is to ensure that offences are dealt with in the place where they can be most effectively prosecuted. Where the main witnesses and the main evidence are in another state, then it makes sense for the defendants to be extradited to face justice there.

Taking all these matters into account, I am satisfied that the right balance has been struck between the need to safeguard the rights of defendants against the need to uphold the rule of law.

(HC Deb 3 December 2007 Vol 468 c770W–771W)

19/24
(See also **8/2**)

The Attorney-General wrote:

On 1 November 2006, my noble friend Lady Scotland informed the House that I had opened discussions with the Attorney General of the United States of America on jurisdictional issues in criminal cases.

I am pleased to inform the House that the Attorney General of the US, the Lord Advocate of Scotland and I have agreed guidance for handling cross-border cases between the UK and US.

I believe that the guidance will improve communication by facilitating the early sharing of case information and consultation between prosecutors in those jurisdictions. International co-operation in fighting transnational crime is essential. Further, this guidance should assist prosecutors to have the earliest notice of cases that could be of interest to them for possible investigation and prosecution in the UK. The guidance retains the UK prosecutor's powers to decide that a case should be tried in the UK when this is possible and in accordance with the law and public interest.

The guidance agreed between the UK and US is augmented by domestic guidance for prosecutors in England, Wales and Northern Ireland. The domestic guidance will enable my office to ensure that each of my prosecuting departments is informed of cross-border cases in which it may have an interest.

(HL Deb 25 January 2007 Vol 688 cWS68)

19/25

Mutual Assistance

A Minister wrote:

Requests for mutual legal assistance are received by the UK central authority within the Home Office. They are considered under the relevant UK legislation, namely the Crime (International Co-operation) Act 2003, in conjunction with international convention or treaty obligations that may be pertinent. The central authority receives approximately 5,000 such requests from other states per annum.

Requests are checked to ensure that they come from a competent judicial authority and that they relate to criminal investigations or proceedings being conducted by the requesting state. Checks are also conducted on the requests to ensure there are no issues relating to double jeopardy or human rights considerations such as the death penalty.

While the majority of these cases are straightforward and can be processed relatively quickly, some of the more complex cases require more consideration.

(HC Deb 17 December 2007 Vol 469 c947W)

19/26

OECD Bribery Treaty—BAE—Al Yamamah

The Attorney-General said:

I shall make a Statement which relates to the investigation by the Serious Fraud Office into BAE Systems plc concerning payments made in relation to the Al Yamamah programme with Saudi Arabia. This afternoon, the Serious Fraud Office has announced that it is discontinuing this investigation. Its statement says:

> "The Director of the Serious Fraud Office has decided to discontinue the investigation into the affairs of BAe Systems plc as far as they relate to the Al Yamamah defence contract. This decision has been taken following representations that have been made both to the Attorney General and the Director concerning the need to safeguard national and international security. It has been necessary to balance the need to maintain the rule of law against the wider public interest. No weight has been given to commercial interests or to the national economic interest".

Given the intense interest in this issue and its market sensitivity, I have decided to inform the House this afternoon of this decision and to give a further brief explanation. The SFO has divided its investigation of these matters into three periods. The first period, which it has termed phase one, runs from the mid-1980s until the coming into force of the Anti-terrorism, Crime and Security Act 2001. This Act extended the pre-existing law of corruption to the bribery of overseas officials. The view of the SFO in relation to these payments is that no prosecution should be brought before the coming into force of the new Act. That is a view with which I concur.

The other phases concern the period after the coming into force of the new Act. Phase two covers payments made at about the time of the termination of the arrangements under which payments had previously been made by BAE. Phase three covers a longer period in relation to which at the moment there is little hard evidence that payments were made. In the SFO's view, there is no guarantee that this investigation would lead to prosecution and there are real issues to be determined. In order to complete this investigation, significant further inquiries would be necessary, which would last in the SFO's judgment a further 18 months. It accordingly has concluded that in these circumstances the potential damage to the public interest which such a further period of investigation would cause is such that it should discontinue that investigation now. I agree that there are considerable uncertainties that a prosecution could be brought; indeed, my view goes somewhat further as I consider, having carefully considered the present evidence, that there are obstacles to a successful prosecution so that it is likely that it would not in the end go ahead.

As to the public interest considerations, there is a strong public interest in upholding and enforcing the criminal law, in particular against international corruption, which Parliament specifically legislated to prohibit in 2001. In addition I have, as is normal practice in any sensitive case, obtained the views of the Prime Minister and the Foreign and Defence Secretaries as to the public interest considerations raised by this investigation. They have expressed the clear view that continuation of the investigation would cause serious damage to UK/Saudi security, intelligence and diplomatic co-operation, which is likely to have seriously negative consequences for the United Kingdom public interest in terms of both national security and our highest priority foreign policy objectives in the Middle East. The heads of our security and intelligence agencies and our ambassador to Saudi Arabia share this assessment.

Article 5 of the OECD Convention on Combating Bribery of Foreign Public Officials in International Business Transactions precludes me and the Serious Fraud Office from taking into account considerations of the national economic interest or the potential effect upon relations with another state, and we have not done so. Noble Lords will understand that further public comment about the case must inevitably be limited in order to avoid causing unfairness to individuals who have been the subject of investigation or any damage to the wider public interest. It is also appropriate that I should add that the company and individuals involved deny any wrongdoing.

(HL Deb 14 December 2006 Vol 687 c1711–1713)

19/27

The Government were asked under what statutory or prerogative power the Attorney-General gave instructions to the Serious Fraud Office not to pursue its investigation of offences of corruption in relation to Saudi Arabian arms contracts; what limits there were, if any, on the exercise of this power to halt investigations; and into what classes of offence. The Attorney-General wrote:

No such instructions were given. The SFO itself decided to discontinue its investigation but not as a result of any instructions from me.

Further, the Government were asked whether the Attorney-General had received representations from BAE Systems warning of the adverse impact on business from the loss of a Eurofighter Typhoon agreement unless the Serious Fraud Office investigation into alleged bribery of Saudi officials was halted.

The Attorney-General wrote:

BAE Systems made such representations to me in November 2005, which I passed on to the Serious Fraud Office. However, in reaching the decision to discontinue the investigation, in accordance with Article 5 of the OECD Convention on Combating Bribery of Foreign Public Officials in International Business Transactions, the SFO took no account of such considerations.

(HL Deb 8 January 2007 Vol 688 cWA9–WA10)

19/28
And the Government were asked what were the respective roles and responsibilities of the Prime Minister and the Attorney-General in reaching the decision to halt the Serious Fraud Office investigation into alleged bribery by BAE Systems of Saudi officials.
The Attorney-General wrote:

The decision to discontinue the investigation was made by the Serious Fraud Office, which exercises its functions under my statutory superintendence. As I explained in my Statement of 14 December 2006, I obtained views from the Prime Minister and the Foreign and Defence Secretaries as to the public interest considerations raised by the investigation. The nature of those views was set out in my Statement.

And the Government were asked whether the decision to abandon the Serious Fraud Office investigation into the Al Yamamah oil-for-arms contracts was influenced by pressure from Saudi Arabia in relation to the jet fighter contract with Saudi Arabia.

The Attorney-General wrote:

As I explained in my Statement of 14 December 2006, the public interest factors taken into account by the SFO related to national and international security, not commercial or economic considerations.

(HL Deb 8 January 2007 Vol 688 cWA9–WA10)

19/29
The Foreign Secretary was asked if she would make a statement on the UK's record of compliance with the 1999 Organisation for Economic Co-operation and Development (OECD) Anti Bribery Convention; and what enquiries had been made by the OECD regarding UK compliance since the beginning of December 2006. An FCO Minister wrote:

The Working Group on Bribery (WGB) of the Organisation for Economic Co-operation and Development (OECD) monitors implementation of the Anti-Bribery Convention through a system of peer review.

In its December 1999 "phase 1" evaluation of the UK's legislative compliance with the convention, the WGB said that it was

"not in a position to determine that the UK laws are in compliance with the standards under the convention."

The OECD conducted a follow-up review after the introduction of the Anti-Terrorism, Crime and Security Act 2001, whose part 12 amended the scope of UK law as it relates to bribery. The WGB's "phase 1bis" evaluation, published in March 2003, concluded:

"...the UK law now addresses the requirements set forth in the convention".

In a separate cycle of reviews, the WGB assesses all aspects of parties' implementation of the convention—from awareness-raising to administrative processes and legal enforcement. The "phase 2" report on the UK was published in March 2005. It commended a number of aspects of our anti-bribery framework, such as employee whistleblower protection, the ability of the tax authorities to make spontaneous disclosures of suspicious information to law enforcement agencies and the wide scope of the "regulated sector" in our anti-money-laundering reporting regime. The report also noted the Government's support provided to a range of private sector and civil society anti-corruption initiatives. In addition, the report made a number of recommendations for further action, for example in our awareness-raising efforts, on investigation and prosecution and on working with the Crown dependencies and overseas territories. In line with the standard procedure, the UK gave an oral progress report to the WGB in March 2006 and we will be submitting a written report in March this year. I will place a copy of this report in the Library of the House after the WGB plenary discussion in March [http://213.253.134.43/oecd/pdfs/brosweit/2807051E.PDF, Ed.]

The chair of the working group wrote in December 2006 to explore the reasons for the Serious Fraud Office's decision to discontinue its investigation into bribery allegations against British Aerospace with respect to Saudi Arabia. Contacts with the chair continue and the UK delegation will discuss questions other delegations may have at the next plenary meeting on 16–18 January 2007.

(HC Deb 15 January 2007 Vol 455 c828W)

19/30

In a debate about controls on arms exports, a Trade Minister said:

The days are gone when the UK defence industry was largely autonomous. Defence manufacturing is now a complex globalised process, with international collaboration firmly to the fore. Technology crosses borders, often electronically, at all stages of the process, and components and equipment will often leave the UK to be turned into the final product elsewhere. That mirrors what is happening in many industries and it happens for perfectly legitimate business reasons, but it inevitably presents additional challenges for export controls.

Our export controls are graduated on a risk basis: the higher the risk and the greater the potential damage from an unwarranted export proceeding, the greater the stringency of control. Thus in some cases—for example, those in which components are going to the Governments of NATO countries and other trusted allies—we can provide more flexible licensing options. For high-risk transactions, however, we need to apply close scrutiny before a decision is given. For those activities that are inherently undesirable, we want to control not only what happens in the UK, but what UK citizens are doing overseas. That relates to the so-called extraterritorial controls.

For example, we quite rightly apply extraterritorial controls in the field of torture equipment and for supplies to embargoed destinations. In doing so, the UK is sending a clear message that it does not want such things to be exported from its territory, and nor does it want its citizens, wherever they may be located, to be involved in arranging for others to supply them or to provide other services in support of those supplies. However, making extraterritorial controls work in practice is always going to be difficult.

Such controls are likely to lead to conflicts of jurisdiction where other countries take a different view from us on individual cases, causing problems with enforcement. It is difficult to ensure that UK citizens overseas are aware of them, and there is clear potential to confuse those who find themselves operating under two separate, perhaps differing, sets of legislation...

I reiterate that all applications from any destination, including Israel, are rigorously assessed against the consolidated EU and national export licensing criteria on a case-by-case basis. With applications from Israel, the likelihood of an export being used in the occupied territories is a key factor in risk assessment against the consolidated criteria. If a licence is considered to be inconsistent with the criteria, the licence will be refused, as many for Israel have been.

Our overseas posts also have standing instructions to report any misuse of UK-supplied equipment. If such information comes to light—whether through the media, NGOs or intelligence reports—it will be taken into account when assessing future licence applications. This issue may also be raised with the relevant authorities in the country in question... I can say that we recently refused licences for the export of head-up displays to Israel because of concerns that they might be used in the occupied territories...

[I was asked about] extraterritoriality for trafficking and brokering. The British Government controls UK involvement in the movement of any military goods from one overseas country to another if any part of the trading activity takes place in the UK. Fully extraterritorial trade controls would apply to any UK person anywhere in the world and to any act calculated to promote the supply or delivery from one third country to another of restricted goods only—long-range missiles with a range of 300 km or more and their components and torture goods—and to military equipment to embargoed destinations. Whether those controls should be extended to other types of military equipment, particularly small arms and light weapons, or adapted in other ways are key questions for the forthcoming review. The Government will seriously consider all the evidence that is put before them...

[I was asked about] export licensing and sustainable development...DFID is the lead Department for advice on sustainable development considerations, as defined in criterion 8 of the consolidated criteria. The criteria require the Government to consider the compatibility of exports with the economic and technical capacity of the end-user country before issuing or refusing a licence. That ensures that sustainable development must be considered in relation to export licence applications.

The ECO will refer licence applications to DFID for assessment against criterion 8, if the destination is on the list of countries for which sustainable development is most likely to be an issue and—with standard individual export licences and standard individual trade control licences—the value of the licence is above a certain threshold that is determined on a country-by-country basis. The destination list is made up of countries that are eligible for concessional loans from the World Bank's International Development Association and is taken to represent the world's poorest. The list is kept under constant review to take account of changing circumstances.

(HC Deb 22 February 2007 Vol 457 c182–185WH)

19/31
Attorney General's Speech to launch the Justice Assistance Network

The Rule of Law matters. It is not just a slogan. It is necessary for: peace, economic development, human rights and the ability to create efficient and effective social infrastructures that improve health and education; and for the fight against crime, corruption and terrorism.

In putting this network in place we are ensuring that justice is at the heart of making poverty history. The Justice Assistance Network marks an essential step forward in providing assistance and intervention overseas. We have a duty to provide legal assistance to the places that need it most and in doing this we are making it a priority to address poverty and humanitarian causes.

In the 1990s, the World Bank's Consultations with the Poor gathered the views of more than 60,000 people in 60 countries. The messages were clear: poor people care about their safety, security, dignity and respect as much as they care about better access to services and improved livelihoods. Ensuring that people have access to, and confidence in the law is how this is achieved in practice.

And there are strong economic reasons for promoting justice reform. A country cannot function effectively, grow its economy, take care of and develop its population, or take its proper place in the world, if it is not exercising and subject to the Rule of Law. In 2003 the European Commission estimated that stolen African assets equivalent to more than half the continent's external debt were held in foreign bank accounts—a shocking statistic illustrating both the opportunities and degree of threat of corruption unchecked. In the intervening period work between the UK and several African countries, for example, Nigeria, Kenya, and Ghana, concerning asset forfeiture procedure and mutual legal assistance is helping to address the problem...

Importantly, people, particularly foreign investors, will not invest in countries where they cannot look to effective and honest forms of dispute resolution to deal with the problems which may arise as their investment runs its course. If there is not a system worth reporting to they go elsewhere...

The UK has a strong reputation in this field. UK legal advice is in demand and there is great interest in how we do things. The UK legal brand is known and respected. My concern has been that we could do better where formal co-ordination of activity between government departments was concerned...

The Justice Assistance Network and its principles of engagement will satisfy the requirement in terms of government activity. It will draw together, in a virtual network, key personnel with knowledge of their respective departmental capabilities. The application of the agreed principles of engagement by them and the terms of reference they will utilise will lead to better informed decisions about the priority to be afforded to individual initiatives and (crucially) the allocation of the most appropriate resources to fulfil our objectives.

The Network will meet at regular intervals and will report on progress to Ministers. Its Work Plan for the coming year has been established.

As to the effective bridge between the public and private sectors, many of you will know that last year, after consultation between the professional bodies involved I was invited to establish the International Pro Bono Committee. Among other important functions this Committee will act as a forum for the exchange of information between organisations like the Bar Council, Law Society, International Bar Association and others, and as a clearing house matching skills and experience to demand.

Now there will be a direct channel of communication between its work and the activities of the Judicial Assistance Network via officials from my own office who will sit on both. Whilst the work of the international pro bono community will remain wholly independent from that of the public sector, better connections between the two will lead to a more complementary relationship and one that will be mutually beneficial.

One of the outcomes I and ministerial colleagues will be looking for from the more strategic approach the Network and its principles of engagement is the identification, organisation and delivery of more holistic—end-to-end—projects that involve each part of the justice process in a synchronised fashion. For example, by being able to provide judicial, prosecutorial, investigative, general legal and management skills in a co-ordinated programme rather than being committed to only one part of the justice sector. What might be termed 'working smarter' than at present. The routine engagement of Ministers and officials from across government provided for by the Network will mean that this will be easier to put into practice than has hitherto been the case. Add to this the communication with the skills and knowledge of the private sector then I believe we have created a much better platform from which to achieve our aims.

(Speech by the Attorney-General, Justice Assistance Network launch— The Role of UK Law in promoting Justice Overseas, 16 May 2007, www.attorneygeneral.gov.uk/attachments/Justice%20Assistance%20 Project%20Speech.pdf)

19/32
Trafficking

A Minister wrote:

The Government are committed to ratifying the Council of Europe Convention on Action against Trafficking as soon as possible as part of our ongoing anti-trafficking strategy, set out in the comprehensive UK Action Plan on tackling human trafficking. We will not ratify the Convention until it is certain that we have implemented it in full because our legal system, unlike in some other signatory countries, requires full compliance with a Convention before ratification.

(HC Deb 17 December 2007 Vol 469 c960W)

19/33
Transfer of Prisoners

A Justice Minister wrote:

The United Kingdom is a party to two multi-party prisoner transfer agreements, the Council of Europe Convention on the Transfer of Sentenced Persons, and the Commonwealth Scheme for the Transfer of Convicted Offenders. In addition, the United Kingdom has concluded a small number of bilateral prisoner transfer agreements. The following lists those countries and territories with which the United Kingdom has a prisoner transfer arrangement. [The list is not reproduced here, Ed.]

No payments have been made to foreign countries for the transfer of prisoners to serve the remainder of their sentence.

(HC Deb 19 November 2007 Vol 467 c517W)

19/34
A Justice Minister said:

One of the central principles of the Council of Europe Convention on the Transfer of Sentenced Persons, under which Michael [Shields] was transferred to a prison in the United Kingdom, is that the receiving state must respect the findings of the sentencing state [Shields had been convicted in Bulgaria, Ed.]. Indeed, Article 13 of the Convention makes it clear that the sentencing state alone retains the right to review the judgment of its court. Under the terms of that convention there is limited scope for the receiving state, which in this case is the United Kingdom, to change the sentence imposed by the sentencing state. A sentence can be adapted where the sentence imposed exceeds the sentence available to courts in the receiving state for the same offence...Michael is serving a sentence of 10 years for attempted murder. As the maximum sentence available to British courts for attempted murder is life imprisonment, we have no power to reduce Michael's sentence on those grounds.

(HC Deb 20 November 2007 Vol 467 c1165)

Part Nineteen: IX. *Legal Aspects of International Relations and Co-operation in Particular Matters—Military and security matters*

19/35
The Foreign Secretary was asked whether the agreement with the US under which the UK acquires nuclear submarine-related technologies

required by way of reciprocation the UK to support the US in armed conflicts under certain circumstances. An FCO Minister wrote:

No.

(HC Deb 15 January 2007 Vol 455 c828W)

19/36

Arms Trade

An FCO Minister wrote:

The Government are committed to leading work to secure a legally binding treaty to set standards for the international trade in conventional arms, including small arms. On 6 December 2006 we secured agreement to start a UN process to take forward this work, with the backing of 153 states. In March we submitted to the UN the United Kingdom's views on the initiative, making clear we envisage a treaty which will allow the responsible sale of small arms but will prohibit their sale in certain cases, including where they will be used in the commission of serious violations of international humanitarian or human rights law, or to provoke or exacerbate internal or regional conflict.

(HC Deb 2 July 2007 Vol 462 c895W–896W)

19/37
An FCO Minister wrote:

The UK recognises that all countries, including Israel, have a legitimate right to purchase conventional arms for their defence and security needs. However, UK policy dictates that all licences are assessed on a case by case basis against the Consolidated EU and National Export Licensing Criteria. This takes into account respect for human rights and the preservation of regional peace, security and stability. If there is a clear risk that the equipment will be used in a manner inconsistent with the Consolidated Criteria, a licence will not be approved.

(HC Deb 23 July 2007 Vol 463 c708W)

19/38

Arms Trade—Tanzania—Military Air Traffic Control System

In a debate on arms exports (a military air traffic control system to Tanzania), the Secretary of International Development said:

Criterion 8 [of the consolidated EU and national arms export criteria] requires the Government to consider whether the export will "seriously undermine the economy or seriously hamper the sustainable development of the recipient country".

The export licensing process also involves consideration of conflict, human rights and other issues, but criterion 8 is most relevant to this particular case. The Government take their responsibilities on arms export licensing very seriously, and they considered the application of the criterion carefully when the licence for the air traffic control system for Tanzania was considered. The issue was thoroughly discussed by the Departments involved and, in the end, the Secretary of State for Trade and Industry concluded that the licence should be approved. That is not to say that there were no concerns about the system and its suitability—there clearly were, as the World Bank and the ICAO reports made clear—but the test of criterion 8 is whether it is likely seriously to undermine the economy and sustainable development. The Government at the time judged that it would not do so and, looking back from this vantage point, it would be hard to argue that it did.

It was put to the Minister that:

The argument is that criterion 8 should have ruled out the sale of the system because it seriously hampers the sustainable development of the country. I would argue that for a country heavily in debt, that must be the case, but if the [Minister] argues to the contrary, is he saying that criterion 8 needs to be amended?

The Minister replied:

Criterion 8 does not exactly say that. There will be an opportunity to review the Export Control Act 2002 during the year, and the House has the opportunity this evening to debate the issue, as we are doing. We should always reflect on experience. In the end, the Government weighed these matters up and reached a view that the test in criterion 8 was not met.

First, there was a need for clearer guidance within Whitehall. We have now agreed guidance for officials when they look at the impact of proposed arms exports on a recipient country. The principle that sustainable development must be taken into account in licensing decisions was enshrined in the Export Control Act 2002, which is one of the toughest licensing systems in the world. The House should recognise that. DFID continues to play an active part in the licensing process. The Export Control Act is due for review this year. The Department of Trade and Industry will lead the process, consulting widely with other Departments, Parliament and civil society. One important area that we will look at is the activities of arms brokers, how well the current controls are working and whether they need to be strengthened.

The second question that we need to ask ourselves is how we continue to ensure, as a major exporter of defence equipment and as a major international donor, that UK arms exports do not undermine development. That is what we are concerned about. We know that excessive spending on arms can divert money away from health and education, and irresponsible transfers can be used to ignite violence.

Nevertheless, all countries have a right to provide for their legitimate defence and security needs, and those of their citizens. For that they need suitable equipment, and few developing countries have the means to manufacture that equipment. Most are dependent on arms imports. In the circumstances, what we can do is to have the right framework for taking decisions about UK licensing decisions, but to recognise that that is not good enough if other countries do not follow the same approach. That is why the UK has been leading the campaign for an international agreement, in the shape of an arms trade treaty, which would benefit everyone and which would also have the power to stop arms transfers that fuel violent conflict, particularly in the world's poorest countries.

The Minister was then asked whether or not he would press for the registration of brokers.

He said:

...extra-territoriality currently applies to certain brokering activities abroad relating—from memory—to weapons of mass destruction, instruments of torture and brokering that contravenes international arms embargoes. At the time we said that we wanted to see how the new arrangements worked. Part of the purpose of the review of the legislation is to give the House the opportunity to reflect on that. If the world did more to control the flow of small arms and light weapons, which are principally responsible for the terrible death toll in developing countries, I am sure the whole House would welcome that.

On international action, the UK has ratified the UN Convention against Corruption and promoted the very successful extractive industries transparency initiative. We are setting up the governance and transparency fund to help those working to improve transparency, we have established the international corruption group, and we are taking on additional police officers working with the City of London and Metropolitan police. Why? It is to increase our capacity to investigate bribery, corruption and money laundering.

(HC Deb 30 January 2007 Vol 456 c164–166)

19/39
Another Minister then said:

The episode started in 1992, when our high commissioner in Tanzania alerted the then Government to the requirement for a new air traffic control system, and the Defence Export Services Organisation notified BAE Systems of the prospect. The Government's decision to issue export licences in December 2001 for an air traffic control system for Tanzania was taken after careful and lengthy consideration of the application—and clearly some controversy—against the Government's consolidated EU and national arms export licensing criteria... the Government take their responsibility on arms export licensing, including in relation to sustainable development, most seriously. In assessing all applications, we draw on the expertise of several Departments to ensure stringent assessment against the licensing criteria. They ensure that the risks that concern us all, including internal repression, internal or regional conflict, the need to support sustainable development and the risk of diversion to undesirable end users, are rigorously assessed on every occasion.

The Government carried out just such an analysis when they considered the licences for the air traffic control system for Tanzania. We also discussed the issue thoroughly among Departments, and concluded that the licence should be approved. Although there were some concerns about the system and its suitability, ultimately they were matters for the Government of Tanzania to resolve. It was not our place to dictate to the Government of Tanzania which system they thought that they needed. Equally, if the export was not clearly in breach of any of the EU criteria, it would not have been right for us to withhold a licence with a view to blocking the proposed export.

One of the interesting features to come out of this debate is the balance that we need to strike between the criteria that should determine the Government's action and the independence of a sovereign nation. I should like to cite the remarks of Tanzania's Foreign Minister Kikwete—now its President—in 2002:

"We are not a department of the World Bank—we are a country and it's a bit insulting to suggest that we need to wait for the World Bank to prescribe what's best for us . . . The responsibility for Tanzania is in the hands of Tanzanians."

. . .

The issue of whether the Government of Tanzania needed a military air traffic control system—and whether it was, to coin a phrase, fit for purpose—has been a big feature of this debate. The criteria required us to assess whether the export was compatible with the technical and economic capacity of the recipient country. Beyond that, I repeat that it was for the Government of Tanzania to assess whether the system was appropriate for their needs, and whether to purchase it. The fact that the UK Government issued the licences did not oblige the Government of Tanzania to proceed with the purchase.

Why did we authorise this export to Tanzania, one of the world's poorest countries? Was the system too expensive? We have discussed these questions during the debate, and they were specifically considered in the assessment against the consolidated criteria, particularly criterion 8. In assessing the application, the Government were required to consider whether the export would

"seriously undermine the economy or seriously hamper the sustainable development of the recipient country".

Our judgment was that it would not, even in the worst case scenario. If we had assessed that the export was not consistent with any of the criteria, licences would not have been issued.

Asked about the methodology of applying Criterion 8, the Minister said:

. . . we have a clear methodology for applying criterion 8. It is EU-based and is summarised, I am advised, in the Export Control Organisation's 2005 annual report, commencing on page 83, and accessible via the DTI website. That is EU guidance based on UK guidance developed in the light of the Tanzanian case.

Obviously, there were some points arising from the Tanzanian case, which we have subsequently addressed. The need was highlighted for clearer procedures within Whitehall for assessing applications when criterion 8 came into play. We have therefore agreed guidance for officials when they consider the impact of a proposed arms export on the recipient country. That guidance has been incorporated into the EU criteria. Moreover, the principle that sustainable development must be taken into account in licensing decisions was enshrined in the Export Control Act 2002. DFID continues to play an active part in the licensing process, and in all discussions on the arms trade.

... In 2005, 129 licence applications were refused and many others were withdrawn when the stringency of the criteria were understood. I am advised that we actually have the highest refusal rate of any EU country...

We also publish comprehensive details of our policy and decision making in our quarterly and annual reports, and we are of course scrutinised carefully by the Quadripartite Committee. Not least because of the issues raised, we will initiate a review later this year of the controls introduced, in 2004, under the Export Control Act 2002. That is timed to commence three years after the new export control legislation was implemented, in accordance with Cabinet Office better regulation guidelines. There will be full public consultation, and the review is timely.

The Government also have a proud record on attacking corruption. We have ratified the UN Convention against Corruption, and put new legislation in place to allow us to do so. We have also established a new internal corruption group staffed by City of London and Metropolitan police officers...

[CRITERION EIGHT OF THE CONSOLDIATED EU AND NATIONAL GUIDELINES ON ARMS EXPORTS

The compatibility of the arms exports with the technical and economic capacity of the recipient country, taking into account the desirability that states should achieve their legitimate needs of security and defence with the least diversion for armaments of human and economic resources.

The Government will take into account, in the light of information from relevant sources such as United Nations Development Programme, World Bank, IMF and Organisation for Economic Cooperation and Development reports, whether the proposed export would seriously undermine the economy or seriously hamper the sustainable development of the recipient country.

The Government will consider in this context the recipient country's relative levels of military and social expenditure, taking into account also any EU or bilateral aid, and its public finances, balance of payments, external debt, economic and social development and any IMF- or World Bank-sponsored economic reform programme., Ed.]

(HC Deb 30 January 2007 Vol 456 c196–199)

TABLE OF CASES

INDEX